WRITER'S MARKET

DELUXE EDITION

2016

includes a one-year online subscription to

THE ULTIMATE MARKET RESEARCH TOOL FOR WRITERS

To register your *Writer's Market Deluxe Edition 2016* book and **start your one-year online subscription**, scratch off the block below to reveal your activation code*, then go to www.WritersMarket.com. Find the box that says "Purchased a Deluxe Edition?" then click on "Activate Your Account" and enter the activation code. It's that easy!

UPDATED MARKET LISTINGS FOR YOUR INTEREST AREA

EASY-TO-USE SEARCHABLE DATABASE • RECORD-KEEPING TOOLS

PROFESSIONAL TIPS & ADVICE • INDUSTRY NEWS

*valid through 12/31/16

16th ANNUAL EDITION

WRITER'S MARKET

DELUXE EDITION

2016

Robert Lee Brewer, Editor

WRITER'S DIGEST BOOKS

WritersDigest.com

Cincinnati, Ohio

Publisher: Phil Sexton

Writer's Market website: www.writersmarket.com
Writer's Digest website: www.writersdigest.com

Distributed in Canada by Fraser Direct
100 Armstrong Avenue
Georgetown, Ontario, Canada L7G 5S4
Tel: (905) 877-4411

Distributed in the U.K. and Europe by F&W Media International
Brunel House, Newton Abbot, Devon, TQ12 4PU, England
Tel: (+44) 1626-323200, Fax: (+44) 1626-323319
E-mail: postmaster@davidandcharles.co.uk

Distributed in Australia by Capricorn Link
P.O. Box 704, Windsor, NSW 2756 Australia
Tel: (02) 4577-3555

Library of Congress Catalog Number 31-20772
ISSN: 0084-2729
ISBN-13: 978-1-59963-937-6
ISBN-13: 978-1-59963-942-0 (*Writer's Market Deluxe Edition*)
ISBN-10: 1-59963-937-8
ISBN-10: 1-59963-942-4 (*Writer's Market Deluxe Edition*)

Attention Booksellers: This is an annual directory of F + W Media, Inc.
Return deadline for this edition is December 31, 2016.

Edited by: Robert Lee Brewer
Designed by: Alexis Brown
Production coordinated by: Debbie Thomas

CONTENTS

MARKETS

FROM THE EDITOR

It's a common refrain in publishing: The one thing that always remains the same is change.

This is my 10th year as the main editor of *Writer's Market*, and every single year has proven out that refrain: The one thing that always remains the same is change.

For the 2016 edition, change means returning a fan favorite, the Book Publishers Subject Index, to the back of the book. Of course, change also means that we've updated and added thousands of listings in this edition of the book.

Plus, there are new articles, including "9 Secrets of Six-Figure Freelancers," "4 Ways to Create a Productive Home Office," "6 Apps That Make Freelancing Easier," and more.

But don't worry; we didn't change the entire book. We still have listings for literary agents, book publishers, consumer magazines, trade journals, contests, and more. We still include the freelance writing pay rate chart.

And while the topic has changed, we've once again included an exciting webinar intended to help freelance writers find more success with their writing. Learn more at www.writersmarket.com/wm16-webinar.

Until next we meet, keep writing and marketing what you write.

Robert Lee Brewer
Senior Content Editor
Writer's Market and WritersMarket.com
http://writersdigest.com/editor-blogs/poetic-asides
http://blog.writersmarket.com
http://twitter.com/robertleebrewer

HOW TO USE *WRITER'S MARKET*

Writer's Market is here to help you decide where and how to submit your writing to appropriate markets. Each listing contains information about the editorial focus of the market, how it prefers material to be submitted, payment information, and other helpful tips.

WHAT'S INSIDE?

Since 1921, *Writer's Market* has been giving you the information you need to knowledgeably approach a market. We've continued to develop improvements to help you access that information more efficiently.

NAVIGATIONAL TOOLS. We've designed the pages of *Writer's Market* with you, the writer, in mind. Within the pages you will find **readable market listings** and **accessible charts and graphs**. One such chart can be found in the ever-popular "How Much Should I Charge?" article.

We've taken all of the updated information in this feature and put it into an easy-to-read-and-navigate chart, making it convenient for you to find the rates that accompany the freelance jobs you're seeking.

ICONS. There are a variety of icons that appear before each listing. A complete Key to Icons & Abbreviations appears on the right. Icons let you know whether a book publisher accepts only agented writers (Ⓐ), comparative pay rates for a magazine ($-$$$$), and more.

CONTACT NAMES, ROYALTY RATES AND ADVANCES. In every section, we identify key contact people with the boldface word **Contact** to help you get your manuscript to the right person.

EDITORS, PAY RATES, ROYALTIES, ADVANCES, AND PERCENTAGE OF MATERIAL WRITTEN BY FREELANCE WRITERS. For Book Publishers, royalty rates and advances are highlighted in boldface, as is other important information on the percentage of first-time writers and unagented writers the company publishes, the number of books published, and the number of manuscripts received each year. In the Consumer Magazines and Trade Journals sections, we identify the amount (percentage) of material accepted from freelance writers, and the pay rates for features, columns and departments, and fillers in boldface to help you quickly identify the information you need to know when considering whether to submit your work.

QUERY FORMATS. We asked editors how they prefer to receive queries and have indicated in the listings whether they prefer them by mail, e-mail, fax or phone. Be sure to check an editor's individual preference before sending your query.

ARTICLES. Writers who want to improve their submission techniques should read the articles in the **Finding Work** section. The **Managing Work** section is geared more toward post-acceptance topics, such as contract negotiation, organization, and self-promotion.

IF THIS BOOK IS NEW TO YOU . . .

Look at the **Contents** pages to familiarize you with the arrangement of *Writer's Market*. The three largest sections of the book are the market listings of Book Publishers; Consumer Magazines; and Trade Journals. You will also find other sections of market listings for Literary Agents and Contests & Awards. More opportunities can be found on the WritersMarket.com website.

Narrowing your search

After you've identified the market categories that interest you, you can begin researching specific markets within each section.

Consumer Magazines and Trade Journals are categorized by subject within their respective sections to make it easier for you to identify markets for your work.

KEY TO ICONS & ABBREVIATIONS

Ⓐ	market accepts agented submissions only
⊘	market does not accept unsolicited submissions
(maple leaf)	Canadian market
(globe)	market located outside of the U.S. and Canada
$	market pays 0-9¢/word or $0-$150/article
$$	market pays 10-49¢/word or $151-$750/article
$$$	market pays 50-99¢/word or $751-$1,500/article
$$$$	market pays $1/word or over $1,500/article
(speech bubble)	comment from the editor of *Writer's Market*
(key)	tips to break into a specific market
ms, mss	manuscript(s)
b&w	black & white (photo)
SASE	self-addressed, stamped envelope
SAE	self-addressed envelope
IRC	International Reply Coupon, for use when mailing to countries other than your own

IMPORTANT LISTING INFORMATION

1) Listings are based on editorial questionnaires and interviews. They are not advertisements; publishers do not pay for their listings. The markets are not endorsed by *Writer's Market* editors. Writer's Digest Books and its employees go to great effort to ascertain the validity of information in this book. However, transactions between users of the information and individuals and/or companies are strictly between those parties.
2) All listings have been verified before publication of this book. If a listing has not changed from last year, then the editor said the market's needs have not changed and the previous listing continues to accurately reflect its policies.
3) *Writer's Market* reserves the right to exclude any listing.
4) When looking for a specific market, check the index. A market may not be listed for one of these reasons:
    - It doesn't solicit freelance material.
    - It doesn't pay for material.
    - It has gone out of business.
    - It has failed to verify or update its listing for this edition.
    - It hasn't answered *Writer's Market* inquiries satisfactorily.

There is a subject index available for Book Publishers in the back of the book. It is broken into fiction and nonfiction categories and subcategories.

Contests & Awards are categorized by genre of writing. If you want to find journalism contests, you would search the Journalism category; if you have an unpublished novel, check the Fiction category.

Interpreting the markets

Once you've identified companies or publications that cover the subjects in which you're interested, you can begin evaluating specific listings to pinpoint the markets most receptive to your work and most beneficial to you.

In evaluating individual listings, check the location of the company, the types of material it is interested in seeing, submission requirements, and rights and payment policies. Depending on your personal concerns, any of these items could be a deciding factor as you determine which markets you plan to approach. Many listings also include a reporting time.

Whenever possible, obtain submission guidelines before submitting material. You can usually obtain guidelines by sending a SASE to the address in the listing or by checking online. Many of the listings contain instructions on how to obtain sample copies, catalogs or market lists. The more research you do upfront, the better your chances of acceptance, publication and payment.

BEFORE YOUR FIRST SALE

Everything in life has to start somewhere and that somewhere is always at the beginning. Stephen King, Stephenie Meyer, Jeff Kinney, Nora Roberts—they all had to start at the beginning. It would be great to say becoming a writer is as easy as waving a magic wand over your manuscript and "Poof!" you're published, but that's not how it happens. While there's no one true "key" to becoming successful, a long, well-paid writing career *can* happen when you combine four elements:

- Good writing
- Knowledge of writing markets
- Professionalism
- Persistence

Good writing is useless if you don't know which markets will buy your work or how to pitch and sell your writing. If you aren't professional and persistent in your contact with editors, your writing is just that—your writing. But if you are a writer who embraces the above four elements, you have a good chance at becoming a paid, published writer who will reap the benefits of a long and successful career.

As you become more involved with writing, you may read articles or talk to editors and authors with conflicting opinions about the right way to submit your work. The truth is, there are many different routes a writer can follow to get published, but no matter which route you choose, the end is always the same—becoming a published writer.

The following advice on submissions has worked for many writers, but it is by no means the be-all-end-all of proper submission guidelines. It's very easy to get wrapped up in the specifics of submitting (Should I put my last name on every page of my manuscript?) and ignore the more important issues (Will this idea on ice fishing in Alaska be appropriate for a regional magazine in Seattle?). Don't allow yourself to become so blinded by submission procedures that you forget common sense. If you use your common sense and develop professional, courteous relations with editors, you will eventually find your own submission style.

DEVELOP YOUR IDEAS, THEN TARGET THE MARKETS

Writers often think of an interesting story, complete the manuscript, and then begin the search for a suitable publisher or magazine. While this approach is common for fiction, poetry and screenwriting, it reduces your chances of success in many nonfiction writing areas. Instead, choose categories that interest you and study those sections in *Writer's Market*. Select several listings you consider good prospects for your type of writing. Sometimes the individual listings will even help you generate ideas.

Next, make a list of the potential markets for each idea. Make the initial contact with markets using the method stated in the market listings. If you exhaust your list of possibilities, don't give up. Instead, reevaluate the idea or try another angle. Continue developing ideas and approaching markets. Identify and rank potential markets for an idea and continue the process.

As you submit to the various publications listed in *Writer's Market*, it's important to remember that every magazine is published with a particular audience and slant in mind. Probably the number one complaint we receive from editors is the submissions they receive are completely wrong for their magazines or book line. The first mark of professionalism is to know your market well. Gaining that knowledge starts with *Writer's Market*, but you should also do your own detective work. Search out back issues of the magazines you wish to write for, pick up recent issues at your local newsstand, or visit magazines' websites—anything that will help you figure out what subjects specific magazines publish. This research is also helpful in learning what topics have been covered ad nauseum—the topics you should stay away from or approach in a fresh way. Magazines' websites are invaluable as most post the current issue of the magazine, as well as back issues, and most offer writer's guidelines.

The same advice is true for submitting to book publishers. Research publisher websites for their submission guidelines, recently published titles and their backlist. You can use this information to target your book proposal in a way that fits with a publisher's other titles while not directly competing for sales.

Prepare for rejection and the sometimes lengthy wait. When a submission is returned, check your file folder of potential markets for that idea. Cross off the market that rejected the idea. If the editor has given you suggestions or reasons why the manuscript was not accepted, you might want to incorporate these suggestions when revising your manuscript.

After revising your manuscript mail it to the next market on your list.

Take rejection with a grain of salt

Rejection is a way of life in the publishing world. It's inevitable in a business that deals with such an overwhelming number of applicants for such a limited number of positions. Anyone who has published has lived through many rejections, and writers with thin skin are at a distinct disadvantage. A rejection letter is not a personal attack. It simply indicates your submission is not appropriate for that market. Writers who let rejection dissuade them from pursuing their dream or who react to an editor's "No" with indignation or fury do themselves a disservice. Writers who let rejection stop them do not get published. Resign yourself to facing rejection now. You will live through it, and you'll eventually overcome it.

QUERY AND COVER LETTERS

A query letter is a brief, one-page letter used as a tool to hook an editor and get him interested in your idea. When you send a query letter to a magazine, you are trying to get an editor to buy your idea or article. When you query a book publisher, you are attempting to get an editor interested enough in your idea to request your book proposal or your entire manuscript. (Note: Some book editors prefer to receive book proposals on first contact. Check individual listings for which method editors prefer.)

Here are some basic guidelines to help you create a query that's polished and well-organized. For more tips see "Query Letter Clinic" article.

- **LIMIT IT TO ONE PAGE, SINGLE-SPACED**, and address the editor by name (Mr. or Ms. and the surname). *Note*: Do not assume that a person is a Mr. or Ms. unless it is obvious from the name listed. For example, if you are contacting a D.J. Smith, do not assume that D.J. should be preceded by Mr. or Ms. Instead, address the letter to D.J. Smith.
- **GRAB THE EDITOR'S ATTENTION WITH A STRONG OPENING.** Some magazine queries, for example, begin with a paragraph meant to approximate the lead of the intended article.
- **INDICATE HOW YOU INTEND TO DEVELOP THE ARTICLE OR BOOK.** Give the editor some idea of the work's structure and content.
- **LET THE EDITOR KNOW IF YOU HAVE PHOTOS** or illustrations available to accompany your magazine article.
- **MENTION ANY EXPERTISE OR TRAINING THAT QUALIFIES YOU** to write the article or book. If you've been published before, mention it; if not, don't.
- **END WITH A DIRECT REQUEST TO WRITE THE ARTICLE.** Or, if you're pitching a book, ask for the go-ahead to send in a full proposal or the entire manuscript. Give the editor an idea of the expected length and delivery date of your manuscript.

A common question that arises is: If I don't hear from an editor in the reported response time, how do I know when I can safely send the query to another market? Many writers find it helpful to indicate in their queries that if they don't receive a response from the editor (slightly after the listed reporting time), they will assume the editor is not interested. It's best to take this approach, particularly if your topic is timely.

A brief, single-spaced cover letter is helpful when sending a manuscript as it helps personalize the submission. However, if you

QUERY LETTER RESOURCES

The following list of books provides you with more detailed information on writing query letters, cover letters, and book proposals. All titles are published by Writer's Digest Books.

- *Formatting & Submitting Your Manuscript*, 3rd Edition, by Chuck Sambuchino
- *How to Write Attention-Grabbing Query & Cover Letters*, by John Wood
- *How to Write a Book Proposal*, 4th Edition, by Michael Larsen
- *Writer's Market Companion*, 2nd Edition, by Joe Feiertag and Mary Cupito

have previously queried the editor, use the cover letter to politely and briefly remind the editor of that query—when it was sent, what it contained, etc. "Here is the piece on low-fat cooking that I queried you about on December 12. I look forward to hearing from you at your earliest convenience." Do not use the cover letter as a sales pitch.

If you are submitting to a market that accepts unsolicited manuscripts, a cover letter is useful because it personalizes your submission. You can, and should, include information about the manuscript, yourself, your publishing history, and your qualifications.

In addition to tips on writing queries, the "Query Letter Clinic" article offers eight example query letters, some that work and some that don't, as well as comments on why the letters were either successful or failed to garner an assignment or contract.

Querying for fiction

Fiction is sometimes queried, but more often editors prefer receiving material. Many fiction editors won't decide on a submission until they have seen the complete manuscript. When submitting a fiction book idea, most editors prefer to see at least a synopsis and sample chapters (usually the first three). For fiction published in magazines, most editors want to see the complete short story manuscript. If an editor does request a query for fiction, it should include a description of the main theme and story line, including the conflict and resolution. Take a look at individual listings to see what editors prefer to receive.

THE SYNOPSIS

Most fiction books are sold by a complete manuscript, but most editors and agents don't have the time to read a complete manuscript of every wannabe writer. As a result, publishing decision-makers use the synopsis and sample chapters to help the screening process of fiction. The synopsis, on its most basic level, communicates what the book is about.

The length and depth of a synopsis can change from agent to agent or publisher to publisher. Some will want a synopsis that is one to two single-spaced pages; others will want a synopsis that can run up to 25 double-spaced pages. Checking your listings in *Writer's Market*, as well as double-checking with the listing's website, will help guide you in this respect.

The content should cover all the essential points of the novel from beginning to end and in the correct order. The essential points include main characters, main plot points, and, yes, the ending. Of course, your essential points will vary from the editor who wants a one-page synopsis to the editor who wants a 25-page synopsis.

NONFICTION PROPOSALS

Most nonfiction books are sold by a book proposal—a package of materials that details what your book is about, who its intended audience is, and how you intend to write the book. It includes some combination of a cover or query letter, an overview, an outline, author's information sheet, and sample chapters. Editors also want to see information about the audience for your book and about titles that compete with your proposed book.

Submitting nonfiction proposals

A proposal package should include the following items:

- **A COVER OR QUERY LETTER.** This letter should be a short introduction to the material you include in the proposal.
- **AN OVERVIEW.** This is a brief summary of your book. It should detail your book's subject and give an idea of how that subject will be developed.
- **AN OUTLINE.** The outline covers your book chapter by chapter and should include all major points covered in each chapter. Some outlines are done in traditional outline form, but most are written in paragraph form.
- **AN AUTHOR'S INFORMATION SHEET.** This information should acquaint the editor with your writing background and convince him of your qualifications regarding the subject of your book.
- **SAMPLE CHAPTERS.** Many editors like to see sample chapters, especially for a first book. Sample chapters show the editor how you write and develop ideas from your outline.
- **MARKETING INFORMATION.** Facts about how and to whom your book can be successfully marketed are now expected to accompany every book proposal. If you can provide information about the audience for your book and suggest ways the book publisher can reach those people, you will increase your chances of acceptance.
- **COMPETITIVE TITLE ANALYSIS.** Check the *Subject Guide to Books in Print* for other titles on your topic. Write a one- or two-sentence synopsis of each. Point out how your book differs and improves upon existing topics.

For more information on nonfiction book proposals, read Michael Larsen's *How to Write a Book Proposal* (Writer's Digest Books).

A WORD ABOUT AGENTS

An agent represents a writer's work to publishers, negotiates contracts, follows up to see that contracts are fulfilled, and generally handles a writer's business affairs, leaving the writer free to write. Effective agents are valued for their contacts in the publishing industry, their knowledge about who to approach with certain ideas, their ability to guide an author's career, and their business sense.

While most book publishers listed in *Writer's Market* publish books by unagented writers, some of the larger houses are reluctant to consider submissions that have not reached them through a literary agent. Companies with such a policy are noted by an (Ⓐ) icon at the beginning of the listing, as well as in the submission information within the listing.

Writer's Market includes a list of literary agents who are all members of the Association of Authors' Representatives and who are also actively seeking new and established writers.

MANUSCRIPT FORMAT

You can increase your chances of publication by following a few standard guidelines regarding the physical format of your manuscript. It should be your goal to make your manuscript readable. Follow these suggestions as you would any other suggestions: Use what works for you and discard what doesn't.

In general, when submitting a manuscript, you should use white, 8½×11, 20 lb. paper, and you should also choose a legible, professional looking font (i.e., Times New Roman)—no all-italic or artsy fonts. Your entire manuscript should be double-spaced with a 1½-inch margin on all sides of the page. Once you are ready to print your manuscript, you should print either on a laser printer or an ink-jet printer.

MANUSCRIPT FORMATTING SAMPLE

1 Your Name 50,000 Words 3
Your Street Address
City State ZIP Code
Day and Evening Phone Numbers
E-mail Address

Website (if applicable)

2

TITLE

by

4 Your Name

5 You can increase your chances of publication by following a few standard guidelines regarding the physical format of your article or manuscript. It should be your goal to make your manuscript readable. Use these suggestions as you would any other suggestions: Use what works for you and discard what doesn't.

In general, when submitting a manuscript, you should use white, 8½×11, 20-lb. bond paper, and you should also choose a legible, professional-looking font (i.e., Times New Roman)—no all-italic or artsy fonts. Your entire manuscript should be double-spaced with a 1½-inch margin on all sides of the page. Once you are ready to print your article or manuscript, you should print either on a laser printer or an ink-jet printer.

Remember, articles should be written after you send a one-page query letter to an editor, and the editor then asks you to write the article. If, however, you are sending an article "on spec" to an editor, you should send both a query letter and the complete article.

Fiction and poetry is a little different from nonfiction articles, in that it is rarely queried. More often than not, poetry and fiction editors want to review the complete manuscript before making a final decision.

1 Type your real name (even if you use a pseudonym) and contact information 2 Double-space twice 3 Estimated word count 4 Type your title in capital letters, double-space and type "by," double-space again, and type your name (or pseudonym if you're using one) 5 Double-space twice, then indent first paragraph and start text of your manuscript 6 On subsequent pages, type your name, a dash, and the page number in the upper left or right corner

ESTIMATING WORD COUNT

All computers provide you with a word count of your manuscript. Your editor will count again after editing the manuscript. Although your computer is counting characters, an editor or production editor is more concerned about the amount of space the text will occupy on a page. Several small headlines or subheads, for instance, will be counted the same by your computer as any other word of text. However, headlines and subheads usually employ a different font size than the body text, so an editor may count them differently to be sure enough space has been estimated for larger type.

For short manuscripts, it's often quickest to count each word on a representative page and multiply by the number of pages. You can get a very rough count by multiplying the number of pages in your manuscript by 250 (the average number of words on a double-spaced typewritten page).

PHOTOGRAPHS AND SLIDES

In some cases, the availability of photographs and slides can be the deciding factor as to whether an editor will accept your submission. This is especially true when querying a publication that relies heavily on photographs, illustrations or artwork to enhance the article (e.g., craft magazines, hobby magazines, etc.). In some instances, the publication may offer additional payment for photographs or illustrations.

Check the individual listings to find out which magazines review photographs and what their submission guidelines are. Most publications prefer you do not send photographs with your submission. However, if photographs or illustrations are available, you should indicate that in your query. As with manuscripts, never send the originals of your photographs or illustrations. Instead, send digital images, which is what most magazine and book publishers prefer to use.

SEND PHOTOCOPIES

If there is one hard-and-fast rule in publishing, it's this: *Never* send the original (or only) copy of your manuscript. Most editors cringe when they find out a writer has sent the only copy of their manuscript. You should always send copies of your manuscript.

Some writers choose to send a self-addressed, stamped postcard with a photocopied submission. In their cover letter they suggest if the editor is not interested in their manuscript, it may be tossed out and a reply sent on the postcard. This method is particularly helpful when sending your submissions to international markets.

MAILING SUBMISSIONS

No matter what size manuscript you're mailing, always include a self-addressed, stamped envelope (SASE) with sufficient return postage. The website for the U.S. Postal Service (www.usps.com) and the website for the Canadian Post (www.canadapost.ca) both have postage calculators if you are unsure how much postage to affix.

A book manuscript should be mailed in a sturdy, well-wrapped box. Enclose a self-addressed mailing label and paper clip your return postage to the label. However, be aware that some book publishers do not return unsolicited manuscripts, so make sure you know the practice of the publisher before sending any unsolicited material.

Types of mail service

There are many different mailing service options available to you whether you are sending a query letter or a complete manuscript. You can work with the U.S. Postal Service, United Parcel Service, Federal Express, or any number of private mailing companies. The following are the five most common types of mailing services offered by the U.S. Postal Service.

- **FIRST CLASS** is a fairly expensive way to mail a manuscript, but many writers prefer it. First-Class mail generally receives better handling and is delivered more quickly than Standard mail.
- **PRIORITY MAIL** reaches its destination within two or three days.
- **STANDARD MAIL** rates are available for packages, but be sure to pack your materials carefully because they will be handled roughly. To make sure your package will be returned to you if it is undeliverable, print "Return Postage Guaranteed" under your address.
- **CERTIFIED MAIL** must be signed for when it reaches its destination.
- **REGISTERED MAIL** is a high-security method of mailing where the contents are insured. The package is signed in and out of every office it passes through, and a receipt is returned to the sender when the package reaches its destination.

MAILING MANUSCRIPTS

- Fold manuscripts under five pages into thirds, and send in a #10 SASE.
- Mail manuscripts five pages or more unfolded in a 9×12 or 10×13 SASE.
- For return envelope, fold the envelope in half, address it to yourself, and add a stamp, or, if going to Canada or another international destination, International Reply Coupons (available at most post office branches).
- Don't send by Certified Mail—this is a sign of an amateur.

QUERY LETTER CLINIC

Many great writers ask year after year, "Why is it so hard to get published?" In many cases, these writers have spent years developing their craft. They submit to the appropriate markets, yet rejection is always the end result. The culprit? A weak query letter.

The query letter is often the most important piece of the publishing puzzle. In many cases, it determines whether editors or agents will even read your manuscript. A good query makes a good first impression; a bad query earns a swift rejection.

ELEMENTS OF A QUERY

A query letter should sell editors or agents on your idea or convince them to request your finished manuscript. The most effective query letters get into the specifics from the very first line. It's important to remember that the query is a call to action, not a listing of features and benefits.

In addition to selling your idea or manuscript, a query can include information on the availability of photographs or artwork. You can include a working title and projected word count. Depending on the piece, you might also mention whether a sidebar might be appropriate and the type of research you plan to conduct. If appropriate, include a tentative deadline and indicate whether the query is being simultaneously submitted.

Biographical information should be included as well, but don't overdo it unless your background actually helps sell the article or proves that you're the only person who could write your proposed piece.

THINGS TO AVOID IN QUERY

The query is not a place to discuss pay rates. This step comes after an editor has agreed to take on your article or book. Besides making an unprofessional impression, it can also work to your disadvantage in negotiating your fee. If you ask too much, an editor may not even contact you to see if a lower rate works. If you ask for too little, you may start an editorial relationship where you make less than the normal rate.

You should also avoid rookie mistakes, such as mentioning your work is copyrighted or including the copyright symbol on your work. While you want to make it clear that you've researched the market, avoid using flattery as a technique for selling your work. It often has the opposite effect of what you intend. In addition, don't hint that you can re-write the piece, as this only leads the editor to think there will be a lot of work involved in shaping up your writing.

Also, never admit several other editors or agents have rejected the query. Always treat your new audience as if they are the first place on your list.

HOW TO FORMAT A QUERY

It's OK to break writing rules in a short story or article, but you should follow the rules when it comes to crafting an effective query. Here are guidelines for query writing.

- Use a normal font and typeface, such as Courier and 10- or 12-point type.
- Include your name, address, phone number, e-mail address and website.
- Use one-inch margin on paper queries.
- Address a specific editor or agent. (Note: It's wise to double-check contact names online or by calling.)
- Limit query to one single-spaced page.
- Include self-addressed, stamped envelope or postcard for response with post submissions.

HOW TO FOLLOW UP

Accidents do happen. Queries may not reach your intended reader. Staff changes or interoffice mail snafus may end up with your query letter thrown away. Or the editor may have set your query off to the side for further consideration and forgotten it. Whatever the case may be, there are some basic guidelines you should use for your follow-up communication.

Most importantly, wait until the reported response time, as indicated in *Writer's Market* or their submission guidelines, has elapsed before contacting an editor or agent. Then, you should send a short and polite e-mail describing the original query sent, the date it was sent, and asking if they received it or made a decision regarding its fate.

The importance of remaining polite and businesslike when following up cannot be stressed enough. Making a bad impression on an editor can often have a ripple effect—as that editor may share his or her bad experience with other editors at the magazine or publishing company. Also, don't call.

HOW THE CLINIC WORKS

As mentioned earlier, the query letter is the most important weapon for getting an assignment or a request for your full manuscript. Published writers know how to craft a well-written, hard-hitting query. What follows are eight queries: four are strong; four are not. Detailed comments show what worked and what did not. As you'll see, there is no cut-and-dried "good" query format; every strong query works on its own merit.

GOOD NONFICTION MAGAZINE QUERY

Jimmy Boaz, editor
American Organic Farmer's Digest
8336 Old Dirt Road
Macon GA 00000

Dear Mr. Boaz, (1)

There are 87 varieties of organic crops grown in the United States, but there's only one farm producing 12 of these—Morganic Corporation. (2)

Located in the heart of Arkansas, this company spent the past decade providing great organic crops at a competitive price helping them grow into the ninth leading organic farming operation in the country. Along the way, they developed the most unique organic offering in North America.

As a seasoned writer with access to Richard Banks, the founder and president of Morganic, I propose writing a profile piece on Banks for your Organic Shakers department. After years of reading this riveting column, I believe the time has come to cover Morganic's rise in the organic farming industry. (3)

This piece would run in the normal 800-1,200 word range with photographs available of Banks and Morganic's operation.

I've been published in *Arkansas Farmer's Deluxe, Organic Farming Today* and in several newspapers. (4)

Thank you for your consideration of this article. I hope to hear from you soon.

Sincerely,

Jackie Service
34 Good St.
Little Rock AR 00000
jackie.service9867@email.com

(1) My name is only available on our magazine's website and on the masthead. This writer has done her research. (2) Here's a story that hasn't been pitched before. I didn't know Morganic was so unique in the market. I want to know more. (3) The writer has access to her interview subject, and she displays knowledge of the magazine by pointing out the correct section in which her piece would run. (4) While I probably would've assigned this article based on the idea alone, her past credits do help solidify my decision.

BAD NONFICTION MAGAZINE QUERY

Dear Gentlemen, (1)

I'd like to write the next great article you'll ever publish. My writing credits include amazing pieces I've done for local and community newspapers and for my college English classes. I've been writing for years and years. (2)

Your magazine may not be a big one like *Rolling Stone* or *Sports Illustrated,* but I'm willing to write an interview for you anyway. I know you need material, and I need money. (Don't worry. I won't charge you too much.) (3)

Just give me some people to interview, and I'll do the best job you've ever read. It will be amazing, and I can re-write the piece for you if you don't agree. I'm willing to re-write 20 times if needed. (4)

You better hurry up and assign me an article though, because I've sent out letters to lots of other magazines, and I'm sure to be filled up to capacity very soon. (5)

Later gents,

Carl Bighead
76 Bad Query Lane
Big City NY 00000

(1) This is sexist, and it doesn't address any contact specifically. (2) An over-the-top claim by a writer who does not impress me with his publishing background. (3) Insults the magazine and then reassures me he won't charge too much? (4) While I do assign material from time to time, I prefer writers pitch me their own ideas after studying the magazine. (5) I'm sure people aren't going to be knocking down his door anytime soon.

GOOD FICTION MAGAZINE QUERY

Marcus West
88 Piano Drive
Lexington KY 00000

August 8, 2011 (1)

Jeanette Curic, editor
Wonder Stories
45 Noodle Street
Portland OR 00000

Dear Ms. Curic,

Please consider the following 1,200-word story, "Turning to the Melon," a quirky coming-of-age story with a little magical realism thrown in the mix. (2)

After reading *Wonder Stories* for years, I think I've finally written something that would fit with your audience. My previous short story credits include *Stunned Fiction Quarterly* and *Faulty Mindbomb*. (3)

Thank you in advance for considering "Turning to Melon."

Sincerely,

Marcus West
(123) 456-7890
marcusw87452@email.com

Encl: Manuscript and SASE (4)

(1) Follows the format we established in our guidelines. Being able to follow directions is more important than many writers realize. (2) Story is in our word count, and the description sounds like the type of story we would consider publishing. (3) It's flattering to know he reads our magazine. While it won't guarantee publication, it does make me a little more hopeful that the story I'm reading will be a good fit. Also, good to know he's been published before. (4) I can figure it out, but it's nice to know what other materials were included in the envelope. This letter is not flashy, but it gives me the basics and puts me in the right frame of mind to read the actual story.

BAD FICTION MAGAZINE QUERY

To: curic@wonderstories808.com ❶
Subject: A Towering Epic Fantasy

Hello there. ❷

I've written a great fantasy epic novel short story of about 25,000 words that may be included in your magazine if you so desire. ❸

More than 20 years, I've spent chained to my desk in a basement writing out the greatest story of our modern time. And it can be yours if you so desire to have it. ❹

Just say the word, and I'll ship it over to you. We can talk money and movie rights after your acceptance. I have big plans for this story, and you can be part of that success. ❺

Yours forever (if you so desire), ❻

Harold
(or Harry for friends)

❶ We do not consider e-mail queries or submissions. ❷ This is a little too informal. ❸ First off, what did he write? An epic novel or short story? Second, 25,000 words is way over our 1,500-word max. ❹ I'm lost for words. ❺ Money and movie rights? We pay moderate rates and definitely don't get involved in movies. ❻ I'm sure the writer was just trying to be nice, but this is a little bizarre and kind of creepy. I do not so desire more contact with "Harry."

GOOD NONFICTION BOOK QUERY

To: corey@bigbookspublishing.com
Subject: Query: Become a Better Parent in 30 Days (1)

Dear Mr. Corey,

(2) As a parent of six and a high school teacher for more than 20 years, I know first hand that being a parent is difficult work. Even harder is being a good parent. My proposed title, (3) *Taking Care of Yourself and Your Kids: A 30-day Program to Become a Better Parent While Still Living Your Life*, would show how to handle real-life situations and still be a good parent.

This book has been years in the making, as it follows the outline I've used successfully in my summer seminars I give on the topic to thousands of parents every year. It really works, because past participants contact me constantly to let me know what a difference my classes have made in their lives. (4)

In addition to marketing and selling *Taking Care of Yourself and Your Kids* at my summer seminars, I would also be able to sell it through my website and promote it through my weekly e-newsletter with over 25,000 subscribers. Of course, it would also make a very nice trade title that I think would sell well in bookstores and possibly retail outlets, such as Wal-Mart and Target. (5)

Please contact me for a copy of my full book proposal today. (6)

Thank you for your consideration.

Marilyn Parent
8647 Query St.
Norman OK 00000
mparent8647@email.com
www.marilynsbetterparents.com

(1) Effective subject line. Lets me know exactly what to expect when I open the e-mail. (2) Good lead. Six kids and teaches high school. I already trust her as an expert. (3) Nice title that would fit well with others we currently offer. (4) Her platform as a speaker definitely gets my attention. (5) 25,000 e-mail subscribers? She must have a very good voice to gather that many readers. (6) I was interested after the first paragraph, but every paragraph after made it impossible to not request her proposal.

BAD NONFICTION BOOK QUERY

To: info@bigbookspublishing.com
Subject: a question for you (1)

I really liked this book by Mega Book Publishers called *Build Better Trains in Your Own Backyard.* It was a great book that covered all the basics of model train building. My father and I would read from it together and assemble all the pieces, and it was magical like Christmas all through the year. Why wouldn't you want to publish such a book? (2)

Well, here it is. I've already copyrighted the material for 2006 and can help you promote it if you want to send me on a worldwide book tour. As you can see from my attached digital photo, I'm not the prettiest person, but I am passionate. (3)

There are at least 1,000 model train builders in the United States alone, and there might be even more than that. I haven't done enough research yet, because I don't know if this is an idea that appeals to you. If you give me maybe $500, I could do that research in a day and get back to you on it. (4)

Anyway, this idea is a good one that brings back lots of memories for me.

Jacob (5)

(1) The subject line is so vague I almost deleted this e-mail as spam without even opening it. (2) The reason we don't publish such a book is easy—we don't do hobby titles. (3) I'm not going to open an attachment from an unknown sender via e-mail. Also, copyrighting your work years before pitching is the sign of an amateur. (4) 1,000 possible buyers is a small market, and I'm not going to pay a writer to do research on a proposal. (5) Not even a last name? Or contact information? At least I won't feel guilty for not responding.

GOOD FICTION BOOK QUERY

Jeremy Mansfield, editor
Novels R Us Publishing
8787 Big Time Street
New York NY 00000

Dear Mr. Mansfield,

My 62,000-word novel, *The Cat Walk,* is a psychologically complex thriller in the same mold as James Patterson's Alex Cross novels, but with a touch of the supernatural a la Stephenie Meyer. (1)

Rebecca Frank is at the top of the modeling world, posing for magazines in exotic locales all over the world and living life to its fullest. Despite all her success, she feels something is missing in her life. Then she runs into Marcus Hunt, a wealthy bachelor with cold blue eyes and an ambiguous past.

Within 24 hours of meeting Marcus, Rebecca's understanding of the world turns upside down, and she finds herself fighting for her life and the love of a man who may not have the ability to return her the favor.

Filled with demons, serial killers, trolls, maniacal clowns and more, *The Cat Walk* follows Rebecca through a gauntlet of trouble and turmoil, leading up to a final climactic realization that may lead to her own unraveling. (2)

The Cat Walk should fit in well with your other titles, such as *Bone Dead* and *Carry Me Home*, though it is a unique story. Your website mentioned supernatural suspense as a current interest, so I hope this is a good match. (3)

My short fiction has appeared in many mystery magazines, including a prize-winning story in *The Mysterious Oregon Quarterly*. This novel is the first in a series that I'm working on (already half-way through the second). (4)

As stated in your guidelines, I've included the first 30 pages. Thank you for considering *The Cat Walk*.

Sincerely,

Merry Plentiful
54 Willow Road
East Lansing MI 00000
merry865423@email.com

(1) Novel is correct length and has the suspense and supernatural elements we're seeking. (2) The quick summary sounds like something we would write on the back cover of our paperbacks. That's a good thing, because it identifies the triggers that draw a response out of our readers. (3) She mentions similar titles we've done and that she's done research on our website. She's not afraid to put in a little extra effort. (4) At the moment, I'm not terribly concerned that this book could become a series, but it is something good to file away in the back of my mind for future use.

BAD FICTION BOOK QUERY

Jeremy Mansfield
Novels R Us Publishing
8787 Big Time Street
New York NY 00000

Dear Editor,

My novel has an amazing twist ending that could make it a worldwide phenomenon overnight while you are sleeping. It has spectacular special effects that will probably lead to a multi-million dollar movie deal that will also spawn action figures, lunch boxes, and several other crazy subsidiary rights. I mean, we're talking big-time money here. ❶

I'm not going to share the twist until I have a signed contract that authorizes me to a big bank account, because I don't want to have my idea stolen and used to promote whatever new initiative "The Man" has in mind for media nowadays. Let it be known that you will be rewarded handsomely for taking a chance on me. ❷

Did you know that George Lucas once took a chance on an actor named Harrison Ford by casting him as Han Solo in Star Wars? Look at how that panned out. Ford went on to become a big actor in the Indiana Jones series, *The Fugitive, Blade Runner*, and more. It's obvious that you taking a risk on me could play out in the same dramatic way. ❸

I realize that you've got to make money, and guess what? I want to make money too. So we're on the same page, you and I. We both want to make money, and we'll stop at nothing to do so.

If you want me to start work on this amazing novel with an incredible twist ending, just send a one-page contract agreeing to pay me a lot of money if we hit it big. No other obligations will apply. If it's a bust, I won't sue you for millions. ❹

Sincerely,

Kenzel Pain
92 Bad Writer Road
Austin TX 00000

① While I love to hear enthusiasm from a writer about his or her work, this kind of unchecked excitement is worrisome for an editor. ② I need to know the twist to make a decision on whether to accept the manuscript. Plus, I'm troubled by the paranoia and emphasis on making a lot of money. ③ I'm confused. Does he think he's Harrison Ford? ④ So that's the twist: He hasn't even written the novel yet. There's no way I'm going to offer a contract for a novel that hasn't been written by someone with no experience or idea of how the publishing industry works.

LANDING THE SIX-FIGURE DEAL

What Makes Your Proposal Hot

by SJ Hodges

It's the question every first-time author wants to ask:

"If I sell my book, will the advance even cover my rent?"

Authors, I am happy to tell you that, yes, the six-figure book deal for a newbie still exists—even if you're not a celebrity with your own television show! As a ghostwriter, I work with numerous authors and personalities to develop both nonfiction and fiction proposals, and I've seen unknown first-timers land life-changing deals even in a down economy. Is platform the ultimate key to their success? You better believe it's a huge consideration for publishers, but here's the good news: Having a killer platform is only one element that transforms a "nice deal" into a "major deal."

You still have to ensure the eight additional elements of your proposal qualify as major attractions. Daniela Rapp, editor at St. Martin's Press explains, "In addition to platform, authors need to have a fantastic, original idea. They have to truly be an expert in their field and they must be able to write." So how do you craft a proposal that conveys your brilliance, your credentials, your talent and puts a couple extra zeroes on your check?

ONE: NARRATIVE OVERVIEW

Before you've even written word one of your manuscript, you are expected to, miraculously, summarize the entirety of your book in such a compelling and visceral way that a publisher or agent will feel as if they are reading the *New York Times* review. Sound impossible? That's because it is.

That's why I'm going to offer two unorthodox suggestions. First, consider writing the first draft of your overview after you've created your table of contents and your chapter outlines. You'll know much more about the content and scope of your material even if you're not 100 percent certain about the voice and tone. That's why you'll take another pass after you complete your sample chapters. Because then you'll be better acquainted with the voice of your book which brings me to unorthodox suggestion number two… treat your overview as literature.

I believe every proposal component needs to be written "in voice" especially because your overview is the first page the editor sees after the title page. By establishing your voice on the page immediately, your proposal becomes less of a sales document and more of a page-turner. Remember, not everyone deciding your fate works in marketing and sales. Editors still have some buying power and they are readers, first and foremost.

TWO: TABLE OF CONTENTS AND CHAPTER OUTLINES

Television writers call this "breaking" a script. This is where you break your book or it breaks you. This is where you discover if what you plan to share with the world actually merits 80,000 words and international distribution.

Regardless of whether you're writing fiction or nonfiction, this element of your proposal must take your buyer on a journey (especially if it's nonfiction) and once more, I'm a big fan of approaching this component with creativity particularly if you're exploring a specific historical time period, plan to write using a regional dialect, rely heavily on "slanguage," and especially if the material is highly technical and dry.

This means you'll need to style your chapter summaries and your chapter titles as a form of dramatic writing. Think about the arc of the chapters, illuminating the escalating conflict, the progression towards a resolution, in a cinematic fashion. Each chapter summary should end with an "emotional bumper," a statement that simultaneously summarizes and entices in the same way a television show punches you in the gut before they cut to a commercial.

Is it risky to commit to a more creative approach? Absolutely. Will it be perfect the first time you write it? No. The fifth time you write it? No. The tenth time? Maybe. But the contents and chapter summary portion of your proposal is where you really get a chance to show off your skills as an architect of plot and structure and how you make an editor's job much, much easier. According to Lara Asher, acquisitions editor at Globe Pequot Press, it is the single most important component of your proposal. "If I can't easily understand what a book is trying to achieve then I can't present it to my colleagues," Asher says. "It won't make it through the acquisitions process."

THREE: YOUR AUTHOR BIO

Your author bio page must prove that you are more than just a pro, that you are recognized by the world at large as "the definitive expert" on your topic, that you have firsthand experience tackling the problems and implementing your solutions, and that you've seen positive results not only in your personal life but in the lives of others. You have to have walked the walk and talked the talk. You come equipped with a built-in audience, mass media attention, and a strong social network. Your bio assures your buyer that you are the right writer exploring the right topic at the right time.

FOUR: YOUR PLATFORM

Platform, platform, platform. Sit through any writing conference, query any agent, lunch with any editor and you'll hear the "P" word over and over again. What you won't hear is hard-and-fast numbers about just how large this platform has to be in order to secure a serious offer. Is there an audience-to-dollar-amount ratio that seems to be in play? Are publishers paying per head?

"I haven't found this to be the case," says Julia Pastore, former editor for Random House. "It's easier to compel someone to 'Like' you on Facebook or follow you on Twitter than it is to compel them to plunk down money to buy your book. Audience engagement is more important than the sheer number of social media followers."

With that said, if you're shooting for six-figures, publishers expect you'll have big numbers and big plans. Your platform will need to include:

Cross-promotional partnerships

These are organizations or individuals that already support you, are already promoting your brand, your products or your persona. If you host a show on HGTV or Nike designed a tennis racket in your honor, they definitely qualify. If, however, you're not rolling like an A-lister just yet, you need to brainstorm any and every possible connection you have to organizations with reach in the 20,000 + range. Maybe your home church is only 200 people but the larger association serves 40,000 and you often write for their newsletter. Think big. Then think bigger.

Specific, verifiable numbers proving the loyalty of your audience

"Publishers want to see that you have direct contact with a loyal audience," says Maura Teitelbaum, an agent at Folio Literary Management. Meaning a calendar full of face-to-face speaking engagements, a personal mailing list, extensive database and verifiable traffic to your author website.

But how much traffic does there need to be? How many public appearances? How many e-mails in your Constant Contact newsletter? Publishers are loathe to quote concrete numbers for "Likes" and "Followers" so I'll stick my neck out and do it instead. At a minimum, to land a basic book deal, meaning a low five-figure sum, you'll need to prove that you've got 15,000-20,000 fans willing to follow you into hell and through high water.

For a big six-figure deal, you'll need a solid base of 100,000 rabid fans plus access to hundreds of thousands more. If not millions. Depressed yet? Don't be. Because we live in a time when things as trivial as angry oranges or as important as scientific TED talks can go viral and propel a writer out of obscurity in a matter of seconds. It is only your job to become part of the conversation. And once your foot is in the door, you'll be able to gather…

Considerable media exposure

Publishers are risk averse. They want to see that you're a media darling achieving pundit status. Organize and present all your clips, put together a DVD demo reel of your on-air appearances and be able to quote subscriber numbers and demographics about the publications running your articles or features about you.

Advance praise from people who matter

Will blurbs really make a difference in the size of your check? "I would include as many in a proposal as possible," says Teitelbaum. "Especially if those people are willing to write letters of commitment saying they will promote the book via their platform. That shows your efforts will grow exponentially."

FIVE: PROMOTIONAL PLANS

So what is the difference between your platform and your promotional plan? Your promotional plan must demonstrate specifically how you will activate your current platform and the expected sales results of that activation. These are projections starting three to six months before your book release date and continuing for one year after its hardcover publication. They want your guarantee to sell 15,000 books within that first year.

In addition, your promotional plan also issues promises about the commitments you are willing to make in order to promote the book to an even wider market. This is your expansion plan. How will you broaden your reach and who will help you do it? Publishers want to see that your goals are ambitious but doable.

Think about it this way. If you own a nail salon and you apply for a loan to shoot a movie, you're likely to be rejected. But ask for a loan to open your second salon and your odds get much better. In other words, keep your promotional plans in your wheelhouse while still managing to include:

- Television and radio appearances
- Access to print media
- A massive social media campaign
- Direct e-mail solicitations
- E-commerce and back of room merchandising
- New joint partnerships
- Your upcoming touring & speaking Schedule with expected audience

You'll notice that I did not include hiring a book publicist as a requirement. Gone are the days when an advance-sucking, three-month contract with a book publicist makes any difference. For a six-figure author, publishers expect there is a team in place: a powerful agent, a herd of assistants and a more generalized media publicist already managing the day-to-day affairs of building your brand, growing your audience. Hiring a book publicist at the last minute is useless.

SIX: YOUR MARKET ANALYSIS

It would seem the odds against a first-time author hitting the jackpot are slim but that's where market analysis provides a glimmer of hope. There are actually markets considered more desirable to publishers. "Broader is generally better for us," says Rapp. "Niche generally implies small. Not something we [St. Martin's Press] can afford to do these days. Current affairs books, if they are explosive and timely, can work. Neuroscience is hot. Animal books (not so much animal memoirs) still work. Military books sell."

"The health and diet category will always be huge," says Asher. "But in a category like parenting which is so crowded, we look for an author tackling a niche topic that hasn't yet been covered."

Niche or broad, your market analysis must position your book within a larger context, addressing the needs of the publishing industry, the relevant cultural conversations happening in the zeitgeist, your potential audience and their buying power and the potential for both domestic and international sales.

SEVEN: YOUR C.T.A.

Choose the books for your competitive title analysis not only for their topical similarities but also because the author has a comparable profile and platform to your own. Says Pastore, "It can be editorially helpful to compare your book to *Unbroken* by Hillenbrand, but unless your previous book was also a bestseller, this comparison won't be helpful to our sales force."

Limit your C.T.A. to five or six solid offerings then get on BookScan and make sure none of the books sold fewer than 10,000 copies. "Higher sales are preferable," says Rapp. "And you should leave it to the publisher to decide if the market can hold one more title or not. We always do our own research anyway, so just because the book is not mentioned in your line-up doesn't mean we won't know about it."

EIGHT: SAMPLE CHAPTERS

Finally, you have to/get to prove you can… write. Oh yeah, that!

This is the fun part, the pages of your proposal where you really get to shine. It is of upmost importance that these chapters, in harmony with your overview and chapter summaries, allow the beauty, wisdom and/or quirkiness of your voice to be heard. Loud and clear.

"Writing absolutely matters and strong sample chapters are crucial." Pastore explains, "An author must be able to turn their brilliant idea into engaging prose on the page."

Approach the presentation of these chapters creatively. Consider including excerpts from several different chapters and not just offering the standard Introduction, Chapter One and Two. Consider the inclusion of photographs to support the narrative, helping your editor put faces to names. Consider using sidebar or box quotes from the narrative throughout your proposal to build anticipation for the actual read.

NINE: YOUR ONE-PAGER

Lastly, you'll need a one-pager, which is a relatively new addition to the book proposal format. Publishers now expect an author to squeeze a 50- or 60-page proposal down to a one-page summary they can hand to their marketing and sales teams. In its brevity, the one-pager must provide your buyer with "a clear vision of what the book is, why it's unique, why you are the best person to write it, and how we can reach the audience," says Pastore. And it must do that in fewer than 1,000 words. There is no room to be anything but impressive.

And if you're shooting for that six-figure deal, impressive is what each component of your book proposal must be. Easy? No. But still possible? Yes.

SJ HODGES is an 11-time published playwright, ghostwriter and editor. Her most recent book, a memoir co-authored with Animal Planet's "Pit Boss" Shorty Rossi was purchased by Random House/Crown, hit #36 on the Amazon bestseller list and went into its 3rd printing less than six weeks after its release date. As a developmental editor, SJ has worked on books published by Vanguard Press, Perseus Book Group and St. Martin's Press. SJ is a tireless advocate for artists offering a free listing for jobs, grants and fellowships at her Facebook page: facebook.com/constantcreator. She can be reached through her website: sjhodges.com.

HOW TO FIND SUCCESS IN THE MAGAZINE WORLD

by Kerrie Flanagan

Contrary to popular belief, magazines are still going strong. According to the latest study by the Magazine Publishers of America there are over 20,000 magazines in print. This is good news if you are looking to write for magazines. But before you jump in, there are a few things you should know that will increase your chances of getting an acceptance letter.

KNOW THE READER

Every magazine has a certain readership; teenage girl, mother of young children, budget traveler and so on. It is imperative you know as much about that reader as you can before submitting a query to the editor, because the more you know about who reads the magazine, the more you can tailor your query, article, or essay to best reach that audience.

Geoff Van Dyke, deputy editor of the Denver magazine *5280* said, "I wish people would truly read the magazine, like cover to cover, and understand our readership and voice and mission before sending queries. Sometimes—more often than not—writers submit queries that make it clear that they don't really understand *5280*, don't understand our readers or our mission, and, thus, the query is a bad fit. If they just spend a little more time on the front end, it would make all the difference."

So how can you find out who is the target audience for a specific magazine? The key is in the advertising. Companies spend thousands of dollars getting their messages out to their consumers. They are only going to invest their money in a magazine directed at their target market. By paying attention to the ads in a publication (and this goes for online too) you can learn a lot about the reader. What are the ages of the people in the ads? Are they families? Singles? What types of products are highlighted? Expensive clothes? Organic foods? Luxury cars and world travel or family cars and domestic travel?

Another way to find out the demographics of the reader is to locate the media kit on the magazine's website. This is a document intended to provide information to potential advertisers about their readership, but is a gold mine for freelance writers. The media kit provides information like the average age, income, gender, hobbies, home ownership, education and marital status.

This becomes invaluable when looking at ideas and topics to pitch to a magazine. For instance, in the media kit for *5280* magazine, 71 percent of the readers are married, 93 percent own their own home and 78 percent have lived in Colorado for more than 10 years or are natives of the state. With this little bit of information, pitching an article on where to find the best deals on apartments in Denver, is definitely not a good fit since most of their readers own their own home. An article on the best bars in Denver to meet other singles is also not a good idea for this publication, but one on the most romantic weekend getaways in Colorado to take your spouse is a possibility. It is also clear that, when writing the article, time does not have to be spent explaining to the reader things about Colorado that people who live in the state already know since 78 percent of the readers have been there for more than a decade.

KNOW THE MAGAZINE

Once you understand the reader, then you need to familiarize yourself with the actual magazine. Take the time to explore who are the writers, the length of the articles and the departments.

Tom Hess, editor with *Encompass Magazine* wishes more writers would take the time to know his magazine, in all its forms, before querying. "Too few writers make the effort, and those who do, get my immediate attention."

One way to do this with print magazines is to literally take apart the magazine. To see who writes for the magazine, find the masthead, the page in the front of the magazine that lists the editors and contributing writers. Tear it out so you have it as a reference. Now, go through the magazine, page by page and make a note by each article with a byline to find out who wrote the piece. Was it an editor? A contributing editor? If you can't find their names on the masthead, then they are typically freelance writers. A contributing editor is usually not on staff, but writes frequently for the magazine.

Now go through and pay attention to the length of articles and the various departments. How many feature stories are there? Is there a back page essay? Are there short department pieces in the front?

By knowing all of this information, you can better direct your query to the areas of the magazine that are more open to freelance writers and tailor your idea to better fit the type of articles they publish.

KNOW THE STYLE

Each magazine has its own style and tone. It's what makes the difference between *The New Yorker* and *Time*. Some magazines are very literary, others are more informational, so it is important to study the magazines to have a good understanding of their style.

Below are two travel writing examples portraying Ketchikan, Alaska, but with very different styles. As you read over each selection, pay attention to the style by looking at the use of quotes, the point of view (first person, third person…), the descriptions and the overall tone of the article.

Example 1

> *In Ketchikan, there are many great things to see and do. The roots of the three Native Alaskan tribes, the Tlingit, Haida, and Tsimshian run deep on this island where you can find the world's largest collection of totem poles. In a beautiful cove, eight miles north of downtown is Totem Bight State Park where 14 historic totems are found along with a native clanhouse. Totems can also be viewed at the Totem Heritage Center and the Southest Discovery Center. At the Saxman Tribal house and at the Metlakatla Long House, skilled groups bring Native dance to life with regular performances.*

Example 2

> *The rest of the world disappeared when I entered this lush, green rainforest. Stillness and peace embraced me while I strolled on the wooden walkway, in awe of the surrounding beauty: moss hung from trees, foliage so dense it provided shelter from the rain and beautiful rivers flowed, in search of the ocean. Ketchikan, Alaska, is in the heart of the Tongass National Forest, and an unlikely place to find the Earth's largest remaining temperate rainforest.*

The first article provides information and facts about traveling to Ketchikan to see the totem poles. This article would be a good fit for a magazine like *Family Motor Coaching*. The second article definitely has a different style; one that is more poetic and descriptive and more likely to be found in *National Geographic Traveler*.

Both pieces are good but are unique in their style and tone. By understanding this aspect of a magazine, your query or article can better reflect the voice of the publication and increase your chances of an assignment and well-received article.

KNOW THE GUIDELINES

Most magazines put together submission guidelines, spelling out exactly what they are looking for with articles and how to submit your idea to them.

"I wish writers would understand exactly what kind of material we are looking for," said Russ Lumpkin, managing editor of *Gray's Sporting Journal*, "and that they would adhere strictly to our submission guidelines. We publish fly fishing and hunting stories and accept only digital submissions via e-mail. A poem about watching butterflies submitted through the mail creates work that falls out of my ordinary work flow. And that's aggravating."

The submission guidelines are usually found in the "About Us" or "Contact Us" section on a magazine's website as well as in great resources like *Writer's Market*. Read the guidelines carefully and follow them when submitting your query or article.

KNOW HOW TO WRITE AN EFFECTIVE QUERY LETTER

Once you have done all your upfront research and have found a magazine that is a good fit for your idea, it is time to write a good query letter. The letter should be professional and written in a style and tone similar to the article you are pitching.

Robbin Gould, editor of *Family Motor Coaching* believes a writer needs to submit as comprehensive a query as possible and be fully aware of the magazine's focus, particularly when dealing with a niche publication. "A writer who misuses terms or makes erroneous statements about the subject he or she proposes to cover indicates a lack of knowledge to the editor," says Gould. "Or a query that simply states, 'Would you be interested in an article about XXX?' with minimal explanation wastes everyone's time and suggests the writer is looking for any publication to take the article. If the writer doesn't show much attention to detail up front, the editor probably won't spend much time considering the idea."

There are basic components that should be included in every query letter.

- **Salutation (Dear Mr. Smith).** Find out who the correct editor is to direct your query. You should be able to find this information online. If not make a quick phone call to the publishing company and ask, "Who would I direct a travel query to?" Ask for spelling and the editor's e-mail. Unless you know the editor, use a formal salutation with Mr., Mrs., or Ms. If you are not sure if the editor is a man or woman, put their full name.
- **Good Hook.** You have about 10 seconds to catch the attention of an editor. The opening should be about one to three sentences in length and needs to lure the editor in right away.
- **Article Content.** This is the bulk of your query and should be about one paragraph. It will focus on the main points of the article and the topics you plan to cover.
- **Specifics.** Here you will include the specifics of the article: word count, department where you think it will fit, possible experts you are going to interview and other information pertinent to the piece.
- **Purpose.** In one sentence, share the purpose of your article. Will your article inform, educate, inspire, or entertain?
- **Qualifications.** This is not the place to be shy. You need to convince the editor that you are the perfect person to write this article. If you do not have any published clips, then really expand more on your experiences that relate to your article. If you are pitching a parenting article and you have six kids, mention that. It clearly positions you as an expert in the parenting field.
- **Sending.** Most magazines accept and want queries by e-mail. When sending a query via e-mail, include your information in the body of the message, not in an attachment. Make sure your contact information is at the bottom of

the e-mail. Put something noticeable in the subject line. For example: "QUERY: The Benefits of Chocolate and the Creative Process."

By following all the steps in this article you will be ready set off on a magazine-writing journey equipped with the necessary tools and confidence to get your queries noticed, and, in the end, see your articles in print.

KERRIE FLANAGAN has 130+ published articles and essays to her credit. In addition she is the director of Northern Colorado Writers, a group she founded in 2007 that supports and encourages writers of all levels and genres through classes, networking events, retreats and an annual writer's conference. Kerrie is also available for writing coaching. Visit her website for more information about her and NCW. www.KerrieFlanagan.com.

9 SECRETS OF SIX-FIGURE FREELANCERS

by Mridu Khullar Relph

What are some of the things that six-figure freelancers do that regular folks don't? In researching this topic for my book *Secrets of Six-Figure Freelancers* and trying to cross over that magical threshold myself, I made a few surprising discoveries.

Turns out, making a six-figure living as a freelance writer or journalist is not only about strategy, it's also about mindset, lifestyle, and habit.

In talking to more than two dozen six-figure freelancers, here are the commonalities I've found.

SECRET #1: THEY STRETCH THEMSELVES CONSTANTLY.

Ask a six-figure freelancer if they know about content marketing and most of them will list off at least half a dozen clients they have that do exactly that. Crowdsourcing? They've tried it. E-books? Most of them have self-published at least one. Not that the e-books made them any money, mind you, and not even one six-figure freelancer I interviewed said that the e-book added any substantial weight to their income, but they'd tried it. They'd had the willingness to put in the time and effort into something new, even if it didn't eventually add multiple zeroes to their income.

In fact, trying new things and creating additional income streams was a common goal amongst six-figure freelancers. While most of them identified as writers and journalists, they also brought in money (both large and small paychecks) from websites, traditional book deals, books they'd self-published, speaking engagements, teaching, and coaching. None of them were dependent on one income stream to generate all their income, which also ensured that when one part of their business was generating less cash, they were easily able to make up that deficit through other areas.

Most have pitched and been rejected (or met with silence) by *The New Yorker*.

SECRET #2: THEY TAKE RISKS.

Many of the six-figure freelancers I spoke to advised that writers create a safety net—

three to six months of living expenses in the bank—before they quit their jobs to go full-time. Yet, did they do the same when they were starting out? Mostly, no, and ironically, many of them attribute their success to that very fact. Quitting their jobs and taking up freelancing full-time when they had no other source of income forced six-figure freelancers I interviewed to hustle like no one's business. They had no safety net, no plan B, and therefore, many of them felt that they had no choice but to earn money, and earn good money at this chosen career path. By taking away the choice, they forced themselves to come up with creative solutions to problems, write when they didn't particularly feel like it, and contact clients for work even when it felt uncomfortable. They showed up to work every single day and performed because not doing so was never an option.

Many of them attributed their current work ethic to these early days and years of training themselves to write even when they weren't in the mood.

SECRET #3: THEY WORK INCREDIBLY LONG HOURS.

This wasn't particularly inspiring or welcome news, but most of the six-figure freelancers I interviewed worked very long and hard hours. While some managed to hit the magic number despite part-time hours (less than 20 hours a week), most six-figure freelancers work somewhere between 40 and 60 hours, and some even log in as many as 80.

The good news, however, is that many of these six-figure freelancers felt that they were working these long hours not because of economic necessity, but because they really enjoyed their work and liked putting time into helping their business grow. Most felt they could easily scale back if they wanted to without a massive drop in revenue.

SECRET #4: THEY'RE IN STABLE RELATIONSHIPS.

Speaking of happiness, six-figure freelancers are typically in stable, happy relationships—many of them happily married for many years—or at peace with whatever relationship situation they find themselves in. For most, a lack of drama on the home front was an important factor in ensuring that they could work through the challenges in their freelancing careers. Further, a supportive spouse or partner was, for many, essential in getting through the lean times and the encouragement they received at home enabled them to go out confidently and perform at work.

SECRET #5: THEY SET GOALS.

While many six-figure freelancers sailed over the threshold without even realizing it, most actually had that number in their minds for a few years before they hit it. They worked towards the goal, keeping track of their earnings, their most profitable clients, and their hourly rate. They almost always tracked their time, had Excel worksheets filled with data about hours worked, rates per assignment, and most importantly, weekly and monthly income goals that allowed them to stay on track with the big yearly number.

For most freelancers who eventually hit the six-figure mark, it didn't happen the first year they decided to hit this number, not even for the next three. But within five years, most of the freelancers I spoke to had achieved their goal. They stayed committed to it, even when it felt difficult and unachievable, and eventually found that the numbers kept growing, until they were able to hit the $100,000 mark.

SECRET #6: THEY SAY NO. A LOT.

A side effect of setting goals and knowing what they need to bring in each month, week, and day means that six-figure freeancers often have very specific limits of what they won't accept in terms of compensation. Many I spoke to had a minimum hourly rate that they mentally calculate for every assignment they're offered (typically $100 an hour) and several had a $500 baseline, that is, they wouldn't accept any project that fell below that number. Three $200 projects ended up being a lot more work, they found, than one $600 project because of the starting and stopping and mental energy that went into the three projects.

Further, not one six-figure freelancer I spoke to felt any hesitation in turning down projects or assignments that they felt didn't move them towards their financial (or other) goals. They considered it a sign of their professionalism to be able to turn down work that didn't meet their needs than to take on everything that came their way. Almost all had turned down work in the last six months.

SECRET #7: THEY JOIN AND REMAIN A PART OF PROFESSIONAL NETWORKS.

Six-figure freelancers believe in mentorship, in professional networking, in creating supportive communities surrounding their work, and partnering with like-minded people in order to work towards common goals. Most six-figure freelancers are a part of two or more networking organizations, groups, or online forums, and frequently join Facebook and LinkedIn groups they feel will help them connect with other writers in their industries.

They're committed to learning, I found, and a huge chunk of that comes from these professional organizations and associations. A large number of six-figure freelancers I interviewed had attended at least one conference in the last two years and several made it a point each year to set aside money for professional training, coaching, conference travel, and online courses. Most had at least two or three freelancers in their networks that they would consider close personal friends that they could rely on for support and advice.

SECRET #8: THEY'RE OPTIMISTIC ABOUT THE FUTURE.

It could be argued that any writing professional at that level of income would, of course, be optimistic about the future of writing, their careers, and their earning potential, but in most cases, the optimism came first and the money arrived later, most likely a consequence of that optimism and faith. Writers who believed—and continued to believe, in the face of adversity and periods of low income—that there was enough work out there for them, were more likely to actually hit that number.

It's pretty simple, really. The six-figure freelancers who believed that there was work out there that could pay well and keep them happy, were also much more likely to turn down work that didn't pay well, to negotiate harder, and to come up with creative ways to find it. They also were much more likely to market themselves regularly because they believed that this marketing would indeed, lead to rewards. Writers who don't believe that their six-figure share is there for the taking are often operating from a deficit mentality, that is, they think that if they don't accept the low-paying work, they may not get any work at all. They're all much more likely to give up on marketing when it doesn't yield results quickly.

SECRET #9: THEY BUILD RELATIONSHIPS.

Almost all the six-figure freelancers I interviewed had a core group of regular clients that were responsible for a large chunk of their income. Most of them said they had anchor clients, people who came to them repeatedly for work, giving them a guaranteed number each week or month that ensured a steady income and freed up hours for marketing that could be utilized elsewhere. Six-figure freelancers make it a point to keep in touch with former contacts and clients and to continue nurturing those professional relationships in big and little ways, such as calling every now and again, making a trip to New York City to meet all their editors, or sending holiday cards in the mail at the end of the year to each client. These small efforts often led to them being top of mind for clients and got them repeat work.

MRIDU KHULLAR RELPH is a multiple award-winning freelance writer and journalist who divides her time between New Delhi, India, and London, UK. She has lived and worked in Asia, Africa, Europe, and North America, and writes for *The New York Times*, *TIME*, CNN, ABC News (Australia), *The Independent*, *Global Post*, Parade.com, *Ms.*, and *The Christian Science Monitor*, among others. Mridu also runs The International Freelancer at www.TheInternationalFreelancer.com..

EARN A FULL-TIME INCOME FROM BLOGGING

by Carol Tice

It sounds like a dream: Instead of sending query letters and relying on editors to give you paying assignments, you start your own blog and turn it into a money-maker. No matter where in the world you want to live, you're able to earn a good living.

For a growing number of writers, it's not a dream. I'm among the writers who now earn more from their own blogs than they do from freelance assignments.

But it's not easy, by any means. The vast majority of blogs never find an audience and their authors never earn a dime. It's hard to stand out—at the end of 2011, pollster Nielsen reported there were over 181 million blogs, up from 36 million in 2006.

In this vast sea of blogs, how can you write one that stands out and becomes the basis for a money-earning business? It begins with setting up the blog to attract a loyal readership. Once you build an audience, there are a limited number of ways you can earn income from your blog audience—I spotlight the five of the most popular methods below.

SETTING IT UP TO EARN

Many blogs don't attract readers because they lack basic elements of design and usability that make blogs appealing, says Seattle WordPress trainer Bob Dunn (www.bobwp.com). Dunn's own blog is the platform on which he's built his business.

How do you create an attractive blog?

Use a professional platform

Free blog platforms such as Blogger and Moveable Type have limitations that make it hard to look professional (and some free platforms prohibit commerce). If you're serious about blogging, pay for a host and use WordPress—it's now the dominant blogging platform, Technorati reports.

Offer contact information

Many bloggers cultivate an air of mystery, using a pen name and providing no contact info. But readers want to know who you are and be able to e-mail you questions, says Dunn.

Have an "About" page

With a million scams on the Internet, the About page has become a vital blog component—it's usually the most-visited page after the Home page, Dunn says. This is the place where readers get to know you and learn why you write your blog.

"I can't tell you how many times I go on a blog and there's no About page," says, Dunn. "It should be more than a resume, too—tell a story."

Clean up the design

No matter how wonderful your writing is, if your blog is a clutter of tiny type, dark backgrounds, multiple sidebars, and flashing ads, readers will leave, Dunn says. Begin with a simple, graphical header, title, and tagline that quickly communicate what your blog is about. You have just a few seconds in which to convey what you write about before readers leave, so be clear.

Make navigation simple

Many bloggers end up with multiple rows of tabs or long drop-down menus. Try to simplify—for every additional click you require, you will lose some readers, Dunn says.

Pick a niche topic

While most blogs ramble about whatever the author feels like discussing that day, business-focused blogs stick to a subject or a few related topics, notes Dunn. This allows you to attract and keep readers interested in your subject.

Create useful content

Write with your readers' needs in mind, rather than about your own interests, says Mexico-based Jon Morrow. His year-old blog Boost Blog Traffic (boostblogtraffic.com) earned $500,000 in 2012. If you don't know what readers want, Morrow says, take polls and ask questions to find out.

Write strong headlines

If you want readers to find your posts online, your headlines need key words and phrases that relate to your topic, to help them rank well in Google searches for your topic. You can do keyword research free using Google's tool (https://adwords.google.com/o/KeywordTool). Headlines also need to be lively and interesting to draw readers—Morrow offers a Headline Hacks report on his blog that dissects effective headline styles.

Use blog style

Blog posts are different from magazine articles because of how people read—make that skim—online, says Dunn. Good blog-post paragraphs are short, often just one or two sentences. Posts with bold subheads or bulleted or numbered lists are easy to scan and often enjoy higher readership.

Make sharing easy

To grow your audience, you'll need readers to spread the word, says Dunn. Make that easy with one-click sharing buttons for Twitter, Facebook and other popular social-media platforms. You should be active in these platforms, too, building relationships with influential people who might send you readers.

Start guest-posting

One of the fastest ways to build your blog audience is by guest-posting on popular blogs with lots of traffic. Your guest post will give you a link back to your own blog and allow new readers to find you. This is usually not paid work, but think of it as a marketing cost for your blog-based business. Many top blogs do accept guest posts—look for writer's guidelines on their sites.

"The big secret to making money from blogging is to get serious about marketing," Morrow says.

Build an e-mail list

The best way to stay in touch with readers is via an e-mail list visitors are encouraged to join, says Dunn. Subscribers who sign up through real simple syndication, or RSS, don't reveal their e-mail address, so it's hard to sell them anything.

START EARNING

Once your blog is set up to entice readers, you're ready to experiment with ways to generate income off your blog. Among the common approaches:

1. Freelance Gigs

Add a "Hire Me" tab to your site to begin attracting freelance blogging gigs from online businesses and publications. That's the approach U.K.-based writer Tom Ewer took when he quit his job and launched his blog Leaving Work Behind (www.leavingworkbehind.com) in 2011.

A brand-new writer at the time, Ewer quickly got a couple of freelance blogging clients by applying to online job ads. More clients approached him after seeing his guest posts on big blogs and finding his blog from there. Ewer was soon blogging for pay about topics including WordPress and government contracting. By late 2012, he was earning $4,000 a month as a paid blogger at $100 a post and up, working part-time hours.

A similar strategy worked for Nigerian blogger Bamidele Onibalusi, who began his online-earning themed blog YoungPrePro (www.youngprepro.com) in 2010, when he was just 16. By 2012, he was making $50,000 a year writing for blog owners who learned of him from his dozens of guest posts on top blogs including DailyBlogTips and ProBlogger.

He's blogged for paying clients in the United States, United Kingdom, Greece, and elsewhere about real estate, accounting, and weight loss, among other topics. Onibalusi says he impresses prospects with long, highly useful posts with strong key words that attract an ongoing stream of readers.

"Google has sent me most of my business," he says.

2. Books & E-books

Build a major following on your blog, and you can earn well writing and selling your own books and e-books. That strategy has been successful for Jeff Goins of the writing and social-change blog GoinsWriter (goinswriter.com), who has two Kindle e-books and a traditionally published print book under his belt.

Launched in 2010 and now boasting 25,000 subscribers, GoinsWriter has loyal fans who help drive more than $3,500 a month in sales of his two low-priced e-books, including his co-authored *You Are a Writer (So Start Acting Like One)*, which goes for just $2.99.

Goins first creates excitement around his e-books by blogging about the upcoming release first. Then, as the publication date nears, he gives more than 100 diehard fans a free PDF of the e-book in exchange for Amazon reviews. When he officially publishes a few days later on Amazon and elsewhere, the glowing reviews help encourage thousands of purchases. The reviews and frequent downloads keep his e-books ranking highly for the writing category, which drives more sales. Links in the e-book also help bring more blog readers.

E-book sales also kicked off the blog-earning career of Pat Flynn, a southern Californian who first had modest blog-monetizing success with an e-book he wrote on how to pass an architectural exam. He started the Smart Passive Income (www.smartpassiveincome.com) blog in 2008 to dissect that success. This second blog went on to greatly surpass the original project, bringing in over $200,000 its first year alone.

3. Affiliate Sales

Flynn earns primarily through affiliate sales, a strategy in which a blogger receives a commission for selling someone else's product or service. It's an approach that works best with a large audience—Smart Passive Income has 57,000 subscribers and gets 100,000 visitors a month.

His audience includes many bloggers who need to set up their websites, so many of his affiliate products are tools or services that enable bloggers. Flynn's top-selling affiliate product in 2012 was website host Bluehost, from which he now typically earns $20,000 or more monthly. He receives a commission every time someone signs up for website hosting through his unique affiliate links.

"I find products that help them get from A to Z," he says. "They're recommended products I've actually used. You want to be sort of an expert in it."

Flynn builds loyalty by creating free blog posts that offer "high value content that would usually require payment." Rather than slapping up ads that might annoy readers, he simply states that site links earn him a commission. Fans are happy to click, and even send him thank-you notes about the products he sells.

Like many top-earning bloggers, Flynn uses videos and podcasts to help promote his blogs. Flynn's Smart Passive Income Podcast has brought many new readers—it's one of the top business-related podcasts on iTunes and has seen more than 2 million downloads.

4. Courses & Coaching

When you've built your reputation through delivering useful blog posts, you can sell your fans more advanced information on your topic. Courses and coaching are the main earners for Boost Blog Traffic's Morrow, who teaches a guest-blogging class and takes just

10 students at a time in his $10,000-a-head, five-month coaching course. The secret sauce in the guest-blogging class includes personal introductions by Morrow to top blog editors.

Build your authority enough, and customers pay just for the opportunity to learn from someone they respect, says Morrow.

"I'm not really selling products," he says. "I'm selling me."

Morrow attributes part of his earning success to hard work to improve the marketing campaigns for his paid programs. He says he's spent hundreds of hours testing and tinkering with marketing e-mails and promotional videos that help sell the courses. Now that he's refined his process, he says he needs to spend only five hours a week on his guest-blogging course. Affiliates do much of the selling of his blogging course for him.

An extension of this teaching niche is public speaking, for which top presenters can earn tens of thousands of dollars per appearance. Morrow recently presented at the New Media Expo (formerly known as BlogWorld), for instance.

5. Membership Community

Once they're publishing, teaching, speaking, and creating audio and video materials on a topic, bloggers can leverage all that content to earn even more through a paid membership community. Inside the community, members can access large amounts of training materials and their favorite expert's advice via chat forums for one low monthly rate, instead of paying for it piecemeal. The community model allows bloggers to earn more as additional members join without having to do much more work, as members mostly access existing content.

Large communities can be major money generators—for instance, A-List Blogger Club (www.alistbloggingbootcamps.com/alist-blogger-club-join), a blog-building training community started by top blogger Leo Babauta of Zen Habits that I used to learn how to build my own blog, had roughly 900 members in 2012 paying $20 apiece per month. The blog Write to Done (writetodone.com) serves as the main platform that introduces writers to the club.

Blogging is not for every writer. It's a lot of work coming up with post ideas and writing several posts a month or even a week. It can be many months until a blog starts to earn money, and there are no guarantees it will ever catch on. But for writers with the drive to stick with it and a willingness to learn about blog marketing, the rewards can be rich.

CAROL TICE writes the Make a Living Writing (www.makealivingwriting.com) blog and runs the writers learning community Freelance Writers Den (freelancewritersden.com). She has written two nonfiction business books and co-authored the Kindle e-book *13 Ways to Get the Writing Done Faster* (www.amazon.com/Ways-Writing-Done-Faster-ebook/dp/B009XM03SK).

FUNDS FOR WRITERS 101

Find Money You Didn't Know Existed

by C. Hope Clark

When I completed writing my novel over a decade ago, I imagined the next step was simply to find a publisher and watch the book sell. Like most writers, my goal was to earn a living doing what I loved so I could walk away from the day job. No such luck. Between rejection and newfound knowledge that a novel can take years to sell enough for a single house payment, I opened my mind to other writing avenues. I learned that there's no *one* way to find funds to support your writing; instead there are *many.* So many, in fact, that I felt the need to share the volume of knowledge I collected, and I called it FundsforWriters.com.

Funds are money. But obtaining those funds isn't necessarily a linear process, or a one-dimensional path. As a serious writer, you study all options at your fingertips, entertaining financial resources that initially don't make sense as well as the obvious.

GRANTS

Grants come from government agencies, nonprofits, businesses and even generous individuals. They do not have to be repaid, as long as you use the grant as intended. No two are alike. Therefore, you must do your homework to find the right match between your grant need and the grant provider's mission. Grantors like being successful at their mission just as you like excelling at yours. So they screen applicants, ensuring they fit the rules and show promise to follow through.

Don't fear grants. Sure, you're judged by a panel, and rejection is part of the game, but you already know that as a writer. Gigi Rosenberg, author of *The Artist's Guide to Grant Writing*, states, "If one funder doesn't want to invest in your project, find another who does. And if nobody does, then begin it any way you can. Once you've started, that momentum will help your project find its audience and its financial support."

TYPES OF GRANTS

Grants can send you to retreats, handle emergencies, provide mentors, pay for conferences, or cover travel. They also can be called awards, fellowships, residencies, or scholarships. But like any aspect of your writing journey, define how any tool, even a grant, fits into your plans. Your mission must parallel a grantor's mission.

The cream-of-the-crop grants have no strings attached. Winning recipients are based upon portfolios and an application that defines a work-in-progress. You don't have to be a Pulitzer winner, but you must prove your establishment as a writer.

You find most of these opportunities in state arts commissions. Find them at www.nasaa-arts.org or as a partner listed at the National Endowment for the Arts website, www.nea.gov. Not only does your state's arts commission provide funding, but the players can direct you to other grant opportunities, as well as to artists who've gone before you. Speaking to grant winners gives you a wealth of information and a leg up in designing the best application.

Foundations and nonprofits fund the majority of grants. Most writers' organizations are nonprofits. Both the Mystery Writers of America (www.mysterywriters.org) and Society of Children's Book Writers and Illustrators (www.scbwi.org) offer scholarships and grants.

Many retreats are nonprofits. Journalist and freelancer Alexis Grant, (http://alexisgrant.com/) tries to attend a retreat a year. Some ask her to pay, usually on a sliding scale based upon income, and others provide scholarships. Each time, she applies with a clear definition of what she hopes to gain from the two to five-week trips. "It's a great way to get away from the noise of everyday responsibilities, focus on writing well and meet other people who prioritize writing. I always return home with a new perspective." One resource to find writing retreats is the Alliance of Artists Communities (www.artistcommunities.org/).

Laura Lee Perkins won four artist-in-residence slots with the National Park Service (www.nps.gov). The federal agency has 43 locations throughout the United States where writers and artists live for two to four weeks. From Acadia National Park in Maine to Sleeping Bear Dunes National Lakeshore in Michigan, Perkins spoke to tourists about her goals to write a book about Native American music. "Memories of the US National Parks' beauty and profound serenity will continue to enrich my work. Writers find unparalleled inspiration, quietude, housing, interesting staff, and a feeling of being in the root of your artistic desires."

Don't forget writers' conferences. While they may not advertise financial aid, many have funds available in times of need. Always ask as to the availability of a scholarship or work-share program that might enable your attendance.

Grants come in all sizes. FundsforWriters posts emergency grants on its grants page (www.fundsforwriters.com) as well as new grant opportunities such as the Sustainable Arts Foundation (www.sustainableartsfoundation.org) that offers grants to writers and artists with children under the age of 18, or the Awesome Foundation (www.awecomefoundation.org), which gives $1,000 grants to creative projects.

Novelist Joan Dempsey won an Elizabeth George Foundation grant (http://www.elizabethgeorgeonline.com/foundation/index.htm) in early 2012. "I applied to the Foundation for a research grant that included three trips to places relevant to my novel-in-progress, trips I otherwise could not have afforded. Not only does the grant provide travel funds, but it also provides validation that I'm a serious writer worthy of investment, which is great for my psyche and my resume."

FISCAL SPONSORSHIP

Nonprofits have access to an incredibly large number of grants that individuals do not, and have the ability to offer their tax-exempt status to groups and individuals involved in activities related to their mission. By allowing a nonprofit to serve as your grant overseer, you may acquire funds for your project.

Deborah Marshall is President of the Missouri Writers Guild (www.missouriwritersguild.org) and founder of the Missouri Warrior Writers Project, with ample experience with grants in the arts. "Although grant dollars are available for individual writers, writing the grant proposal becomes difficult without significant publication credits. Partnering with a nonprofit organization, whether it is a writing group, service, community organization, or any 501(c)3, can fill in those gaps to make a grant application competitive. Partnering not only helps a writer's name become known, but it also assists in building that all-important platform."

Two excellent groups that offer fiscal sponsorship for writers are The Fractured Atlas (www.fracturedatlas.org) and Artspire (www.artspire.org) sponsored by the New York Foundation for the Arts and open to all US citizens. Visit The Foundation Center (www.foundationcenter.org) for an excellent tutorial guide to fiscal sponsorship.

CROWD SOURCING

Crowd sourcing is a co-op arrangement where people support artists directly, much like the agricultural co-op movement where individuals fund farming operations in exchange for fresh food. Kickstarter (www.kickstarter.com) has made this funding method successful in the arts.

Basically, the writer proposes his project, and for a financial endorsement as low as $1, donors receive some token in return, like an autographed book, artwork, or bookmark. The higher the donation, the bigger the *wow* factor in the gift. Donors do not receive ownership in the project.

Meagan Adele Lopez (www.ladywholunches.net) presented her debut self-published book *Three Questions* to Kickstarter readers, requesting $4,400 to take her book on tour, create a book trailer, pre-order books, and redesign the cover. Eighty-eight backers pledged a total of $5,202. She was able to hire an editor and a company that designed film trailers. For every $750 she received over her plan, she added a new city to her book tour.

Other up-and-coming crowd sourcing companies include Culture 360 (www.culture360.org) that serves Asia and Europe, and Indiegogo (www.indiegogo.com), as well as Rocket Hub (www.rockethub.com). And nothing stops you from simply asking those you know to support your project. The concept is elementary.

CONTESTS

Contests offer financial opportunity, too. Of course you must win, place or show, but many writers overlook the importance that contests have on a career. These days, contests not only open doors to publishing, name recognition, and money, but listing such achievements in a query letter might make an agent or publisher take a second glance. Noting your wins on a magazine pitch might land a feature assignment. Mentioning your accolades to potential clients could clinch a freelance deal.

I used contests as a barometer when fleshing out my first mystery novel, *A Lowcountry Bribe*, Bell Bridge Books. After I placed in several contests, earned a total of $750, and reached the semi-finals of the Amazon Breakthrough Novel Award (www.createspace.com/abna), my confidence grew strong enough to pitch agents. My current agent admits that the contest wins drew her in.

Contests can assist in sales of existing books, not only aiding sales but also enticing more deals for future books . . . or the rest of your writing profession.

Whether writing short stories, poetry, novels, or nonfiction, contests abound. As with any call for submission, study the rules. Double checking with entities that screen, like FundsforWriters.com and WinningWriters.com, will help alleviate concerns when selecting where to enter.

FREELANCING

A thick collection of freelancing clips can make an editor sit up and take notice. You've been vetted and accepted by others in the business, and possibly established a following. The more well known the publications, the brighter your aura.

Sooner or later in your career, you'll write an article. In the beginning, articles are a great way to gain your footing. As your career develops, you become more of an expert, and are expected to enlighten and educate about your journey and the knowledge you've acquired. Articles are, arguably, one of the best means to income and branding for writers.

Trade magazines, national periodicals, literary journals, newsletters, newspapers and blogs all offer you a chance to present yourself, earn money, and gain readers for a platform. Do not discount them as income earners.

Linda Formichelli, of Renegade Writer fame (www.therenegadewriter.com) leaped into freelance magazine writing because she simply loved to write, and that love turned her into an expert. "I never loved working to line someone else's pockets." A full-time freelancer since 1997, with credits like *Family Circle*, *Redbook*, and *Writer's Digest*, she also writes articles, books, e-courses, and e-books about her profession as a magazine writer.

JOBS

Part-time, full-time, temporary or permanent, writing jobs hone your skills, pad your resume, and present avenues to movers and shakers you wouldn't necessarily meet on your own. Government and corporate managers hire writers under all sorts of guises like Social Media Specialist and Communications Specialist, as well as the expected Reporter and Copywriter.

Alexis Grant considers her prior jobs as catapults. "Working at a newspaper (*Houston Chronicle*) and a news magazine (*US News & World Report*) for six years provided the foundation for what I'm doing now as a freelancer. Producing stories regularly on tight deadlines will always make you a better writer."

Joan Dempsey chose to return to full-time work and write her novel on the side, removing worries about her livelihood. "My creative writing was suffering trying to freelance. So, I have a day job that supports me now." She still maintains her Facebook presence to continue building her platform for her pending novel.

DIVERSIFICATION

Most importantly, however, is learning how to collect all your funding options and incorporate them into your plan. The successful writer doesn't perform in one arena. Instead, he thrives in more of a three-ring circus.

Grant states it well: "For a long while I thought of myself as only a journalist, but there are so many other ways to use my skills. Today my income comes from three streams: helping small companies with social media and blogging (the biggest source), writing and selling e-guides and courses (my favorite), and taking freelance writing or editing assignments."

Formichelli is proud of being flexible. "When I've had it with magazine writing, I put more energy into my e-courses, and vice versa. Heck, I'm even a certified personal trainer, so if I get really sick of writing I can work out. But a definite side benefit to diversifying is that I'm more protected from the feast-or-famine nature of writing."

Sometimes pursuing the more common sense or lucrative income opportunity can open doors for the dream. When my novel didn't sell, I began writing freelance articles. Then I established FundsforWriters, using all the grant, contest, publisher and market research I did for myself. A decade later, once the site thrived with over 45,000 readers, I used the very research I'd gleaned for my readers to find an agent and sign a publishing contract . . . for the original novel started so long ago.

You can fight to fund one project or study all resources and fund a career. Opportunity is there. Just don't get so wrapped up in one angle that you miss the chance to invest more fully in your future.

C. HOPE CLARK manages FundsForWriters.com and is the author of several books, including *Lowcountry Bribe* and *Palmetto Poison*. Learn more at http://chopeclark.com.

BUILDING RELATIONSHIPS IN THE PUBLISHING BUSINESS

by Leslie Lee Sanders

There's much talk about establishing relationships in the writing business to market your brand and advance your career. Read on to understand exactly what building relationships mean, why is it important, and how is it done correctly.

WHAT IT MEANS TO BUILD RELATIONSHIPS

To advance your writing career you must build relationships within the industry. The most direct way to do this is by participating in the writing community; working directly with cover artists, agents, publishers, editors, bloggers, and other writers, and engaging your readers.

The more you communicate with others in the business, the better you get to know and respect one another, which can lead to helping each other successfully reach your goals.

A surefire way to make connections in the business is to offer something valuable for free. And the most valued things to offer are advice; volunteer your expertise. If *communication* is a handshake, *giving* is laying out the welcoming mat. We open ourselves up to people who help make achieving our goals easier, faster, and better.

Simple ways to offer assistance:

Learn the kinds of books your author friend writes and recommend works (besides your one) that she might enjoy, or books or articles on the craft of writing she might find useful. Offer to beta read or promote a friend's story, share their blog posts on your social media sites, or give them solutions to problems they're facing.

WHY RELATIONSHIPS ARE IMPORTANT

People are selfish. Sure, we always want to know what we can get out of a relationship. And getting something of importance from another is usually why we hang on to a relationship or value them, but relationships are a two-way street. You must learn to give in order to receive. Don't ask, what am I getting out of it? Ask yourself, what am I adding to the relationship?

Steps to building relationships:

1. Communication. Communication is the main component of a successful relationship. Like any form of communication it's a collaborative effort of give-and-take. It requires speaking and listening. The best relationships exist between people who are good listeners as well as speakers, and are givers as well as takers. If you really want a relationship to work, you can't have one without the other.

2. Professionalism. The key to any business relationship is professionalism. *Professional and business* goes hand in hand. *Personal and professional* does not. Keep your personal feelings, opinions, and business out of the equation unless your relationship develops beyond business. Most times it's better not to mix the two, in order to avoid any awkwardness or embarrassment in the future.

3. Being natural and genuine. Sincerity over flattery will take you a long way as most people can spot false adulation from a distance. Being genuine is one of the first steps to building trust, and trust in every relationship is vital for its success.

4. Building trust. Being honest is important when earning and building trust, but trust also requires consistency, delivering on promises, and delivering beyond expectations when it counts. In other words, you have to prove yourself and your commitment.

5. Being pleasant and helpful. Describe the traits of a person you like. The words friendly, easy to speak to, pleasant to be around, or helpful may come to mind. Be the kind of person you would like to build a relationship with. What draws you to them might draw them to you too.

TYPES OF RELATIONSHIPS

Author-Editor

One of the many important relationships you'll have in the publishing business is the one with your editor. Every editor; the magazine editor who hires you for freelance work, the freelance book editor who you hire to polish your manuscripts, and even the acquisition editor of the publishing house you submit your book to. Each are important to your writing career.

Great first impressions and lasting impressions are critical, especially with this pairing. In many cases, this is the first person you will encounter on your journey to publication. Build a relationship with your editor by doing the following:

- **Make a great first impression.** Your very first piece of correspondence with an editor will most likely be in the form of an e-mail, either as a pitch for a nonfiction piece or a query for your novel or story you hope will be acquired. Most editors have submission guidelines, study them and adhere to them. A good way to leave a gritty taste in an editor's mouth is to disregard the guidelines he sets in place to help make his job easier. Respect his time by following the rules.

- **Deliver on promises.** You ensured that you would rewrite the conclusion to your article, cite your sources, and return it completed by Thursday. Not only did you do exactly as you promised, but you've demonstrated that you are reliable, efficient, and are someone your editor shouldn't hesitate to work with again in the future.
- **Go above and beyond.** Imagine not only doing what you've promised, but also accomplishing more, faster, and better. In some cases it's not wise to go overboard. Maybe turning in a 2,000-word article when the editor specifically asks for 1,000 words, or attaching your complete manuscript when the editor asked for a synopsis, may backfire. The simplest thing can be the most impressive, like providing a list of sources to help manage the editor's time when fact checking, or turning in your article days ahead of the deadline. Determine how going above and beyond can assist the editor and make his job easier.
- **Meet or exceed deadlines.** Almost every professional in the business has deadlines. If you agree to deliver by a deadline, you are then expected to meet it. Get your work in on time. This takes us back to following the guidelines and how important that is. Show your respect by following the rules. Even better is doing the unexpected and get the job done satisfactorily before the deadline. Life happens, so if you believe you won't meet the deadline discuss this with your editor well in advance. Don't wait until the night before the deadline to ask for an extension.

Practicing the above tips is the first steps to becoming a well liked, hardworking writer any editor could depend on to get the job done. If you have excellent ideas and great writing skills, guess who would be more likely to land the next freelancing gig or get welcomed back to submit their work again.

Author-Reader

The most essential relationship is the one you have with your audience. After all, these are the people who are subscribing to your newsletters, sharing your blog posts, buying your books, giving you free advertisement through word of mouth, leaving reviews, and providing you with that all-to-important social proof. They make up your platform, and they deserve your attention. Here are some ways to build a relationship with your readers.

- **Engage on social media.** Go where your readers are and contribute to their conversations. Instead of selling or promoting yourself and your work, actually focus on getting to know them and allowing them to get to know you. The greatest form of self-promotion is when it doesn't feel like selling to either you or the reader. Ask questions, reply to comments, share something entertaining or useful, and comment when they share.

- **Contribute.** Give them what they want. The keyword here is give. Supply them with the information they seek, share their blog posts, comment on their status updates, answer their questions, respond to their e-mails and comments, give them freebies or goodies, provide them with a list of books by other authors they might enjoy, or direct them toward the information they seek, especially if you can't deliver.
- **Be genuine.** Be yourself. You are probably more attractive to your audience than anyone you can imagine being. Share things about yourself, your life, or your work that you think will inspire, aid, or entertain others. Let your audience know as much or as little about you as you choose, but be true to who you are.

Author-Blogger

Bloggers are the perfect people to form relationships with because they help spread the word about you, your business, your product, or your brand to their audience by featuring your guest posts or posting your promotional material like interviews, book excerpts, or reviews. Engage with bloggers who cater to your target audience.

- **Follow and engage with blogs.** Sign up to the blog's mailing list, engage with commenters, leave comments yourself.
- **Familiarize yourself with their content.** What types of posts do they publish? Who is their target audience? How large is their audience? Who hosts the blog?
- **Follow their guest posting guidelines.** Every blog has a specific set of rules to abide, by doing so you help make the guest posting process easy on the host and show your respect for the blog.
- **Be courteous and thankful.** If you're invited to guest post, answer questions from commenters, thank the host, and promote the content.

Author-Author

Authors are a strange breed. We yearn to thrive in a business where rejection and uncertainty are prevalent, strangers judge every single word we write, everything is constantly and quickly changing, and we look at others in the writing community as competition. However, no matter how unreliable the business is, there is room for all of us to flourish and nurture one another.

The author-author relationship can be confusing at times, but that largely depends on your mindset. Instead of looking at each other as rivals, look to other authors as a way to boost your writing career. Here how:

- **Cross promoting.** Remember give-and-take. Do for authors what you'd like them to do for you. Get together with another author or a group of authors in a similar genre to promote each other's works, combining each other's platforms.

- **Co-authoring.** Write a book, or blog post, or an article together. Blending your talent and expertise is a great way to provide a quality product to a collective audience.
- **Beta reading.** Authors make great beat readers. They know what to look for to improve your story and to ready your book for submission.
- **Guest posting.** Most authors are bloggers to, and if your audience is similar to their audience, asking permission to publish a guest post on their blog (or inviting them to guest post on your blog) can help boost your sales, readership, and career by putting you and your work in front of a wider audience.
- **Sharing experience and knowledge.** Many authors in the community spend many years in the business, failing, learning, and becoming experts in their field. Exchanging tips and advice can be helpful.

THE MOST IMPORTANT RELATIONSHIPS

This depends on your goals. However, no matter what your objective is, a relationship with your readers is important. The author-reader relationship will help you build a career before, during and after your work is published. Every relationship has its importance, but your goals will determine which is more essential and when.

GOAL	RELATIONSHIP
Build a following	Author-reader Author-blogger Author-author
Sell more books	Author-reader Author-blogger
Perfect your work before publication	Author-editor Author reader
Be a go-to person in the industry	Author-blogger Author reader

LESLIE LEE SANDERS has been published in the *2014 Guide to Self-Publishing* and online blogs like Be a Freelance Blogger. Learn more at http://LeslieLeeSanders.com.

4 WAYS TO CREATE A PRODUCTIVE HOME OFFICE

by Kylie Jane Wakefield

Working at home is no easy task. You don't need to set an alarm, answer to a boss, or collaborate with colleagues who rely on you to do your part. When you're an independent worker, you're responsible for keeping yourself on task, and your success is completely in your hands.

When you're starting out, it takes time to figure out how you function best. When it comes to creating a great at-home working environment, the same rules apply.

If you're struggling to stick to a schedule, missing deadlines because you're distracted, or feel your career is stagnant, your home office might be the problem. Though it may seem subtle, your surroundings greatly influence your efficiency. But by taking a few steps, you can turn things around.

The following are some tips for creating a productive home office that will help you achieve your freelance writing goals.

MAKE A DEDICATED SPACE

Sometimes you work at the kitchen table while eating your breakfast. Other times you sit on the sofa and turn on the TV in the background. Before you go to sleep at night, you type on your laptop in bed. Though it seems like you're working nonstop, writing in so many different places may actually be the biggest block to your productivity.

"Where possible, have a dedicated home office, such as an actual room that is only used for this purpose, or an area that can be hidden when not in use," said Lise Cartwright, a full-time freelance writer and founder of the website Outsourced Freelancing Success. "A great way to create a home office is to convert a spare room or wardrobe into an office, particularly if they're not in use."

Erin Doland, the editor-in-chief of home-and-office organization website Unclutter, took six months to get into a solid work schedule. She says she needed to make a clear boundary between her career and her professional life. "I found that a door on my office was key to separating my work life from my home life. At the end of the workday, I shut the door and leave work."

Could you declutter your garage to make room for your desk? Is there an extra bedroom or a guesthouse you can makeover? Anywhere that's private will do. If you don't have a door, put up a curtain. Set up a white noise machine at the entrance to your space to drown out any distractions. If you're constantly shuffling from room to room, it's hard to get anything done.

Brie Weiler Reynolds, director of online content at FlexJob.com, a job board for part-time and freelance workers, says, "Whether you set up some office space in a guest bedroom, or cordon off a corner in your living room with a divider, do whatever it takes to give yourself a dedicated, productive space for writing."

DETERMINE YOUR IDEAL WORKING ENVIRONMENT

You probably quit your office job because you didn't like your settings. Now that you're at home, you can put together the perfect work situation for yourself.

Even the smallest details matter when you're working at home, from your wardrobe, to what's on the wall, and the noises going on in and outside of your residency.

"I wear jeans most days, but some people need to put on business attire to be productive," says Doland. "I tried that out for a few weeks and found it had no particular influence on my performance. I couldn't figure out how much coffee to make in the morning, as ridiculous as that sounds. After many rounds of trial and error I discovered that I can't have the television on but I'm OK with music, even though I had a television on my desk for years when I was doing media and lobbying work."

Maybe you find that you're most productive between the hours of 1 p.m. to 7 p.m. Or perhaps you're comfortable with the 9 a.m. to 5 p.m. lifestyle. You find that you have more brainpower after you workout, but around lunchtime, you begin to feel sluggish. If you're in tune with yourself, you can establish a set routine and create the most idyllic working conditions possible.

"It's about figuring out what works best for your working rhythms and then putting steps in place to make the most of those optimal times," says Cartwright. "That's what I try to do."

ORGANIZE YOUR OFFICE

Some writers' home offices are nice and tidy. Folders are labeled with color-coded Post-it notes, papers are tucked away in their drawers, and not a single speck of dust is to be found. Other writers' workspaces look like a tsunami struck them. Papers are scattered everywhere, old banana peels are in the trashcan, and, over the years, several coffee rings found their home on the desk.

If you're in the latter group, you might consider cleaning up your office a bit. "Some people swear they're more productive in a messy or cluttered space," says Reynolds. "My advice is to start with organization, and see how you do. You might think you work better with the mess, but until you try being organized, you'll never know."

Reynolds suggests working in an organized space for a week or two and seeing the results. Then, you should ask yourself whether you were more productive as an organized or messy writer. "Ultimately, it's up to each individual writer to determine what makes him or her efficient," she says.

Doland recommends going over the inventory of office supplies, keeping a calendar handy, and "taking at least 15 minutes at the end of every work day to organize your office and get it ready for the next work day."

If you need help cleaning your space, consider hiring a professional organizer. Look for one on NAPO.net, the National Association of Professional Organizers website, and find one for hire in your area.

PREVENT DISTRACTIONS

Distractions may be the biggest hindrance to your productivity. Since you won't get in trouble for checking your Facebook account or answering personal e-mails on the clock, you're going to be more likely to do it.

Instead of guilting yourself, you need to pinpoint what's really keeping you from getting your work done, and then prevent the interruption before it can occur.

"If you are someone who is easily distracted by social media, shut off your router or enable site blocking programs before you sit down to work," says Doland. "If you are tempted to do chores instead of your project, schedule time to do those chores on your calendar so you know exactly when to do them instead of using them to procrastinate. If people who live with you keep walking in on you when you're concentrating, get a door and lock it. You have to be honest with yourself about your diversion triggers. We all have temptations. Know yours and take steps to keep them from harming your productivity."

Reyonds says to let whomever you reside with know that you're working. "If you live with other people, you have to ask them directly for cooperation when you're working. Ask them to leave you alone unless it's an emergency, tell them when your work hours will be, and let them know how important it is that you remain focused."

She also suggests sticking a note on your front door for visitors to let them know you won't be able to answer it, as well as not checking personal e-mails while you're writing. "Distractions seep in when we let too much of our work and personal lives blur together," she says. "Try to keep those things as separate as possible and you'll be much less distracted."

When Cartwright feels that she isn't getting anything done, she'll go outside and take a quick walk around the block, or head to the local coffee shop. That way, her mind is clear and when she gets back home, she is able to focus on the task at hand once again.

According to DeskTime, a time-tracking app, people get the most done when they work for 52 minutes in a row, and then take 17-minute breaks. The time-off should not be spent in front of your computer, however. Instead, put on your tennis shoes and go for a stroll, or read the newspaper, prepare some food, garden, or play with your pets.

Doland suggests taking that time to get your things in order. "It's the ten-minute mental breaks every hour when the more mindless organizing tasks can be completed," she says.

IT'S NOT SIMPLE, BUT IT IS WORTH IT

You became a freelance writer for a reason. You like the freedom, independence, and working for yourself. When it comes to your home office, you must have a can-do attitude, like you do the rest of the time.

"Working from home requires self-management, self-discipline, and self-organization," said Reynolds. "If you can manage to keep those three traits well-tuned, honing those skills every day, productivity won't be a big issue."

KYLIE JANE WAKEFIELD is a freelance writer based in Los Angeles. She writes about Jewish news, content marketing, legal issues, and tech, and creates content for a variety of brands. She's been published by *Tablet Magazine*, *Legal Management Magazine*, and Forbes.com. Learn more at KylieJaneWakefield.com.

REMOVING INVISIBLE SPLINTERS

For Healthy and Successful Writing

by Ellen Ziegler

Imagine that a writer's block carries the weight of a whisper. And imagine that your ideas flow like streams of consciousness over the paths of least resistance.

Now, imagine the connections between your ideas, characters, and scenes create work that hook and land agents and publishers waiting for you in *Writer's Market.*

What if success were as possible as tweezing a splinter from the surface of your fingertip? Or reading a love story?

This is a love story about two protagonists: you and your writing, and the antagonists irritating your mind and body and triggering inflammation, brain fog, creative blocks, and low energy.

INVISIBLE SPLINTERS

Some irritants are stress, sugar, lack of sleep, prolonged sitting, food sensitivities, toxins, and inflammatory foods. For writers, sharp rejections and stressful deadlines penetrate so deep; they can increase inflammation and throw your mind and body into chaos.

Charles Glassman, M.D., also known as Coach MD, a Holistic Internist and author of the award-winning book *Brain Drain* feels that if we turn negative thoughts into positive ones we can calm the chaos.

Glassman says, "Rejections and deadlines trigger that part of us that reaffirms our vulnerability. Our automatic brain is hard wired to fight and flee such things and when we do it releases chemicals that cause inflammation."

He suggests this mantra: "Rejections make me stronger. I will not take them personally and goals are merely dreams with deadlines."

If you were a sculptor, carving a block of wood, a splinter would be a reminder of your work. It's visible and can be tweezed out. But as a wordsmith, who may be under pressure, eating on the run, sitting for too long and eating and drinking mindlessly or not eating or drinking at all, you are inviting in the "Invisible Splinters" of inflammation.

HOW TO REMOVE SPLINTERS

•Slowly substitute inflammatory foods like gluten, simple carbs, unfermented soy and dairy from your diet. If you react poorly to cow's milk dairy, try raw goat's milk cheese. The new goat goudas are mild and satisfying.

•Avoid fluids with meals as they dilute the digestive enzymes you need to absorb nutrients. *We are what we absorb.*

•Drink water upon awakening and throughout the day as your cells are like sponges, craving hydration.

•Chew slowly and mindfully to help break foods down. Eating on the run is a race toward illness.

•Snack on unsalted nuts or nut butter with organic fruit. An overdose of salt creates sugar cravings. Try whole food bars lightly sweetened with agave, stevia or coconut sugar, homemade trail mix, guacamole or hummus spread on raw vegetables, sugar snap pea pods and unsalted almond butter on slices of organic apples or pears. Add sunflower seeds or butter to balance blood sugar.

•Be aware of cravings for crunchy foods if you're frustrated. Fruit, raw vegetables, nuts are better than biting someone. Millet and flax chips found in health food stores are gluten free and they keep their crunch when you top them with the spreads mentioned above. Nutrient density vs. empty calories is the equation for unblocking your inner muse and motivating him or her to produce stories that sing.

•Drink coffee. The new data on coffee may make coffee lovers smile. Organic, low-acid black coffee, ground fresh from beans is packed with antioxidants. Once you add cream or sugar you negate the benefits; substitute with lite coconut or almond milk and agave.

•Get up and move. When we sit for too long, we neglect our joints and bones. Stretching often and trying a fun, weight-bearing exercise (bouncing and running in place) on an exercise trampoline helps. If you drink filtered water before and after there's the side benefit of ridding your lymphatic system of toxic "Invisible Splinters."

•Go organic. Speaking of toxins, wean yourself off grain-fed beef and antibiotic-and-hormone-filled poultry. Eat grass fed and organic. Organic might be more expensive, but you'll eat less because it's nutrient dense. If you try the ten-minute rule, you'll consume even less: Eat until satisfied, but not full, and wait ten minutes. Watch your growing mindfulness turn you into a superhero or heroine in your own epic.

•Get your D3. Rice bran or coconut oil are the best oils to heat, but save the high heat for your Romantic/Suspense novel. Consider a soy and filler-free organic multivitamin. If you're working indoors you may lack vitamin D3 so have your blood levels checked. The required daily amount has increased. Vitamin D3 is oil based and absorbed well with a salad tossed with organic olive oil and fresh lemon.

•Be alkaline. The salad makes you more alkaline, which helps you avoid disease. Ernest Hemingway, a meat eater, balanced his meals with vegetables, using his five senses to savor foods, described in his writing. He believed an appetite for life and food were inseparable.

The opposite of alkaline is acidic. Silent acid reflux and joint pains are health issues for writers who might be sedentary and under stress. You can Google acid-producing foods and activities and pace yourself in substituting them with healthy, delicious choices. Some people have gone off acid-blocking medications (with the okay of their doctors) by being more mindful.

MAKING CHANGES

Consider how long it took you to get into the shape you're in now, so change gradually and you'll see that every small step in reducing inflammation rewards you with energy as you reduce your "Invisible Splinters" while working on the writing you love. Improving your quality of life helps you improve the quality of your work.

EPILOGUE

The foods we chew and swallow are called *"Secondary Foods."* Eaten organic they transfer their energy to you. Inflammation gets stored in our fat cells. If we don't remove inflammatory foods and stressful lifestyle practices, it's difficult to maintain healthy weight, even after dieting, because fat cells expand while high-energy foods fuel our imagination and endurance and help us lose weight.

Marilyn Benkler, award-winning writer, sculptor, artist, teacher and singer believes that the primary foods exercise, relationships, humor, meditation, forgiveness, career—and the one writers have in abundance, creativity—heighten awareness.

Benkler says, "Spending a lifetime practicing and teaching the arts, I have seen the creative process grow from within when one becomes keenly aware of the details outside oneself – what one sees, hears, smells, tastes, touches, believes. The primary foods, especially meditation, exercise and creativity open up possibilities for higher levels of concentration and focus. Creativity is actually its own meditative state."

Imagine you, the writer changing the world with your creativity—allowing it to flow and work its magic. You are a word-crafter and when you run your mind along the rough edge of an idea and get stuck, it might be an "Invisible Splinter." Be mindful of your day. Is your blood sugar low? Has a stressful incident set you back?

Grow your characters with the truths you discover when you let go and with the writing and marketing advice in this book, stretch your creativity and skills to their full potential.

Now, imagine that a whisper is heard in the windstorm of our world.

Your whisper.

ELLEN ZIEGLER is a Board Certified Holistic Health and Nutrition Counselor (Columbia U Teachers College) and Life Coach who has changed the lives, health, and output of her clients. Her writing has been published in *Hudson Valley Magazine*, *Women's World*, and many literary journals.

CONTRACTS 101

by Cindy Ferraino

After you do a victory dance about getting the book deal you always dreamed about or your article hitting the top of the content list of a popular magazine, the celebration quickly comes to a halt when you realize you are not at the finish line yet. Your heart begins to beat faster because you know the next possible hurdle is just around the corner—the contract. For many, the idea of reviewing a contract is like being back in first grade. You know you have to listen to the teacher when you could be playing outside. You know you have to read this contract but why because there are terms in there that look like an excerpt from a foreign language syllabus.

Before I changed my status to self-employed writer, I was working as a grants and contracts administrator at a large medical university in Philadelphia. I helped shepherd the MD and PhD researchers through the channels of grants and contracts administration. While the researchers provided the technical and scientific pieces that could potentially be the next cure for diabetes, heart disease, or cancer, I was there to make sure they did their magic within the confines of a budget and imposed contractual regulations. The budget process was easy but when it came to contract regulations—oh well, that was a different story. I became familiar with the terms such as indemnifications, property and intellectual rights and conditions of payments. I was an integral part of reviewing and negotiating a grant or contract that had the best interests for every party involved.

After my son was born, I left the university and my contracts background went on a brief hiatus. Once my son went off to school, I began freelance writing. After a few writing gigs sprinkled with a few too many rejection slips, I landed an assignment for *Dog Fancy* magazine. I was thrilled and eagerly anticipated the arrival of a contract in my inbox. As I opened the document, the hiatus had lifted. I read through the contract and was able to send it back within a few hours.

For many new freelancers or writers who have been around the block, contract administration is not something that they can list as a perk on their resume. Instead of searching through the Yellow Pages for a contract lawyer or trying to call in a special favor to a writer friend, there are some easy ways for a newbie writer or even a seasoned writer to review a contract before putting a smiley face next to the dotted line.

TAKE A DEEP BREATH, THEN READ ON

Remember breaking those seals on test booklets and the voice in the background telling you, "Please read the directions slowly." As you tried to drown out the voice because your stomach was in knots, little did you know that those imparting words of wisdom would come in handy as you perspired profusely over the legal jargon that unfolded before your eyes. The same words go for contracts.

Many writers, including myself, are anxious to get an assignment underway, but the contract carrot continues to loom over our creative minds. "I'm surprised by writers who just skim a contract and then sign it without understanding what it means," says Kelly James-Enger. James-Enger is the author of books including *Six Figure Freelancing: The Writer's Guide to Making More* (Random House, 2005) and blog Dollarsanddeadlines.blogspot.com. "Most of the language in magazine contracts isn't that complicated, but it can be confusing when you're new to the business."

When I receive a contract from a new publisher or editor, I make a second copy. My children call it "my sloppy copy." I take out a highlighter and begin to mark up the key points of the contract: beginning and end date, conditions of payment, how my relationship is defined by the publisher and what the outline of the article should look like.

The beginning and end date of a contract is crucial. After I recently negotiated a contract, the editor changed the due date of the article in an e-mail. I made sure the contract was changed to reflect the new due date. The conditions of the payments are important because it will describe when the writer will be paid and by what method. Most publishers have turned to incremental payment schedules or payments to be made online like PayPal. How the publisher considers your contractor status is important. If you're a freelance contract writer, the contract should reflect that as well as identify you as an independent contractor for IRS tax purposes. Finally, the contract will highlight an outline of what your article or proposal should look like.

As you slowly digest the terms you are about to agree to for your assignment or book project, you gain a better understanding of what an editor or publisher expects from you and when.

CUTTING TO THE LEGAL CHASE

Once you have had a chance to review a contract, you may be scratching your head and saying, "Okay, now what does this all mean to me as a writer?" James-Enger describes three key areas where writers should keep sharp on when it comes to contracts—Indemnification, Pay and Exclusivity provisions.

INDEMNIFICATION is a publisher's way of saying if something goes wrong, we are not responsible. If a claim is brought against another writer's work, a publisher does not want to be responsible for the legal aftermath but you could be the one receiving a notice in the mail. James-Enger warns writers to be on the lookout for indemnification clauses. "In the U.S., anyone can sue anyone over just about anything," she says; "I'm okay with agreeing to indemnification clauses that specify breaches of contract because I know I'm not going to plagiarize, libel or misquote anyone. But I can't promise that the publication will never be sued by anyone whether or not I actually breached the contract."

PAY is where you want the publisher "to show you the money." Writers need to be aware of how publishers will discuss the terms of payment in the contract. James-Enger advises to have "payment on acceptance." This means you will be paid when the editor agrees to accept your manuscript or article. If there is "no payment on acceptance," some publishers will pay when the article is published. "Push for payment whenever you can," she says.

EXCLUSIVITY PROVISIONS are where a particular publisher will not allow the writer to publish an article or manuscript that is "about the same or similar subject" during the time the publisher runs the piece. Because of the nature of the writing business, James-Enger feels writers need to negotiate this part of the contract. "I specialize in health, fitness and nutrition, and I'm always writing about a similar subject," she says.

PAYMENT TYPES

There are any number of different arrangements for publishers to pay writers. However, here are three of the most common and what they mean.

- Pays on acceptance. This means a publisher pays (or cuts a check) for the writer upon acceptance of the manuscript. This is usually the best deal a writer can hope to receive. .
- Pays on publication. In these cases, a publisher pays (or cuts a check) for the writer by the publication date of the manuscript. For magazines, this could mean several months after the manuscript was accepted and approved. For books, this could mean more than a year.
- Pays after publication. Sometimes contracts will specify exactly how long after publication. Be wary of contracts that leave it open-ended.

CONTRACT TIPS

Even seasoned freelancers can find themselves intimidated by contracts. Here are a few things to consider with your contract:

- **KEEP COPY ON RECORD.** If the contract is sent via e-mail, keep a digital copy, but also print up a hard copy and keep it in an easy-to-find file folder.
- **CHECK FOR RIGHTS.** It's almost never a good idea to sell all rights. But you should also pay attention to whether you're selling any subsidiary or reprint rights. The more rights you release the more payment you should expect (and demand).
- **WHEN PAYMENT.** Make sure you understand when you are to be paid and have it specified in your contract. You may think that payment will come when the article is accepted or published, but different publishers have different policies. Get it in writing.
- **HOW MUCH PAYMENT.** The contract should specify exactly how much you are going to be paid. If there is no payment listed on the contract, the publisher could use your work for free.
- **TURN IN CONTRACT BEFORE ASSIGNMENT.** Don't start working until the contract is signed, and everything is official. As a freelancer, time is as important as money. Don't waste any of your time and effort on any project that is not yet contracted.

WHEN TO HEAD TO THE BARGAINING TABLE

Recently, I became an independent contractor for the American Composites Manufacturing Association (ACMA). When I reviewed the terms of the contract, I was concerned how my independent contractor status was identified. Although I am not an ACMA employee, I wanted to know if I could include my ACMA publications on my resume. Before I signed the contract, I questioned this issue with my editor. My editor told me I may use this opportunity to put on my resume. I signed the contract and finished my assignment.

Writers should be able to talk to an editor or a publisher if there is a question about a term or clause in a contract. "Don't be afraid to talk to the editor about the changes you'd like to make to a contract," James-Enger says; "You don't know what you'll get or if an editor is willing to negotiate it, until you ask."

When writers have to approach an editor for changes to a contract, James-Enger advises writers to act professionally when it comes to the negotiations. "I start out with saying—I am really excited to be working with you on this story and I appreciate the assignment, but I have a couple of issues with the contract that I'd like to talk to you about," she says. "Sure I want a better contract but I also want to maintain a good working relationship with my editor.

A scorched-earth policy doesn't benefit any freelancer in the long run."

Negotiating payment terms is a tricky subject for some writers. Writers want to get the most bang for their buck but they don't want to lose a great writing assignment. Do your research first before you decide to ask an editor for more money to complete the assignment. Double check the publisher's website or look to see if the pay scale is equivalent to other publishers in the particular industry. Some publishers have a set publishing fee whereas others may have a little more wiggle room depending on the type of the assignment given. In today's economy, writers are a little more reluctant to ask for a higher rate for an article. If the publisher seems to be open to discussion about the pay scale, just make sure you approach the situation in a professional manner so as to not turn the publisher away from giving you another assignment.

WHO OWNS YOUR WRITING?

Besides payment terms, another area that writers may find themselves on the other end of the negotiation table is with ownership rights. We all want to take credit for the work that we have poured our heart and soul into. Unfortunately, the business of publishing has different ways of saying how a writer can classify their work. Ownership rights vary, but the biggest one that writers have a hard time trying to build up a good case against is "all rights." "All rights" is exactly what it means: *hope you are not in love with what you have just written because you will not be able to use it again.* In recent months, I have written for two publications that I had given "all rights" to the company. My rationale is that I knew I would never need to use those articles again but I did make sure I was able to include those articles for my byline to show that I have publishing experience.

If you feel that you want to reuse or recycle an article that you had written a few years ago, you might want to consider negotiating an "all rights" clause or maybe going to another publisher. "We don't take all rights so there is no reason for authors to request we change the rights clause," says Angela Hoy, author and owner of WritersWeekly.com and Booklocker.com. "Our contracts were rated 'Outstanding' by Mark Levine (author of *The Fine Print of Self-Publishing*) and has also been called the clearest and fairest in the industry."

James-Enger is also an advocate of negotiating against contracts with an "all rights" clause. "I hate 'all rights' contracts, and try to avoid signing them as they preclude me from ever reselling the piece as a reprint to other markets," she says. "I explain that to editors, and I have been able to get editors to agree to let me retain nonexclusive reprint rights even when they buy all rights—which still lets me market the piece as a reprint." James-Enger also advises that "if the publisher demands all rights, then negotiate if the payment is sub-standard."

So if you are just receiving a contract in the mail for the first time or you are working with a new publisher, you should not be afraid of the legal lingo that blankets the message "we want to work with you." Contracts are meant to protect both the interests of the publishers and writers. Publishers want the commitment from writers that he or she will provide their best work and writers want to be recognized for their best work. But between those contracts lines, the legal lingo can cause writers to feel they need a law degree to review the contract. No, just sit back and relax and enjoy the prose that will take your writing to the next level.

RIGHTS AND WHAT THEY MEAN

A creative work can be used in many different ways. As the author of the work, you hold all rights to the work in question. When you agree to have your work published, you are granting a publisher the right to use your work in any number of ways. Whether that right is to publish the manuscript for the first time in a publication, or to publish it as many times and in as many ways as a publisher wishes, is up to you—it all depends on the agreed-upon terms. As a general rule, the more rights you license away, the less control you have over your work and the money you're paid. You should strive to keep as many rights to your work as you can.

Writers and editors sometimes define rights in a number of different ways. Below you will find a classification of terms as they relate to rights.

- **FIRST SERIAL RIGHTS.** Rights that the writer offers a newspaper or magazine to publish the manuscript for the first time in any periodical. All other rights remain with the writer. Sometimes the qualifier "North American" is added to these rights to specify a geographical limitation to the license. When content is excerpted from a book scheduled to be published, and it appears in a magazine or newspaper prior to book publication, this is also called first serial rights.
- **ONE-TIME RIGHTS.** Nonexclusive rights (rights that can be licensed to more than one market) purchased by a periodical to publish the work once (also known as simultaneous rights). That is, there is nothing to stop the author from selling the work to other publications at the same time.
- **SECOND SERIAL (REPRINT) RIGHTS.** Nonexclusive rights given to a newspaper or magazine to publish a manuscript after it has already appeared in another newspaper or magazine.
- **ALL RIGHTS.** This is exactly what it sounds like. "All rights" means an author is selling every right he has to a work. If you license all rights to your work, you forfeit the right to ever use the work again. If you think you may want to use the article again, you should avoid submitting to such markets or refuse payment and withdraw your material.

- **ELECTRONIC RIGHTS.** Rights that cover a broad range of electronic media, including websites, CD/DVDs, video games, smart phone apps, and more. The contract should specify if—and which—electronic rights are included. The presumption is unspecified rights remain with the writer.
- **SUBSIDIARY RIGHTS.** Rights, other than book publication rights, that should be covered in a book contract. These may include various serial rights; movie, TV, audio, and other electronic rights; translation rights, etc. The book contract should specify who controls the rights (author or publisher) and what percentage of sales from the licensing of these rights goes to the author.
- **DRAMATIC, TV, AND MOTION PICTURE RIGHTS.** Rights for use of material on the stage, on TV, or in the movies. Often a one-year option to buy such rights is offered (generally for 10 percent of the total price). The party interested in the rights then tries to sell the idea to other people—actors, directors, studios, or TV networks. Some properties are optioned numerous times, but most fail to become full productions. In those cases, the writer can sell the rights again and again.

Sometimes editors don't take the time to specify the rights they are buying. If you sense that an editor is interested in getting stories, but doesn't seem to know what his and the writer's responsibilities are, be wary. In such a case, you'll want to explain what rights you're offering (preferably one-time or first serial rights only) and that you expect additional payment for subsequent use of your work.

The Copyright Law that went into effect January 1, 1978, states writers are primarily selling one-time rights to their work unless they—and the publisher—agree otherwise in writing. Book rights are covered fully by contract between the writer and the book publisher.

CINDY FERRAINO has been blessed with a variety of assignments, including newspaper articles, magazine articles, ghost-written articles, stories for books, and most recently authoring a book on accounting and bookkeeping terminology, *The Complete Dictionary of Accounting & Bookkeeping Terms Explained Simply* (Atlantic Publishing Group).

7 HABITS OF FINANCIALLY SAVVY WRITERS

by Kate Meadows

We all know the stereotype of the starving artist. Fun work, little pay. But just how true is that stereotype?

For the writer, it depends on a few things. First, it depends on how you value yourself as a writer. Are you a hobbyist, writing on the side either strictly for pleasure or for a bit of extra income? Or are you a professional, going at the business of writing as a day job?

Make no mistake: There is nothing wrong with writing for pleasure. But if writing is your profession, or if you strive to make it your profession (goodbye, day job!), managing the financial side of your trade is crucial. How you handle money can make or break that notion of "starving artist."

Many writers don't take time to consider the importance of finances in their profession, acknowledges Hope Clark, an author who heads the popular website and newsletter, Funds for Writers (www.fundsforwriters.com). "If they do consider it," she says, "they treat it with trepidation."

Why? Perhaps it's because so often the creative overrules the practical aspect of making a living. Your burning desire to pen the next great American novel shouldn't be ignored. But writers who can balance the creative with the practical are the true professionals.

This is what "financially savvy" boils down to, says Mridu Khullar Relph, whose freelance articles appear in *The New York Times*, *Time Magazine*, *Christian Science Monitor* and elsewhere: "It's making sure you make the right decisions financially to be able to sustain your career and create time and space for yourself to work on projects you may believe in but that may not be lucrative."

Adds Clark: "We cannot just be artists. Writers have to be businesspeople, as well."

1. MARKET, MARKET, MARKET!

Marketing is crucial for two reasons. First, it pushes your ideas into the world. Second, it pushes you and your skill into the world.

Not only must you market your work; you must also market yourself.

"Marketing is the number one thing you need to do to make it as a writer," says Linda Formichelli, a freelance writer whose articles have appeared in *Redbook*, *Family Circle*, and *Writer's Digest*, among others. "You can be the best writer ever, but if you don't market no one will ever know about it—or pay you."

Marketing is a never-ending process. Relph strives to make one marketing effort a day: an email, a follow-up phone call, a tweet.

"Finding an idea that gets you excited and then writing to an editor with the potential that idea holds, is the honeymoon phase of the project," she says, "when all possibilities exist and anything could happen."

Stay on top of your marketing efforts by having a system in place that tracks your ideas and potential markets for those ideas. I maintain two documents. My "Active Query Tracker" lists ideas I have pitched, the publication to which I sent the query and the appropriate editor's name and contact info, and the expected response date. My "Ideas List" includes all of my story ideas, each followed by a list of potential publications that fit the idea. When I receive a rejection, I delete that idea from my "Active Query Tracker" and strike out the publication on my "Ideas List." Then I pitch the idea to the next publication in line and update the "Active Query Tracker" as necessary.

2. THINK OF YOURSELF AS AN ENTREPRENEUR.

Anyone will concede that it's important for entrepreneurs to be financially savvy.

"The minute a writer decides to sell his work, he shifts from writer to entrepreneur," says Clark.

But too many writers fall short of this realization, focusing only on the creative output. The result? Lots of fantastic words and ideas that go nowhere.

Hate promoting yourself? Join the club. Feel clueless when it comes to the business end of writing? Take a class on accounting, marketing or running a home business. Such classes are often offered through community centers or colleges.

Relph draws these similarities between writers and entrepreneurs: "We come up with big ideas that others may or may not believe in and spend large chunks of time chasing them down and bringing them to fruition."

The difference, she says, is that entrepreneurs have a business model. Writers often don't.

Entrepreneurs invest in their trade. As a writer, it's important to put money into your venture, investing in supplies and experiences that will improve your craft.

Clark points out that many writers are so concerned with saving precious writing dollars that they don't pause to consider what might be reaped from spending. To save a few dollars, they won't pay for a cover design. They won't pay for a class they sorely need to improve a certain skill. They won't hire a professional to design their website, falling back on the mediocre skills of a friend who will do it for free.

Entrepreneurs know that quality upfront investments pay off in the long run. Becoming an entrepreneur means being proactive. It means recognizing opportunities when they arise and going after them wholeheartedly. Yes, there is risk involved. But what pursuit worth chasing doesn't involve some risk?

3. BE YOUR NO. 1 FAN.

You've heard it since grade school: A confident attitude goes a long way.

"A confident writer has no problem putting herself and her work out there," says Formichelli. "And that's where the money comes from."

Editors want to hire people who know what they're doing.

"I really believe that as independent professionals, how well we present ourselves plays a huge role in how much work we get and what we get paid for it," Relph says.

Relph once queried an editor at a UK-based Asian magazine and received a favorable response, under the condition that she would write the first article for free and then be paid a modest fee for each article thereafter. Relph declined the assignment. She couldn't afford to work for free, she explained, and her usual rate was twice what the editor offered for future pay, anyway. The editor responded, saying she would pay Relph that standard rate, for the first story and all stories thereafter.

Similarly, a lack of confidence can directly result in a lack of work. Procrastination and perfectionism are two big career killers, Formichelli says, both results of a lack of confidence.

If you don't believe in yourself, no one else will either.

4. KEEP RECEIPTS AND PAY STUBS, AND TRACK INCOME AND EXPENSES.

Writing is a numbers game.

"You need to know how much money you have coming in versus going out, how much you need to charge to earn what you want, and what your typical hourly rate is," says Formichelli.

Relying on hard numbers is crucial. How else will you know what sort of income you're earning, or where that hard-earned cash is going?

"Lots of writers assume or just want to believe that the only thing they have to do is write, and the rest of the stuff will take care of itself," says author John Scalzi. "It won't, and it doesn't."

Formichelli suggests using an accounting system like Freshbooks to make the in/out record keeping simple. I use an Excel spreadsheet, with one column that tracks income and another that tracks expenses. Allena Tapia, a freelance writer/editor and owner of GardenWall Publications, suggests using the week between Christmas and New Year's Day to prepare a chart for the coming year, so it's ready to go come January 1.

Crucial to your accounting system is sending invoices for every assignment. Many writers miss this important step and therefore chance losing payment for their work. Think about it: If you never received a bill from your utility provider, would you still write a check? A simple invoice takes just a few minutes to write and send.

Maintaining records requires diligence. And diligence is tough. But it is so worth it in the end.

5. DIVERSIFY YOUR PROJECTS.

Writers are wearers of many hats.

"Some things you do for the glamour, some you do for the money, some you do for personal satisfaction," says Relph. "Having that mix is what makes a freelancer successful."

Love to write fiction? Why not pitch to a writing magazine a service piece on how to sketch compelling characters? Have a penchant for realty? Consider offering your services as a copywriter or proofreader of newsletters and web content for realty companies in your area.

I recently started offering services as a freelance editor alongside my writing gigs. I contacted some nearby writing centers and offered to teach a series of workshops in my genre, nonfiction. The extra work keeps my business fund healthy when the writing assignments are slow in coming. What's more, the variety of projects is rewarding and keeps me on my toes.

Yes, you may have to venture into some work that's not as fun, to pad up your bank account. But treat those experiences as chances to expand your portfolio. Work such as technical writing or copywriting often pay better than the more creative end.

"You want to earn enough to create the time and space to work on projects that you truly enjoy," says Relph. "If you're earning great money in half of your working life, then you can dedicate the rest of it to writing whatever you want, without having to worry about the market."

6. ACKNOWLEDGE MISTAKES, AND THEN MOVE ON.

Face it. No one is going to write a winning query every time. Nor is everyone going to nail every assignment on the first draft. Stephen King pounded a nail into his wall, on which he hung every rejection letter he received. When that nail filled up, he got a bigger nail.

Good writers work hard. Good writers fail sometimes. But good writers also learn from their experiences.

I once pitched a strong query to a top children's magazine. Though I had never written for the children's market, the idea interested me, and the editor responded favorably, requesting the article on spec.

I rounded up sources and wrote the story. But, not being a children's writer, I struggled to fit the story to an audience of 6 to 12-year-olds. Consequently, the editor rejected the story, saying it was not suitable to the magazine's readership. Lesson learned? I am not a children's writer. Now I choose to focus on those markets I know I can handle.

7. READ CONTRACTS CAREFULLY, NEGOTIATE FAIR RATES, AND SIGN ONLY IF YOU UNDERSTAND AND AGREE WITH ALL THE TERMS.

Contracts are nothing to fear. They are simply documents that outline both the writer's and the client's terms regarding a specific assignment. In other words, a contract is a communication tool.

Knowing what rights you give up as a writer for what financial return is part of being proactive—and professional. Know the difference between First Serial Rights, which grants a publication the right to be the first to publish your work in a market (giving you the opportunity to sell reprints later on) and All Rights, which grants a publication exclusive rights to your work.

Don't want to give up exclusive rights to your work? Have the courage to say "no," or negotiate a different arrangement. Think five cents a word is not enough? Ask for more.

Negotiating fair rates is an act of confidence, Formichelli points out. It is the writer's way of advocating for himself and valuing his work.

Art must have two components to be professional: It must have a creative side, and it must have a business side. It's easy to fall back into the romanticized image of "starving artist" if you're a writer who just can't make ends meet. But before you toss in the towel and concede that writers are just undervalued professionals, ask yourself how well you practice these 7 habits.

The self-sustaining writers last the longest, says Clark. And being regarded as a self-sufficient wordsmith is a heck of a lot more rewarding than being regarded as a starving artist.

KATE MEADOWS is a freelance writer and editor who specializes in life stories and personal and small business histories. Her work has appeared in *Writer's Digest, Chicken Soup for the Soul, USAA Financial Magazine, Kansas City Parent,* and numerous trade and regional publications. Her book, *Tough Love: A Wyoming Childhood* (Pronghorn Press), was published in 2012.

MAKING THE MOST OF THE MONEY YOU EARN

by Sage Cohen

Writers who manage money well can establish a prosperous writing life that meets their short-term needs and long-term goals. This article will introduce the key financial systems, strategies, attitudes, and practices that will help you cultivate a writing life that makes the most of your resources and sustains you over time.

DIVIDING BUSINESS AND PERSONAL EXPENSES

If you are reporting your writing business to the IRS, it is important that you keep the money that flows from this source entirely separate from your personal finances. Here's what you'll need to accomplish this:

- **BUSINESS CHECKING ACCOUNT:** Only two types of money go into this account: money you have been paid for your writing and/or "capital investments" you make by depositing your own money to invest in the business. And only two types of payments are made from this account: business-related expenses (such as: subscriptions, marketing and advertisement, professional development, fax or phone service, postage, computer software and supplies), and "capital draws" which you make to pay yourself.
- **BUSINESS SAVINGS ACCOUNT OR MONEY MARKET ACCOUNT:** This account is the holding pen where your quarterly tax payments will accumulate and earn interest. Money put aside for your retirement account(s) can also be held here.
- **BUSINESS CREDIT CARD:** It's a good idea to have a credit card for your business as a means of emergency preparedness. Pay off the card responsibly every month and this will help you establish a good business credit record, which can be useful down the line should you need a loan for any reason.

When establishing your business banking and credit, shop around for the best deals, such as highest interest rates, lowest (or no) monthly service fees, and free checking. Mint.com is a good source for researching your options.

EXPENSE TRACKING AND RECONCILING

Once your bank accounts are set up, it's time to start tracking and categorizing what you earn and spend. This will ensure that you can accurately report your income and itemize your deductions when tax time rolls around every quarter. Whether you intend to prepare your taxes yourself or have an accountant help you, immaculate financial records will be the key to speed and success in filing your taxes.

For the most effective and consistent expense tracking, I highly recommend that you use a computer program such as QuickBooks. While it may seem simpler to do accounting by hand, I assure you that it isn't. Even a luddite such as I, who can't comprehend the most basic principles of accounting, can use QuickBooks with great aplomb to plug in the proper categories for income and expenses, easily reconcile bank statements, and with a few clicks prepare all of the requisite reports that make it easy to prepare taxes.

PAYING BILLS ONLINE

While it's certainly not imperative, you might want to check out your bank's online bill pay option if you're not using this already. Once you've set up the payee list, you can make payments in a few seconds every month or set up auto payments for expenses that are recurring. Having a digital history of bills paid can also come in handy with your accounting.

MANAGING TAXES

Self-employed people need to pay quarterly taxes. A quick, online search will reveal a variety of tax calculators and other online tools that can help you estimate what your payments should be. Programs such as TurboTax are popular and useful tools for automating and guiding you step-by-step through tax preparation. An accountant can also be helpful in understanding your unique tax picture, identifying and saving the right amount for taxes each quarter, and even determining SEP IRA contribution amounts (described later in this article). The more complex your finances (or antediluvian your accounting skills), the more likely that you'll benefit from this kind of personalized expertise.

Once you have forecasted your taxes either with the help of a specialized, tax-planning program or an accountant, you can establish a plan toward saving the right amount for quarterly payments. For example, once I figured out what my tax bracket was and the approximate percentage of income that needed to be set aside as taxes, I would immediately transfer a percentage of every deposit to my savings account, where it would sit and grow a little interest until quarterly tax time came around. When I could afford to do so, I would also set aside the appropriate percentage of SEP IRA contribution from each deposit so that I'd be ready at end-of-year to deposit as much as I possibly could for retirement.

THE PRINCIPLE TO COMMIT TO IS THIS: Get that tax-earmarked cash out of your hot little hands (i.e., checking account) as soon as you can, and create whatever deterrents you need to leave the money in savings so you'll have it when you need it.

INTELLIGENT INVESTING FOR YOUR CAREER

Your writing business will require not only the investment of your time but also the investment of money. When deciding what to spend and how, consider your values and your budget in the three, key areas in the chart below: education, marketing and promotion, and keeping the wheels turning.

This is not an absolute formula for spending—just a snapshot of the types of expenses you may be considering and negotiating over time. My general rule would be: start small and modest with the one or two most urgent and/or inexpensive items in each list, and grow slowly over time as your income grows.

The good news is that these legitimate business expenses may all be deducted from your income—making your net income and tax burden less. Please keep in mind that the IRS allows losses as long as you make a profit for at least three of the first five years you are in business. Otherwise, the IRS will consider your writing a non-deductible hobby.

PREPARATION AND PROTECTION FOR THE FUTURE

As a self-employed writer, in many ways your future is in your hands. Following are some of the health and financial investments that I'd recommend you consider as you build and nurture The Enterprise of You. Please

EDUCATION	MARKETING AND PROMOTION	KEEPING THE WHEELS TURNING
Subscriptions to publications in your field	URL registration and hosting for blogs and websites	Technology and application purchase, servicing and back-up
Memberships to organizations in your field	Contact database subscription (such as Constant Contact) for communicating with your audiences	Office supplies and furniture
Books: on topics you want to learn, or in genres you are cultivating	Business cards and stationery	Insurance for you and/or your business
Conferences and seminars	Print promotions (such as direct mail), giveaways and schwag	Travel, gas, parking
Classes and workshops	Online or print ad placement costs	Phone, fax and e-mail

understand that these are a layperson's suggestions. I am by no means an accountant, tax advisor, or financial planning guru. I am simply a person who has educated herself on these topics for the sake of her own writing business, made the choices I am recommending, and benefited from them. I'd like you to benefit from them, too.

SEP IRAS

Individual Retirement Accounts (IRAs) are investment accounts designed to help individuals save for retirement. But I do recommend that you educate yourself about the Simplified Employee Pension Individual Retirement Account (SEP IRA) and consider opening one if you don't have one already.

A SEP IRA is a special type of IRA that is particularly beneficial to self-employed people. Whereas a Roth IRA has a contribution cap of $5,000 or $6,000, depending on your age, the contribution limit for self-employed people in 2011 is approximately 20% of adjusted earned income, with a maximum contribution of $49,000. Contributions for a SEP IRA are generally 100% tax deductible and investments grow tax deferred. Let's say your adjusted earned income this year is $50,000. This means you'd be able to contribute $10,000 to your retirement account. I encourage you to do some research online or ask your accountant if a SEP IRA makes sense for you.

CREATING A 9-MONTH SAVINGS BUFFER

When you're living month-to-month, you are extremely vulnerable to fluctuation in the economy, client budget changes, life emergencies and every other wrench that could turn a good working groove into a frightening financial rut. The best way to prepare for the unexpected is to start (or continue) developing a savings buffer. The experts these days are suggesting that we accumulate nine months of living expenses to help us navigate transition in a way that we feel empowered rather than scared and desperate to take the next thing that comes along.

I started creating my savings buffer by opening the highest-interest money market account I could find and setting up a modest, monthly automatic transfer from my checking account. Then, when I paid off my car after five years of monthly payments, I added my car payment amount to the monthly transfer. (I'd been paying that amount for five years, so I was pretty sure I could continue to pay it to myself.) When I paid off one of my credit cards in full, I added that monthly payment to the monthly savings transfer. Within a year, I had a hefty sum going to savings every month before I had time to think about it, all based on expenses I was accustomed to paying, with money that had never been anticipated in the monthly cash flow.

What can you do today—and tomorrow—to put your money to work for your life, and start being as creative with your savings as you are with language?

DISABILITY INSURANCE

If writing is your livelihood, what happens if you become unable to write? I have writing friends who have become incapacitated and unable to work due to injuries to their brains, backs, hands and eyes. Disability insurance is one way to protect against such emergencies and ensure that you have an income in the unlikely event that you're not physically able to earn one yourself.

Depending on your health, age, and budget, monthly disability insurance payments may or may not be within your means or priorities. But you won't know until you learn more about your coverage options. I encourage you to investigate this possibility with several highly rated insurance companies to get the lay of the land for your unique, personal profile and make an informed decision.

HEALTH INSURANCE

Self-employed writers face tough decisions about health insurance. If you're lucky, there's someone in your family with health coverage also available to you. Without the benefit of group health insurance, chances are that self-costs are high and coverage is low. As in disability insurance, age and health status are significant variables in costs and availability.

Ideally, of course, you'll have reasonably-priced health insurance that helps make preventive care and health maintenance more accessible and protects you in case of a major medical emergency. The following are a few possibilities to check out that could reduce costs and improve access to health coverage:

- Join a group that aggregates its members for group coverage, such as a Chamber of Commerce or AARP. Ask an insurance agent in your area if there are any other group coverage options available to you.
- Consider a high-deductible health plan paired with a Health Savings Account (HSA). Because the deductible is so high, these plans are generally thought to be most useful for a major medical emergency. But an HSA paired with such a plan allows you to put aside a chunk of pre-tax change every year that can be spent on medical expenses or remain in the account where it can be invested and grow.

Establishing effective financial systems for your writing business will take some time and energy at the front end. I suggest that you pace yourself by taking an achievable step or two each week until you have a baseline of financial management that works for you. Then, you can start moving toward some of your bigger, longer-term goals. Once it's established, your solid financial foundation will pay you in dividends of greater efficiency, insight, and peace of mind for the rest of your writing career.

SAGE COHEN is the author of *The Productive Writer* and *Writing the Life Poetic,* both from Writer's Digest Books. She's been nominated for a Pushcart Prize, won first prize in the Ghost Road Press Poetry contest and published dozens of poems, essays and articles on the writing life. Sage holds an MFA in creative writing from New York University and a BA from Brown University. Since 1997, she has been a freelance writer serving clients including Intuit, Blue Shield, Adobe, and Kaiser Permanente..

6 APPS THAT MAKE FREELANCING EASIER

by Jocelyn Kerr

Freelance writing has never been a simple way to make a living, but smartphones have taken us a long way toward streamlining the process. When I started out nearly a decade ago, e-mail was about as high-tech as it got. Now there are more productivity and project management apps at our fingertips than most of us can keep track of.

In the latest 2014 Pew Research findings, 58 percent of American adults own a smartphone, and 44 percent of us sleep with our phones near our beds so we don't miss any messages. (Guilty as charged.) With so many of us attached to our smartphones, shouldn't it make our freelancing lives easier?

As a corporate copywriter and freelance journalist, smartphone apps have helped me stay on track and deliver projects more efficiently over the last couple of years. Everything from time tracking to editing advice to file management is available on your smartphone. You can even send out invoices while you're in line at the grocery store.

There are many, many more free and paid apps out there that will help streamline everything from social media postings to calendar reminders, but these apps are the ones I turn to almost daily.

POMODROIDO (ANDROID)/ FLAT TOMATO (IOS)

Let's start with an app that kills two freelancing birds with one stone: task management and taking all-important breaks during marathon writing days. These apps are loosely based on Francesco Cirillo's Pomadoro Technique. In a nutshell, he recommends using a timer to break tasks into 25-minute chunks, followed by a five-minute break. One of these 30-minute blocks is called a "pomodoro." After four pomadoros, take a 30-minute break.

A 2010 study published in the *Journal of Behavioral Optometry* found that up to 90 percent of computer users suffer from computer vision syndrome (CVS). Symptoms include dry eye, eyestrain and in some cases headaches. Research from a 2006 study published in the Journal of Occupational Rehabilitation found the two most common health issues for people who work on computers are vision problems and "musculoskeletal disorders." In other words, neck, back, and wrist pain. Researchers noted dry eye kicks in after about 25 minutes of screen time, so there might be something to that magic number.

During the five-minute breaks, get up and walk around. Go outside for a few minutes, or do a few quick stretches. It'll help your eyes and help keep your body from being stiff and sore after a day at the desk.

Want to break down your workday into a different block of minutes? There are tons of free timers out there. But, they won't have the cool ticking tomato red interface.

HELP! FOR WRITERS

This is the only paid app on the list, $1.99 as of this writing, but it's one of the only all-encompassing nonfiction writing apps I've ever come across. The app provides practical advice on everything from finding story ideas to building a coherent draft. At some point all writers need advice, and this app is like having a mini nonfiction writing coach in your pocket.

Produced by the Pointer Institute's News University, the app takes Roy Peter Clark's writing advice from his book *Help! For Writers: 210 Solutions to the Problems Every Writer Faces* and condenses it into an easy-to-navigate mobile app. Clark is a renowned writing coach, the author of multiple books on writing, and he teaches workshops through Pointer's NewsU. There's a link to his online workshop within the app, if you're looking for some journalism training.

To use the app, choose one of five problem areas: getting started, hunting and gathering, finding a focus, building a draft or making it better. Then drill down to your specific problem and read one of the 200 tips to solve the problem.

THE WRITER'S STYLE GUIDE

The Writer Ltd is the world's largest language consultancy, which basically means they write and train others to write. They created a free style guide app that works equally well for British and American business writers. If you ever have a project where you need to convert one to the other, this is your app. The company is based in London and New York City, so the guide covers grammar on both sides of the Atlantic and offers clarity on the all-important debate over whether it's okay to start a sentence with a conjunction (they say yes).

Scroll through the style guide for quick answers to grammar and usage questions. While the app is geared toward business writing, the emphasis on clear, focused writing is useful for any writer.

Beyond just being a style guide, The Writer's app has a "readability checker" where you can enter a writing sample and find out how readable your prose is. There's also a fun quiz and polls for when you're standing in line (or procrastinating on a deadline).

DROPBOX

If you have to deliver high-resolution photos, videos, or graphics to a client, Dropbox will save your sanity. Sign up for a free account and create client folders to store your deliverables. When it comes time to submit, send a link to the folder and your client can access the files straight from Dropbox. Add password protection if you'd like, but the link will only be accessible to the person you send it to.

This prevents the drama of having e-mails bounce back because the attachments are too large, or from having to send one file at a time. There are similar file-sharing services like Google Drive, Box, and One-Drive, but I find the interface on Dropbox, both the Web interface and the mobile app, to be the easiest to navigate.

Another great thing is Dropbox functions like a thumb drive. Lose your phone or have a computer meltdown? No problem. Access your files from any computer with Internet access. Just sign into the Web interface.

ASANA

If you have corporate clients, there will come a time when you need to use project management software. Basecamp is a popular choice, but it's a subscription-based service. I have clients who have added me to their Basecamp account and I use the free Basecamp app to manage their tasks and files from my phone.

However, if your client isn't footing the bill for a subscription service, Asana is a good free choice. Sign up for a free account online, set up your projects and add project team members, and then download the app to manage tasks and review team updates.

The benefit of using Asana is everyone on the team has access to all the task lists and relevant project information. When you're working on projects with multiple decision-makers, it helps to have one central place where everyone can see what tasks are due. It's much more efficient than e-mail chains and phone tag, where tasks can slip through the cracks.

Even if you're not working on a corporate project, Asana is a good way to break down any big task. Use it to amp up your marketing efforts or plan out that novel.

QUICKBOOKS OR FRESHBOOKS

Now that the work is done, it's time to invoice and get paid. I've included both QuickBooks and FreshBooks here, because I've used both and while they're very similar, they also have distinct differences. The apps are free, but you'll need an account to use them.

Both apps allow you to create and track invoices directly from your phone. Both apps allow you to accept online payments. That's about where the similarities end. The FreshBooks service is free if you're only invoicing one client and have no staff members. Their paid invoicing service allows you to manage billable staff hours, log project time, and manage multiple clients. QuickBooks is basically a bookkeeping service, so you won't get the team management and timekeeping features.

About two years into my freelance career I started using QuickBooks to manage my accounts, so I use their app. However, I did try the FreshBooks free version for about a year and I found it to be a great service. I just didn't need the project management and time-tracking features. I'm also more familiar with the QuickBooks interface. It's personal preference more than anything. Both services offer the ability to manage client lists and invoices straight from your phone.

For new freelancers who haven't decided whether they need or want a full-featured invoicing and accounting service, FreshBooks is a great place to start. Add a client for free, send invoices and accept online payments through PayPal and Stripe.

WORD PROCESSING APPS

What about actually writing on your smartphone? There are many word processing apps, both free and paid, and I have installed and used several of them. The reason I don't use them is simple: Who wants to type a document on a smartphone? In an absolute emergency, maybe you'll find yourself needing to make an edit on the fly or add a paragraph somewhere, but I've never found it comfortable to compose on a phone screen. A tablet? Maybe. But I don't want to type on a phone.

Call me old fashioned, but I still do all my writing on a computer and use the phone for ideas, file sharing, and overall project management. In any case, freelancing is a lot more efficient with the right apps.

JOCELYN KERR is a freelance writer, editor and journalist who is never without her smartphone. She has run a corporate copywriting company since 2012, and her reporting has appeared in the *Houston Chronicle*, *DRAFT Magazine*, Tiger Oak Publications, Gayot Publications, and others. Connect at linkedin.com/in/jocelynkerr.

HOW MUCH SHOULD I CHARGE?

by Aaron Belz

The first question most aspiring freelance writers ask themselves is, "Where do I find paying gigs?" But once a writer finds that first freelance gig, they often ask, "How much should I charge?"

They ask this question, because often their clients ask them. In the beginning, this can be one of the most stressful parts of the freelancing process: Trying to set rates that don't scare away clients, but that also help put dinner on the table.

Maybe that's why the "How Much Should I Charge?" pay rate chart is one of the most popular and useful pieces of the *Writer's Market*. Freelancers use the rates to justify their worth on the market to potential clients, and clients use the chart as an objective third party authority on what the current market is paying.

Use the following chart to help you get started in figuring out your freelance rates. If you're a beginner, it makes sense to price yourself closer to the lower end of the spectrum, but always use your gut in negotiating rates. The rate on that first assignment often helps set the expectations for future rates.

As you find success in securing work, your rates should naturally increase. If not, consider whether you're building relationships with clients that lead to multiple assignments. Also, take into account whether you're negotiating for higher rates on new assignments with familiar and newer clients.

Remember that smarter freelancers work toward the goal of higher rates, because better rates mean one of two things for writers: Either they're able to earn money, or they're able to earn the same money in less time. For some freelancers, having that extra time is worth more than anything money can buy.

Use the listings in *Writer's Market* to find freelance work for magazines, book publishers, and other traditional publishing markets. But don't restrict your search to the traditional markets if you want to make a serious living as a freelance writer.

As the pay rate chart shows, there are an incredible number of opportunities for writers to make a living doing what they love: writing. Maybe that writing critiques, editing anthologies, blogging, or something else entirely.

While this pay rate chart covers a wide variety of freelance writing gigs, there are some that are just too unique to get a going rate. If you can't find a specific job listed here, try to find something that is similar to use as a guide for figuring out a rate. There are times when you just have to create the going rate yourself.

Thank you, Aaron Belz, for assembling this pay rate chart and sharing your sources in the sidebar below. I know it will help more than one freelance writer negotiate the freelance rates they deserve.

—*Robert Lee Brewer*

PARTICIPATING ORGANIZATIONS

Here are the organizations surveyed to compile the "How Much Should I Charge?" pay rate chart. You can also find Professional Organizations in the Resources.

- American Medical Writers Association (AMWA), www.amwa.org
- American Society of Journalists & Authors (ASJA), www.asja.org
- American Society of Media Photographers (ASMP), www.asmp.org
- American Society of Picture Professionals (ASPP), www.aspp.com
- American Translators Association (ATA), www.atanet.org
- Association of Independents in Radio (AIR), www.airmedia.org
- Educational Freelancers Association (EFA), www.the-efa.org
- Freelance Success (FLX), www.freelancesucess.com
- Investigative Reporters & Editors (IRE), www.ire.org
- Media Communicators Association International (MCA-I), www.mca-i.org
- National Cartoonists Society (NCS), www.reuben.org/main.asp
- National Writers Union (NWU), www.nwu.org
- National Association of Science Writers (NASW), www.nasw.org
- Society of Professional Journalists (SPJ), www.spj.org
- Women in Film (WIF), www.wif.org
- Writer's Guild of America East (WGAE), www.wgaeast.org
- Writer's Guild of America West (WGA), www.wga.org

AARON BELZ is the author of *The Bird Hoverer* (BlazeVOX), *Lovely, Raspberry* (Persea), and *Glitter Bomb* (Persea). A St. Louis native, he now lives and works in Hillsborough, North Carolina. Visit him online at belz.net or follow him on Twitter @aaronbelz..

	PER HOUR			PER PROJECT			OTHER		
	HIGH	LOW	AVG	HIGH	LOW	AVG	HIGH	LOW	AVG
ADVERTISING & PUBLIC RELATIONS									
Advertising copywriting	$156	$36	$84	$9,000	$160	$2,760	$3/word	30¢/word	$1.57/word
Advertising editing	$125	$20	$65	n/a	n/a	n/a	$1/word	30¢/word	66¢/word
Advertorials	$182	$51	$93	$1,890	$205	$285	$3/word	85¢/word	$1.58/word
Business public relations	$182	$30	$85	n/a	n/a	n/a	$500/day	$200/day	$356/day
Campaign development or product launch	$156	$36	$100	$8,755	$1,550	$4,545	n/a	n/a	n/a
Catalog copywriting	$156	$25	$71	n/a	n/a	n/a	$350/item	$30/item	$116/item
Corporate spokesperson role	$182	$72	$107	n/a	n/a	n/a	$1,200/day	$500/day	$740/day
Direct-mail copywriting	$156	$36	$85	$8,248	$500	$2,839	$4/word $400/page	$1/word $200/page	$2.17/word $315/page
Event promotions/publicity	$126	$30	$76	n/a	n/a	n/a	n/a	n/a	$500/day
Press kits	$182	$31	$81	n/a	n/a	n/a	$850/60sec	$120/60sec	$458/60sec
Press/news release	$182	$30	$80	$1,500	$125	$700	$2/word $750/page	50¢/word $150/page	$1.20/word $348/page

	PER HOUR			PER PROJECT			OTHER		
	HIGH	LOW	AVG	HIGH	LOW	AVG	HIGH	LOW	AVG
Radio commercials	$102	$30	$74	n/a	n/a	n/a	$850/60sec	$120/60sec	$456/60sec
Speech writing/editing for individuals or corporations	$168	$36	$92	$10,000	$2,700	$5,036	$355/minute	$105/minute	$208/minute
BOOK PUBLISHING									
Abstracting and abridging	$125	$30	$74	n/a	n/a	n/a	$2/word	$1/word	$1.48/word
Anthology editing	$80	$23	$51	$7,900	$1,200	$4,588	n/a	n/a	n/a
Book chapter	$100	$35	$60	$2,500	$1,200	$1,758	20¢/word	8¢/word	14¢/word
Book production for clients	$100	$40	$67	n/a	n/a	n/a	$17.50/page	$5/page	$10/page
Book proposal consultation	$125	$25	$66	$1,500	$250	$788	n/a	n/a	n/a
Book publicity for clients	n/a	n/a	n/a	$10,000	$500	$2,000	n/a	n/a	n/a
Book query critique	$100	$50	$72	$500	$75	$202	n/a	n/a	n/a
Children's book writing	$75	$35	$50	n/a	n/a	n/a	$5/word $5,000/adv	$1/word $450/adv	$2.75/word $2,286/adv
Content editing (scholarly/textbook)	$125	$20	$51	$15,000	$500	$4,477	$20/page	$3/page	$6.89/page

	PER HOUR			PER PROJECT			OTHER		
	HIGH	LOW	AVG	HIGH	LOW	AVG	HIGH	LOW	AVG
Content editing (trade)	$125	$19	$54	$20,000	$1,000	$6,538	$20/page	$3.75/page	$8/page
Copyediting (trade)	$100	$16	$46	$5,500	$2,000	$2,892	$6/page	$1/page	$4.22/page
Encyclopedia articles	n/a	n/a	n/a	n/a	n/a	n/a	50¢/word $3,000/item	15¢/word $50/item	35¢/word $933/item
Fiction book writing (own)	n/a	n/a	n/a	n/a	n/a	n/a	$40,000/adv	$525/adv	$14,193/adv
Ghostwriting, as told to	$125	$35	$67	$47,000	$5,500	$22,892	$100/page	$50/page	$87/page
Ghostwriting, no credit	$125	$30	$73	n/a	n/a	n/a	$3/word $500/page	50¢/word $50/page	$1.79/word $206/page
Guidebook writing/editing	n/a	n/a	n/a	n/a	n/a	n/a	$14,000/adv	$10,000/adv	$12,000/adv
Indexing	$60	$22	$35	n/a	n/a	n/a	$12/page	$2/page	$4.72/page
Manuscript evaluation and critique	$150	$23	$66	$2,000	$150	$663	n/a	n/a	n/a
Manuscript typing	n/a	n/a	$20	n/a	n/a	n/a	$3/page	95¢/page	$1.67/page
Movie novelizations	n/a	n/a	n/a	$15,000	$5,000	$9,159	n/a	n/a	n/a

	PER HOUR			PER PROJECT			OTHER		
Nonfiction book writing (collaborative)	$125	$40	$80	n/a	n/a	n/a	$110/page $75,000/adv	$50/page $1,300/adv	$80/page $22,684/adv
Nonfiction book writing (own)	$125	$40	$72	n/a	n/a	n/a	$110/page $50,000/adv	$50/page $1,300/adv	$80/page $14,057/adv
Novel synopsis (general)	$60	$30	$45	$450	$150	$292	$100/page	$10/page	$37/page
Personal history writing/editing (for clients)	$125	$30	$60	$40,000	$750	$15,038	n/a	n/a	n/a
Proofreading	$75	$15	$31	n/a	n/a	n/a	$5/page	$2/page	$3.26/page
Research for writers or book publishers	$150	$15	$52	n/a	n/a	n/a	$600/day	$400/day	$525/day
Rewriting/structural editing	$120	$25	$67	$50,000	$2,500	$13,929	14¢/word	5¢/word	10¢/word
Translation—literary	n/a	n/a	n/a	$95,000	$6,500	$8,000	17¢/target word	4¢/target word	8¢/target word
Translation—nonfiction/technical	n/a	n/a	n/a	n/a	n/a	n/a	30¢/target word	5¢/target word	12¢/target word

	PER HOUR			PER PROJECT			OTHER		
	HIGH	LOW	AVG	HIGH	LOW	AVG	HIGH	LOW	AVG
BUSINESS									
Annual reports	$185	$60	$102	$15,000	$500	$5,850	$600	$100	$349
Brochures, booklets, flyers	$150	$45	$91	$15,000	$300	$4,230	$2.50/word $800/page	35¢/word $50/page	$1.21/word $341/page
Business editing (general)	$155	$40	$80	n/a	n/a	n/a	n/a	n/a	n/a
Business letters	$155	$40	$79	n/a	n/a	n/a	$2/word	$1/word	$1.47/word
Business plan	$155	$40	$87	$15,000	$200	$4,115	n/a	n/a	n/a
Business writing seminars	$155	$70	$112	$8,600	$550	$2,919	n/a	n/a	n/a
Consultation on communications	$155	$50	$80	n/a	n/a	n/a	$1,300/day	$530/day	$830/day
Copyediting for business	$155	$35	$65	n/a	n/a	n/a	$4/page	$2/page	$3/page
Corporate histories	$155	$45	$91	160,000	$5,000	$54,525	$2/word	$1/word	$1.50/word
Corporate periodicals, editing	$155	$45	$74	n/a	n/a	n/a	$2.50/word	75¢/word	$1.42/word
Corporate periodicals, writing	$155	$45	$83	n/a	n/a	$1,880	$3/word	$1/word	$1.71/word
Corporate profiles	$155	$45	$93	n/a	n/a	$3,000	$2/word	$1/word	$1.50/word

	PER HOUR			PER PROJECT			OTHER		
	HIGH	LOW	AVG	HIGH	LOW	AVG	HIGH	LOW	AVG
Ghostwriting for business execs	$155	$45	$89	$3,000	$500	$1,400	$2.50/word	50¢/word	$2/word
Ghostwriting for businesses	$155	$45	$114	$3,000	$500	$1,790	n/a	n/a	n/a
Newsletters, desktop publish-ing/production	$155	$45	$75	$6,600	$1,000	$3,490	$750/page	$150/page	$429/page
Newsletters, editing	$155	$35	$72	n/a	n/a	$3,615	$230/page	$150/page	$185/page
Newsletters, writing	$155	$35	$82	$6,600	$800	$3,581	$5/word $1,250/page	$1/word $150/page	$2.31/word $514/page
Translation services for business use	$80	$45	$57	n/a	n/a	n/a	$35/ target word $1.41/ target line	7¢/ target word $1/ target line	$2.31/ target word $1.21/ target line
Resume writing	$105	$70	$77	$500	$150	$295	n/a	n/a	n/a
COMPUTER, INTERNET & TECHNICAL									
Blogging—paid	$150	$35	$100	$2,000	$500	$1,250	$500/post	$6/post	$49/post
E-mail copywriting	$135	$30	$85	n/a	n/a	$300	$2/word	30¢/word	91¢/word

	PER HOUR			PER PROJECT			OTHER		
	HIGH	LOW	AVG	HIGH	LOW	AVG	HIGH	LOW	AVG
Educational webinars	$500	$0	$195	n/a	n/a	n/a	n/a	n/a	n/a
Hardware/Software help screen writing	$95	$60	$81	$6,000	$1,000	$4,000	n/a	n/a	n/a
Hardware/Software manual writing	$165	$30	$80	$23,500	$5,000	$11,500	n/a	n/a	n/a
Internet research	$95	$25	$55	n/a	n/a	n/a	n/a	n/a	n/a
Keyword descriptions	n/a	n/a	n/a	n/a	n/a	n/a	$200/page	$130/page	$165/page
Online videos for clients	$95	$60	$76	n/a	n/a	n/a	n/a	n/a	n/a
Social media postings for clients	$95	$25	$62	n/a	n/a	$500	n/a	n/a	$10/word
Technical editing	$150	$30	$65	n/a	n/a	n/a	n/a	n/a	n/a
Technical writing	$160	$30	$80	n/a	n/a	n/a	n/a	n/a	n/a
Web editing	$100	$25	$57	n/a	n/a	n/a	$10/page	$4/page	$5.67/page
Webpage design	$150	$25	$80	$4,000	$200	$1,278	n/a	n/a	n/a
Website or blog promotion	n/a	$30	n/a	$650	$195	$335	n/a	n/a	n/a

	PER HOUR			PER PROJECT			OTHER		
	HIGH	LOW	AVG	HIGH	LOW	AVG	HIGH	LOW	AVG
Website reviews	n/a	$30	n/a	$900	$50	$300	n/a	n/a	n/a
Website search engine optimization	$89	$30	$76	$50,000	$8,000	$12,000	n/a	n/a	n/a
White papers	$135	$30	$82	$10,000	$2,500	$4,927	n/a	n/a	n/a
EDITORIAL/DESIGN PACKAGES									
Desktop publishing	$150	$18	$67	n/a	n/a	n/a	$750/page	$30/page	$202/page
Photo brochures	$125	$60	$87	$15,000	$400	$3,869	$65/picture	$30/picture	$48/picture
Photography	$100	$45	$71	$10,500	$50	$2,100	$2,500/day	$500/day	$1,340/day
Photo research	$75	$45	$49	n/a	n/a	n/a	n/a	n/a	n/a
Picture editing	$100	$45	$64	n/a	n/a	n/a	$65/picture	$30/picture	$53/picture
EDUCATIONAL & LITERARY SERVICES									
Author appearances at national events	n/a	n/a	n/a	n/a	n/a	n/a	$500/hour $30,000/event	$100/hour $500/event	$285/hour $5,000/event
Author appearances at regional events	n/a	n/a	n/a	n/a	n/a	n/a	$1,500/event	$50/event	$615/event

	PER HOUR			PER PROJECT			OTHER		
	HIGH	LOW	AVG	HIGH	LOW	AVG	HIGH	LOW	AVG
Author appearances at local groups	$63	$40	$47	n/a	n/a	n/a	$400/event	$75/event	$219/event
Authors presenting in schools	$125	$25	$78	n/a	n/a	n/a	$350/class	$50/class	$183/class
Educational grant and proposal writing	$100	$35	$67	n/a	n/a	n/a	n/a	n/a	n/a
Manuscript evaluation for theses/dissertations	$100	$15	$53	$1,550	$200	$783	n/a	n/a	n/a
Poetry manuscript critique	$100	$25	$62	n/a	n/a	n/a	n/a	n/a	n/a
Private writing instruction	$60	$50	$57	n/a	n/a	n/a	n/a	n/a	n/a
Readings by poets, fiction writers	n/a	n/a	n/a	n/a	n/a	n/a	$3,000/event	$50/event	$225/event
Short story manuscript critique	$150	$30	$75	$175	$50	$112	n/a	n/a	n/a
Teaching adult writing classes	$125	$30	$82	n/a	n/a	n/a	$800/class $5,000/course	$115/class $500/course	$450/class $2,667/course
Writer's workshop panel or class	$220	$30	$92	n/a	n/a	n/a	$5,000/day	$60/day	$1,186/day
Writing for scholarly journals	$100	$40	$63	$450	$100	$285	n/a	n/a	n/a

	PER HOUR			PER PROJECT			OTHER		
	HIGH	LOW	AVG	HIGH	LOW	AVG	HIGH	LOW	AVG
FILM, VIDEO, TV, RADIO, STAGE									
Book/novel summaries for film producers	n/a	n/a	n/a	n/a	n/a	n/a	$34/page	$15/page	$23/page $120/book
Business film/video scriptwriting	$150	$50	$97	n/a	n/a	$600	$1,000/run min	$50/run min	$334/run min $500/day
Comedy writing for entertainers	n/a	n/a	n/a	n/a	n/a	n/a	$150/joke $500/group	$5/joke $100/group	$50/joke $283/group
Copyediting audiovisuals	$90	$22	$53	n/a	n/a	n/a	n/a	n/a	n/a
Educational or training film/video scriptwriting	$125	$35	$81	n/a	n/a	n/a	$500/run min	$100/run min	$245/run min
Feature film options	First 18 months, 10% WGA minimum; 10% minimum each 18-month period thereafter.								
TV options	First 180 days, 5% WGA minimum; 10% minimum each 180-day period thereafter.								
Industrial product film/video scriptwriting	$150	$30	$99	n/a	n/a	n/a	$500/run min	$100/run min	$300/run min
Playwriting for the stage	5-10% box office/Broadway, 6-7% box office/off-Broadway, 10% box office/regional theatre.								

	PER HOUR			PER PROJECT			OTHER		
Radio editorials	$70	$50	$60	n/a	n/a	n/a	$200/run min $400/day	$45/run min $250/day	$124/run min $325/day
Radio interviews	n/a	n/a	n/a	$1,500	$110	$645	n/a	n/a	n/a
Screenwriting (original screenplay-including treatment)	n/a	n/a	n/a	n/a	n/a	n/a	$118,745	$63,526	$92,153
Script synopsis for agent or film	$2,344/30 min, $4,441/60 min, $6,564/90 min								
Script synopsis for business	$75	$45	$62	n/a	n/a	n/a	n/a	n/a	n/a
TV commercials	$99	$60	$81	n/a	n/a	n/a	$2,500/30 sec	$150/30 sec	$1,204/30 sec
TV news story/feature	$1,550/5 min, $3,000/10 min, $4,200/15 min								
TV scripts (non-theatrical)	Prime Time: $33,700/60 min, $47,500/90 min Not Prime Time: $12,900/30 min, $23,500/60 min, $35,300/90 min								
TV scripts (teleplay/MOW)	$70,000/120 min								

	PER HOUR			PER PROJECT			OTHER		
	HIGH	LOW	AVG	HIGH	LOW	AVG	HIGH	LOW	AVG
MAGAZINES & TRADE JOURNALS									
Article manuscript critique	$130	$25	$69	n/a	n/a	n/a	n/a	n/a	n/a
Arts query critique	$105	$50	$80	n/a	n/a	n/a	n/a	n/a	n/a
Arts reviewing	$100	$65	$84	$335	$95	$194	$1.25/word	12¢/word	63¢/word
Book reviews	n/a	n/a	n/a	$900	$12	$348	$1.50/word	20¢/word	73¢/word
City magazine calendar	n/a	n/a	n/a	$250	$45	$135	$1/word	35¢/word	75¢/word
Comic book/strip writing	$225 original story, $525 existing story, $50 short script.								
Consultation on magazine editorial	$155	$35	$86	n/a	n/a	n/a	n/a	n/a	$100/page
Consumer magazine column	n/a	n/a	n/a	$2,500	$70	$898	$2.50/word	37¢/word	$1.13/word
Consumer front-of-book	n/a	n/a	n/a	$850	$320	$550	n/a	n/a	n/a
Content editing	$130	$30	$62	$6,500	$2,000	$3,700	15¢/word	6¢/word	11¢/word
Contributing editor	n/a	n/a	n/a	n/a	n/a	n/a	$160,000/ contract	$22,000/ contract	$53,000/ contract
Copyediting magazines	$105	$18	$55	n/a	n/a	n/a	$10/page	$2.90/page	$5.78/page

	PER HOUR			PER PROJECT			OTHER		
	HIGH	LOW	AVG	HIGH	LOW	AVG	HIGH	LOW	AVG
Fact checking	$130	$15	$46	n/a	n/a	n/a	n/a	n/a	n/a
Gag writing for cartoonists	$35/gag; 25% sale on spec.								
Ghostwriting articles (general)	$225	$30	$107	$3,500	$1,100	$2,200	$10/word	65¢/word	$2.50/word
Magazine research	$125	$20	$53	n/a	n/a	n/a	$500/item	$100/item	$200/item
Proofreading	$80	$20	$40	n/a	n/a	n/a	n/a	n/a	n/a
Reprint fees	n/a	n/a	n/a	$1,500	$20	$439	$1.50/word	10¢/word	76¢/word
Rewriting	$130	$25	$74	n/a	n/a	n/a	n/a	n/a	$50/page
Trade journal feature article	$128	$45	$80	$4,950	$150	$1,412	$3/word	20¢/word	$1.20/word
Transcribing interviews	$185	$95	$55	n/a	n/a	n/a	$3/min	$1/min	$2/min
MEDICAL/SCIENCE									
Medical/scientific conference coverage	$125	$50	$85	n/a	n/a	n/a	$800/day	$300/day	$600/day
Medical/scientific editing	$96	$15	$33	n/a	n/a	n/a	$12.50/page $600/day	$3/page $500/day	$4.40/page $550/day
Medical/scientific writing	$91	$20	$46	$4,000	$500	$2,500	$2/word	25¢/word	$1.12/word

	PER HOUR			PER PROJECT			OTHER		
	HIGH	LOW	AVG	HIGH	LOW	AVG	HIGH	LOW	AVG
Medical/scientific multimedia presentations	$100	$50	$75	n/a	n/a	n/a	$100/slide	$50/slide	$77/slide
Medical/scientific proofreading	$80	$18	$50	n/a	n/a	$500	$3/page	$2.50/page	$2.75/page
Pharmaceutical writing	$125	$100	$50	n/a	n/a	n/a	n/a	n/a	n/a
NEWSPAPERS									
Arts reviewing	$69	$30	$53	$200	$15	$101	60¢/word	6¢/word	36¢/word
Book reviews	$69	$45	$58	$350	$15	$140	60¢/word	25¢/word	44¢/word
Column, local	n/a	n/a	n/a	$600	$25	$206	$1/word	38¢/word	50¢/word
Column, self-syndicated	n/a	n/a	n/a	n/a	n/a	n/a	$35/insertion	$4/insertion	$16/insertion
Copyediting	$35	$15	$27	n/a	n/a	n/a	n/a	n/a	n/a
Editing/manuscript evaluation	$75	$25	$35	n/a	n/a	n/a	n/a	n/a	n/a
Feature writing	$79	$40	$63	$1,040	$85	$478	$1.60/word	10¢/word	59¢/word
Investigative reporting	n/a	n/a	n/a	n/a	n/a	n/a	$10,000/grant	$250/grant	$2,250/grant
Obituary copy	n/a	n/a	n/a	$225	$35	$124	n/a	n/a	n/a

	PER HOUR			PER PROJECT			OTHER		
	HIGH	LOW	AVG	HIGH	LOW	AVG	HIGH	LOW	AVG
Proofreading	$45	$15	$23	n/a	n/a	n/a	n/a	n/a	n/a
Stringing	n/a	n/a	n/a	$2,400	$40	$525	n/a	n/a	n/a
NONPROFIT									
Grant writing for nonprofits	$150	$12	$75	$3,000	$400	$1,852	n/a	n/a	n/a
Nonprofit annual reports	$100	$28	$60	n/a	n/a	n/a	n/a	n/a	n/a
Nonprofit writing	$150	$17	$65	$17,600	$100	$4,706	n/a	n/a	n/a
Nonprofit editing	$125	$16	$50	n/a	n/a	n/a	n/a	n/a	n/a
Nonprofit fundraising literature	$110	$35	$74	$3,500	$200	$1,597	$1,000/day	$300/day	$767/day
Nonprofit presentations	$100	$40	$73	n/a	n/a	n/a	n/a	n/a	n/a
Nonprofit public relations	$100	$30	$60	n/a	n/a	n/a	n/a	n/a	n/a

	PER HOUR			PER PROJECT			OTHER		
	HIGH	LOW	AVG	HIGH	LOW	AVG	HIGH	LOW	AVG
POLITICS/GOVERNMENT									
Government agency writing/editing	$110	$25	$64	n/a	n/a	n/a	$1.25/word	25¢/word	75¢/word
Government grant writing/editing	$150	$19	$72	n/a	n/a	n/a	n/a	n/a	n/a
Government-sponsored research	$110	$35	$66	n/a	n/a	n/a	n/a	n/a	$600/day
Public relations for political campaigns	$150	$40	$86	n/a	n/a	n/a	n/a	n/a	n/a
Speechwriting for government officials	$200	$40	$96	$4,550	$1,015	$2,755	$200/run min	$110/run min	$155/run min
Speechwriting for political campaigns	$155	$65	$101	n/a	n/a	n/a	$200/run min	$100/run min	$162/run min

USE VIDEO TO PROMOTE YOUR WORK

by Lorena Beniquez

We writers are a lucky lot that our pursuit can be as low tech as putting pen to paper. However, sometimes we need to tech it up when it comes to promoting our careers. Even books are high tech now so we have to keep pace with technology and learn to embrace it.

Writers already know the importance of maintaining their social media but too often we only do it with words. I am not knocking words (what a traitor I would be), but those words have even more impact when it comes to marketing your career. Take a look at the big publishing houses' websites and you can see why video is crucial for promoting writers. Unfortunately, most writers have yet to warm up to it.

WRITERS ON YOUTUBE

One would think YouTube would be cluttered with writers promoting their careers. However, that is not the case. Maybe production sounds like too much work. It really isn't. A marketing video can be as short as six seconds. That's right: only six seconds.

In addition to being a freelance writer, I am a filmmaker and commercial director. That said, you don't have to be a pro to make video part of your marketing plan. You probably already have the tools to do it. All you need is a smart phone, and, perhaps, video editing software to start on your way. If you want to increase production values, good sound equipment would be nice but let's not overthink this. The best part of the whole production is you already wrote the script (aka manuscript) and have a creative mind. So, off we go to explore the world of video and how it can propel a writer's marketing machine.

Warning: Do not go into production with the thought, "I can't wait for this to go viral!"

Going viral is as elusive as garnering a number one bestseller and there is no formula to make either happen. What you should instead be thinking is, "What story do I want to tell?"

Because we are writers, this isn't a tough question to answer. Just keep in mind, often times only a piece of your story can be explored because of video's time constraints.

For instance, does your book document the accordion's role in cultures around the world? Then isolate how the Polish have embraced the instrument in one video and, in another, focus on how Mexicans have adapted it.

Know what your call to action is. Is your aim to attract people to your next open mic stint? Do you want parents to buy your book for their children? Or, do you want to give a behind-the-scenes look at the making of your travel book? Determine your marketing goal before you start shooting.

POSTING VIDEOS

So where are you going to put these videos? Your blog, website, Facebook, YouTube, LinkedIn, Twitter, Instagram, Pinterest, and any other social media sites you desire.

You should also explore Vine. Each video on Vine is only six seconds in length and that is the beauty of it. This means less editing time or none at all. It also means more preproduction. Since you must tell your story succinctly, put some time into planning the story's arc. If you have never shot video before, Vine is a great way to start. The platform's demands are minimal so you can dip your toe into the sea of video marketing.

So how can I use video to promote my book? The possibilities are limitless but here are some ideas to rev up your imagination.

Put your words to video. You can sit in a room and read a stanza of your poem while your cousin plays guitar. Or, you can hire a couple of actors to perform a scene from your novel.

There are a million ways to liven up the production. For instance, use props. Why not use a puppet if you are promoting a children's book (or even a book on politics for that matter)? Is your book about sailing? Go jump on a yacht! Use visuals to tell the story. Utilizing still photographs in video can even help tremendously.

Tape your next career event. Whether it is a book signing or a public speaking engagement, shoot it so the rest of the world can see what they missed. You can turn a room of 25 audience members into 250,000 fans via the Internet.

DEALING WITH FAILURE

What happens if an event is an epic fail? There might still be some production value to it. I learned that the hard way when I did not bring my camera to a recent book signing of mine. Despite the fact that I did not sell or sign even one book, I should have been shooting the event.

During the book signing, I was sandwiched between several cute kittens from the SPCA and a celebrity with a snake. So, it made sense that people could care less about my tome. Either way, it was great comedy/tragedy and I should have been prepared to capture it.

Would it have been horrible for my image to show me failing? Who cares? People like it when you can laugh at yourself and, let's face it, your video needs to have some entertainment value.

Publicize your publicity. Did a local television station interview you? Use the link from the station's website on your social media platforms. Are you going to be a guest on a radio show? Tape your gab fest so you can use it later to promote your book's debut.

One thing to keep in mind: Ensure you have permission to shoot media hosts and that you are allowed to share it. Many outlets encourage sharing but just make sure of the legalities before you do.

WHEN TO START THINKING OF YOUR VIDEO

While crafting your book, start thinking of video possibilities before you have typed "the end." For instance, did you write a diet book? Shoot an interview with a doctor quoted in your pages. Then, use a short clip from the interview when the book is released. Is your book based on a true story that was covered by the media? Use those media interviews on your platforms with a short written introduction to let people know how it relates to your work. Perhaps you are promoting a book on Elvis sightings. You can use the countless reports already produced to help people understand the scope of the phenomenon.

Do a mock version of a television news package. A package is just a fancy term for a reporter's story. The package consists of interviews, video footage, and a script. Voiceovers and stand-ups (where the reporter directly addresses the camera with copy) are optional. These are easy to craft because they follow a formula which is easy to mimic.

Produce an electronic press kit (EPK). The electronic press kit will not only tell your audience about your work but who you are as an artist. The EPK could illustrate passages from your work using still photos, video, or graphics. In addition, use interview footage of yourself exploring why you wrote the work and how it was developed. For instance, if you had to travel to three different countries to complete research, discuss it and show video, or still photographs, from your travels.

Do a promo for your book. A great example of a book promo is the one produced for Mitch Albom's paperback release of *The First Phone Call from Heaven*. Despite the fact that Albom had a bigger production budget than most of us, his promo is a great template for producing your own. Albom speaks about the book in an outdoors setting (no studio required) and later interviewees are asked to talk about miracles in their lives. It is touching, funny, and well-crafted. My only criticism of the piece is that it is two minutes and thirty seconds long. Because Albom is a bestselling author, he can get away with it. A promo for the rest of us only needs to be two minutes or fewer.

A great attention grabber is the instructional video. Did you write a cookbook? Then head to the kitchen and whip up a recipe for the camera. Then post that video to your blog and link it to Pinterest. Have you written the *Hipster's Handbook*? Produce a piece on the gear needed to be a proper hipster.

A FEW VIDEO TIPS

Are you inspired yet? Good! But before you rush off to start shooting, here are some quick production tips:

- Keep your shots steady. You don't want viewers clicking out because they feel seasick.
- Don't shoot too wide. If your camera frame is too wide, it could end up including visual distractions to your message.
- Put the good stuff up top. Use your most compelling visuals at the beginning of the piece.
- Keep editing simple. You do not need a lot of bells and whistles if you have properly developed your story.
- Enlist a crew, even if it is only one person. Your husband, brother or 15-year-old daughter will do just fine. If you want to get extra fancy, check into a local college's policy on loaning out students for extra credit work.
- Keep most video under two minutes in length. Of course, if you are using Vine, six seconds is all you get.
- Incorporate music into your piece to add depth and sweeten production values.

Ready to get out there and shoot? Then let me leave you with this one last piece of advice, probably the most important piece. Have fun! Video marketing is just one more way to make your words resonate.

LORENA BENIQUEZ has utilized her writing skills as a celebrity publicist, scriptwriter and magazine freelancer. As a professional videographer, her work has been viewed on CNN and NBC's *Today* show. In addition, she founded the Central PA Film Office and the Wilkes-Barre Metro Film Office.

BLOGGING BASICS

Get the Most Out of Your Blog

by Robert Lee Brewer

In these days of publishing and media change, writers have to build platforms and learn how to connect to audiences if they want to improve their chances of publication and overall success. There are many methods of audience connection available to writers, but one of the most important is through blogging.

Since I've spent several years successfully blogging—both personally and professionally—I figure I've got a few nuggets of wisdom to pass on to writers who are curious about blogging or who already are.

Here's my quick list of tips:

1. **START BLOGGING TODAY.** If you don't have a blog, use Blogger, WordPress, or some other blogging software to start your blog today. It's free, and you can start off with your very personal "Here I am, world" post.
2. **START SMALL.** Blogs are essentially simple, but they can get complicated (for people who like complications). However, I advise bloggers start small and evolve over time.
3. **USE YOUR NAME IN YOUR URL.** This will make it easier for search engines to find you when your audience eventually starts seeking you out by name. For instance, my url is http://robertleebrewer.blogspot.com. If you try Googling "Robert Lee Brewer," you'll notice that My Name Is Not Bob is one of the top five search results (behind my other blog: Poetic Asides).
4. **UNLESS YOU HAVE A REASON, USE YOUR NAME AS THE TITLE OF YOUR BLOG.** Again, this helps with search engine results. My Poetic Asides blog includes my name in the title, and it ranks higher than My Name Is Not Bob. However, I felt the play on my name was worth the trade off.
5. **FIGURE OUT YOUR BLOGGING GOALS.** You should return to this step every couple months, because it's natural for your blogging goals to evolve over time. Initially, your blogging goals may be to make a post a week about what you have written, submitted, etc. Over

time, you may incorporate guests posts, contests, tips, etc.

6.BE YOURSELF. I'm a big supporter of the idea that your image should match your identity. It gets too confusing trying to maintain a million personas. Know who you are and be that on your blog, whether that means you're sincere, funny, sarcastic, etc.

7.POST AT LEAST ONCE A WEEK. This is for starters. Eventually, you may find it better to post once a day or multiple times per day. But remember: Start small and evolve over time.

8.POST RELEVANT CONTENT. This means that you post things that your readers might actually care to know.

9.USEFUL AND HELPFUL POSTS WILL ATTRACT MORE VISITORS. Talking about yourself is all fine and great. I do it myself. But if you share truly helpful advice, your readers will share it with others, and visitors will find you on search engines.

10. TITLE YOUR POSTS IN A WAY THAT GETS YOU FOUND IN SEARCH ENGINES. The more specific you can get the better. For instance, the title "Blogging Tips" will most likely get lost in search results. However, the title "Blogging Tips for Writers" specifies which audience I'm targeting and increases the chances of being found on the first page of search results.

11. LINK TO POSTS IN OTHER MEDIA. If you have an e-mail newsletter, link to your blog posts in your newsletter. If you have social media accounts, link to your blog posts there. If you have a helpful post, link to it in relevant forums and on message boards.

12. WRITE WELL, BUT BE CONCISE. At the end of the day, you're writing blog posts, not literary manifestos. Don't spend a week writing each post. Try to keep it to an hour or two tops and then post. Make sure your spelling and grammar are good, but don't stress yourself out too much.

13. FIND LIKE-MINDED BLOGGERS. Comment on their blogs regularly and link to them from yours. Eventually, they may do the same. Keep in mind that blogging is a form of social media, so the more you communicate with your peers the more you'll get out of the process.

14. RESPOND TO COMMENTS ON YOUR BLOG. Even if it's just a simple "Thanks," respond to your readers if they comment on your blog. After all, you want your readers to be engaged with your blog, and you want them to know that you care they took time to comment.

15. EXPERIMENT. Start small, but don't get complacent. Every so often, try something new. For instance, the biggest draw to my Poetic Asides blog are the poetry prompts and challenges I issue to poets. Initially, that was an experiment—one that worked very well. I've tried other experiments that haven't panned out, and that's fine. It's all part of a process.

SEO TIPS FOR WRITERS

Most writers may already know what SEO is. If not, SEO stands for *search engine optimization*. Basically, a site or blog that practices good SEO habits should improve its rankings in search engines, such as Google and Bing. Most huge corporations have realized the importance of SEO and spend enormous sums of time, energy and money on perfecting their SEO practices. However, writers can improve their SEO without going to those same extremes.

In this section, I will use the terms of *site pages* and *blog posts* interchangeably. In both cases, you should be practicing the same SEO strategies (when it makes sense).

Here are my top tips on ways to improve your SEO starting today:

1. **USE APPROPRIATE KEYWORDS.** Make sure that your page displays your main keyword(s) in the page title, content, URL, title tags, page header, image names and tags (if you're including images). All of this is easy to do, but if you feel overwhelmed, just remember to use your keyword(s) in your page title and content (especially in the first and last 50 words of your page).
2. **USE KEYWORDS NATURALLY.** Don't kill your content and make yourself look like a spammer to search engines by overloading your page with your keyword(s). You don't get SEO points for quantity but for quality. Plus, one of the main ways to improve your page rankings is when you...
3. **DELIVER QUALITY CONTENT.** The best way to improve your SEO is by providing content that readers want to share with others by linking to your pages. Some of the top results in search engines can be years old, because the content is so good that people keep coming back. So, incorporate your keywords in a smart way, but make sure it works organically with your content.
4. **UPDATE CONTENT REGULARLY.** If your site looks dead to visitors, then it'll appear that way to search engines too. So update your content regularly. This should be very easy for writers who have blogs. For writers who have sites, incorporate your blog into your site. This will make it easier for visitors to your blog to discover more about you on your site (through your site navigation tools).
5. **LINK BACK TO YOUR OWN CONTENT.** If I have a post on Blogging Tips for Writers, for instance, I'll link back to it if I have a Platform Building post, because the two complement each other. This also helps clicks on my blog, which helps SEO. The one caveat is that you don't go crazy with your linking and that you make sure your links are relevant. Otherwise, you'll kill your traffic, which is not good for your page rankings.
6. **LINK TO OTHERS YOU CONSIDER HELPFUL.** Back in 2000, I remember being ordered by my boss at the time (who didn't last too much longer afterward) to ignore any competitive or complementary websites—no matter how helpful their content—because they were our competitors. You

can try basing your online strategy on these principles, but I'm nearly 100 percent confident you'll fail. It's helpful for other sites and your own to link to other great resources. I shine a light on others to help them out (if I find their content truly helpful) in the hopes that they'll do the same if ever they find my content truly helpful for their audience.

7.GET SPECIFIC WITH YOUR HEADLINES. If you interview someone on your blog, don't title your post with an interesting quotation. While that strategy may help get readers in the print world, it doesn't help with SEO at all. Instead, title your post as "Interview With (insert name here)." If you have a way to identify the person further, include that in the title too. For instance, when I interview poets on my Poetic Asides blog, I'll title those posts like this: Interview With Poet Erika Meitner. Erika's name is a keyword, but so are the terms *poet* and *interview*.

8.USE IMAGES. Many expert sources state that the use of images can improve SEO, because it shows search engines that the person creating the page is spending a little extra time and effort on the page than a common spammer. However, I'd caution anyone using images to make sure those images are somehow complementary to the content. Don't just throw up a lot of images that have no relevance to anything. At the same time...

9.OPTIMIZE IMAGES THROUGH STRATEGIC LABELING. Writers can do this by making sure the image file is labeled using your keyword(s) for the post. Using the Erika Meitner example above (which does include images), I would label the file "Erika Meitner headshot.jpg"—or whatever the image file type happens to be. Writers can also improve image SEO through the use of captions and ALT tagging. Of course, at the same time, writers should always ask themselves if it's worth going through all that trouble for each image or not. Each writer has to answer that question for him (or her) self.

10. USE YOUR SOCIAL MEDIA PLATFORM TO SPREAD THE WORD. Whenever you do something new on your site or blog, you should share that information on your other social media sites, such as Twitter, Facebook, LinkedIn, online forums, etc. This lets your social media connections know that something new is on your site/blog. If it's relevant and/or valuable, they'll let others know. And that's a great way to build your SEO.

Programmers and marketers could get even more involved in the dynamics of SEO optimization, but I think these tips will help most writers out immediately and effectively while still allowing plenty of time and energy for the actual work of writing.

BLOG DESIGN TIPS FOR WRITERS

Design is an important element to any blog's success. But how can you improve your blog's design if you're not a designer? I'm just an editor with an English Lit degree and no formal training in design. However,

I've worked in media for more than a decade now and can share some very fundamental and easy tricks to improve the design of your blog.

Here are my seven blog design tips for writers:

1. **USE LISTS.** Whether they're numbered or bullet points, use lists when possible. Lists break up the text and make it easy for readers to follow what you're blogging.
2. **BOLD MAIN POINTS IN LISTS.** Again, this helps break up the text while also highlighting the important points of your post.
3. **USE HEADINGS.** If your posts are longer than 300 words and you don't use lists, then please break up the text by using basic headings.
4. **USE A READABLE FONT.** Avoid using fonts that are too large or too small. Avoid using cursive or weird fonts. Times New Roman or Arial works, but if you want to get "creative," use something similar to those.
5. **LEFT ALIGN.** English-speaking readers are trained to read left to right. If you want to make your blog easier to read, avoid centering or right aligning your text (unless you're purposefully calling out the text).
6. **USE SMALL PARAGRAPHS.** A good rule of thumb is to try and avoid paragraphs that drone on longer than five sentences. I usually try to keep paragraphs to around three sentences myself.
7. **ADD RELEVANT IMAGES.** Personally, I shy away from using too many images. My reason is that I only like to use them if they're relevant. However, images are very powerful on blogs, so please use them—just make sure they're relevant to your blog post.

If you're already doing everything on my list, keep it up! If you're not, then you might want to re-think your design strategy on your blog. Simply adding a header here and a list there can easily improve the design of a blog post.

GUEST POSTING TIPS FOR WRITERS

Recently, I've broken into guest posting as both a guest poster and as a host of guest posts (over at my Poetic Asides blog). So far, I'm pretty pleased with both sides of the guest posting process. As a writer, it gives me access to an engaged audience I may not usually reach. As a blogger, it provides me with fresh and valuable content I don't have to create. Guest blogging is a rare win-win scenario.

That said, writers could benefit from a few tips on the process of guest posting:

1. **PITCH GUEST POSTS LIKE ONE WOULD PITCH ARTICLES TO A MAGAZINE.** Include what your hook is for the post, what you plan to cover, and a little about who you are. Remember: Your post should somehow benefit the audience of the blog you'd like to guest post.
2. **OFFER PROMOTIONAL COPY OF YOUR BOOK (OR OTHER GIVEAWAYS) AS PART OF YOUR GUEST POST.** Hav-

ing a random giveaway for people who comment on a blog post can help spur conversation and interest in your guest post, which is a great way to get the most mileage out of your guest appearance.

3.CATER POSTS TO AUDIENCE. As the editor of *Writer's Market* and *Poet's Market*, I have great range in the topics I can cover. However, if I'm writing a guest post for a fiction blog, I'll write about things of interest to a novelist—not a poet.

4.MAKE IT PERSONAL, BUT PROVIDE NUGGET. Guest posts are a great opportunity for you to really show your stuff to a new audience. You could write a very helpful and impersonal post, but that won't connect with readers the same way as if you write a very helpful and personal post that makes them want to learn more about you (and your blog, your book, your Twitter account, etc.). Speaking of which...

5.SHARE LINKS TO YOUR WEBSITE, BLOG, SOCIAL NETWORKS, ETC. After all, you need to make it easy for readers who enjoyed your guest post to learn more about you and your projects. Start the conversation in your guest post and keep it going on your own sites, profiles, etc. And related to that...

6.PROMOTE YOUR GUEST POST THROUGH YOUR NORMAL CHANNELS ONCE THE POST GOES LIVE. Your normal audience will want to know where you've been and what you've been doing. Plus, guest posts lend a little extra "street cred" to your projects. But don't stop there...

7.CHECK FOR COMMENTS ON YOUR GUEST POST AND RESPOND IN A TIMELY MANNER. Sometimes the comments are the most interesting part of a guest post (no offense). This is where readers can ask more in-depth or related questions, and it's also where you can show your expertise on the subject by being as helpful as possible. And guiding all seven of these tips is this one:

8.PUT SOME EFFORT INTO YOUR GUEST POST. Part of the benefit to guest posting is the opportunity to connect with a new audience. Make sure you bring your A-game, because you need to make a good impression if you want this exposure to actually help grow your audience. Don't stress yourself out, but put a little thought into what you submit.

ONE ADDITIONAL TIP: Have fun with it. Passion is what really drives the popularity of blogs. Share your passion and enthusiasm, and readers are sure to be impressed.

ROBERT LEE BREWER is an editor with the Writer's Digest Writing Community and author of *Solving the World's Problems* (Press 53). Follow him on Twitter @robertleebrewer.

LITERARY AGENTS

The literary agencies listed in this section are open to new clients and are members of the Association of Authors' Representatives (AAR), which means they do not charge for reading, critiquing, or editing. Some agents in this section may charge clients for office expenses such as photocopying, foreign postage, long-distance phone calls, or express mail services. Make sure you have a clear understanding of what these expenses are before signing any agency agreement.

FOR MORE...

The *2016 Guide to Literary Agents* (Writer's Digest Books) offers more than 800 literary agents, as well as information on writers' conferences. It also offers a wealth of information on the author/agent relationship and other related topics.

SUBHEADS

Each listing is broken down into subheads to make locating specific information easier.

In the first section, you'll find contact information for each agency. Further information is provided which indicates an agency's size, its willingness to work with a new or previously unpublished writer, and its general areas of interest.

⊘ DOMINICK ABEL LITERARY AGENCY, INC.

146 W. 82nd St., #1A, New York NY 10024. (212)877-0710. **E-mail:** agency@dalainc.com. **Website:** dalainc.com/. Estab. 1975. Member AAR. Represents 100 clients. Currently handles: adult fiction and nonfiction.

HOW TO CONTACT Query via e-mail. Check website to learn when this agency reopens to new submissions.

TERMS Agent receives 15% commission on domestic sales. Agent receives 20% commission on foreign sales.

ADAMS LITERARY

7845 Colony Rd., C4 #215, Charlotte NC 28226. (704)542-1440. **Fax:** (704)542-1450. **E-mail:** info@adamsliterary.com. **Website:** www.adamsliterary.com. **Contact:** Tracey Adams, Josh Adams. Member of AAR. Other memberships include SCBWI and WNBA. Currently handles: juvenile books.

MEMBER AGENTS Tracey Adams, Josh Adams, Samantha Bagood (assistant).

REPRESENTS Considers these fiction areas: middle grade, picture books, young adult.

HOW TO CONTACT Contact through online form on website only. Send e-mail if that is not operating correctly. All submissions and queries should first be made through the online form on website. Will not review—and will promptly recycle—any unsolicited submissions or queries received by mail. Before submitting work for consideration, review complete guidelines online, as the agency sometimes shuts off to new submissions. "While we have an established client list, we do seek new talent—and we accept submissions from both published and aspiring authors and artists."

TERMS Agent receives 15% commission on domestic sales; 20% on foreign sales. Offers written contract.

⊘ ALIVE COMMUNICATIONS, INC.

7680 Goddard St., Suite 200, Colorado Springs CO 80920. (719)260-7080. **Fax:** (719)260-8223. **E-mail:** submissions@alivecom.com. **Website:** www.alivecom.com. **Contact:** Rick Christian. Member of AAR. Other memberships include Authors Guild.

MEMBER AGENTS Rick Christian, president (blockbusters, bestsellers); Lee Hough (popular/commercial nonfiction and fiction, thoughtful spirituality, children's); **Andrea Heinecke** (thoughtful/inspirational nonfiction, women's fiction/nonfiction, popular/commercial nonfiction & fiction); **Bryan Norman**; **Lisa Jackson**.

REPRESENTS Nonfiction books, novels, short story collections, novellas. **Considers these nonfiction areas:** autobiography, biography, business, child guidance, economics, how-to, inspirational, parenting, personal improvement, religious, self-help, women's issues, women's studies. **Considers these fiction areas:** adventure, contemporary issues, crime, family saga, historical, humor, inspirational, literary, mainstream, mystery, police, religious, satire, suspense, thriller.

HOW TO CONTACT "Because all our agents have full client loads, they are only considering queries from authors referred by clients and close contacts." New clients come through recommendations from others.

TERMS Agent receives 15% commission on domestic sales. Offers written contract; 2-month notice must be given to terminate contract.

BETSY AMSTER LITERARY ENTERPRISES

6312 SW Capitol Hwy #503, Portland OR 97239. **Website:** www.amsterlit.com. **Contact:** Betsy Amster (adult); Mary Cummings (children's and YA). Estab. 1992. Member of AAR. Represents more than 65 clients. 35% of clients are new/unpublished writers. Currently handles: nonfiction books 65%, novels 35%.

REPRESENTS Nonfiction books, novels. **Considers these nonfiction areas:** art & design, biography, business, child guidance, cooking/nutrition, current affairs, ethnic, gardening, health/medicine, history, memoirs, money, parenting, popular culture, psychology, science/technology, self-help, sociology, travelogues, social issues, women's issues. **Considers these fiction areas:** ethnic, literary, women's, high quality.

HOW TO CONTACT For adult titles: b.amster.assistant@gmail.com. "For fiction or memoirs, please embed the first three pages in the body of your e-mail. For nonfiction, please embed your proposal." For children's and YA: b.amster.kidsbooks@gmail.com. See submission requirements online at website. "For picture books, please embed the entire text in the body of your e-mail. For novels, please embed the first three pages." Accepts simultaneous submissions. Responds in 1 month to queries. Responds in 2 months to mss. Obtains most new clients through recommendations from others, solicitations, conferences.

TERMS Agent receives 15% commission on domestic sales. Agent receives 20% commission on foreign sales. Offers written contract, binding for 1 year; 3-month notice must be given to terminate contract. Charges for photocopying, postage, messengers, galleys/books used in submissions to foreign and film agents and to magazines for first serial rights.

ANDERSON LITERARY MANAGEMENT, LLC

12 W. 19th St., New York NY 10011. (212)645-6045. **Fax:** (212)741-1936. **E-mail:** info@andersonliterary.com; kathleen@andersonliterary.com; adam@andersonliterary.com. **Website:** www.andersonliterary.com. **Contact:** Kathleen Anderson. Estab. 2006. Member of AAR. Represents 100+ clients. 20% of clients are new/unpublished writers. Currently handles: nonfiction books 50%, novels 50%.

MEMBER AGENTS Kathleen Anderson, Claire Wheeler.

REPRESENTS Nonfiction books, novels, short story collections, juvenile. **Considers these nonfiction areas:** anthropology, archeology, architecture, art, autobiography, biography, cultural interests, current affairs, dance, design, education, environment, ethnic, gay, government, history, law, lesbian, memoirs, music, nature, politics, psychology, women's issues, women's studies. **Considers these fiction areas:** action, adventure, ethnic, family saga, feminist, frontier, gay, historical, lesbian, literary, mystery, suspense, thriller, westerns, women's, young adult.

HOW TO CONTACT Query with SASE. Submit synopsis, first 3 sample chapters, proposal (for nonfiction). Snail mail queries only. Accepts simultaneous submissions. Responds in 6 weeks to queries. Obtains most new clients through recommendations from others, solicitations, conferences.

TERMS Agent receives 15% commission on domestic sales. Offers written contract.

ARCADIA

31 Lake Place N., Danbury CT 06810. **E-mail:** arcadialit@sbcglobal.net. **Contact:** Victoria Gould Pryor. Member of AAR.

REPRESENTS Nonfiction books. **Considers these nonfiction areas:** biography, current affairs, health, history, psychology, science, investigative journalism, culture, classical music, life transforming self-help.

HOW TO CONTACT No unsolicited submissions. Query with SASE. This agency accepts e-queries (no attachments).

THE AXELROD AGENCY

55 Main St., P.O. Box 357, Chatham NY 12037. (518)392-2100. **E-mail:** steve@axelrodagency.com. **Website:** www.axelrodagency.com. **Contact:** Steven Axelrod. Member of AAR. Represents 15-20 clients. Currently handles: novels 95%.

REPRESENTS Novels. **Considers these fiction areas:** crime, mystery, new adult, romance, women's.

HOW TO CONTACT Query. Accepts simultaneous submissions. Obtains most new clients through recommendations from others.

TERMS Agent receives 15% commission on domestic sales. Agent receives 20% commission on foreign sales. No written contract.

BARER LITERARY, LLC

20 W. 20th St., Suite 601, New York NY 10011. (212)691-3513. **E-mail:** submissions@barerliterary.com. **Website:** www.barerliterary.com. **Contact:** Julie Barer. Estab. 2004. Member of AAR.

MEMBER AGENTS Julie Barer, Anna Geller, William Boggess (literary fiction and narrative nonfiction).

REPRESENTS Nonfiction books, novels, short story collections., Julie Barer is especially interested in working with emerging writers and developing long-term relationships with new clients. **Considers these nonfiction areas:** biography, ethnic, history, memoirs, popular culture, women's. **Considers these fiction areas:** contemporary issues, ethnic, fantasy, historical, literary, mainstream, science fiction, women's, young adult.

HOW TO CONTACT Query; no attachments if querying by e-mail. "We do not respond to queries via phone or fax."

TERMS Agent receives 15% commission on domestic sales. Agent receives 20% commission on foreign sales. Offers written contract. Charges for photocopying and books ordered.

BOOKENDS, LLC

Website: www.bookends-inc.com. **Contact:** Jessica Faust, Kim Lionetti, Jessica Alvarez, Beth Campbell. Member of AAR. RWA, MWA Represents 50+ clients. 10% of clients are new/unpublished writers. Currently handles: nonfiction books 50%, novels 50%.

MEMBER AGENTS **Jessica Faust**, JFaust@bookends-inc.com (fiction: women's fiction, mysteries and suspense; all other genres accepted by referral only); **Kim Lionetti**, klionetti@bookends-inc.com (only currently considering contemporary romance, women's fiction, cozies, new adult, and contemporary young adult); **Jessica Alvarez** (romance, women's fiction, erotica, romantic suspense); **Beth Campbell** (urban fantasy, science fiction, YA, suspense, romantic suspense, and mystery).

REPRESENTS Nonfiction books, novels. **Considers these nonfiction areas:** business, ethnic, how-to, money, sex. **Considers these fiction areas:** mainstream, mystery, romance, women's.

HOW TO CONTACT Review website for guidelines, as they change. BookEnds is no longer accepting unsolicited proposal packages or snail mail queries. Send query in the body of e-mail to only 1 agent. No attachments.

BOOKS & SUCH LITERARY AGENCY

52 Mission Circle, Suite 122, PMB 170, Santa Rosa CA 95409. **E-mail:** representation@booksandsuch.com. **Website:** www.booksandsuch.com. **Contact:** Janet Kobobel Grant, Wendy Lawton, Rachel Kent, Mary Keeley, Rachelle Gardner. Member of AAR. Member of CBA (associate), American Christian Fiction Writers. Currently handles: nonfiction books 50%, novels 50%.

REPRESENTS Nonfiction books, novels. **Considers these nonfiction areas:** humor, religion, self help, women's. **Considers these fiction areas:** historical, literary, mainstream, new adult, religious, romance, young adult.

HOW TO CONTACT Query via e-mail only; no attachments. Accepts simultaneous submissions. Responds in 1 month to queries. "If you don't hear from us asking to see more of your writing within 30 days after you have sent your e-mail, please know that we have read and considered your submission but determined that it would not be a good fit for us." Obtains most new clients through recommendations from others, conferences.

TERMS Agent receives 15% commission on domestic sales. Agent receives 20% commission on foreign sales. Offers written contract; 2-month notice must be given to terminate contract. No additional charges.

BRANDT & HOCHMAN LITERARY AGENTS, INC.

1501 Broadway, Suite 2310, New York NY 10036. (212)840-5760. **Fax:** (212)840-5776. **Website:** brandthochman.com. **Contact:** Gail Hochman. Member of AAR. Represents 200 clients.

MEMBER AGENTS Gail Hochman; Marianne Merola; Bill Contardi; Emily Forland; Emma Patterson (anything about the Yankees, stories set in Brooklyn); Jody Kahn; Henry Thayer. The e-mail addresses and specific likes of each of these agents is listed on the agency website.

REPRESENTS Considers these nonfiction areas: biography, cooking, creative nonfiction, foods, history, memoirs, music, sports, young adult. **Considers these fiction areas:** crime, family saga, fantasy, historical, literary, middle grade, mystery, suspense, thriller, women's.

HOW TO CONTACT "We accept queries by e-mail and regular mail; however, we cannot guarantee a response to e-mailed queries. For queries via regular mail, be sure to include a self-addressed stamped envelope for our reply. Query letters should be no more than two pages and should include a convincing overview of the book project and information about the author and his or her writing credits. Address queries to the specific Brandt & Hochman agent whom you would like to consider your work. Agent e-mail addresses and query preferences may be found at the end of each agent profile on the 'Agents' page of our website." Accepts simultaneous submissions. Obtains most new clients through recommendations from others.

TERMS Agent receives 15% commission on domestic sales. Agent receives 20% commission on foreign sales.

BARBARA BRAUN ASSOCIATES, INC.

7 E. 14th St., Suite 19F, New York NY 10003. **Fax:** (212)604-9023. **E-mail:** bbasubmissions@gmail.com. **Website:** www.barbarabraunagency.com. **Contact:** Barbara Braun. Member of AAR.

MEMBER AGENTS Barbara Braun; John F. Baker.

REPRESENTS Nonfiction books, novels. **Considers these nonfiction areas:** architecture, art, biography, design, film, history, photography, psychology, women's issues. **Considers these fiction areas:** commercial, literary.

HOW TO CONTACT "We no longer accept submissions by regular mail. Please send all queries via email, marked 'Query' in the subject line. Your query should include: a brief summary of your book, word count, genre, any relevant publishing experience, and the first 5 pages of your manuscript pasted into the body of the email. (NO attachments – we will not open these.)"

TERMS Agent receives 15% commission on domestic sales. Agent receives 20% commission on foreign sales.

BRET ADAMS LTD. AGENCY

448 W. 44th St., New York NY 10036. (212)765-5630. **E-mail:** literary@bretadamsltd.net. **Website:** bretad-

amsltd.net. **Contact:** Aislinn Frantz. Member of AAR. Currently handles: stage plays.

MEMBER AGENTS Bruce Ostler, Mark Orsini; Alexis Williams.

REPRESENTS Theatrical stage play.

HOW TO CONTACT Use the online submission form. Because of this agency's submission policy and interests, it's best to approach with a professional recommendation from a client.

KIMBERLEY CAMERON & ASSOCIATES

1550 Tiburon Blvd., #704, Tiburon CA 94920. **Fax:** (415)789-9191. **Website:** www.kimberleycameron.com. **Contact:** Kimberley Cameron. Member of AAR.

MEMBER AGENTS Kimberley Cameron; Elizabeth Kracht, liz@kimberleycameron.com (literary, commercial, women's, thrillers, mysteries, and YA with crossover appeal); **Pooja Menon**, pooja@kimberleycameron.com (international stories, literary, historical, commercial, fantasy and high-end women's fiction; in nonfiction, she's looking for adventure & travel memoirs, journalism & human-interest stories, and self-help books addressing relationships and the human psychology from a fresh perspective); **Amy Cloughley**, amyc@kimberleycameron.com (literary and upmarket fiction, women's, mystery, narrative nonfiction); **Mary C. Moore** (literary fiction; she also loves a good commercial book; commercially she is looking for unusual fantasy, grounded science fiction, and atypical romance; strong female characters and unique cultures especially catch her eye).

REPRESENTS Considers these nonfiction areas: creative nonfiction, psychology, self-help, travel. **Considers these fiction areas:** commercial, fantasy, historical, literary, mystery, romance, science fiction, thriller, women's, young adult.

HOW TO CONTACT "We accept e-mail queries only. Please address all queries to one agent only. Please send a query letter in the body of the email, written in a professional manner and clearly addressed to the agent of your choice. Attach a one-page synopsis and the first 50 pages of your manuscript as separate Word or PDF documents. We have difficulties opening other file formats. Include 'Author Submission' in the subject line. If submitting nonfiction, attach a nonfiction proposal." Obtains new clients through recommendations from others, solicitations.

TERMS Agent receives 15% on domestic sales; 10% on film sales. Offers written contract, binding for 1 year.

CASTIGLIA LITERARY AGENCY

P.O. Box 1094, Sumerland CA 93067. **E-mail:** castigliaagency-query@yahoo.com. **Website:** www.castigliaagency.com. Member of AAR. Other memberships include PEN. Represents 65 clients. Currently handles: nonfiction books 55%, novels 45%.

MEMBER AGENTS Julie Castiglia (not accepting queries at this time); Win Golden (fiction: thrillers, mystery, crime, science fiction, YA, commercial/literary fiction; nonfiction: narrative nonfiction, current events, science, journalism).

REPRESENTS Nonfiction books, novels. **Considers these nonfiction areas:** creative nonfiction, current affairs, investigative, science. **Considers these fiction areas:** commercial, crime, literary, mystery, science fiction, thriller, young adult.

HOW TO CONTACT Query via e-mail to CastigliaAgency-query@yahoo.com. Send no materials via first contact besides a one-page query. No snail mail submissions accepted. Obtains most new clients through recommendations from others, solicitations, conferences.

TERMS Agent receives 15% commission on domestic sales. Agent receives 25% commission on foreign sales. Offers written contract; 6-week notice must be given to terminate contract.

JANE CHELIUS LITERARY AGENCY

548 Second St., Brooklyn NY 11215. (718)499-0236. **Fax:** (718)832-7335. **E-mail:** Jane@janechelius.com. **E-mail:** queries@janechelius.com. **Website:** www.janechelius.com. Member of AAR.

MEMBER AGENTS Jane Chelius, Mark Chelius.

REPRESENTS Nonfiction books, novels. **Considers these nonfiction areas:** biography, humor, medicine, parenting, popular culture, satire, women's issues, women's studies, natural history; narrative. **Considers these fiction areas:** literary, mystery, suspense, women's.

HOW TO CONTACT E-query. Does not consider email queries with attachments. No unsolicited sample chapters or mss. Responds if interested. Responds in 3-4-weeks usually.

⊘ CINE/LIT REPRESENTATION

P.O. Box 802918, Santa Clarita CA 91380-2918. (661)513-0268. **Fax:** (661)513-0915. **Contact:** Mary Alice Kier. Member of AAR.

MEMBER AGENTS Mary Alice Kier; Anna Cottle.
HOW TO CONTACT Send query letter with SASE. Or e-query to cinelit@att.net. Note this agency's specialized nature.

CORNERSTONE LITERARY, INC.

4525 Wilshire Blvd., Suite 208, Los Angeles CA 90010. (323)930-6039. **Fax:** (323)930-0407. **E-mail:** info@cornerstoneliterary.com. **Website:** www.cornerstoneliterary.com. **Contact:** Helen Breitwieser. Member of AAR. Other memberships include Author's Guild, MWA, RWA, PEN, Poets & Writers. Represents 40 clients. 30% of clients are new/unpublished writers.
REPRESENTS Novels. **Considers these nonfiction areas:** creative nonfiction. **Considers these fiction areas:** commercial, literary.
HOW TO CONTACT "Submissions should consist of a one-page query letter detailing the book as well as the qualifications of the author. For fiction, submissions may also include the first ten pages of the novel pasted in the email or one short story from a collection. We receive hundreds of queries each month, and make every effort to give each one careful consideration. We cannot guarantee a response to queries submitted electronically due to the volume of queries received." Obtains most new clients through recommendations from others.
TERMS Agent receives 15% commission on domestic sales. Agent receives 20% commission on foreign sales. Offers written contract, binding for 1 year; 2-month notice must be given to terminate contract.

CURTIS BROWN, LTD.

10 Astor Place, New York NY 10003-6935. (212)473-5400. **Website:** www.curtisbrown.com. **Contact:** Ginger Knowlton. Alternate address: Peter Ginsberg, president at CBSF, 1750 Montgomery St., San Francisco CA 94111; (415)954-8566. Member of AAR. Signatory of WGA.
MEMBER AGENTS **Ginger Clark** (science fiction, fantasy, paranormal romance, literary horror, and young adult and middle grade fiction); **Katherine Fausset** (adult fiction and nonfiction, including literary and commercial fiction, journalism, memoir, lifestyle, prescriptive and narrative nonfiction); **Holly Frederick**; **Peter Ginsberg**, president; **Elizabeth Harding**, vice president (represents authors and illustrators of juvenile, middle-grade and young adult fiction); **Steve Kasdin** (commercial fiction, including mysteries/thrillers, romantic suspense—emphasis on the suspense, and historical fiction; narrative nonfiction, including biography, history and current affairs; and young adult fiction, particularly if it has adult crossover appeal); **Ginger Knowlton**, executive vice president (authors and illustrators of children's books in all genres); **Timothy Knowlton**, chief executive officer; **Jonathan Lyons** (biographies, history, science, pop culture, sports, general narrative non-fiction, mysteries, thrillers, science fiction and fantasy, and young adult fiction); **Laura Blake Peterson**, Vice President (memoir and biography, natural history, literary fiction, mystery, suspense, women's fiction, health and fitness, children's and young adult, faith issues and popular culture); **Maureen Walters**, Senior Vice President (working primarily in women's fiction and nonfiction projects on subjects as eclectic as parenting & child care, popular psychology, inspirational/motivational volumes as well as a few medical/nutritional book); **Mitchell Waters** (literary and commercial fiction and nonfiction, including mystery, history, biography, memoir, young adult, cookbooks, self-help and popular culture); **Kerry D'Agostino** (a wide range of literary and commercial fiction, as well as narrative nonfiction and memoir); **Noah Ballard** (literary debuts, upmarket thrillers and narrative nonfiction, and he is always on the look-out for honest and provocative new writers).
REPRESENTS Nonfiction books, novels, short story collections, juvenile. **Considers these nonfiction areas:** animals, anthropology, art, biography, business, computers, cooking, crafts, creative nonfiction, current affairs, education, ethnic, film, gardening, government, health, history, how-to, humor, language, memoirs, military, money, multicultural, music, New Age, philosophy, photography, popular culture, psychology, recreation, regional, science, self-help, sex, sociology, software, spirituality, sports, translation, travel, true crime. **Considers these fiction areas:** adventure, confession, detective, erotica, ethnic, experimental, fantasy, feminist, gay, historical, horror, humor, juvenile, literary, mainstream, middle grade, military, multicultural, multimedia, mystery, New Age, occult, picture books, regional, religious, romance, spiritual, sports, thriller, translation, women's, young adult.
HOW TO CONTACT "Send us a query letter, a synopsis of the work, a sample chapter and a brief resume. Illustrators should send 1-2 samples of published work,

along with 6-8 color copies (no original art). Please send all book queries to our address, Attn: Query Department. Please enclose a stamped, self-addressed envelope for our response and return postage if you wish to have your materials returned to you. We typically respond to queries within 6 to 8 weeks." Note that some agents list their e-mail on the agency website and are fine with e-mail submissions. Note in your submission if the query is being considered elsewhere. Responds in 3 weeks to queries; 5 weeks to mss. Obtains most new clients through recommendations from others, solicitations, conferences.

TERMS Agent receives 15% commission on domestic sales; 20% on foreign sales. Offers written contract. 75-day notice must be given to terminate contract. Offers written contract. Charges for some postage (overseas, etc.).

CYNTHIA CANNELL LITERARY AGENCY

833 Madison Ave., New York NY 10021. (212)396-9595. **Website:** www.cannellagency.com. **Contact:** Cynthia Cannell. Estab. 1997. Member of AAR. Other memberships include the Women's Media Group.

REPRESENTS Considers these nonfiction areas: biography, history, memoirs, science, self-help, spirituality. **Considers these fiction areas:** literary.

HOW TO CONTACT "Please query us with an e-mail or letter. If querying by e-mail, send a brief description of your project with relevant biographical information including publishing credits (if any) to info@cannellagency.com. Do not send attachments. If querying by conventional mail, enclose an SASE." Responds if interested.

DARHANSOFF & VERRILL LITERARY AGENTS

133 West 72nd St., Room 304, New York NY 10023. (917)305-1300. **Fax:** (917)305-1400. **E-mail:** submissions@dvagency.com. **Website:** www.dvagency.com. Member of AAR.

MEMBER AGENTS Liz Darhansoff; Chuck Verrill; Michele Mortimer; Catherine Luttinger (science fiction, fantasy, historical fiction, thrillers, mysteries).

REPRESENTS Considers these nonfiction areas: creative nonfiction, memoirs. **Considers these fiction areas:** fantasy, historical, literary, mystery, science fiction, suspense, thriller.

HOW TO CONTACT Send queries via e-mail (submissions@dvagency.com) or by snail mail with SASE. Obtains most new clients through recommendations from others.

DAVID BLACK LITERARY AGENCY

335 Adams St., Suite 2707, Brooklyn NY 11201. (718)852-5500. **Fax:** (718)852-5539. **Website:** www.davidblackagency.com. **Contact:** David Black, owner. Member of AAR. Represents 150 clients.

MEMBER AGENTS David Black; Gary Morris; Joy E. Tutela (general nonfiction, literary fiction, commercial fiction, YA, MG); **Linda Loewenthal; Antonella Iannarino; Susan Raihofer; Sarah Smith.**

REPRESENTS Nonfiction books, novels. **Considers these nonfiction areas:** biography, business, creative nonfiction, current affairs, gay/lesbian, health, history, humor, memoirs, money, parenting, politics, self-help, women's issues. **Considers these fiction areas:** commercial, literary, middle grade, thriller, young adult.

HOW TO CONTACT "To query an individual agent, please follow the specific query guidelines outlined in the agent's profile on our website. Not all agents are currently accepting unsolicited queries. To query the agency, please send a 1-2 page query letter describing your book, and include information about any previously published works, your audience, and your platform." Note that some agents prefer e-queries whereas some prefer snail mail queries. Accepts simultaneous submissions. Responds in 2 months to queries.

TERMS Agent receives 15% commission on domestic sales. Charges clients for photocopying and books purchased for sale of foreign rights.

DEFIORE & CO.

47 E. 19th St., 3rd Floor, New York NY 10003. (212)925-7744. **Fax:** (212)925-9803. **E-mail:** brian@defliterary.com. **E-mail:** info@defliterary.com; submissions@defliterary.com. **Website:** www.defioreandco.com. Member of AAR.

MEMBER AGENTS Brian DeFiore (popular nonfiction, business, pop culture, parenting, commercial fiction); **Laurie Abkemeier** (memoir, parenting, business, how-to/self-help, popular science); **Kate Garrick** (literary fiction, memoir, popular nonfiction); **Matthew Elblonk** (young adult, popular culture, narrative nonfiction); **Caryn Karmatz-Rudy** (popular fiction, self-help, narrative nonfiction); **Adam Schear** (commercial fiction, humor, YA, smart thrillers, historical fiction, and quirky debut literary novels. For nonfiction: popular science, politics, popular culture, and current events); **Meredith Kaffel** (smart upmarket women's fiction, literary fiction [especially debut] and literary thrillers, narrative nonfiction, nonfiction about science and tech, sophisticated pop culture/humor books); **Rebecca Strauss** (literary and commercial fiction, women's fiction, urban fantasy, romance, mystery, YA, memoir, pop culture, and select nonfiction); **Debra Goldstein** (nonfiction books on how to live better).

REPRESENTS Nonfiction books, novels. **Considers these nonfiction areas:** autobiography, biography, business, child guidance, cooking, economics, foods, how-to, inspirational, money, multicultural, parenting, popular culture, politics, psychology, religious, science, self-help, sports, young adult. **Considers these fiction areas:** ethnic, literary, mainstream, middle grade, mystery, paranormal, romance, short story collections, suspense, thriller, women's, young adult.

HOW TO CONTACT Query with SASE or e-mail to submissions@defliterary.com. "Please include the word 'Query' in the subject line. All attachments will be deleted; please insert all text in the body of the e-mail. For more information about our agents, their individual interests, and their query guidelines, please visit our 'About Us' page on our website." There is more information (details, sales) for each agent on the agency website. Accepts simultaneous submissions. Obtains most new clients through recommendations from others.

TERMS Agent receives 15% commission on domestic sales. Agent receives 20% commission on foreign sales. Offers written contract; 10-day notice must be given to terminate contract. Charges clients for photocopying and overnight delivery (deducted only after a sale is made).

DIANA FINCH LITERARY AGENCY

116 W. 23rd St., Suite 500, New York NY 10011. (917)544-4470. **E-mail:** diana.finch@verizon.net. **Website:** dianafinchliteraryagency.blogspot.com. **Contact:** Diana Finch. Member of AAR.

REPRESENTS Nonfiction books, novels, scholarly. **Considers these nonfiction areas:** autobiography, biography, business, child guidance, computers, cultural interests, current affairs, dance, economics, environment, ethnic, film, government, health, history, how-to, humor, investigative, juvenile nonfiction, law, medicine, memoirs, military, money, music, parenting, photography, popular culture, politics, psychology, satire, science, self-help, sports, technology, theater, translation, true crime, war, women's issues, women's studies. **Considers these fiction areas:** action, adventure, crime, detective, ethnic, historical, literary, mainstream, police, thriller, young adult.

HOW TO CONTACT This agency prefers submissions via its online form: https://dianafinchliteraryagency.submittable.com/submit Accepts simultaneous submissions. Obtains most new clients through recommendations from others.

TERMS Agent receives 15% commission on domestic sales. Agent receives 20% commission on foreign sales. Offers written contract. "I charge for overseas postage, galleys, and books purchased, and try to recoup these costs from earnings received for a client, rather than charging outright."

SANDRA DIJKSTRA LITERARY AGENCY

1155 Camino del Mar, PMB 515, Del Mar CA 92014. (858)755-3115. **Fax:** (858)794-2822. **E-mail:** elise@dijkstraagency.com. **Website:** www.dijkstraagency.com. Member of AAR. Other memberships include Authors Guild, PEN West, PEN USA, Organization of American Historians, Poets and Editors, MWA. Represents 100+ clients. 30% of clients are new/unpublished writers.

MEMBER AGENTS Sandra Dijkstra, president (adult only). Acquiring Sub-agents: **Elise Capron** (adult only), **Jill Marr** (adult only), **Thao Le** (adult and YA), **Roz Foster** (adult and YA), **Jessica Watterson** (subgenres of adult and new adult romance, and women's fiction).

REPRESENTS Nonfiction books, novels. **Considers these nonfiction areas:** biography, business, creative nonfiction, design, history, memoirs, psychology, science, self-help, narrative. **Considers these fiction areas:** commercial, horror, literary, middle grade, new adult, romance, science fiction, suspense, thriller, women's, young adult.

HOW TO CONTACT "Please see guidelines on our website, and note that we only accept e-mail submissions. Due to the large number of unsolicited submissions we receive, we are only able to respond those submissions in which we are interested." Accepts simultaneous submissions. Responds to queries of interest within 6 weeks.

TERMS Works in conjunction with foreign and film agents. Agent receives 15% commission on domestic sales and 20% commission on foreign sales. Offers written contract. No reading fee.

DONADIO & OLSON, INC.

121 W. 27th St., Suite 704, New York NY 10001. (212)691-8077. **Fax:** (212)633-2837. **E-mail:** neil@donadio.com. **E-mail:** mail@donadio.com. **Website:** donadio.com. **Contact:** Neil Olson. Member of AAR.

MEMBER AGENTS Neil Olson (no queries); **Edward Hibbert** (no queries); **Carrie Howland** (represents literary fiction and nonfiction as well as young adult fiction; she can be reached at carrie@donadio.com).

REPRESENTS Nonfiction books, novels. **Considers these fiction areas:** literary, young adult.

HOW TO CONTACT Please send a query letter, full synopsis, and the first three chapters/first 25 pages of the manuscript to mail@donadio.com. Please allow a few weeks for a reply. Obtains most new clients through recommendations from others.

DON CONGDON ASSOCIATES INC.

110 William St., Suite 2202, New York NY 10038. (212)645-1229. **Fax:** (212)727-2688. **E-mail:** dca@doncongdon.com. **Website:** doncongdon.com. **Contact:** Michael Congdon, Susan Ramer, Cristina Concepcion, Maura Kye Casella, Katie Kotchman, Katie Grimm. Member of AAR. Represents 100 clients.

REPRESENTS Considers these nonfiction areas: anthropology, archeology, autobiography, biography, child guidance, cooking, creative nonfiction, current affairs, dance, environment, film, foods, government, health, history, humor, language, law, literature, medicine, memoirs, military, music, parenting, popular culture, politics, psychology, satire, science, technology, theater, travel, true crime, war, women's issues, women's studies. **Considers these fiction areas:** action, adventure, contemporary issues, crime, detective, literary, mainstream, middle grade, mystery, police, short story collections, suspense, thriller, women's, young adult.

HOW TO CONTACT "For queries via email, you must include the word 'Query' and the agent's full name in your subject heading. Please also include your query and sample chapter in the body of the email, as we do not open attachments for security reasons. Please query only one agent within the agency at a time." Responds in 3 weeks to queries. Responds in 1 month to mss. Obtains most new clients through recommendations from other authors.

TERMS Agent receives 15% commission on domestic sales. Agent receives 20% commission on foreign sales. Charges client for extra shipping costs, photocopying, copyright fees, book purchases.

JANIS A. DONNAUD & ASSOCIATES, INC.

525 Broadway, Second Floor, New York NY 10012. (212)431-2664. **Fax:** (212)431-2667. **E-mail:** jdonnaud@aol.com; donnaudassociate@aol.com. **Website:** www.publishersmarketplace.com/members/JanisDonnaud/. **Contact:** Janis A. Donnaud. Member of AAR. Signatory of WGA. Represents 40 clients. 5% of clients are new/unpublished writers. Currently handles: nonfiction books 100%.

REPRESENTS Nonfiction books. **Considers these nonfiction areas:** biography, business, creative nonfiction, health, history, memoirs, money, psychology.

HOW TO CONTACT Query. For nonfiction, send a proposal; for fiction, paste a sample chapter into the email. Prefers exclusive submissions. Responds in 1 month to queries and mss. Obtains most new clients through recommendations from others.

TERMS Agent receives 15% commission on domestic and film sales; 20% commission on foreign sales. Offers written contract; 1-month notice must be given to terminate contract.

DREISBACH LITERARY MANAGEMENT

PO Box 5379, El Dorado Hills CA 95762. (916)804-5016. **E-mail:** verna@dreisbachliterary.com. **Website:** www.dreisbachliterary.com. **Contact:** Verna Dreisbach. Estab. 2007.

REPRESENTS Considers these nonfiction areas: animals, biography, business, health, memoirs, multicultural, parenting, travel, true crime, women's issues. **Considers these fiction areas:** commercial, literary, mystery, thriller, young adult.

HOW TO CONTACT E-mail queries only. No attachments in the query; they will not be opened. No unsolicited mss. *Accepting new nonfiction clients only through a writers conference or a personal referral. Not accepting fiction.*

DUNHAM LITERARY, INC.

110 William St., Suite 2202, New York NY 10038. (212)929-0994. **E-mail:** query@dunhamlit.com. **Website:** www.dunhamlit.com. **Contact:** Jennie Dunham. Member of AAR. SCBWI Represents 50 clients. 15% of clients are new/unpublished writers. Currently handles: nonfiction books 25%, novels 25%, juvenile books 50%.

REPRESENTS Considers these nonfiction areas: anthropology, archeology, biography, cultural interests, environment, ethnic, health, history, language, literature, medicine, popular culture, politics, psychology, science, technology, women's issues, women's studies. **Considers these fiction areas:** ethnic, juvenile, literary, mainstream, picture books, young adult.

HOW TO CONTACT Query with SASE. Responds in 3 weeks to queries; 2 months to mss. Obtains most new clients through recommendations from others, solicitations.

TERMS Agent receives 15% commission on domestic sales. Agent receives 20% commission on foreign sales.

DUNOW, CARLSON, & LERNER AGENCY

27 W. 20th St., Suite 1107, New York NY 10011. (212)645-7606. **E-mail:** betsy@dclagency.com; jennifer@dclagency.com. **E-mail:** mail@dclagency.com. **Website:** www.dclagency.com. Member of AAR.

MEMBER AGENTS Jennifer Carlson (narrative nonfiction writers and journalists covering current events and ideas and cultural history, as well as literary and upmarket commercial novelists); **Henry Dunow** (quality fiction - literary, historical, strongly written commercial - and with voice-driven nonfiction across a range of areas - narrative history, biography, memoir, current affairs, cultural trends and criticism, science, sports); **Erin Hosier** (nonfiction: popular culture, music, sociology and memoir); **Betsy Lerner** (nonfiction writers in the areas of psychology, history, cultural studies, biography, current events, business; fiction: literary, dark, funny, voice driven); **Yishai Seidman** (broad range of fiction: literary, postmodern, and thrillers; nonfiction: sports, music, and pop culture); **Amy Hughes** (nonfiction in the areas of history, cultural studies, memoir, current events, wellness, health, food, pop culture, and biography; also literary fiction); **Eleanor Jackson** (literary, commercial, memoir, art, food, science and history); **Julia Kenny** (fiction—adult, middle grade and YA—and is especially interested in dark, literary thrillers and suspense); **Edward Necarsulmer IV** (strong new voices in teen & middle grade as well as picture books).

REPRESENTS Nonfiction books, novels, juvenile. **Considers these nonfiction areas:** art, biography, creative nonfiction, cultural interests, current affairs, foods, health, history, memoirs, music, popular culture, psychology, science, sociology, sports. **Considers these fiction areas:** commercial, literary, mainstream, middle grade, mystery, picture books, thriller, young adult.

HOW TO CONTACT Query via snail mail with SASE, or by e-mail. No attachments. Responds if interested.

DYSTEL & GODERICH LITERARY MANAGEMENT

1 Union Square W., Suite 904, New York NY 10003. (212)627-9100. **Fax:** (212)627-9313. **Website:** www.dystel.com. Estab. 1994. Member of AAR. Other membership includes SCBWI. Represents 600+ clients.

MEMBER AGENTS Jane Dystel; Miriam Goderich, miriam@dystel.com (literary and commercial fiction as well as some genre fiction, narrative nonfiction, pop culture, psychology, history, science, art, business books, and biography/memoir); **Stacey Kendall Glick,** sglick@dystel.com (narrative nonfiction including memoir, parenting, cooking and food, psychology, science, health and wellness, lifestyle, current events, pop culture, YA, middle grade, and select adult contemporary fiction); **Michael Bourret,** mbourret@dystel.com (middle grade and young adult fiction, commercial adult fiction, and all sorts of nonfiction, from practical to narrative; he's especially interested in food and cocktail related books, memoir, popular history, politics, religion (though not spirituality), popular science, and current events); **Jim McCarthy,** jmccarthy@dystel.com (literary women's fiction, underrepresented voices, mysteries, romance, paranormal fiction, narrative nonfiction, memoir, and paranormal nonfiction); **Jessica Papin,** jpapin@dystel.com (literary and smart commercial fiction, narrative nonfiction, history with a thesis, medicine, science and religion, health, psychology, women's issues); **Lauren E. Abramo,** labramo@dystel.com (smart commercial fiction and well-paced literary fiction with a unique voice, including middle grade, YA, and adult and a wide variety of narrative nonfiction including science, interdisciplinary cultural studies, pop culture, psychology, reportage, media, contemporary culture, and history); **John Rudolph,** jrudolph@dystel.com (picture book author/illustrators, middle grade, YA, commercial fiction for men, nonfiction); **Rachel Stout,** rstout@dystel.com (literary fiction, narrative nonfiction, and believable and thought-provoking YA as well as magical realism); **Sharon Pelletier,** spelletier@dystel.com (witty literary fiction and smart commercial fiction featuring female characters, narrative nonfiction).

REPRESENTS Nonfiction books, novels. **Considers these nonfiction areas:** animals, anthropology, archeology, autobiography, biography, business, child guidance, cultural interests, current affairs, economics, ethnic, gay/lesbian, health, history, humor, inspirational, investigative, medicine, metaphysics, military, New Age, parenting, popular culture, psychology, religious, science, technology, true crime, women's issues, women's studies. **Considers these fiction areas:** action, adventure, commercial, crime, detective, ethnic, family saga, gay, lesbian, literary, mainstream, middle grade, mystery, picture books, police, suspense, thriller, women's, young adult.

HOW TO CONTACT Query via e-mail and put "Query" in the subject line. "Synopses, outlines or sample chapters (say, one chapter or the first 25 pages of your manuscript) should either be included below the cover letter or attached as a separate document. We won't open attachments if they come with a blank e-mail." Accepts simultaneous submissions. Responds in 6 to 8 weeks to queries; within 8 weeks to mss. Obtains most new clients through recommendations from others, solicitations, conferences.

TERMS Agent receives 15% commission on domestic sales. Agent receives 19% commission on foreign sales. Offers written contract.

THE LISA EKUS GROUP, LLC

57 North St., Hatfield MA 01038. (413)247-9325. **Fax:** (413)247-9873. **E-mail:** info@lisaekus.com. **Website:** www.lisaekus.com. **Contact:** Lisa Ekus-Saffer. Member of AAR.

MEMBER AGENTS Lisa Ekus; Sally Ekus.

REPRESENTS Nonfiction books. **Considers these nonfiction areas:** cooking, diet/nutrition, foods, occasionally health/well-being and women's issues.

HOW TO CONTACT Submit a one-page query via e-mail or submit complete hard copy proposal with title page, proposal contents, concept, bio, marketing, TOC, etc. Include SASE for the return of materials. The agency shares submissions tips at lisaekus.com/submission-requirements/.

⊘ THE ELAINE P. ENGLISH LITERARY AGENCY

4710 41st St. NW, Suite D, Washington DC 20016. (202)362-5190. **Fax:** (202)362-5192. **Website:** www.elaineenglish.com/. **Contact:** Elaine English. Member of AAR.

MEMBER AGENTS Elaine English (novels).

REPRESENTS Novels. **Considers these fiction areas:** historical, multicultural, mystery, suspense, thriller, women's, romance (single title, historical, contemporary, romantic, suspense, chick lit, erotic), general women's fiction. The agency is slowly but steadily acquiring in all mentioned areas.

HOW TO CONTACT Not accepting queries as of 2015. Keep checking the website for further information and updates. Responds in 4-8 weeks to queries; 3 months to requested submissions. Obtains most new clients through recommendations from others, conferences, submissions.

TERMS Agent receives 15% commission on domestic sales. Agent receives 20% commission on foreign sales. Offers written contract; 30-day notice must be given to terminate contract. Charges only for shipping expenses; generally taken from proceeds.

FAYE BENDER LITERARY AGENCY

19 Cheever Place, Brooklyn NY 11231. **E-mail:** info@fbliterary.com. **Website:** www.fbliterary.com. **Contact:** Faye Bender. Estab. 2004. Member of AAR.

MEMBER AGENTS Faye Bender.

REPRESENTS Nonfiction books, novels, juvenile. **Considers these nonfiction areas:** biography, memoirs, popular culture, women's issues, women's studies, young adult, narrative; health; popular science. **Considers these fiction areas:** commercial, literary, middle grade, women's, young adult.

HOW TO CONTACT Please submit a query letter and ten sample pages to info@fbliterary.com (no attachments). "Due to the volume of e-mails, we can't respond to everything. If we are interested, we will be in touch as soon as we possibly can. Otherwise, please consider it a pass."

FELICIA ETH LITERARY REPRESENTATION

555 Bryant St., Suite 350, Palo Alto CA 94301-1700. **E-mail:** feliciaeth.literary@gmail.com. **Website:** ethliterary.com. **Contact:** Felicia Eth. Member of AAR. Represents 25-35 clients. Currently handles: nonfiction books 75%, novels 25% adult.

REPRESENTS Nonfiction books, novels. **Considers these nonfiction areas:** animals, anthropology, autobiography, biography, business, child guidance, cultural interests, current affairs, economics, health, history, investigative, law, medicine, parenting, popular culture, politics, psychology, science, sociology, technology, women's issues, women's studies. **Considers these fiction areas:** literary, mainstream.

HOW TO CONTACT Query with SASE. Accepts simultaneous submissions. Responds in 3 weeks to queries. Responds in 4-6 weeks to mss.

TERMS Agent receives 15% commission on domestic sales. Agent receives 20% commission on foreign sales. Agent receives 20% commission on film sales. Charges clients for photocopying and express mail service.

FINEPRINT LITERARY MANAGEMENT

115 W. 29th, 3rd Floor, New York NY 10001. (212)279-1282. **Website:** www.fineprintlit.com. Member of AAR.

MEMBER AGENTS **Peter Rubie**, CEO, peter@fineprintlit.com (nonfiction interests include narrative nonfiction, popular science, spirituality, history, biography, pop culture, business, technology, parenting, health, self help, music, and food; fiction interests include literate thrillers, crime fiction, science fiction and fantasy, military fiction and literary fiction, middle grade and YA fiction and nonfiction for boys); **Stephany Evans**, stephany@fineprintlit.com (nonfiction: health and wellness, especially women's health; spirituality, environment/sustainability, food and wine, memoir, and narrative nonfiction; fiction interests include stories with a strong and interesting female protagonist, both literary and upmarket commercial/book club fiction, romance [all subgenres], mysteries); **Janet Reid** (crime fiction and narrative nonfiction); **Laura Wood**, laura@fineprintlit.com (serious nonfiction, especially in the areas of science and nature, along with substantial titles in business, history, religion, and other areas by academics, experienced professionals, and journalists); **June Clark** (see juneclark.com).

REPRESENTS **Considers these nonfiction areas:** biography, business, creative nonfiction, foods, health, history, humor, law, memoirs, music, parenting, popular culture, science, self-help, spirituality, technology. **Considers these fiction areas:** commercial, crime, fantasy, middle grade, military, mystery, romance, science fiction, suspense, thriller, women's, young adult.

HOW TO CONTACT E-query. For fiction, send a query, synopsis, bio, and 30 pages pasted into the e-mail. No attachments. For nonfiction, send a query only; proposal requested later if the agent is interested. Obtains most new clients through recommendations from others, solicitations.

TERMS Agent receives 15% commission on domestic sales. Agent receives 20% commission on foreign sales.

FLETCHER & COMPANY

78 Fifth Ave., 3rd Floor, New York NY 10011. (212)614-0778. **Fax:** (212)614-0728. **E-mail:** info@fletcherandco.com. **Website:** www.fletcherandco.com. **Contact:** Christy Fletcher. Estab. 2003. Member of AAR.

MEMBER AGENTS **Christy Fletcher** (referrals only); **Melissa Chinchillo** (predominantly nonfiction—psychology, popular philosophy, science, history, biography, investigative/narrative journalism, politics, current affairs, pop culture and self-help; some fiction—upmarket, commercial, literary horror/fantasy, mystery; very select children's and young adult); **Rebecca Gradinger** (literary fiction, upmarket commercial fiction, narrative nonfiction, self-help, memoir, women's studies, humor, and pop culture); **Gráinne Fox** (literary fiction and quality commercial authors, award-winning journalists and food writers); **Lisa Grubka** (fiction—literary, upmarket women's, and young adult; and nonfiction—narrative, food, science, and more); **Donald Lamm** (nonfiction—history, biography, investigative journalism, politics, current affairs, and business); **Todd Sattersten** (business books); **Sylvie Greenberg** (literary fiction, business, history, sports writing, science, investigative journalism); **Rachel Crawford** (literary fiction, especially if it's dark, experimental, or quirky; speculative fiction; YA; and great science writing).

REPRESENTS Nonfiction books, novels. **Considers these nonfiction areas:** biography, business, creative nonfiction, foods, history, humor, investigative, memoirs, popular culture, politics, science, self-help, sports, women's issues, women's studies. **Considers these fiction areas:** commercial, fantasy, literary, science fiction, women's, young adult.

HOW TO CONTACT To query, please send a letter, brief synopsis, and an SASE to our address, or you may also send queries to info@fletcherandco.com. Please do not include email attachments with your initial query, as they will be deleted. Address your query to a specific agent. No snail mail queries.

FOLIO LITERARY MANAGEMENT, LLC

The Film Center Building, 630 Ninth Ave., Suite 1101, New York NY 10036. (212)400-1494. **Fax:** (212)967-0977. **Website:** www.foliolit.com. Member of AAR. Represents 100+ clients.

MEMBER AGENTS Claudia Cross, Scott Hoffman, Jeff Kleinman, Frank Weimann, Michelle Brower, Michael Harriot, Erin Harris, Molly Jaffa, Katherine Latshaw, Erin Niumata, Ruth Pomerance, Marcy Posner, Jeff Silberman, Michael Sterling, Steve Troha, Emily van Beek, Melissa Sarver White.

REPRESENTS Nonfiction books, novels, short story collections. **Considers these nonfiction areas:** animals, art, biography, business, child guidance, cooking, creative nonfiction, economics, environment, foods, health, history, how-to, humor, inspirational, memoirs, military, parenting, popular culture, politics, psychology, religious, satire, science, self-help, technology, war, women's issues, women's studies. **Considers these fiction areas:** commercial, erotica, fantasy, horror, literary, middle grade, mystery, picture books, religious, romance, thriller, women's, young adult.

HOW TO CONTACT Query via e-mail only (no attachments). Read agent bios online for specific submission guidelines and email addresses.

FRANCES COLLIN, LITERARY AGENT

P.O. Box 33, Wayne PA 19087-0033. **E-mail:** queries@francescollin.com. **Website:** www.francescollin.com. Member of AAR. Represents 90 clients. 1% of clients are new/unpublished writers.

HOW TO CONTACT Query via e-mail describing project (text in the body of the e-mail only, no attachments) to queries@francescollin.com. "Please note that all queries are reviewed by all agents at the agency." No phone or fax queries. Accepts simultaneous submissions.

TERMS Agent receives 15% commission on domestic sales. Agent receives 20% commission on foreign sales. Offers written contract.

JEANNE FREDERICKS LITERARY AGENCY, INC.

221 Benedict Hill Rd., New Canaan CT 06840. (203)972-3011. **Fax:** (203)972-3011. **E-mail:** jeanne.fredericks@gmail.com. **Website:** www.jeannefredericks.com. **Contact:** Jeanne Fredericks. Estab. 1997. Member of AAR. Other memberships include Authors Guild. Currently handles: nonfiction books 100%.

REPRESENTS Nonfiction books. **Considers these nonfiction areas:** animals, autobiography, biography, child guidance, cooking, decorating, foods, gardening, health, history, how-to, interior design, medicine, parenting, photography, psychology, self-help, women's issues.

HOW TO CONTACT Query first by e-mail, then send outline/proposal, 1-2 sample chapters, if requested. If you do send requested submission materials, note the word "Requested" in the subject line. See submission guidelines online first. Accepts simultaneous submissions. Responds in 3-5 weeks to queries. Responds in 2-4 months to mss. Obtains most new clients through recommendations from others, solicitations, conferences.

TERMS Agent receives 15% commission on domestic sales. Agent receives 25% commission on foreign sales with co-agent. Offers written contract, binding for 9 months; 2-month notice must be given to terminate contract. Charges client for photocopying of whole proposals and mss, overseas postage, priority mail, express mail services.

THE FRIEDRICH AGENCY

19 W. 21st St., Suite 201, New York NY 10010. **E-mail:** mfriedrich@friedrichagency.com; lcarson@friedrichagency.com; nichole@friedrichagency.com. **Website:** www.friedrichagency.com. **Contact:** Molly Friedrich; Lucy Carson. Member of AAR. Signatory of WGA. Represents 50+ clients.

MEMBER AGENTS **Molly Friedrich**, founder and agent (open to queries); **Lucy Carson**, foreign rights director and agent (open to queries); **Nichole LeFebvre** (foreign rights manager; open to queries).

REPRESENTS Full-length fiction and nonfiction. **Considers these nonfiction areas:** creative nonfiction, memoirs. **Considers these fiction areas:** commercial, literary.

HOW TO CONTACT Query by e-mail only. Please query only one agent at this agency.

GELFMAN SCHNEIDER / ICM PARTNERS

850 7th Ave., Suite 903, New York NY 10019. (212)245-1993. **Fax:** (212)245-8678. **E-mail:** mail@gelfmanschneider.com. **Website:** www.gelfmanschneider.com. **Contact:** Jane Gelfman, Deborah Schneider. Member of AAR. Represents 300+ clients. 10% of clients are new/unpublished writers.

MEMBER AGENTS Deborah Schneider, Jane Gelfman, Victoria Marini, Heather Mitchell.

REPRESENTS Fiction and nonfiction books. **Considers these nonfiction areas:** creative nonfiction, popular culture. **Considers these fiction areas:** historical, literary, mainstream, middle grade, mystery, science fiction, suspense, westerns, women's, young adult.

HOW TO CONTACT Query. Send queries via snail mail only. No unsolicited mss. Please send a query letter, a synopsis, and a sample chapter only. Consult website for each agent's submission requirements. Note that Ms. Marini is the only agent at this agency who accepts e-queries: victoria.gsliterary@gmail.com. If querying Marini, put "Query" in the subject line and paste all materials (query, 1-3 sample chapters) in the body of the e-mail. Responds in 1 month to queries. Responds in 2 months to mss.

TERMS Agent receives 15% commission on domestic sales. Agent receives 20% commission on foreign sales. Agent receives 15% commission on film sales. Offers written contract. Charges clients for photocopying and messengers/couriers.

⊘ GEORGES BORCHARDT, INC.

136 E. 57th St., New York NY 10022. (212)753-5785. **Website:** www.gbagency.com. Estab. 1967. Member of AAR. Represents 200+ clients.

MEMBER AGENTS Anne Borchardt; Georges Borchardt; Valerie Borchardt; Samantha Shea.

HOW TO CONTACT *No unsolicited mss.* Obtains most new clients through recommendations from others.

TERMS Agent receives 15% commission on domestic sales. Agent receives 20% commission on foreign sales. Offers written contract.

FRANCES GOLDIN LITERARY AGENCY, INC.

57 E. 11th St., Suite 5B, New York NY 10003. (212)777-0047. **Fax:** (212)228-1660. **Website:** www.goldinlit.com. Estab. 1977. Member of AAR.

MEMBER AGENTS **Frances Goldin**, principal/agent; **Ellen Geiger**, agent (commercial and literary fiction and nonfiction, cutting-edge topics of all kinds); Matt McGowan, agent/rights director (innovative works of fiction and nonfiction); **Sam Stoloff**, agent, (literary fiction, memoir, history, accessible sociology and philosophy, cultural studies, serious journalism, narrative and topical nonfiction with a progressive orientation); **Sarah Bridgins**, agent/office manager, sb@goldinlit.com (voice-driven fiction and narrative nonfiction); **Ria Julien**; **Matt McGowan**.

REPRESENTS Nonfiction books, novels. **Considers these nonfiction areas:** creative nonfiction, cultural interests, investigative, memoirs, philosophy, sociology. **Considers these fiction areas:** literary, mainstream.

HOW TO CONTACT There is an online submission process you can find here: www.goldinlit.com/contact.html Responds in 4-6 weeks to queries.

IRENE GOODMAN LITERARY AGENCY

27 W. 24th St., Suite 700B, New York NY 10010. **Website:** www.irenegoodman.com. Member of AAR.

MEMBER AGENTS **Irene Goodman** (her fiction list includes upmarket women's fiction, middle grade, young adult, thrillers, historical fiction, and mysteries; her nonfiction list includes pop culture, science, Francophilia, and lifestyle); **Beth Vesel** (narrative nonfiction, cultural criticism, psychology, science and memoir; **Miriam Kriss** (commercial fiction and she represents everything from hardcover historical mysteries to all subgenres of romance, from young adult fiction to kick ass urban fantasies, and everything in between); **Barbara Poelle** (thrillers, literary suspense, young adult and upmarket fiction); **Rachel Ekstrom** (young adult, women's fiction, new adult, mysteries, thrillers, romance, and the occasional quirky work of nonfiction).

REPRESENTS Nonfiction, novels. **Considers these nonfiction areas:** narrative nonfiction dealing with social, cultural and historical issues; an occasional memoir and current affairs book, parenting, social issues, francophilia, anglophilia, Judaica, lifestyles, cooking, memoir. **Considers these fiction areas:** crime, detective, historical, mystery, romance, thriller, women's, young adult.

HOW TO CONTACT Query. Submit synopsis, first 10 pages. E-mail queries only! See the website submission page. No e-mail attachments. Query one agent only. Responds in 2 months to queries. Consult website for each agent's submission guidelines.

ASHLEY GRAYSON LITERARY AGENCY

1342 W. 18th St., San Pedro CA 90732. **E-mail:** graysonagent@earthlink.net. **Website:** www.publishersmarketplace.com/members/CGrayson/. Estab. 1976. Member of AAR.

MEMBER AGENTS **Ashley Grayson** (fantasy, mystery, thrillers, young adult); **Carolyn Grayson** (chick lit, mystery, children's, nonfiction, women's fiction, romance, thrillers); **Lois Winston** (women's fiction, chick lit, mystery).

REPRESENTS Nonfiction books, novels. **Considers these nonfiction areas:** business, computers, economics, history, investigative, popular culture, science, self-help, sports, technology, true crime. **Con-**

siders these fiction areas: fantasy, juvenile, middle grade, multicultural, mystery, romance, science fiction, suspense, women's, young adult.

HOW TO CONTACT The agency is temporarily closed to queries from *fiction* writers who are not previously published at book length (self published or print-on-demand do not count). There are only three exceptions to this policy: (1) Unpublished authors who have received an offer from a reputable publisher, who need an agent before beginning contract negotiations; (2) Authors who are recommended by a published author, editor or agent who has read the work in question; (3) Authors whom we have met at conferences and from whom we have requested submissions. Nonfiction authors who are recognized within their field or area may still query with proposals. Note: We cannot review self-published, subsidy-published, and POD-published works to evaluate moving them to mainstream publishers.

TERMS Agent receives 15% commission on domestic sales. Agent receives 20% commission on foreign sales.

SANFORD J. GREENBURGER ASSOCIATES, INC.

55 Fifth Ave., New York NY 10003. (212)206-5600. **Fax:** (212)463-8718. **Website:** www.greenburger.com. Member of AAR. Represents 500 clients.

MEMBER AGENTS Matt Bialer, LRibar@sjga.com (fantasy, science fiction, thrillers, and mysteries as well as a select group of literary writers, and also loves smart narrative nonfiction including books about current events, popular culture, biography, history, music, race, and sports); **Brenda Bowen**, queryBB@sjga.com (literary fiction, writers and illustrators of picture books, chapter books, and middle-grade and teen fiction); **Lisa Gallagher**, lgsubmissions@sjga.com (accessible literary fiction, quality commercial women's fiction, crime fiction, lively narrative nonfiction); **Faith Hamlin**, fhamlin@sjga.com (receives submissions by referral); **Heide Lange**, queryHL@sjga.com; **Daniel Mandel**, querydm@sjga.com (literary and commercial fiction, as well as memoirs and non-fiction about business, art, history, politics, sports, and popular culture); **Courtney Miller-Callihan**, cmiller@sjga.com (YA, middle grade, women's fiction, romance, and historical novels, as well as nonfiction projects on unusual topics, humor, pop culture, and lifestyle books); **Nicholas Ellison**, nellison@sjga.com; **Chelsea Lindman**, clindman@sjga.com (playful literary fiction, upmarket crime fiction, and forward thinking or boundary-pushing nonfiction); **Rachael Dillon Fried**, rfried@sjga.com (both fiction and nonfiction authors, with a keen interest in unique literary voices, women's fiction, narrative nonfiction, memoir, and comedy); **Lindsay Ribar**, co-agents with Matt Bailer (young adult and middle grade fiction); **Thomas Miller** (primarily nonfiction projects in the areas of wellness and health, popular culture, psychology and self-help, business, diet, spirituality, cooking, and narrative nonfiction).

REPRESENTS Nonfiction books and novels. **Considers these nonfiction areas:** art, biography, business, creative nonfiction, current affairs, ethnic, history, humor, memoirs, music, popular culture, politics, sports. **Considers these fiction areas:** crime, fantasy, historical, literary, middle grade, mystery, picture books, romance, science fiction, thriller, women's, young adult.

HOW TO CONTACT E-query. "Please look at each agent's profile page for current information about what each agent is looking for and for the correct email address to use for queries to that agent. Please be sure to use the correct query e-mail address for each agent." Accepts simultaneous submissions. Responds in 2 months to queries and mss. Obtains most new clients through recommendations from others.

TERMS Agent receives 15% commission on domestic sales. Agent receives 20% commission on foreign sales. Charges for photocopying and books for foreign and subsidiary rights submissions.

GREYHAUS LITERARY

3021 20th St., PL SW, Puyallup WA 98373. **E-mail:** scott@greyhausagency.com. **Website:** www.greyhausagency.com. **Contact:** Scott Eagan, member RWA. Estab. 2003.

REPRESENTS Considers these fiction areas: romance, women's.

HOW TO CONTACT Submissions to Greyhaus can be done in one of three ways: 1) Send a query, the first 3 pages and a synopsis of no more than 3 pages (and a SASE), using a snail mail submission. 2) A standard query letter via email. If using this method, do not attach documents or send anything else other than a query letter. Or 3) use the Submission Form found on the website on the Contact page.

THE JOY HARRIS LITERARY AGENCY, INC.

381 Park Avenue S, Suite 428, New York NY 10016. (212)924-6269. **Fax:** (212)725-5275. **E-mail:** submis-

sions@jhlitagent.com. **Website:** joyharrisliterary.com. **Contact:** Joy Harris. Estab. 1990. Member of AAR. Represents more than 100 clients. Currently handles: nonfiction books 50%, novels 50%.

MEMBER AGENTS **Joy Harris** (most interested in literary fiction and narrative nonfiction); **Adam Reed** (arts, literary fiction, science and technology, and pop culture).

REPRESENTS **Considers these nonfiction areas:** art, creative nonfiction, popular culture, science, technology. **Considers these fiction areas:** literary.

HOW TO CONTACT "Please e-mail your submission to submissions@joyharrisliterary.com; however, we will only reply if interested. Do not send your full manuscript before it is requested." Accepts simultaneous submissions. Responds in 2 months to queries. Obtains most new clients through recommendations from clients and editors.

TERMS Agent receives 15% commission on domestic sales. Agent receives 20% commission on foreign sales. Charges clients for some office expenses.

JOHN HAWKINS & ASSOCIATES, INC.

80 Maiden Lane, Suite 1503, New York NY 10038. (212)807-7040. **Fax:** (212)807-9555. **E-mail:** jha@jhalit.com. **Website:** www.jhalit.com. **Contact:** Moses Cardona (rights and translations); Liz Free (permissions); Warren Frazier, literary agent; Anne Hawkins, literary agent. Member of AAR. Represents 100+ clients. 5-10% of clients are new/unpublished writers. Currently handles: nonfiction books 40%, novels 40%, juvenile books 20%.

MEMBER AGENTS **Moses Cardona**, moses@jhalit.com (commercial fiction, suspense, business, science, and multicultural fiction); **Warren Frazier**, frazier@jhalit.com (nonfiction—technology, history, world affairs and foreign policy); **Anne Hawkins** ahawkins@jhalit.com (thrillers to literary fiction to serious nonfiction; she also has particular interests in science, history, public policy, medicine and women's issues).

REPRESENTS Nonfiction books, novels. **Considers these nonfiction areas:** biography, business, history, medicine, politics, science, technology, women's issues. **Considers these fiction areas:** commercial, historical, literary, multicultural, suspense, thriller.

HOW TO CONTACT Query. Include the word "Query" in the subject line. For fiction, include 1-3 chapters of your book as a single Word attachment. For nonfiction, include your proposal as a single attachment. E-mail a particular agent directly if you are targeting one. Accepts simultaneous submissions. Responds in 1 month to queries. Obtains most new clients through recommendations from others.

TERMS Agent receives 15% commission on domestic sales. Agent receives 20% commission on foreign sales. Charges clients for photocopying.

HEACOCK HILL LITERARY AGENCY, INC.

West Coast Office, 1020 Hollywood Way, #439, Burbank CA 91505. (818)951-6788. **E-mail:** agent@heacockhill.com. **Website:** www.heacockhill.com. **Contact:** Catt LeBaigue or Tom Dark. Estab. 2009. Member of AAR. Other memberships include SCBWI.

MEMBER AGENTS **Tom Dark** (adult fiction, nonfiction); **Catt LeBaigue** (juvenile fiction, adult nonfiction including arts, crafts, anthropology, astronomy, nature studies, ecology, body/mind/spirit, humanities, self-help).

REPRESENTS Nonfiction, fiction. **Considers these nonfiction areas:** art, business, gardening, politics. **Considers these fiction areas:** juvenile, middle grade, picture books, young adult.

HOW TO CONTACT E-mail queries only. No unsolicited manuscripts. No e-mail attachments. Responds in 1 week to queries. Obtains most new clients through recommendations from others, solicitations.

TERMS Offers written contract.

RICHARD HENSHAW GROUP

145 W. 28th St., 12th Floor, New York NY 10001. (212)414-1172. **E-mail:** submissions@henshaw.com. **Website:** www.richardhenshawgroup.com. **Contact:** Rich Henshaw. Member of AAR.

MEMBER AGENTS Richard Henshaw; Susannah Taylor.

REPRESENTS Nonfiction books, novels. **Considers these nonfiction areas:** animals, autobiography, biography, business, child guidance, cooking, current affairs, dance, economics, environment, foods, gay/lesbian, health, humor, investigative, money, music, New Age, parenting, popular culture, politics, psychology, science, self-help, sociology, sports, technology, true crime, women's issues, women's studies. **Considers these fiction areas:** crime, detective, fantasy, historical, horror, literary, mainstream, mystery, police, science fiction, supernatural, suspense, thriller, young adult.

HOW TO CONTACT "Please feel free to submit a query letter in the form of an e-mail of fewer than

250 words to submissions@henshaw.com address." No snail mail queries. Responds in 3 weeks to queries. Responds in 6 weeks to mss. Obtains most new clients through recommendations from others, solicitations, conferences.

TERMS Agent receives 15% commission on domestic sales. Agent receives 20% commission on foreign sales. No written contract. Charges clients for photocopying and book orders.

HOPKINS LITERARY ASSOCIATES

2117 Buffalo Rd., Suite 327, Rochester NY 14624-1507. (585)352-6268. **Contact:** Pam Hopkins. Member of AAR. Other memberships include RWA.

REPRESENTS Novels. **Considers these fiction areas:** romance, women's.

HOW TO CONTACT Regular mail with synopsis, 3 sample chapters (or first 50 pages), SASE. Accepts simultaneous submissions. Obtains most new clients through recommendations from others, solicitations, conferences.

TERMS Agent receives 15% commission on domestic sales. Agent receives 20% commission on foreign sales. No written contract.

⊘ ICM PARTNERS

730 Fifth Ave., New York NY 10019. (212)556-5600. **Website:** www.icmtalent.com. **Contact:** Literary Department. Member of AAR. Signatory of WGA.

REPRESENTS Nonfiction, fiction, novels, juvenile books.

HOW TO CONTACT This agency is generally not open to unsolicited submissions. However, some agents do attend conferences and meet writers then. The agents take referrals, as well. Obtains most new clients through recommendations from others.

TERMS Agent receives 15% commission on domestic sales. Agent receives 20% commission on foreign sales.

HARVEY KLINGER, INC.

300 W. 55th St., Suite 11V, New York NY 10019. (212)581-7068. **E-mail:** queries@harveyklinger.com. **Website:** www.harveyklinger.com. **Contact:** Harvey Klinger. Member of AAR. Represents 100 clients. 25% of clients are new/unpublished writers. Currently handles: nonfiction books 50%, novels 50%.

MEMBER AGENTS **Harvey Kliinger; David Dunton** (popular culture, music-related books, literary fiction, young adult, fiction, and memoirs); **Sara Crowe** (children's and young adult authors, adult fiction and nonfiction, foreign rights sales); **Andrea Somberg** (literary fiction, commercial fiction, romance, sci-fi/fantasy, mysteries/thrillers, young adult, middle grade, quality narrative nonfiction, popular culture, how-to, self-help, humor, interior design, cookbooks, health/fitness).

REPRESENTS Nonfiction books, novels. **Considers these nonfiction areas:** autobiography, biography, cooking, diet//nutrition, foods, health, investigative, medicine, psychology, science, self-help, spirituality, sports, technology, true crime, women's issues, women's studies. **Considers these fiction areas:** action, adventure, crime, detective, family saga, glitz, literary, mainstream, mystery, police, suspense, thriller.

HOW TO CONTACT Use online e-mail submission form on the website, or query with SASE via snail mail. No phone or fax queries. Don't send unsolicited manuscripts or e-mail attachments. Make submission letter to the point and as brief as possible. Responds in 2-4 weeks to queries, if interested. Obtains most new clients through recommendations from others.

TERMS Agent receives 15% commission on domestic sales. Agent receives 25% commission on foreign sales. Offers written contract. Charges for photocopying mss and overseas postage for mss.

LINDA KONNER LITERARY AGENCY

10 W. 15th St., Suite 1918, New York NY 10011. (212)691-3419. **E-mail:** ldkonner@cs.com. **Website:** www.lindakonnerliteraryagency.com. **Contact:** Linda Konner. Member of AAR. Signatory of WGA. Other memberships include ASJA. Represents 85 clients. 30-35% of clients are new/unpublished writers. Currently handles: nonfiction books 100%.

REPRESENTS Nonfiction books. **Considers these nonfiction areas:** gay/lesbian, health, medicine, money, parenting, popular culture, psychology, science, self-help, women's issues, biography (celebrity), African American and Latino issues, relationships, popular science.

HOW TO CONTACT Query by e-mail or by mail with SASE, synopsis, author bio, sufficient return postage. Prefers to read materials exclusively for 2 weeks. Accepts simultaneous submissions. Obtains most new clients through recommendations from others, occasional solicitation among established authors/journalists.

TERMS Agent receives 15% commission on domestic sales. Agent receives 25% commission on foreign sales. Offers written contract. Charges one-time fee for domestic expenses; additional expenses may be incurred for foreign sales.

⊘ BARBARA S. KOUTS, LITERARY AGENT

P.O. Box 560, Bellport NY 11713. (631)286-1278. **Fax:** (631) 286-1538. **Contact:** Barbara S. Kouts. Member of AAR. Represents 50 clients. 10% of clients are new/unpublished writers.

REPRESENTS Juvenile.

HOW TO CONTACT Query with SASE. Accepts solicited queries by snail mail only. Accepts simultaneous submissions. Obtains most new clients through recommendations from others, solicitations, conferences.

TERMS Agent receives 10% commission on domestic sales. Agent receives 20% commission on foreign sales. This agency charges clients for photocopying.

STUART KRICHEVSKY LITERARY AGENCY, INC.

381 Park Ave. S., Suite 428, New York NY 10016. (212)725-5288. **Fax:** (212)725-5275. **Website:** www.skagency.com. Member of AAR.

MEMBER AGENTS **Stuart Krichevsky**, query@skagency.com (emphasis on narrative nonfiction, literary journalism and literary and commercial fiction); **Allison Hunter**, AHquery@skagency.com (literary and commercial fiction, memoir, narrative nonfiction, cultural studies and pop culture; she is always looking for funny female writers, great love stories, family epics, and for nonfiction projects that speak to the current cultural climate); **Ross Harris**, RHquery@skagency.com (voice-driven humor and memoir, books on popular culture and our society, narrative nonfiction and literary fiction); **David Patterson**, dp@skagency.com (writers of upmarket narrative nonfiction and literary fiction, historians, journalists and thought leaders); **Shana Cohen**.

REPRESENTS Nonfiction books, novels. **Considers these nonfiction areas:** creative nonfiction, humor, memoirs, popular culture. **Considers these fiction areas:** commercial, contemporary issues, literary.

HOW TO CONTACT Please send a query letter and the first few (up to 10) pages of your manuscript or proposal in the body of an e-mail (not an attachment) to one of the e-mail addresses. No attachments. Responds if interested. Obtains most new clients through recommendations from others, solicitations.

MICHAEL LARSEN/ELIZABETH POMADA, LITERARY AGENTS

1029 Jones St., San Francisco CA 94109. (415)673-0939. **E-mail:** larsenpoma@aol.com. **Website:** www.larsen-pomada.com. **Contact:** Mike Larsen, Elizabeth Pomada. Member of AAR. Other memberships include Authors Guild, ASJA, WNBA, California Writers Club, National Speakers Association. Represents 100 clients. 40-45% of clients are new/unpublished writers. Currently handles: nonfiction books 70%, novels 30%.

MEMBER AGENTS Michael Larsen (nonfiction); Elizabeth Pomada (fiction and narrative nonfiction).

REPRESENTS **Considers these nonfiction areas:** anthropology, archeology, architecture, art, autobiography, biography, business, current affairs, diet//nutrition, design, economics, environment, ethnic, film, foods, gay/lesbian, health, history, how-to, humor, inspirational, investigative, law, medicine, memoirs, metaphysics, money, music, New Age, popular culture, politics, psychology, religious, satire, science, self-help, sociology, sports, travel, women's issues, women's studies, futurism. **Considers these fiction areas:** action, adventure, contemporary issues, crime, detective, ethnic, experimental, family saga, feminist, gay, glitz, historical, humor, inspirational, lesbian, literary, mainstream, mystery, police, religious, romance, satire, suspense.

HOW TO CONTACT **Elizabeth Pomada** handles literary and commercial fiction, romance, thrillers, mysteries, narrative nonfiction and mainstream women's fiction. If you have completed a novel, **please e-mail the first 10 pages and 2-page synopsis to larsenpoma@aol.com**. Use 14-point typeface, double-spaced, as an e-mail letter with no attachments. For nonfiction, please read Michael's *How to Write a Book Proposal* book—available through your library or bookstore, and through our website—so you will know exactly what editors need. Then, before you start writing, send him the title, subtitle, and your promotion plan via conventional mail (with SASE) or e-mail. If sent as e-mail, please include the information in the body of your e-mail with no attachments. Please allow up to 2 weeks for a response. See each agent's page on the website for contact and submission information. Responds in 8 weeks to pages or submissions.

TERMS Agent receives 15% commission on domestic sales. Agent receives 20% (30% for Asia) commission on foreign sales.

LAURA DAIL LITERARY AGENCY, INC.

350 Seventh Ave., Suite 2003, New York NY 10001. (212)239-7477. **Fax:** (212)947-0460. **E-mail:** ldail@ldlainc.com. **E-mail:** queries@ldlainc.com. **Website:** www.ldlainc.com. Member of AAR.

MEMBER AGENTS Laura Dail; Tamar Rydzinski.

REPRESENTS Nonfiction books, novels. **Considers these nonfiction areas:** humor. **Considers these fiction areas:** commercial, historical, young adult.

HOW TO CONTACT "If you would like, you may include a synopsis and no more than 10 pages. If you are mailing your query, please be sure to include a self-addressed, stamped envelope; without it, you may not hear back from us. To save money, time and trees, we prefer queries by e-mail to queries@ldlainc.com. We get a lot of spam and are wary of computer viruses, so please use the word 'Query' in the subject line and include your detailed materials in the body of your message, not as an attachment."

SARAH LAZIN BOOKS

121 W. 27th St., Suite 704, New York NY 10001. (212)989-5757. **Fax:** (212)989-1393. **E-mail:** amanda@lazinbooks.com; slazin@lazinbooks.com. **Website:** www.lazinbooks.com. **Contact:** Sarah Lazin. Estab. 1983. Member of AAR.

MEMBER AGENTS Sarah Lazin; Amanda Hartman (subsidiary rights).

REPRESENTS Nonfiction books, novels. **Considers these nonfiction areas:** biography, history, investigative, memoirs, parenting, popular culture. **Considers these fiction areas:** commercial, literary, short story collections.

HOW TO CONTACT As of 2015: "We accept submissions through referral only." Only accepts queries on referral.

TERMS Agent receives 15% commission on domestic sales. Agent receives 20% commission on foreign sales.

⊘ THE NED LEAVITT AGENCY

70 Wooster St., Suite 4F, New York NY 10012. (212)334-0999. **Website:** www.nedleavittagency.com. **Contact:** Ned Leavitt; Jillian Sweeney. Member of AAR. Represents 40+ clients.

MEMBER AGENTS **Ned Leavitt**, founder and agent; **Britta Alexander**, agent; **Jillian Sweeney**, agent.

REPRESENTS Nonfiction books, novels.

HOW TO CONTACT This agency now only takes queries/submissions through referred clients. Do *not* cold query.

LEVINE GREENBERG ROSTAN LITERARY AGENCY, INC.

307 Seventh Ave., Suite 2407, New York NY 10001. (212)337-0934. **Fax:** (212)337-0948. **E-mail:** submit@levinegreenberg.com. **Website:** www.levinegreenberg.com. Member of AAR. Represents 250 clients. 33% of clients are new/unpublished writers. Currently handles: nonfiction books 70%, novels 30%.

MEMBER AGENTS **Jim Levine**; **Stephanie Rostan** (adult fiction, nonfiction, YA); Melissa Rowland; **Daniel Greenberg** (literary fiction; nonfiction: popular culture, narrative nonfiction, memoir, and humor); **Victoria Skurnick**; **Danielle Svetcov**; **Elizabeth Fisher**; **Lindsay Edgecombe** (narrative nonfiction, memoir, lifestyle and health, illustrated books, as well as literary fiction); **Monika Verma** (nonfiction: humor, pop culture, memoir, narrative nonfiction and style and fashion titles; some young adult fiction); **Kerry Sparks** (young adult and middle grade); **Tim Wojcik** (quirky adventures, as-yet untold oral histories, smart humor, anything sports, music and food-related, thrillers, mysteries, and literary fiction); **Arielle Eckstut** (no queries); **Kirsten Wolf** (adult and children's literature).

REPRESENTS Nonfiction books, novels. **Considers these nonfiction areas:** animals, art, biography, business, computers, cooking, creative nonfiction, gardening, health, humor, memoirs, money, New Age, science, sociology, spirituality, sports. **Considers these fiction areas:** literary, mainstream, middle grade, mystery, thriller, women's, young adult.

HOW TO CONTACT E-query, or online submission form. Do not submit directly to agents. Prefers electronic submissions. Cannot respond to submissions by mail. Do not attach more than 50 pages. Obtains most new clients through recommendations from others.

TERMS Agent receives 15% commission on domestic sales. Agent receives 20% commission on foreign sales. Offers written contract. Charges clients for out-of-pocket expenses—telephone, fax, postage, photocopying—directly connected to the project.

⊘ LITERARY AND CREATIVE ARTISTS, INC.

3543 Albemarle St., N.W., Washington D.C. 20008-4213. (202)362-4688. **Fax:** (202)362-8875. **E-mail:** lca9643@lcadc.com. **Website:** www.lcadc.com. **Contact:** Muriel Nellis. Member of AAR. Other memberships include Authors Guild, American Bar Association, American Booksellers Association. Currently handles: nonfiction books 50%, novels 50%.

MEMBER AGENTS Prior to becoming an agent, Mr. Powell was in sales and contract negotiation.

REPRESENTS Nonfiction books, novels, art, biography, business, photography, popular culture, religion, self help, literary, regional, religious, satire. **Considers these nonfiction areas:** autobiography, biography, business, cooking, diet//nutrition, economics, foods, government, health, how-to, law, medicine, memoirs, philosophy, politics.

HOW TO CONTACT Query via e-mail first and include a synopsis. No attachments. **We do not accept unsolicited manuscripts, faxed manuscripts, manuscripts sent by e-mail, or manuscripts on computer disk.** Accepts simultaneous submissions. Responds in 3 weeks to queries. Responds in 1 week to mss. Obtains new clients through recommendations from others.

TERMS Agent receives 15% commission on domestic sales. Agent receives 25% commission on foreign sales. Offers written contract. Charges clients for long-distance phone/fax, photocopying, shipping.

LIVING WORD LITERARY AGENCY

P.O. Box 40974, Eugene OR 97414. **E-mail:** livingwordliterary@gmail.com. **Website:** livingwordliterary.wordpress.com. **Contact:** Kimberly Shumate, agent. Estab. 2009. Member Evangelical Christian Publishers Association

REPRESENTS **Considers these nonfiction areas:** health, parenting, self-help, relationships. **Considers these fiction areas:** inspirational, adult fiction, Christian living.

HOW TO CONTACT Submit a query with short synopsis and first chapter via Word document. Agency only responds if interested.

LIZA DAWSON ASSOCIATES

350 Seventh Ave., Suite 2003, New York NY 10001. (212)465-9071. **Website:** www.lizadawsonassociates.com. **Contact:** Caitie Flum. Member of AAR. Other memberships include MWA, Women's Media Group. Represents 50+ clients. 30% of clients are new/unpublished writers.

MEMBER AGENTS **Liza Dawson**, queryliza@LizaDawsonAssociates.com (plot-driven literary and popular fiction, historicals, thrillers, suspense, history,psychology [both popular and clinical], politics, narrative nonfiction and memoirs); **Caitlin Blasdell**, queryCaitlin@LizaDawsonAssociates.com (science fiction, fantasy [both adult and young adult], parenting, business, thrillers and women's fiction; **Hannah Bowman**, queryHannah@LizaDawsonAssociates.com; (commercial fiction—especially science fiction and fantasy, women's fiction, cozy mysteries, romance, young adult, also nonfiction in the areas of mathematics, science, and spirituality); **Monica Odom**, querymonica@LizaDawsonAssociates.com (literary fiction, women's fiction, voice-driven memoir, nonfiction in the areas of pop culture, food and cooking, history, politics, and current affairs); **Caitie Flum**, querycaitie@LizaDawsonAssociates.com (commercial fiction, especially historical, women's fiction, mysteries, new adult and young adult, nonfiction in the areas of theater, memoir, current affairs and pop culture).

HOW TO CONTACT Query by e-mail only. No phone calls. Each of these agents has their own specific submission requirements, which you can find online at their website. querymonica@LizaDawsonAssociates.com; queryHannah@LizaDawsonAssociates.com; queryhavis@LizaDawsonAssociates.com; queryanna@LizaDawsonAssociates.com; queryCaitlin@LizaDawsonAssociates.com; queryliza@LizaDawsonAssociates.com. Responds in 4 weeks to queries; 8 weeks to mss. Obtains most new clients through recommendations from others, conferences.

TERMS Agent receives 15% commission on domestic sales. Agent receives 20% commission on foreign sales. Offers written contract.

LOWENSTEIN ASSOCIATES INC.

15 East 23rd St., Floor 4, New York NY 10010. (212)206-1630. **Fax:** (212)727-0280. **E-mail:** assistant@bookhaven.com. **Website:** www.lowensteinassociates.com. **Contact:** Barbara Lowenstein. Member of AAR.

MEMBER AGENTS **Barbara Lowenstein**, president (nonfiction interests include narrative nonfiction, health, money, finance, travel, multicultural, popular culture, and memoir; fiction interests include literary fiction and women's fiction).

REPRESENTS Nonfiction books, novels. **Considers these nonfiction areas:** creative nonfiction, health, memoirs, money, multicultural, popular culture, travel. **Considers these fiction areas:** commercial, fantasy, literary, middle grade, science fiction, women's, young adult.

HOW TO CONTACT "For fiction, please send us a 1-page query letter, along with the first 10 pages pasted in the body of the message by e-mail to assistant@bookhaven.com. If nonfiction, please send a 1-page query letter, a table of contents, and, if available, a proposal pasted into the body of the e-mail. Please put the word 'QUERY' and the title of your project in the subject field of your e-mail and address it to the agent of your choice. Please do not send an attachment as the message will be deleted without being read and no reply will be sent." Accepts simultaneous submissions. Responds in 6 weeks to queries. Obtains most new clients through recommendations from others, solicitations, conferences.

TERMS Agent receives 15% commission on domestic sales. Agent receives 20% commission on foreign sales. Offers written contract. Charges for large photocopy batches, messenger service, international postage.

DONALD MAASS LITERARY AGENCY

121 W. 27th St., Suite 801, New York NY 10001. (212)727-8383. **Website:** www.maassagency.com. Estab. 1980. Member of AAR. Other memberships include SFWA, MWA, RWA. Represents more than 100 clients. 5% of clients are new/unpublished writers. Currently handles: novels 100%.

MEMBER AGENTS **Donald Maass** (mainstream, literary, mystery/suspense, science fiction, romance); **Jennifer Jackson** (commercial fiction, romance, science fiction, fantasy, mystery/suspense); **Cameron McClure** (literary, mystery/suspense, urban, fantasy, narrative nonfiction and projects with multicultural, international, and environmental themes, gay/lesbian); **Stacia Decker** (fiction, memoir, narrative nonfiction, pop-culture [cooking, fashion, style, music, art], smart humor, upscale erotica/erotic memoir and multicultural fiction/nonfiction); **Amy Boggs** (fantasy and science fiction, especially urban fantasy, paranormal romance, steampunk, YA/children's, and alternate history. historical fiction, multicultural fiction, westerns); **Katie Shea Boutillier** (women's fiction/book club; edgy/dark, realistic/contemporary YA; commercial-scale literary fiction; and celebrity memoir); **Jennifer Udden** (speculative fiction (both science fiction and fantasy), urban fantasy, and mysteries, as well as historical, erotic, contemporary, and paranormal romance).

REPRESENTS Nonfiction, novels. **Considers these nonfiction areas:** creative nonfiction, memoirs, popular culture. **Considers these fiction areas:** crime, detective, fantasy, historical, horror, literary, mainstream, multicultural, mystery, paranormal, police, psychic, romance, science fiction, supernatural, suspense, thriller, westerns, women's, young adult.

HOW TO CONTACT E-query. All the agents have different submission addresses and instructions. See the website and each agent's online profile for exact submission instructions. Accepts simultaneous submissions.

TERMS Agent receives 15% commission on domestic sales. Agent receives 20% commission on foreign sales.

CAROL MANN AGENCY

55 Fifth Ave., New York NY 10003. (212)206-5635. **Fax:** (212)675-4809. **E-mail:** submissions@carolmannagency.com. **Website:** www.carolmannagency.com. **Contact:** Lydia Byfield. Member of AAR. Represents roughly 200 clients. 15% of clients are new/unpublished writers.

MEMBER AGENTS **Carol Mann** (health/medical, religion, spirituality, self-help,parenting, narrative nonfiction, current affairs); **Laura Yorke**; **Gareth Esersky**; **Myrsini Stephanides** (nonfiction areas of interest: pop culture and music, humor, narrative nonfiction and memoir, cookbooks; fiction areas of interest: offbeat literary fiction, graphic works, and edgy YA fiction); **Joanne Wyckoff** (nonfiction areas of interest: memoir, narrative nonfiction,personal narrative, psychology, women's issues, education, health and wellness, parenting, serious self-help, natural history; also accepts fiction).

REPRESENTS Nonfiction books, novels. **Considers these nonfiction areas:** anthropology, archeology, architecture, art, autobiography, biography, business, child guidance, cultural interests, current affairs, design, ethnic, government, health, history, law, medicine, money, music, parenting, popular culture, politics, psychology, self-help, sociology, sports, women's issues, women's studies. **Considers these fiction areas:** commercial, literary, young adult, graphic works.

HOW TO CONTACT Please see website for submission guidelines. Responds in 4 weeks to queries.
TERMS Agent receives 15% commission on domestic sales. Agent receives 20% commission on foreign sales. Offers written contract.

MANUS & ASSOCIATES LITERARY AGENCY, INC.

425 Sherman Ave., Suite 200, Palo Alto CA 94306. (650)470-5151. **Fax:** (650)470-5159. **Website:** www.manuslit.com. **Contact:** Jillian Manus, Jandy Nelson, Penny Nelson. NYC address: 444 Madison Ave., 29th Floor, New York, NY 10022 Member of AAR.
MEMBER AGENTS **Jandy Nelson** (currently not taking on new clients); **Jillian Manus**, jillian@manuslit.com (political, memoirs, self-help, history, sports, women's issues, thrillers); **Penny Nelson,** penny@manuslit.com (memoirs, self-help, sports, nonfiction).
REPRESENTS Nonfiction books, novels. **Considers these nonfiction areas:** cooking, history, inspirational, memoirs, politics, psychology, religious, self-help, sports, women's issues. **Considers these fiction areas:** thriller.
HOW TO CONTACT Snail mail submissions welcome. E-queries also accepted. For nonfiction, send a full proposal via snail mail. For fiction, send a query letter and 30 pages (unbound) if submitting via snail mail. Send only an e-query if submitting fiction via e-mail. If querying by e-mail, submit directly to one of the agents. Accepts simultaneous submissions. Responds in 3 months to queries. Responds in 3 months to mss. Obtains most new clients through recommendations from others, solicitations, conferences.
TERMS Agent receives 15% commission on domestic sales. Agent receives 20-25% commission on foreign sales. Offers written contract, binding for 2 years; 60-day notice must be given to terminate contract. Charges for photocopying and postage/UPS.

THE DENISE MARCIL LITERARY AGENCY, LLC

483 Westover Road, Stamford CT 06902. (203)327-9970. **E-mail:** dmla@DeniseMarcilAgency.com; AnneMarie@denisemarcilagency.com. **Website:** www.denisemarcilagency.com. **Contact:** Denise Marcil, Anne Marie O'Farrell. Address for Anne Marie O'Farrell: 86 Dennis Street, Manhasset, NY 11030. Member of AAR.
MEMBER AGENTS **Denise Marcil** (self-help and popular reference books such as wellness, health, women's issues, self-help, and popular reference); **Anne Marie O'Farrell** (books that convey and promote innovative, practical and cutting edge information and ideas which help people increase their self-awareness and fulfillment and maximize their potential in whatever area they choose; she is dying to represent a great basketball book).
REPRESENTS **Considers these nonfiction areas:** business, health, parenting, self-help, women's issues. **Considers these fiction areas:** commercial, suspense, thriller, women's.
HOW TO CONTACT E-query.
TERMS Agent receives 15% commission on domestic sales. Agent receives 20% commission on foreign sales. Offers written contract, binding for 2 years.

MARIA CARVAINIS AGENCY, INC.

Rockefeller Center, 1270 Avenue of the Americas, Suite 2320, New York NY 10020. (212)245-6365. **Fax:** (212)245-7196. **E-mail:** mca@mariacarvainisagency.com. **Website:** mariacarvainisagency.com. Estab. 1977. Member of AAR. Signatory of WGA. Other memberships include Authors Guild, Women's Media Group, ABA, MWA, RWA. Represents 75 clients.
MEMBER AGENTS Maria Carvainis, president/literary agent.
REPRESENTS Nonfiction books, novels. **Considers these nonfiction areas:** biography, business, history, memoirs, popular culture, psychology, science. **Considers these fiction areas:** historical, literary, mainstream, middle grade, mystery, suspense, thriller, women's, young adult.
HOW TO CONTACT You can query via email or snail mail. If by snail mail, send your submission "ATTN: Query Department." Please send a query letter, a synopsis of the work, two sample chapters, and note any writing credentials. Obtains most new clients through recommendations from others, conferences, query letters.
TERMS Agent receives 15% commission on domestic sales. Agent receives 20% commission on foreign sales. Offers written contract. Charges clients for foreign postage and bulk copying.

THE EVAN MARSHALL AGENCY

07068-1121, Roseland NJ 07068-1121. (973)287-6216. **Fax:** (973)488-7910. **E-mail:** evan@evanmarshallagency.com. **Contact:** Evan Marshall. Member of AAR. Currently handles: novels 100%.

REPRESENTS Novels. **Considers these fiction areas:** action, adventure, erotica, ethnic, frontier, historical, horror, humor, inspirational, literary, mainstream, mystery, religious, satire, science fiction, suspense, western, romance (contemporary, gothic, historical, regency).

HOW TO CONTACT Do not query. Currently accepting clients only by referal from editors and our own clients. Responds in 1 week to queries. Responds in 1 month to mss. Obtains most new clients through recommendations from others.

TERMS Agent receives 15% commission on domestic sales. Agent receives 20% commission on foreign sales. Offers written contract.

MARTIN LITERARY MANAGEMENT

7683 SE 27th St., #307, Mercer Island WA 98040. (206)466-1773. **E-mail:** sharlene@martinliterarymanagement.com. **Website:** www.MartinLiteraryManagement.com. **Contact:** Sharlene Martin.

MEMBER AGENTS Sharlene Martin (nonfiction); Clelia Gore (children's, middle grade, young adult).

REPRESENTS Considers these nonfiction areas: autobiography, biography, business, child guidance, current affairs, economics, health, history, how-to, humor, inspirational, investigative, medicine, memoirs, parenting, popular culture, psychology, satire, self-help, true crime, women's issues, women's studies. **Considers these fiction areas:** juvenile, middle grade, young adult.

HOW TO CONTACT Query via e-mail with MS Word only. No attachments on queries; place letter in body of e-mail. Accepts simultaneous submissions. Responds in 2 weeks to queries. Responds in 3-4 weeks to mss. Obtains most new clients through recommendations from others.

TERMS Agent receives 15% commission on domestic sales. Agent receives 25% commission on foreign sales. Offers written contract, binding for 1 year; 1-month notice must be given to terminate contract. Charges author for postage and copying if material is not sent electronically. 99% of materials are sent electronically to minimize charges to author for postage and copying.

MARY EVANS INC.

242 E. Fifth St., New York NY 10003. (212)979-0880. **Fax:** (212)979-5344. **E-mail:** info@maryevansinc.com. **Website:** maryevansinc.com. Member of AAR.

MEMBER AGENTS **Mary Evans** (no unsolicited queries); **Julia Kardon** (literary and upmarket fiction, narrative nonfiction, journalism, and history); **Mary Gaule** (picture books, middle grade, and YA fiction).

REPRESENTS Nonfiction books, novels.

HOW TO CONTACT Query by mail or email. If querying by mail, include a proper SASE. If querying by email, put "Query" in the subject line. For fiction: Include the first few pages, or opening chapter of your novel as a single Word attachment. For nonfiction: Include your book proposal as a single Word attachment. Responds within 8 weeks. Obtains most new clients through recommendations from others, solicitations.

MARGRET MCBRIDE LITERARY AGENCY

P.O. Box 9128, La Jolla CA 92038. (858)454-1550. **Fax:** (858)454-2156. **E-mail:** staff@mcbridelit.com. **Website:** www.mcbrideliterary.com. **Contact:** Michael Daley, submissions manager. Member of AAR. Other memberships include Authors Guild.

MEMBER AGENTS Margret McBride; Faye Atchinson.

REPRESENTS Nonfiction books, novels. **Considers these nonfiction areas:** autobiography, biography, business, cooking, cultural interests, current affairs, economics, ethnic, foods, government, health, history, how-to, law, medicine, money, popular culture, politics, psychology, science, self-help, sociology, technology, women's issues, style. **Considers these fiction areas:** action, adventure, crime, detective, historical, humor, literary, mainstream, mystery, police, satire, suspense, thriller.

HOW TO CONTACT "Submit a query letter to us via e-mail (staff@mcbridelit.com) or snail mail. In your letter, please provide a brief synopsis of your work, as well as any pertinent information about yourself." There are detailed nonfiction proposal guidelines online. Accepts simultaneous submissions. Responds in 8 weeks to queries. Responds in 6-8 weeks to mss.

TERMS Agent receives 15% commission on domestic sales. Agent receives 25% commission on foreign sales. Charges for overnight delivery and photocopying.

THE MCCARTHY AGENCY, LLC

456 Ninth St., No. 28, Hoboken NJ 07030. **E-mail:** McCarthylit@aol.com. **Contact:** Shawna McCarthy. Member of AAR.

MEMBER AGENTS Shawna McCarthy.

REPRESENTS Nonfiction books, novels. **Considers these fiction areas:** fantasy, middle grade, mystery, new adult, science fiction, women's, young adult.

HOW TO CONTACT E-queries only. Accepts simultaneous submissions.

SALLY HILL MCMILLAN & ASSOCIATES, INC.

429 E. Kingston Ave., Charlotte NC 28203. (704)334-0897. **E-mail:** mcmagency@aol.com. **Website:** www.publishersmarketplace.com/members/McMillanAgency/. **Contact:** Sally Hill McMillan. Member of AAR.

REPRESENTS **Considers these nonfiction areas:** creative nonfiction, health, history, women's issues, women's studies. **Considers these fiction areas:** commercial, literary, mainstream, mystery.

HOW TO CONTACT "Please query first with SASE and await further instructions. Email queries will be read, but not necessarily answered."

MENDEL MEDIA GROUP, LLC

115 W. 30th St., Suite 800, New York NY 10001. (646)239-9896. **Fax:** (212)685-4717. **E-mail:** scott@mendelmedia.com. **Website:** www.mendelmedia.com. Member of AAR. Represents 40-60 clients.

REPRESENTS Nonfiction books, novels, scholarly, with potential for broad/popular appeal. **Considers these nonfiction areas:** Americana, animals, anthropology, architecture, art, biography, business, child guidance, cooking, current affairs, dance, diet//nutrition, education, environment, ethnic, foods, gardening, gay/lesbian, government, health, history, how-to, humor, investigative, language, medicine, memoirs, military, money, multicultural, music, parenting, philosophy, popular culture, psychology, recreation, regional, religious, science, self-help, sex, sociology, software, spirituality, sports, true crime, war, women's issues, women's studies, Jewish topics; creative nonfiction. **Considers these fiction areas:** action, adventure, contemporary issues, crime, detective, erotica, ethnic, feminist, gay, glitz, historical, humor, inspirational, juvenile, lesbian, literary, mainstream, mystery, picture books, police, religious, romance, satire, sports, thriller, young adult, Jewish fiction.

HOW TO CONTACT Query with SASE. Do not e-mail or fax queries. For nonfiction, include a complete, fully edited book proposal with sample chapters. For fiction, include a complete synopsis and no more than 20 pages of sample text. Responds in 2 weeks to queries. Responds in 4-6 weeks to mss. Obtains most new clients through recommendations from others.

TERMS Agent receives 15% commission on domestic sales. Agent receives 20% commission on foreign sales.

⊘ DORIS S. MICHAELS LITERARY AGENCY, INC.

1841 Broadway, Suite 903, New York NY 10023. (212)265-9474. **Fax:** (212)265-9480. **Website:** www.dsmagency.com. **Contact:** Doris S. Michaels, President. Member of AAR. Other memberships include WNBA.

REPRESENTS Novels. **Considers these fiction areas:** commercial, literary.

HOW TO CONTACT As of early 2015, they are not taking new clients. Check the website to see if this agency reopens to queries.

⊘ MARTHA MILLARD LITERARY AGENCY

50 W.67th St., #1G, New York NY 10023. **Contact:** Martha Millard. Estab. 1980. Member of AAR. Other memberships include SFWA.

REPRESENTS Nonfiction books, novels. **Considers these nonfiction areas:** architecture, art, autobiography, biography, business, child guidance, cooking, cultural interests, current affairs, design, economics, education, ethnic, film, health, history, how-to, memoirs, metaphysics, money, music, New Age, parenting, photography, popular culture, psychology, self-help, theater, true crime, women's issues, women's studies. **Considers these fiction areas:** fantasy, mystery, romance, science fiction, suspense.

HOW TO CONTACT No unsolicited queries. **Referrals only**. Obtains most new clients through recommendations from others.

TERMS Agent receives 15% commission on domestic sales. Agent receives 20% commission on foreign sales. Offers written contract.

MIRIAM ALTSHULER LITERARY AGENCY

53 Old Post Rd. N, Red Hook NY 12571. (845)758-9408. **E-mail:** query@maliterary.com. **Website:** www.miriamaltshulerliteraryagency.com. **Contact:** Miriam Altshuler. Estab. 1994. Member of AAR. Represents 40 clients.

MEMBER AGENTS **Miriam Altshuler** (literary and commercial fiction, nonfiction, and children's books); **Reiko Davis** (literary fiction, well-told commercial fiction, narrative nonfiction, and young adult).

REPRESENTS Nonfiction books, novels, short story collections, juvenile. **Considers these nonfiction areas:** creative nonfiction, how-to, memoirs, self-help, spirituality, women's issues. **Considers these fiction areas:** commercial, literary, middle grade, picture books, young adult.

HOW TO CONTACT Query through email or snail mail. "A query should include a brief author bio, a synopsis of the work, and the first chapter pasted within the body of the email only. (For security purposes, we do not open attachments.) " Accepts simultaneous submissions. Obtains most new clients through recommendations from others.

TERMS Agent receives 15% commission on domestic sales. Agent receives 20% commission on foreign sales. Charges clients for overseas mailing, photocopies, overnight mail when requested by author.

HOWARD MORHAIM LITERARY AGENCY

30 Pierrepont St., Brooklyn NY 11201. (718)222-8400. **Fax:** (718)222-5056. **Website:** www.morhaimliterary.com. Member of AAR.

MEMBER AGENTS **Howard Morhaim** (no unsolicited submissions), **Kate McKean**, kmckean@morhaimliterary.com (adult fiction: contemporary romance, contemporary women's fiction, literary fiction, historical fiction set in the 20th Century, high fantasy, magical realism, science fiction, middle grade, young adult; in nonfiction, books by authors with demonstrable platforms in the areas of sports, food writing, humor, design, creativity, and craft [sewing, knitting, etc.], narrative nonfiction by authors with or without an established platform. Some memoir); **Paul Lamb**, paul@morhaimliterary.com (nonfiction in a wide variety of genres and subjects, notably business, political science, sociology, memoir, travel writing, sports, pop culture, and music; he is also interested in select literary fiction); **Maria Ribas**, maria@morhaimliterary.com (cookbooks, self-help, health, diet, home, parenting, and humor, all from authors with demonstrable platforms; she's also interested in narrative nonfiction and select memoir).

REPRESENTS **Considers these nonfiction areas:** business, cooking, crafts, creative nonfiction, design, health, humor, memoirs, parenting, self-help, sports. **Considers these fiction areas:** fantasy, historical, literary, middle grade, new adult, romance, science fiction, women's, young adult, LGBTQ young adult, magical realism, fantasy should be high fantasy, historical fiction should be no earlier than the 20th century.

HOW TO CONTACT Query via e-mail with cover letter and three sample chapters. See each agent's listing for specifics.

⊘ WILLIAM MORRIS ENDEAVOR ENTERTAINMENT

1325 Avenue of the Americas, New York NY 10019. (212)586-5100. **Fax:** (212)246-3583. **Website:** www.wma.com. **Contact:** Literary Department Coordinator. Member of AAR.

REPRESENTS Nonfiction books, novels, TV, movie scripts, feature film.

HOW TO CONTACT This agency is generally closed to unsolicited literary submissions. Meet an agent at a conference, or query through a referral. Accepts simultaneous submissions.

TERMS Agent receives 15% commission on domestic sales. Agent receives 20% commission on foreign sales.

JEAN V. NAGGAR LITERARY AGENCY, INC.

216 E. 75th St., Suite 1E, New York NY 10021. (212)794-1082. **E-mail:** jweltz@jvnla.com; atasman@jvnla.com. **Website:** www.jvnla.com. **Contact:** Jean Naggar. Member of AAR. Other memberships include Women's Media Group, SCBWI, Pace University's Masters in Publishing Board Member. Represents 450 clients. 20% of clients are new/unpublished writers.

MEMBER AGENTS **Jennifer Weltz** (well researched and original historicals, thrillers with a unique voice, wry dark humor, and magical realism; enthralling narrative nonfiction; young adult, middle grade); **Jean Naggar** (taking no new clients); **Alice Tasman** (literary, commercial, YA, middle grade, and nonfiction in the categories of narrative, biography, music or pop culture); **Elizabeth Evans** (narrative nonfiction [travel/adventure], memoir, current affairs, pop science, journalism, health and wellness, psychology, history, pop culture, cookbooks and humor); **Laura Biagi** (literary fiction, magical realism, psychological thrillers, young adult novels, middle grade novels, and picture books).

REPRESENTS Nonfiction books, novels. **Considers these nonfiction areas:** biography, creative nonfiction, current affairs, health, history, humor, memoirs, music, popular culture, psychology, science. **Considers these fiction areas:** commercial, fantasy, literary, middle grade, picture books, thriller, young adult.

HOW TO CONTACT "Visit our website, www.jvnla.com, for complete, up-to-date submission guidelines.

Please be advised that Jean Naggar is no longer accepting new clients." Accepts simultaneous submissions.

TERMS Agent receives 15% commission on domestic sales. Agent receives 20% commission on foreign sales. Offers written contract. Charges for overseas mailing, messenger services, book purchases, long-distance telephone, photocopying—all deductible from royalties received.

NELSON LITERARY AGENCY

1732 Wazee St., Suite 207, Denver CO 80202. (303)292-2805. **Website:** www.nelsonagency.com. **Contact:** Kristin Nelson, president. Estab. 2002. Member of AAR. RWA, SCBWI, SFWA.

REPRESENTS Considers these fiction areas: commercial, fantasy, literary, mainstream, middle grade, romance, science fiction, women's, young adult.

HOW TO CONTACT Query by e-mail. Put the word "Query" in the email subject line. No attachments; querykristin@nelsonagency.com. Responds within 1 month.

HAROLD OBER ASSOCIATES

425 Madison Ave., New York NY 10017. (212)759-8600. **Fax:** (212)759-9428. **Website:** www.haroldober.com. **Contact:** Appropriate agent. Member of AAR. Represents 250 clients. 10% of clients are new/unpublished writers. Currently handles: nonfiction books 35%, novels 50%, juvenile books 15%.

MEMBER AGENTS Phyllis Westberg; Pamela Malpas; Craig Tenney (few new clients, mostly Ober backlist); Jake Elwell (previously with Elwell & Weiser).

HOW TO CONTACT Submit concise query letter addressed to a specific agent with the first 5 pages of the ms or proposal and SASE. No fax or e-mail. Does not handle filmscripts or plays. Responds as promptly as possible. Obtains most new clients through recommendations from others.

TERMS Agent receives 15% commission on domestic sales. Agent receives 20% commission on foreign sales. Charges clients for express mail/package services.

THE RICHARD PARKS AGENCY

P.O. Box 693, Salem NY 12865. (518)854-9466. **Fax:** (518)854-9466. **E-mail:** rp@richardparksagency.com. **Website:** www.richardparksagency.com. **Contact:** Richard Parks. Member of AAR. Currently handles: nonfiction 55%, novels 40%, story collections 5%.

REPRESENTS Nonfiction books, novels. **Considers these nonfiction areas:** animals, anthropology, archeology, art, autobiography, biography, business, child guidance, cooking, crafts, cultural interests, current affairs, dance, diet/nutrition, economics, environment, ethnic, film, foods, gardening, gay/lesbian, government, health, history, hobbies, how-to, humor, language, law, memoirs, military, money, music, parenting, popular culture, politics, psychology, science, self-help, sociology, technology, theater, travel, women's issues, women's studies.

HOW TO CONTACT Query with SASE. Does not accept queries by e-mail or fax. Other Responds in 2 weeks to queries. Obtains most new clients through recommendations/referrals.

TERMS Agent receives 15% commission on domestic sales. Agent receives 20% commission on foreign sales. Charges clients for photocopying or any unusual expense incurred at the writer's request.

L. PERKINS AGENCY

5800 Arlington Ave., Riverdale NY 10471. (718)543-5344. **Fax:** (718)543-5354. **E-mail:** submissions@lperkinsagency.com. **Website:** lperkinsagency.com. Member of AAR. Represents 90 clients. 10% of clients are new/unpublished writers.

MEMBER AGENTS Tish Beaty, ePub agent (erotic romance – including paranormal, historical, gay/lesbian/bisexual, and light-BDSM fiction; also, she seeks new adult and YA); **Sandy Lu**, sandy@lperkinsagency.com (fiction: she is looking for dark literary and commercial fiction, mystery, thriller, psychological horror, paranormal/urban fantasy, historical fiction, YA, historical thrillers or mysteries set in Victorian times; nonfiction: narrative nonfiction, history, biography, pop science, pop psychology, pop culture [music/theatre/film], humor, and food writing); **Lori Perkins** (not currently taking new clients); **Leon Husock** (science fiction & fantasy, as well as young adult and middle-grade); **Rachel Brooks** (picture books, all genres of young adult and new adult fiction, as well as adult romance—especially romantic suspense).

REPRESENTS Nonfiction books, novels. **Considers these nonfiction areas:** biography, creative nonfiction, film, foods, history, humor, music, popular culture, psychology, science, theater. **Considers these fiction areas:** commercial, erotica, fantasy, gay, historical, horror, lesbian, middle grade, mystery, new adult, paranormal, picture books, science fiction, thriller, urban fantasy, young adult.

HOW TO CONTACT E-queries only. Include your query, a 1-page synopsis, and the first 5 pages from your novel pasted into the email. No attachments. Submit to only one agent at the agency. No smail mail queries. "If you are submitting to one of our agents, please be sure to check the submission status of the agent by visiting their social media accounts listed [on the agency website]." Accepts simultaneous submissions. Obtains most new clients through recommendations from others, solicitations, conferences.

TERMS Agent receives 15% commission on domestic sales. Agent receives 20% commission on foreign sales. No written contract. Charges clients for photocopying.

AARON M. PRIEST LITERARY AGENCY

708 3rd Ave., 23rd Floor, New York NY 10017. (212)818-0344. **Fax:** (212)573-9417. **E-mail:** info@aaronpriest.com. **Website:** www.aaronpriest.com. Estab. 1974. Member of AAR. Currently handles: nonfiction books 25%, novels 75%.

MEMBER AGENTS **Aaron Priest**, querypriest@aaronpriest.com (thrillers, commercial fiction, biographies); **Lisa Erbach Vance**, queryvance@aaronpriest.com (contemporary fiction, especially women's fiction, thoughtful fiction about families and friends, thrillers/suspense, psychological suspense, contemporary gothic fiction, unique ghost stories, international fiction [not translation], narrative nonfiction, current or historical topics); **Lucy Childs Baker**, querychilds@aaronpriest.com (commercial fiction [women's and mystery], and especially literary fiction [including historical], as well as narrative nonfiction); **Melissa Edwards**, queryedwards@aaronpriest.com (international thrillers with likeable and arresting protagonists, lighthearted women's fiction and YA, female-driven [possibly small-town] suspense, and completely immersive fantasy).

HOW TO CONTACT Query one of the agents using the appropriate e-mail listed on the website. "Please do not submit to more than 1 agent at this agency. We urge you to check our website and consider each agent's emphasis before submitting. Your query letter should be about one page long and describe your work as well as your background. You may also paste the first chapter of your work in the body of the e-mail. Do not send attachments." Accepts simultaneous submissions. Responds in 4 weeks, only if interested.

TERMS Agent receives 15% commission on domestic sales.

REES LITERARY AGENCY

14 Beacon St., Suite 710, Boston MA 02108. (617)227-9014. **Fax:** (617)227-8762. **Website:** reesagency.com. Estab. 1983. Member of AAR. Represents more than 100 clients. 50% of clients are new/unpublished writers.

MEMBER AGENTS **Ann Collette**, Agent10702@aol.com (literary, mystery, thrillers, suspense, vampire, and women's fiction; in nonfiction, she prefers true crime, narrative nonfiction, military and war, work to do with race and class, and work set in or about Southeast Asia); **Lorin Rees**, lorin@reesagency.com (literary fiction, memoirs, business books, self-help, science, history, psychology, and narrative nonfiction); **Rebecca Podos**, rebecca@reesagency.com (young adult fiction of all kinds, including contemporary, emotionally driven stories, mystery, romance, urban and historical fantasy, horror and sci-fi; occasionally, she considers literary and commercial adult fiction, new adult, and narrative nonfiction).

REPRESENTS Nonfiction books, novels. **Considers these nonfiction areas:** business, creative nonfiction, health, history, memoirs, military, psychology, science, self-help, true crime, war. **Considers these fiction areas:** commercial, historical, horror, literary, mystery, new adult, romance, science fiction, suspense, thriller, urban fantasy, women's, young adult.

HOW TO CONTACT Consult website for each agent's submission guidelines and e-mail addresses, as they differ. Obtains most new clients through recommendations from others, conferences, submissions.

TERMS Agent receives 15% commission on domestic sales. Agent receives 20% commission on foreign sales.

REGAL LITERARY AGENCY

236 W. 26th St., #801, New York NY 10001. (212)684-7900. **Fax:** (212)684-7906. **E-mail:** submissions@regal-literary.com. **Website:** www.regal-literary.com. London Office: 36 Gloucester Ave., Primrose Hill, London NW1 7BB, United Kingdom, uk@regal-literary.com Estab. 2002. Member of AAR. Represents 70 clients. 20% of clients are new/unpublished writers.

MEMBER AGENTS **Michelle Andelman** (all categories of children's books); **Claire Anderson-Wheeler**; **Markus Hoffmann** (international and literary fiction, crime, [pop] cultural studies, current affairs, economics, history, music, popular science, and travel literature); **Joseph Regal** (literary fiction, international thrillers, history, science, photography, music, culture, and whimsy).

REPRESENTS **Considers these nonfiction areas:** creative nonfiction, memoirs, psychology, science. **Considers these fiction areas:** literary, middle grade, picture books, thriller, women's, young adult.

HOW TO CONTACT "Query with SASE or via e-mail. No phone calls. Submissions should consist of a 1-page query letter detailing the book in question, as well as the qualifications of the author. For fiction, submissions may also include the first 10 pages of the novel or one short story from a collection." Responds if interested. Accepts simultaneous submissions. Responds in 4-8 weeks.

TERMS Agent receives 15% commission on domestic sales. Agent receives 20% commission on foreign sales. "We charge no reading fees."

THE RIGHTS FACTORY

P.O. Box 499, Station C, Toronto ON M6J 3P6 Canada. (416)966-5367. **Website:** www.therightsfactory.com. Estab. 2004.

MEMBER AGENTS **Sam Hiyate**, **Ali McDonald** (children's literature of all kinds); **Haskell Nussbaum**; **Drea Cohane** (fiction, memoir, crime, nonfiction and YA; her roster consists of British, American, and Canadian clients; international talent is welcome); **Olga Filina** (commercial and historical fiction, great genre fiction in the area of romance and mystery, nonfiction in the field of business, wellness, lifestyle and memoir; and young adult and middle grade novels with memorable characters); **Lydia Moed** (science fiction and fantasy, though she also enjoys magic realism, historical fiction and stories inspired by folklore from around the world; for nonfiction, she is interested in narrative nonfiction on a wide variety of topics, including history, popular science, biography and memoir).

REPRESENTS **Considers these nonfiction areas:** biography, business, history, memoirs, science. **Considers these fiction areas:** commercial, crime, fantasy, historical, literary, mainstream, middle grade, mystery, picture books, romance, science fiction, young adult.

HOW TO CONTACT There is a submission form on this agency's website. You can also query via snail mail.

ANGELA RINALDI LITERARY AGENCY

P.O. Box 7875, Beverly Hills CA 90212-7875. (310)842-7665. **Fax:** (310)837-8143. **E-mail:** amr@rinaldiliterary.com. **Website:** www.rinaldiliterary.com. **Contact:** Angela Rinaldi. Member of AAR.

REPRESENTS Nonfiction books, novels, TV and motion picture rights (for clients only). **Considers these nonfiction areas:** biography, business, cooking, current affairs, health, psychology, self-help, women's issues, food narratives, wine, lifestyle, career, personal finance, prescriptive and proactive self help books by journalists, academics, doctors and therapists, based on their research. **Considers these fiction areas:** commercial, literary, suspense, women's, upmarket women's fiction, book club women's fiction.

HOW TO CONTACT E-queries only. For fiction, please send a brief e-mail inquiry with the first 10 pages pasted into the e-mail—no attachments unless asked for. For nonfiction, query with detailed letter or outline/proposal, no attachments unless asked for. Accepts simultaneous submissions. Responds in 2-4 weeks.

TERMS Agent receives 15% commission on domestic sales. Agent receives 25% commission on foreign sales. Offers written contract.

ANN RITTENBERG LITERARY AGENCY, INC.

15 Maiden Lane, Suite 206, New York NY 10038. **Website:** www.rittlit.com. **Contact:** Ann Rittenberg, president. Member of AAR. Currently handles: fiction 75%, nonfiction 25%.

REPRESENTS **Considers these nonfiction areas:** creative nonfiction, women's issues.

HOW TO CONTACT Query with SASE. Submit outline, 3 sample chapters, SASE. Query via postal mail or e-mail to info@rittlit.com. Accepts simultaneous submissions. Responds in 6 weeks to queries. Responds in 2 months to mss. Obtains most new clients through referrals from established writers and editors.

TERMS Agent receives 15% commission on domestic sales. Agent receives 20% commission on foreign sales. Offers written contract. This agency charges clients for photocopying only.

RLR ASSOCIATES, LTD.

Literary Department, 7 W. 51st St., New York NY 10019. (212)541-8641. **Fax:** (212)262-7084. **E-mail:** sgould@rlrassociates.net. **Website:** www.rlrassociates.net. **Contact:** Scott Gould. Member of AAR. Represents 50 clients. 25% of clients are new/unpublished writers. Currently handles: nonfiction books 70%, novels 25%, story collections 5%.

REPRESENTS Nonfiction books, novels, short-story collections, scholarly. **Considers these nonfiction areas:** creative nonfiction. **Considers these fiction areas:** commercial, literary, mainstream, middle grade, picture books, romance, women's, young adult.

HOW TO CONTACT Query by either e-mail or snail mail. For fiction, send a query and 1-3 chapters (pasted). For nonfiction, send query or proposal. Accepts simultaneous submissions. "If you do not hear from us within 3 months, please assume that your work is out of active consideration." Obtains most new clients through recommendations from others.

TERMS Agent receives 15% commission on domestic sales. Agent receives 20% commission on foreign sales. Offers written contract.

B.J. ROBBINS LITERARY AGENCY

5130 Bellaire Ave., North Hollywood CA 91607-2908. **E-mail:** Robbinsliterary@gmail.com. **Website:** www.publishersmarketplace.com/members/bjrobbins. **Contact:** (Ms.) B.J. Robbins, or Amy Maldonado. Estab. 1992. Member of AAR.

REPRESENTS Nonfiction books, novels. **Considers these nonfiction areas:** autobiography, biography, cultural interests, current affairs, dance, ethnic, film, health, humor, investigative, medicine, memoirs, music, popular culture, psychology, self-help, sociology, sports, theater, travel, true crime, women's issues, women's studies. **Considers these fiction areas:** crime, detective, ethnic, literary, mainstream, mystery, police, sports, suspense, thriller.

HOW TO CONTACT E-query with no attachments. Accepts simultaneous submissions. Only responds to projects if interested. Obtains most new clients through conferences, referrals.

TERMS Agent receives 15% commission on domestic sales. Agent receives 20% commission on foreign sales. Offers written contract; 3-month notice must be given to terminate contract.

THE ROSENBERG GROUP

23 Lincoln Ave., Marblehead MA 01945. (781)990-1341. **Fax:** (781)990-1344. **Website:** www.rosenberggroup.com. **Contact:** Barbara Collins Rosenberg. Estab. 1998. Member of AAR. Recognized agent of the RWA. Represents 25 clients. 15% of clients are new/unpublished writers. Currently handles: nonfiction books 30%, novels 30%, scholarly books 10%, 30% college textbooks.

REPRESENTS Nonfiction books, novels, textbooks, college textbooks only. **Considers these nonfiction areas:** current affairs, foods, popular culture, psychology, sports, women's issues, women's studies, women's health, wine/beverages. **Considers these fiction areas:** romance, women's, chick lit.

HOW TO CONTACT Query via snail mail. Your query letter should not exceed one page in length. It should include the title of your work, the genre and/or sub-genre; the manuscript's word count; and a brief description of the work. If you are writing category romance, please be certain to let her know the line for which your work is intended. Responds in 2 weeks to queries. Responds in 4-6 weeks to mss. Obtains most new clients through recommendations from others, solicitations, conferences.

TERMS Agent receives 15% commission on domestic sales. Agent receives 15% commission on foreign sales. Offers written contract; 1-month notice must be given to terminate contract. Charges maximum of $350/year for postage and photocopying.

RITA ROSENKRANZ LITERARY AGENCY

440 West End Ave., #15D, New York NY 10024. (212)873-6333. **Website:** www.ritarosenkranzliteraryagency.com. **Contact:** Rita Rosenkranz. Member of AAR. Represents 35 clients. 30% of clients are new/unpublished writers. Currently handles: nonfiction books 99%, novels 1%.

REPRESENTS Nonfiction books. **Considers these nonfiction areas:** animals, anthropology, art, autobiography, biography, business, child guidance, computers, cooking, crafts, cultural interests, current affairs, dance, decorating, economics, ethnic, film, gay, government, health, history, hobbies, how-to, humor, inspirational, interior design, language, law, lesbian, literature, medicine, military, money, music, nature, parenting, personal improvement, photography, popular culture, politics, psychology, religious, satire, science, self-help, sports, technology, theater, war, women's issues, women's studies.

HOW TO CONTACT Send query letter only (no proposal) via regular mail or e-mail. Submit proposal package with SASE only on request. No fax queries. Accepts simultaneous submissions. Responds in 2 weeks to queries. Obtains most new clients through directory listings, solicitations, conferences, word of mouth.

TERMS Agent receives 15% commission on domestic sales. Agent receives 20% commission on foreign sales. Offers written contract, binding for 3 years; 3-month written notice must be given to terminate contract. Charges clients for photocopying. Makes referrals to editing services.

ROSS YOON AGENCY

1666 Connecticut Ave. NW, Suite 500, Washington DC 20009. (202)328-3282. **Fax:** (202)328-9162. **E-mail:** submissions@rossyoon.com. **Website:** rossyoon.com. **Contact:** Jennifer Manguera. Member of AAR.

MEMBER AGENTS **Gail Ross** (represents important commercial nonfiction in a variety of areas and counts top doctors, CEO's, prize-winning journalists, and historians among her clients. She and her team work closely with first-time authors; gail@rossyoon.com); **Howard Yoon** (nonfiction topics ranging from current events and politics to culture to religion and history, to smart business; howard@rossyoon.com); **Anna Sproul-Latimer** (pop culture, science, humor, memoir, anything surprising; anna@rossyoon.com).

REPRESENTS Nonfiction books.

HOW TO CONTACT E-query submissions@rossyoon.com with a query letter briefly explaining your idea, media platform, and qualifications for writing on this topic; or send a complete book proposal featuring an overview of your idea, author bio, media and marketing strategy, chapter outline, and 1-3 sample chapters. Please send these as attachments in .doc or .docx format. Accepts simultaneous submissions. Responds in 4-6 weeks to queries. Obtains most new clients through referrals from current clients.

TERMS Agent receives 15% commission on domestic sales. Agent receives 20% commission on foreign sales. Reserves the right to bill clients for office expenses.

JANE ROTROSEN AGENCY LLC

318 E. 51st St., New York NY 10022. (212)593-4330. **Fax:** (212)935-6985. **Website:** www.janerotrosen.com. Estab. 1974. Member of AAR. Other memberships include Authors Guild. Represents more than 100 clients.

MEMBER AGENTS **Jane Rotrosen Berkey** (not taking on clients); **Andrea Cirillo**, acirillo@janerotrosen.com (suspense and women's fiction); **Annelise Robey**, arobey@janerotrosen.com (women's fiction, suspense, mystery, literary fiction and the occasional nonfiction project); **Meg Ruley**, mruley@janerotrosen.com (women's fiction as well as suspense, thrillers, and mystery); **Christina Hogrebe**, chogrebe@janerotrosen.com (young adult, contemporary romance and new adult, women's fiction, historical fiction, mystery, fanfiction); **Amy Tannenbaum**, atannenbaum@janerotrosen.com (contemporary romance and new adult; Amy is particularly interested in those areas, as well as women's fiction that falls into that sweet spot between literary and commercial); **Rebecca Scherer** (women's fiction, mystery, suspense/thriller, romance, upmarket fiction at the cross between commercial and literary).

REPRESENTS Nonfiction books, novels. **Considers these fiction areas:** literary, mystery, new adult, romance, suspense, thriller, women's.

HOW TO CONTACT Agent submission email addresses are different. Send a query letter, a brief synopsis, and up to three chapters of your novel or the proposal for nonfiction. No attachments. Responds in 2 weeks to writers who have been referred by a client or colleague. Responds in 2 months to mss. Obtains most new clients through recommendations from others.

TERMS Agent receives 15% commission on domestic sales. Agent receives 20% commission on foreign sales. Offers written contract, binding for 3 years; 2-month notice must be given to terminate contract. Charges clients for photocopying, express mail, overseas postage, book purchase.

⊘ THE DAMARIS ROWLAND AGENCY

420 E. 23rd St., Suite 6F, New York NY 10010. **Contact:** Damaris Rowland. Member of AAR.

REPRESENTS Nonfiction books, novels.

HOW TO CONTACT Obtains most new clients through recommendations from others, solicitations, conferences.

TERMS Agent receives 15% commission on domestic sales. Agent receives 20% commission on foreign sales. Offers written contract.

THE SAGALYN AGENCY / ICM PARTNERS

1250 Connecticut Ave., 7th Floor, Washington DC 20036. **E-mail:** query@sagalyn.com. **Website:** www.sagalyn.com. Estab. 1980. Member of AAR.

MEMBER AGENTS Raphael Sagalyn.

REPRESENTS **Considers these nonfiction areas:** biography, business, creative nonfiction, economics, popular culture, science, technology.

HOW TO CONTACT Please send e-mail queries only (no attachments).

VICTORIA SANDERS & ASSOCIATES

40 Buck Rd., Stone Ridge NY 12484. (212)633-8811. **Fax:** (212)633-0525. **E-mail:** queriesvsa@gmail.com. **Website:** www.victoriasanders.com. **Contact:** Victoria Sanders. Estab. 1992. Member of AAR. Signatory of WGA. Represents 135 clients. 25% of clients are new/unpublished writers.

MEMBER AGENTS Victoria Sanders, Chris Kepner, Bernadette Baker-Baughman.

REPRESENTS Nonfiction books, novels. **Considers these nonfiction areas:** autobiography, biography, cultural interests, current affairs, ethnic, film, gay/lesbian, government, history, humor, law, literature, music, popular culture, politics, psychology, satire, theater, translation, women's issues, women's studies. **Considers these fiction areas:** action, adventure, contemporary issues, crime, ethnic, family saga, feminist, lesbian, literary, mainstream, mystery, new adult, picture books, thriller, young adult.

HOW TO CONTACT Query by e-mail only. "We will not respond to e-mails with attachments or attached files."

TERMS Agent receives 15% commission on domestic sales. Agent receives 20% commission on foreign/film sales. Offers written contract. Charges for photocopying, messenger, express mail. If in excess of $100, client approval is required.

⊘ HAROLD SCHMIDT LITERARY AGENCY

415 W. 23rd St., #6F, New York NY 10011. **Contact:** Harold Schmidt, acquisitions. Estab. 1984. Member of AAR. Represents 3 clients.

REPRESENTS nonfiction, fiction. **Considers these fiction areas:** contemporary issues, gay, literary, original quality fiction with unique narrative voices, high quality psychological suspense and thrillers, likes offbeat/quirky.

HOW TO CONTACT Query by mail with SASE or e-mail; do not send material without being asked. No telephone or e-mail queries. We will respond if interested. Do not send material unless asked as it cannot be read or returned.

⊙ SUSAN SCHULMAN LITERARY AGENCY

454 W. 44th St., New York NY 10036. (212)713-1633. **Fax:** (212)581-8830. **E-mail:** Susan@Schulmanagency.com. **Website:** www.publishersmarketplace.com/members/Schulman/. **Contact:** Susan Schulman. Estab. 1980. Member of AAR. Signatory of WGA. Other memberships include Dramatists Guild. 10% of clients are new/unpublished writers. Currently handles: nonfiction books 50%, novels 25%, juvenile books 15%, stage plays 10%.

REPRESENTS Considers these nonfiction areas: biography, business, cooking, ethnic, health, history, money, religious, science, travel, women's issues, women's studies. **Considers these fiction areas:** juvenile, literary, mainstream, women's.

HOW TO CONTACT "For fiction: query letter with outline and three sample chapters, resume and SASE. For nonfiction: query letter with complete description of subject, at least one chapter, resume and SASE. Queries may be sent via regular mail or email. Please do not submit queries via UPS or Federal Express. Please do not send attachments with e-mail queries." Accepts simultaneous submissions. Responds in 6 weeks to queries/mss. Obtains most new clients through recommendations from others, solicitations, conferences.

TERMS Agent receives 15% commission on domestic sales. Agent receives 20% commission on foreign sales. Offers written contract; 30-day notice must be given to terminate contract.

SCOVIL GALEN GHOSH LITERARY AGENCY, INC.

276 Fifth Ave., New York NY 10001. (212)679-8686. **Fax:** (212)679-6710. **Website:** www.sgglit.com. **Contact:** Russell Galen. Estab. 1992. Member of AAR. Represents 300 clients.

MEMBER AGENTS **Russell Galen**, russellgalen@sgglit.com (novels that stretch the bounds of reality; strong, serious nonfiction books on almost any subject that teach something new; no books that are merely entertaining, such as diet or pop psych books; serious interests include science, history, journalism, biography, business, memoir, nature, politics, sports, contemporary culture, literary nonfiction, etc.); **Ann Behar**, annbehar@sgglit.com (juvenile books for all ages).

HOW TO CONTACT E-mail queries only. Note how each agent at this agency has their own submission e-mail. Accepts simultaneous submissions.

THE SEYMOUR AGENCY

475 Miner St., Canton NY 13617. (315)386-1831. **E-mail:** marysue@twcny.rr.com; nicole@theseymouragency.com; julie@theseymouragency.com; lane@theseymouragency.com. **Website:** www.theseymoura-

gency.com. Member of AAR. Signatory of WGA. Other memberships include RWA, Authors Guild.

MEMBER AGENTS **Mary Sue Seymour** (accepts queries in Christian, inspirational, romance, and nonfiction); **Nicole Resciniti** (accepts all genres of romance, young adult, middle grade, new adult, suspense, thriller, mystery, sci-fi, fantasy); **Julie Gwinn** (Christian and inspirational fiction and nonfiction, women's fiction [contemporary and historical], new adult, Southern fiction, literary fiction and young adult); Lane Heymont (science fiction, fantasy, nonfiction).

REPRESENTS Nonfiction books, novels. **Considers these nonfiction areas:** business, health, how-to, self help, Christian books; cookbooks; any well-written nonfiction that includes a proposal in standard format and 1 sample chapter. **Considers these fiction areas:** action, fantasy, inspirational, middle grade, mystery, new adult, religious, romance, science fiction, suspense, thriller, young adult.

HOW TO CONTACT For Mary Sue: E-query with synopsis, first 50 pages for romance. Accepts e-mail queries. For Nicole and Julie: E-mail the query plus first 5 pages of the manuscript pasted into the e-mail. Accepts simultaneous submissions. Responds in 1 month to queries. Responds in 3 months to mss.

TERMS Agent receives 12-15% commission on domestic sales.

DENISE SHANNON LITERARY AGENCY, INC.

20 W. 22nd St., Suite 1603, New York NY 10010. (212)414-2911. **Fax:** (212)414-2930. **E-mail:** submissions@deniseshannonagency.com. **Website:** www.deniseshannonagency.com. **Contact:** Denise Shannon. Estab. 2002. Member of AAR.

REPRESENTS Nonfiction books, novels. **Considers these nonfiction areas:** biography, business, health, narrative nonfiction; politics; journalism; memoir; social history. **Considers these fiction areas:** literary.

HOW TO CONTACT "Queries may be submitted by post, accompanied by a SASE, or by e-mail to submissions@deniseshannonagency.com. Please include a description of the available book project and a brief bio including details of any prior publications. We will reply and request more material if we are interested. We request that you inform us if you are submitting material simultaneously to other agencies."

SHEREE BYKOFSKY ASSOCIATES, INC.

PO Box 706, Brigantine NJ 08203. **E-mail:** shereebee@aol.com. **E-mail:** submitbee@aol.com. **Website:** www.shereebee.com. **Contact:** Sheree Bykofsky. Member of AAR. Memberships include Author's Guild, Atlantic City Chamber of Commerce, WNBA. Currently handles: nonfiction books 80%, novels 20%.

MEMBER AGENTS Janet Rosen, associate; Thomas V. Hartmann, associate.

REPRESENTS Nonfiction, novels. **Considers these nonfiction areas:** Americana, animals, architecture, art, autobiography, biography, business, child guidance, cooking, crafts, creative nonfiction, cultural interests, current affairs, dance, design, economics, education, environment, ethnic, film, finance, foods, gardening, gay, government, health, history, hobbies, humor, language, law, lesbian, memoirs, metaphysics, military, money, multicultural, music, nature, New Age, nutrition, parenting, philosophy, photography, popular culture, politics, psychology, recreation, regional, religious, science, sex, sociology, spirituality, sports, translation, travel, true crime, war, anthropology; creative nonfiction. **Considers these fiction areas:** contemporary issues, literary, mainstream, mystery, suspense.

HOW TO CONTACT "We only accept e-queries now and will only respond to those in which we are interested. E-mail short queries to submitbee@aol.com. Please, no attachments, snail mail, or phone calls. One-page query, one-page synopsis, and first page of ms in the body of the e-mail. Nonfiction: One-page query in the body of the e-mail. We cannot open attached Word files or any other types of attached files. These will be deleted." Accepts simultaneous submissions. Responds in 1 month to requested mss. Obtains most new clients through recommendations from others.

TERMS Agent receives 15% commission on domestic sales. Agent receives 15% commission on foreign sales, plus international co-agent receives another 10%. Offers written contract, binding for 1 year. Charges for postage, photocopying, fax.

WENDY SHERMAN ASSOCIATES, INC.

27 W. 24th St., Suite 700B, New York NY 10010. (212)279-9027. **E-mail:** submissions@wsherman.com. **Website:** www.wsherman.com. **Contact:** Wendy Sherman; Kim Perel. Member of AAR.

MEMBER AGENTS **Wendy Sherman** (women's fiction that hits that sweet spot between literary and mainstream, Southern voices, historical dramas, suspense with a well-developed protagonist, and writing that illuminates the multicultural experience); **Kim Perel** (illustrated lifestyle books in the areas of fashion, home décor and food; she also loves unique memoir that reads like fiction, in-depth journalistic no-fiction, "big idea" books about why we think, live or process thoughts the way we do, and fiction that straddles literary and commercial with a strong story and beautifully-crafted prose).

REPRESENTS **Considers these nonfiction areas:** creative nonfiction, foods, humor, memoirs, parenting, popular culture, psychology, self-help, narrative nonfiction. **Considers these fiction areas:** mainstream, Mainstream fiction that hits the sweet spot between literary and commercial.

HOW TO CONTACT Query via e-mail only. "We ask that you include your last name, title, and the name of the agent you are submitting to in the subject line. For fiction, please include a query letter and your first 10 pages copied and pasted in the body of the email. We will not open attachments unless they have been requested. For nonfiction, please include your query letter and author bio. Due to the large number of e-mail submissions that we receive, we can only reply to e-mail queries in the affirmative. We respectfully ask that you do not send queries to our individual e-mail addresses." Accepts simultaneous submissions. Obtains most new clients through recommendations from other writers.

TERMS Agent receives standard 15% commission. Offers written contract.

⊘ ROSALIE SIEGEL, INTERNATIONAL LITERARY AGENCY, INC.

1 Abey Dr., Pennington NJ 08534. (609)737-1007. **Fax:** (609)737-3708. **Website:** rosaliesiegel.com. **Contact:** Rosalie Siegel. Member of AAR.

HOW TO CONTACT "Please note that we are no longer accepting submissions of new material." Obtains most new clients through referrals from writers and friends.

TERMS Agent receives 15% commission on domestic sales. Agent receives 20% commission on foreign sales. Offers written contract; 2-month notice must be given to terminate contract. Charges clients for photocopying.

SPENCERHILL ASSOCIATES

8131 Lakewood Main St., Building M, Suite 2015, Lakewood Ranch FL 34202. (518)392-9293. **Fax:** (518)392-9554. **E-mail:** submissions@spencerhillassociates.com. **Website:** www.spencerhillassociates.com. **Contact:** Karen Solem, Nalini Akolekar or Amanda Leuck. Member of AAR. Represents 96 clients. 10% of clients are new/unpublished writers.

MEMBER AGENTS Karen Solem; Nalini Akolekar; Amanda Leuck.

REPRESENTS Novels. **Considers these fiction areas:** commercial, erotica, literary, mainstream, mystery, paranormal, romance, thriller.

HOW TO CONTACT "We accept electronic submissions and are no longer accepting paper queries. Please send us a query letter in the body of an e-mail, pitch us your project and tell us about yourself: Do you have prior publishing credits? Attach the first three chapters and synopsis preferably in .doc, rtf or txt format to your email. Send all queries to submission@spencerhillassociates.com. We do not have a preference for exclusive submissions, but do appreciate knowing if the submission is simultaneous. We receive thousands of submissions a year and each query receives our attention. Unfortunately, we are unable to respond to each query individually. If we are interested in your work, we will contact you within 8 weeks." Accepts simultaneous submissions.

TERMS Agent receives 15% commission on domestic sales. Agent receives 20% commission on foreign sales. Offers written contract; 3-month notice must be given to terminate contract.

PHILIP G. SPITZER LITERARY AGENCY, INC

50 Talmage Farm Lane, East Hampton NY 11937. (631)329-3650. **Fax:** (631)329-3651. **E-mail:** lukas.ortiz@spitzeragency.com; spitzer516@aol.com. **Website:** www.spitzeragency.com. **Contact:** Luc Hunt. Member of AAR.

MEMBER AGENTS Philip G. Spitzer; Lukas Ortiz.

REPRESENTS Nonfiction books, novels. **Considers these nonfiction areas:** biography, current affairs, history, politics, sports, travel. **Considers these fiction areas:** juvenile, literary, mainstream, suspense, thriller.

HOW TO CONTACT E-mail or snail mail query containing synopsis of work, brief biography, and two sample chapters (pasted into the e-mail). Be aware that this agency openly says their client list is quite full. Obtains most new clients through recommendations from others.

TERMS Agent receives 15% commission on domestic sales. Agent receives 20% commission on foreign sales. Charges clients for photocopying.

STEELE-PERKINS LITERARY AGENCY

26 Island Ln., Canandaigua NY 14424. (585)396-9290. **Fax:** (585)396-3579. **E-mail:** pattiesp@aol.com. **Contact:** Pattie Steele-Perkins. Member of AAR. Other memberships include RWA. Currently handles: novels 100%.

REPRESENTS Novels. **Considers these fiction areas:** romance, women's, category romance, romantic suspense, historical, contemporary, multi-cultural, and inspirational.

HOW TO CONTACT Submit query along with synopsis and one chapter via e-mail (no attachments) or snail mail. Snail mail submissions require SASE. Accepts simultaneous submissions. Obtains most new clients through recommendations from others, queries/solicitations.

TERMS Agent receives 15% commission on domestic sales. Offers written contract, binding for 1 year; 1-month notice must be given to terminate contract.

STERLING LORD LITERISTIC, INC.

65 Bleecker St., 12th Floor, New York NY 10012. (212)780-6050. **Fax:** (212)780-6095. **E-mail:** info@sll.com. **Website:** www.sll.com. Estab. 1987. Member of AAR. Signatory of WGA.

MEMBER AGENTS **Philippa Brophy** (represents journalists, nonfiction writers and novelists, and is most interested in current events, memoir, science, politics, biography, and women's issues); **Laurie Liss** (represents authors of commercial and literary fiction and nonfiction whose perspectives are well developed and unique); **Sterling Lord; Peter Matson; Douglas Stewart** (primarily fiction and memoir, running the gamut from the innovatively literary to the unabashedly commercial); **Neeti Madan** (memoir, journalism, popular culture, lifestyle, women's issues, multicultural books and virtually any intelligent writing on intriguing topics); **Robert Guinsler** (literary and commercial fiction (including YA), journalism, narrative nonfiction with an emphasis on pop culture, science and current events, memoirs and biographies); **Jim Rutman; Celeste Fine** (expert, celebrity, and corporate clients with strong national and international platforms, particularly in the health, science, self-help, food, business, and lifestyle fields); **Judy Heiblum** (literary fiction, narrative nonfiction, history, and popular science); **Erica Rand Silverman** (specializes in representing authors and illustrators of children's literature, picture books through YA, and adult nonfiction, with a special interest in parenting, DIY, emotional health and education); **Caitlin McDonald; Mary Krienke** (literary fiction, creative nonfiction, and realistic YA that pays close attention to craft and voice); **Madeleine Clark** (commercial and literary fiction as well as narrative nonfiction; she is particularly drawn to realistic YA, literary thrillers, novels that can believably introduce a bit of fantasy/sci-fi, and books that draw heavily from their environment whether that is geographical or cultural); **Jenny Stephens** (some fiction, as well as food and travel-related narrative nonfiction, lifestyle, and cookbook projects).

REPRESENTS **Considers these nonfiction areas:** biography, cooking, creative nonfiction, current affairs, education, history, memoirs, multicultural, parenting, popular culture, politics, science, women's issues. **Considers these fiction areas:** commercial, juvenile, literary, middle grade, picture books, young adult.

HOW TO CONTACT Query via snail mail. "Please submit a query letter, a synopsis of the work, a brief proposal or the first three chapters of the manuscript, a brief bio or resume, and a stamped self-addressed envelope for reply. Original artwork is not accepted. Enclose sufficient postage if you wish to have your materials returned to you. We do not respond to unsolicited e-mail inquiries." Responds in approximately 1 month.

TERMS Agent receives 15% commission on domestic sales; 20% commission on foreign sales. Offers written contract.

ROBIN STRAUS AGENCY, INC.

229 E. 79th St., Suite 5A, New York NY 10075. (212)472-3282. **Fax:** (212)472-3833. **E-mail:** info@robinstrausagency.com. **Website:** www.robinstrausagency.com. **Contact:** Ms. Robin Straus. Estab. 1983. Member of AAR.

REPRESENTS **Considers these nonfiction areas:** biography, cooking, creative nonfiction, current affairs, history, memoirs, parenting, popular culture, psychology, mainstream science. **Considers these fiction areas:** commercial, literary, mainstream, women's.

HOW TO CONTACT E-query or query via snail mail with SASE. "Send us a query letter with contact information, an autobiographical summary, a brief synopsis or description of your book project, submission history, and information on competition. If you wish, you may also include the opening chapter of your manuscript (pasted). We do not open attachments from people we don't know. Please let us know if you are showing the manuscript to other agents simultaneously."

TERMS Agent receives 15% commission on domestic sales. Agent receives 20% commission on foreign sales. Offers written contract.

THE STRINGER LITERARY AGENCY, LLC

E-mail: mstringer@stringerlit.com. **Website:** www.stringerlit.com. **Contact:** Marlene Stringer.

REPRESENTS Considers these fiction areas: fantasy, middle grade, mystery, romance, thriller, women's, young adult.

HOW TO CONTACT Electronic submissions through website submission form only. Accepts simultaneous submissions.

THE STROTHMAN AGENCY, LLC

63 East 9th St., 10X, New York NY 10003. **E-mail:** info@strothmanagency.com. **Website:** www.strothmanagency.com. **Contact:** Wendy Strothman, Lauren MacLeod. Member of AAR. Other memberships include Authors' Guild. Represents 50 clients.

MEMBER AGENTS Wendy Strothman; Lauren MacLeod.

REPRESENTS Nonfiction, juvenile books. **Considers these nonfiction areas:** business, current affairs, environment, government, history, language, law, literature, politics, travel. **Considers these fiction areas:** literary, middle grade, young adult.

HOW TO CONTACT Accepts queries only via e-mail at strothmanagency@gmail.com. See submission guidelines online. Accepts simultaneous submissions. Responds in 4 weeks to queries. Responds in 8 weeks to mss. Obtains most new clients through recommendations from others.

TERMS Agent receives 15% commission on domestic sales. Agent receives 20% commission on foreign sales. Offers written contract; 30-day notice must be given to terminate contract.

EMMA SWEENEY AGENCY, LLC

245 E 80th St., Suite 7E, New York NY 10075. **E-mail:** queries@emmasweeneyagency.com. **Website:** www.emmasweeneyagency.com. Member of AAR. Other memberships include Women's Media Group. Represents 80 clients. 5% of clients are new/unpublished writers. Currently handles: nonfiction books 50%, novels 50%.

REPRESENTS Nonfiction books, novels. **Considers these nonfiction areas:** biography, business, history, religious. **Considers these fiction areas:** literary, mainstream, mystery.

HOW TO CONTACT "We accept only electronic queries, and ask that all queries be sent to queries@emmasweeneyagency.com rather than to any agent directly. Please begin your query with a succinct (and hopefully catchy) description of your plot or proposal. Always include a brief cover letter telling us how you heard about ESA, your previous writing credits, and a few lines about yourself. We cannot open any attachments unless specifically requested, and ask that you paste the first 10 pages of your proposal or novel into the text of your e-mail."

TERMS Agent receives 15% commission on domestic sales. Agent receives 10% commission on foreign sales.

TESSLER LITERARY AGENCY, LLC

27 W. 20th St., Suite 1003, New York NY 10011. (212)242-0466. **Fax:** (212)242-2366. **Website:** www.tessleragency.com. **Contact:** Michelle Tessler. Estab. 2004. Member of AAR.

REPRESENTS Considers these nonfiction areas: biography, business, creative nonfiction, foods, memoirs, science, travel. **Considers these fiction areas:** commercial, literary, women's.

HOW TO CONTACT Submit query through online query form only. Accepts simultaneous submissions. New clients by queries/submissions through the website and recommendations from others.

TERMS Receives 15% commission on domestic sales; 20% on foreign sales. Offers written contract.

TRIDENT MEDIA GROUP

41 Madison Ave., 36th Floor, New York NY 10010. (212)333-1511. **Website:** www.tridentmediagroup.com. **Contact:** Ellen Levine. Member of AAR.

MEMBER AGENTS Kimberly Whalen, ws.assistant@tridentmediagroup (commercial fiction and nonfiction, women's fiction, suspense, paranormal, and pop culture); **Scott Miller**, smiller@tridentmediagroup.com (thrillers, crime fiction, women's and book club fiction, and a wide variety of nonfiction, such as military, celebrity and pop culture, narrative, sports, prescriptive, and current events); **Melissa Flashman**, mflashman@tridentmediagroup.

com (pop culture, memoir, wellness, popular science, business and economics, and technology—also fiction in the genres of mystery, suspense or YA); **Alyssa Eisner Henkin**, ahenkin@tridentmediagroup.com (juvenile, children's, young adult); **Don Fehr**, dfehr@tridentmediagroup.com (literary and commercial fiction, narrative nonfiction, memoirs, travel, science, and health); **John Silbersack**, silbersack.assistant@tridentmediagroup.com (commercial and literary fiction, science fiction and fantasy, narrative nonfiction, young adult, thrillers); **Erica Spellman-Silverman**; **Ellen Levine**, levine.assistant@tridentmediagroup.com (popular commercial fiction and compelling nonfiction—memoir, popular culture, narrative nonfiction, history, politics, biography, science, and the odd quirky book); **MacKenzie Fraser-Bub**, MFraserBub@tridentmediagroup.com (many genres of fiction—specializing in women's fiction); **Mark Gottlieb** (in fiction, he seeks science fiction, fantasy, young adult, comics, graphic novels, historical, history, horror, literary, middle grade, mystery, thrillers and new adult; in nonfiction, he seeks arts, cinema, photography, biography, memoir, self-help, sports, travel, world cultures, true crime, mind/body/spirit, narrative nonfiction, politics, current affairs, pop culture, entertainment, relationships, family, science, technology); **Alexander Slater**, aslater@tridentmdiagroup.com (children's, middle grade, and young adult fiction and nonfiction, from new and established authors).

REPRESENTS Considers these nonfiction areas: biography, business, creative nonfiction, current affairs, economics, health, history, memoirs, military, popular culture, politics, science, sports, technology, travel. **Considers these fiction areas:** commercial, crime, fantasy, juvenile, literary, middle grade, mystery, paranormal, science fiction, suspense, thriller, women's, young adult.

HOW TO CONTACT While some agents are open to e-queries, all seem open to submissions through the agency's online submission form on the agency website. Query only one agent at a time. If you e-query, include no attachments.

VERITAS LITERARY AGENCY

601 Van Ness Ave., Opera Plaza, Suite E, San Francisco CA 94102. (415)647-6964. **Fax:** (415)647-6965. **E-mail:** submissions@veritasliterary.com. **Website:** www.veritasliterary.com. **Contact:** Katherine Boyle. Member of AAR. Other memberships include Author's Guild and SCBWI.

MEMBER AGENTS Katherine Boyle, Michael Carr.

REPRESENTS Nonfiction books, novels. **Considers these nonfiction areas:** current affairs, memoirs, popular culture, politics, true crime, women's issues, narrative nonfiction, art and music biography, natural history, health and wellness, psychology, serious religion (no New Age) and popular science. **Considers these fiction areas:** commercial, fantasy, literary, middle grade, mystery, science fiction, young adult.

HOW TO CONTACT This agency accepts short queries or proposals via e-mail only. "If you are sending a proposal or a manuscript after a positive response to a query, please write 'requested material' on the subject line and include the initial query letter." For fiction, send a query, synopsis and the first 2 chapters pasted. For nonfiction, send a full, thorough book proposal. If you have not heard from this agency in 12 weeks, consider that a no.

WALES LITERARY AGENCY, INC.

P.O. Box 9426, Seattle WA 98109. (206)284-7114. **E-mail:** waleslit@waleslit.com. **Website:** www.waleslit.com. **Contact:** Elizabeth Wales; Neal Swain. Member of AAR. Other memberships include Authors Guild, Pacific Northwest Writers Association.

MEMBER AGENTS Elizabeth Wales; Neal Swain.

HOW TO CONTACT E-query with no attachments. Accepts simultaneous submissions. Responds in 2 weeks to queries, 2 months to mss.

TERMS Agent receives 15% commission on domestic sales. Agent receives 20% commission on foreign sales.

WEED LITERARY

55 E. 65th St., Suite 4E, New York NY 10065. **E-mail:** info@weedliterary.com. **Website:** www.weedliterary.com. **Contact:** Elisabeth Weed. Estab. 2007.

REPRESENTS Fiction, novels. **Considers these fiction areas:** literary, mainstream, women's.

HOW TO CONTACT *As of early 2015, this agency was closed to submissions. Check the agency website to see when Ms. Weed reopens to submissions.*

WRITERS HOUSE

21 W. 26th St., New York NY 10010. (212)685-2400. **Fax:** (212)685-1781. **Website:** www.writershouse.com. Estab. 1973. Member of AAR.

MEMBER AGENTS Amy Berkower; Stephen Barr; Susan Cohen; Dan Conaway; Lisa DiMona; Susan Ginsburg; Merrilee Heifetz; Brianne Johnson; Daniel Lazar; Simon Lipskar; Steven Malk; Jodi Reamer, Esq.; Robin Rue; Rebecca Sherman; Geri Thoma; Albert Zuckerman; Alec Shane; Sarah Nagel; Stacy Testa; Lisa DiMona.

REPRESENTS Nonfiction books, novels, juvenile.

HOW TO CONTACT Query with SASE. Do not contact two agents here at the same time. While snail mail is OK for all agents, some agents do accept e-queries (see below). Check the website for individual agent bios. Accepts simultaneous submissions. Obtains most new clients through recommendations from authors and editors.

TERMS Agent receives 15% commission on domestic sales. Agent receives 20% commission on foreign sales. Offers written contract, binding for 1 year. Agency charges fees for copying mss/proposals and overseas airmail of books.

BOOK PUBLISHERS

The markets in this year's Book Publishers section offer opportunities in nearly every area of publishing. Large, commercial houses are here as are their smaller counterparts.

The Book Publishers Subject Index is the best place to start your search. You'll find it in the back of the book, before the General Index. Subject areas for both fiction and nonfiction are broken out for all of the book publisher listings.

When you have compiled a list of publishers interested in books in your subject area, read the detailed listings. Pare down your list by cross-referencing two or three subject areas and eliminating the listings only marginally suited to your book. When you have a good list, send for those publishers' catalogs and manuscript guidelines, or check publishers' websites, which often contain catalog listings, manuscript preparation guidelines, current contact names, and other information helpful to prospective authors. You want to use this information to make sure your book idea is in line with a publisher's list but is not a duplicate of something already published.

You should also visit bookstores and libraries to see if the publisher's books are well represented. When you find a couple of books the house has published that are similar to yours, write or call the company to find out who edited those books. This extra bit of research could be the key to getting your proposal to precisely the right editor.

Publishers prefer different methods of submission on first contact. Most like to see a one-page query, especially for nonfiction. Others will accept a brief proposal package that might include an outline and/or a sample chapter. Some publishers will accept submissions from agents only. Each listing in the Book Publishers section includes specific submission methods, if provided by the publisher. Make sure you read each listing carefully to find out exactly what the publisher wants to receive.

When you write your one-page query, give an overview of your book, mention the intended audience, the competition for your book (check local bookstore shelves), and what sets your book apart from the competition. You should also include any previous publishing experience or special training relevant to the subject of your book. For more on queries, read "Query Letter Clinic."

Personalize your query by addressing the editor individually and mentioning what you know about the company from its catalog or books. Under the heading **Contact**, we list the names of editors who acquire new books for each company, along with the editors' specific areas of expertise. Try your best to send your query to the appropriate editor. Editors move around all the time, so it's in your best interest to look online or call the publishing house to make sure the editor you are addressing your query to is still employed by that publisher.

Author-subsidy publishers' not included

Writer's Market is a reference tool to help you sell your writing, and we encourage you to work with publishers that pay a royalty. Subsidy publishing involves paying money to a publishing house to publish a book. The source of the money could be a government, foundation or university grant, or it could be the author of the book. If one of the publishers listed in this book offers you an author-subsidy arrangement (sometimes called "co-operative publishing," "co-publishing," or "joint venture"); or asks you to pay for part or all of the cost of any aspect of publishing (editing services, manuscript critiques, printing, advertising, etc.); or asks you to guarantee the purchase of any number of the books yourself, we would like you to inform us of that company's practices immediately.

⊘ ABBEVILLE PRESS

137 Varick St., New York NY 10013. (212)366-5585. **Fax:** (212)366-6966. **E-mail:** abbeville@abbeville.com. **Website:** www.abbeville.com. Estab. 1977. Mainstay in the art book publishing world. "Our list is full for the next several seasons." **Publishes 8 titles/year. 10% of books from first-time authors.**

NONFICTION Subjects include art. Not accepting unsolicited book proposals at this time.

FICTION Picture books through imprint Abbeville Family. Not accepting unsolicited book proposals at this time.

ABC-CLIO

Acquisitions Department, P.O. Box 1911, Santa Barbara CA 93116. (805)968-1911. **E-mail:** acquisition_inquiries@abc-clio.com. **Website:** www.abc-clio.com. Estab. 1955. ABC-CLIO is an award-winning publisher of reference titles, academic and general interest books, electronic resources, and books for librarians and other professionals. **Publishes 600 titles/year. 20% of books from first-time authors. 90% from unagented writers. Pays variable royalty on net price.** Accepts simultaneous submissions. Catalog and guidelines online.

IMPRINTS ABC-CLIO; Greenwood Press; Praeger; Linworth and Libraries Unlimited.

NONFICTION Subjects include business, child guidance, education, government, history, humanities, language, music, psychology, religion, social sciences, sociology, sports, women's issues. No memoirs, drama. Query with proposal package, including scope, organization, length of project, whether a complete ms is available or when it will be, CV, and SASE. Check guidelines online for each imprint.

TIPS "Looking for reference materials and materials for educated general readers. Many of our authors are college professors who have distinguished credentials and who have published research widely in their fields."

ABDO PUBLISHING CO.

8000 W. 78th St., Suite 310, Edina MN 55439. (800)800-1312. **Fax:** (952)831-1632. **E-mail:** nonfiction@abdopublishing.com. **E-mail:** fiction@abdopublishing.com; illustration@abdopublishing.com. **Website:** www.abdopub.com. **Contact:** Paul Abdo, editor-in-chief. Estab. 1985. Publishes hardcover originals. ABDO publishes nonfiction children's books (pre-kindergarten to 8th grade) for school and public libraries—mainly history, sports, biography, geography, science, and social studies. "Please specify each submission as either nonfiction, fiction, or illustration." **Publishes 300 titles/year.** Guidelines online.

NONFICTION Subjects include animals, history, science, sports, geography, social studies.

ABINGDON PRESS

Imprint of The United Methodist Publishing House, 201 Eighth Ave. S., P.O. Box 801, Nashville TN 37202. (615)749-6000. **Fax:** (615)749-6512. **Website:** www.abingdonpress.com. Estab. 1789. Publishes hardcover and paperback originals. "Abingdon Press, America's oldest theological publisher, provides an ecumenical publishing program dedicated to serving the Christian community—clergy, scholars, church leaders, musicians, and general readers—with quality resources in the areas of Bible study, the practice of ministry, theology, devotion, spirituality, inspiration, prayer, music and worship, reference, Christian education, and church supplies." **Publishes 120 titles/year. 3,000 queries received/year. 250 mss received/year. 85% from unagented writers. Pays 7½% royalty on retail price.** Publishes ms 2 years after acceptance. Responds in 2 months to queries. Book catalog available free. Guidelines online.

NONFICTION Subjects include education, religion, theology. Query with outline and samples only. The author should retain a copy of any unsolicited material submitted.

FICTION Publishes stories of faith, hope, and love that encourage readers to explore life. Agented submissions only for fiction.

⊘ HARRY N. ABRAMS, INC.

115 W. 18th St., 6th Floor, New York NY 10011. (212)206-7715. **Fax:** (212)519-1210. **E-mail:** abrams@abramsbooks.com. **Website:** www.abramsbooks.com. **Contact:** Managing Editor. Estab. 1951. Publishes hardcover and a few paperback originals. **Publishes 250 titles/year.**

IMPRINTS Stewart, Tabori & Chang: Abrams Appleseed; Abrams Books for Young Readers; Abrams Image; STC Craft; Amulet Books.

Does not accept unsolicited materials.

NONFICTION Subjects include art, architecture, nature, environment, recreation, outdoor.

FICTION Subjects include young adult. Publishes hardcover and "a few" paperback originals. Averages 150 total titles/year.

TIPS "We are one of the few publishers who publish almost exclusively illustrated books. We consider ourselves the leading publishers of art books and high-quality artwork in the U.S. Once the author has signed a contract to write a book for our firm the author must finish the manuscript to agreed-upon high standards within the schedule agreed upon in the contract."

⊘ ABRAMS BOOKS FOR YOUNG READERS

115 W. 18th St., New York NY 10011. **Website:** www.abramsyoungreaders.com.

Abrams no longer accepts unsolicted mss or queries.

ACADEMY CHICAGO PUBLISHERS

814 N. Franklin St., Chicago IL 60610. (312)337-0747. **Fax:** (312)337-5985. **E-mail:** frontdesk@ipgbook.com. **Website:** www.academychicago.com. **Contact:** Anita Miller and Jordan Miller, editors-at-large. Estab. 1975. Publishes hardcover and some paperback originals and trade paperback reprints. "We publish quality fiction and nonfiction. Our audience is literate and discriminating. No novelized biography, history, or science fiction." No electronic submissions. **Publishes 10 titles/year. Pays 7-10% royalty on wholesale price.** Publishes ms 18 months after acceptance. Responds in 3 months. Book catalog online. Guidelines online.

NONFICTION Subjects include history, travel. No religion, cookbooks, or self-help. Submit proposal package, outline, bio, 3 sample chapters.

FICTION Subjects include historical, mainstream, contemporary, military, war, mystery. "We look for quality work, but we do not publish experimental, avant garde, horror, science fiction, thrillers novels." Submit proposal package, synopsis, 3 sample chapters, and short bio.

TIPS "At the moment, we are looking for good nonfiction; we certainly want excellent original fiction, but we are swamped. No fax queries, no disks. No electronic submissions. We are always interested in reprinting good out-of-print books."

Ⓐ⊘ ACE SCIENCE FICTION AND FANTASY

Imprint of the Berkley Publishing Group, Penguin Group (USA), Inc., 375 Hudson St., New York NY 10014. (212)366-2000. **Website:** www.us.penguingroup.com. Estab. 1953. Publishes hardcover, paperback, and trade paperback originals and reprints. Ace publishes science fiction and fantasy exclusively. **Publishes 75 titles/year. Pays royalty. Pays advance.**

As imprint of Penguin, Ace is not open to unsolicited submissions.

FICTION Subjects include fantasy, science fiction. No other genre accepted. No short stories. Due to the high volume of manuscripts received, most Penguin Group (USA) Inc. imprints do not normally accept unsolicited mss.

ACTA PUBLICATIONS

4848 N. Clark St., Chicago IL 60640. **E-mail:** acta@actapublications.com. **Website:** www.actapublications.com. **Contact:** Acquisitions Editor. Estab. 1958. Publishes trade paperback originals. "ACTA publishes nonacademic, practical books aimed at the mainline religious market." **Publishes 12 titles/year. 100 queries received/year. 25 mss received/year. 50% of books from first-time authors. 90% from unagented writers. Pays 10-12% royalty on wholesale price.** Publishes ms 1 year after acceptance. Responds in 2-3 months to proposals. Book catalog and guidelines online.

"While some of ACTA's material is specifically Catholic in nature, most of the company's products are aimed at a broadly ecumenical audience."

NONFICTION Subjects include religion, spirituality. Submit outline, 1 sample chapter. No e-mail submissions. Reviews artwork/photos. Send photocopies.

TIPS "Don't send a submission unless you have examined our catalog, website and several of our books."

ADAMS-BLAKE PUBLISHING

8041 Sierra St. #321, Fair Oaks CA 95628. (916)962-9296. **E-mail:** web@adams-blake.com. **Website:** www.adams-blake.com. **Contact:** Monica Blane, acquisitions editor. Estab. 1992. Publishes only e-books. "We are getting away from doing trade titles and are doing more short-run/high-priced specialized publications targeted to corporations, law, medicine, engineering, computers, etc." **Publishes 5 titles/year. 50 queries received/year. 15 mss received/year. 80% of books from first-time authors. 99% from unagented writers. Pays 15% royalty on wholesale price.** Publishes ms 2 months after acceptance. Accepts simultaneous submissions. Responds in 2 months.

NONFICTION Subjects include business, economics, computers, electronics, counseling, career guidance, labor, money, finance. "We like titles in sales and marketing, but which are targeted to a specific industry. We don't look for retail trade titles but more to special markets where we sell 10,000 copies to a company to give to their employees." Query. Does not review artwork/photos.

TIPS "If you have a book that a large company might buy and give away at sales meetings, send us a query. We like books on sales, especially in specific industries—Like 'How to Sell Annuities' or 'How to Sell High-Tech.' We look for the title that a company will buy several thousand copies of at a time. We often 'personalize' for the company. We especially like short books, 50,000 words (more or less)."

ADAMS MEDIA

Division of F+W Media, Inc., 57 Littlefield St., Avon MA 02322. (508)427-7100. **Fax:** (800)872-5628. **E-mail:** adamsmediasubmissions@fwmedia.com. **Website:** www.adamsmedia.com. **Contact:** Acquisitions Editor. Estab. 1980. Publishes hardcover originals, trade paperback, e-book originals and reprints. Adams Media publishes commercial nonfiction, including self-help, women's issues, pop psychology, relationships, business, careers, pets, parenting, New Age, gift books, cookbooks, how-to, reference, and humor. Does not return unsolicited materials. **Publishes more than 250 titles/year. 5,000 queries received/year. 1,500 mss received/year. 40% of books from first-time authors. Pays standard royalty or makes outright purchase. Pays variable advance.** Publishes ms 12-18 months after acceptance. Accepts simultaneous submissions. Responds in 3 months to queries. Guidelines online.

ADDICUS BOOKS, INC.

P.O. Box 45327, Omaha NE 68145. (402)330-7493. **Fax:** (402)330-1707. **E-mail:** info@addicusbooks.com. **Website:** www.addicusbooks.com. **Contact:** Acquisitions Editor. Estab. 1994. Addicus Books, Inc. seeks mss with strong national or regional appeal. "We are dedicated to producing high-quality nonfiction books. Our focus is on consumer health titles, but we will consider other topics. In addition to working with a master book distributor, IPG Books of Chicago, which delivers books to stores and libraries, we continually seek special sales channels, outside traditional bookstores." **Publishes 10 titles/year. 90% of books from first-time authors. 95% from unagented writers.** Publishes ms 9 months after acceptance. Responds in 1 month to proposals. Catalog and guidelines online.

"Due to the amount of queries we receive our editors are not available for phone inquiries. If we're interested in taking a closer look at your book, we'll contact you after we receive your inquiry."

NONFICTION Subjects include business, economics, consumer health, investing. "We are expanding our line of consumer health titles." Query with a brief e-mail. "Tell us what your book is about, who the audience is, and how that audience would be reached. If we are interested, we may ask for a proposal, outlining the nature of your work. See proposal guidelines on our website. Do not send entire ms unless requested. When querying electronically, send only 1-page e-mail, giving an overview of your book and its market Please do not send hard copies by certified mail or return receipt requested. Additional submission guidelines online."

TIPS "We are looking for compact, concise books on consumer health topics."

AERONAUTICAL PUBLISHERS

1 Oakglade Circle, Hummelstown PA 17036-9525. **E-mail:** info@possibilitypress.com. **Website:** www.aeronauticalpublishers.com. **Contact:** Mike Markowski, publisher. Estab. 1981. Publishes trade paperback originals. "Our mission is to help people learn more about aviation and model aviation through the written word." **Pays variable royalty.** Responds in 2 months to queries. Guidelines online.

IMPRINTS American Aeronautical Archives, Aviation Publishers, Aeronautical Publishers.

NONFICTION Subjects include history, aviation, hobbies, recreation, radio control, free flight, indoor models, micro radio control, home-built aircraft, ultralights, and hang gliders. Prefers submission by mail. Include SASE. See guidelines online. Reviews artwork/photos. Do not send originals.

TIPS "Our focus is on books of short to medium length that will serve the emerging needs of the hobby. We also want to help youth get started, while enhancing everyone's enjoyment of the hobby. We are looking for authors who are passionate about the hobby, and will champion their book and the messages of their books, supported by efforts at promoting and selling their books."

AHSAHTA PRESS

MFA Program in Creative Writing, Boise State University, 1910 University Dr., MS 1525, Boise ID 83725.

(208)426-3414. **E-mail:** ahsahta@boisestate.edu. **E-mail:** jholmes@boisestate.edu. **Website:** ahsahtapress.org. **Contact:** Janet Holmes, director. Estab. 1974. Publishes trade paperback originals. **Publishes 7 titles/year. 1,000 mss received/year. 30% of books from first-time authors. 100% from unagented writers. Pays 8% royalty on retail price for first 1,000 sold; 10% thereafter.** Publishes ms 2 years after acceptance. Accepts simultaneous submissions. Responds in 3 months to mss. Book catalog online. Guidelines online; submit through submissions manager.

POETRY "We hold an open submissions period in May as well as the Sawtooth Poetry Prize competition, from which we publish 2-3 mss per year." Submit complete ms. The press publishes runners-up as well as winners of the Sawtooth Poetry Prize. Forthcoming, new, and backlist titles available on website. Most backlist titles: $9.95; most current titles: $18.

TIPS "Ahsahta's motto is that poetry is art, so our readers tend to come to us for the unexpected—poetry that makes them think, reflect, and even do something they haven't done before."

⊘ ALADDIN

Simon & Schuster, 1230 Avenue of the Americas, 4th Floor, New York NY 10020. (212)698-7000. **Website:** www.simonandschuster.com. **Contact:** Acquisitions Editor. Publishes hardcover/paperback originals and imprints of Simon & Schuster Children's Publishing Children's Division. Aladdin publishes picture books, beginning readers, chapter books, middle grade and tween fiction and nonfiction, and graphic novels and nonfiction in hardcover and paperback, with an emphasis on commercial, kid-friendly titles.

FICTION Simon & Schuster does not review, retain or return unsolicited materials or artwork. "We suggest prospective authors and illustrators submit their mss through a professional literary agent."

ALGONQUIN BOOKS OF CHAPEL HILL

Workman Publishing, P.O. Box 2225, Chapel Hill NC 27515-2225. (919)967-0108. **Website:** www.algonquin.com. **Contact:** Editorial Department. Publishes hardcover originals. "Algonquin Books publishes quality literary fiction and literary nonfiction." **Publishes 24 titles/year.** Guidelines online.

IMPRINTS Algonquin Young Readers.

NONFICTION Query by mail before submitting work. No phone, e-mail or fax queries or submissions. Visit our website for full submission policy to queries.

FICTION Subjects include literary. Query first.

ALGORA PUBLISHING

222 Riverside Dr., 16th Floor, New York NY 10025-6809. (212)678-0232. **Fax:** (212)666-3682. **Website:** www.algora.com. **Contact:** Martin DeMers, editor (sociology/philosophy/economics); Claudiu A. Secara, publisher (philosophy/international affairs). Estab. 1992. Publishes hardcover and trade paperback originals and reprints. Algora Publishing is an academic-type press, focusing on works by North and South American, European, Asian, and African authors for the educated general reader. **Publishes 25 titles/year. 1,500 queries received/year. 800 mss received/year. 20% of books from first-time authors. 85% from unagented writers. Pays $0-1,000 advance.** Publishes ms 10-18 months after acceptance. Accepts simultaneous submissions. Responds in 1 month to queries/proposals; 3 months to mss. Book catalog and guidelines online.

NONFICTION Subjects include anthropology, archeology, creative nonfiction, dance, education, environment, finance, government, history, language, literature, military, money, music, nature, philosophy, politics, psychology, religion, science, sociology, translation, war, womens issues, womens studies, economics. Algora Publishing welcomes proposals for original mss, but "we do not handle self-help, recovery, or children's books." Submit a query or ms by uploading file to our website.

TIPS "We welcome first-time writers; we help craft an author's raw manuscript into a literary work."

IAN ALLAN PUBLISHING, LTD.

Terminal House, Shepperton TW17 8 AS, United Kingdom. (44)(193)226-6600. **E-mail:** info@ianallanpub.co.uk. **Website:** www.ianallanpublishing.com. **Contact:** Peter Waller, publishing manager. Publishes hardcover, trade paperback and mass market paperback originals and reprints. **Publishes 120 titles/year. 300 queries received/year. 50 mss received/year. 5% of books from first-time authors. 95% from unagented writers. Payment is subject to contract and type of publication.** Publishes ms 6 months after acceptance. Accepts simultaneous submissions. Book catalog available free.

NONFICTION Subjects include history, hobbies, military, war, sports, travel. Query with SASE. Reviews artwork/photos.

TIPS "Audience is enthusiasts and historians. We don't publish books with a strong autobiographical bias—e.g., military reminiscences—and no fiction/children's/poetry."

ALLWORTH PRESS

An imprint of Skyhorse Publishing, 307 West 36th St., 11th Floor, New York NY 10018. (212)643-6816. **Fax:** (212)643-6819. **E-mail:** allworthsubmissions@skyhorsepublishing.com. **Website:** www.allworth.com. Estab. 1989. Publishes hardcover and trade paperback originals. "Allworth Press publishes business and self-help information for artists, designers, photographers, authors and film and performing artists, as well as books about business, money and the law for the general public. The press also publishes the best of classic and contemporary writing in art and graphic design. Currently emphasizing photography, graphic and industrial design, performing arts, fine arts and crafts, et al." **Publishes 12-18 titles/year. Pays advance.** Responds in 4-6 weeks.

NONFICTION Subjects include art, architecture, business, economics, film, cinema, stage, music, dance, photography, film, television, graphic design, performing arts, as well as business and legal guides for the public. "We are currently accepting query letters for practical, legal, and technique books targeted to professionals in the arts, including designers, graphic and fine artists, craftspeople, photographers, and those involved in film and the performing arts." Query with 1-2 page synopsis, chapter outline, market analysis, sample chapter, bio, SASE.

TIPS "We are helping creative people in the arts by giving them practical advice about business and success."

ALONDRA PRESS, LLC

4119 Wildacres Dr., Houston TX 77072. **E-mail:** lark@alondrapress.com. **Website:** www.alondrapress.com. **Contact:** Henry Hollenbaugh, fiction editor; Solomon Tager, nonfiction editor. Estab. 2007. Publishes trade paperback originals and reprints. **Publishes 4 titles/year. 75% of books from first-time authors. 75% from unagented writers.** Publishes ms 8 months after acceptance. Accepts simultaneous submissions. Responds in 1 month to queries/proposals; 3 months to mss. Guidelines online.

NONFICTION Subjects include anthropology, archaeology, history, philosophy, psychology, translation. Submit complete ms.

FICTION Subjects include literary, all fiction genres. "Just send us a few pages in an e-mail attachment, or the entire manuscript. We will look at it quickly and tell you if it interests us."

TIPS "Be sure to read our guidelines before sending a submission. We will not respond to authors who do not observe our simple guidelines. Send your submissions in an e-mail attachment only."

ALPINE PUBLICATIONS

38262 Linman Rd., Crawford CO 81415. (970)921-5005. **Fax:** (970)921-5081. **E-mail:** editorialdept@alpinepub.com. **Website:** alpinepub.com. Estab. 1975. Publishes hardcover and trade paperback originals and reprints. **Publishes 6-10 titles/year. 40% of books from first-time authors. 95% from unagented writers. Pays 8-15% royalty on wholesale price. Pays advance.** Publishes ms 18 months after acceptance. Accepts simultaneous submissions. Responds in 1 month. Book catalog available free. Guidelines online.

NONFICTION Subjects include animals. Alpine specializes in books that promote the enjoyment of and responsibility for companion animals with emphasis on dogs and horses. No biographies. Query with a brief synopsis, chapter outline, bio, 1-3 sample chapters, and market analysis.

TIPS "Our audience is pet owners, breeders, exhibitors, veterinarians, animal trainers, animal care specialists, and judges. Our books are in-depth and most are heavily illustrated. Look up some of our titles before you submit. See what is unique about our books. Write your proposal to suit our guidelines."

THE ALTHOUSE PRESS

University of Western Ontario, Faculty of Education, 1137 Western Rd., London ON N6G 1G7, Canada. (519)661-2096. **Fax:** (519)661-3714. **E-mail:** press@uwo.ca. **Website:** www.edu.uwo.ca/althousepress. **Contact:** Katherine Butson, editorial assistant. Publishes trade paperback originals and reprints. "The Althouse Press publishes both scholarly research monographs in education and professional books and materials for educators in elementary schools, secondary schools, and faculties of education. De-emphasizing curricular or instructional materials intended for use by elementary or secondary school students." **Publishes 1-5 titles/year. 50-100 queries received/year. 14 mss received/year. 50% of books from first-time authors. 100% from unagented writers. Pays $300 advance.** Publishes ms 18 months after acceptance.

Accepts simultaneous submissions. Responds in 1-2 months to queries; 4 months to mss. Book catalog available free. Guidelines online.

NONFICTION Subjects include education, scholarly. "Do not send incomplete manuscripts that are only marginally appropriate to our market and limited mandate." Reviews artwork/photos. Send photocopies.

TIPS "Audience is practicing teachers and graduate education students."

AMACOM BOOKS

American Management Association, 1601 Broadway, New York NY 10019. (212)586-8100. **Fax:** (212)903-8083. **E-mail:** ekadin@amanet.org; rnirkind@amanet.org; spower@amanet.org; whelms@amanet.org. **Website:** www.amacombooks.org. **Contact:** Ellen Kadin, executive editor (marketing, career, personal development); Robert Nirkind, senior editor (sales, customer service, project management, finance); Stephen Power, senior editor (leadership, management, human resources); William Helms, associate acquisitions editor (training, science and technology, education). Estab. 1923. Publishes hardcover and trade paperback originals and e-books. AMACOM is the publishing arm of the American Management Association, the world's largest training organization for managers and their organizations—advancing the skills of individuals to drive business success. AMACOM's books are intended to enhance readers' personal and professional growth, and to help readers meet the challenges of the future by conveying emerging trends and cutting-edge thinking.

NONFICTION Publishes nonfiction books for consumer and professional markets, including all business topics, parenting, health & fitness, and popular psychology. Submit proposals including brief book description and rationale, TOC, author bio and platform, intended audience, competing books and sample chapters. Proposals returned with SASE only.

TIPS "Platform reflects author activities that demonstrate author's visibility, authority, and audience reach."

AMADEUS PRESS

Hal Leonard Publishing Group, 33 Plymouth St., Suite 302, Montclair NJ 07402. (973)337-5034. **Fax:** (973)337-5227. **E-mail:** jcerullo@halleonard.com. **Website:** www.amadeuspress.com. **Contact:** John Cerullo, publisher.

NONFICTION "Amadeus Press welcomes submissions pertaining to classical and traditional music and opera. Send proposal including: a letter describing the purpose and audience for your book, along with your background and qualifications; please indicate which word-processing software you use as we ask that final ms be submitted on disk; an outline or table of contents and an estimate of the length of the completed ms in numbers of words or double-spaced pages; a sample chapter or two, printed out (no electronic file transfers, please); sample illustrations as well as an estimate of the total numbers and types (for example, pen-and-ink artwork for line drawings, black-and-white glossy photographic prints, camera-ready music examples) of illustrations planned for your book; your schedule to complete the book. Generally, we ask authors to submit book proposals early in the writing process as this allows us to give editorial advice during the development phase and cuts down the amount of revisions needed later. Due to the large volume of submissions, you may not receive a response from us. If you wish to have the materials you submit returned to you, please so indicate and include return postage."

AMERICAN CATHOLIC PRESS

16565 S. State St., South Holland IL 60473. (312)331-5845. **Fax:** (708)331-5484. **E-mail:** acp@acpress.org. **Website:** www.acpress.org. **Contact:** Rev. Michael Gilligan, PhD, editorial director. Estab. 1967. Publishes hardcover originals and hardcover and paperback reprints. **Publishes 4 titles/year. Makes outright purchase of $25-100.** Guidelines online.

NONFICTION Subjects include education, music, dance, religion, spirituality. "We publish books on the Roman Catholic liturgy—for the most part, books on religious music and educational books and pamphlets. We also publish religious songs for church use, including Psalms, as well as choral and instrumental arrangements. We are interested in new music, meant for use in church services. Books, or even pamphlets, on the Roman Catholic Mass are especially welcome. We have no interest in secular topics and are not interested in religious poetry of any kind."

TIPS "Most of our sales are by direct mail, although we do work through retail outlets."

AMERICAN CHEMICAL SOCIETY

Publications/Books Division, 1155 16th St. NW, Washington DC 20036. (202)452-2120. **Fax:** (202)513-8819. **E-mail:** b_hauserman@acs.org. **Website:** pubs.

acs.org/books/. **Contact:** Bob Hauserman, acquisitions editor. Estab. 1876. Publishes hardcover originals. American Chemical Society publishes symposium-based books for chemistry. **Publishes 35 titles/year. Pays royalty.** Accepts simultaneous submissions. Responds in 2 months to proposals. Book catalog available free. Guidelines online.

NONFICTION Subjects include science. Emphasis is on meeting-based books. Log in to submission site online.

AMERICAN CORRECTIONAL ASSOCIATION

206 N. Washington St., Suite 200, Alexandria VA 22314. (703)224-0194. **Fax:** (703)224-0172. **E-mail:** kellim@aca.org. **Website:** www.aca.org. **Contact:** Kelli McAfee. Estab. 1870. Publishes trade paperback originals. "American Correctional Association provides practical information on jails, prisons, boot camps, probation, parole, community corrections, juvenile facilities and rehabilitation programs, substance abuse programs, and other areas of corrections." **Publishes 18 titles/year. 90% of books from first-time authors. 100% from unagented writers.** Publishes ms 1 year after acceptance. Responds in 4 months. Book catalog free. Guidelines online.

NONFICTION "We are looking for practical, how-to texts or training materials written for the corrections profession. We are especially interested in books on management, development of first-line supervisors, and security-threat group/management in prisons." No autobiographies or true-life accounts by current or former inmates or correctional officers, theses, or dissertations. No fiction or poetry. Query with SASE. Reviews artwork/photos.

TIPS "Authors are professionals in the field of corrections. Our audience is made up of corrections professionals and criminal justice students. No books by inmates or former inmates. This publisher advises out-of-town freelance editors, indexers, and proofreaders to refrain from requesting work from them."

AMERICAN COUNSELING ASSOCIATION

6101 Stevenson Ave., Alexandria VA 22304. (703)823-9800. **Fax:** (703)823-4786. **E-mail:** cbaker@counseling.org. **Website:** www.counseling.org. **Contact:** Carolyn C. Baker, associate publisher. Estab. 1952. Publishes paperback originals. "The American Counseling Association is dedicated to promoting public confidence and trust in the counseling profession. We publish scholarly texts for graduate level students and mental health professionals. We do not publish books for the general public." **Publishes 8-10 titles/year. 1% of books from first-time authors. 90% from unagented writers.** Accepts simultaneous submissions. Responds in 1 month to queries. Guidelines available free.

NONFICTION Subjects include education, psychology, religion, spirituality, womens issues, LGBTQ mental health, school counseling, marriage, family, couples counseling. ACA does not publish self-help books or autobiographies. Query with SASE. Submit proposal package, outline, 2 sample chapters, vitae.

TIPS "Target your market. Your books will not be appropriate for everyone across all disciplines."

AMERICAN FEDERATION OF ASTROLOGERS

6535 S. Rural Rd., Tempe AZ 85283. (480)838-1751. **Fax:** (480)838-8293. **E-mail:** info@astrologers.com. **Website:** www.astrologers.com. Estab. 1938. Publishes trade paperback originals and reprints. American Federation of Astrologers publishes astrology books, calendars, charts, and related aids. **Publishes 10-15 titles/year. 10 queries received/year. 20 mss received/year. 50% of books from first-time authors. 100% from unagented writers. Pays 10% royalty.** Publishes ms 10 months after acceptance. Accepts simultaneous submissions. Responds in 6 months to mss. Book catalog available free. Guidelines online.

NONFICTION "Our market for beginner books, Sun-sign guides, and similar material is limited and we thus publish very few of these. The ideal word count for a book-length manuscript published by AFA is about 40,000 words, although we will consider manuscripts from 20,000 to 60,000 words." Submit complete ms.

TIPS "AFA welcomes articles for *Today's Astrologer*, our monthly journal for members, on any astrological subject. Most articles are 1,500-3,000 words, but we do accept shorter and longer articles. Follow the guidelines online for book manuscripts. You also can e-mail your article to info@astrologers.com, but any charts or illustrations must be submitted as attachments and not embedded in the body of the e-mail or in an attached document."

⊘ AMERICAN PRESS

60 State St., Suite 700, Boston MA 02109. (617)247-0022. **E-mail:** americanpress@flash.net. **Website:** www.americanpresspublishers.com. **Contact:** Jana

Kirk, editor. Estab. 1911. Publishes college textbooks. **Publishes 25 titles/year. 350 queries received/year. 100 mss received/year. 50% of books from first-time authors. 90% from unagented writers. Pays 5-15% royalty on wholesale price.** Publishes ms 9 months after acceptance. Responds in 3 months to queries.

Mss proposals are welcome in all subjects and disciplines.

NONFICTION Subjects include agriculture, anthropology, archeology, art, architecture, business, economics, education, government, politics, health, medicine, history, horticulture, music, dance, psychology, science, sociology, sports. "We prefer that our authors actually teach courses for which the manuscripts are designed." Query, or submit outline with tentative TOC. *No complete mss.*

AMERICAN QUILTER'S SOCIETY

5801 Kentucky Dam Rd., Paducah KY 42003. (270)898-7903. **Fax:** (270)898-1173. **E-mail:** editor@aqsquilt.com. **Website:** www.americanquilter.com. **Contact:** Elaine Brelsford, executive book editor (primarily how-to and patterns, but other quilting books sometimes published, including quilt-related fiction). Estab. 1984. Publishes trade paperbacks. "American Quilter's Society publishes how-to and pattern books for quilters (beginners through intermediate skill level). We are not the publisher for non-quilters writing about quilts. We now publish quilt-related craft cozy romance and mystery titles, series only. Humor is good. Graphic depictions and curse words are bad." **Publishes 20-24 titles/year. 100 queries received/year. 60% of books from first-time authors. Pays 5% royalty on retail price for both nonfiction and fiction.** Publishes ms 9-18 months after acceptance. Fiction published on a different schedule TBD. after acceptance of ms. Responds in 2 months to proposals. Guidelines online.

Accepts simultaneous nonfiction submissions. Does not accept simultaneous fiction submissions.

NONFICTION No queries; proposals only. Note: 1 or 2 completed quilt projects must accompany proposal.

FICTION Submit a synopsis and 2 sample chapters, plus an outline of the next 2 books in the series.

AMERICAN WATER WORKS ASSOCIATION

6666 W. Quincy Ave., Denver CO 80235. (303)347-6260. **Fax:** (303)794-7310. **E-mail:** submissions@awwa.org. **Website:** www.awwa.org. **Contact:** David Plank, manager, business and product development. Estab. 1881. Publishes hardcover and trade paperback originals. "AWWA strives to advance and promote the safety and knowledge of drinking water and related issues to all audiences—from kindergarten through post-doctorate." **Publishes 25 titles/year.** Responds in 4 months to queries. Book catalog and ms guidelines free.

NONFICTION Subjects include nature, environment, science, software, drinking water- and wastewater-related topics, operations, treatment, sustainability. Query with SASE. Submit outline, bio, 3 sample chapters. Reviews artwork/photos. Send photocopies.

TIPS "See website to download submission instructions."

AMG PUBLISHERS

6815 Shallowford Rd., Chattanooga TN 37421-1755. (423)894-6060. **Fax:** (423)894-9511. **E-mail:** ricks@amgpublishers.com. **Website:** www.amgpublishers.com. **Contact:** Rick Steele, Product development/acquisitions. Publishes hardcover and trade paperback originals, electronic originals, and audio Bible and book originals. **Publishes 25-30 titles/year. 2,500 queries received/year. 500 mss received/year. 25% of books from first-time authors. 25% from unagented writers. Pays 10-14% royalty on net sales.** Publishes ms 12-18 months after acceptance. Accepts simultaneous submissions. Responds in 1 month to queries, 4 months to proposals/mss. Book catalog and guidelines online.

IMPRINTS Living Ink Books; God and Country.

NONFICTION Subjects include Reference, Bible Study workbooks, Bibles, commentaries. Looking for books that facilitate interaction with Bible, encourage and facilitate spiritual growth. Subjects include Christian living, women's, men's family issues, marriage and divorce issues, devotionals, contemporary issues, biblical reference, applied theology, and apologetics. Query with letter first, e-mail preferred.

FICTION Young Adult (teen and preteen) contemporary and fantasy; historical fiction for adults to expand God and Country imprint. "We are looking for youth/young adult (teen) fantasy that contains spiritual truths. We are also now looking for historical fiction for adults."

TIPS "AMG is open to well-written, niche books that meet immediate needs in the lives of adults and young adults."

AMHERST MEDIA, INC.

175 Rano St., Suite 200, Buffalo NY 14207. (716)874-4450. **Fax:** (716)874-4508. **E-mail:** submissions@amherstmedia.com. **Website:** www.amherstmedia.com. **Contact:** Craig Alesse, publisher. Estab. 1974. Publishes trade paperback originals and reprints. Amherst Media publishes how-to photography books. **Publishes 30 titles/year. 60% of books from first-time authors. 90% from unagented writers. Pays 6-8% royalty. Pays advance.** Publishes ms 1 year after acceptance. Accepts simultaneous submissions. Responds in 2 months to queries. Book catalog online. Guidelines online.

NONFICTION Subjects include photography. Looking for well-written and illustrated photo books. Query with outline, 2 sample chapters, and SASE. Reviews artwork/photos.

TIPS "Our audience is made up of beginning to advanced photographers. If I were a writer trying to market a book today, I would fill the need of a specific audience and self-edit in a tight manner."

AMIRA PRESS

2721 N. Rosedale St., Baltimore MD 21216. (704)858-7533. **E-mail:** submissions@amirapress.com. **Website:** www.amirapress.com. **Contact:** Yvette A. Lynn, CEO (any sub genre). Estab. 2007. Format publishes in paperback originals, e-books, POD printing. "We are a small press which publishes sensual and erotic romance. Our slogan is 'Erotic and Sensual Romance. Immerse Yourself.' Our authors and stories are diverse." **Publishes 50 titles/year. Pays royalties, 8.5% of cover price (print)—30-40% of cover price (e-books).** Publishes ms 1-4 months after acceptance. Accepts simultaneous submissions. Responds in 3 months. Guildelines online.

FICTION Subjects include erotica. Submit complete ms with cover letter by e-mail. "No snail mail." Include estimated word count, heat level, brief bio, list of publishing credits. Accepts unsolicited mss. Sometimes critiques/comments on rejected mss.

TIPS "Please read our submission guidelines thoroughly and follow them when submitting. We do not consider a work until we have all the requested information and the work is presented in the format we outline."

AMULET BOOKS

115 W. 18th St., New York NY 10001. **Website:** www.amuletbooks.com. Estab. 2004. **10% of books from first-time authors.**

Does not accept unsolicited mss or queries.

FICTION Middle readers: adventure, contemporary, fantasy, history, science fiction, sports. Young adults/teens: adventure, contemporary, fantasy, history, science fiction, sports, suspense.

ANDREWS MCMEEL UNIVERSAL

1130 Walnut St., Kansas City MO 64106. (816)581-7500. **Website:** www.andrewsmcmeel.com. **Contact:** Christine Schillig, vice president/editorial director. Estab. 1973. Publishes hardcover and paperback originals. Andrews McMeel publishes general trade books, humor books, miniature gift books, calendars, and stationery products. **Publishes 300 titles/year. Pays royalty on retail price or net receipts. Pays advance.** Guidelines online.

NONFICTION Subjects include cooking, games, comics, puzzles. Submit proposal.

ANHINGA PRESS

P.O. Box 3665, Tallahassee FL 32315. Phone/**Fax:** (850)577-0745. **E-mail:** info@anhinga.org. **Website:** www.anhinga.org. **Contact:** Kristine Snodgrass, editor. Publishes hardcover and trade paperback originals. Publishes only full-length collections of poetry (60-80 pages). No individual poems or chapbooks. **Publishes 5 titles/year. Pays 10% royalty on retail price.** Accepts simultaneous submissions. Responds in 3 months. Guidelines online.

POETRY Not accepting any unsolicited submissions at this time. Enter Robert Dana-Anhinga Prize for Poetry.

ANKERWYCKE

American Bar Association, 321 N. Clark St., Chicago IL 60654. **Website:** www.ababooks.org. **Contact:** Tim Brandhorst, director of new product development. Estab. 1878. Publishes hardcover and trade paperback originals. "In 1215, the Magna Carta was signed underneath the ancient Ankerwycke Yew tree, starting the process which led to rule by constitutional law—in effect, giving rights and the law to the people. And today, the ABA's Ankerwycke line of books continues to bring the law to the people. With legal fiction, crime books, popular legal histories, public policy handbooks, and prescriptive guides to current legal and business issues, Ankerwycke is a contemporary and innovative line of books for everyone from a trusted and vested authority." **Publishes 30-40 titles/year. 1,000's of queries received/year. 25% of books from first-time authors. 50% from unagented writers.** Publishes ms 12-18 months after acceptance. Accepts simultaneous submissions. Responds in 1 month to queries and proposals; 3 months to mss. Book catalog and ms guidelines online.

NONFICTION Subjects include business, consumer legal. "Extremely high quality nonfiction with a legal aspect; business books specifically for service professionals; consumer legal on a wide range of topics—we're actively acquiring in all these areas." Query with cover letter; outline or TOC; and CV/bio including other credits. Include e-mail address for response.

FICTION "We're actively acquiring legal fiction with extreme verisimilitude." Query with cover letter; outline or TOC; and CV/bio including other credits. Include e-mail address for response.

ANNICK PRESS, LTD.

15 Patricia Ave., Toronto ON M2M 1H9, Canada. (416)221-4802. **Fax:** (416)221-8400. **Website:** www.annickpress.com. **Contact:** The Editors. Publishes picture books, juvenile and YA fiction and nonfiction; specializes in trade books. "Annick Press maintains a commitment to high quality books that entertain and challenge. Our publications share fantasy and stimulate imagination, while encouraging children to trust their judgment and abilities." *Does not accept unsolicited mss.* **Publishes 25 titles/year. 5,000 queries received/year. 3,000 mss received/year. 20% of books from first-time authors. 80-85% from unagented writers. Pays authors royalty of 5-12% based on retail price. Offers advances (average amount: $3,000). Pays illustrators royalty of 5% minimum.** Publishes book Publishes a book 2 years after acceptance. Book catalog and guidelines online.

NONFICTION Works with 20 illustrators/year. Illustrations only: Query with samples.

FICTION Publisher of children's books. Not accepting picture books at this time.

ANVIL PRESS

P.O. Box 3008 MPO, Vancouver BC V6B 3X5, Canada. (604)876-8710. **Fax:** (604)879-2667. **E-mail:** info@anvilpress.com. **Website:** www.anvilpress.com. Estab. 1988. Publishes trade paperback originals. "Anvil Press publishes contemporary adult fiction, poetry, and drama, giving voice to up-and-coming Canadian writers, exploring all literary genres, discovering, nurturing, and promoting new Canadian literary talent. Currently emphasizing urban/suburban themed fiction and poetry; de-emphasizing historical novels." Canadian authors only. No e-mail submissions. **Publishes 8-10 titles/year. 300 queries received/year. 80% of books from first-time authors. 70% from unagented writers. Pays advance. Average advance is $500-2,000, depending on the genre.** Publishes ms 8 months after acceptance. Accepts simultaneous submissions. Responds in 2 months to queries; 6 months to mss. Book catalog for 9×12 SAE with 2 first-class stamps. Guidelines online.

NONFICTION Query with 20-30 pages and SASE.

FICTION Subjects include experimental, literary, short story collections. Contemporary, modern literature; no formulaic or genre. Query with 20-30 pages and SASE.

POETRY "Get our catalog, look at our poetry. We do very little poetry-maybe 1-2 titles per year." Query with 8-12 poems and SASE.

TIPS "Audience is informed, educated, aware, with an opinion, culturally active (films, books, the performing arts). No U.S. authors. Research the appropriate publisher for your work."

APA BOOKS

American Psychological Association, 750 First St., NE, Washington DC 20002. (202)336- 5792. **E-mail:** booksubmissions@apa.org. **Website:** www.apa.org/books. Publishes hardcover and trade paperback originals. Book catalog online. Guidelines online.

IMPRINTS Magination Press (children's books).

NONFICTION Subjects include education, gay, lesbian, multicultural, psychology, science, social sciences, sociology, women's issues, women's studies. Submit cv and prospectus with TOC, intended audience, selling points, and outside competition.

TIPS "Our press features scholarly books on empirically supported topics for professionals and students in all areas of psychology."

APPALACHIAN MOUNTAIN CLUB BOOKS

5 Joy St., Boston MA 02108. (617)523-0636. **Fax:** (617)523-0722. **E-mail:** amcbooks@outdoors.org. **Website:** www.outdoors.org. Estab. 1876. Publishes hardcover and trade paperback originals. "AMC Books are written and published by the experts in the Northeast outdoors. Our mission is to publish au-

thoritative, accurate, and easy-to-use books and maps based on AMC's expertise in outdoor recreation, education, and conservation. We are committed to producing books and maps that appeal to novices and day visitors as well as outdoor enthusiasts in our core activity areas of hiking and paddling. By advancing the interest of the public in outdoor recreation and helping our readers to access backcountry trails and waterways, and by using our books to educate the public about safety, conservation, and stewardship, we support AMC's mission of promoting the protection, enjoyment, and wise use of the Northeast outdoors. We work with the best professional writers possible and draw upon the experience of our programs staff and chapter leaders from Maine to Washington, D.C." Accepts simultaneous submissions. Guidelines online.

NONFICTION Subjects include nature, environment, recreation, regional, Northeast outdoor recreation, literary nonfiction, guidebooks, Maps that are based on our direct work with land managers and our on-the-ground collection of data on trails, natural features, and points of interest. AMC Books also publishes narrative titles related to outdoor recreation, mountaineering, and adventure, often with a historical perspective. "Appalachian Mountain Club publishes hiking guides, paddling guides, nature, conservation, and mountain-subject guides for America's Northeast. We connect recreation to conservation and education." Query with proposal and the first 3 chapters of your ms.

TIPS "Our audience is outdoor recreationists, conservation-minded hikers and canoeists, family outdoor lovers, armchair enthusiasts. Visit our website for proposal submission guidelines and more information."

ARBORDALE PUBLISHING

612 Johnnie Dodds, Suite A2, Mt. Pleasant SC 29464. (843)971-6722. **Fax:** (843)216-3804. **E-mail:** katie@arbordalepublishing.com. **E-mail:** donna@arbordalepublishing.com. **Website:** www.arbordalepublishing.com. **Contact:** Donna German and Katie Hall, editors. Estab. 2004. Publishes hardcover, trade paperback, and electronic originals. "The picture books we publish are usually, but not always, fictional stories with nonfiction woven into the story that relate to science and math and retellings of traditional cultural folklore with an underlying science theme. All books should subtly convey an educational theme through a warm story that is fun to read and that will grab a child's attention. Each book has a 4-page '*For Creative Minds*' section to reinforce the educational component. This section will have a craft and/or game as well as 'fun facts' to be shared by the parent, teacher, or other adult. Authors do not need to supply this information. Mss. should be less than 1,500 words and meet all of the following 4 criteria: Fun to read—mostly fiction with nonfiction facts woven into the story; National or regional in scope; Must tie into early elementary school curriculum; must be marketable through a niche market such as a zoo, aquarium, or museum gift shop." **Publishes 20 titles/year. 1,000 mss received/year. 50% of books from first-time authors. 100% from unagented writers. Pays 6-8% royalty on wholesale price. Pays small advance.** Publishes ms 18 months after acceptance. May hold onto mss of interest for 1 year until acceptance. Accepts simultaneous submissions. Acknowledges receipt of ms submission within 1 month. Book catalog and guidelines online.

NONFICTION Subjects include science, math. "We are not looking for mss. about: pets (dogs or cats in particular); new babies; local or state-specific; magic; biographies; history-related; ABC books; poetry; series; young adult books or novels; holiday-related books. We do not consider mss. that have been previously published in any way, including e-books or self-published." Accepts electronic submissions only. Snail mail submissions are discarded without being opened. Reviews artwork/photos. Send 1-2 JPEGS.

FICTION Subjects include picture books. Picture books: animal, folktales, nature/environment, math-related. Word length—picture books: no more than 1,500. Accepts electronic submissions only. Snail mail submissions are discarded without being opened.

TIPS "Please make sure that you have looked at our website to read our complete submission guidelines and to see if we are looking for a particular subject. Manuscripts must meet all four of our stated criteria. We look for fairly realistic, bright and colorful art-no cartoons. We want the children excited about the books. We envision the books being used at home and in the classroom."

ARCADE PUBLISHING

Skyhorse Publishing, 307 W. 36th St., 11th Floor, New York NY 10018. (212)643-6816. **Fax:** (212)643-6819. **E-mail:** arcadesubmissions@skyhorsepublishing.com. **Website:** www.arcadepub.com. **Contact:** Acquisitions Editor. Estab. 1988. Publishes hardcover originals, trade paperback reprints. "Arcade prides itself on publishing top-notch literary nonfiction and fiction, with a significant proportion of foreign writers." **Publishes 35 titles/year. 5% of books from first-time authors. Pays royalty on retail price and 10 author's copies. Pays advance.** Publishes ms 18 months after acceptance. Responds in 2 months if interested. Book catalog and ms guidelines for #10 SASE.

NONFICTION Subjects include history, memoirs, nature, environment, travel, popular science, current events. Submit proposal with brief query, 1-2 page synopsis, chapter outline, market analysis, sample chapter, bio.

FICTION Subjects include literary, mainstream, contemporary, short story collections, translation. No romance, historical, science fiction. Submit proposal with brief query, 1-2 page synopsis, chapter outline, market analysis, sample chapter, bio.

ARCADIA PUBLISHING

420 Wando Park Blvd., Mt. Pleasant SC 29464. (843)853-2070. **Fax:** (843)853-0044. **E-mail:** publishingnortheast@arcadiapublishing.com; publishingsouth@arcadiapublishing.com; publishingwest@arcadiapublishing.com; publishingmidwest@arcadiapublishing.com; publishingmidatlantic@arcadiapublishing.com; publishingsouthwest@arcadiapublishing.com. **Website:** www.arcadiapublishing.com. Estab. 1993. Publishes trade paperback originals. "Arcadia publishes photographic vintage regional histories. We have more than 3,000 Images of America series in print. We have expanded our California program." **Publishes 600 titles/year. Pays 8% royalty on retail price.** Publishes ms 9 months after acceptance. Accepts simultaneous submissions. Book catalog online. Guidelines available free.

NONFICTION Subjects include history, local, regional. "Arcadia accepts submissions year-round. Our editors seek proposals on local history topics and are able to provide authors with detailed information about our publishing program as well as book proposal submission guidelines. Due to the great demand for titles on local and regional history, we are currently searching for authors to work with us on new photographic history projects. Please contact one of our regional publishing teams if you are interested in submitting a proposal." Specific proposal form to be completed.

TIPS "Writers should know that we only publish history titles. The majority of our books are on a city or region, and contain vintage images with limited text."

ARCHAIA

Imprint of Boom! Studios, 1680 N. Vine St., Hollywood CA 90028. **Website:** www.archaia.com. **Contact:** Mark Smylie, chief creative officer. Use online submission form.

FICTION Subjects include adventure, fantasy, horror, mystery, science fiction. Looking for graphic novel submissions that include finished art. "Archaia is a multi-award-winning graphic novel publisher with more than 75 renowned publishing brands, including such domestic and international hits as *Artesia, Mouse Guard*, and a line of Jim Henson graphic novels including *Fraggle Rock* and *The Dark Crystal*. Publishes creator-shared comic books and graphic novels in the adventure, fantasy, horror, pulp noir, and science fiction genres that contain idiosyncratic and atypical writing and art. *Archaia does not generally hire freelancers or arrange for freelance work, so submissions should only be for completed book and series proposals.*"

ARCH STREET PRESS

1429 S. 9th St., Philadelphia PA 19147. (877)732-ARCH. **E-mail:** contact@archstreetpress.org. **Website:** www.archstreetpress.org. **Contact:** Managing Editor. Estab. 2010. Publishes hardcover, trade paperback, mass market paperback, and electronic originals. **Publishes 4 titles/year. 100 queries received/year. 5 mss received/year. 30% of books from first-time authors. 50% from unagented writers. Pays 6-20% royalty on retail price.** Publishes ms 1 year after acceptance. Accepts simultaneous submissions. Responds in 1-2 months. Book catalog and guidelines online.

NONFICTION Subjects include art, business, communications, community, contemporary culture, creative nonfiction, economics, education, environment, finance, government, health, history, humanities, labor, language, law, literary criticism, literature, memoirs, multicultural, music, nature, philosophy, social sciences, sociology, spirituality, translation, womens studies, world affairs, leadership. Query with SASE. Submit proposal package including outline and 3 sample chapters. Review artwork. Writers should send photocopies.

FICTION Query with SASE. Submit proposal package, including outline and 3 sample chapters.

ARC PUBLICATIONS

Nanholme Mill, Shaw Wood Rd., Todmorden, Lancashire OL14 6DA, England. **E-mail:** editorarcuk@btinternet.com. **E-mail:** international-editor@arcpublications.co.uk. **Website:** www.arcpublications.co.uk. **Contact:** John W. Clarke, domestic editor; James Byrne, international editor (outside Ireland/England). Estab. 1969. Responds in 6 weeks.

POETRY Publishes "contemporary poetry from new and established writers from the UK and abroad, specializing in the work of world poets writing in English, and the work of overseas poets in translation." Send 16-24 pages of poetry and short cover letter.

A-R EDITIONS, INC.

8551 Research Way, Suite 180, Middleton WI 53562. (608)203-2565. **E-mail:** pamela.whitcomb@areditions.com. **Website:** www.areditions.com. **Contact:** Pamela Whitcomb, managing editor (Recent Researches Series). Estab. 1962. "A-R Editions publishes modern critical editions of music based on current musicological research. Each edition is devoted to works by a single composer or to a single genre of composition. The contents are chosen for their potential interest to scholars and performers, then prepared for publication according to the standards that govern the making of all reliable, historical editions." **Publishes 30 titles/year. 40 queries received/year. 30 mss received/year. 75% of books from first-time authors. 100% from unagented writers. Pays royalty or honoraria.** Responds in 1 month to queries; 3 months to proposals; 6 months to mss. Book catalog online. Guidelines online.

NONFICTION Subjects include computers, electronics, music, dance, software, historical music editions. Computer Music and Digital Audio Series titles deal with issues tied to digital and electronic media, and include both textbooks and handbooks in this area. Query with SASE. Submit outline. "All material submitted in support of a proposal becomes the property of A-R Editions. Please send photocopies of all important documents (retain your originals). We suggest that you send your proposal either with delivery confirmation or by a service that offers package tracking to avoid misdirected packages."

ARROW PUBLICATIONS, LLC

20411 Sawgrass Dr., Montgomery Village MD 20886. (301)299-9422. **Fax:** (240)632-8477. **E-mail:** arrow_info@arrowpub.com. **Website:** www.arrowpub.com. **Contact:** Tom King, managing editor; Maryan Gibson, acquisition editor. Estab. 1987. **Publishes 50 e-book titles. Paperback version launched in 2009 with 12 English and 12 Spanish titles/year. titles/year. 150 queries received/year. 100 mss received/year. 80% of books from first-time authors. 100% from unagented writers. Makes outright purchase of accepted completed scripts.** Publishes ms 4-6 months after acceptance. Responds in 2 month to queries; 1 month to mss sent upon request. Guidelines online.

No graphic novels until further notice.

FICTION "We are looking for outlines of stories heavy on romance with elements of adventure/intrigue/mystery. We will consider other romance genres such as fantasy, western, inspirational, and historical as long as the romance element is strong." Query with outline first with SASE. Consult submission guidelines online before submitting.

TIPS "Our audience is primarily women 18 and older. Send query with outline only."

ARSENAL PULP PRESS

#202-211 East Georgia St., Vancouver BC V6A 1Z6, Canada. (604)687-4233. **Fax:** (604)687-4283. **E-mail:** info@arsenalpulp.com. **Website:** www.arsenalpulp.com. **Contact:** Editorial Board. Estab. 1980. Publishes trade paperback originals, and trade paperback reprints. "We are interested in literature that traverses uncharted territories, publishing books that challenge and stimulate and ask probing questions about the world around us." **Publishes 14-20 titles/year. 500 queries received/year. 300 mss received/year. 30% of books from first-time authors. 100% from unagented writers.** Publishes ms 1 year after acceptance. Accepts simultaneous submissions. Responds in 2-4 months. Book catalog for 9×12 SAE with IRCs or online. Guidelines online.

NONFICTION Subjects include art, architecture, cooking, foods, nutrition, creative nonfiction, ethnic, Canadian, cultural studies, aboriginal issues, gay, health, lesbian, history, cultural, language, literature, multicultural, political/sociological studies, regional studies and guides, in particular for British Columbia, sex, sociology, travel, women's issues, women's studies, youth culture, film, visual art. Rarely publishes non-Canadian authors. No poetry at this time. "We do not publish children's books." Each submission must include: "a synopsis of the work, a chapter by chapter outline for nonfiction, writing credentials, a 50-page excerpt from the ms (*do not send more, it will be a waste of postage; if we like what we see, we'll ask for the rest of the manuscript*), and a marketing analysis. If our editorial board is interested, you will be asked to send the entire ms. We do not accept discs or submissions by fax or e-mail, and we do not discuss concepts over the phone." Reviews artwork/photos.

FICTION Subjects include ethnic, general, feminist, gay, lesbian, literary, multicultural, short story collections. No children's books or genre fiction, i.e., westerns, romance, horror, mystery, etc. Submit proposal package, outline, clips, 2-3 sample chapters.

ARTE PUBLICO PRESS

University of Houston, 4902 Gulf Fwy, Bldg 19, Rm 100, Houston TX 77204-2004. **Fax:** (713)743-2847. **E-mail:** submapp@uh.edu. **Website:** artepublicopress.com. **Contact:** Nicolas Kanellos, editor. Estab. 1979. Publishes hardcover originals, trade paperback originals and reprints. Arte Publico Press is the oldest and largest publisher of Hispanic literature for children and adults in the United States. "We are a showcase for Hispanic literary creativity, arts and culture. Our endeavor is to provide a national forum for U.S.-Hispanic literature." **Publishes 25-30 titles/year. 1,000 queries received/year. 2,000 mss received/year. 50% of books from first-time authors. 80% from unagented writers. Pays 10% royalty on wholesale price. Provides 20 author's copies; 40% discount on subsequent copies. Pays $1,000-3,000 advance.** Publishes ms 2 years after acceptance. Accepts simultaneous submissions. Responds in 1 month to queries and proposals; 4 months to mss. Book catalog available free. Guidelines online.

NONFICTION Subjects include ethnic, language, literature, regional, translation, women's issues, women's studies. Hispanic civil rights issues for new series: The Hispanic Civil Rights Series. Submissions made through online submission form.

FICTION Subjects include contemporary, ethnic, literary, mainstream. "Written by U.S.-Hispanics." Submissions made through online submission form.

POETRY Submissions made through online submission form.

TIPS "Include cover letter in which you 'sell' your book—why should we publish the book, who will want to read it, why does it matter, etc. Use our ms submission online form. Format files accepted are: Word, plain/text, rich/text files. Other formats will not be accepted. Manuscript files cannot be larger than 5MB. Once editors review your ms, you will receive an e-mail with the decision. Revision process could take up to 4 months."

ASA, AVIATION SUPPLIES & ACADEMICS

7005 132 Place SE, Newcastle WA 98059. (425)235-1500. **E-mail:** feedback@asa2fly.com. **Website:** www.asa2fly.com. "ASA is an industry leader in the development and sales of aviation supplies, publications, and software for pilots, flight instructors, flight engineers and aviation technicians. All ASA products are developed by a team of researchers, authors and editors." Book catalog available free.

NONFICTION Subjects include education. "We are primarily an aviation publisher. Educational books in this area are our specialty; other aviation books will be considered." All subjects must be related to aviation education and training. Query with outline. Send photocopies or MS Word files.

TIPS "Two of our specialty series include ASA's *Focus Series*, and ASA *Aviator's Library*. Books in our *Focus Series* concentrate on single-subject areas of aviation knowledge, curriculum and practice. The *Aviator's Library* is comprised of titles of known and/or classic aviation authors or established instructor/authors in the industry, and other aviation specialty titles."

ASABI PUBLISHING

Asabi Publishing, (813)671-8827. **E-mail:** submissions@asabipublishing.com. **Website:** www.asabipublishing.com. **Contact:** Tressa Sanders, publisher. Estab. 2004. Publishes hardcover, mass market and trade paperback originals. **Publishes 24 titles/year. Accepts professional queries only. 30% of books from first-time authors. 10% from unagented writers. Pays 10% royalty on wholesale or list price. Pays up to $500 advance.** Publishes ms 1 year after acceptance. Responds in 1 month to queries and proposals, 2-6 months to mss. Book catalog online. Guidelines online.

IMPRINTS Solomon Publishing Group-Sweden.

NONFICTION Subjects include agriculture, environment, ethnic, gay, health, history, house and home, lesbian, medicine, psychology, science, sex, travel, young adult, skilled trades. Wants how-to skilled trades, organic agriculture, how-to renewable energy, alternative homebuilding, natural medicine, psychology, sexual instruction, African history, living abroad, non-religious homeschooling, lesbian romance. Submit professional query letter only. "We do not publish poetry or titles containing religious or spiritual content of any kind." Reviews artwork/photos. Writers should send photocopies.

FICTION Subjects include confession, erotica, lesbian, romance. Submit professional query letter.

ASCE PRESS

American Society of Civil Engineers, 1801 Alexander Bell Dr., Reston VA 20191. (703)295-6275. **Fax:** (703)295-6278. **Website:** www.asce.org/pubs. Estab. 1989. "ASCE Press publishes technical volumes that are useful to practicing civil engineers and civil engineering students, as well as allied professionals. We publish books by individual authors and editors to advance the civil engineering profession. Currently emphasizing geotechnical, structural engineering, sustainable engineering and engineering history. De-emphasizing highly specialized areas with narrow scope." **Publishes 10-15 titles/year. 20% of books from first-time authors. 100% from unagented writers.** Guidelines online.

NONFICTION "We are looking for topics that are useful and instructive to the engineering practitioner." Query with proposal, sample chapters, CV, TOC, and target audience.

TIPS "As a traditional publisher of scientific and technical materials, ASCE Press applies rigorous standards to the expertise, scholarship, readability and attractiveness of its books."

ASHLAND POETRY PRESS

401 College Ave., Ashland OH 44805. (419)289-5098. **Fax:** (419)289-5255. **E-mail:** app@ashland.edu. **Website:** www.ashlandpoetrypress.com. **Contact:** Wendy Hall, managing editor. Estab. 1969. Publishes trade paperback originals. **Publishes 2-3 titles/year. 400 mss received/year in Snyder Prize. 50% of books from first-time authors. 100% from unagented writers. Makes outright purchase of $500-1,000.** Publishes ms 10 months after acceptance. Accepts simultaneous submissions. Responds in 1 month to queries; 6 months to mss. Book catalog online. Guidelines online.

POETRY "We accept unsolicited manuscripts through the Snyder Prize competition each spring-the deadline is April 30. Judges are mindful of dedication to craftsmanship and thematic integrity."

TIPS "We rarely publish a title submitted off the transom outside of our Snyder Prize competition."

ASM PRESS

Book division for the American Society for Microbiology, 1752 N St., NW, Washington DC 20036. (202)737-3600. **Fax:** (202)942-9342. **E-mail:** lwilliams@asmusa.org. **Website:** www.asmscience.org. **Contact:** Lindsay Williams, editorial and rights coordinator. Estab. 1899. Publishes hardcover, trade paperback and electronic originals. **Publishes 30 titles/year. 40% of books from first-time authors. 95% from unagented writers. Pays 5-15% royalty on wholesale price. Pays $1,000-10,000 advance.** Publishes ms 6-9 months after acceptance. Accepts simultaneous submissions. Responds in 2 months. Book catalog online. Guidelines online.

NONFICTION Subjects include agriculture, animals, education, health, medicine, history, horticulture, nature, environment, science, microbiology and related sciences. "Must have bona fide academic credentials in which they are writing." Query with SASE or by e-mail. Submit proposal package, outline, prospectus. Reviews artwork/photos. Send photocopies.

TIPS "Credentials are most important."

ASSOCIATION FOR SUPERVISION AND CURRICULUM DEVELOPMENT

1703 N. Beauregard St., Alexandria VA 22311-1714. (703)578-9600. **Fax:** (703)575-5400. **E-mail:** acquisitions@ascd.org. **Website:** www.ascd.org. **Contact:** Genny Ostertag, acquisitions editor; Allison Scott, acquisitions editor. Estab. 1943. Publishes trade paperback originals. ASCD publishes high-quality professional books for educators. **Publishes 24-30 titles/year. 100 queries received/year. 100 mss received/year. 50% of books from first-time authors. 95% from unagented writers. Pays negotiable royalty on actual monies received.** Publishes ms 1 year after acceptance. Accepts simultaneous submissions. Responds in 2-3 months to proposals. Book catalog and ms guidelines online.

NONFICTION Subjects include education, for professional educators. Submit full proposal, 2 sample chapters. Reviews artwork/photos. Send photocopies.

ASTRAGAL PRESS

Finney Company, 5995 149th St. W., Suite 105, Apple Valley MN 55124. (866)543-3045. **E-mail:** info@finneyco.com. **Website:** www.astragalpress.com. Estab. 1983. Publishes trade paperback originals and reprints. "Our primary audience includes those interested in antique tool collecting, metalworking, carriage building, early sciences and early trades, and railroading." Accepts simultaneous submissions. Responds in 3 months. Book catalog and ms guidelines free.

NONFICTION Wants books on early tools, trades and technology, and railroads. Query with sample chapters, TOC, book overview, illustration descriptions.

TIPS "We sell to niche markets. We are happy to work with knowledgeable amateur authors in developing titles."

Ⓐ⊘ ATHENEUM BOOKS FOR YOUNG READERS

Simon & Schuster, 1230 Avenue of the Americas, New York NY 10020. **Website:** kids.simonandschuster.com. Estab. 1961. Publishes hardcover originals. Accepts simultaneous submissions. Guidelines for #10 SASE.

NONFICTION Subjects include Americana, animals, art, architecture, business, economics, government, politics, health, medicine, history, music, dance, nature, environment, photography, psychology, recreation, religion, science, sociology, sports, travel. Publishes hardcover originals, picture books for young kids, nonfiction for ages 8-12 and novels for middle-grade and young adults. 100% require freelance illustration. Agented submissions only.

FICTION Subjects include adventure, ethnic, experimental, fantasy, gothic, historical, horror, humor, mainstream, contemporary, mystery, science fiction, sports, suspense, western, Animal. All in juvenile versions. "We have few specific needs except for books that are fresh, interesting and well written. Fad topics are dangerous, as are works you haven't polished to the best of your ability. We also don't need safety pamphlets, ABC books, coloring books and board books. In writing picture book texts, avoid the coy and 'cutesy,' such as stories about characters with alliterative names." Agented submissions only. No paperback romance-type fiction.

TIPS "Study our titles."

A.T. PUBLISHING

23 Lily Lake Rd., Highland NY 12528. (845)691-2021. **E-mail:** tjp2@optonline.net. **Contact:** Anthony Prizzia, publisher (education); John Prizzia, publisher. Estab. 2001. Publishes trade paperback originals. **Publishes 1-3 titles/year. 5-10 queries received/year. 100% of books from first-time authors. 100% from unagented writers. Pays 15-25% royalty on retail price. Makes outright purchase of $500-2,500. Pays $500-1,000 advance.** Accepts simultaneous submissions. Responds in 1 month to queries; 2 months to proposals; 4 months to mss.

NONFICTION Subjects include cooking, foods, nutrition, education, recreation, science, sports. Query with SASE. Submit complete ms. Reviews artwork/photos. Send photocopies.

TIPS "Audience is people interested in a variety of topics, general. Submit typed manuscript for consideration, including a SASE for return of ms."

AUTUMN HOUSE PRESS

87½ Westwood St., Pittsburgh PA 15211. (412)381-4261. **E-mail:** info@autumnhouse.org. **Website:** www.autumnhouse.org. **Contact:** Michael Simms, editor-in-chief (fiction). Fiction Editor: Sharon Dilworth. Estab. 1998. Publishes hardcover, trade paperback, and electronic originals. Format: acid-free paper; offset printing; perfect and casebound (cloth) bound; sometimes contains illustrations. Average print order: 1,000. Debut novel print order: 1,000. "We are a non-profit literary press specializing in high-quality poetry, fiction, and nonfiction. Our editions are beautifully designed and printed, and they are distributed nationally. Approximately one-third of our sales are to college literature and creative writing classes." Member CLMP and Academy of American Poets. "We distribute our own titles. We do extensive national promotion through ads, web-marketing, reading tours, bookfairs and conferences. We are open to all genres. The quality of writing concerns us, not the genre." You can also learn about our annual Fiction Prize, Poetry Prize, Nonfiction Prize, and Chapbook Award competitions, as well as our online journal, *Coal Hill Review*. (Please note that Autumn House accepts unsolicited mss *only* through these competitions.) **Publishes 8 titles/year. Receives 1,000 mss/year. 10% of books from first-time authors. 100% from unagented writers. Pays 7% royalty on wholesale price. Pays $0-2,500 advance.** Publishes book Publishes 9 months after acceptance. Accepts simultaneous submissions. Responds in 1-3 days on queries and proposals; 3 months on mss. Catalog free on request. Guidelines online.

NONFICTION Subjects include memoirs. Enter the nonfiction contest.

FICTION Subjects include literary. Holds competition/award for short stories, novels, story collections, memoirs, nonfiction. *We ask that all submissions from authors new to Autumn House come through one of our annual contests.* See website for official guidelines. Responds to queries in 2 days. Accepts mss only through contest. Never critiques/comments on rejected mss. "Submit only through our annual contest. The competition is tough, so submit only your best work!"

POETRY *"We ask that all submissions from authors new to Autumn House come through one of our annual contests."* All finalists will be considered for publication. Submit only through our annual contest. See guidelines online.

TIPS "The competition to publish with Autumn House is very tough. Submit only your best work."

AVALON TRAVEL PUBLISHING

Avalon Publishing Group, 1700 4th St., Berkeley CA 94710. (510)595-3664. **Fax:** (510)595-4228. **E-mail:** avalon.acquisitions@perseusbooks.com. **Website:** www.avalontravelbooks.com. Estab. 1973. Publishes trade paperback originals. "Avalon travel guides feature practicality and spirit, offering a traveler-to-traveler perspective perfect for planning an afternoon hike, around-the-world journey, or anything in between. ATP publishes 7 major series. Each one has a different emphasis and a different geographic coverage. We have expanded our coverage, with a focus on European and Asian destinations. Our main areas of interest are North America, Central America, South America, the Caribbean, and the Pacific. We are seeking only a few titles in each of our major series. Check online guidelines for our current needs. Follow guidelines closely." **Publishes 100 titles/year. 5,000 queries received/year. 25% of books from first-time authors. 95% from unagented writers. Pays up to $17,000 advance.** Publishes ms an average of 9 months after acceptance. Accepts simultaneous submissions. Responds in 4 months. Guidelines online.

NONFICTION Subjects include regional, travel. "We are not interested in fiction, children's books, and travelogues/travel diaries." Submit cover letter, resume, and up to 5 relevant clips.

AVON ROMANCE

Harper Collins Publishers, 10 E. 53 St., New York NY 10022. **E-mail:** info@avonromance.com. **Website:** www.avonromance.com. Estab. 1941. Publishes paperback and digital originals and reprints. "Avon has been publishing award-winning books since 1941. It is recognized for having pioneered the historical romance category and continues to bring the best of commercial literature to the broadest possible audience." **Publishes 400 titles/year.**

FICTION Subjects include historical, literary, mystery, romance, science fiction, young adult. Submit a query and ms via the online submission form at www.avonromance.com/impulse.

⊘ AZRO PRESS

PMB 342, 1704 Llano St. B, Santa Fe NM 87505. (505)989-3272. **Fax:** (505)989-3832. **E-mail:** books@azropress.com. **Website:** www.azropress.com. Estab. 1997. **Pays authors royalty of 5-10% based on wholesale price. Pays illustrators by the project ($2,000) or royalty of 5%.** Publishes ms 1-2 years after acceptance. Accepts simultaneous submissions. Responds in 3-4 months. Catalog online.

NONFICTION Picture books: animal, geography, history. Young readers: geography, history.

FICTION Picture books: animal, history, humor, nature/environment. Young readers: adventure, animal, hi-lo, history, humor. Average word length: picture books—1,200; young readers—2,000-2,500.

TIPS "We are not currently accepting new manuscripts. Please see our website for acceptance date."

BACKBEAT BOOKS

Hal Leonard Publishing Group, 33 Plymouth St., Suite 302, Montclair NJ 07042. (800)637-2852. **E-mail:** jcerullo@halleonard.com. **Website:** www.backbeatbooks.com. **Contact:** John Cerullo, group publisher. Publishes hardcover and trade paperback originals; trade paperback reprints. **Publishes 24 titles/year.**

NONFICTION Subjects include music (rock & roll), pop culture. Query with TOC, sample chapter, sample illustrations.

BACKCOUNTRY GUIDES

Imprint of The Countryman Press, P. O. Box 748, Woodstock VT 05091. (802)457-4826. **Fax:** (802)457-1678. **E-mail:** countrymanpress@wwnorton.com. **Website:** www.countrymanpress.com. **Contact:** Submissions. Estab. 1973. Publishes trade paperback originals. "We publish books of the highest quality that take the reader where they want to go. Our books are promoted and sold to bookstores and to specialty markets throughout the United States, Canada, and other parts of the world." **Publishes 70 titles/year.** Accepts simultaneous submissions. Responds in

3 months to proposals. Book catalog available free. Guidelines online.

NONFICTION Subjects include nature, environment, recreation, bicycling, hiking, canoeing, kayaking, fly fishing, walking, guidebooks, and series, sports, travel, food, gardening, country living, New England history. Query with SASE. Submit proposal package, outline, 2-3 sample chapters, market analysis. Reviews artwork/photos. Send transparencies.

TIPS "Look at our existing series of guidebooks to see how your proposal fits in."

THE BACKWATERS PRESS

3502 N. 52nd St., Omaha NE 68104. **Website:** www.thebackwaterspress.org. **Contact:** James Cihlar, editor.

POETRY Only considers submissions to Backwaters Prize. More details on website.

BAEN BOOKS

P.O. Box 1188, Wake Forest NC 27588. (919)570-1640. **E-mail:** info@baen.com. **Website:** www.baen.com. Estab. 1983. "We publish only science fiction and fantasy. Writers familiar with what we have published in the past will know what sort of material we are most likely to publish in the future: powerful plots with solid scientific and philosophical underpinnings are the sine qua non for consideration for science fiction submissions. As for fantasy, any magical system must be both rigorously coherent and integral to the plot, and overall the work must at least strive for originality." Responds to mss within 12-18 months.

FICTION "Style: Simple is generally better; in our opinion good style, like good breeding, never calls attention to itself. Length: 100,000-130,000 words Generally we are uncomfortable with manuscripts under 100,000 words, but if your novel is really wonderful send it along regardless of length." "Query letters are not necessary. We prefer to see complete manuscripts accompanied by a synopsis. We prefer not to see simultaneous submissions. Electronic submissions are strongly preferred. *We no longer accept submissions by e-mail.* Send ms by using the submission form at: http://ftp.baen.com/Slush/submit.aspx. No disks unless requested. Attach ms as a Rich Text Format (.rtf) file. Any other format will not be considered."

BAILIWICK PRESS

309 East Mulberry St., Fort Collins CO 80524. (970)672-4878. **Fax:** (970)672-4731. **E-mail:** info@bailiwickpress.com. **E-mail:** aldozelnick@gmail.com. **Website:** www.bailiwickpress.com. "We're a micro-press that produces books and other products that inspire and tell great stories. Our motto is 'books with something to say.' We are now considering submissions, agented and unagented, for children's and young adult fiction. We're looking for smart, funny, and layered writing that kids will clamor for. Authors who already have a following have a leg up. We are only looking for humorous children's fiction. Please do not submit work for adults. Illustrated fiction is desired but not required. (Illustrators are also invited to send samples.) Make us laugh out loud, ooh and aah, and cry, 'Eureka!'" Accepts simultaneous submissions. Responds in 6 months.

FICTION "Please read the Aldo Zelnick series to determine if we might be on the same page, then fill out our submission form. Please do not send submissions via snail mail or phone calls. You must complete the online submission form to be considered. If, after completing and submitting the form, you also need to send us an e-mail attachment (such as sample illustrations or excerpts of graphics), you may e-mail them to aldozelnick@gmail.com."

Ⓐ⊘ BAKER ACADEMIC

Division of Baker Publishing Group, 6030 E. Fulton Rd., Ada MI 49301. (616)676-9185. **E-mail:** submissions@bakeracademic.com. **Website:** bakerpublishinggroup.com/bakeracademic. Estab. 1939. Publishes hardcover and trade paperback originals. "Baker Academic publishes religious academic and professional books for students and church leaders. Does not accept unsolicited queries. We will consider unsolicited work only through one of the following avenues. Materials sent to our editorial staff through a professional literary agent will be considered. In addition, our staff attends various writers' conferences at which prospective authors can develop relationships with those in the publishing industry." **Publishes 50 titles/year. 10% of books from first-time authors. 85% from unagented writers. Pays advance.** Publishes ms 1 year after acceptance.

NONFICTION Subjects include anthropology, archeology, education, psychology, religion, women's issues, women's studies, Biblical studies, Christian doctrine, books for pastors and church leaders, contemporary issues. Agented submissions only.

BAKER BOOKS

Division of Baker Publishing Group, 6030 East Fulton Rd., Ada MI 49301. (616)676-9185. **Website:** bakerpublishinggroup.com/bakerbooks. Estab. 1939. Publishes in hardcover and trade paperback originals, and trade paperback reprints. "We will consider unsolicited work only through one of the following avenues. Materials sent through a literary agent will be considered. In addition, our staff attends various writers' conferences at which prospective authors can develop relationships with those in the publishing industry." Book catalog for 9½×12½ envelope and 3 first-class stamps. Guidelines online.

NONFICTION Subjects include childe guidance, psychology, religion, women's issues, women's studies, Christian doctrines.

TIPS "We are not interested in historical fiction, romances, science fiction, biblical narratives or spiritual warfare novels. Do not call to 'pass by' your idea."

BAKER PUBLISHING GROUP

6030 E. Fulton Rd., Ada MI 49301. (616)676-9185. **Fax:** (616)676-2315. **Website:** www.bakerpublishinggroup.com.

IMPRINTS Baker Academic; Baker Books; Bethany House; Brazos Press; Chosen; Fleming H. Revell.

Does not accept unsolicited queries.

BALLANTINE BOOKS

Imprint of Random House, Inc., 1745 Broadway, 18th Floor, New York NY 10019. (212)782-9000. **Website:** www.randomhouse.com. Estab. 1952. Publishes hardcover, trade paperback, mass market paperback originals. Ballantine Books publishes a wide variety of nonfiction and fiction. Guidelines online.

NONFICTION Subjects include animals, child guidance, community, cooking, foods, nutrition, creative nonfiction, education, gay, lesbian, health, medicine, history, language, literature, memoirs, military, war, recreation, religion, sex, spirituality, travel, crime. Agented submissions only. Reviews artwork/photos. Send photocopies.

FICTION Subjects include confession, ethnic, fantasy, feminist, gay, lesbian, historical, humor, literary, mainstream, contemporary, womens, military, war, multicultural, mystery, romance, short story collections, spiritual, suspense, translation, general fiction. Agented submissions only.

JONATHAN BALL PUBLISHERS

P.O. Box 6836, Roggebaai 8012, South Africa. (27)(11)622-2900. **Fax:** (27)(11)601-8183. **E-mail:** shamiela.steyn@jonathanball.co.za. **Website:** www.jonathanball.co.za. **Contact:** Shamiela Steyn. Publishes books about South Africa which enlighten and entertain. Guidelines online.

NONFICTION Subjects include cooking, foods, nutrition, history, military, war, nature, environment, sports, travel, politics.

BALL PUBLISHING

P.O. Box 1660, West Chicago IL 60186. (630)231-3675. **Fax:** (630)231-5254. **E-mail:** cbeytes@ballpublishing.com. **Website:** www.ballpublishing.com. **Contact:** Chris Beytes. Publishes hardcover and trade paperback originals. "We publish for the book trade and the horticulture trade. Books on both home gardening/landscaping and commercial production are considered." **Publishes 4-6 titles/year.** Accepts simultaneous submissions. Book catalog for 8 ½×11 envelope and 3 first-class stamps.

NONFICTION Subjects include agriculture, gardening, floriculture. Query with SASE. Submit proposal package, outline, 2 sample chapters. Reviews artwork/photos. Send photocopies.

TIPS "We are expanding our book line to home gardeners, while still publishing for green industry professionals. Gardening books should be well thought out and unique in the market. Actively looking for photo books on specific genera and families of flowers and trees."

BALZER & BRAY

HarperCollins Children's Books, 10 E. 53rd St., New York NY 10022. **Website:** www.harpercollinschildrens.com. Estab. 2008. "We publish bold, creative, groundbreaking picture books and novels that appeal directly to kids in a fresh way." **Publishes 10 titles/year. Offers advances. Pays illustrators by the project.** Publishes ms 18 months after acceptance.

NONFICTION Subjects include animals, cooking, dance, environment, history, multicultural, music, nature, science, social sciences, sports. "We will publish very few nonfiction titles, maybe 1-2 per year." Agented submissions only.

FICTION Picture Books, Young Readers: adventure, animal, anthology, concept, contemporary, fantasy, history, humor, multicultural, nature/environment, poetry, science fiction, special needs, sports, suspense.

Middle readers, young adults/teens: adventure, animal, anthology, contemporary, fantasy, history, humor, multicultural, nature/environment, poetry, science fiction, special needs, sports, suspense. Agented submissions only.

Ⓐ BANCROFT PRESS

P.O. Box 65360, Baltimore MD 21209-9945. (410)358-0658. **Fax:** (410)764-1967. **E-mail:** bruceb@bancroftpress.com. **Website:** www.bancroftpress.com. **Contact:** Bruce Bortz, editor/publisher (health, investments, politics, history, humor, literary novels, mystery/thrillers, chick lit, young adult). Publishes hardcover and trade paperback originals. "Bancroft Press is a general trade publisher. We publish young adult fiction and adult fiction, as well as occasional nonfiction. Our only mandate is 'books that enlighten.'" **Publishes 4-6 titles/year. Pays 6-8% royalty. Pays various royalties on retail price. Pays $750 advance.** Publishes ms up to 3 years after acceptance. Accepts simultaneous submissions. Responds in 6-12 months. Guidelines online.

NONFICTION Subjects include business, economics, government, politics, health, medicine, money, finance, regional, sports, women's issues, women's studies, popular culture. "We advise writers to visit the website." All quality books on any subject of interest to the publisher. Submit proposal package, outline, 5 sample chapters, competition/market survey.

FICTION Subjects include ethnic, general, feminist, gay, lesbian, historical, humor, literary, mainstream, contemporary, military, war, mystery, amateur sleuth, cozy, police procedural, private eye/hardboiled, regional, science fiction, hard science fiction/technological, soft/sociological, translation, frontier sage, traditional, young adult, historical, problem novels, series, thrillers. "Our current focuses are young adult fiction, women's fiction, and literary fiction." Submit complete ms.

TIPS "We advise writers to visit our website and to be familiar with our previous work. Patience is the number one attribute contributors must have. It takes us a very long time to get through submitted material, because we are such a small company. Also, we only publish 4-6 books per year, so it may take a long time for your optioned book to be published. We like to be able to market our books to be used in schools and in libraries. We prefer fiction that bucks trends and moves in a new direction. We are especially interested in mysteries and humor (especially humorous mysteries)."

Ⓐ⊘ BANTAM BOOKS

Imprint of Random House, Inc., 1745 Broadway, New York NY 10019. (212)782-9000. **Website:** www.bantam-dell.atrandom.com. *Not seeking mss at this time.*

Ⓐ BANTAM DELL PUBLISHING GROUP

1745 Broadway, New York NY 10019. **E-mail:** bdpublicity@randomhouse.com. **Website:** www.bantamdell.com. Estab. 1945. Agented submissions only.

BARBARIAN BOOKS

P.O. Box 170881, Boise ID 83716. **E-mail:** submissions@barbarianbooks.com. **Website:** www.barbarianbooks.com. **Contact:** Conda Douglas, e-talent scout; Kathy McIntosh, e-talent scout. Estab. 2011. Publishes electronic originals. Barbarian Books believes that quality ebooks should be plentiful and affordable. Offers great reads for great readers. By only publishing for digital devices, Barbarian Books believes it can bring more well written stories to more people, faster than ever before. **Publishes 4-5 titles/year. Receives 40 queries and 100 mss per year. 80% of books from first-time authors. 98% from unagented writers. Pays authors 70% royalties on retail price.** Publishes book Publishes 12 months after acceptance. Accepts simultaneous submissions. Responds in 2-6 months on mss. Catalog available online. Ms guidelines available online.

FICTION Subjects include adventure, contemporary, experimental, fantasy, historical, horror, humor, mainstream, mystery, occult, romance, science fiction, suspense, western, cross genre. "Strong plots and compelling characters are more important than easily classified genre. A Barbarian Books title is an excellent and often refreshingly different choice for a reader of crime, fantasy, romance, science fiction, westerns, and cross genre. Our motto is: Great reads for great readers." Submit completed ms. Looking for submissions of entire, completed novel-length mss, around 60,000 words.

⊘ BARBOUR PUBLISHING, INC.

1810 Barbour Dr., P.O. Box 719, Urichsville OH 44683. **E-mail:** editors@barbourbooks.com; aschrock@barbourbooks.com; fictionsubmit@barbourbooks.com. **Website:** www.barbourbooks.com. Estab. 1981. "Barbour Books publishes inspirational/devotional material that is nondenominational and evangelical in nature. We're a Christian evangelical publisher." Specializes in short, easy-to-read Christian bargain books. "Faithfulness to the Bible and Jesus Christ are the bedrock values behind every book Barbour's staff produces."

BARRICADE BOOKS, INC.

185 Bridge Plaza N., Suite 309, Fort Lee NJ 07024. (201)944-7600. **Fax:** (201)917-4951. **Website:** www.barricadebooks.com. **Contact:** Carole Stuart, publisher. Estab. 1991. Publishes hardcover and trade paperback originals, trade paperback reprints. "Barricade Books publishes nonfiction, mostly of the controversial type, and books we can promote with authors who can talk about their topics on radio and television and to the press." **Publishes 12 titles/year. 200 queries received/year. 100 mss received/year. 80% of books from first-time authors. 50% from unagented writers. Pays 10-12% royalty on retail price for hardcover. Pays advance.** Publishes ms 18 months after acceptance. Responds in 1 month to queries.

NONFICTION Subjects include business, economics, ethnic, gay, lesbian, government, politics, health, medicine, history, nature, environment, psychology, sociology, crime. "We look for quality nonfiction mss—preferably with a controversial lean." Query with SASE. Submit outline, 1-2 sample chapters. Material will not be returned or responded to without SASE. "We do not accept proposals on disk or via e-mail." Reviews artwork/photos. Send photocopies.

TIPS "Do your homework. Visit bookshops to find publishers who are doing the kinds of books you want to write. Always submit to a person—not just 'Editor.'"

BASIC BOOKS

Perseus Books, 250 W. 57th St., Suite 1500, New York NY 10107. **E-mail:** basic.books@perseusbooks.com. **Website:** www.basicbooks.com. **Contact:** Editor. Estab. 1952. Publishes hardcover and trade paperback originals and reprints. Accepts simultaneous submissions. Responds in at least 3 months to queries. Book catalog available free. Guidelines online.

NONFICTION Subjects include history, psychology, sociology, politics, current affairs.

BAYLOR UNIVERSITY PRESS

One Bear Place 97363, Waco TX 76798. (254)710-3164. **Fax:** (254)710-3440. **E-mail:** carey_newman@baylor.edu. **Website:** www.baylorpress.com. **Contact:** Dr. Carey C. Newman, director. Estab. 1897. Publishes hardcover and trade paperback originals. "We publish contemporary and historical scholarly works about culture, religion, politics, science, and the arts." **Publishes 30 titles/year. Pays 10% royalty on wholesale price.** Publishes ms 1 year after acceptance. Accepts simultaneous submissions. Responds in 2 months to proposals. Guidelines online.

NONFICTION Submit outline, 1-3 sample chapters via e-mail.

BAYWOOD PUBLISHING CO., INC.

26 Austin Ave., P.O. Box 337, Amityville NY 11701. (631)691-1270. **Fax:** (631)691-1770. **Website:** www.baywood.com. **Contact:** Stuart Cohen, managing editor. Estab. 1964. "Baywood Publishing publishes original and innovative books in the humanities and social sciences, including areas such as health sciences, gerontology, death and bereavement, psychology, technical communications, and archaeology." **Pays 7-15% royalty on retail price.** Publishes ms within 1 year of acceptance. after acceptance of ms. Book catalog and guidelines online.

NONFICTION Subjects include anthropology, archaeology, computers, electronics, education, health, environment, psychology, sociology, women's issues, gerontology, technical writing, death and bereavement, environmental issues, recreational mathematics, health policy, labor relations, workplace rights. Submit proposal package.

BEACON HILL PRESS OF KANSAS CITY

Nazarene Publishing House, P.O. Box 419527, Kansas City MO 64141. (816)931-1900. **Fax:** (816)753-4071. **E-mail:** crm@nph.com. **Website:** beaconhillbooks.com. **Contact:** Judi Perry, consumer editor. Publishes hardcover and paperback originals. "Beacon Hill Press is a Christ-centered publisher that provides authentically Christian resources faithful to God's word and relevant to life." **Publishes 30 titles/year. Pays royalty.** Publishes ms 2 years after acceptance. Responds in 3 months to queries.

NONFICTION "Accent on holy living; encouragement in daily Christian life." No fiction, autobiography, poetry, short stories, or children's picture books. Query or submit proposal electronically.

BEACON PRESS

24 Farnsworth St., Boston MA 02210. **E-mail:** editorial@beacon.org. **Website:** www.beacon.org. **Contact:** Melissa Nasson, acquisitions editor. Estab. 1854. Publishes hardcover originals and paperback reprints. Beacon Press publishes general interest

books that promote the following values: the inherent worth and dignity of every person; justice, equity, and compassion in human relations; acceptance of one another; a free and responsible search for truth and meaning; the goal of world community with peace, liberty, and justice for all; respect for the interdependent web of all existence. Currently emphasizing innovative nonfiction writing by people of all colors. De-emphasizing poetry, children's stories, art books, self-help. **Publishes 60 titles/year. 10% of books from first-time authors. Pays royalty. Pays advance.** Accepts simultaneous submissions. Responds in 3 months to queries.

NONFICTION Subjects include anthropology, archeology, child guidance, education, ethnic, gay, lesbian, nature, environment, philosophy, religion, women's issues, women's studies, world affairs. *Strongly prefers agented submissions.* Query by e-mail only. *Strongly prefers referred submissions, on exclusive.*

TIPS "We probably accept only 1 or 2 manuscripts from an unpublished pool of 4,000 submissions/year. No fiction, children's books, or poetry submissions invited. An academic affiliation is helpful."

BEARMANOR MEDIA

P.O. Box 71426, Albany GA 31708. (800)755-4506. **Fax:** (814)690-1559. **E-mail:** books@benohmart.com. **Website:** www.bearmanormedia.com. **Contact:** Ben Ohmart, publisher. Estab. 2000. Publishes trade paperback originals and reprints. **Publishes 70 titles/year. 90% of books from first-time authors. 90% from unagented writers. Negotiable per project. Pays upon acceptance.** Accepts simultaneous submissions. Responds only if interested. Book catalog available online, or free with a 9 x 12 SASE submission.

NONFICTION Subjects include old-time radio, voice actors, old movies, classic television. Query with SASE. E-mail queries preferred. Submit proposal package, outline, list of credits on the subject.

TIPS "My readers love the past. Radio, old movies, old television. My own tastes include voice actors and scripts, especially of radio and television no longer available. I prefer books on subjects that haven't previously been covered as full books. It doesn't matter to me if you're a first-time author or have a track record. Just know your subject and know how to write a sentence!"

BEAR STAR PRESS

185 Hollow Oak Dr., Cohasset CA 95973. (530)891-0360. **Website:** www.bearstarpress.com. **Contact:** Beth Spencer, publisher/editor. Estab. 1996. Publishes trade paperback originals. "Bear Star is committed to publishing the best poetry it can attract. Each year it sponsors the Dorothy Brunsman contest, open to poets from Western and Pacific states. From time to time we add to our list other poets from our target area whose work we admire." **Publishes 1-3 titles/year. Pays $1,000, and 25 copies to winner of annual Dorothy Brunsman contest.** Publishes ms 9 months after acceptance. Accepts simultaneous submissions. Responds in 2 weeks to queries. Guidelines online.

POETRY Wants well-crafted poems. No restrictions as to form, subject matter, style, or purpose. "Poets should enter our annual book competition. Other books are occasionally solicited by publisher, sometimes from among contestants who didn't win." Online submissions strongly preferred.

TIPS "Send your best work, consider its arrangement. A 'wow' poem early keeps me reading."

BEHRMAN HOUSE INC.

11 Edison Place, Springfield NJ 07081. (973)379-7200. **Fax:** (973)379-7280. **E-mail:** customersupport@behrmanhouse.com. **Website:** www.behrmanhouse.com. Estab. 1921. Publishes books on all aspects of Judaism: history, cultural, textbooks, holidays. "Behrman House publishes quality books of Jewish content—history, Bible, philosophy, holidays, ethics—for children and adults." **12% of books from first-time authors. Pays authors royalty of 3-10% based on retail price or buys ms outright for $1,000-5,000. Offers advance. Pays illustrators by the project (range: $500-5,000).** Publishes ms 18 months after acceptance. Accepts simultaneous submissions. Responds in 1 month to queries; 2 months to mss. Book catalog free on request. Guidelines online.

NONFICTION All levels: Judaism, Jewish educational textbooks. Average word length: young reader—1,200; middle reader—2,000; young adult—4,000. Submit outline/synopsis and sample chapters.

FREDERIC C. BEIL, PUBLISHER, INC.

609 Whitaker St., Savannah GA 31401. (912)233-2446. **Fax:** (912)233-6456. **E-mail:** editor@beil.com. **Website:** www.beil.com. Estab. 1982. Publishes hardcover originals and reprints. Frederic C. Beil publishes in the fields of history, literature, and biography. **Pub-**

lishes 13 titles/year. 3,500 queries received/year. 13 mss received/year. 80% of books from first-time authors. 100% from unagented writers. Pays 7.5% royalty on retail price.** Publishes ms 20 months after acceptance. Accepts simultaneous submissions. Responds in 1 week to queries. Book catalog available free.

NONFICTION Subjects include art, architecture, history, language, literature, book arts. Query with SASE. Reviews artwork/photos. Send photocopies.

FICTION Subjects include historical, literary, regional, short story collections, translation, biography. Query with SASE.

TIPS "Our objectives are (1) to offer to the reading public carefully selected texts of lasting value; (2) to adhere to high standards in the choice of materials and in bookmaking craftsmanship; (3) to produce books that exemplify good taste in format and design; and (4) to maintain the lowest cost consistent with quality."

BELLEVUE LITERARY PRESS

New York University School of Medicine, Dept. of Medicine, NYU School of Medicine, 550 First Avenue, OBV 612, New York NY 10016. (212)263-7802. **E-mail:** blpsubmissions@gmail.com. **Website:** blpress.org. **Contact:** Erika Goldman, publisher/editorial director. Estab. 2005. "Publishes literary and authoritative fiction and nonfiction at the nexus of the arts and the sciences, with a special focus on medicine. As our authors explore cultural and historical representations of the human body, illness, and health, they address the impact of scientific and medical practice on the individual and society."

NONFICTION "If you have a completed ms, a sample of a ms or a proposal that fits our mission as a press feel free to submit it to us by e-mail."

FICTION Subjects include literary. Submit complete ms.

TIPS "We are a project of New York University's School of Medicine and while our standards reflect NYU's excellence in scholarship, humanistic medicine, and science, our authors need not be affiliated with NYU. We are not a university press and do not receive any funding from NYU. Our publishing operations are financed exclusively by foundation grants, private donors, and book sales revenue."

BENBELLA BOOKS

10300 N. Central Expressway, Suite 530, Dallas TX 75231. **E-mail:** glenn@benbellabooks.com. **Website:** www.benbellabooks.com. **Contact:** Glenn Yeffeth, publisher. Estab. 2001. Publishes hardcover and trade paperback originals. **Publishes 30-40 titles/year. Pays 6-15% royalty on retail price.** Publishes ms 10 months after acceptance. Accepts simultaneous submissions. Guidelines online.

NONFICTION Subjects include pop contemporary culture, cooking, foods, nutrition, health, medicine, literary criticism, money, finance, science. Submit proposal package, including: outline, 2 sample chapters (via e-mail).

BENTLEY PUBLISHERS

1734 Massachusetts Ave., Cambridge MA 02138. (617)547-4170. **Fax:** (617)876-9235. **Website:** www.bentleypublishers.com. **Contact:** Michael Bentley, president. Estab. 1950. Publishes hardcover and trade paperback originals and reprints. "Bentley Publishers publishes books for automotive enthusiasts. We are interested in books that showcase good research, strong illustrations, and valuable technical information." Automotive subjects only. Query with SASE. Submit sample chapters, bio, synopsis, target market. Reviews artwork/photos. Book catalog and ms guidelines online.

NONFICTION Subjects include Automotive subjects only. Query with SASE. Submit sample chapters, bio, synopsis, target market. Rreviews artwork/photos.

TIPS "Our audience is composed of serious, intelligent automobile, sports car, and racing enthusiasts, automotive technicians and high-performance tuners."

Ⓐ⊘ BERKLEY BOOKS

Penguin Group (USA) Inc., 375 Hudson St., New York NY 10014. **Website:** us.penguingroup.com/. **Contact:** Leslie Gelbman, president and publisher. Estab. 1955. Publishes paperback and mass market originals and reprints. The Berkley Publishing Group publishes a variety of general nonfiction and fiction including the traditional categories of romance, mystery and science fiction. **Publishes 700 titles/year.**

IMPRINTS Ace; Jove; Heat; Sensation; Berkley Prime Crime; Berkley Caliber.

NONFICTION Subjects include business, economics, child guidance, creative nonfiction, gay, lesbian, health, medicine, history, New Age, psychology, crime, job-seeking communication. No memoirs or personal stories. Prefers agented submissions.

FICTION Subjects include adventure, historical, literary, mystery, romance, spiritual, suspense, western, young adult. No occult fiction. Prefers agented submissions.

BERRETT-KOEHLER PUBLISHERS, INC.

1333 Broadway, Suite #1000, Oakland CA 94612. **E-mail:** bkpub@bkpub.com. **Website:** www.bkconnection.com. **Contact:** Anna Leinberger, editorial assistant. Publishes hardcover and trade paperback originals, mass market paperback originals, hardcover and trade paperback reprints. "Berrett-Koehler Publishers' mission is to publish books that support the movement toward a world that works for all. Our titles promote positive change at personal, organizational and societal levels." Please see proposal guidelines online. **Publishes 40 titles/year. 1,300 queries received/year. 800 mss received/year. 20-30% of books from first-time authors. 70% from unagented writers. Pays 10-20% royalty.** Publishes ms 10 months after acceptance. Accepts simultaneous submissions. Responds in 1 month. Book catalog online.

NONFICTION Subjects include business, economics, community, government, politics, New Age, spirituality. Submit proposal package, outline, bio, 1-2 sample chapters. Hard-copy proposals only. Do not e-mail, fax, or phone please. Reviews artwork/photos. Send photocopies or originals with SASE.

TIPS "Our audience is business leaders. Use common sense, do your research."

⊘ BETHANY HOUSE PUBLISHERS

Division of Baker Publishing Group, 6030 E. Fulton Rd., Ada MI 49301. (616)676-9185. **Fax:** (616)676-9573. **Website:** bakerpublishinggroup.com/bethanyhouse. Estab. 1956. Publishes hardcover and trade paperback originals, mass market paperback reprints. Bethany House Publishers specializes in books that communicate Biblical truth and assist people in both spiritual and practical areas of life. "While we do not accept unsolicited queries or proposals via telephone or e-mail, we will consider 1-page queries sent by fax and directed to adult nonfiction, adult fiction, or young adult/children." *All unsolicited mss returned unopened.* **Publishes 90-100 titles/year. 2% of books from first-time authors. 50% from unagented writers. Pays royalty on net price. Pays advance.** Publishes book Publishes a book 1 year after acceptance. Accepts simultaneous submissions. Responds in 3 months to queries. Book catalog for 9 x 12 envelope and 5 first-class stamps. Guidelines online.

NONFICTION Subjects include child guidance, Biblical disciplines, personal and corporate renewal, emerging generations, devotional, marriage and family, applied theology, inspirational.

FICTION Subjects include historical, young adult, contemporary.

TIPS "Bethany House Publishers' publishing program relates Biblical truth to all areas of life—whether in the framework of a well-told story, of a challenging book for spiritual growth, or of a Bible reference work. We are seeking high-quality fiction and nonfiction that will inspire and challenge our audience."

BETTERWAY HOME BOOKS

Imprint of F+W Media, Inc., 10151 Carver Rd., Suite 200, Cincinnati OH 45242. **E-mail:** jim.schlender@fwcommunity.com. **Website:** www.betterwaybooks.com. **Contact:** Jim Schlender, publisher and community leader. Publishes trade paperback and hardcover originals. **60% of books from first-time authors. 95% from unagented writers. Pays 8-10% royalty on wholesale price. Pays $2,500-3,000 advance.** Publishes ms 18 months after acceptance. Accepts simultaneous submissions. Responds in 3 months.

NONFICTION Subjects include gardening, house and home, preparedness, house and home self-sufficiency, home organization, homemaking, simple living, homesteading skills. Query with SASE. Submit proposal package, outline, 1 sample chapter. Reviews artwork/photos. Send photocopies and PDFs (if submitting electronically).

TIPS "Looking for authors with a savvy online presence in their category and strong interaction via social media outlets."

BETWEEN THE LINES

401 Richmond St. W., Suite 277, Toronto ON M5V 3A8, Canada. (416)535-9914. **Fax:** (416)535-1484. **E-mail:** submissioins@btlbooks.com. **Website:** www.btlbooks.com. **Contact:** Amanda Crocker, managing editor. Publishes trade paperback originals. "Between the Lines publishes nonfiction books in the following subject areas: politics and public policy issues, social issues, development studies, history, education, the environment, health, gender and sexuality, labour, technology, media, and culture. Please note that we do not publish fiction or poetry. We prefer to receive pro-

posals rather than entire manuscripts for consideration." **Publishes 8 titles/year. 350 queries received/year. 50 mss received/year. 80% of books from first-time authors. 95% from unagented writers. Pays 8% royalty.** Publishes ms 1 year after acceptance. Accepts simultaneous submissions. Responds in 2-4 months. Book catalog online. Guidelines online.

NONFICTION Subjects include education, gay, lesbian, government, politics, health, medicine, history, nature, environment, social sciences, sociology, development studies, labor, technology, media, culture. Submit proposal as a PDF by e-mail.

Ⓐ⊘ BEYOND WORDS PUBLISHING, INC.

20827 NW Cornell Rd., Suite 500, Hillsboro OR 97124. (503)531-8700. **Fax:** (503)531-8773. **E-mail:** info@beyondword.com. **Website:** www.beyondword.com. **Contact:** Submissions Department (for agents only). Estab. 1984. Publishes hardcover and trade paperback originals and paperback reprints. "At this time, we are not accepting any unsolicited queries or proposals, and recommend that all authors work with a literary agent in submitting their work." **Publishes 10-15 titles/year.** Accepts simultaneous submissions.

BICK PUBLISHING HOUSE

16 Marion Rd., Branford CT 06405. Phone/**Fax:** (203)208-5253. **E-mail:** bickpubhse@aol.com. **Website:** www.bickpubhouse.com. **Contact:** Dale Carlson, president. Estab. 1994. Publishes trade paperback originals. Bick Publishing House publishes step-by-step, easy-to-read professional information for the general adult public about physical, psychological, and emotional disabilities or special needs. "The mission of Bick Publishing House for Teens/Young Adults is to relate modern science and its ethics, communications arts, philosophy, psychology to the teenager's world, so they can make their own responsible decisions about their own lives and future. The Life Sciences books in the series are presented with accessible texts, with glossary of terms, illustrations, index, resources, bibliography,websites. The mission of Bick Publishing House for Adults is to bring professional information to the general audience in mental illness and recovery, addictions and recovery, in the art of living with disabilities, and in wildlife rehabilitation." Currently emphasizing science, psychology for teens. **Publishes 4 titles/year. 100 queries received/year; 100 mss received/year. 55% of books from first-time authors. 55% from unagented writers. Pays $500-1,000 advance.** Publishes ms 1 year after acceptance. Responds in 1 month to queries; 2 months to proposals; 3 months to mss. Book catalog available free. Guidelines for #10 SASE.

NONFICTION Subjects include health, medicine, disability/special needs, psychology, young adult or teen science, psychology, wildlife rehabilitation. Query with SASE. Submit proposal package, outline, resumè, 3 sample chapters.

BIRCH BOOK PRESS

P.O. Box 81, Delhi NY 13753. **Fax:** (607)746-7453. **E-mail:** birchbrook@copper.net. **Website:** www.birchbrookpress.info. **Contact:** Tom Tolnay, editor/publisher; Leigh Eckmair, art & research editor. Estab. 1982. Occasionally publishes trade paperback originals. Birch Brook Press "is a letterpress book printer/typesetter/designer that uses monies from these activities to publish several titles of its own each year with cultural and literary interest." Specializes in literary work, flyfishing, baseball, outdoors, theme anthologies, and books about books. **Publishes 3 titles/year. 200+ queries received/year; 200+ mss received/year. 95% from unagented writers. Pays modest royalty on acceptance.** Publishes ms 10-18 months after acceptance. Accepts simultaneous submissions. Responds in 3 to 6 months. Book catalog online.

NONFICTION Subjects include film, music (rare), nonfiction of cultural interest, including stage, opera, including outdoors.

FICTION "Mostly we do anthologies around a particular theme generated inhouse. We make specific calls for fiction when we are doing an anthology." Query with SASE and submit sample chapter(s), synopsis.

POETRY Query first with a few sample poems or chapters, or send entire ms. No e-mail submissions; submissions by postal mail only. Must include SASE with submissions. Occasionally comments on rejected poems. Royalty on co-op contracts.

TIPS "Write well on subjects of interest to BBP, such as outdoors, flyfishing, baseball, music, literary stories, fine poetry, and occasional novellas, books about books."

BKMK PRESS

University of Missouri - Kansas City, 5101 Rockhill Rd., Kansas City MO 64110-2499. (816)235-2558. **Fax:** (816)235-2611. **E-mail:** bkmk@umkc.edu. **Website:** newletters.org. Estab. 1971. Publishes trade paperback originals. "BkMk Press publishes fine literature.

Reading period January-June." **Publishes 4 titles/year.** Accepts simultaneous submissions. Responds in 4-6 months to queries. Guidelines online.

NONFICTION Creative nonfiction essays. Submit 25-50 sample pages and SASE.

FICTION Subjects include literary, short story collections. Query with SASE.

POETRY Submit 10 sample poems and SASE.

TIPS "We skew toward readers of literature, particularly contemporary writing. Because of our limited number of titles published per year, we discourage apprentice writers or 'scattershot' submissions."

BLACK DOME PRESS CORP.

649 Delaware Ave., Delmar NY 12054. (518)439-6512. **Fax:** (518)439-1309. **E-mail:** blackdomep@aol.com. **Website:** www.blackdomepress.com. Estab. 1990. Publishes cloth and trade paperback originals and reprints. Do not send the entire work. Mail a cover letter, table of contents, introduction, sample chapter (or 2), and your CV or brief biography to the Editor. Please do not send computer disks or submit your proposal via e-mail. If your book will include illustrations, please send us copies of sample illustrations. Do not send originals. Accepts simultaneous submissions. Book catalog and guidelines online.

NONFICTION Subjects include history, nature, environment, photography, regional, New York state, Native Americans, grand hotels, genealogy, colonial life, French & Indian War (NYS), American Revolution (NYS), quilting, architecture, railroads, hiking and kayaking guidebooks. New York state regional material only. Submit proposal package, outline, bio.

TIPS "Our audience is comprised of New York state residents, tourists, and visitors."

BLACK HERON PRESS

P.O. Box 13396, Mill Creek WA 98082. **Website:** www.blackheronpress.com. Estab. 1984. Publishes hardcover and trade paperback originals, trade paperback reprints. "Black Heron Press publishes primarily literary fiction." **Publishes 4 titles/year. 1,500 queries received/year. 50% of books from first-time authors. 90% from unagented writers. Pays 8% royalty on retail price.** Publishes ms 2 years after acceptance. Accepts simultaneous submissions. Responds in 6 months. Catalog available online.

NONFICTION Subjects include military, war. Submit proposal package, include cover letter and first 30-50 pages of your completed novel. "We do not review artwork."

FICTION Subjects include confession, erotica, literary (regardless of genre), military, war, sci-fi, young adult, Some science fiction—not fantasy, not Dungeons & Dragons—that makes or implies a social statement. "All of our fiction is character driven. We don't want to see fiction written for the mass market. If it sells to the mass market, fine, but we don't see ourselves as a commercial press." Submit proposal package, including cover letter and first 40-50 pages pages of your completed novel.

TIPS "Our Readers love good fiction—they are scattered among all social classes, ethnic groups, and zip code areas. If you can't read our books, at least check out our titles on our website."

BLACK LAWRENCE PRESS

326 Bigham St., Pittsburgh PA 15211. **E-mail:** editors@blacklawrencepress.com. **Website:** www.blacklawrencepress.com. **Contact:** Diane Goettel, executive editor. Estab. 2003. Black Lawrence press seeks to publish intriguing books of literature—novels, short story collections, poetry collections, chapbooks, anthologies, and creative nonfiction. Will also publish the occasional translation from German. Publishes 15-20 books/year, mostly poetry and fiction. Mss are selected through open submission and competition. Books are 20-400 pages, offset-printed or high-quality POD, perfect-bound, with 4-color cover. **Accepts submissions during the months of June and November. Pays royalties.** Responds in 6 months to mss.

FICTION Subjects include literary, short story collections, translation. Submit complete ms.

POETRY Submit complete ms.

BLACK LYON PUBLISHING, LLC

P.O. Box 567, Baker City OR 97814. **E-mail:** info@blacklyonpublishing.com. **E-mail:** queries@blacklyonpublishing.com. **Website:** www.blacklyonpublishing.com. **Contact:** The Editors. Estab. 2007. Publishes paperback and e-book originals. "Black Lyon Publishing is a small, independent publisher. We are very focused on giving new novelists a launching pad into the industry." **Publishes 15-20 titles/year.** Responds in 2-3 months to queries. Guidelines online.

FICTION Subjects include gothic, historical, romance. Prefers e-mail queries.

TIPS "Write a good, solid romance with a setting, premise, character or voice just a little 'different' than what you might usually find on the market. We like unique books—but they still need to be romances."

BLACK OCEAN

P.O. Box 52030, Boston MA 02205. **Fax:** (617)849-5678. **E-mail:** carrie@blackocean.org. **Website:** www.blackocean.org. **Contact:** Carrie Olivia Adams, poetry editor. Estab. 2006. **Publishes 6 titles/year.** Responds in 6 months to mss.

POETRY Wants poetry that is well-considered, risks itself, and by its beauty and/or bravery disturbs a tiny corner of the universe. Mss are selected through open submission. Books are 60+ pages. Book/chapbook mss may include previously published poems. "We have an open submission period in June of each year; specific guidelines are updated and posted on our website in the months preceding."

BLACK VELVET SEDUCTIONS PUBLISHING

E-mail: ric@blackvelvetseductions.com. **Website:** www.blackvelvetseductions.com. **Contact:** Richard Savage, acquisitions editor. Estab. 2005. Publishes trade paperback and electronic originals and reprints. "We publish two types of material: 1) romance novels and short stories and 2) romantic stories involving spanking between consenting adults. We look for well-crafted stories with a high degree of emotional impact. No first person point of view. All material must be in third person point of view." Publishes trade paperback and electronic originals. "We have a high interest in republishing backlist titles in electronic and trade paperback formats once rights have reverted to the author." Accepts only complete mss. Query with SASE. Submit complete ms. **Publishes about 20 titles/year. 500 queries received/year. 1,000 mss received/year. 90% of books from first-time authors. 100% from unagented writers. Pays 10% royalty for paperbacks; 50% royalty for electronic books.** Publishes ms 6-12 months after acceptance. Accepts simultaneous submissions. Responds in 6 months to queries; 8 months to proposals; 8-12 months to mss. Catalog free or online. Guidelines online.

FICTION Subjects include romance, erotic romance, historical romance, multicultural romance, romance, short story collections romantic stories, romantic suspense, western romance. All stories must have a strong romance element. "There are very few sexual taboos in our erotic line. We tend to give our authors the widest latitude. If it is safe, sane, and consensual we will allow our authors latitude to show us the eroticism. However, we will not consider manuscripts with any of the following: bestiality (sex with animals), necrophilia (sex with dead people), pedophillia (sex with children)." Only accepts electronic submissions.

TIPS "We publish romance and erotic romance. We look for books written in very deep point of view. Shallow point of view remains the number one reason we reject manuscripts in which the storyline generally works."

JOHN F. BLAIR, PUBLISHER

1406 Plaza Dr., Winston-Salem NC 27103. (336)768-1374. **Fax:** (336)768-9194. **E-mail:** editorial@blairpub.com. **Website:** www.blairpub.com. **Contact:** Carolyn Sakowski, president. Estab. 1954. **Pays royalties. Pays negotiable advance.** Publishes ms 18 months after acceptance. Responds in 3-6 months.

FICTION "We specialize in regional books, with an emphasis on nonfiction categories such as history, travel, folklore, and biography. We publish only one or two works of fiction each year. Fiction submitted to us should have some connection with the Southeast. We do not publish children's books, poetry, or category fiction such as romances, science fiction, or spy thrillers. We do not publish collections of short stories, essays, or newspaper columns." Accepts unsolicited mss. Any fiction submitted should have some connection with the Southeast, either through setting or author's background. Send a cover letter, giving a synopsis of the book. Include the first 2 chapters (at least 50 pages) of the ms. "You may send the entire ms if you wish. If you choose to send only samples, please include the projected word length of your book and estimated completion date in your cover letter. Send a biography of the author, including publishing credits and credentials."

TIPS "We are primarily interested in nonfiction titles. Most of our titles have a tie-in with North Carolina or the southeastern United States, we do not accept short-story collections. Please enclose a cover letter and outline with the ms. We prefer to review queries before we are sent complete mss. Queries should include an approximate word count."

BLAZEVOX [BOOKS]

131 Euclid Ave., Kenmore NY 14217. **E-mail:** editor@blazevox.org. **Website:** www.blazevox.org. **Contact:** Geoffrey Gatza, editor/publisher. Estab. 2005. "We are a major publishing presence specializing in innovative fictions and wide-ranging fields of innova-

tive forms of poetry and prose. Our goal is to publish works that are challenging, creative, attractive, and yet affordable to individual readers. Articles of submission depend on many criteria, but overall items submitted must conform to one ethereal trait, your work must not suck. This put plainly, bad art should be punished; we will not promote it. However, all submissions will be reviewed and the author will receive feedback. We are human too." **Pays 10% royalties on fiction and poetry books, based on net receipts. This amount may be split across multiple contributors. "We do not pay advances."** Guidelines online.

FICTION Subjects include experimental, short story collections. Submit complete ms via e-mail.

POETRY Submit complete ms via e-mail.

TIPS "We actively contract and support authors who tour, read and perform their work, play an active part of the contemporary literary scene, and seek a readership."

BLOOMBERG PRESS

Imprint of John Wiley & Sons, Professional Development, 111 River St., Hoboken NJ 07030. **Website:** www.wiley.com. Estab. 1995. Publishes hardcover and trade paperback originals. Bloomberg Press publishes professional books for practitioners in the financial markets. "We publish commercially successful, very high-quality books that stand out clearly from the competition by their brevity, ease of use, sophistication, and abundance of practical tips and strategies; books readers need, will use, and appreciate." **Publishes 18-22 titles/year. 200 queries received/year. 20 mss received/year. 45% from unagented writers. Pays negotiable, competitive royalty. Pays negotiable advance for trade books.** Publishes ms 9 months after acceptance. Accepts simultaneous submissions. Responds in 1 month to queries.

NONFICTION Subjects include business, economics, money, finance, professional books on finance, investment and financial services, and books for financial advisors. "We are looking for authorities and for experienced service journalists. Do not send us unfocused books containing general information already covered by books in the marketplace. We do not publish business, management, leadership, or career books." Submit outline, sample chapters, SAE with sufficient postage. Submit complete ms.

Ⓐ BLOOMSBURY CHILDREN'S BOOKS

Imprint of Bloomsbury USA, 1385 Broadway, 5th Floor, New York NY 10008. **Website:** www.bloomsbury.com/us/childrens. No phone calls or e-mails. *Agented submissions only.* **Publishes 60 titles/year. 25% of books from first-time authors. Pays royalty. Pays advance.** Accepts simultaneous submissions. Responds in 6 months. Book catalog online. Guidelines online.

FICTION Subjects include adventure, fantasy, historical, humor, juvenile, multicultural, mystery, picture books, poetry, science fiction, sports, suspense, young adult, animal, anthology, concept, contemporary, folktales, problem novels. Agented submissions only.

BLUEBRIDGE

Imprint of United Tribes Media, Inc., P.O. Box 601, Katonah NY 10536. (914)301-5901. **E-mail:** janguerth@bluebridgebooks.com. **Website:** www.bluebridgebooks.com. **Contact:** Jan-Erik Guerth, publisher (general nonfiction). Estab. 2004. Publishes hardcover and trade paperback originals. BlueBridge is an independent publisher of international nonfiction based near New York City. The BlueBridge mission: Thoughtful Books for Mind and Spirit. **Publishes 6 titles/year. 1,000 queries received/year. Pays variable advance.** Accepts simultaneous submissions. Responds in 1 month.

NONFICTION Subjects include Americana, anthropology, archaeology, art, architecture, business, economics, child guidance, contemporary culture, creative nonfiction, ethnic, gardening, gay, lesbian, government, politics, health, medicine, history, humanities, language, literature, literary criticism, multicultural, music, dance, nature, environment, philosophy, psychology, religion, science, social sciences, sociology, spirituality, travel, women's issues, world affairs. Query with SASE or preferably by e-mail.

TIPS "We target a broad general nonfiction audience."

BLUE LIGHT PRESS

1563 45th Ave., San Francisco CA 94122. **E-mail:** bluelightpress@aol.com. **Website:** www.bluelightpress.com. **Contact:** Diane Frank, chief editor. Estab. 1988. "We like poems that are imagistic, emotionally honest, and push the edge—where the writer pushes through the imagery to a deeper level of insight and understanding. No rhymed poetry." Has published poetry by Rustin Larson, Mary Kay Rummel, Philip Kobylarz, Daniel J. Langton, and K.B. Ballentine. "Books are elegantly designed and artistic. Our books are professionally printed, with original cover art, and we publish full-length books of poetry and chapbooks."

POETRY "We have an online poetry workshop with a wonderful group of American and international poets—open to new members 3 times/year. Send an e-mail for info." Does not accept e-mail submissions. Deadlines: January 30 full-sized ms. and June 15 for chapbooks. "Read our guidelines before sending your ms."

BLUE MOUNTAIN PRESS

Blue Mountain Arts, Inc., P.O. Box 4549, Boulder CO 80306. (800)525-0642. **E-mail:** editorial@sps.com. **Website:** www.sps.com. **Contact:** Patti Wayant, editorial director. Estab. 1971. Publishes hardcover originals, trade paperback originals, electronic originals. *"Please note: We are not accepting works of fiction, rhyming poetry, children's books, chapbooks, or memoirs."* **Pays royalty on wholesale price.** Publishes ms 6-8 months after acceptance. Accepts simultaneous submissions. Responds in 2-4 months. Guidelines by e-mail.

NONFICTION , Personal growth, teens/tweens, family, relationships, motivational, and inspirational but not religious. Query with SASE. Submit proposal package including outline and 3-5 sample chapters.

POETRY "We publish poetry appropriate for gift books, self-help books, and personal growth books. We do not publish chapbooks or literary poetry." Query. Submit 10+ sample poems.

BLUE POPPY PRESS

Imprint of Blue Poppy Enterprises, Inc., 1990 57th Court Unit A, Boulder CO 80301. (303)447-8372. **Fax:** (303)245-8362. **E-mail:** info@bluepoppy.com. **Website:** www.bluepoppy.com. **Contact:** Bob Flaws, editor-in-chief. Estab. 1981. Publishes hardcover and trade paperback originals. "Blue Poppy Press is dedicated to expanding and improving the English language literature on acupuncture and Asian medicine for both professional practitioners and lay readers." **Publishes 3-4 titles/year. 50 queries received/year. 5-10 mss received/year. 30-40% of books from first-time authors. 100% from unagented writers. Pays 8-12% royalty.** Publishes ms 1 year after acceptance. Responds in 1 month to queries. Book catalog available free. Guidelines online.

NONFICTION Subjects include ethnic, health, medicine. "We only publish books on acupuncture and Oriental medicine by authors who can read Chinese and have a minimum of 5 years clinical experience. We also require all our authors to use Wiseman's *Glossary of Chinese Medical Terminology* as their standard for technical terms." Query with SASE. Submit outline, 1 sample chapter.

TIPS "Audience is practicing acupuncturists interested in alternatives in healthcare, preventive medicine, Chinese philosophy, and medicine."

BLUE RIVER PRESS

Cardinal Publishers Group, 2402 N. Shadeland Ave., Suite A, Indianapolis IN 46219. (317)352-8200. **Fax:** (317)352-8202. **E-mail:** tdoherty@cardinalpub.com. **Website:** www.cardinalpub.com. **Contact:** Tom Doherty, president (adult nonfiction). Estab. 2000. Publishes hardcover, trade paperback and electronic originals and reprints. **Publishes 8-12 titles/year. 200 queries received/year. 25% of books from first-time authors. 80% from unagented writers. Pays 10-15% on wholesale price. Outright purchase of $500-5,000. Offers advance up to $5,000.** Publishes ms 6-12 months after acceptance. Accepts simultaneous submissions. Responds to queries in 2 months. Book catalog for #10 SASE or online. Guidelines available by e-mail.

NONFICTION "Most non-religious adult nonfiction subjects are of interest. We like concepts that can develop into series products. Most of our books are paperback or hardcover in the categories of sport, business, health, fitness, lifestyle, yoga, and educational books for teachers and students."

BNA BOOKS

P.O. Box 7814, Edison NJ 08818. (800)960-1220. **Fax:** (723)346-1624. **Website:** www.bnabooks.com. Estab. 1929. Publishes hardcover and softcover originals. BNA Books publishes professional reference books written by lawyers, for lawyers. Accepts simultaneous submissions. Book catalog online. Guidelines online.

NONFICTION No fiction, biographies, bibliographies, cookbooks, religion books, humor, or trade books. Submit detailed TOC or outline, CV, intended market, estimated word length.

TIPS "Our audience is made up of practicing lawyers and law librarians. We look for authoritative and comprehensive treatises that can be supplemented or revised every year or 2 on legal subjects of interest to those audiences."

BOA EDITIONS, LTD.

P.O. Box 30971, Rochester NY 14603. (585)546-3410. **Fax:** (585)546-3913. **E-mail:** contact@boaeditions.org. **Website:** www.boaeditions.org. **Contact:** Peter Conners, publisher; Melissa Hall, development director/office manager. Estab. 1976. Publishes hardcover and trade paperback originals. "BOA Editions publishes distinguished collections of poetry, fiction and poetry in translation. Our goal is to publish the finest American contemporary poetry, fiction and poetry in translation." **Publishes 11-13 titles/year. 1,000 queries received/year. 700 mss received/year. 15% of books from first-time authors. 90% from unagented writers. Negotiates royalties. Pays variable advance.** Publishes ms 18 months after acceptance. Accepts simultaneous submissions. Responds in 1 week to queries; 5 months to mss. Book catalog online. Guidelines online.

FICTION Subjects include literary, poetry, poetry in translation, short story collections. "We now publish literary fiction through our American Reader Series. While aesthetic quality is subjective, our fiction will be by authors more concerned with the artfulness of their writing than the twists and turns of plot. Our strongest current interest is in short story collections (and short-short story collections), although we will consider novels. We strongly advise you to read our first published fiction collections." *Temporarily closed to novel/collection submissions.*

POETRY "Readers who, like Whitman, expect of the poet to 'indicate more than the beauty and dignity which always attach to dumb real objects... They expect him to indicate the path between reality and their souls,' are the audience of BOA's books." BOA Editions, a Pulitzer Prize-winning, not-for-profit publishing house acclaimed for its work, reads poetry mss for the American Poets Continuum Series (new poetry by distinguished poets in mid- and late career), the Lannan Translations Selection Series (publication of 2 new collections of contemporary international poetry annually, supported by The Lannan Foundation of Santa Fe, NM), The A. Poulin, Jr. Poetry Prize (to honor a poet's first book; mss considered through competition), and The America Reader Series (short fiction and prose on poetics). Check website for reading periods for the American Poets Continuum Series and The Lannan Translation Selection Series. "Please adhere to the general submission guidelines for each series." Guidelines online.

BOLD STROKES BOOKS, INC.

P.O. Box 249, Valley Falls NY 12185. (518)677-5127. **Fax:** (518)677-5291. **E-mail:** sandy.boldstrokes@gmail.com. **E-mail:** submissions@boldstrokesbooks.com. **Website:** www.boldstrokesbooks.com. **Contact:** Sandy Lowe, senior editor. Publishes trade paperback originals and reprints; electronic originals and reprints. **Publishes 85+ titles/year. 300 queries/year; 300 mss/year. 10-20% of books from first-time authors. Sliding scale based on sales volume and format.** Publishes ms 6-16 months after acceptance. Responds in 1 month to queries; 2 months to proposals; 4 months to mss. Guidelines online.

IMPRINTS BSB Fiction; Victory Editions Lesbian Fiction; Liberty Editions Gay Fiction; Soliloquy Young Adult; Heat Stroke Erotica.

NONFICTION Subjects include gay, lesbian, memoirs, young adult. Submit completed ms with bio, cover letter, and synopsis electronically only. Does not review artwork.

FICTION Subjects include adventure, erotica, fantasy, gay, gothic, historical, horror, lesbian, literary, mainstream, mystery, romance, science fiction, suspense, western, young adult. "Submissions should have a gay, lesbian, transgendered, or bisexual focus and should be positive and life-affirming." Submit completed ms with bio, cover letter, and synopsis—electronically only.

TIPS "We are particularly interested in authors who are interested in craft enhancement, technical development, and exploring and expanding traditional genre definitions and boundaries and are looking for a long-term publishing relationship."

BOOKOUTURE

StoryFire Ltd., 23 Sussex Rd., Ickenham UB10 8P, United Kingdom. **E-mail:** questions@bookouture.com. **E-mail:** pitch@bookouture.com. **Website:** www.bookouture.com. **Contact:** Oliver Rhodes, founder and publisher. Estab. 2012. Publishes mass market paperback and electronic originals and reprints. **Publishes 40 titles/year. Receives 200 queries/year; 300 mss/year. Pays 45% royalty on wholesale price.** Publishes ms 4 months after acceptance. Accepts simultaneous submissions. Responds in 1 month. Book catalog online.

IMPRINTS Imprint of StoryFire Ltd.

FICTION Subjects include contemporary, erotica, ethnic, fantasy, gay, historical, lesbian, mainstream, mystery, romance, science fiction, suspense, western, crime, thriller, new adult. "We are looking for entertaining fiction targeted at modern women. That can be anything from Steampunk to Erotica, Historicals to thrillers. A distinctive author voice is more important than a particular genre or ms length." Submit complete ms.

TIPS "The most important question that we ask of submissions is why would a reader buy the next book? What's distinctive or different about your storytelling that will mean readers will want to come back for more. We look to acquire global English language rights for e-book and Print on Demand."

⊘✪ BOREALIS PRESS, LTD.

8 Mohawk Crescent, Napean ON K2H 7G6, Canada. (613)829-0150. **Fax:** (613)829-7783. **E-mail:** drt@borealispress.com. **Website:** www.borealispress.com. Estab. 1972. Publishes hardcover and paperback originals and reprints. "Our mission is to publish work that will be of lasting interest in the Canadian book market." Currently emphasizing Canadian fiction, nonfiction, drama, poetry. De-emphasizing children's books. **Publishes 20 titles/year. 80% of books from first-time authors. 95% from unagented writers. Pays 10% royalty on net receipts; plus 3 free author's copies.** Publishes ms 18 months after acceptance. Responds in 2 months to queries; 4 months to mss. Book catalog online. Guidelines online.

IMPRINTS Tecumseh Press.

NONFICTION Subjects include government, politics, history, language, literature, regional. Only material Canadian in content. Looks for style in tone and language, reader interest, and maturity of outlook. Query with SASE. Submit outline, 2 sample chapters. *No unsolicited mss.* Reviews artwork/photos.

FICTION Subjects include adventure, ethnic, historical, juvenile, literary, mainstream, contemporary, romance, short story collections, young adult. Only material Canadian in content and dealing with significant aspects of the human situation. Query with SASE. Submit clips, 1-2 sample chapters. *No unsolicited mss.*

BOTTOM DOG PRESS, INC.

P.O. Box 425, Huron OH 44839. **E-mail:** lsmithdog@smithdocs.net. **Website:** smithdocs.net. **Contact:** Larry Smith, director; Allen Frost, Laura Smith, Susanna Sharp-Schwacke, associate editors. Bottom Dog Press, Inc., "is a nonprofit literary and educational organization dedicated to publishing the best writing and art from the Midwest and Appalachia."

BOYDS MILLS PRESS

Highlights for Children, Inc., 815 Church St., Honesdale PA 18431. (570)253-1164. **Website:** www.boydsmillspress.com. Estab. 1990. Boyds Mills Press publishes picture books, nonfiction, activity books, and paperback reprints. Their titles have been named notable books by the International Reading Association, the American Library Association, and the National Council of Teachers of English. They've earned numerous awards, including the National Jewish Book Award, the Christopher Medal, the NCTE Orbis Pictus Honor, and the Golden Kite Honor. Boyds Mills Press welcomes unsolicited submissions from published and unpublished writers and artists. Submit a ms with a cover letter of relevant information, including experience with writing and publishing. Label the package "Manuscript Submission" and include an SASE. For art samples, label the package "Art Sample Submission." Responds to mss within 3 months. Catalog online. Guidelines online.

POETRY Send a book-length collection of poems. Do not send an initial query. Keep in mind that the strongest collections demonstrate a facility with multiple poetic forms.

NICHOLAS BREALEY PUBLISHING

20 Park Plaza, Suite 610, Boston MA 02116. (617)523-3801. **Fax:** (617)523-3708. **Website:** www.nicholasbrealey.com. **Contact:** Attn: Aquisitions Editor. Estab. 1992. "Nicholas Brealey Publishing has a reputation for publishing high-quality and thought-provoking business books with international appeal. Over time our list has grown to focus also on careers, professional and personal development, travel narratives and crossing cultures. We welcome fresh ideas and new insights in all of these subject areas." Submit via e-mail and follow the guidelines on the website.

BREWERS PUBLICATIONS

Imprint of Brewers Association, 551 Westbury Ln., Georgetown TX 78633. **E-mail:** kristi@brewersassociation.org. **Website:** www.brewerspublications.com. **Contact:** Kristi Switzer, publisher. Estab. 1986. Publishes trade paperback originals. "BP is the largest publisher of contemporary and relevant brewing literature for today's craft brewers and homebrewers." **Publishes 2 titles/year. 50% of books from first-time authors. 100% from unagented writers. Pays advance.** Publishes ms 9 months after acceptance. Accepts simultaneous submissions. Responds in 3 months to relevant queries. "Only those submissions relevant to our needs will receive a response to queries.". Guidelines online.

NONFICTION "We seek to do this in a positive atmosphere, create lasting relationships and shared pride in our contributions to the brewing and beer community. The books we select to carry out this mission include titles relevant to homebrewing, professional brewing, starting a brewery, books on particular styles of beer, industry trends, ingredients, processes and the occasional broader interest title on cooking or the history/impact of beer in our society." Query first with proposal and sample chapter.

BRICK BOOKS

Box 20081, 431 Boler Rd., London ON N6K 4G6, Canada. (519)657-8579. **E-mail:** brick.books@sympatico.ca. **Website:** www.brickbooks.ca. **Contact:** Don McKay, Stan Dragland, Barry Dempster, editors. Estab. 1975. Publishes trade paperback originals. Brick Books has a reading period of January 1-April 30. Mss received outside that period will be returned. No multiple submissions. Pays 10% royalty in book copies only. **Publishes 7 titles/year. 30 queries received/year. 100 mss received/year. 30% of books from first-time authors. 100% from unagented writers.** Publishes ms 2 years after acceptance. Responds in 3-4 months to queries. Book catalog free or online. Guidelines online.

POETRY Submit only poetry.

TIPS "Writers without previous publications in literary journals or magazines are rarely considered by Brick Books for publication."

BRICK ROAD POETRY PRESS, INC.

P.O. Box 751, Columbus GA 31902. (706)649-3080. **Fax:** (706)649-3094. **E-mail:** editor@brickroadpoetrypress.com. **Website:** www.brickroadpoetrypress.com. **Contact:** Ron Self and Keith Badowski, co-editors/founders. Estab. 2009.

POETRY Publishes poetry only: books (single author collections), e-zine, and annual anthology. "We prefer poetry that offers a coherent human voice, a sense of humor, attentiveness to words and language, narratives with surprise twists, persona poems, and/or philosophical or spiritual themes explored through the concrete scenes and images." Does not want overemphasis on rhyme, intentional obscurity or riddling, highfalutin vocabulary, greeting card verse, overt religious statements of faith and/or praise, and/or abstractions. Publishes 10-12 poetry books/year and 1 anthology/year. Accepted poems meeting our theme requirements are published on our website. Mss accepted through open submission and competition. "We accept .doc, .rtf, or .pdf file formats. We prefer electronic submissions but will reluctantly consider hard copy submissions by mail if USPS Flat Rate Mailing Envelope is used and with the stipulation that, should the author's work be chosen for publication, an electronic version (.doc or .rtf) must be prepared in a timely manner and at the poet's expense." Please include cover letter with poetry publication/recognition highlights and something intriguing about your life story or ongoing pursuits. "We would like to develop a connection with the poet as well as the poetry." Please include the collection title in the cover letter. "We want to publish poets who are engaged in the literary community, including regular submission of work to various publications and participation in poetry readings, workshops, and writers' groups. That said, we would never rule out an emerging poet who demonstrates ability and motivation to move in that direction." Pays royalties and 15 author copies. Initial print run of 150, print-on-demand thereafter.

TIPS "The best way to discover all that poetry can be and to expand the limits of your own poetry is to read expansively. We recommend the following poets: Kim Addonizio, Ken Babstock, Coleman Barks, Billy Collins, Morri Creech, Alice Friman, Beth A. Gylys, Jane Hirshfield, Jane Kenyon, Ted Kooser, Stanley Kunitz, Thomas Lux, Barry Marks, Michael Meyerhofer, Linda Pastan, Mark Strand, and Natasha D. Trethewey."

BRIGHT RING PUBLISHING, INC.

P.O. Box 31338, Bellingham WA 98228. (360)592-9201. **Fax:** (360)592-4503. **E-mail:** maryann@brightring.com. **Website:** www.brightring.com. **Contact:** MaryAnn Kohl, editor. Estab. 1985.

Bright Ring is no longer accepting ms submissions.

BROADVIEW PRESS, INC.

P.O. Box 1243, Peterborough ON K9J 7H5, Canada. (705)743-8990. **Fax:** (705)743-8353. **E-mail:** customerservice@broadviewpress.com. **Website:** www.broadviewpress.com. Estab. 1985. "We publish in a broad variety of subject areas in the arts and social sciences. We are open to a broad range of political and philosophical viewpoints, from liberal and conservative to libertarian and Marxist, and including a wide range of feminist viewpoints." **Publishes over 40 titles/year. 500 queries received/year. 200 mss received/year. 10% of books from first-time authors. 99% from unagented writers. Pays royalty.** Publishes ms 12 months after acceptance. Accepts simultaneous submissions. Responds in 1 month to queries; 2 months to proposals; 4 months to mss. Book catalog available free. Guidelines online.

NONFICTION Subjects include language, literature, philosophy, religion, politics. "Our focus is very much on English studies and Philosophy, but within those two core subject areas we are open to a broad range of academic approaches and political viewpoints. We welcome feminist perspectives, and we have a particular interest in addressing environmental issues. Our publishing program is internationally-oriented, and we publish for a broad range of geographical markets-but as a canadian company we also publish a broad range of titles with a canadian emphasis." Query with SASE. Submit proposal package. Reviews artwork/photos. Send photocopies.

TIPS "Our titles often appeal to a broad readership; we have many books that are as much of interest to the general reader as they are to academics and students."

BROADWAY BOOKS

The Crown Publishing Group/Random House, 1745 Broadway, New York NY 10019. (212)782-9000. **Fax:** (212)782-9411. **Website:** crownpublishing.com/imprint/broadway-books. Estab. 1995. Publishes hardcover and trade paperback books. "Broadway publishes high quality general interest nonfiction and fiction for adults." **Receives thousands of mss/year. Pays royalty on retail price. Pays advance.**

IMPRINTS Broadway Books; Broadway Business; Doubleday; Doubleday Image; Doubleday Religious Publishing; Main Street Books; Nan A. Talese.

NONFICTION Subjects include business, economics, child guidance, contemporary culture, cooking, foods, nutrition, gay, lesbian, government, politics, health, medicine, history, memoirs, money, finance, multicultural, New Age, psychology, sex, spirituality, sports, travel, narrative, womens' issues, women's studies, current affairs, motivational/inspirational, popular culture, consumer reference. *Agented submissions only.*

FICTION *Agented submissions only.*

BRONZE MAN BOOKS

Millikin University, 1184 W. Main, Decatur IL 62522. (217)424-6264. **E-mail:** rbrooks@millikin.edu. **Website:** www.bronzemanbooks.com. **Contact:** Dr. Randy Brooks, editorial board; Edwin Walker, editorial board. Estab. 2006. Publishes hardcover, trade paperback, and mass market paperback originals. **Publishes 3-4 titles/year. 80% of books from first-time authors. 100% from unagented writers. Outright purchase based on wholesale value of 10% of a press run.** Publishes ms 6 months after acceptance. Accepts simultaneous submissions. Responds in 1-3 months.

NONFICTION Subjects include architecture, art. Query with SASE.

FICTION Subjects include art, graphic design, exhibits, general. Submit completed ms.

POETRY Submit completed ms.

TIPS "The art books are intended for serious collectors and scholars of contemporary art, especially of artists from the Midwestern US. These books are published in conjunction with art exhibitions at Millikin University or the Decatur Area Arts Council. The children's books have our broadest audience, and the literary chapbooks are intended for readers of contemporary fiction, drama, and poetry."

THE BRUCEDALE PRESS

P.O. Box 2259, Port Elgin ON N0H 2C0, Canada. (519)832-6025. **E-mail:** info@brucedalepress.ca. **Website:** brucedalepress.ca. Publishes hardcover and trade paperback originals. The Brucedale Press publishes books and other materials of regional interest and merit, as well as literary, historical, and/or pictorial works. **Publishes 3 titles/year. 50 queries received/year. 30 mss received/year. 75% of books from first-time authors. 100% from unagented writers. Pays royalty.** Publishes ms 1 year after acceptance. Accepts simultaneous submissions. Book catalog online. Guidelines online.

Accepts works by Canadian authors only. Book submissions reviewed November to January. Submissions to The Leaf Journal accepted in September and March only.

NONFICTION Subjects include history, language, literature, memoirs, military, war, nature, environment, photography. Reviews artwork/photos.

FICTION Subjects include fantasy, feminist, historical, humor, juvenile, literary, mainstream, contemporary, mystery, plays, poetry, romance, short story collections, young adult.

TIPS "Our focus is very regional. In reading submissions, I look for quality writing with a strong connection to the Queen's Bush area of Ontario. All authors should visit our website, get a catalog, and read our books before submitting."

BUCKNELL UNIVERSITY PRESS

Bucknell University, Lewisburg PA 17837. (570)577-3672. **E-mail:** universitypress@bucknell.edu. **Website:** www.bucknell.edu/universitypress. **Contact:** Greg Clingham, director. Estab. 1968. Publishes hardcover, paperback, and e-books on various platforms. 'In all fields, our criteria are scholarly excellence, critical originality, and interdisciplinary and theoretical expertise and sensitivity." **Publishes 35-40 titles/year.** Book catalog available free. Guidelines online.

NONFICTION Subjects include environment, ethnic, history, law, literary criticism, multicultural, philosophy, psychology, sociology, Luso-Hispanic studies, Latin American studies, 18-century studies, ecocriticism, African studies, Irish literature, cultural studies, historiography, legal theory. Series: Transits: Literature, Thought & Culture 1650-1850; Bucknell Series in Latin American Literature and Theory; Eighteenth-Century Scotland; New Studies in the Age of Goethe; Contemporary Irish Writers; Griot Project Book Series; Apercus: Histories Texts Cultures. Submit full proposal and CV by Word attachment.

BULLITT PUBLISHING

P.O. Box, Austin TX 78729. **E-mail:** bullittpublishing@yahoo.com. **E-mail:** submissions@bullittpublishing.com. **Website:** bullittpublishing.com. **Contact:** Pat Williams, editor. Estab. 2012. Publishes trade paperback and electronic originals. "Bullitt Publishing is a royalty-offering publishing house specializing in smart, contemporary romance. We are proud to provide print on demand distribution through the world's most comprehensive distribution channel including Amazon.com and BarnesandNoble.com. Digital distribution is available through the world's largest distibutor of e-books and can be downloaded to reading devices such as the iPhone, Ipod Touch, Amazon Kindle, Sony Reader or Barnes & Noble nook. E-books are distributed to the Apple iBookstore, Barnes & Noble, Sony, Kobo and the Diesel eBook Store. Whether this is your first novel or your 101st novel, Bullitt Publishing will treat you with the same amount of professionalism and respect. While we expect well-written entertaining manuscripts from all of our authors, we promise to provide high quality, professional product in return." **Publishes 12 titles/year.**

IMPRINTS Includes imprint Tempo Romance.

FICTION Subjects include romance.

BULL PUBLISHING CO.

P.O. Box 1377, Boulder CO 80306. (800)676-2855. **Fax:** (303)545-6354. **Website:** www.bullpub.com. **Contact:** James Bull, publisher. Estab. 1974. Publishes hardcover and trade paperback originals. "Bull Publishing publishes health and nutrition books for the public with an emphasis on self-care, nutrition, women's health, weight control and psychology." **Publishes 6-8 titles/year. Pays 10-16% royalty on wholesale price (net to publisher).** Publishes ms 6 months after acceptance. Book catalog available free.

NONFICTION Subjects include cooking, foods, nutrition, education, health, medicine, women's issues, women's studies. Subjects include self-care, nutrition, fitness, child health and nutrition, health education, mental health. "We look for books that fit our area of strength: responsible books on health that fill a substantial public need, and that we can market primarily through professionals." Submit outline, sample chapters. Reviews artwork/photos.

BURFORD BOOKS

101 E. State St., #301, Ithaca NY 14850. (607)319-4373. **E-mail:** info@burfordbooks.com. **Website:** www.burfordbooks.com. **Contact:** Burford Books Editorial Department. Estab. 1997. Publishes hardcover originals, trade paperback originals and reprints. Burford Books publishes books on all aspects of the outdoors, from backpacking to sports, practical and literary. **Publishes 12 titles/year. 300 queries received/year. 200 mss received/year. 30% of books from first-time authors. 60% from unagented writers. Pays royalty on wholesale price.** Publishes ms 18 months after acceptance. Accepts simultaneous submissions. Responds in 1 week to queries; 1 month to proposals; 2 months to mss. Book catalog and ms guidelines online.

NONFICTION Subjects include animals, cooking, foods, nutrition, hobbies, military, war, nature, environment, recreation, sports, travel, fitness. "Burford Books welcomes proposals on new projects, especially in the subject areas in which we specialize: sports, the outdoors, golf, nature, gardening, food and wine, travel, and military history. We are not currently considering fiction or children's books. In general it's sufficient to send a brief proposal letter that outlines your idea, which should be e-mailed to info@burfordbooks.com with the word 'query' in the subject line." Reviews artwork/photos. Send photocopies.

BUSTER BOOKS

9 Lion Yard, Tremadoc Rd., London WA SW4 7NQ, United Kingdom. (020)7720-8643. **Fax:** (022)7720-8953. **E-mail:** enquiries@mombooks.com. **Website:** www.busterbooks.co.uk. "We are dedicated to providing irresistible and fun books for children of all ages. We typically publish black & white nonfiction for children aged 8-12 novelty titles-including doodle books."

NONFICTION Prefers synopsis and sample text over complete ms.

FICTION Submit synopsis and sample text.

TIPS "We do not accept fiction submissions. Please do not send original artwork as we cannot guarantee its safety." Visit website before submitting.

BUTTE PUBLICATIONS, INC.

P.O. Box 1328, Hillsboro OR 97123-1328. (503)648-9791. **E-mail:** service@buttepublications.com. **Website:** www.buttepublications.com. Estab. 1992. Butte Publications, Inc., publishes classroom books related to deafness and language. **Publishes several titles/year.** Accepts simultaneous submissions. Responds in 6 months to mss. Book catalog and ms guidelines for #10 SASE or online.

NONFICTION Subjects include education, all related to field of deafness and education. Not seeking autobiographies or novels. Submit proposal package, including author bio, synopsis, market survey, 2-3 sample chapters, SASE and ms (if completed). Reviews artwork/photos. Send photocopies.

TIPS "Audience is students, teachers, parents, and professionals in the arena dealing with deafness and hearing loss."

BY LIGHT UNSEEN MEDIA

P.O. Box 1233, Pepperell MA 01463. (978)433-8866. **Fax:** (978)433-8866. **E-mail:** vyrdolak@bylightunseenmedia.com. **Website:** www.bylightunseenmedia.com. **Contact:** Inanna Arthen, owner/editor-in-chief. Estab. 2006. Publishes hardcover, paperback and electronic originals; trade paperback reprints. **Publishes 5 titles/year. 20 mss received/year; 5 queries received/year. 80% of books from first-time authors. 100% from unagented writers. Pays royalty of 20-50% on net as explicitly defined in contract. Payment quarterly. Pays $200 advance.** Publishes ms 4 months after acceptance. Accepts simultaneous submissions. Responds in 3 months. Catalog online. Ms guidelines online.

NONFICTION Subjects include alternative lifestyles, contemporary culture, creative nonfiction, history, language, literary criticism, literature, New Age, science, social sciences, folklore, popular media. "We are a niche small press that will *only* consider nonfiction on the theme of vampires (vampire folklore, movies, television, literature, vampires in culture, etc.). We're especially interested in academic or other well-researched material, but will consider self-help/New Age types of books (e.g. the kind of material published by Llewellyn). We use digital printing so all interiors would need to be black and white, including illustrations." Submit proposal package including outline, 3 sample chapters, brief author bio. *All unsolicited mss will be returned unopened.* Reviews artwork. Send photocopies/scanned PDF/jpeg.

FICTION Subjects include fantasy, gay, gothic, horror, lesbian, mystery, occult, science fiction, short story collections, suspense, western, young adult, magical realism, thriller. "We are a niche small press that *only* publishes fiction relating in some way to vampires. Within that guideline, we're interested in almost any genre that includes a vampire trope, the more creative and innovative, the better. Restrictions are noted in the submission guidelines (no derivative fiction based on other works, such as Dracula, no gore-for-gore's-sake 'splatter' horror, etc.) We do not publish anthologies." Submit proposal package including synopsis, 3 sample chapters, brief author bio. *"We encourage electronic submissions." All unsolicited mss will be returned unopened.*

TIPS "We strongly urge authors to familiarize themselves with the vampire genre and not imagine that they're doing something new and amazingly different just because they're not imitating the current fad."

C&T PUBLISHING

1651 Challenge Dr., Concord CA 94520-5206. (925)677-0377. **Fax:** (925)677-0373. **E-mail:** roxanec@ctpub.com. **Website:** www.ctpub.com. **Contact:** Roxane Cerda. Estab. 1983. Publishes hardcover and trade paperback originals. "C&T publishes well-written, beautifully designed books on quilting and fiber crafts, embroidery, dollmaking, knitting and paper crafts." **Publishes 70 titles/year.** Accepts simultaneous submissions. Responds in 3 months to queries. Book catalog free; guidelines online.

IMPRINTS Stash Books.

NONFICTION Subjects include hobbies, quilting books, occasional quilt picture books, quilt-related crafts, wearable art, needlework, fiber and surface embellishments, other books relating to fabric crafting and paper crafting. Extensive proposal guidelines are available on the company's website.

TIPS "In our industry, we find that how-to books have the longest selling life. Quiltmakers, sewing enthusiasts, needle artists, fiber artists and paper crafters are our audience. We like to see new concepts or techniques. Include some great samples, and you'll get our attention quickly. Dynamic design is hard to resist, and if that's your forte, show us what you've done."

⊘ CALAMARI PRESS

Via Titta Scarpetta #28, Rome 00153, Italy. **E-mail:** derek@calamaripress.net. **Website:** www.calamaripress.com. Publishes paperback originals. Calamari Press publishes books of literary text and art. Mss are selected by invitation. Occasionally has open submission period—check website. Helps to be published in *SleepingFish* first. **Publishes 1-2 titles/year. Pays in author's copies.** Publishes book Ms published 2-6 months after acceptance. Responds to mss in 2 weeks. Guidelines online.

FICTION Query with outline/synopsis and 3 sample chapters. Accepts queries by e-mail only. Include brief bio. Send SASE or IRC for return of ms.

CALKINS CREEK

Boyds Mills Press, 815 Church St., Honesdale PA 18431. **Website:** www.calkinscreekbooks.com. Estab. 2004. "We aim to publish books that are a well-written blend of creative writing and extensive research, which emphasize important events, people, and places in U.S. history." **Pays authors royalty or work purchased outright.** Guidelines online.

NONFICTION Subjects include history. Submit outline/synopsis and 3 sample chapters.

FICTION Subjects include historical. Submit outline/synopsis and 3 sample chapters.

TIPS "Read through our recently published titles and review our catalog. When selecting titles to publish, our emphasis will be on important events, people, and places in U.S. history. Writers are encouraged to submit a detailed bibliography, including secondary and primary sources, and expert reviews with their submissions."

Ⓐ⊘ CANDLEWICK PRESS

99 Dover St., Somerville MA 02144. (617)661-3330. **Fax:** (617)661-0565. **E-mail:** bigbear@candlewick.com. **Website:** www.candlewick.com. Estab. 1991. Publishes hardcover and trade paperback originals, and reprints. "Candlewick Press publishes high-quality, illustrated children's books for ages infant through young adult. We are a truly child-centered publisher." **Publishes 200 titles/year. 5% of books from first-time authors. Pays authors royalty of 2½-10% based on retail price. Offers advance.**

Candlewick Press is not accepting queries or unsolicited mss at this time.

NONFICTION Picture books: concept, biography, geography, nature/environment. Young readers: biography, geography, nature/environment.

FICTION Subjects include juvenile, picture books, young adult. Picture books: animal, concept, contemporary, fantasy, history, humor, multicultural, nature/environment, poetry. Middle readers, young adults: contemporary, fantasy, history, humor, multicultural, poetry, science fiction, sports, suspense/mystery. "We currently do not accept unsolicited editorial queries or submissions. If you are an author or illustrator and would like us to consider your work, please read our submissions policy (online) to learn more."

TIPS "*We no longer accept unsolicited mss.* See our website for further information about us."

CANTERBURY HOUSE PUBLISHING, LTD.

4535 Ottawa Trail, Sarasota FL 34233. (941)312-6912. **Website:** www.canterburyhousepublishing.com. **Contact:** Sandra Horton, editor. Estab. 2009. Publishes hardcover, trade paperback, and electronic originals. "Our audience is made up of readers looking for wholesome fiction with good southern stories, with elements of mystery, romance, and inspiration and/or are looking for stories of achievement and triumph over challenging circumstances. We are very strict on our submission guidelines due to our small staff, and our target market of Southern regional settings." **Publishes 3-6 titles/year. 35% of books from first-time authors. 100% from unagented writers. Pays 10-15% royalty on wholesale price.** Publishes ms 9-12 months after acceptance. Accepts simultaneous submissions. Responds in 1 month to queries; 3 months to mss. Book catalog online. Guidelines online.

NONFICTION Subjects include memoirs, regional. Query with SASE and through website e-mail upon request. Reviews artwork. Send photocopies.

FICTION Subjects include contemporary, historical, literary, mainstream, mystery, regional, romance, suspense. Query with SASE and through website.

TIPS "Because of our limited staff, we prefer authors who have good writing credentials and submit edited manuscripts. We also look at authors who are business and marketing savvy and willing to help promote their books."

CAPALL BANN PUBLISHING

Auton Farm, Milverton, Somerset TA4 1NE, United Kingdom. (44)(182)340-1528. **E-mail:** enquiries@capallbann.co.uk. **Website:** www.capallbann.co.uk. **Contact:** Julia Day (MBS, healing, animals); Jon Day (MBS, religion). Publishes trade and mass market paperback originals and trade paperback and mass market paperback reprints. "Our mission is to publish books of real value to enhance and improve readers' lives." **Publishes 46 titles/year. 800 queries received/year. 450 mss received/year. 50% of books from first-time authors. 100% from unagented writers. Pays 10% royalty on net sales.** Publishes ms 4-8 months after acceptance. Accepts simultaneous submissions. Responds in 2-6 weeks to queries; 2 months to proposals and mss. Book catalog free. Guidelines online.

NONFICTION Subjects include animals, anthropology, archeology, gardening, health, medicine, music, dance, nature, environment, philosophy, religion, spirituality, women's issues, witchcraft, paganism, druidry, ritual magic, new age. Submit outline. Reviews artwork/photos. Send photocopies.

CAPSTONE PRESS

Capstone Young Readers, 1710 Roe Crest Dr., North Mankato MN 56003. **E-mail:** nf.il.sub@capstonepub.com. **Website:** www.capstonepub.com. Estab. 1991. The Capstone Press imprint publishes nonfiction with accessible text on topics kids love to capture interest and build confidence and skill in beginning, struggling, and reluctant readers, grades pre-K-9. Responds only if submissions fit needs. Mss and writing samples will not be returned. "If you receive no reply within 6 months, you should assume the editors are not interested.". Catalog available upon request. Guidelines online.

CARCANET PRESS

Alliance House, 4th Floor, 30 Cross St., Manchester England M2 7AQ, United Kingdom. **E-mail:** info@carcanet.co.uk. **E-mail:** schmidt@carcanet.co.uk. **Website:** www.carcanet.co.uk. **Contact:** Michael Schmidt, editorial and managing director. Estab. 1969. Publishes hardcover and trade paperback originals. "Carcanet Press is one of Britain's leading poetry publishers. It provides a comprehensive and diverse list of modern and classic poetry in English and in translation."

POETRY Familiarize yourself with our books, and then submit between 6 and 10 pages or work (poetry or translations) and SASE. Replies are usually sent within 6 weeks. Writers wishing to propose other projects should send a full synopsis and cover letter, with sample pages, having first ascertained that the kind of book proposed is suitable for our programme. Do not call in person.

THE CAREER PRESS, INC.

220 West Parkway, Unit 12, Pompton Lakes NJ 07442. (201)848-0310 or (800)227-3371. **E-mail:** aschwartz@careerpress.com. **Website:** www.careerpress.com. **Contact:** Michael Pye, director of product development, Adam Schwartz, acquisitions editor. Estab. 1985. Publishes hardcover and paperback originals. Career Press publishes books for adult readers seeking practical information to improve themselves in careers, business, HR, sales, entrepreneurship, and other related topics, as well as titles on supervision, management and CEOs. New Page Books publishes in the areas of New Age, new science, paranormal, the unexplained, alternative history, spirituality. Accepts simultaneous submissions. Guidelines online.

NONFICTION Subjects include business, economics, money, finance, recreation, nutrition. Look through our catalog; become familiar with our publications. "We like to select authors who are specialists on their topic." Submit outline, bio, TOC, 2-3 sample chapters, marketing plan, SASE. Or, send complete ms (preferred).

CARNEGIE MELLON UNIVERSITY PRESS

5032 Forbes Ave., Pittsburgh PA 15289-1021. (412)268-2861. **Fax:** (412)268-8706. **E-mail:** carnegiemellonuniversitypress@gmail.com. **Website:** www.cmu.edu/universitypress/. **Contact:** Cynthia Lamb, senior editor. Estab. 1972. Publishes hardcover and trade paperback originals. **Publishes 6 titles/year.** Book catalog and guidelines online.

NONFICTION Subjects include art, architecture, computers, electronics, education, (higher), history, literary criticism, memoirs, music, dance, science, sociology, translation. Query with SASE.

FICTION Subjects include literary, mainstream, contemporary, poetry, poetry in translation, short story collections, drama, epistolary novel.

POETRY Holds annual reading period. "This reading period is only for poets who have not previously been published by CMP." Submit complete ms. **Requires reading fee of $15.**

CAROLINA WREN PRESS

120 Morris St., Durham NC 27701. (919)560-2738. **E-mail:** carolinawrenpress@earthlink.net. **Website:** www.carolinawrenpress.org. **Contact:** Andrea Selch, president. Estab. 1976. "We publish poetry, fiction, and memoirs by, and/or about people of color, women, gay/lesbian issues, and work by writers from, living in, or writing about the U.S. South." Publishes ms 2 year after acceptance. Accepts simultaneous submissions. Responds in 3 months to queries; 6 months to mss. Guidelines online.

Accepts simultaneous submissions, but "let us know if work has been accepted elsewhere."

NONFICTION Subjects include ethnic, gay, lesbian, literature, multicultural, womens issues.

FICTION Subjects include ethnic, experimental, poetry, feminist, gay, lesbian, literary, short story collections. "We are no longer publishing children's literature of any topic." Books: 6×9 paper; typeset; various bindings; illustrations. Distributes titles through Amazon.com, Barnes & Noble, Baker & Taylor, and on their website. "We very rarely accept any unsolicited manuscripts, but we accept submissions for the Doris Bakwin Award for Writing by a Woman in Jan-March of even-numbered years." Query by mail. "We will accept e-mailed queries—a letter in the body of the e-mail describing your project—but please do not send large attachments."

POETRY Publishes 2 poetry books/year, "usually through the Carolina Wren Press Poetry Series Contest. Otherwise we primarily publish women, minorities, and authors from, living in, or writing about the U.S. South." Not accepting unsolicited submissions except through Poetry Series Contest. Accepts e-mail queries, but send only letter and description of work, no large files. Carolina Wren Press Poetry Contest for a First or Second Book takes submissions, electronically, from January to March of odd-numbered years.

TIPS "Best way to get read is to submit to a contest."

CAROLRHODA BOOKS, INC.

1251 Washington Ave. N., Minneapolis MN 55401. **Website:** www.lernerbooks.com. Estab. 1959. "We will continue to seek targeted solicitations at specific reading levels and in specific subject areas. The company will list these targeted solicitations on our website and in national newsletters, such as the SCBWI Bulletin." Interested in "boundary-pushing" teen fiction. *Lerner Publishing Group no longer accepts submissions to any of their imprints except for Kar-Ben Publishing.*

CAROUSEL PRESS

P.O. Box 6038, Berkeley CA 94706-0038. (510)527-5849. **E-mail:** editor@carousel-press.com. **Website:** www.berkeleyandbeyond.com/carousel-press. **Contact:** Carole T. Meyers, editor/publisher. Estab. 1976. Publishes trade paperback originals and reprints. **Publishes 1-2 titles/year. Pays 10-15% royalty on wholesale price.** Responds in 1 month to queries.

NONFICTION Subjects include travel, travel-related. Query with SASE.

CARSON-DELLOSA PUBLISHING CO., INC.

P.O. Box 35665, Greensboro NC 27425-5665. (336)632-0084. **E-mail:** freelancesamples@carson-dellosa.com. **Website:** www.carsondellosa.com. **Publishes 80-90 titles/year. 15-20% of books from first-time authors. 95% from unagented writers. Makes outright purchase.** Accepts simultaneous submissions. Responds in 3 months to proposals. Book catalog online. Guidelines available free.

NONFICTION Subjects include education, including Christian education. "We publish supplementary educational materials, such as teacher resource books, workbooks, and activity books." No textbooks or trade children's books, please. Submit proposal package, sample chapters or pages, SASE. Reviews artwork/photos. Send photocopies.

CARTWHEEL BOOKS

Imprint of Scholastic Trade Division, 557 Broadway, New York NY 10012. (212)343-6100. **Website:** www.scholastic.com. Estab. 1991. Publishes novelty books, easy readers, board books, hardcover and trade paperback originals. Cartwheel Books publishes innovative books for children, up to age 8. "We are looking for 'novelties' that are books first, play objects second. Even without its gimmick, a Cartwheel Book should stand alone as a valid piece of children's literature." Accepts simultaneous submissions. Guidelines available free.

NONFICTION Subjects include animals, history, music, dance, nature, environment, recreation, science, sports. Cartwheel Books publishes for the very young, therefore nonfiction should be written in a manner that is accessible to preschoolers through 2nd grade. Often writers choose topics that are too narrow or "special" and do not appeal to the mass market. Also, the text and vocabulary are frequently too difficult for our young audience. *Accepts mss from agents only.* Reviews artwork/photos. Send Please do not send original artwork.

FICTION Subjects include humor, juvenile, mystery, picture books. Again, the subject should have mass market appeal for very young children. Humor can be helpful, but not necessary. Mistakes writers make are a reading level that is too difficult, a topic of no interest or too narrow, or mss that are too long. *Accepts mss from agents only.*

CATHOLIC UNIVERSITY OF AMERICA PRESS

620 Michigan Ave. NE, 240 Leahy Hall, Washington DC 20064. (202)319-5052. **Fax:** (202)319-4985. **E-mail:** cua-press@cua.edu. **Website:** cuapress.cua.edu. **Contact:** Trevor Lipscombe, director. Estab. 1939. The Catholic University of America Press publishes in the fields of history (ecclesiastical and secular), literature and languages, philosophy, political theory, social studies, and theology. "We have interdisciplinary emphasis on patristics, and medieval studies. We publish works of original scholarship intended for academic libraries, scholars and other professionals and works that offer a synthesis of knowledge of the subject of interest to a general audience or suitable for use in college and university classrooms." **Publishes 30-35 titles/year. 50% of books from first-time authors. 100% from unagented writers. Pays variable royalty on net receipts.** Publishes ms 18 months after acceptance. Responds in 5 days to queries. Book catalog on request. Guidelines online.

NONFICTION Subjects include government, politics, history, language, literature, philosophy, religion, Church-state relations. No unrevised doctoral dissertations. Length: 40,000-120,000 words. Query with outline, sample chapter, CV, and list of previous publications.

TIPS "Scholarly monographs and works suitable for adoption as supplementary reading material in courses have the best chance."

CATO INSTITUTE

1000 Massachusetts Ave. NW, Washington DC 20001. (202)842-0200. **Website:** www.cato.org. **Contact:** Submissions Editor. Estab. 1977. Publishes hardcover originals, trade paperback originals and reprints. Cato Institute publishes books on public policy issues from a free-market or libertarian perspective. **Publishes 12 titles/year. 25% of books from first-time authors. 90% from unagented writers. Makes outright purchase of $1,000-10,000. Pays advance.** Publishes ms 9 months after acceptance. Accepts simultaneous submissions. Responds in 3 months to queries. Book catalog online.

NONFICTION Subjects include business, economics, education, government, politics, health, medicine, money, finance, sociology, public policy. Query with SASE.

CAVE BOOKS

277 Clamer Rd., Trenton NJ 08628. (609)530-9743. **E-mail:** editor@cavebooks.com. **Website:** www.cavebooks.com. **Contact:** Elizabeth Winkler, managing editor. Estab. 1980. Publishes hardcover and trade paperback originals and reprints. Cave Books publishes books only on caves, karst, and speleology. **Publishes 2 titles/year. 20 queries received/year. 10 mss received/year. 75% of books from first-time authors. 100% from unagented writers. Pays 10% royalty on retail price.** Publishes ms 18 months after acceptance. Accepts simultaneous submissions. Responds in 2 weeks to queries; 3 months to mss.

NONFICTION Subjects include Americana, animals, anthropology, archeology, history, nature, environment, photography, recreation, regional, science, sports, cave exploration, travel. Submit complete ms. Reviews artwork/photos. Send photocopies.

FICTION Subjects include adventure, historical, literary, caves, karst, speleology. Must be realistic and centrally concerned with cave exploration. The cave and action in the cave must be central, authentic, and realistic. No gothic, science fiction, fantasy, romance, mystery, or poetry. No novels that are not entirely about caves. Query with SASE. Submit complete ms.

TIPS "Our readers are interested only in caves, karst, and speleology. Please do not send manuscripts on other subjects."

CAVE HOLLOW PRESS

P.O. Drawer J, Warrensburg MO 64093. **E-mail:** gbcrump@cavehollowpress.com. **Website:** www.cavehollowpress.com. **Contact:** G.B. Crump, editor. Estab. 2001. Publishes trade paperback originals. **Publishes 1 titles/year. 85 queries received/year. 6 mss received/year. 80% of books from first-time authors. 100% from unagented writers. Pays 7-12% royalty on wholesale price. Pays negotiable amount in advance.** Publishes ms 1 year after acceptance. Accepts simultaneous submissions. Responds in 1-2 months to queries and proposals; 3-6 months to mss. Book catalog for #10 SASE. Guidelines available free.

FICTION Subjects include contemporary, mainstream. "Our website is updated frequently to reflect the current type of fiction Cave Hollow Press is seeking." Query with SASE.

TIPS "Our audience varies based on the type of book we are publishing. We specialize in Missouri and Midwest regional fiction. We are interested in talented writers from Missouri and the surrounding Midwest. Check our submission guidelines on the website for what type of fiction we are interested in currently."

MARSHALL CAVENDISH

99 White Plains Rd., Tarrytown NY 10591. (914)332-8888. **Fax:** (914)332-1082. **Website:** www.marshallcavendish.us. "Marshall Cavendish is an international publisher that publishes books, directories, magazines and digital platforms. Our philosophy of enriching life through knowledge transcends boundaries of geography and culture. In line with this vision, our products reach across the globe in 13 languages, and our publishing network spans Asia and the USA. Our brands have garnered international awards for educational excellence, and they include Marshall Cavendish Reference, Marshall Cavendish Benchmark, Marshall Cavendish Children, Marshall Cavendish Education and Marshall Cavendish Editions."

Marshall Cavendish is no longer accepting unsolicited mss. However, the company will continue to consider agented mss.

CEDAR FORT, INC.

2373 W. 700 S, Springville UT 84663. (801)489-4084. **Fax:** (801)489-1097. **Website:** www.cedarfort.com. Estab. 1986. Publishes hardcover, trade paperback originals and reprints, mass market paperback and electronic reprints. "Each year we publish well over 100 books, and many of those are by first-time authors. At the same time, we love to see books from established authors. As one of the largest book publishers in Utah, we have the capability and enthusiasm to make your book a success, whether you are a new author or a returning one. We want to publish uplifting and edifying books that help people think about what is important in life, books people enjoy reading to relax and feel better about themselves, and books to help improve lives. Although we do put out several children's books each year, we are extremely selective. Our children's books must have strong religious or moral values, and must contain outstanding writing and an excellent storyline." **Publishes 150 titles/year. Receives 200 queries/year; 600 mss/year. 60% of books from first-time authors. 95% from unagented writers. Pays 10-12% royalty on wholesale price. Pays $2,000-50,000 advance.** Publishes ms 10-14 months after acceptance. Responds in 1 month on queries; 2 months on proposals; 4 months on mss. Catalog and guidelines online.

IMPRINTS Council Press, Sweetwater Books, Bonneville Books, Front Table Books, Hobble Creek Press, CFI, Plain Sight Publishing, Horizon Publishers, Pioneer Plus.

NONFICTION Subjects include agriculture, Americana, animals, anthropology, archeology, business, child guidance, communications, cooking, crafts, creative nonfiction, economics, education, foods, gardening, health, history, hobbies, horticulture, house and home, military, nature, recreation, regional, religion, social sciences, spirituality, war, womens issues, young adult. Query with SASE; submit proposal package, including outline, 2 sample chapters; or submit completed ms. Reviews artwork as part of the ms package. Send photocopies.

FICTION Subjects include adventure, contemporary, fantasy, historical, humor, juvenile, literary, mainstream, military, multicultural, mystery, regional, religious, romance, science fiction, spiritual, sports, suspense, war, western, young adult. Submit completed ms.

TIPS "Our audience is rural, conservative, mainstream. The first page of your ms is very important because we start reading every submission, but good-writing and plot keep us reading."

CENTERSTREAM PUBLISHING

P.O. Box 17878, Anaheim Hills CA 92817. (714)779-9390. **Fax:** (714)779-9390. **E-mail:** centerstrm@aol.com. **Website:** www.centerstream-usa.com. Estab. 1980. Publishes music hardcover and mass market paperback originals, trade paperback and mass market paperback reprints. Centerstream publishes music history and instructional books, all instruments plus DVDs. **Publishes 12 titles/year. 15 queries received/year. 15 mss received/year. 80% of books from first-time authors. 100% from unagented writers. Pays 10-15% royalty on wholesale price. Pays $300-3,000 advance.** Publishes ms 8 months after acceptance. Accepts simultaneous submissions. Responds in 3 months to queries. Book catalog and ms guidelines for #10 SASE.

NONFICTION Query with SASE.

CHALICE PRESS

483 E. Lockwood Ave., Suite 100, St. Louis MO 63119. (314)231-8500. **Fax:** (314)231-8524. **E-mail:** submissions@chalicepress.com. **Website:** www.chalicepress.com. **Contact:** Bradley Lyons, president and publisher. Publishes hardcover and trade paperback originals. **Publishes 20 titles/year. 300 queries received/year. 250 mss received/year. 10% of books from first-time authors. 100% from unagented writers.** Publishes ms 1 year after acceptance. Accepts simultaneous submissions. Responds in 2 months to queries; 3 months to proposals and mss. Book catalog online. Guidelines online.

NONFICTION Subjects include religion, Christian spirituality. Submit query.

TIPS "We publish for lay Christian readers, church ministers, and educators."

S. CHAND & COMPANY LTD.

7361 Ram Nagar, Qutab Rd., New Delhi 110055, India. (91)(11)2367-2080. **Fax:** (91)(11)2367-7446. **E-mail:** editorial@schandgroup.com. **Website:** www.schandgroup.com. Guidelines online.

NONFICTION Subjects include business, economics, history, botany, chemistry, engineering, technical, English, mathematics, physics, political science, zoology. Query through website.

CHANGELING PRESS LLC

315 N. Centre St., Martinsburg WV 25404. **E-mail:** submissions@changelingpress.com. **Website:** www.changelingpress.com. **Contact:** Margaret Riley, publisher. Publishes e-books. Novellas only (8,000-25,000 words). **Pays 35% gross royalties monthly.** Responds in 1 week to queries.

FICTION Subjects include erotica, fantasy, romance, science fiction, suspense, paranormal, BDSM. Accepts unsolicited submissions. E-mail submissions only.

CHARLESBRIDGE PUBLISHING

85 Main St., Watertown MA 02472. (617)926-0329. **Fax:** (617)926-5720. **E-mail:** tradeeditorial@charlesbridge.com. **Website:** www.charlesbridge.com. Estab. 1980. Publishes hardcover and trade paperback nonfiction and fiction, children's books for the trade and library markets. "Charlesbridge publishes high-quality books for children, with a goal of creating lifelong readers and lifelong learners. Our books encourage reading and discovery in the classroom, library, and home. We believe that books for children should offer accurate information, promote a positive worldview, and embrace a child's innate sense of wonder and fun. To this end, we continually strive to seek new voices, new visions, and new directions in children's literature." **Publishes 30 titles/year. 10-20% of books from first-time authors. 80% from unagented writers. Pays royalty. Pays advance.** Publishes ms 2-4 years after acceptance. Responds in 3 months. Guidelines online.

NONFICTION Subjects include animals, creative nonfiction, history, multicultural, nature, environment, science, social science. Strong interest in nature, environment, social studies, and other topics for trade and library markets. *Exclusive submissions only.* "Charlesbridge accepts unsolicited manuscripts submitted exclusively to us for a period of 3 months. 'Exclusive Submission' should be written on all envelopes and cover letters." Please submit only 1 or 2 chapters at a time. For nonfiction books longer than 30 ms pages, send a detailed proposal, a chapter outline, and 1-3 chapters of text.

FICTION Strong stories with enduring themes. Charlesbridge publishes both picture books and transitional bridge books (books ranging from early readers to middle-grade chapter books). Our fiction titles include lively, plot-driven stories with strong, engaging characters. No alphabet books, board books, coloring books, activity books, or books with audiotapes or CD-ROMs. *Exclusive submissions only.* "Charlesbridge accepts unsolicited manuscripts submitted exclusively to us for a period of 3 months. 'Exclusive Submission' should be written on all envelopes and cover letters." Please submit only 1 or 2 mss at a time. For picture books and shorter bridge books, please send a complete ms. For fiction books longer than 30 ms pages, please send a detailed plot synopsis, a chapter outline, and 3 chapters of text.

TIPS "To become acquainted with our publishing program, we encourage you to review our books and visit our website where you will find our catalog."

THE CHARLES PRESS, PUBLISHERS

230 North 21st St., #202, Philadelphia PA 19103. (215)561-2786. **Fax:** (215)561-0191. **E-mail:** submissions@charlespresspub.com. **Website:** www.charlespresspub.com. **Contact:** Lauren Meltzer, publisher. Estab. 1982. Publishes hardcover and trade paperback originals. Currently emphasizing mental and physical health (especially holistic, complementary and alternative healthcare), psychology, animals/pets/veterinary medicine, how-to (especially relating to healthcare and wellness), comparative religion, aging/eldercare/geriatrics, medical reference books. Accepts simultaneous submissions. Responds in 1-2 months. Book catalog online. Guidelines online.

NONFICTION Subjects include child guidance, health, mental health, physical health, medicine, psychology, religion, nursing, health care, how-to, aging/eldercare, criminology, crime. No fiction, autobiographies, children's books, or poetry. Query first, then submit proposal package that includes a description of the book, a few representative sample chapters, intended audience, competing titles, author's qualifications/background and SASE. No e-mailed or faxed submissions. Reviews artwork/photos. Send photocopies or transparencies.

CHELSEA GREEN PUBLISHING CO.

85 N. Main St., Suite 120, White River Junction VT 05001. (802)295-6300. **Fax:** (802)295-6444. **E-mail:** editorial@chelseagreen.com. **E-mail:** submissions@chelseagreen.com. **Website:** www.chelseagreen.com. Estab. 1984. Publishes hardcover and trade paperback originals and reprints. "Since 1984, Chelsea Green has been the publishing leader for books on the politics and practice of sustainable living." **Publishes 18-25 titles/year. 600-800 queries received/year. 200-300 mss received/year. 30% of books from first-time authors. 80% from unagented writers. Pays royalty on publisher's net. Pays $2,500-10,000 advance.** Publishes ms 18 months after acceptance. Responds in 2 weeks to queries; 1 month to proposals/mss. Book catalog online. Guidelines online.

NONFICTION Subjects include agriculture, alternative lifestyles, ethical & sustainable business, environment, foods, organic gardening, health, green building, progressive politics, science, social justice, simple living, renewable energy; and other sustainability topics. "We seldom publish cookbooks." Prefers electronic queries and proposals via e-mail (as a single attachment). If sending via snail mail, submissions will only be returned with SASE. Please review our guidelines carefully before submitting. Reviews artwork/photos.

TIPS "Our readers and our authors are passionate about finding sustainable and viable solutions to contemporary challenges in the fields of energy, food production, economics, and building. It would be helpful for prospective authors to have a look at several of our current books, as well as our website."

CHEMICAL PUBLISHING CO., INC.

P.O. Box 676, Revere MA 02151. (888)439-3976. **Fax:** (888)439-3976. **E-mail:** info@chemical-publishing.com. **Website:** www.chemical-publishing.com. **Contact:** B. Carr, publisher. Estab. 1934. Publishes hardcover originals. Chemical Publishing Co., Inc., publishes professional chemistry-technical titles aimed at people employed in the chemical industry, libraries and graduate courses. **Publishes 10-15 titles/year. 20 queries received/year. 50% of books from first-time authors. 100% from unagented writers. Pays 10% royalty on retail price or makes negotiable outright purchase. Pays negotiable advance.** Publishes ms 8 months after acceptance. Responds in 3 weeks to queries; 5 weeks to proposals; 1 months to mss. Book catalog available free. Guidelines online.

NONFICTION Subjects include agriculture, cooking, foods, nutrition, health, medicine, nature, environment, science, analytical methods, chemical technology, cosmetics, dictionaries, engineering, environmental science, food technology, formularies, industrial technology, medical, metallurgy, textiles. Submit outline, a few pages of 3 sample chapters, SASE. Download CPC submission form online and include with submission. Reviews, artwork and photos should also be part of the manuscript package.

TIPS "Audience is professionals in various fields of chemistry, corporate and public libraries, college libraries. We request a fax letter with an introduction of the author and the kind of book written. Afterwards, we will reply. If the title is of interest, then we will request samples of the manuscript."

CHICAGO REVIEW PRESS

814 N. Franklin St., Chicago IL 60610. (312)337-0747. **Fax:** (312)337-5110. **E-mail:** frontdesk@ipgbook.com. **Website:** www.chicagoreviewpress.com. **Contact:** Cynthia Sherry, publisher; Yuval Taylor, senior editor; Jerome Pohlen, senior editor; Lisa Reardon, senior editor. Estab. 1973. "Chicago Review Press publishes high-quality, nonfiction, educational activity books that extend the learning process through hands-on projects and accurate and interesting text. We look for activity books that are as much fun as they are constructive and informative." **Pays authors royalty of 7.5-12.5% based on retail price. Offers advances of $3,000-6,000. Pays illustrators and photographers by the project (range varies considerably).** Publishes book Publishes a book 1-2 years after acceptance. Accepts simultaneous submissions. Responds in 2 months. Book catalog available for $3. Ms guidelines available for $3.

IMPRINTS Academy Chicago; Ball Publishing; Chicago Review Press; Lawrence Hill Books; Zephyr Press.

NONFICTION Young readers, middle readers and young adults: activity books, arts/crafts, multicultural, history, nature/environment, science. "We're interested in hands-on, educational books; anything else probably will be rejected." Average length: young readers and young adults—144-160 pages. Enclose cover letter and no more than a table of contents and 1-2 sample chapters; prefers not to receive e-mail queries.

TIPS "We're looking for original activity books for small children and the adults caring for them—new themes and enticing projects to occupy kids' imaginations and promote their sense of personal creativity. We like activity books that are as much fun as they are constructive. Please write for guidelines so you'll know what we're looking for."

⊘ CHILDREN'S BRAINS ARE YUMMY (CBAY) BOOKS

P.O. Box 670296, Austin TX 75367. **E-mail:** conflictsubmissions@gmail.com; madeline@cbaybooks.com. **Website:** www.cbaybooks.com. **Contact:** Madeline Smoot, publisher. Estab. 2008. "CBAY Books currently focuses on quality fantasy and science fiction books for the middle grade and teen markets. We are not currently accepting unsolicited submissions." **Publishes 8 titles/year. 30% of books from first-time authors. Pays authors royalty 10%-15% based on wholesale price. Offers advances against royalties. Average amount $500.** Brochure and guidelines online.

FICTION Subjects include adventure, mystery, science fiction, suspense, folktales.

⊘ CHILD'S PLAY (INTERNATIONAL) LTD.

Child's Play, Ashworth Rd. Bridgemead, Swindon, Wiltshire SN5 7YD, United Kingdom. **E-mail:** neil@childs-play.com; office@childs-play.com. **Website:** www.childs-play.com. **Contact:** Sue Baker, Neil Burden, manuscript acquisitions. Art Director: Annie Kubler. Estab. 1972. Specializes in nonfiction, fiction, educational material, multicultural material. Produces 30 picture books/year; 10 young readers/year. "A child's early years are more important than any other. This is when children learn most about the world around them and the language they need to survive and grow. Child's Play aims to create exactly the right material for this all-important time." **Publishes 40 titles/year.** Publishes ms 2 years after acceptance. Accepts simultaneous submissions.

NONFICTION Picture books: activity books, animal, concept, multicultural, music/dance, nature/environment, science. Young readers: activity books, animal, concept, multicultural, music/dance, nature/environment, science. Average word length: picture books—2,000; young readers—3,000.

FICTION Picture books: adventure, animal, concept, contemporary, folktales, multicultural, nature/environment. Young readers: adventure, animal, anthology, concept, contemporary, folktales, humor, multicultural, nature/environment, poetry. Average word length: picture books—1,500; young readers—2,000.

TIPS "Look at our website to see the kind of work we do before sending. Do not send cartoons. We do not publish novels. We do publish lots of books with pictures of babies/toddlers."

CHILD WELFARE LEAGUE OF AMERICA

1726 M St. NW, Suite 500, Washington DC 20036. **E-mail:** cwla@cwla.org. **Website:** www.cwla.org. Publishes hardcover and trade paperback originals. CWLA is a privately supported, nonprofit, membership-based organization committed to preserving, protecting, and promoting the well-being of all children and their families. Accepts simultaneous submissions. Book catalog and guidelines online.

NONFICTION Subjects include child guidance, sociology. Submit complete ms and proposal with outline, TOC, sample chapter, intended audience, and SASE.

TIPS "We are looking for positive, kid-friendly books for ages 3-9. We are looking for books that have a positive message—a feel-good book."

CHOSEN BOOKS

a division of Baker Publishing Group, 3985 Bradwater St., Fairfax VA 22031. (703)764-8250. **E-mail:** jcampbell@chosenbooks.com. **Website:** www.chosenbooks.com. **Contact:** Jane Campbell, editorial director. Estab. 1971. Publishes hardcover and trade paperback originals. "We publish well-crafted books that recognize the gifts and ministry of the Holy Spirit, and help the reader live a more empowered and effective life for Jesus Christ." **Publishes 24 titles/year. 10% of books from first-time authors. 90% from unagented writers. Pays small advance.** Publishes ms 12-18 months after acceptance. Accepts simultaneous submissions. Responds in 2-3 months to queries. Guidelines online.

NONFICTION "We publish books reflecting the current acts of the Holy Spirit in the world, books with a charismatic Christian orientation, or thematic first-person narrative. Query briefly by e-mail first." No New Age, poetry, fiction, autobiographies, biographies, compilations, Bible studies, booklets, academic, or children's books. Submit synopsis, chapter outline, 2 chapters, resume and SASE or e-mail address. No computer disks. E-mail attachments OK.

TIPS "We look for solid, practical advice for the growing and maturing Christian. Platform essential. No chronicling of life events, please. Narratives have to be theme-driven. State the topic or theme of your book clearly in your query."

CHRISTIAN BOOKS TODAY LTD

136 Main St., Buckshaw Village Chorley, Lancashire PR7 7BZ, United Kingdom. **E-mail:** editme@christianbookstoday.com. **Website:** www.christianbookstoday.com. **Contact:** Jason Richardson, MD (nonfiction); Lynda McIntosh, editor (fiction). Estab. 2009. Publishes trade paperback originals/reprints and electronic originals/reprints. **Publishes 39 titles/year. 75% of books from first-time authors. 100% from unagented writers. Pays 10% royalty on Amazon retail price; 15% e-book; 5% wholesale trade.** Publishes ms 6 months after acceptance. Accepts simultaneous submissions. Responds in 1 month to queries; 2 months to proposals and mss. Catalog and guidelines online.

NONFICTION Subjects include spirituality, Christian/Catholic. "We are not looking for nonfiction at this time. Please send us your fiction."

FICTION Subjects include adventure, mainstream, poetry, religious, Catholic, Evangelical, Christian. "Please send us your Christian or 'clean read' fiction. Nondenominational Christian romance, suspense, mystery, and contemporary Christian fiction are always welcome." Submit chapter-by-chapter outline and 3 sample chapters.

TIPS "We are looking particularly for Christian romance. Any other genre will likely not find a place with our publishing house at this time. New and unpublished writers are welcome. We appeal to a general Christian readership. We are interested in 'clean read' mss only. No profanity, sexual content, gambling, substance abuse, or graphic violence. Please do not send us conspiracy-type stories."

CHRISTIAN FOCUS PUBLICATIONS

Geanies House, Fearn, Tain Ross-shire Scotland IV20 1TW, United Kingdom. (44)1862-871-011. **Fax:** (44)1862-871-699. **E-mail:** submissions@christianfocus.com. **Website:** www.christianfocus.com. **Contact:** Director of Publishing. Estab. 1975. Specializes in Christian material, nonfiction, fiction, educational material. **Publishes 22-32 titles/year. 2% of books from first-time authors.** Publishes ms 1 year after acceptance. Responds to queries in 2 weeks; mss in 3 months.

NONFICTION All levels: activity books, biography, history, religion, science. Average word length: picture books—5,000; young readers—5,000; middle readers—5,000-10,000; young adult/teens—10,000-20,000. Query or submit outline/synopsis and 3 sample chapters. Will consider electronic submissions and previously published work.

FICTION Picture books, young readers, adventure, history, religion. Middle readers: adventure, problem novels, religion. Young adult/teens: adventure, history, problem novels, religion. Average word length: young readers—5,000; middle readers—max 10,000; young adult/teen—max 20,000. Query or submit outline/synopsis and 3 sample chapters. Will consider electronic submissions and previously published work.

TIPS "Be aware of the international market as regards writing style/topics as well as illustration styles. Our company sells rights to European as well as Asian countries. Fiction sales are not as good as they were. Christian fiction for youngsters is not a product that is performing well in comparison to nonfiction such as Christian biography/Bible stories/church history, etc."

CHRONICLE BOOKS

680 Second St., San Francisco CA 94107. **E-mail:** submissions@chroniclebooks.com. **Website:** www.chroniclebooks.com. "We publish an exciting range of books, stationery, kits, calendars, and novelty formats. Our list includes children's books and interactive formats; young adult books; cookbooks; fine art, design, and photography; pop culture; craft, fashion, beauty, and home decor; relationships, mind-body-spirit; innovative formats such as interactive journals, kits, decks, and stationery; and much, much more." **Publishes 90 titles/year. Generally pays authors in royalties based on retail price, "though we do occasionally work on a flat fee basis." Advance varies. Illustrators paid royalty based on retail price or flat fee.** Publishes book Publishes a book 1-3 years after acceptance. Responds to queries in 1 month. Book catalog for 9x12 SAE and 8 first-class stamps. Ms guidelines for #10 SASE.

NONFICTION Subjects include art, beauty, cooking, crafts, house and home, New Age, pop culture. "We're always looking for the new and unusual. We do accept unsolicited manuscripts and we review all proposals. However, given the volume of proposals we receive, we are not able to personally respond to unsolicited proposals unless we are interested in pursuing the project." Submit via mail or e-mail (prefers e-mail for adult submissions; only by mail for children's submissions). Submit proposal (guidelines online) and allow 3 months for editors to review and for children's submissions, allow 6 months. If submitting by mail, do not include SASE since our staff will not return materials.

FICTION Only interested in fiction for children and young adults. No adult fiction. Submit complete ms (picture books); submit outline/synopsis and 3 sample chapters (for older readers). Will not respond to submissions unless interested. Will not consider submissions by fax, e-mail or disk. Do not include SASE; do not send original materials. No submissions will be returned.

CHRONICLE BOOKS FOR CHILDREN

680 Second St., San Francisco CA 94107. (415)537-4200. **Fax:** (415)537-4460. **E-mail:** submissions@chroniclebooks.com. **Website:** www.chroniclekids.com. Publishes hardcover and trade paperback originals. "Chronicle Books for Children publishes an eclectic mixture of traditional and innovative children's books. Our aim is to publish books that inspire young readers to learn and grow creatively while helping them discover the joy of reading. We're looking for quirky, bold artwork and subject matter." **Publishes 100-110 titles/year. 30,000 queries received/year. 6% of books from first-time authors. 25% from unagented writers. Pays variable advance.** Publishes book Publishes a book 18-24 months after acceptance. Accepts simultaneous submissions. Responds in 2-4 weeks to queries; 6 months to mss. Book catalog for 9x12 envelope and 3 first-class stamps. Guidelines online.

NONFICTION Subjects include animals, art, architecture, multicultural, nature, environment, science. Query with synopsis. Reviews artwork/photos.

FICTION Subjects include mainstream, contemporary, multicultural, young adult, picture books. Does not accept proposals by fax, via e-mail, or on disk. When submitting artwork, either as a part of a project or as samples for review, do not send original art.

TIPS "We are interested in projects that have a unique bent to them—be it in subject matter, writing style, or illustrative technique. As a small list, we are looking for books that will lend our list a distinctive flavor. Primarily we are interested in fiction and nonfiction picture books for children ages up to 8 years, and nonfiction books for children ages up to 12 years. We publish board, pop-up, and other novelty formats as well as picture books. We are also interested in early chapter books, middle grade fiction, and young adult projects."

CHURCH PUBLISHING INC.

19 E. 34th St., New York NY 10016. (800)223-6602. **Fax:** (212)779-3392. **E-mail:** nabryan@cpg.org. **Website:** www.churchpublishing.org. **Contact:** Nancy Bryan, editorial director. Estab. 1884. "With a religious publishing heritage dating back to 1918 and headquartered today in New York City, CPI is an official publisher of worship materials and resources for

The Episcopal Church, plus a multi-faceted publisher and supplier to the broader ecumenical marketplace. In the nearly 100 years since its first publication, Church Publishing has emerged as a principal provider of liturgical and musical resources for The Episcopal Church, along with works on church leadership, pastoral care and Christian formation. With its growing portfolio of professional books and resources, Church Publishing was recognized in 1997 as the official publisher for the General Convention of the Episcopal Church in the United States. Simultaneously through the years, Church Publishing has consciously broadened its program, reach, and service to the church by publishing books for and about the worldwide Anglican Communion."

IMPRINTS Church Publishing, Morehouse Publishing, Seabury Books.

TIPS "Prefer using freelancers who are located in central Pennsylvania and are available for meetings when necessary."

CLARION BOOKS

Houghton Mifflin Co., 215 Park Ave. S., New York NY 10003. **Website:** www.hmhco.com. Estab. 1965. Publishes hardcover originals for children. "Clarion Books publishes picture books, nonfiction, and fiction for infants through grade 12. Avoid telling your stories in verse unless you are a professional poet. *We are no longer responding to your unsolicited submission unless we are interested in publishing it. Please do not include a SASE. Submissions will be recycled, and you will not hear from us regarding the status of your submission unless we are interested. We regret that we cannot respond personally to each submission, but we do consider each and every submission we receive."* **Publishes 50 titles/year. Pays 5-10% royalty on retail price. Pays minimum of $4,000 advance.** Publishes book Publishes a book 2 years after acceptance. Responds in 2 months to queries. Guidelines online.

NONFICTION Subjects include Americana, history, language, literature, nature, environment, photography, holiday. No unsolicited mss. Query with SASE. Submit proposal package, sample chapters, SASE. Reviews artwork/photos. Send photocopies.

FICTION Subjects include adventure, historical, humor, mystery, suspense, strong character studies, contemporary. "Clarion is highly selective in the areas of historical fiction, fantasy, and science fiction. A novel must be superlatively written in order to find a place on the list. Mss that arrive without an SASE of adequate size will *not* be responded to or returned. Accepts fiction translations." Submit complete ms. No queries, please. Send to only *one* Clarion editor.

TIPS "Looks for freshness, enthusiasm—in short, life."

CLARITY PRESS, INC.

3277 Roswell Rd. NE, Suite 469, Atlanta GA 30305. (404)647-6501. **Fax:** (877)613-7868. **E-mail:** claritypress@usa.net. **Website:** www.claritypress.com. **Contact:** Diana G. Collier, editorial director (contemporary social justice issues). Estab. 1984. Publishes hardcover and trade paperback originals. **Publishes 8 titles/year.** Accepts simultaneous submissions. Responds to queries only if interested.

NONFICTION Subjects include ethnic, world affairs, human rights/socioeconomic and minority issues, globalization, social justice. Publishes books on contemporary global issues in U.S., Middle East and Africa. No fiction. Query by e-mail only with synopsis, TOC, résumé, publishing history.

TIPS "Check our titles on the website."

Ⓐ CLARKSON POTTER

The Crown Publishing Group, Random House, Inc., 1745 Broadway, New York NY 10019. (212)782-9000. **Website:** www.clarksonpotter.com. Estab. 1959. Publishes hardcover and trade paperback originals. Accepts agented submissions only. Clarkson Potter specializes in publishing cooking books, decorating and other around-the-house how-to subjects.

NONFICTION Subjects include art, architecture, child guidance, cooking, foods, nutrition, language, literature, memoirs, nature, environment, photography, psychology, translation. Agented submissions only.

CLEIS PRESS

Cleis Press & Viva Editions, 2246 Sixth St., Berkeley CA 94710. (510)845-8000 or (800)780-2279. **Fax:** (510)845-8001. **E-mail:** cleis@cleispress.com. **E-mail:** bknight@cleispress.com. **Website:** www.cleispress.com. **Contact:** Brenda Knight, publisher. Estab. 1980. Publishes books that inform, enlighten, and entertain. Areas of interest include gift, inspiration, health, family and childcare, self-help, women's issues, reference, cooking. "We do our best to bring readers quality books that celebrate life, inspire the mind, revive the spirit, and enhance lives all around. Our authors are practical visionaries; people who offer deep wisdom in a hopeful and helpful manner.". Cleis Press publishes provocative, intelligent books in the areas of sexuality, gay and lesbian studies, erotica, fiction, gender studies, and human rights. **Publishes 45 titles/year. 10% of books from first-time authors. 90% from unagented writers. Pays royalty on retail price.** Publishes ms 2 years after acceptance. Responds in 2 month to queries.

NONFICTION Subjects include gay, lesbian, women's issues, women's studies, sexual politics. "Cleis Press is interested in books on topics of sexuality, human rights and women's and gay and lesbian literature. Please consult our website first to be certain that your book fits our list." Query or submit outline and sample chapters.

FICTION Subjects include feminist, gay, lesbian, literary. "We are looking for high quality fiction and nonfiction." Submit complete ms. Include brief bio, list of publishing credits. Send SASE for return of ms or send a disposable ms and SASE for reply only.

TIPS "Be familiar with publishers' catalogs; be absolutely aware of your audience; research potential markets; present fresh new ways of looking at your topic; avoid 'PR' language and include publishing history in query letter."

CLEVELAND STATE UNIVERSITY POETRY CENTER

2121 Euclid Ave., RT 1841, Cleveland OH 44115. (216)687-3986. **Fax:** (216)687-6943. **E-mail:** poetrycenter@csuohio.edu. **Website:** www.csupoetrycenter.com. **Contact:** Amber Allen, managing editor. Estab. 1962.

POETRY The Cleveland State University Poetry Center publishes "full-length collections by established and emerging poets, through competition and solicitation, as well as occasional poetry anthologies, texts on poetics, and novellas. Eclectic in its taste and inclusive in its aesthetic, with particular interest in lyric poetry and innovative approaches to craft. Not interested in light verse, devotional verse, doggerel, or poems by poets who have not read much contemporary poetry." Most mss are accepted through the competitions. All mss sent for competitions are considered for publication. Outside of competitions, mss are accepted by solicitation only.

COACHES CHOICE

P.O. Box 1828, Monterey CA 93942. (888)229-5745. **E-mail:** info@coacheschoice.com. **Website:** www.coacheschoice.com. Publishes trade paperback originals and reprints. "We publish books for anyone who coaches a sport or has an interest in coaching a sport—all levels of competition." Detailed descriptions, step-by-step instructions, and easy-to-follow diagrams set our books apart. Accepts simultaneous submissions. Book catalog available free.

NONFICTION Subjects include sports, sports specific training. Submit proposal package, outline, resume, 2 sample chapters. Reviews artwork/photos. Send photocopies and diagrams.

COACH HOUSE BOOKS

80 bpNichol Lane, Toronto ON M5S 3J4, Canada. (416)979-2217. **Fax:** (416)977-1158. **E-mail:** editor@chbooks.com. **Website:** www.chbooks.com. **Contact:** Alana Wilcox, editorial director. Publishes trade paperback originals by Canadian authors. **Publishes 18 titles/year. 80% of books from first-time authors. Pays 10% royalty on retail price.** Publishes ms 1 year after acceptance. Responds in 6 months to queries. Guidelines online.

NONFICTION Query.

FICTION Subjects include experimental, literary, poetry. "Electronic submissions are welcome. Please send your complete ms, along with an introductory letter that describes your work and compares it to at least 2 current Coach House titles, explaining how your book would fit our list, and a literary CV listing your previous publications and relevant experience. If you would like your ms back, please enclose a large enough self-addressed envelope with adequate postage. If you don't want your ms back, a small stamped envelope or e-mail address is fine. We prefer electronic submissions. Please email PDF files to editor@chbooks.com and include the cover letter and CV as a part of the ms. Please send your manuscript only once. Revised and updated versions will not be read, so make sure you're happy with your text before sending. You can also mail your ms. Please do not send it by ExpressPost or Canada Post courier—regular Canada Post mail is much more likely to arrive here. Be patient. We try to respond promptly, but we do receive hundreds of submissions, so it may take us several months to get back to you. Please do not call or email to check on the status of your submission. We will answer you as promptly as possible."

TIPS "We are not a general publisher, and publish only Canadian poetry, fiction, artist books and drama.

We are interested primarily in innovative or experimental writing."

COFFEE HOUSE PRESS

79 13th NE, Suite 110, Minneapolis MN 55413. (612)338-0125. **Fax:** (612)338-4004. **E-mail:** info@coffeehousepress.org. **Website:** www.coffeehousepress.org. **Contact:** Molly Fuller, production editor. Estab. 1984. Publishes hardcover and trade paperback originals. This successful nonprofit small press has received numerous grants from various organizations including the NEA, the McKnight Foundation and Target. Books published by Coffee House Press have won numerous honors and awards. Example: The Book of Medicines by Linda Hogan won the Colorado Book Award for Poetry and the Lannan Foundation Literary Fellowship. **Publishes 16-18 titles/year.** Responds in 4-6 weeks to queries; up to 6 months to mss. Book catalog and ms guidelines online.

NONFICTION Subjects include creative nonfiction, memoirs, book-length essays, collections of essays. Query with outline and sample pages during annual reading periods (March 1-31 and September 1-30).

FICTION Seeks literary novels, short story collections and poetry. Query first with outline and samples (20-30 pages) during annual reading periods (March 1-31 and September 1-30).

POETRY Coffee House Press will not accept unsolicited poetry submissions. Please check our web page periodically for future updates to this policy.

TIPS "Look for our books at stores and libraries to get a feel for what we like to publish. No phone calls, e-mails, or faxes."

THE COLLEGE BOARD

College Entrance Examination Board, 45 Columbus Ave., New York NY 10023. (212)713-8000. **Website:** www.collegeboard.com. Publishes trade paperback originals. The College Board publishes guidance information for college-bound students. **Publishes 2 titles/year. 25% of books from first-time authors. 50% from unagented writers. Pays royalty on retail price. Pays advance.** Publishes ms 9 months after acceptance. Responds in 2 months to queries. Book catalog available free.

NONFICTION Subjects include education, college guidance. "We want books to help students make a successful transition from high school to college." Query with SASE. Submit outline, sample chapters, SASE.

COLLEGE PRESS PUBLISHING CO.

P.O. Box 1132, 2111 N. Main St., Suite C, Joplin MO 64801. (800)289-3300. **Fax:** (417)623-1929. **Website:** www.collegepress.com. **Contact:** Acquisitions Editor. Estab. 1959. Publishes hardcover and trade paperback originals and reprints. College Press is a traditional Christian publishing house. Seeks proposals for Bible studies, topical studies (biblically based), apologetic studies, historical biographies of Christians, Sunday/Bible School curriculum (adult electives). Accepts simultaneous submissions. Responds in 3 months to proposals; 2 months to mss. Book catalog for 9x12 envelope and 5 first-class stamps. Guidelines online.

NONFICTION Seeks Bible studies, topical studies, apologetic studies, historical biographies of Christians, and Sunday/Bible school curriculum. No poetry, games/puzzles, books on prophecy from a premillennial or dispensational viewpoint, or any book without a Christian message. Query with SASE.

TIPS "Our core market is Christian Churches/Churches of Christ and conservative evangelical Christians. Have your material critically reviewed prior to sending it. Make sure that it is non-Calvinistic and that it leans more amillennial (if it is apocalyptic writing)."

COLOURPOINT BOOKS

Jubilee Business Park, 21 Jubilee Rd., Newtownards, Northern Ireland BT23 4YH, United Kingdom. (44)(289)182-0505. **Fax:** (44)(289)182-1900. **E-mail:** info@colourpoint.co.uk. **Website:** www.colourpoint.co.uk. Estab. 1993. **Publishes 25 titles/year. Pays royalty.** Responds in 2-3 months. Guidelines online.

NONFICTION Subjects include education. "Our specialisms are educational textbooks and transport subjects—mainly trains and buses. When e-mailing queries, please put 'submission query' in the subject line." Does not want fiction, poetry or plays. Query with SASE. Submit outline, outline/proposal, resume, publishing history, bio, 2 sample pages, SASE.

TIPS "Before approaching any publisher with a proposal, be sure that you are sending it to the right company. Publishing houses have their own personalities and specialisms and much time can be saved—including yours—by not submitting to a totally unsuitable publisher."

CONARI PRESS

Red Wheel/Weiser, LLC., 665 Third St., Suite 400, San Francisco CA 94107. **E-mail:** info@rwwbooks.

com. **E-mail:** submissions@rwwbooks.com. **Website:** www.redwheelweiser.com. **Contact:** Pat Bryce, acquisitions editor. Estab. 1987. "Conari Press, an imprint of Red Wheel/Weiser, publishes books on topics ranging from spirituality, personal growth, and relationships to women's issues, parenting, and social issues. Our mission is to publish quality books that will make a difference in people's lives—how we feel about ourselves and how we relate to one another. We value integrity, compassion, and receptivity, both in the books we publish and in the way we do business."

NONFICTION Subjects include foods, health, parenting, spirituality, womens issues, womens studies. "Inspire, literally to breathe life into. That's what Conari Press books aim to do—inspire all walks of life, mind, body, and spirit; inspire creativity, laughter, gratitude, good food, good health, and all good things in life." Submit proposal, including: an overview of the book; a complete TOC; a market/audience analysis, including similar titles; an up-to-date listing of your own marketing and publicity experience and/or plans; your vita and/or qualifications to write the book; and 2-3 sample chapters. Send cover letter including author information and brief description of proposed work.

TIPS "Review our website to make sure your work is appropriate."

CONCORDIA PUBLISHING HOUSE

3558 S. Jefferson Ave., St. Louis MO 63118. (314)268-1187. **Fax:** (314)268-1329. **E-mail:** publicity@cph.org. **Website:** www.cph.org. Estab. 1869. Publishes hardcover and trade paperback originals. Concordia Publishing House is the publishing arm of The Lutheran Church—Missouri Synod. "We develop, produce, and distribute (1) resources that support pastoral and congregational ministry, and (2) scholary and professional books in exegetical, historical, dogmatic, and practical theology."

CONSTABLE & ROBINSON, LTD.

55-56 Russell Square, London WC1B 4HP, United Kingdom. (0208)741-3663. **Fax:** (0208)748-7562. **E-mail:** reader@constablerobinson.com. **Website:** constablerobinson.co.uk. Publishes hardcover and trade paperback originals. **Publishes 60 titles/year. 3,000 queries/year; 1,000 mss/year. Pays royalty. Pays advance.** Publishes ms 1 year after acceptance. Accepts simultaneous submissions. Responds in 1-3 months. Book catalog available free.

NONFICTION Subjects include health, history, medicine, military, photography, politics, psychology, science, travel, war. Query with SASE. Submit synopsis. Reviews artwork/photos. Send photocopies.

FICTION Subjects include historical, mystery. Publishes "crime fiction (mysteries) and historical crime fiction." Length 80,000 words minimum; 130,000 words maximum. *Agented submissions only.*

CONTINUUM INTERNATIONAL PUBLISHING GROUP, LTD.

Imprint of Bloomsbury Group, 1385 Broadway, 5th Floor, New York NY 10018. (212)419-5300. **Website:** www.continuumbooks.com. Continuum publishes textbooks, monographs, and reference works in religious studies, the humanities, arts, and social sciences for students, teachers, and professionals worldwide. *Does not accept unsolicited submissions.* Book catalog online.

NONFICTION Subjects include anthropology, archeology, business, economics, education, film, cinema, stage, performance, government, politics, history, language, literature, music, dance, popular, philosophy, religion, sociology, linguistics.

CORNELL UNIVERSITY PRESS

Sage House, 512 E. State St., Ithaca NY 14850. (607)277-2338. **Fax:** (607)277-2374. **Website:** www.cornellpress.cornell.edu. **Contact:** Emily Powers and Max Richman, acquisitions assistants. Estab. 1869. Publishes hardcover and paperback originals. "Cornell Press is an academic publisher of nonfiction with particular strengths in anthropology, Asian studies, biological sciences, classics, history, labor and business, literary criticism, politics and international relations, women's studies, Slavic studies, philosophy, urban studies, health care work, regional titles, and security studies. Currently emphasizing sound scholarship that appeals beyond the academic community." **Publishes 150 titles/year. Pays royalty. Pays $0-5,000 advance.** Publishes ms 1 year after acceptance. Accepts simultaneous submissions. Book catalog and guidelines online.

NONFICTION Subjects include agriculture, anthropology, archeology, art, architecture, business, economics, ethnic, government, politics, history, language, literature, military, war, music, dance, philosophy, regional, sociology, translation, women's issues, women's studies, classics, life sciences. Submit résumé, cover letter, and prospectus.

CORWIN PRESS, INC.

2455 Teller Rd., Thousand Oaks CA 91320. (800)818-7243. **Fax:** (805)499-2692. **E-mail:** lisa.shaw@corwinpress.com. **Website:** www.corwinpress.com. **Contact:** Lisa Shaw, vice president (publishing and professional group); Jessica Allan, senior acquisitions editor (science, special education, gifted education, early childhood education, and counseling); Dan Alpert, program director (equity/diversity, professional learning); Arnis Burvikos, executive editor (educational leadership, technology); Lisa Luedeke, publisher (Corwin Literacy); Erin Null, acquisitions editor (math, science, STEM, general methods). Estab. 1990. Publishes paperback originals. **Publishes 150 titles/year.** Publishes ms 7 months after acceptance. Responds in 1-2 months to queries. Guidelines online.

NONFICTION Subjects include education. Seeking fresh insights, conclusions, and recommendations for action. Prefers theory or research-based books that provide real-world examples and practical, hands-on strategies to help busy educators be successful. Professional-level publications for administrators, teachers, school specialists, policymakers, researchers and others involved with Pre K-12 education. No textbooks that simply summarize existing knowledge or mass-market books. Query with SASE.

COTEAU BOOKS

Thunder Creek Publishing Co-operative Ltd., 2517 Victoria Ave., Regina SK S4P 0T2, Canada. (306)777-0170. **Fax:** (306)522-5152. **E-mail:** coteau@coteaubooks.com. **Website:** www.coteaubooks.com. **Contact:** Geoffrey Ursell, publisher. Estab. 1975. Publishes trade paperback originals and reprints. "Our mission is to publish the finest in Canadian fiction, nonfiction, poetry, drama, and children's literature, with an emphasis on Saskatchewan and prairie writers. De-emphasizing science fiction, picture books." **Publishes 12 titles/year. 200 queries received/year. 40 mss received/year. 25% of books from first-time authors. 90% from unagented writers. Pays 10% royalty on retail price.** Publishes ms 1 year after acceptance. Responds in 3 months. Book catalog available free. Guidelines online.

NONFICTION Subjects include creative nonfiction, ethnic, history, language, literature, memoirs, regional, sports, travel. *Canadian authors only.* Submit hard copy query, bio, 3-4 sample chapters, SASE.

FICTION Subjects include ethnic, fantasy, feminist, gay, lesbian, historical, humor, juvenile, literary, mainstream, contemporary, multicultural, multimedia, mystery, plays, poetry, regional, short story collections, spiritual, sports, teen/young adult, novels/short fiction, adult/middle years. *Canadian authors only.* No science fiction. No children's picture books. Query.

POETRY Submit 20-25 sample poems.

TIPS "Look at past publications to get an idea of our editorial program. We do not publish romance, horror, or picture books but are interested in juvenile and teen fiction from Canadian authors. Submissions, even queries, must be made in hard copy only. We do not accept simultaneous/multiple submissions. Check our website for new submission timing guidelines."

COUNCIL ON SOCIAL WORK EDUCATION

1701 Duke St., Suite 200, Alexandria VA 22314. (703)683-8080. **Fax:** (703)683-8099. **E-mail:** info@cswe.org. **Website:** www.cswe.org. **Contact:** Elizabeth Simon, publications manager. Estab. 1952. Publishes trade paperback originals. "Council on Social Work Education produces books and resources for social work educators, students and practitioners." **Publishes 4 titles/year. 12 queries received/year. 8 mss received/year. 25% of books from first-time authors. 100% from unagented writers. Pays sliding royalty scale, starting at 10%.** Publishes ms 1 year after acceptance. Responds in 2-3 months. Book catalog and guidelines online.

NONFICTION Subjects include education, sociology, social work. Books for social work and other educators. Query via e-mail only with proposal package, including CV, outline, expected audience, and 2 sample chapters.

TIPS "Audience is Social work educators and students and others in the helping professions. Check areas of publication interest on website."

COVENANT COMMUNICATIONS, INC.

920 E. State Rd., Suite F, P.O. Box 416, American Fork UT 84003. (801)756-9966. **Fax:** (801)756-1049. **E-mail:** submissionsdesk@covenant-lds.com. **Website:** www.covenant-lds.com. **Contact:** Kathryn Gordon, managing editor. Estab. 1958. "Currently emphasizing inspirational, doctrinal, historical, biography, and fiction." **Publishes 80-100 titles/year. Receives 1,200 mss/year. 30% of books from first-time authors. 99% from unagented writers. Pays 6-15%**

royalty on retail price. Publishes ms 6-12 months after acceptance. Responds in 1 month on queries; 4-6 months on mss. Guidelines online.

NONFICTION Subjects include history, religion, spirituality. "We target an audience of members of The Church of Jesus Christ of Latter-day Saints, LDS, or Mormon. All mss must be acceptable to that audience." Submit complete ms. Reviews artwork. Send photocopies.

FICTION Subjects include adventure, historical, mystery, regional, religious, romance, spiritual, suspense. "Manuscripts do not necessarily have to include LDS/Mormon characters or themes, but cannot contain profanity, sexual content, gratuitous violence, witchcraft, vampires, and other such material." Submit complete ms.

TIPS "We are actively looking for new, fresh regency romance authors."

CQ PRESS

2300 N St., NW, Suite 800, Washington DC 20037. (202)729-1800. **E-mail:** scalabi@cqpress.com. **Website:** www.cqpress.com. **Contact:** Sarah Calabi, acquisitions editor. Estab. 1945. Publishes hardcover and online paperback titles. CQ Press seeks to educate the public by publishing authoritative works on American and international politics, policy, and people. Accepts simultaneous submissions. Book catalog available free.

NONFICTION Subjects include government, politics, history. "We are interested in American government, public administration, comparative government, and international relations." Submit proposal package, including prospectus, TOC, 1-2 sample chapters.

TIPS "Our books present important information on American government and politics, and related issues, with careful attention to accuracy, thoroughness, and readability."

⊘ CRABTREE PUBLISHING COMPANY

PMB 59051, 350 Fifth Ave., 59th Floor, New York NY 10118. (212)496-5040; (800)387-7650. **Fax:** (800)355-7166. **Website:** www.crabtreebooks.com. Estab. 1978. Crabtree Publishing Company is dedicated to producing high-quality books and educational products for K-8+. Each resource blends accuracy, immediacy, and eye-catching illustration with the goal of inspiring nothing less than a life-long interest in reading and learning in children. The company began building its reputation in 1978 as a quality children's non-fiction book publisher with acclaimed author Bobbie Kalman's first series about the early pioneers. The Early Settler Life Series became a mainstay in schools as well as historic sites and museums across North America.

TIPS "Since our books are for younger readers, lively photos of children and animals are always excellent." Portfolio should be diverse and encompass several subjects rather than just 1 or 2; depth of coverage of subject should be intense so that any publishing company could, conceivably, use all or many of a photographer's photos in a book on a particular subject."

CRAFTSMAN BOOK CO.

6058 Corte Del Cedro, Carlsbad CA 92011. (760)438-7828 or (800)829-8123. **Fax:** (760)438-0398. **E-mail:** jacobs@costbook.com. **Website:** www.craftsman-book.com. **Contact:** Laurence D. Jacobs, editorial manager. Estab. 1957. Publishes paperback originals. Publishes how-to manuals for professional builders. Currently emphasizing construction software. **Publishes 12 titles/year. 85% of books from first-time authors. 98% from unagented writers. Pays 7-12% royalty on wholesale price or retail price.** Publishes ms 2 years after acceptance. Accepts simultaneous submissions. Responds in 2 months to queries. Book catalog and ms guidelines free.

NONFICTION All titles are related to construction for professional builders. Reviews artwork/photos.

TIPS "The book submission should be loaded with step-by-step instructions, illustrations, charts, reference data, forms, samples, cost estimates, rules of thumb, and examples that solve actual problems in the builder's office and in the field. It must cover the subject completely, become the owner's primary reference on the subject, have a high utility-to-cost ratio, and help the owner make a better living in his chosen field."

CRAIGMORE CREATIONS

PMB 114, 4110 SE Hawthorne Blvd., Portland OR 97124. (503)477-9562. **E-mail:** info@craigmorecreations.com. **Website:** www.craigmorecreations.com. Estab. 2009. Accepts simultaneous submissions.

NONFICTION Subjects include animals, anthropology, archeology, creative nonfiction, environment, multicultural, nature, regional, science, young adult, Earth sciences, natural history. "We publish books that make time travel seem possible: nonfiction that explores pre-history and Earth sciences for children."

Submit proposal package. See website for detailed submission guidelines. Send photocopies.

FICTION Subjects include juvenile, picture books, young adult. Submit proposal package. See website for detailed submission guidelines.

CREATIVE COMPANY

P.O. Box 227, Mankato MN 56002. (800)445-6209. **Fax:** (507)388-2746. **E-mail:** info@thecreativecompany.us. **Website:** www.thecreativecompany.us. **Contact:** Kate Riggs, managing editor. Estab. 1932. The Creative Company has two imprints: Creative Editions (picture books), and Creative Education (nonfiction series). **Publishes 140 titles/year.** Publishes book Publishes a book 2 years after acceptance. Responds in 3 months. Guidelines available for SAE.

NONFICTION Picture books, young readers, young adults: animal, arts/crafts, biography, careers, geography, health, history, hobbies, multicultural, music/dance, nature/environment, religion, science, social issues, special needs, sports. Average word length: young readers—500; young adults—6,000. Submit outline/synopsis and 2 sample chapters, along with division of titles within the series.

TIPS "We are accepting nonfiction, series submissions only. Fiction submissions will not be reviewed or returned. Nonfiction submissions should be presented in series (4, 6, or 8) rather than single."

CRESCENT MOON PUBLISHING

P.O. Box 393, Maidstone Kent ME14 5XU, United Kingdom. (44)(162)272-9593. **E-mail:** cresmopub@yahoo.co.uk. **Website:** www.crmoon.com. **Contact:** Jeremy Robinson, director (arts, media, cinema, literature); Cassidy Hushes (visual arts). Estab. 1988. Publishes hardcover and trade paperback originals. "Our mission is to publish the best in contemporary work, in poetry, fiction, and critical studies, and selections from the great writers. Currently emphasizing nonfiction (media, film, music, painting). De-emphasizing children's books." **Publishes 25 titles/year. 300 queries received/year. 400 mss received/year. 1% of books from first-time authors. 1% from unagented writers. Pays royalty. Pays negotiable advance.** Publishes ms 18 months after acceptance. Accepts simultaneous submissions. Responds in 2 months to queries; 4 months to proposals and mss. Book catalog and ms guidelines free.

IMPRINTS *Joe's Press, Pagan America Magazine, Passion Magazine.*

NONFICTION Subjects include Americana, art, architecture, gardening, government, politics, language, literature, music, dance, philosophy, religion, travel, women's issues, women's studies, cinema, the media, cultural studies. Query with SASE. Submit outline, 2 sample chapters, bio. Reviews artwork/photos. Send photocopies.

FICTION Subjects include erotica, experimental, feminist, gay, lesbian, literary, short story collections, translation. "We do not publish much fiction at present but will consider high quality new work." Query with SASE. Submit outline, clips, 2 sample chapters, bio.

POETRY "We prefer a small selection of the poet's very best work at first. We prefer free verse or non-rhyming poetry. Do not send too much material." Query and submit 6 sample poems.

TIPS "Our audience is interested in new contemporary writing."

CRICKET BOOKS

Imprint of Carus Publishing, 70 E. Lake St., Suite 300, Chicago IL 60601. (603)924-7209. **Fax:** (603)924-7380. **Website:** www.cricketmag.com. **Contact:** Submissions Editor. Estab. 1999. Publishes hardcover originals. Cricket Books publishes picture books, chapter books, and middle-grade novels. **Publishes 5 titles/year. Pays up to 10% royalty on retail price. Average advance: $1,500 and up.** Publishes ms 18 months after acceptance. *Currently not accepting queries or mss. Check website for submissions details and updates.*

FICTION Subjects include juvenile, adventure, easy-to-read, fantasy/science fiction, historical, horror, mystery/suspense, problem novels, sports, westerns.

TIPS "Take a look at the recent titles to see what sort of materials we're interested in, especially for nonfiction. Please note that we aren't doing the sort of strictly educational nonfiction that other publishers specialize in."

CRIMSON ROMANCE

Adams Media, a division of F+W Media, Inc., 57 Littlefield St., Avon MA 02322. (508)427-7100. **E-mail:** editorcrimson@gmail.com. **Website:** crimsonromance.com. **Contact:** Jennifer Lawler, editor. Publishes electronic originals. "Direct to e-book imprint of Adams Media."

FICTION Subjects include romance. "We're open to romance submissions in 5 popular subgenres: romantic suspense, contemporary, paranormal, historical, and erotic romance. Within those subgenres, we are flexible about what happens. It's romance, so there must be a happily-ever-after, but we're open to how your characters get there. You won't come up against preconceived ideas about what can or can't happen in romance or what kind of characters you can or can't have. Our only rule is everyone has to be a consenting adult. Other than that, we're looking for smart, savvy heroines, fresh voices, and new takes on old favorite themes." Length: 55,000-90,000 words. Submit brief description of work–please, no attachments.

CROSS-CULTURAL COMMUNICATIONS

239 Wynsum Ave., Merrick NY 11566. (516)869-5635. **Fax:** (516)379-1901. **E-mail:** info@cross-culturalcommunications.com. **Website:** www.cross-culturalcommunications.com. Estab. 1971. Publishes hardcover and trade paperback originals. **Publishes 10 titles/year. 200 queries received/year. 50 mss received/year. 10-25% of books from first-time authors. 100% from unagented writers.** Publishes ms 1 year after acceptance. Responds in 1 month to proposals; 2 months to mss. Book catalog (sample flyers) for #10 SASE.

NONFICTION Subjects include language, literature, memoirs, multicultural. "Query first; we basically do not want the focus on nonfiction." Query with SASE. Reviews artwork/photos. Send photocopies.

FICTION Subjects include historical, multicultural, poetry, poetry in translation, translation, bilingual poetry. Query with SASE.

POETRY For bilingual poetry submit 3-6 short poems in original language with English translation, a brief (3-5 lines) bio of the author and translator(s).

TIPS "Best chance: poetry from a translation."

THE CROSSROAD PUBLISHING COMPANY

83 Chestnut Ridge Rd., Chestnut Ridge NY 10977. **Fax:** (845)517-0181. **E-mail:** submissions@crossroadpublishing.com. **Website:** www.cpcbooks.com. Estab. 1980. Publishes hardcover and trade paperback originals and reprints. **Publishes 45 titles/year. 1,000 queries received/year. 200 mss received/year. 10% of books from first-time authors. 75% from unagented writers. Pays 6-14% royalty on wholesale price.** Publishes ms 14 months after acceptance. Accepts simultaneous submissions. Responds in 6 weeks to queries and proposals; 12 weeks to mss. Book catalog available free. Guidelines online.

IMPRINTS Crossroad (trade); Herder (classroom/academic).

NONFICTION Subjects include creative nonfiction, ethnic, leadership, philosophy, religion, spirituality, spiritual direction, women's issues, leadership, Catholicism. "We want hopeful, well-written books on religion and spirituality." Query with SASE.

TIPS "Refer to our website and catalog for a sense of the range and kinds of books we offer. Follow our application guidelines as posted on our website."

CROSSWAY

A publishing ministry of Good News Publishing, 1300 Crescent St., Wheaton IL 60174. (630)682-4300. **Fax:** (630)682-4785. **E-mail:** info@crossway.org. **E-mail:** submissions@crossway.org. **Website:** www.crossway.org. **Contact:** Jill Carter, editorial administrator. Estab. 1938. "'Making a difference in people's lives for Christ' as its maxim, Crossway Books lists titles written from an evangelical Christian perspective." Member ECPA. Distributes titles through Christian bookstores and catalogs. Promotes titles through magazine ads, catalogs. **Publishes 85 titles/year. Pays negotiable royalty.** Publishes ms 18 months after acceptance.

Does not accept unsolicited mss.

NONFICTION "Send us an e-mail query and, if your idea fits within our acquisitions guidelines, we'll invite a proposal."

CROWN BUSINESS

Random House, Inc., 1745 Broadway, New York NY 10019. (212)572-2275. **Fax:** (212)572-6192. **E-mail:** crownosm@randomhouse.com. **Website:** crownpublishing.com. Estab. 1995. Publishes hardcover and trade paperback originals. *Agented submissions only.* Accepts simultaneous submissions. Book catalog online.

NONFICTION Subjects include business, economics, money, finance.

CROWN PUBLISHING GROUP

Random House, Inc., 1745 Broadway, New York NY 10019. (212)782-9000. **E-mail:** crownosm@randomhouse.com. **Website:** www.randomhouse.com/crown. Estab. 1933. Publishes popular fiction and nonfiction hardcover originals. *Agented submissions only.* See website for more details.

IMPRINTS Amphoto Books; Back Stage Books; Billboard Books; Broadway Books; Clarkson Potter; Crown; Crown Archetype; Crown Business; Crown Forum; Harmony Books; Image Books; Potter Craft;

Potter Style; Ten Speed Press; Three Rivers Press; Waterbrook Multnomah; Watson-Guptill.

CRYSTAL SPIRIT PUBLISHING, INC.

P.O. Box 12506, Durham NC 27709. **E-mail:** crystalspiritinc@gmail.com. **E-mail:** submissions@crystalspiritinc.com. **Website:** www.crystalspiritinc.com. **Contact:** Vanessa S. O'Neal, senior editor. Estab. 2004. Publishes hardcover, trade paperback, mass market paperback, and electronic originals. "Our readers are lovers of high-quality books that are sold as direct sales, in bookstores, gift shops and placed in libraries and schools. They support independent authors and they expect works that will provide them with entertainment, inspiration, romance, and education. Our audience loves to read and will embrace niche authors that love to write." **Publishes 3-5 titles/year. Receives 80 mss/year. 80% of books from first-time authors. 100% from unagented writers. Pays 20-45% royalty on retail price.** Publishes ms 3-6 months after acceptance. Accepts simultaneous submissions. Responds in 3-6 months to mss. Book catalog and ms guidelines online.

NONFICTION Subjects include business, creative nonfiction, economics, ethnic, memoirs, multicultural, religion, sex, spirituality, young adult, inspirational, Christian romance. Submit cover letter, synopsis, and 30 pages by USPS mail or e-mail.

FICTION Subjects include confession, contemporary, erotica, ethnic, feminist, humor, juvenile, literary, mainstream, multicultural, religious, romance, short story collections, spiritual, young adult, inspirational, Christian romance, LGBT. Submit cover letter, synopsis, and 30 pages by USPS mail or e-mail.

TIPS "Submissions are accepted for publication throughout the year. Works should be positive and non-threatening. Typed pages only. Non-typed entries will not be reviewed or returned. Ensure that all contact information is correct, abide by the submission guidelines and do not send follow-up e-mails or calls."

CSLI PUBLICATIONS

Condura Hall, Stanford University, 210 Panama St., Stanford CA 94305. (650)723-1839. **Fax:** (650)725-2166. **E-mail:** pubs@csli.stanford.edu. **Website:** csli-publications.stanford.edu. Publishes hardcover and scholarly paperback originals. CSLI Publications, part of the Center for the Study of Language and Information, specializes in books in the study of language, information, logic, and computation. Book catalog available free. Guidelines online.

NONFICTION Subjects include anthropology, archeology, computers, electronics, language, literature, linguistics, science, logic, cognitive science. Query with SASE or by e-mail.

CUP OF TEA BOOKS

PageSpring Publishing, P.O. Box 21133, Columbus OH 43221. **E-mail:** weditor@pagespringpublishing.com. **Website:** www.cupofteabooks.com. Estab. 2012. Publishes trade paperback and electronic originals. "Cup of Tea Books publishes novel-length women's fiction. We are interested in finely-drawn characters, a compelling story, and deft writing. We accept e-mail queries only; see our website for details." **Pays royalty.** Publishes ms 6 months after acceptance. Accepts simultaneous submissions. Responds in 1 month. Guidelines online.

FICTION Subjects include adventure, contemporary, fantasy, feminist, historical, humor, literary, mainstream, mystery, regional, romance. Submit proposal package via e-mail. Include synopsis and the first 30 pages.

CYCLE PUBLICATIONS, INC.

Van der Plas Publications, 1282 Seventh Ave., San Francisco CA 94112. (415)665-8214. **Fax:** (415)753-8572. **E-mail:** rvdp@cyclepublishing.com. **Website:** www.cyclepublishing.com. Estab. 1985. "Van der Plas Publications/Cycle Publishing was started in 1997 with 4 books. Since then, we have introduced about 4 new books each year, and in addition to our 'mainstay' of cycling books, we now also have books on manufactured housing, golf, baseball, and strength training. Our offices are located in San Francisco, where we do editorial work, as well as administration, publicity, and design. Our books are warehoused in Kimball, Michigan, which is close to the companies that print most of our books and is conveniently located to supply our book trade distributors and the major book wholesalers."

CYCLOTOUR GUIDE BOOKS

160 Harvard St., Rochester NY 14607. (585)244-6157. **E-mail:** cyclotour@cyclotour.com. **Website:** www.cyclotour.com. Estab. 1994. Publishes trade paperback originals. **Publishes 2 titles/year. Receives 25 queries/year and 2 mss/year. 25% of books from first-time authors. 100% from unagented writers.** Publishes ms 2 years after acceptance. Accepts simultane-

ous submissions. Responds in 1 month. Book catalog and ms guidelines online.

NONFICTION Subjects include sports (bicycle only), travel (bicycle tourism). No narrative accounts of their bicycle tour without distance indicators. Query with SASE. Reviews artwork/photos as part of ms package. Send photocopies.

TIPS Bicyclists. Folks with a dream of bicycle touring. "Check your grammar and spelling. Write logically."

DA CAPO PRESS

Perseus Books Group, 44 Farnsworth St., 3rd Floor, Boston MA 02210. (617)252-5200. **Website:** www.dacapopress.com. Estab. 1975. Publishes hardcover originals and trade paperback originals and reprints. **Publishes 115 titles/year. 500 queries received/year. 300 mss received/year. 25% of books from first-time authors. 1% from unagented writers. Pays 7-15% royalty. Pays $1,000-225,000 advance.** Publishes ms 1 year after acceptance. Book catalog and guidelines online.

NONFICTION Subjects include art, architecture, contemporary culture, creative nonfiction, government, politics, history, language, literature, memoirs, military, war, social sciences, sports, translation, travel, world affairs. No unsolicited mss or proposals. Agented submissions only.

DARTON, LONGMAN & TODD

1 Spencer Ct., 140-142 Wandsworth High St., London SW18 4JJ, United Kingdom. (44)(208)875-0155. **Fax:** (44)(208)875-0133. **E-mail:** editorial@darton-longman-todd.co.uk. **Website:** www.dltbooks.com. **Contact:** Editorial Department. Estab. 1959. Darton, Longman and Todd is an internationally-respected publisher of brave, ground-breaking, independent books and e-books on matters of heart, mind, and soul that meet the needs and interests of ordinary people. **Publishes 50 titles/year. Pays royalty.** Accepts simultaneous submissions. Guidelines online.

NONFICTION Subjects include religion, spirituality. Simultaenous submissions accepted, but inform publisher if submitting elsewhere. Does not want poetry, scholarly monographs or children's books. Query by e-mail only.

TIPS "Our books are read by people inside and outside the Christian churches, by believers, seekers and sceptics, and by thoughtful non-specialists as well as students and academics. The books are widely sold throughout the religious and the general trade."

DAW BOOKS, INC.

Penguin Group (USA), 375 Hudson St., New York NY 10014-3658. (212)366-2096. **Fax:** (212)366-2090. **E-mail:** daw@us.penguingroup.com. **Website:** www.dawbooks.com. **Contact:** Peter Stampfel, submissions editor. Estab. 1971. Publishes hardcover and paperback originals and reprints. DAW Books publishes science fiction and fantasy. **Publishes 50-60 titles/year. Pays in royalties with an advance negotiable on a book-by-book basis.** Responds in 3 months. Guidelines online.

FICTION Subjects include fantasy, science fiction. "Currently seeking modern urban fantasy and paranormals. We like character-driven books with appealing protagonists, engaging plots, and well-constructed worlds. We accept both agented and unagented manuscripts." Submit entire ms, cover letter, SASE. "Do not submit your only copy of anything. The average length of the novels we publish varies but is almost never less than 80,000 words."

DAWN PUBLICATIONS

12402 Bitney Springs Rd., Nevada City CA 95959. (530)274-7775. **Fax:** (530)274-7778. **Website:** www.dawnpub.com. **Contact:** Glenn Hovemann, editor. Estab. 1979. Publishes hardcover and trade paperback originals. "Dawn Publications is dedicated to inspiring in children a sense of appreciation for all life on earth. Dawn looks for nature awareness and appreciation titles that promote a relationship with the natural world and specific habitats, usually through inspiring treatment and nonfiction." **Publishes 6 titles/year. 2,500 queries or mss received/year. 15% of books from first-time authors. 90% from unagented writers. Pays advance.** Publishes ms 1-2 years after acceptance. Accepts simultaneous submissions. Responds in 2 months to queries. Book catalog and guidelines online.

Dawn accepts mss submissions by e-mail; follow instructions posted on website. Submissions by mail still OK.

NONFICTION Subjects include animals, nature, environment.

TIPS "Publishes mostly creative nonfiction with lightness and inspiration." Looking for "picture books expressing nature awareness with inspirational quality leading to enhanced self-awareness." Does not publish anthropomorphic works; no animal dialogue.

KATHY DAWSON BOOKS

Penguin Group, 375 Hudson St., New York NY 10014. (212)366-2000. **Website:** kathydawsonbooks.tumblr.com. **Contact:** Kathy Dawson, vice-president and publisher. Estab. 2014. Mission statement: Publish stellar novels with unforgettable characters for children and teens that expand their vision of the world, sneakily explore the meaning of life, celebrate the written word, and last for generations. The imprint strives to publish tomorrow's award contenders: quality books with strong hooks in a variety of genres with universal themes and compelling voices—books that break the modl and the heart. Responds only if interested. Guidelines online.

FICTION Accepts fiction queries via snail mail only. Include cover sheet with one-sentence elevator pitch, main themes, author version of catalog copy for book, first 10 pages of ms (double-spaced, Times Roman, 12 point type), and publishing history. No SASE needed. Responds only if interested.

DELACORTE PRESS

Imprint of Random House Publishing Group, 1745 Broadway, New York NY 10019. (212)782-9000. **Website:** www.randomhouse.com. Publishes middle grade and young adult fiction in hard cover, trade paperback, mass market and digest formats. Publishes middle grade and young adult fiction in hardcover, trade paperback, mass market and digest formats.

All other query letters or ms submissions must be submitted through an agent or at the request of an editor. No e-mail queries.

DEL REY BOOKS

Imprint of Random House Publishing Group, 1745 Broadway, 18th Floor, New York NY 10019. (212)782-9000. **Website:** www.randomhouse.com. Estab. 1977. Publishes hardcover, trade paperback, and mass market originals and mass market paperback reprints. Del Rey publishes top level fantasy, alternate history, and science fiction. **Pays royalty on retail price. Pays competitive advance.**

IMPRINTS Del Rey/Manga, Del Rey/Lucas Books.

FICTION Subjects include fantasy, should have the practice of magic as an essential element of the plot, science fiction, well-plotted novels with good characterizations, exotic locales and detailed alien creatures, alternate history. *Agented submissions only.*

TIPS "Del Rey is a reader's house. Pay particular attention to plotting, strong characters, and dramatic, satisfactory conclusions. It must be/feel believable. That's what the readers like. In terms of mass market, we basically created the field of fantasy bestsellers. Not that it didn't exist before, but we put the mass into mass market."

DIAL BOOKS FOR YOUNG READERS

Imprint of Penguin Group (USA), 345 Hudson St., New York NY 10014. (212)366-2000. **Website:** www.penguin.com/youngreaders. **Contact:** Lauri Hornik, president/publisher. Estab. 1961. Publishes hardcover originals. "Dial Books for Young Readers publishes quality picture books for ages 18 months-6 years; lively, believable novels for middle readers and young adults; and occasional nonfiction for middle readers and young adults." **Publishes 50 titles/year. 5,000 queries received/year. 20% of books from first-time authors. Pays royalty. Pays varies advance.** Responds in 4-6 months to queries. Book catalog and guidelines online.

NONFICTION Only responds if interested. "We accept entire picture book manuscripts and a maximum of 10 pages for longer works (novels, easy-to-reads). When submitting a portion of a longer work, please provide an accompanying cover letter that briefly describes your manuscript's plot, genre (i.e. easy-to-read, middle grade or YA novel), the intended age group, and your publishing credits, if any."

FICTION Subjects include adventure, fantasy, juvenile, picture books, young adult. Especially looking for lively and well-written novels for middle grade and young adult children involving a convincing plot and believable characters. The subject matter or theme should not already be overworked in previously published books. The approach must not be demeaning to any minority group, nor should the roles of female characters (or others) be stereotyped, though we don't think books should be didactic, or in any way message-y. No topics inappropriate for the juvenile, young adult, and middle grade audiences. No plays. Accepts unsolicited queries and up to 10 pages for longer works and unsolicited mss for picture books. Will only respond if interested.

TIPS "Our readers are anywhere from preschool age to teenage. Picture books must have strong plots, lots of action, unusual premises, or universal themes treated with freshness and originality. Humor works well in these books. A very well-thought-out and intelligently presented book has the best chance of being taken on. Genre isn't as much of a factor as presentation."

Ⓐ DISNEY HYPERION BOOKS FOR CHILDREN

114 Fifth Ave., New York NY 10011-5690. **Website:** www.hyperionbooksforchildren.com.

NONFICTION Narrative nonfiction for elementary schoolers. *Agented submissions only.*

FICTION Picture books, early readers, middle readers, young adults: adventure, animal, anthology (short stories), contemporary, fantasy, history, humor, multicultural, poetry, science fiction, sports, suspense/mystery. Middle readers, young adults: commercial fiction. *All submissions must come via an agent.*

DIVERTIR

P.O. Box 232, North Salem NH 03073. **E-mail:** info@divertirpublishing.com; query@divertirpublishing.com. **Website:** www.divertirpublishing.com. **Contact:** Kenneth Tupper, publisher. Estab. 2009. Publishes trade paperback and electronic originals. **Publishes 6-12 titles/year. 80% of books from first-time authors. 100% from unagented writers. Pays 10-15% royalty on wholesale price (for novels and nonfiction).** Publishes ms 6-9 months after acceptance. Accepts simultaneous submissions. Responds in 1-2 months on queries; 3-4 months on proposals and mss. Catalog online. Guidelines online.

NONFICTION Subjects include contemporary culture, crafts, government, history, hobbies, New Age, politics, psychic, world affairs. "We are particularly interested in the following: political/social commentary, current events, history, humor and satire, and crafts and hobbies." Reviews artwork/photos as part of the ms package. Submit electronically.

FICTION Subjects include adventure, contemporary, fantasy, gothic, historical, horror, humor, literary, mainstream, mystery, occult, poetry, religious, romance, science fiction, young adult. "We are particularly interested in the following: science fiction, fantasy, historical, alternate history, contemporary mythology, mystery and suspense, paranormal, and urban fantasy." Electronically submit proposal package, including synopsis and query letter with author's bio.

TIPS "Please see our Author Info page (online) for more information."

Ⓐ DK PUBLISHING

Penguin Random House, 80 Strand, London WC2R 0RL, United Kingdom. **Website:** www.dk.com. "DK publishes photographically illustrated nonfiction for children of all ages." *DK Publishing does not accept unagented mss or proposals.*

DOVER PUBLICATIONS, INC.

31 E. Second St., Mineola NY 11501. (516)294-7000. **Fax:** (516)873-1401. **E-mail:** hr@doverpublications.com. **Website:** www.doverpublications.com. Estab. 1941. Publishes trade paperback originals and reprints. **Publishes 660 titles/year. Makes outright purchase.** Accepts simultaneous submissions. Book catalog online.

NONFICTION Subjects include agriculture, Americana, animals, anthropology, archeology, art, architecture, cooking, foods, nutrition, health, medicine, history, hobbies, language, literature, music, dance, nature, environment, philosophy, photography, religion, science, sports, translation, travel. Publishes mostly reprints. Accepts original paper doll collections, game books, coloring books (juvenile). Query with SASE. Reviews artwork/photos.

DOWN THE SHORE PUBLISHING

P.O. Box 100, West Creek NJ 08092. **Fax:** (609)597-0422. **E-mail:** info@down-the-shore.com. **Website:** www.down-the-shore.com. Publishes hardcover and trade paperback originals and reprints. "Bear in mind that our market is regional-New Jersey, the Jersey Shore, the mid-Atlantic, and seashore and coastal subjects." **Publishes 4-10 titles/year. Pays royalty on wholesale or retail price, or makes outright purchase.** Accepts simultaneous submissions. Responds in 3 months to queries. Book catalog online. Guidelines online.

NONFICTION Subjects include Americana, art, architecture, history, nature, environment, regional. Query with SASE. Submit proposal package, 1-2 sample chapters, synopsis. Reviews artwork/photos. Send photocopies.

FICTION Subjects include regional. Query with SASE. Submit proposal package, clips, 1-2 sample chapters.

POETRY "We do not publish poetry, unless it is to be included as part of an anthology."

TIPS "Carefully consider whether your proposal is a good fit for our established market."

DREAM OF THINGS

P.O. Box 872, Downers Grove IL 60515. **E-mail:** editor@dreamofthings.com. **Website:** dreamofthings.com. **Contact:** Mike O'Mary, owner. Estab. 2009. Publishes trade paperback originals and reprints, electronic originals and reprints. Publishes memoirs, essay collections, and creative nonfiction. **Publishes 3-4 titles/year. 90% of books from first-time authors. 90% from unagented writers. Pays 10% royalties on retail price. No advance.** Publishes book Accept to publish time is 6 months. after acceptance of ms. Accepts simultaneous submissions. Catalog online. Guidelines online.

NONFICTION Subjects include creative nonfiction, memoirs, essay collections. Submit via online form. For memoirs, submit 1 sample chapter. For essay collections, submit 2-3 essays. Does not review artwork.

DUFOUR EDITIONS

P.O. Box 7, 124 Byers Rd., Chester Springs PA 19425. (610)458-5005 or (800)869-5677. **Fax:** (610)458-7103. **Website:** www.dufoureditions.com. Estab. 1948. Publishes hardcover originals, trade paperback originals and reprints. "We publish literary fiction by good writers which is well received and achieves modest sales. De-emphsazing poetry and nonfiction." **Publishes 3-4 titles/year. 200 queries received/year. 15 mss received/year. 20-30% of books from first-time authors. 80% from unagented writers. Pays $100-500 advance.** Publishes ms 18 months after acceptance. Accepts simultaneous submissions. Responds in 3-6 months. Book catalog available free.

NONFICTION Subjects include history, translation. Query with SASE. Reviews artwork/photos. Send photocopies.

FICTION Subjects include literary, short story collections, translation. "We like books that are slightly offbeat, different and well-written." Query with SASE.

POETRY Query.

DUNDURN PRESS, LTD.

3 Church St., Suite 500, Toronto ON M5E 1M2, Canada. (416)214-5544. **E-mail:** info@dundurn.com. **Website:** www.dundurn.com. **Contact:** Acquisitions Editor. Estab. 1972. Publishes hardcover, trade paperback, and e-book originals and reprints. Dundurn publishes books by Canadian authors. **600 queries received/year. 25% of books from first-time authors. 50% from unagented writers.** Publishes ms 1-2 year after acceptance. Accepts simultaneous submissions. Responds in 3 months to queries. Guidelines online.

NONFICTION Subjects include art, architecture, history, Canadian and military, war, music, dance, drama, regional, art history, theater, serious and popular nonfiction. Submit cover letter, synopsis, CV, TOC, writing sample, e-mail contact. Accepts submissions via postal mail only. Do not submit original materials. Submissions will not be returned.

FICTION Subjects include literary, mystery, young adult. No romance, science fiction, or experimental. "Until further notice, we will not be accepting any unsolicited fiction manuscripts."

DUNEDIN ACADEMIC PRESS LTD

Hudson House, 8 Albany St., Edinburgh EH1 3QB, United Kingdom. (44)(131)473-2397. **E-mail:** mail@dunedinacademicpress.co.uk. **Website:** www.dunedinacademicpress.co.uk. **Contact:** Anthony Kinahan, director. Estab. 2001. **Publishes 15-20 titles/year. 10% of books from first-time authors. 90% from unagented writers. Pays royalty.** Book catalog and proposal guidelines online.

NONFICTION , earth science, health and social care, child protection. Reviews artwork/photos.

TIPS "Dunedin's list contains authors and subjects from across the international the academic world DAP's horizons are far broader than our immediate Scottish environment. One of the strengths of Dunedin is that we are able to offer our authors that individual support that comes from dealing with a small independent publisher committed to growth through careful treatment of its authors."

THOMAS DUNNE BOOKS

Imprint of St. Martin's Press, 175 Fifth Ave., New York NY 10010. (212)674-5151. **Website:** www.thomasdunnebooks.com. Estab. 1986. Publishes hardcover and trade paperback originals, and reprints. "Thomas Dunne Books publishes popular trade fiction and nonfiction. With an output of approximately 175 titles each year, his group covers a range of genres including commercial and literary fiction, thrillers, biography, politics, sports, popular science, and more. The list is intentionally eclectic and includes a wide range of fiction and nonfiction, from first books to international bestsellers." Accepts simultaneous submissions. Book catalog and ms guidelines free.

NONFICTION Subjects include government, politics, history, sports, political commentary. *Accepts agented submissions only.*

FICTION Subjects include mainstream, contemporary, mystery, suspense, thrillers, women's. *Accepts agented submissions only.*

DUQUESNE UNIVERSITY PRESS

600 Forbes Ave., Pittsburgh PA 15282. (412)396-6610. **Fax:** (412)396-5984. **E-mail:** wadsworth@duq.edu. **Website:** www.dupress.duq.edu. **Contact:** Susan Wadsworth-Booth, director. Estab. 1927. Publishes hardcover and trade paperback originals. "Duquesne publishes scholarly monographs in the fields of literary studies (medieval and Renaissance), continental philosophy, ethics, religious studies and existential psychology. Interdisciplinary works are also of interest. Duquesne University Press does not publish fiction, poetry, children's books, technical or 'hard' science works, or unrevised theses or dissertations." **Publishes 8-12 titles/year. 400 queries received/year. 65 mss received/year. 30% of books from first-time authors. 95% from unagented writers. Pays royalty on net price. Pays (some) advance.** Publishes ms 1 year after acceptance. Responds in 1-3 months. Book catalog available. Guidelines online.

NONFICTION Subjects include language, literature, philosophy, continental, psychology, existential, religion. "We look for quality of scholarship." For scholarly books, query or submit outline, 1 sample chapter, and SASE.

Ⓐ⊘ DUTTON ADULT TRADE

Imprint of Penguin Group (USA), Inc., 375 Hudson St., New York NY 10014. (212)366-2000. **Website:** us.penguingroup.com. Estab. 1852. Publishes hardcover originals. "Dutton currently publishes 45 hardcovers a year, roughly half fiction and half nonfiction." **Pays royalty. Pays negotiable advance.** Book catalog online.

NONFICTION Agented submissions only. *No unsolicited mss.*

FICTION Subjects include adventure, historical, literary, mainstream, contemporary, mystery, short story collections, suspense. Agented submissions only. *No unsolicited mss.*

TIPS "Write the complete ms and submit it to an agent or agents. They will know exactly which editor will be interested in a project."

DUTTON CHILDREN'S BOOKS

Penguin Group (USA), 375 Hudson St., New York NY 10014. **E-mail:** duttonpublicity@us.penguingroup.com. **Website:** www.penguin.com. **Contact:** Julie Strauss-Gabel, vice president and publisher. Estab. 1852. Publishes hardcover originals as well as novelty formats. Dutton Children's Books publishes high-quality fiction and nonfiction for readers ranging from preschoolers to young adults on a variety of subjects. Currently emphasizing middle grade and young adult novels that offer a fresh perspective. De-emphasizing photographic nonfiction and picture books that teach a lesson. **Publishes 100 titles/year. 15% of books from first-time authors. Pays royalty on retail price. Pays advance.**

NONFICTION Subjects include animals, history, US, nature, environment, science. Query. Only responds if interested.

FICTION Subjects include juvenile, young adult. Dutton Children's Books has a diverse, general interest list that includes picture books; easy-to-read books; and fiction for all ages, from first chapter books to young adult readers. Query. Responds only if interested.

EAGLE'S VIEW PUBLISHING

6756 N. Fork Rd., Liberty UT 84310. (801)393-4555. **Website:** www.eaglesviewpub.com. **Contact:** Denise Knight, editor-in-chief. Estab. 1982. Publishes trade paperback originals. "Eagle's View primarily publishes how-to craft books with a subject related to historical or contemporary Native American/Mountain Man/frontier crafts/bead crafts. Currently emphasizing bead-related craft books. De-emphasizing history except for historical Indian crafts." **Publishes 2-4 titles/year. 40 queries received/year. 20 mss received/year. 90% of books from first-time authors. 100% from unagented writers. Pays 8-10% royalty on net selling price.** Publishes ms 1 year after acceptance. Accepts simultaneous submissions. Responds in 1 year to proposals.

NONFICTION Subjects include anthropology, archaeology, Native American crafts, ethnic, Native American, history, American frontier historical patterns and books, hobbies, crafts, especially beadwork. Submit outline, 1-2 sample chapters. Reviews artwork/photos. Send photocopies and sample illustrations.

EASTLAND PRESS

P.O. Box 99749, Seattle WA 98139. (206)217-0204. **Fax:** (206)217-0205. **E-mail:** info@eastlandpress.com. **Website:** www.eastlandpress.com. **Contact:** John O'Connor, Managing Editor. Estab. 1981. Publishes hardcover and trade paperback originals. "Eastland Press is interested in textbooks for practitioners of alternative medical therapies, primarily Chinese and physical therapies, and related bodywork." **Publish-**

es 3-4 titles/year. 25 queries received/year. 30% of books from first-time authors. 90% from unagented writers. Pays 12-15% royalty on receipts. Publishes ms 1-2 years after acceptance. Accepts simultaneous submissions. Responds in 1 month to queries.

NONFICTION Subjects include health, medicine. "We prefer that a manuscript be completed or close to completion before we will consider publication. Proposals are rarely considered, unless submitted by a published author or teaching institution." Submit outline and 2-3 sample chapters. Reviews artwork/photos. Send photocopies.

THE ECCO PRESS

10 E. 53rd St., New York NY 10022. (212)207-7000. **Fax:** (212)702-2460. **Website:** www.harpercollins.com. **Contact:** Daniel Halpern, editor-in-chief. Estab. 1970. Publishes hardcover and trade paperback originals and reprints. **Publishes 60 titles/year. Pays royalty. Pays negotiable advance.** Publishes ms 1 year after acceptance.

FICTION Literary, short story collections. "We can publish possibly 1 or 2 original novels a year." *Does not accept unsolicited mss.*

TIPS "We are always interested in first novels and feel it's important that they be brought to the attention of the reading public."

ÉCRITS DES FORGES

992-A, rue Royale, Trois-Rivières QC G9A 4H9, Canada. (819)840-8492. **Website:** www.ecritsdesforges.com. **Contact:** Bernard Pozier, director. Estab. 1971. **Pays royalties of 10-20%.** Responds to queries in 6 months.

POETRY Écrits des Forges publishes poetry only that is "authentic and original as a signature. We have published poetry from more than 1,000 poets coming from most of the francophone countries." Publishes 45-50 paperback books of poetry/year. Books are usually 80-88 pages, digest-sized, perfect-bound, with 2-color covers with art. Query first with a few sample poems and a cover letter with brief bio and publication credits. Order sample books by writing or faxing.

EDGE SCIENCE FICTION AND FANTASY PUBLISHING/TESSERACT BOOKS

Hades Publications, Box 1714, Calgary AB T2P 2L7, Canada. (403)254-0160. **Fax:** (403)254-0456. **Website:** www.edgewebsite.com. **Contact:** Editorial Manager. Estab. 1996. Publishes hardcover and trade paperback originals. "We are an independent publisher of science fiction and fantasy novels in hard cover or trade paperback format. We produce high-quality books with lots of attention to detail and lots of marketing effort. We want to encourage, produce and promote thought-provoking and fun-to-read science fiction and fantasy literature by 'bringing the magic alive: one world at a time' (as our motto says) with each new book released." **Pays 10% royalty on wholesale price. Negotiable advance.** Publishes ms 18-20 months after acceptance. Responds in 4-5 months to mss. Guidelines online.

FICTION Subjects include fantasy, science fiction. "We are looking for all types of fantasy and science fiction, horror except juvenile/young adlut, erotica, religious fiction, short stories, dark/gruesome fantasy, or poetry." Length: 75,000-100,000/words. Submit first 3 chapters and synopsis. Check website for guidelines. Include estimated word count.

ÉDITIONS DU NOROÎT

4609 D'Iberville, Bureau 202, Montreal QC H2H 2L9, Canada. (514)727-0005. **Fax:** (514)723-6660. **E-mail:** lenoroit@lenoroit.com. **Website:** www.lenoroit.com. **Contact:** Paul Belanger, director. Publishes trade paperback originals and reprints. "Editions du Noiroît publishes poetry and essays on poetry." **Publishes 20 titles/year. 500 queries received/year. 500 mss received/year. Pays 10% royalty on retail price.** Publishes ms 1 year after acceptance. Responds in 4 months to mss.

POETRY Submit 40 sample poems.

EDUPRESS, INC.

P.O. Box 8610, Madison WI 53708. (608)242-1201. **E-mail:** edupress@highsmith.com; lizb@demco.com. **Website:** www.edupress.com. **Contact:** Liz Bowie. Estab. 1979. Edupress, Inc., publishes supplemental curriculum resources for PK-6th grade. Currently emphasizing Common Core reading and math games and materials. **Work purchased outright from authors.** Publishes ms 1-2 years after acceptance. Responds in 2-4 months. Catalog online.

NONFICTION Submit complete ms via mail or e-mail with "Manuscript Submission" as the subject line.

TIPS "We are looking for unique, research-based, quality supplemental materials for Pre-K through 6th grade. We publish mainly reading and math materials in many different formats, including games. Our materials are intended for classroom and home schooling use. We do not publish picture books."

WILLIAM B. EERDMANS PUBLISHING CO.

2140 Oak Industrial Dr. NE, Grand Rapids MI 49505. (616)459-4591. **Fax:** (616)459-6540. **E-mail:** info@eerdmans.com. **Website:** www.eerdmans.com. **Contact:** Jon Pott, editor-in-chief. Estab. 1911. Publishes hardcover and paperback originals and reprints. "The majority of our adult publications are religious and most of these are academic or semi-academic in character (as opposed to inspirational or celebrity books), though we also publish general trade books on the Christian life. Our nonreligious titles, most of them in regional history or on social issues, aim, similarly, at an educated audience." Accepts simultaneous submissions. Responds in 4 weeks. Book catalog and ms guidelines free.

NONFICTION Subjects include history, religious, language, literature, philosophy, of religion, psychology, regional, history, religion, sociology, translation, Biblical studies. "We prefer that writers take the time to notice if we have published anything at all in the same category as their manuscript before sending it to us." Query with TOC, 2-3 sample chapters, and SASE for return of ms. Reviews artwork/photos.

FICTION Subjects include religious, children's, general, fantasy. Query with SASE.

EDWARD ELGAR PUBLISHING, INC.

The William Pratt House, 9 Dewey Ct., Northampton MA 01060. (413)584-5551. **Fax:** (413)584-9933. **E-mail:** submissions@e-elgar.co.uk. **Website:** www.e-elgar.com. Estab. 1986. "Specializing in research monographs, reference books and upper-level textbooks in highly focused areas, we are able to offer a unique service in terms of editorial, production and worldwide marketing. We have three offices, Cheltenham and Camberley in the UK and Northampton, MA, US. We are actively commissioning new titles and are happy to consider and advise on ideas for monograph books, textbooks, professional law books and academic journals at any stage. Please complete a proposal form in as much detail as possible. We review all prososals with our academic advisors."

ELLORA'S CAVE PUBLISHING, INC.

1056 Home Ave., Akron OH 44310. **E-mail:** submissions@ellorascave.com. **Website:** www.ellorascave.com. Estab. 2000. Publishes electronic originals and reprints; print books. **Pays 45% royalty on amount received.** Accepts simultaneous submissions. Responds in 2-4 months to mss. No queries. Guidelines online. "Read and follow detailed submission instructions.".

FICTION Erotic romance and erotica fiction of every subgenre, including gay/lesbian, menage and more, and BDSM. All must have abundant, explicit, and graphic erotic content. Submit electronically only; cover e-mail as defined in our submission guidelines plus 1 attached .docx file containing full synopsis, first 3 chapters, and last chapter.

TIPS "Our audience is romance readers who want explicit sexual detail. They come to us because we offer sex with romance, plot, emotion. In addition to erotic romance with happy-ever-after endings, we also publish pure erotica, detailing sexual adventure, and experimentation."

EMIS, INC.

P.O. Box 270666, Fort Collins CO 80527. (214)349-0077; (800)225-0694. **Fax:** (970)672-8606. **Website:** www.emispub.com. Publishes trade paperback originals. "Medical text designed for physicians; fit in the lab coat pocket as a quick reference. Currently emphasizing women's health." **Publishes 2 titles/year. Pays 12% royalty on retail price.** Responds in 3 months to queries. Book catalog available free. Guidelines available free.

NONFICTION Subjects include health, medicine, psychology, women's health/medicine. Submit 3 sample chapters with SASE.

Ⓐ⊘ ENCOUNTER BOOKS

900 Broadway, Suite 601, New York NY 10003. (212)871-6310. **Fax:** (212)871-6311. **Website:** www.encounterbooks.com. **Contact:** Roger Kimball, editor and president. Publishes hardcover, trade paperback, and e-book originals and trade paperback reprints. Encounter Books publishes serious nonfiction—books that can alter our society, challenge our morality, stimulate our imaginations—in the areas of history, politics, religion, biography, education, public policy, current affairs, and social sciences. Encounter Books is an activity of Encounter for Culture and Education, a tax-exempt, non profit corporation dedicated to strengthening the marketplace of ideas and engaging in educational activities to help preserve democratic culture. Accepts simultaneous submissions. Book catalog online. Guidelines online.

NONFICTION Subjects include child guidance, education, ethnic, government, politics, health, medicine, history, language, literature, memoirs, military, war, multicultural, philosophy, psychology, religion, science, sociology, women's issues, women's studies, gender studies. Only considers agented submissions.

ENETE ENTERPRISES

6504 N. Omaha Ave., Oklahoma City OK 73116. **E-mail:** eneteenterprises@gmail.com. **Website:** www.eneteenterprises.com. **Contact:** Shannon Enete, editor. Estab. 2011. Publishes trade paperback originals, mass market paperback originals, electronic originals. **Publishes 6 titles/year. 290 queries received/year. 95% of books from first-time authors. 100% from unagented writers. Pays royalties of 10-20%.** Publishes ms 3-6 months after acceptance. Accepts simultaneous submissions. Responds to queries/proposals in 1 month; mss in 1-3 months. Guidelines online.

NONFICTION Subjects include memoirs, multicultural, travel, travel guides, travel memoirs, life abroad, retired living abroad. Submit query, proposal, or ms with marketing plan by e-mail.

TIPS "Send me your best work. Do not rush a draft."

ENSLOW PUBLISHERS, INC.

101 W. 23rd St., Suite 240, New York NY 10011. (973)771-9400. **E-mail:** customerservice@enslow.com. **Website:** www.enslow.com. Estab. 1977. Publishes hardcover originals. 10% require freelance illustration. Enslow publishes nonfiction and fiction series books for young adults and school-age children. **Publishes 250 titles/year. Pays royalty on net price with advance or flat fee. Pays advance.** Publishes ms 1 year after acceptance. Responds in 1 month to queries. Guidelines via e-mail.

NONFICTION Subjects include health, medicine, history, recreation, sports, science, sociology. "Interested in new ideas for series of books for young people." No fiction, fictionalized history, or dialogue.

TIPS "We love to receive resumes from experienced writers with good research skills who can think like young people."

ENTREPRENEUR PRESS

18061 Fitch, Irvine CA 92614. (949)261-2325. **Fax:** (949)622-5274. **E-mail:** press@entrepreneur.com. **Website:** www.entrepreneurbookstore.com. **Contact:** Jillian McTigue, Director of Entrepreneur Press. "We specialize in quality paperbacks and e-books that focus on the entrepreneur in us all. Addressing the diverse challenges at all stages of business, each Entrepreneur Press book aims to provide actionable solutions to help entrepreneurs excel in all ventures they take on." **Publishes 20+ titles/year. Pays competitive net royalty.** Accepts simultaneous submissions. Guidelines online.

NONFICTION Subjects include business, business start-up, small business management, business planning, marketing, finance, careers, personal finance, accounting, motivation, leadership, legal advise, management. When submitting work to us, please send as much of the proposed book as possible. Proposal should include: cover letter, preface, marketing plan, analysis of competition and comparative titles, author bio, TOC, 2 sample chapters. Go to website for more details. Reviews artwork/photos. Send transparencies and all other applicable information.

TIPS "We are currently seeking proposals covering sales, small business, startup, online businesses, marketing, etc."

EPICENTER PRESS, INC.

200 W. 34th Ave. #825, Anchorage AK 99503. **Fax:** (425)481-8253. **E-mail:** slay@epicenterpress.com. **Website:** www.epicenterpress.com. **Contact:** Lael Morgan, acquisitions editor. Estab. 1987. Publishes hardcover and trade paperback originals. "We are a regional press founded in Alaska whose interests include but are not limited to the arts, history, environment, and diverse cultures and lifestyles of the North Pacific and high latitudes." **Publishes 4-8 titles/year. 200 queries received/year. 100 mss received/year. 75% of books from first-time authors. 90% from unagented writers.** Publishes ms 1-2 years after acceptance. Responds in 3 months to queries. Book catalog and guidelines online.

NONFICTION Subjects include animals, ethnic, history, nature, environment, recreation, regional, women's issues. "Our focus is Alaska and the Pacific Northwest. We do not encourage nonfiction titles from outside this region." Submit outline and 3 sample chapters. Reviews artwork/photos. Send photocopies.

F+W, A CONTENT AND ECOMMERCE COMPANY

10151 Carver Rd., Suite 200, Blue Ash OH 45242. (513)531-2690. **Website:** www.fwcommunity.com. President: Sara Domville. Estab. 1913. Publishes content in a variety of formats, in addition to online education, events, and more. **Publishes 650+ titles/year.** Guidelines online.

IMPRINTS Adams Media (general interest series); David & Charles (crafts, equestrian, railroads, soft crafts); HOW Books (graphic design, illustrated, humor, pop culture); IMPACT Books (fantasy art, manga, creative comics and popular culture); Interweave (knitting, beading, crochet, jewelry, sewing); Krause Books (antiques and collectibles, automotive, coins and paper money, comics, crafts, games, firearms, militaria, outdoors and hunting, records and CDs, sports, toys); Memory Makers (scrapbooking); North Light Books (crafts, decorative painting, fine art); Popular Woodworking Books (shop skills, woodworking); Tyrus Books (mystery and literary fiction); Warman's (antiques and collectibles, field guides); Writer's Digest Books (writing and reference).

Please see individual listings for specific submission information about the company's imprints.

FACTS ON FILE, INC.

Infobase Learning, 132 W. 31st St., 17th Floor, New York NY 10001. (800)322-8755. **Fax:** (800)678-3633. **E-mail:** llikoff@factsonfile.com; custserv@factsonfile.com. **Website:** www.factsonfile.com. Estab. 1941. Publishes hardcover originals and reprints. Facts on File produces high-quality reference materials on a broad range of subjects for the school library market and the general nonfiction trade. **Publishes 135-150 titles/year. 25% from unagented writers. Pays 10% royalty on retail price. Pays $5,000-10,000 advance.** Accepts simultaneous submissions. Responds in 2 months to queries. Book catalog available free. Guidelines online.

NONFICTION Subjects include contemporary culture, education, health, medicine, history, language, literature, multicultural, recreation, religion, sports, careers, entertainment, natural history, popular culture. "We publish serious, informational books for a targeted audience. All our books must have strong library interest, but we also distribute books effectively to the trade. Our library books fit the junior and senior high school curriculum." No computer books, technical books, cookbooks, biographies (except YA), pop psychology, humor, fiction or poetry. Query or submit outline and sample chapter with SASE. No submissions returned without SASE.

TIPS "Our audience is school and public libraries for our more reference-oriented books and libraries, schools and bookstores for our less reference-oriented informational titles."

FAIRLEIGH DICKINSON UNIVERSITY PRESS

285 Madison Ave., M-GH2-01, Madison NJ 07940. (973)443-8564. **Fax:** (973)443-8364. **E-mail:** fdupress@fdu.edu. **Website:** www.fdupress.org. **Contact:** Harry Keyishian, director. Estab. 1967. Publishes hardcover originals and occasional paperbacks, and all existing electronic formats. Fairleigh Dickinson publishes scholarly books for the academic market, in the humanities and social sciences through a copublishing partnership that was established in 2010 with The Rowman & Littlefield Publishing Group, Lanham, MD. **Publishes 35-45 titles/year. 33% of books from first-time authors. 95% from unagented writers.** Publishes ms 6-7 months after acceptance. Responds in 2 weeks to queries.

"Contracts are arranged through The Rowman & Littlefield Publishing Group, which also handles editing and production. We are a selection committee."

NONFICTION Subjects include architecture, art, cinema, communications, contemporary culture, dance, economics, ethnic, film, gay, government, history, law, lesbian, literary criticism, multicultural, music, philosophy, psychology, regional, religion, sociology, womens issues, womens studies, world affairs, local, world literature, Italian Studies (series), Communication Studies (series), Willa Cather (series), American history and culture, Civil War, Jewish studies. "The Press discourages submissions of unrevised dissertations. We will consider scholarly editions of literary works in all fields, in English, or translation. We welcome inquiries about essay collections if the the material is previously unpublished, he essays have a unifying and consistent theme, and the editors provide a substantial scholarly introduction." No nonscholarly books. We do not publish textbooks, or original fiction, poetry or plays. Query with outline, detailed abstract, and sample chapters (if possible), and CV. Does not review artwork.

FAMILIUS

1254 Commerce Way, Sanger CA 93657. (559)876-2170. **Fax:** (559)876-2180. **E-mail:** bookideas@familius.com. **Website:** familius.com. **Contact:** Michele Robbins, acquisitions editor. Estab. 2011. Publishes hardcover, trade paperback, and electronic originals and reprints. Familius is all about strengthening families. Collective, the authors and staff have experienced a wide slice of the family-life spectrum.

Some come from broken homes. Some are married and in the throes of managing a bursting household. Some are preparing to start families of their own. Together, they publish books, articles, and videos that help families be happy. **Publishes 40 titles/year. 200 queries received/year. 100 mss received/year. 60% of books from first-time authors. 70% from unagented writers. Authors are paid 10-30% royalty on wholesale price.** Publishes ms 12 months after acceptance. Accepts simultaneous submissions. Responds in 1 month to queries and proposals; 2 months to mss. Catalog online. Guidelines online.

NONFICTION Subjects include Americana, child guidance, cooking, finance, foods, health, medicine, memoirs, money, nutrition, parenting, young adult. All mss must align with Familius mission statement to help families succeed. Submit a proposal package, including an outline, one sample chapter, competition evaluation, and your author platform. Reviews JPEGS if sent as part of the submission package.

FICTION Subjects include juvenile, picture books, young adult. All fiction must align with Familius values statement listed on the website footer. Submit a proposal package, including a synopsis, 3 sample chapters, and your author platform.

FAMILYLIFE PUBLISHING

FamilyLife, a division of Campus Crusade for Christ, P.O. Box 7111, Little Rock AR 72223. (800)358-6329. **Website:** www.familylife.com. Publishes hardcover and trade paperback originals. FamilyLife is dedicated to effectively developing godly families. We publish connecting resources—books, videos, audio resources, and interactive multi-piece packs—that help husbands and wives communicate better, and parents and children build stronger relationships. **Publishes 3-12 titles/year. 250 queries received/year. 50 mss received/year. 1% of books from first-time authors. 90% from unagented writers. Pays 2-18% royalty on wholesale price. Makes outright purchase of 250.** Publishes ms 2 years after acceptance. Accepts simultaneous submissions. Responds in 3 months to queries; 6 months to proposals and mss. Book catalog online.

NONFICTION Subjects include audio, child guidance, education, religion, sex, spirituality, womens issues, womens studies. FamilyLife Publishing exists to create resources to connect your family. "We publish very few books. Become familiar with what we offer. Our resources are unique in the marketplace. Discover what makes us unique, match your work to our style, and then submit." Query with SASE. Submit proposal package, outline, 2 sample chapters. Reviews artwork/photos.

FANTAGRAPHICS BOOKS, INC.

7563 Lake City Way NE, Seattle WA 98115. (206)524-1967. **Fax:** (206)524-2104. **Website:** www.fantagraphics.com. **Contact:** Submissions Editor. Estab. 1976. Publishes original trade paperbacks. Publishes comics for thinking readers. Does not want mainstream genres of superhero, vigilante, horror, fantasy, or science fiction. Responds in 2-3 months to queries. Book catalog online. Guidelines online.

FICTION Subjects include comic books. "Fantagraphics is an independent company with a modus operandi different from larger, factory-like corporate comics publishers. If your talents are limited to a specific area of expertise (i.e. inking, writing, etc.), then you will need to develop your own team before submitting a project to us. We want to see an idea that is fully fleshed-out in your mind, at least, if not on paper. Submit a minimum of 5 fully-inked pages of art, a synopsis, SASE, and a brief note stating approximately how many issues you have in mind."

TIPS "Take note of the originality and diversity of the themes and approaches to drawing in such Fantagraphics titles as *Love & Rockets* (stories of life in Latin America and Chicano L.A.), *Palestine* (journalistic autobiography in the Middle East), *Eightball* (surrealism mixed with kitsch culture in stories alternately humorous and painfully personal), and *Naughty Bits* (feminist humor and short stories which both attack and commiserate). Try to develop your own, equally individual voice; originality, aesthetic maturity, and graphic storytelling skill are the signs by which Fantagraphics judges whether or not your submission is ripe for publication."

FARCOUNTRY PRESS

P.O. Box 5630, Helena MT 59604. (800)821-3874. **Fax:** (406)443-5480. **E-mail:** will@farcountrypress.com. **Website:** www.farcountrypress.com. **Contact:** Will Harmon. Award-winning publisher Farcountry Press specializes in softcover and hardcover color photography books showcasing the nation's cities, states, national parks, and wildlife. Farcountry also publishes several children's series, as well as guidebooks, cookbooks, and regional history titles nationwide. **Pub-**

lishes The staff produces about 30 books annually; the backlist has grown to more than 300 titles titles/year. Submission guidelines available on website.

FARRAR, STRAUS & GIROUX

18 W. 18th St., New York NY 10011. (646)307-5151. **Website:** us.macmillan.com. **Contact:** Editorial Department. Estab. 1946. Publishes hardcover originals and trade paperback reprints. "We publish original and well-written material for all ages." **Publishes 75 titles/year. 6,000 queries and mss received/year. 5% of books from first-time authors. 50% from unagented writers. Pays 2-6% royalty on retail price for paperbacks, 3-10% for hardcovers. Pays $3,000-25,000 advance.** Publishes ms 18 months after acceptance. Accepts simultaneous submissions. Responds in 2-3 months. Catalog available by request. Guidelines online.

NONFICTION All levels. Send cover letter describing submission with first 50 pages.

FICTION Subjects include juvenile, picture books, young adult. Do not query picture books; just send ms. Do not fax or e-mail queries or mss. Send cover letter describing submission with first 50 pages.

POETRY Send cover letter describing submission with 3-4 poems. By mail only.

FARRAR, STRAUS & GIROUX FOR YOUNG READERS

Macmillan Children's Publishing Group, 175 Fifth Ave., New York NY 10010. (212)741-6900. **Fax:.** (212)633-2427. **E-mail:** childrens.editorial@fsgbooks.com. **Website:** www.fsgkidsbooks.com. Estab. 1946. Book catalog available by request. Ms guidelines online.

NONFICTION All levels: all categories. "We publish only literary nonfiction." Submit cover letter, first 50 pages by mail only.

FICTION All levels: all categories. "Original and well-written material for all ages." Submit cover letter, first 50 pages by mail only.

POETRY Submit cover letter, 3-4 poems by mail only.

TIPS "Study our catalog before submitting. We will see illustrators' portfolios by appointment. Don't ask for criticism and/or advice—due to the volume of submissions we receive, it's just not possible. Never send originals. Always enclose SASE."

FATHER'S PRESS

2424 SE 6th St., Lee's Summit MO 64063. (816)600-6288. **E-mail:** mike@fatherspress.com. **Website:** www.fatherspress.com. **Contact:** Mike Smitley, owner (fiction, nonfiction). Estab. 2006. Publishes hardcover, trade paperback, and mass market paperback originals and reprints. **Publishes 6-10 titles/year. Pays 10-15% royalty on wholesale price.** Publishes ms 6 months after acceptance. Responds in 1-3 months. Guidelines online.

NONFICTION Subjects include animals, cooking, foods, nutrition, creative nonfiction, history, military, war, nature, regional, religion, travel, women's issues, world affairs. Query with SASE. Unsolicited mss returned unopened. Call or e-mail first. Reviews artwork/photos. Send photocopies.

FICTION Subjects include adventure, historical, juvenile, literary, mainstream, contemporary, military, war, mystery, regional, religious, suspense, western, young adult. Query with SASE. Unsolicited mss returned unopened. Call or e-mail first.

Ⓐ⊘ FAWCETT

The Ballantine Publishing Group, A Division of Random House, Inc., 1745 Broadway, New York NY 10019. **Website:** www.randomhouse.com. Estab. 1955. Publishes paperback originals and reprints. Major publisher of mystery mass market and trade paperbacks.

FICTION Subjects include mystery. Agented submissions only. *All unsolicited mss returned.*

Ⓐ⊘ FEIWEL AND FRIENDS

Macmillan Children's Publishing Group, 175 Fifth Ave., New York NY 10010. (646)307-5151. **Website:** us.macmillan.com/feiwelandfriends.aspx. Feiwel and Friends is a publisher of innovative children's fiction and nonfiction literature, including hardcover, paperback series, and individual titles. The list is eclectic and combines quality and commercial appeal for readers ages 0-16. The imprint is dedicated to "book by book" publishing, bringing the work of distinctive and oustanding authors, illustrators, and ideas to the marketplace. This market does not accept unsolicited mss due to the volume of submissions; they also do not accept unsolicited queries for interior art. The best way to submit a ms is through an agent. Catalog online.

FENCE BOOKS

Science Library 320, Univ. of Albany, 1400 Washington Ave., Albany NY 12222. (518)591-8162. **E-mail:** fencesubmissions@gmail.com. **E-mail:** peter.n.fence@gmail.com. **Website:** www.fenceportal.org. **Contact:** Submissions Manager. Publishes hardcover originals. Closed to submissions until June 15. Check website for details. Guidelines online.

FICTION Subjects include literary, poetry. Submit via contests and occasional open reading periods.

POETRY Submit via contests and occasional open reading periods.

FERGUSON PUBLISHING CO.

Infobase Publishing, 132 W. 31st St., 17th Floor, New York NY 10001. (800)322-8755. **E-mail:** editorial@factsonfile.com. **Website:** www.infobasepublishing.com. Estab. 1940. Publishes hardcover and trade paperback originals. "We are primarily a career education publisher that publishes for schools and libraries. We need writers who have expertise in a particular career or career field (for possible full-length books on a specific career or field)." **Publishes 50 titles/year. Pays by project.** Responds in 6 months to queries. Guidelines online.

NONFICTION "We publish work specifically for the elementary/junior high/high school/college library reference market. Works are generally encyclopedic in nature. Our current focus is career encyclopedias and young adult career sets and series. We consider manuscripts that cross over into the trade market." No mass market, poetry, scholarly, or juvenile books, please. Query or submit an outline and 1 sample chapter.

TIPS "We like writers who know the market—former or current librarians or teachers or guidance counselors."

FERNWOOD PUBLISHING, LTD.

32 Ocenavista Ln., Black Pointe NS B0J 1B0, Canada. (902)857-1388. **E-mail:** errol@fernpub.ca. **E-mail:** editorial@fernpub.ca. **Website:** www.fernwoodpublishing.ca. **Contact:** Errol Sharpe, publisher. Publishes trade paperback originals. "Fernwood's objective is to publish critical works which challenge existing scholarship." **Publishes 15-20 titles/year. 80 queries received/year. 30 mss received/year. 40% of books from first-time authors. 100% from unagented writers. Pays 7-10% royalty on wholesale price. Pays advance.** Publishes ms 1 year after acceptance. Accepts simultaneous submissions. Responds in 6 weeks to proposals. Guidelines online.

NONFICTION Subjects include agriculture, anthropology, archeology, business, economics, education, ethnic, gay, lesbian, government, politics, health, medicine, history, language, literature, multicultural, nature, environment, philosophy, regional, sex, sociology, sports, translation, women's issues, women's studies, contemporary culture, world affairs. "Our main focus is in the social sciences and humanities, emphasizing labor studies, women's studies, gender studies, critical theory and research, political economy, cultural studies, and social work-for use in college and university courses." Submit proposal package, outline, sample chapters. Reviews artwork/photos. Send photocopies.

DAVID FICKLING BOOKS

31 Beamont St., Oxford OX1 2NP, United Kingdom. (018)65-339000. **Fax:** (018)65-339009. **E-mail:** submissions@davidficklingbooks.com. **Website:** www.davidficklingbooks.co.uk. **Contact:** Simon Mason, managing editor. David Fickling Books is a story house. **Publishes 12-20 titles/year.** Responds to mss in 3 months, if interested. Guidelines online.

FICTION Considers all categories. Submit cover letter and 3 sample chapters as PDF attachment saved in format "Author Name_Full Title."

TIPS "We adore stories for all ages, in both text and pictures. Quality is our watch word."

FIFTH HOUSE PUBLISHERS

Fitzhenry & Whiteside, 195 Allstate Pkwy., Markham ON L3R 4T8, Canada. (403)571-5230; (800)387-9776. **E-mail:** sfitz@fifthhousepublishers.ca. **Website:** www.fifthhousepublishers.ca. **Contact:** Sharon Fitzhenry, publisher. Estab. 1982. "Fifth House Publishers, a Fitzhenry & Whiteside company, is committed to 'bringing the West to the rest' by publishing approximately 15 books a year about the land and people who make this region unique. Our books are selected for their quality and contribution to the understanding of western-Canadian (and Canadian) history, culture, and environment."

FILBERT PUBLISHING

140 3rd St. N., Kandiyohi MN 56251-0326. (320)444-5080. **E-mail:** filbertpublishing@filbertpublishing.com. **Website:** filbertpublishing.com. **Contact:** Maurice Erickson, acquisitions. Estab. 2001. Publishes trade paperback and electronic originals and reprints. "We really like to publish books that creative people can use to help them make a living following their dream. This includes books on marketing, books that encourage living a full life, freelancing, we'll consider a fairly wide range of subjects under this umbrella. We will also give consideration to books on healthy living

and plant-based cooking. Make sure your cookbook has a strong hook. We've got a few awesome books in this category on the horizon and are anxious to extend that line. The people who purchase our books (and visit our website) tend to be in their fifties, female, well-educated; many are freelancers who want to make a lviing writing. Any well-written title that would appeal to that audience is nearly a slam dunk to get added to our catalog. " **Publishes 6-12 titles/year. 95% of books from first-time authors. 99% from unagented writers. Authors receive 10% royalty on retail price. E-books receive 50% net.** Publishes ms 2-3 months after acceptance. Accepts simultaneous submissions. Responds in 1 month. Catalog online. Guidelines online.

NONFICTION Subjects include communications, cooking, foods, health, medicine, nutrition, religion, spirituality, reference books for freelancers and creative people, with an emphasis on marketing. "Our projects tend to be evergreen. If you've got a great project that's as relevant today as it will be 10 years from now, something that you're passionate about, query." Submit a query via SASE with a proposal package, including an outline and 2 sample chapters. Will review artwork. Writers should send photocopies or query about sending electronically.

FICTION Subjects include contemporary, mainstream, mystery, romance, suspense. "We're slow to accept new fiction, however, we are thrilled when we find a story that sweeps us off our feet. Fiction queries have been very sparse the last couple of years, and we're keen on expanding that line in the coming months." Query via SASE with a proposal package, including a synopsis, 5 sample chapters, information regarding your web platform, and a brief mention of your current marketing plan.

TIPS "Get to know us. Subscribe to Writing Etc. to capture our preferred tone. Dig through our website, you'll get many ideas of what we're looking for. We love nurturing new writing careers and most of our authors have stuck with us since our humble beginning. We love words. We really love the publishing business. If you share those passions, feel free to query."

FILTER PRESS, LLC

P.O. Box 95, Palmer Lake CO 80133. (888)570-2663. **Fax:** (719)481-2420. **E-mail:** info@filterpressbooks.com. **Website:** www.filterpressbooks.com. **Contact:** Doris Baker, president. Estab. 1957. Publishes trade paperback originals and reprints. "Filter Press specializes in nonfiction of the West." **Publishes 4-6 titles/year. Pays 10-12% royalty on wholesale price.** Publishes ms 18 months after acceptance.

NONFICTION Subjects include Americana, anthropology, archeology, ethnic, history, regional, crafts and crafts people of the Southwest. Query with outline and SASE. Reviews artwork/photos.

FINDHORN PRESS

Delft Cottage, Dyke, Forres Scotland IV36 2TF, United Kingdom. (44)(1309) 690-582. **Fax:** (44)(131) 777-2711. **E-mail:** submissions@findhornpress.com. **Website:** www.findhornpress.com. **Contact:** Thierry Bogliolo, publisher. Estab. 1971. Publishes trade paperback originals and e-books. **Publishes 20 titles/year. 1,000 queries received/year. 50% of books from first-time authors. 80% from unagented writers. Pays 10-15% royalty on wholesale price.** Publishes ms 12-18 months after acceptance. Responds in 3-4 months to proposals. Book catalog and ms guidelines online.

NONFICTION Subjects include nature, spirituality, alternative health. No autobiographies.

FINNEY COMPANY, INC.

5995 149th St. W., Suite 105, Apple Valley MN 55124. **E-mail:** info@finneyco.com. **Website:** www.finneyco.com. **Contact:** Alan E. Krysan, president. Publishes trade paperback originals. **Publishes 2 titles/year. Pays 10% royalty on wholesale price. Pays advance.** Publishes ms 1 year after acceptance. Responds in 2-3 months to queries.

NONFICTION Subjects include business, economics, education, career exploration/development. Finney publishes career development educational materials. Query with SASE. Reviews artwork/photos.

FIRE ENGINEERING BOOKS & VIDEOS

Imprint of PennWell Corp., 1421 S. Sheridan Rd., Tulsa OK 74112. (918)831-9410. **Fax:** (918)831-9555. **E-mail:** marlap@pennwell.com. **Website:** www.pennwellbooks.com. **Contact:** Marla Patterson, editorial manager. Publishes hardcover and softcover originals. "Fire Engineering publishes textbooks relevant to firefighting and training. Currently emphasizing strategy and tactics, reserve training, preparedness for terrorist threats, natural disasters, first response to fires and emergencies." Responds in 1 month to proposals. Book catalog available free.

NONFICTION Submit proposal via e-mail.

TIPS "No human-interest stories; technical training only."

FIRST SECOND

Macmillan Children's Publishing Group, 175 5th Ave., New York NY 10010. **E-mail:** mail@firstsecondbooks.com. **Website:** www.firstsecondbooks.com. First Second is a publisher of graphic novels and an imprint of Macmillan Children's Publishing Group. First Second does not accept unsolicited submissions. Responds in about 6 weeks. Catalog online.

FITZHENRY & WHITESIDE LTD.

195 Allstate Pkwy., Markham ON L3R 4T8, Canada. (905)477-9700. **Fax:** (905)477-9179. **E-mail:** fitzkids@fitzhenry.ca; godwit@fitzhenry.ca; charkin@fitzhenry.ca. **Website:** www.fitzhenry.ca/. **Contact:** Sharon Fitzhenry (adult books); Cheryl Chen (children's books). Emphasis on Canadian authors and illustrators, subject or perspective. **Publishes 15 titles/year. 10% of books from first-time authors. Pays authors 8-10% royalty with escalations. Offers "respectable" advances for picture books, split 50/50 between author and illustrator. Pays illustrators by project and royalty. Pays photographers per photo.** Publishes ms 1-2 years after acceptance.

TIPS "We respond to quality."

FLARESTACK POETS

69 Beaks Hill Rd., Birmingham B38 8BL, United Kingdom. **E-mail:** flarestackpoets@gmail.com. **Website:** www.flarestackpoets.co.uk. **Contact:** Meredith Andrea and Jacqui Rowe. Estab. 2008. **Pays 25% royalty and 6 contributor's copies.** Responds in 6 weeks.

POETRY Flarestack Poets wants "poems that dare outside current trends, even against the grain." Publishes 6 chapbooks/year. Chapbooks are 20-30 pages, professional photocopy, saddle-stitched, card cover. See website for current submission arrangements.

FLASHLIGHT PRESS

527 Empire Blvd., Brooklyn NY 11225. (718)288-8300. **Fax:** (718)972-6307. **E-mail:** editor@flashlightpress.com. **Website:** www.flashlightpress.com. **Contact:** Shari Dash Greenspan, editor. Estab. 2004. Publishes hardcover and trade paperback originals. **Publishes 2-3 titles/year. 1,200 queries received/year; 120 mss received/year. 50% of books from first-time authors. Pays 8-10% royalty on wholesale price.** Publishes ms up to 3 years after acceptance. Accepts simultaneous submissions. "Only accepts e-mail queries according to submission guidelines." Responds in 3 months to requested mss. Book catalog available online.

FICTION Average word length: 1,000 words. Picture books: contemporary, humor, multicultural. "Query by e-mail only, after carefully reading our submission guidelines: www.flashlightpress.com/submissionguidelines.html. No e-mail attachments. Do not send anything by snail mail."

FLOATING BRIDGE PRESS

909 NE 43rd St., #205, Seattle WA 98105. **E-mail:** floatingbridgepress@yahoo.com. **Website:** www.floatingbridgepress.org. Estab. 1994.

POETRY Floating Bridge Press publishes chapbooks and anthologies by Washington State poets, selected through an annual competition.

FLUX

Llewellyn Worldwide, Ltd., Llewellyn Worldwide, Ltd., 2143 Wooddale Dr., Woodbury MN 55125. (651)312-8613. **Fax:** (651)291-1908. **Website:** www.fluxnow.com. Estab. 2005. "Flux seeks to publish authors who see YA as a point of view, not a reading level. We look for books that try to capture a slice of teenage experience, whether in real or imagined worlds." **Publishes 21 titles/year. 50% of books from first-time authors. Pays royalties of 10-15% based on wholesale price.** Book catalog and guidelines online.

FICTION Young Adults: adventure, contemporary, fantasy, history, humor, problem novels, religion, science fiction, sports, suspense. Average word length: 50,000. *Accepts agented submissions only.*

TIPS "Read contemporary teen books. Be aware of what else is out there. If you don't read teen books, you probably shouldn't write them. Know your audience. Write incredibly well. Do not condescend."

FLYLEAF PRESS

4 Spencer Villas, Glenageary, County Dublin , Ireland. (353)(1)285-4658. **E-mail:** books@flyleaf.ie. **Website:** www.flyleaf.ie. **Contact:** James Ryan, managing editor (family history). Publishes hardcover originals. **Publishes 3 titles/year. 15 queries received/year. 10 mss received/year. 60% of books from first-time authors. 100% from unagented writers. Pays 7-10% royalty on wholesale price.** Publishes ms 6 months after acceptance. Responds in 1 month to mss. Book catalog online.

NONFICTION Subjects include history, hobbies, family history. Submit proposal package, outline, 1 sample chapter.

TIPS "Audience is family history hobbyists, history students, local historians."

FOCAL PRESS

Imprint of Elsevier (USA), Inc., 711 3rd Ave., 8th Floor, New York NY 10017. **Website:** www.focalpress.com. **Contact:** Amorette Petersen, publishing director; for further editorial contacts, visit the contacts page on the company's Website. Estab. US, 1981; UK, 1938. Publishes hardcover and paperback originals and reprints. "Focal Press provides excellent books for students, advanced amateurs, and working professionals involved in all areas of media technology. Topics of interest include photography (digital and traditional techniques), film/video, audio, broadcasting, and cinematography, through to journalism, radio, television, video, and writing. Currently emphasizing graphics, gaming, animation, and multimedia." **Publishes 80-120 UK-US titles/year; entire firm publishes over 1,000 titles/year. 25% of books from first-time authors. 90% from unagented writers.** Publishes ms 6 months after acceptance. Accepts simultaneous submissions. Responds in 2 months to queries. Guidelines online.

NONFICTION Subjects include film, cinema, stage, photography, film, cinematography, broadcasting, theater and performing arts, audio, sound and media technology. Does not publish collections of photographs or books composed primarily of photographs. To submit a proposal for consideration by Elsevier, complete the proposal form online. "Once we have had a chance to review your proposal in line with our publishing plan and budget, we will contact you to discuss the next steps." Reviews artwork/photos.

FODOR'S TRAVEL PUBLICATIONS, INC.

Imprint of Random House, Inc., 1745 Broadway, New York NY 10019. **E-mail:** editors@fodors.com. **Website:** www.fodors.com. Estab. 1936. Publishes trade paperback originals. Fodor's publishes travel books on many regions and countries. "Remember that most Fodor's writers live in the areas they cover. Note that we do not accept unsolicited mss." **Most titles are collective works, with contributions as works for hire. Most contributions are updates of previously published volumes.** Accepts simultaneous submissions. Responds in 2 months to queries. Book catalog available free.

NONFICTION Subjects include travel. "We are interested in unique approaches to favorite destinations. Writers seldom review our catalog or our list and often query about books on topics that we're already covering. Beyond that, it's important to review competition and to say what the proposed book will add. Do not send originals without first querying as to our interest in the project. We're not interested in travel literature or in proposals for general travel guidebooks." Submit writing clips and résumé via mail or e-mail. In cover letter, explain qualifications and areas of expertise.

TIPS "In preparing your query or proposal, remember that it's the only argument Fodor's will hear about why your book will be a good one, and why you think it will sell; and it's also best evidence of your ability to create the book you propose. Craft your proposal well and carefully so that it puts your best foot forward."

FOLDED WORD

79 Tracy Way, Meredith NH 03253. **E-mail:** editors@foldedword.com. **Website:** www.foldedword.com. Editor-in-Chief: J.S. Graustein. Poetry Editor: Rose Auslander. Fiction Editor: Casey Murphy. Estab. 2008. "Folded Word is an independent literary press. Our focus? Connecting new voices to readers. Our goal? To make poetry and fiction accessible for the widest audience possible both on and off the page."

TIPS "We are seeking non-formulaic narratives that have a strong sense of place and/or time, especially the exploration of unfamiliar place/time."

FORDHAM UNIVERSITY PRESS

2546 Belmont Ave., University Box L, Bronx NY 10458. (718)817-4795. **Fax:** (718)817-4785. **Website:** www.fordhampress.com. **Contact:** Tom Lay, acquisitions editor. Editorial Director: Richard W. Morrison. Publishes hardcover and trade paperback originals and reprints. "We are a publisher in humanities, accepting scholarly monographs, collections, occasional reprints and general interest titles for consideration. No fiction." Book catalog and ms guidelines free.

NONFICTION Subjects include anthropology, archeology, art, architecture, education, film, cinema, stage, government, politics, history, language, literature, military, war, World War II, philosophy, regional, New York, religion, science, sociology, translation, business, Jewish studies, media, music. Submit query letter, CV, SASE.

TIPS "We have an academic and general audience."

FOREIGN POLICY ASSOCIATION

470 Park Ave. S., New York NY 10016. (212)481-8100. **Fax:** (212)481-9275. **E-mail:** krohan@fpa.org. **Website:** www.fpa.org. **Contact:** Karen Rohan, editorial department. Publishes 2 periodicals, an annual eight episode PBS Television series with DVD and an occasional hardcover and trade paperback original. The Foreign Policy Association, a nonpartisan, not-for-profit educational organization founded in 1918, is a catalyst for developing awareness, understanding of and informed opinion on US foreign policy and global issues. Through its balanced, nonpartisan publications, FPA seeks to encourage individuals in schools, communities and the workplace to participate in the foreign policy process. Accepts simultaneous submissions. Book catalog available free.

IMPRINTS Headline Series (quarterly); Great Decisions (annual).

NONFICTION Subjects include government, politics, history, foreign policy.

TIPS "Audience is students and people with an interest, but not necessarily any expertise, in foreign policy and international relations."

FORMAC PUBLISHING CO. LTD.

5502 Atlantic St., Halifax NS B3H 1G4, Canada. (902)421-7022. **Fax:** (902)425-0166. **Website:** www.formac.ca. **Contact:** Acquisitions Editor. Estab. 1977. Publishes hardcover and trade paperback originals. **Publishes 15-20 titles/year. 200 queries received/year. 150 mss received/year. 20% of books from first-time authors. 75% from unagented writers. Pays 5-10% royalty on wholesale price.** Publishes ms 1 year after acceptance. Accepts simultaneous submissions. Responds in 2 months to queries and to proposals; 4 months to mss. Book catalog available free. Guidelines online.

NONFICTION Subjects include animals, art, architecture, cooking, foods, nutrition, creative nonfiction, government, politics, history, military, war, multicultural, nature, environment, regional, travel, marine subjects, transportation. Submit proposal package, outline, 2 sample chapters, CV or résumé of author(s).

TIPS "For our illustrated books, our audience includes adults interestsed in regional topics. For our travel titles, the audience is Canadians and visitors looking for cultural and outdoor experiences. Check out our website to see if you think your books fits anywhere in our list before submitting it. We are primarily interested in the work of Canadian authors."

FORTRESS PRESS

P.O. Box 1209, Minneapolis MN 55440. (612)330-3300. **Website:** www.fortresspress.com. Publishes hardcover and trade paperback originals. "Fortress Press publishes academic books in Biblical studies, theology, Christian ethics, church history, and professional books in pastoral care and counseling." **Pays royalty on retail price.** Accepts simultaneous submissions. Book catalog free. Guidelines online.

NONFICTION Subjects include religion, women's issues, women's studies, church history, African-American studies. Use online form. Please study guidelines before submitting.

FORWARD MOVEMENT

412 Sycamore St., Cincinnati OH 45202. (513)721-6659; (800)543-1813. **Fax:** (513)721-0729. **E-mail:** rthompson@forwardmovement.org. **Website:** www.forwardmovement.org. **Contact:** Richelle Thompson, managing editor. Estab. 1934. "Forward Movement was established to help reinvigorate the life of the church. Many titles focus on the life of prayer, where our relationship with God is centered, death, marriage, baptism, recovery, joy, the Episcopal Church and more. Currently emphasizing prayer/spirituality." **Publishes 30 titles/year.** Responds in 1 month. Book catalog free. Guidelines online.

NONFICTION Subjects include religion. "We are an agency of the Episcopal Church. There is a special need for tracts of under 8 pages. (A page usually runs about 200 words.) On rare occasions, we publish a full-length book." Query with SASE or by e-mail with complete ms attached.

FICTION Subjects include juvenile.

TIPS "Audience is primarily Episcopalians and other Christians."

WALTER FOSTER PUBLISHING, INC.

3 Wrigley, Suite A, Irvine CA 92618. (800)426-0099. **Fax:** (949)380-7575. **E-mail:** info@walterfoster.com. **Website:** www.walterfoster.com. **Contact:** Submissions. Estab. 1922. Publishes trade paperback originals. "Walter Foster publishes instructional how-to/craft instruction as well as licensed products." Guidelines online.

NONFICTION Art, craft, activity books. Submit proposal package.

FOUR WAY BOOKS

Box 535, Village Station, New York NY 10014. **E-mail:** editors@fourwaybooks.com. **Website:** www.fourwaybooks.com. **Contact:** Martha Rhodes, director. Estab. 1993. "Four Way Books is a not-for-profit literary press dedicated to publishing poetry and short fiction by emerging and established writers. Each year, Four Way Books publishes the winners of its national poetry competitions, as well as collections accepted through general submission, panel selection, and solicitation by the editors."

FICTION Open reading period: June 1-30. Book-length story collections and novellas. Submission guidelines will be posted online at end of May. Does not want novels or translations.

POETRY Four Way Books publishes poetry and short fiction. Considers full-length poetry mss only. Books are about 70 pages, offset-printed digitally, perfect-bound, with paperback binding, art/graphics on covers. Does not want individual poems or poetry intended for children/young readers. See website for complete submission guidelines and open reading period in June. Book mss may include previously published poems. Responds to submissions in 4 months. Payment varies. Order sample books from Four Way Books online or through bookstores.

FOX CHAPEL PUBLISHING

1970 Broad St., East Petersburg PA 17520. (800)457-9112. **Fax:** (717)560-4702. **E-mail:** acquisitions@foxchapelpublishing.com. **Website:** www.foxchapelpublishing.com. **Contact:** Peg Couch, acquisitions editor. Publishes hardcover and trade paperback originals and trade paperback reprints. Fox Chapel publishes craft, lifestyle, and woodworking titles for professionals and hobbyists. **Publishes 50-90 titles/year. 30% of books from first-time authors. 100% from unagented writers. Pays royalty or makes outright purchase. Pays variable advance.** Accepts simultaneous submissions. Submission guidelines online.

TIPS "We're looking for knowledgeable artists, craftspeople and woodworkers, all experts in their fields, to write books of lasting value."

FRANCES LINCOLN BOOKS

74-77 White Lion St., Islington, London N1 9PF, United Kingdom. (44)(20)7284-4009. **E-mail:** fl@franceslincoln.com. **Website:** www.franceslincoln.com. Estab. 1977. **Publishes 100 titles/year. 6% of books from first-time authors.** Publishes ms 18 months after acceptance. Accepts simultaneous submissions. Responds in 6 weeks to mss.

NONFICTION Subjects include animals, career guidance, cooking, environment, history, multicultural, nature, religion, social issues, special needs. Query by e-mail.

FRANCES LINCOLN CHILDREN'S BOOKS

Frances Lincoln, 74-77 White Lion St., Islington, London N1 9PF, United Kingdom. (44)(20)7284-4009. **E-mail:** fl@franceslincoln.com. **Website:** www.franceslincoln.com. Estab. 1977. "Our company was founded by Frances Lincoln in 1977. We published our first books two years later, and we have been creating illustrated books of the highest quality ever since, with special emphasis on gardening, walking and the outdoors, art, architecture, design and landscape. In 1983, we started to publish illustrated books for children. Since then we have won many awards and prizes with both fiction and nonfiction children's books." **Publishes 100 titles/year. 6% of books from first-time authors.** Publishes ms 18 months after acceptance. Accepts simultaneous submissions. Responds in 6 weeks to mss.

NONFICTION Subjects include animals, career guidance, cooking, environment, history, multicultural, nature, religion, young adult, social issues, special needs. Average word length: picture books—1,000; middle readers—29,768. Query by e-mail.

FICTION Subjects include adventure, fantasy, historical, humor, juvenile, multicultural, picture books, sports, young adult, anthololgy, folktales, nature. Average word length: picture books—1,000; young readers— 9,788; middle readers— 20,653; young adults—35,407. Query by e-mail.

FRANCISCAN MEDIA PRESS

28 W. Liberty St., Cincinnati OH 45202-6498. (513)241-5615. **Fax:** (513)241-0399. **E-mail:** mckendzia@franciscanmedia.org. **Website:** www.americancatholic.org. **Contact:** Mary Carol Kendzia, product development director. Estab. 1970. Publishes trade paperback originals. "St. Anthony Messenger Press/Franciscan Communications seeks to communicate the word that is Jesus Christ in the styles of Saints Francis and Anthony. Through print and electronic media marketed in North America and worldwide, we endeavor to evangelize, inspire, and inform those who search for God and seek a richer Catholic, Christian,

human life. Our efforts help support the life, ministry, and charities of the Franciscan Friars of St. John the Baptist Province, who sponsor our work. Currently emphasizing prayer/spirituality." **Publishes 20-25 titles/year. 300 queries received/year. 50 mss received/year. 5% of books from first-time authors. 99% from unagented writers. Pays $1,000 average advance.** Publishes ms 18 months after acceptance. Responds in 2 months. Guidelines online.

IMPRINTS Servant Books.

NONFICTION Query with SASE. Submit outline. Reviews artwork/photos.

FRANKLIN WATTS

338 Euston Rd., London NW1 3BH, United Kingdom. (44)(20)7873-6000. **Fax:** (44)(20)7873-6024. **E-mail:** ad@hachettechildrens.co.uk. **Website:** www.franklinwatts.co.uk. Estab. 1942. Franklin Watts is well known for its high quality and attractive information books, which support the National Curriculum and stimulate children's enquiring minds. *Generally does not accept unsolicited mss.*

FREE SPIRIT PUBLISHING, INC.

217 Fifth Ave. N., Suite 200, Minneapolis MN 55401-1299. (612)338-2068. **Fax:** (612)337-5050. **E-mail:** acquisitions@freespirit.com. **Website:** www.freespirit.com. Estab. 1983. Publishes trade paperback originals and reprints. "We believe passionately in empowering kids to learn to think for themselves and make their own good choices." **Publishes 12-18 titles/year. 5% of books from first-time authors. 75% from unagented writers. Pays advance.** Responds to proposals in 4-6 months. Book catalog and ms guidelines online.

Free Spirit does not accept general fiction, poetry or storybook submissions.

NONFICTION Subjects include child guidance, education, pre-K-12, study and social sciences skills, special needs, differentiation but not textbooks or basic skills books like reading, counting, etc., health, medicine, mental/emotional health for/about children, psychology for/about children, sociology for/about children. "Many of our authors are educators, mental health professionals, and youth workers involved in helping kids and teens." No general fiction or picture storybooks, poetry, single biographies or autobiographies, books with mythical or animal characters, or books with religious or New Age content. "We are not looking for academic or religious materials, or books that analyze problems with the nation's school systems." Query with cover letter stating qualifications, intent, and intended audience and market analysis (how your book stands out from the field), along with your promotional plan, outline, 2 sample chapters, resume, SASE. Do not send original copies of work.

FICTION "We will consider fiction that relates directly to select areas of focus. Please review catalog and author guidelines (both available online) for details before submitting proposal. If you'd like material returned, enclose a SASE with sufficient postage." Accepts queries only—not submissions—by e-mail.

TIPS "Our books are issue-oriented, jargon-free, and solution-focused. Our audience is children, teens, teachers, parents and youth counselors. We are especially concerned with kids' social and emotional wellbeing and look for books with ready-to-use strategies for coping with today's issues at home or in school—written in everyday language. We are not looking for academic or religious materials, or books that analyze problems with the nation's school systems. Instead, we want books that offer practical, positive advice so kids can help themselves, and parents and teachers can help kids succeed."

FULCRUM PUBLISHING

4690 Table Mountain Dr., Suite 100, Golden CO 80403. **E-mail:** acquisitions@fulcrumbooks.com. **Website:** www.fulcrum-books.com. **Contact:** T. Baker, acquisitions editor. Estab. 1984. **Pays authors royalty based on wholesale price. Offers advances.** Catalog for SASE. Guidelines online.

NONFICTION Middle and early readers: Western history, nature/ environment, Native American. Submit complete ms or submit outline/synopsis and 2 sample chapters. "Publisher does not send response letters unless we are interested in publishing." Do not send SASE.

TIPS "Research our line first. We look for books that appeal to the school market and trade. "

FUTURECYCLE PRESS

Website: www.futurecycle.org. **Contact:** Diane Kistner, director/editor-in-chief. Estab. 2007. Publishes English-language poetry books, chapbooks, and anthologies in print-on-demand and digital editions. Awards the FutureCycle Poetry Book Prize and honorarium for the best full-length book the press publishes each year. **Pays in deeply discounted author copies (no purchase required).** Accepts simultaneous submissions. Responds in 3 months. Guidelines, sample contract, and detailed *Guide for Authors* online.

POETRY Wants "poetry from imaginative, highly skilled poets, whether well known or emerging. We abhor the myopic, self-absorbed, and sloppy, but otherwise are eclectic in our tastes." Does not want concrete or visual poetry. Publishes 15+ poetry books/year and 5+ chapbooks/year. Ms. selected through open submission. Books average 62-110 pages; chapbooks 30-42 pages; anthologies 100+ pages. Submit complete ms. No need to query.

FUTURE HORIZONS

721 W. Abram St., Arlington TX 76013. (817)277-0727. **Fax:** (817)277-2270. **Website:** www.fhautism.com. **Contact:** Jennifer Gilpin-Yacio, editorial director. Publishes hardcover originals, trade paperback originals and reprints. **Publishes 10 titles/year. 250 queries received/year. 125 mss received/year. 75% of books from first-time authors. 95% from unagented writers. Pays 10% royalty. Makes outright purchase.** Publishes ms 2 months after acceptance. Accepts simultaneous submissions. Responds in 1 month to queries; 2 months to proposals. Book catalog available free. Guidelines online.

NONFICTION Subjects include education, about autism/Asperger's syndrome, autism. Submit proposal package, outline by mail (no e-mail). Reviews artwork/photos. Send photocopies.

TIPS "Audience is parents, teachers."

GENEALOGICAL PUBLISHING CO., INC.

3600 Clipper Mill Rd., Suite 260, Baltimore MD 21211. (410)837-8271. **Fax:** (410)752-8492. **E-mail:** info@genealogical.com. **E-mail:** jgaronzi@genealogical.com. **Website:** www.genealogical.com. **Contact:** Joe Garonzik, marketing director. Estab. 1959. Publishes hardcover and trade paperback originals and reprints. **Publishes 50 titles/year. Receives 100 queries/year; 20 mss/year. 10% of books from first-time authors. 99% from unagented writers. Pays 10-15% royalty on wholesale price.** Publishes ms 6 months after acceptance. Accepts simultaneous submissions. Responds in 1 month. Catalog free on request.

NONFICTION Subjects include Americana, ethnic, history, hobbies. Submit outline, 1 sample chapter. Reviews artwork/photos as part of the mss package.

TIPS "Our audience is genealogy hobbyists."

GERTRUDE PRESS

P.O. Box 83948, Portland OR 97283. (503)515-8252. **E-mail:** edelehoy@fc.edu. **Website:** www.gertrudepress.org. **Contact:** Justus Ballard (all fiction). Estab. 2005. "Gertrude Press is a nonprofit organization developing and showcasing the creative talents of lesbian, gay, bisexual, trans, queer-identified and allied individuals. We publish limited-edition fiction and poetry chapbooks plus the biannual literary journal, *Gertrude*." Reads chapbook mss only through contests.

FICTION Subjects include ethnic, experimental, feminist, gay, humor, lesbian, literary, mainstream, multicultural, short story collections.

TIPS Sponsors poetry and fiction chapbook contest. Prize is $50 and 50 contributor's copies. Submission guidelines and fee information on website. "Read the journal and sample published work. We are not impressed by pages of publications; your work should speak for itself."

GIBBS SMITH

P.O. Box 667, Layton UT 84041. (801)544-9800. **Fax:** (801)544-8853. **E-mail:** duribe@gibbs-smith.com. **Website:** www.gibbs-smith.com. **Contact:** Suzanne Taylor, associate publisher and creative director (children's activity books); Jennifer Grillone, art acquisitions. Estab. 1969. **Publishes 3 titles/year. 50% of books from first-time authors. 50% from unagented writers. Pays authors royalty of 2% based on retail price or work purchased outright ($500 minimum). Offers advances (average amount: $2,000).** Publishes ms 1-2 years after acceptance. Accepts simultaneous submissions. Responds in 2 months. Book catalog available for 9×12 SAE and $2.30 postage. Ms guidelines available by e-mail.

NONFICTION Middle readers: activity, arts/crafts, cooking, how-to, nature/environment, science. Average word length: picture books—under 1,000 words; activity books—under 15,000 words. Submit an outline and writing samples for activity books; query for other types of books.

TIPS "We target ages 5-11. We do not publish young adult novels or chapter books."

⊘ GIFTED EDUCATION PRESS

10201 Yuma Ct., Manassas VA 20109. (703)369-5017. **E-mail:** mfisher345@comcast.net. **Website:** www.giftedstemeducation.com. **Contact:** Maurice Fisher, publisher. Estab. 1981. Publishes trade paperback originals. "Searching for rigorous texts on teaching science, math and humanities to gifted students." **Publishes 5 titles/year. 20 queries received/year. 10 mss received/year. 90% of books from first-time authors. 100% from unagented writers. Pays 10% royalty on retail price.** Publishes ms 4 months after acceptance. Accepts simultaneous submissions. Responds in 1 month. Book catalog online. Guidelines online.

NONFICTION Subjects include child guidance, computers, electronics, education, history, humanities, philosophy, science, teaching, math, biology, Shakespeare, chemistry, physics, creativity. Query with SASE. *All unsolicited mss returned unopened.* Reviews artwork/photos.

TIPS "Audience includes teachers, parents, gifted program supervisors, professors. Be knowledgeable about your subject. Write clearly and don't use educational jargon."

GINNINDERRA PRESS

P.O. Box 3461, Port Adelaide 5015, Australia. **E-mail:** stephen@ginninderrapress.com.au. **Website:** www.ginninderrapress.com.au. **Contact:** Stephen Matthews, publisher. Estab. 1996. Ginninderra Press works "to give publishing opportunities to new writers." Has published poetry by Alan Gould and Geoff Page. Books are usually up to 72 pages, A5, laser-printed, saddle-stapled or thermal-bound, with board covers. *Publishes books by Australian authors only.* Responds to queries within 1 week; mss in 2 months.

POETRY Query first, with a few sample poems and a cover letter with brief bio and publication credits. Considers previously published poems.

GIVAL PRESS

Gival Press, LLC, P.O. Box 3812, Arlington VA 22203. (703)351-0079. **E-mail:** givalpress@yahoo.com. **Website:** www.givalpress.com. **Contact:** Robert L. Giron, editor-in-chief (area of interest: literary). Estab. 1998. Publishes trade paperback, electronic originals, and reprints. **Publishes 4-5 titles/year. 200 queries received/year. 60 mss received/year. 50% of books from first-time authors. 70% from unagented writers. Pays royalty.** Publishes ms 12 months after acceptance. Accepts simultaneous submissions. Responds in 3-5 months. Book online. Guidelines online.

NONFICTION Subjects include gay, lesbian, memoirs, multicultural, translation, womens issues, womens studies, scholarly. Submit between May 15-August 15. Always query first via e-mail; provide plan/ms content, bio, and supportive material. Reviews artwork/photos; query first.

FICTION Subjects include gay, lesbian, literary, multicultural, poetry, translation. Always query first via e-mail; provide description, author's bio, and supportive material.

POETRY Query via e-mail; provide description, bio, etc.; submit 5-6 sample poems via e-mail.

TIPS "Our audience is those who read literary works with depth to the work. Visit our website—there is much to be read/learned from the numerous pages."

GLENBRIDGE PUBLISHING, LTD.

19923 E. Long Ave., Centennial CO 80016. (800)986-4135; (720)870-8381. **Fax:** (720)230-1209. **E-mail:** glenbridge10@gmail.com. **Website:** www.glenbridgepublishing.com. Estab. 1986. Publishes hardcover originals and reprints, trade paperback originals. "Glenbridge has an eclectic approach to publishing. We look for titles that have long-term capabilities." **Publishes 6-8 titles/year. Pays 10% royalty.** Publishes ms 1 year after acceptance. Accepts simultaneous submissions. Responds in 2 months to queries. Book catalog online. Guidelines for #10 SASE.

NONFICTION Subjects include Americana, animals, business, economics, education, environment, family, finance, parenting, writing, film, theatre, communication, cooking, foods, nutrition, health, medicine, history, philosophy, politics & government, psychology, sociology. Send e-mail on website. Query with outline/synopsis, sample chapters.

THE GLENCANNON PRESS

P.O. Box 1428, El Cerrito CA 94530. (510)528-4216. **Fax:** (510)528-3194. **E-mail:** merships@yahoo.com. **Website:** www.glencannon.com. **Contact:** Bill Harris (maritime, maritime children's). Estab. 1993. Publishes hardcover and paperback originals and hardcover reprints. "We publish quality books about ships and the sea." Average print order: 1,000. Member PMA, BAIPA. Distributes titles through Baker & Taylor. Promotes titles through direct mail, magazine advertising and word of mouth. Accepts unsolicited mss. Often comments on rejected mss. **Publishes 4-5 titles/year. Pays 10-20% royalty.** Publishes ms 6-24 months after acceptance. Accepts simultaneous submissions. Responds in 1 month to queries; 2 months to mss.

IMPRINTS Smyth: perfect binding; illustrations.

FICTION Subjects include adventure, ethnic, historical, juvenile, mainstream, military, multicultural, mystery, western, young adult. Submit complete ms. Include brief bio, list of publishing credits. Send SASE for return of ms or send a disposable ms and SASE for reply only.

TIPS "Write a good story in a compelling style."

DAVID R. GODINE, PUBLISHER

15 Court Square, Suite 320, Boston MA 02108. (617)451-9600. **Fax:** (617)350-0250. **E-mail:** info@godine.com. **Website:** www.godine.com. Estab. 1970. "We publish books that matter for people who care." This publisher is no longer considering unsolicited mss of any type. Only interested in agented material.

GOLDEN BOOKS FOR YOUNG READERS GROUP

1745 Broadway, New York NY 10019. **Website:** www.randomhouse.com. Estab. 1935. "Random House Books aims to create books that nurture the hearts and minds of children, providing and promoting quality books and a rich variety of media that entertain and educate readers from 6 months to 12 years." *Random House-Golden Books does not accept unsolicited mss, only agented material.* They reserve the right not to return unsolicited material. **2% of books from first-time authors. Pays authors in royalties; sometimes buys mss outright.** Book catalog free on request.

GOLDEN WEST BOOKS

P.O. Box 80250, San Marino CA 91118. (626)458-8148. **Fax:** (626)458-8148. **Website:** www.goldenwestbooks.com. Publishes hardcover originals. "Golden West Books specializes in railroad history. We are always interested in new material. Please use the form online to contact us; we will follow up with you as soon as possible." **Publishes 3-4 titles/year. 8-10 queries received/year. 5 mss received/year. 75% of books from first-time authors. 100% from unagented writers. Pays 8-10% royalty on wholesale price.** Publishes ms 3 months after acceptance. Responds in 3 months to queries. Book catalog and ms guidelines free.

NONFICTION Subjects include Americana, history. Use online form. Reviews artwork/photos.

GOODMAN BECK PUBLISHING

E-mail: info@goodmanbeck.com. **Website:** www.goodmanbeck.com. Estab. 2007. Publishes trade paperback originals. "Our primary interest at this time is mental health, personal growth, aging well, positive psychology, accessible spirituality, and self-help. Our audience is adults trying to cope with this 'upside down world.' With our self-help books, we are trying to improve the world one book at a time." **Publishes 5-6 titles/year. 65% of books from first-time authors. 90% from unagented writers. Pays 10% royalty on retail price.** Publishes ms 6-9 months after acceptance. Accepts simultaneous submissions. "Due to high query volume, response not guaranteed.".

NONFICTION Subjects include creative nonfiction, health, medicine, philosophy, psychology, spirituality,. No religious or political works, textbooks, or how-to books at this time. Query by e-mail only. Reviews artwork/photos. Send photocopies.

POETRY "We are interested in zen-inspired haiku and non-embellished, non-rhyming, egoless poems. Read Mary Oliver." Query, submit 3 sample poems. E-mail submissions only.

TIPS "Your book should be enlightening and marketable. Be prepared to have a comprehensive marketing plan. You will be very involved."

GOOSE LANE EDITIONS

500 Beaverbrook Ct., Suite 330, Fredericton NB E3B 5X4, Canada. (506)450-4251. **Fax:** (506)459-4991. **E-mail:** submissions@gooselane.com. **Website:** www.gooselane.com. **Contact:** Angela Williams, publishing assistant. Estab. 1954. Publishes hardcover and paperback originals and occasional reprints. "Goose Lane publishes literary fiction and nonfiction from well-read and highly skilled Canadian authors." **Publishes 16-20 titles/year. 20% of books from first-time authors. 60% from unagented writers. Pays 8-10% royalty on retail price. Pays $500-3,000, negotiable advance.** Responds in 6 months to queries.

NONFICTION Subjects include art, architecture, history, language, literature, nature, environment, regional, women's issues, women's studies. Query with SASE.

FICTION Subjects include literary, novels, short story collections, contemporary. Our needs in fiction never change: Substantial, character-centered literary fiction. No children's, YA, mainstream, mass market, genre, mystery, thriller, confessional or science fiction. Query with SAE with Canadian stamps or IRCs. No U.S. stamps.

POETRY Considers mss by Canadian poets only. Submit cover letter, list of publications, synopsis, entire ms, SASE.

TIPS "Writers should send us outlines and samples of books that show a very well-read author with highly developed literary skills. Our books are almost all by Canadians living in Canada; we seldom consider submissions from outside Canada. We consider submissions from outside Canada only when the author is Canadian and the book is of extraordinary interest to Canadian readers. We do not publish books for children or for the young adult market."

GRANITE PUBLISHING, LLC

P.O. Box 1429, Columbus NC 28722. (828)894-8444. **Fax:** (828)894-8454. **E-mail:** brian@granitepublishing.us. **Website:** www.granitepublishing.us/index.html. **Contact:** Brian Crissey. Publishes trade paperback originals and reprints. "Granite Publishing strives to preserve the Earth by publishing books that develop new wisdom about our emerging planetary citizenship, bringing information from the outerworlds to our world. Currently emphasizing indigenous ideas, planetary healing. Granite Publishing accepts only a few very fine mss in our niches each year, and those that are accepted must follow our rigid guidelines online. Our Little Granite Books imprint publishes only our own writings for children." **Publishes 4 titles/year. 50 queries received/year. 150 mss received/year. 70% of books from first-time authors. 90% from unagented writers. Pays 7-10% royalty.** Publishes ms 16 months after acceptance. Accepts simultaneous submissions. Responds in 6 months to mss.

NONFICTION Subjects include New Age, planetary paradigm shift. Submit proposal. Reviews artwork/photos. Send photocopies.

Ⓐ⊘ GRAYWOLF PRESS

250 Third Ave. N., Suite 600, Minneapolis MN 55401. **E-mail:** wolves@graywolfpress.org. **Website:** www.graywolfpress.org. **Contact:** Lucia Cowles, editorial and administrative assistant. Estab. 1974. Publishes trade cloth and paperback originals. "Graywolf Press is an independent, nonprofit publisher dedicated to the creation and promotion of thoughtful and imaginative contemporary literature essential to a vital and diverse culture." **Publishes 30 titles/year. Pays royalty on retail price. Pays $1,000-25,000 advance.** Publishes book Publishes 18 months after acceptance. Responds in 3 months to queries. Book catalog free. Guidelines online.

NONFICTION Subjects include contemporary culture, language, literature, culture. Agented submissions only.

FICTION Subjects include short story collections, literary novels. "Familiarize yourself with our list first." No genre books (romance, western, science fiction, suspense) Agented submissions only.

POETRY "We are interested in linguistically challenging work." Agented submissions only.

GREAT POTENTIAL PRESS

1325 N. Wilmot Ave., #300, Tucson AZ 85712. (520)777-6161. **Fax:** (520)777-6217. **Website:** www.greatpotentialpress.com. **Contact:** Janet Gore, editor; James T. Webb, Ph.D., president. Estab. 1986. Publishes trade paperback originals. Specializes in nonfiction books that address academic, social and emotional issues of gifted and talented children and adults. **Publishes 6-10 titles/year. 75 queries received/year. 20-30 mss received/year. 50% of books from first-time authors. 100% from unagented writers. Pays 10% royalty on retail price.** Publishes ms 1 year after acceptance. Accepts simultaneous submissions. Responds in 2 months to queries; 3 months to proposals; 4 months to mss. Book catalog free or on website. Guidelines online.

NONFICTION Subjects include child guidance, education, multicultural, psychology, translation, travel, women's issues, gifted/talented children and adults, misdiagnosis of gifted, parenting gifted, teaching gifted, meeting the social and emotional needs of gifted and talented, and strategies for working with gifted children and adults. Use online submission form.

TIPS "Mss should be clear, cogent, and well-written and should pertain to gifted, talented, and creative persons and/or issues."

GREENHAVEN PRESS

27500 Drake Rd., Farmington Hills MI 48331. **Website:** www.gale.com/greenhaven. Estab. 1970. Publishes 220 young adult academic reference titles/year. 50% of books by first-time authors. Greenhaven continues to print quality nonfiction anthologies for libraries and classrooms. "Our well-known Opposing Viewpoints series is highly respected by students and librarians in need of material on controversial social issues." Greenhaven accepts no unsolicited mss. Send query, resume, and list of published works by e-mail.

Work purchased outright from authors; write-for-hire, flat fee.

NONFICTION Young adults (high school): controversial issues, social issues, history, literature, science, environment, health.

GREENWILLOW BOOKS

HarperCollins Publishers, 10 E. 53rd St., New York NY 10022. (212)207-7000. **Website:** www.greenwillowblog.com. Estab. 1974. Publishes hardcover originals, paperbacks, e-books, and reprints. *Does not accept unsolicited mss.* "Unsolicited mail will not be opened and will not be returned." **Publishes 40-50 titles/year. Pays 10% royalty on wholesale price for first-time authors. Offers variable advance.** Publishes ms 2 years after acceptance.

FICTION Subjects include fantasy, humor, literary, mystery, picture books. *Agented submissions only.*

GREENWOOD PRESS

ABC-CLIO, P.O. Box 1911, Santa Barbara CA 93116. (805)968-1911. **E-mail:** acquisitions_inquiries@abc-clio.com. **Website:** www.abc-clio.com. **Contact:** Vince Burns, vice president of editorial. Publishes hardcover originals. Greenwood Press publishes reference materials for high school, public and academic libraries in the humanities and the social and hard sciences. **Publishes 200 titles/year. 1,000 queries received/year. 25% of books from first-time authors. Pays variable royalty on net price. Pays rare advance.** Publishes ms 1 year after acceptance. Accepts simultaneous submissions. Responds in 6 months to queries. Book catalog and ms guidelines online.

NONFICTION Subjects include humanities, literary criticism, social sciences, humanities and the social and hard sciences. Query with proposal package, including scope, organization, length of project, whether complete ms is available or when it will be, CV or resume and SASE. *No unsolicited mss.*

GREY GECKO PRESS

565 S. Mason Rd., Suite 154, Katy TX 77450. Phone/**Fax:** (866)535-6078. **E-mail:** info@greygeckopress.com. **E-mail:** submissions@greygeckopress.com. **Website:** www.greygeckopress.com. **Contact:** Submissions Coordinator. Estab. 2011. Publishes hardcover, trade paperback, and electronic originals. **Publishes 5-10 titles/year. 200+ queries received/year; 30-40 mss received/year. 100% from unagented writers. Pays 50-75% royalties on net revenue.** Publishes ms 6-12 months after acceptance. Accepts simultaneous submissions. Responds in 3-6 months. Guidelines online.

NONFICTION Subjects include architecture, art, contemporary culture, cooking, creative nonfiction, environment, foods, history, marine subjects, military, nature, photography, travel, war. "All nonfiction submissions are evaluated on a case by case basis. We focus mainly on fiction, but we'll take a look at nonfiction works." Use online submission page. Reviews artwork. Send photocopies or link to photo website.

FICTION Subjects include adventure, contemporary, ethnic, fantasy, feminist, gay, historical, horror, humor, juvenile, lesbian, literary, mainstream, military, multicultural, mystery, occult, regional, romance, science fiction, short story collections, sports, suspense, war, western, young adult. "We do not publish extreme horror, erotica, or religious fiction. New and interesting stories by unpublished authors will always get our attention. Innovation is a core value of our company." Use online submission page.

TIPS "Be willing to be a part of the Grey Gecko family. Publishing with us is a partnership, not indentured servitude. Authors are expected and encouraged to be proactive and contribute to their book's success."

GROSSET & DUNLAP PUBLISHERS

Penguin Putnam Inc., 345 Hudson St., New York NY 10014. **Website:** www.penguin.com. **Contact:** Francesco Sedita, vice president/publisher. Estab. 1898. Publishes hardcover (few) and mass market paperback originals. Grosset & Dunlap publishes children's books that show children that reading is fun, with books that speak to their interests, and that are affordable so that children can build a home library of their own. Focus on licensed properties, series and readers. "Grosset & Dunlap publishes high-interest, affordable books for children ages 0-10 years. We focus on original series, licensed properties, readers and novelty books." **Publishes 140 titles/year. Pays royalty. Pays advance.**

NONFICTION Subjects include nature, environment, science. *Agented submissions only.*

FICTION Subjects include juvenile. *Agented submissions only.*

GROUNDWOOD BOOKS

110 Spadina Ave., Suite 801, Toronto Ontario M5V 2K4, Canada. (416)363-4343. **Fax:** (416)363-1017. **E-mail:** ssutherland@groundwoodbooks.com. **Website:** www.groundwoodbooks.com. Publishes 19 picture

books/year; 2 young readers/year; 3 middle readers/year; 3 young adult titles/year, approximately 2 nonfiction titles/year. **Offers advances.** Accepts simultaneous submissions. Responds to mss in 6-8 months. Visit website for guidelines: www.houseofanansi.com/Groundwoodsubmissions.aspx.

NONFICTION Recently published: *The Amazing Travels of IBN Batutta*, by Fatima Sharafeddine, Illustrated by Intelaq Mohammed Ali. Picture books recently published: *Mr. Frank*, by Irene Luxbacher; *The Tweedles Go Electric*, by Monica Kulling, illustrated by Marie LaFrance; *Morris Micklewhite and the Tangerine Dress*, by Christine Baldacchino, illustrated by Isabelle Malenfant; *Why Are You Doing That?*, by Elisa Amado, illustrated by Manuel Monroy; *Don't*, by Litsa Trochatos, illustrated by Virginia Johnson.

FICTION Recently published: *Lost Girl Found*, by Leah Bassoff and Laura Deluca; *A Simple Case of Angels*, by Carolnie Adderson; *This One Summer*, by Mariko Tamaki and Jillian Tamaki. Submit synopsis and sample chapters via e-mail.

GROUP PUBLISHING, INC.

1515 Cascade Ave., Loveland CO 80539. **Website:** www.group.com. Estab. 1974. Publishes trade paperback originals. "Our mission is to equip churches to help children, youth, and adults grow in their relationship with Jesus." **Publishes 65 titles/year. 500 queries received/year. 500 mss received/year. 40% of books from first-time authors. 95% from unagented writers. Pays up to 10% royalty on wholesale price or makes outright purchase or work for hire. Pays up to $1,000 advance.** Publishes ms 18 months after acceptance. Accepts simultaneous submissions. Responds in 1 month to queries; 6 months to proposals and mss. Book catalog for 9x12 envelope and 2 first-class stamps.

NONFICTION Subjects include education, religion. "We're an interdenominational publisher of resource materials for people who work with adults, youth or children in a Christian church setting. We also publish materials for use directly by youth or children (such as devotional books, workbooks or Bibles stories). Everything we do is based on concepts of active and interactive learning as described in *Why Nobody Learns Much of Anything at Church: And How to Fix It*, by Thom and Joani Schultz. We need new, practical, hands-on, innovative, out-of-the-box ideas—things that no one's doing... yet." Query with SASE. Submit proposal package, outline, 3 sample chapters, cover letter, introduction to book, and sample activities if appropriate.

TIPS "Our audience consists of pastors, Christian education directors, youth leaders, and Sunday school teachers."

Ⓐ⊘ GROVE/ATLANTIC, INC.

841 Broadway, 4th Floor, New York NY 10003. (212)614-7850. **Fax:** (212)614-7886. **E-mail:** info@groveatlantic.com. **Website:** www.groveatlantic.com. Estab. 1917. Publishes hardcover and trade paperback originals, and reprints. "Due to limited resources of time and staffing, Grove/Atlantic cannot accept manuscripts that do not come through a literary agent. In today's publishing world, agents are more important than ever, helping writers shape their work and navigate the main publishing houses to find the most appropriate outlet for a project." **Publishes 100 titles/year. 1,000+ queries received/year. 1,000+ mss received/year. 10% of books from first-time authors. Pays 7 ½-12 ½% royalty. Makes outright purchase of $5-500,000.** Publishes book Book published 9 months after acceptance. Accepts simultaneous submissions. Responds in 1 month to queries; 2 months to proposals; 4 months to mss. Book catalog available online.

IMPRINTS Black Cat, Atlantic Monthly Press, Grove Press.

NONFICTION Subjects include art, architecture, business, economics, creative nonfiction, education, government, politics, language, literature, memoirs, military, war, philosophy, psychology, science, social sciences, sports, translation. Agented submissions only.

FICTION Subjects include erotica, horror, literary, science fiction, short story collections, suspense, western. Agented submissions only.

POETRY Agented submissions only.

GRYPHON HOUSE, INC.

P.O. Box 10, 6848 Leon's Way, Lewisville NC 27023. **Website:** www.gryphonhouse.com. **Contact:** Kathy Charner, editor-in-chief. Estab. 1981. Publishes trade paperback originals. "Gryphon House publishes books that teachers and parents of young children (birth-age 8) consider essential to their daily lives." Publishes parent and teacher resource books, textbooks. Recently published *Reading Games*, by Jackie Silberg; *Primary Art*, by MaryAnn F. Kohl; *Teaching*

Young Children with Autism Spectrum Disorder, by Clarissa Willis; *The Complete Resource Book for Infants*, by Pam Schiller. "At Gryphon House, our goal is to publish books that help teachers and parents enrich the lives of children from birth through age 8. We strive to make our books useful for teachers at all levels of experience, as well as for parents, caregivers, and anyone interested in working with children." Query. Submit outline/synopsis and 2 sample chapters. Responds to queries/mss in 6 months. Publishes a book 18 months after acceptance. Will consider simultaneous submissions, e-mail submissions. Book catalog and ms guidelines available via website or with SASE. "We are looking for books of creative, participatory learning experiences that have a common conceptual theme to tie them together. The books should be on subjects that parents or teachers want to do on a daily basis." **Publishes 12-15 titles/year. Pays royalty on wholesale price.** Responds in 3-6 months to queries. Guidelines available online.

NONFICTION Subjects include child guidance, education, early childhood. Currently emphasizing social-emotional intelligence and classroom management; de-emphasizing literacy after-school activities. "We prefer to receive a letter of inquiry and/or a proposal, rather than the entire manuscript. Please include: the proposed title, the purpose of the book, table of contents, introductory material, 20-40 sample pages of the actual book. In addition, please describe the book, including the intended audience, why teachers will want to buy it, how it is different from other similar books already published, and what qualifications you possess that make you the appropriate person to write the book. If you have a writing sample that demonstrates that you write clear, compelling prose, please include it with your letter."

GUERNICA EDITIONS

1569 Heritage Way, Oakville Ontario L6M 2Z7, Canada. (905)599-5304. **Fax:** (416)981-7606. **E-mail:** michaelmirolla@guernicaeditions.com. **Website:** www.guernicaeditions.com. **Contact:** Michael Mirolla, editor/publisher (poetry, nonfiction, short stories, novels). Estab. 1978. Publishes trade paperback originals and reprints. Guernica Editions is a literary press that produces works of poetry, fiction and nonfiction often by writers who are ignored by the mainstream. **Publishes 25-30 titles/year. Several hundred mss received/year. 20% of books from first-time authors. 99% from unagented writers. Pays 8-10% royalty on retail price, or makes outright purchase of $200-5,000. Pays $450-750 advance.** Publishes book Publishes 24-36 months after acceptance. Responds in 1 month to queries. Responds in 6 months to proposals. Responds in 1 year to manuscripts. Book catalog available online.

NONFICTION Subjects include art, architecture, creative nonfiction, ethnic, film, cinema, stage, gay, lesbian, government, politics, history, language, literature, lit-crit, memoirs, multicultural, music, dance, philosophy, psychology, regional, religion, sex, translation, women's issues. Query by e-mail only. Reviews artwork/photos. Send photocopies.

FICTION Subjects include feminist, gay, lesbian, literary, multicultural, plays, poetry, poetry in translation, translation. "We wish to open up into the fiction world and focus less on poetry. We specialize in European, especially Italian, translations." E-mail queries only.

POETRY Feminist, gay/lesbian, literary, multicultural, poetry in translation. We wish to have writers in translation. Any writer who has translated Italian poetry is welcomed. Full books only. No single poems by different authors, unless modern, and used as an anthology. First books will have no place in the next couple of years. Query.

GULF PUBLISHING COMPANY

2 Greenway Plaza, Suite 1020, Houston TX 77046. (713)529-4301. **Fax:** (713)520-4433. **E-mail:** svb@gulfpub.com. **Website:** www.gulfpub.com. **Contact:** Katie Hammon. Estab. 1916. Publishes hardcover originals and reprints; electronic originals and reprints. "Gulf Publishing Company is the leading publisher to the oil and gas industry. Our specialized publications reach over 100,000 people involved in energy industries worldwide. Our magazines and catalogs help readers keep current with information important to their field and allow advertisers to reach their customers in all segments of petroleum operations. More than half our editorial staff have engineering degrees. The others are thoroughly trained and experienced business journalists and editors." **Publishes 12-15 titles/year. 3-5 queries and mss received in a year. 30% of books from first-time authors. 80% from unagented writers. Royalties on retail price. Pays $1,000-$1,500 advance.** Publishes ms 8-9 months after acceptance. Accepts simultane-

ous submissions. Responds in 2 months to queries; 1 month to proposals and mss. Catalog free on request. Guidelines available by e-mail.

NONFICTION , Engineering. "We don't publish a lot in the year, therefore we are able to focus more on marketing and sales—we are hoping to grow in the future." Submit outline, 1-2 sample chapters, completed ms. Reviews artwork. Send high res file formats with high dpi in b&w.

TIPS "Our audience would be engineers, engineering students, academia, professors, well managers, construction engineers. We recommend getting contributors to help with the writing process—this provides a more comprehensive overview for technical and scientific books. Work harder on artwork. It's expensive and time-consuming for a publisher to redraw a lot of the figures."

Ⓐ GUN DIGEST BOOKS

F+W Media, 700 E. State St., Iola WI 54990. (888)457-2873. **E-mail:** kevin.michalowski@fwmedia.com. **Website:** www.gundigest.com; www.krause.com. **Contact:** Kevin Michalowski, senior editor (all aspects of firearms history, scholarship, nonpolitical literature). Estab. 1944. Hardcover, trade paperback, mass market paperback, and electronic originals (all). **Publishes 25 titles/year. 75 submissions received/year. 30% of books from first-time authors. 80% from unagented writers. 10 min. to 20% max. (rare) royalty on wholesale price. Pays advance between $2,800 and $5,000.** Publishes ms 7 months after acceptance. Accepts simultaneous submissions. Responds immediately to queries; 2 months to proposals/ms. Catalog online at www.krause.com. Guidelines available by e-mail at corrina.peterson@fwmedia.com.

IMPRINTS Gun Digest Books, Krause Publications.

NONFICTION , Firearms, hunting-related titles only. "Must have mainstream appeal and not be too narrowly focused." Submit proposal package, including outline, 2 sample chapters, and author bio; submit completed ms. Review artwork/photos (required); high-res digital only (.jpg, .tif).

TIPS "Our audience is shooters, collectors, hunters, outdoors enthusiasts. We prefer not to work through agents."

HACHAI PUBLISHING

527 Empire Blvd., Brooklyn NY 11225. (718)633-0100. **Fax:** (718)633-0103. **Website:** www.hachai.com. **Contact:** Devorah Leah Rosenfeld, editor. Estab. 1988. Publishes hardcover originals. Hachai is dedicated to producing high quality Jewish children's literature, ages 2-10. Story should promote universal values such as sharing, kindness, etc. **Publishes 4 titles/year. 75% of books from first-time authors. Work purchased outright from authors for $800-1,000.** Accepts simultaneous submissions. Responds in 2 months to mss. Book catalog available free. Guidelines online.

NONFICTION Subjects include ethnic, religion. Submit complete ms. Reviews artwork/photos. Send photocopies.

FICTION Picture books and young readers: contemporary, historical fiction, religion. Middle readers: adventure, contemporary, problem novels, religion. Does not want to see fantasy, animal stories, romance, problem novels depicting drug use or violence. Submit complete ms.

TIPS "We are looking for books that convey the traditional Jewish experience in modern times or long ago; traditional Jewish observance such as Sabbath and holidays and mitzvos such as mezuzah, blessings etc.; positive character traits (middos) such as honesty, charity, respect, sharing, etc. We are also interested in historical fiction for young readers (7-10) written with a traditional Jewish perspective and highlighting the relevance of Torah in making important choices. Please, no animal stories, romance, violence, preachy sermonizing. Write a story that incorporates a moral, not a preachy morality tale. Originality is the key. We feel Hachai publications will appeal to a wider readership as parents become more interested in positive values for their children."

HADLEY RILLE BOOKS

PO Box 25466, Overland Park KS 66225. **E-mail:** subs@hadleyrillebooks.com. **Website:** www.hrbpress.com. **Contact:** Eric T. Reynolds, editor/publisher. Estab. 2005.

Currently closed to submissions. Check website for future reading periods.

FICTION Subjects include fantasy, science fiction, short story collections.

TIPS "We aim to produce books that are aligned with current interest in the genres. Anthology markets are somewhat rare in SF these days, we feel there aren't enough good anthologies being published each year and part of our goal is to present the best that we can. We like stories that fit well within the guidelines of the particular anthology for which we are soliciting manuscripts. Aside from that, we want stories with strong characters (not necessarily characters with strong personalities, flawed characters are welcome). We want a sense of wonder and awe. We want to feel the world around the character and so scene description is important (however, this doesn't always require a lot of text, just set the scene well so we don't wonder where the character is). We strongly recommend workshopping the story or having it critiqued in some way by readers familiar with the genre. We prefer clichés be kept to a bare minimum in the prose and avoid re-working old story lines."

HAMPTON ROADS PUBLISHING CO., INC.

665 Third St., Suite 400, San Francisco CA 94107. **E-mail:** submissions@rwwbooks.com. **Website:** www.redwheelweiser.com. **Contact:** Ms. Pat Bryce, Acquisitions Editor. Estab. 1989. Publishes and distributes hardcover and trade paperback originals on subjects including metaphysics, health, complementary medicine, visionary fiction, and other related topics. "Our reason for being is to impact, uplift, and contribute to positive change in the world. We publish books that will enrich and empower the evolving consciousness of mankind. Though we are not necessarily limited in scope, we are most interested in manuscripts on the following subjects: Body/Mind/Spirit, Health and Healing, Self-Help. Please be advised that at the moment we are not accepting: Fiction or Novelized material that does not pertain to body/mind/spirit, Channeled writing." **Publishes 35-40 titles/year. 1,000 queries received/year. 1,500 mss received/year. 50% of books from first-time authors. 70% from unagented writers. Pays royalty. Pays $1,000-50,000 advance.** Publishes ms 1 year after acceptance. Accepts simultaneous submissions. Responds in 2-4 months to queries; 1 month to proposals; 6-12 months to mss. Guidelines online.

NONFICTION Subjects include New Age, spirituality. Query with SASE. Submit synopsis, SASE. No longer accepting electronic submissions. Reviews artwork/photos. Send photocopies.

FICTION Subjects include literary, spiritual, visionary fiction, past-life fiction based on actual memories. Fiction should have 1 or more of the following themes: spiritual, inspirational, metaphysical, i.e., past-life recall, out-of-body experiences, near-death experience, paranormal. Query with SASE. Submit outline, 2 sample chapters, clips. Submit complete ms.

HANCOCK HOUSE PUBLISHERS

U.S. Office, 1431 Harrison Ave., Blaine WA 98230. (604)538-1114. **Fax:** (604)538-2262. **E-mail:** submissions@hancockhouse.com. **Website:** www.hancockhouse.com. Estab. 1971. Publishes hardcover, trade paperback, and e-book originals and reprints. "Hancock House Publishers is the largest North American publisher of wildlife and Native Indian titles. We also cover Pacific Northwest, fishing, history, Canadiana, biographies. We are seeking agriculture, natural history, and popular science titles with a regional (Pacific Northwest), national, or international focus. Currently emphasizing nonfiction wildlife, cryptozoology, guide books, native history, biography, fishing." **Publishes 12-20 titles/year. 50% of books from first-time authors. 90% from unagented writers. Pays 10% royalty.** Publishes ms 1 year after acceptance. Accepts simultaneous submissions. Responds to proposals in 3-6 months. Book catalog available free. Guidelines online.

NONFICTION Subjects include agriculture, animals, ethnic, history, horticulture, nature, environment, regional. Centered around Pacific Northwest, local history, nature guide books, international ornithology, and Native Americans. Query via e-mail, including outline with word count, a short author bio, table of contents, 3 sample chapters. Accepts double-spaced word .docs or PDFs. Reviews artwork/photos. Send photocopies.

HANSER PUBLICATIONS

6915 Valley Ave., Cincinnati OH 45244. (513)527-8800; (800)950-8977. **Fax:** (513)527-8801. **E-mail:** info@hanserpublications.com. **Website:** www.hanserpublications.com. **Contact:** Development Editor. Estab. 1993. Publishes hardcover and paperback originals, and digital educational and training programs. "Hanser Publications publishes books and electronic media for the manufacturing (both metalworking and plastics) industries. Publications range from basic training materials to advanced reference books." **Publishes 10-15 titles/year. 100 queries received/year. 10-20 mss received/year. 50% of books from first-time authors. 100% from unagented writers.** Publishes ms 10 months after acceptance. Accepts simultaneous submissions. Responds in 2 weeks to queries; 1 month to proposals/mss. Book catalog available free. Guidelines available online.

NONFICTION "We publish how-to texts, references, technical books, and computer-based learning materials for the manufacturing industries. Titles include award-winning management books, encyclopedic references, and leading references." Submit outline, sample chapters, resume, preface, and comparison to competing or similar titles.

TIPS "E-mail submissions speed up response time."

HARCOURT, INC., TRADE DIVISION

Imprint of Houghton Mifflin Harcourt Book Group, 215 Park Ave. S., New York NY 10003. **Website:** www.harcourtbooks.com. Publishes hardcover and trade paperback originals and trade paperback reprints. **Publishes 120 titles/year. 5% of books from first-time authors. 5% from unagented writers. Pays 6-15% royalty on retail price. Pays $2,000 minimum advance.** Accepts simultaneous submissions. Book catalog for 9×12 envelope and first-class stamps. Guidelines available online.

NONFICTION *No unsolicited mss.* Agented submissions only.

FICTION Agented submissions only.

HARKEN MEDIA

4308 201st Ave. NE, Sammamish WA 98074-6120. **E-mail:** info@harkenmedia.com. **E-mail:** manuscripts@harkenmedia.com. **Website:** www.harkenmedia.com. **Contact:** Robert Sappington, editor-in-chief; Sheila Sappington, editor. Publishes hardcover originals, trade paperback originals, and electronic originals. Harken Media publishes original, unpublished novels possessing unique insights on compelling themes for young adult, new adult, or adult audiences. Compelling themes explore our humanity and in the process expand awareness and understand. **Publishes 1-5 titles/year. Receives 1,000 queries and 50 mss from writers/year. 100% of books from first-time authors. 100% from unagented writers. Authors are paid 15-50% royalty on net wholesale price.** Publishes book Publishes in 6-12 months after acceptance. Accepts simultaneous submissions. Responds in 1 month to queries and proposals, 1-3 months to mss. Catalog available online at www.harkenmedia.com/p/catalog.html. Guidelines available online at www.harkenmedia.com/p/submmissions.html.

FICTION Subjects include adventure, fantasy, gay, gothic, historical, humor, lesbian, literary, mainstream, multicultural, multimedia, mystery, science fiction, suspense, young adult. "Our notion of entertainment encompasses a broad range of emotional responses from readers. We're as likely to publish a story that makes us cry as laugh. Manipulate our emotions; we like that. A novel's emotional impact is as important as its message. Thus, a successful story for Harken Media both entertains and enlightens." Submit a proposal package including a synopsis and a detailed description fo theme(s) and unique insight(s).

HARLEQUIN AMERICAN ROMANCE

225 Duncan Mill Rd., Don Mills ON M3B 3K9, Canada. **Website:** www.harlequin.com. **Contact:** Kathleen Scheibling, senior editor. "Upbeat and lively, fast paced and well plotted, American Romance celebrates the pursuit of love in the backyards, big cities and wide-open spaces of America." Publishes paperback originals and reprints. Books: newspaper print paper; web printing; perfect bound. Length: 55,000 words. "American Romance features heartwarming romances with strong family elements. These are stories about the pursuit of love, marriage and family in America today." **Pays royalty. Offers advance.** Guidelines online.

FICTION Subjects include romance. Needs "all-American stories with a range of emotional and sensual content that are supported by a sense of community within the plot's framework. In the confident and caring heroine, the tough but tender hero, and their dynamic relationship that is at the center of this series, real-life love is showcased as the best fantasy of all!" Submit online.

HARLEQUIN BLAZE

225 Duncan Mill Rd., Don Mills ON M3B 3K9, Canada. (416)445-5860. **Website:** www.harlequin.com. Publishes paperback originals. "Harlequin Blaze is a red-hot series. It is a vehicle to build and promote new authors who have a strong sexual edge to their stories. It is also the place to be for seasoned authors who want to create a sexy, sizzling, longer contemporary story." Guidelines online.

FICTION Subjects include romance. "Sensuous, highly romantic, innovative plots that are sexy in premise and execution. The tone of the books can run from fun and flirtatious to dark and sensual. Submissions should have a very contemporary feel—what it's like to be young and single today. We are looking for heroes and heroines in their early 20s and up. There should be a a strong emphasis on the physical relationship between the couples. Fully described love scenes along with a high level of fantasy and playfulness." Length: 55,000-60,000 words.

TIPS "Are you a *Cosmo* girl at heart? A fan of *Sex and the City*? Or maybe you have a sexually adventurous spirit. If so, then Blaze is the series for you!"

HARLEQUIN DESIRE

233 Broadway, Suite 1001, New York NY 10279. (212)553-4200. **Website:** www.harlequin.com. **Contact:** Stacy Boyd, senior editor. Publishes paperback originals and reprints. Always powerful, passionate, and provocative. "Desire novels are sensual reads and a love scene or scenes are still needed. But there is no set number of pages that needs to be fulfilled. Rather, the level of sensuality must be appropriate to the storyline. Above all, every Silhouette Desire novel must fulfill the promise of a powerful, passionate and provocative read." **Pays royalty. Offers advance.** Guidelines online.

FICTION Subjects include romance. Looking for novels in which "the conflict is an emotional one, springing naturally from the unique characters you've chosen. The focus is on the developing relationship, set in a believable plot. Sensuality is key, but lovemaking is never taken lightly. Secondary characters and subplots need to blend with the core story. Innovative new directions in storytelling and fresh approaches to classic romantic plots are welcome." Manuscripts must be 50,000-55,000 words.

HARLEQUIN HQN

Imprint of Harlequin, 225 Duncan Mill Rd., Don Mills ON M3B 3K9, Canada. **Website:** harlequin.com. Publishes hardcover, trade paperback, and mass market paperback originals. "HQN publishes romance in all subgenres—historical, contemporary, romantic suspense, paranormal—as long as the story's central focus is romance. Prospective authors can familiarize themselves with the wide range of books we publish by reading work by some of our current authors. The imprint is looking for a wide range of authors from known romance stars to first-time authors. At the moment, we are accepting only agented submissions—unagented authors may send a query letter to determine if their project suits our needs. Please send your projects to our New York Editorial Office." **Pays royalty. Pays advance.**

FICTION Subjects include romance, contemporary and historical. Accepts unagented material. Length: 90,000 words.

HARLEQUIN INTRIGUE

225 Duncan Mill Rd., Don Mills ON M3B 3K9, Canada. **Website:** www.eharlequin.com. Wants crime stories tailored to the series romance market packed with a variety of thrilling suspense and whodunit mystery. Word count: 55,000-60,000. Guidelines online.

FICTION Subjects include mystery, romance, suspense. Submit online.

HARLEQUIN SUPERROMANCE

225 Duncan Mill Rd., Don Mills ON M3B 3K9, Canada. **Website:** www.harlequin.com. **Contact:** Victoria Curran, senior editor. Publishes paperback originals. "The Harlequin Superromance line focuses on believable characters triumphing over true-to-life drama and conflict. At the heart of these contemporary stories should be a compelling romance that brings the reader along with the hero and heroine on their journey of overcoming the obstacles in their way and falling in love. Because of the longer length relevant subplots and secondary characters are welcome but not required. This series publishes a variety of story types—family sagas, romantic suspense, Westerns, to name a few—and tones from light to dramatic, emotional to suspenseful. Settings also vary from vibrant urban neighborhoods to charming small towns. The unifying element of Harlequin Superromance stories is the realistic treatment of character and plot. The characters should seem familiar to readers—similar to people they know in their own lives—and the circumstances within the realm of possibility. The stories should be layered and complex in that the conflicts should not be easily resolved. The best way to get an idea of we're looking for is to read what we're currently publishing. The aim of Superromance novels is to produce a contemporary, involving read with a mainstream tone in its situations and characters, using romance as the major theme. To achieve this, emphasis should be placed on individual writing styles and unique and topical ideas." **Pays royalties. Pays advance.** Guidelines online.

FICTION Subjects include romance. "The criteria for Superromance books are flexible. Aside from length (80,000 words), the determining factor for publication will always be quality. Authors should strive to break free of stereotypes, clichés and worn-out plot devices to create strong, believable stories with depth and emotional intensity. Superromance novels are intended to appeal to a wide range of romance readers." Submit online.

TIPS "A general familiarity with current Superromance books is advisable to keep abreast of ever-changing trends and overall scope, but we don't want imitations. We look for sincere, heartfelt writing based on true-to-life experiences the reader can identify with. We are interested in innovation."

HARLEQUIN TEEN

Harlequin, 233 Broadway, Suite 1001, New York NY 10279. **Website:** www.harlequin.com. **Contact:** Natashya Wilson, executive editor. Harlequin Teen is a single-title program dedicated to building authors and publishing unique, memorable young-adult fiction. Accepts simultaneous submissions.

FICTION Harlequin Teen looks for fresh, authentic fiction featuring extraordinary characters and extraordinary stories set in contemporary, paranormal, fantasy, science-fiction, and historical worlds. Wants commercial, high-concept stories that capture the teen experience and will speak to readers with power and authenticity. All subgenres are welcome, so long as the book delivers a relevant reading experience that will resonate long after the book's covers are closed. Expects that most stories will include a compelling romantic element. *Agented submissions only.*

HARPERBUSINESS

Imprint of HarperCollins General Books Group, 195 Broadway, New York NY 10007. (212)207-7000. **Website:** www.harpercollins.com. Estab. 1991. Publishes hardcover, trade paperback originals and reprints. HarperBusiness publishes the inside story on ideas that will shape business practices with cutting-edge information and visionary concepts. **Pays royalty on retail price. Pays advance.** Accepts simultaneous submissions.

NONFICTION Subjects include business, economics, marketing subjects. "We don't publish how-to, textbooks or things for academic market; no reference (tax or mortgage guides), our reference department does that. Proposals need to be top notch. We tend not to publish people who have no business standing. Must have business credentials." Agented submissions only.

HARPERCOLLINS

195 Broadway, New York NY 10007. (212)207-7000. **Website:** www.harpercollins.com. Publishes hardcover and paperback originals and paperback reprints. HarperCollins, one of the largest English language publishers in the world, is a broad-based publisher with strengths in academic, business and professional, children's, educational, general interest, and religious and spiritual books, as well as multimedia titles. **Pays royalty. Pays negotiable advance.**

NONFICTION Agented submissions only. Unsolicited mss returned unopened.

FICTION Subjects include adventure, fantasy, gothic, historical, literary, mystery, science fiction, suspense, western. "We look for a strong story line and exceptional literary talent." Agented submissions only. *All unsolicited mss returned.*

TIPS "We do not accept any unsolicited material."

HARPERCOLLINS CANADA, LTD.

2 Bloor St. E., 20th Floor, Toronto ON M4W 1A8, Canada. (416)975-9334. **Fax:** (416)975-5223. **Website:** www.harpercollins.ca. Estab. 1989. *HarperCollins Canada is not accepting unsolicited material at this time.*

HARPERCOLLINS CHILDREN'S BOOKS/ HARPERCOLLINS PUBLISHERS

195 Broadway, New York NY 10007. (212)207-7000. **Website:** www.harpercollins.com. **Contact:** Katherine Tegen, vice president and publisher; Anica Mrose Rissi, executive editor; Claudia Gabel, executive editor; Kathleen Duncan, general design assistant; Erica Dechavez, picture book assistant designer. Publishes hardcover and paperback originals and paperback reprints. HarperCollins, one of the largest English language publishers in the world, is a broad-based publisher with strengths in academic, business and professional, children's, educational, general interest, and religious and spiritual books, as well as multimedia titles. **Publishes 500 titles/year. Negotiates payment upon acceptance.** Accepts simultaneous submissions. Responds in 1 month, will contact only if interested. Does not accept any unsolicted texts. Catalog online.

IMPRINTS **HarperCollins Australia/New Zealand:** Angus & Robertson, Fourth Estate, HarperBusiness, HarperCollins, HarperPerenniel, HarperReligious, HarperSports, Voyager; **HarperCollins Canada:** HarperFlamingoCanada, PerennialCanada; **HarperCollins Children's Books Group:** Amistad, Julie

Andrews Collection, Avon, Joanna Cotler Books, Eos, Laura Geringer Books, Greenwillow Books, HarperAudio, HarperCollins Children's Books, HarperFestival, HarperTempest, HarperTrophy, Rayo, Katherine Tegen Books; **HarperCollins General Books Group:** Access, Amistad, Avon, Caedmon, Ecco, Eos, Fourth Estate, HarperAudio, HarperBusiness, HarperCollins, HarperEntertainment, HarperLargePrint, HarperResource, HarperSanFrancisco, HarperTorch, Harper Design International, Perennial, PerfectBound, Quill, Rayo, ReganBooks, William Morrow, William Morrow Cookbooks; **HarperCollins UK:** Collins Bartholomew, Collins, HarperCollins Crime & Thrillers, Collins Freedom to Teach, HarperCollins Children's Books, Thorsons/Element, Voyager Books; **Zondervan:** Inspirio, Vida, Zonderkidz, Zondervan.

NONFICTION *No unsolicited mss or queries.* Agented submissions only. Unsolicited mss returned unopened.

FICTION Subjects include picture books, young adult, chapter books, middle grade, early readers. "We look for a strong story line and exceptional literary talent." Agented submissions only. *All unsolicited mss returned.*

TIPS "We do not accept any unsolicited material."

Ⓐ HARPERTEEN

195 Broadway, New York NY 10007. (212)207-7000. **Website:** www.harpercollins.com. HarperTeen is a teen imprint that publishes hardcovers, paperback reprints and paperback originals. **Publishes 100 titles/year.**

Ⓐ⊘ HARPER VOYAGER

Imprint of HarperCollins General Books Group, 195 Broadway, New York NY 10007. (212)207-7000. **Website:** www.eosbooks.com. Estab. 1998. Publishes hardcover originals, trade and mass market paperback originals, and reprints. Eos publishes quality science fiction/fantasy with broad appeal. **Pays royalty on retail price. Pays variable advance.** Guidelines online.

FICTION Subjects include fantasy, science fiction. No horror or juvenile. Agented submissions only. *All unsolicited mss returned.*

HARTMAN PUBLISHING, INC.

1313 Iron Ave. SW, Albuquerque NM 87102. **E-mail:** info@hartmanonline.com. **Website:** www.hartmanonline.com. **Contact:** Managing Editor. Publishes trade paperback originals. "We publish educational books for employees of nursing homes, home health agencies, hospitals, and providers of eldercare." **Publishes 5-10 titles/year. 50 queries received/year. 25 mss received/year. 50% of books from first-time authors. 100% from unagented writers. Pays 6-12% royalty on wholesale or retail price, or makes outright purchase of $200-600.** Publishes ms 4-12 months after acceptance. Accepts simultaneous submissions. Responds in 2 months to proposals; 3 months to mss. Book catalog available free. Guidelines online.

IMPRINTS Care Spring.

NONFICTION Subjects include health, medicine. "Writers should request our books-wanted list, as well as view samples of our published material." Submit via online form.

THE HARVARD COMMON PRESS

535 Albany St., 5th Floor, Boston MA 02118. (617)423-5803. **Fax:** (617)695-9794. **E-mail:** info@harvardcommonpress.com. **E-mail:** editorial@harvardcommonpress.com. **Website:** www.harvardcommonpress.com. **Contact:** Submissions. Estab. 1976. Publishes hardcover and trade paperback originals and reprints. "We want strong, practical books that help people gain control over a particular area of their lives. Currently emphasizing cooking, child care/parenting, health. De-emphasizing general instructional books, travel." **Publishes 16 titles/year. 20% of books from first-time authors. 40% from unagented writers. Pays royalty. Pays average $2,500-10,000 advance.** Publishes ms 1 year after acceptance. Accepts simultaneous submissions. Responds in 2 months to queries. Guidelines online.

NONFICTION Subjects include child guidance, cooking, foods, nutrition, health, medicine. "A large percentage of our list is made up of books about cooking, child care, and parenting; in these areas we are looking for authors who are knowledgeable, if not experts, and who can offer a different approach to the subject. We are open to good nonfiction proposals that show evidence of strong organization and writing, and clearly demonstrate a need in the marketplace. First-time authors are welcome." Submit outline. Potential authors may also submit a query letter or e-mail of no more than 300 words, rather than a full proposal; if interested, will ask to see a proposal. Queries and questions may be sent via e-mail. "We will not consider e-mail attachments containing proposals. No phone calls, please."

TIPS "We are demanding about the quality of proposals; in addition to strong writing skills and thorough knowledge of the subject matter, we require a detailed analysis of the competition."

HARVEST HOUSE PUBLISHERS

990 Owen Loop N., Eugene OR 97402. (541)343-0123. **Fax:** (541)302-0731. **Website:** www.harvesthousepublishers.com. Estab. 1974. Publishes hardcover, trade paperback, and mass market paperback originals and reprints. **Publishes 160 titles/year. 1,500 queries received/year. 1,000 mss received/year. 1% of books from first-time authors. Pays royalty.**

NONFICTION Subjects include anthropology, archeology, business, economics, child guidance, health, medicine, money, finance, religion, women's issues, women's studies, Bible studies. *No unsolicited mss.*

FICTION *No unsolicited mss, proposals, or artwork.* Agented submissions only.

TIPS "For first time/nonpublished authors we suggest building their literary résumé by submitting to magazines, or perhaps accruing book contributions."

HAY HOUSE, INC.

P.O. Box 5100, Carlsbad CA 92018. (760)431-7695. **Fax:** (760)431-6948. **E-mail:** editorial@hayhouse.com. **Website:** www.hayhouse.com. Estab. 1985. Publishes hardcover, trade paperback and e-book/POD originals. "We publish books, audios, and videos that help heal the planet." **Publishes 50 titles/year. Pays standard royalty.** Accepts simultaneous submissions. Guidelines online.

IMPRINTS Hay House Lifestyles; Hay House Insights; Hay House Visions; New Beginnings Press; SmileyBooks.

NONFICTION Subjects include cooking, foods, nutrition, education, health, medicine, money, finance, nature, environment, New Age, philosophy, psychology, sociology, women's issues, women's studies, mind/body/spirit. "Hay House is interested in a variety of subjects as long as they have a positive self-help slant to them. No poetry, children's books, or negative concepts that are not conducive to helping/healing ourselves or our planet." Accepts e-mail submissions from agents.

TIPS "Our audience is concerned with our planet, the healing properties of love, and general self-help principles. If I were a writer trying to market a book today, I would research the market thoroughly to make sure there weren't already too many books on the subject I was interested in writing about. Then I would make sure I had a unique slant on my idea. Simultaneous submissions from agents must include SASE's."

HEALTH COMMUNICATIONS, INC.

3201 SW 15th St., Deerfield Beach FL 33442. (954)360-0909, ext. 232. **Fax:** (954)360-0034. **E-mail:** editorial@hcibooks.com. **Website:** www.hcibooks.com. **Contact:** Editorial Committee. Estab. 1976. Publishes hardcover and trade paperback nonfiction only. "While HCI is a best known for recovery publishing, today recovery is only one part of a publishing program that includes titles in self-help and psychology, health and wellness, spirituality, inspiration, women's and men's issues, relationships, family, teens and children, memoirs, mind/body/spirit integration, and gift books." **Publishes 60 titles/year.** Responds in 3-6 months. Guidelines online.

NONFICTION Subjects include child guidance, health, parenting, psychology, women's issues, women's studies, young adult, self-help.

TIPS "Due to the volume of submissions, Health Communications cannot guarantee response times or personalize responses to individual proposals. Under no circumstances do we accept phone calls or e-mails pitching submissions."

HEALTH PROFESSIONS PRESS

P.O. Box 10624, Baltimore MD 21285-0624. (410)337-9585. **Fax:** (410)337-8539. **E-mail:** mmagnus@healthpropress.com. **Website:** www.healthpropress.com. **Contact:** Acquisitions Department. Publishes hardcover and trade paperback originals. "We are a specialty publisher. Our primary audiences are professionals, students, and educated consumers interested in topics related to aging and eldercare." **Publishes 6-8 titles/year. 70 queries received/year. 12 mss received/year. 50% of books from first-time authors. 100% from unagented writers. Pays 8-18% royalty on wholesale price.** Publishes ms 10 months after acceptance. Accepts simultaneous submissions. Responds in 1 month to queries; 3 months to proposals; 4 months to mss. Book catalog free or online. Guidelines online.

NONFICTION Subjects include health, medicine, psychology. Query with SASE. Submit proposal package, outline, resume, 1-2 sample chapters, cover letter.

WILLIAM S. HEIN & CO., INC.

2350 N. Forest Rd., Getzville NY 14068. (716)882-2600. **Fax:** (716)883-8100. **E-mail:** mail@wshein.com.

Website: www.wshein.com. **Contact:** Sheila Jarrett, senior editor. Estab. 1961. "William S. Hein & Co. publishes reference books for law librarians, legal researchers, and those interested in legal writing. Currently emphasizing legal research, legal writing, and legal education." **Publishes 18 titles/year. 30 queries received/year. 20 mss received/year. 30% of books from first-time authors. 99% from unagented writers. Pays 10-20% royalty on net price.** Publishes ms 9 months after acceptance. Accepts simultaneous submissions. Responds in 6 weeks to queries. Book catalog online. Guidelines by e-mail.

NONFICTION Subjects include education, government, politics, women's issues, world affairs, legislative histories.

HEINEMANN EDUCATIONAL PUBLISHERS

P.O. Box 781940, Sandton 2146, South Africa. **E-mail:** customerliaison@heinemann.co.za. **Website:** www.heinemann.co.za. Interested in textbooks for primary schools, literature and textbooks for secondary schools, and technical publishing for colleges/universities.

NONFICTION Subjects include animals, art, architecture, business, economics, education, ethnic, health, medicine, history, humanities, language, literature, music, dance, psychology, regional, religion, science, social sciences, sports, math, engineering, management, nursing, marketing.

HELLGATE PRESS

P.O. Box 3531, Ashland OR 97520. (541)973-5154. **E-mail:** harley@hellgatepress.com. **Website:** www.hellgatepress.com. **Contact:** Harley B. Patrick, editor. Estab. 1996. "Hellgate Press specializes in military history, other military topics, travel adventure, and historical/adventure fiction." **Publishes 15-20 titles/year. 85% of books from first-time authors. 95% from unagented writers. Pays royalty.** Publishes ms 6-9 months after acceptance. Responds in 2 months to queries.

NONFICTION Subjects include history, memoirs, military, war, travel adventure. Query/proposal by e-mail only. *Do not send mss.*

HENDRICK-LONG PUBLISHING CO., INC.

10635 Tower Oaks, Suite D, Houston TX 77070. (832)912-READ. **Fax:** (832)912-7353. **E-mail:** hendrick-long@worldnet.att.net. **Website:** hendricklongpublishing.com. **Contact:** Vilma Long. Estab. 1969. Publishes hardcover and trade paperback originals and hardcover reprints. "Hendrick-Long publishes historical fiction and nonfiction about Texas and the Southwest for children and young adults." **Publishes 4 titles/year. 90% from unagented writers. Pays royalty on selling price. Pays advance.** Publishes ms 18 months after acceptance. Responds in 3 months to queries. Book catalog available. Guidelines online.

NONFICTION Subjects include history, regional. Subject must be Texas related; other subjects cannot be considered. "We are particularly interested in material from educators that can be used in the classroom as workbooks, math, science, history with a Texas theme or twist." Query, or submit outline and 2 sample chapters. Reviews artwork/photos. Send photocopies.

FICTION Subjects include juvenile, young adult. Query with SASE. Submit outline, clips, 2 sample chapters.

HENDRICKSON PUBLISHERS, INC.

P.O. Box 3473, Peabody MA 01961. **Fax:** (978)573-8276. **E-mail:** editorial@hendrickson.com. **Website:** www.hendrickson.com. Estab. 1983. Publishes trade reprints, bibles, and scholarly material in the areas of New Testament; Hebrew Bible; religion and culture; patristics; Judaism; and practical, historical, and Biblical theology. "Hendrickson is an academic publisher of books that give insight into Bible understanding (academically) and encourage spiritual growth (popular trade). Currently emphasizing Biblical helps and reference, ministerial helps, and Biblical studies." **Publishes 35 titles/year. 800 queries received/year. 10% of books from first-time authors. 90% from unagented writers.** Publishes ms 1 year after acceptance. Guidelines online.

NONFICTION Subjects include religion. "No longer accepting unsolicited manuscripts or book proposals. Cannot return material sent or respond to all queries."

HERITAGE BOOKS, INC.

5810 Ruatan St., Berwyn Heights MD 20740. (301)345-2077. **E-mail:** info@heritagebooks.com. **E-mail:** submissions@heritagebooks.com. **Website:** www.heritagebooks.com. Estab. 1978. Publishes hardcover and paperback originals and reprints. "Our goal is to celebrate life by exploring all aspects of American life: settlement, development, wars, and other significant events, including family histories, memoirs, etc. Currently emphasizing early American life, early wars and conflicts, ethnic studies." **Publishes 200 titles/year. 25% of books from first-time authors. 100% from unagented writers. Pays 10% royalty on list price.** Accepts simultaneous submissions. Responds in 3 months to queries. Book catalog and ms guidelines free.

NONFICTION Subjects include Americana, ethnic, origins and research guides, history, memoirs, military, war, regional, history. Query with SASE. Submit outline via e-mail. Reviews artwork/photos.

TIPS "The quality of the book is of prime importance; next is its relevance to our fields of interest."

HERITAGE HOUSE PUBLISHING CO., LTD.

103-1075 Pendergast St., Victoria BC V8V 0A1, Canada. (250)360-0829. **E-mail:** heritage@heritagehouse.ca. **Website:** www.heritagehouse.ca. **Contact:** Lara Kordic, senior editor. Publishes mostly trade paperback and some hardcovers. "Heritage House publishes books that celebrate the historical and cultural heritage of Canada, particularly Western Canada and the Pacific Northwest. We also publish some children's titles, titles of national interest and a series of books aimed at young and casual readers, called *Amazing Stories*. We accept simultaneous submissions, but indicate on your query that it is a simultaneous submission." **Publishes 25-30 titles/year. 200 queries received/year. 100 mss received/year. 50% of books from first-time authors. 90% from unagented writers. Pays 12-15% royalty on net proceeds. Advances are rarely paid.** Publishes ms within 1-2 years of acceptance. after acceptance of ms. Accepts simultaneous submissions. Responds in 6 months to queries. Catalog and guidelines online.

NONFICTION Subjects include history, regional, adventure, contemporary Canadian culture. Query by e-mail. Include synopsis, outline, 2-3 sample chapters with indication of illustrative material available, and marketing strategy.

TIPS "Our books appeal to residents of and visitors to the northwest quadrant of the continent. We're looking for good stories and good storytellers. We focus on work by Canadian authors."

HEYDAY BOOKS

c/o Acquisitions Editor, Box 9145, Berkeley CA 94709. **Fax:** (510)549-1889. **E-mail:** heyday@heydaybooks.com. **Website:** www.heydaybooks.com. **Contact:** Gayle Wattawa, acquisitions and editorial director. Estab. 1974. Publishes hardcover originals, trade paperback originals and reprints. "Heyday Books publishes nonfiction books and literary anthologies with a strong California focus. We publish books about Native Americans, natural history, history, literature, and recreation, with a strong California focus." **Publishes 12-15 titles/year. 50% of books from first-time authors. 90% from unagented writers. Pays 8% royalty on net price.** Publishes ms 18 months after acceptance. Responds in 3 months. Book catalog online. Guidelines online.

NONFICTION Subjects include Americana, ethnic, history, nature, environment, recreation, regional, travel. Books about California only. Query with outline and synopsis. "Query or proposal by traditional post. Include a cover letter introducing yourself and your qualifications, a brief description of your project, a table of contents and list of illustrations, notes on the market you are trying to reach and why your book will appeal to them, a sample chapter, and a SASE if you would like us to return these materials to you." Reviews artwork/photos.

FICTION Publishes picture books, beginning readers, and young adult literature. Submit complete ms for picture books; proposal with sample chapters for longer works. Mark attention: Children's Submission.

HIGHLAND PRESS PUBLISHING

P.O. Box 2292, High Springs FL 32655. **E-mail:** the.highland.press@gmail.com; submissions.hp@gmail.com. **Website:** www.highlandpress.org. **Contact:** Leanne Burroughs, CEO (fiction); she will forward all mss to appropriate editor. Estab. 2005. Publishes paperback originals. "With our focus on historical romances, Highland Press Publishing is known as your 'Passport to Romance.' We focus on historical romances and our award-winning anthologies. Our short stories/novellas are heart warming. As for our historicals, we publish historical novels like many of us grew up with and loved. History is a big part of the story and is tactfully woven throughout the romance. We have opened our submissions up to all genres, with the exception of erotica. Our newest lines are inspirational, regency, and young adult." **Publishes 30 titles/year. 90% from unagented writers. Pays royalties 7.5-8%.** Publishes ms within 18 months of acceptance. after acceptance of ms. Accepts simultaneous submissions. Responds in 3 months to queries; 3-12 months to mss. Catalog and guidelines online.

FICTION Subjects include romance. Query with outline/synopsis and sample chapters. Accepts queries by snail mail, e-mail. Include estimated word count, target market.

TIPS "I don't publish based on industry trends. We buy what we like and what we believe readers are looking for. However, often this proves to be the genres and time-periods larger publishers are not currently interested in. Be professional at all times. Present your manuscript in the best possible light. Be sure you have run spell check and that the manuscript has been vetted by at least one critique partner, preferably more. Many times we receive manuscripts that have wonderful stories involved, but would take far too much time to edit to make it marketable."

HIGH PLAINS PRESS

P.O. Box 123, 403 Cassa Rd., Glendo WY 82213. (307)735-4370. **Fax:** (307)735-4590. **E-mail:** editor@highplainspress.com. **Website:** www.highplainspress.com. **Contact:** Nancy Curtis, publisher. Estab. 1984. Publishes hardcover and trade paperback originals. High Plains Press is a regional book publishing company specializing in books about the American West, with special interest in things relating to Wyoming. **Publishes 4 titles/year. 50 queries; 75 mss received/year. 75% of books from first-time authors. 100% from unagented writers. Pays 10% royalty on wholesale price. Pays $200-1,200 advance.** Publishes ms 2 years after acceptance. Accepts simultaneous submissions. Responds in 1 month to queries and proposals; 12 months on mss. Book catalog and guidelines online.

NONFICTION Subjects include agriculture, Americana, environment, history, horticulture, memoirs, nature, regional. "We consider only books with strong connection to the West." Query with SASE. Reviews artwork/photos. Send photocopies.

POETRY "We publish 1 poetry volume a year. Require connection to West. Consider poetry in August." Submit 5 sample poems.

TIPS "Our audience comprises general readers interested in history and culture of the Rockies."

HILL AND WANG

Farrar Straus & Giroux, Inc., 18 W. 18th St., New York NY 10011. (212)741-6900. **Fax:** (212)633-9385. **Website:** www.fsgbooks.com. Estab. 1956. Publishes hardcover and trade paperbacks. "Hill and Wang publishes serious nonfiction books, primarily in history, science, mathematics and the social sciences. We are not considering new fiction, drama, or poetry." **Publishes 12 titles/year. 1,500 queries received/year. 50% of books from first-time authors. 50% from unagented writers.** Publishes ms 1 year after acceptance. Accepts simultaneous submissions. Book catalog available free.

NONFICTION Subjects include government, politics, history, American. *Agented submissions only.*

LAWRENCE HILL BOOKS

Chicago Review Press, 814 N. Franklin St., 2nd Floor, Chicago IL 60610. (312)337-0747. **Fax:** (312)337-5110. **Website:** www.chicagoreviewpress.com. **Contact:** Yuval Taylor, senior editor. Publishes hardcover originals and trade paperback originals and reprints. **Publishes 3-10 titles/year. 20 queries received/year. 10 mss received/year. 40% of books from first-time authors. 50% from unagented writers. Pays 7-12% royalty on retail price. Pays $3,000-10,000 advance.** Publishes ms 1 year after acceptance. Accepts simultaneous submissions. Responds in 1 month to queries; 2 months to proposals and mss.

NONFICTION Subjects include ethnic, government, politics, history, multicultural. Submit proposal package, outline, 2 sample chapters.

HIPPOCRENE BOOKS, INC.

171 Madison Ave., New York NY 10016. (718)454-2366. **E-mail:** info@hippocrenebooks.com. **Website:** www.hippocrenebooks.com. Estab. 1971. "Over the last forty years, Hippocrene Books has become one of America's foremost publishers of foreign language reference books and ethnic cookbooks. As a small publishing house in a marketplace dominated by conglomerates, Hippocrene has succeeded by continually reinventing its list while maintaining a strong international and ethnic orientation."

HIPPOPOTAMUS PRESS

22 Whitewell Rd., Frome Somerset BA11 4EL, United Kingdom. (44)(173)466-6653. **E-mail:** rjhippopress@aol.com. **Contact:** R. John, editor; M. Pargitter (poetry); Anna Martin (translation). Estab. 1974. Publishes hardcover and trade paperback originals. "Hippopotamus Press publishes first, full collections of verse by those well represented in the mainstream poetry magazines of the English-speaking world." **Publishes 6-12 titles/year. 90% of books from first-time authors. 90% from unagented writers. Pays 7½-10% royalty on retail price. Pays advance.** Publishes ms 10 months after acceptance. Accepts simultaneous

submissions. Responds in 1 month to queries. Book catalog available free.

NONFICTION Subjects include language, literature, translation. Query with SASE. Submit complete ms.

POETRY "Read one of our authors—poets often make the mistake of submitting poetry without knowing the type of verse we publish." Query and submit complete ms.

TIPS "We publish books for a literate audience. We have a strong link to the Modernist tradition. Read what we publish."

HIPSO MEDIA

8151 E. 29th Ave., Denver CO 80238. **Website:** www.hipsomedia.com. Estab. 2012. Publishes trade and mass market paperback and electronic originals. **Publishes 6 titles/year. 10% of books from first-time authors. 100% from unagented writers. Authors receive between 15-30% on royalty.** Publishes book Averages 6 months between acceptance of a book-length ms and publication. after acceptance of ms. Accepts simultaneous submissions. Responds in 1 month. Catalog online. Guidelines online.

NONFICTION Subjects include alternative lifestyles, contemporary culture, cooking, foods, health, medicine, nutrition, travel. Looking for books that can be enhanced with media, video, audio, animation, and interactivity. Query via online form. Reviews artwork as part of the ms package. Artwork or photos must be in JPG form.

FICTION Subjects include erotica, experimental, humor, multicultural, multimedia, mystery, short story collections, young adult. Query via online form.

TIPS Describes ideal audience as "hip readers of e-books. We are going digital first, so tell us why someone would want to read your book."

HISTORY PUBLISHING COMPANY, INC.

P.O. Box 700, Palisades NY 10964. **Fax:** (845)231-6167. **Website:** www.historypublishingco.com. **Contact:** Don Bracken, editorial director. Estab. 2001. Publishes hardcover and trade paperback originals and electronic books. "History Publishing is looking for interesting stories that make up history. If you have a story about an aspect of history that would have an appeal to a large niche or broad readership, History Publishing is interested." **Publishes 20 titles/year. 50% of books from first-time authors. 50% from unagented writers. Pays 7-10% royalty on wholesale list price. Does not pay advances to unpublished authors.** Publishes ms 1 year after acceptance. Responds in 2 months to full mss. Guidelines online.

NONFICTION Subjects include Americana, business, contemporary culture, creative nonfiction, economics, government, history, military, politics, social sciences, sociology, war, world affairs. Query with SASE. Submit proposal package, outline, 3 sample chapters or submit complete ms. Reviews artwork/photos. Send photocopies.

TIPS "We focus on an audience interested in the events that shaped the world we live in and the events of today that continue to shape that world. Focus on interesting and serious events that will appeal to the contemporary reader who likes easy-to-read history that flows from one page to the next."

HOBAR PUBLICATIONS

A division of Finney Co., 5995 149th St. W., Suite 105, Apple Valley MN 55124. (952)469-6699. **Fax:** (952)469-1968. **E-mail:** feedback@finney-hobar.com. **Website:** www.finney-hobar.com. **Contact:** Alan E. Krysan, president. Publishes trade paperback originals. "Hobar publishes career and technical educational materials." **Publishes 4-6 titles/year. 30 queries received/year. 10 mss received/year. 35% of books from first-time authors. 100% from unagented writers. Pays 10% royalty on wholesale price. Pays advance.** Publishes ms 1 year after acceptance. Accepts simultaneous submissions. Responds in 10-12 weeks to queries.

NONFICTION Subjects include agriculture, animals, business, economics, education, gardening, nature, environment, science, building trades. Query with SASE. Reviews artwork/photos.

HOHM PRESS

P.O. Box 4410, Chino Valley AZ 86323. (800)381-2700. **Fax:** (928)717-1779. **Website:** www.hohmpress.com. Estab. 1975. Publishes hardcover and trade paperback originals. "*Hohm Press* publishes a range of titles in the areas of transpersonal psychology and spirituality, herbistry, alternative health methods, and nutrition. Not interested in personal health survival stories." **Publishes 6-8 titles/year. 50% of books from first-time authors. Pays 10% royalty on net sales.** Publishes ms 18 months after acceptance. Accepts simultaneous submissions. Responds in 3 months to queries.

NONFICTION Subjects include health, medicine, natural/alternative health, medicine, philosophy, religion, Hindu, Buddhist, Sufi, or translations of classic texts in major religious traditions, yoga. "We look for writers who have an established record in their field of expertise. The best buy of recent years came from 2 women who fully substantiated how they could market their book. We believed they could do it. We were right." No children's books please. Query with SASE. No e-mail inquiries, please.

POETRY "We are not accepting poetry at this time except for translations of recognized religious/spiritual classics."

HOLIDAY HOUSE, INC.

425 Madison Ave., New York NY 10017. (212)688-0085. **Fax:** (212)421-6134. **E-mail:** info@holidayhouse.com. **Website:** holidayhouse.com. Estab. 1935. Publishes hardcover originals and paperback reprints. "Holiday House publishes children's and young adult books for the school and library markets. We have a commitment to publishing first-time authors and illustrators. We specialize in quality hardcovers from picture books to young adult, both fiction and nonfiction, primarily for the school and library market." **Publishes 50 titles/year. 5% of books from first-time authors. 50% from unagented writers. Pays royalty on list price, range varies.** Publishes book Publishes 1-2 years after acceptance. Responds in 4 months. Guidelines for #10 SASE.

NONFICTION Subjects include Americana, history, science, Judaica. Please send the entire ms, whether submitting a picture book or novel. "We do not accept certified or registered mail. There is no need to include a SASE. We do not consider submissions by e-mail or fax. Please note that you do not have to supply illustrations. However, if you have illustrations you would like to include with your submission, you may send detailed sketches or photocopies of the original art. Do not send original art." Reviews artwork/photos. Send photocopies-no originals.

FICTION Subjects include adventure, historical, humor, literary, mainstream, contemporary, Judaica and holiday, animal stories for young readers. Children's books only. Query with SASE. No phone calls, please.

TIPS "We need manuscripts with strong stories and writing."

Ⓐ⊘ HENRY HOLT

175 Fifth Ave., New York NY 10011. **Website:** www.henryholt.com. *Agented submissions only.*

HOLY CROSS ORTHODOX PRESS

Hellenic College, 50 Goddard Ave., Brookline MA 02445. (617)850-1321. **Fax:** (617)850-1457. **E-mail:** press@hchc.edu. **Contact:** Dr. Anton C. Vrame. Estab. 1974. Publishes trade paperback originals. "Holy Cross publishes titles that are rooted in the tradition of the Eastern Orthodox Church." **Publishes 8 titles/year. 10-15 queries received/year. 10-15 mss received/year. 85% of books from first-time authors. 100% from unagented writers. Pays 8-12% royalty on retail price.** Publishes ms 2 years after acceptance. Accepts simultaneous submissions. Responds in 6 months to mss. Book catalog available online through Holy Cross Bookstore.

IMPRINTS Holy Cross Orthodox Press.

NONFICTION Subjects include ethnic, religion, Greek Orthodox. Holy Cross Orthodox Press publishes scholarly and popular literature in the areas of Orthodox Christian theology and Greek letters. Submissions are often far too technical usually with a very limited audiences. Submit outline. Submit complete ms. Reviews artwork/photos. Send photocopies.

Ⓐ HOPEWELL PUBLICATIONS

P.O. Box 11, Titusville NJ 08560. **Website:** www.hopepubs.com. **Contact:** E. Martin, publisher. Estab. 2002. Format publishes in hardcover, trade paperback, and electronic originals; trade paperback and electronic reprints. "Hopewell Publications specializes in classic reprints—books with proven sales records that have gone out of print—and the occasional new title of interest. Our catalog spans from one to sixty years of publication history. We print fiction and nonfiction, and we accept agented and unagented materials. Submissions are accepted online only." **Publishes 20-30 titles/year. Receives 2,000 queries/year; 500 mss/year. 25% of books from first-time authors. 75% from unagented writers. Pays royalty on retail price.** Publishes ms 6-12 months after acceptance. Accepts simultaneous submissions. Responds in 3 months to queries; 6 months to proposals; 9 months to mss. Catalog online. Guidelines online.

IMPRINTS Egress Books, Legacy Classics.

NONFICTION , All nonfiction subjects acceptable. Query online using online guidelines.

FICTION Subjects include adventure, contemporary, experimental, fantasy, gay, historical, humor, juvenile, literary, mainstream, mystery, plays, short story collections, spiritual, suspense, young adult, All fiction subjects acceptable. Query online using our online guidelines.

HOUGHTON MIFFLIN HARCOURT BOOKS FOR CHILDREN

Imprint of Houghton Mifflin Trade & Reference Division, 222 Berkeley St., Boston MA 02116. (617)351-5000. **Fax:** (617)351-1111. **Website:** www.houghtonmifflinbooks.com. Publishes hardcover originals and trade paperback originals and reprints. Houghton Mifflin Harcourt gives shape to ideas that educate, inform, and above all, delight. *Does not respond to or return mss unless interested.* **Publishes 100 titles/year. 5,000 queries received/year. 14,000 mss received/year. 10% of books from first-time authors. 60% from unagented writers. Pays 5-10% royalty on retail price. Pays variable advance.** Publishes ms 2 years after acceptance. Accepts simultaneous submissions. Responds in 4-6 months to queries. Guidelines online.

NONFICTION Subjects include animals, anthropology, archeology, art, architecture, ethnic, history, language, literature, music, dance, nature, environment, science, sports. Interested in innovative books and subjects about which the author is passionate. Query with SASE. Submit sample chapters, synopsis. Reviews artwork/photos. Send photocopies.

FICTION Subjects include adventure, ethnic, historical, humor, juvenile, early readers, literary, mystery, picture books, suspense, young adult, board books. Submit complete ms.

HOUGHTON MIFFLIN HARCOURT CO.

222 Berkeley St., Boston MA 02116. (617)351-5000. **Website:** www.hmhco.com. Estab. 1832. Publishes hardcover originals and trade paperback originals and reprints. "Houghton Mifflin Harcourt gives shape to ideas that educate, inform and delight. In a new era of publishing, our legacy of quality thrives as we combine imagination with technology, bringing you new ways to know."

NONFICTION "We are not a mass market publisher. Our main focus is serious nonfiction. We do practical self-help but not pop psychology self-help." *Agented submissions only. Unsolicited mss returned unopened.*

HOUSE OF ANANSI PRESS

110 Spadina Ave., Suite 801, Toronto ON M5V 2K4, Canada. (416)363-4343. **Fax:** (416)363-1017. **Website:** www.anansi.ca. Estab. 1967. House of Anansi publishes literary fiction and poetry by Canadian and international writers. **Pays 8-10% royalties. Pays $750 advance and 10 author's copies.** Publishes book Responds to queries within 1 year; to mss (if invited) within 4 months. after acceptance of ms.

NONFICTION Avoids dry, jargon-filled academic prose and has a literary twist that will interest general readers and experts alike. Query with SASE.

FICTION Publishes literary fiction that has a unique flair, memorable characters, and a strong narrative voice. Query with SASE.

POETRY "We seek to balance the list between well-known and emerging writers, with an interest in writing by Canadians of all backgrounds. We publish Canadian poetry only, and poets must have a substantial publication record—if not in books, then definitely in journals and magazines of repute." Does not want "children's poetry or poetry by previously unpublished poets." Canadian poets should query first with 10 sample poems (typed double-spaced) and a cover letter with brief bio and publication credits. Considers simultaneous submissions. Poems are circulated to an editorial board. Often comments on rejected poems.

HOW BOOKS

F+W, a Content + eCommerce Company, 10151 Carver Rd., Suite 200, Blue Ash OH 45242. (513)531-2690. **E-mail:** scott.francis@fwmedia.com. **Website:** www.howdesign.com. **Contact:** Scott Francis, editor. Estab. 1985. Publishes hardcover and trade paperback originals. **Publishes 15 titles/year. 50 queries received/year. 5 mss received/year. 50% of books from first-time authors. 50% from unagented writers. Pays 10% royalty on wholesale price. Pays $2,000-6,000 advance.** Publishes ms 18-24 months after acceptance. Accepts simultaneous submissions. Responds in 1 month to queries and proposals; 3 months to mss. Book catalog available online. Guidelines available online.

NONFICTION , graphic design, web design, creativity, pop culture. "We look for material that reflects the cutting edge of trends, graphic design, and culture. Nearly all HOW Books are intensely visual, and authors must be able to create or supply art/illustration for their books." Query via e-mail. Submit proposal package, outline, 1 sample chapter, sample art or sample design. Reviews artwork/photos. Send as PDF's.

TIPS "Audience comprised of graphic designers. Your art, design, or concept."

HUMAN KINETICS PUBLISHERS, INC.

P.O. Box 5076, Champaign IL 61825-5076. (800)747-4457. **Fax:** (217)351-1549. **E-mail:** acquisitions@hkusa.com. **Website:** www.humankinetics.com. Estab. 1974. Publishes hardcover, ebooks, and paperback text and reference books, trade paperback originals, course software and audiovisual. "*Human Kinetics* publishes books which provide expert knowledge in sport and fitness training and techniques, physical education, sports sciences and sports medicine for coaches, athletes and fitness enthusiasts and professionals in the physical action field." **Publishes 160 titles/year. Pays 10-15% royalty on net income.** Publishes ms up to 18 months after acceptance. Accepts simultaneous submissions. Responds in 2 months to queries. Book catalog available free. Guidelines online.

NONFICTION Subjects include education, health, medicine, psychology, recreation, sports, sciences. "Here is a current listing of our divisions: Amer. Sport Education; Aquatics Edu.; Professional Edu.; HPERD Div., Journal Div.; STM Div., Trade Div." Submit outline, sample chapters. Reviews artwork/photos.

IBEX PUBLISHERS

P.O. Box 30087, Bethesda MD 20824. (301)718-8188. **Fax:** (301)907-8707. **E-mail:** info@ibexpub.com. **Website:** www.ibexpublishers.com. Estab. 1979. Publishes hardcover and trade paperback originals and reprints. "IBEX publishes books about Iran and the Middle East and about Persian culture and literature." **Publishes 10-12 titles/year. Payment varies.** Accepts simultaneous submissions. Book catalog available free.

IMPRINTS Iranbooks Press.

NONFICTION Subjects include cooking, foods, nutrition, language, literature. Query with SASE, or submit proposal package, including outline and 2 sample chapters.

POETRY "Translations of Persian poets will be considered."

ICONOGRAFIX/ENTHUSIAST BOOKS

1830A Hanley Rd., Hudson WI 54016. (715)381-9755. **Fax:** (715)381-9756. **E-mail:** dcfrautschi@iconografixinc.com. **Website:** www.enthusiastbooks.com. **Contact:** Dylan Frautschi, editorial director. Estab. 1992. Publishes trade paperback originals. "Iconografix publishes special, historical-interest photographic books for transportation equipment enthusiasts. Currently emphasizing emergency vehicles, buses, trucks, railroads, automobiles, auto racing, construction equipment, snowmobiles." **Publishes 6-10 titles/year. 50 queries received/year. 20 mss received/year. 50% of books from first-time authors. 100% from unagented writers. Pays 8-12% royalty on wholesale price. Pays $1,000-3,000 advance.** Publishes ms 1 year after acceptance. Accepts simultaneous submissions. Responds in 1 month to queries; 3 months to proposals and mss. Book catalog and ms guidelines free.

NONFICTION Subjects include Americana, photos from archives of historic places, objects, people, history, hobbies, military, war, transportation (older photos of specific vehicles). Interested in photo archives. Query with SASE, or submit proposal package, including outline. Reviews artwork/photos. Send photocopies.

ICS PUBLICATIONS

Institute of Carmelite Studies, 2131 Lincoln Rd. NE, Washington DC 20002. (202)832-8489. **Fax:** (202)832-8967. **E-mail:** editor@icspublications.org. **Website:** www.icspublications.org. **Contact:** Patricia Morrison, editorial director. Publishes hardcover and trade paperback originals and reprints. "Our audience consists of those interested in the Carmelite tradition and in developing their life of prayer and spirituality." **Publishes 3 titles/year. 10-20 queries received/year. 10 mss received/year. 10% of books from first-time authors. 90-100% from unagented writers. Pays 2-6% royalty on retail price or makes outright purchase. Pays $500 advance.** Publishes ms 3 years after acceptance. Responds in 6 months to proposals.

NONFICTION "Too often we receive proposals for works that merely repeat what has already been done, are too technical for a general audience, or have little to do with the Carmelite tradition and spirit. We are looking for significant works on Carmelite history, spirituality, and main figures (Saints Teresa, John of the Cross, Therese of Lisieux, etc.)."

IDEALS CHILDREN'S BOOKS AND CANDYCANE PRESS

2630 Elm Hill Pike, Suite 100, Nashville TN 37214. **Website:** www.idealsbooks.com. **Contact:** Submissions. Estab. 1944.

NONFICTION Ideals publishes for ages 4-8, no longer than 800 words; CandyCane publishes for ages 2-5, no longer than 500 words. Submit complete ms.

FICTION Picture books: animal, concept, history, religion. Board books: animal, history, nature/environment, religion. Ideals publishes for ages 4-8, no longer than 800 words; CandyCane publishes for ages 2-5, no longer than 500 words. Submit complete ms.

IDEALS PUBLICATIONS, INC.

2630 Elm Hill Pike, Suite 100, Nashville TN 37214. (615)333-0478. **E-mail:** idealsinfo@guideposts.org. **Website:** www.idealsbooks.com. Estab. 1944. "Ideals Publications publishes 20-25 new children's titles a year, primarily for 2-8 year-olds. Our backlist includes more than 400 titles, and we publish picture books, activity books, board books, and novelty and sound books covering a wide array of topics, such as Bible stories, holidays, early learning, history, family relationships, and values. Our bestselling titles include *The Story of Christmas*, *The Story of Easter*, *Seaman's Journal*, *How Do I Love You?*, *God Made You Special* and *A View at the Zoo*. Through our dedication to publishing high-quality and engaging books, we never forget our obligation to our littlest readers to help create those special moments with books."

IMPRINTS Ideals, Ideals Children's Books, CandyCane Press, Williamson Books.

FICTION Ideals Children's Books publishes fiction and nonfiction picture books for children ages 4 to 8. Subjects include holiday, inspirational, and patriotic themes; relationships and values; and general fiction. Mss should be no longer than 800 words. CandyCane Press publishes board books and novelty books for children ages 2 to 5. Subject matter is similar to Ideals Children's Books, with a focus on younger children. Mss should be no longer than 250 words.

IDW PUBLISHING

5080 Santa Fe, San Diego CA 92109. **E-mail:** letters@idwpublishing.com. **Website:** www.idwpublishing.com. Estab. 1999. Publishes hardcover, mass market and trade paperback originals. IDW Publishing currently publishes a wide range of comic books and graphic novels including titles based on GI Joe, Star Trek, Terminator: Salvation, and Transformers. Creator-driven titles include Fallen Angel by Peter David and JK Woodward, Locke & Key by Joe Hill and Gabriel Rodriguez, and a variety of titles by writer Steve Niles including Wake the Dead, Epilogue, and Dead, She Said.

IDYLL ARBOR, INC.

39129 264th Ave. SE, Enumclaw WA 98022. (360)825-7797. **Fax:** (360)825-5670. **E-mail:** editors@idyllarbor.com. **Website:** www.idyllarbor.com. **Contact:** Tom Blaschko. Estab. 1984. Publishes hardcover and trade paperback originals, and trade paperback reprints. "Idyll Arbor publishes practical information on the current state and art of healthcare practice. Currently emphasizing therapies (recreational, horticultural), and activity directors in long-term care facilities. Issues Press looks at problems in society from video games to returning veterans and their problems reintegrating into the civilian world. Pine Winds Press publishes books about strange phenomena such as Bigfoot and the life force." **Publishes 6 titles/year. 50% of books from first-time authors. 100% from unagented writers. Pays 8-15% royalty on wholesale price or retail price.** Publishes ms 1 year after acceptance. Accepts simultaneous submissions. Responds in 1 month; 2 months to proposals; 6 months to mss. Book catalog and ms guidelines free.

IMPRINTS Issues Press; Pine Winds Press.

NONFICTION Subjects include health, medicine, for therapists, activity directors, psychology, recreational therapy, horticulture (used in long-term care activities or health care therapy). "Idyll Arbor is currently developing a line of books under the imprint Issues Press, which treats emotional issues in a clear-headed manner. We look for manuscripts from authors with recent clinical experience. Good grounding in theory is required, but practical experience is more important." Query preferred with outline and 1 sample chapter. Reviews artwork/photos. Send photocopies.

TIPS "The books must be useful for the health practitioner who meets face to face with patients or the books must be useful for teaching undergraduate and graduate level classes. Pine Winds Press books should be compatible with the model of the soul found on calculatingsoulconnections.com."

ILIUM PRESS

2407 S. Sonora Dr., Spokane WA 99037. (509)701-8866. **E-mail:** contact@iliumpress.com; submissions@iliumpress.com. **Website:** www.iliumpress.com. **Contact:** John Lemon, owner/editor (literature, epic poetry). Estab. 2010. Publishes trade paperback originals and reprints, electronic originals and reprints. **Publishes 1-3 titles/year. Pays 20-50% royalties on receipts.** Publishes ms up to 1 year after acceptance. Accepts simultaneous submissions. Responds in 6 months. Guidelines online.

FICTION Subjects include adventure, historical, literary, noir. No epic fantasy or paranormal romance.

POETRY "Submit only narrative epic poems in metered or sprung blank non-rhyming verse. All others will be rejected. See submission guidelines on website." Query with first 20 pages and SASE.

ILR PRESS

Cornell University Press, Sage House, 512 E. State St., Ithaca NY 14850. (607)277-2338. **Fax:** (607)277-2374. **E-mail:** fgb2@cornell.edu. **Website:** www.ilr.cornell.edu/ilrpress. **Contact:** Frances Benson, editorial director. Estab. 1945. Publishes hardcover and trade paperback originals and reprints. "We are interested in manuscripts with innovative perspectives on current workplace issues that concern both academics and the general public." **Publishes 10-15 titles/year. Pays royalty.** Responds in 2 months to queries. Book catalog available free.

NONFICTION Subjects include business, economics, government, politics, history, sociology. All titles relate to labor relations and/or workplace issues including relevant work in the fields of history, sociology, political science, economics, human resources, and organizational behavior. Special series: culture and politics of health care work. Query with SASE. Submit outline, sample chapters, CV.

TIPS "Manuscripts must be well documented to pass our editorial evaluation, which includes review by academics in related fields."

IMAGE COMICS

2001 Center St., 6th Floor, Berkeley CA 94704. **E-mail:** submissions@imagecomics.com. **Website:** www.imagecomics.com. **Contact:** Eric Stephenson, publisher. Estab. 1992. Publishes creator-owned comic books, graphic novels. See this company's website for detailed guidelines. Does not accept writing samples without art.

FICTION Query with 1-page synopsis and 5 pages or more of samples. "We do not accept writing (that is plots, scripts, whatever) samples! If you're an established pro, we might be able to find somebody willing to work with you but it would be nearly impossible for us to read through every script that might find its way our direction. Do not send your script or your plot unaccompanied by art—it will be discarded, unread."

TIPS "We are not looking for any specific genre or type of comic book. We are looking for comics that are well written and well drawn, by people who are dedicated and can meet deadlines."

IMMEDIUM

P.O. Box 31846, San Francisco CA 94131. (415)452-8546. **Fax:** (360)937-6272. **Website:** www.immedium.com. Estab. 2005. Publishes hardcover and trade paperback originals. "Immedium focuses on publishing eye-catching children's picture books, Asian American topics, and contemporary arts, popular culture, and multicultural issues." **Publishes 4 titles/year. 50 queries received/year. 25 mss received/year. 50% of books from first-time authors. 90% from unagented writers. Pays 5% royalty on wholesale price. Pays on publication.** Publishes ms 2 years after acceptance. Accepts simultaneous submissions. Responds in 1-3 months. Catalog online. Guidelines online.

NONFICTION Subjects include art, architecture, multicultural. Submit complete ms. Reviews artwork/photos. Send photocopies.

FICTION Subjects include comic books, picture books. Submit complete ms.

TIPS "Our audience is children and parents. Please visit our site."

IMPACT BOOKS

F+W Media, Inc., 10151 Carver Rd., Suite 200, Blue Ash OH 45242. **Fax:** (513)531-2686. **E-mail:** mona.clough@fwcommunity.com. **Website:** www.northlightshop.com; www.impact-books.com. **Contact:** Mona Clough, content director (art instruction for fantasy, comics, manga, anime, popular culture, graffiti, science fiction, cartooning and body art). Estab. 2004. Publishes trade paperback originals and reprints. **Publishes 8-9 titles/year. 50 queries received/year. 10-12 mss received/year. 80% of books from first-time authors. 80% from unagented writers.** Publishes book 11 months after acceptance of ms. Accepts simultaneous submissions. Responds in 4 months to queries. Responds in 4 months to proposals. Responds in 4 months to manuscripts. Visit website for booklist. Guidelines available at www.artistsnetwork.com/contactus.

IMPACT Books publishes titles that emphasize illustrated how-to-draw-manga, graffiti, fantasy and comics art instruction. Currently emphasizing manga and anime art, traditional American comics styles, including humor, and pop art. Looking for good science fiction art instruction. This market is for experienced artists who are willing to work with an IMPACT editor to produce a step-by-step how-to book about how to create the art and the artist's creative process. See also separate listing for F+W Media in this section.

NONFICTION Subjects include art, art instruction, contemporary culture, creative nonfiction, hobbies. Submit proposal package, outline, 1 sample chapter, at least 20 examples of sample art. Reviews artwork/photos. Send digital art.

TIPS "Audience comprised primarily of 12- to 18-year-old beginners along the lines of comic buyers, in general—mostly teenagers—but also appealing to a broader audience of young adults 19-30 who need basic techniques. Art must appeal to teenagers and be submitted in a form that will reproduce well. Authors need to know how to teach beginners step-by-step. A sample step-by-step demonstration is important."

IMPACT PUBLISHERS, INC.

P.O. Box 6016, Atascadero CA 93423. **E-mail:** submissions@impactpublishers.com. **Website:** www.impactpublishers.com. **Contact:** Freeman Porter, submissions editor. Estab. 1970. "Our purpose is to make the best human services expertise available to the widest possible audience. We publish only popular psychology and self-help materials written in everyday language by professionals with advanced degrees and significant experience in the human services." **Publishes 3-5 titles/year. 20% of books from first-time authors. Pays authors royalty of 10-12%. Offers advances.** Accepts simultaneous submissions. Responds in 3 months. Book catalog for #10 SASE with 2 first-class stamps. Guidelines for SASE.

IMPRINTS Little Imp Books, Rebuilding Books, The Practical Therapist Series.

NONFICTION Young readers, middle readers, young adults: self-help. Query or submit complete ms, cover letter, résumé.

TIPS "Please do not submit fiction, poetry or narratives."

INCENTIVE PUBLICATIONS, INC.

233 N. Michigan Ave., Suite 2000, Chicago IL 60601. **E-mail:** incentive@worldbook.com. **Website:** www.incentivepublications.com. **Contact:** Paul Kobasa, editor-in-chief. Estab. 1970. Publishes paperback originals. "Incentive publishes developmentally appropriate teacher/school administrator/parent resource materials and supplementary instructional materials for children in grades K-12. Actively seeking proposals for student workbooks, all grades/all subjects, and professional development resources for pre K-12 classroom teachers and school administrators." **Publishes 10-15 titles/year. 25% of books from first-time authors. 100, but agent proposals welcome% from unagented writers. Pays royalty, or makes outright purchase.** Publishes book an average of 1 year after acceptance of ms. Responds in 1 month to queries.

NONFICTION Subjects include education. Instructional, teacher/administrator professional development books in pre-K through 12th grade. Query with synopsis and detailed outline.

INDIANA HISTORICAL SOCIETY PRESS

450 W. Ohio St., Indianapolis IN 46202-3269. (317)233-6073. **Fax:** (317)233-0857. **E-mail:** hspress@indianahistory.org. **Website:** www.indianahistory.org. **Contact:** Submissions Editor. Estab. 1830. Publishes hardcover and paperback originals. **Publishes 10 titles/year.** Responds in 1 month to queries.

NONFICTION Subjects include agriculture, art, architecture, business, economics, ethnic, government, politics, history, military, war, sports, family history, children's books. All topics must relate to Indiana. "We seek book-length manuscripts that are solidly researched and engagingly written on topics related to Indiana: biography, history, literature, music, politics, transportation, sports, agriculture, architecture, and children's books." Query with SASE.

INFORMATION TODAY, INC.

143 Old Marlton Pike, Medford NJ 08055. (609)654-6266. **Fax:** (609)654-4309. **E-mail:** jbryans@infotoday.com. **Website:** www.infotoday.com. **Contact:** John B. Bryans, editor-in-chief/publisher. Publishes hardcover and trade paperback originals. "We look for highly-focused coverage of cutting-edge technology topics. Written by established experts and targeted to a tech-savvy readership. Virtually all our titles focus on how information is accessed, used, shared, and transformed into knowledge that can benefit people, business, and society. Currently emphasizing Internet/online technologies, including their social significance: biography, how-to, technical, reference, scholarly. De-emphasizing fiction." **Publishes 15-20 titles/year. 200 queries received/year. 30 mss received/year. 30% of books from first-time authors. 90% from unagented writers. Pays 10-15% royalty on wholesale price. Pays $500-2,500 advance.** Publishes ms 9 months after acceptance. Accepts simultaneous submissions. Responds in 1 month to queries; 2 months to propos-

als; 3 months to mss. Book catalog free or on website. Proposal guidelines free or via e-mail as attachment.

IMPRINTS ITI (academic, scholarly, library science); CyberAge Books (high-end consumer and business technology books-emphasis on Internet/WWW topics including online research).

NONFICTION Subjects include business, economics, computers, electronics, education, science, Internet and cyberculture. Query with SASE. Reviews artwork/photos. Send photocopies.

TIPS "Our readers include scholars, academics, educators, indexers, librarians, information professionals (ITI imprint), as well as high-end consumer and business users of Internet/WWW/online technologies, and people interested in the marriage of technology with issues of social significance (i.e., cyberculture)."

INNOVATIVE PUBLISHERS INC.

133 Clarendon St., Box 170021, Boston MA 02117. (617)963-0886. **Fax:** (617)861-8533. **E-mail:** admin@innovative-publishers.com. **Website:** www.innovative-publishers.com. Estab. 2000. Publishes hardcover, trade paperback, mass market, and electronic originals; trade paperback and mass market reprints. **Publishes 350-600 titles/year. Receives 4,500 queries/year; 800-1,000 mss/year. 45% of books from first-time authors. 50% from unagented writers. Pays 5-17% royalty on retail price. Offers $1,500-125,000 advance.** Publishes ms 2 years after acceptance. Responds in 3 months to queries; 4-6 months to mss and proposals. Book catalog for 9x12 SASE with 7 first-class stamps. Guidelines for #10 SASE.

NONFICTION Subjects include Americana, anthropology, archeology, architecture, art, business, career guidance, child guidance, communications, community, contemporary culture, cooking, counseling, crafts, creative nonfiction, economics, education, entertainment, finance, foods, games, gardening, government, health, history, hobbies, house and home, humanities, language, law, literary criticism, literature, memoirs, money, multicultural, music, New Age, philosophy, photography, psychology, real estate, religion, science, social sciences, sociology, spirituality, translation, transportation, travel, womens issues, womens studies, world affairs, young adult. "We want books from dedicated writers and not those who are writing on the latest trend. Our audience is broad, educated, and insightful." Query with SASE. Reviews artwork.

FICTION Subjects include adventure, comic books, confession, contemporary, erotica, ethnic, experimental, fantasy, feminist, gothic, historical, horror, humor, juvenile, literary, mainstream, multicultural, mystery, picture books, plays, poetry, religious, romance, science fiction, short story collections, spiritual, suspense, translation, young adult. "Primarily seeking artists that are immersed in their topic. If you live, eat, and sleep your topic, it will show. Our focus is a wide demographic." See submission requirements online.

POETRY "Some works may be slated for anthologies. Readers are from diverse demographic. Seeking innovative styles. Especially seeking emerging ethnic poets from Asia, Europe, and Spanish-speaking countries."

INSOMNIAC PRESS

520 Princess Ave., London ON N6B 2B8, Canada. (416)504-6270. **E-mail:** mike@insomniacpress.com. **Website:** www.insomniacpress.com. **Contact:** Mike O'Connor, publisher. Estab. 1992. Publishes trade paperback originals and reprints, mass market paperback originals, and electronic originals and reprints. **Publishes 20 titles/year. 250 queries received/year. 1,000 mss received/year. 50% of books from first-time authors. 80% from unagented writers. Pays 10-15% royalty on retail price. Pays $500-1,000 advance.** Publishes ms 6 months after acceptance. Accepts simultaneous submissions. Guidelines online.

NONFICTION Subjects include business, creative nonfiction, gay, lesbian, government, politics, health, medicine, language, literature, money, finance, multicultural, religion, crime. Very interested in areas such as crime and well-written and well-researched nonfiction on topics of wide interest. Query via e-mail, submit proposal package including outline, 2 sample chapters, or submit complete ms. Reviews artwork/photos. Send photocopies.

FICTION Subjects include comic books, ethnic, experimental, gay, lesbian, humor, literary, mainstream, multicultural, mystery, poetry, suspense. "We publish a mix of commercial (mysteries) and literary fiction." Query via e-mail, submit proposal.

POETRY "Our poetry publishing is limited to 2-4 books per year and we are often booked up a year or two in advance." Submit complete ms.

TIPS "We envision a mixed readership that appreciates up-and-coming literary fiction and poetry as well as solidly researched and provocative nonfiction. Peruse our website and familiarize yourself with what we've published in the past."

INTERLINK PUBLISHING GROUP, INC.

46 Crosby St., Northampton MA 01060. (413)582-7054. **Fax:** (413)582-7057. **E-mail:** info@interlinkbooks.com. **Website:** www.interlinkbooks.com. Estab. 1987. Publishes hardcover and trade paperback originals. Interlink is an independent publisher of general trade adult fiction and nonfiction with an emphasis on books that have a wide appeal while also meeting high intellectual and literary standards. **Publishes 90 titles/year. 30% of books from first-time authors. 50% from unagented writers. Pays 6-8% royalty on retail price. Pays small advance.** Publishes ms 18 months after acceptance. Accepts simultaneous submissions. Responds in 3-6 months to queries. Book catalog and guidelines online.

NONFICTION Subjects include world travel, world literature, world history and politics, art, world music & dance, international cooking, children's books from around the world. Submit outline and sample chapters.

FICTION Subjects include ethnic, international. "We are looking for translated works relating to the Middle East, Africa or Latin America." No science fiction, romance, plays, erotica, fantasy, horror. Query with SASE. Submit outline, sample chapters.

TIPS "Any submissions that fit well in our publishing program will receive careful attention. A visit to our website, your local bookstore, or library to look at some of our books before you send in your submission is recommended."

INTERNATIONAL FOUNDATION OF EMPLOYEE BENEFIT PLANS

18700 W. Bluemound Rd., Brookfield WI 53045. (262)786-6700. **Fax:** (262)786-8780. **E-mail:** bookstore@ifebp.org. **Website:** www.ifebp.org. **Contact:** Kelli Kolsrud, director, information services and publications. Estab. 1954. Publishes trade paperback originals. IFEBP publishes general and technical monographs on all aspects of employee benefits—pension plans, health insurance, etc. **Publishes 6 titles/year. 15% of books from first-time authors. 80% from unagented writers. Pays 5-15% royalty on wholesale and retail price.** Publishes ms 1 year after acceptance. Responds in 3 months to queries. Book catalog online. Guidelines online.

NONFICTION Subjects limited to health care, pensions, retirement planning and employee benefits and compensation. Query with outline.

TIPS "Be aware of interests of employers and the marketplace in benefits topics, for example, pension plan changes, healthcare cost containment."

INTERNATIONAL MARINE

The McGraw-Hill Companies, 90 Mechanic St., Camden ME 04843. (207)236-4838. **Fax:** (207)236-6314. **Website:** www.internationalmarine.com. **Contact:** Acquisitions Editor. Estab. 1969. Publishes hardcover and paperback originals. International Marine publishes the best books about boats. **Publishes 50 titles/year. 500-700 mss received/year. 30% of books from first-time authors. 60% from unagented writers. Pays standard royalties based on net price. Pays advance.** Publishes ms 1 year after acceptance. Responds in 2 months to queries. Guidelines online.

IMPRINTS Ragged Mountain Press (sports and outdoor books that take you off the beaten path).

NONFICTION All books are illustrated. Material in all stages welcome. Publishes a wide range of subjects include: sea stories, seamanship, boat maintenance, etc. Query first with outline and 2-3 sample chapters. Reviews artwork/photos.

TIPS "Writers should be aware of the need for clarity, accuracy and interest. Many progress too far in the actual writing."

INTERNATIONAL PRESS

P.O. Box 502, Somerville MA 02143. (617)623-3855. **Fax:** (617)623-3101. **E-mail:** ipb-mgmt@intlpress.com. **Website:** www.intlpress.com. **Contact:** Brian Bianchini, general manager (research math and physics). Estab. 1992. Publishes hardcover originals and reprints. International Press of Boston, Inc. is an academic publishing company that welcomes book publication inquiries from prospective authors on all topics in Mathematics and Physics. International Press also publishes high-level mathematics and mathematical physics book titles and textbooks. **Publishes 12 titles/year. 200 queries received/year. 500 mss received/year. 10% of books from first-time authors. 100% from unagented writers. Pays 3-10% royalty.** Publishes ms 6 months after acceptance. Responds in 5 months to queries and proposals; 1 year to mss. Book catalog available free. Guidelines online.

NONFICTION Subjects include science. All our books will be in research mathematics. Authors need to provide ready to print latex files. Submit complete ms. Reviews artwork/photos. Send EPS files.

TIPS "Audience is PhD mathematicians, researchers and students."

INTERNATIONAL SOCIETY FOR TECHNOLOGY IN EDUCATION (ISTE)

180 W. 8th St., Suite 300, Eugene OR 97401. (541)434-8928. **E-mail:** iste@iste.org. **Website:** www.iste.org. Publishes trade paperback originals. "Currently emphasizing books on educational technology standards, curriculum integration, professional development, and assessment. De-emphasizing software how-to books." **Publishes 10 titles/year. 100 queries received/year. 40 mss received/year. 75% of books from first-time authors. 95% from unagented writers. Pays 10% royalty on retail price.** Publishes ms 6-9 months after acceptance. Accepts simultaneous submissions. Responds in 2 weeks to queries; 1 month to proposals and mss. Book catalog and guidelines online.

NONFICTION Submit proposal package, outline, sample chapters, TOC, vita. Reviews artwork/photos. Send photocopies.

TIPS "Our audience is K-12 teachers, teacher educators, technology coordinators, and school and district administrators."

INTERNATIONAL WEALTH SUCCESS

P.O. Box 186, Merrick NY 11570. (516)766-5850. **Fax:** (516)766-5919. **E-mail:** admin@iwsmoney.com. **Website:** www.iwsmoney.com. **Contact:** Tyler G. Hicks, editor. Estab. 1967. "Our mission is to publish books, newsletters, and self-study courses aimed at helping beginners and experienced business people start, and succeed in, their own small business in the fields of real estate, import-export, mail order, licensing, venture capital, financial brokerage, etc. The large number of layoffs and downsizings have made our publications of greater importance to people seeking financial independence in their own business, free of layoff threats and snarling bosses." **Publishes 10 titles/year. 100% of books from first-time authors. 100% from unagented writers. Pays 10% royalty on wholesale or retail price. Offers usual advance of $1,000, but this varies depending on author's reputation and nature of book. Buys all rights.** Publishes ms 4 months after acceptance. Responds in 1 month to queries.

NONFICTION Subjects include business, economics, financing, business success, venture capital, etc. Techniques, methods, sources for building wealth. Highly personal, how-to-do-it with plenty of case histories. Books are aimed at wealth builders and are highly sympathetic to their problems. These publications present a wide range of business opportunities while providing practical, hands-on, step-by-step instructions aimed at helping readers achieve their personal goals in as short a time as possible while adhering to ethical and professional business standards. Length: 60,000-70,000 words. Query. Reviews artwork/photos.

INTERVARSITY PRESS

P.O. Box 1400, Downers Grove IL 60515. **E-mail:** email@ivpress.com. **Website:** www.ivpress.com/submissions. **Contact:** Cindy Bunch, senior editor (IVP Books, IVP Connect, IVP Formatio, IVP Cresendo); David Congdon, associate editor (academic, reference); Dan Reid, senior editor (reference, academic); Al Hsu, senior editor (IVP Books, IVP Praxis); Andy Le Peau, editorial director (academic); Helen Lee, associate editor (IVP Books, IVP Crescendo); David McNutt, associate editor (academic, reference). Estab. 1947. Publishes hardcover originals, trade paperback and mass market paperback originals. "InterVarsity Press publishes a full line of books from an evangelical Christian perspective targeted to an open-minded audience. We serve those in the university, the church, and the world, by publishing books from an evangelical Christian perspective." **Publishes 115 titles/year. 1,000 queries received/year. 900 mss received/year. 13% of books from first-time authors. 86% from unagented writers. Pays 14-16% royalty on retail price. Outright purchase is $75-1,500. Pays negotiable advance.** Publishes ms 18 months after acceptance. Accepts simultaneous submissions. "We are unable to provide updates on the review process or personalized responses to unsolicited proposals. We regret that submissions will not be returned.". Book catalog online. Guidelines online.

IMPRINTS IVP Academic; IVP Connect; IVP Books.

NONFICTION Subjects include business, child guidance, contemporary culture, economics, ethnic, history, multicultural, philosophy, psychology, religion, science, social sciences, sociology, spirituality. "InterVarsity Press publishes a full line of books from an evangelical Christian perspective targeted to an open-minded audience. We serve those in the university, the church, and the world, by publishing books from an evangelical Christian perspective." Submit proposal that includes chapter-by-chapter summary, 2 complete sample chapters, and bio. Does not review artwork.

TIPS "The best way to submit to us is to go to a conference where one of our editors are. Networking is key. We're seeking writers who have good ideas and a presence/platform where they've been testing their ideas out (a church, university, on a prominent blog). We need authors who will bring resources to the table for helping to publicize and sell their books (speaking at seminars and conferences, writing for national magazines or newspapers, etc.)."

INTERWEAVE PRESS

201 E. Fourth St., Loveland CO 80537. (970)669-7672. **Fax:** (970)667-8317. **E-mail:** kbogert@interweave.com. **Website:** www.interweave.com. **Contact:** Kerry Bogert, acquisitions editor. Estab. 1975. Publishes hardcover and trade paperback originals. Interweave Press publishes instructive titles relating to the fiber arts and beadwork topics. **Publishes 40-45 titles/year. 60% of books from first-time authors. 90% from unagented writers.** Publishes ms 6-18 months after acceptance. Accepts simultaneous submissions. Responds in 2 months to queries. Book catalog and guidelines online.

NONFICTION Subjects limited to fiber arts (spinning, knitting, dyeing, weaving, sewing/stiching, art quilting, mixed media/collage) and jewelrymaking (beadwork, stringing, wireworking, metalsmithing). Submit outline, sample chapters. Accepts simultaneous submissions if informed of non-exclusivity. Reviews artwork/photos.

TIPS "We are looking for very clear, informally written, technically correct manuscripts, generally of a how-to nature, in our specific fiber and beadwork fields only. Our audience includes a variety of creative self-starters who appreciate inspiration and clear instruction. They are often well educated and skillful in many areas."

INVERTED-A

P.O. Box 267, Licking MO 65542. **E-mail:** amnfn@well.com. **Contact:** Aya Katz, chief editor (poetry, novels, political); Nets Katz, science editor (scientific, academic). Estab. 1985. Publishes paperback originals. Books: offset printing. Average print order: POD. Distributes through Baker & Taylor, Amazon, Bowker. **Pays 10 author's copies.** Publishes ms 1 year after acceptance. Accepts simultaneous submissions. Responds in 1 month to queries; 3 months to mss. Guidelines for SASE.

FICTION Utopian, political. Does not accept unsolicited mss. Query with SASE. Reading period open from January 2 to March 15. Accepts queries by e-mail. Include estimated word count.

TIPS "Read our books. Read the *Inverted-A Horn*. We are different. We do not follow industry trends."

IRISH ACADEMIC PRESS

8 Chapel Lane, Sallins Co. Kildare , Ireland. (353)(1)2989937. **Fax:** (353)(1)2982783. **E-mail:** info@iap.ie. **E-mail:** lisa.hyde@iap.ie. **Website:** www.iap.ie. **Contact:** Conor Graham. Estab. 1974. **Publishes 15 titles/year. Pays royalty.** Accepts simultaneous submissions. Guidelines online.

NONFICTION Subjects include art, architecture, government, politics, history, literary criticism, military, war, womens issues, womens studies, genealogy, Irish history. Does not want fiction or poetry. Query with SASE. Submit proposal package, outline, publishing history, bio, target audience, competing books, 2-3 sample chapters, SASE.

IRON GATE PUBLISHING

P.O. Box 999, Niwot CO 80544. (303)530-2551. **Fax:** (303)530-5273. **E-mail:** editor@irongate.com. **Website:** www.irongate.com. **Contact:** Dina C. Carson, publisher (how-to, genealogy, local history). Publishes hardcover and trade paperback originals. "Our readers are people who are looking for solid, how-to advice on planning reunions or self-publishing a genealogy." **Publishes 6-10 titles/year. 100 queries received/year. 20 mss received/year. 30% of books from first-time authors. 10% from unagented writers. Pays royalty on a case-by-case basis.** Publishes ms 1 year after acceptance. Accepts simultaneous submissions. Responds in 2 months to proposals. Book catalog and writer's guidelines free or online.

NONFICTION , hobbies, genealogy, local history, reunions, party planning. Query with SASE, or submit proposal package, including outline, 2 sample chapters, and marketing summary. Reviews artwork/photos. Send photocopies.

TIPS "Please look at the other books we publish and tell us in your query letter why your book would fit into our line of books."

ITALICA PRESS

595 Main St., Suite 605, New York NY 10044-0047. (917)371-0563. **E-mail:** inquiries@italicapress.com. **Website:** www.italicapress.com. **Contact:** Ronald G. Musto and Eileen Gardiner, publishers. Estab. 1985. Publishes hardcover and trade paperback originals. "Italica Press publishes English translations of modern Italian fiction and medieval and Renaissance nonfiction." **Publishes 6 titles/year. 600 queries received/year. 60 mss received/year. 5% of books from first-time authors. 100% from unagented writers. Pays 7-15% royalty on wholesale price; author's copies.** Publishes ms 1 year after acceptance. Accepts simultaneous submissions. Responds in 1 month to queries; 4 months to mss. Book catalog and guidelines online.

NONFICTION Subjects include translation. "We publish English translations of medieval and Renaissance source materials and English translations of modern Italian fiction." Query via e-mail. Reviews artwork/photos.

FICTION "First-time translators published. We would like to see translations of Italian writers who are well-known in Italy who are not yet translated for an American audience." Query via e-mail.

POETRY Poetry titles are always translations and generally dual language. Query with 10 sample translations of medieval and Renaissance Italian poets. Include cover letter, bio, and list of publications.

TIPS "We are interested in considering a wide variety of medieval and Renaissance topics (not historical fiction), and for modern works we are only interested in translations from Italian fiction by well-known Italian authors. *Only* fiction that has been previously published in Italian. A *brief* e-mail saves a lot of time. 90% of proposals we receive are completely off base—but we are very interested in things that are right on target."

JAIN PUBLISHING CO.

P.O. Box 3523, Fremont CA 94539. (510)659-8272. **E-mail:** mail@jainpub.com. **Website:** www.jainpub.com. **Contact:** M. Jain, editor-in-chief. Estab. 1989. Publishes hardcover and paperback originals and reprints. Jain Publishing Co. is a humanities and social sciences publisher that publishes college textbooks and supplements, professional and scholarly references, as well as trade books in both print and electronic formats. It also publishes in the areas of humanities and societies pertaining specifically to Asia, commonly categorized as "Asian Studies." **Publishes 8-10 titles/year. 300 queries received/year. 100% from unagented writers. Pays 5-10% royalty on net sales.** Publishes ms 1-2 years after acceptance. Responds in 3 months to mss. Book catalog and ms guidelines online.

NONFICTION Subjects include humanities, social sciences, Asian studies. Submit proposal package, publishing history. Reviews artwork/photos. Send photocopies.

ALICE JAMES BOOKS

114 Prescott St., Farmington ME 04938. (207)778-7071. **Fax:** (207)778-7766. **E-mail:** alicejamesea@alicejamesbooks.org. **Website:** www.alicejamesbooks.org. **Contact:** Alyssa Neptune, managing editor; Carey Salerno, executive director; Nicole Wakefield, senior editorial assistant. Estab. 1973. Publishes trade paperback originals. "Alice James Books is a nonprofit cooperative poetry press. The founders' objectives were to give women access to publishing and to involve authors in the publishing process. The cooperative selects mss for publication through both regional and national competitions." **Publishes 6 titles/year. Approximately 1,000 mss received/year. 50% of books from first-time authors. 100% from unagented writers. Pays through competition awards.** Publishes ms 1 year after acceptance. Accepts simultaneous submissions. Responds promptly to queries; 4 months to mss. Book catalog online. Guidelines online.

POETRY "Alice James Books is a nonprofit cooperative poetry press. The founders' objectives were to give women access to publishing and to involve authors in the publishing process. The cooperative selects mss for publication through both regional and national competitions." Does not want children's poetry or light verse.

TIPS "Send SASE for contest guidelines or check website. Do not send work without consulting current guidelines."

JEWISH LIGHTS PUBLISHING

LongHill Partners, Inc., Sunset Farm Offices, Rt. 4, P.O. Box 237, Woodstock VT 05091. (802)457-4000. **Fax:** (802)457-4004. **Website:** www.jewishlights.com. **Contact:** Acquisitions Editor. Estab. 1990. Publishes hardcover and trade paperback originals, trade paperback reprints. "Jewish Lights publishes books for people of all faiths and all backgrounds who yearn for books that attract, engage, educate and spiritually inspire. Our authors are at the forefront of spiritual thought and deal with the quest for the self and for meaning in life by drawing on the Jewish wisdom tradition. Our books cover topics including history, spirituality, life cycle, children, self-help, recovery, theology and philosophy. We do not publish autobiography, biography, fiction, haggadot, poetry or cookbooks. At this point we plan to do only two books for children annually, and one will be for younger children (ages 4-10)." **Publishes 30 titles/year. 50% of books from first-time authors. 75% from unagented writers. Pays authors royalty of 10% of revenue received; 15% royalty for subsequent printings.** Publishes ms 1 year after acceptance. Accepts simultaneous submissions. Responds in 3 months to queries. Book catalog and guidelines online.

NONFICTION Subjects include business, economics, with spiritual slant, finding spiritual meaning in one's work, health, medicine, healing/recovery, wellness, aging, life cycle, history, nature, environment, philosophy, religion, theology, spirituality, and inspiration, women's issues, women's studies. Picture book, young readers, middle readers: activity books, spirituality. "We do *not* publish haggadot, biography, poetry, or cookbooks." Query. Reviews artwork/photos. Send photocopies.

FICTION Picture books, young readers, middle readers: spirituality. "We are not interested in anything other than spirituality." Query with outline/synopsis and 2 sample chapters; submit complete ms for picture books.

TIPS "We publish books for all faiths and backgrounds that also reflect the Jewish wisdom tradition. Explain in your cover letter why you're submitting your project to us in particular. Make sure you know what we publish."

JIST PUBLISHING

875 Montreal Way, St. Paul MN 55102. **E-mail:** info@jist.com. **Website:** www.jist.com. Estab. 1981. Publishes hardcover and trade paperback originals. "Our purpose is to provide quality job search, career development, occupational, and life skills information, products, and services that help people manage and improve their lives and careers-and the lives of others. Publishes practical, self-directed tools and training materials that are used in employment and training, education, and business settings. Whether reference books, trade books, assessment tools, workbooks, or videos, JIST products foster self-directed job-search attitudes and behaviors." **Publishes 60 titles/year. Receives 40 submissions/year. 25% of books from first-time authors. 75% from unagented writers. Pays 8-10% royalty on net receipts.** Accepts simultaneous submissions. Responds in 6 months. Book catalog and guidelines online.

NONFICTION Subjects include business, economics, education. "We want text/workbook formats that would be useful in a school or other institutional setting. We also publish trade titles for all reading levels. Will consider books for professional staff and educators, appropriate software and videos." Submit proposal package, including outline, 1 sample chapter, and author resume, competitive analysis, marketing ideas. Does not review artwork/photos.

TIPS "Our audiences are students, job seekers, and career changers of all ages and occupations who want to find good jobs quickly and improve their futures. We sell materials through the trade as well as to institutional markets like schools, colleges, and one-stop career centers."

THE JOHNS HOPKINS UNIVERSITY PRESS

2715 N. Charles St., Baltimore MD 21218. (410)516-6900. **Fax:** (410)516-6968. **E-mail:** gb@press.jhu.edu. **Website:** www.press.jhu.edu. **Contact:** Jacqueline C. Wehmueller, executive editor (consumer health, psychology and psychiatry, and history of medicine; jcw@press.jhu.edu); Matthew McAdam, editor (mxm@jhu.press.edu); Robert J. Brugger, senior acquisitions editor (American history; rjb@press.jhu.edu); Vincent J. Burke, exec. editor (biology; vjb@press.jhu.edu). Estab. 1878. Publishes hardcover originals and reprints, and trade paperback reprints. **Publishes 140 titles/year. Pays royalty.** Publishes ms 1 year after acceptance.

NONFICTION Subjects include government, politics, health, medicine, history, humanities, literary criticism, regional, religion, science. Submit proposal package, outline, 1 sample chapter, CV. Reviews artwork/photos. Send photocopies.

POETRY "One of the largest American university presses, Johns Hopkins publishes primarily scholarly books and journals. We do, however, publish short fiction and poetry in the series Johns Hopkins: Poetry and Fiction, edited by John Irwin."

JOHNSON BOOKS

Imprint of Big Earth Publishing, 3005 Center Green Dr., Suite 225, Boulder CO 80301. (303)443-9766. **Fax:** (303)443-9687. **E-mail:** books@bigearthpublishing.com. **Website:** bigearthpublishing.com/johnson-books. Estab. 1979. Publishes hardcover and paperback originals and reprints. Johnson Books specializes in books on the American West, primarily outdoor, useful titles that will have strong national appeal. **Publishes 20-25 titles/year. 30% of books from first-time authors. 90% from unagented writers. Royalties vary.** Publishes ms 1 year after acceptance. Responds in 3 months to queries. Book catalog for 9 x 12 SAE with 5 first-class stamps.

NONFICTION Subjects include anthropology, archeology, history, nature, environment, environmental subjects, recreation, outdoor, regional, science, travel, regional, general nonfiction. "We are primarily interested in books for the informed popular market, though we will consider vividly written scholarly works. Looks for good writing, thorough research, professional presentation, and appropriate style. Marketing suggestions from writers are helpful." Submit outline/synopsis and 3 sample chapters.

⊘ JONATHAN DAVID PUBLISHERS, INC.

68-22 Eliot Ave., Middle Village NY 11379. (718)456-8611. **Fax:** (718)894-2818. **Website:** www.jdbooks.com. **Contact:** David Kolatch, editorial director. Estab. 1948. Publishes hardcover and trade paperback originals and reprints. Jonathan David publishes popular Judaica. **Publishes 20-25 titles/year. 50% of books from first-time authors. 90% from unagented writers. Pays royalty, or makes outright purchase.** Publishes ms 18 months after acceptance. Responds in 1-2 months. Book catalog and guidelines online.

NONFICTION Subjects include cooking, foods, nutrition, creative nonfiction, ethnic, multicultural, religion, sports. Unsolicited mss are not being accepted at this time.

JOSSEY-BASS

John Wiley & Sons, Inc., One Montgomery St., San Francisco CA 94104. **Website:** www.wiley.com. Jossey-Bass is an imprint of Wiley, specializing in books and periodicals for thoughtful professionals and researchers in the areas of business and management, leadership, human resource development, education, health, psychology, religion, and the public and nonprofit sectors. **Publishes 250 titles/year. Pays variable royalties. Pays occasional advance.** Publishes ms 1 year after acceptance. Accepts simultaneous submissions. Responds in 2-3 months to queries. Guidelines online.

NONFICTION Subjects include business, economics, education, health, medicine, money, finance, psychology, religion. Jossey-Bass publishes first-time and unagented authors. Publishes books on topics of interest to a wide range of readers: business and management, conflict resolution, mediation and negotiation, K-12 education, higher and adult education, healthcare management, psychology/behavioral healthcare, nonprofit and public management, religion, human resources and training. Also publishes 25 periodicals. See guidelines online.

JOURNEYFORTH

Imprint of BJU Press, 1700 Wade Hampton Blvd., Greenville SC 29614. (864)242-5100, ext. 4350. **Fax:** (864)298-0268. **E-mail:** journeyforth@bjupress.com. **Website:** www.journeyforth.com. Estab. 1974. Publishes paperback originals. "Small independent publisher of trustworthy novels and biographies for readers pre-school through high school from a conservative Christian perspective, Christian living books, and Bible studies for adults." **Publishes 25 titles/year. 10% of books from first-time authors. 8% from unagented writers. Pays royalty.** Publishes ms 12-18 months after acceptance. Does accept simultaneous submissions. Responds in 1 month to queries; 3 months to mss. Book catalog available free. Guidelines online.

NONFICTION Subjects include animals, contemporary culture, creative nonfiction, environment, history, music, nature, religion, spirituality, sports, young adult. Christian living, Bible studies, church and ministry, church history. "We produce books for the adult Christian market that are from a conservative Christian worldview."

FICTION Subjects include adventure, historical, animal, easy-to-read, series, mystery, sports, children's/juvenile, suspense, young adult, western. "Our fiction is all based on a moral and Christian worldview." Does not want short stories. Submit 5 sample chapters, synopsis, SASE.

TIPS "Study the publisher's guidelines. No picture books and no submissions by e-mail."

JUDAICA PRESS

123 Ditmas Ave., Brooklyn NY 11218. (718)972-6200. **Fax:** (718)972-6204. **E-mail:** submissions@judaicapress.com. **Website:** www.judaicapress.com. Estab. 1963. Publishes hardcover and trade paperback originals and reprints. "We cater to the Orthodox Jewish market." **Publishes 12 titles/year.** Responds in 3 months to queries. Book catalog in print and online.

NONFICTION Subjects include religion, Bible commentary, prayer, holidays, life cycle. Looking for Orthodox Judaica in all genres. Submit ms with SASE.

JUDSON PRESS

P.O. Box 851, Valley Forge PA 19482. (610)768-2127. **Fax:** (610)768-2441. **E-mail:** acquisitions@judsonpress.com. **Website:** www.judsonpress.com. Estab. 1824. Publishes hardcover and paperback originals. "Our audience is comprised primarily of pastors, leaders, and Christians who seek a more fulfilling personal spiritual life and want to serve God in their churches, communities, and relationships. We have a large African-American readership. Currently emphasizing small group resources. De-emphasizing biography, children's books, poetry." **Publishes 12-15 titles/year. 750 queries received/year. Pays royalty or makes outright purchase.** Publishes ms 12 months after acceptance. Accepts simultaneous submissions. Responds in 3-6 months to queries. Book catalog for 9 x 12 SAE with 4 first-class stamps. Guidelines online.

NONFICTION Subjects include multicultural, religion. Adult religious nonfiction of 30,000-80,000 words. Query with SASE or by e-mail. Submit annotated outline, sample chapters, CV, competing titles, marketing plan.

TIPS "Writers have the best chance selling us practical books assisting clergy or laypersons in their ministry and personal lives. Our audience consists of Protestant church leaders and members. Be informed about the market's needs and related titles. Be clear about your audience, and be practical in your focus. Books on multicultural issues are very welcome. Also seeking books that respond to real (felt) needs of pastors and churches."

⊘ JUPITER GARDENS PRESS

Jupiter Gardens, LLC, PO Box 191, Grimes IA 50111. **Website:** www.jupitergardens.com. **Contact:** Mary Wilson, publisher. Estab. 2007. Format publishes in trade paperback originals and reprints; electronic originals and reprints. **Publishes 30+ titles/year. Pays 40% royalty on retail price.** Publishes ms 4 months after acceptance. Accepts simultaneous submissions. Responds in 1 month on proposals; 2 months on mss. Catalog online. Guidelines online.

NONFICTION Subjects include alternative lifestyles, animals, astrology, environment, gay, health, lesbian, medicine, nature, psychic, religion, sex, spirituality, womens issues, world affairs, young adult, romance, science fiction, fantasy, and metaphysical fiction & nonfiction. "We only publish metaphysical/New Age nonfiction, or nonfiction related to science fiction and fantasy." Use online form. Currently closed to submissions.

FICTION Subjects include fantasy, gay, lesbian, occult, religious, romance, science fiction, spiritual, young adult, New Age/metaphysical. "We only publish romance (all sub-genres), science fiction & fantasy & metaphysical fiction. Our science fiction and fantasy covers a wide variety of topics, such as feminist fantasy, or more hard science fiction and fantasy which looks at the human condition. Our young adult imprint, Jupiter Storm, with thought provoking reads that explore the full range of speculative fiction, includes science fiction or fantasy and metaphysical fiction. These readers would enjoy edgy contemporary works. Our romance readers love seeing a couple, no matter the gender, overcome obstacles and grow in order to find love. Like our readers, we believe that love can come in many forms." Use online submission form. Currently closed to submissions.

TIPS "No matter which line you're submitting to, know your genre and your readership. We publish a diverse catalog, and we're passionate about our main focus. We want romance that takes your breath away and leaves you with that warm feeling that love does conquer all. Our science fiction takes place in wild and alien worlds, and our fantasy transports readers to mythical realms and finds strange worlds within our own. And our metaphysical non-fiction will help readers gain new skills and awareness for the coming age. We want authors who engage with their readers and who aren't afraid to use social media to connect. Read and follow our submission guidelines."

KAEDEN BOOKS

P.O. Box 16190, Rocky River OH 44116. **Website:** www.kaeden.com. Estab. 1986. Publishes paperback originals. "Children's book publisher for education K-3 market: reading stories, fiction/nonfiction, chapter books, science, and social studies materials." **Publishes 12-20 titles/year. 1,000 mss received/year. 30% of books from first-time authors. 95% from unagented writers. Work purchased outright from authors. Pays royalties to previous authors.** Publishes ms 6-9 months after acceptance. Accepts simultaneous submissions. Responds only if interested. Book catalog and guidelines online.

NONFICTION Subjects include animals, creative nonfiction, science, social sciences. Mss should have interesting topics and information presented in language comprehensible to young students. Content should be supported with details and accurate facts. Submit complete ms. "Can be as minimal as 25 words for the earliest reader or as much as 2,000 words for the fluent reader. Beginning chapter books are welcome. Our readers are in kindergarten to third grade, so vocabulary and sentence structure must be appropriate for young readers. Make sure that all language used in the story is of an appropriate level for the students to read independently. Sentences should be complete and grammatically correct." Reviews artwork/photos. Send photocopies.

FICTION Subjects include adventure, fantasy, historical, humor, mystery, short story collections, sports, suspense. "We are looking for stories with humor, surprise endings, and interesting characters that will appeal to children in kindergarten through third grade." No sentence fragments. Please do not submit: queries, ms summaries, or résumés, mss that stereotype or demean individuals or groups, mss that present violence as acceptable behavior. Submit complete ms. "Can be as minimal as 25 words for the earliest reader or as much as 2,000 words for the fluent reader. Beginning chapter books are welcome. Our readers are in kindergarten to third grade, so vocabulary and sentence structure must be appropriate for young readers. Make sure that all language used in the story is of an appropriate level for the students to read independently. Sentences should be complete and grammatically correct."

TIPS "Our audience ranges from kindergarten-third grade school children. We are an educational publisher. We are particularly interested in humorous stories with surprise endings and beginning chapter books."

KALMBACH PUBLISHING CO.

21027 Crossroads Circle, P.O. Box 1612, Waukesha WI 53187. (262)796-8776. **Fax:** (262)798-6468. **Website:** www.kalmbach.com. Estab. 1934. Publishes paperback originals and reprints. **Publishes 40-50 titles/year. 50% of books from first-time authors. 99% from unagented writers. Pays 7% royalty on net receipts. Pays $1,500 advance.** Publishes ms 18 months after acceptance. Responds in 2 months to queries.

NONFICTION "Focus on beading, wirework, and one-of-a-kind artisan creations for jewelry-making and crafts and in the railfan, model railroading, plastic modeling and toy train collecting/operating hobbies. Kalmbach publishes reference materials and how-to publications for hobbyists, jewelry-makers, and crafters." Query with 2-3 page detailed outline, sample chapter with photos, drawings, and how-to text. Reviews artwork/photos.

TIPS "Our how-to books are highly visual in their presentation. Any author who wants to publish with us must be able to furnish good photographs and rough drawings before we'll consider his or her book."

Ⓐ KANE/MILLER BOOK PUBLISHERS

4901 Morena Blvd., Suite 213, San Diego CA 92117. (858)456-0540. **Fax:** (858)456-9641. **E-mail:** submissions@kanemiller.com. **Website:** www.kanemiller.com. **Contact:** Editorial Department. Estab. 1985. "Kane/Miller Book Publishers is a division of EDC Publishing, specializing in award-winning children's books from around the world. Our books bring the children of the world closer to each other, sharing stories and ideas, while exploring cultural differences and similarities. Although we continue to look for books from other countries, we are now actively seeking works that convey cultures and communities within the US. We are looking for picture book fiction and nonfiction on those subjects that may be defined as particularly American: sports such as baseball, historical events, American biographies, American folk tales, etc. We are committed to expanding our early and middlegrade fiction list. We're interested in great stories with engaging characters in all genres (mystery, fantasy, adventure, historical, etc.) and, as with picture books, especially those with particularly American subjects." Responds in 90 days to queries.

NONFICTION Subjects include Americana, history, sports, young adult.

FICTION Subjects include adventure, fantasy, historical, juvenile, mystery, picture books. Picture Books: concept, contemporary, health, humor, multicultural. Young Readers: contemporary, multicultural, suspense. Middle Readers: contemporary, humor, multicultural, suspense.

TIPS "We like to think that a child reading a Kane/Miller book will see parallels between his own life and what might be the unfamiliar setting and characters of the story. And that by seeing how a character who is somehow or in some way dissimilar—an outsider—finds a way to fit comfortably into a culture or community or situation while maintaining a healthy sense of self and self-dignity, she might be empowered to do the same."

KAR-BEN PUBLISHING

Lerner Publishing Group, 241 First Ave. N, Minneapolis MN 55401. (612)215-6229. **Fax:** 612-332-7615. **E-mail:** Editorial@Karben.com. **Website:** www.karben.com. Estab. 1974. Publishes hardcover, trade paperback and electronic originals. **Publishes 10-15 titles/year. 800 mss received/year. 20% of books from first-time authors. 70% from unagented writers. Pays 5% royalty on NET sale. Pays $500-2,500 advance.** Publishes book Most manuscripts published within 2 years. after acceptance of ms. Accepts simultaneous submissions. Responds in 6 weeks. Book catalog available online; free upon request. Guidelines available online.

NONFICTION Subjects include Jewish content children's books only. "In addition to traditional Jewish-themed stories about Jewish holidays, history, folktales and other subjects, we especially seek stories that reflect the rich diversity of the contemporary Jewish community." Picture books, young readers: activity books, arts/crafts, biography, careers, concept, cooking, history, how-to, multicultural, religion, social issues, special needs; must be of Jewish interest. No textbooks, games, or educational materials. Submit completed ms. Reviews artwork separately. Works with 10-12 illustrators/year. Prefers four-color art in any medium that is scannable. Reviews illustration packages from artists. Submit sample of art or online portfolio (no originals).

FICTION Subjects include juvenile; Jewish content only. "We seek picture book mss of about 1,000 words on Jewish-themed topics for children." Picture books: Adventure, concept, folktales, history, humor, multicultural, religion, special needs; must be on a Jewish theme. Average word length: picture books–1,000. Recently published titles: *The Count's Hanukkah Countdown, Sammy Spider's First Book of Jewish Holidays, The Cats of Ben Yehuda Street.* Submit full ms. Picture books only.

TIPS "Authors: Do a literature search to make sure similar title doesn't already exist. Illustrators: Look at our online catalog for a sense of what we like—bright colors and lively composition."

KAYA PRESS

USC ASE, 3620 S. Vermont Ave. KAP 462, Los Angeles CA 90089. (213)740-2285. **E-mail:** info@kaya.com. **Website:** www.kaya.com. **Contact:** Sunyoung Lee, editor. Publishes hardcover originals and trade paperback originals and reprints. Kaya is an independent literary press dedicated to the publication of innovative literature from the Asian diaspora. "We are looking for innovative writers with a commitment to quality literature." Accepts simultaneous submissions. Responds in 6 months to mss. Book catalog available free. Guidelines online.

NONFICTION Subjects include multicultural. Submit proposal package, outline, sample chapters, previous publications, SASE. Reviews artwork/photos. Send photocopies.

FICTION Submit 2-4 sample chapters, clips, SASE.

POETRY Submit complete ms.

TIPS "Audience is people interested in a high standard of literature and who are interested in breaking down easy approaches to multicultural literature."

KELSEY STREET PRESS

Poetry by Women, 2824 Kelsey St., Berkeley CA 94705. **E-mail:** amber@kelseyst.com. **Website:** www.kelseyst.com. Estab. 1974. Hardcover and trade paperback originals and electronic originals. "A Berkeley, California press publishing collaborations between women poets and artists. Many of the press's collaborations focus on a central theme or conceit, like the sprawl and spectacle of New York in *Arcade* by Erica Hunt and Alison Saar."

FICTION Subjects include experimental, gay, lesbian, horror, multicultural, mystery, poetry, prose, women of color.

POETRY Query.

KENSINGTON PUBLISHING CORP.

850 Third Ave., 16th Floor, New York NY 10022. (212)407-1500. **Fax:** (212)935-0699. **E-mail:** jscognamiglio@kensingtonbooks.com. **Website:** www.kensingtonbooks.com. **Contact:** John Scognamiglio, editorial director, fiction (historical romance, Regency romance, women's contemporary fiction, gay and

lesbian fiction and nonfiction, mysteries, suspense, mainstream fiction); Michaela Hamilton, editor-in-chief, Citadel Press (thrillers, mysteries, mainstream fiction, crime, current events); Selena James, executive editor, Dafina Books (African American fiction and nonfiction, inspirational, young adult, romance); Peter Senftleben, assistant editor (mainstream fiction, women's contemporary fiction, gay and lesbian fiction, mysteries, suspense, thrillers, romantic suspense, paranormal romance). Estab. 1975. Publishes hardcover and trade paperback originals, mass market paperback originals and reprints. "Kensington focuses on profitable niches and uses aggressive marketing techniques to support its books." **Publishes over 500 titles/year. 5,000 queries received/year. 2,000 mss received/year. 10% of books from first-time authors. Pays 6-15% royalty on retail price. Makes outright purchase. Pays $2,000 and up advance.** Publishes ms 9-12 months after acceptance. Accepts simultaneous submissions. Responds in 1 month to queries and proposals; 4 months to mss. Book catalog and guidelines online.

NONFICTION Subjects include alternative, Americana, animals, business, economics, child guidance, contemporary culture, cooking, foods, nutrition, gay, lesbian, health, medicine, history, hobbies, memoirs, military, war, money, finance, multicultural, nature, environment, philosophy, psychology, recreation, regional, sex, sports, travel, crime, pop culture. Query.

FICTION Subjects include ethnic, gay, lesbian, historical, horror, mainstream, multicultural, mystery, occult, romance, contemporary, historical, regency, suspense, western, epic, thrillers, women's. No science fiction/fantasy, experimental fiction, business texts or children's titles. Query.

TIPS "Agented submissions only, except for submissions to romance lines. For those lines, query with SASE or submit proposal package including 3 sample chapters, synopsis."

KENT STATE UNIVERSITY PRESS

P.O. Box 5190, 1118 University Library, 1125 Risman Dr., Kent OH 44242. **Fax:** (330)672-3104. **E-mail:** ksupress@kent.edu. **Website:** www.kentstateuniversitypress.com. **Contact:** Joyce Harrison, acquiring editor. Estab. 1965. Publishes hardcover and paperback originals and some reprints. "Kent State publishes primarily scholarly works and titles of regional interest. Currently emphasizing US history, US literary criticism." **Publishes 30-35 titles/year. Nonauthor subsidy publishes 20% of books. Standard minimum book contract on net sales.** Responds in 4 months to queries. Book catalog available free.

NONFICTION Subjects include anthropology, archeology, art, architecture, history, language, literature, literary criticism, regional, crime, literary criticism, material culture, textile/fashion studies, US foreign relations. "Especially interested in scholarly works in history (US and world) and US literary studies of high quality, any titles of regional interest for Ohio, scholarly biographies and general nonfiction. Send a letter of inquiry before submitting mss. Decisions based on in-house readings and 2 by outside scholars in the field of study." Please, no faxes, phone calls, or e-mail submissions.

KIDS CAN PRESS

25 Dockside Dr., Toronto ON M5A 0B5, Canada. (416)479-7000. **Fax:** (416)960-5437. **Website:** www.kidscanpress.com. **Contact:** Corus Quay, acquisitions. Estab. 1973. Publishes ms 18-24 months after acceptance. Responds in 6 months only if interesed.

Kids Can Press is currently accepting unsolicited mss from Canadian adult authors only.

NONFICTION Picture books: activity books, animal, arts/crafts, biography, careers, concept, health, history, hobbies, how-to, multicultural, nature/environment, science, social issues, special needs, sports. Young readers: activity books, animal, arts/crafts, biography, careers, concept, history, hobbies, how-to, multicultural. Middle readers: cooking, music/dance. Average word length: picture books 500-1,250; young readers 750-2,000; middle readers 5,000-15,000. Submit outline/synopsis and 2-3 sample chapters. For picture books submit complete ms.

FICTION Picture books, young readers: concepts. "We do not accept young adult fiction or fantasy novels for any age." Adventure, animal, contemporary, folktales, history, humor, multicultural, nature/environment, special needs, sports, suspense/mystery. Average word length: picture books 1,000-2,000; young readers 750-1,500; middle readers 10,000-15,000; young adults over 15,000. Submit outline/synopsis and 2-3 sample chapters. For picture books submit complete ms.

KIRKBRIDE BIBLE CO., INC.

1102 Deloss St., Indianapolis IN 46203. (800)428-4385. **Fax:** (317)633-1444. **E-mail:** info@kirkbride.

com. **Website:** www.kirkbride.com. Estab. 1915. Publishes Thompson Chain-Reference Bible hardcover originals and quality leather bindings styles and translations of the Bible. Types of books include reference and religious. Specializes in reference and study material.

DENIS KITCHEN PUBLISHING CO., LLC

P.O. Box 2250, Amherst MA 01004. (413)259-1627. **Fax:** (413)259-1812. **E-mail:** help@deniskitchen.com. **Website:** www.deniskitchen.com. **Contact:** Denis Kitchen, publisher. Publishes hardcover and trade paperback originals and reprints. **Publishes 4 titles/year. 15% of books from first-time authors. 50% from unagented writers. Pays 6-10% royalty on retail price. Occasionally makes deals based on percentage of wholesale if idea and/or bulk of work is done in-house. Pays $1-5,000 advance.** Publishes ms 9-12 months after acceptance. Responds in 4-6 weeks.

This publisher strongly discourages e-mail submissions.

NONFICTION Query with SASE. Submit proposal package, outline, illustrative matter. Submit complete ms. Reviews artwork/photos. Send photocopies and transparencies.

FICTION Subjects include adventure, erotica, historical, horror, humor, literary, mystery, occult, science fiction, only if in graphic novel form. "We do not want pure fiction. We seek cartoonists or writer/illustrator teams who can tell compelling stories with a combination of words and pictures." No pure fiction (meaning text only). Query with SASE. Submit sample illustrations/comic pages. Submit complete ms.

TIPS "Our audience is readers who embrace the graphic novel revolution, who appreciate historical comic strips and books, and those who follow popular and alternative culture. We like to discover new talent. The artist who has a day job but a great idea is encouraged to contact us. The pop culture historian who has a new take on an important figure is likewise encouraged. We have few preconceived notions about manuscripts or ideas, though we are decidedly selective. Historically, we have published many first-time authors and artists, some of whom developed into award-winning creators with substantial followings. Artists or illustrators who do not have confidence in their writing should send us self-promotional postcards (our favorite way of spotting new talent)."

KNOPF

Imprint of Random House, 1745 Broadway, New York NY 10019. **Fax:** (212)940-7390. **Website:** knopfdoubleday.com/imprint/knopf. **Contact:** The editors. Estab. 1915. Publishes hardcover and paperback originals. **Publishes 200 titles/year. Royalties vary. Offers advance.** Publishes ms 1 year after acceptance. Responds in 2-6 months to queries.

NONFICTION Usually only accepts mss submitted by agents. However, writers may submit sample 25-50 pages with SASE.

FICTION Publishes book-length fiction of literary merit by known or unknown writers. Length: 40,000-150,000 words. Usually only accepts mss submitted by agents. However, writers may submit sample 25-50 pages with SASE.

KNOX ROBINSON PUBLISHING

244 Fifth Ave., Suite 1861, New York NY 10001. **E-mail:** subs@knoxrobinsonpublishing.com. **Website:** www.knoxrobinsonpublishing.com. **Contact:** Dana Celeste Robinson, managing director (historical fiction, historical romance, fantasy). Estab. 2010. Knox Robinson Publishing started as an international, independent, specialist publisher of historical fiction, historical romance and fantasy. Now open to well-written literature in all genres. **Publishes 5 titles/year. Pays royalty.** Accepts simultaneous submissions. Responds in 2 months to submissions of first 3 chapters. "We do not accept proposals.". Guidelines online.

NONFICTION Subjects include history, humanities, religion, general nonfiction, scholarly, history monographs. "Our goal is to publish history books, monographs and historical fiction that satisfies history buffs and encourages general readers to learn more." Submit first 3 chapters and author questionnaire found on website. Reviews artwork/photos. Send photocopies. Does not accept printed submissions; electronic only.

FICTION Subjects include adventure, contemporary, fantasy, historical, horror, literary, mainstream, romance, science fiction. "We are seeking historical fiction featuring obscure historical figures." Submit first 3 chapters and author questionnaire found on website.

KRAUSE PUBLICATIONS

A Division of F+W Media, Inc., 700 E. State St., Iola WI 54990. (715)445-2214. **Fax:** (715)445-4087. **Website:** www.krausebooks.com. **Contact:** Paul Kennedy (antiques and collectibles, music, sports, militaria, humor, numismatics); Corrina Peterson (firearms);

Chris Berens (outdoors); Brian Earnest (automotive). Publishes hardcover and trade paperback originals. "We are the world's largest hobby and collectibles publisher." **Publishes 80 titles/year. 200 queries received/year. 150 mss received/year. 50% of books from first-time authors. 95% from unagented writers. Pays advance. Photo budget.** Publishes ms 18 months after acceptance. Responds in 3 months to proposals; 2 months to mss. Book catalog for free or on website. Guidelines available free upon request.

NONFICTION Submit proposal package, including outline, TOC, a sample chapter, and letter explaining your project's unique contributions. Reviews artwork/photos. Accepts only digital photography. Send sample photos.

TIPS Audience consists of serious hobbyists. "Your work should provide a unique contribution to the special interest."

⊘ KREGEL PUBLICATIONS

2450 Oak Industrial Dr. NE, Grand Rapids MI 49505. (616)451-4775. **Fax:** (616)451-9330. **E-mail:** kregelbooks@kregel.com. **Website:** www.kregelpublications.com. **Contact:** Dennis R. Hillman, publisher. Estab. 1949. Publishes hardcover and trade paperback originals and reprints. "Our mission as an evangelical Christian publisher is to provide—with integrity and excellence—trusted, Biblically based resources that challenge and encourage individuals in their Christian lives. Works in theology and Biblical studies should reflect the historic, orthodox Protestant tradition." **Publishes 90 titles/year. 20% of books from first-time authors. 35% from unagented writers. Pays royalty on wholesale price. Pays negotiable advance.** Publishes ms 16 months after acceptance. Guidelines online.

NONFICTION "We serve evangelical Christian readers and those in career Christian service." Finds works through The Writer's Edge and Christian Manuscript Submissions ms screening services.

FICTION Subjects include religious, children's, general, inspirational, mystery/suspense, relationships, young adult. Fiction should be geared toward the evangelical Christian market. Wants books with fast-paced, contemporary storylines presenting a strong Christian message in an engaging, entertaining style. Finds works through The Writer's Edge and Christian Manuscript Submissions ms screening services.

TIPS "Our audience consists of conservative, evangelical Christians, including pastors and ministry students."

KRIEGER PUBLISHING CO.

P.O. Box 9542, Melbourne FL 32902-9542. (321)724-9542. **Fax:** (321)951-3671. **E-mail:** info@krieger-publishing.com. **Website:** www.krieger-publishing.com. **Contact:** Sharan B. Merriam and Ronald M. Cervero, series editor (adult education); David E. Kyvig, series director (local history); James B. Gardner, series editor (public history). Also publishes in the fields of natural sciences, history and space sciences. Estab. 1969. Publishes hardcover and paperback originals and reprints. "We are a short-run niche publisher providing accurate and well-documented scientific and technical titles for text and reference use, college level and higher." **Publishes 30 titles/year. 30% of books from first-time authors. 100% from unagented writers. Pays royalty on net price.** Publishes ms 9-18 months after acceptance. Responds in 3 months to queries. Book catalog available free.

IMPRINTS Anvil Series; Orbit Series; Public History; Professional Practices in Adult Education and Lifelong Learning Series.

NONFICTION Subjects include agriculture, animals, education, adult, history, nature, environment, science, space, herpetology. Query with SASE. Reviews artwork/photos.

KWELA BOOKS

Imprint of NB Publishers, P.O. Box 6525, Roggebaai 8012, South Africa. (27)(21)406-3605. **Fax:** (27)(21)406-3712. **E-mail:** kwela@kwela.com. **Website:** www.kwela.com. Estab. 1994.

NONFICTION Subjects include ethnic, contemporary culture, history, memoirs, social sciences.

FICTION Subjects include literary.

LAKE CLAREMONT PRESS

P.O. Box 711, Chicago IL 60690. (312)226-8400. **Fax:** (312)226-8420. **E-mail:** sharon@lakeclaremont.com. **Website:** www.lakeclaremont.com. **Contact:** Sharon Woodhouse, publisher. Estab. 1994. Publishes trade paperback originals. "We specialize in nonfiction books on the Chicago area and its history, particularly by authors with a passion or organizations with a mission." **Publishes 2-3 titles/year. 250 queries received/year. 100 mss received/year. 50% of books from first-time authors. 100% from unagented writers. Pays 10-15% royalty on net sales. Pays $500-1,000 ad-**

vance. Publishes ms 12-18 months after acceptance. Accepts simultaneous submissions. Responds in 1 month to queries; 2 months to proposals; 2-6 months to mss. Book catalog online.

NONFICTION Subjects include Americana, ethnic, history, nature, environment, regional, travel, women's issues, film/cinema/stage (regional)—as long as it is primarily a Chicago book. Query with SASE, or submit proposal package, including outline and 2 sample chapters, or submit complete ms (e-mail queries and proposals preferred).

TIPS "Please include a market analysis in proposals (who would buy this book and where) and an analysis of similar books available for different regions. Please know what else is out there."

LANGMARC PUBLISHING

P.O. Box 90488, Austin TX 78709-0488. (512)394-0989. **Fax:** (512)394-0829. **E-mail:** langmarc@booksails.com. **Website:** www.langmarc.com. **Contact:** Lois Qualben, president (inspirational). Publishes trade paperback originals. **Publishes 3-5 titles/year. 150 queries received/year. 80 mss received/year. 60% of books from first-time authors. 80% from unagented writers. Pays 14% royalty on sales price.** Publishes ms 8-14 months after acceptance. Accepts simultaneous submissions. Responds in 3 months to queries. Book catalog available free. Guidelines online.

NONFICTION Subjects include child guidance, education. Query with SASE. Reviews artwork/photos. Send photocopies.

LAPWING PUBLICATIONS

1 Ballysillan Dr., Belfast BT14 8HQ, Northern Ireland. (44)2890-500-796. **Fax:** (44)2890-295-800. **E-mail:** lapwing.poetry@ntlworld.com. **Website:** www.lapwingpoetry.com. **Contact:** Dennis Greig, editor. Estab. 1989. **Pays 20 author's copies, no royalties.** Responds to queries in 1 month; mss in 2 months.

Lapwing will produce work only if and when resources to do so are available.

POETRY Lapwing publishes "emerging Irish poets and poets domiciled in Ireland, plus the new work of a suitable size by established Irish writers. Non-Irish poets are also published. Poets based in continental Europe have become a major feature. Emphasis on first collections preferrably not larger than 80 pages. "Submit 6 poems in the first instance; depending on these, an invitation to submit more may follow." Considers simultaneous submissions. Accepts e-mail submissions in body of message or in DOC format. Cover letter is required. "All submissions receive a first reading. If these poems have minor errors or faults, the writer is advised. Those which appeal at first reading are retained, and a conditional offer is sent." Often comments on rejected poems. "After initial publication, irrespective of the quantity, the work will be permanently available using 'print-on-demand' production; such publications may not always be printed exactly as the original, although the content will remain the same."

TIPS "We are unable to accept new work from beyond mainland Europe and the British Isles due to delivery costs."

LARSON PUBLICATIONS

4936 Rt. 414, Burdett NY 14818-9729. (607)546-9342. **Fax:** (607)546-9344. **Website:** www.larsonpublications.com. **Contact:** Paul Cash, director. Estab. 1982. Publishes hardcover and trade paperback originals. **Publishes 4-5 titles/year. 5% of books from first-time authors. Pays variable royalty. Seldom offers advance.** Publishes ms 1-2 years after acceptance. Accepts simultaneous submissions. Responds in 8 weeks to queries. Visit website for book catalog. Guidelines online.

NONFICTION Subjects include philosophy, psychology, religion, spirituality. Query with SASE and outline. Use snail mail.

TIPS "We look for original studies of comparative spiritual philosophy or personal fruits of independent (transsectarian viewpoint) spiritual research/practice."

LEAPFROG PRESS

Box 505, Fredonia NY 14063. (508)274-2710. **E-mail:** leapfrog@leapfrogpress.com; acquisitions@leapfrogpress.com. **Website:** www.leapfrogpress.com. **Contact:** Sarah Murphy, acquisitions editor. Estab. 1996. **Pays 10% royalty on net receipts. Average advance: negotiable.** Publishes ms 1-2 years after acceptance.

FICTION "We search for beautifully written literary titles and market them aggressively to national trade and library accounts. We also sell film, translation, foreign, and book club rights." Publishes paperback originals. Books: acid-free paper; sewn binding. Average print order: 3,000. First novel print order: 2,000 (average). Member, Publishers Marketing Association, PEN. Distributes titles through Consortium

Book Sales and Distribution, St. Paul, MN. Promotes titles through all national review media, bookstore readings, author tours, website, radio shows, chain store promotions, advertisements, book fairs. "Genres often blur; look for good writing. We are most interested in works that are quirky, that fall outside of any known genre,and of course well written and finely crafted. We are most interested in literary fiction." Query by e-mail only. Send letter and first 5 to 10 ms pages within e-mail message. No attachments. Responds in 2-3 weeks to queries by e-mail; 6 months to mss. May consider simultaneous submissions.

TIPS "We like anything that is superbly written and genuinely original. We like the idiosyncratic and the peculiar. We rarely publish nonfiction. Send only your best work, and send only completed work that is ready. That means the completed ms has already been through extensive editing and is ready to be judged. We consider submissions from both previously published and unpublished writers. We are uninterested in an impressive author bio if the work is poor; if the work is excellent, the author bio is equally unimportant."

LEE & LOW BOOKS

95 Madison Ave., #1205, New York NY 10016. (212)779-4400. **E-mail:** general@leeandlow.com. **Website:** www.leeandlow.com. **Contact:** Louise May, vice president/editorial director (multicultural children's fiction/nonfiction). Jessica Echeverria, associate editor; Samantha Wolf, editorial assistant Estab. 1991. Publishes hardcover originals and trade paperback reprints. "Our goals are to meet a growing need for books that address children of color, and to present literature that all children can identify with. We only consider multicultural children's books. Sponsors a yearly New Voices Award for first-time picture book authors of color. Contest rules online at website or for SASE." **Publishes 12-14 titles/year. Receives 100 queries/year; 1,200 mss/year. 20% of books from first-time authors. 50% from unagented writers. Pays net royalty. Pays authors advances against royalty. Pays illustrators advance against royalty. Photographers paid advance against royalty.** Publishes ms 2 years after acceptance. Responds in 6 months to mss if interested. Book catalog available online. Guidelines available online or by written request with SASE.

NONFICTION Picture books: concept. Picture books, middle readers: biography, history, multicultural, science and sports. Average word length: picture books-1,500-3,000. Submit complete ms. Reviews artwork/photos only if writer is also a professional illustrator or photographer. Send photocopies and nonreturnable art samples only.

FICTION Subjects include contemporary and historical fiction featuring people of color. Also accepts thematic or narrative poetry collections with a multicultural focus. Picture books, young readers: anthology, contemporary, history, multicultural, poetry. Picture book, middle reader: contemporary, history, multicultural, nature/environment, poetry, sports. Average word length: picture books—1,000-1,500 words. "We do not publish folklore or animal stories." Submit complete ms.

POETRY Submit complete ms.

TIPS "Check our website to see the kinds of books we publish. Do not send mss that don't fit our mission."

LEGACY PRESS

P.O. Box 261129, San Diego CA 92196. (858)277-1167. **E-mail:** john.gregory@rainbowpublishers.com. **Website:** www.rainbowpublishers.com. Estab. 1979. Publishes 4 young readers/year; 4 middle readers/year; 4 young adult titles/year. 50% of books by first-time authors. "Our mission is to publish Bible-based, teacher resource materials that contribute to and inspire spiritual growth and development in kids ages 2-12." **For authors work purchased outright (range: $500 and up). Pays illustrators by the project (range: $300 and up). Sends galleys to authors.** Accepts simultaneous submissions. Responds to queries in 6 weeks, mss in 3 months.

NONFICTION Young readers, middle readers, young adult/teens: activity books, arts/crafts, how-to, reference, religion. Works with 10 illustrators/year. Reviews ms/illustration packages from artists. Submit ms with 2-5 pieces of final art. Illustrations only: Query with samples. Responds in 6 weeks. Samples returned with SASE; samples filed.

TIPS "Our Rainbow imprint publishes reproducible books for teachers of children in Christian ministries, including crafts, activities, games and puzzles. Our Legacy imprint publishes titles for children such as devotionals, fiction and Christian living. Please see website and study the market before submitting material."

LEHIGH UNIVERSITY PRESS

B040 Christmas-Saucon Hall, 14 E. Packer Ave., Lehigh University, Bethlehem PA 18015. (610)758-3933. **Fax:** (610)758-6331. **E-mail:** inlup@lehigh.edu. **Website:** www.lehigh.edu/library/lup. **Contact:** Kate Crassons. Estab. 1985. Publishes nonfiction hardcover originals. Currently emphasizing works on 18th-century studies, history of technology, literary criticism, and topics involving Asian Studies. **Publishes 10 titles/year. 90-100 queries received/year. 50-60 mss received/year. 70% of books from first-time authors. 100% from unagented writers. Pays royalty.** Publishes ms 18 months after acceptance. Responds in 3 months to queries. Book catalog available free. Guidelines online.

NONFICTION Subjects include Americana, art, architecture, history, language, literature, science. Lehigh University Press is a conduit for nonfiction works of scholarly interest to the academic community. Submit proposal package with cover letter, several sample chapters, current CV and SASE.

HAL LEONARD BOOKS

Hal Leonard Publishing Group, 33 Plymouth St., Suite 302, Montclair NJ 07042. (973)337-5034. **Fax:** (973)337-5227. **Website:** www.halleonardbooks.com. **Contact:** John Cerullo, publisher. **Publishes 30 titles/year.**

NONFICTION Subjects include music. Query with SASE.

LES ÉDITIONS DU VERMILLON

305 Saint Patrick St., Ottawa ON K1N 5K4, Canada. (613)241-4032. **Fax:** (613)241-3109. **E-mail:** leseditionsduvermillon@rogers.com. **Website:** www.leseditionsduvermillon.ca. **Contact:** Jacques Flamand, editorial director. Publishes trade paperback originals. **Publishes 15-20 titles/year. Pays 10% royalty.** Publishes ms 18 months after acceptance. Responds in 6 months to mss. Book catalog available free.

FICTION Subjects include juvenile, literary, religious, short story collections, young adult.

LES FIGUES PRESS

P.O. Box 7736, Los Angeles CA 90007. **E-mail:** info@lesfigues.com. **Website:** www.lesfigues.com. **Contact:** Teresa Carmody and Vanessa Place, co-directors. Les Figues Press is an independent, nonprofit publisher of poetry, prose, visual art, conceptual writing, and translation. With amission is to create aesthetic conversations between readers, writers, and artists, Les Figues Press favors projects which push the boundaries of genre, form, and general acceptability. Submissions are only reviewed through its annual NOS Book Contest.

LETHE PRESS

118 Heritage Ave., Maple Shade NJ 08052. (609)410-7391. **E-mail:** editor@lethepressbooks.com. **Website:** www.lethepressbooks.com. **Contact:** Steve Berman, publisher. Estab. 2001. "Welcomes submissions from authors of any sexual or gender identity." Guidelines online.

NONFICTION Query via e-mail.

FICTION Subjects include gay, lesbian, occult, science fiction. "Named after the Greek river of memory and forgetfulness (and pronounced Lee-Thee), Lethe Press is a small press devoted to ideas that are often neglected or forgotten by mainstream, profit-oriented publishers." Distributes/promotes titles. Lethe Books are distributed by Ingram Publications and Bookazine, and are available at all major bookstores, as well as the major online retailers. Query via e-mail.

POETRY "Lethe Press is a small press seeking gay and lesbian themed poetry collections." Lethe Books are distributed by Ingram Publications and Bookazine, and are available at all major bookstores, as well as the major online retailers. Query with 7-10 poems, list of publications.

ARTHUR A. LEVINE BOOKS

Scholastic, Inc., 557 Broadway, New York NY 10012. (212)343-4436. **Fax:** (212)343-6143. **Website:** www.arthuralevinebooks.com. **Contact:** Arthur A. Levine, VP/publisher. Estab. 1996. Publishes hardcover, paperback, and e-book editions. Publishes book Publishes a book 18 months after acceptance. Responds in 1 month to queries; 5 months to mss. Guidelines online.

NONFICTION Please follow submission guidelines. Works with 8 illustrators/year. Will review ms/illustration packages from artists. Query first. Illustrations only: Send postcard sample with tearsheets. Samples not returned.

FICTION Subjects include juvenile, picture books, young adult. "Arthur A. Levine is looking for distinctive literature, for children and young adults, for whatever's extraordinary." Averages 18-20 total titles/year. Query.

LEXISNEXIS CANADA, INC.

123 Commerce Valley Dr. E., Suite 700, Markham ON L3T 7W8, Canada. (905)479-2665. **Fax:** (905)479-2826. **Website:** www.lexisnexis.ca. **Contact:** Product Development Director. LexisNexis Canada, Inc., publishes professional reference material for the legal, business, and accounting markets under the Butterworths imprint and operates the Quicklaw and LexisNexis online services. **Publishes 100 titles/year. 50% of books from first-time authors. 100% from unagented writers. Pays 5-15% royalty on wholesale price.** Publishes ms 4 months after acceptance. Accepts simultaneous submissions. Responds in 1 month to queries. Book catalog available free. Guidelines online.

TIPS "Audience is legal community, business, medical, accounting professions."

LIFE CYCLE BOOKS

P.O. Box 799, Fort Collins CO 80522. **Website:** www.lifecyclebooks.com. **Contact:** Paul Broughton, general manager. Estab. 1973. Publishes trade paperback originals and reprints, and mass market reprints. **Publishes 6 titles/year. 100+ queries received/year. 50% of books from first-time authors. 100% from unagented writers. Pays 8-10% royalty on wholesale price. Pays $250-1,000 advance.** Publishes ms 1 year after acceptance. Responds in 1 month. Book catalog online.

NONFICTION Subjects include health, medicine, religion, social sciences, womens issues, womens studies. "We specialize in human life issues." Query with SASE. Submit complete ms. Reviews artwork/photos.

LIGUORI PUBLICATIONS

One Liguori Dr., Liguori MO 63057. (636)464-2500. **Fax:** (636)464-8449. **E-mail:** manuscript_submission@liguori.org. **Website:** www.liguori.org. Estab. 1947. Publishes paperback originals and reprints under the Ligouri and Libros Ligouri imprints. Liguori Publications, faithful to the charism of St. Alphonsus, is an apostolate within the mission of the Denver Province. Its mission, a collaborative effort of Redemptorists and laity, is to spread the gospel of Jesus Christ primarily through the print and electronic media. It shares in the Redemptorist priority of giving special attention to the poor and the most abandoned. Currently emphasizing practical spirituality, prayers and devotions, how-to spirituality. **Publishes 20-25 titles/year. Pays royalty. Makes outright purchase. Pays varied advance.** Publishes ms 2 years after acceptance. Responds in 2-3 months. Guidelines online.

NONFICTION Subjects include religion, spirituality. Mostly adult audience; limited children/juvenile. Mss with Catholic sensibility. Query with SASE. Submit outline, 1 sample chapter.

TIPS "As a rule, Liguori Publications does not accept unsolicited fiction, poetry, art books, biography, autobiography, private revelations."

LILLENAS PUBLISHING CO.

Imprint of Lillenas Drama Resources, P.O. Box 419527, Kansas City MO 64141. (816)931-1900. **Fax:** (816)412-8390. **E-mail:** drama@lillenas.com. **Website:** www.lillenasdrama.com. Publishes mass market paperback and electronic originals. "We purchase only original, previously unpublished materials. Also, we require that all scripts be performed at least once before it is submitted for consideration. We do not accept scripts that are sent via fax or e-mail. Direct all manuscripts to the Drama Resources Editor." **Publishes 50+ titles/year. Pays royalty on net price. Makes outright purchase.** Responds in 4-6 months to material. Guidelines online.

NONFICTION Subjects include religion, life issues. No musicals. Query with SASE. Submit complete ms.

FICTION "Looking for sketch and monologue collections for all ages – adults, children and youth. For these collections, we request 12 - 15 scripts to be submitted at one time. Unique treatments of spiritual themes, relevant issues and biblical messages are of interest. Contemporary full-length and one-act plays that have conflict, characterization, and a spiritual context that is neither a sermon nor an apologetic for youth and adults. We also need wholesome so-called secular full-length scripts for dinner theatres and schools." No musicals.

TIPS "We never receive too many manuscripts."

LINDEN PUBLISHING, INC.

2006 S. Mary, Fresno CA 93721. (559)233-6633. **Fax:** (559)233-6933. **E-mail:** richard@lindenpub.com. **Website:** www.lindenpub.com. **Contact:** Richard Sorsky, president; Kent Sorsky, vice president. Estab. 1976. Publishes trade paperback originals; hardcover and trade paperback reprints. **Publishes 10-12 titles/year. 30+ queries received/year. 5-15 mss received/year. 40% of books from first-time authors. 50% from unagented writers. Pays 7½ -12% royalty on wholesale price. Pays $500-6,000 advance.** Publishes ms 18 months after acceptance. Responds in 1 month. Book catalog online. Guidelines available via e-mail.

NONFICTION Subjects include history, regional, hobbies, woodworking, Regional California history. Submit proposal package, outline, 3 sample chapters, bio. Reviews artwork/photos. Send electronic files, if available.

R.C. LINNELL PUBLISHING

2100 Tyler Ln., Louisville KY 40205. **E-mail:** info@linnellpublishing.com. **Website:** www.linnellpublishing.com. **Contact:** Cheri Powell, owner. Estab. 2010. Publishes print on demand paperbacks. "We are currently very small and have published a limited number of books. We would review books on other subjects on a case-by-case basis. If a book is well-written and has an audience we would consider it." **Publishes 3 titles/year. 5 queries received/year. 5 mss received/year. 83% of books from first-time authors. 100% from unagented writers. Pays 10-40% royalty on retail price.** Publishes ms 3 months after acceptance. Accepts simultaneous submissions. Responds in 1 month to mss. Book catalog and guidelines online.

NONFICTION Subjects include alternative lifestyles, Americana, astrology, career guidance, contemporary culture, cooking, counseling, creative nonfiction, ethnic, foods, language, literature, memoirs, multicultural, New Age, philosophy, psychic, psychology, regional, religion, sociology, spirituality, translation, travel, womens issues, womens studies, young adult. Submit complete ms.

FICTION Subjects include adventure, confession, contemporary, experimental, fantasy, feminist, gay, gothic, hi-lo, historical, humor, lesbian, literary, mainstream, multicultural, mystery, occult, regional, religious, romance, science fiction, short story collections, spiritual, suspense, translation, western, young adult. Submit complete ms.

TIPS "Visit our website to understand the business model and the relationship with authors. All sales are through the internet. Author should have a marketing plan in mind. We can help expand the plan but we do not market books. Author should be comfortable with using the internet and should know their intended readers. We are especially interested in books that inspire, motivate, amuse and challenge readers."

LIQUID SILVER BOOKS

10509 Sedgegrass Dr., Indianapolis IN 46235. **E-mail:** submissions@liquidsilverbooks.com. **Website:** www.lsbooks.com. **Contact:** Terri Schaefer, editorial director. Estab. 1999. Liquid Silver Books is an imprint of Atlantic Bridge Publishing, a royalty paying, full-service ePublisher. Atlantic Bridge has been in business since June 1999. Liquid Silver Books is dedicated to bringing high quality erotic romance to our readers. Liquid Silver Books, Romance's Silver Lining. Publishes ms 105 days after contract. after acceptance of ms. Accepts simultaneous submissions. Responds to mss in 10-15 days.

FICTION Needs contemporary, gay and lesbian, paranormal, supernatural, sci-fi, fantasy, historical, suspense, and western romances. "We do not accept literary erotica submissions." E-mail entire ms as an attachment in .RTF format in Arial 12 pt. "Include in the body of the e-mail: author bio, your thoughts on ePublishing, a blurb of your book, including title and series title if applicable. Ms must include Pen name, real name, snail mail and email contact information on the first page, top left corner."

LISTEN & LIVE AUDIO

1700 Manhattan Ave., Union City NJ 07087. **E-mail:** alfred@listenandlive.com. **Website:** www.listenandlive.com. **Contact:** Alfred C. Martino, president. Independent audiobook publisher. "We also license audiobooks for the download market. We specialize in the following genres: fiction, mystery, nonfiction, self-help, business, children's, and teen." **Publishes 10+ titles/year.** Catalog online.

Ⓐ⊘ LITTLE, BROWN AND CO. ADULT TRADE BOOKS

1290 Avenue of the Americas, New York NY 10104. **E-mail:** publicity@littlebrown.com. **Website:** www.hachettebookgroup.com. Estab. 1837. Publishes hardcover originals and paperback originals and reprints. "The general editorial philosophy for all divisions continues to be broad and flexible, with high quality and the promise of commercial success as always the first considerations." **Publishes 100 titles/year. Pays royalty. Offer advance.** Guidelines online.

NONFICTION *Agented submissions only.*

FICTION Subjects include contemporary, literary, mainstream. *Agented submissions only.*

Ⓐ⊘ LITTLE, BROWN BOOKS FOR YOUNG READERS

Hachette Book Group USA, 1290 Avenue of the Americas, New York NY 10104. (212)364-1100. **Fax:** (212)364-0925. **E-mail:** publicity@lbchildrens.com.

Website: hachettebookgroup.com. Estab. 1837. "Little, Brown and Co. Children's Publishing publishes all formats including board books, picture books, middle grade fiction, and nonfiction YA titles. We are looking for strong writing and presentation, but no predetermined topics." *Only interested in solicited agented material.* **Publishes 100-150 titles/year. Pays authors royalties based on retail price. Pays illustrators and photographers by the project or royalty based on retail price. Sends galleys to authors; dummies to illustrators. Pays negotiable advance.** Publishes ms 2 years after acceptance. Accepts simultaneous submissions. Responds in 1-2 months.

NONFICTION Subjects include animals, art, architecture, ethnic, gay, lesbian, history, hobbies, nature, environment, recreation, science, sports. "Writers should avoid looking for the 'issue' they think publishers want to see, choosing instead topics they know best and are most enthusiastic about/inspired by." *Agented submissions only.*

FICTION Subjects include adventure, fantasy, feminist, gay, lesbian, historical, humor, mystery, science fiction, suspense, chick lit, multicultural. Average word length: picture books—1,000; young readers—6,000; middle readers—15,000- 50,000; young adults—50,000 and up. *Agented submissions only.*

TIPS "In order to break into the field, authors and illustrators should research their competition and try to come up with something outstandingly different."

LITTLE SIMON

Imprint of Simon & Schuster, 1230 Avenue of the Americas, New York NY 10020. (212)698-1295. **Fax:** (212)698-2794. **Website:** www.simonsayskids.com. Publishes novelty and branded books only. "Our goal is to provide fresh material in an innovative format for preschool to age 8. Our books are often, if not exclusively, format driven." **Offers advance and royalties.**

NONFICTION "We publish very few nonfiction titles." No picture books. *Currently not accepting unsolicited mss.*

FICTION Novelty books include many things that do not fit in the traditional hardcover or paperback format, such as pop-up, board book, scratch and sniff, glow in the dark, lift the flap, etc. Children's/juvenile. No picture books. Large part of the list is holiday-themed. *Currently not accepting unsolicited mss.*

LITTLE TIGER PRESS

1 The Coda Centre, 189 Munster Rd., London SW6 6AW, United Kingdom. (44)(20)7385-6333. **Website:** www.littletigerpress.com. Little Tiger Press is a dynamic and busy independent publisher.

FICTION Picture books: animal, concept, contemporary, humor. Average word length: picture books—750 words or less.

TIPS "Every reasonable care is taken of the manuscripts and samples we receive, but we cannot accept responsibility for any loss or damage. Try to read or look at as many books on the Little Tiger Press list before sending in your material. Refer to our website for further details."

LIVINGSTON PRESS

University of West Alabama, Station 22, Livingston AL 35470. **E-mail:** jwt@uwa.edu. **Website:** www.livingstonpress.uwa.edu. **Contact:** Joe Taylor, director. Estab. 1974. Publishes hardcover and trade paperback originals. "Livingston Press, as do all literary presses, looks for authorial excellence in style. Currently emphasizing novels." Reading in June only. Check back for details. **Publishes 8-10 titles/year. 50% of books from first-time authors. 100% from unagented writers. Pays 100 contributor's copies, after sales of 1,500, standard royalty.** Publishes ms 18 months after acceptance. Accepts simultaneous submissions. Responds in 2 months to queries; 6-12 months to mss. Book catalog online. Guidelines online.

IMPRINTS Swallow's Tale Press.

FICTION Subjects include experimental, literary, short story collections, off-beat or Southern. "We are interested in form and, of course, style."

TIPS "Our readers are interested in literature, often quirky literature that emphasizes form and style. Please visit our website for current needs."

LLEWELLYN PUBLICATIONS

Imprint of Llewellyn Worldwide, Ltd., 2143 Wooddale Dr., Woodbury MN 55125. (651)291-1970. **Fax:** (651)291-1908. **E-mail:** submissions@llewellyn.com. **Website:** www.llewellyn.com. Estab. 1901. Publishes trade and mass market paperback originals. "Llewellyn publishes New Age fiction and nonfiction exploring new worlds of mind and spirit. Currently emphasizing astrology, alternative health and healing, tarot. De-emphasizing fiction, channeling." **Publishes 100+ titles/year. 30% of books from first-time authors. 50% from unagented writers. Pays 10% roy-**

alty on wholesale or retail price. Accepts simultaneous submissions. Responds in 3 months to queries. Book catalog online.

NONFICTION Subjects include cooking, foods, nutrition, health, medicine, nature, environment, New Age, psychology, women's issues, women's studies. Submit outline, sample chapters. Reviews artwork/photos.

LONELY PLANET PUBLICATIONS

150 Linden St., Oakland CA 94607-2538. (510)893-8555. **Fax:** (510)893-8563. **Website:** www.lonelyplanet.com. Estab. 1973. Publishes trade paperback originals. "Lonely Planet publishes travel guides, atlases, travel literature, phrasebooks, condensed pocket guides, diving and snorkeling guides." **Work-for-hire: on contract, 1/3 on submission, 1/3 on approval. Pays advance.** Accepts simultaneous submissions. Responds in 3 months to queries. Book catalog online. Guidelines online.

NONFICTION Subjects include travel. "We only work with contract writers on book ideas that we originate. We do not accept original proposals. Request our writer's guidelines. Send resume and clips of travel writing." Query with SASE.

LOOSE ID

P.O. Box 806, San Francisco CA 94104. **E-mail:** submissions@loose-id.com. **Website:** www.loose-id.com. **Contact:** Treva Harte, editor-in-chief. Estab. 2004. "*Loose Id* is love unleashed. We're taking romance to the edge." Publishes e-books and some print books. Distributes/promotes titles. "The company promotes itself through web and print advertising wherever readers of erotic romance may be found, creating a recognizable brand identity as the place to let your id run free and the people who unleash your fantasies. It is currently pursuing licensing agreements for foreign translations, and has a print program of 2 to 5 titles per month." **Pays e-book royalties of 40%.** Publishes ms within 1 year after acceptance. Responds to queries in 1 month. Guidelines online.

FICTION Subjects include erotica, romance. Wants nontraditional erotic romance stories, including gay, lesbian, heroes and heroines, multi-culturalism, cross-genre, fantasy, and science fiction, straight contemporary or historical romances. Query with outline/synopsis and 3 sample chapters. Accepts queries by e-mail. Include estimated word count, list of publishing credits, and why your submission is love unleashed. "Before submitting a query or proposal, please read the guidelines on our website. Please don't hesitate to contact us by e-mail for any information you don't see there."

LOST HORSE PRESS

105 Lost Horse Lane, Sandpoint ID 83864. (208)255-4410. **E-mail:** losthorsepress@mindspring.com. **Website:** www.losthorsepress.org. **Contact:** Christine Holbert, publisher. Estab. 1998. Publishes hardcover and paperback originals. Distributed by University of Washington Press. **Publishes 8-10 titles/year.** Publishes ms 3-9 months after acceptance.

⊘ LOVING HEALING PRESS INC.

5145 Pontiac Trail, Ann Arbor MI 48105. (888)761-6268. **Fax:** (734)663-6861. **E-mail:** info@lovinghealing.com. **Website:** www.lovinghealing.com. **Contact:** Victor R. Volkman, senior editor (psychology, self-help, personal growth, trauma recovery). Estab. 2003. Publishes hardcover and trade paperback originals and reprints. **Publishes 20 titles/year. Receives 200 queries/year; 100 mss/year. 50% of books from first-time authors. 80% from unagented writers. Pays 6-12% royalty on retail price.** Publishes ms 10 months after acceptance. Accepts simultaneous submissions. Responds in 1 month on queries and proposals. Catalog and guidelines online.

IMPRINTS Modern History Press, Marvelous Spirit Press.

Currently not accepting mss.

NONFICTION Subjects include child guidance, health, memoirs, psychology, social work. "We are primarily interested in self-help books which are person-centered and non-judgmental." Submit proposal package, including outline, 3 sample chapters. Reviews artwork/photos as part of the ms package; send JPEG files.

LOYOLA PRESS

3441 N. Ashland Ave., Chicago IL 60657. (773)281-1818. **Fax:** (773)281-0152. **E-mail:** durepos@loyolapress.com. **Website:** www.loyolapress.org. **Contact:** Joseph Durepos, acquisitions editor. Publishes hardcover and trade paperback. **Publishes 20-30 titles/year. 500 queries received/year. Pays standard royalties. Offers reasonable advance.** Accepts simultaneous submissions. Book catalog online. Guidelines online.

NONFICTION Subjects include religion, spirituality, inspirational, prayer, Catholic life, parish and adult faith formation resources with a special focus on Ignatian spirituality and Jesuit history. Query with SASE.

TIPS "We're looking for motivated authors who have a passion for the Catholic tradition, to prayer and spirituality, and to helping readers respond to the existence of God in their lives."

LRP PUBLICATIONS, INC.

360 Hiatt Dr., Palm Beach Gardens FL 33418. **Website:** www.lrp.com. Estab. 1977. Publishes hardcover and trade paperback originals. "LRP publishes two industry-leading magazines, *Human Resource Executive*® and *Risk & Insurance*®, as well as hundreds of newsletters, books, videos and case reporters in the fields of: human resources, federal employment, workers' compensation, public employment law, disability, bankruptcy, education administration and law." **Pays royalty.** Book catalog free. Guidelines free.

NONFICTION Subjects include business, economics, education. Submit proposal package, outline.

LUCKY MARBLE BOOKS

PageSpring Publishing, P.O. Box 21133, Columbus OH 43221. **E-mail:** yaeditor@pagespringpublishing.com. **Website:** www.luckymarblebooks.com. Estab. 2012. Publishes trade paperback and electronic originals. "Lucky Marble Books publishes novel-length young adult and middle grade fiction. We are looking for engaging characters and well-crafted plots that keep our readers turning the page. We accept e-mail queries only; see our website for details." **Pays royalty.** Publishes ms 9-12 months after acceptance. Accepts simultaneous submissions. Responds in 3 months. Guidelines online.

FICTION Subjects include adventure, contemporary, fantasy, feminist, historical, humor, juvenile, literary, mainstream, multicultural, mystery, regional, romance, science fiction, sports, suspense, young adult. Does not want picture books. Submit proposal package via e-mail. Include synopsis and 30 sample pages.

TIPS "We are particularly interested in books that integrate education content into a great story with vivid characters."

⊘ LUNA BISONTE PRODS

137 Leland Ave., Columbus OH 43214-7505. **E-mail:** bennettjohnm@gmail.com. **Website:** www.johnmbennett.net. **Contact:** John M. Bennett, editor/publisher. Estab. 1967.

POETRY "Interested in avant-garde and highly experimental work only." Has published poetry by Jim Leftwich, Sheila E. Murphy, Al Ackerman, Richard Kostelanetz, Carla Bertola, Olchar Lindsann, and many others. Query first, with a few sample poems and cover letter with brief bio and publication credits. "Keep it brief. Chapbook publishing usually depends on grants or other subsidies, and is usually by solicitation. **Will also consider subsidy arrangements on negotiable terms.**" A sampling of various Luna Bisonte Prods products is available for $20.

⊘ THE LYONS PRESS

The Globe Pequot Press, Inc., Box 480, 246 Goose Ln., Guilford CT 06437. (203)458-4500. **Fax:** (203)458-4668. **Website:** www.lyonspress.com. Estab. 1984 (Lyons & Burford), 1997 (The Lyons Press). Publishes hardcover and trade paperback originals and reprints. The Lyons Press publishes practical and literary books, chiefly centered on outdoor subjects—natural history, all sports, gardening, horses, fishing, hunting, survival, self-reliant living, plus cooking, memoir, bio, nonfiction. "At this time, we are not accepting unsolicited mss or proposals." Check back for updates. **Pays $3,000-25,000 advance.** Book catalog online. Guidelines online.

NONFICTION Subjects include agriculture, Americana, animals, art & reference, cooking, foods & wine, nutrition, history, military, war, nature, environment, recreation, sports, adventure, fitness, the sea, woodworking.

MAGENTA PUBLISHING FOR THE ARTS

151 Winchester St., Toronto ON M4X 1B5, Canada. **E-mail:** info@magentafoundation.org. **Website:** www.magentafoundation.org. **Contact:** Submissions. Estab. 2004. "Established in 2004, The Magenta Foundation is Canada's pioneering non-profit, charitable arts publishing house. Magenta was created to organize promotional opportunities for artists, in an international context, through circulated exhibitions and publications. Projects mounted by Magenta are supported by credible international media coverage and critical reviews in all mainstream-media formats (radio, television and print). Magenta works with respected individuals and international organizations to help increase recognition for artists while uniting the global photography community."

MAGE PUBLISHERS, INC.

(202)342-1642. **Fax:** (202)342-9269. **E-mail:** as@mage.com. **Website:** www.mage.com. Estab. 1985. Publishes hardcover originals and reprints, trade paperback originals. Mage publishes books relating to Persian/Iranian culture. **Pays royalty.** Accepts simultaneous submissions. Responds in 1 month to queries. Book catalog available free. Guidelines online.

NONFICTION Subjects include anthropology, archeology, art, architecture, cooking, foods, nutrition, ethnic, history, language, literature, music, dance, sociology, translation. Submit outline, bio, SASE. Query via mail or e-mail. Reviews artwork/photos. Send photocopies.

FICTION Subjects include ethnic, feminist, historical, literary, mainstream, contemporary, short story collections. Must relate to Persian/Iranian culture. Submit outline, SASE. Query via mail or e-mail.

POETRY Must relate to Persian/Iranian culture. Query.

TIPS "Audience is the Iranian-American community in America and Americans interested in Persian culture."

MAGINATION PRESS

750 First St. NE, Washington DC 20002. (202)336-5618. **Fax:** (202)336-5624. **E-mail:** magination@apa.org. **Website:** www.apa.org. Estab. 1988. Magination Press is an imprint of the American Psychological Association. "We publish books dealing with the psycho/therapeutic resolution of children's problems and psychological issues with a strong self-help component." Submit complete ms. Materials returned only with SASE. **Publishes 12 titles/year. 75% of books from first-time authors.** Publishes book Publishes a book 18-24 months after acceptance. Accepts simultaneous submissions. Responds to queries in 1-2 months; mss in 2-6 months.

NONFICTION All levels: psychological and social issues, self-help, health, multicultural, special needs.

FICTION All levels: psychological and social issues, self-help, health, parenting concerns and, special needs. Picture books, middle school readers.

MAGNUS PRESS

1647 Shire Ave., Oceanside CA 92057. (760)806-3743. **Fax:** (760)806-3689. **E-mail:** magnuspress@cox.net. **Website:** www.magnuspress.com. Estab. 1997. Publishes trade paperback originals and reprints. **Publishes 1-3 titles/year. 120 queries received/year. 75 mss received/year. 44% of books from first-time authors. 89% from unagented writers. Pays 6-15% royalty on retail price.** Publishes ms 1 year after acceptance. Accepts simultaneous submissions. Responds in 1 month. Book catalog and ms guidelines for #10 SASE.

NONFICTION Subjects include religion, from a Christian perspective. "Writers must be well-grounded in Biblical knowledge and must be able to communicate effectively with the lay person." Submit proposal package, outline, sample chapters, bio.

TIPS "Magnus Press's audience is mainly Christian lay persons, but also includes anyone interested in spirituality and/or Biblical studies and the church. Study our listings and catalog; learn to write effectively for an average reader; read any one of our published books."

MANDALA PUBLISHING

Mandala Publishing and Earth Aware Editions, 800 A St., San Rafael CA 94901. **E-mail:** info@mandalapublishing.com. **Website:** www.mandalapublishing.com. Estab. 1989. Publishes hardcover, trade paperback, and electronic originals. "In the traditions of the East, wisdom, truth, and beauty go hand in- hand. This is reflected in the great arts, music, yoga, and philosophy of India. Mandala Publishing strives to bring to its readers authentic and accessible renderings of thousands of years of wisdom and philosophy from this unique culture-timeless treasures that are our inspirations and guides. At Mandala, we believe that the arts, health, ecology, and spirituality of the great Vedic traditions are as relevant today as they were in sacred India thousands of years ago. As a distinguished publisher in the world of Vedic literature, lifestyle, and interests today, Mandala strives to provide accessible and meaningful works for the modern reader." **Publishes 12 titles/year. 200 queries received/year. 100 mss received/year. 40% of books from first-time authors. 100% from unagented writers. Pays 3-15% royalty on retail price.** Publishes ms 8 months after acceptance. Accepts simultaneous submissions. Responds in 6 months. Book catalog online.

NONFICTION Subjects include alternative, cooking, foods, nutrition, education, health, medicine, philosophy, photography, religion, spirituality. Query with SASE. Reviews artwork/photos. Send photocopies and thumbnails.

FICTION Subjects include juvenile, religious, spiritual. Query with SASE.

MANOR HOUSE PUBLISHING, INC.

452 Cottingham Crescent, Ancaster ON L9G 3V6, Canada. **E-mail:** mbdavie@manor-house.biz. **Web-**

site: www.manor-house.biz. **Contact:** Mike Davie, president (novels, poetry, and nonfiction). Estab. 1998. Publishes hardcover, trade paperback, and mass market paperback originals reprints. **Publishes 5-6 titles/year. 30 queries received/year; 20 mss received/year. 90% of books from first-time authors. 90% from unagented writers. Pays 10% royalty on retail price.** Publishes ms 1 year after acceptance. Accepts simultaneous submissions. Queries and mss to be sent by e-mail only. "We will respond in 30 days if interested-if not, there is no response. Do not follow up unless asked to do so.". Book catalog online. Guidelines available via e-mail.

NONFICTION Subjects include alternative, anthropology, business, community, history, sex, social sciences, sociology, spirituality. "We are a Canadian publisher, so mss should be Canadian in content and aimed as much as possible at a wide, general audience. At this point in time, we are only publishing books by Canadian citizens residing in Canada." Query via e-mail. Submit proposal package, outline, bio, 3 sample chapters. Submit complete ms. Reviews artwork/photos. Send photocopies.

FICTION Subjects include adventure, experimental, gothic, historical, horror, humor, juvenile, literary, mystery, occult, poetry, regional, romance, short story collections, young adult. Stories should have Canadian settings and characters should be Canadian, but content should have universal appeal to wide audience. Query via e-mail. Submit proposal package, clips, bio, 3 sample chapters. Submit complete ms.

POETRY Poetry should engage, provoke, involve the reader.

TIPS "Our audience includes everyone-the general public/mass audience. Self-edit your work first, make sure it is well written with strong Canadian content."

MARINE TECHNIQUES PUBLISHING

126 Western Ave., Suite 266, Augusta ME 04330. (207)622-7984. **E-mail:** info@marinetechpublishing.com. **Website:** www.marinetechpublishing.com. **Contact:** James L. Pelletier, president/owner(commercial maritime); Maritime Associates Globally (commercial maritime). Estab. 1983. Trade paperback originals and reprints. "Publishes only books related to the commercial marine/maritime industry." **Publishes 2-5 titles/year. 20+ queries received/year. 40+ mss received/year. 50% of books from first-time authors. 75% from unagented writers. Pays 25-55% royalty on wholesale or retail price. Makes outright purchase.** Publishes ms 1 year after acceptance. Accepts simultaneous submissions. Responds in 2 months. Book catalog online. Guidelines available by e-mail.

NONFICTION Subjects include maritime education, marine subjects, counseling, career guidance, maritime labor, marine engineering, global water transportation, marine subjects, water transportation. "We are concerned with 'maritime related works' and not recreational boating, but rather commercial maritime industries, such as deep-sea water transportation, offshore oil & gas, inland towing, coastal tug boat, 'water transportation industries.'" Submit proposal package, including all sample chapters; submit completed ms. Reviews artwork/photos as part of the ms package; send photocopies.

FICTION Subjects include adventure, military, war, maritime. Must be commercial maritime/marine related. Submit proposal package, including all sample chapters. Submit complete ms.

TIPS "Audience consists of commercial marine/maritime firms, persons employed in all aspects of the marine/maritime commercial water-transportation-related industries and recreational fresh and salt water fields, persons interested in seeking employment in the commercial marine industry; firms seeking to sell their products and services to vessel owners, operators, and managers; shipyards, vessel repair yards, recreational and yacht boat building and national and international ports and terminals involved with the commercial marine industry globally worldwide, etc."

MARTIN SISTERS PUBLISHING, LLC

P.O. Box 1154, Barbourville KY 40906-1499. **E-mail:** submissions@martinsisterspublishing.com. **Website:** www.martinsisterspublishing.com. **Contact:** Melissa Newman, Publisher/Editor (Fiction/nonfiction). Estab. 2011. Firm/imprint publishes trade and mass market paperback originals; electronic originals. **Publishes 12 titles/year. 75% of books from first-time authors. 100% from unagented writers. Pays 7.5% royalty/max on retail price. No advance offered.** Publishes ms 6 months after acceptance. Accepts simultaneous submissions. Responds in 1 month on queries, 2 months on proposals, 3-6 months on mss. Catalog and guidelines online.

IMPRINTS Ivy House Books; Rainshower Books; Skyvine Books; Martin Sisters Books; Barefoot Books. Query Ms. Newman for all imprints listed.

NONFICTION Subjects include Americana, child guidance, contemporary culture, cooking, creative nonfiction, education, gardening, history, house and home, humanities, labor, language, law, literature, memoirs, money, nutrition, parenting, psychology, regional, sociology, spirituality, womens issues, womens studies, western. Send query letter only. Does not review artwork.

FICTION Subjects include adventure, confession, fantasy, historical, humor, juvenile, literary, mainstream, military, mystery, poetry in translation, regional, religious, romance, science fiction, short story collections, spiritual, sports, suspense, war, western, young adult. Send query letter only.

MARVEL COMICS

135 W. 50th St., 7th Floor, New York NY 10020. **Website:** www.marvel.com. Publishes hardcover originals and reprints, trade paperback reprints, mass market comic book originals, electronic reprints. **Pays on a per page work for hire basis or creator-owned which is then contracted. Pays negotiable advance.** Responds in 3-5 weeks to queries. Guidelines online.

FICTION Subjects include adventure, comic books, fantasy, horror, humor, science fiction, young adult. Our shared universe needs new heroes and villains; books for younger readers and teens needed. Submit inquiry letter, idea submission form (download from website), SASE.

MASTER BOOKS

P.O. Box 726, Green Forest AR 72638. (870)438-5288. **Fax:** (870)438-5120. **E-mail:** submissions@newleafpress.net. **Website:** www.masterbooks.net. **Contact:** Craig Froman, acquisitions editor. Estab. 1975. Publishes 3 middle readers/year; 2 young adult nonfiction titles/year; 10 homeschool curriculum titles; 20 adult trade books/year. **10% of books from first-time authors. Pays authors royalty of 3-15% based on wholesale price.** Publishes ms 1 year after acceptance. Responds in 6 months. Book catalog available upon request. Guidelines online.

NONFICTION Picture books: activity books, animal, nature/environment, creation. Young readers, middle readers, young adults: activity books, animal, biography Christian, nature/environment, science, creation. Submission guidelines on website.

TIPS "All of our children's books are creation-based, including topics from the Book of Genesis. We look also for home school educational material that would be supplementary to a home school curriculum, especially elementary material."

MAUPIN HOUSE PUBLISHING, INC.

1710 Roe Crest Dr., North Mankato MN 56003. **Website:** www.maupinhouse.com. **Contact:** Julie Graddy, publisher (areas of interest: education, professional development). Publishes trade paperback originals and reprints. "Maupin House publishes professional resource books for language arts teachers K-12." **Publishes 6-8 titles/year. 60% of books from first-time authors. 100% from unagented writers. Pays 10% royalty on retail price.** Publishes ms 18 months after acceptance. Accepts simultaneous submissions. Responds in less than 1 month. Catalog and guidelines online.

NONFICTION Subjects include education, language arts, literacy and the arts, reading comprehension, writing workshop. "Study the website to understand our pubilshing preferences. Successful authors are all teachers or former teachers." Query with SASE or via e-mail. Submit proposal package, including outline, 1-2 sample chapters, and TOC/marketing ideas. Reviews artwork/photos as part of the mss package. Writers should send photocopies, digital.

TIPS "Our audience is K-12 educators, teachers. Be familiar with our publishing areas and tell us why your book idea is better/different than what is out there. How do you plan to promote it? Successful authors help promote books via speaking engagements, conferences, etc."

MAVEN HOUSE PRESS

4 Snead Ct., Palmyra VA 22963. (610)883-7988. **Fax:** (888)894-3403. **E-mail:** jim@mavenhousepress.com. **Website:** www.mavenhousepress.com. **Contact:** Jim Pennypacker, publisher. Estab. 2012. Publishes hardcover, trade paperback, and electronic originals. Maven House Press publishes business books for executives and managers to help them lead their organizations to greatness. **Publishes 6 titles/year. Pays 10-50% royalty based on wholesale price.** Publishes ms 9 months after acceptance. Accepts simultaneous submissions. Responds in 1 month.

NONFICTION Subjects include business, economics, Business/management. Submit proposal package including: outline, 1-2 sample chapters. See submission form online.

MAVERICK DUCK PRESS

E-mail: maverickduckpress@yahoo.com. **Website:** www.maverickduckpress.com. **Contact:** Kendall A. Bell, editor. Assistant Editors: Kayla Marie Middlebrook and Brielle Kelton. Estab. 2005. Maverick Duck Press is a "publisher of chapbooks from undiscovered talent. We are looking for fresh and powerful work that shows a sense of innovation or a new take on passion or emotion. Previous publication in print or online journals could increase your chances of us accepting your manuscript." Does not want "unedited work." **Pays 20 author's copies (out of a press run of 50).**

POETRY Send ms in Microsoft Word format with a cover letter with brief bio and publication credits. Chapbook mss may include previously published poems. "Previous publication is always a plus, as we may be more familiar with your work. Chapbook mss should have 16-24 poems, but no more than 24 poems."

MAVERICK MUSICALS AND PLAYS

89 Bergann Rd., Maleny QLD 4552, Australia. Phone/**Fax:** (61)(7)5494-4007. **E-mail:** gail@maverickmusicals.com. **Website:** www.maverickmusicals.com. Estab. 1978. Guidelines online.

FICTION Subjects include plays and musicals. "Looking for two-act musicals and one- and two-act plays. See website for more details."

MCBOOKS PRESS

ID Booth Building, 520 N. Meadow St., Ithaca NY 14850. (607)272-2114. **Fax:** (607)273-6068. **E-mail:** mcbooks@mcbooks.com. **Website:** www.mcbooks.com. **Contact:** Alexander G. Skutt, publisher. Estab. 1979. Publishes trade paperback and hardcover originals and reprints. **Publishes 5 titles/year.** Accepts simultaneous submissions. Guidelines online.

Currently not accepting submissions or queries for fiction or nonfiction.

FICTION Publishes Julian Stockwin, John Biggins, Colin Sargent, and Douglas W. Jacobson. Distributes titles through Independent Publishers Group.

TIPS "We are currently only publishing authors with whom we have a pre-existing relationship. If this policy changes, we will announce the change on our website."

MCCLELLAND & STEWART, LTD.

The Canadian Publishers, One Toronto St., Unit 300, Toronto ON M5A 2P9, Canada. (416)364-4449. **Fax:** (416)598-7764. **Website:** www.mcclelland.com. Publishes hardcover, trade paperback, and mass market paperback originals and reprints. **Publishes 80 titles/year. 1,500 queries received/year. 10% of books from first-time authors. 30% from unagented writers. Pays 10-15% royalty on retail price (hardcover rates). Pays advance.** Publishes ms 1 year after acceptance. Responds in 3 months to proposals.

NONFICTION Subjects include art, architecture, business, economics, gay, lesbian, government, politics, health, medicine, history, language, literature, military, war, music, dance, nature, environment, philosophy, photography, psychology, recreation, religion, science, sociology, sports, translation, travel, women's issues, women's studies, Canadiana. "We publish books primarily by Canadian authors." Submit outline. *All unsolicited mss returned unopened.*

FICTION "We publish work by established authors, as well as the work of new and developing authors." Query. *All unsolicited mss* returned unopened.

POETRY Only Canadian poets should apply. We publish only 4 titles each year. Query. *No unsolicted mss.*

THE MCDONALD & WOODWARD PUBLISHING CO.

431 E. College St., Granville OH 43023. (740)641-2691. **Fax:** (740)321-1141. **E-mail:** mwpubco@mwpubco.com. **Website:** www.mwpubco.com. **Contact:** Jerry N. McDonald, publisher. Estab. 1986. Publishes hardcover and trade paperback originals. McDonald & Woodward publishes books in natural history, cultural history, and natural resources. Currently emphasizing travel, natural and cultural history, and natural resource conservation. **Publishes 5 titles/year. 25 queries received/year. 20 mss received/year. Pays 10% royalty.** Accepts simultaneous submissions. Responds in less than 1 month. Book catalog online. Guidelines free on request; by e-mail.

NONFICTION Subjects include animals, architecture, environment, history, nature, science, travel, natural history. Query with SASE. Reviews artwork/photos. Photos are not required.

FICTION Subjects include historical. Query with SASE.

TIPS "Our books are meant for the curious and educated elements of the general population."

⊘ MARGARET K. MCELDERRY BOOKS

Imprint of Simon & Schuster Children's Publishing Division, 1230 Sixth Ave., New York NY 10020. (212)698-7200. **Website:** www.simonsayskids.com. Estab. 1971. "Margaret K. McElderry Books publishes hardcover and paperback trade books for children from pre-school age through young adult. This list includes picture books, middle grade and teen fiction, poetry, and fantasy. The style and subject matter of the books we publish is almost unlimited. We do not publish textbooks, coloring and activity books, greeting cards, magazines, pamphlets, or religious publications." **Publishes 30 titles/year. 15% of books from first-time authors. 50% from unagented writers. Pays authors royalty based on retail price. Pays illustrator royalty of by the project. Pays photographers by the project. Original artwork returned at job's completion. Offers $5,000-8,000 advance for new authors.** Guidelines for #10 SASE.

NONFICTION Subjects include history, adventure. *No unsolicited mss. Agented submissions only.*

FICTION Subjects include adventure, fantasy, historical, mainstream, contemporary, mystery, picture books, young adult, or middle grade. *No unsolicited mss. Agented submissions only.*

TIPS "Read! The children's book field is competitive. See what's been done and what's out there before submitting. We look for high quality: an originality of ideas, clarity and felicity of expression, a well organized plot, and strong character-driven stories. We're looking for strong, original fiction, especially mysteries and middle grade humor. We are always interested in picture books for the youngest age reader. Study our titles."

MCFARLAND & CO., INC., PUBLISHERS

Box 611, Jefferson NC 28640. (336)246-4460. **Fax:** (336)246-5018. **E-mail:** info@mcfarlandpub.com. **Website:** www.mcfarlandpub.com. **Contact:** Editorial Department. Estab. 1979. Publishes hardcover and quality paperback originals. "McFarland publishes serious nonfiction in a variety of fields, including general reference, performing arts, popular culture, sports (particularly baseball); women's studies, librarianship, literature, Civil War, history and international studies. Currently emphasizing medieval history, automotive history. De-emphasizing memoirs." **Publishes 350 titles/year. 50% of books from first-time authors. 95% from unagented writers.** Publishes ms 10 months after acceptance. Responds in 1 month to queries. Guidelines online.

NONFICTION Subjects include art, architecture, automotive, health, medicine, history, military, war/war, popular contemporary culture, music, dance, recreation, sociology, world affairs, sports (very strong), African-American studies (very strong). Reference books are particularly wanted—fresh material (i.e., not in head-to-head competition with an established title). "We prefer manuscripts of 250 or more double-spaced pages or at least 75,000 words." No fiction, New Age, exposes, poetry, children's books, devotional/inspirational works, Bible studies, or personal essays. Query with SASE. Submit outline, sample chapters. Reviews artwork/photos.

TIPS "We want well-organized knowledge of an area in which there is not information coverage at present, plus reliability so we don't feel we have to check absolutely everything. Our market is worldwide and libraries are an important part."

MCGRAW-HILL PROFESSIONAL BUSINESS

Imprint of The McGraw-Hill Companies, 2 Penn Plaza, New York NY 10121-2298. **E-mail:** tania_loghmani@mcgraw-hill.com. **Website:** www.books.mcgraw-hill.com. McGraw Hill Professional is a publishing leader in business/investing, management, careers, self-help, consumer health, language reference, test preparation, sports/recreation, and general interest titles. Publisher not responsible for returning mss or proposals. Accepts simultaneous submissions. Guidelines online.

NONFICTION Subjects include business, economics, child guidance, education, study guides, health, medicine, money, finance, sports, fitness, management, consumer reference, English and foreign language reference. Current, up-to-date, original ideas are needed. Good self-promotion is key. Submit proposal package, outline, concept of book, competition and market info, CV.

MC PRESS

3695 W. Quail Heights Ct., Boise ID 83703. **Fax:** (208)639-1231. **E-mail:** duptmor@mcpressonline.com. **Website:** www.mc-store.com. **Contact:** David Uptmor, publisher. Estab. 2001. Publishes trade paperback originals. **Publishes 12 titles/year. 50 queries received/year. 15 mss received/year. 50% of books from first-time authors. 100% from unagented writers. Pays 10-16% royalty on wholesale price.**

Publishes ms 5 months after acceptance. Accepts simultaneous submissions. Responds in 1 month. Book catalog and ms guidelines free.

IMPRINTS MC Press, IBM Press.

NONFICTION Subjects include computers, electronics. "We specialize in computer titles targeted at IBM technologies." Submit proposal package, outline, 2 sample chapters, abstract. Reviews artwork/photos. Send photocopies.

MEDALLION MEDIA GROUP

4222 Meridian Pkwy., Aurora IL 60504. (630)513-8316. **E-mail:** emily@medallionmediagroup.com. **E-mail:** submissions@medallionmediagroup.com. **Website:** medallionmediagroup.com. **Contact:** Emily Steele, editorial director. Estab. 2003. Publishes trade paperback, hardcover, e-book originals, book apps, and TREEbook. "We are an independent, innovative publisher looking for compelling, memorable stories told in distinctive voices." **Offers advance.** Publishes ms 1-2 years after acceptance. Responds in 2-3 months to mss. Guidelines online.

NONFICTION Subjects include art, health, celebrity, design, fitness. *Agented only.* Please query.

FICTION Subjects include fantasy, historical, horror, literary, mainstream, mystery, romance, science fiction, suspense, young adult, thriller, YA-YA (YA written by young adults). Word count: 40,000-90,000 for YA; 60,000-120,000 for all others. No short stories, anthologies, erotica. Submit first 3 consecutive chapters and a synopsis through our online submission form.

TIPS "We are not affected by trends. We are simply looking for well-crafted, original, compelling works of fiction and nonfiction. Please visit our website for the most current guidelines prior to submitting anything to us."

MEDICAL GROUP MANAGEMENT ASSOCIATION

104 Inverness Terrace E., Englewood CO 80112. (303)799-1111. **E-mail:** support@mgma.com; connexion@mgma.com. **Website:** www.mgma.org. Estab. 1926. Publishes professional and scholarly hardcover, paperback, and electronic originals, and trade paperback reprints. **Publishes 6 titles/year. 18 queries received/year. 6 mss received/year. 30% of books from first-time authors. 100% from unagented writers. Pays 8-17% royalty on net sales (twice a year). Pays $2,000-5,000 advance.** Publishes ms 6 months after acceptance. Accepts simultaneous submissions. Responds in less than 3 weeks to queries. Book catalog online. Guidelines online.

NONFICTION Subjects include audio, business, economics, education, health. Submit proposal package, outline, 3 sample chapters. Submit complete ms. Reviews artwork/photos. Send photocopies.

TIPS "Audience includes medical practice managers and executives. Our books are geared at the business side of medicine."

MEDICAL PHYSICS PUBLISHING

4555 Helgesen Dr., Madison WI 53718. (608)224-4508. **Fax:** (608)224-5016. **E-mail:** todd@medicalphysics.org. **Website:** www.medicalphysics.org. **Contact:** Todd Hanson, editor. Estab. 1985. Publishes hardcover and paperback originals and reprints. "We are a nonprofit, membership organization publishing affordable books in medical physics and related fields. Currently emphasizing biomedical engineering. De-emphasizing books for the general public." **Publishes 5-6 titles/year. 10-20 queries received/year. 100% from unagented writers. Pays 10% royalty on wholesale price.** Publishes book Publsihes ms 1 year after acceptance. Accepts simultaneous submissions. Responds in 6 months to mss. Book catalog available via website or upon request.

NONFICTION Subjects include health, medicine, symposium proceedings in the fields of medical physics and radiology. Submit complete ms. Reviews artwork/photos. Send disposable copies.

MELANGE BOOKS, LLC

White Bear Lake MN 55110-5538. **E-mail:** melangebooks@melange-books.com. **E-mail:** submissions@melange-books.com. **Website:** www.melange-books.com. **Contact:** Nancy Schumacher, publisher and acquiring editor for Melange and Satin Romance; Caroline Andrus, acquiring editor for Fire and Ice for Young Adult. Estab. 2011. Publishes trade paperback originals and electronic originals. Melange is a royalty-paying company publishing e-books and print books. **Publishes 75 titles/year. Receives 1,000 queries/year. Receives 700 mss/year. 65% of books from first-time authors. 75% from unagented writers. Authors receive a minimum of 20% royalty on print sales, 40% on electronic book sales. Does not offer an advance.** Publishes ms 12-15 months after acceptance. Accepts simultaneous submissions. Responds in 1 month on queries; 2 months on proposals; 4-6 months on mss. Send SASE for book catalog. Guidelines online.

IMPRINTS Imprints include Fire and Ice for Young and New Adults and Satin Romance.

FICTION Subjects include adventure, contemporary, erotica, fantasy, gay, gothic, historical, lesbian, mainstream, multicultural, mystery, romance, science fiction, suspense, western, young adult. Submit a clean mss by following guidelines on website. Query electronically by clicking on "submissions" on website. Include a synopsis and 4 chapters.

MELBOURNE UNIVERSITY PUBLISHING, LTD.

Subsidiary of University of Melbourne, Level 1, 11-15 PL STH., Carlton VIC 3053, Australia. (61)(3)934-20300. **Fax:** (61)(3)9342-0399. **E-mail:** mup-info@unimelb.edu.au. **Website:** www.mup.com.au. **Contact:** The Executive Assistant. Estab. 1922. **Publishes 80 titles/year.** Responds to queries in 4 months if interested. Guidelines online.

IMPRINTS Melbourne University Press; The Miegunyah Press (strong Australian content); Victory Books.

NONFICTION Subjects include art, politics, philosophy, science, social sciences, Aboriginal studies, cultural studies, gender studies, natural history. Submit using MUP Book Proposal Form available online.

MENASHA RIDGE PRESS

2204 First Ave. S., Suite 102, Birmingham AL 35233. (205)322-0439. **E-mail:** tim@keencommunication.com. **Website:** www.menasharidge.com. **Contact:** Tim Jackson, acquisitions editor. Publishes hardcover and trade paperback originals. Menasha Ridge Press publishes distinctive books in the areas of outdoor sports, travel, and diving. "Our authors are among the best in their fields." **Publishes 20 titles/year. 30% of books from first-time authors. 85% from unagented writers. Pays varying royalty. Pays varying advance.** Publishes ms 1 year after acceptance. Accepts simultaneous submissions. Responds in 2 months to queries.

NONFICTION Subjects include recreation, outdoor, sports, adventure, travel, outdoors. Most concepts are generated in-house, but a few come from outside submissions. Submit proposal package, resume, clips. Reviews artwork/photos.

MERRIAM PRESS

133 Elm St., Suite 3R, Bennington VT 05201. (802)447-0313. **E-mail:** ray@merriam-press.com. **Website:** www.merriam-press.com. Estab. 1988. Publishes hardcover and softcover trade paperback originals and reprints. "Merriam Press specializes in military history, particularly World War II history. We are also branching out into other genres." **Publishes 20+ titles/year. 70-90% of books from first-time authors. 100% from unagented writers. Pays 10% royalty on actual selling price.** Publishes ms 6 months or less after acceptance. Responds quickly (e-mail preferred) to queries. Book catalog and guidelines online.

NONFICTION Especially but not limited to military history. Query with SASE or by e-mail first. Send copies of sample chapters or entire ms by mail or on disk/flash drive or as an e-mail attachment (preferred in Word .doc/.docx file format). Reviews artwork/photos.

FICTION Especially but not limited to military history. Query with SASE or by e-mail first.

POETRY Especially but not limited to military topics. Query with SASE or by e-mail first.

TIPS "Our military history books are geared for military historians, collectors, model kit builders, wargamers, veterans, general enthusiasts. We now publish some historical fiction and poetry and will consider well-written books on a variety of non-military topics."

MESSIANIC JEWISH PUBLISHERS

6120 Day Long Ln., Clarksville MD 21029. (410)531-6644. **E-mail:** editor@messianicjewish.net. **Website:** www.messianicjewish.net. Publishes hardcover and trade paperback originals and reprints. **Publishes 6-12 titles/year. Pays 7-15% royalty on wholesale price.** Guidelines via e-mail.

NONFICTION Subjects include religion, Messianic Judaism, Jewish roots of the Christian faith. Text must demonstrate keen awareness of Jewish culture and thought, and Biblical literacy. Jewish themes only. Query with SASE. Unsolicited mss are not returned.

FICTION Subjects include religious. "We publish very little fiction. Jewish or Biblical themes are a must. Text must demonstrate keen awareness of Jewish culture and thought." Query with SASE. Unsolicited mss are not return.

METAL POWDER INDUSTRIES FEDERATION

105 College Rd. E., Princeton NJ 08540. (609)452-7700. **Fax:** (609)987-8523. **Website:** www.mpif.org. Estab. 1946. Publishes hardcover originals. "Metal Powder Industries publishes monographs, textbooks, handbooks, design guides, conference proceedings,

standards, and general titles in the field of powder metallurgy or particulate materials." **Publishes 10 titles/year. Pays 3-12% royalty on wholesale or retail price. Pays $3,000-5,000 advance.** Responds in 1 month to queries.

NONFICTION Work must relate to powder metallurgy or particulate materials.

METHUEN PUBLISHING LTD

Editorial Department, 11-12 Buckingham Gate, London SW1E 6LB, United Kingdom. (44)(207)798-1600. **Fax:** (44)(207)828-2098. **E-mail:** editorial@metheun.co.uk. **Website:** www.methuen.co.uk. Estab. 1889. **Pays royalty.** Guidelines online.

No unsolicited mss; synopses and ideas welcome. Prefers to be approached via agents or a letter of inquiry. No first novels, cookery books or personal memoirs.

NONFICTION Subjects include contemporary culture, film, cinema, stage, government, politics, history, psychology, sports. No cookbooks or memoirs. Query with SASE. Submit outline, resume, publishing history, clips, bio, SASE.

FICTION No first novels. Query with SASE. Submit proposal package, outline, outline/proposal, resume, publishing history, clips, bio, SASE.

TIPS "We recommend that all prospective authors attempt to find an agent before submitting to publishers and we do not encourage unagented submissions."

MIAMI UNIVERSITY PRESS

356 Bachelor Hall, Miami University, Oxford OH 45056. **E-mail:** tumakw@miamioh.edu. **Website:** www.miamioh.edu/mupress. **Contact:** Keith Tuma, editor; Amy Toland, managing editor. Estab. 1992. Publishes 1-2 books of poetry/year and 1 novella, in paperback editions.

POETRY Miami University Press is unable to respond to unsolicited mss and queries.

MICHIGAN STATE UNIVERSITY PRESS

1405 S. Harrison Rd., Suite 25, East Lansing MI 48823-5202. (517)355-9543. **Fax:** (517)432-2611. **E-mail:** msupress@msu.edu. **Website:** msupress.org. **Contact:** Alex Schwartz and Julie Loehr, acquisitions. Estab. 1947. Publishes hardcover and softcover originals. Michigan State University Press has notably represented both scholarly publishing and the mission of Michigan State University with the publication of numerous award-winning books and scholarly journals. In addition, they publish nonfiction that addresses, in a more contemporary way, social concerns, such as diversity and civil rights. They also publish literary fiction and poetry. **Pays variable royalty.** Book catalog and ms guidelines online.

NONFICTION Subjects include Americana, American Studies, business, economics, creative nonfiction, ethnic, Afro-American studies, government, politics, history, contemporary civil rights, language, literature, literary criticism, regional, Great Lakes regional, Canadian studies, women's studies, environmental studies, and American Indian Studies. Distributes books for: University of Calgary Press, University of Alberta Press, and University of Manitoba Press. Submit proposal/outline and sample chapter. Hard copy is preferred but email proposals are also accepted. Initial submissions to MSU Press should be in the form of a short letter of inquiry and a sample chapter(s), as well as our preliminary Marketing Questionnaire, which can be downloaded from their website. We do not accept: Festschrifts, conference papers, or unrevised dissertations. Reviews artwork/photos.

FICTION Subjects include literary. Publishes literary fiction. Submit proposal.

POETRY Publishes poetry collections. Submit proposal with sample poems.

MICROSOFT PRESS

E-mail: 4bkideas@microsoft.com. **Website:** www.microsoft.com/learning/en/us/microsoft-press-books.aspx. **Publishes 80 titles/year. 25% of books from first-time authors. 90% from unagented writers.** Book proposal guidelines online.

NONFICTION Subjects include software. A book proposal should consist of the following information: TOC, a resume with author biography, a writing sample, and a questionnaire. "We place a great deal of emphasis on your proposal. A proposal provides us with a basis for evaluating the idea of the book and how fully your book fulfills its purpose."

MILKWEED EDITIONS

1011 Washington Ave. S., Suite 300, Minneapolis MN 55415. (612)332-3192. **Fax:** (612)215-2550. **Website:** www.milkweed.org. **Contact:** Patrick Thomas, editor and program director. Estab. 1979. Publishes hardcover, trade paperback, and electronic originals; trade paperback and electronic reprints. "Milkweed Editions publishes with the intention of making a humane impact on society, in the belief that literature is a transformative art uniquely able to convey the essential experiences of the human heart and spirit. To that end, Milkweed Editions publishes distinctive voices of literary merit in handsomely designed, visually dynamic books, exploring the ethical, cultural, and esthetic issues that free societies need continually to address." **Publishes 15-20 titles/year. 25% of books from first-time authors. 75% from unagented writers. Pays authors variable royalty based on retail price. Offers advance against royalties. Pays varied advance from $500-10,000.** Publishes ms in 18 months. after acceptance of ms. Accepts simultaneous submissions. Responds in 6 months. Book catalog online. Guidelines online.

NONFICTION Subjects include agriculture, animals, archaeology, art, contemporary culture, creative nonfiction, environment, gardening, gay, government, history, humanities, language, literature, multicultural, nature, politics, literary, regional, translation, women's issues, world affairs. Does not review artwork.

FICTION Subjects include experimental, short story collections, translation, young adult. Novels for adults and for readers 8-13. High literary quality. For adult readers: literary fiction, nonfiction, poetry, essays. Middle readers: adventure, contemporary, fantasy, multicultural, nature/environment, suspense/mystery. Average length: middle readers—90-200 pages. No romance, mysteries, science fiction. Query with SASE, submit completed ms.

POETRY Milkweed Editions is "looking for poetry manuscripts of high quality that embody humane values and contribute to cultural understanding." Not limited in subject matter. Open to writers with previously published books of poetry or a minimum of 6 poems published in nationally distributed commercial or literary journals. Considers translations and bilingual mss. Query with SASE; submit completed ms.

TIPS "We are looking for excellent writing with the intent of making a humane impact on society. Please read submission guidelines before submitting and acquaint yourself with our books in terms of style and quality before submitting. Many factors influence our selection process, so don't get discouraged. Nonfiction is focused on literary writing about the natural world, including living well in urban environments."

MILKWEED FOR YOUNG READERS

Milkweed Editions, Open Book Building, 1011 Washington Ave. S., Suite 300, Minneapolis MN 55415. (612)332-3192. **Fax:** (612)215-2550. **Website:** www.milkweed.org. **Contact:** Patrick Thomas, managing director. Estab. 1984. Publishes hardcover and trade paperback originals. "We are looking first of all for high quality literary writing. We publish books with the intention of making a humane impact on society." **Publishes 3-4 titles/year. 25% of books from first-time authors. 50% from unagented writers. Pays 7% royalty on retail price. Pays variable advance.** Publishes ms 1 year after acceptance. Accepts simultaneous submissions. Responds in 6 months to queries. Book catalog for $1.50. Guidelines online.

FICTION Subjects include adventure, fantasy, historical, humor, mainstream, contemporary, animal, environmental. "Milkweed Editions now accepts manuscripts online through our Submission Manager. If you're a first-time submitter, you'll need to fill in a simple form and then follow the instructions for selecting and uploading your manuscript. Please make sure that your manuscript follows the submission guidelines."

⊘ THE MILLBROOK PRESS

Lerner Publishing Group, 1251 Washington Ave N, Minneapolis MN 55401. **Website:** www.lernerbooks.com. "Millbrook Press publishes informative picture books, illustrated nonfiction titles, and inspiring photo-driven titles for grades K–5. Our authors approach curricular topics with a fresh point of view. Our fact-filled books engage readers with fun yet accessible writing, high-quality photographs, and a wide variety of illustration styles. We cover subjects ranging from the parts of speech and other language arts skills; to history, science, and math; to art, sports, crafts, and other interests. Millbrook Press is the home of the best-selling Words Are CATegorical® series and Bob Raczka's Art Adventures. We do not accept unsolicited manuscripts from authors. Occasionally, we may put out a call for submissions, which will be announced on our website."

MINNESOTA HISTORICAL SOCIETY PRESS

Minnesota Historical Society, 345 Kellogg Blvd. W., St. Paul MN 55102. (651)259-3200. **Fax:** (651)297-1345. **E-mail:** ann.regan@mnhs.org. **Website:** shop.mnhs.org. **Contact:** Ann Regan, editor-in-chief. Estab. 1852. Publishes hardcover, trade paperback and electronic originals; trade paperback and electronic reprints. "Minnesota Historical Society Press publishes both scholarly and general interest books that contribute to the understanding of the Midwest." **Publishes 30 titles/year. 300 queries received/year. 150 mss received/year. 60% of books from first-time authors. 95% from unagented writers. Royalties are negotiated; 5-10% on wholesale price. Pays $1,000 and up.** Publishes ms 16 months after acceptance. Accepts simultaneous submissions. Responds in 1-4 months. Book catalog online. Guidelines online.

NONFICTION Subjects include scholarly, Americana, anthropology, archaeology, art, architecture, community, cooking, foods, nutrition, creative nonfiction, ethnic, government, politics, history, memoirs, multicultural, nature, environment, photography, regional, women's issues, women's studies, Native American studies. Books must have a connection to the Midwest. Regional works only. Submit proposal package, outline, 1 sample chapter and other materials listed in our online website in author guidelines: CV, brief description, intended audience, readership, length of ms, schedule. Reviews artwork/photos. Send photocopies.

MISSOURI HISTORICAL SOCIETY PRESS

The Missouri Historical Society, P.O. Box 11940, St. Louis MO 63112-0040. (314)746-4558 or (314)746-4556. **Fax:** (314)746-4548. **E-mail:** vwmonks@mohistory.org. **Website:** www.mohistory.org. **Contact:** Victoria Monks, publications manager. Publishes hardcover and trade paperback originals and reprints. **Publishes 2-4 titles/year. 30 queries received/year. 20 mss received/year. 10% of books from first-time authors. 80% from unagented writers. Pays 5-10% royalty.** Responds in 1-2 months.

NONFICTION Subjects include art, architecture, history, language, literature, multicultural, regional, sports, women's issues, women's studies, popular culture, photography, children's nonfiction. Query with SASE and request author-proposal form.

TIPS "We're looking for new perspectives, even if the topics are familiar. You'll get our attention with nontraditional voices and views."

MITCHELL LANE PUBLISHERS, INC.

P.O. Box 196, Hockessin DE 19707. (302)234-9426. **Fax:** (866)834-4164. **E-mail:** barbaramitchell@mitchelllane.com. **Website:** www.mitchelllane.com. **Contact:** Barbara Mitchell, publisher. Estab. 1993. Publishes hardcover and library bound originals. **Publishes 80 titles/year. 100 queries received/year. 5 mss received/year. 0% of books from first-time authors. 90% from unagented writers. Work purchased outright from authors (range: $350-2,000). Pays illustrators by the project (range: $40-400).** Publishes ms 1 year after acceptance. Responds only if interested to queries. Book catalog available free.

NONFICTION Subjects include ethnic, multicultural. Young readers, middle readers, young adults: biography, nonfiction, and curriculum-related subjects. Average word length: 4,000-50,000 words. Recently published: *My Guide to US Citizenship*, *Rivers of the World* and *Vote America*. Query with SASE. *All unsolicited mss discarded.*

TIPS "We hire writers on a 'work-for-hire' basis to complete book projects we assign. Send résumé and writing samples that do not need to be returned."

MONDIAL

203 W. 107th St., Suite 6C, New York NY 10025. (212)851-3252. **Fax:** (208)361-2863. **E-mail:** contact@mondialbooks.com. **Website:** www.mondialbooks.com; www.librejo.com. **Contact:** Andrew Moore, editor. Estab. 1996. Publishes hard cover, trade paperback originals and reprints. **Publishes 20 titles/year. 2,000 queries received/year. 500 mss received/year. 20%% of books from first-time authors. Pays 10% royalty on wholesale price.** Publishes ms 4 months after acceptance. Accepts simultaneous submissions. Responds to queries in 3 months. Responds only if interested. Guidelines available online.

NONFICTION Subjects include alternative, ethnic, gay, lesbian, history, language, literature, literary criticism, memoirs, multicultural, philosophy, psychology, sex, sociology, translation. Submit proposal package, outline, 1 sample chapters. Send only electronically by e-mail.

FICTION Subjects include adventure, erotica, ethnic, gay, lesbian, historical, literary, mainstream, contemporary, multicultural, mystery, poetry, romance, short story collections, translation. Query through online submission form.

MONTANA HISTORICAL SOCIETY PRESS

225 N. Roberts St., Helene MT 59620-1201. (406)444-4741. **E-mail:** mholz@mt.gov. **Website:** www.montanahistoricalsociety.org. **Contact:** Molly Holz, editor. Estab. 1956. Publishes hardcover originalsand trade paperback originals and reprints. **Publishes 4 titles/**

year. 24 queries received/year. 16 mss received/year. 50% of books from first-time authors. 100% from unagented writers. Pays 5-10% royalty on wholesale price. Publishes ms 1 year after acceptance. Responds in 1 month to queries; 2 months to proposals; 4 months to mss. Book catalog online. Guidelines online.

NONFICTION Subjects include anthropology, archeology, history, military, war, nature, environment, regional, travel. "We publish history and environmental studies books focusing on the northern plains and Rocky Mountains." Query with SASE.

TIPS "Audience includes history buffs; people with an interest in Yellowstone National Park."

Ⓐ⊘ MOODY PUBLISHERS

Moody Bible Institute, 820 N. LaSalle Blvd., Chicago IL 60610. (800)678-8812. **Fax:** (312)329-4157. **E-mail:** authors@moody.edu. **Website:** www.moodypublishers.org. Estab. 1894. Publishes hardcover, trade, and mass market paperback originals. "The mission of Moody Publishers is to educate and edify the Christian and to evangelize the non-Christian by ethically publishing conservative, evangelical Christian literature and other media for all ages around the world, and to help provide resources for Moody Bible Institute in its training of future Christian leaders." **Publishes 60 titles/year. 1,500 queries received/year. 2,000 mss received/year. 1% of books from first-time authors. 80% from unagented writers. Royalty varies.** Publishes ms 1 year after acceptance. Responds in 2-3 months to queries. Book catalog for 9×12 envelope and 4 first-class stamps. Guidelines online.

NONFICTION Subjects include child guidance, money, finance, religion, spirituality, women's issues, women's studies. "We are no longer reviewing queries or unsolicited manuscripts unless they come to us through an agent. Unsolicited proposals will be returned only if proper postage is included. We are not able to acknowledge the receipt of your unsolicited proposal." Does not accept unsolicited nonfiction submissions.

FICTION Subjects include fantasy, historical, mystery, religious, children's religious, inspirational, religious mystery/suspense, science fiction, young adult, adventure, fantasy/science fiction, historical, mystery/suspense, series. *Agented submissions only.*

TIPS "In our fiction list, we're looking for Christian storytellers rather than teachers trying to present a message. Your motivation should be to delight the reader. Using your skills to create beautiful works is glorifying to God."

MOREHOUSE PUBLISHING CO.

Church Publishing Incorporated, 19 E. 34th St., New York NY 10016. **Fax:** (717)541-8136. **E-mail:** dperkins@cpg.org. **Website:** www.morehousepublishing.org. **Contact:** Davis Perkins. Estab. 1884. Publishes hardcover and paperback originals. Morehouse Publishing publishes mainline Christian books, primarily Episcopal/Anglican works. Currently emphasizing Christian spiritual direction. **Publishes 35 titles/year. 50% of books from first-time authors. Pays small advance.** Publishes ms 18 months after acceptance. Accepts simultaneous submissions. Responds in 2-3 months to queries. Guidelines online.

NONFICTION Subjects include religion, Christian, women's issues, women's studies, Christian spirituality, liturgies, congregational resources, issues around Christian life. Submit outline, résumé, 1-2 sample chapters, market analysis.

MOTORBOOKS

Quayside Publishing Group, Motorbooks, 400 First Ave. N., Suite 400, Minneapolis MN 55401. (612)344-8100. **Fax:** (612)344-8691. **E-mail:** zmiller@quartous.com. **Website:** www.motorbooks.com. **Contact:** Zack Miller. Estab. 1973. Publishes hardcover and paperback originals. "Motorbooks is one of the world's leading transportation publishers, covering subjects from classic motorcycles to heavy equipment to today's latest automotive technology. We satisfy our customers' high expectations by hiring top writers and photographers and presenting their work in handsomely designed books that work hard in the shop and look good on the coffee table." **Publishes 200 titles/year. 300 queries received/year. 50 mss received/year. 95% from unagented writers. Pays $5,000 average advance.** Publishes ms 1 year after acceptance. Accepts simultaneous submissions. Responds in 6-8 months to proposals. Book catalog available free. Guidelines online.

NONFICTION Subjects include Americana, history, hobbies, military, war, photography, translation, nonfiction. State qualifications for doing book. Transportation-related subjects. Query with SASE. Reviews artwork/photos. Send photocopies.

THE MOUNTAINEERS BOOKS

1001 SW Klickitat Way, Suite 201, Seattle WA 98134-1162. (206)223-6303. **Fax:** (206)223-6306. **E-mail:** submissions@mountaineersbooks.org. **Website:** www.mountaineersbooks.org. **Contact:** Kate Rogers, editor in chief. Estab. 1961. Publishes hardcover and trade paperback originals and reprints. "Mountaineers Books specializes in expert, authoritative books dealing with mountaineering, hiking, backpacking, skiing, snowshoeing, etc. These can be either how-to-do-it or where-to-do-it (guidebooks). Currently emphasizing regional conservation and natural history." **Publishes 40 titles/year. 25% of books from first-time authors. 98% from unagented writers. Pays advance.** Publishes ms 1 year after acceptance. Responds in 3 months to queries. Guidelines online.

NONFICTION Subjects include nature, environment, recreation, regional, sports, non-competitive self-propelled, translation, travel, natural history, conservation. Accepts nonfiction translations. Looks for expert knowledge, good organization. Also interested in nonfiction adventure narratives. Does *not* want to see anything dealing with hunting, fishing or motorized travel. Submit outline, 2 sample chapters, bio.

TIPS "The type of book the writer has the best chance of selling to our firm is an authoritative guidebook (*in our field*) to a specific area not otherwise covered; or a how-to that is better than existing competition (again, *in our field*)."

MOUNTAIN PRESS PUBLISHING CO.

P.O. Box 2399, Missoula MT 59806. (406)728-1900 or (800)234-5308. **Fax:** (406)728-1635. **E-mail:** info@mtnpress.com. **Website:** www.mountain-press.com. **Contact:** Jennifer Carey, editor. Estab. 1948. Publishes hardcover and trade paperback originals. "We are expanding our Roadside Geology, Geology Underfoot, and Roadside History series (done on a state-by-state basis). We are interested in well-written regional field guides—plants and flowers—and readable history and natural history." **Publishes 15 titles/year. 50% of books from first-time authors. 90% from unagented writers. Pays 7-12% royalty on wholesale price.** Publishes ms 2 years after acceptance. Responds in 3 months to queries. Book catalog online.

Expanding children's/juvenile nonfiction titles.

NONFICTION Subjects include animals, history, Western, nature, environment, regional, science, Earth science. No personal histories or journals, poetry or fiction. Query with SASE. Submit outline, sample chapters. Reviews artwork/photos.

TIPS "Find out what kind of books a publisher is interested in and tailor your writing to them; research markets and target your audience. Research other books on the same subjects. Make yours different. Don't present your manuscript to a publisher—sell it. Give the information needed to make a decision on a title. Please learn what we publish before sending your proposal. We are a 'niche' publisher."

MOVING PARTS PRESS

10699 Empire Grade, Santa Cruz CA 95060. (831)427-2271. **E-mail:** frice@movingpartspress.com. **Website:** www.movingpartspress.com. **Contact:** Felicia Rice, poetry editor. Estab. 1977. Moving Part Press publishes handsome, innovative books, broadsides, and prints that "explore the relationship of word and image, typography and the visual arts, the fine arts and popular culture."

POETRY *Does not accept unsolicited mss.*

MSI PRESS

1760-F Airline Hwy, #203, Hollister CA 95023. **E-mail:** editor@msipress.com. **Website:** www.msipress.com. **Contact:** Betty Leaver, managing editor (foreign culture, self-help, spirituality, religion, memoir, mind/body/spirit). Estab. 2003. Publishes trade paperback originals and corresponding e-books. **Publishes 8-12 titles/year. 10% of books from first-time authors. 100% from unagented writers. Pays 10% royalty on retail price.** Publishes ms 6-12 months after acceptance. Accepts simultaneous submissions. Responds in 1 month to queries and proposals; 2 months to mss. Catalog online. Guidelines available by e-mail.

NONFICTION Subjects include education, health, humanities, language, medicine, psychology, spirituality. "We are hoping to expand our spirituality, psychology, and self-help line." Submit proposal package, including: outline, 1 sample chapter, and professional resume. Prefers electronic submissions. Reviews artwork/photos; send computer disk, or, preferably, e-file.

TIPS "We are interested in helping to develop new writers who have good literacy skills and a strong story. We also have the capacity to work with authors with limited English skills whose first language is Arabic, Russian, Spanish, French, German, or Czech."

MUSSIO VENTURES PUBLISHING LTD.

106 - 1500 Hartley Ave., Coquitlam BC V3K 7A1, Canada. **E-mail:** info@backroadmapbooks.com. **Website:** www.backroadmapbooks.com. Estab. 1993. "We are in the business of producing, publishing, distributing and marketing Outdoor Recreation guidebooks and maps. We are also actively looking to advance our digital side of the business including making our products Google Earth, cell phone or iPhone and GPS compatible." **Publishes 5 titles/year. 5 queries received/year. 2 mss received/year. 25% of books from first-time authors. Makes outright purchase of $2,000-4,800. Pays $1,000 advance.** Publishes ms 12 months after acceptance. Accepts simultaneous submissions. Responds in 1 month. Book catalog available free.

NONFICTION Subjects include nature, environment, maps and guides. Submit proposal package, outline/proposal, 1 sample chapter. Reviews artwork/photos. Send photocopies and digital files.

TIPS "Audience includes outdoor recreation enthusiasts and travellers. Provide a proposal including an outline and samples."

MVP BOOKS

MBI Publishing and Quayside Publishing Group, 400 First Ave. N, Suite 400, Minneapolis MN 55401. (612)344-8160. **Website:** www.mvpbooks.com. Estab. 2009. Publishes hardcover and trade paperback originals. "We publish books for enthusiasts in a wide variety of sports, recreation, and fitness subjects, including heavily illustrated celebrations, narrative works, and how-to instructional guides. We seek authors who are strongly committed to helping us promote and sell their books. Please present as focused an idea as possible in a brief submission. Note your credentials for writing the book. Tell all you know about the market niche, existing competition, and marketing possibilities for proposed book." **Publishes 15-20 titles/year. Pays royalty or fees. Pays advance.** Publishes ms 1 year after acceptance. Responds in 3 months to queries.

NONFICTION Subjects include sports (baseball, football, basketball, hockey, surfing, golf, bicycling, martial arts, etc.); outdoor activities (hunting and fishing); health and fitness. No children's books. Query with SASE. "We consider queries from both first-time and experienced authors as well as agented or unagented projects. Submit outline." Reviews artwork/photos. Send sample digital images or transparencies (duplicates and tearsheets only).

NATIONAL ASSOCIATION FOR MUSIC EDUCATION

1806 Robert Fulton Dr., Reston VA 20191-4348. **Fax:** (703)860-1531. **E-mail:** ellaw@nafme.org. **Website:** www.nafme.org. **Contact:** Ella Wilcox, editor. Estab. 1907. Publishes hardcover and trade paperback originals. "Our mission is to advance music education by encouraging the study and making of music by all." **Publishes 5 titles/year. 75 queries received/year. 50 mss received/year. 40% of books from first-time authors. 100% from unagented writers. Pays royalty on retail price.** Publishes ms 1-2 years after acceptance. Responds in 2 months to queries; 4 months to proposals. Catalog and guidelines online.

NONFICTION Subjects include child guidance, education, multicultural, music, dance, music education. Mss evaluated by professional music educators. Submit proposal package, outline, 1-3 sample chapters, bio, CV, marketing strategy. For journal articles, submit electronically to http://mc.manuscriptcentral.com/mej. Authors will be required to set up an online account on the SAGETRACK system powered by ScholarOne (this can take about 30 minutes). From their account, a new submission can be initiated.

TIPS "Look online for book proposal guidelines. No telephone calls. We are committed to music education books that will serve as the very best resources for music educators, students and their parents."

NATIONAL GEOGRAPHIC CHILDREN'S BOOKS

1145 17th St. NW, Washington DC 20090-8199. (800)647-5463. **Website:** www.ngchildrensbooks.org. National Geographic CHildren's Books provides quality nonfiction for children and young adults by award-winning authors. *This market does not currently accept unsolicited mss.*

NATUREGRAPH PUBLISHERS, INC.

P.O. Box 1047, Happy Camp CA 96039. **Fax:** (530)493-5240. **E-mail:** nature@sisqtel.net. **Website:** www.naturegraph.com. **Contact:** Barbara Brown, owner. Estab. 1946. Publishes trade paperback originals. **Publishes 2 titles/year. 300 queries received/year. 12 mss received/year. 80% of books from first-time authors.** Publishes ms 2 years after acceptance. Accepts simultaneous submissions. Responds in 1 month to queries; 2 months to mss. Book catalog for #10 SASE.

NONFICTION Subjects include anthropology, archaeology, multicultural, nature, environment, science, natural history: biology, geology, ecology, astronomy, crafts.
TIPS "Please-always send a stamped reply envelope. Publishers get hundreds of manuscripts yearly."

THE NAUTICAL & AVIATION PUBLISHING CO.

845 A Low Country Blvd., Mt. Pleasant SC 29464. (843)856-0561. **Fax:** (843)856-3164. **E-mail:** nauticalaviationpublishing@comcast.net. **Website:** www.nauticalaviation.bizland.com. Estab. 1979. Publishes hardcover and trade paperback originals and reprints. **Publishes 6 titles/year. 200 queries received/year. Pays royalty.** Accepts simultaneous submissions. Book catalog and guidelines available free.
NONFICTION Subjects include military, war, American, naval history. Query with SASE. Submit 3 sample chapters, synopsis.
FICTION Subjects include historical, military, war. Submit complete ms with cover letter and brief synopsis.
TIPS "We are primarily a nonfiction publisher, but we will review historical fiction of military interest with strong literary merit."

NAVAL INSTITUTE PRESS

US Naval Institute, 291 Wood Rd., Annapolis MD 21402. (410)268-6110. **Fax:** (410)295-1084. **E-mail:** books@usni.org. **Website:** www.usni.org. Estab. 1873. "The Naval Institute Press publishes trade and scholarly nonfiction. We are interested in national and international security, naval, military, military jointness, intelligence, and special warfare, both current and historical." **Publishes 80-90 titles/year. 50% of books from first-time authors. 90% from unagented writers.** Guidelines online.
NONFICTION Submit proposal package with outline, author bio, TOC, description/synopsis, sample chapter(s), page/word count, number of illustrations, ms completion date, intended market; or submit complete ms. Send SASE with sufficient postage for return of ms. Send by postal mail only. No e-mail submissions, please.

⊘ NAVPRESS

351 Executive Dr., Carol Stream IL 60188. **Website:** www.navpress.com. Estab. 1975. Publishes hardcover, trade paperback, direct and mass market paperback originals and reprints; electronic books and Bible studies. **Pays royalty. Pays low or no advances.** Book catalog available free.
NONFICTION Subjects include child guidance, parenting, sociology, spirituality and contemporary culture, Christian living, marriage.

NBM PUBLISHING

160 Broadway, Suite 700, East Bldg., New York NY 10038. **E-mail:** nbmgn@nbmpub.com. **Website:** nbmpub.com. **Contact:** Terry Nantier, editor/art director. Estab. 1976. Publishes graphic novels for an audience of YA/adults. Types of books include fiction, mystery and social parodies.

Ⓐ⊘ THOMAS NELSON, INC.

HarperCollins Christian Publishing, Box 141000, Nashville TN 37214-1000. (615)889-9000. **Website:** www.thomasnelson.com. Publishes hardcover and paperback orginals. Thomas Nelson publishes Christian lifestyle nonfiction and fiction, and general nonfiction. **Publishes 100-150 titles/year. Rates negotiated for each project. Pays advance.** Publishes ms 1-2 years after acceptance. Accepts simultaneous submissions.
NONFICTION Subjects include business, economics, business, economics development, cooking, foods, nutrition, gardening, health, medicine, and fitness, religion, spirituality, adult inspirational, motivational, devotional, Christian living, prayer and evangelism, Bible study, personal development, political, biography/autobiography. *Does not accept unsolicited mss.* No phone queries.
FICTION Publishes authors of commercial fiction who write for adults from a Christian perspective. *Does not accept unsolicited mss.* No phone queries.

⊘ TOMMY NELSON

Imprint of Thomas Nelson, Inc., P.O. Box 141000, Nashville TN 37214-1000. (615)889-9000. **Fax:** (615)902-2219. **Website:** www.tommynelson.com. Publishes hardcover and trade paperback originals. "Tommy Nelson publishes children's Christian nonfiction and fiction for boys and girls up to age 14. We honor God and serve people through books, videos, software and Bibles for children that improve the lives of our customers." **Publishes 50-75 titles/year.** Guidelines online.
NONFICTION Subjects include religion, Christian evangelical. *Does not accept unsolicited mss.*

FICTION Subjects include adventure, juvenile, mystery, picture books, religious. No stereotypical characters. *Does not accept unsolicited mss.*

TIPS "Know the Christian Booksellers Association market. Check out the Christian bookstores to see what sells and what is needed."

NEW AMERICAN LIBRARY

Penguin Putnam, Inc., 375 Hudson St., New York NY 10014. (212)366-2000. **Fax:** (212)366-2889. **Website:** www.penguinputnam.com. Estab. 1948. Publishes mass market and trade paperback originals and reprints. NAL publishes commercial fiction and nonfiction for the popular audience. **Pays negotiable royalty. Pays negotiable advance.** Book catalog for SASE.

NONFICTION Subjects include animals, child guidance, ethnic, health, medicine, military, war, psychology, sports, movie tie-in. *Agented submissions only.*

FICTION Subjects include erotica, ethnic, fantasy, historical, horror, mainstream, contemporary, mystery, romance, science fiction, suspense, western, chicklit. All kinds of commercial fiction. *Agented submissions only.*

NEW DIRECTIONS

80 Eighth Ave., New York NY 10011. **Fax:** (212)255-0231. **E-mail:** editorial@ndbooks.com. **Website:** www.ndpublishing.com. **Contact:** Editorial Assistant. Estab. 1936. Hardcover and trade paperback originals. "Currently, New Directions focuses primarily on fiction in translation, avant garde American fiction, and experimental poetry by American and foreign authors. If your work does not fall into one of those categories, you would probably do best to submit your work elsewhere." **Publishes 30 titles/year.** Responds in 3-4 months to queries. Book catalog and guidelines online.

FICTION Subjects include ethnic, experimental, historical, humor, literary, poetry, poetry in translation, regional, short story collections, suspense, translation. No juvenile or young adult, occult or paranormal, genre fiction (formula romances, sci-fi or westerns), arts & crafts, and inspirational poetry. Brief query only.

POETRY Query.

TIPS "Our books serve the academic community."

NEWEST PUBLISHERS LTD.

201, 8540-109 St., Edmonton AB T6G 1E6, Canada. (780)432-9427. **Fax:** (780)433-3179. **E-mail:** submissions@newestpress.com. **Website:** www.newestpress.com. Estab. 1977. Publishes trade paperback originals. NeWest publishes Western Canadian fiction, nonfiction, poetry, and drama. **Publishes 13-16 titles/year. 40% of books from first-time authors. 85% from unagented writers. Pays 10% royalty.** Publishes ms 2-3 years after acceptance. Accepts simultaneous submissions. Responds in 6-8 months to queries. Book catalog for 9×12 SASE. Guidelines online.

NONFICTION Subjects include ethnic, government, politics, Western Canada, history, Western Canada, nature, environment, northern, Canadian. Query.

FICTION Subjects include literary. Submit complete ms.

NEW FORUMS PRESS

New Forums, 1018 S. Lewis St., Stillwater OK 74074. (405)372-6158. **Fax:** (405)377-2237. **E-mail:** contact@newforums.com. **E-mail:** submissions@newforums.com. **Website:** www.newforums.com. **Contact:** Doug Dollar, president (interests: higher education, Oklahoma-Regional). Estab. 1981. Hardcover and trade paperback originals. "New Forums Press is an independent publisher offering works devoted to various aspects of professional development in higher education, home and office aides, and various titles of a regional interest. We welcome suggestions for thematic series of books and thematic issues of our academic journals—addressing a single issue, problem, or theory." **60% of books from first-time authors. 100% from unagented writers.** Use online guidelines or call (800)606-3766 with any questions.

NONFICTION Subjects include business, finance, history, literature, money, music, politics, regional, sociology, young adult. "We are actively seeking new authors—send for review copies and author guidelines, and visit our website." Mss should be submitted as a Microsoft Word document, or a similar standard word processor document (saved in RTF rich text), as an attachment to an e-mail sent to submissions@newforums.com. Otherwise, submit your manuscript on 8 ½ x 11 inch white bond paper (one original). The name and complete address, telephone, fax number, and e-mail address of each author should appear on a separate cover page, so it can be removed for the blind review process.

NEW HARBINGER PUBLICATIONS

5674 Shattuck Ave., Oakland CA 94609. (510)652-0215. **Fax:** (510)652-5472. **E-mail:** proposals@newharbinger.com. **Website:** www.newharbinger.com.

Estab. 1973. "We look for psychology and health self-help books that teach readers how to master essential life skills. Mental health professionals who want simple, clear explanations or important psychological techniques and health issues also read our books. Thus, our books must be simple ane easy to understand but also complete and authoritative. Most of our authors are therapists or other helping professionals." **Publishes 55 titles/year. 1,000 queries received/year. 300 mss received/year. 60% of books from first-time authors. 75% from unagented writers.** Publishes ms 1 year after acceptance. Accepts simultaneous submissions. Responds in 2 weeks to queries; 1 month to proposals; 2 months to mss. Book catalog free. Guidelines online.

NONFICTION Subjects include health, medicine, psychology, women's issues, women's studies, psycho spirituality, anger management, anxiety, coping, mindfulness skills. Authors need to be qualified psychotherapists or health practitioners to publish with us. Submit proposal package, outline, 2 sample chapters, TOC, competing titles, and a compelling, supported reason why the book is unique.

TIPS "Audience includes psychotherapists and lay readers wanting step-by-step strategies to solve specific problems. Our definition of a self-help psychology or health book is one that teaches essential life skills. The primary goal is to train the reader so that, after reading the book, he or she can deal more effectively with health and/or psychological challenges."

NEW HOPE PUBLISHERS

Woman's Missionary Union, P.O. Box 12065, Birmingham AL 35202-2065. (205)991-4950. **Fax:** (205)991-4015. **E-mail:** new_hope@wmu.org. **Website:** www.newhopepublishers.com. **Contact:** Acquisitions Editor. "Our vision is to challenge believers to understand and be radically involved in the missions of God. This market does not accept unsolicited mss. We encourage you to post your proposal at ChristianManuscriptSubmissions.com." **Publishes 20-28 titles/year. 25% of books from first-time authors.** Publishes ms 2 years after acceptance.

NONFICTION Subjects include child guidance, from Christian perspective, education, Christian church, health, medicine, Christian, multicultural, religion, spiritual development, Bible study, life situations from Christian perspective, ministry, women's issues, women's studies, Christian, church leadership. "We publish books dealing with all facets of Christian life for women and families, including health, discipleship, missions, ministry, Bible studies, spiritual development, parenting, and marriage. We currently do not accept adult fiction or children's picture books. We are particularly interested in niche categories and books on lifestyle development and change." Prefers a query and prospectus.

NEW HORIZON PRESS

P.O. Box 669, Far Hills NJ 07931. (908)604-6311. **Fax:** (908)604-6330. **E-mail:** nhp@newhorizonpressbooks.com. **Website:** www.newhorizonpressbooks.com. **Contact:** Dr. Joan S. Dunphy, publisher (nonfiction, social issues, crime). Estab. 1983. Publishes hardcover and trade paperback originals. "New Horizon publishes adult nonfiction featuring stories of uncommon heroes, crime, social issues, and self help." **Publishes 12 titles/year. 90% of books from first-time authors. 50% from unagented writers. Pays standard royalty on net receipts. Pays advance.** Publishes ms within 2 years of acceptance. after acceptance of ms. Accepts simultaneous submissions. Book catalog available free. Guidelines online.

IMPRINTS Small Horizons.

NONFICTION Subjects include child guidance, creative nonfiction, government, politics, health, medicine, nature, environment, psychology, women's issues, women's studies, crime. Submit proposal package, outline, résumé, bio, 3 sample chapters, photo, marketing information.

TIPS "We are a small publisher, thus it is important that the author/publisher have a good working relationship. The author must be willing to promote his book."

NEW ISSUES POETRY & PROSE

Western Michigan University, 1903 W. Michigan Ave., Kalamazoo MI 49008-5463. (269)387-8185. **Fax:** (269)387-2562. **E-mail:** new-issues@wmich.edu. **Website:** wmich.edu/newissues. **Contact:** Managing Editor. Estab. 1996. **50% of books from first-time authors. 95% from unagented writers.** Publishes book Publishes 18 months after acceptance. Accepts simultaneous submissions. Guidelines online.

FICTION Subjects include literary, poetry. Only considers submissions to book contests.

POETRY New Issues Poetry & Prose offers two contests annually. The Green Rose Prize is awarded to an author who has previously published at least one full-length book of poems. The New Issues Poetry Prize, an award for a first book of poems, is chosen by a guest judge. Past judges have included Philip Levine, C.K. Williams, C.D. Wright, and Campbell McGrath. New Issues does not read mss outside our contests. Graduate students in the Ph.D. and M.F.A. programs of Western Michigan Univ. often volunteer their time reading mss. Finalists are chosen by the editors. New Issues often publishes up to 2 additional mss selected from the finalists.

NEW LIBRI PRESS

4230 95th Ave. SE, Mercer Island WA 98040. **E-mail:** query@newlibri.com. **Website:** www.newlibri.com. **Contact:** Michael Muller, editor; Stanislav Fritz, editor. Estab. 2011. Publishes trade paperback, electronic original, electronic reprints. **Publishes 10 titles/year. 80% of books from first-time authors. 100% from unagented writers. Pays 20-35% royalty on wholesale price. No advance.** Publishes ms 9-12 months after acceptance. Responds in 3 months to mss. Catalog online. Guidelines online. Electronic submissions only.

NONFICTION Subjects include agriculture, automotive, business, child guidance, computers, cooking, creative nonfiction, economics, electronics, environment, gardening, hobbies, house and home, nature, parenting, recreation, science, sex, software, translation, travel. "Writers should know we embrace e-books. This means that some formats and types of books work well and others don't." Prefers e-mail. Submit proposal package, including outline, 2 sample chapters, and summary of market from author's perspective. Prefers complete ms.

FICTION Subjects include adventure, experimental, fantasy, historical, horror, literary, mainstream, military, mystery, science fiction, translation, war, western, young adult. "Open to most ideas right now; this will change as we mature as a press. As a new press, we are more open than most and time will probably shape the direction. That said, trite as it is, we want good writing that is fun to read. While we currently are not looking for some sub-genres, if it is well written and a bit off the beaten path, submit to us. We are e-book focused. We may not create a paper version if the e-book does not sell, which means some fiction may be less likely to currently sell (e.g. picture books would work only on an iPad or Color Nook as of this writing)." Submit proposal package, including synopsis. Prefers complete ms.

TIPS "Our audience is someone who is comfortable reading an e-book,or someone who is tired of the recycled authors of mainstream publishing, but still wants a good, relatively fast, reading experience. The industry is changing, while we accept for the traditional model, we are searching for writers who are interested in sharing the risk and controlling their own destiny. We embrace writers with no agent."

NEW RIVERS PRESS

MSU Moorhead, 1104 Seventh Ave. S., Moorhead MN 56563. **E-mail:** kelleysu@mnstate.edu. **Website:** www.newriverspress.com. **Contact:** Suzzanne Kelley, managing editor. Estab. 1968. New Rivers Press publishes collections of poetry, novels, nonfiction, translations of contemporary literature, and collections of short fiction and nonfiction. "We continue to publish books regularly by new and emerging writers, but we also welcome the opportunity to read work of every character and to publish the best literature available nationwide. Each fall through the Many Voices Project competition, we choose 2 books: 1 poetry and 1 prose."

FICTION Sponsors American Fiction Prize to find best unpublished short stories by American writers.

POETRY The Many Voices Project awards $1,000, a standard book contract, publication of a book-length ms by New Rivers Press, and national distribution. All previously published poems must be acknowledged. "We will consider simultaneous submissions if noted as such. If your manuscript is accepted elsewhere during the judging, you must notify New Rivers Press immediately. If you do not give such notification and your manuscript is selected, your entry gives New Rivers Press permission to go ahead with publication." Guidelines online.

NEWSAGE PRESS

P.O. Box 607, Troutdale OR 97060-0607. (503)695-2211. **E-mail:** info@newsagepress.com. **Website:** www.newsagepress.com. Estab. 1985. Publishes trade paperback originals. "We focus on nonfiction books. No 'how-to' books or cynical, despairing books. Photo-essay books in large format are no longer published by Newsage Press. No novels or other forms of fiction." Guidelines online.

NONFICTION Subjects include animals, multicultural, nature, environment, womens issues, womens studies, death/dying. Submit 2 sample chapters, proposal (no more than 1 page), SASE.

NEW SOCIETY PUBLISHERS

P.O. Box 189, Gabriola Island BC V0R 1X0, Canada. (250)247-9737. **Fax:** (250)247-7471. **E-mail:** editor@newsociety.com. **Website:** www.newsociety.com. Publishes trade paperback originals and reprints and electronic originals. **Publishes 25 titles/year. 400 queries received/year. 300 mss received/year. 50% of books from first-time authors. 80% from unagented writers. Pays 10-12% royalty on wholesale price. Pays $0-5,000 advance.** Publishes ms about 9 months after acceptance. Accepts simultaneous submissions. Responds in 1-2 months. Book catalog and guidelines online.

NONFICTION Subjects include business, economics, child guidance, creative nonfiction, education, government, politics, memoirs, nature, environment, philosophy, regional, sustainability, open building, peak oil, renewable energy, post carbon prep, sustainable living, gardening & cooking, green building, natural building, ecological design & planning, environment & economy. Query with SASE. Submit proposal package, outline, 2 sample chapters. Reviews artwork/photos. Send photocopies.

TIPS "Audience is activists, academics. Don't get an agent!"

NEW WORLD LIBRARY

14 Pamaron Way, Novato CA 94949. (415)884-2100. **Fax:** (415)884-2199. **E-mail:** submit@newworldlibrary.com. **Website:** www.newworldlibrary.com. **Contact:** Jonathan Wichmann, submissions editor. Estab. 1979. Publishes hardcover and trade paperback originals and reprints. "NWL is dedicated to publishing books that inspire and challenge us to improve the quality of our lives and our world." Prefers e-mail submissions. No longer accepting children's mss. **Publishes 35-40 titles/year. 10% of books from first-time authors. 40% from unagented writers.** Accepts simultaneous submissions. Responds in 3 months to queries. Book catalog free. Guidelines online.

NONFICTION Submit outline, bio, 2-3 sample chapters, SASE.

NEW YORK UNIVERSITY PRESS

838 Broadway, 3rd Floor, New York NY 10003. (212)998-2575. **Fax:** (212)995-3833. **E-mail:** information@nyupress.org. **Website:** www.nyupress.org. **Contact:** Ellen Chodosh, director. Estab. 1916. Hardcover and trade paperback originals. "New York University Press embraces ideological diversity. We often publish books on the same issue from different poles to generate dialogue, engender and resist pat categorizations." **Publishes 100 titles/year. 800-1,000 queries received/year. 30% of books from first-time authors. 90% from unagented writers.** Publishes ms 9-11 months after acceptance. Accepts simultaneous submissions. Responds in 1-4 months (peer reviewed) to proposals. Guidelines online.

NONFICTION Subjects include business, economics, ethnic, gay, lesbian, government, politics, language, literature, military, war, psychology, regional, religion, sociology, women's issues, women's studies, American history, anthropology. New York University Press is a publisher primarily of academic books and is a department of the New York University Division of Libraries. NYU Press publishes in the humanities and social sciences, with emphasis on sociology, law, cultural and American studies, religion, American history, anthropology, politics, criminology, media and film, and psychology. The Press also publishes books on New York regional history, politics, and culture. Query with SASE. Submit proposal package, outline, 1 sample chapter. Reviews artwork/photos. Send photocopies.

NINETY-SIX PRESS

Furman University, 3300 Poinsett Hwy., Greenville SC 29613. (864)294-3152. **Fax:** (864)294-2224. **E-mail:** gil.allen@furman.edu. **Website:** library.furman.edu/specialcollections/96Press/index.htm. **Contact:** Gilbert Allen, editor. Estab. 1991. For a sample, send $10.

TIPS "South Carolina poets only. Check our website for guidelines."

NODIN PRESS

5114 Cedar Lake Rd., Minneapolis MN 55416. (952)546-6300. **Fax:** (952)546-6303. **E-mail:** nstill4402@aol.com. **Contact:** Norton Stillman, publisher. Publishes hardcover and trade paperback originals. "Nodin Press publishes Minnesota regional titles: nonfiction, memoir, sports, poetry." **Publishes 9 titles/year. 40 queries received/year. 40 mss received/year. 50% of books from first-time authors. 100% from unagented writers. Pays 5% royalty.** Publishes ms 6 months after acceptance. Accepts simultaneous submissions. Responds in 6 months to queries. Book catalog and ms guidelines free.

NONFICTION Subjects include history, ethnic, regional, sports, travel. Query with SASE.

POETRY Regional (Minnesota poets). Submit 10 sample poems.

NOLO

950 Parker St., Berkeley CA 94710. (510)549-1976. **Fax:** (510)859-0025. **E-mail:** mantha@nolo.com. **Website:** www.nolo.com. **Contact:** Editorial Department. Estab. 1971. Publishes trade paperback originals. "We publish practical, do-it-yourself books, software and various electronic products on financial and legal issues that affect individuals, small business, and nonprofit organizations. We specialize in helping people handle their own legal tasks; i.e., write a will, file a small claims lawsuit, start a small business or nonprofit, or apply for a patent." **Publishes 75 new editions and 15 new titles/year. 20% of books from first-time authors. Pays advance.** Accepts simultaneous submissions. Responds in 3 weeks to queries. Responds in 5 weeks to proposals. Guidelines online.

NONFICTION Subjects include business, economics, money, finance, legal guides in various topics including employment, small business, intellectual property, parenting and education, finance and investment, landlord/tenant, real estate, and estate planning. Query with SASE. Submit outline, 1 sample chapter.

NOMAD PRESS

2456 Christain St., White River Junction VT 05001. (802)649-1995. **Fax:** (802)649-2667. **E-mail:** rachel@nomadpress.net; info@nomadpress.net. **Website:** www.nomadpress.net. **Contact:** Alex Kahan, publisher. Estab. 2001. "We produce nonfiction children's activity books that bring a particular science or cultural topic into sharp focus. Nomad Press does not accept unsolicited manuscripts. If authors are interested in contributing to our children's series, please send a writing resume that includes relevant experience/expertise and publishing credits." **Pays authors royalty based on retail price or work purchased outright. Offers advance against royalties.** Publishes ms 1 year after acceptance. Responds to queries in 3-4 weeks. Catalog online.

Nomad Press does not accept picture books or fiction.

NONFICTION Middle readers: activity books, history, science. Average word length: middle readers—30,000.

TIPS "We publish a very specific kind of nonfiction children's activity book. Please keep this in mind when querying or submitting."

NORTH ATLANTIC BOOKS

2526 MLK Jr. Way, Berkeley CA 94704. **Website:** www.northatlanticbooks.com. **Contact:** Acquisitions Board. Estab. 1974. Publishes hardcover, trade paperback, and electronic originals; trade paperback and electronic reprints. **Publishes 60 titles/year. Receives 200 mss/year. 50% of books from first-time authors. 75% from unagented writers. Pays royalty percentage on wholesale price.** Publishes ms 14 months after acceptance. Accepts simultaneous submissions. Responds in 3-6 months. Book catalog free on request (if available). Guidelines online.

IMPRINTS Evolver Editions, Blue Snake Books.

NONFICTION Subjects include agriculture, anthropology, archeology, architecture, art, astrology, business, child guidance, community, contemporary culture, cooking, economics, electronics, environment, finance, foods, gardening, gay, health, horticulture, lesbian, medicine, memoirs, money, multicultural, nature, New Age, nutrition, philosophy, politics, psychic, psychology, public affairs, religion, science, social sciences, sociology, spirituality, sports, travel, womens issues, womens studies, world affairs. Submit proposal package including an outline, 3-4 sample chapters, and "a 75-word statement about the book, your qualifications as an author, marketing plan/audience, for the book, and comparable titles." Reviews artwork with ms package.

FICTION Subjects include adventure, literary, multicultural, mystery, regional, science fiction, spiritual. "We only publish fiction on rare occasions." Submit proposal package including an outline, 3-4 sample chapters, and "a 75-word statement about the book, your qualifications as an author, marketing plan/audience, for the book, and comparable titles."

POETRY Submit 15-20 sample poems.

NORTH CAROLINA OFFICE OF ARCHIVES AND HISTORY

Historical Publications Section, 4622 Mail Service Center, Raleigh NC 27699. (919)733-7442. **Fax:** (919)733-1439. **E-mail:** historical.publications@ncdcr.gov. **Website:** www.ncpublications.com. **Contact:** Michael Hill, supervisor (michael.hill@ncdcr.gov). Publishes hardcover and trade paperback originals. "We publish *only* titles that relate to North Carolina.

The North Carolina Office of Archives and History also publishes the *North Carolina Historical Review*, a quarterly scholarly journal of history." **Publishes 1 titles/year. 10 queries received/year. 5 mss received/year. 5% of books from first-time authors. 100% from unagented writers. Makes one-time payment upon delivery of completed ms.** Publishes ms 2 years after acceptance. Accepts simultaneous submissions. Responds in 1 week to queries and to proposals; 2 months to mss. Guidelines for $3.

NONFICTION Subjects include history, related to North Carolina, military, war, related to North Carolina, regional, North Carolina and Southern history. Query with SASE. Reviews artwork/photos. Send photocopies.

NORTHERN ILLINOIS UNIVERSITY PRESS

2280 Bethany Rd., DeKalb IL 60115-2854. (815)753-1075. **Fax:** (815)753-1845. **E-mail:** afarranto@niu.edu. **E-mail:** lmanning2@niu.edu. **Website:** www.niupress.niu.edu. **Contact:** Amy Farranto, editor; Linda Manning, director. Estab. 1965. The NIU Press publishes nonfiction on a variety of topics in the humanities, arts, and social sciences. With more than 400 books in print, each year it brings out about 20 new books on aspects of history, politics, anthropology, and literature. In fulfilling its broadly educational mission, the Press publishes books for inquiring general readers as well as for specialists. **Publishes 20-22 titles/year. Pays 10-15% royalty on wholesale price. Pays advance.** Book catalog available free.

IMPRINTS Switchgrass Books.

NONFICTION Subjects include anthropology, archeology, government, politics, history, language, literature, literary criticism, philosophy, regional, translation. No collections of previously published essays or unsolicited poetry. Submit (preferably via e-mail) a brief prospectus, consisting of a table of contents, an introduction, a sample chapter, and vita to the appropriate editor.

Ⓐ NORTHFIELD PUBLISHING

Imprint of Moody Publishers, 820 N. La Salle Blvd., Chicago IL 60610. (800)678-8001. **Fax:** (312)329-2019. **Website:** www.moodypublishers.org. **Contact:** Acquisitions Coordinator. Northfield publishes a line of books for non-Christians or those exploring the Christian faith. "While staying to Biblical principles, we eliminate some of the Christian wording and scriptual references to avoid confusion." **Publishes 5-10 titles/year. Pays $500-50,000 advance.** Publishes ms 1 year after acceptance. Accepts simultaneous submissions.

NONFICTION Subjects include business, economics, child guidance, money, finance, religion. Agented submissions only.

NORTH LIGHT BOOKS

F+W Media, a Content + eCommerce Company, 10151 Carver Rd., Suite 200, Blue Ash OH 45242. **Fax:** (513)891-7153. **E-mail:** mona.clough@fwcommunity.com. **Website:** www.fwcommunity.com; www.artistsnetwork.com; www.createmixedmedia.com. **Contact:** Mona Clough, content director art and mixed media. Publishes hardcover and trade paperback how-to books. "North Light Books publishes art books, including watercolor, drawing, mixed media, acrylic that emphasize illustrated how-to art instruction. Currently emphasizing drawing including traditional, zen, doodle and creativity and inspiration." **Publishes 50 titles/year. Pays 8% royalty on net receipts and $3,000 advance.** Accepts simultaneous submissions. Responds in approx. 2 months to queries. visit www.northlightshop.com. Does not return submissions.

> This market is for experienced fine artists who are willing to work with an North Light editor to produce a step-by-step how-to book that teaches readers how to accomplish art techniques. See also separate listing for F+W Media, Inc., in this section.

NONFICTION Subjects include hobbies, watercolor, realistic drawing, creativity, decorative painting, paper arts, collage and other craft instruction books. Interested in books on acrylic painting, basic drawing and sketching, journaling, pen and ink, colored pencil, decorative painting, art and how-to. Do not submit coffee table art books without how-to art instruction. Query via e-mail only. Submit outline with JPEG low-resolution images. Submissions via snail mail will not be returned.

Ⓐ⊘ NORTH POINT PRESS

Imprint of Farrar Straus & Giroux, Inc., 175 Fifth Ave., New York NY 10010. **Website:** www.fsgbooks.com. Estab. 1980. Publishes hardcover and paperback originals. "We are a broad-based literary trade publisher-high quality writing only." **Pays standard royalty. Pays varied advance.** Accepts simultaneous submissions.

NONFICTION Subjects include history, nature, environment, religion;no New Age, travel, cultural criticism, music, cooking/food. Be familiar with our list. No genres. *Agented submissions only.*

NORTIA PRESS

Santa Ana CA **E-mail:** acquisitions@nortiapress.com. **Website:** www.nortiapress.com. Estab. 2009. Publishes trade paperback and electronic originals. **Publishes 6 titles/year. 0% of books from first-time authors. 80% from unagented writers. Pays negotiable royalties on wholesale price.** Publishes ms 7 months after acceptance. Accepts simultaneous submissions. Responds in 1 month.

NONFICTION Subjects include ethnic, government, humanities, military, public affairs, religion, social sciences, sociology, war, womens issues.

FICTION Subjects include ethnic, historical, literary, military, war. "We focus mainly on nonfiction as well as literary and historical fiction, but are open to other genres. No vampire stories, science fiction, or erotica, please." Submit a brief e-mail query. Please include a short bio, approximate word count of book, and expected date of completion (fiction titles should be completed before sending a query, and should contain a sample chapter in the body of the e-mail). All unsolicited snail mail or attachments will be discarded without review.

TIPS "We specialize in working with experienced authors who seek a more collaborative and fulfilling relationship with their publisher. As such, we are less likely to accept pitches form first-time authors, no matter how good the idea. As with any pitch, please make your e-mail very brief and to the point, so the reader is not forced to skim it. Always include some biographic information. Your life is interesting."

Ⓐ⊘ W.W. NORTON & COMPANY, INC.

500 Fifth Ave., New York NY 10110. (212)354-5500. **Fax:** (212)869-0856. **Website:** www.wwnorton.com. Estab. 1923. "W. W. Norton & Company, the oldest and largest publishing house owned wholly by its employees, strives to carry out the imperative of its founder to 'publish books not for a single season, but for the years' in fiction, nonfiction, poetry, college textbooks, cookbooks, art books and professional books. Due to the workload of our editorial staff and the large volume of materials we receive, *Norton is no longer able to accept unsolicited submissions.* If you are seeking publication, we suggest working with a literary agent who will represent you to the house."

NO STARCH PRESS, INC.

245 8th St., San Francisco CA 94103. (415)863-9900. **Fax:** (415)863-9950. **E-mail:** editors@nostarch.com. **Website:** www.nostarch.com. **Contact:** William Pollock, publisher. Estab. 1994. Publishes trade paperback originals. "No Starch Press publishes the finest in geek entertainment—unique books on technology, with a focus on open source, security, hacking, programming, alternative operating systems, LEGO, science, and math. Our titles have personality, our authors are passionate, and our books tackle topics that people care about." **Publishes 20-25 titles/year. 100 queries received/year. 5 mss received/year. 80% of books from first-time authors. 90% from unagented writers. Pays 10-15% royalty on wholesale price. Pays advance.** Publishes ms 4 months after acceptance. Accepts simultaneous submissions. Book catalog online.

NONFICTION Subjects include science, technology, computing, lego. Submit outline, bio, 1 sample chapter, market rationale. Reviews artwork/photos. Send photocopies.

TIPS "Books must be relevant to tech-savvy, geeky readers."

NOVA PRESS

9058 Lloyd Place, West Hollywood CA 90069. (310)275-3513. **Fax:** (310)281-5629. **E-mail:** novapress@aol.com. **Website:** www.novapress.net. **Contact:** Jeff Kolby, president. Estab. 1993. Publishes trade paperback originals. "Nova Press publishes only test prep books for college entrance exams (SAT, GRE, GMAT, LSAT, etc.), and closely related reference books, such as college guides and vocabulary books." **Publishes 4 titles/year.** Publishes ms 6 months after acceptance. Book catalog available free.

NONFICTION Subjects include education, software.

NURSESBOOKS.ORG

American Nurses Association, 8515 Georgia Ave., Suite 400, Silver Spring MD 20901. (800)274-4ANA. **Fax:** (301)628-5003. **E-mail:** anp@ana.org. **E-mail:** joseph.vanilla@ana.org. **Website:** www.nursesbooks.org. **Contact:** Joseph Vanilla, publisher. Publishes professional paperback originals and reprints. "Nursebooks.org publishes books designed to help professional nurses in their work and careers. Through the publishing program, Nursebooks.org provides nurses in all practice settings with publications that address cutting edge issues and form a basis for debate and exploration of this century's most critical health care trends." **Publishes 10 titles/year. 50 queries received/year. 8-10 mss received/year. 75% of books from first-time authors. 100% from unagented writers.** Publishes ms 4 months after acceptance. Responds in 3 months. Book catalog online. Guidelines available free.

NONFICTION Subjects include advanced practice, computers, continuing education, ethics, health care policy, nursing administration, psychiatric and mental health, quality, nursing history, workplace issues, key clinical topics, such as geriatrics, pain management, public health, spirituality and home health. Submit outline, 1 sample chapter, CV, list of 3 reviewers and paragraph on audience and how to reach them. Reviews artwork/photos. Send photocopies.

OAK KNOLL PRESS

310 Delaware St., New Castle DE 19720. (302)328-7232. **Fax:** (302)328-7274. **E-mail:** publishing@oakknoll.com. **Website:** www.oakknoll.com. **Contact:** Robert D. Fleck, president. Estab. 1976. Publishes hardcover and trade paperback originals and reprints. "Oak Knoll specializes in books about books and manuals on the book arts: preserving the art and lore of the printed word." **Publishes 40 titles/year. 250 queries received/year. 100 mss received/year. 50% of books from first-time authors. 100% from unagented writers.** Publishes ms 1 year after acceptance. Accepts simultaneous submissions. Guidelines online.

NONFICTION Reviews artwork/photos. Send photocopies.

OAK TREE PRESS

1820 W. Lacy Blvd., #220, Hanford CA 93230. **E-mail:** query@oaktreebooks.com. **Website:** www.oaktreebooks.com. **Contact:** Billie Johnson, publisher. Estab. 1998. Publishes trade paperback and hardcover books. Oak Tree Press is an independent publisher that celebrates writers, and is dedicated to the many great unknowns who are just waiting for the opportunity to break into print. "We're looking for mainstream, genre fiction, narrative nonfiction, how-to. Sponsors 3 contests annually: Dark Oak Mystery, Timeless Love Romance and CopTales for crime and other stories of law enforcement professionals." **Royalties based on sales. No advance.** Publishes ms 9-18 months after acceptance. Responds in 4-6 weeks. Catalog and guidelines online.

FICTION Subjects include adventure, confession, contemporary, ethnic, fantasy, feminist, humor, mainstream, mystery, picture books, suspense, young adult. Emphasis on mystery and romance novels. "No science fiction or fantasy novels, or stories set far into the future. Next, novels substantially longer than our stated word count are not considered, regardless of genre. We look for manuscripts of 70-90,000 words. If the story really charms us, we will bend some on either end of the range. No right-wing political or racist agenda, gratuitous sex or violence, especially against women, or depict harm of animals." Does not accept or return unsolicited mss. Query with SASE. Accepts queries by e-mail. Include estimated word count, brief bio, list of publishing credits, brief description of ms.

TIPS "Perhaps my most extreme pet peeve is receiving queries on projects which we've clearly advertised we don't want: science fiction, fantasy, epic tomes, bigoted diatribes and so on. Second to that is a practice I call 'over-taping,' or the use of yards and yards of tape, or worse yet, the filament tape so that it takes forever to open the package. Finding story pitches on my voice mail is also annoying."

OBERLIN COLLEGE PRESS

50 N. Professor St., Oberlin College, Oberlin OH 44074. (440)775-8408. **Fax:** (440)775-8124. **E-mail:** oc.press@oberlin.edu. **Website:** www.oberlin.edu/ocpress. **Contact:** Marco Wilkinson, managing editor. Estab. 1969. Publishes hardcover and trade paperback originals. **Publishes 2-3 titles/year. Pays 7½-10% royalty.** Accepts simultaneous submissions. Responds promptly to queries; 2 months to mss.

POETRY *FIELD Magazine*—submit 2-6 poems through website "submissions" tab; FIELD Translation Series—query with SASE and sample poems; FIELD Poetry Series—*no unsolicited mss.* Enter mss in FIELD Poetry Prize ($1,000 and a standard royalty contract) held annually in May. Submit complete ms.

TIPS "Queries for the FIELD Translation Series: send sample poems and letter describing project. Winner of the annual FIELD poetry prize determines publication. Do not send unsolicited manuscripts."

OCEANVIEW PUBLISHING

595 Bay Isles Rd., Suite 120-G, Longboat Key FL 34228. **E-mail:** submissions@oceanviewpub.com. **Website:** www.oceanviewpub.com. **Contact:** Robert

Gussin, CEO. Estab. 2006. Publishes hardcover and electronic originals. "Independent publisher of nonfiction and fiction, with primary interest in original mystery, thriller and suspense titles. Accepts new and established writers." Responds in 3 months on mss. Catalog and guidelines online.

NONFICTION Accepts nonfiction but specializes in original mystery, thriller and suspense titles. Query first.

FICTION Subjects include mystery, suspense, thriller. Accepting adult mss with a primary interest in the mystery, thriller and suspense genres—from new and established writers. No children's or YA literature, poetry, cookbooks, technical manuals or short stories. Within body of e-mail only, include author's name and brief bio (Indicate if this is an agent submission), ms title and word count, author's mailing address, phone number and e-mail address. Attached to the e-mail should be the following: A synopsis of 750 words or fewer. The first 30 pages of the ms. Please note that we accept only Word documents as attachments to the submission e-mail. Do not send query letters or proposals.

OHIO STATE UNIVERSITY PRESS

1070 Carmack Rd., 180 Pressey Hall, Columbus OH 43210-1002. (614)292-6930. **Fax:** (614)292-2065. **E-mail:** eugene@osupress.org. **E-mail:** lindsay@osupress.org. **Website:** www.ohiostatepress.org. **Contact:** Eugene O'Connor, acquisitions editor (medieval studies and classics); Lindsay Martin, acquisitions editor (literary studies). Estab. 1957. The Ohio State University Press publishes scholarly nonfiction, and offers short fiction and short poetry prizes. Currently emphasizing history, literary studies, political science, women's health, classics, Victoria studies. **Publishes 30 titles/year. Pays royalty. Pays advance.** Responds in 3 months to queries. Guidelines online.

NONFICTION Subjects include business, economics, education, government, politics, history, American, language, literature, literary criticism, multicultural, regional, sociology, women's issues, women's studies, criminology, literary criticism, women's health. Query.

POETRY Offers poetry competition through *The Journal*.

OHIO UNIVERSITY PRESS

215 Columbus Rd., Suite 101, Athens OH 45701. (740)593-1155. **Fax:** (740)593-4536. **Website:** www.ohioswallow.com. **Contact:** Gillian Berchowitz, director. Estab. 1964. Publishes hardcover and trade paperback originals and reprints. "Ohio University Press publishes and disseminates the fruits of research and creative endeavor, specifically in the areas of literary studies, regional works, philosophy, contemporary history, and African studies. Its charge to produce books of value in service to the academic community and for the enrichment of the broader culture is in keeping with the university's mission of teaching, research and service to its constituents." **Publishes 45-50 titles/year. 500 queries received/year. 50 mss received/year. 20% of books from first-time authors. 95% from unagented writers.** Publishes ms 1 year after acceptance. Responds in 1-3 months. Book catalog available free. Guidelines online.

NONFICTION Subjects include Americana, anthropology, archaeology, government, history, language, literature, military, nature, politics, regional, sociology, women's issues, women's studies, African studies. "We prefer queries or detailed proposals, rather than manuscripts, pertaining to scholarly projects that might have a general interest." Proposals should explain the thesis and details of the subject matter, not just sell a title. Query with SASE. Reviews artwork/photos. Send photocopies.

TIPS "Rather than trying to hook the editor on your work, let the material be compelling enough and well-presented enough to do it for you."

ONEWORLD PUBLICATIONS

10 Bloomsbury St., London WC1B 3SR, United Kingdom. (44)(20)7307-8900. **E-mail:** submissions@oneworld-publications.com. **Website:** www.oneworld-publications.com. Estab. 1986. Publishes hardcover and trade paperback originals and mass market paperback reprints. "We publish general trade nonfiction, which must be accessible but authoritative, mainly by academics or experts for a general readership and where appropriate a cross-over student market. Currently emphasizing current affairs, popular science, history, psychology, politics and business; de-emphasizing self-help. We also publish literary fiction by international authors, both debut and established, throughout the English language world as well as selling translation rights. Our focus is on well-written literary and high-end commercial fiction from a variety of cultures and periods, many exploring interesting themes and issues. In addition we publish fiction in

translation and YA fiction." **Publishes 80 titles/year. 300 queries received/year; 200 mss received/year. 20% of books from first-time authors. 20% from unagented writers. Pays 10% royalty on wholesale price for academic books; standard royalties for trade titles. Pays $1,000-50,000 advance.** Publishes ms 12-15 months after acceptance. Book catalog online. Guidelines online.

NONFICTION Subjects include business, economics. Submit through online proposal form.

FICTION Subjects include politics, history, multicultural, philosophy, psychology, religion, science, sociology, women's issues, women's studies. Submit through online proposal forms.

TIPS "We don't require agents—just good proposals with enough hard information."

ONSTAGE PUBLISHING

190 Lime Quarry Rd., Suite 106-J, Madison AL 35758-8962. (256)461-0661. **E-mail:** onstage123@knology.net. **Website:** www.onstagepublishing.com. **Contact:** Dianne Hamilton, senior editor. Estab. 1999. "At this time, we only produce fiction books for ages 8-18. We have added an eBook only side of the house for mysteries for grades 6-12. See our website for more information. We will not do anthologies of any kind. Query first for nonfiction projects as nonfiction projects must spark our interest. Now accepting e-mail queries and submissions. For submissions: Put the first 3 chapters in the body of the e-mail. Do not use attachments! We will no longer return any mss. Only an SASE envelope is needed. Send complete ms if under 20,000 words, otherwise send synopsis and first 3 chapters." **80% of books from first-time authors. Pays authors/illustrators/photographers advance plus royalties.**

FICTION Middle readers: adventure, contemporary, fantasy, history, nature/environment, science fiction, suspense/mystery. Young adults: adventure, contemporary, fantasy, history, humor, science fiction, suspense/mystery. Average word length: chapter books—4,000-6,000 words; middle readers—5,000 words and up; young adults—25,000 and up. Recently published *Mission: Shanghai* by Jamie Dodson (an adventure for boys ages 12+); *Birmingham, 1933: Alice* (a chapter book for grades 3-5). "We do not produce picture books."

TIPS "Study our titles and get a sense of the kind of books we publish, so that you know whether your project is likely to be right for us."

ON THE MARK PRESS

15 Dairy Ave., Napanee ON K7R 1M4, Canada. (800)463-6367. **Fax:** (800)290-3631. **Website:** www.onthemarkpress.com. Estab. 1986. Publishes books for the Canadian curriculum. **15% of books from first-time authors.**

OOLICHAN BOOKS

P.O. Box 2278, Lantzville BC V0R 1M0, Canada. (250)390-4839. **Fax:** (866)299-0026. **E-mail:** oolichanbooks@telus.net. **Website:** www.oolichan.com. Estab. 1974. Publishes hardcover and trade paperback originals and reprints. **Publishes 8 titles/year. 2,000 mss received/year. 30% of books from first-time authors. Pays royalty on retail price.** Publishes ms 6-12 months after acceptance. Accepts simultaneous submissions. Responds in 1-3 months. Book catalog online. Guidelines online.

Only publishes Canadian authors.

NONFICTION Subjects include history, regional, community. "We try to publish creative nonfiction titles each year which are of regional, national, and international interest." Submit proposal package, publishing history, bio, cover letter, 3 sample chapters, SASE.

FICTION Subjects include literary. "We try to publish at least 2 literary fiction titles each year. We receive many more deserving submissions than we are able to publish, so we publish only outstanding work. We try to balance our list between emerging and established writers, and have published many first-time writers who have gone on to win or be shortlisted for major literary awards, both nationally and internationally." Submit proposal package, publishing history, clips, bio, cover letter, 3 sample chapters, SASE.

POETRY "We are one of the few small literary presses in Canada that still publishes poetry. We try to include 2-3 poetry titles each year. We attempt to balance our list between emerging and established poets. Our poetry titles have won or been shortlisted for major national awards, including the Governor General's Award, the BC Book Prizes, and the Alberta Awards." Submit 10 sample poems.

TIPS "Our audience is adult readers who love good books and good literature. Our audience is regional and national, as well as international. Follow our submission guidelines. Check out some of our titles at your local library or bookstore to get an idea of what we publish. Don't send us the only copy of your manuscript. Let us know if your submission is simultaneous, and inform us if it is accepted elsewhere. Above all, keep writing!"

OOLIGAN PRESS

369 Neuberger Hall, 724 SW Harrison St., Portland OR 97201. (503)725-9410. **E-mail:** acquisitions@ooliganpress.pdx.edu. **Website:** ooligan.pdx.edu. Estab. 2001. Publishes trade paperback, and electronic originals and reprints. **Publishes 4-6 titles/year. 250-500 queries received/year. 200 mss received/year. 90% of books from first-time authors. 90% from unagented writers. Pays negotiable royalty on retail price.** Book catalog online. Guidelines online.

NONFICTION Subjects include agriculture, alternative, anthropology, archeology, art, architecture, community, contemporary culture, cooking, foods, nutrition, creative nonfiction, education, ethnic, film, cinema, stage, gay, lesbian, government, politics, history, humanities, language, literature, literary criticism, memoirs, multicultural, music, dance, nature, environment, philosophy, regional, religion, social sciences, sociology, spirituality, translation, travel, women's issues, women's studies, world affairs, young adult. Young adult: open to all categories. Query with SASE. Submit proposal package, outline, 4 sample chapters, projected page count, audience, marketing ideas and a list of similar titles. Reviews artwork/photos.

FICTION Subjects include adventure, ethnic, experimental, fantasy, feminist, historical, horror, humor, literary, multicultural, mystery, plays, regional, science fiction, short story collections, spiritual, suspense, middle grade. "Ooligan Press is a general trade press at Portland State University. As a teaching press, Ooligan makes as little distinction as possible between the press and the classroom. Under the direction of professional faculty and staff, the work of the press is done by students enrolled in the Book Publishing graduate program at PSU. We are especially interested in works with social, literary, or educational value. Though we place special value on regional authors, we are open to all submissions, including translated works and writings by children and young adults. We do not currently publish picture books, board books, easy readers, or pop-up books or middle grade readers." Query with SASE. *"At this time we cannot accept science fiction or fantasy submissions."*

POETRY Ooligan is a not-for-profit general trade press that publishes books honoring the cultural and natural diversity of the Pacific Northwest. "We are limited in the number of poetry titles that we publish as poetry represents only a small percentage of our overall acquisitions. We are open to all forms of style and verse; however, we give special preference to prose poetry and traditional verse. Although spoken word, slam, and rap poetry are of interest to the press, we will consider such work if it does not translate well to the written page." Ooligan does not publish chapbooks. Query, submit 20 sample poems, submit complete ms.

TIPS "For children's books, our audience will be middle grades and young adult, with marketing to general trade, libraries, and schools. Good marketing ideas increase the chances of a manuscript succeeding."

OPEN COURT PUBLISHING CO.

70 E. Lake St., Suite 800, Chicago IL 60601. **E-mail:** opencourt@cricketmedia.com. **Website:** www.opencourtbooks.com. **Contact:** Acquisitions Editor. Estab. 1887. Publishes hardcover and trade paperback originals. **Publishes 20 titles/year. Pays 5-15% royalty on wholesale price.** Publishes ms 2 years after acceptance. Book catalog online. Guidelines online.

NONFICTION Subjects include philosophy, Asian thought, religious studies and popular culture. Query with SASE. Submit proposal package, outline, 1 sample chapter, TOC, author's cover letter, intended audience.

TIPS "Audience consists of philosophers and intelligent general readers. Only accepting submissions to Popular Culture and Philosophy series."

OPEN ROAD TRAVEL GUIDES

P.O. Box 284, Cold Spring Harbor NY 11724. (631)692-7172. **E-mail:** jonathan@openroadguides.com. **Website:** www.openroadguides.com. **Contact:** Jonathan Stein, publisher. Estab. 1993. Publishes trade paperback originals. "Open Road publishes travel guides and, in its Cold Spring Press imprint, now publishes genealogy books (8 in print to date) and welcomes submissions in this area." **Publishes 20-22 titles/year. 200 queries received/year. 75 mss received/year. 30% of books from first-time authors. 98% from unagented writers. Pays 5-6% royalty on retail price. Pays $1,000-3,500 advance.** Publishes ms

3 months after acceptance. Accepts simultaneous submissions. Responds in 1 month to queries; 2 months to proposals. Book catalog online.

NONFICTION Subjects include travel guides and travelogues. Query.

ORCA BOOK PUBLISHERS

P.O. Box 5626, Stn. B, Victoria BC V8R 6S4, Canada. **Fax:** (877)408-1551. **E-mail:** orca@orcabook.com. **Website:** www.orcabook.com. **Contact:** Amy Collins, editor (picture books); Sarah Harvey, editor (young readers); Andrew Wooldridge, editor (juvenile and teen fiction); Bob Tyrrell, publisher (YA, teen); Ruth Linka, associate editor (rapid reads). Estab. 1984. Publishes hardcover and trade paperback originals, and mass market paperback originals and reprints. **Publishes 30-50 titles/year. 2,500 queries received/year. 1,000 mss received/year. 20% of books from first-time authors. 75% from unagented writers. Pays 10% royalty.** Publishes ms 12-18 months after acceptance. Responds in 1 month to queries; 2 months to proposals and mss. Book catalog for 8½x11 SASE. Guidelines online.

Only publishes Canadian authors.

NONFICTION Subjects include multicultural, picture books. Only publishes Canadian authors. Query with SASE.

FICTION Subjects include hi-lo, juvenile (5-9), literary, mainstream, contemporary, young adult (10-18). Picture books: animals, contemporary, history, nature/environment. Middle readers: contemporary, history, fantasy, nature/environment, problem novels, graphic novels. Young adults: adventure, contemporary, hi-lo (Orca Soundings), history, multicultural, nature/environment, problem novels, suspense/mystery, graphic novels. Average word length: picture books—500-1,500; middle readers—20,000-35,000; young adult—25,000-45,000; Orca Soundings—13,000-15,000; Orca Currents—13,000-15,000. No romance, science fiction. Query with SASE. Submit proposal package, outline, clips, 2-5 sample chapters, SASE.

TIPS "Our audience is students in grades K-12. Know our books, and know the market."

ORCHARD BOOKS

557 Broadway, New York NY 10012. **E-mail:** mcroland@scholastic.com. **Website:** www.scholastic.com. **Contact:** Ken Geist, vice president/editorial director; David Saylor, vice president/creative director. *Orchard is not accepting unsolicited mss.* **Publishes 20 titles/year. 10% of books from first-time authors. Most commonly offers an advance against list royalties.**

FICTION Picture books, early readers, and novelty: animal, contemporary, history, humor, multicultural, poetry.

ORCHISES PRESS

P.O. Box 320533, Alexandria VA 22320. (703)683-1243. **E-mail:** lathbury@gmu.edu. **Website:** mason.gmu.edu/~lathbury. **Contact:** Roger Lathbury, editor-in-chief. Estab. 1983. Publishes hardcover and trade paperback originals and reprints. Orchises Press is a general literary publisher specializing in poetry with selected reprints and textbooks. No new fiction or children's books. **Publishes 2-3 titles/year. 1% of books from first-time authors. 95% from unagented writers. Pays 36% of receipts after Orchises has recouped its costs.** Publishes ms 1 year after acceptance. Accepts simultaneous submissions. Responds in 3 months to queries. Guidelines online.

NONFICTION No real restrictions on subject matter. Query with SASE. Reviews artwork/photos. Send photocopies.

POETRY Poetry must have been published in respected literary journals. *Orchises Press no longer reads unsolicited mss.* Publishes free verse, but has strong formalist preferences. Query and submit 5 sample poems.

OREGON STATE UNIVERSITY PRESS

121 The Valley Library, Corvallis OR 97331. (541)737-3873. **Fax:** (541)737-3170. **E-mail:** mary.braun@oregonstate.edu. **Website:** osupress.oregonstate.edu. **Contact:** Mary Elizabeth Braun, acquisitions editor. Estab. 1962. Publishes hardcover, paperback, and e-book originals. **Publishes 20-25 titles/year. 40% of books from first-time authors.** Publishes ms 1 year after acceptance. Responds in 3 months to queries. Book catalog for 6x9 SAE with 2 first-class stamps. Guidelines online.

NONFICTION Subjects include regional, science. Publishes scholarly books in history, biography, geography, literature, natural resource management, with strong emphasis on Pacific or Northwestern topics and Native American and indigenous studies. Submit outline, sample chapters.

O'REILLY MEDIA

1005 Gravenstein Highway N., Sebastopol CA 95472. (707)827-7000. **Fax:** (707)829-0104. **E-mail:** workwithus@oreilly.com. **Website:** www.oreilly.com. **Contact:** Acquisitions Editor. "We're always looking for new authors and new book ideas. Our ideal author has real technical competence and a passion for explaining things clearly." Guidelines online.

NONFICTION Subjects include computers, electronics. "At the same time as you might say that our books are written 'by and for smart people,' they also have a down to earth quality. We like straight talk that goes right to the heart of what people need to know." Submit proposal package, outline, publishing history, bio.

TIPS "It helps if you know that we tend to publish 'high end' books rather than books for dummies, and generally don't want yet another book on a topic that's already well covered."

OUR SUNDAY VISITOR, INC.

200 Noll Plaza, Huntington IN 46750. **E-mail:** jlindsey@osv.com. **Website:** www.osv.com. **Contact:** Jacquelyn Lindsey; David Dziena; Bert Ghezzi; Cindy Cavnar; Tyler Ottinger, art director. Publishes paperback and hardbound originals. "We are a Catholic publishing company seeking to educate and deepen our readers in their faith. Currently emphasizing devotional, inspirational, Catholic identity, apologetics, and catechetics." **Publishes 40-50 titles/year. Pays authors royalty of 10-12% net. Pays illustrators by the project (range: $25-1,500).** Publishes ms 1-2 years after acceptance. Accepts simultaneous submissions. Responds in 2 months. Book catalog for 9×12 envelope and first-class stamps; ms guidelines available online.

Our Sunday Visitor, Inc. is publishing only those children's books that are specifically Catholic. See website for submission guidelines.

NONFICTION Prefers to see well-developed proposals as first submission with annotated outline and definition of intended market; Catholic viewpoints on family, prayer, and devotional books, and Catholic heritage books. Picture books, middle readers, young readers, young adults. Query, submit complete ms, or submit outline/synopsis and 2-3 sample chapters. Reviews artwork/photos.

TIPS "Stay in accordance with our guidelines."

THE OVERMOUNTAIN PRESS

P.O. Box 1261, Johnson City TN 37605. (423)926-2691. **Fax:** (423)232-1252. **E-mail:** submissions@overmtn.com. **Website:** www.overmtn.com. Estab. 1970. Publishes hardcover and trade paperback originals and reprints. "The Overmountain Press publishes primarily Appalachian history. Audience is people interested in history of Tennessee, Virginia, North Carolina, Kentucky, and all aspects of this region—Revolutionary War, Civil War, county histories, historical biographies, etc." Publishes ms 1-2 years after acceptance. Accepts simultaneous submissions. Responds in 3-6 months to mss. Book catalog available free. Guidelines online.

NONFICTION Subjects include Americana, cooking, foods, nutrition, ethnic, history, military, war, nature, environment, photography, regional, women's issues, women's studies, Native American, ghostlore, guidebooks, folklore. Regional works only. Submit proposal package, outline, 3 sample chapters, marketing suggestions. Reviews artwork/photos. Send photocopies.

FICTION Subjects include picture books, must have regional flavor. Submit complete ms.

RICHARD C. OWEN PUBLISHERS, INC.

P.O. Box 585, Katonah NY 10536. (914)232-3903; (800)262-0787. **E-mail:** richardowen@rcowen.com. **Website:** www.rcowen.com. **Contact:** Richard Owen, publisher. Estab. 1982. "We publish child-focused books, with inherent instructional value, about characters and situations with which 5, 6, and 7-year-old children can identify—books that can be read for meaning, entertainment, enjoyment and information. We include multicultural stories that present minorities in a positive and natural way. Our stories show the diversity in America." Not interested in lesson plans, or books of activities for literature studies or other content areas. Submit complete ms and cover letter. **Pays authors royalty of 5% based on net price or outright purchase (range: $25-500). Offers no advances. Pays illustrators by the project (range: $100-2,000) or per photo (range: $50-150).** Publishes ms 2-3 years after acceptance. Accepts simultaneous submissions. Responds to mss in 1 year. Book catalog available with SASE. Ms guidelines with SASE or online.

NONFICTION Subjects include art, architecture, history, nature, environment, recreation, science, sports, women's issues, women's studies, music, diverse culture, nature. "Our books are for kindergarten, first- and second-grade children to read on their own. The stories are very brief—up to 2,000 words—yet well structured and crafted with memorable characters, language, and plots. Picture books, young readers:

animals, careers, history, how-to, music/dance, geography, multicultural, nature/environment, science, sports. Multicultural needs include: Good stories respectful of all heritages, races, cultural—African-American, Hispanic, American Indian, Asian, European, Middle Eastern." Wants lively stories. No "encyclopedic" type of information stories. Average word length: under 500 words.

PETER OWEN PUBLISHERS

20 Holland Park Ave., London W11 3 QU, United Kingdom. (44)(208)350-1775. **Fax:** (44)(208)340-9488. **E-mail:** admin@peterowen.com. **Website:** www.peterowen.com. **Contact:** Antonia Owen, editorial director. Publishes hardcover originals and trade paperback originals and reprints. "We are far more interested in proposals for nonfiction than fiction at the moment. No poetry or short stories." **Publishes 20-30 titles/year. 3,000 queries received/year. 800 mss received/year. 70% from unagented writers. Pays 7½-10% royalty. Pays negotiable advance.** Publishes ms 1 year after acceptance. Responds in 2 months to queries; 3 months to proposals and mss. Book catalog for SASE, SAE with IRC or on website.

NONFICTION Subjects include history, literature, memoirs, translation, travel, art, drama, literary, biography. Query with synopsis, sample chapters.

FICTION Subjects include literary and translation. "No first novels. Authors should be aware that we publish very little new fiction these days." Query with synopsis, sample chapters.

OXFORD UNIVERSITY PRESS

198 Madison Ave., New York NY 10016. (212)726-6000. **E-mail:** custserv.us@oup.com. **Website:** www.oup.com/us. World's largest university press with the widest global audience. Guidelines online.

NONFICTION Query with outline, proposal, sample chapters.

OXFORD UNIVERSITY PRESS: SOUTHERN AFRICA

P.O. Box 12119, NI City Cape Town 7463, South Africa. (27)(21)596-2300. **Fax:** (27)(21)596-1234. **E-mail:** oxford.za@oup.com. **Website:** www.oup.com/za. Academic publisher known for its educational books for southern African schools. Also publishes general and reference titles. **Publishes 150 titles/year.** Book catalog online. Guidelines online.

NONFICTION Submit cover letter, synopsis, first few chapters, and submission form (available online) via mail.

FICTION Submit cover letter, synopsis.

OZARK MOUNTAIN PUBLISHING, LLC

P.O. Box 754, Huntsville AR 72740. (479)738-2348. **Fax:** (479)738-2448. **E-mail:** kristy@ozarkmt.com. **Website:** www.ozarkmt.com. **Contact:** Nancy Garrison, general manager. Estab. 1992. Publishes trade paperback originals. **Publishes 8-10 titles/year. 50-75 queries; 150-200 mss received/year. 50% of books from first-time authors. 95% from unagented writers. Pays 10-15% royalty on retail or wholesale price. Pays $250-500 advance.** Publishes ms within 18 months after acceptance. Accepts simultaneous submissions. Responds in 6 months to queries; 7 months to mss. Book catalog free on request. Guidelines online.

NONFICTION Subjects include new age/metaphysical/body-mind-spirit, philosophy, spirituality. No phone calls please. Query with SASE. Submit 4-5 sample chapters.

TIPS "We envision our audience to be open minded, spiritually expanding. Please do not call to check on submissions. Do not submit electronically. Send hard copy only."

P & R PUBLISHING CO.

P.O. Box 817, Phillipsburg NJ 08865. **Fax:** (908)859-2390. **E-mail:** editorial@prpbooks.com. **Website:** www.prpbooks.com. Estab. 1930. Publishes hardcover originals and trade paperback originals and reprints. **Publishes 40 titles/year. Up to 300 queries received/year. 100 mss received/year. 5% of books from first-time authors. 95% from unagented writers. Pays 10-16% royalty on wholesale price.** Accepts simultaneous submissions. Responds in 3 months to proposals. Guidelines online.

NONFICTION Subjects include history, religion, spirituality, translation. Only accepts electronic submission with completion of online Author Guidelines. Hard copy mss will not be returned.

TIPS "Our audience is evangelical Christians and seekers. All of our publications are consistent with Biblical teaching, as summarized in the Westminster Standards."

PACIFIC PRESS PUBLISHING ASSOCIATION

Trade Book Division, 1350 N. Kings Rd., Nampa ID 83687. (208)465-2500. **Fax:** (208)465-2531. **E-mail:**

booksubmissions@pacificpress.com. **Website:** www.pacificpress.com. **Contact:** Scott Cady, acquisitions editor (children's stories, biography, Christian living, spiritual growth); David Jarnes, book editor (theology, doctrine, inspiration). Estab. 1874. Publishes hardcover and trade paperback originals and reprints. "We publish books that fit Seventh-day Adventist beliefs only. All titles are Christian and religious. For guidance, see www.adventist.org/beliefs/index.html. Our books fit into the categories of this retail site: www.adventistbookcenter.com." **Publishes 35 titles/year. 35% of books from first-time authors. 100% from unagented writers. Pays 8-16% royalty on wholesale price.** Publishes ms 2 years after acceptance. Responds in 3 months to queries. Guidelines online.

NONFICTION Subjects include child guidance, cooking, foods, nutrition, vegetarian only, health, history, nature, environment, philosophy, religion, spirituality, women's issues, family living, Christian lifestyle, Bible study, Christian doctrine, prophecy. Query with SASE or e-mail, or submit 3 sample chapters, cover letter with overview of book. Electronic submissions accepted. Reviews artwork/photos.

FICTION Subjects include religious. "Pacific Press rarely publishes fiction, but we're interested in developing a line of Seventh-day Adventist fiction in the future. Only proposals accepted; no full manuscripts."

TIPS "Our primary audience is members of the Seventh-day Adventist denomination. Almost all are written by Seventh-day Adventists. Books that do well for us relate the Biblical message to practical human concerns and focus more on the experiential rather than theoretical aspects of Christianity. We are assigning more titles, using less unsolicited material—although we still publish manuscripts from freelance submissions and proposals."

PAGESPRING PUBLISHING

P.O. Box 2113, Columbus OH 43221. **E-mail:** ps@pagespringpublishing.com. **E-mail:** yaeditor@pagespringpublishing.com; weditor@pagespringpublishing.com. **Website:** www.pagespringpublishing.com. Estab. 2012. Publishes trade paperback and electronic originals. "PageSpring Publishing publishes young adult and middle grade titles under the Lucky Marble Books imprint and women's fiction under the Cup of Tea imprint. See imprint websites for submission details." **Publishes 10-20 titles/year. Pays royalty on wholesale price.** Publishes ms 6 months after acceptance. Accepts simultaneous submissions. Responds to queries in 1 month. Guidelines online.

IMPRINTS Lucky Marble Books, Cup of Tea Books.

FICTION Subjects include adventure, contemporary, fantasy, feminist, historical, humor, literary, mainstream, mystery, regional, romance, young adult. Submit proposal package including synopsis and 3 sample chapters.

PALADIN PRESS

7077 Winchester Circle, Boulder CO 80301. (303)443-7250. **Fax:** (303)442-8741. **E-mail:** editorial@paladin-press.com. **Website:** www.paladin-press.com. Estab. 1970. Publishes hardcover originals and paperback originals and reprints, videos. "Paladin Press publishes the action library of nonfiction in military science, police science, weapons, combat, personal freedom, self-defense, survival." **Publishes 50 titles/year. 50% of books from first-time authors. 95% from unagented writers. "We pay royalties in full and on time." Pays advance.** Publishes book 1 year after acceptance of ms. Accepts simultaneous submissions. Responds in 2 months to proposals. Book catalog available free.

IMPRINTS Sycamore Island Books; Flying Machines Press; Outer Limits Press; Romance Book Classics.

NONFICTION Subjects include government, politics, military, war. If applicable, send sample photographs and line drawings with complete outline and sample chapters. Paladin Press primarily publishes original manuscripts on military science, weaponry, self-defense, personal privacy, financial freedom, espionage, police science, action careers, guerrilla warfare, and fieldcraft. To submit a book proposal to Paladin Press, send an outline or chapter description along with 1-2 sample chapters (or the entire ms) to the address below. If applicable, samples of illustrations or photographs are also useful. Do not send a computer disk at this point, and be sure keep a copy of everything you send us. We are not accepting mss as electronic submissions at this time. Please allow 2-6 weeks for a reply. If you would like your sample material returned, a SASE with proper postage is required. Editorial Department, Paladin Press Gunbarrel Tech Center,7077 Winchester Circle, Boulder, CO 80301, or email us at: editorial@paladin-press.com. Query with SASE. Submitting a proposal for a video project is not much different than a book proposal. See guidelines online and send to: All materials related to video proposals should be addressed directly to: David Dubrow, Video Production Manager.

TIPS "We need lucid, instructive material aimed at our market and accompanied by sharp, relevant illustrations and photos. As we are primarily a publisher of 'how-to' books, a manuscript that has step-by-step instructions, written in a clear and concise manner (but not strictly outline form) is desirable. No fiction, first-person accounts, children's, religious, or joke books. We are also interested in serious, professional videos and video ideas (contact Michael Rigg)."

PALARI PUBLISHING

107 S. West St., PMB 778, Alexandria VA 22314. (866)570-6724. **Fax:** (866)570-6724. **E-mail:** dave@palaribooks.com. **Website:** www.palaribooks.com. **Contact:** David Smitherman, publisher/editor. Estab. 1998. Publishes hardcover and trade paperback originals. "Palari provides authoritative, well-written nonfiction that addresses topical consumer needs and fiction with an emphasis on intelligence and quality. We accept solicited and unsolicited manuscripts, however we prefer a query letter and SASE, describing the project briefly and concisely. This letter should include a complete address and telephone number. Palari Publishing accepts queries or any other submissions by e-mail, but prefers queries submitted by US mail. All queries must be submitted by mail according to our guidelines. Promotes titles through book signings, direct mail and the Internet." **Pays royalty.** Publishes ms 1 year after acceptance. Responds in 1 month to queries; 2-3 months to mss. Guidelines online.

Member of Publishers Marketing Association.

NONFICTION Subjects include business, economics, memoirs.

FICTION Subjects include adventure, ethnic, gay, lesbian, historical, literary, mainstream, contemporary, multicultural. "Tell why your idea is unique or interesting. Make sure we are interested in your genre before submitting." Query with SASE. Submit bio, estimated word count, list of publishing credits. Accepts queries via e-mail (prefer US Mail), fax.

TIPS "Send a good bio. I'm interested in a writer's experience and unique outlook on life."

PALETTES & QUILLS

1935 Penfield Road, Penfield NY 14526. (585)456-0217. **E-mail:** palettesnquills@gmail.com. **Website:** www.palettesnquills.com. **Contact:** Donna M. Marbach, publisher/owner. Estab. 2002.

NONFICTION Does not want political and religious diatribes.

POETRY Palettes & Quills "is at this point, a poetry press only, and produces only a handful of publications each year, specializing in anthologies, individual chapbooks, and broadsides." Wants "work that should appeal to a wide audience." Does not want "poems that are sold blocks of text, long-lined and without stanza breaks. Wildly elaborate free-verse would be difficult and in all likelihood fight with art background, amateurish rhyming poem, overly sentimental poems, poems that use excessive profanity, or which denigrate other people, or political and religious diatribes." Query first with 3-5 poems and a cover letter with brief bio and publication credits for individual unsolicited chapbooks. May include previously published poems. Chapbook poets would get 20 copies of a run; broadside poets and artists get 5-10 copies and occasionally paid $10 for reproduction rights. Anthology poets get 1 copy of the anthology. All poets and artists get a discount on purchases that include their work.

PALGRAVE MACMILLAN

St. Martin's Press, 175 Fifth Ave., New York NY 10010. (212)982-3900. **Fax:** (212)777-6359. **Website:** www.palgrave.com. **Contact:** Airié Stuart (history, business, economics, current events, psychology, biography); Anthony Wahl (political science, current events, Asian studies, international relations); Farideh Koohi-Kamali (literature, anthropology, cultural studies, performing arts, Islamic World & Middle East); Amanda Johnson (education, religion, women's studies/history); Ella Pearce (African studies, Latin American studies); Alessandra Bastagli (American history, American studies, world history); Heather Van Dusen (political science, political economy, political theory). Publishes hardcover and trade paperback originals. "Palgrave wishes to expand on our already successful academic, trade, and reference programs so that we will remain at the forefront of publishing in the global information economy of the 21st century. We publish high-quality academic works and a distinguished range of reference titles, and we expect to see many of our works available in electronic form. We do not accept fiction or poetry." Accepts simultaneous submissions. Book catalog and ms guidelines online.

Palgrave Macmillan is a cross-market publisher specializing in cutting edge academic and trade non-fiction titles. Our list consists of top authors ranging from academics making original contributions in their disciplines to trade authors, including journalists and experts, writing news-making books for a broad, educated readership.

NONFICTION Subjects include business, economics, creative nonfiction, education, ethnic, gay, lesbian, government, politics, history, language, literature, military, war, money, finance, multicultural, music, dance, philosophy, regional, religion, sociology, spirituality, translation, women's issues, women's studies, humanities. We are looking for good solid scholarship. Query with proposal package including outline, 3-4 sample chapters, prospectus, cv and SASE. Reviews artwork/photos.

PANTHEON BOOKS

Random House, Inc., 1745 Broadway, 3rd Floor, New York NY 10019. **E-mail:** pantheonpublicity@randomhouse.com. **Website:** www.pantheonbooks.com. Estab. 1942. Publishes hardcover and trade paperback originals and trade paperback reprints.

Pantheon Books publishes both Western and non-Western authors of literary fiction and important nonfiction.

NONFICTION *Does not accept unsolicited mss.* Agented submissions only.

FICTION *Does not accept unsolicited mss.* Agented submissions only.

PANTS ON FIRE PRESS

2062 Harbor Cove Way, Winter Garden FL 34787. **E-mail:** editor@pantsonfirepress.com. **E-mail:** submission@pantsonfirepress.com. **Website:** www.pantsonfirepress.com. **Contact:** Becca Goldman, senior editor; Emily Gerety, editor. Estab. 2012. Publishes hardcover originals and reprints, trade paperback originals and reprints, and electronic originals and reprints. Pants On Fire Press is an award-winning book publisher of picture, middle-grade, young adult, and adult books. They are a digital-first book publisher, striving to follow a high degree of excellence while maintaining quality standards. **Publishes 10-15 titles/year. Receives 2,500 queries and mss per year. 60% of books from first-time authors. 80% from unagented writers. Pays 10-50% royalties on wholesale price.** Publishes ms approximately 7 months after acceptance. Accepts simultaneous submissions. Responds in 3 months to queries, proposals, and mss. Catalog available on website. Mss guidelines available on website.

FICTION Subjects include juvenile, young adult. Publishes big story ideas with high concepts, new worlds, and meaty characters for children, teens, and discerning adults. Always on the lookout for Action, Adventure, Animals, Comedic, Dramatic, Dystopian, Fantasy, Historical, Paranormal, Romance, Sci-Fi, Supernatural, and Suspense stories. Submit a proposal package including a synopsis, 3 sample chapters, and a query letter via e-mail.

PAPERCUTZ

160 Broadway, Suite 700E, New York NY 10038. (646)559-4681. **Fax:** (212)643-1545. **Website:** www.papercutz.com. Estab. 2004. Publisher of graphic novels. **Publishes 10 titles/year.**

FICTION "Independent publisher of graphic novels based on popular existing properties aimed at the teen and tween market."

TIPS "Be familiar with our titles—that's the best way to know what we're interested in publishing. If you are somehow attached to a successful tween or teen property and would like to adapt it into a graphic novel, we may be interested."

PARACLETE PRESS

P.O. Box 1568, Orleans MA 02653. (508)255-4685. **Fax:** (508)255-5705. **E-mail:** jsweeney@paracletepress.com. **Website:** www.paracletepress.com. **Contact:** Editorial Review Committee. Estab. 1981. Publishes hardcover and trade paperback originals. Publisher of devotionals, new editions of classics, books on prayer, Christian living, spirituality, fiction, compact discs, and videos. **Publishes 40 titles/year. 250 mss received/year.** Publishes ms up to 2 years after acceptance. Responds in 2 months.

NONFICTION Subjects include religion. Query with SASE. Submit 2-3 sample chapters, TOC, chapter summaries.

PARADISE CAY PUBLICATIONS

P.O. Box 29, Arcata CA 95518-0029. (800)736-4509. **Fax:** (707)822-9163. **E-mail:** info@paracay.com; james@paracay.com. **Website:** www.paracay.com. **Contact:** Matt Morehouse, publisher. Publishes hardcover and trade paperback originals and reprints. "Paradise Cay Publications, Inc. is a small independent publisher specializing in nautical books, videos, and art prints. Our primary interest is in manuscripts that deal with the instructional and technical aspects of ocean sailing. We also publish and will consider fiction if it has a strong nautical theme." **Publishes 5 titles/year. 360-480 queries received/year. 240-360 mss received/year. 10% of books from first-time authors. 100% from unagented writers. Pays 10-15% royalty on wholesale price. Makes outright purchase of $1,000-10,000. Does not normally pay advances to first-time or little-known authors.** Publishes ms 4 months after acceptance. Responds in 1 month to queries/proposals; 2 months to mss. Book catalog and ms guidelines free on request or online.

IMPRINTS Pardey Books.

NONFICTION Subjects include cooking, foods, nutrition, recreation, sports, travel. Must have strong nautical theme. Include a cover letter containing a story synopsis and a short bio, including any plans to promote their work. The cover letter should describe the book's subject matter, approach, distinguishing characteristics, intended audience, author's qualifications, and why the author thinks this book is appropriate for Paradise Cay. Call first. Reviews artwork/photos. Send photocopies.

FICTION Subjects include adventure, nautical, sailing. All fiction must have a nautical theme. Query with SASE. Submit proposal package, clips, 2-3 sample chapters.

TIPS "Audience is recreational sailors. Call Matt Morehouse (publisher)."

PARADISE RESEARCH PUBLICATIONS, INC.

P.O. Box 837, Kihei HI 96753. (808)874-4876. **Fax:** (808)874-4876. **E-mail:** dickb@dickb.com. **Website:** www.dickb.com/index.shtml. Publishes trade paperback originals. Paradise Research Publications wants only books on Alcoholics Anonymous and its spiritual roots. **Publishes 3 titles/year. 5 queries received/year. 1 mss received/year. 20% of books from first-time authors. 100% from unagented writers. Pays 10% royalty.** Publishes ms 3 months after acceptance. Accepts simultaneous submissions. Responds in 1 month to queries. Book catalog available online.

NONFICTION Subjects include health, medicine, psychology, religion, spirituality, recovery, alcoholism, addictions, Christian recovery, history of Alcoholics Annonymous. Query with SASE.

PARAGON HOUSE PUBLISHERS

3600 Labore Rd., Suite 1, St. Paul MN 55110. (651)644-3087. **Fax:** (651)644-0997. **E-mail:** paragon@paragonhouse.com. **Website:** www.paragonhouse.com. **Contact:** Gordon Anderson, acquisitions editor. Estab. 1962. Publishes hardcover and trade paperback originals and trade paperback reprints and eBooks. "We publish general-interest titles and textbooks that provide the readers greater understanding of society and the world. Currently emphasizing religion, philosophy, economics, and society." **Publishes 5-10 titles/year. 1,500 queries received/year. 150 mss received/year. 7% of books from first-time authors. 90% from unagented writers. Pays $500-1,000 advance.** Publishes ms 1 year after acceptance. Accepts simultaneous submissions. Guidelines online.

IMPRINTS Omega Books.

NONFICTION Subjects include government, politics, multicultural, environment, philosophy, psychology, religion, sociology, women's issues, world affairs, economics, integral studies. Submit proposal package, outline, 2 sample chapters, market breakdown, SASE.

PARALLAX PRESS

P.O. Box 7355, Berkeley CA 94707. (510)525-0101, ext. 113. **Fax:** (510)525-7129. **E-mail:** rachel.neumann@parallax.org. **Website:** www.parallax.org. **Contact:** Rachel Neumann, publisher. Estab. 1985. Publishes hardcover and trade paperback originals. "We focus primarily on engaged Buddhism." **Publishes 5-8 titles/year.** Responds in 6-8 weeks to queries. Guidelines online.

NONFICTION Subjects include multicultural, religion, Buddhism, spirituality. Query with SASE. Submit 1 sample chapter, 1-page proposal. Reviews artwork/photos. Send photocopies.

PASSKEY PUBLICATIONS

27762 Antonio Parkway, Suite L1, #238, Ladera Ranch CA 92694. (916)712-7446. **Fax:** (916)427-5765. **Website:** www.passkeypublications.com. **Contact:** Christine P. Silva, president. Estab. 2007. Publishes trade paperback originals. **Publishes 15 titles/year. Receives 375 queries/year; 120 mss/year. 15% of books from first-time authors. 90% from unagented writers. Pay varies on retail price.** Publishes ms 1 year after acceptance. Accepts simultaneous submissions. Responds in 1 month. Catalog and guidelines online.

IMPRINTS Passkey Publications, PassKey EA Review.

NONFICTION Subjects include business, economics, finance, money, real estate, accounting, taxation, study guides for professional examinations. "Books on taxation and accounting are generally updated every year to reflect tax law changes, and the turn-around on a ms must be less than 3 months for accounting and tax subject matter. Books generally remain in publication only 11 months and are generally published every year for updates." Submit complete ms. Nonfiction mss only. Reviews artwork/photos as part of ms package. Send electronic files on disk, via e-mail, or jump drive.

TIPS "Accepting business, accounting, tax, finance and other related subjects only."

PAUL DRY BOOKS

1700 Sansom St., Suite 700, Philadelphia PA 19103. (215)231-9939. **Fax:** (215)231-9942. **E-mail:** pdry@pauldrybooks.com; editor@pauldrybooks.com. **Website:** pauldrybooks.com. Hardcover and trade paperback originals, trade paperback reprints. "We publish fiction, both novels and short stories, and nonfiction, biography, memoirs, history, and essays, covering subjects from Homer to Chekhov, bird watching to jazz music, New York City to shogunate Japan." Book catalog available online. Guidelines available online.

NONFICTION Subjects include agriculture, contemporary culture, history, literary criticism, memoirs, multicultural, philosophy, religion, translation, popular mathematics. Submit proposal package.

FICTION Subjects include literary, short story collections, translation, young adult, novels. Submit sample chapters, clips, bio.

TIPS "Our aim is to publish lively books 'to awaken, delight, and educate'—to spark conversation. We publish fiction and nonfiction, and essays covering subjects from Homer to Chekhov, bird watching to jazz music, New York City to shogunate Japan."

PAULINE BOOKS & MEDIA

50 St. Paul's Ave., Boston MA 02130. (617)522-8911. **Fax:** (617)541-9805. **E-mail:** design@paulinemedia.com; editorial@paulinemedia.com. **Website:** www.pauline.org. Estab. 1932. Publishes trade paperback originals and reprints. "Submissions are evaluated on adherence to Gospel values, harmony with the Catholic faith tradition, relevance of topic, and quality of writing." For board books and picture books, the entire manuscript should be submitted. For easy-to-read, young readers, and middle reader books and teen books, please send a cover letter accompanied by a synopsis and two sample chapters. "Electronic submissions are encouraged. We make every effort to respond to unsolicited submissions within 2 months." **Publishes 40 titles/year. 15- for adult books; about 40% for children's books% of books from first-time authors. 5% from unagented writers. Varies by project, but generally are royalties with advance. Flat fees sometimes considered for smaller works.** Publishes book Publishes a book approximately 11-18 months after acceptance. Responds in 2 months to queries, proposals, & mss. Book catalog available online. Guidelines available online & by e-mail.

NONFICTION Subjects include child guidance, religion, spirituality. Picture books, young readers, middle readers, teen: religion and fiction. Average word length: picture books—500-1,000; young readers—8,000-10,000; middle readers—15,000-25,000; teen—30,000-50,000. Recently published children's titles: *Bible Stores for Little Ones* by Genny Monchapm; *I Forgive You: Love We Can Hear, Ask For and Give* by Nicole Lataif; *Shepherds To the Rescue* (first place Catholic Book Award Winner) by Maria Grace Dateno; *FSP*; *Jorge from Argentina*; *Prayers for Young Catholics*. Teen Titles: *Teens Share the Mission* by Teens; *Martyred: The Story of Saint Lorenzo Ruiz*; *Ten Commandmenst for Kissing Gloria Jean* by Britt Leigh; *A.K.A. Genius* (2nd Place Catholic Book Award Winner) by Marilee Haynes; *Tackling Tough Topics* with Faith and Fiction by Diana Jenkins. No memoir/autobiography, poetry, or strictly nonreligious works currently considered. Submit proposal package, including outline, 1- 2 sample chapters, cover letter, synopsis, intended audience and proposed length.

FICTION Subjects include juvenile. Children's and teen fiction only. We are now accepting submissions for easy-to-read and middle reader chapter, and teen well documented historical fiction. We would also consider well-written fantasy, fairy tales, myths, science fiction, mysteries, or romance if approached from a Catholic perspective and consistent with church teaching. Please see our Writer's Guidelines. "Submit proposal package, including synopsis, 2 sample chapters, and cover letter; complete ms."

TIPS "Manuscripts may or may not be explicitly catechetical, but we seek those that reflect a positive worldview, good moral values, awareness and appreciation of diversity, and respect for all people. All material must be relevant to the lives of readers and must conform to Catholic teaching and practice."

PAULIST PRESS

997 MacArthur Blvd., Mahwah NJ 07430. (201)825-7300. **Fax:** (201)825-8345. **Website:** www.paulistpress.

com. **Contact:** Trace Murphy, editorial director. Estab. 1865. "Paulist Press publishes ecumenical theology, Roman Catholic studies, and books on scripture, liturgy, spirituality, church history, and philosophy, as well as works on faith and culture. Our publishing is oriented toward adult-level nonfiction. We do not publish poetry or works of fiction, and we have scaled back our involvement in children's publishing." **Receives 250 submissions/year. Royalties and advances are negotible. Illustrators sometimes receive a flat fee when all we need are spot illustrations.** Publishes book Publishes a book 18-24 months after acceptance. Responds in 3 months to queries and proposals; 3-4 months on mss. Book catalog available online. Guidelines available online and by e-mail.

NONFICTION Accepts submissions via e-mail. Hard copy submissions returned only if accompanied by self-addressed envelope with adequate postage.

PAYCOCK PRESS

3819 N. 13th St., Arlington VA 22201. (703)525-9296. **E-mail:** rchrdpeabody9@gmail.com. **Website:** www.gargoylemagazine.com. **Contact:** Richard Peabody. Estab. 1976. "Too academic for the underground, too outlaw for the academic world. We tend to be edgy and look for ultra-literary work." Publishes paperback originals. Books: POD printing. Average print order: 500. Averages 1 total title/year. Member CLMP. Distributes through Amazon and website. Publishes ms 1 year after acceptance. Accepts simultaneous submissions. Responds to queries in 1 month; mss in 4 months.

FICTION Subjects include experimental, literary, poetry, short story collections. Accepts unsolicited mss. Accepts queries by e-mail. Include brief bio. Send SASE for return of ms or send a disposable ms and SASE for reply only.

POETRY Considers experimental, edgy poetry collections. Accepts unsolicited mss. Accepts queries by e-mail. Include brief bio. Send SASE for return of ms or send a disposable ms and SASE for reply only.

TIPS "Check out our website. Two of our favorite writers are Paul Bowles and Jeanette Winterson."

A ⊘ PEACE HILL PRESS

Affiliate of W.W. Norton, 18021 The Glebe Ln., Charles City VA 23030. (804)829-5043. **Fax:** (804)829-5704. **E-mail:** info@peacehillpress.com. **Website:** www.peacehillpress.com. Estab. 2001. Publishes hardcover and trade paperback originals. **Publishes 4-8 titles/year. Pays 6-10% royalty on retail price. Pays $500-1,000 advance.** Publishes book Publishes a book 18 months after acceptance.

NONFICTION Subjects include education, history, language, literature. Does not take submissions. Reviews artwork/photos. Send photocopies.

FICTION Subjects include historical, juvenile, picture books, young adult. Does not take submissions.

PEACHTREE CHILDREN'S BOOKS

Peachtree Publishers, Ltd., 1700 Chattahoochee Ave., Atlanta GA 30318-2112. (404)876-8761. **Fax:** (404)875-2578. **E-mail:** hello@peachtree-online.com. **Website:** www.peachtree-online.com. **Contact:** Helen Harriss, submissions editor. Publishes hardcover and trade paperback originals. "We publish a broad range of subjects and perspectives, with emphasis on innovative plots and strong writing." **Publishes 30 titles/year. 25% of books from first-time authors. 25% from unagented writers. Pays royalty on retail price.** Publishes ms 1 year after acceptance. Accepts simultaneous submissions. Responds in 6 months and mss. Book catalog for 6 first-class stamps. Guidelines online.

NONFICTION Subjects include animals, child guidance, creative nonfiction, education, ethnic, gardening, health, medicine, history, language, literature, literary criticism, multicultural, music, dance, nature, environment, recreation, regional, science, social sciences, sports, travel. No e-mail or fax queries of mss. Submit complete ms with SASE, or summary and 3 sample chapters with SASE.

FICTION Subjects include juvenile, picture books, young adult. Looking for very well-written middle grade and young adult novels. No adult fiction. No collections of poetry or short stories; no romance or science fiction. Submit complete ms with SASE.

PEACHTREE PUBLISHERS, LTD.

1700 Chattahoochee Ave., Atlanta GA 30318. (404)876-8761. **Fax:** (404)875-2578. **E-mail:** hello@peachtree-online.com. **Website:** www.peachtree-online.com. **Contact:** Helen Harriss, acquisitions editor; Loraine Joyner, art director; Melanie McMahon Ives, production manager. Estab. 1977. **Publishes 30-35 titles/year.** Publishes ms 1-2 years after acceptance. Accepts simultaneous submissions. Responds in 6-7 months.

NONFICTION Picture books: animal, history, nature/environment. Young readers, middle readers, young adults: animal, biography, nature/environment. Does not want to see religion. Submit complete ms or 3 sample chapters by postal mail only.

FICTION Picture books, young readers: adventure, animal, concept, history, nature/environment. Middle readers: adventure, animal, history, nature/environment, sports. Young adults: fiction, mystery, adventure. Does not want to see science fiction, romance. Submit complete ms or 3 sample chapters by postal mail only.

PEDLAR PRESS

113 Bond St., St. John's NL A16 1T6, Canada. (709)738-6702. **E-mail:** feralgrl@interlog.com. **Website:** www.pedlarpress.com. **Contact:** Beth Follett, owner/editor. Distributes in Canada through LitDistCo. **Publishes 7 titles/year. Pays 10% royalty on retail price. Average advance: $200-400.** Publishes ms 1 year after acceptance.

FICTION Experimental, feminist, gay/lesbian, literary, short story collections. Canadian writers only. Query with SASE, sample chapter(s), synopsis.

TIPS "I select manuscripts according to my taste, which fluctuates. Be familiar with some if not most of Pedlar's recent titles."

PELICAN PUBLISHING COMPANY

1000 Burmaster St., Gretna LA 70053. (504)368-1175. **Fax:** (504)368-1195. **E-mail:** editorial@pelicanpub.com. **Website:** www.pelicanpub.com. Estab. 1926. Publishes hardcover, trade paperback and mass market paperback originals and reprints. "We believe ideas have consequences. One of the consequences is that they lead to a best-selling book. We publish books to improve and uplift the reader. Currently emphasizing business and history titles." Publishes 20 young readers/year; 1 middle reader/year. "Our children's books (illustrated and otherwise) include history, biography, holiday, and regional. Pelican's mission is to publish books of quality and permanence that enrich the lives of those who read them." **Pays authors in royalties; buys ms outright "rarely." Illustrators paid by "various arrangements." Advance considered.** Publishes book Publishes a book 9-18 months after acceptance. Responds in 1 month to queries; 3 months to mss. Book catalog and ms guidelines online.

NONFICTION Subjects include Americana, especially Southern regional, Ozarks, Texas, Florida, and Southwest, art, architecture, ethnic, government, politics, special interest in conservative viewpoint, history, popular, multicultural, American artforms, but will consider others: jazz, blues, Cajun, R&B, regional, religion, for popular audience mostly, but will consider others, sports, motivational (with business slant). "We look for authors who can promote successfully. We require that a query be made first. This greatly expedites the review process and can save the writer additional postage expenses." Young readers: biography, history, holiday, multicultural. Middle readers: Louisiana history, holiday, regional. No multiple queries or submissions. Query with SASE. Reviews artwork/photos.

FICTION Subjects include historical, juvenile, regional or historical focus. We publish no adult fiction. Young readers: history, holiday, science, multicultural and regional. Middle readers: Louisiana History. Multicultural needs include stories about African-Americans, Irish-Americans, Jews, Asian-Americans, and Hispanics. Does not want animal stories, general Christmas stories, "day at school" or "accept yourself" stories. Maximum word length: young readers—1,100; middle readers—40,000. No young adult, romance, science fiction, fantasy, gothic, mystery, erotica, confession, horror, sex, or violence. Also no psychological novels. Query with SASE. Submit outline, clips, 2 sample chapters, SASE.

POETRY Considers poetry for "hardcover children's books only (1,100 words maximum), preferably with a regional focus. However, our needs for this are very limited; we publish 20 juvenile titles per year, and most of these are prose, not poetry." Books are 32 pages, magazine-sized, include illustrations.

TIPS "We do extremely well with cookbooks, popular histories, and business. We will continue to build in these areas. The writer must have a clear sense of the market and knowledge of the competition. A query letter should describe the project briefly, give the author's writing and professional credentials, and promotional ideas."

PENGUIN CANADA, LTD.

The Penguin Group, 90 Eglinton Ave. E., Suite 700, Toronto ON M4P 2Y3, Canada. (416)925-2249. **Fax:** (416)925-0068. **Website:** www.penguin.ca. Estab. 1974. **Pays advance.**

NONFICTION Any Canadian subject by any Canadian authors. Agented submissions only.

PENGUIN GROUP: SOUTH AFRICA

P.O. Box 9, Parklands 2121, South Africa. (27)(11)327-3550. **Fax:** (27)(11)327-3660. **E-mail:** publishing@za.penguingroup.com. **Website:** www.penguinbooks.co.za. Seeks adult fiction (literary and mass market titles) and adult nonfiction (travel, sports, politics, current affairs, business). No children's, young adult, poetry, or short stories. **Publishes 20 titles/year. Pays royalty.**

NONFICTION Subjects include business, economics, cooking, foods, nutrition, history, sports, travel, health/fitness, politics/current affairs. Submit info letter, synopsis, SASE. No e-mail/fax queries.

FICTION Subjects include literary, mass market. Submit intro letter, 3 sample chapters.

PENGUIN GROUP USA

375 Hudson St., New York NY 10014. (212)366-2000. **Website:** www.penguin.com. General interest publisher of both fiction and nonfiction. *No unsolicited mss.* Submit work through a literary agent. DAW Books is the lone exception. Guidelines online.

PENGUIN RANDOM HOUSE, LLC

Division of Bertelsmann Book Group, 1745 Broadway, New York NY 10019. (212)782-9000. **Website:** www.randomhouse.com. Estab. 1925. Penguin Random House LLC is the world's largest English-language general trade book publisher. *Agented submissions only. No unsolicited mss.*

IMPRINTS Crown Publishing Group; Knopf Doubleday Publishing Group; Random House Publishing Group; Random House Children's Books; RH Digital Publishing Group; RH International.

PENNY-FARTHING PRODUCTIONS

1 Sugar Creek Center Blvd., Suite 820, Sugar Land TX 77478. (713)780-0300 or (800)926-2669. **Fax:** (713)780-4004. **E-mail:** corp@pfpress.com. **Website:** www.pfpress.com. Estab. 1998. Publishes graphic novels. "Penny Farthing Productions is not currently accepting submissions and submission messages will not receive a response." Guidelines online.

THE PERMANENT PRESS

Attn: Judith Shepard, 4170 Noyac Rd., Sag Harbor NY 11963. (631)725-1101. **Fax:** (631)725-8215. **E-mail:** judith@thepermanentpress.com; shepard@thepermanentpress.com. **Website:** www.thepermanentpress.com. **Contact:** Judith and Martin Shepard, acquisitions/co-publishers. Estab. 1978. Publishes hardcover originals. Mid-size, independent publisher of literary fiction. "We keep titles in print and are active in selling subsidiary rights." Average print order: 1,000-2,500. Averages 16 total titles. Accepts unsolicited mss. Pays 10-15% royalty on wholesale price. Offers $1,000 advance. **Pays 10-15% royalty on wholesale price. Offers $1,000 advance.** Publishes ms within 18 months after acceptance. Responds in weeks or months.

Will not accept simultaneous submissions.

FICTION Promotes titles through reviews. Literary, mainstream/contemporary, mystery. Especially looking for high-line literary fiction, "artful, original and arresting." Accepts any fiction category as long as it is a "well-written, original full-length novel."

TIPS "We are looking for good books—be they 10th novels or first ones, it makes little difference. The fiction is more important than the track record. Send us the first 25 pages; it's impossible to judge something that begins on page 302. Also, no outlines—let the writing present itself."

PERSEA BOOKS

277 Broadway, Suite 708, New York NY 10007. (212)260-9256. **Fax:** (212)267-3165. **E-mail:** info@perseabooks.com. **Website:** www.perseabooks.com. Estab. 1975. The aim of Persea is to publish works that endure by meeting high standards of literary merit and relevance. "We have often taken on important books other publishers have overlooked, or have made significant discoveries and rediscoveries, whether of a single work or writer's entire oeuvre. Our books cover a wide range of themes, styles, and genres. We have published poetry, fiction, essays, memoir, biography, titles of Jewish and Middle Eastern interest, women's studies, American Indian folklore, and revived classics, as well as a notable selection of works in translation." Responds in 8 weeks to proposals; 10 weeks to mss. Guidelines online.

NONFICTION Subjects include contemporary culture, literary criticism, literature, memoirs, translation, travel, young adult. Queries should include a cover letter, author background and publication history, a detailed synopsis of the proposed work, and a sample chapter. Please indicate if the work is simultaneously submitted.

FICTION Subjects include contemporary, literary, short story collections, translation, young adult. Queries should include a cover letter, author background and publication history, a detailed synopsis of the proposed work, and a sample chapter. Please indicate if the work is simultaneously submitted.

POETRY "We have a longstanding commitment to publishing extraordinary contemporary poetry and maintain an active poetry program. At this time, due to our commitment to the poets we already publish, we are limited in our ability to add new collections." Send an e-mail to poetry@perseabooks.com describing current project and publication history, attaching a pdf or Word document with up to 12 sample pages of poetry. "If the timing is right and we are interested in seeing more work, we will contact you."

⊘ PERUGIA PRESS

P.O. Box 60364, Florence MA 01062. **Website:** www.perugiapress.com. **Contact:** Susan Kan, director. Estab. 1997. Celebrating poetry by women since 1997. "Contact us through our website."

PETER PAUPER PRESS, INC.

202 Mamaroneck Ave., 4th Floor, White Plains NY 10601. **Website:** www.peterpauper.com. Estab. 1928. Publishes hardcover originals. "PPP publishes small and medium format, illustrated gift books for occasions and in celebration of specific relationships such as mom, sister, friend, teacher, grandmother, granddaughter. PPP has expanded into the following areas: books for teens and tweens, activity books for children, organizers, books on popular topics of nonfiction for adults and licensed books by best-selling authors." **Publishes 40-50 titles/year. 100 queries received/year. 150 mss received/year. 5% from unagented writers. Makes outright purchase only. Pays advance.** Publishes ms 1 year after acceptance. Responds in 2 months to queries.

NONFICTION "We do not publish fiction or poetry. We publish brief, original quotes, aphorisms, and wise sayings. Please do not send us other people's quotes." Submit cover letter and hard copy ms.

TIPS "Our readers are primarily female, age 10 and over, who are likely to buy a 'gift' book or gift book set in a stationery, gift, book, or boutique store or national book chain. Writers should become familiar with our previously published work. We publish only small- and medium-format, illustrated, hardcover gift books and sets of between 1,000-4,000 words. We have much less interest in work aimed at men."

PETERSON'S

461 From Rd., Paramus NJ 07652. **E-mail:** support@petersons.com. **Website:** www.petersons.com. Estab. 1966. Publishes trade and reference books. Peterson's publishes guides to graduate and professional programs, colleges and universities, financial aid, distance learning, private schools, summer programs, international study, executive education, job hunting and career opportunities, educational and career test prep, as well as online products and services offering educational and career guidance and information for adult learners and workplace solutions for education professionals. **Pays royalty. Pays advance.** Book catalog available free.

NONFICTION Subjects include business, economics, education, careers. Looks for appropriateness of contents to our markets, author's credentials, and writing style suitable for audience.

PFEIFFER

John Wiley & Sons, Inc., 989 Market St., San Francisco CA 94103. **Website:** www.wiley.com. Pfeiffer is an imprint of Wiley. **Publishes 250 titles/year. Pays variable royalties. Pays occasional advance.** Publishes ms 1 year after acceptance. Accepts simultaneous submissions. Responds in 2-3 months to queries. Guidelines online.

NONFICTION Subjects include business, economics, education, health, medicine, money, finance, psychology, religion. See proposal guidelines online.

PFLAUM PUBLISHING GROUP

2621 Dryden Rd., Suite 300, Dayton OH 45439. **Website:** www.pflaum.com. "Pflaum Publishing Group, a division of Peter Li, Inc., serves the specialized market of religious education, primarily Roman Catholic. We provide high quality, theologically sound, practical, and affordable resources that assist religious educators of and ministers to children from preschool through senior high school." **Publishes 20 titles/year. Payment by outright purchase.** Book catalog and ms guidelines free.

NONFICTION Query with SASE.

PHAIDON PRESS

65 Bleecker St., New York NY 10012. (212)652-5400. **Fax:** (212)652-5410. **E-mail:** submissions@phaidon.com. **Website:** www.phaidon.com. Estab. 1923. Publishes hardcover and trade paperback originals and reprints. Phaidon Press is the world's leading publisher of books on the visual arts, with offices in London, Paris, Berlin, Barcelona, Milan, New York and Tokyo. Their books are recognized worldwide for the highest quality of content, design, and production. They cover

everything from art, architecture, photography, design, performing arts, decorative arts, contemporary culture, fashion, film, travel, cookery and children's books. **Publishes 100 titles/year. 500 mss received/year. 40% of books from first-time authors. 90% from unagented writers. Pays royalty on wholesale price, if appropriate. Offers advance, if appropriate.** Publishes ms 1 year after acceptance. Accepts simultaneous submissions. Responds in 3 months to proposals. Book catalog available free. Guidelines online.

NONFICTION Subjects include art, architecture, photography, design. Submit proposal package and outline, or submit complete ms. Submissions by e-mail or fax will not be accepted. Reviews artwork/photos. Send photocopies.

TIPS "Please do not contact us to obtain an update on the status of your submission until we have had your submission for at least three months, as we will not provide updates before this period of time has elapsed. Phaidon does not assume any responsibility for any unsolicited submissions, or any materials included with a submission."

PHILOMEL BOOKS

Imprint of Penguin Group (USA), Inc., 375 Hudson St., New York NY 10014. (212)414-3610. **Website:** www.penguin.com. **Contact:** Michael Green, president/publisher. Estab. 1980. Publishes hardcover originals. "We look for beautifully written, engaging manuscripts for children and young adults." **Publishes 8-10 titles/year. 5% of books from first-time authors. 20% from unagented writers. Pays authors in royalties. Average advance payment "varies." Illustrators paid by advance and in royalties. Pays negotiable advance.** Accepts simultaneous submissions.

NONFICTION Picture books. *Agented submissions only.*

FICTION Subjects include adventure, ethnic, fantasy, historical, juvenile, literary, picture books, regional, short story collections, translation, western, young adult. *No unsolicited mss.*

PHILOSOPHY DOCUMENTATION CENTER

P.O. Box 7147, Charlottesville VA 22906-7147. (434)220-3300. **Fax:** (434)220-3301. **E-mail:** leaman@pdcnet.org. **Website:** www.pdcnet.org. **Contact:** Dr. George Leaman, director. Estab. 1966. The Philosophy Documentation Center works in cooperation with publishers, database producers, software developers, journal editors, authors, librarians, and philosophers to create an electronic clearinghouse for philosophical publishing. **Publishes 4 titles/year. 4-6 queries received/year. 4-6 mss received/year. 50% of books from first-time authors. Pays 2-10% royalty. Pays advance.** Publishes ms 1 year after acceptance. Responds in 2 months to queries.

NONFICTION Subjects include philosophy, software. "We want to increase our range of philosophical titles and are especially interested in electronic publishing." Query with SASE. Submit outline.

PIANO PRESS

P.O. Box 85, Del Mar CA 92014. (619)884-1401. **Fax:** (858)755-1104. **E-mail:** pianopress@pianopress.com. **Website:** www.pianopress.com. **Contact:** Elizabeth C. Axford, editor. Estab. 1998. "We publish music-related books, either fiction or nonfiction, coloring books, songbooks, and poetry." **Pays authors, illustrators, and photographers royalty of 5-10% based on retail price.** Publishes ms 1 year after acceptance. Accepts simultaneous submissions. Responds to queries in 3 months; mss in 6 months. Book catalog available for #10 SASE and 2 first-class stamps.

NONFICTION Picture books, young readers, middle readers, young adults: multicultural, music/dance. Average word length: picture books—1,500-2,000.

FICTION Picture books, young readers, middle readers, young adults: folktales, multicultural, poetry, music. Average word length: picture books—1,500-2,000.

TIPS "We are looking for music-related material only for any juvenile market. Please do not send non-music-related materials. Query first before submitting anything."

PIATKUS BOOKS

Little, Brown Book Group, 100 Victoria Embankment, London WA EC4Y 0DY, United Kingdom. (20)7911-8000. **Fax:** (20)7911-8100. **E-mail:** info@littlebrown.co.uk. **Website:** piatkus.co.uk. Estab. 1979. Publishes hardcover originals, paperback originals, and paperback reprints. **10% from unagented writers.** Publishes ms 1 year after acceptance. Guidelines online.

NONFICTION *Agented submissions only.*

FICTION Quality family saga, historical, literary. *Agented submissions only.*

PICADOR USA

MacMillan, 175 Fifth Ave., New York NY 10010. (212)674-5151. **Website:** www.picadorusa.com. Estab. 1994. Picador publishes high-quality literary fiction and nonfiction. "We are open to a broad range of subjects, well written by authoritative authors." Publishes hardcover and trade paperback originals and reprints. Does not accept unsolicited mss. *Agented submissions only.* **Publishes 70-80 titles/year. Pays 7-15% on royalty. Advance varies.** Publishes ms 18 months after acceptance. Accepts simultaneous submissions.

PICCADILLY BOOKS, LTD.

P.O. Box 25203, Colorado Springs CO 80936. (719)550-9887. **Fax:** (719) 550-8810. **E-mail:** info@piccadillybooks.com. **Website:** www.piccadillybooks.com. Estab. 1985. Publishes hardcover originals and trade paperback originals and reprints. "Picadilly publishes nonfiction, diet, nutrition, and health-related books with a focus on alternative and natural medicine." **Publishes 5-8 titles/year. 70% of books from first-time authors. 95% from unagented writers. Pays 6-10% royalty on retail price.** Publishes ms 1 year after acceptance. Accepts simultaneous submissions. Responds only if interested, unless accompanied by a SASE to queries.

NONFICTION Subjects include cooking, foods, nutrition, health, medicine, performing arts. "Do your research. Let us know why there is a need for your book, how it differs from other books on the market, and how you will promote the book. No phone calls. We prefer to see the entire ms, but will accept a minimum of 3 sample chapters on your first inquiry. A cover letter is also required; please provide a brief overview of the book, information about similar books already in print and explain why yours is different or better. Tell us the prime market for your book and what you can do to help market it. Also, provide us with background information on yourself and explain what qualifies you to write this book."

TIPS "We publish nonfiction, general interest, self-help books currently emphasizing alternative health."

PICTON PRESS

Picton Corp., 814 E. Elkcam Circle, Marco Island FL 34145. **E-mail:** sales@pictonpress.com. **Website:** www.pictonpress.com. Publishes hardcover and mass market paperback originals and reprints, DVDs, and CDs. "Picton Press is one of America's oldest, largest, and most respected publishers of genealogical and historical books specializing in research tools for the 17th, 18th, and 19th centuries." **Publishes 15 titles/year. 30 queries received/year. 15 mss received/year. 20% of books from first-time authors. 100% from unagented writers. Pays 0-10% royalty on wholesale price. Makes outright purchase.** Publishes ms 6 months after acceptance. Responds in 1 month. Book catalog available free.

IMPRINTS Cricketfield Press; New England History Press; Penobscot Press; Picton Press.

NONFICTION Subjects include Americana, history, genealogy. Query with SASE. Submit outline.

⊘ THE PILGRIM PRESS

700 Prospect Ave. E., Cleveland OH 44115-1100. (216)736-3755. **Fax:** (216)736-2207. **Website:** www.thepilgrimpress.com. Publishes hardcover and trade paperback originals. No longer accepting unsolicited ms proposals. **Publishes 25 titles/year. 60% of books from first-time authors. 80% from unagented writers. Pays standard royalties. Pays advance.** Publishes ms an average of 18 months after acceptance. Responds in 3 months to queries. Book catalog and ms guidelines online.

NONFICTION Subjects include business, economics, gay, lesbian, government, politics, nature, environment, religion, ethics, social issues with a strong commitment to justice—addressing such topics as public policy, sexuality and gender, human rights and minority liberation—primarily in a Christian context, but not exclusively.

PIÑATA BOOKS

Imprint of Arte Publico Press, University of Houston, 4902 Gulf Fwy., Bldg. 19, Room 100, Houston TX 77204-2004. (713)743-2845. **Fax:** (713)743-3080. **E-mail:** submapp@uh.edu. **Website:** www.artepublicopress.com. Estab. 1994. Publishes hardcover and trade paperback originals. "Piñata Books is dedicated to the publication of children's and young adult literature focusing on U.S. Hispanic culture by U.S. Hispanic authors. Arte Publico's mission is the publication, promotion and dissemination of Latino literature for a variety of national and regional audiences, from early childhood to adult, through the complete gamut of delivery systems, including personal performance as well as print and electronic media." **Publishes 10-15 titles/year. 80% of books from first-time authors. Pays 10% royalty on wholesale price. Pays $1,000-3,000 advance.** Publishes ms 2 years after acceptance. Accepts simultaneous submissions. Responds in 2-3 months to queries; 4-6 months to mss. Book catalog and guidelines online.

NONFICTION Subjects include ethnic. Piñata Books specializes in publication of children's and young adult literature that authentically portrays themes, characters and customs unique to U.S. Hispanic culture. Submissions made through online submission form.

FICTION Subjects include adventure, juvenile, picture books, young adult. Submissions made through online submission form.

POETRY Appropriate to Hispanic theme. Submissions made through online submission form.

TIPS "Include cover letter with submission explaining why your manuscript is unique and important, why we should publish it, who will buy it, etc."

PINEAPPLE PRESS, INC.

P.O. Box 3889, Sarasota FL 34230. (941)706-2507. **Fax:** (800)746-3275. **E-mail:** info@pineapplepress.com. **Website:** www.pineapplepress.com. **Contact:** June Cussen, executive editor. Estab. 1982. Publishes hardcover and trade paperback originals. "We are seeking quality nonfiction on diverse topics for the library and book trade markets. Our mission is to publish good books about Florida." **Publishes 25 titles/year. 1,000 queries received/year. 500 mss received/year. 50% of books from first-time authors. 95% from unagented writers. Pays authors royalty of 10-15%.** Publishes book Publishes a book 1 year after acceptance. Accepts simultaneous submissions. Responds in 2 months. Book catalog for 9×12 SAE with $1.25 postage. Guidelines online.

NONFICTION Subjects include regional, Florida. Picture books: animal, history, nature/environmental, science. Young readers, middle readers, young adults: animal, biography, geography, history, nature/environment, science. Query or submit outline/synopsis and intro and 3 sample chapters. Reviews artwork/photos. Send photocopies.

FICTION Subjects include regional, Florida. Picture books, young readers, middle readers, young adults: animal, folktales, history, nature/environment. Query or submit outline/synopsis and 3 sample chapters.

TIPS "Quality first novels will be published, though we usually only do one or two novels per year and they must be set in Florida. We regard the author/editor relationship as a trusting relationship with communication open both ways. Learn all you can about the publishing process and about how to promote your book once it is published. A query on a novel without a brief sample seems useless."

⊘ PLAN B PRESS

2714 Jefferson Dr., Alexandria VA 22303. (215)732-2663. **E-mail:** planbpress@gmail.com. **Website:** www.planbpress.com. **Contact:** Steven Allen May, president. Estab. 1999. Plan B Press is a "small publishing company with an international feel. Our intention is to have Plan B Press be part of the conversation about the direction and depth of literary movements and genres. Plan B Press's new direction is to seek out authors rarely-to-never published, sharing new voices that might not otherwise be heard. Plan B Press is determined to merge text with image, writing with art." Publishes poetry and short fiction. Wants "experimental poetry, concrete/visual work." **Pays author's copies.** Responds to queries in 1 month; mss in 3 months.

POETRY Wants to see: experimental, concrete, visual poetry. Does not want "sonnets, political or religious poems, work in the style of Ogden Nash."

PLANNERS PRESS

Imprint of the American Planning Association, 205 N. Michigan Ave., Suite 1200, Chicago IL 60601. (312)431-9100. **Fax:** (312)786-6700. **E-mail:** plannerspress@planning.org. **Website:** www.planning.org/plannerspress. **Contact:** Camille Fink (planning practice, urban issues, land use, transportation). Estab. 1970. Publishes hardcover, electronic, and trade paperback originals; and trade paperback and electronic reprints. "Our books often have a narrow audience of city planners and frequently focus on the tools of city planning." **Publishes 10 titles/year. 50 queries received/year. 35 mss received/year. 25% of books from first-time authors. 100% from unagented writers. Pays 10-15% royalty on net receipts. Pays advance against royalties.** Publishes ms 15 months after acceptance. Accepts simultaneous submissions. Responds in 1 month to queries; 2 months to proposals and mss. Book catalog online. Guidelines online.

NONFICTION Subjects include agriculture, business, economics, community, contemporary culture, economics, environment, finance, government, politics, history, horticulture, law, money, finance, nature, environment, politics, real estate, science, social sciences, sociology, transportation, world affairs. Submit proposal package, including: outline, 1 sample chapter and c.v. Submit completed ms. Reviews artwork/photos. Send photocopies.

TIPS "Our audience is professional planners but also anyone interested in community development, urban affairs, sustainability, and related fields."

PLAYLAB PRESS

P.O. Box 3701, South Brisbane BC 4101, Australia. **E-mail:** info@playlab.org.au. **Website:** www.playlab.org.au. Estab. 1978. **Publishes 1 titles/year.** Responds in 3 months to mss. Guidelines online.

NONFICTION Subjects include literary criticism.

FICTION Subjects include plays. Submit 2 copies of ms, cover letter.

TIPS "Playlab Press is committed to the publication of quality writing for and about theatre and performance, which is of significance to Australia's cultural life. It values socially just and diverse publication outcomes and aims to promote these outcomes in local, national, and international contexts."

PLEXUS PUBLISHING, INC.

143 Old Marlton Pike, Medford NJ 08055. (609)654-6500. **Fax:** (609)654-4309. **E-mail:** jbryans@plexuspublishing.com. **Website:** www.plexuspublishing.com. **Contact:** John B. Bryans, editor-in-chief/publisher. Estab. 1977. Publishes hardcover and paperback originals. Plexus publishes regional-interest (southern New Jersey and the greater Philadelphia area) fiction and nonfiction including mysteries, field guides, nature, travel and history. **Pays $500-1,000 advance.** Accepts simultaneous submissions. Responds in 3 months to proposals. Book catalog and book proposal guidelines for 10x13 SASE.

NONFICTION Query with SASE.

FICTION Mysteries and literary novels with a strong regional (southern New Jersey) angle. Query with SASE.

POCKET BOOKS

Simon & Schuster, 1230 Avenue of the Americas, New York NY 10020. (212)698-7000. **Website:** www.simonandschuster.com. Estab. 1939. Publishes paperback originals and reprints, mass market and trade paperbacks. Pocket Books publishes commercial fiction and genre fiction (WWE, Downtown Press, Star Trek). Book catalog available free. Guidelines online.

NONFICTION Subjects include cooking, foods, nutrition. *Agented submissions only.*

FICTION Subjects include mystery, romance, suspense, psychological suspense, thriller, western. *Agented submissions only.*

POCOL PRESS

Box 411, Clifton VA 20124. (703)830-5862. **Website:** www.pocolpress.com. **Contact:** J. Thomas Hetrick, editor. Estab. 1999. Publishes trade paperback originals. "Pocol Press is dedicated to producing high-quality print books and e-books from first-time, non-agented authors. However, all submissions are welcome. We're dedicated to good storytellers and to the written word, specializing in short fiction and baseball. Several of our books have been used as literary texts at universities and in book group discussions around the nation. Pocol Press does not publish children's books, romance novels, or graphic novels." **Publishes 6 titles/year. 90 queries received/year. 20 mss received/year. 90% of books from first-time authors. 100% from unagented writers. Pays 10-12% royalty on wholesale price.** Publishes ms less than 1 year after acceptance. Responds in 1 month to queries; 2 months to mss. Book catalog and guidelines online.

FICTION Subjects include historical, horror, literary, mainstream, contemporary, military, war, mystery, short story collections, thematic, spiritual, sports, western, baseball fiction. "We specialize in thematic short fiction collections by a single author and baseball fiction. Expert storytellers welcome." Does not accept or return unsolicited mss. Query with SASE or submit 1 sample chapter.

TIPS "Our audience is aged 18 and over. Pocol Press is unique; we publish good writing and great storytelling. Write the best stories you can. Read them to you friends/peers. Note their reaction. Publishes some of the finest fiction by a small press."

THE POISONED PENCIL

Poisoned Pen Press, 6962 E. 1st Ave., Suite 103, Scottsdale AZ 85251. (480)945-3375. **Fax:** (480)949-1707. **E-mail:** info@thepoisonedpencil.com. **E-mail:** ellen@thepoisonedpencil.com. **Website:** www.thepoisonedpencil.com. **Contact:** Ellen Larson, editor. Estab. 2012. Publishes trade paperback and electronic originals. **Publishes 4-6 titles/year. 150 submissions received/year. Pays 9-15% for trade paperback; 25-35% for e-books. Pays advance of $1,000.** Publishes ms 15 months after acceptance. Responds in 6 weeks to mss. Guidelines online.

Accepts young adult mysteries only.

FICTION Subjects include mystery, young adult. "We publish only young adult mystery novels, 45,000 to 90,000 words in length. For our purposes, a young adult book is a book with a protagonist between the ages of 13 and 18. We are looking for both traditional and cross-genre young adult mysteries. We encourage off-beat approaches and narrative choices that reflect the complexity and ambiguity of today's world. Submissions from teens are very welcome. Avoid serial killers, excessive gore, and vampires (and other heavy supernatural themes). We only consider authors who live in the US or Canada, due to practicalities of marketing promotion. Avoid coincidence in plotting. Avoid having your sleuth leap to conclusions rather than discover and deduce. Pay attention to the resonance between character and plot; between plot and theme; between theme and character. We are looking for clean style, fluid storytelling, and solid structure. Unrealistic dialogue is a real turn-off." Submit proposal package including synopsis, complete ms, and cover letter.

TIPS "Our audience includes young adults and adults who love YA mysteries."

POISONED PEN PRESS

6962 E. 1st Ave., Suite 103, Scottsdale AZ 85251. (480)945-3375. **Fax:** (480)949-1707. **E-mail:** submissions@poisonedpenpress.com. **Website:** www.poisonedpenpress.com. **Contact:** Robert Rosenwald, publisher; Barbara Peters, editor-in-chief. Estab. 1996. Publishes hardcover originals, and hardcover and trade paperback reprints. "Our publishing goal is to offer well-written mystery novels of crime and/or detection where the puzzle and its resolution are the main forces that move the story forward." **Publishes 36 titles/year. 1,000 queries received/year. 300 mss received/year. 35% of books from first-time authors. 65% from unagented writers. Pays 9-15% royalty on retail price.** Publishes ms 10-12 months after acceptance. Responds in 2-3 months to queries and proposals; 6 months to mss. Book catalog and guidelines online.

IMPRINTS The Poisoned Pencil (Young adult titles. Contact: Ellen Larson).

Not currently accepting submissions. Check website.

FICTION Subjects include mystery. Mss should generally be longer than 65,000 words and shorter than 100,000 words. Member Publishers Marketing Associations, Arizona Book Publishers Associations, Publishers Association of West. Distributes through Ingram, Baker & Taylor, Brodart. Does not want novels centered on serial killers, spousal or child abuse, drugs, or extremist groups, although we do not entirely rule such works out. Accepts unsolicited mss. Electronic queries only. "Query with SASE. Submit clips, first 3 pages. We must receive both the synopsis and ms pages electronically as separate attachments to an e-mail message or as a disk or CD which we will not return."

TIPS "Audience is adult readers of mystery fiction and young adult readers."

POPULAR WOODWORKING BOOKS

Imprint of F+W Media, Inc., 10151 Carver Rd., Suite 200, Blue Ash OH 45242. (513)531-2690. **Website:** www.popularwoodworking.com. **Contact:** David Thiel, executive editor. Publishes trade paperback and hardcover originals and reprints. "Popular Woodworking Books is one of the largest publishers of woodworking books in the world. From perfecting a furniture design to putting on the final coat of finish, our books provide step-by-step instructions and trusted advice from the pros that make them valuable tools for both beginning and advanced woodworkers. Currently emphasizing woodworking jigs and fixtures, furniture and cabinet projects, smaller finely crafted boxes, all styles of furniture. De-emphasizing woodturning, woodcarving, scroll saw projects." **Publishes 6-8 titles/year. 20 queries received/year. 10 mss received/year. 20% of books from first-time authors. 95% from unagented writers.** Accepts simultaneous submissions. Responds in 1 month to queries.

NONFICTION Subjects include hobbies, woodworking/wood crafts. "We publish heavily illustrated how-to woodworking books that show, rather than tell, our readers how to accomplish their woodworking goals." Query with SASE, or electronic query. Proposal package should include an outline and digital photos.

TIPS "Our books are for beginning to advanced woodworking enthusiasts."

POSSIBILITY PRESS

1 Oakglade Circle, Hummelstown PA 17036. **E-mail:** info@possibilitypress.com. **Website:** www.possibilitypress.com. **Contact:** Mike Markowski, publisher. Estab. 1981. Publishes trade paperback originals. "Our mission is to help the people of the world grow and become the best they can be, through the written and spoken word." **Publishes 2-3 titles/year. 90% of books from first-time authors. 100% from unagent-**

ed writers. Royalties vary. Responds in 1 month to queries. Catalog online. Guidelines online.

IMPRINTS Aeronautical Publishers; Possibility Press; Markowski International Publishers.

NONFICTION Subjects include psychology, pop psychology, self-help, leadership, relationships, attitude, business, success/motivation, inspiration, entrepreneurship, sales marketing, MLM and home-based business topics, and human interest success stories. Prefers submissions to be mailed. Include SASE. Submit ms in Microsoft Word. Your submission needs to be made both in hard copy and on a CD. Label it clearly with the book title and your name. Be sure to keep a backup CD for yourself. See guidelines online. Reviews artwork/photos. Do not send originals.

FICTION Needs: parables that teach lessons about life and success.

TIPS "Our focus is on co-authoring and publishing short (15,000-40,000 words) bestsellers. We're looking for kind and compassionate authors who are passionate about making a difference in the world, and will champion their mission to do so, especially by public speaking. Our dream author writes well, knows how to promote, will champion their mission, speaks for a living, has a following and a platform, is cooperative and understanding, humbly handles critique and direction, is grateful, intelligent, and has a good sense of humor."

POTOMAC BOOKS, INC.

22841 Quicksilver Dr., Dulles VA 20166. (703)661-1548. **Fax:** (703)661-1547. **E-mail:** editorial@potomacbooksinc.com. **Website:** www.potomacbooksinc.com. **Contact:** Kristen Elias Rowley (military history); Alicia Christensen (intelligence, military affairs, current affairs). Estab. 1984. Publishes hardcover and trade paperback originals and reprints. "Potomac Books specializes in national and international affairs, history (especially military and diplomatic), intelligence, biography, reference, and sports. We are particularly interested in authors who can communicate a sophisticated understanding of their topic to general readers, as well as specialists." **Publishes 60 titles/year. 900 queries received/year. 20% of books from first-time authors. 70% from unagented writers. Pays royalty on wholesale price. Pays five figure maximum advance.** Publishes ms 1 year after acceptance. Accepts simultaneous submissions. Responds in 2 months to queries. Book catalog available free. Guidelines online.

NONFICTION Subjects include government, politics, history, military, war, sports, world affairs, national and international affairs. When submitting nonfiction, be sure to include sufficient biographical information (e.g., track records of previous publications), and make clear in the query letter how your work might differ from other such works already published and with which yours might compete. Query.

TIPS "Our audience consists of general nonfiction readers, as well as students, scholars, policymakers and the military."

PPI (PROFESSIONAL PUBLICATIONS, INC.)

1250 Fifth Ave., Belmont CA 94002. (650)593-9119. **Fax:** (650)592-4519. **E-mail:** info@ppi2pass.com. **Website:** www.ppi2pass.com. Estab. 1975. Publishes hardcover, paperback, and electronic products, CD-ROMs and DVDs. "PPI publishes professional, reference, and licensing preparation materials. PPI wants submissions from both professionals practicing in the field and from experienced instructors. Currently emphasizing engineering, interior design, architecture, landscape architecture and LEED exam review." **Publishes 10 titles/year. 5% of books from first-time authors. 100% from unagented writers.** Publishes ms 4-18 months after acceptance. Accepts simultaneous submissions. Responds in 1 month to queries. Book catalog and ms guidelines free.

NONFICTION Subjects include architecture, science, landscape architecture, engineering mathematics, engineering, surveying, interior design, greenbuilding, sustainable development, and other professional licensure subjects. Especially needs review and reference books for all professional licensing examinations. Please submit ms and proposal outlining market potential, etc. Proposal template available upon request. Reviews artwork/photos.

TIPS "We specialize in books for those people who want to become licensed and/or accredited professionals: engineers, architects, surveyors, interior designers, LEED APs, etc. Demonstrating your understanding of the market, competition, appropriate delivery methods, and marketing ideas will help sell us on your proposal."

PRAKKEN PUBLICATIONS, INC.

P.O. Box 8623, Ann Arbor MI 48107. (734)975-2800. **Fax:** (734)975-2787. **E-mail:** pam@eddigest.com. **E-**

mail: susanne@eddigest.com. **Contact:** Susanne Peckham, book editor; Sharon K. Miller, art/design/production manager. Estab. 1934. Publishes educational hardcover and paperback originals, as well as educational magazines. "We publish books for educators in career/vocational and technology education, as well as books for the machine trades and machinists' education. Currently emphasizing machine trades." **Publishes 3 titles/year.** Accepts simultaneous submissions. Responds in 2 months to queries. Book catalog for #10 SASE.

NONFICTION Subjects include education. "We are currently interested in manuscripts with broad appeal in any of the specific subject areas of machine trades, technology education, career-technical education, and reference for the general education field." Submit outline, sample chapters.

TIPS "We have a continuing interest in magazine and book manuscripts which reflect emerging issues and trends in education, especially career-technical, industrial, and technology education."

PRESA PRESS

P.O. Box 792, 8590 Belding Rd. NE, Rockford MI 49341. **E-mail:** presapress@aol.com. **Website:** www.presapress.com. **Contact:** Roseanne Ritzema, editor. Estab. 2003. Presa Press publishes perfect-bound paperbacks and saddle-stitched chapbooks of poetry. Wants "imagistic poetry where form is an extension of content, surreal, experimental, and personal poetry." Does not want "overtly political or didactic material." **Pays 10-25 author/quotes copies.** Publishes book Time between acceptance and publication is 8-12 weeks. after acceptance of ms. Responds to queries in 2-4 weeks; to mss in 8-12 weeks.

POETRY Acquires first North American serial rights and the right to reprint in anthologies. Rights include e-book publishing rights. Rights revert to poets upon publication. Accepts postal submissions only. Cover letter is preferred. Reads submissions year round. Poems are circulated to an editorial board. Send materials for review consideration to Roseanne Ritzema. Query first, with a few sample poems and a cover letter with brief bio and publication credits. Book/chapbook mss may include previously published poems.

PRESS 53

560 N. Trade St., Suite 103, Winston-Salem NC 27101. **E-mail:** kevin@press53.com. **Website:** www.press53.com. **Contact:** Kevin Morgan Watson, publisher. "Press 53 was founded in October 2005 and quickly began earning a reputation as a quality publishing house of short story and poetry collections." **Publishes 14-15 titles/year.** Responds in 6 months to mss. Guidelines online.

FICTION Subjects include literary, short story collections. "We publish roughly 4 short story collections each year by writers who are active and earning recognition through publication and awards, plus the winner of our Press 53 Award for Short Fiction." Collections should include 10-15 short stories with 70% or more of those stories previously published. Does not want novels. Finds mss through contest and referrals.

POETRY "We love working with poets who have been widely published and are active in the poetry community. We publish roughly 4-6 full-length poetry collections of around 70 pages or more each year, plus the winner of our Press 53 Award for Poetry." Prefers that at least 30-40% of the poems in the collection be previously published. Finds mss through contest and referrals.

TIPS "We are looking for writers who are actively involved in the writing community, writers who are submitting their work to journals, magazines and contests, and who are getting published, building readership, and earning a reputation for their work."

PRESSES DE L'UNIVERSITÉ DE MONTREAL

C.P. 6128, succ. Centre-ville, Montreal QC H3C 3J7, Canada. (514)343-6933. **Fax:** (514)343-2232. **E-mail:** sb@editionspum.ca. **Website:** www.pum.umontreal.ca. **Contact:** Sylvie Brousseau, rights and sales. Publishes hardcover and trade paperback originals. **Publishes 40 titles/year.** Publishes ms 6 months after acceptance. Responds in 1 month. Book catalog and ms guidelines free.

NONFICTION Subjects include education, health, medicine, history, language, literature, philosophy, psychology, sociology, translation. Submit outline, 2 sample chapters.

PRESS HERE

22230 NE 28th Place, Sammamish WA 98074-6408. **Website:** www.gracecuts.com/press-here. Estab. 1989. Press Here publishes award-winning books of haiku, tanka, and related poetry by the leading poets of these genres, as well as essays, criticism, and interviews about these genres. "We publish work only by those poets who are already frequently published in the leading haiku and tanka journals." Publishes 1-2 poetry books/year, plus occasional books of essays or interviews. Mss are selected through open submission. **Pays a negotiated percentage of author's copies (out of a press run of 200-1,000).** Responds to queries in up to 1 month; to mss in up to 2 months. Catalog available for #10 SASE.

Press Here publications have won the 1st-place Merit Book Award and other awards from the Haiku Society of America.

POETRY Does not want any poetry other than haiku, tanka, and related genres. Has published poetry by Lee Gurga, paul m., Paul O. Williams, Pat Shelley, Cor van den Heuvel, and William J. Higginson. Query first, with a few sample poems and a cover letter with brief bio and publication credits. Book mss may include previously published poems ("previous publication strongly preferred"). "All proposals must be by well-established haiku or tanka poets, and must be for haiku or tanka poetry, or criticism/discussion of these genres. If the editor does not already know your work well from leading haiku and tanka publications, then he is not likely to be interested in your manuscript."

PRESTWICK HOUSE, INC.

P.O. Box 658, Clayton DE 19938. **E-mail:** info@prestwickhouse.com. **Website:** www.prestwickhouse.com. Estab. 1980.

NONFICTION Submit proposal package, outline, resume, 1 sample chapter, TOC.

TIPS "We market our books primarily for middle and high school English teachers. Submissions should address a direct need of grades 7-12 language arts teachers. Current and former English teachers are encouraged to submit materials developed and used by them successfully in the classroom."

PRICE STERN SLOAN, INC.

Penguin Group, 375 Hudson St., New York NY 10014. (212)366-2000. **Website:** www.penguin.com. **Contact:** Francesco Sedita, vice-president/publisher. Estab. 1963. "Price Stern Sloan publishes quirky mass market novelty series for childrens as well as licensed movie tie-in books." Price Stern Sloan only responds to submissions it's interested in publishing. Book catalog online.

FICTION Publishes picture books and novelty/board books. *Agented submissions only.*

TIPS "Price Stern Sloan publishes unique, fun titles."

PRINCETON ARCHITECTURAL PRESS

37 E. 7th St., New York NY 10003. (212)995-9620. **Fax:** (212)995-9454. **E-mail:** submissions@papress.com. **Website:** www.papress.com. Publishes hardcover and trade paperback originals. **Publishes 50 titles/year. 300 queries received/year. 150 mss received/year. 65% of books from first-time authors. 95% from unagented writers. Pays royalty on wholesale price.** Publishes ms 1 year after acceptance. Accepts simultaneous submissions. Responds in 2 months. Book catalog online. Guidelines online.

NONFICTION Subjects include art, architecture. Submit proposal package, outline, 1 sample chapter, TOC, sample of art, and survey of competitive titles. Reviews artwork/photos. Do not send originals.

TIPS "Princeton Architecture Press publishes fine books on architecture, design, photography, landscape, and visual culture. Our books are acclaimed for their strong and unique editorial vision, unrivaled design sensibility, and high production values at affordable prices."

PRINCETON BOOK CO.

614 Route 130, Hightstown NJ 08520. (609)426-0602. **Fax:** (609)426-1344. **E-mail:** pbc@dancehorizons.com. **Website:** www.dancehorizons.com. **Contact:** Charles Woodford, president. Publishes hardcover and trade paperback originals and reprints. **Publishes 5-6 titles/year. 50 queries received/year. 100 mss received/year. 80% of books from first-time authors. 100% from unagented writers. Pays negotiable royalty on net receipts.** Publishes ms 9-12 months after acceptance. Accepts simultaneous submissions. Responds in 1 week. Book catalog and guidelines online.

IMPRINTS Dance Horizons, Elysian Editions.

NONFICTION Subjects include music, dance. "We publish all sorts of dance-related books including those on fitness and health." Does not accept memoir. Submit proposal package, outline, 3 sample chapters. Reviews artwork/photos. Send photocopies.

PRINCETON UNIVERSITY PRESS

41 William St., Princeton NJ 08540. (609)258-4900. **Fax:** (609)258-6305. **Website:** www.pupress.princeton.edu. **Contact:** Brigitta van Rheinberg, editor-in-chief. "The Lockert Library of Poetry in Translation embraces a wide geographic and temporal range, from Scandinavia to Latin America to the subcontinent of India, from the Tang Dynasty to Europe of the modern day. It especially emphasizes poets who are

established in their native lands and who are being introduced to an English-speaking audience. Manuscripts are judged with several criteria in mind: the ability of the translation to stand on its own as poetry in English; fidelity to the tone and spirit of the original, rather than literal accuracy; and the importance of the translated poet to the literature of his or her time and country." Responds in 3-4 months. Guidelines online.

NONFICTION Query with SASE.

POETRY Submit hard copy of proposal with sample poems or full ms. Cover letter is required. Reads submissions year round. Mss will not be returned. Comments on finalists only.

PRINTING INDUSTRIES OF AMERICA

200 Deer Run Rd., Sewickley PA 15143. (412)741-6860. **Fax:** (412)741-2311. **E-mail:** jdeemer@printing.org. **Website:** www.printing.org. **Contact:** Joe Deemer, manager. Estab. 1921. Publishes trade paperback originals and reference texts. "Printing Industries of America, along with its affiliates, delivers products and services that enhance the growth and profitability of its members and the industry through advocacy, education, research, and technical information." Printing Industries of America's mission is to serve the graphic communications community as the major resource for technical information and services through research and education. **Publishes 8-10 titles/year. 20 mss received/year; 30 queries received/year. 50% of books from first-time authors. 100% from unagented writers. Pays 15% royalty on wholesale price.** Publishes ms 18 months after acceptance. Accepts simultaneous submissions. Responds in 1 month to queries.

NONFICTION Subjects include business, communications, economics, education, printing and graphic arts reference, technical, textbook. Currently emphasizing technical textbooks as well as career guides for graphic communications and turnkey training curricula. Query with SASE, or submit outline, sample chapters, and SASE. Reviews artwork. Send photocopies.

PROMETHEUS BOOKS

59 John Glenn Dr., Amherst NY 14228-2119. (800)421-0351. **Fax:** (716)564-2711. **E-mail:** editorial@prometheusbooks.com. **Website:** www.prometheusbooks.com. **Contact:** Steven L. Mitchell, editor-in-chief. Estab. 1969. Publishes hardcover originals, trade paperback originals and reprints. "Prometheus Books is a leading independent publisher in philosophy, social science, popular science, and critical thinking. We publish authoritative and thoughtful books by distinguished authors in many categories. Currently emphasizing popular science, health, psychology, social science, current events, business and economics, atheism and critiques of religion." **Publishes 90-100 titles/year. 30% of books from first-time authors. 40% from unagented writers.** Accepts simultaneous submissions. Responds in 2 months to queries; 3 months to proposals; 4 months to mss. Book catalog and guidelines online.

NONFICTION Subjects include education, government, politics, health, medicine, history, language, literature, New Age, critiquing of, philosophy, psychology, religion, contemporary issues. Ask for a catalog, go to the library or our website, look at our books and others like them to get an idea of what our focus is. Submit proposal package including outline, synopsis, potential market, tentative ms length, résumé, and a well-developed query letter with SASE, two or three of author's best chapters. Reviews artwork/photos. Send photocopies.

TIPS "Audience is highly literate with multiple degrees; an audience that is intellectually mature and knows what it wants. They are aware, and we try to provide them with new information on topics of interest to them in mainstream and related areas."

PRUFROCK PRESS, INC.

P.O. Box 8813, Waco TX 76714. (800)988-2208. **Fax:** (800)240-0333. **E-mail:** info@prufrock.com. **Website:** www.prufrock.com. **Contact:** Joel McIntosh, publisher and marketing director. "Prufrock Press offers award-winning products focused on gifted education, gifted children, advanced learning, and special needs learners. For more than 20 years, Prufrock has supported gifted children and their education and development. The company publishes more than 300 products that enhance the lives of gifted children and the teachers and parents who support them." **50 queries received/year. 40 mss received/year. 20% of books from first-time authors. 100% from unagented writers.** Publishes ms 1-2 year after acceptance. Accepts simultaneous submissions. Book catalog available. Guidelines online.

Accepts simultaneous submissions, but must be notified about it.

NONFICTION Subjects include education, language, literature. "We are always looking for truly original, creative materials for teachers." Query with SASE. Submit outline, 1-3 sample chapters.

FICTION Prufrock Press "offers award-winning products focused on gifted education, gifted children, advanced learning, and special needs learners. For more than 20 years, Prufrock has supported gifted children and their education and development. The company publishes more than 300 products that enhance the lives of gifted children and the teachers and parents who support them." No picture books. "Prufrock Press does not consider unsolicited manuscripts."

PUFFIN BOOKS

Imprint of Penguin Group (USA), Inc., 375 Hudson St., New York NY 10014. (212)366-2000. **Website:** www.penguin.com. **Contact:** Eileen Bishop Kreit, publisher. Publishes trade paperback originals and reprints. "Puffin Books publishes high-end trade paperbacks and paperback reprints for preschool children, beginning and middle readers, and young adults." **Publishes 175-200 titles/year.** Publishes ms 1 year after acceptance.

NONFICTION Subjects include education, history, womens issues, womens studies. "Women in history books interest us." *No unsolicited mss. Agented submissions only.*

FICTION Subjects include fantasy, picture books, science fiction, young adult, middle grade, easy-to-read grades 1-3, graphic novels, classics. *No unsolicited mss. Agented submissions only.*

TIPS "Our audience ranges from little children 'first books' to young adult (ages 14-16). An original idea has the best luck."

PURDUE UNIVERSITY PRESS

504 West State St., West Lafayette IN 47907-2058. (765)494-2038. **E-mail:** pupress@purdue.edu. **Website:** www.thepress.purdue.edu. **Contact:** Rebecca Corbin, administrative assistant. Estab. 1960. Purdue University Press is administratively a unit of Purdue University Libraries and its Director reports to the Dean of Libraries. There are 3 full-time staff and 2 part-time staff, as well as student assistants. Dedicated to the dissemination of scholarly and professional information, the Press provides quality resources in several key subject areas including business, technology, health, veterinary sciences, and other selected disciplines in the humanities and sciences. As well as publishing 30 books a year, and 5 subscription-based journals, the Press is committed to broadening access to scholarly information using digital technology. As part of this initiative, the Press distributes a number of Open Access electronic-only journals. An editorial board of 9 Purdue faculty members is responsible for the imprint of the Press and meets twice a semester to consider mss and proposals, and guide the editorial program. A management advisory board advises the Director on strategy, and meets twice a year. Purdue University Press is a member of the Association of American University Presses.

PURICH PUBLISHING

Box 23032, Market Mall Post Office, Saskatoon SK S7J 5H3, Canada. (306)373-5311. **Fax:** (306)373-5315. **E-mail:** purich@sasktel.net. **Website:** www.purichpublishing.com. **Contact:** Donald Purich, publisher; Karen Bolstad, publisher. Estab. 1992. Publishes trade paperback originals. "Purich publishes books on law, Aboriginal/Native American issues, and Western Canadian history for the academic and professional trade reference market." **Publishes 3-5 titles/year. 20% of books from first-time authors. 100% from unagented writers. Pays 8-12% royalty on retail price.** Publishes ms 4 months after acceptance. Responds in 1 month to queries. Book catalog available free.

NONFICTION , Aboriginal and social justice issues, Western Canadian history. "We are a specialized publisher and only consider work in our subject areas." Query with SASE.

PUSH

Scholastic, 557 Broadway, New York NY 10012. **E-mail:** dlevithan@scholastic.com. **Website:** www.thisispush.com. Estab. 2002. PUSH publishes new voices in teen literature. PUSH does not accept unsolicited mss or queries, only agented or referred fiction/memoir. **Publishes 6-9 titles/year. 50% of books from first-time authors.**

NONFICTION Subjects include memoirs, young adult.

FICTION Subjects include contemporary, multicultural, poetry, young adult. *Does not accept unsolicited mss.*

G.P. PUTNAM'S SONS, PENGUIN YOUNG READERS GROUP

345 Hudson St., 14th Floor, New York NY 10014. (212)366-2000. **Website:** us.penguingroup.com. **Contact:** Annie Ericsson, designer.

Ⓐ⊘ G.P. PUTNAM'S SONS HARDCOVER

Imprint of Penguin Group (USA), Inc., 375 Hudson, New York NY 10014. (212)366-2000. **Fax:** (212)366-2664. **Website:** www.penguinputnam.com. **Contact:** Christine Pepe, vice president/executive editor; Kerri Kolen, executive editor. Publishes hardcover originals. **Pays variable royalties on retail price. Pays varies advance.** Accepts simultaneous submissions. Request book catalog through mail order department.

NONFICTION Subjects include animals, business, economics, child guidance, contemporary culture, cooking, foods, nutrition, health, medicine, military, war, nature, environment, religion, science, sports, travel, women's issues, women's studies, celebrity-related topics. *Agented submissions only. No unsolicited mss.*

FICTION Subjects include adventure, literary, mainstream, mystery, suspense, women's. *Agented submissions only.*

QUE

Pearson Education, 800 E. 96th St., Indianapolis IN 46240. (317)581-3500. **E-mail:** greg.wiegand@pearson.com. **Website:** www.quepublishing.com. **Contact:** Greg Wiegand, associate publisher. Estab. 1981. Publishes hardcover, trade paperback and mass market paperback originals and reprints. **Publishes 100 titles/year. 80% from unagented writers. Pays variable royalty on wholesale price or makes work-for-hire arrangements. Pays varying advance.** Accepts simultaneous submissions. Book catalog and guidelines online.

NONFICTION Subjects include computers, electronics, technology, certification. Submit proposal package, resume, TOC, writing sample, competing titles.

QUEST BOOKS

Imprint of Theosophical Publishing House, 306 W. Geneva Rd., P.O. Box 270, Wheaton IL 60187. **E-mail:** submissions@questbooks.net. **Website:** www.questbooks.net. **Contact:** Richard Smoley, editor. Estab. 1965. Publishes hardcover and trade paperback originals and reprints. "Quest Books is the imprint of the Theosophical Publishing House, the publishing arm of the Theosophical Society in America. Since 1965, Quest books has sold millions of books by leading cultural thinkers on such increasingly popular subjects as transpersonal psychology, comparative religion, spiritual growth, the development of creativity, and the interface between science and spirituality." **Publishes 10 titles/year. 150 mss received/year; 350 queries received/year. 20% of books from first-time authors. 80% from unagented writers. Pays royalty on retail price. Pays varying advance.** Publishes ms 1 year after acceptance. Accepts simultaneous submissions. Responds in 2 months. Book catalog available free. Guidelines online.

NONFICTION Subjects include philosophy, psychology, religion, spirituality, New Age, astrology/psychic. "Our speciality is high-quality spiritual nonfiction. Great writing is a must. We seldom publish 'personal spiritual awakening' stories. No submissions accepted that do not fit the needs outlined above. No fiction, poetry, children's books, or any literature based on channeling or personal psychic impressions." Submit proposal package, including outline, 1 sample chapter. Prefer online submissions; attachments must be sent as a single file in Microsoft Word, Rich Text, or PDF formats. Reviews artwork/photos. Hard copies of mss. and artwork will not be returned. Reviews artwork/photos. Writers should send photocopies or transparencies, but note that none will be returned.

TIPS "Our audience includes readers interested in spirituality, particularly the world's mystical traditions. Read a few recent Quest titles and submission guidelines before submitting. Know our books and our company goals. Explain how your book or proposal relates to other Quest titles. Quest gives preference to writers with established reputations/successful publications. Please be advised that proposals or manuscripts will not be accepted if they fall into any of the following categories: Works intended for or about children, teenagers, or adolescents; Fiction or literary works (novels, short stories, essays, or poetry); Autobiographical material (memoirs, personal experiences, or family stories; Works received through mediumship, trance, or channeling; Works related to UFOs or extraterrestrials; Works related to self-aggrandizement (e.g., 'how to make a fortune') or 'how-to' books. Nor do we publish books from fundamentalist Christian perspectives."

QUILL DRIVER BOOKS

2006 S. Mary St., Fresno CA 93721. **E-mail:** kent@lindenpub.com. **Website:** www.quilldriverbooks.com. **Contact:** Kent Sorsky. Publishes hardcover and trade paperback originals and reprints. "We publish a modest number of books per year, each of which, we hope, makes a worthwhile contribution to the human community, and we have a little fun along the way. We are strongly emphasizing our book series: The Best Half of Life series—on subjects which will serve to enhance the lifestyles, life skills, and pleasures of living for those over 50." **Publishes 10-12 titles/year. 50% of books from first-time authors. 95% from unagented writers. Pays 4-10% royalty on retail price. Pays $500-5,000 advance.** Publishes ms 12 months after acceptance. Accepts simultaneous submissions. Responds in 1 month to queries and proposals; 3 months to mss. Book catalog and ms guidelines for #10 SASE.

NONFICTION Subjects include regional, California, writing, aging. Query with SASE. Submit proposal package. Reviews artwork/photos. Send photocopies.

⊘ QUITE SPECIFIC MEDIA GROUP, LTD.

7373 Pyramid Place, Hollywood CA 90046. **E-mail:** info@quitespecificmedia.com. **Website:** www.quitespecificmedia.com. Estab. 1967. Publishes hardcover originals, trade paperback originals and reprints. "Quite Specific Media Group is an umbrella company of 5 imprints specializing in costume and fashion, theater and design." **Publishes 12 titles/year. 75 queries received/year. 30 mss received/year. 75% of books from first-time authors. 85% from unagented writers. Pays royalty on wholesale price. Pays varies advance.** Publishes ms 18 months after acceptance. Accepts simultaneous submissions. Responds to queries. Book catalog online.

NONFICTION Subjects include fashion, film, cinema, stage, history, literary criticism, translation. Query by e-mail please. Reviews artwork/photos.

RADCLIFFE PUBLISHING LTD

St. Mark's House, Shepherdess Walk, London N1 7BQ, United Kingdom. (44)(0)1908-326-941. **Fax:** (44)(0)-1908-326-960. **E-mail:** jonathan.mckenna@radcliffepublishing.com. **Website:** www.radcliffe-oxford.com. **Contact:** Jonathan McKenna, publishing director. Estab. 1987. "Unsolicited manuscripts, synopses and ideas welcome. We are not interested in non-medical or medical books aimed at lay people. Every proposal we receive is discussed at length in-house, and most are sent out for external review (usually by experts in the field who also fit the intended market profile). The reviewers' comments are passed back to you anonymously for your reference. Often reviewer feedback will elicit further development of the proposal." **Publishes 90 titles/year. Pays royalty.** Guidelines via e-mail.

NONFICTION Subjects include health, medicine, sociology, nursing, midwifery, health services management and policy. Submit proposal package, outline, resume, publishing history, bio.

TIPS "Receive book proposal guidelines by e-mail and study them."

RAGGED SKY PRESS

P.O. Box 312, Annandale NJ 08801. **E-mail:** raggedskyanthology@gmail.com. **Website:** www.raggedsky.com. **Contact:** Ellen Foos, publisher; Vasiliki Katsarou, managing editor; Arlene Weiner, editor. Produces poetry anthologies and single-author poetry collections along with occasional inspired prose. Ragged Sky is a small, highly selective cooperative press. "We work with our authors closely." Individual poetry collections currently by invitation only. Learn more online.

RAINBOW PUBLISHERS

P.O. Box 261129, San Diego CA 92196. (858)277-1167. **E-mail:** editor@rainbowpublishers.com. **Website:** www.rainbowpublishers.com; www.legacypresskids.com. Estab. 1979. "Our mission is to publish Bible-based, teacher resource materials that contribute to and inspire spiritual growth and development in kids ages 2-12." **For authors work purchased outright (range: $500 and up).** Accepts simultaneous submissions. Responds to queries in 6 weeks; mss in 3 months.

NONFICTION Young readers, middle readers, young adult/teens: activity books, arts/crafts, how-to, reference, religion.

TIPS "Our Rainbow imprint publishes reproducible books for teachers of children in Christian ministries, including crafts, activities, games and puzzles. Our Legacy imprint publishes titles for children such as devotionals, fiction and Christian living. Please write for guidelines and study the market before submitting material."

RANDOM HOUSE CHILDREN'S BOOKS

1745 Broadway, New York NY 10019. (212)782-9000. **Website:** www.randomhouse.com. Estab. 1925. "Producing books for preschool children through young adult readers, in all formats from board to activity books to picture books and novels, Random House Children's Books brings together world-famous franchise characters, multimillion-copy series and top-flight, award-winning authors, and illustrators." Submit mss through a literary agent.

IMPRINTS Kids@Random; Golden Books; Princeton Review; Sylvan Learning.

FICTION "Random House publishes a select list of first chapter books and novels, with an emphasis on fantasy and historical fiction." Chapter books, middle-grade readers, young adult. *Does not accept unsolicited mss.*

TIPS "We look for original, unique stories. Do something that hasn't been done before."

RANDOM HOUSE CHILDREN'S PUBLISHERS UK

61-63 Uxbridge Rd., London En W5 5SA, United Kingdom. (44)(208)579-2652. **Fax:** (44)(208)231-6737. **E-mail:** enquiries@randomhouse.co.uk. **Website:** www.kidsatrandomhouse.co.uk. **Contact:** Francesca Dow, managing director. **Publishes 250 titles/year. Pays authors royalty. Offers advances.**

IMPRINTS Bantam, Doubleday, Corgi, Johnathan Cape, Hutchinson, Bodley Head, Red Fox, Tamarind Books.

Only interested in agented material.

FICTION Picture books: adventure, animal, anthology, contemporary, fantasy, folktales, humor, multicultural, nature/environment, poetry, suspense/mystery. Young readers: adventure, animal, anthology, contemporary, fantasy, folktales, humor, multicultural, nature/environment, poetry, sports, suspense/mystery. Middle readers: adventure, animal, anthology, contemporary, fantasy, folktales, humor, multicultural, nature/environment, problem novels, romance, sports, suspense/mystery. Young adults: adventure, contemporary, fantasy, humor, multicultural, nature/environment, problem novels, romance, science fiction, suspense/mystery. Average word length: picture books—800; young readers—1,500-6,000; middle readers—10,000-15,000; young adults—20,000-45,000.

TIPS "Although Random House is a big publisher, each imprint only publishes a small number of books each year. Our lists for the next few years are already full. Any book we take on from a previously unpublished author has to be truly exceptional. Manuscripts should be sent to us via literary agents."

RANDOM HOUSE PUBLISHING GROUP

Division of Random House, Inc., 1745 Broadway, New York NY 10019. (212)782-9000. **Website:** www.randomhouse.com. Estab. 1925. Publishes hardcover and paperback trade books. Random House is the world's largest English-language general trade book publisher. It includes an array of prestigious imprints that publish some of the foremost writers of our time. **Publishes 120 titles/year.**

IMPRINTS Ballantine Books; Bantam; Delacorte; Dell; Del Rey; Modern Library; One World; Presidio Press; Random House Trade Group; Random House Trade Paperbacks; Spectra; Spiegel & Grau; Triumph Books; Villard.

NONFICTION *Agented submissions only.*

FICTION *Agented submissions only.*

RAZORBILL

Penguin Young Readers Group, 375 Hudson St., New York NY 10014. (212)414-3600. **Fax:** (212)414-3343. **E-mail:** mgrossman@penguinrandomhouse.com; bschrank@penguinrandomhouse.com. **Website:** www.razorbillbooks.com. **Contact:** Gillian Levinson, editor; Jessica Almon, editor; Elizabeth Tingue, associate editor; Casey McIntyre, associate publisher; Deborah Kaplan, vice president and executive art director. Estab. 2003. "This division of Penguin Young Readers is looking for the best and the most original of commercial contemporary fiction titles for middle grade and YA readers. A select quantity of nonfiction titles will also be considered." **Publishes 30 titles/year. Offers advance against royalties.** Publishes ms 1-2 after acceptance. Responds in 1-3 months.

NONFICTION Middle readers and young adults/teens: concept. Submit cover letter with up to 30 sample pages.

FICTION Middle Readers: adventure, contemporary, graphic novels, fantasy, humor, problem novels. Young adults/teens: adventure, contemporary, fantasy, graphic novels, humor, multicultural, suspense, paranormal, science fiction, dystopian, literary, romance. Average word length: middle readers—40,000; young adult—60,000. Submit cover letter with up to 30 sample pages.

TIPS "New writers will have the best chance of acceptance and publication with original, contemporary material that boasts a distinctive voice and well-articulated world. Check out website to get a better idea of what we're looking for."

REBELIGHT PUBLISHING, INC.

23-845 Dakota St., Suite 314, Winnipeg Manitoba R2M 5M3, Canada. **E-mail:** submit@rebelight.com. **Website:** www.rebelight.com. **Contact:** Editor. Estab. 2014. Publishes trade paperback and electronic originals. Rebelight Publishing is interested in mss for middle grade, young adult and new adult novels. **Publishes 10-15 titles/year. Receives 520 queries/year, 35 mss/year. 25% of books from first-time authors. 100% from unagented writers. Pays 12-30% royalties on retail price. Does not offer an advance.** Publishes ms 12 months after acceptance. Accepts simultaneous submissions. Responds in 3 months to queries and mss. Catalog available online. Guidelines available online.

Only considers submissions from Canadian writers.

FICTION Subjects include adventure, contemporary, fantasy, horror, humor, juvenile, mainstream, mystery, science fiction, sports, suspense, young adult. All genres are considered, providered they are for a middle grade, young adult, or new adult audience. "Become familiar with our books. Study our website. Stick within the guidelines. Our tag line is 'crack the spine, blow your mind'—we are looking for well-written, powerful, fresh, fast-paced fiction. Keep us turning the pages. Give us something we just have to spread the word about." Submit proposal package, including a synopsis and 3 sample chapters. Read guidelines carefully.

RED DEER PRESS

195 Allstate Pkwy., Markham ON L3R 4TB, Canada. (905)477-9700. **Fax:** (905)477-9179. **E-mail:** rdp@reddeerpress.com. **Website:** www.reddeerpress.com. **Contact:** Richard Dionne, publisher. Estab. 1975. **Pays 8-10% royalty.** Publishes ms 18 months after acceptance. Accepts simultaneous submissions. Responds to queries in 6 months. Book catalog for 9 x 12 SASE.

Red Deer Press is an award-winning publisher of children's and young adult literary titles.

NONFICTION Submit query with outline and sample chapter.

FICTION Publishes young adult, adult science fiction, fantasy, and paperback originals "focusing on books by, about, or of interest to Canadians." Books: offset paper; offset printing; hardcover/perfect-bound. Average print order: 5,000. First novel print order: 2,500. Distributes titles in Canada and the US, the UK, Australia and New Zealand. Young adult (juvenile and early reader), contemporary. No romance or horror. Accepts unsolicited mss. Query with SASE. No submissions on disk.

TIPS "We're very interested in young adult and children's fiction from Canadian writers with a proven track record (either published books or widely published in established magazines or journals) and for manuscripts with regional themes and/or a distinctive voice. We publish Canadian authors exclusively."

RED HEN PRESS

P.O. Box 40820, Pasadena CA 91114. (818)831-0649. **Fax:** (818)831-6659. **Website:** www.redhen.org. **Contact:** Mark E. Cull, publisher/editor (fiction). Estab. 1993. Publishes trade paperback originals. "At this time, the best opportunity to be published by Red Hen is by entering one of our contests. Please find more information in our award submission guidelines." **Publishes 22 titles/year. 2,000 queries received/year. 500 mss received/year. 10% of books from first-time authors. 90% from unagented writers.** Publishes ms 1 year after acceptance. Accepts simultaneous submissions. Responds in 1-2 months. Book catalog available free. Guidelines online.

NONFICTION Subjects include ethnic, gay, lesbian, language, literature, memoirs, women's issues, women's studies, political/social interest. Query with synopsis and either 20-30 sample pages or complete ms using online submission manager.

FICTION Subjects include ethnic, experimental, feminist, gay, lesbian, historical, literary, mainstream, contemporary, poetry, poetry in translation, short story collections. Query with synopsis and either 20-30 sample pages or complete ms using online submission manager.

POETRY Submit to Benjamin Saltman Poetry Award.

TIPS "Audience reads poetry, literary fiction, intelligent nonfiction. If you have an agent, we may be too small since we don't pay advances. Write well. Send queries first. Be willing to help promote your own book."

RED MOON PRESS

P.O. Box 2461, Winchester VA 22604. (540)722-2156. **E-mail:** jim.kacian@redmoonpress.com. **Website:** www.redmoonpress.com. **Contact:** Jim Kacian, editor/publisher. Estab. 1993. Red Moon Press "is the largest and most prestigious publisher of English-language haiku and related work in the world." Publishes 6-8 volumes/year, usually 3-5 anthologies and individual collections of English-language haiku, as well as 1-3 books of essays, translations, or criticism of haiku. Under other imprints, the press also publishes chapbooks of various sizes and formats.

POETRY Query with book theme and information, and 30-40 poems or draft of first chapter. Responds to queries in 2 weeks, to mss (if invited) in 3 months. "Each contract separately negotiated."

RED ROCK PRESS

205 W. 57th St., Suite 8B, New York NY 10024. **Fax:** (212)362-6216. **E-mail:** info@redrockpress.com. **Website:** www.redrockpress.com. **Contact:** Ilene Barth. Estab. 1998. Publishes hardcover and trade paperback originals. **Publishes 6-8 titles/year. Pays royalty on wholesale price. The amount of the advance offered depends on the project.** Responds in 3-4 months to queries.

NONFICTION Subjects include creative nonfiction. All of our books are pegged to gift-giving holidays.

RED SAGE PUBLISHING, INC.

P.O. Box 4844, Seminole FL 33775. (727)391-3847. **E-mail:** submissions@eredsage.com. **Website:** www.eredsage.com. **Contact:** Alexandria Kendall, publisher; Theresa Stevens, managing editor. Estab. 1995. Publishes books of romance fiction, written for the adventurous woman. **Publishes 4 titles/year. 50% of books from first-time authors. Pays advance.** Guidelines online.

FICTION Read guidelines.

RED TUQUE BOOKS, INC.

477 Martin St., Unit #6, Penticton BC V2A 5L2, Canada. (778)476-5750. **Fax:** (778)476-5651. **E-mail:** dave@redtuquebooks.ca. **Website:** www.redtuquebooks.ca. **Contact:** David Korinetz, executive editor. Publishes Canadian authors only, other than in the Annual Canadian Tales Anthology, which will accept stories written about Canada or Canadians by non-Canadians. Publication in the anthology is only through submissions to the Canadian Tales writing contest. See website for details. **Pays 5-7% royalties on net sales. Pays $250 advance.** Publishes ms 1 year after acceptance. Responds in 3 weeks.

FICTION Subjects include adventure, fantasy, science fiction, short story collections, young adult. Submit a query letter, 1-page synopsis, and first 5 pages only. Include total word count. Accepts queries by e-mail and mail. Accepts ms only by mail. SASE for reply only.

TIPS "Well-plotted, character-driven stories, preferably with happy endings, will have the best chance of being accepted. Keep in mind that authors who like to begin sentences with 'and, or, and but' are less likely to be considered. Don't send anything gruesome or overly explicit; tell us a good story, but think PG."

RED WHEEL/WEISER

665 Third St., Suite 400, San Francisco CA 94107. (415)978-2665. **Fax:** (415)359-0142. **E-mail:** submissions@rwwbooks.com. **Website:** www.redwheelweiser.com. **Contact:** Pat Bryce, acquisitions editor. Estab. 1956. Publishes hardcover and trade paperback originals and reprints. **Publishes 60-75 titles/year. 2,000 queries received/year; 2,000 mss received/year. 20% of books from first-time authors. 50% from unagented writers. Pays royalty.** Publishes ms 1 year after accceptance. after acceptance of ms. Accepts simultaneous submissions. Responds in 3-6 months. Book catalog available free. Guidelines online.

NONFICTION Subjects include New Age, spirituality, womens issues, womens studies, parenting. Query with SASE. Submit proposal package, outline, 2 sample chapters, TOC. Reviews artwork/photos. Send photocopies.

ROBERT D. REED PUBLISHERS

P.O. Box 1992, Bandon OR 97411. (541)347-9882. **Fax:** (541)347-9883. **E-mail:** cleonelreed@gmail.com. **Website:** www.rdrpublishers.com. **Contact:** Cleone L. Reed. Estab. 1991. Publishes hardcover and trade paperback originals. **Publishes 25-35 titles/year. 75% of books from first-time authors. 90% from unagented writers. Pays 12-17% royalty on wholesale price.** Publishes ms 5 months after acceptance. Accepts simultaneous submissions. Responds in 1 month. Catalog and guidelines online.

NONFICTION Subjects include alternative lifestyles, business, career guidance, child guidance, communications, contemporary culture, counseling, education, ethnic, gay, health, history, language, lesbian, literature, memoirs, military, money, multicultural, New Age, philosophy, psychology, sex, sociology, spirituality, travel, womens issues, womens studies, world affairs. "We want titles that have a large audience with at least 10-year sales potential, and author's workshop, speaking and seminar participation. We like titles that are part of author's career." Submit proposal package with outline. Reviews artwork.

TIPS "Target trade sales and sales to corporations, organizations, and groups. Read over our website and see what we have done."

REFERENCE SERVICE PRESS

2310 Homestead Road, Suite C1 #219, Los Altos CA 94024. (650)861-3170. **Fax:** (650)861-3171. **E-mail:** info@rspfunding.com. **Website:** www.rspfunding.com. **Contact:** Stuart Hauser, acquisitions editor. Estab. 1977. Publishes hardcover originals. "Reference Service Press focuses on the development and publication of financial aid resources in any format (print, electronic, e-book, etc.). We are interested in financial aid publications aimed at specific groups (e.g., minorities, women, veterans, the disabled, undergraduates majoring in specific subject areas, specific types of financial aid, etc.)." **Publishes 10-20 titles/year. 100% from unagented writers. Pays 10% royalty. Pays advance.** Publishes ms 6 months after acceptance. Accepts simultaneous submissions. Responds in 2 months to queries. Book catalog for #10 SASE.

NONFICTION Subjects include agriculture, art, architecture, business, economics, education, ethnic, health, medicine, history, religion, science, sociology, women's issues, women's studies, disabled. Submit outline, sample chapters.

TIPS "Our audience consists of librarians, counselors, researchers, students, re-entry women, scholars, and other fundseekers."

RENAISSANCE HOUSE

465 Westview Ave., Englewood NJ 07631. (201)408-4048. **E-mail:** info@renaissancehouse.net. **Website:** www.renaissancehouse.net. "We specialize in the development and management of educational and multicultural materials for young readers, Bilingual and Spanish. Our titles are suitable for the school, library, trade markets and reading programs. Publishes biographies, legends and multicultural with a focus on the Hispanic market. Specializes in multicultural and bilingual titles, Spanish-English." Submit manuscript; e-mail submissions. Children's, educational, and multicultural. Represents 80 illustrators. 95% of artwork handled is children's book illustration. Currently open to illustrators seeking representation. Open to both new and established illustrators. Publishes ms 1 year after acceptance. Accepts simultaneous submissions. Responds to queries/mss in 2 weeks.

REVELL

Division of Baker Publishing Group, 630 E. Fulton Rd., Ada MI 49301. **Website:** www.bakerbooks.com. Estab. 1870. Publishes hardcover, trade paperback and mass market paperback originals. "Revell publishes to the heart (rather than to the head). For 125 years, Revell has been publishing evangelical books for the personal enrichment and spiritual growth of general Christian readers." Book catalog and ms guidelines online.

No longer accepts unsolicited mss.

NONFICTION Subjects include child guidance, religion, Christian living, marriage.

FICTION Subjects include historical, religious, suspense, contemporary.

RING OF FIRE PUBLISHING LLC

6523 California Ave. SW #409, Seattle WA 98136. **E-mail:** contact@ringoffirebooks.com. **Website:** www.ringoffirebooks.com. Estab. 2011. Publishes trade paperback and electronic originals. "We are currently closed to submissions." Check website for updates. **Publishes 6-12 titles/year. 75% of books from first-time authors. 100% from unagented writers. Pays royalties.** Publishes ms 6 months after acceptance. Accepts simultaneous submissions. Book catalog and ms guidelines online.

FICTION Subjects include adventure, contemporary, experimental, fantasy, gothic, horror, juvenile, literary, mainstream, mystery, occult, romance, science fiction, short story collections, suspense, western, young adult.

RIO NUEVO PUBLISHERS

Imprint of Treasure Chest Books, P.O. Box 5250, Tucson AZ 85703. **Fax:** (520)624-5888. **E-mail:** info@rionuevo.com. **Website:** www.rionuevo.com. Estab. 1975. Publishes hardcover and trade paperback originals and reprints. **Publishes 12-20 titles/year. 30 queries received/year. 10 mss received/year. 30% of books from first-time authors. 100% from unagented writers. Pays $1,000-4,000 advance.** Publishes ms

1 year after acceptance. Accepts simultaneous submissions. Responds in 6 months. Book catalog online. Guidelines online.

NONFICTION Subjects include animals, cooking, foods, nutrition, gardening, history, nature, environment, regional, religion, spirituality, travel. "We cover the Southwest but prefer titles that are not too narrow in their focus. We want our books to be of broad enough interest that people from other places will also want to read them." Query with SASE or via e-mail. Submit proposal package, outline, 2 sample chapters. Reviews artwork/photos. Send photocopies.

TIPS "We have a general audience of intelligent people interested in the Southwest-nature, history, culture. Many of our books are sold in gift shops throughout the region. Look at our books and website for inspiration and to see what we do."

RIPPLE GROVE PRESS

P.O. Box 86740, Portland OR 97286. **E-mail:** submit@ripplegrovepress.com. **Website:** www.ripplegrovepress.com. Estab. 2013. Publishes hardcover originals. "We started Ripple Grove Press because we have a passion for well-written and beautifully illustrated children's picture books. Each story selected has been read dozens of times, then slept on, then walked away from, then talked about again and again. If the story has the same intrigue and the same interest that it had when we first read it, we move forward." **Publishes 3-6 titles/year. Authors receive between 10-12% royalty on net receipt.** Publishes book Average length of time between acceptance of a book-length ms and publication is 12-18 months. after acceptance of ms. Accepts simultaneous submissions. Responds to queries within 4 months. Guidelines online.

NONFICTION Submit completed mss only. Accepts submissions by mail and e-mail. Please submit a cover letter including a summary of your story, the age range of the story, a brief biography of yourself, and contact information. Does review artwork. Writers should send photo copies or links to their website and online portfolio.

FICTION Subjects include contemporary, humor, juvenile, literary, mainstream, multicultural, picture books. "Our focus is picture books for children age 2-6. We want something unique, sweet, funny, touching, offbeat, colorful, surprising, charming, different, and creative." Submit completed ms. Accepts submissions by mail and e-mail. Please submit a cover letter including a summary of your story, the age range of the story, a brief biography of yourself, and contact information.

TIPS Also targeting the adults reading to the children. "We create books that children and adults want to read over and over again. Our books showcase art as well as stories and tie them together to create a unique and creative product."

RIVER CITY PUBLISHING

1719 Mulberry St., Montgomery AL 36106. **E-mail:** fnorris@rivercitypublishing.com. **Website:** www.rivercitypublishing.com. **Contact:** Fran Norris, editor. Estab. 1989. Publishes hardcover and trade paperback originals. Midsize independent publisher. River City publishes literary fiction, regional, short story collections. No poetry, memoir, or children's books. "We are looking mainly for narrative histories, sociological accounts, and travel. Only biographies and memoirs from noted persons will be considered." **Publishes 6 titles/year.** Accepts simultaneous submissions. Responds to mss in 9 months.

NONFICTION "We do not publish self-help, how-to, business, medicine, religion, education, or psychology." Accepts unsolicited submissions and submissions from unagented authors, as well as those from established and agented writers. Submit 5 consecutive sample chapters or entire ms for review. "Please include a short biography that highlights any previous writing and publishing experience, sales opportunities the author could provide, ideas for marketing the book, and why you think the work would be appropriate for River City." Send appropriate-sized SASE or IRC, "otherwise, the material will be recycled." Also accepts queries by e-mail.

FICTION Subjects include literary, regional, short story collections. No poetry, memoir, or children's books. Send appropriate-sized SASE or IRC, "otherwise, the material will be recycled." Also accepts queries by e-mail. "Please include your electronic query letter as inline text and not an as attachment; we do not open unsolicited attachments of any kind." No multiple submissions. Rarely comments on rejected mss.

TIPS "Only send your best work after you have received outside opinions. From approximately 1,000 submissions each year, we publish no more than 8 books and few of those come from unsolicited material. Competition is fierce, so follow the guidelines exactly. All first-time novelists should submit their work to the Fred Bonnie Award contest."

RIVERHEAD BOOKS

Penguin Putnam, 375 Hudson St., New York NY 10014. **Website:** www.penguin.com. **Contact:** Rebecca Saletan, vice president/editorial director.

FICTION Subjects include contemporary, literary, mainstream. *Submit through agent only. No unsolicited mss.*

ROARING BROOK PRESS

Macmillan Children's Publishing Group, 175 Fifth Ave., New York NY 10010. (646)307-5151. **Website:** us.macmillan.com. Estab. 2000. Roaring Brook Press is an imprint of MacMillan, a group of companies that includes Henry Holt and Farrar, Straus & Giroux. *Roaring Brook is not accepting unsolicited mss.* **Pays authors royalty based on retail price.**

NONFICTION Picture books, young readers, middle readers, young adults: adventure, animal, contemporary, fantasy, history, humor, multicultural, nature/environment, poetry, religion, science fiction, sports, suspense/mystery. *Not accepting unsolicited mss or queries.*

FICTION Picture books, young readers, middle readers, young adults: adventure, animal, contemporary, fantasy, history, humor, multicultural, nature/environment, poetry, religion, science fiction, sports, suspense/mystery. *Not accepting unsolicited mss or queries.*

TIPS "You should find a reputable agent and have him/her submit your work."

ROCKY MOUNTAIN BOOKS

414 13th Ave. NE, Calgary AB T2E 1C2, Canada. (403)249-9490. **Fax:** (403)249-2968. **E-mail:** don@rmbooks.com. **Website:** www.rmbooks.com. **Contact:** Don Gorman, publisher. Publishes trade paperback and hardcover books. "RMB is a dynamic book publisher located in western Canada. We specialize in quality nonfiction on the outdoors, travel, environment, social and cultural issues." **Rarely offers advance.** Accepts simultaneous submissions. Responds in 2-6 months to queries. Book catalog and ms guidelines online.

NONFICTION Subjects include nonfiction outdoors, environment, travel & tourism and international mountain culture/history. "Our main area of publishing is outdoor recreation guides to Western and Northern Canada."

RODALE BOOKS

400 S. Tenth St., Emmaus PA 18098. (610)967-5171. **Fax:** (610)967-8961. **Website:** www.rodaleinc.com. Estab. 1932. "Rodale Books publishes adult trade titles in categories such health & fitness, cooking, spirituality and pet care."

RONSDALE PRESS

3350 W. 21st Ave., Vancouver BC V6S 1G7, Canada. (604)738-4688. **Fax:** (604)731-4548. **E-mail:** ronsdale@shaw.ca. **Website:** ronsdalepress.com. **Contact:** Ronald B. Hatch (fiction, poetry, nonfiction, social commentary); Veronica Hatch (YA novels and short stories). Estab. 1988. Publishes trade paperback originals. "Ronsdale Press is a Canadian literary publishing house that publishes 12 books each year, four of which are young adult titles. Of particular interest are books involving children exploring and discovering new aspects of Canadian history." **Publishes 12 titles/year. 40 queries received/year. 800 mss received/year. 40% of books from first-time authors. 95% from unagented writers. Pays 10% royalty on retail price.** Publishes ms 1 year after acceptance. Accepts simultaneous submissions. Responds to queries in 2 weeks; mss in 2 months. Book catalog for #10 SASE. Guidelines online.

NONFICTION Subjects include history, Canadian, language, literature, nature, environment, regional. Middle readers, young adults: animal, biography, history, multicultural, social issues. Average word length: young readers—90; middle readers—90. "We publish a number of books for children and young adults in the age 10 to 15 range. We are especially interested in YA historical novels. We regret that we can no longer publish picture books." Submit complete ms.

FICTION Subjects include literary, short story collections, novels. Young adults: Canadian novels. Average word length: middle readers and young adults—50,000. Submit complete ms.

POETRY Poets should have published some poems in magazines/journals and should be well-read in contemporary masters. Submit complete ms.

TIPS "Ronsdale Press is a literary publishing house, based in Vancouver, and dedicated to publishing books from across Canada, books that give Canadians new insights into themselves and their country. We aim to publish the best Canadian writers."

ROSE ALLEY PRESS

4203 Brooklyn Ave. NE, #103A, Seattle WA 98105. (206)633-2725. **E-mail:** rosealleypress@juno.com. **Website:** www.rosealleypress.com. **Contact:** David D. Horowitz. Estab. 1995. "Rose Alley Press primarily publishes books featuring rhymed metrical poetry and an annually updated booklet about writing and publication. We do not read or consider unsolicited manuscripts."

ROSEN PUBLISHING

29 E. 21st St., New York NY 10010. (800)237-9932. **Fax:** (888)436-4643. **Website:** www.rosenpublishing.com. Estab. 1950. Rosen Publishing is an independent educational publishing house, established to serve the needs of students in grades Pre-K-12 with high interest, curriculum-correlated materials. Rosen publishes more than 700 new books each year and has a backlist of more than 7,000.

ROTOVISION

Sheridan House, 114 Western Rd., Hove East Sussex BN3 IDD, England. (44)(127)371-6010. **Fax:** (44) (127)372-7269. **E-mail:** isheetam@rotovision.com. **Website:** www.rotovision.com. **Contact:** Isheeta Mustafi. Publishes hardcover and trade paperback originals, and trade paperback reprints. Accepts simultaneous submissions. Book catalog available free. Guidelines available free.

NONFICTION Subjects include art, creative nonfiction, design, fashion, graphic design, photography. "Our books are aimed at keen amateurs and professionals who want to improve their skills." Submit an e-mail with "Book Proposal" in the subject line. Reviews artwork/photos. Send transparencies and PDFs.

TIPS "Our audience includes professionals, keen amateurs, and students of visual arts including graphic design, general design, advertising, and photography. Make your approach international in scope. Content not to be less than 35% US."

ROWMAN & LITTLEFIELD PUBLISHING GROUP

4501 Forbes Blvd., Suite 200, Lanham MD 20706. (301)459-3366. **Fax:** (301)429-5748. **Website:** www.rowmanlittlefield.com. **Contact:** Customer service to get submission guidelines. Estab. 1949. Publishes hardcover and trade paperback originals and reprints. "We are an independent press devoted to publishing scholarly books in the best tradition of university presses; innovative, thought-provoking texts for college courses; and crossover trade books intended to convey scholarly trends to an educated readership. Our approach emphasizes substance and quality of thought over ephemeral trends. We offer a forum for responsible voices representing the diversity of opinion on college campuses, and take special pride in several series designed to provide students with the pros and cons of hotly contested issues." **Pays advance.** Book catalog online. Guidelines online.

NONFICTION "Rowman & Littlefield is seeking proposals in the serious nonfiction areas of history, politics, current events, religion, sociology, philosophy, communication and education. All proposal inquiries can be e-mailed or mailed to the respective acquisitions editor listed on the contacts page on our website."

RUKA PRESS

P.O. Box 1409, Washington DC 20013. **E-mail:** contact@rukapress.com. **E-mail:** submissions@rukapress.com. **Website:** www.rukapress.com. **Contact:** Daniel Kohan, owner. Estab. 2010. Publishes in trade paperback originals, electronic. "We publish nonfiction books with a strong environmental component for a general audience. We are looking for books that explain things, that make an argument, that demystify. We are interested in economics, science, nature, climate change, and sustainability. We like building charts and graphs, tables and timelines. Our politics are progressive, but our books need not be political." **Publishes 2-4 titles/year. Pays advance. Royalties are 10-25% on wholesale price.** Publishes ms an average of 9-12 months after acceptance. Accepts simultaneous submissions. Responds in 1 month to queries and proposals. Book catalog online. Guidelines online.

NONFICTION Subjects include environment, nature, science. Submit proposal package, including outline, resume, bio, or CV, and 1 sample chapter.

TIPS "We appeal to an audience of intelligent, educated readers with broad interests. Be sure to tell us why your proposal is unique, and why you are especially qualified to write this book. We are looking for originality and expertise."

RUTGERS UNIVERSITY PRESS

106 Somerset St., 3rd Floor, New Brunswick NJ 08901. (732)445-7762. **Fax:** (732)445-7039. **E-mail:** lmitch@rutgers.edu. **Website:** rutgerspress.rutgers.edu. **Contact:** Leslie Mitchner, editor-in-chief/associate di-

rector (humanities); Peter Micklaus, editor (social sciences); Dana Dreibelbis, editor (science, health & medicine); Marlie Wasserman, associate editor (Jewish studies). Estab. 1936. Publishes hardcover and trade paperback originals, and reprints. Our Press aims to reach audiences beyond the academic community with accessible scholarly and regional books. **Publishes 100 titles/year. 1,500 queries received/year. 300 mss received/year. 30% of books from first-time authors. 70% from unagented writers. Pays 7 1/2-15% royalty. Pays $1,000-10,000 advance.** Publishes ms 1 year after acceptance. Responds in 1 month to proposals. Book catalog online. Guidelines online.

NONFICTION Subjects include art, architecture, art, architecture history, ethnic, film, cinema, stage, gay, lesbian, government, politics, health, medicine, history, multicultural, nature, environment, regional, religion, sociology, womens issues, womens studies, African-American studies. Books for use in undergraduate courses. Submit outline, 2-3 sample chapters. Reviews artwork/photos. Send photocopies.

TIPS "Both academic and general audiences. Many of our books have potential for undergraduate course use. We are more trade-oriented than most university presses. We are looking for intelligent, well-written, and accessible books. Avoid overly narrow topics."

SAE INTERNATIONAL

400 Commonwealth Dr., Warrendale PA 15096-0001. (724)776-4841. **E-mail:** writeabook@sae.org. **Website:** www.sae.org/writeabook. Estab. 1905. Publishes hardcover and trade paperback originals, e-books. Automotive means anything self-propelled. "We are a professional society serving engineers, scientists, and researchers in the automobile, aerospace, and off-highway industries." **Publishes approximately 10 titles/year. 50 queries received/year. 20 mss received/year. 70% of books from first-time authors. 100% from unagented writers. Pays royalty. Pays possible advance.** Publishes ms 9-10 months after acceptance. Accepts simultaneous submissions. Responds in 4 months to queries. Book catalog free. Guidelines online.

NONFICTION Query with proposal.

TIPS "Audience is automotive and aerospace engineers and managers, automotive safety and biomechanics professionals, students, educators, enthusiasts, and historians."

SAFARI PRESS, INC.

15621 Chemical Ln., Building B, Huntington Beach CA 92649. (714)894-9080. **Fax:** (714)894-4949. **E-mail:** info@safaripress.com. **Website:** www.safaripress.com. Estab. 1985. Publishes hardcover originals and reprints, and trade paperback reprints. Safari Press publishes books only on big-game hunting, sporting, firearms, and wingshooting; this includes African, North American, European, Asian, and South American hunting and wingshooting. Does not want books on 'outdoors' topics (hiking, camping, canoeing, etc.). **Publishes 25-30 titles/year. 70% of books from first-time authors. 80% from unagented writers. Pays 8-15% royalty on wholesale price.** Book catalog for $1. Guidelines online.

NONFICTION "We discourage autobiographies, unless the life of the hunter or firearms maker has been exceptional. We routinely reject manuscripts along the lines of 'Me and my buddies went hunting for... and a good time was had by all!" No outdoors topics (hiking, camping, canoeing, fishing, etc.). Query with SASE. Submit outline.

TIPS The editor notes that she receives many mss outside the areas of big-game hunting, wingshooting, and sporting firearms, and these are always rejected.

SAFER SOCIETY PRESS

P.O. Box 340, Brandon VT 05733. (802)247-3132. **Fax:** (802)247-4233. **Website:** www.safersociety.org. **Contact:** Mary Falcon, editorial director. Estab. 1985. Publishes trade paperback originals. "Our mission is the prevention and treatment of sexual abuse." **Publishes 3-4 titles/year. 15-20 queries received/year. 15-20 mss received/year. 90% of books from first-time authors. 100% from unagented writers. Pays 10% royalty on retail price.** Publishes ms 1 year after acceptance. Accepts simultaneous submissions. Book catalog available free. Guidelines online.

NONFICTION Subjects include psychology, sexual abuse. "We are a small, nonprofit, niche press. We want well-researched books dealing with any aspect of sexual abuse: treatment, prevention, understanding; works on subject in Spanish." Memoirs generally not accepted. Query with SASE, submit proposal package, or complete ms Reviews artwork/photos. Send photocopies.

TIPS "Audience is persons working in mental health/persons needing self-help books. Pays small fees or low royalties."

ST. AUGUSTINE'S PRESS

P.O. Box 2285, South Bend IN 46680. (574)-291-3500. **Fax:** (574)291-3700. **E-mail:** bruce@staugustine.net. **Website:** www.staugustine.net. **Contact:** Bruce Fingerhut, president (philosophy). Publishes hardcover originals and trade paperback originals and reprints. "Our market is scholarly in the humanities. We publish in philosophy, religion, cultural history, and history of ideas only." **Publishes 30+ titles/year. 350 queries received/year. 300 mss received/year. 2% of books from first-time authors. 95% from unagented writers. Pays 6-15% royalty. Pays $500-5,000 advance.** Publishes ms 8-18 months after acceptance. Accepts simultaneous submissions. Responds in 2-6 months to queries; 3-8 months to proposals; 4-8 months to mss. Book catalog available free.

IMPRINTS Carthage Reprints.

NONFICTION Query with SASE. Reviews artwork/photos. Send photocopies.

TIPS "Scholarly and college student audience."

ST. JOHANN PRESS

P.O. Box 241, Haworth NJ 07641. (201)387-1529. **E-mail:** d.biesel@verizon.net. **Website:** www.stjohannpress.com. Estab. 1991. Publishes hardcover originals, trade paperback originals and reprints. **Publishes 6-8 titles/year. Receives 15 submissions/year. 50% of books from first-time authors. 95% from unagented writers. Pays 10-15% royalty on wholesale price.** Publishes ms 15 months after acceptance. Accepts simultaneous submissions. Responds in 1 month on queries. Catalog online. Guidelines free on request.

NONFICTION Subjects include cooking, crafts, foods, history, hobbies, memoirs, military, nutrition, religion, sports (history), war (USMC), Black history in sports. "We are a niche publisher with interests in titles that will sell over a long period of time. For example, the World Football League Encyclopedia, Chicago Showcase of Basketball, will not need to be redone. We do baseball but prefer soccer, hockey, etc." Query with SASE. Reviews artwork/photos as part of the ms package. Send photocopies.

TIPS "Our readership is libraries, individuals with special interests, (e.g. sports historians); we also do specialized reference."

Ⓐ⊘ ST. MARTIN'S PRESS, LLC

Holtzbrinck Publishers, 175 Fifth Ave., New York NY 10010. (212)674-5151. **Fax:** (212)420-9314. **Website:** www.stmartins.com. Estab. 1952. Publishes hardcover, trade paperback and mass market originals. General interest publisher of both fiction and nonfiction. **Publishes 1,500 titles/year. Pays royalty. Pays advance.**

NONFICTION Subjects include business, economics, cooking, foods, nutrition, sports, general nonfiction. *Agented submissions only. No unsolicited mss.*

FICTION Subjects include fantasy, historical, horror, literary, mainstream, contemporary, mystery, science fiction, suspense, western, contemporary, general fiction. *Agented submissions only. No unsolicited mss.*

SAINT MARY'S PRESS

702 Terrace Heights, Winona MN 55987. (800)533-8095. **Fax:** (800)344-9225. **E-mail:** submissions@smp.org. **Website:** www.smp.org. Ms guidelines online or by e-mail.

NONFICTION Subjects include religion, prayers, spirituality. Titles for Catholic youth and their parents, teachers, and youth ministers. High school Catholic religious education textbooks and primary source readings. Query with SASE. Submit proposal package, outline, 1 sample chapter, SASE. Brief author biography.

TIPS "Request product catalog and/or do research online of Saint Mary Press book lists before submitting proposal."

ST PAULS

Society of St. Paul, 2187 Victory Blvd., Staten Island NY 10314. (718)761-0047. **Fax:** (718)761-0057. **E-mail:** edmund_lane@juno.com. **Website:** www.stpauls.us. **Contact:** Edmund C. Lane, SSP, acquisitions editor. Estab. 1957. Publishes trade paperback and mass market paperback originals and reprints. **Publishes 22 titles/year. 250 queries received/year. 150 mss received/year. 10% of books from first-time authors. 100% from unagented writers. Pays 5-10% royalty.** Publishes ms 10 months after acceptance. Responds in 1 month to queries and proposals; 2 months to mss. Book catalog and ms guidelines free.

NONFICTION Subjects include philosophy, religion, spirituality. Alba House is the North American publishing division of the Society of St. Paul, an International Roman Catholic Missionary Religious Congregation dedicated to spreading the Gospel message via the media of communications. Does not want fiction, children's books, poetry, personal testimonies, or autobiographies. Submit complete ms. Reviews artwork/photos. Send photocopies.

TIPS "Our audience is educated Roman Catholic readers interested in matters related to the Church, spirituality, Biblical and theological topics, moral concerns, lives of the saints, etc."

SAKURA PUBLISHING & TECHNOLOGIES

P.O. Box 1681, Hermitage PA 16148. (330)360-5131. **E-mail:** skpublishing124@gmail.com. **Website:** www.sakura-publishing.com. **Contact:** Derek Vasconi, talent finder and CEO. Estab. 2007. Publishes hardcover, trade paperback, mass market paperback and electronic originals and reprints. Mss that don't follow guidelines will not be considered. **Publishes 10-12 titles/year. 90% of books from first-time authors. 80% from unagented writers. Pays royalty of 20-60% on wholesale price or retail price.** Publishes ms 6 months after acceptance. Accepts simultaneous submissions. Responds in 1 week. Book catalog available for #10 SASE. Guidelines online.

NONFICTION Subjects include alternative lifestyles, Americana, animals, architecture, art, contemporary culture, creative nonfiction, entertainment, games, gay, history, hobbies, humanities, memoirs, military. Follow guidelines online.

FICTION Subjects include horror, poetry. Follow guidelines online.

POETRY Follow guidelines online.

TIPS "Please make sure you visit our submissions page at our website and follow all instructions exactly as written. Also, Sakura Publishing has a preference for fiction/nonfiction books specializing in Asian culture."

SALEM PRESS, INC.

P.O. Box 56, Amenia NY 12501. **E-mail:** lmars@greyhouse.com. **Website:** www.salempress.com. **Contact:** Laura Mars, editorial director. **Publishes 20-22 titles/year. 15 queries received/year. Work-for-hire pays 5-15¢/word.** Responds in 3 months to queries; 1 month to proposals. Book catalog online.

NONFICTION Subjects include business, economics, ethnic, government, politics, health, medicine, history, language, literature, military, war, music, dance, nature, environment, philosophy, psychology, science, sociology, women's issues, women's studies. "We accept vitas for writers interested in supplying articles/entries for encyclopedia-type entries in library reference books. Will also accept multi-volume book ideas from people interested in being a general editor." Query with SASE.

SALINA BOOKSHELF

3120 N. Caden Ct., Suite 4, Flagstaff AZ 86004. (928)527-0070. **Fax:** (928)526-0386. **Website:** www.salinabookshelf.com. Publishes trade paperback originals and reprints. **Publishes 4-5 titles/year. 50% of books from first-time authors. 100% from unagented writers. Pays varying royalty. Pays advance.** Publishes ms 1 year after acceptance. Accepts simultaneous submissions. Responds in 3 months to queries.

NONFICTION Subjects include education, ethnic, science. "We publish children's bilingual readers." Nonfiction should be appropriate to science and social studies curriculum grades 3-8. Query with SASE.

FICTION Subjects include juvenile. Submissions should be in English or Navajo. "All our books relate to the Navajo language and culture." Query with SASE.

POETRY "We accept poetry in English/Southwest language for children." Submit 3 sample poems.

SALMON POETRY

Knockeven, Cliffs of Moher, County Clare , Ireland. 353(0)65-7081941. **E-mail:** info@salmonpoetry.com. **E-mail:** jessie@salmonpoetry.com. **Website:** www.salmonpoetry.com. **Contact:** Jessie Lendennie, editor. Estab. 1981. Publishes mass market paperback originals and e-books.

POETRY "Salmon Press has become one of the most important publications in the Irish literary world, specialising in the promotion of new poets, particularly women poets. Established as an alternative voice. Walks tightrope between innovation and convention. Was a flagship for writers in the west of Ireland. Salmon has developed a cross-cultural, internatonal literary dialog, broadening Irish Literature and urging new perspectives on established traditions." E-mail query with short biographical note and 5-10 sample poems.

TIPS "If we are broad minded and willing to nurture the individual voice inherent in the work, the artist will emerge."

SALVO PRESS

E-mail: info@salvopress.com. **E-mail:** submissions@start-media.com. **Website:** www.salvopress.com. **Contact:** Scott Schmidt, publisher. Estab. 1998. **Publishes 6-12 titles/year. 75% from unagented writers. Pays 10% royalty.** Publishes ms 9-12 months after acceptance. Responds in 5 minutes to 1 month to queries; 2 months to mss. Book catalog and ms guidelines online.

FICTION Subjects include adventure, literary, mystery, science fiction, suspense, thriller/espionage. "We are a small press specializing in mystery, suspense, espionage and thriller fiction. Our press publishes in trade paperback and most e-book formats." Query by e-mail.

SAMHAIN PUBLISHING, LTD

11821 Mason Montgomery Rd., Cincinnati OH 45249. (478)314-5144. **Fax:** (478)314-5148. **E-mail:** horror@samhainpublishing.com; retroromance@samhainpublishing.com. **E-mail:** romance@samhainpublishing.com. **Website:** www.samhainpublishing.com. **Contact:** Christina Brashear, president/publisher. Estab. 2005. Publishes e-books and paperback originals. POD/offset printing; line illustrations. "A small, independent publisher, Samhain's motto is 'It's all about the story.' We look for fresh, unique voices who have a story to share with the world. We encourage our authors to let their muse have its way and to create tales that don't always adhere to current trends. One never knows what the next hot genre will be or when it will start, so write what's in your soul. These are the books that, whether the story is based on formula or is an original, when written from the heart will earn you a life-time readership." **Pays royalties 30-40% for e-books, average of 8% for trade paper, and author's copies (quantity varies).** Publishes ms 18 months after acceptance. Responds in 4 months. Guidelines online.

FICTION Needs erotica and all genres and all heat levels of romance (contemporary, futuristic/time travel, gothic, historical, paranormal, regency period, romantic suspense, fantasy, action/adventure, etc.), as well as fantasy, urban fantasy or science fiction with strong romantic elements, with word counts between 12,000 and 120,000 words. Accepts unsolicited mss. Query with outline/synopsis and either 3 sample chapters or the full ms. Accepts queries by e-mail only. Include estimated word count, brief bio, list of publishing credits, and "how the author is working to improve craft: association, critique groups, etc."

TIPS "Because we are an e-publisher first, we do not have to be as concerned with industry trends and can publish less popular genres of fiction if we believe the story and voice are good and will appeal to our customers. Please follow submission guidelines located on our website, include all requested information and proof your query/manuscript for errors prior to submission."

SANTA MONICA PRESS LLC

P.O. Box 850, Solana Beach CA 92075. (858)793-1890; (800)784-9553. **E-mail:** books@santamonicapress.com. **Website:** www.santamonicapress.com. Estab. 1994. Publishes hardcover and trade paperback originals. "At Santa Monica Press, we're not afraid to cast a wide editorial net. Our eclectic list of lively and modern nonfiction titles includes books in such categories as popular culture, film history, photography, humor, biography, travel, and reference." **Publishes 15 titles/year. 25% of books from first-time authors. 75% from unagented writers. Pays 6-10% royalty on net price. Pays $500-10,000+ advance.** Publishes ms 1 year after acceptance. Accepts simultaneous submissions. Responds in 1-2 months to proposals. Guidelines online.

NONFICTION Subjects include Americana, architecture, art, contemporary culture, creative nonfiction, education, entertainment, film, games, humanities, language, literature, memoirs, regional, social sciences, sports, travel, Biography, coffee table book, general nonfiction, gift book, humor, illustrated book, reference. Submit proposal package, including outline, 2-3 sample chapters, biography, marketing and publicity plans, analysis of competitive titles, SASE with appropriate postage. Reviews artwork/photos. Send photocopies.

TIPS "Visit our website before submitting to view our author guidelines and to get a clear idea of the types of books we publish. Carefully analyze your book's competition and tell us what makes your book different—and what makes it better. Also let us know what promotional and marketing opportunities you, as the author, bring to the project."

SARABANDE BOOKS, INC.

2234 Dundee Rd., Suite 200, Louisville KY 40205. (502)458-4028. **Fax:** (502)458-4065. **E-mail:** info@sarabandebooks.org. **Website:** www.sarabandebooks.org. **Contact:** Sarah Gorham, editor-in-chief. Estab. 1994. Publishes trade paperback originals. "Sarabande Books was founded to publish poetry, short fiction, and creative nonfiction. We look for works of lasting literary value. Please see our titles to get an idea of our taste. Accepts submissions through contests and open submissions." **Publishes 10 titles/year. 1,500 queries received/year. 3,000 mss received/year. 35% of books from first-time authors. 75% from unagented writers. Pays royalty. 10% on actual income received. Also pays in author's copies. Pays $500-1,000 advance.** Publishes ms 18 months after acceptance. Accepts simultaneous submissions. Book catalog available free. Contest guidelines for #10 SASE or on website.

Charges $15 handling fee with alternative option of purchase of book from website (e-mail confirmation of sale must be included with submission).

FICTION Subjects include literary, short story collections, novellas, short novels (300 pages maximum, 150 pages minimum). "We consider novels and nonfiction in a wide variety of genres. We do not consider genre fiction such as science fiction, fantasy, or horror. Our target length is 70,000-90,000 words." Queries can be sent via e-mail, fax, or regular post.

POETRY Poetry of superior artistic quality; otherwise no restraints or specifications. Sarabande Books publishes books of poetry of 48 pages minimum. Wants "poetry that offers originality of voice and subject matter, uniqueness of vision, and a language that startles because of the careful attention paid to it—language that goes beyond the merely competent or functional." Mss selected through literary contests, invitation, and recommendation by a well-established writer.

TIPS "Sarabande publishes for a general literary audience. Know your market. Read-and buy-books of literature. Sponsors contests for poetry and fiction. Make sure you're not writing in a vacuum, that you've read and are conscious of contemporary literature. Have someone read your manuscript, checking it for ordering, coherence. Better a lean, consistently strong manuscript than one that is long and uneven. We like a story to have good narrative, and we like to be engaged by language."

SAS PUBLISHING

100 SAS Campus Dr., Cary NC 27513-2414. (919)531-0585. **Fax:** (919)677-4444. **E-mail:** saspress@sas.com. **Website:** support.sas.com/saspress. Estab. 1976. Publishes hardcover and trade paperback originals. "SAS publishes books for SAS and JMP software users, both new and experienced." **Publishes 40 titles/year. 50% of books from first-time authors. 100% from unagented writers. Payment negotiable. Pays negotiable advance.** Responds in 2 weeks to queries. Book catalog and ms guidelines online.

NONFICTION Subjects include software, statistics. SAS Publishing jointly Wiley and SAS Business Series titles. "Through SAS, we also publish books by SAS users on a variety of topics relating to SAS software. SAS titles enhance users' abilities to use SAS effectively. We're interested in publishing manuscripts that describe or illustrate using any of SAS products, including JMP software. Books must be aimed at SAS or JMP users, either new or experienced." Mss must reflect current or upcoming software releases, and the author's writing should indicate an understanding of SAS and the technical aspects covered in the ms. Query with SASE. Submit outline, sample chapters. Reviews artwork/photos.

SASQUATCH BOOKS

1904 Third Ave., Suite 710, Seattle WA 98101. (206)467-4300. **Fax:** (206)467-4301. **E-mail:** custserv@sasquatchbooks.com. **Website:** www.sasquatchbooks.com. Estab. 1986. Publishes regional hardcover and trade paperback originals. "Sasquatch Books publishes books for and from the Pacific Northwest, Alaska, and California is the nation's premier regional press. Sasquatch Books' publishing program is a veritable celebration of regionally written words. Undeterred by political or geographical borders, Sasquatch defines its region as the magnificent area that stretches from the Brooks Range to the Gulf of California and from the Rocky Mountains to the Pacific Ocean. Our top-selling Best Places® travel guides serve the most popular destinations and locations of the West. We also publish widely in the areas of food and wine, gardening, nature, photography, children's books, and regional history, all facets of the literature of place. With more than 200 books brimming with insider information on the West, we offer an energetic eye on the lifestyle, landscape, and worldview of our region. Considers queries and proposals from authors and agents for new projects that fit into our West Coast regional publishing program. We can evaluate query letters, proposals, and complete mss." **Publishes 30 titles/year. 20% of books from first-time authors. 75% from unagented writers. Pays royalty on cover price. Pays wide range advance.** Publishes ms 6-9 months after acceptance. Accepts simultaneous submissions. Responds to queries in 3 months. Guidelines online.

NONFICTION Subjects include animals, art, architecture, business, economics, cooking, foods, nutrition, gardening, history, nature, environment, recreation, regional, sports, travel, women's issues, women's studies, outdoors. "We are seeking quality nonfiction works about the Pacific Northwest and West Coast regions (including Alaska to California). The literature of place includes how-to and where-to as well as history and narrative nonfiction." Picture books: activity books, animal, concept, nature/environment. Query first, then submit outline and sample chapters with SASE. Send submissions to The Editors. E-mailed submissions and queries are not recommended. Please include return postage if you want your materials back.

FICTION Young readers: adventure, animal, concept, contemporary, humor, nature/environment.

TIPS "We sell books through a range of channels in addition to the book trade. Our primary audience consists of active, literate residents of the West Coast."

SATURNALIA BOOKS

105 Woodside Rd., Ardmore PA 19003. (267) 278-9541. **E-mail:** info@saturnaliabooks.com. **Website:** www.saturnaliabooks.org. **Contact:** Henry Israeli, publisher. Estab. 2002. Publishes trade paperback originals and digital versions for e-readers. "We do not accept unsolicited submissions. We hold a contest, the Saturnalia Books Poetry Prize, annually in which 1 anonymously submitted title is chosen by a poet with a national reputation for publication. Submissions are accepted during the month of March. The submission fee is $30, and the prize is $2,000 and 20 copies of the book. See website for details." **Publishes 4 titles/year. Receives 500 mss/year. 33% of books from first-time authors. 100% from unagented writers. Pays authors 4-6% royalty on retail price. Pays $400-2,000 advance.** Accepts simultaneous submissions. Responds in 4 months on mss. Catalog online. Guidelines online.

POETRY "Saturnalia Books has no bias against any school of poetry, but we do tend to publish writers who take chances and push against convention in some way, whether it's in form, language, content, or musicality." Submit complete ms to contest only.

TIPS "Our audience tend to be young avid readers of contemporary poetry. Read a few sample books first."

SCARECROW PRESS, INC.

Imprint of Rowman & Littlefield Publishing Group, 4501 Forbes Blvd., Suite 200, Lanham MD 20706. (301)459-3366. **Fax:** (301)429-5748. **Website:** www.scarecrowpress.com. Estab. 1955. Publishes hardcover originals. Scarecrow Press publishes several series: Historical Dictionaries (includes countries, religions, international organizations, and area studies); Studies and Documentaries on the History of Popular Entertainment (forthcoming); Society, Culture and Libraries. Emphasis is on any title likely to appeal to libraries. Currently emphasizing jazz, Africana, and educational issues of contemporary interest. **Publishes 165 titles/year. 70% of books from first-time authors. 99% from unagented writers. Pays 8% royalty on net of first 1,000 copies; 10% of net price thereafter.** Publishes ms 18 months after acceptance. Responds in 2 months to queries. Catalog and ms guidelines online.

NONFICTION Subjects include film, cinema, stage, language, literature, religion, sports, annotated bibliographies, handbooks and biographical dictionaries in the areas of women's studies and ethnic studies, parapsychology, fine arts and handicrafts, genealogy, sports history, music, movies, stage, library and information science. Query with SASE.

SCHIFFER PUBLISHING, LTD.

4880 Lower Valley Rd., Atglen PA 19310. (610)593-1777. **Fax:** (610)593-2002. **E-mail:** info@schifferbooks.com. **Website:** www.schifferbooks.com. Estab. 1975. **Publishes 10-20 titles/year. Pays royalty on wholesale price.** Responds in 2 weeks to queries. Book catalog available free. Guidelines online.

NONFICTION Art-quality illustrated regional histories. Looking for informed, entertaining writing and lots of subject areas to provide points of entry into the text for non-history buffs who buy a beautiful book because they are from, or love, an area. Full color possible in the case of historic postcards. Fax or e-mail outline, photos, and book proposal.

TIPS "We want to publish books for towns or cities with relevant population or active tourism to support book sales. A list of potential town vendors is a helpful start toward selling us on your book idea."

Ⓐ⊘ SCHOCKEN BOOKS

Imprint of Knopf Publishing Group, Division of Random House, Inc., 1745 Broadway, New York NY 10019. (212)572-9000. **Fax:** (212)572-6030. **Website:** www.

schocken.com. Estab. 1945. Publishes hardcover and trade paperback originals and reprints. "Schocken publishes quality Judaica in all areas-fiction, history, biography, current affairs, spirituality and religious practices, popular culture, and cultural studies." *Does not accept unsolicited mss. Agented submissions only.* **Publishes 9-12 titles/year. Pays varied advance.** Accepts simultaneous submissions.

SCHOLASTIC, INC.

557 Broadway, New York NY 10012. (212)343-6100. **Website:** www.scholastic.com.

IMPRINTS Arthur A. Levine Books, Cartwheel Books®, Chicken House®, Graphix™, Little Scholastic™, Little Shepherd™, Michael di Capua Books, Orchard Books®, Point™, PUSH, Scholastic en Español, Scholastic Licensed Publishing, Scholastic Nonfiction, Scholastic Paperbacks, Scholastic Press, Scholastic Reference™, and The Blue Sky Press® are imprints of the Scholastic Trade Books Division. In addition, Scholastic Trade Books included Klutz®, a highly innovative publisher and creator of "books plus" for children.

Scholastic Trade Books is an award-winning publisher of original children's books. Scholastic publishes more than 600 new hardcover, paperback and novelty books each year. The list includes the phenomenally successful publishing properties Harry Potter®, Goosebumps®, The 39 Clues™, I Spy™, and *The Hunger Games*; best-selling and award-winning authors and illustrators, including Blue Balliett, Jim Benton, Meg Cabot, Suzanne Collins, Christopher Paul Curtis, Ann M. Martin, Dav Pilkey, J.K. Rowling, Pam Muñoz Ryan, Brian Selznick, David Shannon, Mark Teague, and Walter Wick, among others; as well as licensed properties such as Star Wars® and Rainbow Magic®.

SCHOLASTIC CHILDREN'S BOOKS UK

Euston House, 24 Eversholt St., London VI NW1 1DB, United Kingdom. **Website:** www.scholastic.co.uk.

Scholastic UK does not accept unsolicited submissions. Unsolicited illustrations are accepted, but please do not send any original artwork as it will not be returned.

TIPS "Getting work published can be a frustrating process, and it's often best to be prepared for disappointment, but don't give up."

SCHOLASTIC LIBRARY PUBLISHING

90 Old Sherman Turnpike, Danbury CT 06816. (203)797-3500. **Fax:** (203)797-3197. **E-mail:** slpservice@scholastic.com. **Website:** www.scholastic.com/librarypublishing. **Contact:** Phil Friedman, vice president/publisher; Kate Nunn, editor-in-chief; Marie O'Neil, art director. Estab. 1895. Publishes hardcover and trade paperback originals. "Scholastic Library is a leading publisher of reference, educational, and children's books. We provide parents, teachers, and librarians with the tools they need to enlighten children to the pleasure of learning and prepare them for the road ahead. Publishes informational (nonfiction) for K-12; picture books for young readers, grades 1-3." **Pays authors royalty based on net or work purchased outright. Pays illustrators at competitive rates.**

IMPRINTS Grolier; Children's Press; Franklin Watts; Grolier Online.

Accepts agented submissions only.

NONFICTION Photo-illustrated books for all levels: animal, arts/crafts, biography, careers, concept, geography, health, history, hobbies, how-to, multicultural, nature/environment, science, social issues, special needs, sports. Average word length: young readers—2,000; middle readers—8,000; young adult—15,000. Query; submit outline/synopsis, resume, and/or list of publications, and writing sample. SASE required for response.

FICTION Publishes 1 picture book series, Rookie Readers, for grades 1-2. Does not accept unsolicited mss. *Does not accept fiction proposals.*

SCHOLASTIC PRESS

Imprint of Scholastic, Inc., 557 Broadway, New York NY 10012. (212)343-6100. **Fax:** (212)343-4713. **Website:** www.scholastic.com. Publishes hardcover originals. Scholastic Press publishes fresh, literary picture book fiction and nonfiction; fresh, literary nonseries or nongenre-oriented middle grade and young adult fiction. Currently emphasizing subtly handled treatments of key relationships in children's lives; unusual approaches to commonly dry subjects, such as biography, math, history, or science. De-emphasizing fairy tales (or retellings), board books, genre, or series fiction (mystery, fantasy, etc.). **Publishes 60 titles/year. 2,500 queries received/year. 1% of books from first-time authors. Pays royalty on retail price. Pays vari-**

able advance. Publishes ms 2 years after acceptance. Responds in 3 months to queries; 6-8 months to mss.

NONFICTION Agented submissions and previously published authors only.

FICTION Subjects include juvenile, picture books, novels. Looking for strong picture books, young chapter books, appealing middle grade novels (ages 8-11) and interesting and well-written young adult novels. Wants fresh, exciting picture books and novels—inspiring, new talent. *Agented submissions only.*

TIPS "Read *currently* published children's books. Revise, rewrite, rework and find your own voice, style and subject. We are looking for authors with a strong and unique voice who can tell a great story and have the ability to evoke genuine emotion. Children's publishers are becoming more selective, looking for irresistible talent and fairly broad appeal, yet still very willing to take risks, just to keep the game interesting."

SCRIBE PUBLICATIONS

18-20 Edward St., Brunswick VIC 3056, Australia. (61)(3)9388-8780. **Fax:** (61)(3)9388-8787. **E-mail:** info@scribepub.com.au. **Website:** www.scribepublications.com.au. Estab. 1976. **Publishes 70 titles/year. 10-20% from unagented writers.** Guidelines online.

NONFICTION Subjects include environment, history, memoirs, psychology, current affairs, social history. "Please refer first to our website before contacting us or submitting anything, because we explain there who we will accept proposals from."

FICTION Submit synopsis, sample chapters, CV.

TIPS "We are only able to consider unsolicited submissions if you have a demonstrated background of writing and publishing for general readers."

SCRIBNER

Imprint of Simon & Schuster Adult Publishing Group, 1230 Avenue of the Americas, 12th Floor, New York NY 10020. (212)698-7000. **Website:** www.simonsays.com. Publishes hardcover originals. **Publishes 70-75 titles/year. Thousands queries received/year. 20% of books from first-time authors. Pays 7-15% royalty. Pays variable advance.** Publishes ms 9 months after acceptance. Accepts simultaneous submissions. Responds in 3 months to queries.

NONFICTION Subjects include education, ethnic, gay, lesbian, health, medicine, history, language, literature, nature, environment, philosophy, psychology, religion, science, criticism. *Agented submissions only.*

FICTION Subjects include literary, mystery, suspense. *Agented submissions only.*

SEAL PRESS

1700 4th St., Berkeley CA 94710. (510)595-3664. **E-mail:** seal.press@perseusbooks.com. **E-mail:** emma.rose@perseusbooks.com. **Website:** www.sealpress.com. Estab. 1976. Publishes hardcover and trade paperback originals. "Seal Press is an imprint of the Perseus Book Group, a feminist book publisher interested in original, lively, radical, empowering and culturally diverse nonfiction by women addressing contemporary issues with the goal of informing women's lives. Currently emphasizing women outdoor adventurists, young feminists, political issues, health and fitness, parenting, personal finance, sex and relationships, and LGBT and gender topics. *Not accepting fiction at this time.*" **Publishes 30 titles/year. 1,000 queries received/year. 750 mss received/year. 25% of books from first-time authors. 50% from unagented writers. Pays 7-10% royalty on retail price. Pays variable royalty on retail price. Pays wide ranging advance.** Publishes ms 1 year after acceptance. Accepts simultaneous submissions. Responds in 2 months to queries. Book catalog and ms guidelines for SASE or online.

NONFICTION Subjects include Americana, child guidance, contemporary culture, creative nonfiction, ethnic, gay, lesbian, memoirs, multicultural, nature, environment, sex, travel, women's issues, women's studies, popular culture, politics, domestic violence, sexual abuse. Query with SASE. Reviews artwork/photos. Send photocopies. No original art or photos accepted.

TIPS "Seeking empowering and progressive nonfiction that can impact a woman's life across categories."

SEARCH INSTITUTE PRESS

Search Institute, 615 First Ave. NE, Suite 125, Minneapolis MN 55413. (612)399-0200. **Fax:** (612)692-5553. **E-mail:** si@search-institute.org. **Website:** www.search-institute.org. Estab. 1958. Publishes trade paperback originals. **Publishes 12-15 titles/year. Pays royalty.** Publishes ms 1 year after acceptance. Accepts simultaneous submissions. Responds in 6 months. Catalog and guidelines online.

NONFICTION Subjects include career guidance, child guidance, community, counseling, education, entertainment, games, parenting, public affairs, social sciences, youth leadership, prevention, activities. Does not want children's picture books, poetry, New

Age and religious-themes, memoirs, biographies, and autobiographies. Query with SASE. Does not review artwork/photos.

TIPS "Our audience is educators, youth program leaders, mentors, parents."

SEAWORTHY PUBLICATIONS, INC.

2023 N. Atlantic Ave., #226, Cocoa Beach FL 32931. (321)610-3634. **Fax:** (321)400-1006. **E-mail:** queries@seaworthy.com. **Website:** www.seaworthy.com. **Contact:** Joseph F. Janson, publisher. Publishes trade paperback originals, hardcover originals, and reprints. "Seaworthy Publications is a nautical book publisher that primarily publishes books of interest to recreational boaters and bluewater cruisers, including cruising guides, how-to books about boating. Currently emphasizing cruising guides." **Publishes 8 titles/year. 150 queries received/year. 40 mss received/year. 60% of books from first-time authors. 100% from unagented writers. Pays 15% royalty on wholesale price. Pays $1,000 advance.** Publishes ms 6 months after acceptance. Responds in 1 month to queries. Book catalog and guidelines online.

NONFICTION Subjects include regional, sailing, boating, regional, boating guide books. Regional guide books, first-person adventure, reference, technical—all dealing with boating. Query with SASE. Submit 3 sample chapters, TOC. Prefers electronic query via e-mail. Reviews artwork/photos. Send photocopies or color prints.

TIPS "Our audience consists of sailors, boaters, and those interested in the sea, sailing, or long-distance cruising."

SECOND STORY PRESS

20 Maud St., Suite 401, Toronto ON M5V 2M5, Canada. (416)537-7850. **Fax:** (416)537-0588. **E-mail:** info@secondstorypress.ca. **Website:** www.secondstorypress.ca.

NONFICTION Picture books: biography. Accepts appropriate material from residents of Canada only. Submit complete ms or submit outline and sample chapters by postal mail only. No electronic submissions or queries.

FICTION Considers non-sexist, non-racist, and nonviolent stories, as well as historical fiction, chapter books, picture books.

SEEDLING CONTINENTAL PRESS

520 E. Bainbridge St., Elizabethtown PA 17022. **Website:** www.continentalpress.com. Publishes books for classroom use only for the beginning reader in English. "Natural language and predictable text are requisite. Patterned text is acceptable, but must have a unique story line. Poetry, books in rhyme and full-length picture books are not being accepted. Illustrations are not necessary." **Work purchased outright from authors.** Publishes ms 1-2 years after acceptance. Accepts simultaneous submissions. Responds to mss in 6 months.

NONFICTION Young readers: animal, arts/crafts, biography, careers, concept, multicultural, nature/environment, science. Does not accept texts longer than 12 pages or over 300 words. Average word length: young readers—100. Submit complete ms.

FICTION Young readers: adventure, animal, folktales, humor, multicultural, nature/environment. Does not accept texts longer than 12 pages or over 300 words. Average word length: young readers—100. Submit complete ms.

TIPS "See our website. Follow writers' guidelines carefully and test your story with children and educators."

SELF-COUNSEL PRESS

1704 N. State St., Bellingham WA 92225. (360)676-4530. **Website:** www.self-counsel.com. Estab. 1971. Publishes trade paperback originals. Self-Counsel Press publishes a range of quality self-help books written in practical, nontechnical style by recognized experts in the fields of business, financial, or legal guidance for people who want to help themselves. **Publishes 30 titles/year. 1,500 queries received/year. 30% of books from first-time authors. 90% from unagented writers. Pays rare advance.** Publishes ms 8 months after acceptance. Accepts simultaneous submissions. Responds in 2 months to queries. Book catalog online. Guidelines online.

NONFICTION Subjects include business, economics, computers, electronics, money, finance, legal issues for lay people. Submit proposal package, outline, resume, 2 sample chapters.

SENTIENT PUBLICATIONS

1113 Spruce St., Boulder CO 80302. **E-mail:** contact@sentientpublications.com. **Website:** www.sentientpublications.com. **Contact:** Connie Shaw, acquisitions editor. Estab. 2001. Publishes hardcover and trade paperback originals; trade paperback reprints. **Publishes 4 titles/year. 200 queries received/year. 100 mss received/year. 70% of books from first-time**

authors. 50% from unagented writers. Pays royalty on wholesale price. Sometimes pays advance. Publishes ms 6 months after acceptance. Accepts simultaneous submissions. Responds in 1 month to queries; 2 months to proposals and mss. Book catalog online.

NONFICTION Subjects include child guidance, contemporary culture, creative nonfiction, education, environment, gardening, history, philosophy, photography, psychology, science, social sciences, sociology, spirituality, travel. "We're especially looking for holistic health or sustainability books that have something new to say." Submit proposal package or complete ms. Does not review artwork/photos.

SERIOUSLY GOOD BOOKS

999 Vanderbilt Beach Rd., Naples FL 34119. **E-mail:** seriouslygoodbks@aol.com. **Website:** www.seriouslygoodbks.net. Estab. 2010. Publishes trade paperback and electronic originals. Publishes historial fiction only. **Publishes 2-5 titles/year. Pays 15% minimum royalties.** Responds in 1 month to queries. Book catalog and guidelines online.

FICTION Subjects include historical. Query by e-mail.

TIPS "Looking for historial fiction with substance. We seek well-researched historical fiction in the vein of Rutherfurd, Mary Renault, Maggie Anton, Robert Harris, etc. Please don't query with historical fiction mixed with other genres (romance, time travel, vampires, etc.)."

SEVEN STORIES PRESS

140 Watts St., New York NY 10013. (212)226-8760. **Fax:** (212)226-1411. **E-mail:** info@sevenstories.com. **Website:** www.sevenstories.com. **Contact:** Daniel Simon; Anna Lui. Estab. 1995. Publishes hardcover and trade paperback originals. Founded in 1995 in New York City, and named for the seven authors who committed to a home with a fiercely independent spirit, Seven Stories Press publishes works of the imagination and political titles by voices of conscience. While most widely known for its books on politics, human rights, and social and economic justice, Seven Stories continues to champion literature, with a list encompassing both innovative debut novels and National Book Award–winning poetry collections, as well as prose and poetry translations from the French, Spanish, German, Swedish, Italian, Greek, Polish, Korean, Vietnamese, Russian, and Arabic. **Publishes 40-50 titles/year. 15% of books from first-time authors. 50% from unagented writers. Pays 7-15% royalty on retail price. Pays advance.** Publishes ms 1-3 years after acceptance. Accepts simultaneous submissions. Responds in 1 month. Book catalog and ms guidelines free.

NONFICTION Responds only if interested. Submit cover letter with 2 sample chapters.

FICTION Subjects include literary. Submit cover letter with 2 sample chapters.

SEVERN HOUSE PUBLISHERS

Salatin House, 19 Cedar Rd., Sutton, Surrey SM2 5DA, United Kingdom. (44)(208)770-3930. **Fax:** (44) (208)770-3850. **Website:** www.severnhouse.com. Publishes hardcover and trade paperback originals and reprints. Severn House is currently emphasizing suspense, romance, mystery. Large print imprint from existing authors. **Publishes 150 titles/year. 400-500 queries received/year. 50 mss received/year. Pays 7-15% royalty on retail price. Pays $750-5,000 advance.** Accepts simultaneous submissions. Responds in 3 months to proposals. Book catalog available free.

FICTION Subjects include adventure, fantasy, historical, horror, mainstream, contemporary, mystery, romance, short story collections, suspense. *Agented submissions only.*

SHAMBHALA PUBLICATIONS, INC.

300 Massachusetts Ave., Boston MA 02115. (617)424-0030. **Fax:** (617)236-1563. **E-mail:** editors@shambhala.com. **Website:** www.shambhala.com. Estab. 1969. Publishes hardcover and trade paperback originals and reprints. **Publishes 90-100 titles/year. 500 queries received/year. 1,200 mss/proposals received/year. 30% of books from first-time authors. 70% from unagented writers. Pays 8% royalty on retail price.** Publishes ms 1 year after acceptance. Accepts simultaneous submissions. Responds in 4 months. Book catalog and ms guidelines free.

IMPRINTS Roost Books; Snow Lion.

NONFICTION Subjects include cooking, crafts, parenting, Buddhism, martial arts, yoga, natural health, Eastern philosophy, creativity, green living, nature writing. To send a book proposal, include a synopsis of the book, TOC or outline, a copy of the author's resume or some other brief biographical statement, along with two or three sample chapters (they do not need to be in consecutive order). The chapters should be double-spaced. Include SASE. Publishes very little fiction or poetry.

FICTION Submit proposal package, outline, résumé, 2 sample chapters, TOC.

SHEARSMAN BOOKS, LTD

50 Westons Hills Dr., Emersons Green Bristol BS16 7DF, United Kingdom. **E-mail:** editor@shearsman.com. **Website:** www.shearsman.com. **Contact:** Tony Frazer, editor. Estab. 1981. Publishes trade paperback originals. **Publishes 45-60 titles/year. Pays 10% royalty on retail price after 150 copies have sold; authors also receive 10 free copies of their books.** Responds in 2-3 months to mss. Book catalog online. Guidelines online.

NONFICTION Subjects include memoirs, translation, essays.

POETRY "Shearsman only publishes poetry, poetry collections, and poetry in translation (from any language but with an emphasis on work in Spanish & in German). Some critical work on poetry and also memoirs and essays by poets. Mainly poetry by British, Irish, North American, and Australian poets." No children's books.

TIPS "Book ms submission: most of the ms must have already appeared in the UK or USA magazines of some repute, and it has to fill 70-72 pages of half letter or A5 pages. You must have sufficient return postage. Submissions can also be made by email. It is unlikely that a poet with no track record will be accepted for publication as there is no obvious audience for the work. Try to develop some exposure to UK and US magazines and try to assemble a ms only later."

SHIPWRECKT BOOKS PUBLISHING COMPANY LLC

P.O. Box 20, Lanesboro MN 55949. (507)458-8190. **E-mail:** editor@shipwrecktbooks.com. **E-mail:** contact@shipwrecktbooks.com. **Website:** www.shipwrecktbooks.com. **Contact:** Tom Driscoll, managing editor. Publishes trade paperback originals, mass market paperback originals, and electronic originals. **Publishes 6 titles/year. 50% of books from first-time authors. 100% from unagented writers. Authors receive a maximum of 35% royalties.** Publishes book Average length of time between acceptance of a book-length ms and publication is 6 months. after acceptance of ms. Accepts simultaneous submissions. Responds to queries within 2 months. Catalog and guidelines online.

IMPRINTS Rocket Science Press (literary); Up On Big Rock Poetry Series; Lost Lake Folk Art (memoir, biography, essays, and nonfiction).

NONFICTION Subjects include agriculture, alternative lifestyles, Americana, animals, creative nonfiction, environment, ethnic, foods, gardening, gay, government, health, history, hobbies, horticulture, house and home, lesbian, medicine, memoirs, military, multicultural, nature, nutrition, politics, recreation, regional, spirituality, sports, war, womens issues, world affairs, young adult. E-mail query first. All unsolicited mss returned unopened. Does not review artwork.

FICTION Subjects include adventure, comic books, ethnic, experimental, fantasy, historical, humor, literary, multicultural, mystery, poetry, regional, science fiction, suspense, young adult. E-mail query first. All unsolicited mss returned unopened.

POETRY Submit 3 sample poems by e-mail.

TIPS "Quality writing. Query first. Development and full editorial services available."

SIERRA CLUB BOOKS

85 Second St., 2nd Floor, San Francisco CA 94105. (415)977-5500. **Fax:** (415)977-5792. **E-mail:** books.publishing@sierraclub.org. **Website:** www.sierraclub.org/books. Estab. 1962. Publishes hardcover and paperback originals and reprints. "The Sierra Club was founded to help people to explore, enjoy, and preserve the nation's forests, waters, wildlife, and wilderness. The books program publishes quality trade books about the outdoors and the protection of the natural world." **Publishes approximately 15 titles/year. 50% from unagented writers. Pays royalty. Pays $5,000-15,000 average advance.** Publishes ms 1 year after acceptance. Accepts simultaneous submissions. Responds in 1 month to queries; 2 months to proposals; 3 months to mss. Book catalog online. Guidelines online.

NONFICTION Subjects include nature, environment. A broad range of environmental subjects: outdoor adventure, women in the outdoors; literature, including travel and works on the spiritual aspects of the natural world; natural history and current environmental issues. Does not want proposals for large, color-photographic books without substantial text; how-to books on building things outdoors; books on motorized travel; or any but the most professional studies of animals. No fiction or poetry. Query with SASE. Reviews artwork/photos. Send photocopies.

SILMAN-JAMES PRESS

3624 Shannon Rd., Los Angeles CA 90027. (323)661-9922. **Fax:** (323)661-9933. **Website:** www.silmanjamespress.com. Publishes trade paperback originals and reprints. **Pays variable royalty on retail price.** Book catalog available free.

NONFICTION Pertaining to film, theatre, music, performing arts. Submit proposal package, outline, 1+ sample chapters. Will accept phone queries. Reviews artwork/photos. Send photocopies.

TIPS "Our audience ranges from people with a general interest in film (fans, etc.) to students of film and performing arts to industry professionals. We will accept 'query' phone calls."

SILVERFISH REVIEW PRESS

P.O. Box 3541, Eugene OR 97403. (541)344-5060. **E-mail:** sfrpress@earthlink.net. **Website:** www.silverfishreviewpress.com. Estab. 1978. Publishes trade paperback originals. "Sponsors the Gerald Cable Book Award. This prize is awarded annually to a book length manuscript of original poetry by an author who has not yet published a full-length collection. There are no restrictions on the kind of poetry or subject matter; translations are not acceptable. Winners will receive $1,000, publication, and 25 copies of the book. Entries must be postmarked by October 15. Entries may be submitted by e-mail. See website for instructions." **Publishes 2-3 titles/year. 50% of books from first-time authors. 100% from unagented writers.** Guidelines online.

TIPS "Read recent Silverfish titles."

SILVER LAKE PUBLISHING

P.O. Box 173, Aberdeen WA 98520. (360)532-5758. **Fax:** (360)532-5728. **E-mail:** publisher@silverlakepub.com. **Website:** www.silverlakepub.com. Estab. 1998. Publishes hardcover and trade paperback originals and reprints. **Pays royalty.** Accepts simultaneous submissions. Responds in 6-8 weeks to proposals. Book catalog available free. Guidelines available free.

NONFICTION Subjects include business, economics, money, finance. No fiction or poetry. Submit outline, resume, 2 sample chapters, cover letter, synopsis. Submit via mail only.

Ⓐ⊘ SIMON & SCHUSTER

1230 Avenue of the Americas, New York NY 10020. (212)698-7000. **Website:** www.simonandschuster.com. *Accepts agented submissions only.*

IMPRINTS Aladdin; Atheneum Books for Young Readers; Atria; Beach Lane Books; Folger Shakespeare Library; Free Press; Gallery Books; Howard Books; Little Simon; Margaret K. McElderry Books; Pocket; Scribner; Simon & Schuster; Simon & Schuster Books for Young Readers; Simon Pulse; Simon Spotlight; Threshold; Touchstone; Paula Wiseman Books.

Ⓐ⊘ SIMON & SCHUSTER BOOKS FOR YOUNG READERS

Imprint of Simon & Schuster Children's Publishing, 1230 Avenue of the Americas, New York NY 10020. (212)698-7000. **Fax:** (212)698-2796. **Website:** www.simonsayskids.com. Publishes hardcover originals. "Simon and Schuster Books For Young Readers is the Flagship imprint of the S&S Children's Division. We are committed to publishing a wide range of contemporary, commercial, award-winning fiction and nonfiction that spans every age of children's publishing. BFYR is constantly looking to the future, supporting our foundation authors and franchises, but always with an eye for breaking new ground with every publication. We publish high-quality fiction and nonfiction for a variety of age groups and a variety of markets. Above all, we strive to publish books that we are passionate about." *No unsolicited mss.* All unsolicited mss returned unopened. **Publishes 75 titles/year. Pays variable royalty on retail price.** Publishes ms 2-4 years after acceptance. Accepts simultaneous submissions. Guidelines online.

NONFICTION Subjects include history, nature, environment, biography. Picture books: concept. All levels: narrative, current events, biography, history. "We're looking for picture books or middle grade nonfiction that have a retail potential. No photo essays." *Agented submissions only.*

FICTION Subjects include fantasy, historical, humor, juvenile, mystery, picture books, science fiction, young adult, adventure, historical, mystery, contemporary fiction. *Agented submissions only.*

TIPS "We're looking for picture books centered on a strong, fully-developed protagonist who grows or changes during the course of the story; YA novels that are challenging and psychologically complex; also imaginative and humorous middle-grade fiction. And we want nonfiction that is as engaging as fiction. Our imprint's slogan is 'Reading You'll Remember.' We aim to publish books that are fresh, accessible and family-oriented; we want them to have an impact on the reader."

SKINNER HOUSE BOOKS

The Unitarian Universalist Association, 24 Farnsworth St., Boston MA 02210. (617)742-2100 ext. 603. **Fax:** (617)948-6466. **E-mail:** bookproposals@uua.org. **Website:** www.uua.org/publications/skinnerhouse. **Contact:** Betsy Martin. Estab. 1975. Publishes trade paperback originals and reprints. "We publish titles in Unitarian Universalist faith, liberal religion, history, biography, worship, and issues of social justice. Most of our children's titles are intended for religious education or worship use. They reflect Unitarian Universalist values. We also publish inspirational titles of poetic prose and meditations. Writers should know that Unitarian Universalism is a liberal religious denomination committed to progressive ideals. Currently emphasizing social justice concerns." **Publishes 10-20 titles/year. 30% of books from first-time authors. 100% from unagented writers.** Publishes ms 1 year after acceptance. Accepts simultaneous submissions. Responds to queries in 1 month. Book catalog for 6×9 SAE with 3 first-class stamps. Guidelines online.

NONFICTION Subjects include gay, lesbian, memoirs, religion, women's issues, women's studies, inspirational, church leadership. All levels: activity books, multicultural, music/dance, nature/environment, religion. Query or submit proposal with cover letter, TOC, 2 sample chapters. Reviews artwork/photos. Send photocopies.

FICTION Only publishes fiction for children's titles for religious instruction. Query.

TIPS "From outside our denomination, we are interested in manuscripts that will be of help or interest to liberal churches, Sunday School classes, parents, ministers, and volunteers. Inspirational/spiritual and children's titles must reflect liberal Unitarian Universalist values."

Ⓐ⊘ LIZZIE SKURNICK BOOKS

Ig Publishing, 392 Clinton Ave., Brooklyn NY 11238. (718)797-0676. **Website:** lizzieskurnickbooks.com. Estab. 2013. Lizzie Skurnick Books, an imprint of Ig Publishing, is devoted to reissuing the very best in young adult literature, from the classics of the 1930s and 1940s to the social novels of the 1970s and 1980s. Ig does not accept unsolicited mss, either by e-mail or regular mail. If you have a ms that you would like Ig to take a look at, send a query throught online contact form. If interested, they will contact. All unsolicited mss will be discarded. Accepts simultaneous submissions.

SLACK, INC.

6900 Grove Rd., Thorofare NJ 08086. (856)848-1000. **Fax:** (856)853-5991. **E-mail:** editor@healio.com. **Website:** www.healio.com. Estab. 1960. Publishes hardcover and paperback originals. SLACK INC. publishes academic textbooks and professional reference books on various medical topics in an expedient manner. **Publishes 35 titles/year. 80 queries received/year. 23 mss received/year. 75% of books from first-time authors. 100% from unagented writers. Pays 10% royalty. Pays advance.** Publishes ms 8 months after acceptance. Accepts simultaneous submissions. Responds in 1 month to queries/proposals; 3 months to mss. Book catalog and ms guidelines free.

NONFICTION Subjects include health, medicine, ophthalmology. Submit proposal package, outline, 2 sample chapters, market profile and CV. Reviews artwork/photos. Send photocopies.

SLEEPING BEAR PRESS

315 E. Eisenhower Pkwy., Suite 200, Ann Arbor MI 48108. (800)487-2323. **Fax:** (734)794-0004. **E-mail:** submissions@sleepingbearpress.com. **Website:** www.sleepingbearpress.com. **Contact:** Manuscript Submissions. Estab. 1998. Book catalog available via e-mail.

FICTION Picture books: adventure, animal, concept, folktales, history, multicultural, nature/environment, religion, sports. Young readers: adventure, animal, concept, folktales, history, humor, multicultural, nature/environment, religion, sports. Average word length: picture books—1,800. Query with sample of work (up to 15 pages) and SASE.

SMALL BEER PRESS

150 Pleasant St., #306, Easthampton MA 01027. (413)203-1636. **Fax:** (413)203-1636. **E-mail:** info@smallbeerpress.com. **Website:** www.smallbeerpress.com. Estab. 2000. Small Beer Press also publishes the zine *Lady Churchill's Rosebud Wristlet*. "SBP's books have recently received the Tiptree and Crawford Awards." **Publishes 6-10 titles/year.**

FICTION Subjects include experimental, literary, short story collections, speculative. Does not accept unsolicited novel or short story collection mss. Send queries with first 10-20 pages and SASE.

TIPS "Please be familiar with our books first to avoid wasting your time and ours, thank you. E-mail queries will be deleted. Really."

GIBBS SMITH, PUBLISHER

P.O. Box 667, Layton UT 84041. (801)544-9800. **Fax:** (801)546-8853. **E-mail:** duribe@gibbs-smith.com. **Website:** www.gibbs-smith.com. Estab. 1969. Publishes hardcover and trade paperback originals. "We publish books that enrich and inspire humankind. Currently emphasizing interior decorating and design, home reference. De-emphasizing novels and short stories." **Publishes 80 titles/year. 3,000-4,000 queries received/year. 50% of books from first-time authors. 75% from unagented writers. Pays 8-14% royalty on gross receipts. Offers advance based on first year saleability projections.** Publishes ms 1-2 years after acceptance. Accepts simultaneous submissions. Responds in 1 month to queries; 10 weeks to proposals and mss. Guidelines online.

NONFICTION Subjects include art, architecture, nature, environment, regional, interior design, cooking, business, western, outdoor/sports/recreation. Query by e-mail only.

SMITH AND KRAUS PUBLISHERS, INC.

177 Lyme Rd., Hanover NH 03755. **E-mail:** editor@smithandkraus.com. **Website:** smithandkraus.com. Estab. 1990. Publishes hardcover and trade paperback originals. **Publishes 35-40 titles/year. 10% of books from first-time authors. 10-20% from unagented writers. Pays 7% royalty on retail price. Pays $500-2,000 advance.** Publishes ms 1 year after acceptance. Responds in 1 month to queries; 2 months to proposals; 4 months to mss. Book catalog available free.

NONFICTION Subjects include film, cinema, stage, drama. Does not return submissions. Query with SASE.

FICTION Does not return submissions. Query with SASE.

SOFT SKULL PRESS INC.

Counterpoint, 2650 Ninth St., Suite 318, Berkeley CA 94710. (510)704-0230. **Fax:** (510)704-0268. **E-mail:** info@softskull.com. **Website:** www.softskull.com. Publishes hardcover and trade paperback originals. "Here at Soft Skull we love books that are new, fun, smart, revelatory, quirky, groundbreaking, cage-rattling and/or/otherwise unusual." **Publishes 40 titles/year. Pays 7-10% royalty. Average advance: $100-15,000.** Publishes ms 6 months after acceptance. Responds in 2 months to proposals; 3 months to mss. Book catalog and guidelines online.

NONFICTION Subjects include contemporary culture, creative nonfiction, entertainment, literature, pop culture. Send a cover letter describing your project and a full proposal along with 2 sample chapters.

FICTION Subjects include comic books, confession, contemporary, erotica, experimental, gay, lesbian, literary, mainstream, multicultural, short story collections. Does not consider poetry. Soft Skull Press no longer accepts digital submissions. Send a cover letter describing your project in detail and a completed ms. For graphic novels, send a minimum of five fully inked pages of art, along with a synopsis of your storyline. "Please do not send original material, as it will not be returned."

TIPS "See our website for updated submission guidelines."

SOHO PRESS, INC.

853 Broadway, New York NY 10003. **E-mail:** soho@sohopress.com. **Website:** www.sohopress.com. **Contact:** Bronwen Hruska, publisher; Mark Doten, editor. Estab. 1986. Publishes hardcover and trade paperback originals; trade paperback reprints. Soho Press publishes primarily fiction, as well as some narrative literary nonfiction and mysteries set abroad. No electronic submissions, only queries by e-mail. **Publishes 60-70 titles/year. 15-25% of books from first-time authors. 10% from unagented writers. Pays 10-15% royalty on retail price (varies under certain circumstances).** Publishes ms 18 months after acceptance. Accepts simultaneous submissions. Responds in 3 months. Guidelines online.

NONFICTION Subjects include creative nonfiction, ethnic, memoirs. "Independent publisher known for sophisticated fiction, mysteries set abroad, women's interest (no genre) novels and multicultural novels." Publishes hardcover and trade paperback originals and reprint editions. Books: perfect binding; halftone illustrations. First novel print order varies. We do not buy books on proposal. We always need to see a complete ms before we buy a book, though we prefer an initial submission of 3 sample chapters. We do not publish books with color art or photographs or a lot of graphical material." No self-help, how-to, or cookbooks. Submit 3 sample chapters and a cover letter with a synopsis and author bio; SASE. Send photocopies.

FICTION Subjects include ethnic, historical, humor, literary, mystery, In mysteries, we only publish series with foreign or exotic settings, usually procedurals. Adventure, ethnic, feminist, historical, literary, mainstream/contemporary, mystery (police procedural), suspense, multicultural. Submit 3 sample chapters and cover letter with synopsis, author bio, SASE. *No e-mailed submissions.*

TIPS "Soho Press publishes discerning authors for discriminating readers, finding the strongest possible writers and publishing them. Before submitting, look at our website for an idea of the types of books we publish, and read our submission guidelines."

SOURCEBOOKS, INC.

1935 Brookdale Rd., Suite 139, Naperville IL 60563. (630)961-3900. **Fax:** (630)961-2168. **E-mail:** editorialsubmissions@sourcebooks.com. **Website:** www.sourcebooks.com. Estab. 1987. Publishes hardcover and trade paperback originals. "Sourcebooks publishes many forms of fiction and nonfiction titles, including books on parenting, self-help/psychology, business, and health. Focus is on practical, useful information and skills. It also continues to publish in the reference, New Age, history, current affairs, and humor categories. Currently emphasizing gift, women's interest, history, reference, historical fiction, romance genre, and children's." **Publishes 300 titles/year. 30% of books from first-time authors. 25% from unagented writers. Pays royalty on wholesale or list price. Pays advance.** Publishes ms 1 year after acceptance. Accepts simultaneous submissions. Responds in 3 months to queries. Book catalog online. Guidelines online.

NONFICTION Subjects include biography, gift book, how-to, illustrated book, multimedia, reference, self-help, business, economics, child guidance, history, military, war, money, finance, psychology, science, sports, women's issues, women's studies, contemporary culture. Books for small business owners, entrepreneurs, and students. A key to submitting books to us is to explain how your book helps the reader, why it is different from the books already out there (please do your homework), and the author's credentials for writing this book. Books likely to succeed with us are self-help, parenting and childcare, psychology, women's issues, how-to, history, reference, biography, humor, gift books, or books with strong artwork. "We seek unique books on traditional subjects and authors who are smart and aggressive." Query with SASE, 2-3 sample chapters (not the first). *No complete mss.* Reviews artwork/photos.

TIPS "Our market is a decidedly trade-oriented bookstore audience. We also have very strong penetration into the gift-store market. Books which cross over between these 2 very different markets do extremely well with us. Our list is a solid mix of unique and general audience titles and series-oriented projects. We are looking for products that break new ground either in their own areas or within the framework of our series of imprints."

SOURCEBOOKS CASABLANCA

Sourcebooks, Inc., 232 Madison Ave., Suite 1100, New York NY 10016. **E-mail:** romance@sourcebooks.com. **Website:** www.sourcebooks.com. **Contact:** Deb Werksman. "Our romance imprint, Sourcebooks Casablanca, publishes single title romance in all subgenres." Responds in 2-3 months. Guidelines online.

FICTION "Our editorial criteria call for: a heroine the reader can relate to, a hero she can fall in love with, a world gets created that the reader can escape into, there's a hook that we can sell within 2-3 sentences, and the author is out to build a career with us."

TIPS "We are actively acquiring single-title and single-title series romance fiction (90,000-100,000 words) for our Casablanca imprint. We are looking for strong writers who are excited about marketing their books and building their community of readers, and whose books have something fresh to offer in the genre of romance."

SOURCEBOOKS LANDMARK

Sourcebooks, Inc., 232 Madison Ave., Suite 1100, New York NY 10016. **E-mail:** editorialsubmissions@sourcebooks.com. **Website:** www.sourcebooks.com. **Contact:** Shana Drehs, Stephanie Bowen, Deb Werksman, Anna Klenke. "Our fiction imprint, Sourcebooks Landmark, publishes a variety of commercial fiction, including specialties in historical fiction and Austenalia. We are interested first and foremost in books that have a story to tell." Responds in 2-3 months.

FICTION "We are actively acquiring contemporary, book club, and historical fiction for our Landmark imprint. We are looking for strong writers who are excited about marketing their books and building their community of readers." Submit synopsis and full ms preferred. Receipt of e-mail submissions acknowledged within 3 weeks of e-mail.

SOUTHERN ILLINOIS UNIVERSITY PRESS

1915 University Press Dr., SIUC Mail Code 6806, Carbondale IL 62901. (618)453-6626. **Fax:** (618)453-1221. **E-mail:** kageff@siu.edu. **Website:** www.siupress.com. **Contact:** Karl Kageff, editor-in-chief. Estab. 1956. Publishes hardcover and trade paperback originals and reprints. Scholarly press specializes in film and theater studies, rhetoric and composition studies, American history, Civil War, regional and nonfiction trade, poetry. No fiction. Currently emphasizing film, theater and American history, especially Civil War. **Publishes 50-60 titles/year. 700 queries received/year. 300 mss received/year. 40% of books from first-time authors. 99% from unagented writers. Pays 5-10% royalty on wholesale price. Rarely offers advance.** Publishes ms 1 year after acceptance. Responds in 2 months to queries. Book catalog and ms guidelines free.

POETRY Crab Orchard Series in Poetry. Guidelines online.

SPINNER BOOKS

University Games, 2030 Harrison St., San Francisco CA 94110. (415)503-1600. **Fax:** (415)503-0085. **E-mail:** info@ugames.com. **Website:** www.ugames.com. Estab. 1985. "Spinners Books publishes books of puzzles, games and trivia." Publishes ms 6 months after acceptance. Responds to queries in 3 months; mss in 2 months only if interested.

NONFICTION Picture books: games and puzzles. Query.

SQUARE ONE PUBLISHERS, INC.

115 Herricks Rd., Garden City Park NY 11040. (516)535-2010. **Fax:** (516)535-2014. **E-mail:** sq1publish@aol.com. **Website:** www.squareonepublishers.com. **Contact:** Acquisitions Editor. Publishes trade paperback originals. **Publishes 20 titles/year. 500 queries received/year. 100 mss received/year. 95% of books from first-time authors. 95% from unagented writers. Pays 10-15% royalty on wholesale price. Pays variable advance.** Publishes ms 10 months after acceptance. Accepts simultaneous submissions. Responds in 1 month. Book catalog and ms guidelines online.

NONFICTION Subjects include business, economics, child guidance, health, medicine, hobbies, money, finance, nature, environment, psychology, religion, spirituality, sports, travel, writers' guides, cooking/foods, gaming/gambling. Query with SASE. Submit proposal package, outline, bio, introduction, synopsis, SASE. Reviews artwork/photos. Send photocopies.

TIPS "We focus on making our books accessible, accurate, and interesting. They are written for people who are looking for the best place to start, and who don't appreciate the terms 'dummy,' 'idiot,' or 'fool,' on the cover of their books. We look for smartly written, informative books that have a strong point of view, and that are authored by people who know their subjects well."

STACKPOLE BOOKS

5067 Ritter Rd., Mechanicsburg PA 17055. **Fax:** (717)796-0412. **E-mail:** jschnell@stackpolebooks.com. **E-mail:** dreisch@stackpolebooks.com; mallison@stackpolebooks.com; jnichols@stackpolebooks.com. **Website:** www.stackpolebooks.com. **Contact:** Judith Schnell, editorial director (outdoor sports); Mark Allison, editor (nature); David Reisch, editor (regional/Pennsylvania); Jay Nichols, editor (fly fishing). Estab. 1935. Publishes hardcover and trade paperback originals, reprints, and e-books. "Stackpole maintains a growing and vital publishing program by featuring authors who are experts in their fields." **Publishes 100 titles/year. Pays industry standard advance.** Publishes ms 1 year after acceptance. Responds in 1 month to queries. Catalog and guidelines online.

NONFICTION Subjects include history, military, outdoor sports. "First of all, send your query to an individual editor. The more information you can supply, the better." Reviews artwork/photos.

TIPS "Stackpole seeks well-written, authoritative mss for specialized and general trade markets. Proposals should include chapter outline, sample chapter, illustrations, and author's credentials."

STANDARD PUBLISHING

Standex International Corp., 8805 Governor's Hill Dr., Suite 400, Cincinnati OH 45249. (800)543-1353. **E-mail:** customerservice@standardpub.com. **Website:** www.standardpub.com. Estab. 1866. Publishes resources that meet church and family needs in the area of children's ministry. Guidelines online.

STANFORD UNIVERSITY PRESS

425 Broadway St., Redwood City CA 94063. (650)723-9434. **Fax:** (650)725-3457. **E-mail:** kwahl@stanford.

edu. **Website:** www.sup.org. **Contact:** Eric Brandt (Asian studies, US foreign policy, Asian-American studies); Kate Wahl (law, political science, public policy); Margo Beth Fleming (economics, finance, business). Estab. 1925. "Stanford University Press publishes scholarly books in the humanities and social sciences, along with professional books in business, economics and management science; also high-level textbooks and some books for a more general audience." *Submit to specific editor.* **Pays variable royalty (sometimes none). Pays occasional advance.** Guidelines online.

NONFICTION Subjects include anthropology, archeology, business, economics, ethnic, studies, gay, lesbian, government, politics, history, humanities, language, literature, literary criticism, and literary theory, nature, environment, philosophy, psychology, religion, science, social sciences, sociology, political science, law, education, history and culture of China, Japan and Latin America, European history, linguistics, geology, medieval and classical studies. Query with prospectus and an outline. Reviews artwork/photos.

TIPS "The writer's best chance is a work of original scholarship with an argument of some importance."

STARCHERONE BOOKS

P.O. Box 303, Buffalo NY 14201. (716)885-2726. **E-mail:** starcheroneacquisitions@gmail.com. **Website:** www.starcherone.com. **Contact:** Ed Taylor, managing editor. Estab. 2000. Non-profit publisher of literary and experimental fiction. Publishes paperback originals and reprints. Submission period at specific time each year. Check website for updates. **Pays 10-12.5% royalty.** Publishes ms 18 months after acceptance. Responds in 2 months to queries; 6-10 months to mss. Catalog and guidelines online.

STC CRAFT

Imprint of Abrams, 115 W. 18th St., New York NY 10011. **E-mail:** stccraft@abramsbooks.com. **Website:** www.abramsbooks.com. **Contact:** STC Craft Editorial. Publishes a vibrant collection of exciting and visually stunning craft books specializing in knitting, sewing, quilting, felting and other popular craft genres. Accepts simultaneous submissions. Guidelines online.

NONFICTION Subjects include crafts. Please submit via e-mail.

STEEL TOE BOOKS

Department of English, Western Kentucky University, 1906 College Heights Blvd. #11086, Bowling Green KY 42101. (270)745-5769. **E-mail:** tom.hunley@wku.edu. **Website:** www.steeltoebooks.com. **Contact:** Dr. Tom C. Hunley, director. Estab. 2003. Steel Toe Books publishes "full-length, single-author poetry collections. Our books are professionally designed and printed. We look for workmanship (economical use of language, high-energy verbs, precise literal descriptions, original figurative language, poems carefully arranged as a book); a unique style and/or a distinctive voice; clarity; emotional impact; humor (word plays, hyperbole, comic timing); performability (a Steel Toe poet is at home on the stage as well as on the page)." Does not want "dry verse, purposely obscure language, poetry by people who are so wary of being called 'sentimental' they steer away from any recognizable human emotions, poetry that takes itself so seriously that it's unintentionally funny." Has published poetry by Allison Joseph, Susan Browne, James Doyle, Martha Silano, Mary Biddinger, John Guzlowski, Jeannine Hall Gailey, and others. Publishes 1-3 poetry books/year. Mss are normally selected through open submission.

POETRY "Check the website for news about our next open reading period." Book mss may include previously published poems. Responds to mss in 3 months. Pays $500 advance on 10% royalties and 10 author's copies. Order sample books by sending $12 to Steel Toe Books. *Must purchase a manuscript in order to submit.* See website for submission guidelines.

STENHOUSE PUBLISHERS

480 Congress St., Floor 2, Portland ME 04101. **E-mail:** editors@stenhouse.com. **Website:** www.stenhouse.com. **Contact:** Philippa Stratton, editorial director. Estab. 1993. Publishes paperback originals. Stenhouse publishes exclusively professional books for teachers, K-12. **Publishes 15 titles/year. 300 queries received/year. 30% of books from first-time authors. 99% from unagented writers. Pays royalty on wholesale price.** Accepts simultaneous submissions. Responds in 2 weeks to queries; 1 month to mss. Book catalog free or online. Guidelines online.

NONFICTION Subjects include education, specializing in literary with offerings in elementary and middle level math and science. All of our books are a combination of theory and practice. No children's books or student texts. Query by e-mail (preferred) or SASE. Reviews artwork/photos. Send photocopies.

STERLING PUBLISHING CO., INC.

1166 Avenue of the Americas, 17th Floor, New York NY 10036. (212)532-7160. **Fax:** (212)981-0508. **Website:** www.sterlingpublishing.com. Publishes hardcover and paperback originals and reprints. "Sterling publishes highly illustrated, accessible, hands-on, practical books for adults and children. Our mission is to publish high-quality books that educate, entertain, and enrich the lives of our readers." **15% of books from first-time authors. Pays royalty or work purchased outright. Offers advances (average amount: $2,000).** Accepts simultaneous submissions. Catalog online. Guidelines online.

NONFICTION Subjects include alternative, animals, art, architecture, ethnic, gardening, health, medicine, hobbies, New Age, recreation, science, sports, fiber arts, games and puzzles, children's humor, children's science, nature and activities, pets, wine, home decorating, dolls and puppets, ghosts, UFOs, woodworking, crafts, medieval, Celtic subjects, alternative health and healing, new consciousness. Proposals on subjects such as crafting, decorating, outdoor living, and photography should be sent directly to Lark Books at their Asheville, North Carolina offices. Complete guidelines can be found on the Lark site: www.larkbooks.com/submissions. Publishes nonfiction only. Submit outline, publishing history, 1 sample chapter (typed and double-spaced), SASE. "Explain your idea. Send sample illustrations where applicable. For children's books, please submit full mss. We do not accept electronic (e-mail) submissions. Be sure to include information about yourself with particular regard to your skills and qualifications in the subject area of your submission. It is helpful for us to know your publishing history—whether or not you've written other books and, if so, the name of the publisher and whether those books are currently in print." Reviews artwork/photocopies.

FICTION Publishes fiction for children. Submit to attention of "Children's Book Editor."

TIPS "We are primarily a nonfiction activities-based publisher. We have a picture book list, but we do not publish chapter books or novels. Our list is not trend-driven. We focus on titles that will backlist well. "

STIPES PUBLISHING LLC

P.O. Box 526, Champaign IL 61824. (217)356-8391. **Fax:** (217)356-5753. **E-mail:** stipes01@sbcglobal.net. **Website:** www.stipes.com. **Contact:** Benjamin H. Watts, (engineering, science, business); Robert Watts (agriculture, music, and physical education). Estab. 1925. Publishes hardcover and paperback originals. "Stipes Publishing is oriented towards the education market and educational books with some emphasis in the trade market." **Publishes 15-30 titles/year. 50% of books from first-time authors. 95% from unagented writers. Pays 15% maximum royalty on retail price.** Publishes ms 4 months after acceptance. Responds in 2 months to queries. Guidelines online.

NONFICTION Subjects include agriculture, business, economics, music, dance, nature, environment, recreation, science. "All of our books in the trade area are books that also have a college text market. No books unrelated to educational fields taught at the college level." Submit outline, 1 sample chapter.

STONE ARCH BOOKS

1710 Roe Crest Rd., North Mankato MN 56003. **E-mail:** author.sub@capstonepub.com. **Website:** www.stonearchbooks.com. **Work purchased outright from authors.** Catalog online.

FICTION Young readers, middle readers, young adults: adventure, contemporary, fantasy, humor, light humor, mystery, science fiction, sports, suspense. Average word length: young readers—1,000-3,000; middle readers and early young adults—5,000-10,000. Submit outline/synopsis and 3 sample chapters. Electronic submissions preferred.

TIPS "A high-interest topic or activity is one that a young person would spend their free time on without adult direction or suggestion."

STONE BRIDGE PRESS

P.O. Box 8208, Berkeley CA 94707. **E-mail:** sbp@stonebridge.com. **Website:** www.stonebridge.com. **Contact:** Peter Goodman, publisher. Estab. 1989. "Independent press focusing on books about Japan and Asia in English (business, language, culture, literature, animation)." Publishes hardcover and trade paperback originals. Books: 60-70 lb. offset paper; web and sheet paper; perfect bound; some illustrations. Distributes titles through Consortium. Promotes titles through Internet announcements, special-interest magazines and niche tie-ins to associations. **Publishes 12 titles/year. 75% from unagented writers. Pays**

royalty on wholesale price. Publishes ms 2 years after acceptance. Responds to queries in 4 months; mss in 8 months. Book catalog for 2 first-class stamps and SASE. Ms guidelines online.

FICTION Experimental, gay/lesbian, literary, Japan-themed. "Primarily looking at material relating to Japan. Translations only." Does not accept unsolicited mss. Query with SASE. Accepts queries by e -mail, fax.

TIPS "Fiction translations only for the time being. No poetry."

STONESLIDE BOOKS

Stoneslide Media LLC, P.O. Box 8331, New Haven CT 06530. **E-mail:** editors@stoneslidecorrective.com. **E-mail:** submissions@stoneslidecorrective.com. **Website:** www.stoneslidecorrective.com. **Contact:** Jonathan Weisberg, editor; Christopher Wachlin, editor. Estab. 2012. Publishes trade paperback and electronic originals. **Publishes 3-5 titles/year. Receives 300 queries/year; 150 mss/year. Pays 20-80% royalty.** Publishes ms 8 months after acceptance. Responds in 1-2 months. Book catalog and guidelines online.

FICTION Subjects include adventure, contemporary, experimental, fantasy, gothic, historical, humor, literary, mainstream, mystery, science fiction, short story collections, suspense. "We will look at any genre. The important factor for us is that the story use plot, characters, emotions, and other elements of storytelling to think and move the mind forward." Submit proposal package via online submission form including: synopsis and 3 sample chapters.

TIPS "Read the Stoneslide Corrective to see if your work fits with our approach."

STOREY PUBLISHING

210 MASS MoCA Way, North Adams MA 01247. (800)793-9396. **Fax:** (413)346-2196. **E-mail:** feedback@storey.com. **Website:** www.storey.com. **Contact:** Deborah Balmuth, editorial director (building and mind/body/spirit). Estab. 1983. Publishes hardcover and trade paperback originals and reprints. "The mission of Storey Publishing is to serve our customers by publishing practical information that encourages personal independence in harmony with the environment. We seek to do this in a positive atmosphere that promotes editorial quality, team spirit, and profitability. The books we select to carry out this mission include titles on gardening, small-scale farming, building, cooking, homebrewing, crafts, part-time business, home improvement, woodworking, animals, nature, natural living, personal care, and country living. We are always pleased to review new proposals, which we try to process expeditiously. We offer both work-for-hire and standard royalty contracts." **Publishes 40 titles/year. 600 queries received/year. 150 mss received/year. 25% of books from first-time authors. 60% from unagented writers. We offer both work-for-hire and standard royalty contracts. Pays advance.** Publishes ms 2 years after acceptance. Accepts simultaneous submissions. Responds in 1-3 months. Book catalog available free. Guidelines online.

NONFICTION Subjects include animals, gardening, nature, environment, home, mind/body/spirit, birds, beer and wine, crafts, building, cooking. Submit a proposal. Reviews artwork/photos.

STRATEGIC MEDIA BOOKS

782 Wofford St., Rock Hill SC 29730. (803)366-5440. **E-mail:** contact@strategicmediabooks.com. **Website:** strategicmediabooks.com. **Contact:** Ron Chepesiuk, president. Estab. 2010. Publishes hardcover, trade paperback, and electronic originals. "Strategic Media Books, LLC is an independent U.S. publisher that aims to bring extraordinary true-life stories to the widest possible audience. Founded in 2010, Strategic Media Books intends to be one of the most energetic and hard-hitting nonfiction publishers in the business. While we currently specialize in crime, we plan to expand and publish great books in any nonfiction genre." **Publishes 16-20 titles/year. 100 queries received/year. 30-35 mss received/year. 20% of books from first-time authors. 85% from unagented writers. Authors receive 15-20% royalty on retail price.** Publishes ms 9 months after acceptance. Accepts simultaneous submissions. Responds in 1-2 months. Catalog online. Guidelines via e-mail.

NONFICTION Subjects include Americana, contemporary culture, environment, ethnic, government, history, memoirs, military, multicultural, nature, politics, regional, war, world affairs, crime. Planning to increase the number of books for the 2014 and 2015 seasons. Query with SASE. Will review artwork. Writers should send photocopies.

FICTION Subjects include mystery, suspense. "We are very selective in our publication of fiction. If writers want to submit, make sure mss fits the mystery or suspense genres." Query with SASE.

STYLUS PUBLISHING, LLC

22883 Quicksilver Dr., Sterling VA 20166. **E-mail:** stylusinfo@styluspub.com. **Website:** styluspub.com. Estab. 1996. Publishes hardcover and trade paperback originals. "We publish in higher education (diversity, professional development, distance education, teaching, administration)." **Publishes 10-15 titles/year. 50 queries received/year. 6 mss received/year. 50% of books from first-time authors. 100% from unagented writers. Pays 5-10% royalty on wholesale price. Pays advance.** Publishes ms 6 months after acceptance. Responds in 1 month to queries. Book catalog available free. Guidelines online.

NONFICTION Query or submit outline, 1 sample chapter with SASE. Reviews artwork/photos. Send photocopies.

SUBITO PRESS

University of Colorado at Boulder, Dept. of English, 226 UCB, Boulder CO 80309-0226. **E-mail:** subitopressucb@gmail.com. **Website:** www.subitopress.org. Publishes trade paperback originals. Subito Press is a non-profit publisher of literary works. Each year Subito publishes one work of fiction and one work of poetry through its contest. Accepts simultaneous submissions. Guidelines online.

FICTION Subjects include experimental, literary, translation. Submit complete ms to contest.

POETRY Submit complete ms to contest.

TIPS "We publish 2 books of innovative writing a year through our poetry and fiction contests. All entries are also considered for publication with the press."

SUN BOOKS / SUN PUBLISHING

P.O. Box 5588, Santa Fe NM 87502. (505)471-5177. **E-mail:** info@sunbooks.com. **Website:** www.sunbooks.com. **Contact:** Skip Whitson, director. Estab. 1973. Publishes trade paperback originals and reprints. **Publishes 10-15 titles/year. 5% of books from first-time authors. 90% from unagented writers. Pays 5% royalty on retail price. Occasionally makes outright purchase.** Publishes ms 16-18 months after acceptance. "Will respond within 2 months, via e-mail, to queries if interested.". Book catalog online. Queries via e-mail only, please.

NONFICTION , self-help, leadership, motivational, recovery, inspirational.

SUNBURY PRESS, INC.

P.O. Box 548, Boiling Springs PA 17007. **E-mail:** info@sunburypress.com. **E-mail:** proposals@sunburypress.com. **Website:** www.sunburypress.com. Estab. 2004. Publishes trade paperback originals and reprints; electronic originals and reprints. "Please use our online submission form." **Publishes 75 titles/year. 750 queries/year; 500 mss/year. 40% of books from first-time authors. 90% from unagented writers. Pays 10% royalty on wholesale price.** Publishes ms 3 months after acceptance. Accepts simultaneous submissions. Responds in 2 months. Catalog and guidelines online.

NONFICTION Subjects include Americana, animals, anthropology, archeology, architecture, art, astrology, business, career guidance, child guidance, communications, computers, contemporary culture, counseling, crafts, creative nonfiction, dance, economics, education, electronics, entertainment, ethnic, government, health, history, hobbies, house and home, humanities, language, literature, memoirs, military, money, multicultural, music, nature, New Age, photography, regional, religion, science, sex, spirituality, sports, transportation, travel, war, world affairs, young adult. "We are currently seeking Civil War era memoirs and unpublished or new material regarding the Civil War. We are also seeking biographies / histories of local/regional figures who were noteworthy but unpublished or sparsely published." Reviews artwork.

FICTION Subjects include adventure, confession, contemporary, ethnic, experimental, fantasy, gothic, historical, horror, humor, juvenile, mainstream, military, multicultural, mystery, occult, picture books, poetry, regional, religious, romance, science fiction, short story collections, spiritual, sports, suspense, western, young adult. "We are especially seeking historical fiction regarding the Civil War and books of regional interest."

POETRY Submit complete ms.

TIPS "Our books appeal to very diverse audiences. We are building our list in many categories, focusing on many demographics. We are not like traditional publishers—we are digitally adept and very creative. Don't be surprised if we move quicker than you are accustomed to!"

SUNRISE RIVER PRESS

39966 Grand Ave., North Branch MN 55056. (800)895-4585. **Fax:** (651)277-1203. **E-mail:** editorial@sunriseriverpress.com. **Website:** www.sunriseriverpress.com. Estab. 1992. "E-mail is preferred method of contact." **Publishes 30 titles/year. Pays advance.** Accepts simultaneous submissions. Guidelines online.

Sunrise River Press is part of a 3-company publishing house that also includes CarTech Books and Specialty Press. "Sunrise River Press is currently seeking book proposals from health/medical writers or experts who are interested in authoring consumer-geared trade paperbacks on healthcare, fitness, and nutrition topics."

NONFICTION Subjects include cooking, foods, nutrition, health, medicine, genetics, immune system maintenance, fitness; also some professional healthcare titles. Check website for submission guidelines. No phone calls, please; no originals.

SUPERCOLLEGE

2713 Newlands Ave., Belmont CA 94002. Phone/**Fax:** (650)618-2221. **E-mail:** supercollege@supercollege.com. **Website:** www.supercollege.com. Estab. 1998. Publishes trade paperback originals. "We only publish books on admission, financial aid, scholarships, test preparation, student life, and career preparation for college and graduate students." **Publishes 8-10 titles/year. 50% of books from first-time authors. 70% from unagented writers. Pays royalty on wholesale price or makes outright purchase.** Publishes ms 7-9 months after acceptance. Book catalog and writers guidelines online.

NONFICTION Subjects include education, admissions, financial aid, scholarships, test prep, student life, career prep. Submit complete ms. Reviews artwork/photos. Send photocopies.

TIPS "We want titles that are student and parent friendly, and that are different from other titles in this category. We also seek authors who want to work with a small but dynamic and ambitious publishing company."

SWAN ISLE PRESS

P.O. Box 408790, Chicago IL 60640. (773)728-3780. **E-mail:** info@swanislepress.com. **Website:** www.swanislepress.com. Estab. 1999. Publishes hardcover and trade paperback originals. *"We do not accept unsolicited mss."* **Publishes 3 titles/year. 1,500 queries received/year. Pays 7-10% royalty on wholesale price.** Publishes ms 18 months after acceptance. Responds in 6-12 months. Book catalog online. Guidelines online.

NONFICTION Subjects include art, architecture, creative nonfiction, ethnic, history, humanities, language, literature, literary criticism, memoirs, multicultural, translation. Query with SASE.

FICTION Subjects include ethnic, historical, literary, multicultural, poetry, poetry in translation, short story collections, translation. Query with SASE.

POETRY Query with SASE.

SWAN SCYTHE PRESS

1468 Mallard Way, Sunnyvale CA 94087. **E-mail:** robert.pesich@gmail.com. **Website:** www.swanscythe.com. **Contact:** Robert Pesich, editor. Estab. 1999.

POETRY "After publishing 25 chapbooks, a few full-sized poetry collections, and 1 anthology, then taking a short break from publishing, Swan Scythe Press is now re-launching its efforts with some new books, under a new editorship. We have also begun a new series of books, called Poetas/Puentes, from emerging poets writing in Spanish, translated into English. We will also consider mss in indigenous languages from North, Central and South America, translated into English." Query first before submitting a ms via e-mail or through website.

SWEDENBORG FOUNDATION

320 N. Church St., West Chester PA 19380. (610)430-3222. **Fax:** (610)430-7982. **E-mail:** editor@swedenborg.com. **Website:** www.swedenborg.com. **Contact:** Lisa Lapp, editor. Estab. 1849. Publishes trade paperback originals and reprints. The Swedenborg Foundation publishes books by and about Emanuel Swedenborg (1688-1772), his ideas, how his ideas have influenced others, and related topics. Appropriate topics include Swedenborgian concepts, such as: near-death experience, angels, Biblical interpretation, mysteries of good and evil, etc. A work must actively engage the thought of Emanuel Swedenborg and show an understanding of his philosophy in order to be accepted for publication. **Publishes 5 titles/year.** Responds in 1 month to queries; 3 months to proposals and mss. Book catalog available free. Guidelines online.

NONFICTION Subjects include philosophy, psychology, religion, science. Query with SASE. Submit proposal package, outline, sample chapters, synopsis. "I personally prefer e-mail." Reviews artwork/photos. Send photocopies.

SYRACUSE UNIVERSITY PRESS

621 Skytop Rd., Suite 110, Syracuse NY 13244. (315)443-5534. **Fax:** (315)443-5545. **E-mail:** seguiod@syr.edu; dhmccay@syr.edu; dmmanion@syr.edu. **Website:** syracuseuniversitypress.syr.edu. **Con-**

tact: Suzanne Guiod, editor-in-chief; Deanna McCay, acquisitions editor; Deborah Manion, acquisitions editor. Estab. 1943. "Currently emphasizing Middle East studies, Jewish studies, Irish studies, peace studies, disability studies, television and popular culture, sports and entertainment, Native American studies, gender and ethnic studies, New York State." **Publishes 50 titles/year. 25% of books from first-time authors. 95% from unagented writers.** Publishes ms 15 months after acceptance. Book catalog online. Guidelines online.

NONFICTION "Special opportunity in our nonfiction program for books on New York state, sports history, Jewish studies, Irish studies, the Middle East, religion and politics, television, and popular culture, disability studies, peace studies, Native American studies. Provide precise descriptions of subjects, along with background description of project. The author must make a case for the importance of his or her subject." Submit query via e-mail with the book proposal form found on our website and a copy of your CV. Reviews artwork/photos.

TIPS "We're seeking well-written and thoroughly researched books that will make a significant contribution to the subject areas listed above and will be favorably received in the marketplace."

TAFELBERG PUBLISHERS

Imprint of NB Publishers, P.O. Box 879, Cape Town 8000, South Africa. (27)(21)406-3033. **Fax:** (27) (21)406-3812. **E-mail:** kristin@nb.co.za. **Website:** www.tafelberg.com. **Contact:** Kristin Paremoer. General publisher best known for Afrikaans fiction, authoritative political works, children's/youth literature, and a variety of illustrated and nonillustrated nonfiction. **Publishes 10 titles/year. Pays authors royalty of 15-18% based on wholesale price.** Publishes ms 1 year after acceptance. Responds to queries in 2 weeks; mss in 6 months.

NONFICTION Subjects include health, medicine, memoirs, politics. Submit outline, information on intended market, bio, and 1-2 sample chapters.

FICTION Subjects include juvenile, romance. Picture books, young readers: animal, anthology, contemporary, fantasy, folktales, hi-lo, humor, multicultural, nature/environment, scient fiction, special needs. Middle readers, young adults: animal (middle reader only), contemporary, fantasy, hi-lo, humor, multicultural, nature/environment, problem novels, science fiction, special needs, sports, suspense/mystery. Average word length: picture books—1,500-7,500; young readers—25,000; middle readers—15,000; young adults—40,000. Submit complete ms.

TIPS "Writers: Story needs to have a South African or African style. Illustrators: I'd like to look, but the chances of getting commissioned are slim. The market is small and difficult. Do not expect huge advances. Editorial staff attended or plans to attend the following conferences: IBBY, Frankfurt, SCBWI Bologna."

NAN A. TALESE

Imprint of Doubleday, Random House, 1745 Broadway, New York NY 10019. (212)782-8918. **Fax:** (212)782-8448. **Website:** www.nanatalese.com. Publishes hardcover originals. Nan A. Talese publishes nonfiction with a powerful guiding narrative and relevance to larger cultural interests, and literary fiction of the highest quality. **Publishes 15 titles/year. 400 queries received/year. 400 mss received/year. Pays variable royalty on retail price. Pays varying advance.**

NONFICTION Subjects include contemporary culture, history, philosophy, sociology. *Agented submissions only.*

FICTION Subjects include literary. Well-written narratives with a compelling story line, good characterization and use of language. We like stories with an edge. *Agented submissions only.*

TIPS "Audience is highly literate people interested in story, information and insight. We want well-written material submitted by agents only. See our website."

TANTOR MEDIA

2 Business Park Rd., Old Saybrook CT 06475. (860)395-1155. **Fax:** (860)395-1154. **E-mail:** rightsemail@tantor.com. **Website:** www.tantor.com. **Contact:** Ron Formica, director of acquisitions. Estab. 2001. Publishes hardcover, trade paperback, mass market paperback, and electronic originals and reprints. Also publishes audiobooks. Tantor is a leading independent audiobook publisher, producing more than 90 new titles every month. **Publishes 1,000 titles/year. Pays 5-15% royalty on wholesale price.** Publishes ms 3 months after acceptance. Accepts simultaneous submissions. Responds in 2 months. Catalog online.

NONFICTION Subjects include agriculture, alternative lifestyles, Americana, animals, anthropology, astrology, business, child guidance, communications, contemporary culture, cooking, creative nonfiction, economics, education, entertainment, foods, games, gay, government, health, history, horticulture, law, lesbian, literary criticism, marine subjects, memoirs, military, money, multicultural, music, New Age, philosophy, psychology, religion, science, sex, social sciences, sociology, spirituality, sports, womens issues, womens studies, world affairs, young adult. Query with SASE, or submit proposal package, including outline and 3 sample chapters.

FICTION Subjects include adventure, contemporary, erotica, experimental, fantasy, feminist, gay, gothic, historical, horror, humor, juvenile, lesbian, literary, mainstream, military, multicultural, multimedia, mystery, occult, religious, romance, science fiction, short story collections, spiritual, sports, suspense, western, young adult. Query with SASE, or submit proposal package including synopsis and 3 sample chapters.

TARPAULIN SKY PRESS

P.O. Box 189, Grafton VT 05146. **E-mail:** editors@tarpaulinsky.com. **Website:** www.tarpaulinsky.com. **Contact:** Resh Daily, managing editor. Estab. 2006. Tarpaulin Sky Press publishes cross- and trans-genre works as well as innovative poetry and prose. Produces full-length books and chapbooks, hand-bound books and trade paperbacks, and offers both hand-bound and perfect-bound paperback editions of full-length books. "We're a small, author-centered press endeavoring to create books that, as objects, please our authors as much their texts please us."

POETRY Writers whose work has appeared in or been accepted for publication in *Tarpaulin Sky* may submit chapbook or full-length mss at any time, with no reading fee. Tarpaulin Sky Press also considers chapbook and full-length mss from writers whose work has not appeared in the journal, but **asks for a $20 reading fee**. Make checks/money orders to Tarpaulin Sky Press. Cover letter is preferred. Reading periods may be found on the website.

TEACHERS COLLEGE PRESS

1234 Amsterdam Ave., New York NY 10027. (212)678-3929. **Fax:** (212)678-4149. **E-mail:** tcpress@tc.columbia.edu. **Website:** www.teacherscollegepress.com. Estab. 1904. Publishes hardcover and paperback originals and reprints. "Teachers College Press publishes a wide range of educational titles for all levels of students: early childhood to higher education. Publishing books that respond to, examine, and confront issues pertaining to education, teacher training, and school reform." **Publishes 60 titles/year. Pays industry standard royalty. Pays advance.** Publishes ms 1 year after acceptance. Responds in 2 months to queries. Book catalog available free. Guidelines online.

NONFICTION Subjects include computers, electronics, education, film, cinema, stage, government, politics, history, philosophy, sociology, women's issues, women's studies. This university press concentrates on books in the field of education in the broadest sense, from early childhood to higher education: good classroom practices, teacher training, special education, innovative trends and issues, administration and supervision, film, continuing and adult education, all areas of the curriculum, computers, guidance and counseling, and the politics, economics, philosophy, sociology, and history of education. We have recently added women's studies to our list. The Press also issues classroom materials for students at all levels, with a strong emphasis on reading and writing and social studies. Submit outline, sample chapters.

TEBOT BACH

P.O. Box 7887, Huntington Beach CA 92615. (714)968-0905. **E-mail:** info@tebotbach.org. **Website:** www.tebotbach.org. **Contact:** Mifanwy Kaiser, editor/publisher. Publishes book Publishes mss 2 years after acceptance. Responds in 3 months.

POETRY Offers 2 contests per year. The Patricia Bibby First Book Contest and The Clockwise Chapbook contest. Go online for more information. Query first via e-mail, with a few sample poems and cover letter with brief bio.

Ⓐ ⊘ KATHERINE TEGEN BOOKS

HarperCollins, 10 E. 53rd St., New York NY 10022. **Website:** www.harpercollins.com. **Contact:** Katherine Tegen, vice-president and publisher. Estab. 2003. Katherine Tegen Books publishes high-quality, commercial literature for children of all ages, including teens. Talented authors and illustrators who offer powerful narratives that are thought-provoking, well-written, and entertaining are the core of the Katherine Tegen Books imprint. *Katherine Tegen Books accepts agented work only.*

TEMPLE UNIVERSITY PRESS

1852 N. 10th St., Philadelphia PA 19122. (215)926-2140. **Fax:** (215)926-2141. **E-mail:** sara.cohen@temple.edu. **Website:** www.temple.edu/tempress/. **Contact:**

Sara Cohen, assistant editor. Estab. 1969. "Temple University Press has been publishing path-breaking books on Asian-Americans, law, gender issues, film, women's studies and other interesting areas for nearly 40 years." **Publishes 60 titles/year. Pays advance.** Publishes ms 10 months after acceptance. Responds in 2 months to queries. Book catalog available free. Guidelines online.

NONFICTION Subjects include ethnic, government, politics, health, medicine, history, photography, regional, Philadelphia, sociology, labor studies, urban studies, Latin American/Latino, Asian American, African American studies, public policy, women's studies. No memoirs, fiction or poetry. Query with SASE. Reviews artwork/photos.

TEN SPEED PRESS

The Crown Publishing Group, Attn: Acquisitions, 2625 Alcatraz Ave. #505, Berkeley CA 94705. (510)559-1600. **Fax:** (510)524-1052. **E-mail:** crownbiz@randomhouse.com. **Website:** crownpublishing.com/imprint/ten-speed-press. Estab. 1971. Publishes trade paperback originals and reprints. "Ten Speed Press publishes authoritative books for an audience interested in innovative ideas. Currently emphasizing cookbooks, career, business, alternative education, and offbeat general nonfiction gift books." **Publishes 120 titles/year. 40% of books from first-time authors. 40% from unagented writers. Pays $2,500 average advance.** Publishes ms 1 year after acceptance. Accepts simultaneous submissions. Responds in 3 months to queries; 6-8 weeks to proposals. Book catalog for 9×12 envelope and 6 first-class stamps. Guidelines online.

NONFICTION Subjects include business, career guidance, cooking, crafts, relationships, how-to, humor, and pop culture. *Agented submissions only.*

TIPS "We like books from people who really know their subject, rather than people who think they've spotted a trend to capitalize on. We like books that will sell for a long time, rather than 9-day wonders. Our audience consists of a well-educated, slightly weird group of people who like food, the outdoors, and take a light, but serious, approach to business and careers. Study the backlist of each publisher you're submitting to and tailor your proposal to what you perceive as their needs. Nothing gets a publisher's attention like someone who knows what he or she is talking about, and nothing falls flat like someone who obviously has no idea who he or she is submitting to."

TEXAS TECH UNIVERSITY PRESS

3003 15th St., Suite 901, Lubbock TX 79409. (806)834-5821. **Fax:** (806)742-2979. **E-mail:** ttup.editorial@ttu.edu. **Website:** www.ttupress.org. **Contact:** Joanna Conrad, editor-in-chief. Estab. 1971. Texas Tech University Press, the book publishing office of the university since 1971 and an AAUP member since 1986, publishes nonfiction titles in the areas of natural history and the natural sciences; 18th century and Joseph Conrad studies; studies of modern Southeast Asia, particularly the Vietnam War; costume and textile history; Latin American literature and culture; and all aspects of the Great Plains and the American West, especially history, biography, memoir, sports history, and travel. In addition, the Press publishes several scholarly journals, acclaimed series for young readers, an annual invited poetry collection, and literary fiction of Texas and the West. Guidelines online.

NONFICTION Subjects include environment, ethnic, history, law, literary criticism, literature, regional, sports. Submit proposal that includes introduction, 2 sample chapters, cover letter, working title, anticipated ms length, description of audience, comparison of book to others published on the subject, brief bio or CV.

FICTION Subjects include ethnic, multicultural, religious, western. Fiction rooted in the American West and Southwest, Jewish literature, Latin American and Latino fiction (in translation or English).

POETRY "TTUP publishes an annual invited first-book poetry manuscript (please note that we cannot entertain unsolicited poetry submissions)."

TEXAS WESTERN PRESS

The University of Texas at El Paso, 500 W. University Ave., El Paso TX 79968. (915)747-5688. **Fax:** (915)747-5345. **E-mail:** ctavarez@utep.edu. **Website:** twp.utep.edu. **Contact:** Carmen P. Tavarez. Estab. 1952. Publishes hardcover and paperback originals. "Texas Western Press publishes books on the history and cultures of the American Southwest, particularly historical and biographical works about West Texas, New Mexico, northern Mexico, and the U.S. borderlands." **Publishes 1 titles/year. Pays standard 10% royalty. Pays advance.** Responds in 2 months to queries. Book catalog available free. Guidelines online.

IMPRINTS Southwestern Studies.

NONFICTION Subjects include education, health, medicine, history, language, literature, nature, environment, regional, science, social sciences. "Historic and cultural accounts of the Southwest (West Texas, New Mexico, northern Mexico). Also art, photographic books, Native American and limited regional fiction reprints." *Not currently seeking mss.*

TIPS "We try to treat our authors professionally, produce handsome, long-lived books and aim for quality, rather than quantity of titles carrying our imprint."

THISTLEDOWN PRESS LTD.

410 2nd Ave., Saskatoon SK S7K 2C3, Canada. (306)244-1722. **Fax:** (306)244-1762. **E-mail:** editorial@thistledownpress.com. **Website:** www.thistledownpress.com. **Contact:** Allan Forrie, publisher. "Thistledown originates books by Canadian authors only, although we have co-published titles by authors outside Canada. We do not publish children's picture books." **Pays authors royalty of 10-12% based on net dollar sales. Pays illustrators and photographers by the project (range: $250-750).** Publishes ms 1 year after acceptance. Responds to queries in 4 months. Book catalog free on request.

FICTION Middle readers, young adults: adventure, anthology, contemporary, fantasy, humor, poetry, romance, science fiction, suspense/mystery, short stories. Average word length: young adults—40,000. Submit outline/synopsis and sample chapters. *Does not accept mss.* Do not query by e-mail.

POETRY "We do not publish cowboy poetry, inspirational poetry, or poetry for children."

TIPS "Send cover letter including publishing history and SASE."

THOMSON CARSWELL

One Corporate Plaza, 2075 Kennedy Rd., Toronto ON M1T 3V4, Canada. (416)298-5024. **Fax:** (416)298-5094. **Website:** www.carswell.com. Publishes hardcover originals. "Thomson Carswell is Canada's national resource of information and legal interpretations for law, accounting, tax and business professionals." **Publishes 150-200 titles/year. 30-50% of books from first-time authors. Pays 5-15% royalty on wholesale price.** Publishes ms 6 months after acceptance. Accepts simultaneous submissions. Responds in 3 months to queries. Book catalog and ms guidelines free.

NONFICTION Canadian information of a regulatory nature is our mandate. Submit proposal package, outline, resume.

TIPS "Audience is Canada and persons interested in Canadian information; professionals in law, tax, accounting fields; business people interested in regulatory material."

THUNDERSTONE BOOKS

6575 Horse Dr., Las Vegas NV 89131. **E-mail:** info@thunderstonebooks.com. **Website:** www.thunderstonebooks.com. **Contact:** Rachel Noorda, editorial director. Estab. 2014. Publishes hardcover, trade paperback, mass market paperback, and electronic originals. "At ThunderStone Books, we aim to publish children's books that have an educational aspect. We are not looking for curriculum for learning certain subjects, but rather stories that encourage learning for children, whether that be learning about a new language/culture or learning more about science and math in a fun, fictional format. We want to help children to gain a love for other languages and subjects so that they are curious about the world around them. We are currently accepting fiction and non-fiction submissions." **Publishes 2-5 titles/year. Receives 30 queries and mss/year. 100% of books from first-time authors. 100% from unagented writers. Pays 5-15% royalties on retail price. Pays $300-1,000 advance.** Publishes ms 6 months after acceptance. Accepts simultaneous submissions. Responds in 3 months to queries, proposals, and mss. Catalog available for SASE. Guidelines available on website.

NONFICTION Subjects include creative nonfiction, education, language, literature, multicultural, regional, science, translation. Looking for engaging educational materials, not a set curriculum, but books that teach as well as have some fun. Open to a variety of educational subjects, but specialty and main interest lies in language exposure/learning, science, math, and history. Query with SASE. Reviews photocopies of artwork.

FICTION Subjects include multicultural, picture books, regional. Interested in multicultural stories with an emphasis on authentic culture and language (these may include mythology). Query with SASE.

TIA CHUCHA PRESS

P.O. Box 328, San Fernando CA 91341. **E-mail:** info@tiachucha.com. **Website:** www.tiachucha.com. **Contact:** Luis Rodriguez, director. Estab. 1989. Publishes hardcover and trade paperback originals. Tia Chucha's Centro Cultural is a nonprofit learning and cultural arts center. "We support and promote the continued growth, development and holistic learning of our community through the many powerful means of the arts. Tia Centra provides a positive space for people to activate what we all share as humans: the capacity to create, to imagine and to express ourselves in an effort to improve the quality of life for our community." **Publishes 2-4 titles/year. 25-30 queries received/year. 150 mss received/year. Pays 10% royalty on wholesale price.** Publishes ms 1 year after acceptance. Responds in 9 months to mss. Guidelines online.

POETRY No restrictions as to style or content. "We only publish poetry at this time. We do cross-cultural and performance-oriented poetry. It has to work on the page, however." Query and submit complete ms.

TIPS "We will cultivate the practice. Audience is those interested."

TIGHTROPE BOOKS

#207-2 College St., Toronto ON M5G 1K3, Canada. (416)928-6666. **E-mail:** tightropeasst@gmail.com. **Website:** www.tightropebooks.com. **Contact:** Jim Nason, publisher. Estab. 2005. Publishes hardcover and trade paperback originals. **Publishes 12 titles/year. 70% of books from first-time authors. 100% from unagented writers. Pays 5-15% royalty on retail price. Pays advance of $200-300.** Publishes ms 1 year after acceptance. Accepts simultaneous submissions. Responds if interested. Catalog and guidelines online.

Accepting submissions for new mystery imprint, Mysterio.

NONFICTION Subjects include alternative lifestyles, architecture, art, contemporary culture, creative nonfiction, ethnic, gay, language, lesbian, literary criticism, literature, multicultural, womens issues.

FICTION Subjects include contemporary, ethnic, experimental, fantasy, feminist, gay, horror, juvenile, lesbian, literary, mainstream, multicultural, poetry, poetry in translation, short story collections, translation, young adult.

TIPS "Audience is young, urban, literary, educated, unconventional."

TILBURY HOUSE PUBLISHERS

WordSplice Studio, Inc., 12 Starr St., Thomaston ME 04861. (800)582-1899. **Fax:** (207)582-8772. **E-mail:** tilbury@tilburyhouse.com. **Website:** www.tilburyhouse.com. **Contact:** Audrey Maynard, children's book editor; Jonathan Eaton, publisher. Estab. 1990. **Publishes 10 titles/year. Pays royalty based on wholesale price.** Publishes ms 1 year after acceptance. Responds to mss in 3 months. Guidelines and catalog online.

NONFICTION Regional adult biography/history/maritime/nature, and children's picture books that deal with issues, such as bullying, multiculturalism, etc., science/nature. Submit complete ms for picture books or outline/synopsis for longer works. Reviews artwork/photos. Send photocopies.

FICTION Picture books: multicultural, nature/environment. Special needs include books that teach children about tolerance and honoring diversity. Send art/photography samples and/or complete ms to Audrey Maynard, children's book editor.

TIPS "We are always interested in stories that will encourage children to understand the natural world and the environment, as well as stories with social justice themes. We really like stories that engage children to become problem solvers as well as those that promote respect, tolerance and compassion." We do not publish books with personified animal characters; historical fiction; YA or middle grade fiction or chapter books; fantasy."

TIN HOUSE BOOKS

2617 NW Thurman St., Portland OR 97210. (503)473-8663. **Fax:** (503)473-8957. **E-mail:** meg@tinhouse.com. **Website:** www.tinhouse.com. **Contact:** Meg Storey, editor; Tony Perez, editor; Masie Cochran, editor. Publishes hardcover originals, paperback originals, paperback reprints. "We are a small independent publisher dedicated to nurturing new, promising talent as well as showcasing the work of established writers." Distributes/promotes titles through Publishers Group West. **Publishes 10-12 titles/year. 20% from unagented writers.** Publishes ms 1 year after acceptance. Accepts simultaneous submissions. Responds to queries in 2-3 weeks; mss in 2-3 months. Guidelines online.

NONFICTION *Agented mss only.* "We no longer read unsolicited submissions by authors with no representation. We will continue to accept submissions from agents."

FICTION *Agented mss only.* "We no longer read unsolicited submissions by authors with no representation. We will continue to accept submissions from agents."

TITAN PRESS

PMB 17897, Encino CA 91416. **E-mail:** titan91416@yahoo.com. **Website:** www.calwriterssfv.com. **Contact:** Stefanya Wilson, editor. Estab. 1981. Publishes hardcover and paperback originals. **Publishes 12 titles/year. 50% from unagented writers. Pays 20-40% royalty.** Publishes ms 1 year after acceptance. Responds to queries in 3 months. Ms guidelines for #10 SASE.

FICTION Subjects include contemporary, literary, mainstream, short story collections. Does not accept unsolicited mss. Query with SASE. Include brief bio, social security number, list of publishing credits.

TIPS "Look, act, sound, and *be* professional."

⊘ TOP COW PRODUCTIONS, INC.

3812 Dunn Dr., Culver City CA 90232. **E-mail:** fanmail@topcow.com. **Website:** www.topcow.com. Guidelines online.

FICTION *No unsolicited submissions.* Prefers submissions from artists. See website for details and advice on how to break into the market.

TOP PUBLICATIONS, LTD.

12221 Merit Dr., Suite 950, Dallas TX 75251. (972)628-6414. **Fax:** (972)233-0713. **E-mail:** info@toppub.com. **E-mail:** submissions@toppub.com. **Website:** www.toppub.com. Estab. 1999. Publishes paperback originals and e-books. Primarily a mainstream fiction publisher. **Publishes 2-3 titles/year. 200 queries received/year. 5 mss received/year. 100% of books from first-time authors. 95% from unagented writers. Pays 15% royalty on wholesale price. Pays $250-$1,000 advance.** Publishes ms 6 months after acceptance. Accepts simultaneous submissions. Acknowledges receipt of queries but only responds if interested in seeing ms. Responds in 6 months to mss. Guidelines online.

FICTION Subjects include adventure, contemporary, historical, horror, juvenile, military, mystery, regional, romance, science fiction, suspense, young adult.

TIPS "We recommend that our authors write books that appeal to a large mainstream audience to make marketing easier and increase the chances of success. We only publish a few titles a year so the odds at getting published at TOP are slim. If we don't offer you a contract it doesn't mean we don't like your submission. We have to pass on a lot of good material each year simply by the limitations of our time and budget."

TOR BOOKS

Tom Doherty Associates, 175 Fifth Ave., New York NY 10010. **Website:** www.tor-forge.com. Tor Books is the "world's largest publisher of science fiction and fantasy, with strong category publishing in historical fiction, mystery, western/Americana, thriller, YA." **Publishes 10-20 titles/year. Pays author royalty. Pays illustrators by the project.** Book catalog available. Guidelines online.

FICTION Subjects include adventure, fantasy, historical, humor, mystery, picture books, science fiction, suspense, young adult. Submit first 3 chapters, 3-10 page synopsis, dated cover letter, SASE.

TORQUERE PRESS

1380 Rio Rancho Blvd., #1319, Rio Rancho NM 87124. **E-mail:** editor@torquerepress.com. **E-mail:** submissions@torquerepress.com. **Website:** www.torquerepress.com. **Contact:** Kristi Boulware, submissions editor (homoerotica, suspense, gay/lesbian); Lorna Hinson, senior editor (gay/lesbian romance, historicals). Estab. 2003. Publishes trade paperback originals and electronic originals and reprints. "We are a gay and lesbian press focusing on romance and genres of romance. We particularly like paranormal and western romance." **Publishes 140 titles/year. 500 queries received/year. 200 mss received/year. 25% of books from first-time authors. 100% from unagented writers. Pays 8-40% royalty. Pays $35-75 for anthology stories.** Publishes ms 6 months after acceptance. Responds in 1 month to queries and proposals; 2-4 months to mss. Book catalog online. Guidelines online.

FICTION Subjects include adventure, erotica, gay, lesbian, historical, horror, mainstream, contemporary, multicultural, mystery, occult, romance, science fiction, short story collections, suspense, western. All categories gay and lesbian themed. Submit proposal package, 3 sample chapters, clips.

TIPS "Our audience is primarily people looking for a familiar romance setting featuring gay or lesbian protagonists. Please read guidelines carefully and familiarize yourself with our lines."

TORREY HOUSE PRESS, LLC

2806 Melony Dr., Salt Lake City UT 84124. (801)810-9THP. **E-mail:** mark@torreyhouse.com. **Website:** torreyhouse.com. **Contact:** Mark Bailey, publisher. Estab. 2010. Publishes hardcover, trade paperback, and electronic originals. "Torrey House Press

(THP) publishes literary fiction and creative nonfiction about the world environment with a tilt toward the American West. Want submissions from experienced and agented authors only." **Publishes 10 titles/year. 500 queries/year; 200 mss/year. 50% of books from first-time authors. 80% from unagented writers. Pays 5-15% royalty on retail price.** Publishes ms 12-18 months after acceptance. Accepts simultaneous submissions. Responds in 3 months. Catalog online. Guidelines online.

NONFICTION Subjects include creative nonfiction, environment, nature. Query; submit proposal package, including: outline, ms, bio. Does not review artwork.

FICTION Subjects include historical, literary. "Torrey House Press publishes literary fiction and creative nonfiction about the world environment and the American West." Submit proposal package including: synopsis, complete ms, bio.

POETRY Query; submit complete ms.

TIPS "Include writing experience (none okay)."

TOUCHWOOD EDITIONS

The Heritage Group, 103-1075 Pendergast St., Victoria BC V8V 0A1, Canada. (250)360-0829. **Fax:** (250)386-0829. **E-mail:** edit@touchwoodeditions.com. **Website:** www.touchwoodeditions.com. **Contact:** Marlyn Horsdal, editor. Publishes trade paperback originals and reprints. **Publishes 20-25 titles/year. 40% of books from first-time authors. 70% from unagented writers. Pays 15% royalty on net price.** Publishes ms 12-24 months after acceptance. Accepts simultaneous submissions. Responds in 3 months to queries. Book catalog and guidelines online.

NONFICTION Subjects include anthropology, archeology, art, architecture, creative nonfiction, government, politics, history, nature, environment, recreation, regional, nautical. Submit TOC, outline, word count, 2-3 sample chapters, synopsis. Reviews artwork/photos. Send photocopies.

FICTION Subjects include historical, mystery. Submit TOC, outline, word count.

TIPS "Our area of interest is Western Canada. We would like more creative nonfiction and books about people of note in Canada's history."

TOWER PUBLISHING

588 Saco Rd., Standish ME 04084. (207)642-5400. **Fax:** (207)642-5463. **E-mail:** info@towerpub.com. **E-mail:** michaell@towerpub.com. **Website:** www.towerpub.com. **Contact:** Michael Lyons, president. Estab. 1772. Publishes hardcover originals and reprints, trade paperback originals. Tower Publishing specializes in business and professional directories and legal books. **Publishes 22 titles/year. 60 queries received/year. 30 mss received/year. 10% of books from first-time authors. 90% from unagented writers.** Publishes ms 6 months after acceptance. Accepts simultaneous submissions. Responds in 1 month to queries; 2 months to proposals and mss. Book catalog and ms guidelines online.

NONFICTION Subjects include business, economics. Looking for legal books of a national stature. Query with SASE. Submit outline.

TRADEWIND BOOKS

202-1807 Maritime Mews, Granville Island, Vancouver BC V6H 3W7, Canada. (604)662-4405. **Website:** www.tradewindbooks.com. **Contact:** R. David Stephens, senior editor. Publishes hardcover and trade paperback originals. "Tradewind Books publishes juvenile picture books and young adult novels. Requires that submissions include evidence that author has read at least 3 titles published by Tradewind Books." **Publishes 5 titles/year. 15% of books from first-time authors. 50% from unagented writers. Pays 7% royalty on retail price. Pays variable advance.** Publishes ms 3 years after acceptance. Accepts simultaneous submissions. Responds to mss in 2 months. Book catalog and ms guidelines online.

FICTION Subjects include juvenile, multicultural, picture books. Average word length: 900 words. Send complete ms for picture books. *YA novels by Canadian authors only. Chapter books by US authors considered.*

POETRY Please send a book-length collection only.

TRAFALGAR SQUARE BOOKS

P.O. Box 257, 388 Howe Hill Rd., North Pomfret VT 05053. (802)457-1911. **Website:** www.horseandriderbooks.com. **Contact:** Martha Cook, managing director; Rebecca Didier, senior editor. Estab. 1985. Publishes hardcover and trade paperback originals. "We publish high quality instructional books for horsemen and horsewomen, always with the horse's welfare in mind." **Publishes 12 titles/year. 50% of books from first-time authors. 80% from unagented writers. Pays royalty. Pays advance.** Publishes ms 18 months after acceptance. Responds in 1 month to queries; 2 months to proposals; 2-3 months to mss. Catalog free on request and by e-mail.

NONFICTION Subjects include animals, horses/dogs. "We rarely consider books for complete novices." Query with SASE. Submit proposal package including outline, 1-3 sample chapters, letter of introduction including qualifications for writing on the subject and why the proposed book is an essential addition to existing publications. Reviews artwork/photos as part of the ms package. We prefer color laser thumbnail sheets or duplicate prints (do not send original photos or art!).

TIPS "Our audience is comprised of horse lovers and riders interested in pursuing their passion and/or sport while doing what is best for horses."

TRAVELERS' TALES

2320 Bowdoin St., Palo Alto CA 94306. (650)462-2110. **Fax:** (650)462-6305. **E-mail:** submit@travelerstales.com. **Website:** www.travelerstales.com. **Contact:** James O'Reilly; Larry Habegger; Sean O'Reilly, series editors. Publishes inspirational travel books, mostly anthologies and travel advice books. "Due to the volume of submissions, we do not respond unless the material submitted meets our immediate editorial needs. All stories are read and filed for future use contingent upon meeting editorial guidelines." **Publishes 8-10 titles/year. Pays $100 honorarium for anthology pieces.** Accepts simultaneous submissions. Guidelines online.

NONFICTION Subjects include all aspects of travel.

TIPS "We publish personal nonfiction stories and anecdotes—funny, illuminating, adventurous, frightening, or grim. Stories should reflect that unique alchemy that occurs when you enter unfamiliar territory and begin to see the world differently as a result. Stories that have already been published, including book excerpts, are welcome as long as the authors retain the copyright or can obtain permission from the copyright holder to reprint the material."

TRENTHAM BOOKS, LTD.

20 Bedford Way, London WC1H 0AL, United Kingdom. **E-mail:** g.klein@ioe.ac.uk. **Website:** www.trentham-books.co.uk. **Contact:** Gillian Klein, commissioning editor (education, race). Publishes hardcover and trade paperback originals. "Our mission is to enhance the work of professionals in education, law, and social work. Currently emphasizing curriculum, professional behavior. De-emphasizing theoretical issues." **Publishes 32 titles/year. 1,000 queries received/year. 600 mss received/year. 60% of books from first-time authors. 70% from unagented writers. Pays 7½% royalty on wholesale price.** Publishes ms 4 months after acceptance. Responds in 1 month to queries. Guidelines online.

NONFICTION Subjects include education, ethnic, multicultural, language/literacy, psychology, women's issues. Query with SASE.

THE TRINITY FOUNDATION

P.O. Box 68, Unicoi TN 37692. (423)743-0199. **Fax:** (423)743-2005. **E-mail:** tjtrinityfound@aol.com. **Website:** www.trinityfoundation.org. **Contact:** Thomas W. Juodaitis, editor. Publishes hardcover and paperback originals and reprints. **Publishes 5 titles/year.** Publishes ms 9 months after acceptance. Responds in 1 month to queries and proposals; 3 months to mss. Book catalog online.

NONFICTION Only books that conform to the philosophy and theology of the Westminster Confession of Faith. Textbooks subjects include business/economics, education, government/politics, history, philosophy, religion, science. Query with SASE.

TRISTAN PUBLISHING

2355 Louisiana Ave. N, Golden Valley MN 55427. (763)545-1383. **Fax:** (763)545-1387. **E-mail:** info@tristanpublishing.com; manuscripts@tristanpublishing.com. **Website:** www.tristanpublishing.com. **Contact:** Brett Waldman, publisher. Estab. 2002. Publishes hardcover originals. **Publishes 6-10 titles/year. 1,000 queries and mss/year. 15% of books from first-time authors. 100% from unagented writers. Pays royalty on wholesale or retail price; outright purchase.** Publishes ms 2 years after acceptance. Accepts simultaneous submissions. Responds in 3 months. Catalog and guidelines online.

NONFICTION , inspirational. "Our mission is to create books with a message that inspire and uplift in typically 1,000 words or less." Query with SASE; submit completed mss. Reviews artwork/photos; send photocopies.

FICTION , inspirational, gift books. Query with SASE; submit completed mss.

TIPS "Our audience is adults and children."

TRIUMPH BOOKS

814 N. Franklin St., Chicago IL 60610. (312)939-3330; (800)335-5323. **Fax:** (312)663-3557. **Website:** www.triumphbooks.com. Estab. 1990. Publishes hardcover

originals and trade paperback originals and reprints. Accepts simultaneous submissions. Book catalog available free.

NONFICTION Subjects include recreation, sports, health, sports business/motivation. Query with SASE. Reviews artwork/photos. Send photocopies.

TRUMAN STATE UNIVERSITY PRESS

100 E. Normal Ave., Kirksville MO 63501. (660)785-7336. **Fax:** (660)785-4480. **E-mail:** tsup@truman.edu. **E-mail:** bsm@truman.edu. **Website:** tsup.truman.edu. **Contact:** Barbara Smith-Mandell, editor-in-chief. Estab. 1986. Truman State University Press (TSUP) publishes peer-reviewed research in the humanities for the scholarly community and the broader public, and publishes creative literary works. Guidelines online.

NONFICTION , contemporary nonfiction, early modern, American studies, poetry. Submit book ms proposals in American Studies to Barbara Smith-Mandell, at bsm@truman.edu; nonfiction to Monica Barron at tsupnonfiction@truman.edu; early modern studies to wolfem1@stjohns.edu.

POETRY Not accepting unsolicited mss. Submit to annual T.S. Eliot Prize for Poetry.

TU BOOKS

Lee & Low Books, 95 Madison Ave., Suite #1205, New York NY 10016. (212)779-4400. **Fax:** (212)683-1894. **Website:** www.leeandlow.com/imprints/3. **Contact:** Stacy Whitman, publisher. The Tu imprint spans many genres: science fiction, fantasy, mystery, and more. "We don't believe in labels or limits, just great stories. Join us at the crossroads where fantasy and real life collide. You'll be glad you did." Accepts simultaneous submissions. Responds only if interested. Guidelines online. Electronic submissions can be submitted here (only): https://tubooks.submittable.com/submit.

FICTION Focuses on well-told, exciting, adventurous fantasy, science fiction, and mystery novels featuring people of color and/or set in worlds inspired by non-Western folklore or culture. Looking specifically for stories for both middle grade (ages 8-12) and young adult (ages 12-18) readers. Mss should be sent through postal mail only. Mss should be accompanied by a cover letter that includes a brief biography of the author, including publishing history. The letter should also state if the ms is a simultaneous or an exclusive submission. Include a synopsis and the first 3 chapters of the novel. Include full contact information on the cover letter and the first page of the ms.

TUMBLEHOME LEARNING

P.O. Box 71386, Boston MA 02117. **E-mail:** info@tumblehomelearning.com. **Website:** www.tumblehomelearning.com. **Contact:** Pendred Noyce, editor. Estab. 2011. Publishes hardcover, trade paperback, and electronic originals. Tumblehome Learning helps kids imagine themselves as young scientists or engineeers and encourages them to experience science through adventure and discovery. "We do this with exciting mystery and adventure tales as well as experiments carefully designed to engage students from ages 8 and up." **Publishes 8-10 titles/year. Receives 20 queries and 20 mss/year. 50% of books from first-time authors. 100% from unagented writers. Pays authors 8-12% royalties on retail price. Pays $500 advance.** Publishes ms 8 months after acceptance. Accepts simultaneous submissions. Responds in 1 month to queries and proposals, and 2 months to mss. Catalog available online. Guideliens available on request for SASE.

NONFICTION Subjects include science. Rarely publishes nonfiction. Book would need to be sold to trade, not just the school market.

FICTION Subjects include adventure, juvenile. "All our fiction has science at its heart. This can include using science to solve a mystery (see *The Walking Fish* by Rachelle Burk or *Something Stinks!* by Gail Hedrick), realistic science fiction, books in our Galactic Academy of Science series, science-based adventure tales, and the occasional picture book with a science theme, such as appreciation of the stars and constellations in *Elizabeth's Constellation Quilt* by Olivia Fu. A graphic novel about science would also be welcome." Submit completed ms electronically.

TIPS "Please don't submit to us if your book is not about science. We don't accept generic books about animals or books with glaring scientific errors in the first chapter. That said, the book should be fun to read and the science content can be subtle. We work closely with authors, including first-time authors, to edit and improve their books. As a small publisher, the greatest benefit we can offer is this friendly and respectful partnership with authors."

TUPELO PRESS

P.O. Box 1767, North Adams MA 01247. (413)664-9611. **E-mail:** publisher@tupelopress.org. **E-mail:**

www.tupelopress.org/submissions. **Website:** www.tupelopress.org. **Contact:** Jeffrey Levine, publish/editor-in-chief; Jim Schley, managing editor. Estab. 2001. "We're an independent nonprofit literary press. We accept book-length poetry, poetry collections (48+ pages), short story collections, novellas, literary nonfiction/memoirs and up to 80 pages of a novel." Guidelines online.

NONFICTION Subjects include memoirs. No cookbooks, children's books, inspirational books, graphic novels, or religious books. **Charges $45 reading fee.**

FICTION Subjects include poetry, short story collections, novels. "For Novels—submit no more than 100 pages along with a summary of the entire book. If we're interested we'll ask you to send the rest. We accept very few works of prose (1 or 2 per year)." Submit complete ms. **Charges a $45 reading fee.**

POETRY "Our mission is to publish thrilling, visually and emotionally and intellectually stimulating books of the highest quality, inside and out. We want contemporary poetry, etc. by the most diverse list of emerging and established writers in the U.S." Submit complete ms. **Charges $28 reading fee.**

TURNING POINT

WordTech Communications LLC, P.O. Box 541106, Cincinnati OH 45254. **E-mail:** connect@wordtech-communications.com. **Website:** www.turningpoint-books.com. **Pays in royalties.** Catalog and guidelines online.

POETRY "Dedicated to the art of story in poetry. We seek to publish collections of narrative poetry that tell the essential human stories of our times." No e-mail submissions. No calls for book-length poetry right now.

TURNSTONE PRESS

Artspace Building, 206-100 Arthur St., Winnipeg MB R3B 1H3, Canada. (204)947-1555. **Fax:** (204)942-1555. **Website:** www.turnstonepress.com. **Contact:** Submissions Assistant. Estab. 1976. "Turnstone Press is a literary publisher, not a general publisher, and therefore we are only interested in literary fiction, literary nonfiction—including literary criticism—and poetry. We do publish literary mysteries, thrillers, and noir under our Ravenstone imprint. We publish only Canadian authors or landed immigrants, we strive to publish a significant number of new writers, to publish in a variety of genres, and to have 50% of each year's list be Manitoba writers and/or books with Manitoba content." Publishes ms 2 years after acceptance. Responds in 4-7 months. Guidelines online.

NONFICTION "Samples must be 40 to 60 pages, typed/printed in a minimum 12 point serif typeface such as Times, Book Antiqua, or Garamond."

FICTION "Samples must be 40 to 60 pages, typed/printed in a minimum 12 point serif typeface such as Times, Book Antiqua, or Garamond."

POETRY Poetry mss should be a minimum 70 pages. Submit complete ms. Include cover letter.

TIPS "As a Canadian literary press, we have a mandate to publish Canadian writers only. Do some homework before submitting works to make sure your subject matter/genre/writing style falls within the publishers area of interest."

TUTTLE PUBLISHING

364 Innovation Dr., North Clarendon VT 05759. (802)773-8930. **Fax:** (802)773-6993. **E-mail:** submissions@tuttlepublishing.com. **Website:** www.tuttlepublishing.com. Estab. 1832. Publishes hardcover and trade paperback originals and reprints. Tuttle is America's leading publisher of books on Japan and Asia. "Familiarize yourself with our catalog and/or similar books we publish. Send complete book proposal with cover letter, table of contents, 1-2 sample chapters, target audience description, SASE. No e-mail submissions." **Publishes 125 titles/year. 1,000 queries received/year. 20% of books from first-time authors. 40% from unagented writers. Pays 5-10% royalty on net or retail price, depending on format and kind of book. Pays advance.** Publishes ms 18 months after acceptance. Accepts simultaneous submissions. Responds in 2-3 months to proposals.

NONFICTION Publishes Asian cultures, language, martial arts, textbooks, art and design, craft books and kits, cookbooks, religion, philosophy, and more. Query with SASE.

TWILIGHT TIMES BOOKS

P.O. Box 3340, Kingsport TN 37664. **E-mail:** publisher@twilighttimesbooks.com. **Website:** www.twilighttimesbooks.com. **Contact:** Andy M. Scott, managing editor. Estab. 1999. "We publish compelling literary fiction by authors with a distinctive voice." Published 5 debut authors within the last year. Averages 120 total titles; 15 fiction titles/year. Member: AAP, PAS, SPAN, SLF. **90% from unagented writers. Pays 8-15% royalty.** Responds in 4 weeks to queries; 2 months to mss. Guidelines online.

FICTION Accepts unsolicited mss. Do not send complete mss. Queries via e-mail only. Include estimated word count, brief bio, list of publishing credits, marketing plan.

TIPS "The only requirement for consideration at Twilight Times Books is that your novel must be entertaining and professionally written."

TWO DOLLAR RADIO

Website: www.twodollarradio.com. **Contact:** Eric Obenauf, editorial director. Estab. 2005. Two Dollar Radio is a boutique family-run press, publishing bold works of literary merit, each book, individually and collectively, providing a sonic progression that "we believe to be too loud to ignore." Targets readers who admire ambition and creativity. Range of print runs: 2,000-7,500 copies. **Publishes 5-6 (plus a biannual journal of nonfiction essays, *Frequencies*) titles/year. Advance: $500-$1,000.**

FICTION Submit entire, completed ms with a brief cover letter, via Submittable. No previously published work. No proposals. No excerpts. There is a $2 reading fee per submission. Accepts submissions every other month (January, March, May, July, September, November).

TIPS "We want writers who show an authority over language and the world that is being created, from the very first sentence on."

Ⓐ ⊘ TYNDALE HOUSE PUBLISHERS, INC.

351 Executive Dr., Carol Stream IL 60188. (800)323-9400. **Fax:** (800)684-0247. **Website:** www.tyndale.com. **Contact:** Katara Washington Patton, acquisitions; Talinda Iverson, art acquisitions. Estab. 1962. Publishes hardcover and trade paperback originals and mass paperback reprints. "Tyndale House publishes practical, user-friendly Christian books for the home and family." **Publishes 15 titles/year. Pays negotiable royalty. Pays negotiable advance.** Accepts simultaneous submissions. Guidelines online.

NONFICTION Subjects include child guidance, religion, devotional/inspirational. *Agented submissions only. No unsolicited mss.*

FICTION Subjects include juvenile, romance, Christian (children's, general, inspirational, mystery/suspense, thriller, romance). "Christian truths must be woven into the story organically. No short story collections. Youth books: character building stories with Christian perspective. Especially interested in ages 10-14. We primarily publish Christian historical romances, with occasional contemporary, suspense, or standalones." *Agented submissions only. No unsolicited mss.*

TIPS "All accepted manuscripts will appeal to Evangelical Christian children and parents."

⊘ TYRUS BOOKS

F+W Media, 1213 N. Sherman Ave., #306, Madison WI 53704. (508)427-7100. **Fax:** (508)427-6790. **E-mail:** submissions@tyrusbooks.com. **Website:** tyrusbooks.com. "We publish crime and literary fiction. We believe in the life changing power of the written word." Accepts simultaneous submissions.

FICTION Subjects include literary, mystery. Submissions currently closed; check website for updates.

UMI (URBAN MINISTRIES, INC.)

1551 Regency Ct., Calumet City IL 60409. **Fax:** (708)868-6759. **Website:** www.urbanministries.com. Estab. 1970. Publishes trade paperback originals and reprints. **Publishes 2-3 titles/year.**

NONFICTION Subjects include education, religious/Christian, religion, Christian, spirituality, Christian, Christian living, Christian doctrine, theology. "The books we publish are generally those we have a specific need for (i.e., Vacation Bible School curriculum topics); to complement an existing resource or product line; or those with a potential to develop into a curriculum." Query with SASE. Submit proposal package, outline, 2-3 sample chapters, letter why UMI should publish the book and why the book will sell.

UNBRIDLED BOOKS

8201 E. Highway WW, Columbia MO 65201. **E-mail:** michalsong@unbridledbooks.com. **Website:** unbridledbooks.com. **Contact:** Greg Michalson. Estab. 2004. "Unbridled Books is a premier publisher of works of rich literary quality that appeal to a broad audience."

FICTION Please query first by e-mail. "Due to the heavy volume of submissions, we regret that at this time we are not able to consider uninvited mss."

TIPS "We try to read each ms that arrives, so please be patient."

⊘ UNITY HOUSE

1901 N.W. Blue Pkwy., Unity Village MO 64065-0001. (816)524-3550. **Fax:** (816)347-5518. **E-mail:** unity@unityonline.org. **E-mail:** sartinson@unityonline.org. **Website:** www.unityonline.org. **Contact:** Sharon Sartin, executive assistant. Estab. 1889. Publishes hardcover, trade paperback, and electronic originals. Unity House publishes metaphysical Christian books based on Unity principles, as well as inspirational books on metaphysics and practical spirituality. All manuscripts must reflect a spiritual foundation and express the Unity philosophy, practical Christianity, universal principles, and/or metaphysics. **Publishes 5-7 titles/year. 50 queries received/year. 5% of books from first-time authors. 95% from unagented writers. Pays 10-15% royalty on retail price. Pays advance.** Publishes ms 13 months after acceptance. Responds in 6-8 months. Catalog and guidelines online.

NONFICTION Subjects include religion, spirituality, metaphysics, new thought. "Writers should be familiar with principles of metaphysical Christianity but not feel bound by them. We are interested in works in the related fields of holistic health, spiritual psychology, and the philosophy of other world religions." *Not accepting mss for new books at this time.* Reviews artwork/photos. Writers should send photocopies.

FICTION Subjects include spiritual, inspirational, metaphysical, visionary fiction. "We are a bridge between traditional Christianity and New Age spirituality. Unity is based on metaphysical Christian principles, spiritual values and the healing power of prayer as a resource for daily living." *Not accepting mss for new books at this time.*

TIPS "We target an audience of spiritual seekers."

THE UNIVERSITY OF AKRON PRESS

120 E. Mill St., Suite 415, Akron OH 44325. (330)972-6953. **Fax:** (330)972-8364. **E-mail:** uapress@uakron.edu. **Website:** www.uakron.edu/uapress. **Contact:** Thomas Bacher, director and acquisitions. Estab. 1988. Publishes hardcover and paperback originals and reissues. "The University of Akron Press is the publishing arm of The University of Akron and is dedicated to the dissemination of scholarly, professional, and regional books and other content." **Publishes 10-12 titles/year. 100 queries received/year. 50-75 mss received/year. 40% of books from first-time authors. 80% from unagented writers. Pays 7-15% royalty.** Publishes ms 9-12 months after acceptance. Accepts simultaneous submissions. Responds in 2 weeks to queries/proposals; 3-4 months to solicited mss. Query prior to submitting. Guidelines online.

NONFICTION Subjects include Applied politics, early American literature, emerging technologies, history of psychology, history of technology, interdisciplinary studies, Northeast Ohio history and culture, Ohio politics, poetics. Query by e-mail. Mss cannot be returned unless SASE is included.

POETRY Follow the guidelines and submit mss only for the contest: www.uakron.edu/uapress/poetry.html. "We publish two books of poetry annually, one of which is the winner of The Akron Poetry prize. We also are interested in literary collections based around one theme, especially collections of translated works." If you are interested in publishing with The University of Akron Press, please fill out form online.

THE UNIVERSITY OF ALABAMA PRESS

200 Hackberry Lane, 2nd Floor, Tuscaloosa AL 35487. (205)348-5180 or (205)348-1571. **Fax:** (205)348-9201. **E-mail:** waterman@uapress.ua.edu. **Website:** www.uapress.ua.edu. **Contact:** Daniel Waterman, editor-in-chief. Publishes nonfiction hardcover and paperbound originals. **Publishes 70-75 titles/year. 70% of books from first-time authors. 95% from unagented writers. Pays advance in very limited number of circumstances.** Responds in 2-3 weeks to queries. Book catalog available free.

NONFICTION Subjects include anthropology, archeology, politics, history, language, literature, literary criticism, religion. Considers upon merit almost any subject of scholarly interest, but specializes in communications, military history, public administration, literary criticism and biography, history, Judaic studies, and American archaeology. Accepts nonfiction translations. Query with SASE.

TIPS "Please direct inquiry to appropriate acquisitions editor. University of Alabama Press responds to an author within 2-3 weeks upon receiving the ms or proposal. If they think it is unsuitable for Alabama's program, they tell the author as soon as possible. If the ms warrants it, they begin the peer-review process, which may take 2-4 months to complete. During that process, they keep the author fully informed."

UNIVERSITY OF ALASKA PRESS

P.O. Box 756240, Fairbanks AK 99775-6240. (907)474-5831 or (888)252-6657. **Fax:** (907)474-5502. **E-mail:** james.engelhardt@alaska.edu. **Website:** www.uaf.edu/uapress. **Contact:** James Engelhardt, acquisitions editor. Estab. 1967. Publishes hardcover originals, trade paperback originals and reprints. "The mission of the University of Alaska Press is to encourage, publish, and disseminate works of scholarship that will enhance the store of knowledge about Alaska and the North Pacific Rim, with a special emphasis on the circumpolar regions." **Publishes 10 titles/year.** Publishes ms within 2 years of acceptance. after acceptance of ms. Responds in 2 months to queries. Book catalog available free. Guidelines online.

NONFICTION Subjects include Americana, Alaskana, animals, anthropology, archeology, art, architecture, education, ethnic, government, politics, health, medicine, history, language, literature, military, war, nature, environment, regional, science, translation, women's issues, women's studies. Northern or circumpolar only. Query with SASE and proposal. Reviews artwork/photos.

FICTION Subjects include literary. Alaska literary series with Peggy Shumaker as series editor. Publishes 1-3 works of fiction/year. Submit proposal.

TIPS "Writers have the best chance with scholarly nonfiction relating to Alaska, the circumpolar regions and North Pacific Rim. Our audience is made up of scholars, historians, students, libraries, universities, individuals, and the general Alaskan public."

THE UNIVERSITY OF ALBERTA PRESS

Ring House 2, Edmonton AB T6G 2E1, Canada. (780)492-3662. **Fax:** (780)492-0719. **E-mail:** pmidgley@ualberta.ca. **Website:** www.uap.ualberta.ca. **Contact:** Peter Midgley. Estab. 1969. Publishes originals and reprints. "We do not accept unsolicited novels, short story collections, or poetry. Please see our website for details." **Publishes 18-25 titles/year. Royalties are negotiated.** Publishes ms within 2 years after acceptance. Responds in 3 months to queries. Guidelines online.

NONFICTION Subjects include history, language, literature, nature, environment, regional, natural history, social policy. Submit cover letter, word count, CV, 1 sample chapter, TOC.

UNIVERSITY OF ARIZONA PRESS

Main Library Building, 5th Floor, 1510 E. University Blvd., Tucson AZ 85721. (520)621-1441. **Fax:** (520)621-8899. **E-mail:** kbuckles@uapress.arizona.edu. **Website:** www.uapress.arizona.edu. **Contact:** Kristen Buckles, acquiring editor. Estab. 1959. Publishes hardcover and paperback originals and reprints. "University of Arizona is a publisher of scholarly books and books of the Southwest." **Royalty terms vary; usual starting point for scholarly monography is after sale of first 1,000 copies. Pays advance.** Responds in 3 months to queries. Book catalog online. Guidelines online.

NONFICTION Subjects include Americana, anthropology, archeology, ethnic, nature, environment, regional, environmental studies, western, and environmental history. Scholarly books about anthropology, Arizona, American West, archeology, Native American studies, Latino studies, environmental science, global change, Latin America, Native Americans, natural history, space sciences, and women's studies. Submit sample chapters, resume, TOC, ms length, audience, comparable books. Reviews artwork/photos.

TIPS "Perhaps the most common mistake a writer might make is to offer a book manuscript or proposal to a house whose list he or she has not studied carefully. Editors rejoice in receiving material that is clearly targeted to the house's list ('I have approached your firm because my books complement your past publications in') and presented in a straightforward, businesslike manner."

THE UNIVERSITY OF ARKANSAS PRESS

McIlroy House, 105 N. McIlroy Ave., Fayetteville AR 72701. (479)575-3246. **Fax:** (479)575-6044. **E-mail:** mbieker@uark.edu. **Website:** uapress.com. **Contact:** Mike Bieker, director. Estab. 1980. Publishes hardcover and trade paperback originals and reprints. "The University of Arkansas Press publishes series on Ozark studies, the Civil War in the West, poetry and poetics, and sport and society." **Publishes 30 titles/year. 30% of books from first-time authors. 95% from unagented writers.** Publishes ms 1 year after acceptance. Responds in 3 months to proposals. Book catalog and ms guidelines online.

NONFICTION Subjects include government, politics, history, Southern, humanities, literary criticism, nature, environment, regional, Arkansas. Accepted mss must be submitted on disk. Query with SASE. Submit outline, sample chapters, resume.

POETRY University of Arkansas Press publishes 4 poetry books per year through the Miller Williams Poetry Prize.

UNIVERSITY OF CALGARY PRESS

2500 University Dr. NW, Calgary AB T2N 1N4, Canada. (403)220-7578. **Fax:** (403)282-0085. **Website:** www.uofcpress.com. **Contact:** Peter Enman, editor. Publishes scholarly and trade paperback originals and reprints. **Publishes 10 titles/year.** Publishes ms

20 months after acceptance. Book catalog available for free. Guidelines online.

NONFICTION Subjects include art, architecture, philosophy women's studies, world affairs, Canadian studies, post-modern studies, native studies, history, international relations, arctic studies, Africa, Latin American and Caribbean studies, and heritage of the Canadian and American heartland.

UNIVERSITY OF CALIFORNIA PRESS

155 Grand Ave., Suite 400, Oakland CA 94612. **E-mail:** askucp@ucpress.edu. **Website:** www.ucpress.edu. **Contact:** Kate Marshall, acquisitions editor. Estab. 1893. Publishes hardcover and paperback originals and reprints. "University of California Press publishes mostly nonfiction written by scholars." **Pays advance.** Response time varies, depending on the subject. Enclose return postage to queries. Guidelines online.

NONFICTION Subjects include history, nature, environment, translation, art, literature, natural sciences, some high-level popularizations. No length preference. Submit proposal package.

FICTION Publishes fiction only in translation.

⊘ THE UNIVERSITY OF CHICAGO PRESS

1427 E. 60th St., Chicago IL 60637. Voicemail: (773)702-7700. **Fax:** (773)702-9756. **Website:** www.press.uchicago.edu. **Contact:** Randolph Petilos, poetry and medieval studies editor. Estab. 1891. "The University of Chicago Press has been publishing scholarly books and journals since 1891. Annually, we publish an average of four books in our Phoenix Poets series and two books of poetry in translation. Occasionally, we may publish a book of poetry outside Phoenix Poets, or as a paperback reprint from another publisher." Has recently published work by Peter Balakian, Charles Bernstein, Peg Boyers, Killarney Clary, Milo De Angelis, Nate Klug, Robert Pack, Pier Paolo Pasolini, Vanesha Pravin, and Connie Voisine.

UNIVERSITY OF GEORGIA PRESS

Main Library, Third Floor, 320 S. Jackson St., Athens GA 30602. (706)369-6130. **Fax:** (706)369-6131. **E-mail:** books@ugapress.uga.edu. **Website:** www.ugapress.org. Estab. 1938. Publishes hardcover originals, trade paperback originals, and reprints. University of Georgia Press is a midsized press that publishes fiction only through the Flannery O'Connor Award for Short Fiction competition. **Publishes 85 titles/year. Pays 7-10% royalty on net receipts. Pays rare, varying advance.** Publishes ms 1 year after acceptance. Responds in 2 months to queries. Book catalog and guidelines online.

NONFICTION Subjects include government, politics, history, American, nature, environment, regional, environmental studies, literary nonfiction. Query with SASE. Submit bio, 1 sample chapter. Reviews artwork/photos. Send if essential to book.

FICTION Short story collections published in Flannery O'Connor Award Competition.

TIPS "Please visit our website to view our book catalogs and for all manuscript submission guidelines."

UNIVERSITY OF ILLINOIS PRESS

1325 S. Oak St., Champaign IL 61820-6903. (217)333-0950. **Fax:** (217)244-8082. **E-mail:** uipress@uillinois.edu. **Website:** www.press.uillinois.edu. **Contact:** Willis Regier, director (literature, classics, ancient religion, sports history); Laurie Matheson, senior acquisitions editor (history, appalachian studies, labor studies, music, folklore); Daniel Nasset, acquisitions editor (film studies, anthropology, communication studies). Estab. 1918. Publishes hardcover and trade paperback originals and reprints. University of Illinois Press publishes scholarly books and serious nonfiction with a wide range of study interests. Currently emphasizing American history, especially immigration, labor, African-American, and military; American religion, music, women's studies, and film. **Publishes 150 titles/year. 35% of books from first-time authors. 95% from unagented writers. Pays $1,000-1,500 (rarely) advance.** Publishes ms 1 year after acceptance. Responds in 1 month to queries. Guidelines online.

NONFICTION Subjects include Americana, animals, cooking, foods, nutrition, government, politics, history, especially American history, language, literature, military, war, music, especially American music, dance, philosophy, regional, sociology, sports, translation, film/cinema/stage. "Always looking for solid, scholarly books in American history, especially social history; books on American popular music, and books in the broad area of American studies." Query with SASE. Submit outline.

TIPS "As a university press, we are required to submit all mss to rigorous scholarly review. Mss need to be clearly original, well written, and based on solid and thorough research. We cannot encourage memoirs or autobiographies."

UNIVERSITY OF IOWA PRESS

100 Kuhl House, 119 W. Park Rd., Iowa City IA 52242. (319)335-2000. **Fax:** (319)335-2055. **E-mail:** james-mccoy@uiowa.edu; elisabeth-chretien@uiowa.edu; cath-campbell@uiowa.edu. **Website:** www.uiowa-press.org. **Contact:** James McCoy, director (short fiction, poetry, general trade); Elisabeth Chretien, acquisitions editor (literary criticism, literary and general nonfiction, military and veterans' studies); Catherine Cocks, acquisitions editor (book arts, fan studies, food studies, midwestern history and culture, theatre history and culture). Estab. 1969. Publishes hardcover and paperback originals. "We publish authoritative, original nonfiction that we market mostly by direct mail to groups with special interests in our titles, and by advertising in trade and scholarly publications." **Publishes 35 titles/year. 30% of books from first-time authors. 95% from unagented writers. Pays 7-10% royalty on net receipts.** Publishes ms 1 year after acceptance. Book catalog available free. Guidelines online.

NONFICTION Subjects include anthropology, archeology, creative nonfiction, history, regional, language, literature, nature, environment, American literary studies, medicine and literature. "Looks for evidence of original research, reliable sources, clarity of organization, complete development of theme with documentation, supportive footnotes and/or bibliography, and a substantive contribution to knowledge in the field treated. Use *Chicago Manual of Style*." Query with SASE. Submit outline. Reviews artwork/photos.

FICTION Currently publishes the Iowa Short Fiction Award selections.

POETRY Currently publishes winners of the Iowa Poetry Prize Competition, Kuhl House Poets, poetry anthologies. Competition guidelines available on website.

UNIVERSITY OF MAINE PRESS

126A College Ave., Orono ME 04473. (207)866-0573. **Fax:** (207)866-2084. **E-mail:** michael.alpert@umit.maine.edu. **Website:** www.umaine.edu/umpress. **Contact:** Michael Alpert, editorial director. Publishes hardcover and trade paperback originals and reprints. **Publishes 4 titles/year. 50 queries received/year. 25 mss received/year. 50% of books from first-time authors. 90% from unagented writers.** Publishes ms 1 year after acceptance.

NONFICTION Subjects include history, regional, science. "We are an academic book publisher, interested in scholarly works on regional history, regional life sciences, Franco-American studies. Authors should be able to articulate their ideas on the potential market for their work." Query with SASE.

UNIVERSITY OF MICHIGAN PRESS

839 Greene St., Ann Arbor MI 48106. **Website:** www.press.umich.edu. "In partnership with our authors and series editors, we publish in a wide range of humanities and social sciences disciplines." Guidelines online.

NONFICTION Submit proposal.

FICTION Subjects include literary, regional. In addition to the annual Michigan Literary Fiction Awards, this publishes literary fiction linked to the Great Lakes region. Submit cover letter and first 30 pages.

UNIVERSITY OF NEVADA PRESS

Morrill Hall, Mail Stop 0166, Reno NV 89557. (775)784-6573. **Fax:** (775)784-6200. **Website:** www.unpress.nevada.edu. **Contact:** Joanne O'Hare, director. Estab. 1961. Publishes hardcover and paperback originals and reprints. "Small university press. Publishes fiction that primarily focuses on the American West." Member: AAUP **Publishes 25 titles/year.** Publishes ms 18 months after acceptance. Responds in 2 months. Guidelines online.

NONFICTION Subjects include anthropology, archeology, ethnic, studies, history, regional and natural, nature, environment, regional, history and geography, western literature, current affairs, gambling and gaming, Basque studies. No juvenile books. Submit proposal. No online submissions. Reviews artwork/photos. Send photocopies.

FICTION "We publish in Basque Studies, Gambling Studies, Western literature, Western history, Natural science, Environmental Studies, Travel and Outdoor books, Archeology, Anthropology, and Political Studies, all focusing on the West". The Press also publishes creative nonfiction and books on regional topics for a general audience. *Does not publish unsolicited fiction.*

UNIVERSITY OF NEW MEXICO PRESS

1717 Roma Ave., Albuquerque NM 87106. **Fax:** (505)277-3343. **E-mail:** clarkw@unm.edu. **Website:** www.unmpress.com. **Contact:** W. Clark Whitehorn, editor-in-chief. Estab. 1929. Publishes hardcover originals and trade paperback originals and reprints. "The Press is well known as a publisher in the fields of anthropology, archeology, Latin American studies, art and photography, architecture and the history and culture of the American West, fiction, some poetry, Chicano/a studies and works by and about American Indians. We focus on American West, Southwest and Latin American regions." **Pays variable royalty. Pays advance.** Book catalog available free. Guidelines online.

NONFICTION Subjects include Americana, anthropology, archeology, art, architecture, biography, creative nonfiction, ethnic, gardening, gay, lesbian, government, politics, history, language, literature, memoirs, military, war, multicultural, music, dance, nature, environment, photography, regional, religion, science, translation, travel, women's issues, women's studies, contemporary culture, cinema/stage, crime, general nonfiction. No how-to, humor, juvenile, self-help, software, technical or textbooks. Query with SASE. Reviews artwork/photos. Send photocopies.

THE UNIVERSITY OF NORTH CAROLINA PRESS

116 S. Boundary St., Chapel Hill NC 27514. (919)966-3561. **Fax:** (919)966-3829. **E-mail:** uncpress@unc.edu. **Website:** www.uncpress.unc.edu. **Contact:** Mark Simpson-Vos, editorial director. Publishes hardcover originals, trade paperback originals and reprints. "UNC Press publishes nonfiction books for academic and general audiences. We have a special interest in trade and scholarly titles about our region. We do not, however, publish original fiction, drama, or poetry, memoirs of living persons, or festshriften." **Publishes 90 titles/year. 500 queries received/year. 200 mss received/year. 50% of books from first-time authors. 90% from unagented writers. Pays variable royalty on wholesale price. Offers variable advance.** Publishes ms 1 year after acceptance. Responds in 3-4 weeks. Book catalog and guidelines online.

NONFICTION Subjects include Americana, anthropology, archeology, art, architecture, cooking, foods, nutrition, gardening, government, politics, health, medicine, history, language, literature, military, war, multicultural, music, dance, nature, environment, philosophy, photography, regional, religion, translation, womens issues, women's studies, African-American studies, American studies, cultural studies, Latin-American studies, American-Indian studies, media studies, gender studies, social medicine, Appalachian studies. Submit proposal package, outline, CV, cover letter, abstract, and TOC. Reviews artwork/photos. Send photocopies.

UNIVERSITY OF NORTH TEXAS PRESS

1155 Union Circle, #311336, Denton TX 76203. (940)565-2142. **Fax:** (940)565-4590. **E-mail:** ronald.chrisman@unt.edu; karen.devinney@unt.edu. **Website:** untpress.unt.edu. **Contact:** Ronald Chrisman, director; Karen De Vinney, assistant director; Lori Belew, administrative assistant. Estab. 1987. Publishes hardcover and trade paperback originals and reprints. "We are dedicated to producing the highest quality scholarly, academic, and general interest books. We are committed to serving all peoples by publishing stories of their cultures and experiences that have been overlooked. Currently emphasizing military history, Texas history, music, Mexican-American studies." **Publishes 14-16 titles/year. 500 queries received/year. 50% of books from first-time authors. 95% from unagented writers.** Publishes ms 1-2 years after acceptance. Responds in 1 month to queries. Book catalog for 8 ½x11 SASE. Guidelines online.

NONFICTION Subjects include Americana, ethnic, government, history, military, music, nature, politics, regional, womens issues, womens studies. Query by e-mail. Reviews artwork/photos. Send photocopies.

FICTION "The only fiction we publish is the winner of the Katherine Anne Porter Prize in Short Fiction, an annual, national competition with a $1,000 prize, and publication of the winning ms each Fall."

POETRY "The only poetry we publish is the winner of the Vassar Miller Prize in Poetry, an annual, national competition with a $1,000 prize and publication of the winning ms each Spring." Query.

TIPS "We publish series called War and the Southwest; Texas Folklore Society Publications; the Western Life Series; Practical Guide Series; Al-Filo: Mexican-American studies; North Texas Crime and Criminal Justice; Katherine Anne Porter Prize in Short Fiction; and the North Texas Lives of Musicians Series."

UNIVERSITY OF OKLAHOMA PRESS

2800 Venture Dr., Norman OK 73069. **E-mail:** cerankin@ou.edu. **Website:** www.oupress.com. **Contact:** Charles E. Rankin, editor-in-chief. Estab. 1928. Publishes hardcover and paperback originals and reprints. University of Oklahoma Press publishes books for both scholarly and nonspecialist readers. **Publishes 90 titles/year. Pays standard royalty.** Responds promptly to queries. Book catalog for 9×12 SAE with 6 first-class stamps.

IMPRINTS Plains Reprints.

NONFICTION Subjects include political science (Congressional, area and security studies), history (regional, military, natural), language/literature (American Indian, US West), American Indian studies, classical studies. Query with SASE or by e-mail. Submit outline, resume, 1-2 sample chapters. Use *Chicago Manual of Style* for ms guidelines. Reviews artwork/photos.

UNIVERSITY OF OTTAWA PRESS

542 King Edward Ave., Ottawa ON K1N 6N5, Canada. (613)562-5246. **Fax:** (613)562-5247. **E-mail:** puo-uop@uottawa.ca. **Website:** www.press.uottawa.ca. Estab. 1936. "UOP publishes books and journals, in French and English, and in any and all editions and formats, that touch upon the human condition: anthropology, sociology, political science, psychology, criminology, media studies, economics, education, language and culture, law, history, literature, translation studies, philosophy, public administration, health sciences, and religious studies." Accepts simultaneous submissions. Book catalog and ms guidelines online.

NONFICTION Submit outline, proposal form (please see website), CV, 1-2 sample chapters (for monographs only), ms (for collected works only), TOC, 2-5 page proposal/summary, contributor names, short bios, and citizenships (for collected works only).

TIPS "Please note that the University of Ottawa Press does not accept: bilingual works (texts must be either entirely in English or entirely in French), undergraduate or masters theses, or doctoral theses that have not been substantially revised."

UNIVERSITY OF PENNSYLVANIA PRESS

3905 Spruce St., Philadelphia PA 19104. (215)898-6261. **Fax:** (215)898-0404. **Website:** www.pennpress.org. **Contact:** Peter Agree, editor-in-chief. Estab. 1890. Publishes hardcover and paperback originals, and reprints. "Manuscript submissions are welcome in fields appropriate for Penn Press's editorial program. The Press's acquiring editors, and their fields of responsibility, are listed in the Contact Us section of our Web site. Although we have no formal policies regarding manuscript proposals and submissions, what we need minimally, in order to gauge our degree of interest, is a brief statement describing the manuscript, a copy of the contents page, and a reasonably current vita. Initial inquiries are best sent by letter, in paper form, to the appropriate acquiring editor." **Publishes 100+ titles/year. 20-30% of books from first-time authors. 95% from unagented writers. Royalty determined on book-by-book basis. Pays advance.** Publishes ms 10 months after acceptance. Responds in 3 months to queries. Book catalog online. Guidelines online.

NONFICTION Subjects include Americana, art, architecture, history, American, art, architecture, literary criticism, sociology, anthropology, literary criticism, cultural studies, ancient studies, medieval studies, urban studies, human rights. Follow the *Chicago Manual of Style*. "Serious books that serve the scholar and the professional, student and general reader." Query with SASE. Submit outline, resume.

UNIVERSITY OF SOUTH CAROLINA PRESS

1600 Hampton St., 5th Floor, Columbia SC 29208. (803)777-5243. **Fax:** (803)777-0160. **Website:** www.sc.edu/uscpress. **Contact:** Linda Fogle, assistant director for operations (trade books); Jim Denton, acquisitions editor (literature, religious studies, rhetoric, communication, social work); Alexander Moore, acquisitions editor (history, regional studies). Estab. 1944. Publishes hardcover originals, trade paperback originals and reprints. "We focus on scholarly monographs and regional trade books of lasting merit." **Publishes 50 titles/year. 500 queries received/year. 150 mss received/year. 30% of books from first-time authors. 95% from unagented writers.** Publishes ms 1 year after acceptance. Accepts simultaneous submissions. Responds in 3 months to mss. Book catalog available free. Guidelines online.

NONFICTION Subjects include art, architecture, history, American, Civil War, culinary, maritime, women's studies, language, literature, regional, religion, rhetoric, communication. Query with SASE, or submit proposal package and outline, and 1 sample chapter and resume with SASE Reviews artwork/photos. Send photocopies.

POETRY Palmetto Poetry Series, a South Carolina-based original poetry series edited by Nikky Finney. Director: Jonathan Haupt, director (jhaupt@mailbox.sc.edu).

UNIVERSITY OF TAMPA PRESS

University of Tampa, 401 W. Kennedy Blvd., Tampa FL 33606. (813)253-6266. **Fax:** (813)258-7593. **E-mail:** utpress@ut.edu. **Website:** www.utpress.ut.edu. **Contact:** Richard Mathews, editor. Publishes hardcover originals and reprints; trade paperback originals and reprints. Responds in 3-4 months to queries. Book catalog online.

NONFICTION , Florida history. Reviews artwork/photos.

FICTION Subjects include literary, poetry.

POETRY Submit to the Tampa Review Prize for Poetry.

THE UNIVERSITY OF TENNESSEE PRESS

110 Conference Center, 600 Henley St., Knoxville TN 37996. (865)974-3321. **Fax:** (865)974-3724. **E-mail:** twells@utk.edu. **Website:** www.utpress.org. **Contact:** Scot Danforth, acquisitions editor; Thomas Wells, acquisitions editor. Estab. 1940. "Our mission is to stimulate scientific and scholarly research in all fields; to channel such studies, either in scholarly or popular form, to a larger number of people; and to extend the regional leadership of the University of Tennessee by stimulating research projects within the South and by nonuniversity authors." **Publishes 35 titles/year. 35% of books from first-time authors. 99% from unagented writers. Pays negotiable royalty on net receipts.** Guidelines online.

NONFICTION Subjects include Americana, anthropology, archeology, historical, art, architecture, vernacular, history, language, literature, literary criticism, regional, religion, history sociology, anthropology, archeology, biography only, women's issues, women's studies, African-American studies, Appalachian studies, folklore/folklife, material culture. Prefers scholarly treatment and a readable style. Authors usually have PhDs. Submissions in other fields, and submissions of poetry, textbooks, plays and translations are not invited Submit outline, bio, 2 sample chapters. Reviews artwork/photos.

UNIVERSITY OF TEXAS PRESS

P.O. Box 7819, Austin TX 78713-7819. (512)471-4278, ext. 3. **Fax:** (512)232-7178. **E-mail:** rdevens@utpress.utexas.edu. **Website:** www.utexaspress.com. **Contact:** Robert Devens, editor-in-chief. Estab. 1952. "In addition to publishing the results of advanced research for scholars worldwide, UT Press has a special obligation to the people of its state to publish authoritative books on Texas. We do not publish fiction or poetry, except as invited by a series editor, and some Latin American and Middle Eastern literature in translation." **Publishes 90 titles/year. 50% of books from first-time authors. 99% from unagented writers. Pays occasional advance.** Publishes ms 18-24 months after acceptance. Responds in 3 months to queries. Guidelines online.

NONFICTION Subjects include anthropology, archeology, art, architecture, ethnic, film, cinema, stage, history, language, literature, literary criticism, nature, environment, regional, science, translation, women's issues, women's studies, natural history, American, Latin American, Native American, Latino, and Middle Eastern studies; classics and the ancient world, film, contemporary regional architecture, geography, ornithology, biology. Also uses specialty titles related to Texas and the Southwest, national trade titles and regional trade titles. Submit cover letter, TOC, CV, sample chapter.

UNIVERSITY OF WASHINGTON PRESS

P.O. Box 359570, Seattle WA 98195. (206)543-4050. **Fax:** (206)543-3932. **E-mail:** lmclaugh@uw.edu. **Website:** www.washington.edu/uwpress/. **Contact:** Laurin McLaughlin, editor-in-chief. Publishes in hardcover originals. **Publishes 70 titles/year.** Book catalog guidelines online.

NONFICTION Subjects include anthropology, archeology, art, architecture, ethnic, Groups in China, history, Western, multicultural, nature, environment, photography, regional, social sciences. Go to our Book Search page for complete subject listing. We publish academic and general books, especially in anthropology, Asian studies, art, environmental studies, Middle Eastern Studies & regional interests. International Studies with focus on Asia; Jewish Studies; Art & Culture of the Northwest coast; Indians & Alaskan Eskimos; The Asian-American Experience; Southeast Asian Studies; Korean and Slavic Studies; Studies in Modernity & National Identity; Scandinavian Studies. Query with SASE. Submit proposal package, outline, sample chapters.

UNIVERSITY OF WISCONSIN PRESS

1930 Monroe St., 3rd Floor, Madison WI 53711. (608)263-1110. **Fax:** (608)263-1132. **E-mail:** gcwalker@wisc.edu. **E-mail:** kadushin@wisc.edu. **Website:** uwpress.wisc.edu. **Contact:** Raphael Kadushin, senior acquisitions editor; Gwen Walker, acquisitions editor. Estab. 1937. Publishes hardcoveroriginals, paperback originals, and paperback reprints. **Publishes 98 titles/year. Pays royalty.** Publishes ms 9-18 months after acceptance. Responds in 2 weeks to queries; 8 weeks to mss. Rarely comments on rejected mss. Guidelines online.

NONFICTION Subjects include anthropology, dance, environment, film, foods, gay, history, lesbian, memoirs, travel, African Studies, classical studies, human rights, Irish studies, Jewish studies, Latin American studies, Latino/a memoirs, modern Western European history, performance studies, Slavic studies, Southeast Asian studies. Does not accept unsolicited mss. Query with SASE or submit outline, 1-2 sample chapter(s), synopsis.

FICTION Subjects include gay, hi-lo, lesbian, mystery, regional, short story collections. Query with SASE or submit outline, 1-2 sample chapter(s), synopsis.

POETRY The University of Wisconsin Press Awards the Brittingham Prize in Poetry and Felix Pollack Prize in Poetry. More details online.

TIPS "Make sure the query letter and sample text are well-written, and read guidelines carefully to make sure we accept the genre you are submitting."

UNIVERSITY PRESS OF KANSAS

2502 Westbrooke Circle, Lawrence KS 66045. (785)864-4154. **Fax:** (785)864-4586. **E-mail:** upress@ku.edu. **Website:** www.kansaspress.ku.edu; www.facebook.com/kansaspress. **Contact:** Michael J. Briggs, editor-in-chief; Fred Woodward, director emeritus; Kim Hogeland, acquisitions editor; Charles T. Myers, director. Estab. 1946. Publishes hardcover originals, trade paperback originals and reprints. "The University Press of Kansas publishes scholarly books that advance knowledge and regional books that contribute to the understanding of Kansas, the Great Plains, and the Midwest." **Publishes 55 titles/year. 600 queries received/year. 20% of books from first-time authors. 98% from unagented writers. Pays selective advance.** Publishes ms 10 months after acceptance. Responds in 1 month to proposals. Book catalog and ms guidelines free.

NONFICTION Subjects include Americana, archeology, environment, government, military, nature, politics, regional, war, American History, Native Studies, American Cultural Studies. "We are looking for books on topics of wide interest based on solid scholarship and written for both specialists and informed general readers. Do not send unsolicited, complete manuscripts." Submit outline, sample chapters, cover letter, CV, prospectus. Reviews artwork/photos. Send photocopies.

UNIVERSITY PRESS OF KENTUCKY

663 S. Limestone St., Lexington KY 40508. (859)257-8434. **Fax:** (859)323-1873. **E-mail:** adwatk0@email.uky.edu. **Website:** www.kentuckypress.com. **Contact:** Anne Dean Dotson, senior acquisitions editor. Estab. 1943. Publishes hardcover and paperback originals and reprints. "We are a scholarly publisher, publishing chiefly for an academic and professional audience, as well as books about Kentucky, the upper South, Appalachia, and the Ohio Valley." **Publishes 60 titles/year. Royalty varies.** Publishes ms 1 year after accceptance. after acceptance of ms. Responds in 2 months to queries. Book catalog available free. Guidelines online.

NONFICTION Subjects include history, military, war, history, regional, political science. No textbooks, genealogical material, lightweight popular treatments, how-to books, or books unrelated to our major areas of interest. The Press does not consider original works of fiction or poetry. Query with SASE.

UNIVERSITY PRESS OF MISSISSIPPI

3825 Ridgewood Rd., Jackson MS 39211. (601)432-6205. **Fax:** (601)432-6217. **E-mail:** press@mississippi.edu. **Website:** www.upress.state.ms.us. **Contact:** Craig Gill, editor-in-chief (regional studies, history, folklore, music). Estab. 1970. Publishes hardcover and paperback originals and reprints and e-books. "University Press of Mississippi publishes scholarly and trade titles, as well as special series, including: American Made Music; Conversations with Comic Artists; Conversations with Filmmakers; Faulkner and Yoknapatawpha; Literary Conversations; Hollywood Legends; Caribbean Studies." **Publishes 70 titles/year. 80% of books from first-time authors. 90% from unagented writers. Competitive royalties and terms. Pays advance.** Publishes ms 1 year after acceptance. Responds in 3 months to queries.

NONFICTION Subjects include Americana, art, architecture, ethnic, minority studies, politics, history, literature, literary criticism, music, photography, regional, Southern, folklife, literary criticism, popular culture with scholarly emphasis, literary studies. "We prefer a proposal that describes the significance of the work and a chapter outline." Submit outline, sample chapters, CV.

URJ PRESS

633 Third Ave., 7th Floor, New York NY 10017. (212)650-4120. **Fax:** (212)650-4119. **E-mail:** press@

urj.org. **Website:** www.urjbooksandmusic.com. **Contact:** Michael H. Goldberg, editor-in-chief. Publishes hardcover and trade paperback originals. "URJ publishes textbooks for the religious classroom, children's tradebooks and scholarly work of Jewish education import—no adult fiction and no YA fiction." *URJ Press publishes books related to Judaism.* **Publishes 22 titles/year. 500 queries received/year. 400 mss received/year. 70% of books from first-time authors. 90% from unagented writers. Pays 3-5% royalty on retail price. Makes outright purchase of $500-2,000. Pays $500-2,000 advance.** Publishes ms 18-24 months after acceptance. Responds in 4 months. Book catalog and ms guidelines online.

NONFICTION Subjects include art, architecture, synagogue, child guidance, cooking, foods, nutrition, Jewish, education, ethnic, Judaism, government, politics, Israeli/Jewish, history, language, literature, Hebrew, military, war, as relates to Judaism, music, dance, nature, environment, philosophy, Jewish, religion, Judaism only, sex, as it relates to Judaism, spirituality, Jewish. Picture books, young readers, middle readers: religion. Average word length: picture books—1,500. Submit proposal package, outline, bio, 1-2 sample chapters.

TIPS "Look at some of our books. Have an understanding of the Reform Judaism community. In addition to bookstores, we sell to Jewish congregations and Hebrew day schools."

USBORNE PUBLISHING

83-85 Saffron Hill, London En EC1N 8RT, United Kingdom. (44)207430-2800. **Fax:** (44)207430-1562. **E-mail:** mail@usborne.co.uk. **Website:** www.usborne.com. "Usborne Publishing is a multiple-award winning, world-wide children's publishing company publishing almost every type of children's book for every age from baby to young adult." **Pays authors royalty.**

FICTION Young readers, middle readers: adventure, contemporary, fantasy, history, humor, multicultural, nature/environment, science fiction, suspense/mystery, strong concept-based or character-led series. Average word length: young readers—5,000-10,000; middle readers—25,000-50,000; young adult—50,000-100,000. *Agented submissions only.*

TIPS "Do not send any original work and, sorry, but we cannot guarantee a reply."

UTAH STATE UNIVERSITY PRESS

3078 Old Main Hill, Logan UT 84322. **Website:** www.usu.edu/usupress. Estab. 1972. Publishes hardcover and trade paperback originals and reprints. Utah State University Press publishes scholarly works in the academic areas noted below. Currently interested in book-length scholarly mss dealing with folklore studies, composition studies, Native American studies, and history. **Publishes 18 titles/year. 8% of books from first-time authors.** Publishes ms 18 months after acceptance. Responds in 1 month to queries. Book catalog available free. Guidelines online.

NONFICTION Subjects include history, of the West, regional, folklore, the West, Native-American studies, studies in composition and rhetoric. Query via online submission form. Reviews artwork/photos. Send photocopies.

TIPS "Utah State University Press also sponsors the annual May Swenson Poetry Award."

VANDERBILT UNIVERSITY PRESS

PMB 351813, 2301 Vanderbilt Place, Nashville TN 37235. (615)322-3585. **Fax:** (615)343-8823. **E-mail:** vupress@vanderbilt.edu. **Website:** www.vanderbiltuniversitypress.com. **Contact:** Michael Ames, director. Publishes hardcover originals and trade paperback originals and reprints. "Vanderbilt University Press publishes books on healthcare, social sciences, education, and regional studies, for both academic and general audiences that are intellectually significant, socially relevant, and of practical importance." **Publishes 20-25 titles/year. 500 queries received/year. 25% of books from first-time authors. 90% from unagented writers. Pays rare advance.** Publishes ms 10 months after acceptance. Accepts simultaneous submissions. Responds in 2 weeks to proposals. Book catalog online. Guidelines online.

NONFICTION Subjects include Americana, anthropology, archeology, education, ethnic, government, politics, health, medicine, history, language, literature, multicultural, music, dance, nature, environment, philosophy, women's issues, women's studies. Submit cover letter, TOC, CV, 1-2 sample chapters.

TIPS "Our audience consists of scholars and educated, general readers."

VAN SCHAIK PUBLISHERS

1059 Francis Baard St., Hatfield 0083, South Africa. **E-mail:** jread@vanschaiknet.com. **Website:** www.

vanschaiknet.com. **Contact:** Julia Read. Guidelines online.

NONFICTION Subjects include business, economics, management, education, social sciences, nursing/medicine, language, accounting, public administration. Submit proposal package, outline, sample text.

VÉHICULE PRESS

P.O.B. 42094 BP Roy, Montreal QC H2W 2T3, Canada. (514)844-6073. **Fax:** (514)844-7543. **E-mail:** vp@vehiculepress.com. **E-mail:** esplanade@vehiculepress.com. **Website:** www.vehiculepress.com. **Contact:** Simon Dardick, president/publisher. Estab. 1973. Publishes trade paperback originals by Canadian authors mostly. "Montreal's Véhicule Press has published the best of Canadian and Quebec literature-fiction, poetry, essays, translations, and social history." **Publishes 15 titles/year. 20% of books from first-time authors. 95% from unagented writers. Pays 10-15% royalty on retail price. Pays $200-500 advance.** Publishes ms 1 year after acceptance. Responds in 4 months to queries. Book catalog for 9 x 12 SAE with IRCs.

IMPRINTS Signal Editions (poetry); Esplanade Editions (fiction).

NONFICTION Subjects include government, politics, history, language, literature, memoirs, regional, sociology. Especially looking for Canadian social history. Query with SASE. Reviews artwork/photos.

FICTION Subjects include feminist, literary, regional, translation, literary novels. No romance or formula writing. Query with SASE.

POETRY Vehicule Press is a "literary press with a poetry series, Signal Editions, publishing the work of Canadian poets only." Publishes flat-spined paperbacks. Publishes Canadian poetry that is "first-rate, original, content-conscious."

TIPS "Quality in almost any style is acceptable. We believe in the editing process."

VELÁZQUEZ PRESS

Division of Academic Learning Press, 9682 Telstar Ave., Suite 110, El Monte CA 91731. (626)448-3448. **Website:** www.velazquezpress.com. Publishes hardcover and trade paperback originals and reprints. **Publishes 5-10 titles/year. Pays 10% royalty on retail price.** Publishes ms 6 months after acceptance. Accepts simultaneous submissions. Responds in 2 months. Book catalog and guidelines via e-mail.

IMPRINTS WBusiness Books; ZHealth.

NONFICTION Subjects include education. "We are interested in publishing bilingual educational materials." Submit proposal package, outline, 2 sample chapters, cover letter. Submit complete ms. Reviews artwork/photos. Send photocopies.

VENTURE PUBLISHING, INC.

1999 Cato Ave., State College PA 16801. (814)234-4561. **Fax:** (814)234-1651. **Website:** www.venturepublish.com. Estab. 1978. Publishes hardcover and paperback originals and reprints. "Venture Publishing produces quality educational publications, also workbooks for professionals, educators, and students in the fields of recreation, parks, leisure studies, therapeutic recreation and long term care." **Pays royalty on wholesale price. Pays advance.** Book catalog and ms guidelines online.

NONFICTION Subjects include nature, environment, outdoor recreation management and leadership texts, recreation, sociology, leisure studies, long-term care nursing homes, therapeutic recreation. Textbooks and books for recreation activity leaders high priority. Submit 1 sample chapter, book proposal, competing titles.

VERSO

20 Jay St., 10th Floor, Brooklyn NY 11201. (718)246-8160. **Fax:** (718)246-8165. **E-mail:** verso@versobooks.com. **Website:** www.versobooks.com. **Contact:** Editorial Department. Estab. 1970. Publishes hardcover and trade paperback originals. "Our books cover economics, politics, cinema studies, and history (among other topics), but all come from a critical, Leftist viewpoint, on the border between trade and academic." **Publishes 100 titles/year. Pays royalty. Pays advance.** Accepts simultaneous submissions. Book catalog available free. Guidelines online.

NONFICTION Subjects include business, economics, government, politics, history, philosophy, sociology, women's issues, women's studies. Submit proposal package.

VERTIGO

DC Universe, Vertigo-DC Comics, 1700 Broadway, New York NY 10019. **Website:** www.vertigocomics.com. At this time, DC Entertainment does not accept unsolicited artwork or writing submissions.

VIKING

Imprint of Penguin Group (USA), Inc., 375 Hudson St., New York NY 10014. (212)366-2000. **Website:**

www.penguin.com. Estab. 1925. Publishes hardcover and originals. Viking publishes a mix of academic and popular fiction and nonfiction. **Publishes 100 titles/year. Pays 10-15% royalty on retail price.** Publishes ms 18 months after acceptance. Accepts simultaneous submissions.

NONFICTION Subjects include business, economics, child guidance, cooking, foods, nutrition, health, medicine, history, language, literature, music, dance, philosophy, womens issues, womens studies. *Agented submissions only.*

FICTION Subjects include literary, mainstream, contemporary, mystery, suspense. *Agented submissions only.*

Ⓐ⊘ VIKING CHILDREN'S BOOKS

375 Hudson St., New York NY 10014. **Website:** www.penguin.com. **Contact:** Kenneth Wright, publisher. Publishes hardcover originals. "Viking Children's Books is known for humorous, quirky picture books, in addition to more traditional fiction. We publish the highest quality fiction, nonfiction, and picture books for pre-schoolers through young adults." *Does not accept unsolicited submissions.* **Publishes 70 titles/year. Pays 2-10% royalty on retail price or flat fee. Pays negotiable advance.** Publishes ms 1-2 years after acceptance. Responds in 6 months.

NONFICTION All levels: biography, concept, history, multicultural, music/dance, nature/environment, science, and sports. *Agented submissions only.*

FICTION All levels: adventure, animal, contemporary, fantasy, history, humor, multicultural, nature/environment, poetry, problem novels, romance, science fiction, sports, suspense/mystery. *Accepts agented mss only.*

TIPS "No 'cartoony' or mass-market submissions for picture books."

Ⓐ⊘ VILLARD BOOKS

Imprint of Random House Publishing Group, 1745 Broadway, New York NY 10019. (212)572-2600. **Website:** www.atrandom.com. Estab. 1983. "Villard Books is the publisher of savvy and sometimes quirky, best-selling hardcovers and trade paperbacks." **Pays negotiable royalty. Pays negotiable advance.**

NONFICTION *Agented submissions only.*

FICTION Commercial fiction. *Agented submissions only.*

Ⓐ⊘ VINTAGE ANCHOR PUBLISHING

Imprint of Random House, 1745 Broadway, New York NY 10019. **Website:** www.randomhouse.com. **Pays 4-8% royalty on retail price. Average advance: $2,500 and up.** Publishes ms 1 year after acceptance.

FICTION Subjects include contemporary, literary, mainstream, short story collections. *Agented submissions only.*

VIVISPHERE PUBLISHING

675 Dutchess Turnpike, Poughkeepsie NY 12603. (845)463-1100, ext. 314. **Fax:** (845)463-0018. **E-mail:** cs@vivisphere.com. **Website:** www.vivisphere.com. **Contact:** Submissions. Estab. 1995. Publishes trade paperback originals and reprints and e-books. Vivisphere Publishing is now considering new submissions from any genre as follows: game of bridge (cards), nonfiction, history, military, new age, fiction, feminist/gay/lesbian, horror, contemporary, self-help, science fiction and cookbooks. **Pays royalty.** Publishes ms 6 months-2 years after acceptance. Accepts simultaneous submissions. Responds in 6-12 months. Book catalog and ms guidelines online.

"Cookbooks should have a particular slant or appeal to a certain niche. Also publish out-of-print books."

NONFICTION Subjects include history, military, New Age, game of bridge. Query with SASE. Please submit a proposal package (printed paper copy) including: outline and 1st chapter along with your contact information. If submitting, please use above guidelines and e-mail cs@vivisphere.com.

FICTION Subjects include feminist, gay, lesbian, historical, horror, literary, contemporary, military, science fiction. Query with SASE.

⊘ VIZ MEDIA LLC

P.O. Box 77010, San Francisco CA 94107. (415)546-7073. **Website:** www.viz.com. "VIZ Media, LLC is one of the most comprehensive and innovative companies in the field of manga (graphic novel) publishing, animation and entertainment licensing of Japanese content. Owned by three of Japan's largest creators and licensors of manga and animation, Shueisha Inc., Shogakukan Inc., and Shogakukan-Shueisha Productions, Co., Ltd., VIZ Media is a leader in the publishing and distribution of Japanese manga for English speaking audiences in North America, the United Kingdom, Ireland, and South Africa and is a global ex-Asia licensor of Japanese manga and animation.

The company offers an integrated product line including magazines such as *Shonen Jump* and *Shojo Beat*, graphic novels, and DVDs, and develops, markets, licenses, and distributes animated entertainment for audiences and consumers of all ages."

FICTION "At the present, all of the manga that appears in our magazines come directly from manga that has been serialized and published in Japan."

VOLCANO PRESS, INC.

P.O. Box 270, Volcano CA 95689-0270. (209)296-7989. **Fax:** (209)296-4995. **Website:** www.volcanopress.com. Estab. 1969. Publishes trade paperback originals. **Publishes 4-6 titles/year. Pays $500-1,000 advance.** Responds in 1 month to queries. Book catalog available free.

NONFICTION Subjects include health, medicine, multicultural, womens issues, womens studies. "We publish women's health and social issues, particularly in the field of domestic violence." Query with SASE. No e-mail or fax submissions

TIPS "Look at our titles on the Web or in our catalog, and submit materials consistent with what we already publish."

VOYAGEUR PRESS

Quayside Publishing Group, 400 First Ave. N., Suite 400, Minneapolis MN 55401. (800)458-0454. **Fax:** (612)344-8691. **Website:** voyageurpress.com. Estab. 1972. Publishes hardcover and trade paperback originals. "Voyageur Press (and its sports imprint MVP Books) is internationally known as a leading publisher of quality music, sports, country living, crafts, natural history, and regional books. No children's or poetry books." **Publishes 80 titles/year. 1,200 queries received/year. 500 mss received/year. 10% of books from first-time authors. 90% from unagented writers. Pays royalty. Pays advance.** Publishes ms 1 year after acceptance. Accepts simultaneous submissions. Responds in 3 months to queries.

NONFICTION Subjects include Americana, cooking, environment, history, hobbies, music, nature, regional, sports, collectibles, country living, knitting and quilting, outdoor recreation. Query with SASE. Submit outline. Send sample digital images or transparencies (duplicates and tearsheets only).

TIPS "We publish books for an audience interested in regional, natural, and cultural history on a wide variety of subjects. We seek authors strongly committed to helping us promote and sell their books. Please present as focused an idea as possible in a brief submission (1-page cover letter; 2-page outline or proposal). Note your credentials for writing the book. Tell all you know about the market niche and marketing possibilities for proposed book. We use more book designers than artists or illustrators, since most of our books are illustrated with photographs."

⊘ WAKE FOREST UNIVERSITY PRESS

P.O. Box 7333, Winston-Salem NC 27109. (336)758-5448. **Fax:** (336)758-5636. **E-mail:** wfupress@wfu.edu. **Website:** wfupress.wfu.edu. **Contact:** Jefferson Holdridge, director/poetry editor; Dillon Johnston, advisory editor. Estab. 1976. "We publish only poetry from Ireland. I am able to consider only poetry written by native Irish poets. I must return, unread, poetry from American poets." Query with 4-5 samples and cover letter. Sometimes sends prepublication galleys. Buys North American or U.S. rights. **Publishes 4-6 titles/year. Pays on 8% list royalty contract, plus 6-8 author's copies. Negotiable advance.** Responds to queries in 1-2 weeks; to submissions (*if invited*) in 2-3 months.

WALCH PUBLISHING

40 Walch Dr., Portland ME 04103. (207)772-3105. **Fax:** (207)774-7167. **Website:** www.walch.com. Estab. 1927. "We focus on English/language arts, math, social studies and science teaching resources for middle school through adult assessment titles." **Publishes 100 titles/year. 10% of books from first-time authors. 95% from unagented writers. Pays 5-8% royalty on flat rate.** Publishes ms 6 months after acceptance. Accepts simultaneous submissions. Responds in 2 months to queries.

NONFICTION Subjects include education, mathematics, middle school, social sciences studies, remedial and special education, government, politics, history, language, literature, science, technology. "Most titles are assigned by us, though we occasionally accept an author's unsolicited submission. We have a great need for author/artist teams and for authors who can write at third- to seventh-grade levels." Looks for sense of organization, writing ability, knowledge of subject, skill of communicating with intended audience. Formats include teacher resources, reproducibles. "We do *not* want textbooks or anthologies. All authors should have educational writing experience." Query first.

WANNABEE BOOKS

750 Pinehurst Dr., Rio Vista CA 94571-9757. **E-mail:** books@wannabeebooks.com. **Website:** www.wannabeebooks.com. **Contact:** Joanne McCoy, senior editor. Estab. 2014. Publishes trade paperback originals. Wannabee Books publishes full-color, digitally enhanced, and acoustically supplemented children's picture books on CDs that explore exciting subjects that stimulate young minds. **Publishes 6 titles/year. Receives 12-20 queries/year. Receives 12 mss/year. 100% of books from first-time authors. 100% from unagented writers. Pays 15% royalties or makes an outright purchase between $250-500.** Publishes book Publishes mss in 3-4 months upon acceptance. after acceptance of ms. Accepts simultaneous submissions. Responds in 1 month to queries, proposals, and mss. Catalog available online. Guidelines available online or by e-mail.

NONFICTION Subjects include anthropology, archeology, architecture, art, automotive, dance, education, environment, gardening, health, house and home, law, literary criticism, marine subjects, medicine, music, nature, photography, psychology, science, sports, transportation. Interested in topics that explore exciting subjects that stimulate young minds. Wannabee Books helps kids decide what they "wannabee." Do they "wannabee" astronauts, chemists, architects, engineers, etc.? Submit completed ms. Writers should sent artwork/photographs.

WASHINGTON STATE UNIVERSITY PRESS

P.O. Box 645910, Pullman WA 99164-5910. (800)354-7360. **Fax:** (509)335-8568. **E-mail:** wsupress@wsu.edu. **Website:** wsupress.wsu.edu. **Contact:** Robert A. Clark, acquisitions editor. Estab. 1928. Publishes hardcover originals, trade paperback originals, and reprints. WSU Press publishes scholarly nonfiction books on the history, pre-history, culture, and politics of the West, particularly the Pacific Northwest. **Publishes 8-10 titles/year. 40% of books from first-time authors. 95% from unagented writers. Pays 5% royalty graduated according to sales.** Publishes ms 18 months after acceptance. Responds in 2 months to queries. Guidelines online.

NONFICTION Subjects include archaeology, cultural studies, cooking and food history, environment, government, history, politics, nature, railroads, science, essays. "We welcome engaging and thought-provoking mss that focus on the greater Pacific Northwest (primarily Washington, Oregon, Idaho, British Columbia, western Montana, and southeastern Alaska). Currently we are not accepting how-to books, literary criticism, memoirs, novels, or poetry." Submit outline, sample chapters. Reviews artwork/photos.

TIPS "We have developed our marketing in the direction of regional and local history, and use this as the base upon which to expand our publishing program. For history, the secret is to write strong narratives on significant topics or events. Stories should be told in imaginative, clever ways and be substantiated factually. Have visuals (photos, maps, etc.) available to help the reader envision what has happened."

WASHINGTON WRITERS' PUBLISHING HOUSE

P.O. Box 15271, Washington DC 20003. **E-mail:** wwphpress@gmail.com. **Website:** www.washingtonwriters.org. **Contact:** Kathleen Wheaton, president. Estab. 1975. **Offers $1,000 and 50 copies of published book plus additional copies for publicity use.** Guidelines online.

FICTION Washington Writers' Publishing House considers book-length mss for publication by fiction writers living within 75 driving miles of the U.S. Capitol, Baltimore area included, through competition only. Mss may include previously published stories and excerpts. "Author should indicate where they heard about WWPH." Submit an electronic copy by e-mail (use PDF, .doc, or rich text format) or 2 hard copies by snail mail of a short story collection or novel (no more than 350 pages, double or 1-1/2 spaced; author's name should not appear on any ms pages). Include separate page of publication acknowledgments plus 2 cover sheets: one with ms title, poet's name, address, telephone number, and e-mail address, the other with ms title only. Include SASE for results only; mss will not be returned (will be recycled).

POETRY Washington Writers' Publishing House considers book-length mss for publication by poets living within 75 driving miles of the U.S. Capitol (Baltimore area included) through competition only. Publishes 1-2 poetry books/year. "No specific criteria, except literary excellence."

Ⓐ⊘ WATERBROOK MULTNOMAH PUBLISHING GROUP

Random House, 12265 Oracle Blvd., Suite 200, Colorado Springs CO 80921. (719)590-4999. **Fax:** (719)590-8977. **E-mail:** info@waterbrookmultnomah.com.

Website: www.waterbrookmultnomah.com. Estab. 1996. Publishes hardcover and trade paperback originals. **Publishes 70 titles/year. 2,000 queries received/year. 15% of books from first-time authors. Pays royalty.** Publishes ms 1 year after acceptance. Accepts simultaneous submissions. Responds in 2-3 months. Book catalog online.

NONFICTION Subjects include child guidance, money, finance, religion, spirituality, marriage, Christian living. "We publish books on unique topics with a Christian perspective." *Agented submissions only.*

FICTION Subjects include adventure, historical, literary, mainstream, contemporary, mystery, religious, inspirational, religious mystery/suspense, religious thriller, religious romance, romance, contemporary, historical, science fiction, spiritual, suspense. *Agented submissions only.*

WAVE BOOKS

1938 Fairview Ave. E., Suite 201, Seattle WA 98102. (206)676-5337. **E-mail:** info@wavepoetry.com. **Website:** www.wavepoetry.com. **Contact:** Charlie Wright, publisher; Joshua Beckman and Matthew Zapruder, editors; Heidi Broadhead, managing editor. Estab. 2005. Publishes hardcover and trade paperback originals. "Wave Books is an independent poetry press based in Seattle, Washington, dedicated to publishing the best in contemporary American poetry, poetry in translation, and writing by poets. The Press was founded in 2005, merging with established publisher Verse Press. By publishing strong innovative work in finely crafted trade editions and handmade ephemera, we hope to continue to challenge the values and practices of readers and add to the collective sense of what's possible in contemporary poetry." Catalog online.

POETRY "Please no unsolicited mss or queries. We will post calls for submissions on our website."

WAVELAND PRESS, INC.

4180 Illinois Rt. 83, Suite 101, Long Grove IL 60047. (847)634-0081. **Fax:** (847)634-9501. **E-mail:** info@waveland.com. **Website:** www.waveland.com. Estab. 1975. Waveland Press, Inc. is a publisher of college textbooks and supplements. "We are committed to providing reasonably priced teaching materials for the classroom and actively seek to add new titles to our growing lists in a variety of academic disciplines. If you are currently working on a project you feel serves a need and would have promise as an adopted text in the college market, we would like to hear from you."

WESLEYAN PUBLISHING HOUSE

P.O. Box 50434, Indianapolis IN 46250. **E-mail:** submissions@wesleyan.org. **Website:** www.wesleyan.org/wg. **Contact:** Rachael Stevenson, production editor. Estab. 1843. Publishes hardcover and trade paperback originals. **150-175 submissions received/year. Pays royalty on wholesale price.** Publishes ms 11 months after acceptance. Accepts simultaneous submissions. Responds within 2 months to proposals. Catalog online. Guidelines online.

NONFICTION Subjects include Christianity/religion. No hard-copy submissions. Submit proposal package, including outline, 5 sample chapters, bio. See writer's guidelines. Does not review artwork.

RECENT TITLE(S) *Light in the Darkness*, by Gary H. Lovejoy and Gregory M. Knopf; *Faultlines*, by Steve Deneff; *Real Love*, by Thaddeus Barnum.

TIPS "Our books help evangelical Christians learn about the faith or grow in their relationship with God."

⊘ WESLEYAN UNIVERSITY PRESS

215 Long Ln., Middletown CT 06459. (860)685-7711. **Fax:** (860)685-7712. **E-mail:** stamminen@wesleyan.edu. **E-mail:** psmathers@wesleyan.edu. **Website:** www.wesleyan.edu/wespress. **Contact:** Suzanna Tamminen, director and editor-in-chief; Parker Smathers, editor. Estab. 1959. Publishes hardcover originals and paperbacks. "Wesleyan University Press is a scholarly press with a focus on poetry, music, dance and cultural studies." Wesleyan University Press is one of the major publishers of poetry in the nation. Poetry publications from Wesleyan tend to get widely (and respectfully) reviewed. **"We are accepting manuscripts by invitation only until further notice." Pays royalties, plus 10 author's copies.** Accepts simultaneous submissions. Responds to queries in 2 months; to mss in 4 months. Book catalog available free. Guidelines online.

NONFICTION Subjects include music, dance, film/TV & media studies, science fiction studies, dance and poetry. *Does not accept unsolicited mss.*

POETRY *Does not accept unsolicited mss.*

WESTERN PSYCHOLOGICAL SERVICES

625 Alaska Ave., Torrance CA 90503. (424)201-8800 or (800)648-8857. **Fax:** (424)201-6950. **Website:** www.wpspublish.com. Estab. 1948. Publishes psychological and educational assessments and some trade pa-

perback originals. "Western Psychological Services publishes psychological and educational assessments that practitioners trust. Our products allow helping professionals to accurately screen, diagnose, and treat people in need. WPS publishes practical books and games used by therapists, counselors, social workers, and others in the helping professionals who work with children and adults." **Publishes 2 titles/year. 60 queries received/year. 30 mss received/year. 90% of books from first-time authors. 95% from unagented writers. Pays 5-10% royalty on wholesale price.** Publishes ms 1 year after acceptance. Accepts simultaneous submissions. Responds in 2 months to queries. Book catalog available free. Guidelines online.

NONFICTION Subjects include child guidance, psychology, autism, sensory processing disorders. "We publish children's books dealing with feelings, anger, social skills, autism, family problems." Submit complete ms. Reviews artwork/photos. Send photocopies.

WESTMINSTER JOHN KNOX PRESS

Division of Presbyterian Publishing Corp., 100 Witherspoon St., Louisville KY 40202. **Fax:** (502)569-5113. **E-mail:** jkelley@wjkbooks.com. **Website:** www.wjkbooks.com. **Contact:** Jessica Miller Kelley, acquisitions editor. Publishes hardcover and paperback originals and reprints. "All WJK books have a religious/spiritual angle, but are written for various markets-scholarly, professional, and the general reader. Westminster John Knox is affiliated with the Presbyterian Church USA. No phone queries. We do not publish fiction, poetry, memoir, children's books, or dissertations. We will not return or respond to submissions without an accompanying SASE with sufficient postage." **Publishes 70 titles/year. 2,500 queries received/year. 750 mss received/year. 10% of books from first-time authors. Pays royalty on net price.** Responds in 3 months. Proposal guidelines online.

NONFICTION Subjects include religion, spirituality. Submit proposal package according to the WJK book proposal guidelines found online.

WHITAKER HOUSE

1030 Hunt Valley Circle, New Kensington PA 15068. **E-mail:** publisher@whitakerhouse.com. **Website:** www.whitakerhouse.com. **Contact:** Editorial Department. Estab. 1970. Publishes hardcover, trade paperback, and mass market originals. **Publishes 70 titles/year. 600 queries received/year. 200 mss received/year. 15% of books from first-time authors. 60% from unagented writers. Pays 5-15% royalty on wholesale price.** Publishes ms 9 months after acceptance. Accepts simultaneous submissions. Responds in 3 months. Book catalog available online. Guidelines online.

NONFICTION Subjects include religion, Christian. Accepts submissions on topics with a Christian perspective. Query with SASE. Does not review artwork/photos.

FICTION Subjects include religious, Christian, historical romance, African American romance and Amish fiction. All fiction must have a Christian perspective. Query with SASE.

TIPS "Audience includes those seeking uplifting and inspirational fiction and nonfiction."

WHITECAP BOOKS, LTD.

210 - 314 W. Cordova St., Vancouver BC V6B 1 E8, Canada. (604)681-6181. **Fax:** (905)477-9179. **E-mail:** steph@whitecap.ca. **Website:** www.whitecap.ca. Publishes hardcover and trade paperback originals. "Whitecap Books is a general trade publisher with a focus on food and wine titles. Although we are interested in reviewing unsolicited ms submissions, please note that we only accept submissions that meet the needs of our current publishing program. Please see some of most recent releases to get an idea of the kinds of titles we are interested in." **Publishes 30 titles/year. 500 queries received/year; 1,000 mss received/year. 20% of books from first-time authors. 90% from unagented writers. Pays royalty. Pays negotiated advance.** Publishes ms 1 year after acceptance. Accepts simultaneous submissions. Responds in 2-3 months to proposals. Catalog and guidelines online.

NONFICTION Subjects include animals, cooking, foods, nutrition, gardening, history, nature, environment, recreation, regional, travel. Young children's and middle reader's nonfiction focusing mainly on nature, wildlife and animals. "Writers should take the time to research our list and read the submission guidelines on our website. This is especially important for children's writers and cookbook authors. We will only consider submissions that fall into these categories: cookbooks, wine and spirits, regional travel, home and garden, Canadian history, North American natural history, juvenile series-based fiction. At this time, we are not accepting the following categories: self-help or inspirational books, political, social commentary, or issue books, general how-to books, biographies or memoirs, business and finance, art and architecture, religion and spirituality." Submit cover letter, synopsis, SASE via ground mail. See guidelines online. Reviews artwork/photos. Send photocopies.

FICTION No children's picture books or adult fiction. See guidelines.

TIPS "We want well-written, well-researched material that presents a fresh approach to a particular topic."

WHITE MANE KIDS

73 W. Burd St., P.O. Box 708, Shippensburg PA 17257. (717)532-2237. **Fax:** (717)532-6110. **E-mail:** marketing@whitemane.com. **Website:** www.whitemane.com. **Contact:** Harold Collier, acquisitions editor. Estab. 1987. **Pays authors royalty of 7-10%. Pays illustrators and photographers by the project.** Publishes ms 18 months after acceptance. Accepts simultaneous submissions. Responds to queries in 1 month, mss in 6-9 months. Book catalog and writer's guidelines available for SASE.

IMPRINTS White Mane Books, Burd Street Press, White Mane Kids, Ragged Edge Press.

NONFICTION Middle readers, young adults: history. Average word length: middle readers—30,000. Does not publish picture books. Submit outline/synopsis and 2-3 sample chapters.

FICTION Middle readers, young adults: history (primarily American Civil War). Average word length: middle readers—30,000. Does not publish picture books. Query.

TIPS "Make your work historically accurate. We are interested in historically accurate fiction for middle and young adult readers. We do *not* publish picture books. Our primary focus is the American Civil War and some America Revolution topics."

⊘ WHITE PINE PRESS

P.O. Box 236, Buffalo NY 14201. (716)627-4665. **Fax:** (716)627-4665. **E-mail:** wpine@whitepine.org. **Website:** www.whitepine.org. **Contact:** Dennis Maloney, editor. Estab. 1973. Publishes trade paperback originals. **Publishes 8-10 titles/year. Receives 500 queries/year. 1% of books from first-time authors. 100% from unagented writers. Pays contributor's copies.** Publishes ms 18 months after acceptance. Accepts simultaneous submissions. Responds in 1 month to queries and proposals; 4 months to mss. Catalog online. Guidelines online.

NONFICTION Subjects include language, literature, multicultural, translation, poetry. *"We are currently not considering nonfiction mss."*

POETRY "Only considering submissions for our annual poetry contest."

ALBERT WHITMAN & COMPANY

250 S. Northwest Hwy., Suite 320, Park Ridge IL 60068. (800)255-7675. **Fax:** (847)581-0039. **E-mail:** submissions@awhitmanco.com. **Website:** www.albertwhitman.com. Estab. 1919. Publishes in original hardcover, paperback, boardbooks. Albert Whitman & Company publishes books for the trade, library, and school library market. Interested in reviewing the following types of projects: Picture book manuscripts for ages 2-8; novels and chapter books for ages 8-12; young adult novels; nonfiction for ages 3-12 and YA; art samples showing pictures of children. Best known for the classic series The Boxcar Children® Mysteries. "We are no longer reading unsolicited queries and manuscripts sent through the US mail. We now require these submissions to be sent by e-mail. You must visit our website for our guidelines, which include instructions for formatting your e-mail. E-mails that do not follow this format may not be read. We read every submission within 4 months of receipt, but we can no longer respond to every one. If you do not receive a response from us after four months, we have declined to publish your submission." **Publishes 60 titles/year. 10% of books from first-time authors. 50% from unagented writers.** Accepts simultaneous submissions. Guidelines online.

NONFICTION Picture books up to 1,000 words. Submit cover letter, brief description.

FICTION Picture books (up to 1,000 words); middle grade (up to 35,000 words); young adult (up to 70,000 words). For picture books, submit cover letter and brief description. For middle grade and young adult, send query, synopsis, and first 3 chapters.

WILD CHILD PUBLISHING

P.O. Box 4897, Culver City CA 90231. (310) 721-4461. **E-mail:** mgbaun@wildchildpublishing.com. **Website:** www.wildchildpublishing.com. **Contact:** Marci Baun, editor-in-chief. Estab. 1999. "We are known for working with newer/unpublished authors and editing to the standards of NYC publishers." **Publishes 12 titles/year. Pays royalties 10-40%.** Publishes ms 2-4 months after acceptance. Responds in 1 month to queries and mss. Book catalogs on website.

FICTION Subjects include adventure, erotica, ethnic, experimental, fantasy, feminist, gay, historical, horror, humor, juvenile, lesbian, literary, mainstream, military, mystery, romance, science fiction, short story collections, suspense, western, young adult. Multiple anthologies planned. Query with outline/synopsis and 1 sample chapter. Accepts queries by e-mail only. Include estimated word count, brief bio. Often critiques/comments on rejected mss.

TIPS "Read our submission guidelines thoroughly. Send in entertaining, well-written stories. Be easy to work with and upbeat."

WILDERNESS PRESS

2204 First Ave. S., Suite 102, Birmingham AL 35233. (510)558-1666. **Fax:** (510)558-1696. **E-mail:** tim@keencommunications.com. **Website:** www.wildernesspress.com. **Contact:** Tim Jackson, acquisitions editor. Estab. 1967. Publishes paperback originals. "Wilderness Press has a long tradition of publishing the highest quality, most accurate hiking and other outdoor activity guidebooks." **Publishes 12 titles/year.** Publishes ms 8-12 months after acceptance. Responds in 2 months to queries. Book catalog and ms guidelines online.

NONFICTION Subjects include nature, environment, recreation, trail guides for hikers and backpackers. "We publish books about the outdoors and some general travel guides. Many are trail guides for hikers and backpackers, but we also publish climbing, kayaking, and other outdoor activity guides, how-to books about the outdoors and urban walking books. The manuscript must be accurate. The author must research an area in person. If writing a trail guide, you must walk all the trails in the area your book is about. Outlook must be strongly conservationist. Style must be appropriate for a highly literate audience." Download proposal guidelines from website.

JOHN WILEY & SONS, INC.

Wiley-Blackwell, 111 River St., Hoboken NJ 07030. (201)748-6000. **Fax:** (201)748-6088. **Website:** www.wiley.com. **Contact:** Editorial Department. Estab. 1807. Publishes hardcover originals, trade paperback originals and reprints. "The General Interest group publishes nonfiction books for the consumer market. There is also a Higher Education Division. See proposal guideines online." **Pays competitive rates. Pays advance.** Accepts simultaneous submissions. Book catalog online. Guidelines online.

NONFICTION Subjects include history, memoirs, psychology, science, popular, African-American interest, health/self-improvement, technical, medical. "If you have an idea for a new book, journal, or electronic product that falls into the chemistry, the life sciences, medicine, mathematical and physical sciences, humanities, and social sciences arena, please send your proposal or manuscript to Wiley-Blackwell." See website for more details.

TIPS "Include a brief description of the publication and overall objective. Describe exactly what the publication will be about. What will there be about your selection, organization, or treatment of the subject that will make the readers buy the publication? Address why there is a need for the proposed publication."

WILLIAM MORROW

HarperCollins, 195 Broadway, New York NY 10007. (212)207-7000. **Fax:** (212)207-7145. **Website:** www.harpercollins.com. Estab. 1926. "William Morrow publishes a wide range of titles that receive much recognition and prestige—a most selective house." **Pays standard royalty on retail price. Pays varying advance.** Book catalog available free.

NONFICTION Subjects include art, architecture, cooking, foods, nutrition, history. Length 50,000-100,000 words. *No unsolicited mss or proposals. Agented submissions only.*

FICTION Publishes adult fiction. Morrow accepts only the highest quality submissions in adult fiction. *No unsolicited mss or proposals. Agented submissions only.*

WILLIAMSON BOOKS

2630 Elm Hill Pike, Suite 100, Nashville TN 37214. **Website:** www.idealsbooks.com. Estab. 1983. Publishes "very successful nonfiction series (Kids Can! Series) on subjects such as history, science, arts/crafts, geography, diversity, multiculturalism. Little Hands series for ages 2-6, Kaleidoscope Kids series (age 7 and up) and Quick Starts for Kids! series (ages 8 and up). Our goal is to help every child fulfill his/her potential and experience personal growth." **Pays authors advance against future royalties based on wholesale price or purchases outright. Pays illustrators by the project. Pays photographers per photo.** Publishes ms 1 year after acceptance. Responds in 4 months. Guidelines online.

NONFICTION Hands-on active learning books, animals, African-American, arts/crafts, Asian, biography, diversity, careers, geography, health, history, hobbies, how-to, math, multicultural, music/dance, nature/environment, Native American, science, writing and journaling. Does not want to see textbooks, picture books, fiction. "Looking for all things African American, Asian American, Hispanic, Latino, and Native American including crafts and traditions, as well as their history, biographies, and personal retrospectives of growing up in U.S. for grades pre K-8th. We are looking for books in which learning and doing are inseparable." Query with annotated TOC/synopsis and 1 sample chapter.

WILLOW CREEK PRESS

P.O. Box 147, Minocqua WI 54548. (715)358-7010. **Fax:** (715)358-2807. **Website:** www.willowcreekpress.com. **Contact:** Managing Editor. Estab. 1986. Publishes hardcover and trade paperback originals and reprints. "We specialize in nature, outdoor, and sporting topics, including gardening, wildlife, and animal books. Pets, cookbooks, and a few humor books and essays round out our titles. Currently emphasizing pets (mainly dogs and cats), wildlife, outdoor sports (hunting, fishing). De-emphasizing essays, fiction." **Publishes 25 titles/year. 400 queries received/year. 150 mss received/year. 15% of books from first-time authors. 50% from unagented writers. Pays 6-15% royalty on wholesale price. Pays $2,000-5,000 advance.** Publishes ms 18 months after acceptance. Accepts simultaneous submissions. Responds in 2 months to queries. Guidelines online.

NONFICTION Subjects include animals, cooking, foods, nutrition, gardening, nature, environment, recreation, sports, travel, wildlife, pets. Submit cover letter, chapter outline, 1-2 sample chapters, brief bio, SASE. Reviews artwork/photos.

WINDWARD PUBLISHING

Finney Company, 5995 149th St. W., Suite 105, Apple Valley MN 55124. **E-mail:** info@finneyco.com. **Website:** www.finneyco.com. **Contact:** Alan E. Krysan, president. Estab. 1973. Publishes trade paperback originals. Windward publishes illustrated natural history, recreation books, and children's books. "Covers topics of natural history and science, outdoor recreation, and children's literature. Its principal markets are book, retail, and specialty stores. While primarily a nonfiction publisher, we will occasionally accept fiction books with educational value." **Publishes 6-10 titles/year. 120 queries received/year. 50 mss received/year. 50% of books from first-time authors. 100% from unagented writers. Pays 10% royalty on wholesale price. Pays advance.** Publishes ms 1 year after acceptance. Accepts simultaneous submissions. Responds in 8-10 weeks to queries.

NONFICTION Subjects include agriculture, animals, gardening, nature, environment, recreation, science, sports, natural history. Young readers, middle readers, young adults: activity books, animal, careers, nature/environment, science. Young adults: textbooks. Query with SASE. Does not accept e-mail or fax submissions. Reviews artwork/photos.

WISCONSIN HISTORICAL SOCIETY PRESS

816 State St., Madison WI 53706. (608)264-6465. **Fax:** (608)264-6486. **E-mail:** whspress@wisconsinhistory.org. **Website:** www.wisconsinhistory.org/whspress/. **Contact:** Kate Thompson, editor. Estab. 1855. Publishes hardcover and trade paperback originals; trade paperback reprints. **Publishes 12-14 titles/year. 60-75 queries received/year. 20% of books from first-time authors. 90% from unagented writers. Pays royalty on wholesale price.** Publishes ms 2 years after acceptance. Book catalog available free. Guidelines online.

NONFICTION Subjects include Wisconsin history and culture: archaeology, architecture, cooking, foods, ethnic, history (Wisconsin), memoirs, regional, sports. Submit book proposal, form from website. Reviews artwork/photos. Send photocopies.

TIPS "Our audience reads about Wisconsin. Carefully review the book."

WISDOM PUBLICATIONS

199 Elm St., Somerville MA 02144. (617)776-7416, ext. 28. **Fax:** (617)776-7841. **E-mail:** editors@wisdompubs.org. **Website:** www.wisdompubs.org. **Contact:** David Kittelstrom, senior editor. Estab. 1976. Publishes hardcover originals and trade paperback originals and reprints. "Wisdom Publications is dedicated to making available authentic Buddhist works for the benefit of all. We publish translations, commentaries, and teachings of past and contemporary Buddhist masters and original works by leading Buddhist scholars. Currently emphasizing popular applied Buddhism, scholarly titles." **Publishes 20-25 titles/year. 300 queries received/year. 50% of books from first-time authors. 95% from unagented writers. Pays 4-8% royalty on wholesale price. Pays advance.** Publishes ms within 2 years of acceptance. af-

ter acceptance of ms. Book catalog and ms guidelines online.

NONFICTION Subjects include philosophy, psychology, religion, Buddhism, Tibet. Submissions should be made electronically.

TIPS "Wisdom Publications is the leading publisher of contemporary and classic Buddhist books and practical works on mindfulness. Please see our catalog or our website before you send anything to us to get a sense of what we publish."

Ⓐ⊘ PAULA WISEMAN BOOKS

1230 Sixth Ave., New York NY 10020. (212)698-7272. **Fax:** (212)698-2796. **E-mail:** paula.wiseman@simonandschuster.com; sylvie.frank@simonandschuster.com; sarahjane.abbott@simonandschuster.com. **Website:** kids.simonandschuster.com. **Publishes 30 titles/year. 15% of books from first-time authors.**

NONFICTION Picture books: animal, biography, concept, history, nature/environment. Young readers: animal, biography, history, multicultural, nature/environment, sports. Average word length: picture books—500; others standard length. Does not accept unsolicited or unagented mss.

FICTION Considers all categories. Average word length: picture books—500; others standard length.

WOODBINE HOUSE

6510 Bells Mill Rd., Bethesda MD 20817. (301)897-3570. **Fax:** (301)897-5838. **E-mail:** info@woodbinehouse.com. **Website:** www.woodbinehouse.com. Estab. 1985. Publishes trade paperback originals. Woodbine House publishes books for or about individuals with disabilities to help those individuals and their families live fulfilling and satisfying lives in their homes, schools, and communities. **Publishes 10 titles/year. 15% of books from first-time authors. 90% from unagented writers. Pays 10-12% royalty.** Publishes ms 18 months after acceptance. Accepts simultaneous submissions. Responds in 3 months to queries. Guidelines online.

NONFICTION Subjects include specific issues related to a given disability (e.g., communication skills, social sciences skills, feeding issues) and practical guides to issues of concern to parents of children with disabilities (e.g., special education, sibling issues). Publishes books for and about children with disabilities. No personal accounts or general parenting guides. Submit outline, and at least 3 sample chapters. Reviews artwork/photos.

FICTION Subjects include picture books, children's. Receptive to stories re: developmental and intellectual disabilities, e.g., autism and cerebral palsy. Submit complete ms with SASE.

TIPS "Do not send us a proposal on the basis of this description. Examine our catalog or website and a couple of our books to make sure you are on the right track. Put some thought into how your book could be marketed (aside from in bookstores). Keep cover letters concise and to the point; if it's a subject that interests us, we'll ask to see more."

Ⓐ WORDSONG

815 Church St., Honesdale PA 18431. **Fax:** (570)253-0179. **Website:** www.wordsongpoetry.com. Estab. 1990. "We publish fresh voices in contemporary poetry." **Pays authors royalty or work purchased outright.** Responds to mss in 3 months.

POETRY *Agented submissions only.*

TIPS "Collections of original poetry, not anthologies, are our biggest need at this time. Keep in mind that the strongest collections demonstrate a facility with multiple poetic forms and offer fresh images and insights. Check to see what's already on the market and on our website before submitting."

WORKMAN PUBLISHING CO.

225 Varick St., New York NY 10014. **E-mail:** submissions@workman.com. **Website:** www.workman.com. Estab. 1967. Publishes hardcover and trade paperback originals, as well as calendars. "We are a trade paperback house specializing in a wide range of popular nonfiction. We publish no adult fiction and very little children's fiction. We also publish a full range of full-color wall and Page-A-Day calendars." **Publishes 40 titles/year. thousands of queries received/year. Open to first-time authors. Pays variable royalty on retail price. Pays variable advance.** Publishes ms approximately 1 year after acceptance. Accepts simultaneous submissions. Responds in 5 months to queries. Guidelines online.

NONFICTION Subjects include business, economics, child guidance, cooking, foods, nutrition, gardening, health, medicine, sports, travel. Query.

TIPS "We prefer electronic submissions."

WORLD BOOK, INC.

233 N. Michigan Ave., Suite 2000, Chicago IL 60601. (312)729-5800. **Fax:** (312)729-5600. **Website:** www.worldbook.com. World Book, Inc. (publisher of The World Book Encyclopedia), publishes reference

sources and nonfiction series for children and young adults in the areas of science, mathematics, English-language skills, basic academic and social skills, social studies, history, and health and fitness. "We publish print and non-print material appropriate for children ages 3-14. WB does not publish fiction, poetry, or wordless picture books." **Payment negotiated on project-by-project basis.** Publishes ms 18 months after acceptance. Responds to queries in 2 months.

NONFICTION Young readers: animal, arts/crafts, careers, concept, geography, health, reference. Middle readers: animal, arts/crafts, careers, geography, health, history, hobbies, how-to, nature/environment, reference, science. Young adult: arts/crafts, careers, geography, health, history, hobbies, how-to, nature/environment, reference, science. Query.

WRITER'S DIGEST BOOKS

Imprint of F+W Media, Inc., 10151 Carver Rd., Suite #200, Cincinnati OH 45242. **E-mail:** writersdigest@fwcommunity.com. **Website:** www.writersdigest.com. **Contact:** Rachel Randall. Estab. 1920. Publishes hardcover originals and trade paperbacks. "Writer's Digest Books is the premiere source for instructional books on writing and publishing for an audience of aspirational writers. Typical mss are 80,000 words. E-mail queries strongly preferred; no phone calls please." **Publishes 18-20 titles/year. 300 queries received/year. 50 mss received/year. 30% from unagented writers. Pays average $3,000 advance.** Publishes ms 1 year after acceptance. Accepts simultaneous submissions. Responds in 3 months to queries. "Our catalog of titles is available to view online at www.WritersDigestShop.com.".

Writer's Digest Books accepts query letters and complete proposals via e-mail at writersdigest@fwcommunity.com.

NONFICTION "Our instruction books stress results and how to achieve them. Should be well-researched, yet lively and readable. We do not want to see books telling readers how to crack specific nonfiction markets: *Writing for the Computer Market* or *Writing for Trade Publications*, for instance. We are most in need of fiction-technique books written by published authors. Be prepared to explain how the proposed book differs from existing books on the subject." No fiction or poetry. Query with SASE. Submit outline, sample chapters, SASE.

TIPS "Most queries we receive are either too broad (how to write fiction) or too niche (how to write erotic horror), and don't reflect a knowledge of our large backlist of 150 titles. We rarely publish new books on journalism, freelancing, magazine article writing or marketing/promotion. We are actively seeking fiction and nonfiction writing technique books with fresh perspectives, interactive and visual writing instruction books, similar to *The Pocket Muse* by Monica Wood, and general reference works that appeal to an audience beyond writers."

YALE UNIVERSITY PRESS

P.O. Box 209040, New Haven CT 06520. (203)432-0960. **Fax:** (203)432-0948. **E-mail:** christopher.rogers@yale.edu. **Website:** yalepress.yale.edu/yupbooks. **Contact:** Christopher Rogers, editorial director. Estab. 1908. Publishes hardcover and trade paperback originals. "Yale University Press publishes scholarly and general interest books." Accepts simultaneous submissions. Book catalog and ms guidelines online.

NONFICTION Subjects include Americana, anthropology, archeology, art, architecture, business, economics, education, health, medicine, history, language, literature, military, war, music, dance, philosophy, psychology, religion, science, sociology, women's issues, women's studies. "Our nonfiction has to be at a very high level. Most of our books are written by professors or journalists, with a high level of expertise. *Submit proposals only.* We'll ask if we want to see more. *No unsolicited mss.* We won't return them." Submit sample chapters, cover letter, prospectus, CV, TOC, SASE. Reviews artwork/photos. Send photocopies.

POETRY Submit to Yale Series of Younger Poets Competition. Guidelines online.

TIPS "Audience is scholars, students and general readers."

YELLOW SHOE FICTION SERIES

P.O. Box 25053, Baton Rouge LA 70894. **Website:** www.lsu.edu/lsupress. **Contact:** Michael Griffith, editor. Estab. 2004. **Publishes 2 titles/year. Pays royalty. Offers advance.**

FICTION Does not accept unsolicited mss. Accepts queries by mail, Attn: Rand Dotson. No electronic submissions.

YMAA PUBLICATION CENTER

P.O. Box 480, Wolfeboro NH 03894. (603)569-7988. **Fax:** (603)569-1889. **E-mail:** info@ymaa.com. **Contact:** David Ripianzi, director. Estab. 1982. Publishes trade paperback originals and reprints. Publishes 6-8 DVD titles/year. YMAA publishes books on Chinese Chi Kung (Qigong), Taijiquan, (Tai Chi) and Asian martial arts. We are expanding our focus to include books on healing, wellness, meditation and subjects related to Asian culture and Asian medicine. **Publishes 6-8 titles/year. 50 queries received/year. 20 mss received/year. 25% of books from first-time authors. 100% from unagented writers.** Publishes ms 18 months after acceptance. Accepts simultaneous submissions. Responds in 3 months to proposals. Book catalog online. Guidelines available free.

NONFICTION Subjects include ethnic, health, medicine, Chinese, history, philosophy, spirituality, sports, Asian martial arts, Chinese Qigong. "We no longer publish or solicit books for children. We also produce instructional DVDs and videos to accompany our books on traditional Chinese martial arts, meditation, massage, and Chi Kung. We are most interested in Asian martial arts, Chinese medicine, and Chinese Qigong. We publish Eastern thought, health, meditation, massage, and East/West synthesis." Submit proposal package, outline, bio, 1 sample chapter, SASE. Reviews artwork/photos. Send Send photocopies and 1-2 originals to determine quality of photo/line art.

FICTION "We are seeking mss that bring the venerated tradition of Asian martial arts to readers. Your novel length ms should be a thrilling story that conveys insights into martial techniques and philosophies."

TIPS "If you are submitting health-related material, please refer to an Asian tradition. Learn about author publicity options as your participation is mandatory."

YOGI IMPRESSIONS BOOKS PVT. LTD.

1711, Centre 1, World Trade Centre, Cuffe Parade Mumbai 400 005, India. **E-mail:** yogi@yogiimpressions.com. **Website:** www.yogiimpressions.com. Estab. 2000. "Yogi Impressions are Self-help, Personal Growth and Spiritual book publishers based in Mumbai, India. Established at the turn of the millennium, at Mumbai, Yogi Impressions publishes books which seek to revive interest in spirituality, enhance the quality of life and, thereby, create the legacy of a better world for future generations." Guidelines online.

NONFICTION Subjects include audio, child guidance, multicultural, religion, spirituality, alternative health, enlightened business, self-improvement/personal growth. Submit outline/proposal, bio, 2-3 sample chapters, market assessment, SASE.

ZEBRA BOOKS

Kensington, 119 W. 40th St., New York NY 10018. (212)407-1500. **E-mail:** esogah@kensingtonbooks.com. **Website:** www.kensingtonbooks.com. **Contact:** Esi Sogah, senior editor. Publishes hardcover originals, trade paperback and mass market paperback originals and reprints. Zebra Books is dedicated to women's fiction, which includes, but is not limited to romance. Publishes ms 12-18 months after acceptance. Accepts simultaneous submissions. Book catalog online.

FICTION Query.

ZENITH PRESS

Quayside Publishing Group, 400 First Ave. N., Suite 300, Minneapolis MN 55401. (612)344-8100; (800)328-0590. **Fax:** (612)344-8691. **E-mail:** egilg@quaysidepub.com. **Website:** www.qbookshop.com; zenithpress.com. **Contact:** Erik Gilg, editorial director. Estab. 2004. Publishes hardcover and trade paperback originals, electronic originals and reprints, hardcover and trade paperback reprints. "Zenith Press publishes an eclectic collection of historical nonfiction and current affairs in both narrative and illustrated formats. Building on a core of military history, particularly from World War II forward, Zenith reaches out to other historical, aviation, and science topics with compelling narrative hooks or eye-catching photography. From a history of WWII aviation wrecks to an illustrated celebration of the space shuttle program, Zenith books are engaging stories with historical, military, or science foundations—sometimes all 3 at once." **Publishes 210 titles/year. Receives 250 queries/year; 100 mss/year. 25% of books from first-time authors. 50% from unagented writers. Pays authors 8-15% royalty on wholesale price.** Publishes ms 1 year after acceptance. Accepts simultaneous submissions. Responds in 1 month. Catalog and guidelines online.

NONFICTION Subjects include history, military, politics, science, world affairs, aviation. Submit proposal package, including outline, 1-3 sample chapters, and author biography. Reviews artwork. Send digital files.

ZUMAYA PUBLICATIONS, LLC

3209 S. Interstate 35, Austin TX 78741. **E-mail:** business@zumayapublications.com. **E-mail:** acquisitions@zumayapublications.com. **Website:** www.zumayapublications.com. **Contact:** Rie Sheridan Rose, acquisitions editor. Estab. 1999. Publishes trade paperback and electronic originals and reprints. **Publishes 20-25 titles/year. 1,000 queries received/year. 100 mss received/year. 5% of books from first-time authors. 98% from unagented writers.** Publishes ms 2 years after acceptance. Responds in 6 months to queries and proposals; 9 months to mss. Guidelines online.

IMPRINTS Zumaya Arcane (New Age, inspirational fiction & nonfiction), Zumaya Boundless (GLBT); Zumaya Embraces (romance/women's fiction); Zumaya Enigma (mystery/suspense/thriller); Zumaya Thresholds (YA/middle grade); Zumaya Otherworlds (SF/F/H), Zumaya Yesterdays (memoirs, historical fiction, fiction, western fiction); Zumaya Fabled Ink (graphic and illustrated novels).

NONFICTION Subjects include creative nonfiction, memoirs, New Age, spirituality, ghost stories. "The easiest way to figure out what we're looking for is to look at what we've already done. Our main nonfiction interests are in collections of ghost stories, ones that have been investigated or thoroughly documented, memoirs that address specific regions and eras from a 'normal person' viewpoint and books on the craft of writing. That doesn't mean we won't consider something else." Electronic query only. Reviews artwork/photos. Send digital format.

FICTION Subjects include adventure, fantasy, bisexual, gay, lesbian, historical, horror, humor, juvenile, literary, mainstream, contemporary, multicultural, mystery, occult, romance, science fiction, short story collections, spiritual, suspense, transgender, western, young adult. "We are currently oversupplied with speculative fiction and are reviewing submissions in SF, fantasy and paranormal suspense by invitation only. We are much in need of GLBT and YA/middle grade, historical and western, New Age/inspirational (no overtly Christian materials, please), non-category romance, thrillers. As with nonfiction, we encourage people to review what we've already published so as to avoid sending us more of the same, at least, insofar as the plot is concerned. While we're always looking for good specific mysteries, we want original concepts rather than slightly altered versions of what we've already published."

TIPS "We're catering to readers who may have loved last year's best seller but not enough to want to read 10 more just like it. Have something different."

CONSUMER MAGAZINES

Selling your writing to consumer magazines is as much an exercise of your marketing skills as it is of your writing abilities. Editors of consumer magazines are looking for good writing which communicates pertinent information to their readers.

Marketing skills will help you successfully discern a magazine's editorial slant, and write queries and articles that prove your knowledge of the magazine's readership. You can gather clues about a magazine's readership—and establish your credibility with the editor—in a number of ways:

- **Read** the listing in *Writer's Market.*
- **Study** a magazine's writer's guidelines.
- **Check** a magazine's website.
- **Read** current issues of the magazine.

Writers who can correctly and consistently discern a publication's audience and deliver stories that speak to that target readership will win out every time over writers who submit haphazardly.

In nonfiction, editors continue to look for short feature articles covering specialized topics. Editors want crisp writing and expertise. If you are not an expert in the area about which you are writing, make yourself one through research. Always query before sending your manuscript.

Fiction editors prefer to receive complete manuscripts. Writers must keep in mind that fiction is competitive, and editors receive far more material than they can publish. For this reason, they often do not respond to submissions unless they are interested in using the story.

Most magazines listed here have indicated pay rates; some give very specific payment-per-word rates, while others state a range. Any agreement you come to with a magazine, whether verbal or written, should specify the payment you are to receive and when you are to receive it.

ANIMAL

COONHOUND BLOODLINES

United Kennel Club, Inc., 100 E. Kilgore Rd., Kalamazoo MI 49002-5584. (269)343-9020. **Fax:** (269)343-7037. **E-mail:** vrand@ukcdogs.com. **Website:** www.ukcdogs.com. **Contact:** Vicki Rand, editor. **40% freelance written.** Monthly magazine covering all aspects of the 7 Coonhound dog breeds. Estab. 1925. Circ. 10,000. Byline given. Pays on publication. No kill fee. Publishes ms an average of 6 months after acceptance. Please include e-mail address with submissions. Editorial lead time 6 months. Submit seasonal material 6 months in advance. Accepts queries by mail, e-mail, fax, phone. Accepts simultaneous submissions. Responds in 6 weeks to queries. Sample copy: $7.

"Writers must retain the 'slang' particular to dog people and to our readers—many of whom are from the South."

NONFICTION Needs general interest, historical, humor, interview, new product, personal experience, photo feature; breed-specific. Special issues: Seven of the magazine's 12 issues are each devoted to a specific breed of Coonhound. American Leopard Hound (January); Treeing Walker (February); English (July); Black & Tan (April); Bluetick (May); Redbone (June); Plott Hound (August), 1,000-3,000 words and photos. **Buys 12-36 mss/year.** Query. Length: 1,000-5,000 words. **Pays variable amount.** Sometimes pays expenses of writers on assignment.

PHOTOS State availability. Captions, identification of subjects required. Reviews contact sheets. Negotiates payment individually.

FICTION Must be about the Coonhound breeds or hunting with hounds. Needs adventure, historical, humorous, mystery. **Buys 3-6 mss/year.** Query. Length: 1,000-3,000 words. **Pay varies.**

DOG SPORTS MAGAZINE

Cher Car Kennels, 4215 S. Lowell Rd., St. Johns MI 48879. (989)224-7225. **E-mail:** info@chercarkennels.com. **Website:** www.dogsports.com. **Contact:** Cheryl Carlson, editor. **5% freelance written.** Monthly tabloid covering working dogs. *Dog Sports* online magazine is for all dog trainers. Focuses on the "how" of dog training. You will find articles on police K-9 training, narcotics detection, herding, weight pull, tracking, search and rescue, and how to increase your dog-training business. Brings the latest in techniques from the field, actual dog trainers that are out there, working, titling, and training. French Ring, Mondio, Schutzhund, N.A.P.D. PPDA, K-9 Pro Sports all are featured, as well as spotlight articles on breeds, trainers, judges, or events. Estab. 1979. Circ. 2,000. Byline given. Pays on publication. Publishes ms an average of 1 month after acceptance. Editorial lead time 1 month. Submit seasonal material 1 month in advance. Accepts queries by mail, e-mail. Accepts simultaneous submissions. Sample copy free or online.

NONFICTION Needs essays, general interest, how-to, working dogs, humor, interview, technical. **Buys 5 mss/year.** Send complete ms. **Pays $50.**

PHOTOS State availability of photos. Captions, identification of subjects required. Reviews prints. Offers no additional payment for photos accepted with ms.

TIPS "If you have ideas about topics, articles, or areas of interest, please drop us an e-mail and let us know how we can make this online magazine the best training tool you've ever had!"

EQUINE JOURNAL

83 Leicester St., North Oxford MA 01537. (508)987-5886. **Fax:** (508)987-5887. **E-mail:** editorial@equinejournal.com. **Website:** www.equinejournal.com. **Contact:** Kelly Ballou, editor. **90% freelance written.** Monthly tabloid covering horses—all breeds, all disciplines. *Equine Journal* is a monthly, all-breed/discipline regional publication for horse enthusiasts. "The purpose of our editorial is to educate, entertain, and enable amateurs and professionals alike to stay on top of new developments in the field. Every month, the *Equine Journal* presents feature articles and columns spanning the length and breadth of horse-related activities and interests from all corners of the country." Estab. 1988. Circ. 26,000. Byline given. Pays on publication. Editorial lead time 4 months. Accepts queries by mail, e-mail, fax, phone. Responds in 2 months to queries. Guidelines available online.

NONFICTION Needs general interest, how-to, interview. **Buys 100 mss/year.** Send complete ms. Length: 1,200-1,800 words for features; 300-500 words for event write-ups.

PHOTOS Send photos. Reviews prints. Pays $10.

COLUMNS/DEPARTMENTS Horse Health (health-related topics), 1,200-1,500 words. **Buys 12 mss/year.** Query.

FIDO FRIENDLY MAGAZINE

Fido Friendly, Inc., P.O. Box 160, Marsing ID 83639. **E-mail:** fieldeditor@fidofriendly.com. **Website:** www.fidofriendly.com. **Contact:** Susan Sims, publisher. **95% freelance written.** Quarterly magazine covering travel with your dog. "We want articles about all things travel related with your dog." Estab. 2000. Circ. 50,000. Byline given. Pays on publication. 25% kill fee. Publishes ms an average of 2 months after acceptance. Editorial lead time 1-3 months. Submit seasonal material 3 months in advance. Accepts queries by e-mail. Accepts simultaneous submissions. Responds in 2 weeks to queries; in 1 month to mss. Sample copy: $7. Guidelines free.

NONFICTION Needs essays, general interest, how-to, travel with your dog, humor, inspirational, interview, personal experience, travel. No articles from dog's point of view or in dog's voice. **Buys 24 mss/yr mss/year.** Query with published clips. Length: 600-1,200 words. **Pays 10-20¢ for assigned articles and unsolicited articles.**

PHOTOS Send photos. Captions, identification of subjects, model releases required. Reviews GIF/JPEG files. Offers no additional payment for photos accepted with ms.

COLUMNS/DEPARTMENTS Fido Friendly City (city where dogs have lots of options to enjoy restaurants, dog retail stores, dog parks, sports activity). **Buys 6 mss/yr mss/year.** Query with published clips. **Pays 10-20¢/word.**

FICTION Needs adventure, (dog). Nothing from dog's point of view. Query. Length: 600-1,200 words. **Pays 10-20¢/word.**

TIPS "Accept copies in lieu of payment. Our readers treat their pets as part of the family. Writing should reflect that."

HORSEPOWER

Box 670, Aurora ON L4G 4J9 Canada. (800)505-7428. **Fax:** (905)841-1530. **E-mail:** ftdesk@horse-canada.com. **Website:** www.horse-canada.com. **Contact:** Susan Stafford-Pooley, managing editor. Bimonthly 16-page magazine, bound into *Horse Canada*, a bimonthly family horse magazine. "*Horsepower* offers how-to articles and stories relating to horse care for kids ages 6-16, with a focus on safety." Estab. 1988. Circ. 17,000. Pays on publication. Responds to mss in 3 months. Guidelines available for SASE.

Horsepower no longer accepts fiction.

NONFICTION Needs Middle grade readers, young adults: arts/crafts, biography, careers, fashion, games/puzzles, health, history, hobbies, how-to, humorous, interview/profile, problem-solving, travel. **Buys 6-10 mss/year.** Submit complete ms. Length: 500-1,200 words.

TIPS "Articles must be easy to understand, yet detailed and accurate. How-to or other educational features must be written by, or in conjunction with, a riding/teaching professional. Fiction is not encouraged, unless it is outstanding and teaches a moral or practical lesson. Note: Preference will be given to Canadian writers and photographers due to Canadian content laws. Non-Canadian contributors accepted on a very limited basis."

JUST LABS

VP Demand Creation Services, 2779 Aero Park Dr., Traverse City MI 49686. (231)946-3712; (800)447-7367. **E-mail:** jillian.lacross@vpdemandcreation.com. **Website:** www.justlabsmagazine.com. **Contact:** Jason Smith, editor; Jill LaCross, managing editor. **50% freelance written.** Bimonthly magazine covering all aspects of the Labrador Retriever. "*Just Labs* is targeted toward the family Labrador Retriever, and all of our articles help people learn about, live with, train, take care of, and enjoy their dogs. We do not look for articles that pull at the heart strings (those are usually staff-written), but rather we look for articles that teach, inform, and entertain." Estab. 2001. Circ. 15,000. Byline given. Pays on publication. Offers 40% kill fee. Publishes ms an average of 6 months after acceptance. Editorial lead time 6 months. Submit seasonal material 6-8 months in advance. Accepts queries by mail. Responds in 4-6 weeks to queries.; in 2 months to mss. Guidelines for #10 SASE.

NONFICTION Needs essays, how-to, (train, health, lifestyle), humor, inspirational, interview, photo feature, technical, travel. "We don't want tributes to dogs that have passed on. This is a privilege we reserve for our subscribers." **Buys 30 mss/year.** Query. Length: 1,000-1,800 words. **Pays $250-400 for assigned articles. Pays $250-400 for unsolicited articles.**

PHOTOS Send photos. Captions required. Reviews contact sheets, transparencies, prints, GIF/JPEG files. Offers no additional payment for photos accepted with ms.

TIPS "Be professional, courteous, and understanding of our time. Please be aware that we have been around for several years and have probably published an article on almost every 'dog topic' out there. Those queries providing fresh, unique, and interesting angles on common topics will catch our eye."

$ MINIATURE DONKEY TALK

Miniature Donkey Talk, Inc., P.O. Box 982, Cripple Creek CO 80813. (719)689-2904. **E-mail:** mike@donkeytalk.info. **Website:** www.web-donkeys.com. **Contact:** Mike Gross. **65% freelance written.** Quarterly magazine covering donkeys, with articles on healthcare, promotion, and management of donkeys for owners, breeders, and donkey lovers. Estab. 1987. Circ. 4,925. Byline given. Pays on acceptance. Publishes ms an average of 4 months after acceptance. Editorial lead time 2 months. Submit seasonal material 3 months in advance. Accepts queries by mail, e-mail. Responds in 2 weeks to queries. Responds in 1 month to mss. Sample copy for $5. Guidelines free.

NONFICTION Needs book excerpts, humor, interview, personal experience. **Buys 6 mss/year.** Query with published clips. Length: 700-5,000 words. **Pays $25-150.**

PHOTOS State availability. Identification of subjects required. Reviews 3x5 prints. Offers no additional payment for photos accepted with ms.

COLUMNS/DEPARTMENTS Columns: Humor: 2,000 words; Healthcare: 2,000-5,000 words; Management: 2,000 words. **Buys 50 mss/year.** Query. **Pays $25-100.**

TIPS "Simply send your ms. If on topic and appropriate, good possibility it will be published. No fiction or poetry."

$$ PAINT HORSE JOURNAL

American Paint Horse Association, P.O. Box 961023, Ft. Worth TX 76161-0023. (817)834-2742. **Fax:** (817)834-3152. **E-mail:** jhein@apha.com. **Website:** www.phj.apha.com. **Contact:** Jessica Hein, editor. **10% freelance written. Works with a small number of new/unpublished writers each year.** Monthly magazine for people who raise, breed, and show Paint Horses. Estab. 1966. Circ. 12,000. Byline given. Pays on acceptance. Offers negotiable kill fee. Submit seasonal material 3 months in advance. Accepts queries by mail, e-mail, fax. Sample copy for $7 (includes shipping). Guidelines available online.

NONFICTION Needs general interest, personality pieces on well-known owners of Paints, historical, Paint Horses in the past—particular horses and the breed in general, how-to, train and show horses, photo feature of Paint Horses. **Buys 4-5 mss/year.** Query. Length: 1,000-2,000 words. **Pays $100-500.**

PHOTOS Photos must illustrate article and must include registered Paint Horses. Send photos. Captions required. Offers no additional payment for photos accepted with accompanying ms.

POETRY No poetry.

TIPS "Well-written articles are welcomed. Submit items that show a definite understanding of the horse business. Be sure you understand precisely what a Paint Horse is as defined by the American Paint Horse Association. Use proper equine terminology. Photos with copy are almost always essential."

$$ USDF CONNECTION

United States Dressage Federation, 4051 Iron Works Pkwy., Lexington KY 40511. **E-mail:** connection@usdf.org. **E-mail:** editorial@usdf.org. **Website:** www.usdf.org. **40% freelance written.** Magazine published 10 times/year covering dressage (an equestrian sport). All material must relate to the sport of dressage in the U.S. Estab. 2000. Circ. 35,000. Byline given. Pays on acceptance. Offers 50% kill fee. Publishes ms an average of 6 months after acceptance. Editorial lead time 3 months. Submit seasonal material 6 months in advance. Accepts queries by mail, e-mail. Responds in 1 month to queries; in 1-2 months to mss. Sample copy: $5. Guidelines available online.

NONFICTION Needs book excerpts, essays, how-to, interview, opinion, personal experience. Does not want general-interest equine material or stories that lack a U.S. dressage angle. **Buys 20 mss/year.** Query. Length: 500-2,000 words. **Pays $100-400 for assigned articles. Pays $100-300 for unsolicited articles.** Sometimes pays expenses of writers on assignment.

PHOTOS State availability. Captions, identification of subjects required. Reviews JPEG files. Negotiates payment individually.

COLUMNS/DEPARTMENTS Amateur Hour (profiles of and service pieces of interest to USDF's adult amateur members), 1,200-1,500 words; Under 21 (profiles of and service pieces of interest to USDF's young members), 1,200-1,500 words; Horse-Health Connection (dressage-related horse health), 1,200-1,800 words. **Buys 12 mss/year.** Query with published clips. **Pays $150-300.**

TIPS "Know the organization and the sport. Most successful contributors are active in the horse industry and bring valuable perspectives and insights to their stories and images."

YOUNG RIDER

P.O. Box 8237, Lexington KY 40533. (859)260-9800. **Fax:** (859)260-9814. **E-mail:** yreditor@i5publishing.com. **Website:** www.youngrider.com. "*Young Rider* magazine teaches young people, in an easy-to-read and entertaining way, how to look after their horses properly, and how to improve their riding skills safely." Estab. 1994. Byline given. Pays on publication. Publishes ms 6-12 months after acceptance. Rsponds in 2 weeks to queries. Sample copy: $3.50. Guidelines online.

NONFICTION Needs young adults: animal, careers, famous equestrians, health (horse), horse celebrities, riding. Special issues: Wants "'horsey-interest type stories. Stories or events that will interest kids ALL over the country that the editor is not able to personally attend. We need 4-5 good color photos with stories like this; the pictures must be color and tack sharp." Query with published clips. Length: 800-1,000 words. **Pays $200/story.**

FICTION Needs young adults: adventure, animal, horses. "We would prefer funny stories, with a bit of conflict, which will appeal to the 13-year-old age group. They should be written in the third person, and about kids." Query. Length: 800-1,000 words. **Pays $150.**

TIPS "Fiction must be in third person. Read magazine before sending in a query. No 'true story from when I was a youngster.' No moralistic stories. Fiction must be up-to-date and humorous, teen-oriented. No practical or how-to articles—all done in-house."

ART AND ARCHITECTURE

EASTERN ART REPORT

EAPGROUP International Media, P.O. Box 13666, London England SW14 8WF United Kingdom. (44)208-392-1122. **Website:** www.eapgroup.com. *EAR* has a worldwide readership—from scholars to connoisseurs—with varying knowledge of or interest in the historical, philosophical, practical, or theoretical aspects of Eastern art. Estab. 1989. No kill fee. Accepts queries by online submission form. No

NONFICTION Query via online submission form.

PHOTOS Reviews illustrations, electronic images of at least 300 dpi.

METROPOLIS

Bellerophon Publications, 61 W. 23rd St., 4th Floor, New York NY 10010. (212)627-9977. **Fax:** (212)627-9988. **E-mail:** edit@metropolismag.com. **Website:** www.metropolismag.com. **Contact:** Shannon Sharpe, managing editor. **80% freelance written.** Monthly magazine (combined issue July/August) for consumers interested in architecture and design. "*Metropolis* examines contemporary life through design—architecture, interior design, product design, graphic design, crafts, planning, and preservation. Subjects range from the sprawling urban environment to intimate living spaces to small objects of everyday use. In looking for why design happens in a certain way, *Metropolis* explores the economic, environmental, social, cultural, political, and technological context. With its innovative graphic presentation and its provocative voice, *Metropolis* shows how richly designed our world can be." Estab. 1981. Circ. 45,000. Byline given. Pays 60-90 days after acceptance. No kill fee. Publishes ms an average of 3 months after acceptance. Submit seasonal material 3 months in advance. Accepts queries by e-mail. Responds in 8 months to queries. Sample copy: $7. Guidelines online.

NONFICTION Needs essays, design, architecture, urban planning issues and ideas, interview, of multidisciplinary designers/architects. No profiles on individual architectural practices, information from public relations firms, or fine arts. **Buys 30 mss/year.** Send query via e-mail; no mss. "Describe your idea and why it would be good for our magazine. Be concise, specific, and clear. Also, please include clips or links to a few of your recent stories. The ideal *Metropolis* story is based on strong reporting and includes an examination of current critical issues. A design firm's newest work isn't a story, but the issues that its work brings to light might be." Length: 1,500-4,000 words. **Pays $1,500-4,000.**

PHOTOS Captions required. Reviews contact sheets, 35mm or 4x5 transparencies, 8x10 b&w prints. Payment offered for certain photos.

COLUMNS/DEPARTMENTS The Metropolis Observed (architecture, design, and city planning news features), 100-1,200 words, pays $100-1,200; Perspective (opinion or personal observation of architecture and design), 1,200 words, pays $1,200; Enterprise (the business/development of architecture and design), 1,500 words, pays $1,500; In Review (architecture and book review essays), 1,500 words, pays $1,500. **Buys 40 mss/year.** Query with published clips.

TIPS "*Metropolis* strives to tell the story of design to a lay person with an interest in the built environment, while keeping the professional designer engaged. The magazine examines the various design disciplines (architecture, interior design, product design, graphic design, planning, and preservation) and their social/cultural context. We're looking for the new, the obscure, or the wonderful. Also, be patient, and don't expect an immediate answer after submission of query."

SOUTHWEST ART

10901 W. 120th Ave., Suite 340, Broomfield CO 80021. (303)442-0427. **Fax:** (303)449-0279. **E-mail:** southwestart@fwmedia.com. **Website:** www.southwestart.com. **Contact:** Kristin Hoerth, editor-in-chief. **60% freelance written.** Monthly magazine directed to art collectors interested in artists, market trends, and art history of the American West. Estab. 1971. Circ. 60,000. Byline given. Pays on acceptance. Publishes ms an average of 1 year after acceptance. Submit seasonal material 8 months in advance. Accepts queries by mail, fax. Responds in 6 months to mss.

NONFICTION Needs book excerpts, interview. No fiction or poetry. **Buys 70 mss/year.** Query with published clips. Length: 1,400-1,600 words.

PHOTOS Photographs, color print-outs, and videotapes will not be considered. Captions, identification of subjects required. Reviews 35mm, 2¼x2¼, 4x5 transparencies.

TIPS "Research the Southwest art market, send slides or transparencies with queries, and send writing samples demonstrating knowledge of the art world."

ASSOCIATIONS

$$ THE ELKS MAGAZINE

The Elks Magazine, 425 W. Diversey Pkwy., Chicago IL 60614. (773)755-4740. **E-mail:** magnews@elks.org. **Website:** www.elks.org/elksmag. **Contact:** Anna L. Idol, editor/publisher. **25% freelance written.** Magazine covers nonfiction only; published 10 times/year with basic mission of being the voice of the elks. All fraternal is written in-house. Estab. 1922. Circ. 800,000. Pays on acceptance. No kill fee. Accepts queries by mail, e-mail. Responds in 1 month with a yes/no on ms purchase. Guidelines available online.

Each year, the editors buy 20 to 30 articles. These articles consist of previously unpublished, informative, upbeat, entertaining writing on a variety of subjects, including science, technology, travel, nature, Americana, sports, history, health, retirement, personal finance, leisure-time activities, and seasonal topics. Articles should be authoritative (please include sources) and appeal to the lay person.

NONFICTION No fiction, religion, controversial issues, first-person, fillers, or verse. **Buys 20-30 mss/year.** Send complete ms. Length: 1,500-2,000 words. **Pays 25¢/word.**

PHOTOS "If possible, please advise where photographs may be found. Photographs taken and submitted by the writer are paid for separately at $35 each. Send transparencies, slides. Pays $475 for one-time cover rights." Pays $25/photo.

COLUMNS/DEPARTMENTS "The invited columnists are already selected."

TIPS "Please try us first. We'll get back to you soon."

$$ HUMANITIES

National Endowment for the Humanities, 1100 Pennsylvania Ave. NW, Washington DC 20506. (202)606-8435. **Fax:** (202)606-8451. **E-mail:** dskinner@neh.gov; info@neh.gov. **Website:** www.neh.gov/humanities. **Contact:** David Skinner, editor. **50% freelance written.** Bimonthly magazine covering news in the humanities focused on projects that receive financial support from the agency. Estab. 1980. Circ. 7,500. Byline given. Pays on publication. Publishes ms an average of 2 months after acceptance. Editorial lead time 3 months. Submit seasonal material 4 months in advance. Accepts queries by mail, e-mail, fax, phone. Sample copy available online.

NONFICTION Needs book excerpts, historical, interview, photo feature. **Buys 25 mss/year.** Query with published clips. Length: 400-2,500 words. **Pays $300-600.** Sometimes pays expenses of writers on assignment.

PHOTOS Contact: Contact mbiernik@neh.gov. Identification of subjects, model releases required. Offers no additional payment for photos accepted with ms; negotiates payment individually.

COLUMNS/DEPARTMENTS In Focus (directors of state humanities councils), 700 words; Breakout (special activities of state humanities councils), 750 words. **Buys 12 mss/year.** Query with published clips. **Pays $300.**

LION

Lions Clubs International, 300 W. 22nd St., Oak Brook IL 60523-8842. (630)468-6909. **Fax:** (630)571-1685. **E-mail:** magazine@lionsclubs.org. **Website:** www.lionsclubs.org. **Contact:** Jay Copp, senior editor. **35% freelance written. Works with a small number of new/unpublished writers each year.** Monthly magazine covering service club organization for Lions Club members and their families. Estab. 1918. Circ. 490,000. Byline given. Pays on acceptance. No kill fee. Publishes ms an average of 5 months after acceptance. Accepts queries by mail, e-mail, fax, phone. Responds in 1 month to queries. Sample copy and writer's guidelines free.

LION magazine welcomes freelance article submissions with accompanying photos that depict the service goals and projects of Lions clubs on the local, national, and international level. Contributors may also submit general interest articles that reflect the humanitarian, community betterment, and service activism ideals of the worldwide association. Lions Clubs International is the world's largest service club organization. Lions are recognized globally for their commitment to projects that benefit the blind, visually impaired, and people in need.

NONFICTION Needs photo feature, must be of a Lions Club service project, informational (issues of interest to civic-minded individuals). No travel, biography, or personal experiences. **Buys 40 mss/year.** "Article length should not exceed 2,000 words, and is subject to editing. No gags, fillers, quizzes or poems are accepted. Photos must be color prints or sent digitally. *LION* magazine pays upon acceptance of material. Advance queries save your time and ours. Address all submissions to Jay Copp, senior editor, by mail or e-mail text and .tif or .jpg (300 dpi) photos." Length: 500-2,000 words. **Pays $100-750.** Sometimes pays expenses of writers on assignment.

PHOTOS Purchased with accompanying ms. Photos should be at least 5x7 glossies; color prints or slides are preferred. "We also accept digital photos by e-mail. Be sure photos are clear and as candid as possible." Captions required. Total purchase price for ms includes payment for photos accepted with ms.

TIPS "Send detailed description of proposed article. Query first and request writer's guidelines and sample copy. Incomplete details on how the Lions involved actually carried out a project and poor quality photos are the most frequent mistakes made by writers in completing an article assignment for us. No gags, fillers, quizzes, or poems are accepted. We are geared increasingly to an international audience. Writers who travel internationally could query for possible assignments, although only locally related expenses could be paid."

NEW MOBILITY

United Spinal Association, 120-34 Queens Blvd., #320, Kew Gardens NY 11415. (718)803-3782. **E-mail:** info@unitedspinal.org. **Website:** www.spinalcord.org/. **Contact:** Ian Ruder, editor. **50% freelance written.** Bimonthly magazine covering living with spinal cord injury/disorder (SCI/D). The bimonthly membership magazine for the National Spinal Cord Injury Association, a program of United Spinal Association. Members include people with spinal cord injury or disorder, as well as caregivers, parents, and some spinal cord injury/disorder professionals. All articles should reflect this common interest of the audience. Assume that your audience is better educated in the subject of spinal cord injury than average, but be careful not to be too technical. Each issue has a theme (available from editor) that unites features in addition to a series of departments focused on building community and providing solutions for the SCI/D community. Articles that feature members, chapters or the organization are preferred, but any article that deals with issue pertinent to SCI/D community will be considered. Estab. 2011. Circ. 35,000. Byline given. Pays on publication. No kill fee. Publishes ms an average of 1-2 months after acceptance. Accepts queries by e-mail. Sample copy and guidelines available on website.

NONFICTION Needs essays, general interest, how-to, humor, interview, new product, personal experience, photo feature, travel, medical research. Does not want "articles that treat disabilities as an affliction or cause for pity, or that show the writer does not get that people with disabilities are people like anyone else." **Buys 36 mss/year.** Query. Length: 800-1,600 words. **Pays $200-400.**

PHOTOS Send photos. Identification of subjects required. Reviews high-quality GIF/JPEG files. Offers no additional payment for photos accepted with ms.

COLUMNS/DEPARTMENTS Travel (report on access of a single travel destination based on conversations with disabled travelers), Access (hands-on look at how to improve access for a specific type of area), Ask Anything (tap members and experts to answer community question relating to life w/SCI/D), Advocacy (investigation of ongoing advocacy issue related to SCI/D). **Buys 40 mss/year.** Length: 800 words. Query with published clips. **Pays $200.**

TIPS "It helps (though is not necessary) if you have a disability, or if you are comfortable with people with disabilities; they are the subjects of most of our articles as well as the bulk of our readership. Our readers are looking for tips on how to live well with mobility impairment. They're concerned with access to jobs, travel, recreation, education, etc. They like to read about how others deal with like situations and hear about resources or ideas that will help them in their daily lives. They are sophisticated about spinal cord injuries and don't need to be 'inspired' by the typical stories about people with disabilities that appear in the human interest section of most newspapers."

$$ PENN LINES

Pennsylvania Rural Electric Association, P.O. Box 1266, Harrisburg PA 17108. **E-mail:** editor@prea.com. **Website:** www.prea.com/content/pennlines.asp. Monthly magazine covering rural life in Pennsylvania. News magazine of Pennsylvania electric cooperatives. Features should be balanced, and they should have a rural focus. Electric cooperative sources (such as consumers) should be used. Estab. 1966. Circ. 165,000. Byline given. Pays on publication. No kill fee. Publishes ms an average of 3 months after acceptance. Editorial lead time 4 months. Submit seasonal material 4 months in advance. Accepts queries by mail, e-mail. Sample copy available online.

NONFICTION Needs general interest, historical, how-to, interview, travel; rural PA only. Query or send complete ms. Length: 500-2,000 words. **Negotiates payment individually.**

PHOTOS Captions required. Reviews prints and GIF/JPEG files. Negotiates payment individually.

TIPS "Find topics of statewide interest to rural residents. Detailed information on *Penn Lines*' readers, gleaned from a reader survey, is available online."

THE ROTARIAN

Rotary International, One Rotary Center, 1560 Sherman Ave., Evanston IL 60201. (847)866-3000. **Fax:** (847)328-8554. **E-mail:** rotarian@rotary.org. **Website:** www.rotary.org. **40% freelance written.** Monthly magazine for Rotarian business and professional men and women and their families, schools, libraries, hospitals, etc. "Articles should appeal to an international audience and in some way help Rotarians help other people. The organization's rationale is one of hope, encouragement, and belief in the power of individuals talking and working together." Estab. 1911. Circ. 510,000. Byline sometimes given. Pays on acceptance. Offers kill fee. Kill fee negotiable. Editorial lead time 4-8 months. Accepts queries by mail, e-mail. Sample copy for $1 (edbrookc@rotaryintl.org). Guidelines available online.

NONFICTION Needs general interest, humor, inspirational, photo feature, technical, science, travel, lifestyle, sports, business/finance, environmental, health/medicine, social issues. No fiction, religious, or political articles. Query with published clips. Length: 1,500-2,500 words. **Pays negotiable rate.** Answer.

REPRINTS "Send tearsheet, photocopy or typed ms with rights for sale noted and information about when and where the material previously appeared." Negotiates payment.

PHOTOS State availability. Reviews contact sheets, transparencies.

COLUMNS/DEPARTMENTS Health; Management; Finance; Travel, all 550-900 words. Query.

TIPS "The chief aim of *The Rotarian* is to report Rotary international news. Most of this information comes through Rotary channels and is staff written or edited. The best field for freelance articles is in the general interest category. We prefer queries with a Rotary angle. These stories run the gamut from humor pieces and how-to stories to articles about such significant concerns as business management, technology, world health, and the environment."

$$$ SCOUTING

Boy Scouts of America, 1325 W. Walnut Hill Lane, P.O. Box 152079, Irving TX 75015-2079. **Website:** www.scoutingmagazine.org. **80% freelance written.** Magazine published 6 times/year covering Scouting activities for adult leaders of the Boy Scouts, Cub Scouts, and Venturing. Estab. 1913. Circ. 1 million. Byline given. Pays on acceptance for major features and some shorter features. Publishes ms an average of 18 months after acceptance. Editorial lead time 1 year. Submit seasonal material 1 year in advance. Accepts queries by mail. Accepts simultaneous submissions. Responds in 3 weeks to queries; in 2 months to mss. Sample copy: $2.50 and 9x12 SAE with 4 first-class stamps, or online.

NONFICTION Needs inspirational, interview. **Buys 20-30 mss/year.** Query with SASE. Length: short features, 500-700 words; some longer features, up to 1,200 words, usually the result of a definite assignment to a professional writer. **Pays $650-800 for major articles, $300-500 for shorter features. Rates depend on professional quality of article.** Pays expenses of writers on assignment.

REPRINTS Send photocopy of article and information about when and where the article previously appeared. First-person accounts of meaningful Scouting experiences (previously published in local newspapers, etc.) are a popular subject.

PHOTOS State availability. Identification of subjects required. Reviews transparencies, prints.

COLUMNS/DEPARTMENTS Way It Was (Scouting history), 600-750 words; Family Talk (family, raising kids, etc.), 600-750 words. **Buys 8-12 mss/year.** Query. **Pays $300-500.**

FILLERS Limited to personal accounts of humorous or inspirational Scouting experiences. Needs anecdotes, short humor. **Buys 15-25 mss/year.** Length: 50-150 words. **Pays $25 on publication.**

TIPS "*Scouting* magazine articles are mainly about successful program activities conducted by or for Cub Scout packs, Boy Scout troops, and Venturing crews. We also include features on winning leadership techniques and styles, profiles of outstanding individual leaders, and inspirational accounts (usually first person) of *Scouting*'s impact on an individual, either as a youth or while serving as a volunteer adult leader. Because most volunteer Scout leaders are also parents of children of Scout age, *Scouting* is also considered a family magazine. We publish material we feel will help parents in strengthening their families (because they often deal with communicating and interacting with young people, many of these features are useful to a reader in both roles as parent and Scout leader)."

TRAIL & TIMBERLINE

The Colorado Mountain Club, 710 Tenth St., Suite 200, Golden CO 80401. (303)279-3080. **E-mail:** editor@cmc.org. **Website:** www.cmc.org/about/newsroom/trailandtimberline.aspx. **Contact:** Editor. **80% freelance written.** Official quarterly publication for the Colorado Mountain Club. "Articles in *Trail & Timberline* conform to the mission statement of the Colorado Mountain Club to unite the energy, interest, and knowledge of lovers of the Colorado mountains, to collect and disseminate information 'regarding the Colorado mountains in the areas of art, science, literature, and recreation,' to stimulate public interest, and to encourage preservation of the mountains of Colorado and the Rocky Mountain region." Estab. 1918. Circ. 10,500. Byline given. Pays on acceptance. No kill fee. Publishes ms an average of 2 months after acceptance. Editorial lead time 6 months. Submit seasonal material 6 months in advance. Accepts queries by mail, e-mail. Responds in 1 week to queries.; in 1 month to mss. Sample copy: online, or $3 plus catalog-sized SASE. Make checks payable to CMC. Guidelines online.

"We encourage submissions from freelance writers who are familiar with our subject matter and our mission statement. Please be sure your article conforms to style and word usage as detailed in *The Associated Press Stylebook*."

NONFICTION Needs essays, humor, opinion, Switchbacks, personal experience, photo feature, travel, trip reports. **Buys 10-15 mss/year.** Send complete ms. Length: 500-2,000 words. **Pays $50.**

PHOTOS Send photos. Captions, identification of subjects, model releases required. Send images at 72 dpi, 5x7 in. "If possible, please post images on a website for us to view." Offers no additional payment for photos accepted with ms.

TIPS "Writers should be familiar with the purposes and ethos of the Colorado Mountain Club before querying. Writers guidelines are available and should be consulted. All submissions must conform to the mission statement of the Colorado Mountain Club."

ASTROLOGY & NEW AGE

FATE MAGAZINE

Fate Magazine, Inc., P.O. Box 460, Lakeville MN 55044. (952)431-2050. **Fax:** (952)891-6091. **E-mail:** fate@fatemag.com. **Website:** www.fatemag.com. **Contact:** Phyllis Galde, editor-in-chief; David Godwin, managing editor. **75% freelance written.** Covering the paranormal, ghosts, ufos, strange science. "Reports a wide variety of strange and unknown phenomena. We are open to receiving any well-written, well-documented article. Our readers especially like reports of current investigations, experiments, theories, and experiences. See topics on website at http://www.fatemag.com/fatemagold/WritersGuidelines.pdf." Estab. 1948. Circ. 15,000. Byline given. Pays after publication. Publishes ms 3-6 months after acceptance. Editorial lead time 3-6 months. Accepts queries by mail, e-mail, fax. Accepts simultaneous submissions. Responds in 1-3 months to queries. Sample copy available for free online, by e-mail. Guidelines available online.

"*Fate* prefers first-person accounts and investigations of the topics we cover. We do not publish fiction or opinion pieces or book-length mss."

NONFICTION Contact: Editor. Needs general interest, historical, how-to, personal experience, photo feature, technical. "We do not publish poetry, fiction, editorial/opinion pieces, or book-length mss." **Buys 100 mss/year mss/year.** Query. Length: 500-3,000 words, depending on features, briefs and fillers. **Pays $50 per feature article, $10 per short fillers.** Pays with merchandise or ad space if requested.

PHOTOS Contact: Editor. Buys slides, prints, or digital photos/illustrations with ms. Send photos with submission. GIF/JPEG files; prints (4 x 6). Pays $10.

COLUMNS/DEPARTMENTS Contact: Editor. True Mystic Experiences: Short reader-submitted stories of strange experiences; My Proof of Survival: Short, reader-submitted stories of proof of life after death, 300-1,000 words. Writer should query. **$25**

FILLERS Fillers are especially welcomed and must be be fully authenticated also, and on similar topics. Needs anecdotes and facts. Length: 100-1,000 words. **Pays 5¢/word.**

TIPS "*Fate* is looking for exciting, first-hand accounts of UFO and paranormal experiences and investigations."

WHOLE LIFE TIMES

Whole Life Media, LLC, 23705 Vanowen St., #306, West Hills CA 91307. (877)807-2599. **Fax:** (310)933-1693. **E-mail:** editor@wholelifemagazine.com. **Website:** www.wholelifemagazine.com. Bimonthly regional glossy on holistic living. *Whole Life Times* relies almost entirely on freelance material. Open to stories on natural health, alternative healing, green living, sustainable and local food, social responsibility, conscious business, the environment, spirituality and personal growth—anything relevant to a progressive, healthy lifestyle. Estab. 1978. Circ. 40,000 (print); 5,000 (digital). Byline given. Pays within 30-45 days of publication. 50% kill fee on assigned stories. No kill fee to first-time *WLT* writers or for unsolicited submissions. Publishes ms 2-4 months after acceptance. Accepts queries by e-mail only. Sample copy and writer's guidelines available online.

"We are a regional publication and favor material that somehow links to our area via topics, sources, and relevance."

NONFICTION Special issues: Special issues include: Healing Arts, Food and Nutrition, Spirituality, New Beginnings, Relationships, Longevity, Arts/Cultures Travel, Vitamins and Supplements, Women's Issues, Sexuality, Science and Metaphysics, Eco Lifestyle. **Buys 60 mss/year.** Send complete ms. Submissions are accepted via e-mail. Artwork should also be sent via e-mail as hard copies will not be returned. "Queries should be professionally written and show an awareness of our style and current topics of interest in our subject area. We welcome investigative reporting and are happy to see queries that address topics in a political context. We are especially looking for articles on health and nutrition. No regular columns sought. Submissions should be double-spaced in AP style as an attached unformatted MS Word file (.docx). If you do not have Microsoft Word and must e-mail in another program, please also copy and paste your story in the message section of your e-mail." **Payment varies. "*WLT* accepts up to 3 longer stories (800-1,100 words) per issue, and pay ranges from $100-175 depending on topic, research required, and writer experience. In addition, we have a number of regular departments that pay $35-150 depending on topic, length, research required, and writer experience. We pay by invoice, so please be sure to submit one and to name the file with your name."**

REPRINTS Rarely publishes reprints.

COLUMNS/DEPARTMENTS Local News, Taste of Health (food), Yoga & Spirit, Whole Living, Success Track, Art & Soul (media reviews). Length: 600-750 words. Send complete ms or well-developed query and links to previously published work. Submissions are accepted via e-mail. Artwork should also be sent via e-mail as hard copies will not be returned. **"City of Angels is our FOB section featuring short, newsy blurbs on our coverage topics, generally in the context of Los Angeles. These are generally 350-450 words and pay $25-35 depending on length and**

topic. This is a great section for writers who are new to us. BackWords is a 650-word personal essay that often highlights a seminal moment or event in the life of the writer and pays $100. We pay by invoice, so please be sure to submit one, and name the file with your name."

TIPS "We accept articles at any time by e-mail. If you would like your article to be considered for a specific issue, we should have it in hand 2-4 months before the issue of publication."

WITCHES AND PAGANS

BBI Media, Inc., P.O. Box 687, Forest Grove OR 97116. (888)724-3966. **E-mail:** editor2@bbimedia.com. **Website:** www.witchesandpagans.com. Quarterly magazine covering paganism, wicca, and earth religions. "*Witches and Pagans* is dedicated to witches, wiccans, neo-pagans, and various other earth-based, pre-Christian, shamanic, and magical practitioners. We hope to reach not only those already involved in what we cover but the curious and completely new as well." Estab. 2002. Circ. 10,000. Byline given. No cash payment, but 4 contributor copies and one-year subscription given for published submissions. Editorial lead time is 3-4 months. Submit seasonal material 6 months in advance. Accepts queries by mail, e-mail, fax, phone. Responds in 1-2 weeks to querie; 1 month to mss. Sample copy: $6. Guidelines available online.

"Devoted exclusively to promoting and covering contemporary Pagan culture, *W&P* features exclusive interviews with the teachers, writers, and activists who create and lead our traditions, visits to the sacred places and people who inspire us, and in-depth discussions of our ever-evolving practices. You'll also find practical daily magic, ideas for solitary ritual and devotion, God/dess-friendly craft-projects, Pagan poetry and short fiction, reviews, and much more in every 88-page issue. *W&P* is available in either traditional paper copy sent by postal mail or as a digital PDF e-zine download that is compatible with most computers and readers."

NONFICTION Needs book excerpts, essays, historical, how-to, humor, inspirational, interview, new product, opinion, personal experience, photo feature, religious, travel. Special issues: Features (articles, essays, fiction, interviews, and rituals) should range between 1,000-5,000 words. "We most often publish items between 1,500-3000 words; we prefer in-depth coverage to tidbits in most cases, and the upper ranges are usually reserved for lead pieces assigned to specific writers." Send complete ms. "Submit all written material in electronic format. Our first choice is Open Office writer file attachments e-mailed directly to editor2@bbimedia.com. This e-mail address is being protected from spambots. You need JavaScript enabled to view it; other acceptable file attachment formats include text files and commonly used word processing programs; you may also paste the text of your ms directly into an e-mail message. Use a plain, legible font or typeface large enough to read easily. Sidebars can be 500-1,300 words or so. Reviews have specific lengths and formats; e-mail editor2@bbimedia.com." Length: 1,000-4,000 words.

FICTION Needs adventure, erotica, ethnic, fantasy, historical, horror, humorous, mainstream, mystery, novel concepts, religious, romance, suspense. Does not want faction (fictionalized retellings of real events). Avoid gratuitous sex, violence, sentimentality, and pagan moralizing. Don't beat our readers with the Rede or the Threefold Law. **Buys 3-4 mss/year.** Send complete ms. Length: 1,000-5,000 words.

POETRY Needs avant-garde, free verse, haiku, light verse, traditional. Submit maximum 3-5 poems.

TIPS "Read the magazine, do your research, write the piece, send it in. That's really the only way to get started as a writer; everything else is window dressing."

AUTOMOTIVE AND MOTORCYCLE

AUTO RESTORER

BowTie, Inc., 3 Burroughs, Irvine CA 92618. (213)385-2222. **Fax:** (213)385-8565. **E-mail:** tkade@i5publishing.com. **Website:** www.autorestorermagazine.com. **Contact:** Ted Kade, editor. **85% freelance written.** Monthly magazine covering auto restoration. "Our readers own old cars, and they work on them. We help our readers by providing as much practical, how-to information as we can about restoration and old cars." Estab. 1989. Circ. 60,000. Pays on publication. Publishes mss 3 months after acceptance. Submit seasonal material 4 months in advance. Accepts queries by mail, e-mail, fax. Responds in 2 months to queries. Sample copy: $7. Guidelines free.

NONFICTION Needs how-to, auto restoration, new product, photo feature, technical product evaluation.

Buys 60 mss/year. Query first. Length: 250-2,000 words. **Pays $150/published page, including photos and illustrations.**

PHOTOS Emphasizes restoration of collector cars and trucks. Readers are 98% male, professional/technical/managerial, ages 35-65. Buys 47 photos from freelancers/issue; 564 photos/year. Send photos. Model/property release preferred. Photo captions required; include year, make, and model of car; identification of people in photo. Reviews photos with accompanying ms only. Reviews contact sheets, transparencies, 5x7 prints. Looks for "technically proficient or dramatic photos of various automotive subjects, auto portraits, detail shots, action photos, good angles, composition, and lighting. We're also looking for photos to illustrate how-to articles such as how to repair a damaged fender or how to repair a carburetor." Pays $50 for b&w cover; $35 for b&w inside. Pays on publication. Credit line given.

TIPS "Interview the owner of a restored car. Present advice to others on how to do a similar restoration. Seek advice from experts. Go light on history and nonspecific details. Make it something that the magazine regularly uses. Do automotive how-tos."

$$$$ AUTOWEEK

Crain Communications, Inc., 1155 Gratiot Ave., Detroit MI 48207. (313)446-6000. **Fax:** (313)446-1027. **Website:** www.autoweek.com. **5% freelance written, most by regular contributors.** *AutoWeek* is a biweekly magazine for auto enthusiasts. Estab. 1958. Circ. 300,000. Byline given. Pays on publication. Publishes ms an average of 1 month after acceptance. Accepts queries by e-mail.

NONFICTION Needs historical, interview. **Buys 5 mss/year.** Query. Length: 100-400 words. **Pays $1/word.**

Ø$$$$ CAR AND DRIVER

Hearst Communications, Inc., 1585 Eisenhower Place, Ann Arbor MI 48108. (734)971-3600. **Fax:** (734)971-9188. **E-mail:** editors@caranddriver.com. **Website:** www.caranddriver.com. **Contact:** Eddie Alterman, editor-in-chief; Mike Fazioli, managing editor. Monthly magazine for auto enthusiasts; college-educated, professional, median 24-35 years of age. Estab. 1956. Circ. 1,212,555. Byline given. Pays on acceptance. Offers 25% kill fee. Accepts queries by mail, e-mail. Responds in 2 months to queries.

NONFICTION Query with story and published clips before submitting. Pays expenses of writers on assignment.

PHOTOS Color slides and b&w photos sometimes purchased with accompanying ms.

TIPS "It is best to start off with an interesting query and to stay away from nuts-and-bolts ideas, because that will be handled in-house or by an acknowledged expert. Our goal is to be absolutely without flaw in our presentation of automotive facts, but we strive to be every bit as entertaining as we are informative. We do not print this sort of story: 'My Dad's Wacky, Lovable Beetle.'"

$$ RIDER MAGAZINE

1227 Flynn Rd., Ste. 304, Camarillo CA 93010. (805)987-5500. **Website:** www.ridermagazine.com. **60% freelance written.** Monthly magazine covering motorcycling. *Rider* serves the all-brand motorcycle lifestyle/enthusiast with a slant toward travel and touring. Estab. 1974. Circ. 135,000. Byline given. Pays on publication. Publishes ms an average of 6-18 months after acceptance. Editorial lead time 3 months. Submit seasonal material 6 months in advance. Accepts queries by mail, e-mail. Responds in 2 months to queries. Sample copy: $2.95. Guidelines on website.

NONFICTION Needs general interest, historical, how-to, humor, interview, personal experience, travel. Does not want to see fiction or "How I Began Motorcycling" articles. **Buys 40-50 mss/year.** Query. Length: 750-1,800 words. **Pays $150-750.**

PHOTOS Send photos. Captions required. Reviews high-resolution (4MP+) digital images. Offers no additional payment for photos accepted with ms.

COLUMNS/DEPARTMENTS Favorite Rides (short trip), 850-1,000 words. **Buys Buys 12 mss/year mss/year.** Query. **Pays $150-750.**

TIPS "We rarely accept mss without photos. Query first. Follow guidelines available on request. We are most open to favorite rides, feature stories (must include excellent photography), and material for Rides, Rallies and Clubs. Include a map, information on routes, local attractions, restaurants, and scenery in favorite ride submissions."

AVIATION

$ AFRICAN PILOT

Wavelengths 10 (Pty) Ltd., 6 Barbeque Heights, 9 Dytchley Rd., Barbeque Downs, Midrand 1684 South

Africa. +27 11 466-8524. **Fax:** +27 11 466 8496. **E-mail:** editor@africanpilot.co.za. **Website:** www.africanpilot.co.za. **Contact:** Athol Franz, editor. **50% freelance written.** "*African Pilot* is southern Africa's premier monthly aviation magazine. It publishes a high-quality magazine that is well known and respected within the aviation community of southern Africa. The magazine offers a number of benefits to readers and advertisers, including a weekly e-mail, Aviation News, annual service guide, aviation training supplement, executive wall calendar, and an extensive website. The monthly aviation magazine is also available online as an exact replica of the paper edition but where all major advertising pages are hyperlinked to the advertisers website. The magazine offers clean layouts with outstanding photography and reflects editorial professionalism as well as a responsible approach to journalism. The magazine offers a complete and tailored promotional solution for all aviation businesses operating in the African region." Estab. 2001. Circ. 7,000+ online; 6,600+ print. Byline given. No kill fee. Editorial lead time 2-3 months. Accepts queries by e-mail. Accepts simultaneous submissions. Responds only if interested; send nonreturnable samples. Sample copies available upon request. Writer's guidelines online or via e-mail.

NONFICTION Needs general interest, historical, interview, new product, personal experience, photo feature, technical. No articles on aircraft accidents. **Buys up to 60 mss/year.** Send complete ms. Length: 1,200-2,800 words. Sometimes pays expenses of writers on assignment.

PHOTOS Send photos. Captions required. Negotiates payment individually.

TIPS "The website is updated monthly, and all articles are fully published online."

$$ AVIATION HISTORY

Weider History Group, 19300 Promenade Dr., Leesburg VA 20176. **E-mail:** aviationhistory@weiderhistorygroup.com. **Website:** www.historynet.com/aviation-history. **Contact:** Carl Von Wodtke, editor. **95% freelance written.** Bimonthly magazine covering military and civilian aviation from first flight to the space age. "*Aviation History* aims to make aeronautical history not only factually accurate and complete but also enjoyable to a varied subscriber and newsstand audience." Estab. 1990. Circ. 40,000. Byline given. Pays on publication. No kill fee. Publishes ms an average of 2 years after acceptance. Editorial lead time 6 months. Submit seasonal material 1 year in advance. Accepts queries by mail, e-mail. Accepts simultaneous submissions. Responds in 2 months to queries; in 3 months to mss. Sample copy: $6. Guidelines with #10 SASE or online.

NONFICTION Needs historical, interview, personal experience. **Buys 24 mss/year.** Query. Length: 3,000-3,500 words, each with a 500-word sidebar where appropriate, author's biography, and book suggestions for further reading. **Pays $300 and up.**

COLUMNS/DEPARTMENTS Aviators; Restored; Extremes, all 1,500 words or less. **Pays $150 and up. Book reviews, 250-500 words, pays minimum $50.**

TIPS "Choose stories with strong narrative and art possibilities. Write an entertaining, informative, and unusual story that grabs the reader's attention and holds it. All stories must be true. We do not publish fiction or poetry."

$$ CESSNA OWNER MAGAZINE

Jones Publishing, Inc., N7528 Aanstad Rd., Iola WI 54945. (715)445-5000. **Fax:** (715)445-4053. **E-mail:** editor@cessnaowner.org. **Website:** www.cessnaowner.org. **Contact:** Dennis Piotrowski, editor. **50% freelance written.** Monthly magazine covering Cessna single and twin-engine aircraft. *Cessna Owner Magazine* is the official publication of the Cessna Owner Organization (C.O.O.). Readers are Cessna aircraft owners, renters, pilots, and enthusiasts. Articles should deal with buying/selling, flying, maintaining, or modifying Cessnas. The purpose of magazine is to promote safe, fun, and affordable flying. Estab. 1975. Circ. 6,000. Byline given. Pays on publication. No kill fee. Publishes ms an average of 3 months after acceptance. Editorial lead time 1 month. Submit seasonal material 3 months in advance. Accepts queries by mail, e-mail. Responds in 2 weeks to queries. Responds in 1 month to mss. Sample copy on website.

NONFICTION Needs historical of specific Cessna models, how-to, aircraft repairs and maintenance, new product, personal experience, photo feature, technical, aircraft engines and airframes. Special issues: Engines (maintenance, upgrades); Avionics (purchasing, new products). **Buys 48 mss/year.** Query. Length: 1,500-2,000 words. **Pays 12¢/word.**

REPRINTS Send mss via e-mail with rights for sale noted and information about when and where the material previously appeared.

PHOTOS Send photos. Captions, identification of subjects required. Reviews 3x5 and larger prints.

FLIGHT JOURNAL

Air Age Media, 88 Danbury Rd., Wilton CT 06897. (203)431-9000. **E-mail:** flightjournal@airage.com. **Website:** www.flightjournal.com. Bimonthly magazine covering aviation-oriented material, for the most part with a historical overtone, but also with some modern history in the making reporting. "*Flight Journal* is like no other aviation magazine in the world, covering the world of flight from its simple beginnings to its high-tech, no-holds-barred future. We put readers in the cockpit and let them live the thrill and adventure of the aviation experience, narrated by those who know the technology and made the history. Each issue brings the stories of flight—past, present and future—to life." No kill fee. Accepts queries by mail, e-mail.

NONFICTION Needs exposé, historical, humor, interview, new product, personal experience, photo feature, technical. "We do not want any general aviation articles as in 'My Flight to Baja in my 172,' nor detailed recitations of the technical capabilities of an aircraft. Avoid historically accurate but bland chronologies of events." Send a single page outline of your idea. Provide 1 or more samples of prior articles, if practical. Length: 2,500-3,000 words. Lengthier pieces should be discussed in advance with the editors. **Pays $600.**

PHOTOS See submission guidelines. Reviews 5x7 prints. Negotiates payment individually.

TIPS "Use an unusual slant that makes your story idea unique; unusual pictures for an exciting presentation; fantastic but true accounts; lots of human interest. The designers, builders, pilots, and mechanics are what aviation is all about. We like an upbeat style, with humor, where it fits. Use sidebars to divide content of technically dense subjects. If you have a good personal story but aren't a professional-quality writer, we'll help with the writing."

FLYING ADVENTURES

Aviation Publishing Corporation, El Monte Airport (EMT), P.O. Box 93613, Pasadena CA 91109-3613. (626)618-4000. **E-mail:** editor@flyingadventures.com; info@flyingadventures.com. **Website:** www.flyingadventures.com. **Contact:** Lyn Freeman, editor-in-chief. **20% freelance written.** Bimonthly magazine covering lifestyle travel for owners and passengers of private aircraft. Articles cover upscale travelers. Estab. 1994. Circ. 135,000. Byline given for features. Pays on acceptance. No kill fee. Editorial lead time 2 weeks to 2 months. Accepts queries by e-mail. Accepts simultaneous submissions. Responds immediately. Sample copy and guidelines free.

NONFICTION Needs travel, lifestyle. "Nothing nonrelevant or not our style. See magazine." Query with published clips. Length: 500-1,500 words. **Pays $150-300 for assigned and unsolicited articles.** Sometimes pays expenses of writers on assignment.

PHOTOS Contact: Photography director. State availability. Captions, identification of subjects, model releases required. Reviews GIF/JPEG files. Negotiates payment individually.

COLUMNS/DEPARTMENTS Contact: Editor. Numerous departments; see magazine. **Buys Buys 100+ mss/yr. mss/year.** Query with published clips. **Pays $-$150.**

TIPS "Send clip that fits our content and style. Must fit our style!"

BUSINESS AND FINANCE

BUSINESS NATIONAL

DOLLARS & SENSE: THE MAGAZINE OF ECONOMIC JUSTICE

Economic Affairs Bureau, Inc., One Milk St., 5th Floor, Boston MA 02109. (617)447-2177. **Fax:** (617)477-2179. **E-mail:** dollars@dollarsandsense.org. **Website:** www.dollarsandsense.org. **Contact:** Alejandro Reuss and Chris Sturr, co-editors. **10% freelance written.** Bimonthly magazine covering economic, environmental, and social justice. *Dollars & Sense* publishes economic news and analysis, reports on economic justice activism, primers on economic topics, and critiques of the mainstream media's coverage of the economy. Our readers include professors, students, and activists who value our smart and accessible economic coverage. "We explain the workings of the U.S. and international economics and provide left perspectives on current economic affairs." Estab. 1974. Circ. 8,000. Byline given. Pays on publication. No kill fee. Publishes ms an average of 4 months after acceptance. Editorial lead time 3 months. Submit seasonal material 2 months in advance. Accepts queries by mail, e-mail (preferred). Sample copy: $5 or on website. Guidelines online.

NONFICTION Needs exposé, political economics. Special issues: Wants in-depth articles on a broad range of topics. **Buys 6 mss/year.** Query with published clips. Length: 1,500-3,000 words. **Pays $0-200.** Sometimes pays expenses of writers on assignment.
PHOTOS State availability. Captions, identification of subjects required. Negotiates payment individually.
COLUMNS/DEPARTMENTS Active Culture (briefs on activism), 250-400 words; Reviews (coverage of recent books, movies, and other media), 700 words. Query with published clips.
TIPS "Be familiar with our magazine and the types of communities interested in reading us. *Dollars & Sense* is a progressive economics magazine that explains in a popular way both the workings of the economy and struggles to change it. Articles may be on the environment, the World Bank, community organizing, urban conflict, inflation, unemployment, union reform, welfare, changes in government regulation—a broad range of topics that have an economic theme. Find samples of our latest issue on our homepage."

$$ ENTREPRENEUR MAGAZINE

Entrepreneur Media Inc., 18061 Fitch, Irvine CA 92614. (949)261-2325. **E-mail:** queries@entrepreneur.com; pitches@entrepreneur.com. **Website:** www.entrepreneur.com. **Contact:** Carolyn Horwitz, executive editor. **60% freelance written.** "*Entrepreneur* readers already run their own businesses. They have been in business for several years and are seeking innovative methods and strategies to improve their business operations. They are also interested in new business ideas and opportunities, as well as current issues that affect their companies." Circ. 600,000. Byline given. Pays on acceptance. No kill fee. Publishes ms an average of 5 months after acceptance. Submit seasonal material 6 months in advance. Accepts queries by e-mail. Responds in 3 months to queries. Sample copy for $7.20.
NONFICTION Needs how-to, information on running a business, dealing with the psychological aspects of running a business, profiles of unique entrprenuers, current news/trends (and their effect on small business). **Buys 10-20 mss/year.** Query with published clips. Length: 1,800 words. **Payment varies.**
PHOTOS Ask for photos or transparencies when interviewing entrepreneurs; send them with the article.
COLUMNS/DEPARTMENTS Snapshots (profiles of interesting entrepreneurs who exemplify innovation in their marketing/sales technique, financing method or management style, or who have developed an innovative product/service or technology); Money Smarts (financial management); Marketing Smarts; Web Smarts (Internet news); Tech Smarts; Management Smarts; Viewpoint (first-person essay on entrepreneurship), all 300 words. **Pays $1/word.**
TIPS "Read several issues of the magazine! Study the feature articles versus the columns. Probably 75 % of our freelance rejections are for article ideas covered in 1 of our regular columns. Go beyond the typical, flat 'business magazine query'—how to write a press release, how to negotiate with vendors, etc.—and instead investigate a current trend and develop a story on how that trend affects small business. In your query, mention companies you'd like to use to illustrate examples and sources who will provide expertise on the topic."

FORTUNE

Time, Inc., 1271 Avenue of the Americas, New York NY 10020. (212)522-1212. **Fax:** (212)522-0810. **E-mail:** letters@fortune.com. **Website:** www.fortune.com. **Contact:** Eric Danetz, publisher; Michael Schneider, associate publisher. Biweekly magazine covering business and finance. Edited primarily for high-demographic business people. Specializes in big stories about companies, business personalities, technology, managing, Wall Street, media, marketing, personal finance, politics, and policy. Circ. 1,066,000. No kill fee. Editorial lead time 6 weeks.

Query before submitting.

$$$ MYBUSINESS MAGAZINE

Imagination Publishing, 600 W. Fulton St., 6th Floor, Chicago IL 60661. (615)872-5800; (800)634-2669. **E-mail:** nfib@imaginepub.com. **Website:** www.nfib.com/business-resources/mybusiness-magazine. **75% freelance written.** Bimonthly magazine for small businesses. "We are a guide to small business success, however that is defined in the new small business economy. We explore the methods and minds behind the trends and celebrate the men and women leading the creation of the new small business economy." Estab. 1999. Circ. 400,000. Byline given. Pays on publication. Offers 30% kill fee. Publishes ms an average of 4 months after acceptance. Editorial lead time 4-6 months. Submit seasonal material 5 months in advance. Accepts queries by e-mail. Accepts simultaneous submissions. Responds in 3 weeks to queries.

NONFICTION Needs how-to, new product. **Buys 8 mss/year.** "Query with résumé and 2 published clips. We accept pitches for feature stories, which fall under 1 of 3 categories: Own, Operate, and Grow. Story ideas should be small-business focused, with an emphasis on timely problems that small business owners face and real, workable solutions. Trend pieces are also of interest. Copy should be submitted as a Microsoft Word enclosure. Deadlines are 90 days before publication." Length: 200-1,800 words. **Pays $75-1,000.**

TIPS "*MyBusiness* is sent bimonthly to the 400,000 members of the National Federation of Independent Business. We're here to help small business owners by giving them a range of how-to pieces that evaluate, analyze, and lead to solutions."

PROFIT

Rogers Media, 1 Mt. Pleasant Rd., 11th Floor, Toronto ON M4Y 2Y5 Canada. (416)764-1402. **Fax:** (416)764-1404. **E-mail:** profit@profit.rogers.com. **Website:** www.profitguide.com. **80% freelance written.** Magazine published 6 times/year covering small and medium businesses. Profit is Canada's guide to business success. The most-read and best-targeted publication in Canada for entrepreneurs and small business executives. "We specialize in specific, useful information that helps our readers manage their businesses better. We want Canadian stories only." Estab. 1982. Circ. 84,632. Byline given. Pays on acceptance. Offers variable kill fee. Publishes ms an average of 2 months after acceptance. Submit seasonal material 6 months in advance. Accepts queries by e-mail. Responds in 1 month to queries; in 6 weeks to mss.

NONFICTION Needs how-to, business management tips, strategies, Canadian business profiles. **Buys 50 mss/year.** Query with published clips. Length: 800-2,000 words. **Pays $500-2,000.** Pays expenses of writers on assignment.

COLUMNS/DEPARTMENTS Finance (info on raising capital in Canada), 700 words; Marketing (marketing strategies for independent business), 700 words. **Buys 80 mss/year.** Query with published clips. **Pays $150-600.**

TIPS "We're wide open to freelancers with good ideas and some knowledge of business. Read the magazine and understand it before submitting your ideas—which should have a Canadian focus."

TECHNICAL ANALYSIS OF STOCKS & COMMODITIES

4757 California Ave. SW, Seattle WA 98116. (206)938-0570. **E-mail:** editor@traders.com. **Website:** www.traders.com. **90% freelance written.** "Magazine covers methods of investing and trading stocks, bonds and commodities (futures), options, mutual funds, and precious metals using technical analysis." Estab. 1982. Circ. 60,000. Byline given. Pays on publication. No kill fee. Publishes ms an average of 4 months after acceptance. Responds in 2 months to queries. Sample copy: $5. Guidelines available online.

"Eager to work with new/unpublished writers."

NONFICTION Needs how-to, product reviews, real-word trading (actual case studies of trades and their results), trade, technical, cartoons, trading and software aids to trading, utilities. No newsletter-type, buy-sell recommendations. The article subject must relate to technical analysis, charting, or a numerical technique used to trade securities or futures. Almost universally requires graphics with every article. **Buys 150 mss/year.** Send complete ms. Length: 1,000-4,000 words. **Pays $3/column inch (two-column format) or $2/column inch (three-column format); $50 minimum.**

REPRINTS Send tearsheet with rights for sale noted and information about when and where the material previously appeared.

PHOTOS State availability. Captions, identification of subjects, model releases required. Pays $60-350 for b&w or color negatives with prints or positive slides.

FILLERS "Must relate to trading stocks, bonds, options, mutual funds, commodities, or precious metals." **Buys 20 mss/year.** Length: 500 words. **Pays $20-50.**

TIPS "Describe how to use technical analysis, charting, or computer work in day-to-day trading of stocks, bonds, commodities, options, mutual funds, or precious metals. A blow-by-blow account of how a trade was made, including the trader's thought processes, is the best-received story by our subscribers. One of our primary considerations is to instruct in a manner that the layperson can comprehend. We are not hypercritical of writing style."

BUSINESS REGIONAL

ATLANTIC BUSINESS MAGAZINE

Communications Ten, Ltd., P.O. Box 2356, Station C, St. John's NL A1C 6E7 Canada. (709)726-9300. **Fax:** (709)726-3013. **E-mail:** dchafe@atlanticbusinessmagazine.com. **Website:** www.atlanticbusinessmagazine.com. **Contact:** Dawn Chafe, executive editor. **80% freelance written.** Bimonthly magazine covering business in Atlantic Canada. "We discuss positive business developments, emphasizing that the 4 Atlantic provinces are a great place to do business." Estab. 1989. Circ. 30,000. Byline given. Pays within 30 days of publication. No kill fee. Publishes ms an average of 2 months after acceptance. Editorial lead time 6 months. Accepts queries by e-mail. Sample copy free. Guidelines online.

NONFICTION Needs exposé, general interest, interview, new product. "We don't want religious, technical, or scholarly material. We are not an academic magazine. We are interested only in stories concerning business topics specific to the 4 Canadian provinces of Nova Scotia, New Brunswick, Prince Edward Island, and Newfoundland and Labrador." **Buys 36 mss/year.** Query with published clips. Length: 1,000-1,200 words for features; 3,500-4,000 for cover stories. **Pays 40¢/word.** Sometimes pays expenses of writers on assignment.

PHOTOS Send photos. Captions, identification of subjects required. Reviews contact sheets, transparencies, prints. Negotiates payment individually.

COLUMNS/DEPARTMENTS Query with published clips.

TIPS "Writers should submit their areas of interest as well as samples of their work and, if possible, suggested story ideas."

BUSINESS NH MAGAZINE

55 S. Commercial St., Manchester NH 03101. (603)626-6354. **Fax:** (603)626-6359. **E-mail:** hcopeland@BusinessNHmagazine.com. **Website:** www.millyardcommunications.com. **Contact:** Heidi Copeland, publisher. **25% freelance written.** Monthly magazine covering business, politics, and people of New Hampshire. "Our audience consists of the owners and top managers of New Hampshire businesses." Estab. 1983. Circ. 15,000. Byline given. Pays on publication. No kill fee. Publishes ms an average of 2 months after acceptance. Accepts queries by e-mail, fax.

NONFICTION Needs how-to, interview. No unsolicited mss; interested in New Hampshire writers only. **Buys 24 mss/year.** Query with published clips and résumé. Length: 750-2,500 words. **Payment varies.**

PHOTOS Both b&w and color photos are used. Model/property release preferred. Photo captions required; include names, locations, contact phone number. Payment varies. Pays $450 for color cover; $100 for color or b&w inside. Credit line given. Buys one-time rights. Pays on publication.

TIPS "We always want clips and résumés with queries. Freelance stories are almost always assigned. Stories must be local to New Hampshire."

CRAIN'S DETROIT BUSINESS

Crain Communications, Inc., 1155 Gratiot, Detroit MI 48207. (313)446-0419. **Fax:** (313)446-1687. **Website:** www.crainsdetroit.com. **10% freelance written.** Weekly tabloid covering business in the Detroit metropolitan area—specifically Wayne, Oakland, Macomb, Washtenaw, and Livingston counties. "*Crain's Detroit Business* has been covering non-automotive business news in Southeast Michigan since 1985. Our focus is Wayne, Oakland, Macomb, Washtenaw, and Livingston counties. Our stories read differently from stories in the metro Detroit dailies or regional weeklies. Our audience is narrower. A lot of general media stories use 1 or 2 sources. We like to include competitors and customers in our company profiles. And we focus on details: Where is the financing coming from? What will this do to the competition? Is this a trend? Who owns the company?" Estab. 1985. Circ. 150,000. Byline given. Pays on publication. No kill fee. Publishes ms an average of 1 month after acceptance. Accepts queries by e-mail, online submission form. Sample copy: $1.50. Guidelines online.

Crain's Detroit Business uses only area writers and local topics.

NONFICTION Needs new product, technical, business. **Buys 20 mss/year.** Query the appropriate editor with published clips. E-mail cdbdepartments@crain.com for People and Business Diary items. 30-40 words/column inch **Pays $10-15/column inch.** Pays expenses of writers on assignment.

PHOTOS State availability.

TIPS Contact special sections editor in writing with background and, if possible, specific story ideas relating to our type of coverage and coverage area.

$$ INGRAM'S

Show-Me Publishing, Inc., 2049 Wyandotte, Kansas City MO 64108. (816)268-6402. **Fax:** (816)268-6402. **E-mail:** editorial@ingramsonline.com. **Website:** www.ingramsonline.com. **Contact:** Dennis Boone, managing editor. **10% freelance written.** Monthly magazine covering Kansas City business and economic development. *"Ingram's* readers are top-level corporate executives and community leaders, officials and decision makers. Our editorial content must provide such readers with timely, relevant information and insights." Estab. 1975. Circ. 105,000. Byline given. Pays on publication. No kill fee. Publishes ms an average of 1 month after acceptance. Editorial lead time 1 month. Submit seasonal material 5 months in advance. Accepts queries by e-mail. Sample copy free.

Only accepts local writers; guest columnist are not paid articles.

NONFICTION Needs interview, technical. Does not want humor, inspirational, or anything not related to Kansas City business. **Buys 4-6 mss/year.** Query. Length: 500-1,500 words. **Pays $75-200 depending on research/feature length.** Sometimes pays expenses of writers on assignment.

COLUMNS/DEPARTMENTS Say So (opinion), 1,500 words. **Buys 12 mss/year. Pays $75-100 maximum.**

TIPS "Demonstrate familiarity with the magazine and its purpose and audience in an e-mail query."

$$ THE LANE REPORT

Lane Communications Group, 201 E. Main St., 14th Floor, Lexington KY 40507. (859)244-3500. **Fax:** (859)244-3555. **E-mail:** markgreen@lanereport.com. **E-mail:** editorial@lanereport.com. **Website:** www.lanereport.com. **Contact:** Mark Green, editorial director. **70% freelance written.** Monthly magazine covering statewide business. *The Lane Report* is an intelligent, enterprising magazine that informs readers and drives a statewide dialogue by highlighting important business stories in Kentucky. Estab. 1985. Circ. 15,000. Byline given. Pays on publication. No kill fee. Editorial lead time 6 weeks. Submit seasonal material 3 months in advance. Accepts queries by mail, e-mail, fax. Accepts simultaneous submissions. Responds in 1 month to queries. Sample copy and writer's guidelines free.

NONFICTION Needs essays, interview, new product, photo feature. **Buys 30-40 mss/year.** Query with published clips. Do not send unsolicited mss. Looking for major trends shaping the state; noteworthy business and practices; stories with sweeping implications across industry sectors and state regions. Length: 750-3,000 words. **Pays $150-375. Pays on publication.** Sometimes pays expenses of writers on assignment.

PHOTOS State availability. Identification of subjects required. Reviews contact sheets, negatives, transparencies, prints, digital images. Negotiates payment individually.

COLUMNS/DEPARTMENTS Fast Lane Briefs: (100-400 words) recent news and trends and how they might shape the future; Opinion: (750 words) opinion on a business or economic issue about which you, the writer, feel passionate and qualified to write; Entrepreneurs: (750-1,400 words) profile of a particularly interesting or quirky member of the business community. Submit a query via e-mail. No unsolicited mss.

TIPS "As Kentucky's only statewide business and economics publication, we look for stories that incorporate perspectives from the Commonwealth's various regions and prominent industries—tying it into the national picture when appropriate. We also look for insightful profiles and interviews of Kentucky's entrepreneurs and business leaders."

$$$$ OREGON BUSINESS

MEDIAmerica, Inc., 715 SW Morrison St, Suite 800, Portalnd OR 97205. (503)223-0304. **Fax:** (503)221-6544. **E-mail:** lindab@oregonbusiness.com. **E-mail:** editor@oregonbusiness.com. **Website:** www.oregonbusiness.com. **Contact:** Linda Baker, editor. **15-25% freelance written.** Monthly magazine covering business in Oregon. Subscribers inlcude owners of small and medium-sized businesses, government agencies, professional staffs of banks, insurance companies, ad agencies, attorneys, and other service providers. Accepts *only* stories about Oregon businesses, issues, and trends. Estab. 1981. Circ. 50,000. Byline given. Pays on publication. No kill fee. Editorial lead time 2 months. Accepts queries by mail, e-mail. Sample copy for $4. Guidelines available online.

NONFICTION Query with résumé and 2-3 published clips. Length: 1,200-3,000 words.

COLUMNS/DEPARTMENTS First Person (opinion piece on an issue related to business), 750 words; Around the State (recent news and trends, and how they might shape the future), 100-600 words; Business Tools (practical, how-to suggestions for business managers and owners), 400-600 words; In

Character (profile of interesting or quirky member of the business community), 850 words. Query with résumé and 2-3 published clips.

$$ VERMONT BUSINESS MAGAZINE

365 Dorset St., South Burlington VT 05403. (802)863-8038. **Fax:** (802)863-8069. **Website:** www.vermontbiz.com. **Contact:** Tim McQuiston, editor. **80% freelance written.** Monthly tabloid covering business in Vermont. Circ. 8,000. Byline given. Pays on publication. No kill fee. Publishes ms an average of 1 month after acceptance. Responds in 2 months to queries. Sample copy for SAE with 11x14 envelope and 7 first-class stamps.

Magazine accepts Vermont-specific material only.

NONFICTION Buys 200 mss/year. Query with published clips. Length: 800-1,800 words. **Pays $100-200.**

REPRINTS Send tearsheet and information about when and where the material previously appeared.

PHOTOS Send photos. Identification of subjects required. Reviews contact sheets. Offers $10-35/photo.

TIPS "Read daily papers and look for business angles for a follow-up article. We look for issue and trend articles rather than company or businessman profiles."

CAREER, COLLEGE AND ALUMNI

$$ AMERICAN CAREERS

Career Communications, Inc., 6701 W. 64th St., Suite 210, Overland Park KS 66202. (800)669-7795. **E-mail:** ccinfo@carcom.com. **Website:** www.carcom.com; www.americancareersonline.com. **Contact:** Mary Pitchford, editor-in-chief; Jerry Kanabel, art director. **10% freelance written.** *American Careers* provides career, salary, and education information to middle school and high school students. Self-tests help them relate their interests and abilities to future careers. Estab. 1989. Circ. 500,000. Byline given. Pays 1 month after acceptance. No kill fee. Accepts queries by mail. Accepts simultaneous submissions. Sample copy for $4. Guidelines for #10 SASE.

NONFICTION No "preachy" advice to teens or articles that talk down to students. **Buys 5 mss/year.** Query by mail only with published clips. Length: 300-1,000 words. **Pays $100-450.**

PHOTOS State availability. Captions, identification of subjects, model releases required. Negotiates payment individually.

TIPS "Letters of introduction or query letters with samples and résumés are ways we get to know writers. Samples should include how-to articles and career-related articles. Articles written for teenagers also would make good samples. Short feature articles on careers, career-related how-to articles, and self-assessment tools (10-20 point quizzes with scoring information) are primarily what we publish."

$$ HISPANIC CAREER WORLD

Equal Opportunity Publications, Inc., 445 Broad Hollow Rd., Suite 425, Melville NY 11747. (631)421-9421, ext. 12. **Fax:** (631)421-1352. **E-mail:** info@eop.com. **Website:** www.eop.com. **Contact:** James Schneider, editorial and production director. **60% freelance written.** Semiannual magazine aimed at Hispanic students and professionals in all disciplines. Estab. 1969. Byline given. Pays on publication. No kill fee. Publishes ms an average of 3 months after acceptance. Editorial lead time 3 months. Accepts queries by mail, e-mail, fax, phone. Accepts simultaneous submissions. Responds in 2 weeks to queries; 2 months to mss. Sample copy free. Guidelines free.

NONFICTION Needs how-to, find jobs, interview, personal experience. Query. Length: 1,500-2,500 words. **Pays $350 for assigned articles.**

TIPS "Gear articles to our audience."

$$$$ NOTRE DAME MAGAZINE

University of Notre Dame, 500 Grace Hall, Notre Dame IN 46556-5612. (574)631-5335. **E-mail:** ndmag@nd.edu. **Website:** magazine.nd.edu. **Contact:** Kerry Temple, editor; Kerry Prugh, art director. **50% freelance written.** "We are a university magazine with a scope as broad as that found at a university, but we place our discussion in a moral, ethical, and spiritual context reflecting our Catholic heritage." Estab. 1972. Circ. 150,000. Byline given. Pays on acceptance. No kill fee. Publishes ms an average of 1 year after acceptance. Accepts queries by mail, e-mail, fax. Responds in 2 months to queries. Sample copy available online and by request. Guidelines available online.

NONFICTION Needs opinion, personal experience, religious. **Buys 35 mss/year.** Query with published clips. Length: 600-3,000 words. **Pays $250-3,000.** Sometimes pays expenses of writers on assignment.

PHOTOS State availability. Identification of subjects, model releases required.

COLUMNS/DEPARTMENTS CrossCurrents (essays, deal with a wide array of issues—some topical, some personal, some serious, some light). Query with or without published clips or send complete ms.

TIPS "The editors are always looking for new writers and fresh ideas. However, the caliber of the magazine and frequency of its publication dictate that the writing meet very high standards. The editors value articles strong in storytelling quality, journalistic technique, and substance. They do not encourage promotional or nostalgia pieces, stories on sports, or essays that are sentimentally religious."

THE PENN STATER

Penn State Alumni Association, Hintz Family Alumni Center, University Park PA 16802. (814)865-2709. **Fax:** (814)863-5690. **E-mail:** pennstater@psu.edu; tmh1@psu.edu. **Website:** www.pennstatermag.com; www.alumni.psu.edu. **Contact:** Tina Hay, editor. **60% freelance written.** Bimonthly magazine covering Penn State and Penn Staters. Estab. 1910. Circ. 130,000. Byline given. Pays on acceptance. Offers 50% kill fee. Publishes ms an average of 4 months after acceptance. Editorial lead time 3 months. Submit seasonal material 8 months in advance. Accepts queries by mail, e-mail, fax. Accepts simultaneous submissions. Responds in 3 months to queries. Sample copy and writer's guidelines free.

NONFICTION Needs book excerpts, by or about Penn Staters, general interest, historical, interview, personal experience, photo feature, book reviews, science/research. No unsolicited mss. **Buys 20 mss/year.** Query with published clips. Length: 200-3,000 words. **Pays competitive rates.** Pays expenses of writers on assignment.

REPRINTS Send photocopy and information about when and where the material previously appeared. Payment varies

PHOTOS Send photos. Captions required.

TIPS "We are especially interested in attracting writers who are savvy in creative nonfiction/literary journalism. Most stories must have a Penn State tie-in. No phone calls, please."

$$$ UAB MAGAZINE

UAB Office of Public Relations and Marketing (University of Alabama at Birmingham), AB 340, 1720 2nd Ave. S., Birmingham AL 35294-0103. (205)975-6577. **E-mail:** charlesb@uab.edu; uabmagazine@uab.edu. **Website:** www.uab.edu/uabmagazine. **Contact:** Charles Buchanan, editor. **70% freelance written.** University magazine published 3 times/year covering University of Alabama at Birmingham. *UAB Magazine* informs readers about the innovation and creative energy that drives UAB's renowned research, educational, and health care programs. The magazine reaches active alumni, faculty, friends and donors, patients, corporate and community leaders, media, and the public. Estab. 1980. Circ. 33,000. Byline given. Pays on acceptance. Offers 50% kill fee. Publishes ms an average of 3-4 months after acceptance. Editorial lead time 3 months. Accepts queries by mail, e-mail. Sample copy available online.

NONFICTION Needs general interest/interview, science/research. **Buys 40-50 mss/year.** Query with published clips. Length: 500-5,000 words. **Pays $100-1,200.** Sometimes pays expenses of writers on assignment.

CHILD CARE & PARENTAL GUIDANCE

$$$ AMERICAN BABY

Meredith Corp., 375 Lexington Ave., 9th Floor, New York NY 10017. **E-mail:** abletters@americanbaby.com. **Website:** www.americanbaby.com. **Contact:** Dana Points, editor-in-chief. **70% freelance written.** Monthly magazine covering health, medical, and child care concerns for expectant and new parents, particularly those having their first child or those whose child is between the ages of birth and 2 years old. Mothers are the primary readers, but fathers' issues are equally important. Estab. 1938. Circ. 2,000,000. Byline given. Pays on acceptance. Offers 25% kill fee. Publishes ms an average of 6 months after acceptance. Editorial lead time 5 months. Submit seasonal material 6 months in advance. Accepts queries by mail. Responds in 3 months to queries. Responds in 3 months to mss. Sample copy for 9x12 SAE with 6 first-class stamps. Guidelines for #10 SASE.

Prefers to work with published/established writers; works with a small number of new/unpublished writers each year.

NONFICTION Needs book excerpts, essays, general interest, how-to, some aspect of pregnancy or child care, humor, new product, personal experience, fitness, beauty, health. No "hearts and flowers" or fantasy pieces. **Buys 60 mss/year.** Send complete ms. Length: 1,000-2,000 words. **Pays $750-1,200 for assigned articles. Pays $600-800 for unsolicited articles.** Pays expenses of writers on assignment.

REPRINTS Send photocopy and information about when and where the material previously appeared. Pays 50% of original price.

PHOTOS State availability. Identification of subjects, model releases required. Reviews transparencies, prints.

COLUMNS/DEPARTMENTS Personal essays (700-1,000 words) and shorter items for Crib Notes (news and features) and Health Briefs (50-150 words) are also accepted. **Pays $200-1,000.**

TIPS "Get to know our style by thoroughly reading a recent issue of the magazine. Don't send something we recently published. Our readers want to feel connected to other parents, both to share experiences and to learn from one another. They want reassurance that the problems they are facing are solvable and not uncommon. They want to keep up with the latest issues affecting their new family, particularly health and medical news, but they don't have a lot of spare time to read. We forgo the theoretical approach to offer quick-to-read, hands-on information that can be put to use immediately. A simple, straightforward, clear approach is mandatory."

$ ATLANTA PARENT

2346 Perimeter Park Dr., Atlanta GA 30341. (770)454-7599. **E-mail:** editor@atlantaparent.com. **Website:** www.atlantaparent.com. **Contact:** Editor. **50% freelance written.** Monthly magazine for parents in the Atlanta metro area with children from birth to 18 years old. "*Atlanta Parent* magazine has been a valuable resource for Atlanta families since 1983. It is the only magazine in the Atlanta area providing pertinent, local, and award-winning family-oriented articles and information. Atlanta parents rely on us for features that are timely, informative, and reader-friendly on important issues such as childcare, family life, education, adolescence, motherhood, health, and teens. Fun, easy, and inexpensive family activities and crafts as well as the humorous side of parenting are also important to our readers." Estab. 1983. Byline given. Pays on publication. Publishes ms an average of 3 months after acceptance. Submit seasonal material 6 months in advance. Accepts queries by mail, e-mail. Responds in 4 months to queries. Sample copy: $3.

NONFICTION Needs general interest, how-to, humor, interview, travel. No religious or philosophical discussions. **Buys 60 mss/year.** Send complete ms by mail or e-mail. Length: 800-1,200 words. **Pays $5-50.** Sometimes pays expenses of writers on assignment.

REPRINTS Send tearsheet or photocopy with rights for sale noted and information about when and where the material previously appeared. Pays $30-50.

PHOTOS State availability of or send photos. Reviews 3x5 photos. Offers $10/photo.

TIPS "Articles should be geared to problems or situations of families and parents. Should include down-to-earth tips and be clearly written. No philosophical discussions. We're also looking for well-written humor."

$$ CHICAGO PARENT

141 S. Oak Park Ave., Oak Park IL 60302. (708)386-5555. **Website:** www.chicagoparent.com. **Contact:** Tamara O'Shaughnessy, editor. **80% freelance written.** Monthly. *Chicago Parent* has a distinctly local approach. Offers information, inspiration, perspective, and empathy to Chicago-area parents. Lively editorial mix has a "we're all in this together" spirit, and articles are thoroughly researched and well written. Estab. 1988. Circ. 100,000, covering the 6-county Chicago metropolitan area. Byline given. Pays on publication. Offers 10-50% kill fee. Publishes ms an average of 2 months after acceptance. Editorial lead time 4 months. Submit seasonal material 4 months in advance. Accepts queries by e-mail. Responds in 6 weeks to queries. Sample copy for $4.95 and 11×17 SAE with $1.65 postage direct to circulation. Guidelines available on website.

NONFICTION Needs essays, expose, how-to, parent-related, humor, interview, travel. No pot-boiler parenting pieces or nonlocal writers (from outside the 6-county Chicago metropolitan area). **Buys 40-50 mss/year.** Query with links published clips. Length: 200-2,500 words. **Pays $25-450 for assigned articles.**

$ GRAND RAPIDS FAMILY MAGAZINE

Gemini Publications, 549 Ottawa Ave. NW, Suite 201, Grand Rapids MI 49503-1444. (616)459-4545. **Fax:** (616)459-4800. **E-mail:** cvalade@geminipub.com. **Website:** www.grfamilymag.com. **Contact:** Carole Valade, editor. Monthly magazine covering local parenting issues. *Grand Rapids Family* seeks to inform, instruct, amuse, and entertain its readers and their families. Circ. 30,000. Byline given. Pays on publication. Offers $25 kill fee. Editorial lead time 3 months. Submit seasonal material 4 months in advance. Accepts simultaneous submissions. Responds in 2 months to queries. Responds in 6 months to mss. Guidelines with #10 SASE.

NONFICTION Query. **Pays $25-50.**

PHOTOS State availability. Captions, identification of subjects, model releases required. Reviews contact sheets. Offers $25/photo.

COLUMNS/DEPARTMENTS All local: law, finance, humor, opinion, mental health. **Pays $25.**

HOMESCHOOLING TODAY

Paradigm Press, LLC, P.O. Box 1092, Somerset KY 42502. (606)485-4105. **E-mail:** editor@homeschoolingtoday.com. **Website:** www.homeschooltoday.com. **Contact:** Alex Wiggers, publisher; Ashley Wiggers and Debbie Strayer, executive editors. **75% freelance written.** Bimonthly magazine covering homeschooling. "We are a practical magazine for homeschoolers with a broadly Christian perspective." Estab. 1992. Circ. 13,000. Byline given. Pays on publication. Offers 25% kill fee. Publishes ms an average of 1 year after acceptance. Editorial lead time 6 months. Submit seasonal material 1 year in advance. Accepts simultaneous submissions. Responds in 4 months to mss. Sample copy free. Guidelines online.

NONFICTION Needs book excerpts, how-to, interview, new product. No fiction. **Buys 30 mss/year.** Send complete ms. Length: 500-2,000 words. **Pays 10¢/word.**

PHOTOS State availability. Captions, identification of subjects required. Offers no additional payment for photos accepted with ms.

MEDIA FOR LIVING, VALLEY LIVING MAGAZINE

Shalom Foundation, 1251 Virginia Ave., Harrisonburg VA 22802. (540)433-5351. **E-mail:** mediaforliving@gmail.com. **Website:** www.valleyliving.org. **90% freelance written.** Quarterly tabloid covering family living. Articles focus on giving general encouragement for families of all ages and stages. Estab. 1985. Circ. 11,000. Byline given. Pays on publication. No kill fee. Publishes ms an average of 6-12 months after acceptance. Editorial lead time 4-6 months. Submit seasonal material 6 months in advance. Accepts queries by mail, e-mail. Accepts simultaneous submissions. Responds in 2 months to queries; in 2-4 months to mss. Sample copy for SAE with 9x12 envelope and 4 first-class stamps.

"Our bias is to use articles 'showing' rather than telling readers how to raise families (stories rather than how-to). We aim for articles that are well written, understandable, challenging (not the same old thing you've read elsewhere); they should stimulate readers to dig a little deeper but not too deep with academic or technical language; that are interesting and fit our theological perspective (Christian) but are not preachy or overly patriotic. No favorable mentions of smoking, drinking, cursing, etc."

NONFICTION Needs general interest, how-to, humor, inspirational, personal experience. "We do not use devotional materials intended for Christian audiences. We seldom use pet stories and receive way too many grief/death/dealing with serious illness stories to use. We publish in March, June, September, and December, so holidays that occur in other months are not usually the subject of articles." **Buys 48-52 mss/year.** Query. Length: 500-1,200 words. **Pays $35-60.**

PHOTOS Contact: Lindsey Shantz. State availability. Captions, identification of subjects, model releases required. Reviews 4x6 prints, GIF/JPEG files. Offers $15-25/photo.

TIPS "We prefer 'good news' stories that are uplifting and noncontroversial in nature. We want articles that tell stories of people solving problems and dealing with personal issues rather than essays or 'preaching.' If you submit electronically, it is very helpful if you put the specific title of the submission in the subject line and please include your e-mail address in the body of the e-mail or on your manuscript. Also, always include your address and phone number."

METROKIDS

Kidstuff Publications, Inc., 1412-1414 Pine St., Philadelphia PA 19102. (215)291-5560, ext. 102. **Fax:** (215)291-5563. **E-mail:** editor@metrokids.com. **Website:** www.metrokids.com. **Contact:** Cheryl Krementz, managing editor. **25% freelance written.** Monthly magazine providing information for parents and kids in Philadelphia and surrounding counties, South Jersey, and Delaware. "*MetroKids*, a free monthly magazine, is a resource for parents living in the greater Delaware Valley. The Pennsylvania, South Jersey, and Delaware editions of *MetroKids* are available in supermarkets, libraries, daycares, and hundreds of other locations. The magazine and website feature the area's most extensive calendar of day-by-day family events; child-focused camp, day care, and party directories; local family fun suggestions; and articles that offer parenting advice and insights. Other *MetroKids* publications include *The Ultimate Family Guide*, a guide to area attractions, service providers and community resources; SpecialKids, a resource guide for families of children with special needs; and Educator's Edition, a directory of field trips, assemblies, and school enrichment programs." Estab. 1990. Circ. 115,000. Byline given. Pays on publication. Submit seasonal material 4 months in advance. Accepts queries by e-mail. YesGuidelines available by e-mail.

Responds only if interested.

NONFICTION Needs general interest, how-to, new product, travel, parenting, health. Special issues: See editorial calendar online for current needs. **Buys 40 mss/year.** Query with published clips. Length: 575-1,500 words. **Pays $50.**

REPRINTS E-mail summary or complete article and information about when and where the material previously appeared. Pays $35, or $50 if localized after discussion.

COLUMNS/DEPARTMENTS Tech Talk, Mom Matters, Health, Money, Your Home, Parenting, Toddlers, Tweens/Teens, Education, Food & Nutrition, Play, Toddlers, Camp, Classes, Features, all 650-850 words. **Buys 25 mss/year.** Query. **Pays $25-50.**

TIPS "We prefer e-mail queries or submissions. Because they're so numerous, we don't reply unless interested. We are interested in feature articles (on specified topics) or material for our regular departments (with a regional/seasonal base). Articles should cite expert sources, preferably from the Philadelphia/South Jersey/Delaware area, and the most up-to-date theories and facts. We are looking for a journalistic style of writing. We are also interested in finding local writers for assignments."

PARENTGUIDE

PG Media, 101 E. Park Ave., #358, Long Beach NY 11561. (212)213-8840. **Fax:** (646)224-9682. **E-mail:** rachel@parentguidenews.com. **Website:** www.parentguidenews.com. **Contact:** Rachel Kalina, editor; Donald McDermott, managing editor. **80% freelance written.** Monthly magazine covering parenting and family issues. "We are a tabloid-sized publication catering to the needs and interests of parents who have children under the age of 12. Our print publication is distributed in New York City, New Jersey, Long Island, Westchester County, Rockland County, and Queens. Our website (one of the most popular online parenting sites) is read by parents, psychologists, teachers, caretakers, and others concerned about family matters worldwide. Our columns and feature articles cover health, education, child-rearing, current events, parenting issues, recreational activities and social events. We also run a complete calendar of local events. We welcome articles from professional authors as well as never-before-published writers." Estab. 1982. Circ. 285,000. Byline given. Does not offer financial compensation. No kill fee. Publishes ms an average of 5 months after acceptance. Editorial lead time is 3 months. Submit seasonal material 6 months in advance. Accepts queries by e-mail. Accepts simultaneous submissions. Sample copy available online. Guidelines free.

NONFICTION Needs how-to, (family-related service pieces), inspirational, interview, personal experience, travel, (education, health, fitness, special needs, parenting). Length: 750 words max. Include a 3 sentence bio.

FICTION Needs confession, humorous, slice-of-life vignettes. Query. Length: 700-1,000 words.

PARENTS

Meredith Corp., 805 Third Ave., New York NY 10022. (212)499-2000. **Website:** www.parents.com. **Contact:** See masthead for specific department editors. Monthly magazine that focuses on the daily needs and concerns of mothers with young children. Provides high-quality content that informs, entertains, and joins parents in celebrating the joys of parenthood. Features information about child health, safety, behavior, discipline, and education. There are also stories on women's health, nutrition, pregnancy, marriage, and beauty. Estab. 1926. Circ. 2,215,645. Pays on acceptance. Offers 25% kill fee. Submit seasonal material 6-8 months in advance. Accepts queries by mail, e-mail. Responds in 4-6 weeks to queries.

NONFICTION Query before submitting. "Include one-page letter detailing the topic you'd like to address as well as your strategy for writing the story. Demonstrate that you are adept at doing research by mentioning the kinds of sources you intend to use. Keep in mind that all of our articles include expert advice and real-parent examples as well as study data." Include SASE.

TIPS "We're a national publication, so we're mainly interested in stories that will appeal to a wide variety of parents. We're always looking for compelling human-interest stories, so you may want to check your local newspaper for ideas. Keep in mind that we can't pursue stories that have appeared in competing national publications."

SACRAMENTO PARENT

Family Publishing Inc., 457 Grass Valley Hwy., Suite 5, Auburn CA 95603. (530)888-0573. **Fax:** (530)888-1536. **E-mail:** shelly@sacramentoparent.com. **E-mail:** shannon@sacramentoparent.com. **Website:** www.sacramentoparent.com. **Contact:** Shelly Bokman, editor-in-chief; Shannon Smith, editor. **50% freelance written.** Monthly magazine covering parenting in the Sacramento region. "We look for articles that promote a developmentally appropriate, healthy, and peaceful environment for children." Estab. 1992. Circ. 50,000. Byline given. Pays on publication. Offers 10% kill fee. Publishes ms an average of 2 months after acceptance. Editorial lead time 3 months. Submit seasonal material 4 months in advance. Accepts queries by e-mail. Sample copy free. Guidelines by e-mail.

NONFICTION Needs book excerpts, general interest, how-to, humor, interview, opinion, personal experience. **Buys 36 mss/year.** Query. Length: 300-1,000 words. **Pays $50-200 for original articles.**

COLUMNS/DEPARTMENTS Let's Go! (Sacramento regional family-friendly day trips/excursions/activities), 600 words. **Pays $25-45.**

TOLEDO AREA PARENT NEWS

Adams Street Publishing, Co., 1120 Adams St., Toledo OH 43604. (419)244-9859. **E-mail:** cjacobs@adamsstreetpublishing.com; editor@adamsstreetpublishing.com. **Website:** www.toledoparent.com. **Contact:** Collette Jacobs, editor in chief and publisher; Nadine Hariri, assignment editor. Monthly tabloid for Northwest Ohio/Southeast Michigan parents. Estab. 1992. Circ. 40,000. Byline given. Pays on publication. No kill fee. Publishes ms an average of 1 month after acceptance. Editorial lead time 3 months. Accepts queries by mail, e-mail, fax. Responds in 1 month to queries. Sample copy: $1.50.

NONFICTION Needs general interest, interview, opinion. **Buys 10 mss/year.** Length: 1,000-2,500 words. **Pays $75-125.**

PHOTOS State availability. Identification of subjects required. Negotiates payment individually.

TIPS "We love humorous stories that deal with common parenting issues or features on cutting-edge issues."

CONTEMPORARY CULTURE

ADBUSTERS

Adbusters Media Foundation, 1243 W. 7th Ave., Vancouver BC V6H 1B7 Canada. (604)736-9401. **Fax:** (604)737-6021. **E-mail:** editor@adbusters.org. **Website:** www.adbusters.org. **50% freelance written.** Bimonthly magazine on consumerism. "We are an activist journal of the mental environment." Estab. 1989. Circ. 90,000. Byline given. Pays 1 month after publication. Accepts queries by mail, e-mail, fax. Accepts simultaneous submissions. Guidelines available online.

NONFICTION Needs essays, expose, interview, opinion. **Buys variable mss/year.** Query. Length: 250-3,000 words. **Pays $100/page for unsolicited articles; 50¢/word for solicited articles.**

FICTION Inquire about themes.

POETRY Inquire about themes.

BOSTON REVIEW

P.O. Box 425786, Cambridge MA 02142. (617)324-1360. **Fax:** (617)452-3356. **E-mail:** review@bostonreview.net. **Website:** www.bostonreview.net. **90% freelance written.** Bimonthly magazine of cultural and political analysis, reviews, fiction, and poetry. "The editors are committed to a society and culture that foster human diversity and a democracy in which we seek common grounds of principle amidst our many differences. In the hope of advancing these ideals, the *Review* acts as a forum that seeks to enrich the language of public debate." Estab. 1975. Circ. 20,000. Byline given. Publishes ms an average of 4 months after acceptance. Accepts queries by online submission form. Accepts simultaneous submissions. Responds in 4 months to queries. Sample copy for $6.95 plus shipping or online. Guidelines available online.

Boston Review is a recipient of the Pushcart Prize in Poetry.

NONFICTION Needs essays (book reviews). "*We do not accept unsolicited book reviews.* If you would like to be considered for review assignments, please send your résumé along with several published clips." **Buys 50 mss/year.** Query with published clips. "You may submit query letters and unsolicited nonfiction up to 5,000 words via the online submissions system."

FICTION Looking for "stories that are emotionally and intellectually substantive and also interesting on the level of language. Things that are shocking, dark, lewd, comic, or even insane are fine so long as the fiction is *controlled* and purposeful in a masterly way. Subtlety, delicacy, and lyricism are attractive, too. Simultaneous submissions are fine as long as we are notified of the fact." Needs ethnic, experimental, contemporary, prose poem. No romance, erotica, genre fiction. **Buys 5 mss/year.** Send complete ms. Length: 1,200-5,000 words. Average length: 2,000 words. **Pays $25-300 and contributor's copies.**

POETRY "We are open to both traditional and experimental forms. What we value most is originality and a strong sense of voice." Send materials for review consideration. Reads poetry between September 15 and May 15 each year. Submit maximum 6 poems. **Payment varies.**

TIPS "The best way to get a sense of the kind of material *Boston Review* is looking for is to read the magazine. "

BRIARPATCH MAGAZINE

Briarpatch, Inc., 2138 McIntyre St., Regina SK S4P 2R7 Canada. (306)525-2949. **E-mail:** editor@briarpatchmagazine.com. **Website:** www.briarpatchmagazine.com. **Contact:** Adrew Loewen, editor. **90% freelance written.** Magazine published 6 times/year covering Canadian politics, indigenous, labor, environment, women. Readers are socially progressive and politically engaged. "*Briarpatch Magazine* publishes writing and artwork on a wide range of topics, including current events, grassroots activism, electoral politics, economic justice, ecology, labour, food security, gender equity, indigenous struggles, international solidarity, and other issues of political importance." Estab. 1973. Circ. 2,000. Byline given. No kill fee. Editorial lead time 3 months. Submit seasonal material 3 months in advance. Accepts queries by e-mail. Accepts simultaneous submissions. Responds in 1-2 weeks to queries; in 1 month to mss. Sample copy available online. Guidelines available online.

NONFICTION Needs profiles, short essays, features, photo essays, research-based articles and investigative reportage, reviews, interviews. Special issues: Special issues: Labor issue (November/December). **Buys 1-2 mss/year.** "Unsolicited submissions are, but we encourage you to first send us a query via e-mail. Your query should outline what ground your contribution will cover and demonstrate your writing style and tone. Please include your contact information, an estimated word count, a list of recent publications (if applicable), and a short writing sample." Length: 600-3,000 words.

COLUMNS/DEPARTMENTS Parting Shots: Provocative back-page opinion essay, 700 words. Send complete ms.

TIPS "We welcome queries from unpublished writers, seasoned freelancers, front-line activists, and anyone else with a story to tell and a desire to tell it compellingly."

BROKEN PENCIL

P.O. Box 203, Station P, Toronto ON M5S 2S7 Canada. **E-mail:** editor@brokenpencil.com. **Website:** www.brokenpencil.com. **80% freelance written.** Quarterly magazine covering arts and culture. "*Broken Pencil* is one of the few magazines in the world devoted exclusively to underground culture and the independent arts. We are a great resource and a lively read! *Broken Pencil* reviews the best zines, books, websites, videos, and artworks from the underground and reprints the best articles from the alternative press. From the hilarious to the perverse, *Broken Pencil* challenges conformity and demands attention." Estab. 1995. Circ. 5,000. Byline given. Pays on publication. Publishes ms an average of 2-3 months after acceptance. Accepts queries by mail, e-mail. Guidelines available online.

NONFICTION Needs essays, general interest, historical, humor, interview, opinion, personal experience, photo feature, travel, reviews. Does not want anything about mainstream art and culture. **Buys 8 mss/year.** Query with published clips. Length: 400-2,500 words. **Pays $30-300.** Sometimes pays expenses of writers on assignment.

PHOTOS Send photos. Identification of subjects required. Reviews prints, GIF/JPEG files. Negotiates payment individually.

COLUMNS/DEPARTMENTS Books (book reviews and feature articles); Music (music reviews and feature articles); Film (film reviews and feature articles), all 200-300 words for reviews and 1,000 words for features. **Buys 8 mss/year.** Query with published clips. **Pays $30-300.**

FICTION "We're particularly interested in work from emerging writers." Reads fiction submissions only between February 1 and September 15. Needs adventure, erotica, ethnic, experimental, fantasy, historical, horror, humorous, mystery, romance, science fiction, short stories. Submit using online submissions manager. Length: 50-3,000 words. **Pays $30-300.**

TIPS "Remember, we are a guide to alternative and independent culture. We don't want your thoughts on Hollywood movies or your touching tale about coming of age on the prairies! Make sure you have some sense of the kind of work we use before getting in touch. Never send us something if you haven't at least read *Broken Pencil*. Always include your address, phone number, and e-mail, so we know where to find you, and a little something about yourself, so we know who you are."

$$$ COMMENTARY

561 7th Ave., 16th Floor, New York NY 10018. (212)891-1400. **E-mail:** submissions@commentarymagazine.com. **Website:** www.commentarymagazine.com. **Contact:** John Podhoretz, editor. Monthly magazine covering Judaism, politics, and culture. "*Commentary* is America's premier monthly magazine of opinion and a pivotal voice in American intellectual life. Since its inception in 1945, and increasingly after it emerged as the flagship of neoconservatism in the 1970s, the magazine has been consistently engaged with several large, interrelated questions: the fate of democracy and of democratic ideas in a world threatened by totalitarian ideologies; the state of American and Western security; the future of the Jews, Judaism, and Jewish culture in Israel, the United States, and around the world; and the preservation of high culture in an age of political correctness and the collapse of critical standards." Estab. 1945. Byline given. Pays on publication. No kill fee. Publishes ms an average of 2 months after acceptance. Accepts queries by mail, e-mail.

NONFICTION Needs essays, opinion. **Buys 4 mss/year.** Query or submit complete ms by e-mail or mail (include SASE). Length: 2,000-8,000 words. **Pays $400-1,200.**

TIPS "Unsolicited mss must be accompanied by SASE."

$$$ FLAUNT

1422 N. Highland Ave., Los Angeles CA 90028. (323)836-1000. **E-mail:** info@flauntmagazine.com. **Website:** www.flaunt.com. **Contact:** Luis Barajas, editor in chief. **40% freelance written.** Monthly magazine covering culture, arts, entertainment, music, fashion, and film. "*Flaunt* features the bold work of emerging photographers, writers, artists, and musicians. The quality of the content is mirrored in the sophisticated, interactive format of the magazine, using advanced printing techniques, fold-out articles, beautiful papers, and inserts to create a visually stimulating, surprisingly readable, and intelligent book that pushes the magazine into the realm of art-object. *Flaunt* has, since 1998, made it a point to break new ground, earning itself a reputation as an engine of the avant-garde and an outlet for the culture of the cutting edge. *Flaunt* takes pride in reinventing itself each month, while consistently representing a hybrid of all that is interesting in entertaiment, fashion, music, design, film, art, and literature." Estab. 1998. Circ. 100,000. Byline given. No kill fee. Publishes ms an average of 3 months after acceptance. Editorial lead time 3 months. Submit seasonal material 3 months in advance. Accepts queries by mail, e-mail. Accepts simultaneous submissions. Responds in 2 weeks to queries; in 1 month to mss.

NONFICTION Needs book excerpts, essays, exposé, general interest, historical, humor, interview, new product, opinion, personal experience, photo feature, travel. Special issues: Special issues: September and March (fashion issues); February (men's issue); May (music issue). **Buys 20 mss/year.** Query with published clips. Length: 500-5,000 words. **Pays up to $500.** Sometimes pays expenses of writers on assignment.

PHOTOS State availability. Identification of subjects, model releases required. Reviews contact sheets, transparencies, prints, GIF/JPEG files.

$$$$ MOTHER JONES

Foundation for National Progress, 222 Sutter St., Suite 600, San Francisco CA 94108. (415)321-1700. **E-mail:** mmurrmann@motherjones.com; query@motherjones.com. **Website:** www.motherjones.com. **Contact:** Mark Murrmann, photo editor; Ivylise Simones, creative director; Monika Bauerlein and Clara Jeffery, editors. **80% freelance written.** Bimonthly magazine covering politics, investigative reporting, social issues, and pop culture. "*Mother Jones* is a 'progressive' magazine—but the core of its editorial well is reporting (i.e., fact-based). No slant required. Estab. 1976. Circ. 240,000. Byline given. Pays on publication. Offers 33% kill fee. Publishes ms an average of 4 months after acceptance. Editorial lead time 4 months. Submit seasonal material 6 months in advance. Responds in 2 months to queries. Sample copy for $6 and 9x12 SASE. Guidelines available online.

"*Mother Jones* magazine and *MotherJones.com* will consider solidly reported, hard-hitting, groundbreaking news stories. We're also open to thought-provoking, timely opinion and analysis pieces on important current issues. We're interested in just about anything that will raise our readers' eyebrows, but we focus especially on these areas: national politics, environmental issues, corporate wrongdoing, human rights, and political influence in all spheres.

NONFICTION Needs exposè, interview, photo feature, current issues, policy, investigative reporting. **Buys 70-100 mss/year.** Query with published clips. "Please also include your rèsumè and two or three of your most relevant clips. If the clips are online, please provide the complete URLs. Web pieces are generally less than 1,500 words. Because we have staff reporters it is extremely rare that we will pay for a piece whose timeliness or other qualities work for the Web only. Magazine pieces can range up to 5,000 words. There is at least a two-month lead time. No phone calls please." Length: 2,000-5,000 words. **Pays $1/word.** Sometimes pays expenses of writers on assignment.

COLUMNS/DEPARTMENTS Outfront (short, newsy and/or outrageous and/or humorous items), 200-800 words; Profiles of Hellraisers, 500 words. **Pays $1/word.**

TIPS "We're looking for hard-hitting, investigative reports exposing government cover-ups, corporate malfeasance, scientific myopia, institutional fraud or hypocrisy; thoughtful, provocative articles which challenge the conventional wisdom (on the right or the left) concerning issues of national importance; and timely, people-oriented stories on issues such as the environment, labor, the media, healthcare, consumer protection, and cultural trends. Send a great, short query and establish your credibility as a reporter. Explain what you plan to cover and how you will proceed with the reporting. The query should convey your approach, tone and style, and should answer the following: What are your specific qualifications to write on this topic? What 'ins' do you have with your sources? Can you provide full documentation so that your story can be fact-checked?"

NATURALLY

Internaturally, Inc., P.O. Box 317, Newfoundland NJ 07435. (973)697-3552. **Fax:** (973)697-8313. **E-mail:** naturally@internaturally.com. **Website:** www.internaturally.com. **80% freelance written.** Quarterly magazine covering nudism and naturism. "A full-color, glossy magazine with online editions, and the foremost naturist/nudist magazine in the U.S. with international distribution, *Naturally* focuses on the clothes-free lifestyle, publishing articles about worldwide destinations, first-time nudist experiences, and news information pertaining to the clothes-free lifestyle. Our mission is to demystify the human form and allow each human to feel comfortable in their own skin, in a nonsexual environment. We offer a range of books, DVDs, magazines, and other products useful to naturists/nudists in their daily lives and for the education of nonnaturists. Travel DVDs featuring resorts to visit; books on Christianity and nudity, nudist plays, memoirs, cartoons, and novellas; and also towels, sandals, calendars, and more." Estab. 1980. Circ. 30,000. Byline given. Pays on publication. No kill fee. Publishes ms an average of 3 months after acceptance. Editorial lead time 3-6 months. Submit seasonal material 6 months in advance. Accepts queries by mail, phone. Accepts simultaneous submissions. Responds in 2 weeks to queries; in 3 months to mss. Sample copy available online.

Write about nudists and naturists. Wants more people stories than travel.

NONFICTION Needs book excerpts, essays, exposé, general interest, historical, how-to, reviews for first-time visitors to nudist parks, humor, inspirational, interview, new product, personal experience, photo feature, travel. Special issues: Free-beach activities, public nude events. "We don't want opinion pieces and religious slants." **Buys 50 mss/year.** Send complete ms. Length: 500-2,000 words. **Pays $80 per page, text or photos minimum; $300 maximum for assigned articles.**

PHOTOS Send photos. Model releases required. Pays $80 per page minimum; $200 front cover maximum.

COLUMNS/DEPARTMENTS Health (nudism/naturism), Travel (nudism/naturism), Celebrities (nudism/naturism). **Buys 8 mss/year.** Send complete ms.

FICTION Needs humorous. No science fiction. **Buys 6-8 mss/year.** Send complete ms. Length: 800-2,000 words. **Pays up to $80 per page.**

POETRY Needs avant-garde, free verse, haiku, light verse, traditional. Buys 3-6 poems/year. Submit maximum 3 poems.

FILLERS Needs anecdotes, facts, gags, newsbreaks, short humor. **Buys 4 mss/year.**

TIPS "Become a nudist/naturist. Appreciate human beings in their natural state."

$$$ THE SUN

107 N. Roberson St., Chapel Hill NC 27516. (919)942-5282. **Fax:** (919)932-3101. **Website:** www.thesunmagazine.org. **Contact:** Sy Safransky, editor. **90% freelance written.** *The Sun* publishes essays, interviews, fiction, and poetry. "We are open to all kinds of writing, though we favor work of a personal nature." Estab. 1974. Circ. 72,000. Byline given. Pays on publication. Publishes ms an average of 6-12 months after acceptance. Accepts queries by mail. Responds in 3-6 months to queries and mss. Sample copy: $7. Guidelines online.

Magazine: 8.5x11; 48 pages; offset paper; glossy cover stock; photos.

NONFICTION Needs essays, interview, memoir, personal experience, Also needs spiritual fields; in-depth philosophical; thoughtful essays on political, cultural, and philosophical themes. **Buys 50 mss/year.** Send complete ms. No fax or e-mail submissions. Length: up to 7,000 words. **Pays $300-2,000.** True

REPRINTS For reprints, send photocopy and information about when and where the material previously appeared. Pays 50% of standard pay.

PHOTOS Model releases required. Offers $100-500/ photo.

FICTION Open to all fiction. Receives 800 unsolicited mss/month. Accepts 20 short stories/year. Recently published work by Sigrid Nunez, Susan Straight, Lydia Peelle, Stephen Elliott, David James Duncan, Linda McCullough Moore, and Brenda Miller. No science fiction, horror, fantasy, or other genre fiction. "Read an issue before submitting." **Buys 20 mss/year.** Send complete ms. Accepts reprint submissions. Length: up to 7,000 words. **Pays $300-1,500.**

POETRY Needs free verse. Submit up to 6 poems at a time. Considers previously published poems but strongly prefers unpublished work. "Poems should be typed and accompanied by a cover letter and SASE." Recently published poems by Tony Hoagland, Ellen Bass, Steve Kowit, Brian Doyle, and Alison Luterman. Rarely publishes poems that rhyme. **Pays $100-500 on publication plus contributor's copies and subscription.**

TIPS "Do not send queries except for interviews. We're open to unusual work. Read the magazine to get a sense of what we're about. Our submission rate is extremely high. Please be patient after sending us your work and include return postage."

VANITY FAIR

Conde Nast Publications, Inc., 1472 Broadway, New York NY 10036. **E-mail:** letters@vf.com. **Website:** www.vanityfair.com. Monthly magazine. *Vanity Fair* is edited for readers with an interest in contemporary society. No kill fee.

Does not buy freelance material, use freelance writers, or respond to queries.

DISABILITIES

$ DIALOGUE

Blindskills, Inc., P.O. Box 5181, Salem OR 97304. **E-mail:** magazine@blindskills.com. **Website:** www.blindskills.com. **60% freelance written.** Quarterly journal covering visually impaired people. Estab. 1962. Circ. 1,100. Byline given. Pays on publication. Publishes ms an average of 6 months after acceptance. Editorial lead time 3 months. Accepts queries by e-mail. Sample copy: 1 free copy on request. Available in large print, Braille, digital audio cassette, and e-mail. Guidelines available online.

NONFICTION Needs essays, general interest, historical, how-to, life skills methods used by visually impaired people, humor, interview, personal experience, sports, recreation, hobbies. No controversial, explicit sex, religious, or political topics. **Buys 50-60 mss/year.** Send complete ms. Length: 200-1,200/ words. **Pays $15-35 for assigned articles. Pays $15-25 for unsolicited articles.**

COLUMNS/DEPARTMENTS All material should be relative to blind and visually impaired readers. Living with Low Vision, 1,000 words; Hear's How (dealing with sight loss), 1,000 words. Technology Answer Book, 1,000 words. **Buys 80 mss/year.** Send complete ms. **Pays $10-25.**

HEARING HEALTH

Hearing Health, 363 Seventh Ave., 10th Floor, New York NY 10001. (212)257-6140. **E-mail:** info@hhf.org. **Website:** www.hearinghealthfoundation.org. Magazine covering issues and concerns pertaining to hearing health and hearing loss. Byline given. Accepts queries by mail, e-mail. Accepts simultaneous submissions. Guidelines available online.

NONFICTION Send complete ms. **Pays with contributor copies.**

REPRINTS "Please do not submit a previously published article unless permission has been obtained in writing that allows the article's use in *Hearing Health*."

PHOTOS State availability. Captions required. Reviews high-resolution digital images.

COLUMNS/DEPARTMENTS Features (800-1,500 words); First-person stories (500-1,500 words); Humor (500-750 words); Viewpoints/Op-Ed (350-500 words). Send complete ms.

KALEIDOSCOPE

Kaleidoscope, 701 S. Main St., Akron OH 44311-1019. (330)762-9755. **Fax:** (330)762-0912. **E-mail:** kaleidoscope@udsakron.org. **Website:** www.kaleidoscope-online.org. **Contact:** Gail Willmott, editor in chief. **75% freelance written. Eager to work with new/unpublished writers.** Semiannual free online magazine. "*Kaleidoscope* magazine creatively focuses on the experiences of disability through literature and the fine arts. Unique to the field of disability studies, this award-winning publication expresses the diversity of the disablity experience from a variety of perspectives including: individuals, families, friends, caregivers, educators, and healthcare professionals, among others." Estab. 1979. Byline given. Pays on publication. No kill fee. Accepts simultaneous submissions. Responds within 6-9 months. Guidelines available online. Submissions and queries electronically via website and e-mail.

> *Kaleidoscope* has received awards from the Great Lakes Awards Competition and Ohio Public Images; received the Ohioana Award of Editorial Excellence.

NONFICTION Needs essays, interview, personal experience, reviews, articles relating to both literary and visual arts. For book reviews: "Reviews that are substantive, timely, powerful works about publications in the field of disability and/or the arts. The writer's opinion of the work being reviewed should be clear. The review should be a literary work in its own right." **Buys 40-50 mss/year.** Length: no more than 5,000 words. **Pays $10-100.**

REPRINTS Send double-spaced typed ms with complete author's/artist's contact information, rights for sale noted, and information about when and where the material previously appeared. Reprints permitted with credit given to original publication. All rights revert to author upon publication

PHOTOS Send digital images.

FICTION Short stories with a well-crafted plot and engaging characters. Needs short stories. No fiction that is stereotypical, patronizing, sentimental, erotic, or maudlin. No romance, religious or dogmatic fiction; no children's literature. Submit complete ms by website or e-mail. Include cover letter. Length: no more than 5,000 words. All rights revert to author upon publication. **Pays $10-100.**

POETRY Wants poems that have strong imagery, evocative language. Submit up to 5 poems. "Do not get caught up in rhyme scheme. We want high quality with strong imagery and evocative language." Reviews any style.

TIPS "The material chosen for *Kaleidoscope* challenges and overcomes stereotypical, patronizing, and sentimental attitudes about disability. We accept the work of writers with and without disabilities; however the work of a writer without a disability must focus on some aspect of disability. The criteria for good writing apply: effective technique, thought-provoking subject matter, and, in general, a mature grasp of the art of storytelling. Writers should avoid using offensive language and always put the person before the disability."

SPORTS 'N SPOKES

The Magazine for Wheelchair Sports and Recreation, PVA Publications, 2111 E. Highland Ave., Suite 180, Phoenix AZ 85016-4702. (602)224-0500. **Fax:** (602)224-0507. **E-mail:** john@pvamag.com; andy@pvamag.com. **Website:** www.pvamag.com. **Contact:** Richard Hoover, editor; Tom Fjerstad, deputy editor; Andy Nemann, assistant editor; John Groth, editorial coordinator. Bimonthly magazine covering wheelchair sports and recreation. Writing must pertain to wheelchair sports and recreation. Estab. 1974. Circ. 25,000. Byline given. Pays on publication. Publishes ms an average of 2-3 months after acceptance. Editorial lead time 2-3 months. Submit seasonal material 2-3 months in advance. Accepts queries by mail, e-mail. Sample copy and guidelines free.

> "*SPORTS 'N SPOKES* is committed to providing a voice for the wheelchair sporting and recreation community."

NONFICTION Needs general interest, interview, new product. **Buys 5-6 mss/year.** Query before submitting. Length: 1,200-2,500 words. **Pays $20-250.**

ENTERTAINMENT

CINEASTE

Cineaste Publishers, Inc., 708 Third Avenue, 5th Floor, New York NY 10017-4201. (212)209-3856. **E-mail:** cineaste@cineaste.com. **Website:** www.cineaste.com. **30% freelance written.** Quarterly magazine covering motion pictures with an emphasis on social and political perspective on cinema. Estab. 1967. Circ. 11,000. Byline given. Pays on publication. Offers 50% kill fee. Publishes ms an average of 4 months after acceptance. Editorial lead time 3 months. Submit seasonal material 4 months in advance. Accepts queries by mail, e-mail, fax. Responds in 1 month to queries. Sample copy: $7. Writer's guidelines on website.

NONFICTION Needs book excerpts, essays, expose, historical, humor, interview, opinion. **Buys 20-30 mss/year.** Query with published clips. Length: 2,000-5,000 words. **Pays $30-100.**

PHOTOS State availability. Identification of subjects required. Reviews transparencies, 8x10 prints. Offers no additional payment for photos accepted with ms.

COLUMNS/DEPARTMENTS Homevideo (topics of general interest or a related group of films); A Second Look (new interpretation of a film classic or a reevaluation of an unjustly neglected release of more recent vintage); Lost and Found (film that may or may not be released or otherwise seen in the U.S. but which is important enough to be brought to the attention of our readers); all 1,000-1,500 words. Query with published clips. **Pays $50 minimum.**

TIPS "We dislike academic jargon, obtuse Marxist terminology, film buff trivia, trendy 'buzz' phrases, and show biz references. We do not want our writers to speak of how they have 'read' or 'decoded' a film but to view, analyze, and interpret. Warning the reader of problems with specific films is more important to us than artificially 'puffing' a film because its producers or politics are agreeable. One article format we encourage is an omnibus review of several current films, preferably those not reviewed in a previous issue. Such an article would focus on films that perhaps share a certain political perspective, subject matter, or generic concerns (i.e., films on suburban life or urban violence or revisionist Westerns). Like individual film reviews, these articles should incorporate a very brief synopsis of plots for those who haven't seen the films. The main focus, however, should be on the social issues manifested in each film and how it may reflect something about the current political/social/esthetic climate."

DANCE INTERNATIONAL

Scotiabant Dance Centre, Level 6 - 677 Davie St., Vancouver BC V6B 2G6 Canada. (604)681-1525. **Fax:** (604)681-7732. **E-mail:** editor@danceinternational.org; info@danceinternational.org; danceint@direct.ca. **Website:** www.danceinternational.org. **100% freelance written.** Quarterly magazine covering dance arts. Articles and reviews on current activities in world dance, with occasional historical essays; reviews of dance films, DVDs, and books. Estab. 1973. Circ. 3,000. Byline given. Pays on publication. Offers 50% kill fee. Publishes ms an average of 3 months after acceptance. Editorial lead time 3 months. Submit seasonal material 6 weeks in advance. Accepts queries by mail, e-mail. Responds in 2 weeks to queries. Responds in 1 month to mss. Sample copy for $7.50 plus p&p.

Submission deadlines are January 5, April 5, July 5, and October 5.

NONFICTION Needs book excerpts, essays, historical, interview, personal experience, photo feature. **Buys 100 mss/year.** Query with a brief proposal and short bio. Length: 1,200-2,200 words. **Pays $40-150.**

PHOTOS Send photos. Identification of subjects required. Reviews prints. Offers no additional payment for photos accepted with ms.

COLUMNS/DEPARTMENTS Mediawatch (recent books, DVDs, media reviewed), 700-800 words; Regional Reports (events in each region), 800 words. **Buys 100 mss/year.** Query. **Pays $80.**

TIPS Send résumé and samples of recent writings.

METRO MAGAZINE (AUSTRALIA)

P.O. Box 2040, St. Kilda West VIC 3182 Australia. (61)(3)9525-5302. **Fax:** (61)(3)9537-2325. **E-mail:** metro@atom.org.au. **Website:** www.metromagazine.com.au. Quarterly magazine specializing in critical essays on film, TV, and media from Australia, New Zealand, and the Asia-Pacific region. Estab. 1968. Guidelines available online.

NONFICTION Needs essays, general interest, interview, reviews. Send complete ms via e-mail. Length: 1,000-3,000 words.

PHOTOS Send photos. Reviews TIFF/JPEG files.

$$$ OK! MAGAZINE

American Media, Inc., 4 NewYork Plaza, New York NY 10004. (212)545-4800. **E-mail:** tips@okmagazine.com. **Website:** www.okmagazine.com. **Contact:** James Heidenry, editor-in-chief. **10% freelance written.** Weekly magazine covering entertainment news. "We are a celebrity friendly magazine. We strive not to show celebrities in a negative light. We consider ourselves a cross between *People* and *In Style*." Estab. 2005. Circ. 4,800,000. Byline sometimes given. Pays after publication. Publishes ms an average of 1 month after acceptance. Editorial lead time 2 weeks. Accepts queries by mail, e-mail.

NONFICTION Needs interview, photo feature. **Buys 50 mss/year.** Query with published clips. Length: 500-2,000 words. **Pays $100-1,000.**

○$$ RUE MORGUE

Marrs Media, Inc., 1411 Dufferin St., Toronto ON M6H 4C7 Canada. **E-mail:** dave@rue-morgue.com. **Website:** www.rue-morgue.com. **Contact:** Dave Alexander, editor in chief. **50% freelance written.** Monthly magazine covering horror entertainment. "A knowledge of horror entertainment (films, books, games, toys, etc.)." Estab. 1997. Byline given. Pays on publication. No kill fee. Publishes ms an average of 2-4 months after acceptance. Editorial lead time 2 months. Submit seasonal material 4 months in advance. Accepts queries by e-mail. Responds in 6 weeks to queries; in 2 months to mss. Guidelines available by e-mail.

NONFICTION Needs essays, exposé, historical, interview, travel, new product. No reviews. Query with published clips or send complete ms. Length: 500-3,500 words.

COLUMNS/DEPARTMENTS Classic Cut (historical essays on classic horror films, books, games, comic books, music), 500-700 words. Query with published clips.

TIPS "The editors are most responsive to special-interest articles and analytical essays on cultural/historical topics relating to the horror genre. Published examples: Leon Theremin, Soren Kierkegaard, Horror in Fine Art, Murderbilia, The History of the Werewolf."

$$$$ SOUND & VISION

Source Interlink Media, 2 Park Ave., 10th Floor, New York NY 10016. (212)767-5000. **Fax:** (212)767-5200. **E-mail:** rsabin@enthusiastnetwork.com. **Website:** www.soundandvision.com. **Contact:** Rob Sabin, editor. **40% freelance written.** Magazine published 10 times/year covering home theater consumer products. "Provides readers with authoritative information on the home entertainment technologies and products that will impact their lives." Estab. 1958. Circ. 105,000. Byline given. Pays on acceptance. Publishes ms an average of 4 months after acceptance. Accepts queries by mail, e-mail. Sample copy for SAE with 9x12 envelope and 11 first-class stamps.

NONFICTION Buys 25 mss/year. Query with published clips. Length: 1,500-3,000 words. **Pays $1,000-1,500.**

TIPS "Send proposals or outlines, rather than complete articles, along with published clips to establish writing ability. Publisher assumes no responsibility for return or safety of unsolicited art, photos, or mss."

ETHNIC AND MINORITY

AFRICAN VOICES

African Voices Communications, Inc., 270 W. 96th St., New York NY 10025. (212)865-2982. **Fax:** (212)316-3335. **E-mail:** info@africanvoices.com. **Website:** www.africanvoices.com. **Contact:** Maitefa Angaza, managing editor; Mariahadessa Ekere Tallie, poetry editor. **85% freelance written.** Quarterly magazine covering art, film, culture. *African Voices*, published quarterly, is an "art and literary magazine that highlights the work of people of color. We publish ethnic literature and poetry on any subject. We also consider all themes and styles: avant-garde, free verse, haiku, light verse, and traditional. We do not wish to limit the reader or author." Estab. 1992. Circ. 20,000. Byline given. Pays on publication. No kill fee. Publishes ms an average of 3-6 months after acceptance. Editorial lead time 3 months. Submit seasonal material 3 months in advance. Accepts queries by mail. Accepts simultaneous submissions. Responds in 3 months to queries. Sample copy: $6. Subscription: $20.

African Voices is about 48 pages, magazine-sized, professionally printed, saddle-stapled, with paper cover. Receives about 100 submissions/year, accepts about 30%. Press run is 20,000.

NONFICTION Needs book excerpts, essays, historical, humor, inspirational, interview, photo feature, travel. Query with published clips. Length: 500-2,500 words. **Pays in contributor's copies.**

PHOTOS State availability. Pays in contributor copies.

FICTION Needs adventure, erotica, ethnic, experimental, fantasy, historical, horror, humorous, mainstream, mystery, religious, romance, science fiction, slice-of-life vignettes, suspense, African-American. **Buys 4 mss/year.** Send complete ms. Include short bio. Accepts submissions by e-mail (in text box), by fax, and by postal mail. Send SASE for return of ms. Length: 500-2,500 words. **Pays $25-50.**

POETRY Needs avant-garde, free verse, haiku, traditional. Submit no more than 2 poems at a time. Accepts submissions by e-mail (in text box), by fax, and by postal mail. Cover letter and SASE required. Seldom comments on rejected poems. Reviews books of poetry in 500-1,000 words. Send materials for review consideration to Ekere Tallie. Considers poetry written by children. Has published poetry by Reg E. Gaines, Maya Angelou, Jessica Care Moore, Asha Bandele, Tony Medina, and Louis Reyes Rivera. Buys 10 poems/year. Submit maximum 5 poems. Length: 5-100 lines. **Pays 2 contributor copies.**

TIPS "A manuscript stands out if it is neatly typed with a well-written and interesting storyline or plot. Originality is encouraged. We are interested in more horror, erotic, and drama pieces. *AV* wants to highlight the diversity in our culture. Stories must touch the humanity in us all. We strongly encourage new writers/poets to send in their work. Accepted contributors are encouraged to subscribe."

CELTIC LIFE INTERNATIONAL

Clansman Publishing, Ltd., P.O. Box 8805, Station A, Halifax NS B3K 5M4 Canada. (902)835-2358. **Fax:** (902)835-0080. **E-mail:** editor@celticlife.ca. **Website:** www.celticlifeintl.com. **Contact:** Carels Mandel, editor. **95% freelance written.** Quarterly magazine covering culture of those with an interest in Celtic culture around the world. Celtic Life International is a global community for a living, breathing Celtic culture. Home to an extensive collection of feature stories, interviews, history, heritage, news, views, reviews, recipes, events, trivia, humour and tidbits from across all Seven Celtic Nations and beyond. The flagship publication, *Celtic Life International Magazine*, is published four times a year in both print and digital formats, and is distributed around the world. Theonline home, CelticLife.ca, is an informative and interactive community that engages Celts from all walks of life. Estab. 1987. Circ. distribution: 201,340; readership: 1,026,834. Byline given. Pays after publication. No kill fee. Editorial lead time 2 months. Submit seasonal material 3 months in advance. Accepts queries by e-mail only. Responds in 1 week to queries. Responds in 1 month to mss.

NONFICTION Needs essays, general interest, historical, interview, opinion, personal experience, travel, Gaelic language, Celtic music reviews, profiles of Celtic musicians, Celtic history, traditions, and folklore. Also buys short fiction. No fiction, poetry, historical stories already well publicized. **Buys 100 mss/year.** Query or send complete ms. Length: 800-2,500 words. **All writers receive a complimentary subscription.**

PHOTOS State availability. Captions, identification of subjects, model releases required. Reviews 35mm transparencies, 5x7 prints, JPEG files (300 dpi). "We pay for photographs."

COLUMNS/DEPARTMENTS Query.

GERMAN LIFE

Zeitgeist Publishing, Inc., 1068 National Hwy., LaVale MD 21502. (301)729-6190. **Fax:** (301)729-1720. **E-mail:** mslider@germanlife.com. **Website:** www.germanlife.com. **Contact:** Mark Slider. **80% freelance written.** Bimonthly magazine covering German-speaking Europe. "*German Life* is for all interested in the diversity of German-speaking culture—past and present—and in the various ways that the US (and North America in general) has been shaped by its German immigrants. The magazine is dedicated to solid reporting on cultural, historical, social, genealogical, culinary and political topics." Estab. 1994. Circ. 40,000. Byline given. Pays on publication. Editorial lead time 4 months. Submit seasonal material 6 months in advance. Accepts queries by mail, e-mail. Responds in 2 months to queries. Responds in 3 months to mss. Sample copy for $4.95 and SASE with 4 first-class stamps. Guidelines available online.

NONFICTION Needs general interest, historical, interview, photo feature, travel. Special issues: Oktoberfest-related (October); Seasonal Relative to Germany, Switzerland, or Austria (December); Travel to German-speaking Europe (April). **Buys 50 mss/year.** Query with published clips. Length: 800-1,500 words. **Pays $200-500 for assigned articles. Pays $200-350 for unsolicited articles.**

PHOTOS State availability. Identification of subjects required. Reviews color transparencies, 5×7 color or b&w prints, and digital images. Offers no additional payment for photos accepted with ms.

COLUMNS/DEPARTMENTS German-Americana (regards specific German-American communities, organizations, and/or events past or present), 1,200 words; Profile (portrays prominent Germans, Americans, or German-Americans), 1,000 words; At Home (cuisine, etc. relating to German-speaking Europe), 800 words; Library (reviews of books, videos, CDs, etc.), 300 words. **Buys 30 mss/year.** Query with published clips. **Pays $50-150.**

FILLERS Needs facts, newsbreaks. Length: 100-300 words. **Pays $50-150.**

TIPS "The best queries include several informative proposals. Writers should avoid overemphasizing autobiographical experiences/stories. Please avoid 'superficial' travel articles- GL has been in publication for 20+ years and readers are savvy travelers so we look for articles with substance."

$$ HADASSAH MAGAZINE

50 W. 58th St., New York NY 10019. (212)688-0227. **Fax:** (212)446-9521. **E-mail:** magazine@hadassah.org. **Website:** www.hadassah.org/magazine. **Contact:** Elizabeth Barnea. **90% freelance written.** Monthly magazine. Circ. 255,000. Pays on acceptance. Responds in 4 months to mss. Sample copy and writer's guidelines with 9x12 SASE.

NONFICTION Buys 10 unsolicited mss/year. Query. Length: 1,500-2,000 words. Sometimes pays expenses of writers on assignment.

PHOTOS "We buy photos only to illustrate articles. Always interested in striking cover photos." Offers $50 for first photo, $35 for each additional photo.

COLUMNS/DEPARTMENTS "We have a family column and a travel column, but a query for topic or destination should be submitted first to make sure the area is of interest and the story follows our format."

FICTION Contact: Zelda Shluker, managing editor. Short stories with strong plots and positive Jewish values. Needs ethnic, Jewish. Length: 1,500-2,000 words. **Pays $500 minimum.**

TIPS "Stories on a Jewish theme should be neither self-hating nor schmaltzy."

$ INTERNATIONAL EXAMINER

622 S. Washington St., Seattle WA 98104. (206)624-3925. **Fax:** (206)624-3046. **E-mail:** editor@iexaminer.org. **Website:** www.iexaminer.org. **Contact:** Travis Quezon, editor in chief. **75% freelance written.** Biweekly journal of Asian American news, politics, and arts. "*International Examiner* is about Asian American issues and things of interest to Asian Americans. We do not want stuff about Asian things (stories on your trip to China, Japanese Tea Ceremony, etc. will be rejected). Yes, we are in English." Estab. 1974. Circ. 12,000. Pays on publication. No kill fee. Publishes ms an average of 1 month after acceptance. Editorial lead time 1 month. Submit seasonal material 2 months in advance. Accepts queries by mail, e-mail, fax. Accepts simultaneous submissions. Guidelines for #10 SASE.

NONFICTION Needs essays, exposé, general interest, historical, humor, interview, opinion, personal experience, photo feature. **Buys 100 mss/year.** Query by mail, fax, or e-mail with published clips. 750-5,000 words, depending on subject. **Pays $25-100.** Sometimes pays expenses of writers on assignment.

REPRINTS Accepts previously published submissions (as long as published in same area). Send typed ms with rights for sale noted and information about when and where the material previously appeared. Payment negotiable.

PHOTOS State availability. Captions, identification of subjects required. Reviews contact sheets. Negotiates payment individually.

FICTION Asian American authored fiction by or about Asian Americans only. Needs novel concepts. **Buys 1-2 mss/year.** Query.

TIPS "Write decent, suitable material on a subject of interest to the Asian American community. All submissions are reviewed; all good ones are contacted. It helps to call and run an idea by the editor before or after sending submissions."

$$ ITALIAN AMERICA

219 E St. NE, Washington DC 20002. (202)547-2900. **Fax:** (202)546-8168. **E-mail:** ddesanctis@osia.org. **Website:** www.osia.org. **Contact:** Dona De Sanctis, editor. **20% freelance written.** Quarterly magazine. *Italian America* provides timely information about OSIA, while reporting on individuals, institutions, issues, and events of current or historical significance in the Italian-American community. Estab. 1996. Circ. 65,000. Byline given. Pays on publication. Offers 50% kill fee. Publishes ms an average of 3 months after acceptance. Editorial lead time 3 months. Accepts queries by mail, e-mail, fax. Accepts simultaneous

submissions. Sample copy free. Guidelines available online.

NONFICTION Needs historical, little known historical facts that must relate to Italian Americans, interview, opinion, current events. **Buys 8 mss/year.** Query with published clips. Length: 750-1,000 words. **Pays $50-250.**

TIPS "We pay particular attention to the quality of graphics that accompany the stories. We are interested in little known facts about historical/cultural Italian America."

JEWISH CURRENTS

P.O. Box 111, Accord NY 12404. (845)626-2427. **E-mail:** editor@jewishcurrents.org. **Website:** www.jewishcurrents.org. *Jewish Currents*, published 4 times/year, is a progressive Jewish bimonthly magazine that carries on the insurgent tradition of the Jewish left through independent journalism, political commentary, and a 'countercultural' approach to Jewish arts and literature. Estab. 1946. Circ. 4,000. Publishes mss 6-9 months after acceptance. Responds in 3 months. Subscription: $30/year.

Jewish Currents is 80 pages, magazine-sized, offset-printed, saddle-stapled with a full-color arts section, "Jcultcha & Funny Pages." "Our Winter issue is a 12-month arts calendar."

FICTION Needs Jewish, historical, multicultural, feminist, humor, satire, translations, contemporary. Send complete ms with cover letter. "Writers should include brief biographical information." **Pays contributor's copies or small honoraria.**

POETRY Submit 4 poems at a time with a cover letter. "Writers should include brief biographical information." Poems should be typed, double-spaced; include SASE. **Pays contributor's copies.**

JEWISH WOMEN'S LITERARY ANNUAL

Eleanor Leff Jewish Women's Resource Center, 241 W. 72nd St., New York NY 10023. (212)687-5030. **E-mail:** info@ncjwny.org. **Website:** www.ncjwny.org/services_annual.htm. **Contact:** Henny Wenkart, editor. *Jewish Women's Literary Annual*, published in April, prints poetry, fiction, and creative nonfiction by Jewish women. Estab. 1994. Sample copy: $15. Subscription: $48 for 3 issues. Make checks payable to NCJW New York Section.

Jewish Women's Literary Annual is 230 pages, digest-sized, perfect-bound, with laminated card cover. Press run is 1,500.

NONFICTION Needs humor, memoir. Submit complete ms by postal mail.

FICTION Needs Wants prose written by Jewish women on any topic. Submit complete ms by postal mail.

POETRY Needs Wants "poems by Jewish women on any topic, but of the highest literary quality." Submit poems by postal mail. Receives about 1,500 poems/year, accepts about 10%. Has published poetry by Linda Zisquit, Merle Feld, Helen Papell, Enid Dame, Marge Piercy, and Lesléa Newman.

TIPS "Send only your very best. We are looking for humor, as well as other things, but nothing cutesy or smart-aleck. We do no politics and prefer topics other than 'Holocaust'."

LILITH MAGAZINE: INDEPENDENT, JEWISH & FRANKLY FEMINIST

Attn: Submissions, 250 W. 57th St., Suite 2432, New York NY 10107. (212)757-0818. **Fax:** (212)757-5705. **E-mail:** info@lilith.org; naomi@lilith.org. **Website:** www.lilith.org. **Contact:** Susan Weidman Schneider, editor in chief; Naomi Danis, managing editor. *Lilith Magazine: Independent, Jewish & Frankly Feminist*, published quarterly, welcomes submissions of high-quality, lively writing: reportage, opinion pieces, memoirs, fiction, and poetry on subjects of interest to Jewish women. Estab. 1976. Accepts queries by mail, e-mail, online submission form. Responds in 3 months. Sample copy: $7. Guidelines online.

Lilith Magazine is 48 pages, magazine-sized, with glossy color cover. Press run is about 10,000 (about 6,000 subscribers). Subscription: $26/year. For all submissions: Make sure name and contact information appear on each page of mss. Include a short bio (1-2 sentences), written in third person. Accepts submissions year round.

NONFICTION Send complete ms via online submissions form or mail. Length: up to 2,500 words for features, up to 500 words for news briefs.

FICTION Send complete ms via online submissions form or mail. Length: up to 3,000 words.

POETRY Has published poetry by Irena Klepfisz, Lyn Lifshin, Marcia Falk, Adrienne Rich, and Muriel Rukeyser. Send up to 3 poems at a time via online submissions form or mail; no e-mail submissions. Copy should be neatly typed and proofread for typos and spelling errors. Buys 4 poems/year.

TIPS "Read a copy of the publication before you submit your work. Please be patient."

FOOD AND DRINK

AMERICAN WINE SOCIETY JOURNAL

American Wine Society, 2800 S. Lake Leelanau Dr., Lake Leelanau MI 49653. (586)946-0049. **E-mail:** rink@americanwinesociety.org. **Website:** www.americanwinesociety.org. **Contact:** Jim Rink, editor. **100% freelance written.** The nonprofit American Wine Society is the largest consumer-based wine education organization in the U.S. The *Journal* reflects the varied interests of AWS members, which may include wine novices, experts, grape growers, amateur and professional winemakers, chefs, wine appreciators, wine educators, restauranteurs, and anyone wanting to learn more about wine and gastronomy. Estab. 1967. Circ. 5,000. Byline given. Pays on publication. No kill fee. Publishes 3 months after acceptance. Editorial lead time 3 months. Accepts queries by mail, e-mail. Accepts simultaneous submissions. Responds in 2 weeks to queries, 3 months to mss. Sample copy available on website. Writer's guidelines available by e-mail at rink@americanwinesociety.org.

NONFICTION Needs general interest, historical, how-to, nostalgic, technical, travel. Submit query with published clips.

PHOTOS Freelancers should send photos with submission. Requires captions and identification of subjects. Reviews GIF/JPEG files. Offers no additional payment for photos accepted with ms.

COLUMNS/DEPARTMENTS Columns include wine reviews, book reviews, food and wine articles. Writer should send query with published clips.

TIPS "Request a sample copy, which we can provide in PDF format. The readership is diverse, and you may see a travel piece next to a technical piece on malolactic fermentation. Use proper grammar and spelling. Please proofread copy before sending. We're always looking for engaging pieces related to winemaking, grape growing, food and wine, wine and travel, book reviews, recipes, and new developments in the field."

THE DAILY TEA

1000 Germantown Pike, Suite F2, Plymouth Meeting PA 19462. (484)688-0299. **E-mail:** dawnl@thedailytea.com. **Website:** www.thedailytea.com. **Contact:** Dawn L., editor and content manager. **75% freelance written.** Annual magazine covering anything tea related. "Around the office, we have a saying—'It's not just about dry brown leaves, or hot brown liquid.' For sure *The Daily Tea* is for tea lovers of all levels, but we aim to be much more than a text book. It's the culture that surrounds tea that we find even more fascinating—the lives of the people who grow it, the rituals and traditions around tea, the peace we find in drinking it, and the fact that tea is a common denominator to so many around the world. This is what *The Daily Tea* is all about." Estab. 1994. Circ. 9,500. Byline given. Pays on publication. Publishes ms an average of 1 year after acceptance. Editorial lead time 9 months. Submit seasonal material 6 months in advance. Responds in 6 months to mss. Guidelines by e-mail.

NONFICTION Needs book excerpts, essays, general interest, historical, how-to, humor, interview, personal experience, photo feature, travel. Send complete ms or query with proprosal. **Pays negotiable amount.** Sometimes pays expenses of writers on assignment.

PHOTOS Send photos. Captions, identification of subjects required. Reviews prints, GIF/JPEG files (300 dpi). Negotiates payment individually.

COLUMNS/DEPARTMENTS Readers' Stories (personal experience involving tea); Book Reviews (review on tea books). Send complete ms. **Pays negotiable amount.**

TASTE OF HOME

Reader's Digest Association, Inc., 1610 N. 2nd St., Suite 102, Milwaukee WI 53207. (414)423-0100. **Fax:** (414)423-8463. **E-mail:** feedback@tasteofhome.com. **Website:** www.tasteofhome.com. Bimonthly magazine. *Taste of Home* is dedicated to home cooks, from beginners to the very experienced. Editorial includes recipes and serving suggestions, interviews and ideas from the publication's readers and field editors based around the country, and reviews of new cooking tools and gadgets. Circ. 3.5 million. No kill fee.

Query before submitting.

VEGETARIAN JOURNAL

P.O. Box 1463, Baltimore MD 21203-1463. (410)366-8343. **E-mail:** vrg@vrg.org. **Website:** www.vrg.org. **Contact:** Debra Wasserman, editor. Quarterly nonprofit vegetarian magazine that examines the health, ecological and ethical aspects of vegetarianism. "Highly-educated audience including health professionals." Estab. 1982. Circ. 20,000. Sample: $4.

Vegetarian Journal is 36 pages, magazine-sized, professionally printed, saddle-stapled, with glossy card cover. Press run is 20,000.

POETRY "Please, no submissions of poetry from adults; 18 and under only."

TIPS Areas most open to freelancers are recipe section and feature articles. "Review magazine first to learn our style. Send query letter with photocopy sample of line drawings of food."

$$$$ WINE ENTHUSIAST MAGAZINE

Wine Enthusiast Media, 333 North Bedford Rd., Mt. Kisco NY 10549. **E-mail:** editor@wineenthusiast.net. **E-mail:** mdawson@wineenthusiast.net; jczerwin@wineenthusiast.net;. **Website:** www.winemag.com. **Contact:** Mike Dawson, deputy editor; Joe Czerwinski, managing editor; Marina Vataj, digital editorial manager. **40% freelance written.** Monthly magazine covering the lifestyle of wine. "Our readers are upscale and educated, but not necessarily super-sophisticated about wine itself. Our informal, irreverent approach appeals to savvy enophiles and newbies alike." Estab. 1988. Circ. 80,000. Byline given. Pays on acceptance. Offers 25% kill fee. Editorial lead time 4 months. Submit seasonal material 5 months in advance. Accepts queries by e-mail. Responds in 2 weeks to queries. Responds in 2 months to mss.

NONFICTION Needs essays, humor, interview, new product, personal experience. **Buys 5 mss/year.** Submit a proposal (1 or 2 paragraphs) with clips and a resume. Submit short, front-of-book items to Mike Dawson; submit feature stories aimed at the Pairings department and short items for the back of book to Joe Czerwinski; submit web items to Marina Vataj. Back of book stories (anywhere from 200-800 words) can fall into any of the following categories: How to Make the Most of Your Day in: [city, region]; The Wine Trail (true travel tales and observations, profiles; arcane food and wine origins; unusual tasting rooms, museums, roadside attractions, restaurants and the arts in general; weird meals, recipes, customs; wine & culinary history; stories behind wine labels); Q&A (accent on celebrities); humor essay or light, funny op-ed; a chef and his/her favorite ingredient or recipe; quiz, puzzle, game. **Pays $750-2,500 for assigned articles. Pays $750-2,000 for unsolicited articles. Pays 50¢/word for website articles.**

PHOTOS Send photos. Reviews GIF/JPEG files. Offers $135-400/photo.

GAMES AND PUZZLES

$$ CHESS LIFE

P.O. Box 3967, Crossville TN 38557. (931)787-1234. **Fax:** (931)787-1200. **E-mail:** dlucas@uschess.org; fbutler@uschess.org. **Website:** www.uschess.org. **Contact:** Daniel Lucas, editor; Francesca "Frankie" Butler, art director. **15% freelance written. Works with a small number of new/unpublished writers/year.** Monthly magazine. "*Chess Life* is the official publication of the United States Chess Federation, covering news of most major chess events, both here and abroad, with special emphasis on the triumphs and exploits of American players." Estab. 1939. Circ. 85,000. Byline given. No kill fee. Publishes ms an average of 6 months after acceptance. Submit seasonal material 6 months in advance. Accepts queries by e-mail only to dlucas@uschess.org. Accepts simultaneous submissions. Responds in 3 months to mss. Sample copy via PDF is available.

NONFICTION Needs general interest, historical, humor, interview, of a famous chess player or organizer, photo feature, chess centered, technical. No stories about personal experiences with chess. **Buys 30-40 mss/year.** Query with samples if new to publication. 3,000 words maximum. **Pays $100/page (800-1,000 words).** Sometimes pays expenses of writers on assignment.

PHOTOS Uses about 15 photos/issue; 7-8 supplied by freelancers. No answer. Captions, identification of subjects, model releases required. Reviews b&w contact sheets and prints, and color prints and slides. Pays $25-100 inside; covers negotiable. Pays $25-100 for b&w inside; cover payment negotiable. Pays on publication. Buys one-time rights; "we occasionally purchase all rights for stock mug shots." Credit line given.

FILLERS Submit with samples and clips. Buys first or negotiable rights to cartoons and puzzles. **Pays $25 upon acceptance.**

TIPS "Articles must be written from an informed point of view. Freelancers in major population areas (except NY and LA) who are interested in short personality profiles and perhaps news reporting have the best opportunities. We're looking for more personality pieces on chess players around the country; not just the stars, but local masters, talented youths, and dedicated volunteers. Freelancers interested in such pieces might let us know of their interest and their range. Could be we know of an interesting story in their territory that needs covering. Examples of published articles include a locally produced chess television program, a meeting of chess set collectors from around the world, chess in our prisons, and chess in the works of several famous writers."

POKER PRO MAGAZINE

Poker Pro Media, 2101 NE Corporate Blvd., Boca Raton FL 33432. **E-mail:** jwenzel@pokerpromedia.com. **Website:** www.pokerpromagazine.com. **Contact:** John Wenzel, editor. **75% freelance written.** Monthly magazine covering poker, gambling, and nightlife. "We want articles about poker and gambling-related articles only; also nightlife in gaming cities and articles on gaming destinations." Estab. 2005. Circ. 150,000. Byline given. Pays on publication. No kill fee. Publishes ms an average of 1 month after acceptance. Editorial lead time 1.5 months. Submit seasonal material 2 months in advance. Accepts queries by e-mail. Responds in 1 week to queries; in 1 month to mss. Sample copy and guidelines by e-mail.

NONFICTION Needs book excerpts, essays, expose, general interest, historical, how-to, humor, interview, new product, opinion, personal experience, photo feature, travel. **Buys 125 mss/year.** Query. Length: 800-2,500 words. **Pays $100-$200 for assigned or unsolicited articles.** Sometimes pays expenses of writers on assignment.

PHOTOS State availability. Captions, identification of subjects, model releases required. Reviews GIF/JPEG files. Negotiates payment individually.

WOMAN POKER PLAYER MAGAZINE

915 Chestnut St., New Westminster BC V3L 5S6 Canada. **E-mail:** editorial@womanpokerplayer.com. **Website:** www.womanpokerplayer.com. **80% freelance written.** Bimonthly magazine covering poker. *Woman Poker Player* is for the woman who enjoys poker. We are a lifestyle publication that also covers fashion and wellness. Estab. 2005. Circ. 35,000. Byline sometimes given. Pays on publication. No kill fee. Publishes ms an average of 2 months after acceptance. Editorial lead time 1 month. Submit seasonal material 1 month in advance. Accepts queries by online submission form. Accepts simultaneous submissions. Sample copy free.

NONFICTION Needs poker, health, fitness, self-image, relationships, beauty, parenting, love, cooking, green living, gaming. Submit complete ms using online submission form. Length: 250-1,000 words. **Pays variable amount.**

FICTION Needs cond novels, poker. Query. Length: 1,000-2,000 words.

GAY & LESBIAN INTEREST

THE ADVOCATE

Here Media, Inc., 10990 Wilshire Blvd., Penthouse, Los Angeles CA 90024. (310)943-5858. **Fax:** (310)806-6350. **E-mail:** newsroom@advocate.com. **Website:** www.advocate.com. **Contact:** Neal Broverman, managing editor. Biweekly magazine covering national news events with a gay and lesbian perspective on the issues. Estab. 1967. Circ. 120,000. Byline given. Pays on publication. Responds in 1 month to queries. Sample copy for $3.95. Guidelines on website.

NONFICTION Needs expose, interview, news reporting, investigating. Query. Length: 800 words. **Pays $550.**

COLUMNS/DEPARTMENTS Arts & Media (news and profiles of well-known gay or lesbians in entertainment) is most open to freelancers; 750 words. Query. **Pays $100-500.**

TIPS "*The Advocate* is a unique newsmagazine. While we report on gay and lesbian issues and are published by 1 of the country's oldest and most established gay-owned companies, we also play by the rules of mainstream-not-gay-community journalism."

MENSBOOK JOURNAL

CQS Media, Inc., P.O. Box 418, Sturbridge MA 01566. **Fax:** (508)347-8150. **E-mail:** features@mensbook.com. **Website:** www.mensbook.com. **Contact:** P.C. Carr, editor/publisher. **100% freelance written.** Online anthology updated with offerings as they come in and are accepted by our editors. "We target bright, inquisitive, discerning gay men who want more noncommercial substance from gay media. We seek primarily first-person autobiographical pieces—then: biographies, political and social analysis, cartoons, short fiction, commentary, travel, and humor." Estab. 2008. Circ. variable. Byline given. Editorial lead time 4 months. Accepts queries by e-mail. Responds in 8 weeks to queries. Sample copy sent free by PDF. Publisher splits download fee with authors 50/50. Submit finished material anytime by e-mail. Do not call. Guidelines online at www.mensbook.com/writersguidelines.htm.

NONFICTION Special issues: Wants first-person pieces, essays, think-pieces, exposé, humor, inspirational profiles of courage and triumph over adversity, interview/profile, religion/philosophy vis-à-vis the gay experience, opinion, travel. "We do not want celebrity profiles/commentary, chatty, campy gossip; sexual conjecture about famous people; or film reviews." Buys variably throughout the year. Query by e-mail. Length: 750-3,500 words.

FICTION Needs adventure, erotica, fantasy, mystery/suspense, slice-of-life vignettes. Buys variable amounts of fiction mss/year. Send complete ms. Length: 750-3,500 words.

POETRY Needs avant-garde, free verse, haiku, light verse, traditional. Buys 8 poems/year.

TIPS "Be a tight writer with a cogent, potent message. Structure your work with well-organized progressive sequencing. Edit everything down before you send it over so we know it is the best you can do, and we'll work together from there."

RAINBOW RUMPUS

P.O. Box 6881, Minneapolis MN 55406. **Website:** www.rainbowrumpus.org. **Contact:** Beth Wallace, editor in chief and fiction editor. "*Rainbow Rumpus* is the world's only online literary magazine for children and youth with lesbian, gay, bisexual, and transgender (LGBT) parents. We are creating a new genre of children's and young adult fiction. Please carefully read and observe the guidelines on our website." Estab. 2005. Circ. 300 visits/day. Byline given. Pays on publication. Guidelines online.

FICTION "Stories should be written from the point of view of children or teens with lesbian, gay, bisexual, or transgender parents or other family members, or who are connected to the LGBT community. Stories featuring families of color, bisexual parents, transgender parents, family members with disabilities, and mixed-race families are particularly welcome." Needs All levels: adventure, animal, contemporary, fantasy, folktales, history, humorous, multicultural, nature/environment, problem solving, science fiction, sports, suspense/mystery. Query editor through website's Contact page. Be sure to select the Submissions category. Length: 800-2,500 words for stories for 4- to 12-year-olds; up to 5,000 words for stories for 13- to 18-year-olds. **Pays $300/story.**

TIPS "Emerging writers encouraged to submit. You do not need to be a member of the LGBT community to participate."

THE WASHINGTON BLADE

P.O. Box 53352, Washington DC 20009. (202)747-2077. **Fax:** (202)747-2070. **E-mail:** knaff@washblade.com. **Website:** www.washblade.com. **Contact:** Kevin Naff, editor. **20% freelance written.** Nation's oldest and largest weekly newspaper covering the lesbian, gay, bisexual and transgender issues. Articles (subjects) should be written from or directed to a gay perspective. Estab. 1969. Circ. 30,000. Byline given. No kill fee. Submit seasonal material one month in advance. Accepts queries by mail, e-mail, fax. Responds in within one month to queries.

REPRINTS Send typed manuscript with rights for sale noted and information about when and where the material previously appeared.

PHOTOS A photo or graphic with feature articles is particularly important. Photos with news stories are appreciated. Send photos by mail or e-mail to mkey@washblade.com. No Answer. Captions required. Pay varies. Photographers on assignment are paid mutually agreed upon fee.

COLUMNS/DEPARTMENTS Send feature submissions to Joey DiGuglielmo, arts editor (joeyd@washblade.com). Sent opinion submissions to Kevin Naff, editor (knaff@washblade.com). Pay varies. No sexually explicit material.

TIPS "We maintain a highly competent and professional staff of news reporters, and it is difficult to break in here as a freelancer covering news. Include a résumé, good examples of your writing, and know the paper before you send a manuscript for publication. We look for writers who are credible and professional, and for copy that is accurate, fair, timely, and objective in tone. We do not work with writers who play fast and loose with the facts, or who are unprofessional in presentation. Before you send anything, become familiar with our publication. Do not send sexually explicit material."

GENERAL INTEREST

THE ATLANTIC MONTHLY

The Watergate, 600 New Hampshire Ave., NW, Washington DC 20037. **E-mail:** submissions@theatlantic.com; pitches@theatlantic.com. **Website:** www.theatlantic.com. **Contact:** Scott Stossel, magazine editor;

Ann Hulbert, literary editor. Covers poetry, fiction, and articles of the highest quality. General magazine for an educated readership with broad cultural and public-affairs interests. "*The Atlantic* considers unsolicited mss, either fiction or nonfiction. A general familiarity with what we have published in the past is the best guide to our needs and preferences." Estab. 1857. Circ. 500,000. Byline given. Pays on acceptance. No kill fee. Accepts queries by mail, e-mail. Responds in 4-6 weeks to mss. Guidelines online.

NONFICTION Needs book excerpts, essays, general interest, humor, travel. Query with or without published clips to pitches@theatlantic.com, or send complete ms to "Editorial Department" at address above. All unsolicited mss must be accompanied by SASE. "A general familiarity with what we have published in the past is the best guide to our needs and preferences." Length: 1,000-6,000 words **Payment varies.** Sometimes pays expenses.

FICTION "Seeks fiction that is clear, tightly written with strong sense of 'story' and well-defined characters." No longer publishes fiction in the regular magazine. Instead, it will appear in a special newsstand-only fiction issue. Receives 1,000 unsolicited mss/month. Accepts 7-8 mss/year. **Publishes 3-4 new writers/year.** Needs literary, contemporary. Submit via e-mail with Word document attachment to submissions@theatlantic.com. Mss submitted via postal mail must be typewritten and double-spaced. Preferred length: 2,000-6,000 words. **Payment varies.**

POETRY *The Atlantic Monthly* publishes some of the most distinguished poetry in American literature. "We read with interest and attention every poem submitted to the magazine and, quite simply, we publish those that seem to us to be the best." Has published poetry by Maxine Kumin, Stanley Plumly, Linda Gregerson, Philip Levine, Ellen Bryant Voigt, and W.S. Merwin. Receives about 60,000 poems/year. Submit 2-6 poems by e-mail or mail. Buys 30-35 poems/year.

TIPS "Writers should be aware that this is not a market for beginner's work (nonfiction and fiction), nor is it truly for intermediate work. Study this magazine before sending only your best, most professional work. When making first contact, cover letters are sometimes helpful, particularly if they cite prior publications or involvement in writing programs. Common mistakes: melodrama, inconclusiveness, lack of development, unpersuasive characters and/or dialogue."

CAPPER'S FARMER/GRIT

Ogden Publications, Inc., 1503 SW 42nd St., Topeka KS 66609-1265. (800)678-5779. **E-mail:** editor@cappersfarmer.com; editor@grit.com. **Website:** www.cappersfarmer.com; www.grit.com. **Contact:** Caleb Regan, managing editor. **80% freelance written.** "*GRIT* is a bimonthly rural lifestyle magazine that focuses on small-town life, country and rural lifestyles, and small-scale farms." Estab. 1879. Circ. 250,000. Byline given. Pays for articles on publication. Publishes mss an average of 2-15 months after acceptance. Submit seasonal queries 6-8 months in advance. Accepts queries by e-mail only, with "Query" and the subject of the query in the subject line. Responds in 2-3 weeks to queries. Sample copies and guidelines available online or by e-mailing ireid@grit.com.

Does not publish poetry or fiction.

NONFICTION Needs feature-length articles (1,000-1,750 words with photos) on topics of interest to those living in rural areas, on farms or ranches, or those simply interested in the rural lifestyle; department articles (500-1,500 words with photos) on nostalgia, farm equipment and animals, DIY projects, gardening and cooking. Send queries via e-mail (cregan@grit.com). Include complete contact information. Articles (except Heart of the Home) are assigned in most cases; no editorial calendar is published."

PHOTOS Photos paid upon publication. Pay is negotiable. Photo captions required. E-mail managing editor Caleb Regan (cregan@grit.com) to be added to the photo call-out list. Image requests sent for each issue. Send low-res digital images or lightboxes in response to call-out to jteller@grit.com. If images are purchased, send digital images via e-mail, one at a time as JPEG files at 300 dpi resolution to jteller@grit.com. Buys shared rights.

COLUMNS/DEPARTMENTS Departments include Gazette (news and quirky briefs of interest to lifestyle farmers); Heart of the Home (nostalgic remembrances on specific topics asked for in each issue); Country Tech (looking at equipment necessary for the farm life); Looking Back (nostalgic look at life on the farm); and In the Shop (how-to for those specialty farm items). Other departments are Comfort Foods, Recipe Box, In the Wild, and Sow Hoe (gardening topics). A query should be sent via e-mail to cregan@grit.com for all departments except Heart of the Home. Send complete article via e-mail to tsmith@cappers.com or mail them to GRIT/Capper's Farmer Editorial

Department, 1503 SW 42nd St., Topeka, KS 66609. **Payment varies depending on experience and expertise. Payment will also include 2 contributor's copies. For Heart of the Home articles, we pay a standard $25 rate and a standard $5 payment for Heart of the Home articles that appear on our website but not in the magazines.**

TIPS "Study a few issues of the magazine. Most rejections are for material that is unsuitable or out of character for our magazine. Do not try to write for *GRIT* if you know nothing about rural life, gardening, or urban farming. We intend to be an authoritative and sometimes playful voice for rural lifestyle farmers and country or small-town dwellers, and we require our freelance writers to be informed about that way of life. On occasion, we must cut material to fit column space. Electronic submissions preferred."

THE CHRISTIAN SCIENCE MONITOR

210 Massachussetts Ave., Boston MA 02115. **E-mail:** homeforum@csmonitor.com. **Website:** www.csmonitor.com; http://www.csmonitor.com/About/Contributor-guidelines. *The Christian Science Monitor*, an international daily newspaper, regularly features poetry in The Home Forum section. Wants finely crafted poems that explore and celebrate daily life; that provide a respite from daily news and from the bleakness that appears in so much contemporary verse. Considers free verse and fixed forms. Has published poetry by Diana Der-Hovanessian, Marilyn Krysl, and Michael Glaser. Publishes 1-2 poems/week. Estab. 1908.

POETRY Submit up to 5 poems at a time. Accepts submissions via online form. Pays $20/haiku; $40/poem. Does not want "work that presents people in helpless or hopeless states; poetry about death, aging, or illness; or dark, violent, sensual poems. No poems that are overtly religious or falsely sweet." Length: under 20 lines.

EBONY

Johnson Publishing Co., Inc., 820 S. Michigan Ave., Chicago IL 60605. **E-mail:** editors@ebony.com. **Website:** www.ebony.com. **Contact:** Amy D. Barnett, editorial director. Monthly magazine covering topics ranging from education and history to entertainment, art, government, health, travel, sports, and social events. "*Ebony* is the top source for an authoritative perspective on the Black-American community. *Ebony* features the best thinkers, trendsetters, hottest celebrities, and next-generation leaders of Black America. It ignites conversation, promotes empowerment, and celebrates aspiration." Circ. 11,000,000. No kill fee. Editorial lead time 3 months.

Query before submitting.

$$ FORUM

Business Journals, Inc., 1384 Broadway, 11th Floor, New York NY 10018. (212)710-7442. **E-mail:** jillianl@busjour.com. **Website:** www.forum. busjour.com. Lisa Montemorra, project manager. **Contact:** Jillian LaRochelle, managing editor. **80% freelance written.** Semiannual magazine covering luxury fashion (men's 70%, women's 30%), luxury lifestyle. *Forum* directly targets a very upscale reader interested in profiles and service pieces on upscale designers, new fashion trends, and traditional suiting. Lifestyle articles—including wine and spirits, travel, cars, boating, sports, collecting, etc.—are upscale top of the line (i.e., don't write how expensive taxis are). Circ. 150,000. Byline given. Pays on publication. Publishes ms an average of 3-4 months after acceptance. Editorial lead time 6 months. Submit seasonal material 6 months in advance. Accepts queries by mail, e-mail. Responds in 2-3 weeks to queries. Guidelines by e-mail.

NONFICTION Needs general interest, interview, travel, , luxury lifestyle trends, fashion service pieces. Does not want personal essays ("we run a few but commission them"). No fiction or single product articles; "in other words, an article should be on what's new in Italian wines, not about 1 superspecial brand." **Buys 20-25 mss/year.** Query. Length: 300-1,500 words. **Pays $300-500.**

PHOTOS State availability. Reviews GIF/JPEG files. Offers no additional payment for photos accepted with ms.

COLUMNS/DEPARTMENTS Travel, 1,000-1,500 words; Wine + Spirits, 600-1,200 words; Gourmet, 600-1,200 words; Wheels, 600 words. **Buys 10-15 mss/year.** Query. **Pays $300-500.**

TIPS "Be prepared to write like you know the upscale lifestyle. Even if you only own 1 jacket or stay in hostels, remember our readers, for the most part, don't even know about hostels! Experience in a specific category, or direct access to designers for profiles is a huge in!"

$$$$ HARPER'S MAGAZINE

666 Broadway, 11th Floor, New York NY 10012. (212)420-5720. **Fax:** (212)228-5889. **E-mail:** readings@harpers.org; scg@harpers.org. **Website:** www.

harpers.org. **Contact:** Ellen Rosenbush, editor. **90% freelance written.** Monthly magazine for well-educated, socially concerned, widely read men and women who value ideas and good writing. *Harper's Magazine* encourages national discussion on current and significant issues in a format that offers arresting facts and intelligent opinions. By means of its several shorter journalistic forms—Harper's Index, Readings, Forum, and Annotation—as well as with its acclaimed essays, fiction, and reporting, *Harper's* continues the tradition begun with its first issue in 1850: to inform readers across the whole spectrum of political, literary, cultural, and scientific affairs. Estab. 1850. Circ. 230,000. Pays on acceptance. Offers negotiable kill fee. Publishes ms an average of 3 months after acceptance. Responds in 6 weeks to queries.

Harper's Magazine will neither consider nor return unsolicited nonfiction manuscripts that have not been preceded by a written query. *Harper's* will consider unsolicited fiction. Unsolicited poetry will not be considered or returned. No queries or manuscripts will be considered unless they are accompanied by a SASE. All submissions and written queries (with the exception of Readings submissions) must be sent by mail to above address.

NONFICTION Needs humor. No interviews; no profiles. **Buys 2 mss/year.** Query. Length: 4,000-6,000 words.

REPRINTS Reprints accepted for Readings section. Send typed ms with rights for sale and information about when and where the article previously appeared.

PHOTOS Occasionally purchased with ms; others by assignment. State availability. Pays $50-500.

FICTION Will consider unsolicited fiction. Has published work by Rebecca Curtis, George Saunders, Haruki Murakami, Margaret Atwood, Allan Gurganus, Evan Connell, and Dave Bezmosgis. Needs humorous. **Buys 12 mss/year.** Submit complete ms by postal mail. Length: 3,000-5,000 words. **Generally pays 50¢-$1/word.**

TIPS "Some readers expect their magazines to clothe them with opinions in the way that Bloomingdale's dresses them for the opera. The readers of *Harper's Magazine* belong to a different crowd. They strike me as the kind of people who would rather think in their own voices and come to their own conclusions."

$ JOURNAL PLUS

654 Osos St., San Luis Obispo CA 93401. (805)544-8711; (805)546-0609. **Fax:** (805)546-8827. **E-mail:** slojournal@fix.net. **Website:** slojournal.com. **Contact:** Steve Owens, publisher. **60% freelance written.** Monthly magazine that can be read online covering the 25-year old age group and up, but young-at-heart audience. Estab. 1981. Circ. 25,000. Byline given. Pays on publication. No kill fee. Publishes ms an average of 2 months after acceptance. Editorial lead time 2 months. Submit seasonal material 2 months in advance. Accepts queries by mail. Accepts simultaneous submissions. Responds in 2 weeks to queries. Responds in 1 month to mss. Sample copy for 9x12 SAE with $2 postage. Guidelines available online.

NONFICTION Needs historical, humor, interview, personal experience, travel, book reviews, entertainment, health. Special issues: Christmas (December); Travel (October, April). No finance, automotive, heavy humor, poetry, or fiction. **Buys 60-70 mss/year.** Send complete ms. Length: 600-1,400 words. **Pays $50-75.**

PHOTOS Send photos.

TIPS "Review an issue on the website before submitting."

$$$$ NATIONAL GEOGRAPHIC

P.O. Box 98199, Washington DC 20090-8199. (202)857-7000. **Fax:** (202)828-5460. **Website:** www.nationalgeographic.com. **Contact:** Susan Goldberg, editor-in-chief; David Brindley, managing editor. **60% freelance written. Prefers to work with published/established writers.** Monthly magazine for members of the National Geographic Society. Looking for timely articles written in a compelling, "eyewitness" style. Arresting photographs that speak to the beauty, mystery, and harsh realities of life on earth. Maps of unprecedented detail and accuracy. These are the hallmarks of *National Geographic* magazine. Estab. 1888. Circ. 6,800,000. Accepts queries by mail. Guidelines available online.

NONFICTION Query (500 words with clips of published articles) by mail to editor. Do not send mss. Length: 2,000-8,000 words. Pays expenses of writers on assignment.

PHOTOS Query in care of the Photographic Division.

TIPS "State the theme(s) clearly, let the narrative flow, and build the story around strong characters and a vivid sense of place. Give us rounded episodes, logically arranged."

THE NEW YORKER

1 World Trade Center, New York NY 10007. **Website:** www.newyorker.com. **Contact:** David Remnick, editor in chief. A quality weekly magazine of distinct news stories, articles, essays, and poems for a literate audience. Estab. 1925. Circ. 938,600. Pays on acceptance. No kill fee. Accepts queries by mail, e-mail. Responds in 3 months to mss. Subscription: $59.99/year (47 issues), $29.99 for 6 months (23 issues).

The New Yorker receives approximately 4,000 submissions per month.

NONFICTION Submissions should be sent as PDF attachments. Do not paste them into the message field. Due to volume, cannot consider unsolicited "Talk of the Town" stories or other nonfiction.

FICTION Contact: fiction@newyorker.com. Publishes 1 ms/issue. Send complete ms by e-mail (as PDF attachment) or mail (address to Fiction Editor). **Payment varies.**

POETRY Contact: poetry@newyorker.com. Submit up to 6 poems at a time by e-mail (as PDF attachment) or mail (address to Poetry Department). **Pays top rates.**

TIPS "Be lively, original, not overly literary. Write what you want to write, not what you think the editor would like."

$$$$ OUTSIDE

Mariah Media, Inc., 400 Market St., Santa Fe NM 87501. (505)989-7100. **Fax:** (505)989-4700. **Website:** www.outsidemag.com. **Contact:** Axie Navas, associate managing editor. **60% freelance written.** Monthly magazine covering active lifestyle. "*Outside* is a monthly national magazine dedicated to covering the people, sports and activities, politics, art, literature, and hardware of the outdoors. Although our features are usually assigned to a regular stable of experienced and proven writers, we're always interested in new authors and their ideas. In particular, we look for articles on outdoor events, regions, and activities; informative seasonal service pieces; sports and adventure travel pieces; profiles of engaging outdoor characters; and investigative stories on environmental issues." Estab. 1977. Circ. 665,000. Byline given. Pays on acceptance. Offers 25% kill fee. Publishes ms an average of 3-6 months after acceptance. Accepts queries by mail. Responds is 6-8 weeks. Guidelines on website.

NONFICTION Needs book excerpts, new product, travel. **Buys 300 mss/year.** Query with 2 or 3 relevant clips along with a SASE to: Editorial Department at address above. "Queries should present a clear, original, and provocative thesis, not merely a topic or idea, and should reflect familiarity with the magazine's content and tone. Features are generally 1,500-5,000 words in length. Dispatches articles (100-800 words) cover timely news, events, issues, and short profiles. Destinations pieces (300-1,000 words) include places, news, and advice for adventurous travelers. Review articles (200-1,500 words) examine and evaluate outdoor gear and equipment." Length: 100-5,000 words. **Pays $1.50-2/word for assigned articles. Pays $1-1.50/word for unsolicited articles.** Pays expenses of writers on assignment.

COLUMNS/DEPARTMENTS Pays $1.50-$2/word.

$$$$ PARADE

ParadeNet, Inc., 60 E. 42nd St., New York NY 10165-1910. (212)478-1910. **Website:** parade.com. **95% freelance written.** Weekly magazine for a general interest audience. *Parade* magazine is distributed by more than 600 Sunday newspapers, including the *Atlanta Journal & Constitution, The Baltimore Sun, Boston Globe, Chicago Tribune, Dallas Morning News, Houston Chronicle, The Los Angeles Times, The Miami Herald,* the *New York Post, The Philadelphia Inquirer, San Francisco Chronicle, Seattle Times & Post Intelligencer,* and *The Washington Post.* Estab. 1941. Circ. 22,000,000. Pays on acceptance. Offers kill fee. Kill fee varies in amount. Publishes ms an average of 5 months after acceptance. Editorial lead time 1 month. Accepts queries by mail, online submission form. Accepts simultaneous submissions. Sample copy and guidelines available online.

NONFICTION Spot news events are not accepted, as *Parade* has a 2-month lead time. No fiction, fashion, travel, poetry, cartoons, nostalgia, regular columns, personal essays, quizzes, or fillers. Unsolicited queries concerning celebrities, politicians or sports figures are rarely assigned. **Buys 150 mss/year.** Query with published clips. Length: 1,200-1,500 words. **Pays very competitive amount.** Pays expenses of writers on assignment.

TIPS "If the writer has a specific expertise in the proposed topic, it increases the chances of breaking in. Send a well-researched, well-written one-page proposal and enclose a SASE. Do not submit completed mss."

$$$$ ROBB REPORT

CurtCo Robb Media, LLC, 29160 Heathercliff Rd., Suite #200, Malibu CA 90265. (310)589-7700. **Fax:** (310)589-7701. **E-mail:** editorial@robbreport.com. **Website:** www.robbreport.com. **60% freelance written.** Monthly lifestyle magazine geared toward active, affluent readers. Addresses upscale autos, luxury travel, boating, technology, lifestyles, watches, fashion, sports, investments, collectibles. "For over 30 years, *Robb Report* magazine has served as the definitive authority on connoisseurship for ultra-affluent consumers. *Robb Report* not only showcases the products and services available from the most prestigious luxury brands around the globe, but it also provides its sophisticated readership with detailed insight into a range of these subjects, which include sports and luxury automobiles, yachts, real estate, travel, private aircraft, fashion, fine jewelry and watches, art, wine, state-of-the-art home electronics, and much more. For connoisseurs seeking the very best that life has to offer, *Robb Report* remains the essential luxury resource." Estab. 1976. Circ. 104,000. Byline given. Pays on publication. Offers 25% kill fee. Submit seasonal material 5 months in advance. Accepts queries by mail, fax. Responds in 2 months to queries; in 1 month to mss. Sample copy: $14, plus s&h.

NONFICTION Needs new product, autos, boats, aircraft, watches, consumer electronics, travel, international and domestic, dining. Special issues: Home (October); Recreation (March). **Buys 60 mss/year.** Query with published clips. Length: 500-2,000 words. **Pays $1/word.** Sometimes pays expenses of writers on assignment.

PHOTOS State availability. Payment depends on article.

TIPS "Show zest in your writing, immaculate research, and strong thematic structure, and you can handle most any assignment. We want to put the reader there, whether the article is about test driving a car, fishing for marlin, or touring a luxury home. The best articles will be those that tell compelling stories. Anecdotes should be used liberally, especially for leads, and the fun should show in your writing."

$ SENIOR LIVING

Stratis Publishing Ltd., 153, 1581-H Hillside Ave., Victoria BC V8T 2CI Canada. (250)479-4705. **Fax:** (250)479-4808. **E-mail:** editor@seniorlivingmag.com. **Website:** www.seniorlivingmag.com. **Contact:** Bobbie Jo Reid, managing editor. **100% freelance written.** Magazine published 12 times/year covering active 50+ living. "Inspiring editorial profiling 'seniors' (50+) who are active and lead interesting lives. Includes articles on health, housing, accessibility, sports, travel, recipes, etc." Estab. 2004. Circ. 41,000. Byline given. Pays quarterly. No kill fee. Publishes an average of 2-3 months after acceptance. Editorial lead time 3 months. Submit seasonal material 6 months in advance. Accepts queries by e-mail. Accepts simultaneous submissions. Sample copy available online. Guidelines available.

NONFICTION Needs historical, how-to, humor, inspirational, interview, personal experience, travel, active living for 50+. All editorial must be about or reflect the lifestyles of people living in British Columbia. Does not want politics, religion, promotion of business, service or products, humor that demeans 50+ demographic or aging process. **Buys 150 mss/year.** Query. Does not accept previously published material. Length: 500-1,200 words. **Pays $35-150 for assigned articles. Pays $35-150 for unsolicited articles.** Sometimes pays expenses (limit agreed upon in advance).

PHOTOS Send photos. Identification of subjects, model releases required. Reviews GIF/JPEG files. Offers $10-75 per photo.

COLUMNS/DEPARTMENTS Buys 5-6 mss/yr mss/year. Query with published clips. **Pays $25-$50.**

TIPS "All editorial must be about or reflect the lifestyles of people living in British Columbia."

$ SPOON

315 Eastern SE, Grand Rapids MI 49503. (616)245-8633; (616)328-4090. **E-mail:** edholman@rocketmail.com. **Contact:** Ed Holman, poetry editor. "A creative newsletter by and for homeless and disempowered people in the Heartside area of Grand Rapids. We accept material from everywhere." Estab. 2004. Publishes ms 2 months after acceptance. Accepts queries by mail, e-mail. Responds in 1 month. Sometimes comments on rejected poems. Sample copy for $1.50. Guidelines available by e-mail.

Bimonthly. Magazine-size with offset printing, no binding; rarely includes ads. Receives 140 poems/year, accepts about 15-20%. Press run is 1,000. No reading fees. Never publishes theme issues. Never sends prepublication galleys. Single copy: $3; subscription: $15/year. Sample copy for $1.50. Make checks payable to: Cathy Needham, memo: *Spoon.* as published poetry by Edward Holman, Cathy Bousma Richa, Walter Mathews, Tammy Reindle. Considers poetry by children/teens. Reads submissions year round.

POETRY "Does not want vulgar poetry 'for shock value;' however, if a poem has a serious meaning we won't silence it." Submit maximum 3 poems. **Pays $5 per accepted submission.**

TIPS "Read, write, and be passionate."

HEALTH AND FITNESS

$$ CLIMBING

Cruz Bay Publishing, Inc., 2520 55th St., Suite 210, Boulder CO 80302. (303)625-1600. **Fax:** (303)440-3618. **E-mail:** sdavis@climbing.com. **E-mail:** contribute@climbing.com. **Website:** www.climbing.com. Magazine published 9 times/year covering climbing and mountaineering. Provides features on rock climbing and mountaineering worldwide. Estab. 1970. Circ. 51,000. Pays on publication. No kill fee. Editorial lead time 6 weeks. Accepts queries by e-mail. Sample copy for $4.99. Guidelines available online.

"We pride ourselves on running the best, most exciting, and most experimental climbing photography and writing in the world. We're glad that you are interested in helping us convey passion and creativity for the sport."

NONFICTION Needs interview, interesting climbers, personal experience, climbing adventures, surveys of different areas. Query. Length: 1,500-3,500 words. **Pays 35¢/word.**

PHOTOS State availability. Reviews negatives, 35mm transparencies, prints, digital submissions on CD. Pays $25-800.

COLUMNS/DEPARTMENTS Query. **Payment varies.**

$$$$ FITNESS MAGAZINE

Meredith Corp., 805 Third Ave., 25th Floor, New York NY 10022. **E-mail:** fitquestions@fitnessmagazine.com. **Website:** www.fitnessmagazine.com. **Contact:** Kathy Green, managing editor. Monthly magazine for women in their 20s and 30s who are interested in fitness and living a healthy life. Fitness magazine motivates women to move—for fun, for health, for life. With workouts and diet plans that get results, plus inspiring beauty and health tips, *Fitness* empowers women to be fierce about reaching for and achieving body success, however they define it. Circ. 1.5 million. Byline given. Pays on acceptance. Offers 20% kill fee. Responds in 2 months to queries.

NONFICTION Buys 60-80 mss/year. Query. Length: 1,500-2,500 words. Pays expenses of writers on assignment.

REPRINTS Send photocopy. Negotiates fee.

COLUMNS/DEPARTMENTS Length: 600-1,200 words. **Buys 30 mss/year.** Query.

TIPS "Our pieces must get inside the mind of the reader and address her needs, hopes, fears, and desires. *Fitness* acknowledges that getting and staying fit is difficult in an era when we are all time-pressured."

MUSCLEMAG

Robert Kennedy Publishing, Inc., 400 Matheson Blvd. W., Mississauga ON L5R 3M1. **E-mail:** editorial@musclemag.com. **Website:** www.musclemag.com. **80% freelance written.** Covers hardcore bodybuilding. Monthly magazine on building health, fitness, and physique. Byline given. Pays on acceptance. No kill fee. Publishes ms an average of 6 months after acceptance. Accepts queries by mail, e-mail. Responds in 4 months to queries.; in 4 months to mss.

NONFICTION Needs how-to, interview, new product, personal experience, photo feature, bodybuilding, strenth training, health, nutrition, fitness. **Pays $80-400 for assigned, accepted articles submitted on spec.**

PHOTOS Send photos. Captions, identification of subjects required. Reviews 35mm transparencies, 8x10 prints, and hi-res digital images 300 dpi or higher.

FILLERS Needs anecdotes, facts, gags, newsbreaks, fitness, nutrition, health, short humor. **Buys 50-100 mss/year.** Length: 100-200 words.

TIPS "Send in unedited sample articles on training or nutrition to be assessed. Those writers accepted may be added to our roster of freelance writers for future article assignments."

$$$ OXYGEN

Robert Kennedy Publishing, 400 Matheson Blvd. W., Mississauga ON L5R 3M1 Canada. (905)507-3545; (888)254-0767. **Fax:** (905)507-2372. **Website:** www.oxygenmag.com. **70% freelance written.** Monthly magazine covering women's health and fitness. *Oxygen* encourages various exercise, good nutrition to shape, and condition the body. Estab. 1997. Circ. 340,000. Byline given. Pays on acceptance. Offers 25% kill fee. Publishes ms an average of 4 months after acceptance. Editorial lead time 3 months. Submit seasonal material 6 months in advance. Accepts queries by mail, fax. Responds in 5 weeks to queries. Responds in 2 months to mss. Sample copy for $5.

NONFICTION Needs expose, how-to, training and nutrition, humor, inspirational, interview, new product, personal experience, photo feature. No poorly researched articles that do not genuinely help the readers toward physical fitness, health, and physique. **Buys 100 mss/year.** Send complete ms with SASE and $5 for return postage. Length: 1,400-1,800 words. **Pays $250-1,000.** Sometimes pays expenses of writers on assignment.

PHOTOS State availability of or send photos. Identification of subjects required. Reviews contact sheets, 35mm transparencies, prints. Offers $35-500.

COLUMNS/DEPARTMENTS Nutrition (low-fat recipes), 1,700 words; Weight Training (routines and techniques), 1,800 words; Aerobics (how-tos), 1,700 words. **Buys 50 mss/year.** Send complete ms. **Pays $150-500.**

TIPS "Every editor of every magazine is looking, waiting, hoping and praying for the magic article. The beauty of the writing has to spring from the page; the edge imparted has to excite the reader because of its unbelievable information."

REMEDYMD HEALTH GUIDES

Remedy Health Media, 750 Third Ave., 6th Floor, New York NY 10017. (212)695-2223. **Fax:** (212)695-2936. **Website:** www.remedyhealthmedia.com. Magazine published 8 times/year, dealing with specific and current health issues in each issue. See editorial calendar online for details.

This magazine is closed to submissions.

WOMEN'S HEALTH & FITNESS

Blitz Publications, P.O. Box 4075, Mulgrave VIC 3170 Australia. (61)(3)9574-8999. **Fax:** (61)(3)9574-8899. **E-mail:** rebecca@blitzmag.com.au. **Website:** www.womenshealthandfitness.com.au. **Contact:** Rebecca Long, editor. Monthly glossy magazine covering health, fitness, beauty, sex, and travel. *Women's Health & Fitness Magazine* is a holistic guide to a happier and healthier lifestyle, offering information on weight training, nutrition, mental well-being, health, beauty, fat loss, life coaching, home workouts, low-fat recipes, fitness fashion, fitness tips, diet, supplementation, natural remedies, pregnancy, and body shaping. Estab. 1994.

NONFICTION Needs general interest, how-to, new product. Query.

YOGA JOURNAL

Active Interest Media, Healthy Living Group, 475 Sansome St., Suite 850, San Francisco CA 94111. (415)591-0555. **Fax:** (415)591-0733. **E-mail:** queries@yjmag.com. **Website:** www.yogajournal.com. **Contact:** Kaitlin Quistgaard, editor-in-chief. **75% freelance written.** Magazine published 9 times a year covering the practice and philosophy of yoga. Estab. 1975. Circ. 300,000. Byline given. Pays within 90 days of acceptance. Offers kill fee. Offers kill fee on assigned articles. Publishes ms an average of 10 months after acceptance. Submit seasonal material 7 months in advance. Accepts queries by e-mail. Responds in 6 weeks to queries if interested. Sample copy for $4.99. Guidelines on website.

NONFICTION Needs book excerpts, how-to, yoga, exercise, inspirational, yoga or related, interview, opinion, photo feature, travel, yoga-related. Does not want unsolicited poetry or cartoons. "Please avoid New Age jargon and in-house buzz words as much as possible." **Buys 50-60 mss/year.** Query with SASE. Length: 3,000-5,000 words. **Pays $800-2,000.**

REPRINTS Send tearsheet or photocopy with rights for sale noted and information about when and where the material previously appeared.

COLUMNS/DEPARTMENTS Om: Covers myriad aspects of the yoga lifestyle (150-400 words). This department includes Yoga Diary, a 250-word story about a pivotal moment in your yoga practice. Eating Wisely: A popular, 1,400-word department about relationship to food. Most stories focus on vegetarian and whole-foods cooking, nutritional healing, and contemplative pieces about the relationship between yoga and food. Yoga Scene:Featured on the back page of the magazine, this photo depicts some expression of your yoga practice. Please tell us where the photo is from, what was going on during the moment the photo was taken, and any other information that will help put the photo into context. E-mail a well-written query.

TIPS "Please read several issues of *Yoga Journal* before submitting a query. Pitch your article idea to the appropriate department with the projected word count, and what sources you'd use. In your query letter, please indicate your writing credentials. If we are interested in your idea, we will require writing samples. Please note that we do not accept unsolicited mss for any departments except Yoga Diary, a first person, 250-word story that tells about a pivotal moment in the writer's yoga experience (diary@yjmag.com). Please read our writer's guidelines before submission. Do not e-mail or fax unsolicited mss."

HISTORY

AMERICAN HISTORY

Weider History Group, 19300 Promenade Dr., Leesburg VA 20176. **E-mail:** americanhistory@historynet.com. **Website:** www.historynet.com/magazines/american_history. **Contact:** Roger L. Vance, editor. **60% freelance written.** Bimonthly magazine of cultural, social, military, and political history published for a general audience. "Presents the history of America to a broad spectrum of general-interest readers in an authoritative, informative, thought-provoking, and entertaining style. Lively narratives take readers on an adventure with history, complemented by rare photographs, paintings, illustrations, and maps." Estab. 1966. Circ. 95,000. Byline given. Pays on acceptance. No kill fee. Responds in 10 weeks to queries. Sample copy: $6. Guidelines for #10 SASE or by e-mail.

NONFICTION Needs Key prerequisites for publication are thorough research and accurate presentation, precise English usage, and sound organization, a lively style, and a high level of human interest. *Unsolicited manuscripts not considered.* Inappropriate materials include: book reviews, travelogues, personal/family narratives not of national significance, articles about collectibles/antiques, living artists, local/individual historic buildings/landmarks, and articles of a current editorial nature. **Buys 20 mss/year.** Query by mail or e-mail with published clips. Length: 2,000-4,000 words depending on type of article.

PHOTOS Welcomes suggestions for illustrations.

TIPS "We feel that the best guidelines for writing for our magazines are our magazines themselves. If you are interested in submitting a query or writing for our magazines, please pick up several issues from the past few months and read through them. By doing this, you can gain a better sense of the type of writing we are looking for here at the Weider History Group."

ⓈⓈ AMERICA'S CIVIL WAR

Weider History Group, 19300 Promenade Dr., Leesburg VA 20176-6500. (703)771-9400. **Fax:** (703)779-8345. **E-mail:** acw@weiderhistorygroup.com. **Website:** www.historynet.com/americas-civil-war. **Contact:** Tamela Baker, editor. **60% freelance written.** Bimonthly magazine covering popular history and straight historical narrative for both the general reader and the American Civil War buff featuring firsthand accounts, remarkable photos, expert commentary, and maps in making the whole story of the most pivotal era in American history accessible and showing why it still matters in the 21st century. Estab. 1988. Circ. 78,000. Byline given. Pays on publication. No kill fee. Accepts queries by e-mail. Sample copy for $5.99. Guidelines available by e-mail.

NONFICTION Needs historical, book notices, preservation news. **Buys 18 mss/year.** "Query. Submit a page outlining the subject and your approach to it, and why you believe this would be an important article for the magazine. Briefly summarize your prior writing experience in a cover note." Length: 3,500 words; 250-word sidebar. **Pays $300 and up.**

PHOTOS Send photos with submission or cite sources. Captions, identification of subjects required.

TIPS "All stories must be true. We do not publish fiction or poetry. Write an entertaining, well-researched, informative and unusual story that grabs the reader's attention and holds it. Submit queries or mss by e-mail. All submissions are on speculation."

Ⓢ THE ARTILLERYMAN

Historical Publications, Inc., 234 Monarch Hill Rd., Tunbridge VT 05077. (802)889-3500. **Fax:** (802)889-5627. **E-mail:** mail@artillerymanmagazine.com. **Website:** www.artillerymanmagazine.com. **Contact:** Kathryn Jorgensen, editor. **60% freelance written.** Quarterly magazine covering antique artillery, fortifications, and crew-served weapons 1750-1900 for competition shooters, collectors, and living history reenactors using artillery. Estab. 1979. Circ. 1,200. Byline given. Pays on publication. Publishes ms an average of 6 months after acceptance. Accepts queries by mail, e-mail, fax. Accepts simultaneous submissions. Responds in 3 weeks to queries. Sample copy and writer's guidelines for 9x12 SAE with 4 first-class stamps.

NONFICTION Needs historical, how-to, interview, photo feature, technical, travel. **Buys 12 mss/year.** Send complete ms. Length: 300 words minimum. **Pays $40-60.**

PHOTOS Send photos. Captions, identification of subjects required. Pays $15 for color or b&w digital prints.

TIPS "We regularly use freelance contributions for Places-to-Visit and Unit Profiles departments and welcome pieces on unusual cannon or cannon with a known and unique history. Writers should ask themselves if they could knowledgeably talk artillery with an expert."

$$$ CIVIL WAR TIMES

Weider History Group, 19300 Promenade Dr., Leesburg VA 20176-6500. **E-mail:** civilwartimes@weiderhistorygroup.com; cwt@weiderhistorygroup.com. **Website:** www.historynet.com. **Contact:** Dana B. Shoaf, editor. **90% freelance written. Works with a small number of new/unpublished writers each year.** Magazine published 6 times/year covering the history of the American Civil War. "*Civil War Times* is the full-spectrum magazine of the Civil War. Specifically, we look for nonpartisan coverage of battles, prominent military and civilian figures, the home front, politics, military technology, common soldier life, prisoners and escapes, period art and photography, the naval war, blockade-running, specific regiments, and much more." Estab. 1962. Circ. 108,000. Pays on acceptance and on publication. Publishes ms an average of 18 months after acceptance. Submit seasonal material 1 year in advance. Responds in 3-6 months to queries. Sample copy: $6. Guidelines for #10 SASE or by e-mail.

NONFICTION Needs interview, photo feature, Civil War historical material. "Don't send us a comprehensive article on a well-known major battle. Instead, focus on some part or aspect of such a battle, or some group of soldiers in the battle. Similar advice applies to major historical figures like Lincoln and Lee. Positively no fiction or poetry." **Buys 20 freelance mss/year.** Query by mail or e-mail with published clips. **Pays $75-800.**

TIPS "We're very open to new submissions. Send query after examining writer's guidelines and several recent issues. Include photocopies of photos that could feasibly accompany the article. Confederate soldiers' diaries and letters are especially welcome."

$ GOOD OLD DAYS

Annie's, 306 E. Parr Rd., Berne IN 46711. **Fax:** (260)589-8093. **E-mail:** editor@goodolddaysmagazine.com. **Website:** www.goodolddaysmagazine.com. **Contact:** Mary Beth Weisenburger, editor. **75% freelance written.** Bimonthly magazine of first-person nostalgia, 1935-1965. "We look for strong narratives showing life as it was in the middle decades of the 20th century. Our readership is composed of nostalgia buffs, history enthusiasts, and the people who actually lived and grew up in this era." Byline given. Pays on contract. No kill fee. Publishes ms an average of 8 months after acceptance. Submit seasonal material 10 months in advance. Accepts queries by e-mail, fax. Responds in 2 months to queries. Sample copy: $2. Guidelines available online.

Queries accepted but are not necessary.

NONFICTION Needs historical, humor, personal experience, photo feature, favorite food/recipes, year-round seasonal material, biography, memorable events, fads, fashion, sports, music, literature, entertainment. No fiction accepted. **Buys 350 mss/year.** Query or send complete ms. Length: 500-1,500 words. **Pays $15-50, depending on quality and photos.**

PHOTOS Do not send original photos until we ask for them. You may send photocopies or duplicates. Do not submit laser-copied prints. Send photos. Identification of subjects required.

TIPS "Most of our writers are not professionals. We prefer the author's individual voice, warmth, humor, and honesty over technical ability."

$ LEBEN

City Seminary Press, 2150 River Plaza Dr., Suite 150, Sacramento CA 95833. **Website:** www.leben.us. **40% freelance written.** Quarterly magazine presenting the people and events of Christian history from a Reformation perspective. Not a theological journal, per se, but rather a popular history magazine. Estab. 2004. Circ. 5,000. Byline given. Pays on acceptance. Offers 25% kill fee. Publishes ms an average of 6 months after acceptance. Editorial lead time 6 months. Submit seasonal material 6 months in advance. Accepts queries by online submission form. Accepts simultaneous submissions. Responds in 3 weeks to queries; in 2 months to mss. Sample copy: $1.50 (order online or request via e-mail). Guidelines by e-mail.

NONFICTION Needs historical and biographical material related to Protestant and Reformation subjects. Does not want articles that argue theological issues. "There is a place for that, but not in a popular history/biography magazine aimed at general readership." Query. Length: 500-2,500 words. **Pays 5¢/word for original material.**

TIPS "Visit our website and read our publication. We are a niche magazine, but a person knowledgeable about the Reformation should be able to write for us."

MHQ: THE QUARTERLY JOURNAL OF MILITARY HISTORY

Weider History Group, 19300 Promenade Dr., Leesburg VA 20176-6500. **E-mail:** mhq@historynet.com. **Website:** www.historynet.com/magazines/mhq. **Contact:** Dr. Michael W. Robbins, editor. **100% freelance written.** Quarterly journal covering military history. "*MHQ* offers readers in-depth articles on the history of warfare from ancient times into the 21st century. Authoritative features and departments cover military strategies, philosophies, campaigns, battles, personalities, weaponry, espionage, and perspectives, all written in a lively and readable style. Articles are accompanied by classic works of art, photographs, and maps. Readers include serious students of military tactics, strategy, leaders, and campaigns, as well as general world history enthusiasts. Many readers are currently in the military or retired officers." Estab. 1988. Circ. 22,000. Byline given. Pays on publication. No kill fee. Editorial lead time 1 year. Submit seasonal material 1 year in advance. Accepts queries by mail, e-mail. Accepts simultaneous submissions. Sample copy: $6. Writer's guidelines for #10 SASE or via e-mail.

NONFICTION Needs historical, personal experience, photo feature. No fiction or stories pertaining to collectibles or reenactments. **Buys 36 mss/year.** Query by mail or e-mail with published clips. Length: 1,500-6,000 words.

PHOTOS Send photos/art with submission. Identification of subjects required. Reviews transparencies, prints. Negotiates payment individually.

COLUMNS/DEPARTMENTS Artists on War (description of artwork of a military nature); Experience of War (first-person accounts of military incidents); Strategic View (discussion of military theory, strategy); Arms & Men (description of military hardware or unit), all up to 2,500 words. **Buys 16 mss/year.** Send complete ms.

TIPS "Less common topic areas—medieval, Asian, or South American military history, for example—are more likely to attract our attention. The likelihood that articles can be effectively illustrated often determines the ultimate fate of mss. Many otherwise excellent articles have been rejected due to a lack of suitable art or photographs. While the information we publish is scholarly and substantive, we prefer writing that is anecdotal, and, above all, engaging rather than didactic."

MILITARY HISTORY

Weider History Group, 19300 Promenade Dr., Leesburg VA 20176. **E-mail:** militaryhistory@historynet.com. **Website:** www.historynet.com/magazines/military_history. **Contact:** Stephen Harding, editor. **70% freelance written.** Magazine published 6 times/year covering world military history of all ages. "We strive to give the general reader accurate, highly readable, often narrative popular history, richly accompanied by period art." Byline given. Pays upon publication. No kill fee. Submit seasonal material 1 year in advance. Accepts queries by mail, e-mail. Sample copy: $6. Guidelines for #10 SASE or by e-mail.

NONFICTION Needs historical, interview, military figures of commanding interest, personal experience (only occasionally). **Buys 20-30 mss/year.** Query by mail or e-mail with published clips. Length: 2,000-3,000 words with a 200- to 500-word sidebar.

COLUMNS/DEPARTMENTS Interview; What We Learned (lessons from history); Valor (those who have earned medals/awards); Hallowed Ground (battlegrounds of significance); and Reviews (books, video, games, all relating to military history). Length: 700-1,300 words.

TIPS "We seek professional submissions that are thoroughly researched and fact-checked and adhere to the *Associated Press Stylebook*."

$$ PERSIMMON HILL

1700 NE 63rd St., Oklahoma City OK 73111. (405)478-2250, ext. 213. **Fax:** (405)478-4714. **E-mail:** editor@nationalcowboymuseum.org. **Website:** www.nationalcowboymuseum.org. **Contact:** Judy Hilovsky. **70% freelance written. Prefers to work with published/established writers; works with a small number of new/unpublished writers each year.** Biannual magazine for an audience interested in Western art, Western history, ranching, and rodeo, including historians, artists, ranchers, art galleries, schools, and libraries. Publication of the National Cowboy and Western Heritage Museum. Estab. 1970. Circ. 7,500. Byline given. Pays on publication. No kill fee. Publishes ms an average of 18 months after acceptance. Responds in 3 months to queries. Sample copy for $11. Writer's guidelines available on website.

NONFICTION **Buys 50-75 mss/year.** Query with clips. Length: 1,500 words. **Pays $150-300.**

PHOTOS Purchased with ms or on assignment. Captions required. Reviews digital images and b&w prints. Pays according to quality and importance for b&w and color photos.

TIPS "Send us a story that captures the spirit of adventure and indvidualism that typifies the Old West or reveals a facet of the Western lifestyle in comtemporary society. Excellent illustrations for articles are essential! We lean towards scholarly, historical, well-researched articles. We're less focused on Western celebrities than some of the other contemporary Western magazines."

PRESERVATION MAGAZINE

National Trust for Historic Preservation, 2600 Virginia Ave. NW, Suite 1000, Washington DC 20037. (202)588-6388. **E-mail:** preservation@savingplaces.org. **Website:** www.preservationonline.org. **Contact:** Dennis Hockman, editor in chief. **75% freelance written. Prefers to work with published/established writers.** Bimonthly magazine covering preservation of historic buildings and neighborhoods in the U.S. "We cover subjects related in some way to place. Most entries are features, department, or opinion pieces." Circ. 250,000. Byline given. Pays on publication. Offers variable kill fee. Publishes ms an average of 2 months after acceptance. Accepts queries by e-mail, phone. Responds in 2 months to queries.

NONFICTION Needs book excerpts, essays, historical, humor, interview, opinion, photo feature, travel, news. **Buys 30 mss/year.** Query with published clips. Length: 500-3,500 words. Sometimes pays expenses of writers on assignment.

TIPS "Do not send or propose histories of buildings, descriptive accounts of cities or towns, or long-winded treatises. Best bet for breaking in is via Preservation Online, Reporter (news features, 500-1,000 words), House Rules (brief profile or article, 500-800 words)."

TOMBIGBEE COUNTRY MAGAZINE

P.O. Box 621, Gu-Win AL 35563. (205)412-1272. **E-mail:** tombigbeecountrymagazine@yahoo.com. **Website:** www.tombigbeecountry.com. **Contact:** Bo Webster, editor. **50% freelance written.** Monthly magazine covering nostalgia and history. *Tombigbee Country* is a magazine dedicated to the old time tales, history, and humor of northeast Mississippi and northwest Alabama. *Tombigbee Country* is a regional, nostalgia, monthly magazine which features human-interest articles concerning the area surrounding the Upper Tombigbee River (Tenn-Tom Waterway). "We take pride in being a country magazine that uses a mixture of irony, wit, and humor with good folk history." Estab. 2,000. Circ. 10,000. Byline given. Pays on publication. No kill fee. Publishes ms an average of 1 month after acceptance. Editorial lead time 2 months. Submit seasonal material 2 months in advance. Accepts queries by mail, e-mail. Accepts simultaneous submissions. Responds in 1 week to queries. Responds in 1 month to mss. Sample copy $2. Guidelines free.

NONFICTION Needs book excerpts, essays, general interest, historical, humor, inspirational, personal experience, religious. "We do not want tributes to family members." **Buys 24+ mss/year.** Query. "We are eager for stories on personal experience with celebrities—country musicians, famous southerners." Length: 800-2,000 words. **Pays $24 for assigned articles. Pays $24 for unsolicited articles.**

FILLERS Needs short humor. Length: 25-800 words.

TIPS "Ask yourself, would this article be of interest to an elder southerner?"

TRAINS

Kalmbach Publishing Co., P.O. Box 1612, Waukesha WI 53187-1612. (262)796-8776. **Fax:** (262)796-1142. **E-mail:** editor@trainsmag.com; photoeditor@trainsmag.com. **Website:** www.trn.trains.com. **Contact:** Jim Wrinn, editor; Tom Danneman, art director. Monthly magazine covering railroading. "Appeals to consumers interested in learning about the function and history of the railroad industry." Estab. 1940. Circ. 92,419. No kill fee. Editorial lead time 2 months.

Query before submitting.

NONFICTION *Trains* buys news stories and feature articles covering railroading's past and present, including first-person recollections. Before submitting a feature-length article, send a written query via e-mail. Send a brief paragraph explaining the story, its theme, and highlights. Queries should include a possible headline. **Payment: 10¢/word.**

VIETNAM

Weider History Group, 19300 Promenade Dr., Leesburg VA 20176-6500. **E-mail:** vietnam@historynet.com. **Website:** www.historynet.com/vietnam-war. **Contact:** Chuck Springston, editor. **90% freelance written.** Bimonthly magazine providing in-depth and authoritative accounts of the many complexities that made the war in Vietnam unique, including the people, battles, strategies, perspectives, analysis, and weaponry. Estab. 1988. Circ. 46,000. Byline given. Pays on publication. No kill fee. Accepts queries by mail, e-mail. Sample copy: $6. Guidelines for #10 SASE or by e-mail.

NONFICTION Needs historical, military, interview, personal experience. "Absolutely no fiction or poetry; we want straight history, as much personal narrative as possible, but not the gung-ho, shoot-'em-up variety, either." **Buys 24 mss/year.** Query by mail or e-mail with published clips. Length: up to 4,000 words with 500-word sidebar.

PHOTOS Send photos with submission, or state availability and cite sources. Identification of subjects required.

COLUMNS/DEPARTMENTS Arsenal (about weapons used, all sides); Personality (profiles of the players, all sides); Fighting Forces (various units or types of units: air, sea, rescue); Perspectives. Length: 2,000 words. Query.

TIPS "Choose stories with strong art possibilities. All stories must be true, carefully researched third-person articles or firsthand accounts that give the reader a sense of experiencing historical events."

$$ WILD WEST

Weider History Group, 19300 Promenade Dr., Leesburg VA 20176-6500. **E-mail:** wildwest@weiderhistorygroup.com. **Website:** www.historynet.com. **Contact:** Gregory J. Lalire, editor. **95% freelance written.** Bimonthly magazine covering the history of the American frontier, from its eastern beginnings to its western terminus. "*Wild West* covers the popular (narrative) history of the American West—events, trends, personalities, anything of general interest." Estab. 1988. Circ. 83,500. Byline given. Pays on publication. No kill fee. Publishes ms an average of 2 years after acceptance. Editorial lead time 10 months. Submit seasonal material 1 year in advance. Accepts queries by mail, e-mail. Accepts simultaneous submissions. Responds in 3 months to queries; in 6 months to mss. Sample copy: $6. Writer's guidelines for #10 SASE or online.

NONFICTION Needs historical, Old West. No excerpts, travel, etc. Articles can be adapted from book. No fiction or poetry. Nothing current. **Buys 36 mss/year.** Query. Length: 3,500 words with a 500-word sidebar. **Pays $300.**

PHOTOS State availability. Captions, identification of subjects required. Reviews negatives, transparencies. Offers no additional payment for photos accepted with ms.

COLUMNS/DEPARTMENTS Gunfighters & Lawmen, 2,000 words; Westerners, 2,000 words; Warriors & Chiefs, 2,000 words; Western Lore, 2,000 words; Guns of the West, 1,500 words; Artists West, 1,500 words; Books Reviews, 250 words. **Buys 36 mss/year.** Query. **Pays $150 for departments; book reviews paid by the word, minimum $40.**

TIPS "Always query the editor with your story idea. Successful queries include a description of sources of information and suggestions for color and b&w photography or artwork. The best way to break into our magazine is to write an entertaining, informative, and unusual story that grabs the reader's attention and holds it. We favor carefully researched, third-person articles that give the reader a sense of experiencing historical events."

$$$ WORLD WAR II

Weider History Group, 19300 Promenade Dr., Leesburg VA 20176. **E-mail:** worldwar2@weiderhistorygroup.com. **Website:** www.historynet.com/world-war-ii. **Contact:** Karen Jensen, editor. **25% freelance written. "Most of our stories are assigned by our staff to professional writers. However, we do accept written proposals for features and for our Time Travel department."** Bimonthly magazine covering military operations in World War II—events, personalities, strategy, the home front, etc. Estab. 1986. Circ. 146,000. Byline given. Pays on acceptance. Offers kill fee. Accepts queries by mail, e-mail. Writer's guidelines available on website or for SASE.

NONFICTION No fiction. **Buys 24 mss/year.** Query by mail or e-mail with published clips. "Your proposal should convince the editors to cover the subject, describe how you would treat the subject, and give the editors an opportunity to judge your writing ability. Please include your writing credentials and background with your proposal. A familiarity with recent issues of the magazine is the best guide to our editorial needs." Length: 2,500-4,000 words.

HOBBY AND CRAFT

$$$$ AMERICAN CRAFT

American Craft Council, 1224 Marshall St. NE, Suite 200, Minneapolis MN 55413. (612)206-3115. **E-mail:** mmoses@craftcouncil.org. **E-mail:** query@craftcouncil.org. **Website:** www.americancraftmag.org. **Contact:** Monica Moses, editor in chief. **75% freelance written.** Bimonthly magazine covering art, craft, design. Estab. 1943. Circ. 40,000. Byline given. Pays 30 days after acceptance. Offers 25% kill fee. Publishes ms an average of 2 months after acceptance. Editorial lead time 3 months. Submit seasonal material 3 months in advance. Accepts queries by mail, e-mail. Accepts simultaneous submissions. Responds in 1 month to queries; in 2 months to mss. Guidelines online.

NONFICTION Needs craft artist profiles and stories, craft shows, craft theory or history. Query with images. Include medium (glass, clay, fiber, metal, wood, paper, etc.) and department in subject line. Length: 1,200-3,000 words. Pays expenses of writers on assignment.

COLUMNS/DEPARTMENTS On Our Radar (profiles of emerging artists doing remarkable work); Product Placement (stylish, inventive, practical, and generally affordable goods in production and the people who design them); Shop Talk (Q&A with owners of galleries); Material Matters (an artist using unusual material to make amazing craft); Personal Paths (an artist doing very individual—even idiosyncratic—work from a personal motivation), Spirit of Craft (art forms that might not typically be considered fine craft but may entail the sort of devotion generally associated with craft); Craft in Action (artists or organizations using craft to make the world better); Crafted Lives (photo-driven Q&A with a person or people living in a particularly creative space); Ideas (Q&A with a thinker or practitioner whose views represent a challenge to the status quo); Wide World of Craft (foreign or U.S. travel destination for craft lovers). **Buys 10-12 mss/year.** Query with published clips.

TIPS "Keep pitches short and sweet, a paragraph or 2 at most. Please include visuals with any pitches."

$$ BEAD & BUTTON

Kalmbach Publishing, P.O. Box 1612, 21027 Crossroads Circle, Waukesha WI 53187-1612. **E-mail:** editor@beadandbutton.com. **Website:** www.beadandbutton.com. **Contact:** Julia Gerlach, editor. **50% freelance written.** "*Bead & Button* is a bimonthly magazine devoted to techniques, projects, designs, and materials relating to making beaded jewelry. Our readership includes both professional and amateur bead and button makers, hobbyists, and enthusiasts who find satisfaction in making beautiful things." Estab. 1994. Circ. 100,000. Byline given. Pays on acceptance. Offers $75 kill fee. Publishes ms an average of 4-12 months after acceptance. Editorial lead time 4-5 months. Accepts queries by e-mail. Guidelines online.

NONFICTION Needs beaded jewelry history, how-to make beaded jewelry and accessories, humor, inspirational, interview. **Buys 20-25 mss/year.** E-mail complete ms as a Word attachment, or submit through postal mail. Length: 1,000-1,200 words. **Pays $75-400.**

PHOTOS Send photos. Identification of subjects required. Offers no additional payment for photos accepted with ms.

$$ BLADE MAGAZINE

F+W, A Content and Ecommerce Company, 700 E. State St., Iola WI 54990-0001. (715)445-2214. **Fax:** (715)445-4087. **E-mail:** joe.kertzman@fwcommunity.com. **Website:** www.blademag.com. **Contact:** Joe Kertzman, managing editor. **5% freelance written.** Monthly magazine covering working and using collectible, popular knives. *Blade* prefers in-depth articles focusing on groups of knives, whether military, collectible, high-tech, pocket knives, or hunting knives, and how they perform. Estab. 1973. Circ. 39,000. Byline given. Pays on publication. No kill fee. Publishes ms an average of 9 months after acceptance. Editorial lead time 9 months. Submit seasonal material 9 months in advance. Accepts queries by mail, e-mail, fax. Responds in 3 months to queries; in 6 months to mss. Sample copy: $4.99. Guidelines for SAE with 8x11 envelope and 3 first-class stamps.

NONFICTION Needs general interest, historical, how-to, interview, new product, photo feature, technical. "We assign profiles, show stories, hammer-in stories, etc. We don't need those. If you've seen the story on the Internet or in another knife or knife/gun magazine, we don't need it. We don't do stories on knives used for self-defense." Send complete ms. Length: 700-1,400 words. **Pays $150-300.**

PHOTOS Send photos. Captions, identification of subjects required. Reviews transparencies, prints, digital images (300 dpi at 1200x1200 pixels). Offers no additional payment for photos accepted with ms.

FILLERS Needs anecdotes, facts, newsbreaks. **Buys 1-2 mss/year.** Length: 50-200 words. **Pays $25-50.**

TIPS "We are always willing to read submissions from anyone who has read a few copies and studied the market. The ideal article for us is a piece bringing out the romance, legend, and love of man's oldest tool—the knife. We like articles that place knives in peoples' hands—in life-saving situations, adventure modes, etc. (Nothing gory or with the knife as the villain.) People and knives are good copy. We are getting more well-written articles from writers who are reading the publication beforehand. That makes for a harder sell for the quickie writer not willing to do his homework. Go to knife shows and talk to the makers and collectors. Visit knifemakers' shops and knife factories. Read anything and everything you can find on knives and knifemaking."

BREW YOUR OWN

Battenkill Communications, 5515 Main St., Manchester Center VT 05255. (802)362-3981. **Fax:** (802)362-2377. **E-mail:** edit@byo.com. **Website:** www.byo.com. **Contact:** Betsy Parker, editor. **85% freelance written.** Magazine published 8 times/year covering home brewing. "Our mission is to provide practical information in an entertaining format. We try to capture the spirit and challenge of brewing while helping our readers brew the best beer they can." Estab. 1995. Circ. 50,000. Byline given. Pays on acceptance. Offers 25% kill fee. Publishes ms an average of 4 months after acceptance. Editorial lead time 3 months. Submit seasonal material 3 months in advance. Accepts queries by mail, e-mail, fax. Responds in 2 months to queries. Guidelines online.

NONFICTION Needs historical, how-to, home brewing, humor, related to home brewing, interview, of professional brewers who can offer useful tips to home hobbyists, personal experience, trends. **Buys 75 mss/year.** Query with published clips or description of brewing expertise, or submit complete ms. Length: 1,500-3,000 words. **Pays $25-200, depending on length, complexity of article, and experience of writer.** Sometimes pays expenses of writers on assignment.

PHOTOS State availability. Captions required. Reviews contact sheets, transparencies, 5x7 prints, slides, and electronic images. Negotiates payment individually.

COLUMNS/DEPARTMENTS Homebrew Nation (short first-person brewing stories and photos of homemade equipment); Last Call (humorous stories about homebrewing), 600-750 words. **Buys 12 mss/year.** Query with or without published clips. **Pays $75 for Last Call; no payment for Homebrew Nation.**

TIPS "*Brew Your Own* is for anyone who is interested in brewing beer, from beginners to advanced all-grain brewers. We seek articles that are straightforward and factual, not full of esoteric theories or complex calculations. Our readers tend to be intelligent, upscale, and literate."

CANADIAN WOODWORKING AND HOME IMPROVEMENT

Sawdust Media, Inc., 51 Maple Ave. N., RR #3, Burford ON N0E 1A0 Canada. (519)449-2444. **Fax:** (519)449-2445. **E-mail:** pfulcher@canadianwoodworking.com. **Website:** www.canadianwoodworking.com. **20% freelance written.** Bimonthly magazine covering woodworking; only accepts work from Canadian writers. Estab. 1999. Byline given. Pays on publication. Offers 50% kill fee. Accepts queries by e-mail. Sample copy available online. Guidelines by e-mail.

NONFICTION Needs how-to, humor, inspirational, new product, personal experience, photo feature, technical. Does not want profile on a woodworker. Query. Length: 500-4,000 words. **Pays $100-600 for assigned articles. Pays $50-400 for unsolicited articles.**

PHOTOS State availability. Negotiates payment individually.

CLOTH PAPER SCISSORS

Interweave Press, ATTN: CPS Submissions, 490 Boston Post Road, Suite 15, Sudbury MA 01776. **E-mail:** submissions@clothpaperscissors.com. **Website:** www.clothpaperscissors.com. "*Cloth Paper Scissors* is most interested in publishing articles that cover unique collage and mixed-media techniques geared to beginner, intermediate, or advanced artists. Feature articles may explore motifs and methods that will inspire and inform collage, fiber, and mixed-media artists. We are interested in articles focusing on fabric and paper collage techniques; paint and dye applications; handmade books; creative sketchbook keeping; art journaling; altered books techniques; ways of working with polymer clay; stitching on paper, fabric, and other media; crafting as a business and way of life; embossing techniques; digital imagery for collage; working with found objects; crafting 'green'; and stories about creating inspired studios for mixed-media artists." Accepts queries by mail, e-mail. Responds in 3 months to queries. Guidelines online.

NONFICTION Query by e-mail or mail (include SASE). Include contact information and photographs of the art or process.

TIPS "If you have a technique, project, or body of work to share, *Cloth Paper Scissors* would like to know about it. We want to show other artists—from beginners to the advanced—the latest, edgiest, most unusual collage and mixed-media techniques and applications."

$$ DOLLHOUSE MINIATURES

68132 250th Ave., Kasson MN 55944. (507)634-3143. **E-mail:** auralea@ashdown.co.uk. **Website:** www.dhminiatures.com. **70% freelance written.** Monthly magazine covering dollhouse scale miniatures. *Dollhouse Miniatures* is America's best-selling miniatures magazine and the definitive resource for artisans, collectors, and hobbyists. It promotes and supports the large national and international community of miniaturists through club columns, short reports, and by featuring reader projects and ideas. Estab. 1971. Circ. 25,000. Byline given. Pays on acceptance. Editorial lead time 6 months. Submit seasonal material 6 months in advance. Accepts queries by mail. Responds in 1 month to queries, in 2 months to mss. Sample copy: $6.95, plus shipping. Guidelines available by e-mailing submissions editor at traci@ashdown.co.uk.

NONFICTION Needs how-to, miniature projects of various scales in variety of media, interview, artisans, collectors, photo feature, dollhouses, collections, museums. No articles on miniature shops or essays. **Buys 50-60 mss/year.** Send complete ms. Length: 500-1,500 words. **Pays $30-250 for assigned articles and $0-150 for unsolicited articles.**

PHOTOS Send digital photos. Captions, identification of subjects required. Reviews 3x5 prints. Photos are paid for with ms. Seldom buys individual photos.

TIPS "Familiarity with the miniatures hobby is very helpful. Accuracy to scale is extremely important to our readers. A complete digital package (ms/photos) has a better chance of publication."

$$ DOLLS

Jones Publishing, Inc., P.O. Box 5000, N7528 Aanstad Rd., Iola WI 54945. (715)445-5000. **Fax:** (715)445-4053. **E-mail:** joyceg@jonespublishing.com; jonespub@jonespublishing.com. **Website:** www.dollsmagazine.com. **Contact:** Joyce Greenholdt, editor. **75% freelance written.** Magazine published 10 times/year covering dolls, doll artists, and related topics of interest to doll collectors and enthusiasts. "*Dolls* enhances the joy of collecting by introducing readers to the best new dolls from around the world, along with the artists and designers who create them. It keeps readers up to date on shows, sales, and special events in the doll world. With beautiful color photography, *Dolls* offers an array of easy-to-read, informative articles that help our collectors select the best buys." Estab. 1982. Circ. 100,000. Byline given. Pays on publication. No kill fee. Accepts queries by mail, e-mail. Responds in 1 month to queries.

NONFICTION Needs historical, how-to, interview, new product, photo feature. **Buys 55 mss/year.** Send complete ms. Length: 750-1,200 words. **Pays $75-300.**

PHOTOS Send photos. Captions, identification of subjects, model releases required. Reviews transparencies. Offers no additional payment for photos accepted with ms.

TIPS "Know the subject matter and artists. Having quality artwork and access to doll artists for interviews are big pluses. We need original ideas of interest to doll lovers."

F+W, A CONTENT + ECOMMERCE COMPANY (MAGAZINE DIVISION)

(formerly F+W Media, Inc.), 10151 Carver Rd., Suite 200, Cincinnati OH 45242. (513)531-2690. **E-mail:** dave.pulvermacher@fwcommunity.com. **Website:** www.fwcommunity.com. **Contact:** Dave Pulvermacher, marketing research supervisor. "Each month, millions of enthusiasts turn to the magazines from F+W for inspiration, instruction, and encouragement. Readers are as varied as our categories, but all are assured of getting the best possible coverage of their favorite hobby." Publishes magazines in the following categories: **antiques and collectibles** (*Antique Trader*); **astronomy** (*Sky & Telescope*); **automo-**

tive (*Military Vehicles, Old Cars Report Price Guide, Old Cars Weekly*); **beading** (*Beadwork*); **coins and paper money** (*Bank Note Reporter, Coins Magazine, Numismatic News, World Coin News*); **construction** (*Frame Building News, Metal Roofing Magazine, Rural Builder*); **crocheting** (*Interweave Crochet, Love of Crochet*); **fine art** (*Collector's Guide, Drawing, Pastel Journal, Southwest Art, The Artist's Magazine, Watercolor Artist*); **firearms and knives** (*Blade, Gun Digest*); **genealogy** (*Family Tree Magazine*); **graphic design** (*HOW Magazine, PRINT*); **horticulture** (*Horticulture*); **jewelry** (*Jewelry Stringing, Lapidary Journal Jewelry Artist, Step by Step Wire Jewelry*); **knitting** (*Interweave Knits, Knitscene, Love of Knitting*) **militaria** (*Military Trader*); **mixed media** (*Cloth Paper Scissors*); **outdoors and hunting** (*Deer & Deer Hunting, Trapper & Predator Caller*); **quilting** (*Fons & Porter's Easy Quilts, Fons & Porter's Love of Quilting, McCall's Quick Quilts, McCall's Quilting, Quilters Newsletter, Quilting Arts Magazine, Quiltmaker, Quilty*); **records and CDs** (*Goldmine*); **sewing** (*Burdastyle, Creative Machine Embroidery, Interweave Stitch, Piecework, Sew It All, Sew News*); **spinning** (*Spin-off*); **sports** (*Sports Collectors Digest*); **woodworking** (*Popular Woodworking Magazine*); **weaving** (*Handwoven*); **writing** (*Writer's Digest*).

Please see individual listings in the Consumer Magazines and Trade Journals sections for specific submission information about each magazine.

$$$ FAMILY TREE MAGAZINE

F+W, a Content and eCommerce Company, 10151 Carver Rd., Suite 200, Cincinnati OH 45242. (513)531-2690. **Fax:** (513)891-7153. **E-mail:** ftmedit@fwpubs.com. **Website:** www.familytreemagazine.com. **75% freelance written.** Magazine covering family history, heritage, and genealogy research. "*Family Tree Magazine* is a special-interest consumer magazine that helps readers discover, preserve, and celebrate their family's history. We cover genealogy, ethnic heritage, genealogy websites and software, photography and photo preservation, and other ways that families connect with their past." Estab. 1999. Circ. 75,000. Byline given. Pays on acceptance. Offers 25% kill fee. Publishes ms an average of 6 months after acceptance. Editorial lead time 8 months. Submit seasonal material 8 months in advance. Accepts queries by mail, e-mail. Responds in 6-8 weeks to queries. Sample copy: $8 from website. Guidelines online.

NONFICTION Needs book excerpts, historical, how-to, genealogy, new product, photography, computer, technical, genealogy software, photography equipment. Does not publish personal experience stories (except brief stories in Everything's Relative column) or histories of specific families. **Buys 60 mss/year.** Query with a specific story idea and published clips. Length: 250-4,500 words. **Pays $25-800.**

PHOTOS State availability. Captions required. Reviews color transparencies. Negotiates payment individually.

TIPS "Always query with a specific story idea. Look at sample issues before querying to get a feel for appropriate topics and angles. We see too many broad, general stories on genealogy or records and personal accounts of 'How I found great-aunt Sally' without how-to value."

$ FIBRE FOCUS

Magazine of the Ontario Handweavers & Spinners, 17 Robinson Rd., RR4, Waterford ON N0E 1Y0 Canada. (519)443-7104. **E-mail:** ffeditor@ohs.on.ca. **Website:** www.ohs.on.ca. **Contact:** Dawna Beatty, editor. **90% freelance written.** Quarterly magazine covering handweaving, spinning, basketry, beading, and other fibre arts. "Our readers are weavers and spinners who also do dyeing, knitting, basketry, feltmaking, papermaking, sheep raising, and craft supply. All articles deal with some aspect of these crafts." Estab. 1957. Circ. 1,000. Byline given. Pays within 30 days after publication. Editorial lead time 6 months. Submit seasonal material 6 months in advance. Responds in 1 month to queries. Sample copy for $8 (Canadian). Guidelines available online.

NONFICTION Needs how-to, interview, new product, opinion, personal experience, technical, travel, book reviews. **Buys 40-60 mss/year.** Contact the *Fibre Focus* editor before undertaking a project or an article. Mss may be submitted c/o Dawna Beatty by e-mail for anything you have to contribute for upcoming issues. Feature article deadlines: December 31, March 31, June 30, and September 15. Word length varies. **Pays $30 (Canadian) per published page.**

PHOTOS Send photos. Captions, identification of subjects required. Offers additional payment for photos accepted with ms.

TIPS "Visit the OHS website for current information."

FINE WOODWORKING

The Taunton Press, Inc., 63 South Main St., P.O. Box 5506, Newtown CT 06470-5506. (203)426-8171. **Fax:** (203)426-3434. **E-mail:** fw@taunton.com. **Website:** www.finewoodworking.com. **Contact:** Tom McKenna, senior editor. Bimonthly magazine on woodworking in the small shop. Estab. 1975. Circ. 270,000. Byline given. Pays on acceptance. Offers variable kill fee. Submit seasonal material 6 months in advance. Accepts simultaneous submissions. Responds in 1 month to queries. Guidelines online at www.finewoodworking.com/pages/fw_authorguideline.asp.

NONFICTION Needs how-to, woodworking. **Buys 120 mss/year.** Send article outline, helpful drawings or photos, and proposal letter. **Pays $150/magazine page.** Sometimes pays expenses of writers on assignment.

COLUMNS/DEPARTMENTS Fundamentals (basic how-to and concepts for beginning woodworkers); Master Class (advanced techniques); Finish Line (finishing techniques); Question & Answer (woodworking Q&A); Methods of Work (shop tips); Tools & Materials (short reviews of new tools). **Buys 400 mss/year. Pays $50-150/published page.**

TIPS "Look for authors guidelines and follow them. Stories about woodworking reported by non-woodworkers are *not* used. Our magazine is essentially reader-written by woodworkers."

HANDWOVEN

Interweave Press, 24520 Melott Rd., Hillsboro OR 97123. **E-mail:** aosterhaug@interweave.com. **Website:** www.weavingtoday.com. **Contact:** Anita Osterhaug. "The main goal of *Handwoven* articles is to inspire our readers to weave. Articles and projects should be accessible to weavers of all skill levels, even when the material is technical. The best way to prepare an article for *Handwoven* is to study the format and style of articles in recent issues." Pays on publication. Editorial lead time is 6-12 months. Responds in 6 weeks to queries. Guidelines available on website.

NONFICTION Special issues: Query or submit full ms by e-mail or mail. Include written intro, relevant photos or other visuals (include photo credits), 25-word author bio and photo.

THE HOME SHOP MACHINIST

P.O. Box 629, Traverse City MI 49685. (231)946-3712. **Fax:** (231)946-6180. **E-mail:** george.bulliss@vpdemandcreation; kelly.wagner@vpdemandcreation.com. **Website:** www.homeshopmachinist.net. **Contact:** George Bulliss, editor; Kelly Shugart Wagner, managing editor. **95% freelance written.** Bimonthly magazine covering machining and metalworking for the hobbyist. Circ. 34,000. Byline given. Pays on publication. Publishes ms an average of 2 years after acceptance. Responds in 2 months to queries. Sample copy free. Guidelines for 9x12 SASE.

NONFICTION Needs how-to, projects designed to upgrade present shop equipment or hobby model projects that require machining, technical, should pertain to metalworking, machining, drafting, layout, welding or foundry work for the hobbyist. No fiction or people features. **Buys 40 mss/year.** Send complete ms. Length: open—"whatever it takes to do a thorough job." **Pays $40/published page, plus $9/published photo.**

PHOTOS Send photos. Captions, identification of subjects required. Pays $9-40 for 5x7 b&w prints; $70/page for camera-ready art; $40 for b&w cover photo.

COLUMNS/DEPARTMENTS "Become familiar with our magazine before submitting." Book Reviews; New Product Reviews; Micro-Machining; Foundry. Length: 600-1,500 words. **Buys 25-30 mss/year.** Query. **Pays $40-70.**

FILLERS Buys 12-15 mss/year. Length: 100-300 words. **Pays $30-48.**

TIPS "The writer should be experienced in the area of metalworking and machining; should be extremely thorough in explanations of methods and processes—always with an eye to safety; and should provide good quality b&w photos and/or clear dimensioned drawings to aid in description. Visuals are of increasing importance to our readers. Carefully planned photos, drawings and charts will carry a submission to our magazine much farther along the path to publication."

INTERWEAVE CROCHET

Interweave Press, 4868 Innovation Dr., Fort Collins CO 80525. **E-mail:** rachel.koon@fwmedia.com; crochet@interweave.com (general e-mail address). **Website:** www.crochetme.com. "*Interweave Crochet* is a quarterly publication of Interweave for all those who love to crochet. In each issue we present beautifully finished projects, accompanied by clear step-by-step instructions, as well as stories and articles of interest to crocheters. The projects range from quick but intriguing projects that can be accomplished in a weekend to complex patterns that may take months to complete. Engaging and informative feature articles come from around the country and around the world. Fashion sensibility and striking examples of craft technique are important to us." Pays on publication. Guidelines available on website.

NONFICTION Special issues: "We are interested in- articles on a broad range of topics, including: technical pieces, profiles of inspiring crochet designers, and features about regions of the world where crochet has played or continues to play an important role." Query by mail. Include submission form (available online). "Please send a detailed proposal—complete outline, written description—to give us a clear idea of what to expect in the finished piece."

KITPLANES

P.O. Box 1295, Dayton NV 89403. (832)851-6665. **E-mail:** editorial@kitplanes.com. **Website:** www.kitplanes.com. **Contact:** Paul Dye, editor-in-chief; Mark Schrimmer, managing editor. **50% freelance written. Eager to work with new/unpublished writers.** Monthly magazine covering self-construction of private aircraft for pilots and builders. Estab. 1984. Circ. 72,000. Byline given. Pays on publication. Publishes ms an average of 3 months after acceptance. Submit seasonal material 6 months in advance. Accepts queries by mail, e-mail. Responds in 4 weeks to queries. Responds in 6 weeks to mss. Sample copy for $6. Guidelines available online.

NONFICTION Needs general interest, how-to, interview, new product, personal experience, photo feature, technical. No general-interest aviation articles, or "My First Solo" type of articles. **Buys 80 mss/year.** Query. Interested in articles on all phases of aircraft construction, from basic design, to flight trials, to construction technique in wood, metal and composite. Length: 500-3,000 words. Feature articles average about 2,000 words. **Pays $250-1,000, including story photos.**

PHOTOS State availability of or send photos. Captions, identification of subjects required. Pays $300 for cover photos.

TIPS "*Kitplanes* contains very specific information—a writer must be extremely knowledgeable in the field. Major features are entrusted only to known writers. We cannot emphasize enough that articles must be directed at the individual aircraft builder. We need more 'how-to' photo features in all areas of home-built aircraft."

THE LEATHER CRAFTERS & SADDLERS JOURNAL

315 S Oneida Ave., Suite 104, Rhinelander WI 54501. **E-mail:** charil@leathercraftersjournal.com. **Website:** leathercraftersjournal.com. **Contact:** Charil Reis, editor. **100% freelance written.** Bimonthly magazine covering leatherwork. "A leather-working publication with how-to, step-by-step instructional articles using patterns for leathercraft, leather art, custom saddle, boot, etc. A complete resource for leather, tools, machinery, and allied materials, plus leather industry news." Estab. 1990. Circ. 8,000. Byline given. Pays on publication. Publishes ms an average of 4 months after acceptance. Submit seasonal material 6 months in advance. Accepts queries by mail, e-mail. Accepts simultaneous submissions. Responds in 1 month to mss. Sample copy: $7. Guidelines online.

NONFICTION Needs how-to (step-by-step articles on how to make things with leather). **Buys 75 mss/year.** Send complete ms by e-mail: photos (see online guidelines); text (short introduction, step-by-step instructions, and a list of materials and tools used); patterns (see online guidelines). If patterns are too large to e-mail, send by mail. Length: 500-2,500 words. **Pays $20-250 for assigned articles. Pays $25-150 for unsolicited articles.**

REPRINTS Send tearsheet or photocopy. Pays 50% of amount paid for an original article.

PHOTOS Send good contrast color print photos and full-size patterns and/or full-size photo-carve patterns with submission. If by e-mail, send instructions in Word document format, photos and patterns as attachments. Lack of these reduces payment amount. Captions required.

TIPS "We want to work with people who understand and know leathercraft and are interested in passing on their knowledge to others. We would prefer to interview people who have achieved a high level in leathercraft skill."

MILITARY VEHICLES

F+W Media, Inc., 700 E. State St., Iola WI 54990-0001. (715)445-4612. **Fax:** (715)445-4087. **E-mail:** john.adams-graf@fwmedia.com. **Website:** www.military-trader.com. **Contact:** John Adams-Graf, editor. **50% freelance written.** Bimonthly magazine covering historic military vehicles. Dedicated to serving people who collect, restore, and drive historic military vehicles. Estab. 1987. Circ. 18,500. Byline given. Pays on publication. No kill fee. Publishes ms an average of 1 month after acceptance. Accepts queries by mail, e-mail. Accepts simultaneous submissions. Responds in 1 week to queries. Responds in 1 month to mss. Sample copy for $5.

NONFICTION Needs historical, how-to, technical. **Buys 20 mss/year.** Send complete ms. Length: 1,300-2,600 words. **Pays $0-200.**

COLUMNS/DEPARTMENTS Pays $0-75.

TIPS "Be knowledgeable about military vehicles. This magazine is for a very specialized audience. General automotive journalists will probably not be able to write for this group. The bulk of our content addresses U.S.-manufactured and used vehicles. Plenty of good photos will make it easier to be published in our publication. Write for the collector/restorer: Assume that they already know the basics of historical context. Articles that show how to restore or repair military vehicles are given the highest priority."

$ MODEL CARS MAGAZINE

Golden Bell Press, 2403 Champa St., Denver CO 80205. (808)754-1378. **E-mail:** gregg@modelcarsmag.com. **Website:** www.modelcarsmag.com. **25% freelance written.** Magazine published 9 times year covering model cars, trucks, and other automotive models. *Model Cars Magazine* is the how-to authority for the automotive modeling hobbiest. This magazine is on the forefront of the hobby, the editorial staff are model car builders, and every single one of the writers has a passion for the hobby that is evident in the articles and stories that we publish. This is the model car magazine written by and for model car builders. Estab. 1999. Circ. 7,000. Byline given. Pays on publication. Publishes ms an average of 2-3 months after acceptance. Editorial lead time 2-3 months. Accepts queries by mail, e-mail. Sample copy online.

NONFICTION Needs how-to. Length: 600-3,000 words. **Pays $50/page. Pays $25/page for unsolicited articles.**

$ NATIONAL COMMUNICATIONS

Norm Schrein, Inc., P.O. Box 1, Aledo IL 61231-0001. (937)299-7226. **Fax:** (937)299-1323. **E-mail:** norm@bearcat1.com; service@natcommag.com. **Website:** www.nat-com.org. **Contact:** Norm Schrein, editor. **100% freelance written.** Bimonthly magazine covering radio as a hobby. *National Communications* is the magazine for every radio user. Estab. 1990. Circ. 5,000. Byline given. Pays on publication. No kill fee. Publishes ms an average of 2 months after acceptance. Editorial lead time 2 months. Submit seasonal material 2 months in advance. Accepts queries by phone. Accepts simultaneous submissions. Sample copy for $4.

NONFICTION Needs how-to, interview, new product, personal experience, photo feature, technical. Does not want articles off topic of the publication's audience (radio hobbyists). **Buys 2-3 mss/year.** Query. Length: 300 words. **Pays $75+.**

PHOTOS Send photos. Captions, identification of subjects required. Reviews GIF/JPEG files. Offers no additional payment for photos accepted with ms.

$ PIECEWORK MAGAZINE

Interweave/F+W Media, 4868 Innovation Dr., Fort Collins CO 80537. (800) 272-2193. **Fax:** (970)669-6117. **E-mail:** piecework@interweave.com. **Website:** www.interweave.com. **90% freelance written.** Bimonthly magazine covering needlework history. *PieceWork* celebrates the rich tradition of needlework and the history of the people behind it. Stories and projects on embroidery, cross-stitch, knitting, crocheting, and quilting, along with other textile arts, are featured in each issue. Estab. 1993. Circ. 30,000. Byline given. Pays on publication. Offers 25% kill fee. Editorial lead time 6 months. Submit seasonal material 6 months in advance. Accepts queries by mail, e-mail. Responds in 6 months to queries. Writer's guidelines available at pieceworkmagazine.com.

NONFICTION Needs historical articles, book excerpts, new product information. No contemporary needlework articles. **Buys 25-30 mss/year.** Send complete ms. Length: 1,500-4,000 words.

TIPS Submit a well-researched article on a historical aspect of needlework complete with information on visuals and suggestion for accompanying project.

$$ POPULAR WOODWORKING MAGAZINE

F+W, A Content + Ecommerce Company, 8469 Blue Ash Rd., Suite 100, Cincinnati OH 45236. (513)531-2690, ext. 11348. **E-mail:** mike.wallace@fwcommunity.com. **Website:** www.popularwoodworking.com. **Contact:** Michael Wallace. **75% freelance written.** Magazine published 7 times/year. "*Popular Woodworking Magazine* invites woodworkers of all skill levels into a community of professionals who share their hard-won shop experience through in-depth projects and technique articles, which help readers hone their existing skills and develop new ones for both hand

and power tools. Related stories increase the readers' understanding and enjoyment of their craft. Any project submitted must be aesthetically pleasing, of sound construction, and offer a challenge to readers. On the average, we use 5 freelance features per issue. Our primary needs are 'how-to' articles on woodworking. Our secondary need is for articles that will inspire discussion concerning woodworking. Tone of articles should be conversational and informal but knowledgeable, as if the writer is speaking directly to the reader. Our readers are the woodworking hobbyist and small woodshop owner. Writers should have an extensive knowledge of woodworking and excellent woodworking techniques and skills." Estab. 1981. Circ. 150,000. Byline given. Pays on acceptance. No kill fee. Publishes ms an average of 10 months after acceptance. Submit seasonal material 6 months in advance. Accepts queries by mail, e-mail, phone. Responds in 2 months to queries. Sample copy: $5.99 plus 9x12 SAE with 6 first-class stamps, or online. Guidelines available online.

NONFICTION Needs how-to (on woodworking projects, with plans), humor (woodworking anecdotes), technical (woodworking techniques). No tool reviews. **Buys 12 mss/year.** Query first; see guidelines and sample query on website. Length: 1,200-2,500 words. **Pay starts at $250/published page.**

REPRINTS For previously published material, send photocopy with rights for sale noted and information about when and where the material previously appeared. Pays 25% of amount paid for an original article.

PHOTOS Photographic quality affects acceptance. Need professional quality, high-resolution digital images of step-by-step construction process. Send photos. Captions, identification of subjects required. Pays $75/image.

COLUMNS/DEPARTMENTS Tricks of the Trade (helpful techniques), End Grain (thoughts on woodworking as a profession or hobby, can be humorous or serious), both 500-550 words. **Buys 20 mss/year.** Query. **Pays $350 for End Grain and $50-100 for Tricks of the Trade.**

TIPS "Write an 'End Grain' column for us and then follow up with photos of your projects. Submissions should include materials list, complete diagrams (blueprints not necessary), and discussion of the step-by-step process. We select attractive, practical projects with quality construction for which the authors can supply quality digital photography."

QST

American Radio Relay League, 225 Main St., Newington CT 06111. (860)594-0200. **Fax:** (860)594-0259. **E-mail:** qst@arrl.org. **Website:** www.arrl.org. **Contact:** Steve Ford, editor. **90% freelance written.** Monthly magazine covering amateur radio. "*QST* is the monthly membership journal of ARRL, the national association for amateur radio, covering subjects of interest to amateur ('ham') radio operators." Estab. 1915. Circ. 150,000. Byline given. Pays on publication. No kill fee. Publishes ms an average of 6 months after acceptance. Editorial lead time 6 months. Submit seasonal material 6 months in advance. Accepts queries by mail, e-mail, fax, phone. Responds in 1 week to queries; in 1 month to mss. Guidelines available online at: www.arrl.org/qst-author-guide.

NONFICTION Needs general interest, how-to, technical. Send complete ms by mail or e-mail. Length: 900-3,000 words. **Pays $65/published page.**

PHOTOS Send photos. Captions, identification of subjects required. Reviews color prints, slides, GIF/JPEG files. Offers no additional payment for photos accepted with ms.

TIPS "A conversational style will make your article stand out among the candidates."

QUILTING ARTS MAGAZINE

Interweave Press, 201 E. Fourth St., Loveland CO 80537. **E-mail:** submissions@quiltingarts.com. **Website:** www.quiltingdaily.com. "At *Quilting Arts*, we celebrate contemporary art quilting, surface design, mixed media, fiber art trends, and more. We are always looking for new techniques, innovative processes, and unique approaches to the art of quilting." Pays on publication. Editorial lead time is 12 months. Responds in 3 months to queries. Guidelines available on website.

NONFICTION Special issues: Wants "beautiful and inspiring contemporary quilts and exhibits; sketchbook-inspired quilts for our Off The Page series; artists with inspiring portfolios of work to be featured in our In The Spotlight, Artist Profile, and Q&A articles; unique techniques, new ways to use existing tools and supplies, and ideas we've never featured before." Query by e-mail. Include brief description of idea and contact info.

SEWNEWS

Creative Crafts Group, 741 Corporate Circle, Suite A, Golden CO 80401. **E-mail:** sewnews@sewnews.com. **Website:** www.sewnews.com. **Contact:** Ellen March, editor-in-chief. **70% freelance written. Works with a small number of new/unpublished writers each year.** Monthly magazine covering fashion, gift, and home-dec sewing. "*Sew News* magazine is a monthly publication devoted to the enthusiastic and creative people who wants to sew. We provide them with accurate, helpful, step-by-step information for personalizing ready-to-wear and creating original fashions, accessories, gifts, and home décor that express her personal style." Estab. 1980. Circ. 185,000. Byline given. Pays on publication. No kill fee. Publishes ms an average of 6 months after acceptance. Submit seasonal material 6 months in advance. Accepts queries by mail, e-mail. Responds in 2 months to mss. Sample copy: $5.99. Guidelines online.

NONFICTION Needs how-to, sewing techniques, interview, interesting personalities in home-sewing field. **Buys 200-240 mss/year.** Query with published clips if available. Length: 500-2,000 words. **Pays $50-500.**

PHOTOS Prefers digital images, color photos, or slides. Send photos. Identification of subjects required. Payment included in ms price.

TIPS "Query first with writing sample and outline of proposed story. Areas most open to freelancers are how-to and sewing techniques; give explicit, step-by-step instructions, plus rough art. We're using more home decorating and soft craft content."

SPIN-OFF

Interweave Press, 4868 Innovation Dr., Fort Collins CO 80625. **E-mail:** spinoff@interweave.com. **Website:** www.spinningdaily.com. "*Spin-Off* is a quarterly magazine devoted to the interests of handspinners at all skill levels. Informative articles in each issue aim to encourage the novice, challenge the expert, and increase every spinner's working knowledge of this ancient and complex craft." Pays on publication. Editorial lead time is 6-12 months. Responds in 6 weeks to queries. Guidelines available on website.

Spin-Off is published 4 times/year, in March, June, September, and December.

NONFICTION Special issues: Wants articles on the following subjects: spinning tips (400 words or less); spinning basics (1,200 words); back page essay (650 words); methods for dyeing with natural and chemical dyes; tools for spinning and preparing fibers; fiber basics (2,000 words); ideas for using handspun yarn in a variety of techniques; profiles of people who spin; a gallery of your work; tips on blending fibers; the history and/or cultural role of spinning. Query or submit full ms by e-mail or mail. Length: 200-2,700 words. **Pay varies with length, complexity, provided imagery, and author experience.**

STEP BY STEP WIRE JEWELRY

620 W. Sedgwick St., Philadelphia PA 19119. **E-mail:** denise.peck@fwcommunity.com. **Website:** www.jewelrymakingdaily.com. **Contact:** Denise Peck. *Step by Step Wire Jewelry* is published 6 times/year by Interweave/FW Media. The magazine is project-oriented, with step-by-step instructions for creating wire jewelry, as well as tips, tools, and techniques. Articles range from beginner to expert level. Writers must be able to substantiate that material submitted is an original design, accurate, and must make sure that all steps involved in the creation of the piece are feasible using the tools listed. Pays 30 days post publication. Editorial lead time is 6-12 months. Responds in 6 weeks to queries. Guidelines available on website.

NONFICTION Needs step-by-step, how-to jewelry projects. Submit photos by e-mail for review for possible publication. Include name, contact info, level of experience required. Once accepted- Length: 700-2,500 words. **Pays nominal fee for article based on length and complexity and determined by editor.**

TEDDY BEAR & FRIENDS

P.O. Box 5000, Iola WI 54945-5000. (800)331-0038, ext. 150. **Fax:** (715)445-4053. **E-mail:** joyceg@jonespublishing.com. **Website:** www.teddybearandfriends.com. **Contact:** Joyce Greenholdt, editor. **65% freelance written. Works with a small number of new/unpublished writers each year.** Bimonthly magazine on teddy bears for collectors, enthusiasts, and bearmakers. Estab. 1985. Byline given. Payment upon publication on the last day of the month the issue is mailed. Submit seasonal material 6 months in advance. Sample copy and writer's guidelines for $2 and 9x12 SAE.

NONFICTION Needs historical, how-to, interview. No articles from the bear's point of view. **Buys 30-40 mss/year.** Query with published clips. Length: 900-1,500 words. **Pays $100-350.**

PHOTOS Send photos. Captions required. Reviews transparencies, prints. Offers no additional payment for photos accepted with ms.

TIPS "We are interested in good, professional writers around the country with a strong knowledge of teddy bears. Historical profile of bear companies, profiles of contemporary artists, and knowledgeable reports on museum collections are of interest."

$$ TOY FARMER

Toy Farmer Publications, 7496 106 Ave. SE, LaMoure ND 58458-9404. (701)883-5206. **Fax:** (701)883-5209. **E-mail:** info@toyfarmer.com. **Website:** www.toyfarmer.com. **70% freelance written.** Monthly magazine covering farm toys. Estab. 1978. Circ. 27,000. Byline given. Pays on publication. Editorial lead time 2 months. Submit seasonal material 3 months in advance. Accepts queries by mail, e-mail, fax. Responds in 1 month to queries. Responds in 2 months to mss. Guidelines available upon request.

Youth involvement is strongly encouraged.

NONFICTION Needs general interest, historical, interview, new product, personal experience, technical, book introductions. **Buys 100 mss/year.** Query with published clips. Length: 800-1,500 words. **Pays 10¢/word.** Sometimes pays expenses of writers on assignment.

PHOTOS Must be 35mm originals or very high resolution digital images. State availability.

VOGUE KNITTING

Soho Publishing Co., Inc., 161 Avenue of the Americas, Suite 1301, New York NY 10013. (212)937-2555. **Fax:** (646)336-3960. **E-mail:** editors@vogueknitting.com. **Website:** www.vogueknitting.com. Quarterly magazine created for participants in and enthusiasts of high-fashion knitting. Circ. 175,000. No kill fee.

Query before submitting. Include "editorial submission" in the subject line.

$ WESTERN & EASTERN TREASURES

People's Publishing Co., Inc., P.O. Box 37, Sausalito CA 94965-0037. **E-mail:** editor@wetreasures.com. **Website:** www.wetreasures.com. **100% freelance written.** Monthly magazine covering hobby/sport of metal detecting/treasure hunting. "*Western & Eastern Treasures* provides concise yet comprehensive coverage of every aspect of the sport/hobby of metal detecting and treasure hunting with a strong emphasis on current, accurate information; innovative, field-proven advice and instruction; and entertaining, effective presentation." Estab. 1966. Circ. 50,000. Byline given. Pays on publication. No kill fee. Publishes ms an average of 4+ months after acceptance. Editorial lead time 4 months. Submit seasonal material 3-4 months in advance. Responds in 2 months to mss. Sample copy for SAE with 9x12 envelope and 5 first-class stamps. Guidelines for #10 SASE or online.

NONFICTION Needs how-to, tips and finds for metal detectorists, interview (only people in metal detecting), personal experience, positive metal detector experiences, technical (only metal detecting hobby-related), helping in local community with metal detecting skills (i.e., helping local police locate evidence at crime scenes—all volunteer basis). Special issues: *Silver & Gold Annual* (editorial deadline February each year)—looking for articles 1,500+ words, plus photos on the subject of locating silver and/or gold using a metal detector. No fiction, poetry, or puzzles. **Buys 150+ mss/year.** Send complete ms by e-mail or mail (include SASE). Length: 1,000-2,000 words. **Pays 5¢/word.**

PHOTOS Send photos. Captions, identification of subjects required. Reviews 35mm transparencies, prints, digital scans (minimum 300 dpi). Offers $5/photo.

HOME AND GARDEN

$$ THE AMERICAN GARDENER

7931 E. Boulevard Dr., Alexandria VA 22308-1300. (703)768-5700. **Fax:** (703)768-7533. **E-mail:** editor@ahs.org; myee@ahs.org. **Website:** www.ahs.org. **Contact:** Mary Yee, art director. **60% freelance written.** Bimonthly, 64-page, four-color magazine covering gardening and horticulture. "This is the official publication of the American Horticultural Society (AHS), a national, nonprofit, membership organization for gardeners, founded in 1922. The AHS mission is 'to open the eyes of all Americans to the vital connection between people and plants, and to inspire all Americans to become responsible caretakers of the earth, to celebrate America's diversity through the art and science of horticulture, and to lead this effort by sharing the society's unique national resources with all Americans.' All articles are also published on members-only website." Estab. 1922. Circ. 20,000. Byline given. Pays on publication. Offers 25% kill fee. Publishes ms an average of 6 months after acceptance. Editorial lead time 6 months. Submit seasonal material at least 1 year in advance. Accepts queries by mail with SASE. Responds in 3 months to queries. Sample copy for $5. Writer's guidelines by e-mail and online.

"*The American Gardener* goes out bimonthly to about 20,000 members of the American Horticultural Society. *The American Gardener* is primarily free-lance written, and its content differs considerably from that of other gardening publications. Our readers are mainly experienced amateur gardeners; about 20 percent are horticultural professionals. Articles are intended to bring this knowledgeable group new information, ranging from the latest scientific findings that affect plants, to the history of gardening and gardens in America. We introduce readers to unusual plants, personalities, and issues that will enrich what we assume is already a passionate commitment to gardening."

NONFICTION **Buys 20 mss/year.** Query with published clips. No fax, phone, or e-mail submissions. Length: 1,500-2,500 words. **Pays $300-500, depending on complexity and author's experience.**

REPRINTS Rarely purchases second rights. Send photocopy of article with information about when and where the material previously appeared. Payment varies.

PHOTOS E-mail or check website for guidelines before submitting. It is very important to include some kind of plant list for your stock so we can determine if you specialize in the types of plants we cover. The list does not have to be comprehensive, but it should give some idea of the breadth of your photo archive. If, for instance, your list contains mostly tulips, pansies, roses, and other popular plants like these, your stock will not be a good match for our articles. Also, if your list does not include the botanical names for all plants, we will not be able to use the photos. Identification of subjects required. Photo captions required; include complete botanical names of plants including genus, species and botanical variety or cultivar. Pays $350 maximum for color cover; $80-130 for color inside. Pays on publication. Credit line given. Buys one-time North American and nonexclusive rights.

COLUMNS/DEPARTMENTS Natural Connections (explains a natural phenomenon—plant and pollinator relationships, plant and fungus relationships, parasites—that may be observed in nature or in the garden), 750-1,200 words. Homegrown Harvest (articles on edible plants delivered in a personal, reassuring voice. Each issue focuses on a single crop, such as carrots, blueberries, or parsley), 800-900 words; Plant in the Spotlight (profiles of a single plant species or cultivar, including a personal perspective on why it's a favored plant), 600 words. **Buys 5 mss/year.** Query with published clips. **Pays $100-250.**

TIPS "The majority of our readers are advanced, passionate amateur gardeners; about 20 percent are horticultural professionals. Most prefer not to use synthetic chemical pesticides. Our articles are intended to bring this knowledgeable group new information, ranging from the latest scientific findings that affect plants, to in-depth profiles of specific plant groups and leading horticulturalists, and the history of gardening and gardens in America."

ATLANTA HOMES AND LIFESTYLES

Network Communications, Inc., 1117 Perimeter Center West, Suite N118, Atlanta GA 30338. (404)252-6670. **E-mail:** editor@atlantahomesmag.com. **Website:** www.atlantahomesmag.com. **Contact:** Elizabeth Ralls, editor in chief; Elizabeth Anderson, art director. **65% freelance written.** Magazine published 12 times/year. *Atlanta Homes and Lifestyles* is designed for the action-oriented, well-educated reader who enjoys his/her shelter, its design and construction, its environment, and living and entertaining in it. Estab. 1983. Circ. 30,000. Byline given. Pays on publication. Publishes ms an average of 6 months after acceptance. Accepts queries by mail, fax. Responds in 3 months to queries. Sample copy online.

NONFICTION Needs interview, new product, photo feature, well-designed homes, gardens, local art, remodeling, food, preservation, entertaining. "We do not want articles outside the respective market area, not written for magazine format, or that are excessively controversial, investigative, or that cannot be appropriately illustrated with attractive photography." **Buys 35 mss/year.** Query with published clips. Length: 500-1,200 words. **Pays $100-500.** Sometimes pays expenses of writer on assignment.

PHOTOS Most photography is assigned. State availability. Captions, identification of subjects, model releases required. Reviews transparencies. Pays $40-50/photo.

COLUMNS/DEPARTMENTS **Pays $50-200.**

TIPS "Query with specific new story ideas rather than previously published material."

$$ BIRDS & BLOOMS

Reiman Media Group, 1610 N. 2nd St., Suite 102, Milwaukee WI 53212. (414)423-0100. **E-mail:** editors@birdsandblooms.com. **Website:** www.birdsandblooms.com. **15% freelance written.** Bimonthly magazine focusing on "the beauty in your own backyard." *Birds & Blooms* is a sharing magazine that lets backyard enthusiasts chat with each other by exchanging personal experiences. This makes *Birds & Blooms* more like a conversation than a magazine, as readers share tips and tricks on producing beautiful blooms and attracting feathered friends to their backyards. Estab. 1995. Circ. 1,900,000. Byline given. Pays on publication. No kill fee. Publishes ms an average of 7 months after acceptance. Editorial lead time 2 months. Submit seasonal material 4 months in advance. Accepts queries by mail, online submission form. Accepts simultaneous submissions. Responds in 2 months to queries and mss. Sample copy: $2, plus 9x12 SAE and $1.95 postage. Guidelines online.

NONFICTION Needs essays, how-to, humor, inspirational, personal experience, photo feature, natural crafting and plan items for building backyard accents. No bird rescue or captive bird pieces. **Buys 12-20 mss/year.** Query or send complete ms, along with full name, daytime phone number, e-mail address, and mailing address. If submitting for a particular column, note that as well. Each reader contributor whose story, photo, or short item is published receives a *Birds & Blooms* tote bag. See guidelines online. Length: up to 1,000 words. **Pays $100-400.**

PHOTOS Send photos. Identification of subjects required. Reviews transparencies, prints.

COLUMNS/DEPARTMENTS Bird Tales (birding experiences); Front Porch (gardening and birding tips and tricks, reader-created gardening, birding DIYs, etc.); From Your Backyard (more casual writing). **Buys 12-20 mss/year.** Send complete ms. **Pays $50-75.**

FILLERS Needs anecdotes, facts, gags. **Buys 25 mss/year.** Length: 10-250 words. **Pays $10-75.**

TIPS "Focus on conversational writing, like you're chatting with a neighbor over your fence. Mss full of tips and ideas that people can use in backyards across the country have the best chance of being used. Photos that illustrate these points also increase chances of being used."

THE FAMILY HANDYMAN

Reader's Digest Association, 2915 Commers Dr., #700, Eagan MN 55121. **E-mail:** editors@thefamilyhandyman.com. **Website:** www.familyhandyman.com. *The Family Handyman* is an American home-improvement magazine. Estab. 1951. Circ. 1.1 million. Byline given. Pays on acceptance. Accepts queries by online submission form.

NONFICTION Submit to *Family Handyman* via online submission form. Accepts mss for home projects that writers want to share. **Pays $100/ms.**

COLUMNS/DEPARTMENTS Accepts mss for Handy Hint, Great Goof, and Shop Tips. Accepts submissions online. **Pays $100/ms.**

GREENPRINTS

P.O. Box 1355, Fairview NC 28730. (828)628-1902. **E-mail:** pat@greenprints.com. **Website:** www.greenprints.com. **Contact:** Pat Stone, managing editor. **90% freelance written.** "GreenPrints is the 'Weeder's Digest.' We share the human, NOT how-to, side of gardening. We publish true personal gardening stories and essays: humorous, heartfelt, insightful, inspiring." Estab. 1990. Circ. 11,000. Byline given. No editorial lead time. Accepts queries by mail, e-mail. Accepts simultaneous submissions. Responds in 3 months to mss. Sample copy for $5. Guidelines online.

"All must be about gardening!"

NONFICTION Needs essays, general interest, historical, humor, inspirational, nostalgic, personal experience. Does not want how-to. **Buys 60 mss/year.** Submit complete ms. Length: 250-2,500 words. **Pays $50-200 for unsolicited articles.**

COLUMNS/DEPARTMENTS Broken Trowel: The story of your funniest garden mistake. Average word length is 300 words. **Buys 12 mss/year.** Submit complete ms. **Pays between $50 and $75 for columns.**

FICTION "We run very little fiction." **Buys 2 mss/year.** Submit complete ms. **Pays $75-200 maximum.**

POETRY Needs Free verse, light verse, traditional. "If it's not hands-on gardening based, please, please don't send it." Buys 4 poems/year. Submit maximum 3 poems. **Pays $25 for poems.**

FILLERS Wants anecdotes, short humor. Length: 100-300 words. **Pays between $50 and $75 for fillers.**

TIPS Wants "a great, true, *unique* personal *story* with dialogue, a narrative, and something special that happens to make it truly stand out."

$$$$ HOUSE BEAUTIFUL

The Hearst Corp., 300 W. 57th St., 27th Floor, New York NY 10019. **E-mail:** readerservices@housebeautiful.com. **Website:** www.housebeautiful.com. **Contact:** Jeffrey Bauman, executive managing editor. Monthly magazine covering home decoration and design. Targeted toward affluent, educated readers ages 30-40. Covers home design and decoration, gardening and entertaining, interior design, architecture, and travel. Circ. 865,352. No kill fee. Editorial lead time 3 months.

Query before submitting.

LOG HOME LIVING

Home Buyer Publications, Inc., 4125 Lafayette Center Dr., Suite 100, Chantilly VA 20151. (703)222-9411; (800)826-3893. **Fax:** (703)222-3209. **E-mail:** editor@timberhomeliving.com. **Website:** www.loghome.com. **90% freelance written.** Monthly magazine for enthusiasts who are dreaming of, planning for, or actively building a log home. Estab. 1989. Circ. 132,000. Byline given. Pays on acceptance. Offers $100 kill fee. Publishes ms an average of 6 months after acceptance. Editorial lead time 6 months. Submit seasonal material 6 months in advance. Accepts queries by mail, e-mail. Responds in 6 weeks to queries. Sample copy for $4. Guidelines available online.

Also publishes *Timber Home Living, Log Home Design Ideas* and *Building Systems.*

NONFICTION Needs how-to (build or maintain log home), interview of log home owners, personal experience, photo feature (log homes), technical, design/decor topics, travel. **Buys 60 mss/year.** Query with SASE. Length: 1,000-2,000 words. **Payment depends on length, nature of the work, and writer's expertise.** Pays expenses of writers on assignment.

REPRINTS Send tearsheet, photocopy or typed ms and information about when and where the material previously appeared.

PHOTOS State availability. Reviews contact sheets, 4x5 transparencies, 4x6 prints. Negotiates payment individually.

TIPS "*Log Home Living* is devoted almost exclusively to modern manufactured and handcrafted kit log homes. Our interest in historical or nostalgic stories of very old log cabins, reconstructed log homes, or one-of-a-kind owner-built homes is secondary and should be queried first."

$$ MOUNTAIN LIVING

Wiesner Media Network Communications, Inc., 1780 S. Bellaire St., Suite 505, Denver CO 80222. (303)248-2060. **Fax:** (303)248-2066. **E-mail:** greatideas@mountainliving.com; hscott@mountainliving.com; cdeorio@mountainliving.com. **Website:** www.mountainliving.com. **Contact:** Holly Scott, publisher; Christine DeOrio, editor-in-chief. **50% freelance written.** Magazine published 7 times/year covering architecture, interior design, and lifestyle issues for people who live in, visit, or hope to live in the mountains. Estab. 1994. Circ. 40,000. Byline given. Pays on acceptance. Offers 15% kill fee. Publishes ms an average of 4 months after acceptance. Editorial lead time 6 months. Submit seasonal material 8-12 months in advance. Accepts queries by e-mail only. Responds in 6-8 weeks to queries. Responds in 2 months to mss. Sample copy for $7. Guidelines by e-mail.

NONFICTION Needs photo feature, travel, home features. **Buys 30 mss/year.** Query with published clips. Length: 200-600 words. **Pays $250-600.** Sometimes pays expenses of writers on assignment.

PHOTOS Provide photos (digital files only, saved as JPEG or TIFF and at least 300 dpi). State availability. All features photography is assigned to photographers who specialize in architectural and interior photography. Negotiates payment individually.

COLUMNS/DEPARTMENTS ML Recommends; Short Travel Tips; New Product Information; Art; Insider's Guide; Entertaining. Length: 150-400 words.

TIPS "*Mountain Living* is an image-driven magazine and selects its featured homes for their exceptional architecture and interior design. The editorial staff will not consider queries that are not accompanied by professional or scouting photos. Story angles are determined by the editorial staff and assigned to freelance writers. To be considered for freelance assignments, please send your résumé and 4 published clips. Before you query, please read the magazine to get a sense of who we are and what we do."

$$$$ ORGANIC GARDENING

Rodale, 400 S. 10th St., Emmaus PA 18098-0099. **E-mail:** og@rodale.com. **Website:** www.organicgardening.com. **Contact:** Jim Oseland, editor in chief. **75% freelance written.** Bimonthly magazine covering gardening. "*Organic Gardening* is for gardeners who enjoy gardening as an integral part of a healthy lifestyle. Editorial shows readers how to grow flowers, edibles, and herbs, as well as information on ecological landscaping. Also covers organic topics including soil building and pest control." Estab. 1942. Circ. 300,000. Byline given. Pays between acceptance and publication. No kill fee. Accepts queries by mail. Responds in 3 months to queries.

NONFICTION Query with published clips and outline. **Pays up to $1/word for experienced writers.**

TIPS "If you have devised a specific technique that's worked in your garden, have insight into the needs and uses of a particular plant or small group of plants, or have designed whole gardens that integrate well with their environment, and, if you have the capacity to clearly describe what you've learned to other gardeners in a simple but engaging manner, please send us your article ideas. Read a recent issue of the magazine thoroughly before you submit your ideas. If you have an idea that you believe fits with our content, send us a one-page description of it that will grab our attention in the same manner you intend to entice readers into your article. Be sure to briefly explain why your idea is uniquely suited to our magazine. (We will not publish an article that has already appeared elsewhere. Also, please tell us if you are simultaneously submitting your idea to another magazine.) Tell us about the visual content of your idea—that is, what photographs or illustrations would you suggest be included with your article to get the ideas and information across to readers? If you have photographs, let us know. If you have never been published before, consider whether your idea fits into our Gardener to Gardener department. The shorter, narrowly focused articles in the department and its conversational tone make for a more accessible avenue into the magazine for inexperienced writers."

MARTHA STEWART LIVING

Omnimedia, 601 W. 26th St., New York NY 10001. (212)827-8000. **Fax:** (212)827-8204. **Website:** http://livingblog.marthastewart.com; www.marthastewart.com. Monthly magazine for gardening, entertaining, renovating, cooking, collecting, and creating. Magazine, featuring Martha Stewart, that focuses on the domestic arts. Estab. 1990. Circ. 2,000,000.

Query before submitting. Difficult market to break into.

$$ TEXAS GARDENER

Suntex Communications, Inc., P.O. Box 9005, 10566 N. River Crossing, Waco TX 76714. (254)848-9393. **Fax:** (254)848-9779. **E-mail:** info@texasgardener.com. **Website:** www.texasgardener.com. **80% freelance written. Works with a small number of new/unpublished writers each year.** Bimonthly magazine covering vegetable and fruit production, ornamentals, and home landscape information for home gardeners in Texas. Estab. 1981. Circ. 20,000. Byline given. Pays on publication. No kill fee. Publishes ms an average of 4 months after acceptance. Submit seasonal material 6 months in advance. Accepts queries by mail, e-mail, fax. Responds in 2 months to queries. Sample copy for $4.25 and SAE with 5 first-class stamps. Writers' guidelines available online at website.

NONFICTION Needs how-to, humor, interview, photo feature. **Buys 50-60 mss/year.** Query with published clips. Length: 800-2,400 words. **Pays $50-200.**

PHOTOS "We prefer superb color and b&w photos; 90% of photos used are color. Send low resolution jpgs files for review to info@texasgardener.com. High resolution jpg files are required for publication if photos are accepted." Send photos. Identification of subjects, model releases required. Reviews contact sheets, 2 1/4x2 1/4 or 35mm color transparencies, 8x10 b&w prints. Pays negotiable rates.

COLUMNS/DEPARTMENTS Between Neighbors. **Pays $25.**

TIPS First, be a Texan. Then come up with a good idea of interest to home gardeners in this state. Be specific. Stick to feature topics like 'How Alley Gardening Became a Texas Tradition.' Leave topics like 'How to Control Fire Blight' to the experts. High quality photos could make the difference. We would like to add several writers to our group of regular contributors and would make assignments on a regular basis. Fillers are easy to come up with in-house. We want good writers who can produce accurate and interesting copy. Frequent mistakes made by writers in completing an article assignment for us are that articles are not slanted toward Texas gardening, show inaccurate or too little gardening information, or lack good writing style.

$$$$ THIS OLD HOUSE

Time Inc., 135 W. 50th St., 10th Floor, New York NY 10020. (212)522-9465. **Fax:** (212)522-9435. **E-mail:** toh_letters@thisoldhouse.com. **Website:** www.thisoldhouse.com. **40% freelance written.** Magazine published 10 times/year covering home design, renovation, and maintenance. "*This Old House* is the ultimate resource for readers whose homes are their passions. The magazine's mission is threefold: to inform with lively service journalism and reporting on innovative new products and materials, to inspire with beautiful examples of fine craftsmanship and elegant architectural design, and to instruct with clear step-by-step projects that will enhance a home or help a homeowner maintain one. The voice of the magazine is not that of a rarefied design maven or a linear Mr. Fix It but rather that of an eyes-wide-open, in-the-trenches homeowner who's eager for advice, tools, and techniques that'll help him realize his dream of a home." Estab. 1995. Circ. 960,000. Byline given. Pays on acceptance. Publishes ms an average of 3-6 months after acceptance. Editorial lead time 3-12 months. Submit seasonal material 1 year in advance. Accepts queries by mail, e-mail.

NONFICTION Needs essays, how-to, new product, technical; must be house-related. **Buys 70 mss/year.** Query with published clips. Length: 250-2,500 words. **Pays $1/word.** Sometimes pays expenses of writers on assignment.

COLUMNS/DEPARTMENTS Around the House (news, new products), 250 words. **Pays $1/word.**

TRADITIONAL HOME

Meredith Corp., 1716 Locust St., Des Moines IA 50309-3023. **E-mail:** traditionalhome@meredith.com. **Website:** www.traditionalhome.com. Magazine published 8 times/year. Features articles on building, renovating, and decorating homes in the traditional style. From home, garden, and green living to fashion, beauty, entertaining, and travel, *Traditional Home* is a celebration of quality, craftsmanship, authenticity, and family. Estab. 1989. Circ. 950,000. No kill fee. Editorial lead time 6 months.

Query before submitting.

NONFICTION Query.

VICTORIAN HOMES

Beckett Media, 22840 Savi Ranch Pkwy., Suite 200, Yorba Linda CA 92887. (714)939-9991. **Fax:** (714)939-9909. **E-mail:** ephillips@beckett.com. **Website:** www.victorianhomesmag.com. **Contact:** Elaine K. Phillips, editor; Jacqueline deMontravel, editorial director. **90% freelance written.** Quarterly magazine covering Victorian home restoration and decoration. *Victorian Homes* is read by Victorian home owners, restorers, house museum management, and others interested in the Victorian revival. Feature articles cover home architecture, interior design, furnishings, and the home's history. Photography is very important to the feature. Estab. 1981. Circ. 100,000. Byline given. Pays on acceptance. Offers $50 kill fee. Publishes ms an average of 1 year after acceptance. Editorial lead time 4 months. Submit seasonal material 1 year in advance. Accepts queries by e-mail only. Accepts simultaneous submissions. Responds in 6 weeks to queries; in 2 months to mss. Sample copy and writer's guidelines for SAE.

NONFICTION Needs how to create period décor, renovation tutorials, photo-based features. **Buys 30-35 mss/year.** Query. Length: 500-1,200 words. **Pays $50-150.** Sometimes pays expenses of writers on assignment.

PHOTOS State availability. Captions required. Send low-res photos with query. Final image specs 300 dpi, at least 5x7 inches. Negotiates payment individually.

HUMOR

FUNNY TIMES

Funny Times, Inc., P.O. Box 18530, Cleveland Heights OH 44118. (216)371-8600. **Fax:** (216)371-8696. **E-mail:** info@funnytimes.com. **Website:** www.funnytimes.com. **Contact:** Ray Lesser and Susan Wolpert, editors. **50% freelance written.** Monthly tabloid for humor. "*Funny Times* is a monthly review of America's funniest cartoonists and writers. We are the *Reader's Digest* of modern American humor with a progressive/peace-oriented/environmental/politically activist slant." Estab. 1985. Circ. 65,000. Byline given. Pays on publication. Publishes ms an average of 3 months after acceptance. Editorial lead time 2 months. Accepts simultaneous submissions. Responds in 3 months to mss. Sample copy for $3 or 9x12 SAE with 3 first-class stamps ($1.61 postage). Guidelines available online.

NONFICTION Needs essays, funny, humor, interview, opinion, humorous, personal experience, absolutely funny. **Buys 60 mss/year.** Send complete ms. Length: 500-700 words. **Pays $60 minimum.**

COLUMNS/DEPARTMENTS Query with published clips.

FICTION Wants anything funny. Needs humorous. **Buys 6 mss/year.** Query with published clips. Length: 500-700 words. **Pays $50-150.**

TIPS "Send us a small packet (1-3 items) of only your very funniest stuff. If this makes us laugh, we'll be glad to ask for more. We particularly welcome previously published material that has been well received elsewhere."

JUVENILE

APPLESEEDS

Cobblestone Publishing, 30 Grove St., Suite C, Peterborough NH 03458. **E-mail:** mlusted@cricketmedia.com. **Website:** www.cricketmag.com. **Contact:** Marcia Amidon Lusted, editor. *AppleSeeds* is a 36-page, multidisciplinary, nonfiction social studies magazine from Cobblestone Publishing for ages 6-9 (primarily grades 3 and 4). Each issue focuses on 1 theme. Accepts queries by e-mail only. Sample copy for $6.95 + $2 s&h. Guidelines available on website.

Does not accept unsolicited mss.

NONFICTION Special issues: "We are looking for articles that are lively, age-appropriate, and exhibit an original approach to the theme. Scientific and historical accuracy is extremely important." Query only (via e-mail). See website for submission guidelines and theme list.

COLUMNS/DEPARTMENTS Fun Stuff (games or activities relating to the theme, 2 pages); Reading Corner (literature piece, 2-4 pages); By the Numbers (math activities relating to the theme, 1 page); Where in the World (map activities, 2 pages); Your Turn (theme-related opportunities for children to take action, 1 page); Experts in Action (short profile of professional in field related to theme, 1 page); The Artist's Eye (fine or folk art relating to theme, 1 page); From the Source (age-appropriate primary source material, 1-2 pages). Assume 150 words/page. **Pays $50/page.**

TIPS "Submit queries specifically focused on the theme of an upcoming issue. We generally work 6 months ahead on themes. We look for unusual perspectives, original ideas, and excellent scholarship. Writers should check our website for current guidelines, topics, and query deadlines. We use very little fiction. Illustrators should not submit unsolicited art."

AQUILA

Studio 2, 67A Willowfield Rd., Eastbourne BN22 8AP United Kingdom. (44)(132)343-1313. **Fax:** (44) (132)373-1136. **E-mail:** info@aquila.co.uk. **Website:** www.aquila.co.uk. **Contact:** Jackie Berry, editor. "*Aquila* is an educational magazine for readers ages 8-13 including factual articles (no pop/celebrity material), arts/crafts, and puzzles." Entire publication aimed at juvenile market. Estab. 1993. Circ. 40,000. Pays on publication. Publishes ms 1 year after acceptance. Editorial lead time is 1 year. Responds to queries in 6-8 weeks. Sample copy: £5. Guidelines online.

NONFICTION Needs Young Readers: animal, arts/crafts, concept, cooking, games/puzzles, health, history, how-to, interview/profile, math, nature/environment, science, sports. Middle Readers: animal, arts/crafts, concept, cooking, games/puzzles, health, history, interview/profile, math, nature/environment, science, sports. **Buys 48 mss/year.** Query. Length: 600-800 words. **Pays £50-75.**

FICTION Needs Young Readers: animal, contemporary, fantasy, folktales, health, history, humorous, multicultural, nature/environment, problem solving, religious, science fiction, sports, suspense/mystery. Middle Readers: animal, contemporary, fantasy, folktales, health, history, humorous, multicultural, nature/environment, problem solving, religious, romance, science fiction, sports, suspense/mystery. **Buys 6-8 mss/year.** Query with published clips. Length: 1,000-1,150 words. **Pays £90/short story and £80/episode for serial.**

TIPS "We only accept a high level of educational material for children ages 8-13 with a good standard of literacy and ability."

ASK

Cricket Magazine Group, 70 E. Lake St., Suite 800, Chicago IL 60601. **E-mail:** ask@askmagkids.com. **Website:** www.cricketmag.com. **Contact:** Liz Huyck, editor. Magazine published 9 times/year covering science for children ages 7-10. "*Ask* is a magazine of arts and sciences for curious kids who like to find out how the world works." Estab. 2002. Byline given. Visit www.cricketmag.com/19-Submission-Guidelines-for-ASK-magazine-for-children-ages-6-9 or cricketmag.submittable.com for current issue theme list and calendar.

NONFICTION Needs young readers, middle readers: science, engineering, invention, machines, archaeology, animals, nature/environment, history, history of science. "*ASK* commissions most articles but welcomes queries from authors on all nonfiction subjects. Particularly looking for odd, unusual, and interesting stories likely to interest science-oriented kids. Writers interested in working for *ASK* should send a résumé and writing sample (including at least 1 page unedited) for consideration." Average word length: 150-1,600.

PHOTOS Buys 10 illustrations/issue; 60 illustrations/year. Works on assignment only. For illustrations, send query with samples.

$ BABYBUG

Cricket Magazine Group, 70 East Lake St., Suite 800, Chicago IL 60601. **E-mail:** babybug@babybugmagkids.com. **Website:** www.cricketmag.com/babybug; www.babybugmagkids.com. **Contact:** submissions editor. **50% freelance written.** *Babybug* is a look-and-listen magazine for babies and toddlers ages 6 months-3 years. Publishes 9 issues per year. Estab. 1994. Circ. 45,000. Byline given. Pays on publication. Accepts simultaneous submissions. Responds in 3-6 months to mss. Guidelines available online: www.cricketmag.com/submissions.

NONFICTION Needs very short clear fiction. **Buys 10-20 mss/year.** Submit through online submissions manager: submittable.cricketmag.com. Length: up to 6 sentences. **Pays up to 25¢ per word.**

PHOTOS Pays $500/spread; $250/page.

FICTION Wants very short, clear fiction. Needs rhythmic, rhyming. **Buys 10-20 mss/year.** Length: up to 6 sentences. **Up to 25¢/word.**

POETRY "We are especially interested in rhythmic and rhyming poetry. Poems may explore a baby's day, or they may be more whimsical." **Pays up to $3/line; $25 minimum.**

TIPS "Imagine having to read your story or poem—out loud—50 times or more! That's what parents will have to do. Babies and toddlers demand, 'Read it again!' Your material must hold up under repetition. And humor is much appreciated by all."

$$$$ BOYS' LIFE

Boy Scouts of America, P.O. Box 152079, 1325 W. Walnut Hill Ln., Irving TX 75015. **Website:** www.boyslife.org. **Contact:** Paula Murphey, senior editor; Clay Swartz, associate editor. **75% freelance written. Prefers to work with published/established writers; works with small number of new/unpublished writers each year.** *Boys' Life* is a monthly 4-color general interest magazine for boys 7-18, most of whom are Cub Scouts, Boy Scouts, or Venturers. Estab. 1911. Circ. 1.1 million. Byline given. Pays on acceptance. Publishes ms approximately 1 year after acceptance. Accepts queries by mail. Responds to queries/mss in 2 months. Sample copy: $3.95 plus 9x12 SASE. Guidelines online.

NONFICTION Needs scouting activities and general interests. **Buys 60 mss/year.** Query senior editor with SASE. No phone or e-mail queries. Length: 500-1,500 words. **Pay ranges from $400-1,500.** Pays expenses of writers on assignment.

PHOTOS Photo guidelines free with SASE. Pays $500 base editorial day rate against placement fees, plus expenses. **Pays on acceptance.** Buys one-time rights.

COLUMNS/DEPARTMENTS Science; Nature; Earth; Health; Sports; Space and Aviation; Cars; Computers; Entertainment; Pets; History; Music, all 600 words. Query associate editor. **Pays $100-400.**

FICTION Needs All fiction is assigned.

TIPS "We strongly recommend reading at least 12 issues of the magazine before submitting queries. We are a good market for any writer willing to do the necessary homework. Write for a boy you know who is 12. Our readers demand punchy writing in relatively short, straightforward sentences. The editors demand well-reported articles that demonstrate high standards of journalism. We follow the *Associated Press* manual of style and usage. Learn and read our publications before submitting anything."

BOYS' QUEST

P.O. Box 227, Bluffton OH 45817-0227. (419)358-4610, ext. 101. **Fax:** (419)358-8020. **Website:** www.funforkidzmagazines.com. **Contact:** Marilyn Edwards, editor. Bimonthly magazine. "*Boys' Quest* is a magazine created for boys from 5 to 14 years, with youngsters 8, 9 and 10 the specific target age. Our point of view is that every young boy deserves the right to be a young boy for a number of years before he becomes a young adult." Estab. 1995. Circ. 10,000. Byline given. Pays on publication. Accepts queries by mail. Responds to queries in 2 weeks; mss in 2 weeks (if rejected); 6 weeks (if scheduled). Guidelines and open themes available for SASE, or visit www.funforkidz.com and click on 'Writers' at the bottom of the homepage.

NONFICTION Needs Needs nonfiction pieces that are accompanied by clear photos. Articles accompanied by photos with high resolution are far more likely to be accepted than those that need illustrations. Query or send complete ms (preferred). Send SASE with correct postage. No faxed or e-mailed material. Length: 350 words per page.

PHOTOS "We use a number of photos, printed in b&w, inside the magazine. These photos support the articles." $5/photo.

FICTION Picture-oriented material, young readers, middle readers: adventure, animal, history, humorous, multicultural, nature/environment, problem-solving, sports. Does not want to see violence, teenage themes. Buys 30 mss/year. Query or send complete ms (preferred). Send SASE with correct postage. No faxed or e-mailed material. Length: 350 words per page

POETRY Reviews poetry. Limit submissions to 6 poems. Length: 21 lines maximum.

TIPS "First be familiar with our magazines. We are looking for lively writing, most of it from a young boy's point of view—with the boy or boys directly involved in an activity that is both wholesome and unusual. We need nonfiction with photos and fiction stories—around 500 words—puzzles, poems, cooking, carpentry projects, jokes and riddles. Nonfiction pieces that are accompanied by b&w photos are far more likely to be accepted than those that need illustrations. We will entertain simultaneous submissions as long as that fact is noted on the ms."

$ BREAD FOR GOD'S CHILDREN

P.O. Box 1017, Arcadia FL 34265. (863)494-6214. **E-mail:** bread@breadministries.org. **Website:** www.breadministries.org. **Contact:** Judith M. Gibbs, editor. **10% freelance written.** An interdenominational Christian teaching publication published 6-8 times/year written to aid children and youth in leading a Christian life. Estab. 1972. Circ. 10,000 (U.S. and Canada). Byline given. No kill fee. Publishes ms an average of 6 months after acceptance. Accepts queries by mail. Accepts simultaneous submissions. Responds in 6 months to mss. Sample copy for 9x12 SAE and 5 first-class stamps. Guidelines for #10 SASE.

NONFICTION Needs All levels: how-to. "We do not want anything detrimental to solid family values. Most topics will fit if they are slanted to our basic needs." **Buys 3-4 mss/year.** Send complete ms. Length: 500-800 words.

REPRINTS Send tearsheet and information about when and where the material previously appeared.

COLUMNS/DEPARTMENTS Freelance columns: Let's Chat (children's Christian values), 500-700 words; Teen Page (youth Christian values), 600-800 words; Idea Page (games, crafts, Bible drills). **Buys 5-8 mss/year.** Send complete ms. **Pays $30.**

FICTION "We are looking for writers who have a solid knowledge of Biblical principles and are concerned for the youth of today living by those principles. Stories must be well written, with the story itself getting the message across—no preaching, moralizing, or tag endings." Needs Young readers, middle readers, young adult/teen: adventure, religious, problem-solving, sports. Looks for "teaching stories that portray Christian lifestyles without preaching." **Buys 10-15 mss/year.** Send complete ms. Length: 600-800 words for young children; 900-1,500 words for older children. **Pays $40-50.**

TIPS "We want stories or articles that illustrate overcoming obstacles by faith and living solid, Christian lives. Know our publication and what we have used in the past. Know the readership and publisher's guidelines. Stories should teach the value of morality and honesty without preaching. Edit carefully for content and grammar."

$ CADET QUEST MAGAZINE

P.O. Box 7259, Grand Rapids MI 49510-7259. (616)241-5616. **Fax:** (616)241-5558. **E-mail:** submissions@calvinistcadets.org. **Website:** www.calvinistcadets.org. **Contact:** G. Richard Broene, editor. Magazine published 7 times/year. *Cadet Quest Magazine* shows boys 9-14 how God is at work in their lives and in the world around them. Estab. 1958. Circ. 6,000. Byline given. Pays on acceptance. No kill fee. Publishes ms an average of 4-11 months after acceptance. Accepts simultaneous submissions. Responds in 2 months to mss. Sample copy for 9x12 SASE and $1.45 postage. Guidelines online.

NONFICTION Needs how-to, humor, inspirational, interview, personal experience, informational. Special issues: Write for new themes list in January. "Articles about Christian athletes, coaching tips, and developing Christian character through sports are appreciated. Photos of these sports or athletes are also welcomed. Be original in presenting these topics to boys. Articles about camping, nature, and survival should be practical—the 'how-to' approach is best. 'God in nature' articles, if done without being preachy, are appreciated." Send complete ms via postal mail or e-mail (in body of e-mail; no attachments). Length: up to 1,500 words. **Pays 5¢/word and 1 contributor's copy.**

REPRINTS For reprints, send typed ms with rights for sale noted. Payment varies.

PHOTOS Pays $5 each for photos purchased with ms.

COLUMNS/DEPARTMENTS Project/Hobby articles (simple projects boys 9-14 can do on their own, made with easily accessible materials; must provide clear, accurate instructions); Cartoons and Puzzles (wholesome and boy-oriented logic puzzles, crosswords, and hidden pictures).

FICTION "Fast-moving, entertaining stories that appeal to a boy's sense of adventure or to his sense of humor are welcomed. Stories must present Christian life realistically and help boys relate Christian values to their own lives. Stories must have action without long dialogues. Favorite topics for boys include sports and athletes, humor, adventure, mystery, friends, etc. They must also fit the theme of that issue of *Cadet Quest*. Stories with preachiness and/or clichés are not of interest to us." Needs middle readers, boys/early teens: adventure, arts/craft, games/puzzles, hobbies, humorous, multicultural, religious, science, sports. No fantasy, science fiction, fashion, horror, or erotica. Send complete ms by postal mail or e-mail (in body of e-mail; no attachments). Length: 1,000-1,300 words. **Pays 5¢/word and 1 contributor's copy.**

TIPS "The best time to submit stories/articles is early in the year (January-April). Also remember readers are boys ages 9-14. Stories must reflect or add to the theme of the issue and be from a Christian perspective."

CALLIOPE

30 Grove St., Suite C, Peterborough NH 03458-1454. (603)924-7209. **Fax:** (603)924-7380. **E-mail:** customerservice@caruspub.com. **Website:** www.cobblestonepub.com. **Contact:** Rosalie Baker and Charles Baker, co-editors; Lou Waryncia, editorial director; Ann Dillon, art director. **50% freelance written.** Magazine published 9 times/year covering world history (East and West) through 1800 AD for 9- to 14-year-old kids. Estab. 1990. Circ. 13,000. Byline given. Pays on publication. Kill fee. Accepts queries by mail. If interested, responds 5 months before publication date. Sample copy for $5.95, $2 shipping and handling, and 10x13 SASE. Guidelines available online.

Articles must relate to the issue's theme. Lively, original approaches to the subject are the primary concerns of the editors in choosing material.

NONFICTION Needs in-depth nonfiction, plays, biographies. No religious, pornographic, biased, or sophisticated submissions. **Buys 30-40 mss/year.** Query with cover letter, one-page outline, bibliography, SASE. Length: 700-800 words for feature articles; 300-600 words for supplemental nonfiction. **Pays 20-25¢/word.**

PHOTOS If you have photographs pertaining to any upcoming theme, please contact the editor by mail or fax, or send them with your query. You may also send images on speculation. Model/property release preferred. Reviews b&w prints, color slides. Reviews photos with or without accompanying manuscript. "We buy one-time use. Our suggested fee range for professional quality photographs follows: ¼ page to full page b&w, $15-100; color, $25-100. Please note that fees for non-professional quality photographs are negotiated. Cover fees are set on an individual basis for one-time use, plus promotional use. All cover images are color. Prices set by museums, societies, stock photography houses, etc., are paid or negotiated. Photographs that are promotional in nature (e.g., from tourist agencies, organizations, special events, etc.) are usually submitted at no charge." Pays on publication. Credit line given.

FICTION Material must relate to forthcoming themes. Needs authentic historical and biographical fiction, adventure, retold legends, all relating to theme. **Buys 10 mss/year.** Query with cover letter, one-page outline, bibliography, SASE. Length: no more than 800 words. **Pays 20-25¢/word.**

FILLERS Crossword and other word puzzles (no word finds), mazes, and picture puzzles that use the vocabulary of the issue's theme or otherwise relate to the theme. **Pays on an individual basis.**

COBBLESTONE

Cobblestone Publishing, 30 Grove St., Suite C, Peterborough NH 03458. **Website:** www.cobblestonepub.com. **Contact:** Meg Chorlian. **50% freelance written.** "*Cobblestone* is interested in articles of historical accuracy and lively, original approaches to the subject at hand." American history magazine for ages 8-14. Circ. 15,000. Byline given. Pays on publication. Offers 50% kill fee. Accepts queries by mail. Accepts simultaneous submissions. Sample copy: $6.95, plus $2 s&h. Guidelines online.

"*Cobblestone* stands apart from other children's magazines by offering a solid look at one subject and stressing strong editorial content, color photographs throughout, and original illustrations." *Cobblestone* themes and deadline are available on website or with SASE.

NONFICTION Needs historical, humor, interview, personal experience, photo feature, travel, crafts, recipes, activities. No material that editorializes rather than reports. **Buys 45-50 mss/year.** Query with writing sample, one-page outline, bibliography, SASE. Length: 700-800 words for feature articles; 300-600 words for supplemental nonfiction; up to 700 words for activities. **Pays 20-25¢/word.**

PHOTOS Captions, identification of subjects, model release required. Reviews contact sheets, transparencies, prints. Pays $15-100/b&w. Pays on publication. Credit line given. Buys one-time rights. "Our suggested fee range for professional-quality photographs follows: ¼ page to full page b&w, $15-100; color, $25-100. Please note that fees for non-professional-quality photographs are negotiated."

FICTION Needs adventure, historical, biographical, retold legends, folktales, multicultural. **Buys 5 mss/year.** Query. Length: up to 800 words. **Pays 20-25¢/word.**

POETRY Needs free verse, light verse, traditional. Serious and light verse considered. Must have clear, objective imagery. Buys 3 poems/year. Length: up to 100 lines/poem. **Pays on an individual basis.**

FILLERS "Crossword and other word puzzles (no word finds), mazes, and picture puzzles that use the vocabulary of the issue's theme or otherwise relate to the theme." **Pays on an individual basis.**

TIPS "Review theme lists and past issues to see what we're looking for."

$$ CRICKET

Cricket Magazine Group, 70 E. Lake St., Suite 800, Chicago IL 60601. **Website:** www.cricketmag.com/ckt-cricket-magazine-for-kids-ages-9-14; www.cricketmagkids.com. **Contact:** Submissions editor. Monthly magazine for children ages 9-14. *Cricket* is a monthly literary magazine for ages 9-14. Publishes 9 issues per year. Estab. 1973. Circ. 73,000. Byline given. Pays on publication. Accepts queries by mail. Responds in 3-6 months to mss. Guidelines available online at submittable.cricketmag.com or www.cricketmag.com/submissions.

NONFICTION *Cricket* publishes thought-provoking nonfiction articles on a wide range of subjects: history, biography, true adventure, science and technology, sports, inventors and explorers, architecture and engineering, archaeology, dance, music, theater, and art. Articles should be carefully researched and include a solid bibliography that shows that research has gone beyond reviewing websites. Length: 1,200-1,800 words. **Pays up to 25¢/word.**

FICTION Needs realistic, contemporary, historic, humor, mysteries, fantasy, science fiction, folk/fairy tales, legend, myth. No didactic, sex, religious, or horror stories. **Buys 75-100 mss/year.** Submit complete ms. *Cricket* readers want to read about characters who are actively meeting their own challenges - not passively relying on the intervention of adults to solve problems of friends, family, and school. Even if not fully successful, characters in *Cricket* at least progress in coming to terms with themselves and life. Length: 1,200-1,800 words. **Pays up to 25¢/word.**

POETRY *Cricket* publishes both serious and humorous poetry. Poems should be well-crafted, with precise and vivid language and images. Poems can explore a variety of themes, from nature, to family and friendships, to whatever you can imagine that will delight our readers and invite their wonder and emotional response. Buys 20-30 poems/year. Submit maximum 6 poems. Length: 35 lines maximum. Most poems run 8-15 lines. **Pays up to $3/line.**

FILLERS Crossword puzzles, logic puzzles, math puzzles, crafts, recipes, science experiments, games and activities from other countries, plays, music, art.

TIPS Writers: "Read copies of back issues and current issues. Adhere to specified word limits. *Please* do not query." Would currently like to see more fantasy and science fiction. Illustrators: "Send only your best work and be able to reproduce that quality in assignments. Put name and address on *all* samples. Know a publication before you submit."

$ DEVOZINE

1908 Grand Ave., P.O. Box 340004, Nashville TN 37203-0004. **E-mail:** devozine@upperroom.org. **Website:** www.devozine.org. **Contact:** Sandi Miller, editor. *devozine,* published bimonthly, is an 80-page devotional magazine for youth (ages 12-18) and adults who care about youth. Offers meditations, scripture, prayers, poems, stories, songs, and feature articles to "aid youth in their prayer life, introduce them to spiritual disciplines, help them shape their concept of God, and encourage them in the life of discipleship."

NONFICTION Special issues: Submit by postal mail with SASE or by e-mail. Include name, age/birth date (if younger than 25), mailing address, e-mail address, phone number, and fax number (if available). Always publishes theme issues (available for SASE or online). Indicate theme you are writing for. Submit devotionals by mail or e-mail listed above. Submit feature article **queries** by e-mail to smiller@upperroom.org. Length: 150-250 words for devotionals; 500-600 words for feature articles. **Pays $25-100.**

POETRY Needs religious. Considers poetry by teens. Submit by postal mail with SASE or by e-mail. Include name, age/birth date (if younger than 25), mailing address, e-mail address, phone number, and fax number (if available). Always publishes theme issues (available for SASE or online). Indicate theme you are writing for. Length: 10-20 lines/poem. **Pays $25.**

DIG INTO HISTORY

Cobblestone Publishing, Editorial Dept., 30 Grove St., Suite C, Peterborough NH 03458. **Website:** www.cobblestonepub.com. **Contact:** Rosalie Baker, editor. *Dig into History* is an archaeology magazine for kids ages 10-14. Publishes entertaining and educational stories about discoveries, artifacts, and archaeologists. Estab. 1999. Pays on publication. Sample copy for $6.95 + $2 s&h.

NONFICTION Special issues: Wants feature articles ("in-depth nonfiction, plays, and biographies"); supplemental nonfiction (subjects directly and indirectly related to the theme; editors want little-known information but encourage writers not to overlook the obvious"); activities ("crafts, recipes, woodworking, or any other interesting projects that can be done either by children alone or with adult supervision; sketches and description of how activity relates to theme should accompany queries"); puzzles and games (crossword and other word puzzles using vocabulary of edition's theme; mazes and picture puzzles that relate to the theme"). Query. "A query must consist of all of the following to be considered: a brief cover letter stating the subject and word length of the proposed article, a detailed one-page outline explaining the information to be presented in the article, a bibliography of materials the author intends to use in preparing the article, and a SASE. Writers new to *Dig* should send a writing sample with query." Multiple queries accepted; may not be answered for many months. Length: 700-800 words for feature articles; 300-600 words for supplemental nonfiction; up to 700 words for activities. **Pays 20-25¢/printed word for feature articles and supplemental nonfiction. Pays activities, puzzles, and games on an individual basis.**

PHOTOS Uses anything related to archaeology, history, artifacts, and current archaeological events that relate to kids. Uses color prints and 35mm transparencies, and 300 dpi digital images. Provide résumé, promotional literature, or tearsheets to be kept on file. Responds only if interested.

FICTION Query. "Writers new to *Dig* should send a writing sample with query." Multiple queries accepted but may not be answered for many months. Length: up to 800 words. **Pays 20-25¢/printed word.**

TIPS "We are looking for writers who can communicate archaeological concepts in a conversational, interesting, informative, and *accurate* style for kids. Writers should have some idea of where photography can be located to support their articles."

FACES

Cobblestone Publishing, 30 Grove St., Peterborough NH 03458. **E-mail:** ecarpentiere@caruspub.com. **Website:** www.cobblestonepub.com. **Contact:** Elizabeth Crooker Carpentiere. **90-100% freelance written.** "Published 9 times/year, *Faces* covers world culture for ages 9-14. It stands apart from other children's magazines by offering a solid look at 1 subject and stressing strong editorial content, color photographs throughout, and original illustrations. *Faces* offers an equal balance of feature articles and activities, as well as folktales and legends." Estab. 1984. Circ. 15,000. Byline given. Pays on publication. Offers 50% kill fee. Accepts queries by mail, e-mail. Accepts simultaneous submissions. Sample copy: $6.95, plus $2 s&h. Guidelines online.

NONFICTION Needs historical, humor, interview, personal experience, photo feature, travel, recipes, activities, crafts. **Buys 45-50 mss/year.** Query with writing sample, one-page outline, bibliography, SASE. Length: 800 words for feature articles; 300-600 for supplemental nonfiction; up to 700 words for activities. **Pays 20-25¢/word.**

PHOTOS "Contact the editor by mail or e-mail, or send photos with your query. You may also send images on speculation." Captions, identification of subjects, model releases required. Reviews contact sheets, transparencies, prints. Pays $15-100 for b&w; $25-100 for color; cover fees are negotiated.

FICTION Needs ethnic, historical, retold legends and folktales, original plays. Query. Length: up to 800 words. **Pays 20-25¢/word.**

POETRY Serious and light verse considered. Must have clear, objective imagery. Length: up to 100 lines/poem. **Pays on an individual basis.**

FILLERS Needs "crossword and other word puzzles (no word finds), mazes, and picture puzzles that use the vocabulary of the issue's theme or otherwise relate to the theme." **Pays on an individual basis.**

TIPS "Writers are encouraged to study past issues of the magazine to become familiar with our style and content. Writers with anthropological and/or travel experience are particularly encouraged; *Faces* is about world cultures. All feature articles, recipes, and activities are freelance contributions."

THE FRIEND MAGAZINE

The Church of Jesus Christ of Latter-day Saints, 50 E. North Temple St., Salt Lake City UT 84150. (801)240-2210. **Fax:** (801)240-2270. **E-mail:** friend@ldschurch.org. **Website:** www.lds.org/friend. **Contact:** Paul B. Pieper, editor; Mark W. Robison, art director. Monthly magazine for 3-12 year olds. "The *Friend* is published by The Church of Jesus Christ of Latter-day Saints for boys and girls up to 3-12 years of age." Estab. 1971. Circ. 275,000. Pays on acceptance. Submit seasonal material at least 1 year in advance. Responds in 2 months to mss. Sample copy for $1.50, 9x12 envelope, and 4 first-class stamps.

NONFICTION Needs historical, humor, inspirational, religious, adventure, ethnic, nature, family- and gospel-oriented puzzles, games, cartoons. Special issues: Wants photo stories, activities, and games. Send complete ms by mail or e-mail. Length: up to 1,000 words. **Pays $100-150 (400 words and up) for stories; $20 minimum for activities and games.**

FICTION Wants illustrated stories and "For Little Friends" stories. See guidelines online.

POETRY "We are looking for easy-to-illustrate poems with catchy cadences. Poems should convey a sense of joy and reflect gospel teachings. Also brief poems that will appeal to preschoolers." **Pays $30 for poems.**

FUN FOR KIDZ

P.O. Box 227, Bluffton OH 45817. (419)358-4610. **Website:** funforkidz.com. **Contact:** Marilyn Edwards, articles editor. "*Fun for Kidz* is a magazine created for boys and girls ages 6-13, with youngsters 8, 9, and 10 the specific target age. The magazine is designed as an activity publication to be enjoyed by both boys and girls on the alternative months of *Hopscotch* and *Boys' Quest* magazines." Estab. 2002. Byline given. Pays on acceptance. Accepts queries by mail. Accepts simultaneous submissions. Responds in 2 weeks to queries; 6 weeks to mss. Sample copy: $6 in U.S., $9 in Canada, and $12.25 internationally. Guidelines online.

NONFICTION Needs picture-oriented material, young readers, middle readers: animal, arts/crafts, cooking, games/puzzles, history, hobbies, how-to, humorous, problem-solving, sports, carpentry projects. Submit complete ms with SASE, contact info, and notation of which upcoming theme your content should be considered for. Length: 300-750 words. **Pays minimum 5¢/word for articles; variable rate for games and projects, etc.**

TIPS "Our point of view is that every child deserves the right to be a child for a number of years before he or she becomes a young adult. As a result, *Fun for Kidz* looks for activities that deal with timeless topics, such as pets, nature, hobbies, science, games, sports, careers, simple cooking, and anything else likely to interest a child."

GIRLS' LIFE

Monarch Publishing, 3 S. Frederick St., Suite 806, Baltimore MD 21202. (410)426-9600. **Fax:** (866)793-1531. **E-mail:** writeforGL@girlslife.com. **Website:** www.girlslife.com. **Contact:** Karen Bokram, founding editor and publisher; Jessica D'Argenio Waller, fashion editor; Chun Kim, art director. Bimonthly magazine covering girls ages 9-15. Estab. 1994. Circ. 2.16 million. Byline given. Pays on publication. Publishes ms an average of 3 months after acceptance. Editorial lead time 4 months. Submit seasonal material 5 months in advance. Accepts queries by mail, e-mail. Responds in 1 month to queries. Sample copy for $5 or online. Guidelines available online.

NONFICTION Needs book excerpts, essays, general interest, how-to, humor, inspirational, interview, new product, travel. Special issues: Special issues: Back to School (August/September); Fall, Halloween (October/November); Holidays, Winter (December/January); Valentine's Day, Crushes (February/March); Spring, Mother's Day (April/May); and Summer, Father's Day (June/July). **Buys 40 mss/year.** Query by mail with published clips. Submit complete mss on spec only. "Features and articles should speak to young women ages 10-15 looking for new ideas about relationships, family, friends, school, etc. with fresh, savvy advice. Front-of-the-book columns and quizzes are a good place to start." Length: 700-2,000 words. **Pays $350/regular column; $500/feature.**

PHOTOS State availability. Captions, identification of subjects, model releases required. Reviews contact sheets, negatives, transparencies. Negotiates payment individually.

COLUMNS/DEPARTMENTS Buys 20 mss/year. Query with published clips. **Pays $150-450.**

FICTION "We accept short fiction. They should be stand-alone stories and are generally 2,500-3,500 words."

TIPS "Send thought-out queries with published writing samples and detailed résumé. Have fresh ideas and a voice that speaks to our audience-not down to them. And check out a copy of the magazine or visit girlslife.com before submitting."

HIGHLIGHTS FOR CHILDREN

803 Church St., Honesdale PA 18431. (570)253-1080. **Fax:** (570)251-7847. **Website:** www.highlights.com. **Contact:** Christine French Cully, editor-in-chief. **80% freelance written.** Monthly magazine for children up to ages 6-12. "This book of wholesome fun is dedicated to helping children grow in basic skills and knowledge, in creativeness, in ability to think and reason, in sensitivity to others, in high ideals, and worthy ways of living—for children are the world's most important people. We publish stories for beginning and advanced readers. Up to 500 words for beginning readers, up to 800 words for advanced readers." Estab. 1946. Circ. approximately 1.5 million. Pays on acceptance. Accepts queries by mail. Responds in 2 months to queries. Sample copy free. Guidelines on website in "Company" area.

NONFICTION "Generally we prefer to see a manuscript rather than a query. However, we will review queries regarding nonfiction." Length: 800 words maximum. **Pays $25 for craft ideas and puzzles; $25 for fingerplays; $150 and up for articles.**

PHOTOS Reviews electronic files, color 35mm slides, photos.

FICTION Meaningful stories appealing to both girls and boys, up to age 12. Vivid, full of action. Engaging plot, strong characterization, lively language. Prefers stories in which a child protagonist solves a dilemma through his or her own resources. Seeks stories that the child ages 8-12 will eagerly read, and the younger child will like to hear when read aloud (500-800 words). Stories require interesting plots and a number of illustration possiblities. Also need rebuses (picture stories 100 words), stories with urban settings, stories for beginning readers (100-500 words), sports and humorous stories, adventures, holiday stories, and mysteries. We also would like to see more material of 1-page length (300 words), both fiction and factual. Needs adventure, fantasy, historical, humorous, animal, contemporary, folktales, multi-cultural, problem-solving, sports. No stories glorifying war, crime or violence. Send complete ms. **Pays $150 minimum plus 2 contributor's copies.**

POETRY Lines/poem: 16 maximum ("most poems are shorter"). Considers simultaneous submissions ("please indicate"); no previously published poetry. No e-mail submissions. "Submit typed manuscript with very brief cover letter." Occasionally comments on submissions "if manuscript has merit or author seems to have potential for our market." Guidelines available for SASE. Responds "generally within 2 months." Always sends prepublication galleys. Pays 2 contributor's copies; "money varies." Acquires all rights.

TIPS "Know the magazine's style before submitting. Send for guidelines and sample issue if necessary." Writers: "At *Highlights* we're paying closer attention to acquiring more nonfiction for young readers than we have in the past." Illustrators: "Fresh, imaginative work encouraged. Flexibility in working relationships a plus. Illustrators presenting their work need not confine themselves to just children's illustrations as long as work can translate to our needs. We also use animal illustrations, real and imaginary. We need crafts, puzzles and any activity that will stimulate children mentally and creatively. Know our publication's standards and content by reading sample issues, not just the guidelines. Avoid tired themes, or put a fresh twist on an old theme so that its style is fun and lively. Write what inspires you, not what you think the market needs. We are pleased that many authors of children's literature report that their first published work was in the pages of *Highlights*. It is not our policy to consider fiction on the strength of the reputation of the author. We judge each submission on its own merits. Query with simple letter to establish whether the nonfiction subject is likely to be of interest. Expert reviews and complete bibliography required for nonfiction. A beginning writer should first become familiar with the type of material that *Highlights* publishes. Include special qualifications, if any, of author. Write for the child, not the editor. Write in a voice that children understand and relate to. Speak to today's kids, avoiding didactic, overt messages. Even though our general principles haven't changed over the years, we are contemporary in our approach to issues. Avoid worn themes."

$ HOPSCOTCH

Fun for Kidz Magazines, P.O. Box 227, Bluffton OH 45817. (419)358-4610. **Website:** www.hopscotchmagazine.com. **Contact:** Marilyn Edwards, editor. "For girls from ages 6-13, featuring traditional subjects—pets, games, hobbies, nature, science, sports, etc.—with an emphasis on articles that show girls actively involved in unusual and/or worthwhile activities." Estab. 1989. Circ. 14,000. Byline given. Pays on publication. Responds in 2 weeks to queries; 5 weeks to mss. Sample copy: $6 in U.S.; $9 in Canada; $12.25 internationally.

NONFICTION Needs picture-oriented material, young readers, middle readers: animal, arts/crafts, biography, cooking, games/puzzles, geography, hobbies, how-to, humorous, math, nature/environment, science. "Need more nonfiction with quality photos about a *Hopscotch*-age girl involved in a worthwhile activity." Does not want to see pieces dealing with dating, sex, fashion, hard rock music. **Buys 30-36 mss/year.** Query or submit complete ms with SASE, contact info, and notation of which upcoming theme the content should be considered for. Length: 350-750 words. **Pays minimum 5¢/word; pays minimum $10/puzzle; pays variable rate for games, crafts, cartoons, etc.**

FICTION **Buys 9-10 mss/year.** Query or submit complete ms with SASE, contact info, and notation of which upcoming theme the content should be considered for. Length: 350-750 words. **Pays minimum 5¢/word.**

POETRY Query or submit poems with SASE, contact info, and notation of which upcoming theme the content should be considered for. Buys 18 poems/year. **Pays minimum $10/poem.**

TIPS "Remember that we publish only 6 issues a year, which means our editorial needs are extremely limited. Please look at our guidelines and our magazine. Remember, we use far more nonfiction than fiction. Guidelines and current theme list can be downloaded from our website. If decent photos accompany the piece, it stands an even better chance of being accepted. We believe it is the responsibility of the contributor to come up with photos. Please remember, our readers are 6-12 years—most are 8-10—and your text should reflect that. Many magazines try to entertain first and educate second. We try to do the reverse. Our magazine is more simplistic, like a book to be read from cover to cover. We are looking for wholesome, nondated material."

$$ JACK AND JILL

U.S. Kids, P.O. Box 567, Indianapolis IN 46206. (317)634-1100. **E-mail:** jackandjill@uskidsmags.com. **Website:** www.jackandjillmag.org. **50% freelance written.** Bimonthly magazine published for children ages 8-12. Estab. 1938. Circ. 200,000. Byline given. Pays on publication. Publishes ms an average of 8 months after acceptance. Submit seasonal material 8 months in advance. Responds to mss in 3 months. Guidelines available online.

"Please do not send artwork. We prefer to work with professional illustrators of our own choosing."

NONFICTION Needs young readers, middle readers: animal, arts, crafts, cooking, games, puzzles, history, hobbies, how-to, humorous, interviews, profile, nature, science, sports. **Buys 8-10 mss/year.** Submit complete ms via postal mail; no e-mail submissions. Queries not accepted. "We are especially interested in features or Q&As with regular kids (or groups of kids) in the *Jack and Jill* age group who are engaged in unusual, challenging, or interesting activities. No celebrity pieces please." Length: up to 700 words. **Pays 25$ and up.**

FICTION Submit complete ms via postal mail; no e-mail submissions. "The tone of the stories should be fun and engaging. Stories should hook readers right from the get-go and pull them through the story. Humor is very important! Dialogue should be witty instead of just furthering the plot. The story should convey some kind of positive message. Possible themes could include self-reliance, being kind to others, appreciating other cultures, and so on. There are a million positive messages, so get creative! Kids can see preachy coming from a mile away, though, so please focus on telling a good story over teaching a lesson. The message—if there is one—should come organically from the story and not feel tacked on." Needs young readers and middle readers: adventure, contemporary, folktales, health, history, humorous, nature, sports. **Buys 30-35 mss/year.** Length: 600-800 words. **Pays $25 and up.**

POETRY Submit via postal mail; no e-mail submissions. Wants light-hearted poetry appropriate for the age group. Mss must be typewritten with poet's contact information in upper right-hand corner of each poem's page. SASE required. Length: up to 30 lines/poem. **Pays $25 and up.**

TIPS "We are constantly looking for new writers who can tell good stories with interesting slants—stories that are not full of outdated and time-worn expressions. We like to see stories about kids who are smart and capable but not sarcastic or smug. Problem-solving skills, personal responsibility, and integrity are good topics for us. Obtain current issues of the magazine and study them to determine our present needs and editorial style."

$ KEYS FOR KIDS

Box 1001, Grand Rapids MI 49501-1001. (616)647-4500. **Fax:** (616)647-4950. **E-mail:** editorial@keysforkids.org. **Website:** www.cbhministries.org. **Contact:** Hazel Marett, fiction editor. *Keys for Kids*, published by CBH Ministries, features stories and Key Verses of the Day for children ages 6-12 teaching about God's love. Estab. 1982. Pays on acceptance. Accepts simultaneous submissions. Sample copy for 6x9 SAE and 3 first-class stamps. Guidelines online.

FICTION "Propose a title and suggest an appropriate Scripture passage, generall 3-10 verses, to reinforce the theme of your story. Tell a story (not a Bible story) with a spiritual application. Avoid Pollyanna-type children—make them normal, ordinary kids, not goody-goodies. Avoid fairy-tale endings and minced oaths (gee, golly, gosh, darn). Include some action—not conversation only. Some humor is good." Needs religious. Submit complete ms. Length: up to 350 words. **Pays $25.**

TIPS "Be sure to follow guidelines after studying sample copy of the publication."

$$ LADYBUG

Cricket Magazine Group, 700 E. Lake St., Suite 800, Chicago IL 60601. **Website:** www.cricketmag.com/ladybug; ladybugmagkids.com. **Contact:** submissions editor. Monthly magazine for children ages 3-6. *Ladybug* magazine is an imaginative magazine with art and literature for young children (ages 3-6). Publishes 9 issues per year. Estab. 1990. Circ. 125,000. Byline given. Pays on publication. Responds in 6 months to mss. Guidelines available online at submittable.cricketmag.com or www.cricketmag.com/submissions.

NONFICTION Needs gentle nonfiction, action rhymes, finger plays, crafts and activities. **Buys 35 mss/year.** Submit via online submissions manager: cricketmag.submittable.com. Length: up to 400 words. **Pays up to 25¢/word.**

FICTION Needs imaginative contemporary stories, original retellings of fairy and folk tales, multicultural stories. **Buys 30 mss/year.** Submit via online submissions manager: cricket.submittable.com. Length: up to 800 words. **Pays up to 25¢/word.**

POETRY Needs light verse, traditional. Wants poetry that is "rhythmic, rhyming; serious, humorous." Submit via online submissions manager: cricket.submittable.com. Length: up to 20 lines/poem. **Pays up to $3/line ($25 minimum).**

FILLERS Learning activities, games, crafts, songs, finger games. See back issues for types, formats, and length.

$$$Ø MUSE

Cricket Magazine Group, 70 E. Lake St., Suite 800, Chicago IL 60601. **E-mail:** muse@musemagkids.com. **Website:** www.cricketmag.com. **Contact:** submissions editor. "The goal of *Muse* is to give as many children as possible access to the most important ideas and concepts underlying the principal areas of human knowledge. Articles should meet the highest possible standards of clarity and transparency, aided, wherever possible, by a tone of skepticism, humor, and irreverence." All articles are commissioned. To be considered for assignments, experienced science writers may send a résumé and 3 published clips. Estab. 1996. Circ. 40,000. Accepts queries by mail, e-mail.

Muse is not accepting unsolicited mss.

NONFICTION Needs middle readers, young adult: animal, arts, history, math, nature/environment, problem-solving, science, social issues. Query with published clips.

$$$$ NATIONAL GEOGRAPHIC KIDS

National Geographic Society, 1145 17th St. NW, Washington DC 20036. **E-mail:** ashaw@ngs.org. **E-mail:** chughes@ngs.org; asilen@ngs.org; kboatner@ngs.org. **Website:** www.kids.nationalgeographic.com. **Contact:** Catherine Hughes, science editor; Andrea

Silen, associate editor; Kay Boatner, associate editor; Jay Sumner, photo director. **70% freelance written.** Magazine published 10 times/year. "It's our mission to find fresh ways to entertain children while educating and exciting them about their world." Estab. 1975. Circ. 1.3 million. Byline given. Pays on acceptance. Offers 10% kill fee. Publishes ms an average of 6 months after acceptance. Editorial lead time 6+ months. Submit seasonal material 6+ months in advance. Accepts queries by mail. Accepts simultaneous submissions. Sample copy for #10 SASE. Guidelines online.

"We do not want poetry, sports, fiction, or story ideas that are too young—our audience is between ages 6-14."

NONFICTION Needs general interest, humor, interview, technical, travel, animals, human interest, science, technology, entertainment, archaeology, pets, history, paleontology. Query with published clips and résumé. Length: 100-1,000 words. **Pays $1/word for assigned articles.** Pays expenses of writers on assignment.

PHOTOS State availability. Captions, identification of subjects, model releases required. Reviews contact sheets, negatives, transparencies, prints. Negotiates payment individually.

COLUMNS/DEPARTMENTS Freelance columns: Amazing Animals (animal heroes, stories about animal rescues, interesting/funny animal tales), 100 words; Inside Scoop (fun, kid-friendly news items), 50-70 words. Query with published clips. **Pays $1/word.**

TIPS "Submit relevant clips. Writers must have demonstrated experience writing for kids. Read the magazine before submitting."

NATURE FRIEND MAGAZINE

4253 Woodcock Lane, Dayton VA 22821. (540)867-0764. **E-mail:** info@naturefriendmagazine.com; editor@naturefriendmagazine.com; photos@naturefriendmagazine.com. **Website:** www.naturefriendmagazine.com. **Contact:** Kevin Shank, editor. **80% freelance written.** Monthly children's magazine covering creation-based nature. "*Nature Friend* includes stories, puzzles, science experiments, nature experiments—all submissions need to honor God as creator." Estab. 1982. Circ. 13,000. Byline given. Pays on publication. No kill fee. Editorial lead time 4 months. Submit seasonal material 6 months in advance. Accepts simultaneous submissions. Responds in 6 months to mss. Sample copy: $5, postage paid. Guidelines available on website.

Picture-oriented material and conversational material needed.

NONFICTION Needs how-to, nature, photo feature, science experiments (for ages 8-12), articles about interesting/unusual animals. No poetry, evolution, animals depicted in captivity, talking animal stories, or evolutionary material. **Buys 50 mss/year.** Send complete ms. Length: 250-900 words. **Pays 5¢/word.**

PHOTOS Send photos. Captions, identification of subjects required. Reviews prints. Offers $20-75/photo.

COLUMNS/DEPARTMENTS Learning By Doing, 500-900 words. **Buys 12 mss/year.** Send complete ms.

FILLERS Needs facts, puzzles, short essays on something current in nature. **Buys 35 mss/year.** Length: 150-250 words. **5¢/word.**

TIPS "We want to bring joy and knowledge to children by opening the world of God's creation to them. We endeavor to create a sense of awe about nature's Creator and a respect for His creation. We'd like to see more submissions on hands-on things to do with a nature theme (not collecting rocks or leaves—real stuff). Also looking for good stories that are accompanied by good photography."

NEW MOON GIRLS

New Moon Girl Media, P.O. Box 161287, Duluth MN 55816. (218)728-5507. **Fax:** (218)728-0314. **E-mail:** submissions@newmoon.com. **Website:** www.newmoon.com. **25% freelance written.** Bimonthly magazine covering girls ages 8-14, edited by girls ages 8-14. "*New Moon Girls* is for every girl who wants her voice heard and her dreams taken seriously. *New Moon* celebrates girls, explores the passage from girl to woman, and builds healthy resistance to gender inequities. The *New Moon* girl is true to herself, and *New Moon Girls* helps her as she pursues her unique path in life, moving confidently into the world." Estab. 1992. Circ. 30,000. Byline given. Pays on publication. Publishes ms an average of 6 months after acceptance. Editorial lead time 6 months. Submit seasonal material 8 months in advance. Accepts queries by mail, e-mail, fax. Accepts simultaneous submissions. Responds in 2 months to mss. Sample copy: $7.50 or online. Guidelines available at website.

In general, all material should be pro-girl and feature girls and women as the primary focus.

NONFICTION Needs essays, general interest, humor, inspirational, interview, opinion, personal experience, written by girls, photo feature, religious, travel, multicultural/girls from other countries. No fashion, beauty, or dating. **Buys 20 mss/year.** Send complete ms by e-mail. Publishes nonfiction by adults in Herstory and Women's Work departments only. Length: 600 words. **Pays 6-12¢/word.**

PHOTOS State availability. Captions, identification of subjects required. Negotiates payment individually.

COLUMNS/DEPARTMENTS Women's Work (profile of a woman and her job relating the the theme), 600 words; Herstory (historical woman relating to theme), 600 words. **Buys 10 mss/year.** Query. **Pays 6-12¢/word.**

FICTION Prefers girl-written material. All girl-centered. Needs adventure, fantasy, historical, humorous, slice-of-life vignettes. **Buys 6 mss/year.** Send complete ms by e-mail. Length: 900-1,600 words. **Pays 6-12¢/word.**

POETRY No poetry by adults.

TIPS "We'd like to see more girl-written feature articles that relate to a theme. These can be about anything the girl has done personally, or she can write about something she's studied. Please read *New Moon Girls* before submitting to get a sense of our style. Writers and artists who comprehend our goals have the best chance of publication. We love creative articles—both nonfiction and fiction—that are not condescending to our readers. Keep articles to suggested word lengths; avoid stereotypes. Refer to our guidelines and upcoming themes online."

POCKETS

The Upper Room, P.O. Box 340004, Nashville TN 37203. (615)340-7333. **E-mail:** pockets@upperroom.org. **Website:** pockets.upperroom.org. **Contact:** Lynn W. Gilliam, editor. **60% freelance written.** Magazine published 11 times/year. "*Pockets* is a Christian devotional magazine for children ages 6-12. All submissions should address the broad theme of the magazine. Each issue is built around a theme with material which can be used by children in a variety of ways. Scripture stories, fiction, poetry, prayers, art, graphics, puzzles and activities are included. Submissions do not need to be overtly religious. They should help children experience a Christian lifestyle that is not always a neatly wrapped moral package but is open to the continuing revelation of God's will. Seasonal material, both secular and liturgical, is desired." Estab. 1981. Byline given. Pays on acceptance. No kill fee. Publishes ms an average of 1 year after acceptance. Submit seasonal material 1 year in advance. Responds in 8 weeks to mss. Each issue reflects a specific theme. Guidelines online.

Does not accept e-mail or fax submissions.

NONFICTION Needs Picture-oriented, young readers, middle readers: cooking, games/puzzles. Special issues: "*Pockets* seeks biographical sketches of persons, famous or unknown, whose lives reflect their Christian commitment, written in a way that appeals to children." Does not accept how-to articles. "Nonfiction should read like a story." Multicultural needs include stories that feature children of various racial/ethnic groups and do so in a way that is true to those depicted. **Buys 10 mss/year.** Submit complete ms by mail. No e-mail submissions. Length: 400-1,000 words. **Pays 14¢/word.**

REPRINTS Accepts one-time previously published submissions. Send ms with rights for sale noted and information about when and where the material previously appeared.

PHOTOS Send 4-6 close-up photos of children actively involved in peacemakers at work activities. Send photos, contact sheets, prints, or digital images. Must be 300 dpi. Pays $25/photo.

COLUMNS/DEPARTMENTS Family Time, 200-300 words; Peacemakers at Work (profiles of children working for peace, justice, and ecological concerns), 400-600 words. **Pays 14¢/word**. Activities/Games (related to themes). **Pays $25 and up**. Kids Cook (simple recipes children can make alone or with minimal help from an adult). **Pays $25.**

FICTION "Stories should contain lots of action, use believable dialogue, be simply written, and be relevant to the problems faced by this age group in everyday life." Submit complete ms by mail. No e-mail submissions. Length: 600-1,000 words.

POETRY Both seasonal and theme poems needed. Considers poetry by children. Buys 14 poems/year. Length: up to 20 lines. **Pays $25 minimum.**

TIPS "Theme stories, role models, and retold scripture stories are most open to freelancers. Poetry is also open. It is very helpful if writers read our writers' guidelines and themes on our website."

SHINE BRIGHTLY

GEMS Girls' Clubs, 1333 Alger St., SE, Grand Rapids MI 49507. (616)241-5616. **Fax:** (616)241-5558. **E-mail:** shinebrightly@gemsgc.org. **Website:** www.gemsgc.org. **Contact:** Kristine Palosaari, executive director; Kelli Gilmore, managing editor. **80% freelance written. Works with new and published/established writers.** Monthly magazine (with combined June/July, August summer issue). "Our purpose is to lead girls into a living relationship with Jesus Christ and to help them see how God is at work in their lives and the world around them. Puzzles, crafts, stories, and articles for girls ages 9-14." Estab. 1970. Circ. 17,000. Byline given. Pays on publication. No kill fee. Publishes ms an average of 1 year after acceptance. Submit seasonal material 1 year in advance. Accepts simultaneous submissions. Responds in 2 months to mss. Sample copy with 9x12 SASE with 3 first class stamps and $1. Guidelines available online.

NONFICTION Needs humor, inspirational, seasonal and holiday, interview, personal experience, photo feature, religious, travel, adventure, mystery. Avoid the testimony approach. **Buys 35 unsolicited mss/year.** Submit complete ms in body of e-mail. No attachments. Length: 100-800 words. **Pays up to $35, plus 2 copies.**

REPRINTS Send typed manuscript with rights for sale noted and information about when and where the material previously appeared.

PHOTOS Purchased with or without ms. Appreciate multicultural subjects. Reviews 5x7 or 8x10 clear color glossy prints. Pays $25-50 on publication.

COLUMNS/DEPARTMENTS How-to (crafts); puzzles and jokes; quizzes. Length: 200-400 words. Send complete ms. **Pay varies.**

FICTION Does not want "unrealistic stories and those with trite, easy endings. We are interested in manuscripts that show how girls can change the world." Needs adventure experiences girls could have in their hometowns or places they might realistically visit, ethnic, historical, humorous, mystery, religious, omance, slice-of-life vignettes, suspense,. Believable only. Nothing too preachy. **Buys 30 mss/year.** Submit complete ms in body of e-mail. No attachments. Length: 700-900 words. **Pays up to $35, plus 2 copies.**

POETRY Needs free verse, haiku, light verse, traditional. **Limited need for poetry. Pays $5-15.**

TIPS Writers: "Please check our website before submitting. We have a specific style and theme that deals with how girls can impact the world. The stories should be current, deal with pre-adolescent problems and joys, and help girls see God at work in their lives through humor as well as problem-solving." Prefers not to see anything on the adult level, secular material, or violence. Writers frequently oversimplify the articles and often write with a Pollyanna attitude. An author should be able to see his/her writing style as exciting and appealing to girls ages 9-14. The style can be fun, but also teach a truth. Subjects should be current and important to *SHINE brightly* readers. Use our theme update as a guide. We would like to receive material with a multicultural slant."

SPARKLE

GEMS Girls' Clubs, 1333 Alger St. SE, Grand Rapids MI 49507. (616)241-5616. **Fax:** (616)241-5558. **E-mail:** kelli@gemsgc.org. **Website:** www.gemsgc.org. **Contact:** Kelli Gilmore, managing editor; Lisa Hunter, art director/photo editor. **80% freelance written.** Bimonthly magazine for girls ages 6-9. Mission is to prepare young girls to live out their faith and become world-changers. Strives to help girls make a difference in the world. Looks at the application of scripture to everyday life. Also strives to delight the reader and cause the reader to evalute her own life in light of the truth presented. Finally, attempts to teach practical life skills. Estab. 2002. Circ. 9,000. Byline given. Pays on publication. Offers $20 kill fee. Editorial lead time 3 months. Submit seasonal material 1 year in advance. Accepts queries by mail, e-mail. Accepts simultaneous submissions. Responds in 3 weeks to queries; 3 months to mss. Sample copy for 9x13 SAE, 3 first-class stamps, and $1 for coverage/publication cost. Writer's guidelines for #10 SASE or online.

NONFICTION Needs Young readers: animal, arts/crafts, biography, careers, cooking, concept, games/puzzles, geography, health, history, hobbies, how-to, humor, inspirational, interview/profile, math, multicultural, music/drama/art, nature/environment, personal experience, photo feature, problem-solving, quizzes, recipes, religious, science, social issues, sports, travel. Looking for inspirational biographies, stories from Zambia, and ideas on how to live a green lifestyle. Constant mention of God is not necessary if the moral tone of the story is positive. **Buys 15 mss/year.** Send complete ms. Length: 100-400 words. **Pays $35 maximum.**

PHOTOS Send photos. Identification of subjects required. Reviews at least 5X7 clear color glossy prints, GIF/JPEG files on CD. Offers $25-50/photo.

COLUMNS/DEPARTMENTS Crafts; puzzles and jokes; quizzes, all 200-400 words. Send complete ms. **Payment varies.**

FICTION Needs Young readers: adventure, animal, contemporary, ethnic/multicultural, fantasy, folktale, health, history, humorous, music and musicians, mystery, nature/environment, problem-solving, religious, recipes, service projects, slice-of-life, sports, suspense/mystery, vignettes, interacting with family and friends. **Buys 10 mss/year.** Send complete ms. Length: 100-400 words. **Pays $35 maximum.**

POETRY Prefers rhyming. "We do not wish to see anything that is too difficult for a first grader to read. We wish it to remain light. The style can be fun but should also teach a truth." No violence or secular material. Buys 4 poems/year. Submit maximum 4 poems.

FILLERS Needs facts, short humor. **Buys 6 mss/year.** Length: 50-150 words. **Pays $10-15.**

TIPS "Keep it simple. We are writing to first to third graders. It must be simple yet interesting. Mss should build girls up in Christian character but not be preachy. They are just learning about God and how He wants them to live. Mss should be delightful as well as educational and inspirational. Writers should keep stories simple but not write with a 'Pollyanna' attitude. Authors should see their writing style as exciting and appealing to girls ages 6-9. Subjects should be current and important to *Sparkle* readers. Use our theme as a guide. We would like to receive material with a multicultural slant."

SPIDER

Cricket Magazine Group, 70 East Lake St., Suite 300, Chicago IL 60601. **Website:** www.cricketmag.com. **Contact:** Marianne Carus, editor in chief; Suzanne Beck, managing art director. **85% freelance written.** Monthly reading and activity magazine for children ages 6-9. "*Spider* introduces children to the highest-quality stories, poems, illustrations, articles, and activities. It was created to foster in beginning readers a love of reading and discovery that will last a lifetime. We're looking for writers who respect children's intelligence." Estab. 1994. Circ. 70,000. Byline given. Pays on publication. Accepts simultaneous submissions. Responds in 6 months to mss. Guidelines online.

NONFICTION Special issues: Wants "well-researched articles about animals, kids their own age doing amazing things, and cool science discoveries (such as wetsuits for penguins and real-life invisibility cloaks). Nonfiction articles should rise above a simple list of facts; we look for kid-friendly nonfiction shaped into an engaging narrative." Submit complete ms via online submissions manager (cricketmag.submittable.com). Length: 300-800 words. **Pays up to 25¢/word.**

REPRINTS Send photocopy with rights for sale noted and information about when and where the material previously appeared.

PHOTOS For art samples, it is especially helpful to see pieces showing children, animals, action scenes, and several scenes from a narrative showing a character in different situations. Send photocopies/tearsheets. Also considers photo essays (prefers color, but b&w is also accepted). Captions, identification of subjects, model releases required. Reviews contact sheets, transparencies, 8×10 prints.

FICTION Stories should be easy to read. Has published work by Polly Horvath, Andrea Cheng, and Beth Wagner Brust. Needs fantasy, humorous, science fiction, folk tales, fairy tales, fables, myths. No romance, horror, religious. Submit complete ms via online submissions manager (cricketmag.submittable.com). Length: 300-1,000 words. **Pays up to 25¢/word.**

POETRY Needs free verse, traditional. Submit up to 5 poems via online submissions manager (cricketmag.submittable.com). Length: up to 20 lines/poem. **Pays up to $3/line.**

FILLERS Needs recipes, crafts, puzzles, games, brainteasers, math and word activities. Submit via online submissions manager (cricketmag.submittable.com). Length: 1-4 pages. **Pays for fillers.**

TIPS "We'd like to see more of the following: engaging nonfiction, fillers, and 'takeout page' activities; folktales, fairy tales, science fiction, and humorous stories. Most importantly, do not write down to children."

STONE SOUP

Children's Art Foundation, P.O. Box 83, Santa Cruz CA 95063-0083. (831)426-5557. **E-mail:** editor@stonesoup.com. **Website:** http://stonesoup.com. **Contact:** Ms. Gerry Mandel, editor. **100% freelance written.** Bimonthly magazine of writing and art by children age 13 under, including fiction, poetry, book reviews, and art. *Stone Soup* is 48 pages, 7x10, professionally printed in color on heavy stock, saddle-stapled, with coated cover with full-color illustration. Receives 5,000 poetry submissions/year, accepts about 12. Press run is 15,000. Subscription: $37/year (U.S.). "We have a preference for writing and art based on real-life experiences; no formula stories or poems. We only publish writing by children ages 8 to 13. We do not publish writing by adults." Estab. 1973. Pays on publication. Publishes ms an average of 4 months after acceptance. Submit seasonal material 6 months in advance. Sample copy by phone only. Guidelines available online.

"Stories and poems from past issues are available online."

NONFICTION Needs historical, personal experience, book reviews. **Buys 12 mss/year.** Submit complete ms; no SASE. **Pays $40, a certificate and 2 contributor's copies, plus discounts.**

FICTION Needs adventure, ethnic, experimental, fantasy, historical, humorous, mystery, science fiction, slice-of-life vignettes, suspense. "We do not like assignments or formula stories of any kind." **Buys 60 mss/year.** Send complete ms; no SASE. Length: 150-2,500 words. **Pays $40 for stories, a certificate and 2 contributor's copies, plus discounts.**

POETRY Needs avant-garde, free verse. Wants free verse poetry. Does not want rhyming poetry, haiku, or cinquain. Buys 12 poems/year. **Pays $40/poem, a certificate, and 2 contributor's copies, plus discounts.**

TIPS "All writing we publish is by young people ages 13 and under. We do not publish any writing by adults. We can't emphasize enough how important it is to read a couple of issues of the magazine. You can read stories and poems from past issues online. We have a strong preference for writing on subjects that mean a lot to the author. If you feel strongly about something that happened to you or something you observed, use that feeling as the basis for your story or poem. Stories should have good descriptions, realistic dialogue, and a point to make. In a poem, each word must be chosen carefully. Your poem should present a view of your subject, and a way of using words that are special and all your own."

LITERARY & LITTLE

ABLE MUSE

467 Saratoga Ave., #602, San Jose CA 95129-1326. **Website:** www.ablemuse.com. **Contact:** Alex Pepple, editor. "*Able Muse: A Review of Poetry, Prose & Art* published twice/year, predominantly publishes metrical poetry complemented by art and photography, fiction, and nonfiction including essays, book reviews, and interviews with a focus on metrical and formal poetry. We are looking for well-crafted poems of any length or subject that employ skillful and imaginative use of meter and rhyme, executed in a contemporary idiom, that reads as naturally as your free-verse poems." Estab. 1999. Time between acceptance and publication is 3 months. Sometimes comments on rejected poems. Sometimes publishes theme issues. Responds in 4 months. Sometimes sends prepublication galleys. Subscription: $24 for 1 year.

Considers poetry by teens. "High levels of craft still required even for teen writers." Also sponsors 2 annual contests: The Able Muse Write Prize for Poetry & Fiction, and The Able Muse Book Award for Poetry (in collaboration with Able Muse Press at www.ablemusepress.com). See website for details.

POETRY Has published poetry by Mark Jarman, A.E. Stallings, Annie Finch, Rhina P. Espaillat, Rachel Hadas, and R.S. Gwynn. Receives about 1,500 poems/year, accepts about 5%. Submit 1-5 poems and short bio. Electronic submissions only welcome through the online form at www.ablemuse.com/submit, or by e-mail to editor@ablemuse.com. "The e-mail submission method is being phased out. We strongly encourage using the online submission method." Will not accept postal submissions. Reviews books of poetry. Send materials for review consideration.

ACM (ANOTHER CHICAGO MAGAZINE)

P.O. Box 408439, Chicago IL 60640. **E-mail:** editors@anotherchicagomagazine.net. **Website:** www.anotherchicagomagazine.net. **Contact:** Jacob S. Knabb, editor-in-chief; Caroline Eick, managing editor. "*Another Chicago Magazine* is a biannual literary magazine that publishes work by both new and established writers. We look for work that goes beyond the artistic and academic to include and address the larger world. The editors read submissions in fiction, poetry, and creative nonfiction year round. The best way to know what we publish is to read what we publish. If you haven't read *ACM* before, order a sample copy to know if your work is appropriate." Sends prepublication galleys. Estab. 1977. Circ. 2,000. Byline given. Accepts simultaneous submis-

CONSUMER MAGAZINES

sions. Responds in 3 months to queries; 6 months to mss. Submit online through website.

Work published in *ACM* has been included frequently in *The Best American Poetry* and *The Pushcart Prize*.

NONFICTION Wants creative nonfiction. Length: usually no more than 20 pages.

FICTION Submit short stories and novel excerpts. Length: 15-20 pages or less.

POETRY Length: No more than 4 pages.

TIPS "Support literary publishing by subscribing to at least one literary journal—if not ours, another. Get used to rejection slips, and don't get discouraged. Keep introductory letters short. Make sure ms has name and address on every page, and that it is clean, neat, and proofread. We are looking for stories with freshness and originality in subject angle and style and work that encounters the world."

ACORN

Spare Poems Press, 115 Conifer Lane, Walnut Creek CA 94598. **E-mail:** acornhaiku@gmail.com. **Website:** www.acornhaiku.com. **Contact:** Susan Antolin, editor. "Biannual magazine dedicated to publishing the best of contemporary English-language haiku and in particular to showcasing individual poems that reveal the extraordinary moments found in everyday life." Estab. 1998. Publishes ms an average of 1-3 months after acceptance. Responds in 3 weeks to mss. Guidelines and sample poems available online at www.acornhaiku.com.

Reads submissions in January-February and July-August only.

POETRY Needs haiku. "Decisions made by editor on a rolling basis. Poems judged purely on merit." Sometimes acceptance conditional on minor edits. Often comments on rejected poems. Accepts submissions via mail or e-mail, however e-mail is preferred. "Does *not* want epigrams, musings, and overt emotion poured into 17 syllables; surreal, science fiction, or political commentary 'ku;' strong puns or raunchy humor. A 5-7-5 syllable count is not necessary or encouraged." Length: 1-5 lines; 17 or fewer syllables.

TIPS "This is primarily a journal for those with a focused interest in *haiku*. It is a much richer genre than one might surmise from many of the recreational websites that claim to promote '*haiku*.'"

ACUMEN MAGAZINE

Ember Press, 6 The Mount, Higher Furzeham, Brixham, South Devon TQ5 8QY United Kingdom. **E-mail:** patriciaoxley6@gmail.com. **Website:** www.acumen-poetry.co.uk. **Contact:** Patricia Oxley, general editor. *Acumen*, published 3 times/year in January, May, and September, is "a general literary magazine with emphasis on good poetry." Wants "well-crafted, high-quality, imaginative poems showing a sense of form." Does not want "experimental verse of an obscene type." Has published poetry by Ruth Padel, William Oxley, Hugo Williams, Peter Porter, Danielle Hope, and Leah Fritz. Estab. 1971. Accepts queries by mail. Accepts simultaneous submissions. Responds in 3 months. Submission guidelines online at website.

Acumen is 120 pages, A5, perfect-bound.

NONFICTION Needs "*Acumen* is always on the look out for new and unusual articles, etc. However, the magazine likes quality writing in its prose. It will consider articles on poetry and poetry-related subjects (eg. criticism, use of language, poetry from past-masters re-evaluated, etc.) , the main criteria being they are relevant, well-written, interesting and readable (ie. with a minimum of jargon throughout the text)." Length: 1,500-3,500 words.

POETRY Submit 5-6 poems at a time. All submissions should be accompanied by SASE. Include name and address on each separate sheet. Accepts e-mail submissions, but see guidelines on the website. Will send rejections, acceptances, proofs, and other communications via e-mail overseas to dispense with IRCs and other international postage. Any poem that may have chance of publication is shortlisted, and from list final poems are chosen. All other poems returned within 2 months. "If a reply is required, please send IRCs. One IRC for a decision, 3 IRCs if work is to be returned." Willing to reply by e-mail to save IRCs. Buys 150 poems/year. **Pays "by negotiation" and 1 contributor's copy.**

TIPS "Read *Acumen* carefully to see what kind of poetry we publish. Also, read widely in many poetry magazines, and don't forget the poets of the past—they can still teach us a great deal."

THE ADIRONDACK REVIEW

Black Lawrence Press, 8405 Bay Parkway, Apt C8, Brooklyn NY 11214. **E-mail:** editors@theadirondackreview.com. **Website:** www.adirondackreview.homestead.com. **Contact:** Angela Leroux-Lindsey, editor; Amanda Himmelmann, fiction editor; Nicholas Samaras, poetry editor. *The Adirondack Review*, published quarterly online, is a literary journal dedicated to quality free verse poetry and short fiction as well as book and film reviews, art, photography, and interviews. "We are open to both new and established writers. Our only requirement is excellence. We would like to publish more French and German poetry translations as well as original poems in these languages. We publish an eclectic mix of voices and styles, but all poems should show attention to craft. We are open to beginners who demonstrate talent, as well as established voices. The work should speak for itself." Estab. 2000. Accepts queries by online submission form. Responds to queries in 1-2 months; in 2-4 months.

NONFICTION Needs essays, interview, reviews. Special issues: "Interested in nonfiction essays and interviews related to the intersections of art and literature with politics, economics, education, music, and science." Submit via online submissions manager. "For book reviews, include the publisher's information and release date of the reviewed title." Length: up to 5,000 words.

FICTION "We like modern tales with a quality of timelessness: stories with realistic, powerful dialogue and dynamic characters." Needs adventure, experimental, historical. Submit via online submissions manager. Length: up to 4,000 words.

POETRY Submit 2-5 poems at a time; include brief bio. Submit via online submissions manager. Does not want "religious, overly sentimental, horror/gothic, rhyming, greeting card, pet-related, humor, or science fiction poetry."

TIPS "*The Adirondack Review* accepts submissions all year long, so send us your poetry, fiction, nonfiction, translation, reviews, interviews, and art and photography."

AGNI

Creative Writing Program, Boston University, 236 Bay State Rd., Boston MA 02215. (617)353-7135. **Fax:** (617)353-7134. **E-mail:** agni@bu.edu. **Website:** www.agnimagazine.org. **Contact:** Sven Birkerts, editor. Biannual literary magazine. "Eclectic literary magazine publishing first-rate poems, essays, translations, and stories." Estab. 1972. Circ. 3,000 in print, plus more than 60,000 distinct readers online per year. Byline given. Pays on publication. Publishes ms an average of 6 months after acceptance. Editorial lead time 1 year. Accepts queries by mail. Accepts simultaneous submissions. Responds in 2 weeks to queries; in 4 months to mss. Sample copy: $10 or online. Guidelines available online.

Reading period is September 1-May 31 only. Online magazine carries original content not found in print edition. All submissions are considered for both. Founding editor Askold Melnyczuk won the 2001 Nora Magid Award for Magazine Editing. Work from *AGNI* has been included and cited regularly in the *Pushcart Prize* and *Best American* anthologies.

FICTION Buys stories, prose poems. "No science fiction or romance." **Buys 20+ mss/year.** Query by mail. **Pays $10/page up to $150; a one-year subscription; and, for print publication, 2 contributor's copies and 4 gift copies.**

POETRY Submit no more than 5 poems at a time. No e-mail submissions. Cover letter is required ("brief, sincere"). "No fancy fonts, gimmicks. Include SASE or e-mail address; no preformatted reply cards." Buys 120+ poems/year. **Pays $20/page up to $150.**

TIPS "We're also looking for extraordinary translations from little-translated languages. It is important to read work published in *AGNI* before submitting, to see if your own might be compatible."

ALASKA QUARTERLY REVIEW

University of Alaska Anchorage, 3211 Providence Dr. (ESH 208), Anchorage AK 99508. **Fax:** 907-786-6916. **E-mail:** aqr@uaa.alaska.edu. **Website:** www.uaa.alaska.edu/aqr. **Contact:** Ronald Spatz, editor in chief. **95% freelance written.** Semiannual magazine publishing fiction, poetry, literary nonfiction, and short plays in traditional and experimental styles. "*Alaska Quarterly Review* is a literary journal devoted to contemporary literary art, publishing fiction, short plays, poetry, photo essays, and literary nonfiction in traditional and experimental styles. The editors encourage new and emerging writers, while continuing to publish award-winning and established writers." Estab. 1982. Circ. 2,700. Byline given. Publishes ms an average of 6 months after acceptance. Accepts queries by mail. Accepts simultaneous submissions. Responds in 4 months to queries; in 6 weeks-4 months to mss. Sample copy: $6. Guidelines online.

Magazine: 6×9; 232-300 pages; 60 lb. Glatfelter paper; 12 pt. C15 black ink or 4-color; varnish cover stock; photos on cover and photo essays. Reads mss August 15-May 15.

NONFICTION Needs literary nonfiction in traditional and experimental styles. Submit complete ms by postal mail. Include cover letter with contact information and SASE for return of ms. Length: up to 50 pages. **Pays contributor's copies and honoraria when funding is available.**

FICTION "Works in *AQR* have certain characteristics: freshness, honesty, and a compelling subject. The voice of the piece must be strong—idiosyncratic enough to create a unique persona. We look for craft, putting it in a form where it becomes emotionally and intellectually complex. Many pieces in *AQR* concern everyday life. We're not asking our writers to go outside themselves and their experiences to the absolute exotic to catch our interest. We look for the experiential and revelatory qualities of the work. We will champion a piece that may be less polished or stylistically sophisticated if it engages me, surprises me, and resonates for me. The joy in reading such a work is in discovering something true. Moreover, in keeping with our mission to publish new writers, we are looking for voices our readers do not know, voices that may not always be reflected in the dominant culture and that, in all instances, have something important to convey." Needs experimental and traditional literary forms., contemporary, prose poem, novel excerpts, drama: experimental and traditional one-acts. No romance, children's, or inspirational/religious. Submit complete ms by postal mail. Include cover letter with contact information and SASE for return of ms. Length: up to 50 pages. **Pays contributor's copies and honoraria when funding is available.**

POETRY Needs avant-garde, free verse, traditional. Submit poetry by postal mail. Include cover letter with contact information and SASE for return of ms. No light verse. Length: up to 20 pages. **Pays contributor's copies and honoraria when funding is available.**

TIPS "Although we respond to e-mail queries, we cannot review electronic submissions."

THE AMERICAS

3250-60 Chestnut St., Rm. 3025, Philadelphia PA 19104. **E-mail:** americas@drexel.edu. **Website:** www.drexel.edu/theamericas. **Contact:** Ben Vinson III, editor. Quarterly magazine. "*The Americas* has been one of the principal English-language journals of Latin American history since 1944. We publish articles and reviews in history and ethnohistory about all geographical regions of the Americas and their Iberian background. Articles may be submitted in any language. Foreign-language articles accepted for publication will be translated into English by the journal. Founded by the Academy of American Franciscan History, the journal prides itself on providing a bridge between scholars of all the Americas and on presenting a range of subjects and perspectives." Estab. 1944. No kill fee. Accepts queries by mail, e-mail. Guidelines online at www.drexel.edu/theamericas/submissions.

NONFICTION Needs essays, exposé, historical, opinion, religious, translations. Special issues: The Inter-American Notes section is an important part of *The Americas*. It includes short reports on archives, research projects, conferences, scholarly competitions and awards, and cultural news. Other features include publication of translations of documents that may be of use in classroom teaching. "We do not accept unsolicited book reviews." Submit complete ms by mail or e-mail, ATTN: Ben Vinson III. Send mailed submissions of Inter-American Notes to James M. Krippner.

THE ANTIGONISH REVIEW

St. Francis Xavier University, P.O. Box 5000, Antigonish NS B2G 2W5 Canada. (902)867-3962. **Fax:** (902)867-5563. **E-mail:** tar@stfx.ca. **Website:** www.antigonishreview.com. **Contact:** Bonnie McIsaac, office manager. **100% freelance written.** Quarterly literary magazine for educated and creative readers. *The Antigonish Review*, published quarterly, tries "to produce the kind of literary and visual mosaic that the modern sensibility requires or would respond to." Estab. 1970. Circ. 850. Byline given. Pays on publication. Offers variable kill fee. Publishes ms an average of 8 months after acceptance. Editorial lead time 4 months. Submit seasonal material 4 months in advance. Accepts queries by mail, fax. Responds in 1 month to queries; in 6 months to mss. Sample copy: $7 or online. Guidelines for #10 SASE or online.

NONFICTION Needs essays, interview, book reviews/articles. No academic pieces. **Buys 15-20 mss/year.** Query. Length: 1,500-5,000 words **Pays $50 and 2 contributor's copies.**

FICTION Send complete ms. Accepts submissions by fax. Accepts electronic (disk compatible with WordPerfect/IBM and Windows) submissions. Prefers hard copy. Needs literary, translations, contemporary, prose poem. No erotica. **Buys 35-40 mss/year.** Send complete ms. Length: 500-5,000 words. **Pays $50 and 2 contributor's copies for stories.**

POETRY Open to poetry on any subject written from any point of view and in any form. However, writers should expect their work to be considered within the full context of old and new poetry in English and other languages. Has published poetry by Andy Wainwright, W.J. Keith, Michael Hulse, Jean McNeil, M. Travis Lane, and Douglas Lochhead. Buys 100-125 poems/year. Submit 6-8 poems at a time. A preferable submission would be 3-4 poems. Lines/poem: not over 80, i.e., 2 pages. **Pays $10/page to a maximum of $50 and 2 contributor's copies.**

TIPS "Send for guidelines and/or sample copy. Send ms with cover letter and SASE with submission."

ANTIOCH REVIEW

P.O. Box 148, Yellow Springs OH 45387-0148. **E-mail:** mkeyes@antiochreview.org. **Website:** www.antiochreview.org. **Contact:** Robert S. Fogarty, editor; Judith Hall, poetry editor. Quarterly magazine for general, literary, and academic audience. Literary and cultural review of contemporary issues and literature for general readership. *The Antioch Review* "is an independent quarterly of critical and creative thought. For well over 70 years, creative authors, poets, and thinkers have found a friendly reception—regardless of formal reputation. We get far more poetry than we can possibly accept, and the competition is keen. Here, where form and content are so inseparable and reaction is so personal, it is difficult to state requirements or limitations. Studying recent issues of *The Antioch Review* should be helpful." Estab. 1941. Circ. 3,000. Byline given. Pays on publication. Publishes ms an average of 10 months after acceptance. Responds in 3-6 months to mss. Sample copy: $7. Guidelines available online.

Work published in *The Antioch Review* has been included frequently in *The Best American Stories, Best American Essays,* and *The Best American Poetry.* Finalist for National Magazine Award for essays in 2009 and 2011, and for fiction in 2010.

NONFICTION Nonfiction submissions are not accepted between June 1-September 1. Length: 2,000-8,000 words. **Pays $20/printed page, plus 2 contributor's copies.**

FICTION Quality fiction only, distinctive in style with fresh insights into the human condition. Needs experimental, contemporary. No science fiction, fantasy, or confessions. Send complete ms with SASE, preferably mailed flat. Fiction submissions are not accepted between June 1-September 1. Length: generally under 8,000 words. **Pays $20/printed page, plus 2 contributor's copies.**

POETRY Has published poetry by Richard Howard, Jacqueline Osherow, Alice Fulton, Richard Kenney, and others. Receives about 3,000 submissions/year. Submit 3-6 poems at a time. No previously published poems or simultaneous submissions. Include SASE with all submissions. No light or inspirational verse. Poetry submissions are not accepted between between May 1-September 1. Submit maximum 3-6 poems. **Pays $20/printed page, plus 2 contributor's copies.**

ARC

Arc Poetry Society, P.O. Box 81060, Ottawa ON K1P 1B1 Canada. **E-mail:** managingeditor@arcpoetry.ca; coordinatingeditor@arcpoetry.ca. **Website:** www.arcpoetry.ca. **Contact:** Monty Reid, managing editor; Chris Johnson, coordinating editor. Semiannual magazine featuring poetry, poetry-related articles, and criticism. Focus is poetry, and Canadian poetry in general, although *Arc* publishes writers from elsewhere. Looking for the best poetry from new and established writers. Often have special issues. Send a SASE for upcoming special issues and contests. Estab. 1978. Circ. 1,500. Byline given. Pays on publication. Publishes ms an average of 6 months after acceptance. Accepts queries by online submission form. Responds in 4 months. Guidelines for #10 SASE.

Only accepts submissions via online submissions manager. Include brief biographical note with submission. Accepts unsolicited mss each year from September 1-May 31.

NONFICTION Needs essays, interview, book reviews. Query first. Length: 500-4,000 words. **Pays $40/printed page (Canadian), and 2 copies.**

PHOTOS Query first. Pays $300 for 10 photos.

POETRY Needs avant-garde, free verse. Buys 60 poems/year. Submit maximum 3 poems. **Pays $40/printed page (Canadian).**

ART TIMES

A Literary Journal and Resource for All the Arts, P.O. Box 730, Mount Marion NY 12456. (845)246-6944. **Fax:** (845)246-6944. **E-mail:** info@ArtTimesJournal.

com. **Website:** www.arttimesjournal.com. **Contact:** Raymond J. Steiner, editor. **10% freelance written.** Prints quarterly with circulation of 18,000 online monthly. "*Art Times* covers the art fields and is distributed in locations most frequented by those enjoying the arts. Our copies are distributed throughout the lower part of the northeast as well as the metropolitan New York area; locations include theaters, galleries, museums, schools, art clubs, cultural centers, and the like. Our readers are mostly over 40, affluent, art-conscious and sophisticated. Subscribers are located across US and abroad (Italy, France, Germany, Greece, Russia, etc.)." Estab. 1984. Byline given. Pays on publication. No kill fee. Publishes ms an average of 3 years after acceptance. Submit seasonal material 8 months in advance. Accepts simultaneous submissions. Responds in 6 months; in 6 months to mss. Sample copy for SAE with 9x12 envelope and 6 first-class stamps. Writer's guidelines for #10 SASE or online.

FICTION Looks for quality short fiction that aspires to be literary. Publishes 1 story each issue. Needs adventure, ethnic, fantasy, historical, humorous, mainstream, science fiction, contemporary. "Nothing violent, sexist, erotic, juvenile, racist, romantic, political, off-beat, or related to sports or juvenile fiction." **Buys 8-10 mss/year.** Send complete ms. Length: up to 1,500 words. **Pays $25 and a one-year subscription.**

POETRY Needs avant-garde, free verse, haiku, light verse, traditional. Wants "poetry that strives to express genuine observation in unique language. All topics, all forms. We prefer well-crafted 'literary' poems. No excessively sentimental poetry." Publishes 2-3 poems each issue. Buys 30-35 poems/year. Submit maximum 6 poems. Length: no more than 20 lines. **Offers contributor copies and one-year subscription.**

TIPS "Competition is greater (more submissions received), but keep trying. We print new as well as published writers. Be advised that we are presently on an approximate three-year lead for short stories, two-year lead for poetry. We are now receiving 300-400 poems and 40-50 short stories per month. Be familiar with *Art Times* and its special audience."

BELLINGHAM REVIEW

Mail Stop 9053, Western Washington University, Bellingham WA 98225. (360)650-4863. **E-mail:** bellingham.review@wwu.edu. **Website:** wwww.bhreview.org. **Contact:** Brenda Miller, editor in chief; Kaitlyn Teer, managing editor. **100% freelance written.** Annual small-press literary magazine covering poems, stories, and essays. No limitations on form or subject matter. Nonprofit magazine published once/year in the spring. Seeks "literature of palpable quality: poems, stories, and essays so beguiling they invite us to touch their essence. *Bellingham Review* hungers for a kind of writing that nudges the limits of form or executes traditional forms exquisitely." Estab. 1977. Circ. 2,000. Byline given. Pays on publication when funding allows. No kill fee. Publishes ms an average of 6 months after acceptance. Editorial lead time 6 months. Accepts simultaneous submissions. Responds in 1-6 months to mss. Sample copy: $12. Guidelines online.

The editors are actively seeking submissions of creative nonfiction, as well as stories that push the boundaries of the form. Open submission period is from September 15-December 1.

NONFICTION Needs essays, personal experience. Does not want anything nonliterary. Submit complete ms via online submissions manager. Length: up to 6,000 words. **Pays as funds allow, plus contributor copies.**

FICTION Does not want anything nonliterary. Needs experimental, humorous, regional (Northwest). **Buys 4-6 mss/year.** Submit complete ms via online submissions manager. Length: up to 6,000 words. **Pays as funds allow, plus contributor's copies.**

POETRY Needs avant-garde, free verse, traditional. Wants "well-crafted poetry, but is open to all styles." Has published poetry by David Shields, Tess Gallagher, Gary Soto, Jane Hirshfield, Albert Goldbarth, and Rebecca McClanahan. Submit up to 3 poems via online submissions manager. Will not use light verse. Buys 10-30 poems/year. **Pays as funds allow, plus contributor's copies.**

TIPS "The *Bellingham Review* holds 3 annual contests: the 49th Parallel Award for poetry, the Annie Dillard Award for Nonfiction, and the Tobias Wolff Award for Fiction. See the individual listings for these contests under Contests & Awards for full details."

BIG PULP

Exter Press, P.O. Box 92, Cumberland MD 21501. **E-mail:** editors@bigpulp.com. **Website:** www.bigpulp.com. **Contact:** Bill Olver, editor. Quarterly literary magazine. Submissions accepted by e-mail only. *Big Pulp* defines "pulp fiction" very broadly: It's lively, challenging, thought-provoking, thrilling, and fun, regardless of how many or how few genre elements are packed in. Doesn't subscribe to the theory that genre fiction is disposable; a great deal of literary fiction could easily fall under one of their general categories. Places a higher value on character and story than genre elements. Byline given. Pays on publication. Offers 100% kill fee. Publishes ms 1 year after acceptance. Accepts simultaneous submissions. Responds in 2 months to mss. Sample copy: $10; excerpts available online at no cost. Guidelines available online at website.

Currently accepting submissions for themed collections only. See website for details on current needs. Submissions are only accepted during certain reading periods; check website to see if magazine is currently open.

FICTION Needs adventure, fantasy, horror, mystery, romance, science fiction, suspense, western, superhero. Does not want generic slice-of-life, memoirs, inspirational, political, pastoral odes. **Buys 70 mss/year.** Submit complete ms. Length: up to 10,000 words. **Pays $5-25.**

POETRY Needs avant-garde, free verse, haiku, light verse, traditional. All types of poetry are considered, but poems should have a genre connection. Buys 20 poems/year. Submit maximum 5 poems. Length: up to 100 lines/poem. **Pays $5/poem.**

TIPS "We like to be surprised, and we have few boundaries. Fantasy writers may focus on the mundane aspects of a fantastical creature's life or the magic that can happen in everyday life. Romances do not have to be requited or have happy endings, and the object of one's obsession may not be a person. Mysteries need not focus on 'whodunit?' We're always interested in science or speculative fiction focusing on societal issues, but writers should avoid being partisan or shrill. We also like fiction that crosses genre; for example, a science fiction romance or a fantasy crime story. We have an online archive for fiction and poetry and encourage writers to check it out. That said, *Big Pulp* has a strong editorial bias in favor of stories with monkeys. Especially talking monkeys."

BLACKBIRD

Virginia Commonwealth University Department of English, P.O. Box 843082, Richmond VA 23284. (804)827-4729. **E-mail:** blackbird@vcu.edu. **Website:** www.blackbird.vcu.edu. *Blackbird* is published twice a year. Estab. 2001. Accepts queries by mail, online submission form. Accepts simultaneous submissions. Responds in 6 months. Guidelines online at website.

NONFICTION Needs essays, memoir. No book reviews or criticism. "We primarily look for personal essays, but memoir excerpts are acceptable if self-contained."

FICTION "We primarily look for short stories, but novel excerpts are acceptable if self-contained." Needs novel excerpts, short stories. Submit using online submissions manager or by postal mail. Online submission is preferred.

POETRY Submit 2-6 poems at a time. "If submitting online, put all poems into 1 document." Submit maximum 6 poems.

TIPS "We like a story that invites us into its world, that engages our senses, soul, and mind. We are able to publish long works in all genres, but query *Blackbird* before you send a prose piece over 8,000 words or a poem exceeding 10 pages."

BLACK WARRIOR REVIEW

P.O. Box 862936, Tuscaloosa AL 35486. (205)348-4518. **E-mail:** interns.bwr@gmail.com. **Website:** www.bwr.ua.edu. **Contact:** Kirby Johnson, editor. **90% freelance written.** Semiannual magazine covering fiction, poetry, essays, art, comics, and reviews. "We publish contemporary fiction, poetry, reviews, essays, and art for a literary audience. We publish the freshest work we can find." Estab. 1974. Circ. 2,000. Byline given. Pays on publication. Publishes ms 6 months after acceptance. Accepts queries by online submission form. Accepts simultaneous submissions. Responds in 3-6 months. Sample copy: $10. Guidelines available online.

Work that appeared in the *Black Warrior Review* has been included in the *Pushcart Prize* anthology, *Harper's Magazine, Best American Short Stories, Best American Poetry,* and *New Stories from the South.*

NONFICTION Needs essays, interview, "We are looking for essays that offer a new perspective, an unvoiced thought, an overlooked association—and we hope that you will send us pieces that not only challenge us with their content, but also with their form. We prize the lyric and the language driven, both the sparsely stated and the indulgently ruminative." **Buys 5 mss/year.** No queries; send complete ms. Length: no more than 7,000 words. **Pays a one-year subscription and a nominal lump-sum fee for all works published.**

FICTION "We are open to good experimental writing and short-short fiction. No genre fiction please." Publishes novel excerpts if under contract to be published. Needs experimental, short stories. **Buys 10 mss/year.** One story/chapter per envelope. Wants work that is conscious of form and well-crafted. Length: no more than 7,000 words. **Pays a one-year subscription and a nominal lump-sum fee for all works published.**

POETRY "We welcome most styles and forms, and we favor poems that take risks—whether they be quiet or audacious." Submit poems in 1 document. Accepts up to 5 poems per submission at a maximum of 10 pages. **Pays a one-year subscription and a nominal lump-sum fee for all works published.**

TIPS "We look for attention to language, freshness, honesty, a convincing and sharp voice. Send us a clean, well-printed, proofread manuscript. Become familiar with the magazine prior to submission."

BOMB MAGAZINE

New Arts Publications, 80 Hanson Place, Suite 703, Brooklyn NY 11217. (718)636-9100. **Fax:** (718)636-9200. **E-mail:** generalinquiries@bombsite.com. **Website:** www.bombmagazine.com. **Contact:** Mónica de la Torre, senior editor. Quarterly magazine providing interviews between artists, writers, musicians, directors, and actors. "Written, edited, and produced by industry professionals and funded by those interested in the arts, *BOMB Magazine* publishes work which is unconventional and contains an edge, whether it be in style or subject matter." Estab. 1981. Circ. 36,000. Pays on publication. No kill fee. Publishes ms an average of 3-6 months after acceptance. Editorial lead time 3-4 months. Accepts queries by online submission form. Responds in 3-5 months to mss. Sample copy: $10. Guidelines by e-mail.

FICTION Needs experimental, novel concepts, contemporary. No genre fiction: romance, science fiction, horror, western. *BOMB Magazine* accepts unsolicited poetry and prose submissions for our literary supplement *First Proof* by online submission manager in January and August. Submissions sent outside these months will not be read. Submit complete ms via online submission manager. E-mailed submissions will not be considered. Length: up to 25 pages. **Pays $100 and contributor's copies.**

POETRY *BOMB Magazine* accepts unsolicited poetry and prose submissions for our literary supplement *First Proof* by online submission manager in January and August. Submissions sent outside these months will not be read. Submit 4-6 poems via online submission manager. E-mailed submissions will not be considered. **Pays $100 and contributor's copies.**

TIPS "Manuscripts should be typed, double-spaced, and proofread, and should be final drafts. Purchase a sample issue before submitting work."

BOULEVARD

Opojaz, Inc., 6614 Clayton Rd., Box 325, Richmond Heights MO 63117. (314)324-3351. **Fax:** (314)862-2982. **E-mail:** richardburgin@netzero.com; jessicarogen@boulevardmagazine.org. **E-mail:** https://boulevard.submittable.com/submit. **Website:** www.boulevardmagazine.org. **Contact:** Richard Burgin, editor; Jessica Rogen, managing editor. **100% freelance written.** "*Boulevard* is a diverse literary magazine presenting original creative work by well-known authors, as well as by writers of exciting promise." Triannual magazine featuring fiction, poetry, and essays.Sometimes comments on rejected mss. *Boulevard* has been called 'one of the half-dozen best literary journals' by Poet Laureate Daniel Hoffman in *The Philadelphia Inquirer.* We strive to publish the finest in poetry, fiction, and nonfiction. We frequently publish writers with previous credits, we are very interested in publishing less experienced or unpublished writers with exceptional promise. We've published everything from John Ashbery to Donald Hall to a wide variety of styles from new or lesser known poets. We're eclectic. We are interested in original, moving poetry written from the head as well as the heart. It can be about any topic." Estab. 1985. Circ. 11,000. Byline given. Pays on publication. Offers no kill fee. Publishes ms an average of 9 months after acceptance. Accepts queries by mail, e-mail. Accepts simultaneous submissions. Responds in 2 weeks to queries; 4-5 months to mss. Sample copy: $10. Subscription: $15 for 3 issues, $27 for 6 issues, $30 for 9 issues. Foreign subscribers, please add $10. Make checks payable to Opojaz, Inc. Subscriptions are available online at www.boulevardmagazine.org/subscribe.html. Publishes short fiction, poetry, and nonfiction, including critical and culture essays. Submit by mail or via Submittable. Accepts multiple submissions. Does not accept mss between May 1 and October 1. SASE for reply.

Boulevard is 175-250 pages, digest-sized, flat-spined, with glossy card cover. Receives over 600 unsolicited mss/month. Accepts about 10 mss/issue. Publishes 10 new writers/year. Recently published work by Joyce Carol Oates, Floyd Skloot, John Barth, Stephen Dixon, David Guterson, Albert Goldbarth, Molly Peacock, Bob Hicok, Alice Friman, Dick Allen, and Tom Disch.

NONFICTION Needs book excerpts, essays, interview, opinion, photo feature. **Buys 10 mss/year.** Length: up to 8,000 words. **Pays $100-300.**

FICTION Needs confession, experimental, mainstream, novel excerpts. "We do not want erotica, science fiction, romance, western, horror, or children's stories." **Buys 20 mss/year.** Length: up to 8,000 words. **Pays $50-500 (sometimes higher) for accepted work.**

POETRY Needs avant-garde, free verse, haiku, traditional. Does not consider book reviews. "Do not send us light verse." Does not want "poetry that is uninspired, formulaic, self-conscious, unoriginal, insipid." Buys 80 poems/year. Submit maximum 5 poems. Length: up to 200 lines/poem. **Pays $25-250.**

TIPS "Read the magazine first. The work *Boulevard* publishes is generally recognized as among the finest in the country. We continue to seek more good literary or cultural essays. Send only your best work."

BRAIN, CHILD

Erielle Media, LLC, 341 Newtown Turnpike, Wilton CT 06897. (203)563-9149. **E-mail:** submissions@brainchildmag.com. **Website:** www.brainchildmag.com. **Contact:** Marcelle Soviero, editor in chief. **75% freelance written.** Quarterly magazine covering the experience of motherhood. "*Brain, Child: The Magazine for Thinking Mothers,* reflects modern motherhood—the way it really is. It is the largest print literary magazine devoted to motherhood. *Brain, Child* as a community for and by mothers who like to think about what raising kids does for (and to) the mind and soul. *Brain, Child* isn't your typical parenting magazine. We couldn't cupcake-decorate our way out of a paper bag. We are more 'literary' than 'how-to,' more *New Yorker* than *Parents.* We shy away from expert advice on childrearing in favor of first-hand reflections by great writers (Jane Smiley, Barbara Ehrenreich, Anne Tyler) on life as a mother. Each quarterly issue is full of essays, features, humor, reviews, fiction, art, cartoons, and our readers' own stories. Our philosophy is pretty simple: Motherhood is worthy of literature. And there are a lot of ways to mother, all of them interesting. We're proud to be publishing articles and essays that are smart, down to earth, sometimes funny, and sometimes poignant." Estab. 2000. Circ. 36,000. Byline given. Pays on publication. 20% kill fee. Publishes ms an average of 3-4 months after acceptance. Editorial lead time 3 months. Submit seasonal material 6 months in advance. Accepts queries by mail, e-mail. Accepts simultaneous submissions. Responds in 1 month to queries; in 1-3 months to mss. Sample copy available online. Guidelines available online.

NONFICTION Needs essays, including debate, humor, in-depth features. No how-to articles, advice, or tips. **Buys 40-50 mss/year.** Query with published clips for features, new items, and debate essays; send complete ms for essays. "Simultaneous submissions are okay—just let us know immediately if the manuscript is accepted elsewhere." Length: 800-5,000 words. **Payment varies.** Sometimes pays expenses of writers on assignment.

PHOTOS State availability. Model releases required. Reviews contact sheets, prints, GIF/JPEG files.

FICTION "We publish fiction that has a strong motherhood theme." Needs mainstream, literary. No genre fiction. **Buys 4 mss/year.** Send complete ms. Length: 800-5,000 words. **Payment varies.**

TIPS Prefers e-mail submissions. No attachments.

⊙$$ BRICK

Brick, P.O. Box 609, Station P, Toronto ON M5S 2Y4 Canada. **E-mail:** info@brickmag.com. **Website:** www.brickmag.com. **Contact:** Nadia Szilvassy, publisher and managing editor. **90% freelance written.** Semiannual magazine covering literature and the arts. "We publish literary nonfiction of a very high quality on a range of arts and culture subjects." Estab. 1977. Circ. 4,000. Byline given. Pays on publication. No kill fee. Publishes ms 3-5 months after acceptance. Editorial lead time 5 months. Responds in 6 months to mss. Sample copy: $15 plus shipping. Guidelines available online.

NONFICTION Needs essays, historical, interview, opinion, travel. No fiction, poetry, personal memoir, or art. **Buys 30-40 mss/year.** Send complete ms. Length: 250-3,000 words. **Pays $75-500 (Canadian).**

PHOTOS State availability. Reviews transparencies, prints, TIFF/JPEG files. Offers $25-50/photo.

TIPS "*Brick* is interested in polished work by writers who are widely read and in touch with contemporary culture. The magazine is serious but not fusty. We like to feel the writer's personality in the piece, too."

BURNSIDE REVIEW

P.O. Box 1782, Portland OR 97207. **E-mail:** sid@burnsidereview.org. **Website:** www.burnsidereview.org. **Contact:** Sid Miller, founder and editor; Dan Kaplan, managing editor. *Burnside Review*, published every 9 months, prints "the best poetry and short fiction we can get our hands on." Each issue includes 1 featured poet with an interview and new poems. "We tend to publish writing that finds beauty in truly unexpected places; that combines urban and natural imagery; that breaks the heart." Estab. 2004. Pays on publication. Publishes ms 9 months after acceptance. Submit seasonal poems 3-6 months in advance. Accepts queries by online submission form. Accepts simultaneous submissions. Responds in 1-6 months. Single copy: $8; subscription: $13. Make checks payable to *Burnside Review* or order online.

Burnside Review is 80 pages, 6x6, professionally printed, perfect-bound. Charges a $3 submission fee to cover printing costs.

FICTION "Send anything from a group of flash-fiction pieces to a traditional short story, so long as the word count doesn't exceed 5,000 words. We like story. We like character. We don't like hobgoblins. Barthelme, Munro, Carver, and Bender are some of the folks whose work we love." Needs experimental, short stories. Submit 1 short story at a time. Accepts submissions through online submission manager only. **Pays $25 plus 1 contributor's copy.**

POETRY Needs avant-garde, free verse, traditional. Open to all forms. Translations are encouraged. "Would like to see more lyric poetry". Has published poetry by Linda Bierds, Dorianne Laux, Ed Skoog, Campbell McGrath, Paul Guest, and Larissa Szporluk. Reads submissions year-round. "Editors read all work submitted." Seldom comments on rejected work. Submit electronically on website. Submit maximum 5 poems. **Pays $25 plus 1 contributor's copy.**

TIPS "*Burnside Review* accepts submissions of poetry and fiction. If you have something else that you think would be a perfect fit for our journal, please query the editor before submitting. We like work that breaks the heart. That leaves us in a place that we don't expect to be. We like the lyric. We like the narrative. We like when the two merge. We like whiskey. We like hourglass figures. We like crying over past mistakes. We like to be surprised. Surprise us. Read a past issue and try to understand our tastes. At the least, please read the sample poems that we have linked from our prior issues."

BUTTON

P.O. Box 77, Westminster MA 01473. **E-mail:** sally@moonsigns.net. **Website:** www.moonsigns.net. **30% freelance written.** Annual literary magazine. "*Button* is New England's tiniest magazine of poetry, fiction, and gracious living, published once a year. As 'gracious living' is on the cover, we like wit, brevity, cleverly-conceived essays/recipes, poetry that isn't sentimental, or song lyrics. I started *Button* so that a century from now, when people read it in landfills or, preferably, libraries, they'll say, 'Gee, what a great time to have lived. I wish I lived back then." Estab. 1993. Circ. 750. Byline given. Pays on publication. No kill fee. Publishes ms 3-9 months after acceptance. Editorial lead time 6 months. Responds in 1 month to queries. Responds in 2 months to mss. Sometimes comments on rejected mss. Subscription: $5 for 4 issues. Sample copy for $2.50. Guidelines available online. "We don't take e-mail submissions, unless you're living overseas, in which case we respond electronically. But we strongly suggest you request writers' guidelines (send an SASE)."

Receives 20-40 unsolicited mss/month. Accepts 3-6 mss/issue; 3-6mss/year. *Button* is 16-24 pages, saddle-stapled, with cardstock offset cover with illustrations that incorporate 1 or more buttons. Has published poetryby Amanda Powell, Brendan Galvin, Jean Monahan, Mary Campbell, KevinMcGrath, and Ed Conti.

NONFICTION Needs personal experience, cooking stories. Does not want "the tired, the trite, the sexist, the multiply-folded, the single-spaced, the sentimental, the self-pitying, the swaggering, the infantile (i.e., coruscated whimsy and self-conscious quaint), poems about Why You Can't Be Together and stories about How Complicated Am I. Before you send us anything, sit down and read a poem by Stanley Kunitz or a story by Evelyn Waugh, Louisa May Alcott, or anyone who's visited the poles, and if you still think you've written a damn fine thing, have at it. A word count on the top of the page is fine—a copyright or 'all rights reserved' reminder makes you look like a beginner."

Buys 3-6 mss/year. Length: 300-2,000 words. **Pays small honorarium and copies.**

FICTION Seeks quality fiction. No genre fiction, science fiction, techno-thriller. "Wants more of anything Herman Melville, Henry James, or Betty MacDonald would like to read." **Buys 1-2 mss/year.** Send complete ms with bio, list of publications, and explain how you found the magazine. Include SASE. Length: 300-2,000 words. **Pays honorarium and subscriptions.**

POETRY Needs free verse, traditional. Wants quality poetry; "poetry that incises a perfect figure-8 on the ice, but also cuts beneath that mirrored surface. Minimal use of vertical pronoun. Do not submit more than twice in 1 year." Cover letter is required. Does not want "sentiment; no 'musing' on who or what done ya wrong." Buys 2-4 poems/year. Submit maximum 3 poems. **Pays honorarium and at least 2 contributor's copies.**

TIPS "*Button* writers have been widely published elsewhere, in virtually all the major national magazines. They include Ralph Lombreglia, Lawrence Millman, They Might Be Giants, Combustible Edison, Sven Birkerts, Stephen McCauley, Amanda Powell, Wayne Wilson, David Barber, Romayne Dawnay, Brendan Galvin, and Diana DerHovanessian. Follow the guidelines, make sure you read your work aloud, and don't inflate or deflate your publications and experience. We've published plenty of new folks, but on the merits of the work."

THE CAPILANO REVIEW

2055 Purcell Way, North Vancouver BC V7J 3H5 Canada. (604)984-1712. **E-mail:** tcr@capilanou.ca. **Website:** www.thecapilanoreview.ca. **Contact:** Todd Nickel, managing editor. **100% freelance written.** Triannual visual and literary arts magazine that "publishes only what the editors consider to be the very best fiction, poetry, drama, or visual art being produced. *TCR* editors are interested in fresh, original work that stimulates and challenges readers. Over the years, the magazine has developed a reputation for pushing beyond the boundaries of traditional art and writing. We are interested in work that is new in concept and in execution." Estab. 1972. Circ. 800. Byline given. Pays on publication. Publishes ms an average of within 1 year after acceptance. Accepts queries by mail. Responds in 4-6 months to mss. Sample copy: $10 (outside of Canada, USD). Guidelines with #10 SASE with IRC or Canadian stamps.

PHOTOS Pays $50 for cover and $50/page to maximum of $200 Canadian. Additional payment for electronic rights; negotiable. Pays on publication. Credit line given.

FICTION Needs experimental, novel concepts, literary. No traditional, conventional fiction. Wants to see more innovative, genre-blurring work. **Buys 10-15 mss/year.** Send complete ms with SASE and Canadian postage or IRCs. Does not accept submissions through e-mail or on disks. Length: up to 5,000 words **Pays $50-300.**

POETRY Needs avant-garde, free verse, previously unpublished poetry. Submit up to 8 pages of poetry. Buys 40 poems/year. Submit maximum 8 poems. **Pays $50-300.**

THE CHARITON REVIEW

Truman State University Press, 100 E Normal Ave., Kirksville MO 63501. (660)785-8336. **E-mail:** chariton@truman.edu. **Website:** http://tsup.truman.edu/aboutChariton.asp. **Contact:** James D'Agostino, editor; Barbara Smith-Mandell and Jen Creer, managing editors. *The Chariton Review* is an international literary journal publishing the best in short fiction, essays, poetry, and translations in 2 issues each year. Estab. 1975. No kill fee. Guidelines available on website. Send a printout of the submission via snail mail; overseas authors may send submissions as email attachments. See also *The Chariton Review* Short Fiction Prize at http://tsup.truman.edu/prizes.asp.

POETRY Poetry collections are published through TSUP's annual T.S. Eliot Prize for Poetry. Deadline is October 31 of each year. See competition guidelines at http://tsup.truman.edu/prizes.asp.

CHICKEN SOUP FOR THE SOUL PUBLISHING, LLC

Chicken Soup for the Soul Publishing, LLC, **E-mail:** webmaster@chickensoupforthesoul.com (for all inquires). **Website:** www.chickensoup.com. **95% freelance written.** Paperback with 12 publications/year featuring inspirational, heartwarming, uplifting short stories. Estab. 1993. Circ. Over 200 titles; 100 million books in print. Byline given. Pays on publication. No kill fee. Accepts simultaneous submissions. Responds upon consideration. Guidelines available online.

"Stories must be written in the first person."

NONFICTION No sermon, essay, eulogy, term paper, journal entry, political, or controversial issues. **Buys**

1,000 mss/year. Send complete ms. Length: 300-1,200 words. **Pays $200.**

POETRY Needs traditional. No controversial poetry.

TIPS "We no longer accept submissions by mail or fax. Stories and poems can only be submitted on our website. Select the 'Submit Your Story' tab on the left toolbar. The submission form can be found there."

COLORADO REVIEW

Center for Literary Publishing, Colorado State University, 9105 Campus Delivery, Fort Collins CO 80523. (970)491-5449. **E-mail:** creview@colostate.edu. **Website:** coloradoreview.colostate.edu. **Contact:** Stephanie G'Schwind, editor in chief and nonfiction editor; Steven Schwartz, fiction editor; Don Revell, Sasha Steensen, and Matthew Cooperman, poetry editors; Dan Beachy-Quick, book review editor. Literary magazine published 3 times/year. Circ. 1,000. Byline given. Pays on publication. No kill fee. Publishes ms an average of 6 months after acceptance. Editorial lead time 1 year. Accepts simultaneous submissions. Responds in 2 months to mss. Sample copy: $10. Guidelines available online.

Work published in *Colorado Review* has been included in *Best American Poetry*, *Best New American Voices*, *Best Travel Writing*, *Best Food Writing*, and the *Pushcart Prize Anthology*.

NONFICTION Buys 6-9 mss/year. Mss for nonfiction stories are read year round. Send no more than 1 story at a time. **Pays $200 for essays.**

FICTION Needs contemporary, ethnic, experimental, mainstream, short fiction. No genre fiction. Send complete ms. Fiction mss are read August 1-April 30. Mss received May 1-July 31 will be returned unread. Send no more than 1 story at a time. Length: under 30 ms pages. **Pays $200 for short stories.**

POETRY Considers poetry of any style. Poetry mss are read August 1-April 30. Mss received May 1-July 31 will be returned unread. Has published poetry by Sherman Alexie, Laynie Browne, John Gallaher, Mathias Svalina, Craig Morgan Teicher, Pam Rehm, Elizabeth Robinson, Elizabeth Willis, and Rosmarie Waldrop. Buys 60-100 poems/year. Submit maximum 5 poems. **Pays minimum of $30 or $10/page for poetry.**

CONFRONTATION

English Department, LIU Post, Brookville NY 11548. (516)299-2720. **E-mail:** confrontationmag@gmail.com. **Website:** www.confrontationmagazine.org. **Contact:** Jonna Semeiks, editor in chief; Belinda Kremer, poetry editor. **75% freelance written.** Semiannual magazine comprising all forms and genres of stories, poems, essays, memoirs, and plays. A special section contains book reviews. "We also publish the work of 1 visual artist per issue, selected by the editors." "*Confrontation* has been in continuous publication since 1968. Our taste and our magazine is eclectic, but we always look for excellence in style, an important theme, a memorable voice. We enjoy discovering and fostering new talent. Each issue contains work by both well-established and new writers. We read August 16-April 15. Do not send mss or e-mail submissions between April 16 and August 15." Estab. 1968. Circ. 2,000. Byline given. Pays on publication. Offers kill fee. Publishes work in the first or second issue after acceptance. Accepts simultaneous submissions. Responds in 8-10 weeks to mss. "We prefer single submissions. Clear copy. No e-mail submissions unless writer resides outside the U.S. Mail submissions with a SASE."

Confrontation has garnered a long list of awards and honors, including the Editor's Award for Distinguished Achievement from CLMP (given to Martin Tucker, the founding editor of the magazine) and NEA grants. Work from the magazine has appeared in numerous anthologies, including the *Pushcart Prize*, *Best Short Stories*, and *The O. Henry Prize Stories*.

NONFICTION Needs essays, personal experience. Special issues: "We publish personal, cultural, political, and other kinds of essays as well as (self-contained) sections of memoirs." **Buys 5-10 mss/year.** Send complete ms. Length: 1,500-5,000 words. **Pays $100-150; more for commissioned work.**

FICTION "We judge on quality of writing and thought or imagination, so we will accept genre fiction. However, it must have literary merit or must transcend or challenge genre." Needs experimental as well as more traditional fiction, self-contained novel excerpts, slice-of-life vignettes, lyrical or philosophical fiction. No "proselytizing" literature or conventional genre fiction. **Buys 10-15 mss/year.** Send complete ms. Length: Up to 7,200 words. **Pays $175-250; more for commissioned work.**

POETRY Needs avant-garde or experimental as well as traditional poems (and forms), lyric poems, dramatic monologues, satiric or philosophical poems. In short, a wide range of verse. "*Confrontation* is interested in all poetic forms. Our only criterion is high literary merit. We think of our audience as an educated, lay group of intelligent readers." Has published poetry by David Ray, T. Alan Broughton, David Ignatow, Philip Appleman, Jane Mayhall, and Joseph Brodsky. Submit no more than 12 pages at a time (up to 6 poems). *Confrontation* also offers the annual Confrontation Poetry Prize. No sentimental verse. No previously published poems. Buys 20 poems/year. Length should generally be kept to 2 pages. **Pays $25-75; more for commissioned work.**

TIPS "We look for literary merit. Keep honing your skills and keep trying."

CONTRARY

P.O. Box 806363, Chicago IL 60616-3299 (no submissions). **E-mail:** chicago@contrarymagazine.com (no submissions). **Website:** www.contrarymagazine.com. **Contact:** Jeff McMahon, editor; Frances Badgett, fiction editor; Shaindel Beers, poetry editor. *Contrary* publishes fiction, poetry, and literary commentary, and prefers work that combines the virtues of all those categories. Founded at the University of Chicago, it now operates independently and not-for-profit on the South Side of Chicago. "We like work that is not only contrary in content, but contrary in its evasion of the expectations established by its genre. Our fiction defies traditional story form. For example, a story may bring us to closure without ever delivering an ending. We don't insist on the ending, but we do insist on the closure. And we value fiction as poetic as any poem." Quarterly. Member CLMP. Estab. 2003. Circ. 38,000. Pays on publication. Mss published no more than 21 days after acceptance. Responds to queries in 2 weeks; 3 months to mss. Rarely comments on/critiques rejected mss. Guidelines available on website.

FICTION Receives 650 mss/month. Accepts 6 mss/issue; 24 mss/year. Publishes 1 new writer/year. Has published Sherman Alexie, Andrew Coburn, Amy Reed, Clare Kirwan, Stephanie Johnson, Laurence Davies, and Edward McWhinney. Needs literary. Accepts submissions through website only: www.contrarymagazine.com/Contrary/Submissions.html. Include estimated word count, brief bio, list of publications. Considers simultaneous submissions. Length: 2,000 words (maximum); average length: 750 words. Publishes short shorts. Average length of short shorts: 750 words. **Pays $20-60.**

POETRY No mail or e-mail submissions; submit work via the website. Considers simultaneous submissions; no previously published poems. Accepts submissions through online form only. Often comments on rejected poems. Submit maximum 3 poems. **$20 per byline, $60 for featured work."**

TIPS "Beautiful writing catches our eye first. If we realize we're in the presence of unanticipated meaning, that's what clinches the deal. Also, we're not fond of expository fiction. We prefer to be seduced by beauty, profundity, and mystery than to be presented with the obvious. We look for fiction that entrances, that stays the reader's finger above the mouse button. That is, in part, why we favor microfiction, flash fiction, and short shorts. Also, we hope writers will remember that most editors are looking for very particular species of work. We try to describe our particular species in our mission statement and our submission guidelines, but those descriptions don't always convey nuance. That's why many editors urge writers to read the publication itself, in the hope that they will intuit an understanding of its particularities. If you happen to write that particular species of work we favor, your submission may find a happy home with us. If you don't, it does not necessarily reflect on your quality or your ability. It usually just means that your work has a happier home somewhere else."

$ CRAB ORCHARD REVIEW

Dept. of English, Southern Illinois University Carbondale, Faner Hall 2380, Mail Code 4503, 1000 Faner Dr., Carbondale IL 62901. (618)453-6833. **Fax:** (618)453-8224. **Website:** www.craborchardreview.siu.edu. **Contact:** Jon Tribble, managing editor. "We are a general-interest literary journal published twice/year. We strive to be a journal that writers admire and readers enjoy. We publish fiction, poetry, creative nonfiction, fiction translations, interviews, and reviews." Estab. 1995. Circ. 2,500. No kill fee. Publishes ms an average of 9-12 months after acceptance. Accepts simultaneous submissions. Responds in 3 weeks to queries. Responds in 9 months to mss. Always comments on rejected work. Sample copy for $12. Guidelines available online.

Reads submissions February 15-April 1(Winter/Spring issue) and October-November 15 (special Summer/Fall issue).

NONFICTION Send SASE for reply, return of ms. Length: up to 25 pages double-spaced. **Pays $25/pub-**

lished magazine page, $100 minimum, 2 contributor's copies and 1-year subscription.

FICTION Needs ethnic, excerpted novel. No science fiction, romance, western, horror, gothic, or children's. Wants more novel excerpts that also stand alone as pieces. Send SASE for reply, return of ms. Length: up to 25 pages double-spaced. **Pays $25/published magazine page, $100 minimum, 2 contributor's copies and 1-year subscription.**

POETRY Wants all styles and forms from traditional to experimental. Does not want greeting card verse; literary poetry only. Has published poetry by Luisa A. Igloria, Erinn Batykefer, Jim Daniels, and Bryan Tso Jones. Postal submissions only. Cover letter is preferred. "Indicate stanza breaks on poems of more than 1 page. Poems that are under serious consideration are discussed and decided on by the managing editor and poetry editor." Submit maximum 5 poems. **Pays $25/published magazine page, $50 minimum, 2 contributor's copies and 1-year subscription.**

CRAZYHORSE

College of Charleston, Department of English, 66 George St., Charleston SC 29424. (843)953-4470. **E-mail:** crazyhorse@cofc.edu. **Website:** http://crazyhorse.cofc.edu. **Contact:** Jonathan Bohr Heinen, managing editor; Emily Rosko, poetry editor; Anthony Varallo, fiction editor; Bret Lott, nonfiction editor. Semiannual magazine. "We like to print a mix of writing regardless of its form, genre, school, or politics. We're especially on the lookout for original writing that doesn't fit the categories and that engages in the work of honest communication." Estab. 1960. Circ. 1,500. No kill fee. Publishes ms an average of 6-12 months after acceptance. Accepts simultaneous submissions. Responds in 1 week to queries. Responds in 3-4 months to mss. Sample copy for $5. Guidelines for SASE or by e-mail.

Reads submissions September 1-May 31.

NONFICTION "*Crazyhorse* publishes 4-6 stories essays year, so we call for the vey best writing, period. We believe literary nonfiction can take any form, from the letter to the list, from the biography to the memoir, from the journal to the obituary. All we call for is precision of word and vision, and that the truth of the matter be the flag of the day." Length: 2,500-8,500 words. **Pays $20 per page ($200 maximum).**

FICTION Accepts all fiction of fine quality, including short shorts and literary essays. **Buys 12-15 mss/year.** Length: 2,500-8,500 words. **Pays 2 contributor's copies and $20 per page ($200 maximum).**

POETRY Submit 3-5 poems at a time. No fax, e-mail or disk submissions. Cover letter is preferred. Buys 80 poems/year. Submit maximum 5 poems. **Pays $20 per page ($200 maximum) and 2 contributor's copies.**

TIPS "Write to explore subjects you care about. The subject should be one in which something is at stake. Before sending, ask, 'What's reckoned with that's important for other people to read?'"

CREAM CITY REVIEW

c/o UWM Department of English, P.O. Box 413, Milwaukee WI 53201. **E-mail:** info@creamcityreview.org. **Website:** www.creamcityreview.org. **Contact:** Ching-In Chen, editor in chief; Loretta McCormick, managing editor. Semiannual magazine covering poetry, fiction, and nonfiction by new and established writers. *Cream City Review* publishes "memorable and energetic fiction, poetry, and creative nonfiction. Features reviews of contemporary literature and criticism as well as author interviews and artwork. We are interested in camera-ready art depicting themes appropriate to each issue." No kill fee. Accepts queries by online submission form. Accepts simultaneous submissions. Responds in 2-8 months to mss. Sample back issue: $7. Guidelines available online at www.creamcityreview.org/submit. Check for regular updates at www.facebook.com/creamcityreview. Submit using online submissions manager ONLY.

NONFICTION Contact: nonfiction@creamcityreview.org. Needs essays, (book reviews, 1-10 pages), interview, personal experience. Submit ms via online submissions manager only.

PHOTOS Reviews prints, slides.

FICTION Contact: fiction@creamcityreview.org. Needs ethnic, experimental, humorous, literary, regional, flash fiction. "Would like to see more quality fiction. No horror, formulaic, racist, sexist, pornographic, homophobic, science fiction, romance." Submit ms via online submissions manager only.

POETRY Contact: poetry@creamcityreview.org. Submit poems via online submissions manager only. Submit maximum 5 poems.

TIPS "Please include a few lines about your publication history. *CCR* seeks to publish a broad range of writings and a broad range of writers with diverse backgrounds. We accept submissions for our annual theme issue from August 1-November 1 and general submissions from December 1-April 1. No e-mail submissions, please."

CRUCIBLE

Barton College, Wilson NC 27893. **E-mail:** crucible@barton.edu. **Website:** www.barton.edu/crucible. *Crucible*, published annually in the fall, publishes poetry and fiction as part of its Poetry and Fiction Contest run each year. Deadline for submissions: May 1. Estab. 1964. Circ. 500. Notifies winners by October each year. Sample: $8. Guidelines online.

Crucible is under 100 pages, digest-sized, professionally printed on high-quality paper, with matte card cover. Press run is 500.

FICTION Needs ethnic, experimental, feminist, literary, regional. Submit ms by e-mail. Ms accepted only through May 1. Do not include name on ms. Include separate bio. Length: up to 8,000 words. **Pays $150 for 1st prize, $100 for 2nd prize, contributor's copies.**

POETRY Submit "poetry that demonstrates originality and integrity of craftsmanship as well as thought. Traditional metrical and rhyming poems are difficult to bring off in modern poetry. The best poetry is written out of deeply felt experience which has been crafted into pleasing form." Wants "free verse with attention paid particularly to image, line, stanza, and voice." Does not want "very long narratives, poetry that is forced." Has published poetry by Robert Grey, R.T. Smith, and Anthony S. Abbott. Submit up to 5 poems by e-mail. Ms accepted only through May 1. Do not include name on poems. Include separate bio. **Pays $150 for 1st prize, $100 for 2nd prize, contributor's copies.**

DENVER QUARTERLY

University of Denver, 2000 E. Asbury, Denver CO 80208. (303)871-2892. **E-mail:** denverquarterly@gmail.com. **Website:** www.du.edu/denverquarterly/. **Contact:** Laird Hunt, editor. Publishes fiction, articles, and poetry for a generally well-educated audience, primarily interested in literature and the literary experience. Audience reads *DQ* to find something a little different from a stictly academic quarterly or a creative writing outlet. Quarterly. Reads between September 15 and May 15. Estab. 1965. Circ. 2,000. Publishes ms 1 year after acceptance. Accepts simultaneous submissions. Responds in 3 months. Sample copy for $10.

Denver Quarterly received an Honorable Mention for Content from the American Literary Magazine Awards and selections have been anthologized in the *Pushcart Prize* anthologies.

FICTION "We are interested in experimental fiction (minimalism, magic realism, etc.) as well as in realistic fiction and in writing about fiction. No sentimental, science fiction, romance, or spy thrillers." Submit ms by mail, include SASE. Length: up to 15 pages. **Pays $5/page for fiction and poetry and 2 contributor's copies.**

POETRY Contact: Bin Ramke, poetry editor. Poetry submissions should be comprised of 3-5 poems. Submit ms by mail, include SASE. **Pays $5/page for fiction and poetry and 2 contributor's copies.**

TIPS "We look for serious, realistic, and experimental fiction; stories which appeal to intelligent, demanding readers who are not themselves fiction writers. Nothing so quickly disqualifies a manuscript as sloppy proofreading and mechanics. Read the magazine before submitting to it. We try to remain eclectic, but the odds for beginners are bound to be small considering the fact that we receive nearly 10,000 mss per year and publish only about 10 short stories."

DESCANT

P.O. Box 314, Station P, Toronto ON M5S 2S8 Canada. (416)593-2557. **Fax:** (416)593-9362. **E-mail:** info@descant.ca. **E-mail:** submit@descant.ca; managingeditor@descant.ca. **Website:** www.descant.ca. **Contact:** Karen Mulhallen, editor-in-chief; Vera DeWaard, managing editor. *Descant* is a quarterly journal publishing new and established contemporary writers and visual artists from Canada and around the world. *Descant* is devoted to the discovery and development of new writers, and to placing their work in the company of celebrated writers. Estab. 1970. Circ. 1,200. Pays on publication. No kill fee. Publishes ms an average of 16 months after acceptance. Editorial lead time 1 year. Accepts queries by mail, e-mail, phone. Sample copy for $8.50 plus postage. Guidelines available online.

Pays $100 honorarium, plus 1-year's subscription for accepted submissions of any kind.

NONFICTION Needs book excerpts, essays, historical, personal experience, historical.

PHOTOS State availability. Reviews contact sheets, prints. Offers no additional payment for photos accepted with ms.

FICTION Contact: Karen Mulhallen, editor. Short stories or book excerpts. Maximum length 6,000 words; 3,000 words or less preferred. Needs ethnic, experimental, historical, humorous. No erotica, fantasy, gothic, horror, religious, romance, beat. Send complete ms with cover letter. Include estimated word count and brief bio. **Pays $100 (Canadian).**

POETRY Needs free verse, light verse, traditional. "*Descant* seeks high quality poems and stories in both traditional and innovative form." Member CLMP. Literary. Submit maximum 6 poems. **Pays $100.**

TIPS "Familiarize yourself with our magazine before submitting."

DIAGRAM

Department of English, University of Arizona, P.O. Box 210067, Tucson AZ 85721-0067. **E-mail:** editor@thediagram.com. **Website:** www.thediagram.com. **Contact:** Ander Monson, editor; T. Fleischmann and Nicole Walker, nonfiction editors; Sarah Blackman and Lauren Slaughter, fiction editors; Heidi Gotz and E.A. Ramey, poetry editors. Online journal covers poetry, fiction, and nonfiction. Sponsors a yearly chapbook competition. "*DIAGRAM* is an electronic journal of text and art, found and created. We're interested in representations, naming, indicating, schematics, labeling and taxonomy of things; in poems that masquerade as stories; in stories that disguise themselves as indices or obituaries. We specialize in work that pushes the boundaries of traditional genre or work that is in some way schematic. We do publish traditional fiction and poetry, too, but hybrid forms (short stories, prose poems, indexes, tables of contents, etc.) are particularly welcome! We also publish diagrams and schematics (original and found)." Circ. 1,500/day unique visitors online; 300,000+ hits/month. No kill fee. Time between acceptance and publication is 1-10 months. Accepts queries by e-mail. Accepts simultaneous submissions. Responds in 2 weeks to queries; 1-2 months to mss. Often comments on rejected mss. Print version sample copy: $12. Writer's guidelines online.

Publishes 6 new writers/year. Bimonthly. Member CLMP. "We sponsor yearly contests for unpublished hybrid essays and innovative fiction. Guidelines on website."

NONFICTION Send complete ms. Accepts submissions by online submissions manager; no e-mail. If sending by snail mail, send SASE for return of the ms or send disposable copy of the ms and #10 SASE for reply only.

PHOTOS Reviews prints, slides, zip disks, magnetic tapes, DCs, punch cards.

FICTION Receives 100 unsolicited mss/month. Accepts 2-3 mss/issue; 15 mss/year. Needs experimental, literary. "We don't publish genre fiction unless it's exceptional and transcends the genre boundaries." Send complete ms. Accepts submissions by online submissions manager; no e-mail. If sending by snail mail, send SASE for return of the ms or send disposable copy of the ms and #10 SASE for reply only. Average length: 250-2,000 words.

POETRY Submit 3-6 poems at a time. Electronic submissions accepted through submissions manager; no e-mail, disk, or fax submissions. Electronic submissions much preferred; print submissions must include SASE if response is expected. Cover letter is preferred. Reads submissions year round. Poems are circulated to an editorial board. Sometimes comments on rejected poems. Sometimes publishes theme issues. Receives about 1,000 poems/year, accepts about 5%. Does not want light verse. Length: no limit.

TIPS "Submit interesting text, images, sound, and new media. We value the insides of things, vivisection, urgency, risk, elegance, flamboyance, work that moves us, language that does something new, or does something old—well. We like iteration and reiteration. Ruins and ghosts. Mechanical, moving parts, balloons, and frenzy. We want art and writing that demonstrates interaction; the processes of things; how functions are accomplished; how things become or expire, move or stand. We'll consider anything."

EPOCH

251 Goldwin Smith Hall, Cornell University, Ithaca NY 14853-3201. (607)255-3385. **Fax:** (607)255-6661. **Website:** http://english.arts.cornell.edu/publications/epoch. **Contact:** Michael Koch, editor; Heidi E. Marschner, managing editor. **100% freelance written.** Literary magazine published 3 times/year. Looking for well-written literary fiction, poetry, personal essays. Newcomers welcome. Open to mainstream and avant-garde writing. Estab. 1947. Circ. 1,000. Byline given. Pays on publication. Offers 100% kill fee. Publishes ms an average of 6 months after acceptance. Editorial lead time 6 months. Submit seasonal material 8 months in advance. Accepts queries by mail. Responds in 2 weeks to queries. Responds in 6 weeks to mss. Sometimes comments on rejected mss. Sample copy for $5. Guidelines online and for #10 SASE.

Magazine: 6×9; 128 pages; good quality paper; good cover stock. Receives 500 unsolicited mss/month. Accepts 15-20 mss/issue. Reads submissions September 15-April 15. Publishes 3-4 new writers/year. Has published work by Antonya Nelson, Doris Betts, Heidi Jon Schmidt.

NONFICTION Needs essays, interview. No inspirational. **Buys 6-8 mss/year.** Send complete ms. **Pays $5 and up/printed page.**

PHOTOS Send photos. Reviews contact sheets, transparencies, any size prints. Negotiates payment individually.

FICTION Needs ethnic, experimental, mainstream, novel concepts, literary short stories. No genre fiction. Would like to see more Southern fiction (Southern U.S). **Buys 25-30 mss/year.** Send complete ms. Considers fiction in all forms, short short to novella length. **Pays $5 and up/printed page (maximum of $150/story).**

POETRY Needs avant-garde, free verse, haiku, light verse, traditional. Mss not accompanied by SASE will be discarded unread. Occasionally provides criticism on poems. Considers poetry in all forms. Buys 30-75 poems/year. Submit maximum 5 poems. **Pays $5 and up/printed page (maximum of $50/poem).**

TIPS "Tell your story, speak your poem, straight from the heart. We are attracted to language and to good writing, but we are most interested in what the good writing leads us to, or where."

FICTION

Dept. of English, The City College of New York, 138th St. & Covenant Ave., New York NY 10031. **Website:** www.fictioninc.com. **Contact:** Mark J. Mirsky, editor. "As the name implies, we publish only fiction; we are looking for the best new writing available, leaning toward the unconventional. *Fiction* has traditionally attempted to make accessible the inaccessible, to bring the experimental to a broader audience." Reading period for unsolicited mss is September 15-May 15. Estab. 1972. Circ. 4,000. No kill fee. Publishes ms an average of 1 year after acceptance. Accepts simultaneous submissions. Responds in 3-6 months to mss. Sample copy: $7. Guidelines available online.

Stories first published in *Fiction* have been selected for the *Pushcart Prize: Best of the Small Presses, O. Henry Prize Stories*, and *Best American Short Stories.*

FICTION Needs experimental, humorous, satire, Also needs contemporary, literary, translations. No romance, science fiction, etc. Submit complete ms via online submissions manager. Length: up to 5,000 words.

TIPS "The guiding principle of *Fiction* has always been to go to terra incognita in the writing of the imagination and to ask that modern fiction set itself serious questions, if often in absurd and comedic voices, interrogating the nature of the real and the fantastic. It represents no particular school of fiction, except the innovative. Its pages have often been a harbor for writers at odds with each other. As a result of its willingness to publish the difficult, experimental, and unusual, while not excluding the well known, *Fiction* has a unique reputation in the U.S. and abroad as a journal of future directions."

THE FIDDLEHEAD

University of New Brunswick, Campus House, 11 Garland Court, Box 4400, Fredericton NB E3B 5A3 Canada. (506)453-3501. **Fax:** (506) 453-5069. **E-mail:** fiddlehd@unb.ca. **Website:** www.thefiddlehead.ca. Mark Anthony Jarman and Gerard Beirne, fiction editors; Phillip Crymble, Claire Kelly, and Ian LeTourneau, poetry editors. **Contact:** Kathryn Taglia, managing editor. "Canada's longest living literary journal, *The Fiddlehead* is published 4 times/year at the University of New Brunswick, with the generous assistance of the University of New Brunswick, the Canada Council for the Arts, and the Province of New Brunswick. It is experienced, wise enough to recognize excellence, and always looking for freshness and surprise. *The Fiddlehead* publishes short stories, poems, book reviews, and a small number of personal essays. Our full-color covers have become collectors' items and feature work by New Brunswick artists and from New Brunswick museums and art galleries. The journal is open to good writing in English from all over the world, looking always for freshness and surprise. Our editors are always happy to see new unsolicited works in fiction and poetry. Work is read on an ongoing basis; the acceptance rate is around 1-2%. Apart from our annual contest, we have no deadlines for submissions." Estab. 1945. Circ. 1,500. Pays on publication for first or one-time serial rights. Responds in 3-9 months to mss. Occasionally comments on rejected mss. Sample copy: $15 (U.S.).

"No criteria for publication except quality. For a general audience, including many poets and writers." Has published work by George Elliott Clarke, Kayla Czaga, Daniel Woodrell, and Clea Young. *The Fiddlehead* also sponsors an annual writing contest.

FICTION Receives 100-150 unsolicited mss/month. Accepts 4-5 mss/issue; 20-40 mss/year. Agented fiction: small percentage. Publishes high percentage of new writers/year. Needs literary. Send SASE and *Canadian* stamps or IRCs for return of mss. No e-mail, fax, or disc submissions. Simultaneous submissions only if stated on cover letter; must contact immediately if accepted elsewhere. Length: up to 6,000 words. Also publishes short shorts. **Pays up to $40 (Canadian)/published page and 2 contributor's copies.**

POETRY Send SASE and *Canadian* stamps or IRCs for return of mss. No e-mail, fax, or disc submissions. Simultaneous submissions only if stated on cover letter; must contact immediately if accepted elsewhere. Submit maximum 10 poems. **Pays up to $40 (Canadian)/published page and 2 contributor's copies.**

TIPS "If you are serious about submitting to *The Fiddlehead*, you should subscribe or read several issues to get a sense of the journal. Contact us if you would like to order sample back issues ($10-15 plus postage)."

FIELD: CONTEMPORARY POETRY & POETICS

Oberlin College Press, 50 N. Professor St., Oberlin OH 44074-1095. (440)775-8408. **Fax:** (440)775-8124. **E-mail:** oc.press@oberlin.edu. **Website:** www.oberlin.edu/ocpress. **Contact:** Marco Wilkinson, managing editor. **60% freelance written.** Biannual magazine of poetry, poetry in translation, and essays on contemporary poetry by poets. *FIELD: Contemporary Poetry and Poetics*, published semiannually in April and October, is a literary journal with "emphasis on poetry, translations, and essays by poets. See electronic submission guidelines." Estab. 1969. Circ. 1,500. Byline given. Pays on publication. Editorial lead time 4 months. Accepts queries by mail, e-mail, fax, phone, online submission form. Responds in 6-8 weeks to mss. Sample copy for $8. Guidelines available online and for #10 SASE.

FIELD is 100 pages, digest-sized, printed on rag stock, flat-spined, with glossy color card cover. Subscription: $16/year, $28 for 2 years. Sample: $8 postpaid. Has published poetry by Michelle Glazer, Tom Lux, Carl Phillips, Betsy Sholl, Charles Simic, Jean Valentine and translations by Marilyn Hacker and Stuart Friebert.

POETRY Needs contemporary, prose poems, free verse, traditional. Submissions are read August 1 through May 31. Submit 2-6 of your best poems. No e-mail submissions. Include cover letter and SASE. Submit using submission manager. Buys 120 poems/year. Submit maximum 5 poems. **Pays $15/page and 2 contributor's copies.**

TIPS "Keep trying!"

THE FOURTH RIVER

Chatham College, Woodland Rd., Pittsburgh PA 15232. **E-mail:** 4thriver@gmail.com. **Website:** fourthriver.chatham.edu. **100% freelance written.** *The Fourth River*, an annual publication of Chatham University's MFA in Creative Writing Programs, features literature that engages and explores the relationship between humans and their environments. Wants writings that are richly situated at the confluence of place, space, and identity, or that reflect upon or make use of landscape and place in new ways. Estab. 2005. Byline given. Pays with contributor copies only. No kill fee. Publishes mss in 5-8 months after acceptance. Accepts queries by mail. Accepts simultaneous submissions. Responds in 3-5 months to mss. Sample copy: $5 (back issue). Single copy: $10; subscription: $16 for 2 years. Guidelines online.

The Fourth River is digest-sized, perfect-bound, with full-color cover by various artists. *The Fourth River*'s contributors have been published in *Glimmer Train, Alaska Quarterly Review, The Missouri Review, The Best American Short Stories, The O. Henry Prize Stories*, and *The Best American Travel Writing*.

NONFICTION Needs book excerpts, essays, exposé, general interest, historical, humor, opinion, personal experience, travel. Submit complete ms via online submissions manager. Length: up to 7,000 words.

FICTION Needs adventure, condensed novels, ethnic, experimental, fantasy, historical, horror, humorous, mainstream, mystery, romance, science fiction, slice-of-life vignettes, suspense, literary. Submit complete ms via online submissions manager. Length: up to 7,000 words.

POETRY Needs avant-garde, free verse, haiku, light verse, traditional. Submit 3-5 poems via online submissions manager.

FREEFALL MAGAZINE

Freefall Literary Society of Calgary, 922 Ninth Ave. SE, Calgary AB T2G 0S4 Canada. **E-mail:** editors@freefallmagazine.ca. **Website:** www.freefallmagazine.ca. **Contact:** Ryan Stromquist, managing editor. **100% freelance written.** "Magazine published triannually containing fiction, poetry, creative nonfiction, essays on writing, interviews, and reviews. We are looking for exquisite writing with a strong narrative." Estab. 1990. Circ. 1,000. Pays on publication. Accepts queries by e-mail. Guidelines and submission forms on website.

NONFICTION Needs essays, interview, creative nonfiction. Submit via e-mail. E-mail subject line should include your name and type of submission (poetry, fiction, nonfiction, creative nonfiction, flash fiction, short fiction, photo, art work, etc.). Include name, contact information, and description of the type of work you are querying about. **Pays $10/printed page in the magazine, to a maximum of $100, and 1 contributor's copy.**

FICTION Submit via website form. Attach submission file (file name format is lastname_firstname_storytitle.doc or .docx or .pdf). Length: no more than 4,000 words. **Pays $10 per printed page in the magazine, to a maximum of $100, and 1 contributor's copy.**

POETRY Submit 2-5 poems via website. Attach submission file (file name format is lastname_firstname_storytitle.doc or .docx or .pdf). Accepts any style of poetry. Length: no more than 6 pages. **Pays $25 per poem and 1 contributor's copy.**

TIPS "Our mission is to encourage the voices of new, emerging, and experienced Canadian writers and provide a platform for their quality work."

FUGUE LITERARY MAGAZINE

200 Brink Hall, University of Idaho, P.O. Box 44110, Moscow ID 83844. **E-mail:** fugue@uidaho.edu. **Website:** www.fuguejournal.org. **Contact:** Alexandra Teague, faculty advisor. Biannual literary magazine. "Submissions are accepted online only. Poetry, fiction, and nonfiction submissions are accepted September 1-April 1. All material received outside of this period will not be read." $3 submission fee per entry. See website for submission instructions. Estab. 1990. Circ. 500. Accepts queries by online submission form. Accepts simultaneous submissions. Responds in 3-6 months to mss. Sample copy: $8. Guidelines online.

Work published in *Fugue* has won the Pushcart Prize and has been cited in *Best American Essays*.

NONFICTION Needs essays. Submit 1 essay using online submissions manager. **Pays 2 contributor's copies and additional payment.**

FICTION Submit complete ms via online submissions manager. "Please send no more than 2 short shorts or 1 story at a time. Submissions in more than 1 genre should be submitted separately. All multiple submissions will be returned unread. Once you have submitted a piece to us, wait for a response on this piece before submitting again." **Pays 2 contributor's copies and additional payment.**

POETRY Submit up to 3 poems using online submissions manager. **Pays 2 contributor's copies and additional payment.**

TIPS "The best way, of course, to determine what we're looking for is to read the journal. As the name *Fugue* indicates, our goal is to present a wide range of literary perspectives. We like stories that satisfy us both intellectually and emotionally, with fresh language and characters so captivating that they stick with us and invite a second reading. We are also seeking creative literary criticism which illuminates a piece of literature or a specific writer by examining that writer's personal experience."

GARGOYLE

Paycock Press, 3819 N. 13th St., Arlington VA 22201. (703)525-9296. **E-mail:** rchrdpeabody9@gmail.com. **E-mail:** gargoyle@gargoylemagazine.com. **Website:** www.gargoylemagazine.com. **Contact:** Richard Peabody, editor, Lucinda Ebersole, co-editor. **75% freelance written.** "*Gargoyle* has always been a scallywag magazine, a maverick magazine, a bit too academic for the underground and way too underground for the academics. We are a writer's magazine in that we are read by other writers and have never worried about reaching the masses." Annual. Estab. 1976. Circ. 2,000. Publishes ms 1 year after acceptance. Accepts queries by online submission form. Accepts simultaneous submissions. Responds in 1 month to queries, proposals, and mss. Sample copy: $12.95. Catalog available online at FAQ link. "We don't have guidelines; we have never believed in them." Query in an e-mail. "We prefer electronic submissions. Please use submission engine online." For snail mail, send SASE for reply and return of ms, or send a disposable copy of ms.

NONFICTION Needs memoir, photo feature, creative nonfiction, literary criticism. **Pays 10% of print run and 50-50 split (after/if we break even). Sends galleys to author.**

FICTION Wants "edgy realism or experimental works. We run both." Wants to see more Canadian, British, Australian, and Third World fiction. Receives 200 unsolicited mss/week during submission period. Accepts 20-50 mss/issue. Agented fiction 5%. **Publishes 2-3 new writers/year.** Publishes 2 titles/year. Format: trade paperback originals. Needs experimental, poetry, literary, short story collections. No romance, horror, science fiction. **Buys 10-15 mss/year.** Length: 1,000-4,500 words.

POETRY Pays contributor's copies.

TIPS "We have to fall in love with a particular fiction."

THE GEORGIA REVIEW

The University of Georgia, Main Library, Room 706A, 320 S. Jackson St., Athens GA 30602. (706)542-3481. **Fax:** (706)542-0047. **E-mail:** garev@uga.edu. **Website:** thegeorgiareview.com. **Contact:** Stephen Corey, editor. **99% freelance written.** Quarterly journal. "Our readers are educated, inquisitive people who read a lot of work in the areas we feature, so they expect only the best in our pages. All work submitted should show evidence that the writer is at least as well educated and well read as our readers. Essays should be authoritative but accessible to a range of readers." Estab. 1947. Circ. 3,500. Byline given. Pays on publication. No kill fee. Publishes ms an average of 6 months after acceptance. Accepts queries by mail. Responds in 2 weeks to queries; in 2-3 months to mss. Sample copy: $10. Guidelines available online.

Electronic submissions available for $3 fee. Reading period: August 15-May 15.

NONFICTION Needs essays. **Buys 12-20 mss/year.** "For the most part we are not interested in scholarly articles that are narrow in focus and/or overly burdened with footnotes. The ideal essay for *The Georgia Review* is a provocative, thesis-oriented work that can engage both the intelligent general reader and the specialist. Send complete ms." Submit ms via online submissions manager or postal mail. **Pays $50/published page.**

PHOTOS Send photos. Reviews 5x7 prints or larger. Offers no additional payment for photos accepted with ms.

FICTION "We seek original, excellent writing not bound by type." "Ordinarily we do not publish novel excerpts or works translated into English, and we strongly discourage authors from submitting these." **Buys 12-20 mss/year.** Send complete ms via online submissions manager or postal mail. **Pays $50/published page.**

POETRY "We seek original, excellent poetry. Submit 3-5 poems at a time." Buys 60-75 poems/year. **Pays $4/line.**

THE GETTYSBURG REVIEW

Gettysburg College, Gettysburg PA 17325. (717)337-6770. **Fax:** (717)337-6775. **E-mail:** pstitt@gettysburg.edu; mdrew@gettysburg.edu. **Website:** www.gettysburgreview.com. **Contact:** Peter Stitt, editor; Ellen Hathaway, managing editor; Mark Drew, assistant editor. Published quarterly, *The Gettysburg Review* considers unsolicited submissions of poetry, fiction, and essays. "Our concern is quality. Manuscripts submitted here should be extremely well written. Reading period September 1-May 31." Estab. 1988. Circ. 3,000. Byline given. Pays on publication. Publishes ms an average of 6 months after acceptance. Editorial lead time 1 year. Submit seasonal material 9 months in advance. Accepts queries by mail, fax. Accepts simultaneous submissions. Responds in 1 month to queries; in 3-5 months to mss. Sample copy: $10. Guidelines available online.

NONFICTION Needs essays. **Buys 20 mss/year.** Send complete ms. Length: up to 25 pages. **Pays $30/page and 1 contributor's copy.**

FICTION Wants high-quality literary fiction. Needs experimental, historical, humorous, mainstream, novel concepts, serialized, contemporary. "We require that fiction be intelligent and esthetically written." No genre fiction. **Buys 20 mss/year.** Send complete ms with SASE. Length: 2,000-7,000 words. **Pays $30/page and 1 contributor's copy.**

POETRY Considers "well-written poems of all kinds." Has published poetry by Rita Dove, Alice Friman, Philip Schultz, Michelle Boisseau, Bob Hicok, Linda Pastan, and G.C. Waldrep. Buys 50 poems/year. Submit maximum 5 poems. **Pays $2.50/line and 1 contributor's copy.**

GINOSKO LITERARY JOURNAL

P.O. Box 246, Fairfax CA 94978. **E-mail:** editorginosko@aol.com. **Website:** www.ginoskoliteraryjournal.com. **Contact:** Robert Paul Cesaretti, editor. "*Ginos-*

ko (ghin-océ-koe): To perceive, understand, realize, come to know; knowledge that has an inception, a progress, an attainment. The recognition of truth by experience." Accepting short fiction and poetry, creative nonfiction, interviews, social justice concerns, and literary insights for www.GinoskoLiteraryJournal.com. Estab. 2002. Circ. 9,000+. Website receives 800-1,200 hits/month. No kill fee. Editorial lead time 1-2 months. Accepts queries by mail, e-mail. Accepts simultaneous submissions. Guidelines available online at website.

Reads year round. Length of articles flexible; accepts excerpts. Publishing as semiannual ezine. Check downloadable issues on website for tone and style. Downloads free; accepts donations. Also looking for books, art, and music to post on website, and links to exchange. Member CLMP.

NONFICTION Needs essays, interview. Submit via postal mail, e-mail (prefers attachments: .wps, .doc, or .rtf), or online submissions manager (https://ginosko.submittable.com/submit).

FICTION Submit via postal mail, e-mail (prefers attachments: .wps, .doc, or .rtf), or online submissions manager (https://ginosko.submittable.com/submit).

POETRY Submit via postal mail, e-mail (prefers attachments: .wps, .doc, or .rtf), or online submissions manager (https://ginosko.submittable.com/submit).

GLIMMER TRAIN STORIES

Glimmer Train Press, Inc., P.O. Box 80430, Portland OR 97280. **Fax:** (503)221-0837. **E-mail:** eds@glimmertrain.org. **Website:** www.glimmertrain.org. **100% freelance written.** Triannual magazine of literary short fiction. "We are interested in literary short stories, particularly by new and emerging writers." Estab. 1991. Circ. 12,000. Byline given. Pays on acceptance. Publishes ms an average of 15 months after acceptance. Accepts simultaneous submissions. Responds in 2 months to mss. Sometimes comments on rejected mss. Sample copy: $15 on website. For guidelines and to submit online: www.glimmertrain.org.

Recently published work by Benjamin Percy, Laura van den Berg, Manuel Muñoz, Claire Vaye Watkins, Abby Geni, Peter Ho Davies, William Trevor, Thisbe Nissen, and Yiyun Li.

FICTION Submit via the website at www.glimmertrain.org. "In a pinch, send a hard copy and include SASE for response." Receives 36,000 unsolicited mss/year. Accepts 15 mss/issue; 45 mss/year. Agented fiction 2%. Publishes 20 new writers/year. Length: 1,200-12,000 words. **Pays $700 for standard submissions, up to $2,500 for contest-winning stories.**

TIPS "In the last 2 years over half of the first-place stories have been their authors' very first publications. See our contest listings in Contests & Awards section."

GRAIN

P.O. Box 67, Saskatoon SK S7K 3K1 Canada. (306)244-2828. **Fax:** (306)565-8554. **E-mail:** grainmag@skwriter.com. **Website:** www.grainmagazine.ca. **Contact:** Rilla Friesen, editor. Quarterly magazine covering poetry, fiction, creative nonfiction. "*Grain, The Journal Of Eclectic Writing* is a literary quarterly that publishes engaging, diverse, and challenging writing and art by some of the best Canadian and international writers and artists. Every issue features superb new writing from both developing and established writers. Each issue also highlights the unique artwork of a different visual artist. *Grain* has garnered national and international recognition for its distinctive, cutting-edge content and design." Estab. 1973. Circ. 1,600. Byline given. Pays on publication. Typically responds in 3-6 months. Sample: $13 CAD. Subscription: $35 CAD/year, $55 CAD for 2 years. (See website for U.S. and foreign postage fees.). Guidelines available by SASE (or SAE and IRC), e-mail, or on website.

NONFICTION No academic papers or reportage. "No fax or e-mail submissions; postal submissions only. Send typed, unpublished material only (we consider work published online to be previously published). Please only submit work in 1 genre at 1 time." Length: up to 5,000 words. **Pays $50-250 CAD (depending on number of pages) and 2 contributor's copies.**

FICTION Needs experimental, literary, mainstream, contemporary. No romance, confession, science fiction, vignettes, mystery. "Submissions must be typed in readable font (ideally 12 point, Times Roman or Courier), free of typos, printed on 1 side only. No staples. Your name and address must be on every page. Pieces of more than 1 page must be numbered. Cover letter with all contact information, title(s), and genre of work is required." Postal mail submissions only. Length: up to 5,000 words. "Stories at the longer end of the word count must be of exceptional quality." **Pays $50-250 CAD (depending on number of pages) and 2 contributor's copies.**

POETRY Needs individual poems, sequences, suites. Has published poetry by Lorna Crozier, Don Domanski, Cornelia Haeussler, Patrick Lane, Karen Solie, and Monty Reid. Wants "high-quality, imaginative, well-crafted poetry." Submit up to 12 pages of poetry, typed in readable font on 1 side only. No fax or e-mail submissions; postal submissions only. Cover letter with all contact information, title(s), and genre of work is required. "No staples. Your name and address must be on every page. Pieces of more than 1 page must be numbered. Please only submit work in 1 genre at a time." **Pays $50-250 CAD (depending on number of pages) and 2 contributor's copies.**
TIPS "Only work of the highest literary quality is accepted. Read several back issues."

GULF COAST: A JOURNAL OF LITERATURE AND FINE ARTS

4800 Calhoun Road, Houston TX 77204-3013. (713)743-3223. **E-mail:** editors@gulfcoastmag.org. **Website:** www.gulfcoastmag.org. **Contact:** Adrienne Perry, editor; Martin Rock, managing editor; Carlos Hernandez, digital editor; Conor Bracken, Katie Condon, Sam Mansfield, poetry editors; Julia Brown, Laura Jok, Dino Piacentini, fiction editors; Talia Mailman, Steve Sanders, nonfiction editors; Matthew Salesses, online fiction editor; Christopher Murray, online poetry editor; Talia Mailman, online nonfiction editor. Biannual magazine covering innovative fiction, nonfiction, poetry, visual art, and critical art writing. Estab. 1986. No kill fee. Publishes ms 6 months-1 year after acceptance. Accepts queries by mail, phone. Accepts simultaneous submissions. Responds in 4-6 months to mss. Sometimes comments on rejected mss. Back issue: $8, plus 7x10 SASE with 4 first-class stamps. Writer's guidelines for #10 SASE or on website.

Magazine: 7x9; approximately 300 pages; stock paper, gloss cover; illustrations; photos.

NONFICTION Needs interview, reviews. *Gulf Coast* reads general submissions, submitted by post or through the online submissions manager, September 1-March 1. Submissions e-mailed directly to the editors or postmarked March 1-September 1 will not be read or responded to. "Please visit our contest page for contest submission guidelines." **Pays $100 per review and $200 per interview.** Sometimes pays expenses of writers on assignment.

FICTION "Please do not send multiple submissions; we will read only 1 submission per author at a given time, except in the case of our annual contests." Needs ethnic, experimental, multicultural, literary, regional, translations, contemporary. No children's, genre, religious/inspirational. *Gulf Coast* reads general submissions, submitted by post or through the online submissions manager September 1-March 1. Submissions e-mailed directly to the editors or postmarked March 1-September 1 will not be read or responded to. "Please visit our contest page for contest submission guidelines." Receives 500 unsolicited mss/month. Accepts 6-8 mss/issue; 12-16 mss/year. Agented fiction: 5%. Publishes 2-8 new writers/year. Recently published work by Alan Heathcock, Anne Carson, Bret Anthony Johnston, John D'Agata, Lucie Brock-Broido, Clancy Martin, Steve Almond, Sam Lipsyte, Carl Phillips, Dean Young, and Eula Biss. Publishes short shorts. **Pays $50/page.**

POETRY Submit up to 5 poems at a time. Considers simultaneous submissions with notification; no previously published poems. Cover letter is required. List previous publications and include a brief bio. Reads submissions September-April. **Pays $50/page.**

TIPS "Submit only previously unpublished works. Include a cover letter. Online submissions are strongly preferred. Stories or essays should be typed, double-spaced, and paginated with your name, address, and phone number on the first page and the title on subsequent pages. Poems should have your name, address, and phone number on the first page of each." The Annual Gulf Coast Prizes award publication and $1,500 each in poetry, fiction, and nonfiction; opens in December of each year. Honorable mentions in each category will receive a $250 second prize. Postmark/online entry deadline: March 22 of each year. Winners and honorable mentions will be announced in May. **Entry fee:** $23 (includes one-year subscription). Make checks payable to *Gulf Coast*. Guidelines available on website.

HANGING LOOSE

Hanging Loose Press, 231 Wyckoff St., Brooklyn NY 11217. **E-mail:** editor@hangingloosepress.com. **Website:** www.hangingloosepress.com. **Contact:** Robert Hershon, Dick Lourie, and Mark Pawlak, poetry editors. *Hanging Loose*, published in April and October, concentrates on the work of new writers. Wants excellent, energetic poems. Estab. 1966. Responds in 3 months. Sample: $14.

Hanging Loose is 120 pages, offset-printed on heavy stock, flat-spined, with 4-color glossy card cover. Considers poetry by teens (one section contains poems by high-school-age poets).

POETRY Submit up to 6 poems at a time. No fax or e-mail submissions; postal submissions only. "Would-be contributors should read the magazine first." Has published poetry by Sherman Alexie, Paul Violi, Donna Brook, Kimiko Hahn, Harvey Shapiro, and Ha Jin. **Pays small fee and 2 contributor's copies.**

HARVARD REVIEW

Houghton Library of the Harvard College Library, Lamont Library, Harvard University, Cambridge MA 02138. (617)495-9775. **Fax:** (617)496-3692. **E-mail:** info@harvardreview.org. **Website:** harvardreview.fas.harvard.edu. **Contact:** Christina Thompson, editor; Suzanne Berne, fiction editor; Major Jackson, poetry editor. Semiannual magazine covering poetry, fiction, essays, drama, graphics, and reviews in the spring and fall by an eclectic range of international writers. "Previous contributors include John Updike, Alice Hoffman, Joyce Carol Oates, Miranda July, and Jim Crace. We also publish the work of emerging and previously unpublished writers." Estab. 1992. No kill fee. Accepts queries by mail, online submission form. Accepts simultaneous submissions. Responds in 6 months to mss.

Does not accept e-mail submissions. Reading period: September 1-May 31.

NONFICTION Needs essays, reviews. Special issues: If you are interested in reviewing for the *Harvard Review*, write to the editor and enclose 2 or more recent clips. No unsolicited book reviews or genre fiction (romance, horror, detective, etc.). Submit using online submissions manager or by mail. Length: up to 7,000 words.

PHOTOS Contact: Judith Larsen, visual arts editor.

FICTION Submit using online submissions manager or by mail. Length: up to 7,000 words.

POETRY Submit up to 5 poems via online submissions manager or postal mail. Submit maximum 5 poems.

TIPS "Writers at all stages of their careers are invited to apply, however, we can only publish a very small fraction of the material we receive. We recommend that you familiarize yourself with *Harvard Review* before you submit your work."

HAWAII REVIEW

University of Hawaii Board of Publications, 2445 Campus Rd., Hemenway Hall 107, Honolulu HI 96822. (808)956-3030. **Fax:** (808)956-3083. **E-mail:** hawaiireview@gmail.com. **Website:** www.kaleo.org/hawaii_review. **100% freelance written.** Semiannual magazine covering fiction, poetry, reviews, and art. *Hawai'i Review* is a student run biannual literary and visual arts print journal featuring national and international writing and visual art, as well as regional literature and visual art of Hawai'i and the Pacific. Estab. 1973. Circ. 500. Byline given. Publishes ms an average of 3 months after acceptance. Accepts queries by e-mail, fax, phone. Accepts simultaneous submissions. Responds in 3 months to mss. Sample copy: free, plus $5 shipping (back issue). Single copy: $12.50. Guidelines available online.

Accepts submissions online through Submittable only. Offers yearly award with $500 prizes in poetry and fiction.

NONFICTION Needs essays, interviews, book reviews. Send 1 complete ms via online submission manager. Length: up to 7,000 words.

FICTION Needs confession, experimental, humorous, short shorts. Send 1 short story or 2 pieces of flash fiction via online submission manager. Length: up to 7,000 words for short stories, up to 2,500 words for flash fiction.

POETRY Needs avant-garde, free verse, haiku, traditional. Submit up to 6 poems via online submission manager. Length: up to 500 lines/poem (though space limitations are taken into account for longer poems).

TIPS "Make it new."

HOBART

P.O. Box 1658, Ann Arbor MI 48103. **E-mail:** aaron@hobartpulp.com. **Website:** www.hobartpulp.com. **Contact:** Aaron Burch, editor. Website covering short stories, personal essays, short interviews, comics, roundtable discussions. "We tend to like quirky stories like truck driving, mathematics, and vagabonding. We like stories with humor (humorous but engaging, literary but not stuffy). We want to get excited about your story and hope you'll send your best work." No kill fee. Accepts queries by online submission form. Accepts simultaneous submissions. Responds in 1-3 months. "If our response time is longer than 3 months, feel free to inquire." Guidelines on website.

All submissions must go through online submissions manager. Only accepting submissions for online journal.

NONFICTION Needs essays, food and drink, short interviews. Special issues: "We tend to like our nonfiction to be more about something and less 'short memoir-y' pieces." Submit complete ms via online submissions manager. Length: up to 2,000 words.

FICTION "We publish nonstuffy, unpretentious, high-quality fiction that never takes itself too serious and always entertains." Also publishes erotica. Needs erotica, mainstream. Submit complete ms via online submissions manager. Length: up to 2,000 words; prefers submissions of about 1,000 words.

POETRY "There's no one type of poem that we prefer of the other, although we're interested in poetry that doesn't necessarily know it's poetry: work that the uncareful reader might mistake for prose. Send us your barroom promises, your church pew utterances, your missives from that broken place between language and experience. We are looking to be moved by the beauty in what is common. Also, we like poems about dogs, possums, and ugly babies. Submit 3-5 poems as single document via online submissions manager.

TIPS "We'd love to receive fewer run-of-the-mill relationship stories and more stories concerning truck drivers, lumberjacks, carnival workers, and gunslingers. In other words: surprise us. Show us a side of life rarely depicted in literary fiction."

THE HOLLINS CRITIC

P.O. Box 9538, Hollins University, Roanoke VA 24020-1538. **E-mail:** acockrell@hollins.edu. **Website:** www.hollins.edu/who-we-are/news-media/hollins-critic. **Contact:** Cathryn Hankla. **100% freelance written.** Magazine published 5 times/year. *The Hollins Critic*, published 5 times a year, presents the first serious surveys of the whole bodies of contemporary writers' work, with complete checklists. In past issues, you'll find essays on such writers as John Engels (by David Huddle), James McCourt (by David Rollow), Jane Hirshfield (by Jeanne Larsen), Edwidge Danticat (by Denise Shaw), Vern Rutsala (by Lewis Turco), Sarah Arvio (by Lisa Williams), and Milton Kessler (by Liz Rosenberg). Estab. 1964. Circ. 400. Byline given. Pays on publication. No kill fee. Publishes ms an average of 1 year after acceptance. Accepts queries by online submission form. Accepts simultaneous submissions. Responds in 2 months to mss. Sample copy for $3. Guidelines for #10 SASE.

Uses a few short poems in each issue, interesting in form, content, or both. *The Hollins Critic* is 24 pages, magazine-sized. Press run is 500. Subscription: $12/year ($17 outside US). No postal or e-mail submissions. Has published poetry by Natasha Trethewey, Carol Moldaw, David Huddle, Margaret Gibson, and Julia Johnson.

POETRY Needs avant-garde, free verse, traditional. Submit up to 5 poems at a time using the online submission form at www.hollinscriticsubmissions.com, available September 15-December 1. Submissions received at other times will be returned unread. Reading period: September 15-December 15. Publishes 16-20 poems/year. **Pays $25/poem plus 5 contributor's copies.**

TIPS "We accept unsolicited poetry submissions; all other content is by prearrangement."

HOOT

A postcard review of {mini} poetry and prose, 1413 Academy Lane, Elkins Park PA 19027. **E-mail:** info@hootreview.com. **E-mail:** onlinesubmissions@hootreview.com. **Website:** www.hootreview.com. **Contact:** Amanda Vacharat and Dorian Geisler, editors/co-founders. **100% freelance written.** *HOOT* publishes 1 piece of writing, designed with original art/photographs, on the front of a postcard every month, as well as 2-3 pieces online. The postcards are intended for sharing, to be hung on the wall, etc. Therefore, *HOOT* looks for very brief, surprising-yet-gimmick-free writing that can stand on its own, that also follows "The Refrigerator Rule"—something that you would hang on your refrigerator and would want to read and look at for a whole month. This rule applies to online content as well. Estab. 2011. Pays on publication. Publishes ms 2 months after acceptance. Accepts queries by e-mail. Accepts simultaneous submissions. Sample copy: $2. Writer's guidelines available on website.

Costs $2 to submit up to 2 pieces of work. Submit through online submissions manager.

NONFICTION Needs personal experience, creative nonfiction. **Buys 6 mss/year.** Submit complete ms. Length: 150 words maximum. **Pays $10-100 for assigned and unsolicited pieces.**

PHOTOS Send photos (GIF/JPEG files) with submission.

FICTION Needs experimental, literary, flash/short short. **Buys 14 mss/year.** Submit complete ms. Length: 150 words maximum. **Pays $10-100 for print publication.**

POETRY Needs avant-garde, free verse, haiku, light verse, traditional, prose. Buys 14 poems/year. Submit maximum 2 poems. Length: up to 10 lines. **Pays $10-100 for print publication.**

TIPS "We look for writing with audacity and zest from authors who are not afraid to take risks. We appreciate work that is able to go beyond mere description in its 150 words. We offer free online workshops every otherWednesday for authors who would like feedback on their work from the *HOOT* editors. We also often give feedback with our rejections. We publish roughly 6-10 new writers each year."

HUBBUB

5344 SE 38th Ave., Portland OR 97202. **E-mail:** lisa.steinman@reed.edu. **Website:** www.reed.edu/hubbub. J. Shugrue and Lisa M. Steinman, co-editors. *Hubbub*, published once/year, is designed "to feature a multitude of voices from interesting, contemporary American poets." Wants "poems that are well crafted, with something to say. We have no single style, subject, or length requirement and in particular will consider long poems." Estab. 1983. Responds in 4 months. Sample copy: $3.35 (back issues), $7 (current issue). Subscription: $7/year. Guidelines available for SASE.

Hubbub is 50-70 pages, digest-sized, offset-printed, perfect-bound, with cover art. Receives about 1,200 submissions/year, accepts up to 2%. Press run is 350.

POETRY Submit 3-6 typed poems at a time. Include SASE. "We review 2-4 poetry books/year in short (3-page) reviews; all reviews are solicited. We do, however, list books received/recommended." Send materials for review consideration. Has published poetry by Madeline DeFrees, Cecil Giscombe, Carolyn Kizer, Primus St. John, Shara McCallum, and Alice Fulton. Does not want light verse. **Pays $20/poem.**

THE HUDSON REVIEW

The Hudson Review, Inc., 684 Park Ave., New York NY 10065. (212)650-0020. **E-mail:** info@hudsonreview.com. **Website:** hudsonreview.com. **Contact:** Paula Deitz, editor. **100% freelance written.** Quarterly magazine publishing fiction; poetry; essays; book reviews; criticism of literature, art, theatre, dance, film and music; and articles on contemporary cultural developments. Estab. 1948. Circ. 2,000. Byline given. Pays on publication. No kill fee. Publishes ms an average of 6 months after acceptance. Editorial lead time 3 months. Accepts queries by mail. Responds in 6 months to mss. Sample copy: $11. Guidelines online.

Send with SASE. Mss sent outside accepted reading period will be returned unread if SASE contains sufficient postage.

NONFICTION Needs essays, general interest, historical, opinion, personal experience, travel. **Buys 4-6 mss/year.** Send complete ms by postal mail between **January 1-March 31** only. Length: up to 10,000 words.

FICTION Buys 4 mss/year. Send complete ms by postal mail between **September 1-November 30** only. Length: up to 10,000 words.

POETRY Submit up to 7 poems by postal mail between **April 1-June 30** only. Buys 12-20 poems/year.

TIPS "We do not specialize in publishing any particular 'type' of writing; our sole criterion for accepting unsolicited work is literary quality. The best way for you to get an idea of the range of work we publish is to read a current issue. Unsolicited mss submitted outside of specified reading times will be returned unread. Do not send submissions via e-mail."

HUNGER MOUNTAIN

Vermont College of Fine Arts, 36 College St., Montpelier VT 05602. (802)828-8517. **E-mail:** hungermtn@vcfa.edu. **Website:** www.hungermtn.org. **Contact:** Miciah Bay Gault, editor. Monthly online publication and annual perfect-bound journal covering high-quality fiction, poetry, creative nonfiction, craft essays, writing for children, and artwork. Accepts high-quality work from unknown, emerging, or successful writers. No genre fiction, drama, or academic articles, please. Estab. 2002. Byline given. Pays on publication. No kill fee. Publishes ms an average of 1 year after acceptance. Submit seasonal material 1 year in advance. Accepts queries by online submission form. Accepts simultaneous submissions. Responds in 4 months to mss. Single copy: $10; subscription: $12/year, $22 for 2 years. Make checks payable to Vermont College of Fine Arts. Guidelines online.

Hunger Mountain is about 200 pages, 7x10, professionally printed, perfect-bound, with full-bleed color artwork on cover. Press run is

1,000; 10,000 visits online monthly. Uses online submissions manager. Member: CLMP.

NONFICTION Needs "We welcome an array of traditional and experimental work, including, but not limited to, personal, lyrical, and meditative essays, memoirs, collages, rants, and humor. The only requirements are recognition of truth, a unique voice with a firm command of language, and an engaging story with multiple pressure points." No informative or instructive articles, please. Prose for children and young adults is acceptable. Payment varies. Submit complete ms using online submissions manager. Length: up to 10,000 words.

PHOTOS Send photos. Reviews contact sheets, transparencies, prints, GIF/JPEG files. Slides preferred. Negotiates payment individually.

FICTION "We look for work that is beautifully crafted and tells a good story, with characters that are alive and kicking, storylines that stay with us long after we've finished reading, and sentences that slay us with their precision." Needs adventure, high-quality short stories, short shorts. No genre fiction, meaning science fiction, fantasy, horror, erotic, etc. Submit ms using online submissions manager. Length: up to 10,000 words. **Pays $25-100.**

POETRY Needs avant-garde, free verse, traditional. Submit 3-10 poems at a time. All poems should be in 1 file. "We look for poetry that is as much about the world as about the self, that's an invitation, an opening out, a hand beckoning. We like poems that name or identify something essential that we may have overlooked. We like poetry with acute, precise attention to both content and diction." Submit using online submissions manager. No light verse, humor/quirky/catchy verse, greeting card verse. Buys 10 poems/year.

TIPS "Mss must be typed, prose double-spaced. Poets submit at least 3 poems. No multiple genre submissions. Fresh viewpoints and human interest are very important, as is originality. We are committed to publishing an outstanding journal of the arts. Do not send entire novels, mss, or short story collections. Do not send previously published work."

IMAGE

3307 Third Ave. W., Seattle WA 98119. (206)281-2988. **Fax:** (206)281-2979. **E-mail:** image@imagejournal.org. **Website:** www.imagejournal.org. **Contact:** Gregory Wolfe, publisher and editor in chief. **50% freelance written.** Quarterly magazine covering the intersection between art and faith. "*Image* is a unique forum for the best writing and artwork that is informed by—or grapples with—religious faith. We have never been interested in art that merely regurgitates dogma or falls back on easy answers or didacticism. Instead, our focus has been on writing and visual artwork that embody a spiritual struggle, that seek to strike a balance between tradition and a profound openness to the world. Each issue explores this relationship through outstanding fiction, poetry, painting, sculpture, architecture, film, music, interviews, and dance. *Image* also features 4-color reproductions of visual art." Estab. 1989. Circ. 4,500. Byline given. Pays on acceptance. No kill fee. Publishes ms an average of 8 months after acceptance. Accepts queries by mail, e-mail. Accepts simultaneous submissions. Responds in 1 month to queries; in 5 months to mss. Sample copy: $16 or available online. Guidelines online.

Magazine: 7×10; 136 pages; glossy cover stock; illustrations; photos.

NONFICTION "No sentimental, preachy, moralistic, or obvious essays." **Buys 10 mss/year.** Send complete ms. Send SASE for reply, return of ms, or send disposable copy of ms. Does not accept e-mail submissions. Length: up to 6,000 words. **Pays $10/page ($150 maximum) and 4 contributor's copies.**

FICTION "No sentimental, preachy, moralistic, obvious stories, or genre stories (unless they manage to transcend their genre)." **Buys 8 mss/year.** Send complete ms. Send SASE for reply, return of ms, or send disposable copy of ms. Does not accept e-mail submissions. Length: up to 6,000 words. **Pays $10/page ($150 maximum) and 4 contributor's copies.**

POETRY Wants poems that grapple with religious faith, usually Judeo-Christian. Submit by mail. Send SASE for reply, return of ms, or send disposable copy of ms. Does not accept e-mail submissions. **Pays $2/line ($150 maximum) and 4 contributor's copies.**

TIPS "Fiction must grapple with religious faith, though subjects need not be overtly religious."

INDIANA REVIEW

Ballantine Hall 465, 1020 E. Kirkwood, Indiana University, Bloomington IN 47405. (812)855-3439. **E-mail:** inreview@indiana.edu. **Website:** indianareview.org. **Contact:** Britt Ashley, editor; Justin Wolfe, nonfiction editor; Joe Hiland, fiction editor; Michael Mlekoday, poetry editor. **100% freelance written.** Biannual magazine. "*Indiana Review,* a nonprofit organization run by IU graduate students, is a journal of previously unpublished poetry and fiction. Literary interviews and essays are also considered. We publish innovative fiction, nonfiction, and poetry. We're interested in energy, originality, and careful attention to craft. While we publish many well-known writers, we also welcome new and emerging poets and fiction writers." Estab. 1976. Circ. 5,000. Byline given. Pays on publication. Publishes ms an average of 3-6 months after acceptance. Accepts simultaneous submissions. Responds in 2 or more weeks to queries; in 4 or more months to mss. Sample copy: $12. Guidelines available online. "We no longer accept hard-copy submissions. All submissions must be made online."

NONFICTION Needs essays, interview, creative nonfiction. No coming-of-age/slice of life pieces or book reviews. **Buys 5-7 mss/year.** Submit complete ms through online submissions manager. Length: up to 8,000. **Pays $5/page ($10 minimum), plus 2 contributor's copies.**

FICTION "We look for daring stories which integrate theme, language, character, and form. We like polished writing, humor, and fiction which has consequence beyond the world of its narrator." Needs ethnic, experimental, mainstream, novel concepts, literary, short fictions, translations. No genre fiction. **Buys 14-18 mss/year.** Submit via online submissions manager. Length: up to 8,000 words. **Pays $5/page ($10 minimum), plus 2 contributor's copies.**

POETRY "We look for poems that are skillful and bold, exhibiting an inventiveness of language with attention to voice and sonics." Wants experimental, free verse, prose poem, traditional form, lyrical, narrative. Buys 80 poems/year. Submit maximum 6 poems. Length: 5 lines minimum. **Pays $5/page ($10 minimum), plus 2 contributor's copies.**

TIPS "We're always looking for nonfiction essays that go beyond merely autobiographical revelation and utilize sophisticated organization and slightly radical narrative strategies. We want essays that are both lyrical and analytical where confession does not mean nostalgia. Read us before you submit. Often reading is slower in summer and holiday months. Only submit work to journals you would proudly subscribe to, then subscribe to a few. Take care to read the latest 2 issues and specifically mention work you identify with and why. Submit work that 'stacks up' with the work we've published. Offers annual poetry, fiction, short short/prose poem prizes. See website for full guidelines."

THE IOWA REVIEW

308 EPB, The University of Iowa, Iowa City IA 52242. (319)335-0462. **Website:** www.iowareview.org. **Contact:** Harilaos Stecopoulos. Triannual magazine. *The Iowa Review*, published 3 times/year, prints fiction, poetry, essays, reviews, and, occasionally, interviews. Receives about 5,000 submissions/year, accepts up to 100. Press run is 2,900; 1,500 distributed to stores. Subscription: $25. Stories, essays, and poems for a general readership interested in contemporary literature. Estab. 1970. Circ. 3,500. Pays on publication. Publishes ms an average of 12-18 months after acceptance. Accepts queries by mail, online submission form. Accepts simultaneous submissions. Responds in 4 months to mss. Sample copy for $9.95 and online. Guidelines available online.

This magazine uses the help of colleagues and graduate assistants. Its reading period for unsolicited work is September 1-December 1. From January through April, they read entries to their annual Iowa Awards competition. Check the website for further information.

FICTION "We are open to a range of styles and voices and always hope to be surprised by work we then feel we need." Receives 600 unsolicited mss/month. Accepts 4-6 mss/issue; 12-18 mss/year. Does not read mss January-August. Publishes ms an average of 12-18 months after acceptance. Agented fiction less than 2%. **Publishes some new writers/year.** Recently published work by Johanna Hunting, Bennett Sims, and Pedro Mairal. Send complete ms with cover letter. "Don't bother with queries." SASE for return of ms. SASE required. Accepts mss by snail mail and online submission form at https://iowareview.submittable.com/submit; no e-mail submissions. **Pays 8¢ per word ($100 minimum), plus 2 contributor's copies.**

POETRY Submit up to 8 pages at a time. Online submissions accepted, but no e-mail submissions. Cover letter (with title of work and genre) is encouraged. SASE required. Reads submissions "only during the fall semester, September through November, and then contest entries in the spring." Time between acceptance and publication is "around a year." Occasionally comments on rejected poems or offers suggestions on accepted poems. "We simply look for poems that, at the time we read and choose, we find we admire. No specifications as to form, length, style, subject matter, or purpose. Though we print work from established writers, we're always delighted when we discover new talent." **Pays $1.50/line of poetry, $40 minimum.**

TIPS "We publish essays, reviews, novel excerpts, stories, poems, and photography. We have no set guidelines as to content or length but strongly recommend that writers read a sample issue before submitting."

ISLAND

P.O. Box 4703, Bathurst St. Post Office, Hobart Tasmania 7000 Australia. **E-mail:** matthew@islandmag.com. **Website:** www.islandmag.com. **Contact:** Matthew Lamb, editorial director and features editor. Quarterly magazine. *Island* seeks quality fiction, poetry, and essays. It is "one of Australia's leading literary magazines, tracing the contours of our national, and international culture, while still retaining a uniquely Tasmanian perspective." Estab. 1979. Circ. 1,500. Accepts queries by e-mail and submissions only online via website. Subscriptions and sample copies available for purchase online. Guidelines available online.

Only publishes the work of subscribers; you can submit if you are not currently a subscriber, but if your piece is chosen, the subscription will be taken from the fee paid for the piece.

NONFICTION Needs essays. Query first with brief overview of essay and description of why you think it is suitable for *Island*. **Pay varies.**

FICTION Submit 1 piece at a time. **Pay varies.**

POETRY Submit maximum 3 poems. **Pay varies.**

THE JOURNAL

The Ohio State University, 164 W. 17th Ave., Columbus OH 43210. (614)292-6065. **Fax:** (614)292-7816. **E-mail:** managingeditor@thejournalmag.org. **Website:** thejournalmag.org. Quarterly magazine. "We are interested in quality fiction, poetry, nonfiction, art, and reviews of new books of poetry, fiction, and nonfiction. We impose no restrictions on category, type, or length of submission for fiction, poetry, and nonfiction. We are happy to consider long stories and self-contained excerpts of novels. Please double-space all prose submissions. Please send 3-5 poems in 1 submission. We only accept online submissions and will not respond to mailed submissions." Estab. 1973. Circ. 1,500. Byline given. Payment for art contributors only. All other contributors receive 2 contributor's copies and a one-year subscription. Publishes ms an average of 1 year after acceptance. Accepts queries by online submission form. Accepts simultaneous submissions. Responds in 3-4 months to mss. Sample copy: $8 on Submittable or free online spring and fall issues. Guidelines available online: thejournalmag.org/submit. Submit online only at thejournal.submittable.com/submit.

"We're open to all forms; we tend to favor work that gives evidence of a mature and sophisticated sense of the language."

NONFICTION Needs essays, interview. Does not accept queries. Send full ms via online submission system at thejournal.submittable.com. Publishes about 8 essays/year.

COLUMNS/DEPARTMENTS Publishes reviews of contemporary poetry, fiction, and nonfiction, 1,500 words maximum. Publishes around 12 reviews/year.

FICTION Needs novel concepts, literary short stories. No romance, science fiction, or religious/devotional. Does not accept queries. Send full ms via online submission system at thejournal.submittable.com. "Mss are rejected because of lack of understanding of the short story form, shallow plots, undeveloped characters. Cure: Read as much well-written fiction as possible. Our readers prefer 'psychological' fiction rather than stories with intricate plots. Take care to present a clean, well-typed submission."

POETRY Needs avant-garde, free verse, traditional. "However else poets train or educate themselves, they must do what they can to know our language. Too much of the writing we see indicates poets do not, in many cases, develop a feel for the possibilities of language and do not pay attention to craft. Poets should not be in a rush to publish—until they are ready." Publishes about 100 poems/year. Submit maximum 5 poems.

THE KENYON REVIEW

Finn House, 102 W. Wiggin, Gambier OH 43022. (740)427-5208. **Fax:** (740)427-5417. **E-mail:** kenyonreview@kenyon.edu. **Website:** www.kenyonreview.org. **Contact:** Marlene Landefeld. **100% freelance written.** Bimonthly magazine covering contemporary literature and criticism. "An international journal of literature, culture, and the arts, dedicated to an inclusive representation of the best in new writing (fiction, poetry, essays, interviews, criticism) from established and emerging writers." Estab. 1939. Circ. 6,000. Byline given. Pays on publication. No kill fee. Publishes ms an average of 1 year after acceptance. Editorial lead time 1 year. Submit seasonal material 1 year in advance. Accepts simultaneous submissions. Responds in 4 months to mss. Sample copy: $10; includes postage and handling. Call or e-mail to order. Guidelines available online.

The Kenyon Review receives about 8,000 submissions/year. Also now publishes *KR Online*, a separate and complementary literary magazine.

NONFICTION Needs essays, interview, criticism. Only accepts mss via online submissions program; visit website for instructions. Do not submit via e-mail or snail mail. Receives 130 unsolicited mss/month. Unsolicited mss read September 15-January 15 only. Length: 3-15 typeset pages preferred. **Pays $30/page.**

FICTION Receives 800 unsolicited mss/month. Unsolicited mss read September 15-January 15 only. Recently published work by Alice Hoffman, Beth Ann Fennelly, Romulus Linney, John Koethe, Albert Goldbarth, Erin McGraw. Needs condensed novels, ethnic, experimental, historical, humorous, mainstream, contemporary, excerpts from novels, gay/lesbian, literary, translations. Only accepts mss via online submissions program; visit website for instructions. Do not submit via e-mail or snail mail. Length: 3-15 typeset pages preferred. **Pays $30/page.**

POETRY Features all styles, forms, lengths, and subject matters. Considers translations. Has published poetry by Billy Collins, D.A. Powell, Jamaal May, Rachel Zucker, Diane di Prima, and Seamus Heaney. Submit up to 6 poems at a time. No previously published poems. Only accepts mss via online submissions program; visit website for instructions. Do not submit via e-mail or snail mail. Reads submissions September 15-January 15. **Pays $40/page.**

TIPS "We no longer accept mailed or e-mailed submissions. Work will only be read if it is submitted through our online program on our website. Reading period is September 15-January 15. We look for strong voice, unusual perspective, and power in the writing."

LITERAL LATTÉ

200 E. 10th St., Suite 240, New York NY 10003. (212)260-5532. **E-mail:** litlatte@aol.com. **Website:** www.literal-latte.com. **Contact:** Jenine Gordon Bockman, editor and publisher. **99% freelance written.** Bimonthly online publication with an annual print anthology featuring the best of the website. "We want great writing in all styles and subjects. A feast is made of a variety of flavors." Estab. 1994. No kill fee. Editorial lead time 3 months. Submit seasonal material 3 months in advance. Accepts queries by mail, e-mail. Accepts simultaneous submissions. Responds in 6 months to mss. Writer's guidelines online, via e-mail, or for #10 SASE.

NONFICTION Contact: Jeff Bockman, editor. Needs essays, personal experience. No scholarly reviews or essays. They must be personal. **Buys 10 mss/year.** Send complete ms via postal mail. Length: no more than 6,000 words. **Pays minimum of anthology copies and maximum of $1,000.**

FICTION Needs adventure, condensed novels, confessions, erotica, ethnic, experimental, fantasy, historical, horror, humorous, mainstream, mystery, novel excerpts, religious, romance, science fiction, serialized novels, short stories, slice-of-life vignettes, suspense, western. **Buys 12 mss/year.** Send complete ms via postal mail. Length: no more than 6,000 words. **Pays minimum of anthology copies and maximum of $1,000.**

POETRY "We want any poem that captures the magic of the form." Buys 12 poems/year. Submit maximum 6 poems. Length: no more than 4,000 words.

TIPS "Keeping free thought free and challenging entertainment are not mutually exclusive. Words make a manuscript stand out, words beautifully woven together in striking and memorable patterns."

LITERARY MAMA

SC 29843. **E-mail:** lminfo@literarymama.com. **Website:** www.literarymama.com. **Contact:** Maria Scala, editor-in-chief. Website offering writing about the complexities and many faces of motherhood in a variety of genres. "Departments include columns, creative nonfiction, fiction, Literary Reflections, poetry, and Profiles & Reviews. We are interested in reading pieces that are long, complex, ambiguous, deep, raw, irreverent, ironic, and body conscious." Estab. 2003. Circ. 40,000. Accepts queries by e-mail. Accepts simultaneous submissions. Responds in 3 weeks-3 months to mss. "We correspond via e-mail only." Guidelines available at www.literarymama.com/submissions.

NONFICTION Contact: lmnonfiction@literarymama.com. "We don't want pieces that read like columns or intellectual reflections on personal experiences; work that would be accepted by the glossy parenting magazines." Length: 500-7,000 words.

COLUMNS/DEPARTMENTS Contact: lmcolumns@literarymama.com.

FICTION Contact: lmfiction@literarymama.com.

POETRY Contact: lmpoetry@literarymama.com. Submit maximum 4 poems.

TIPS "We seek top-notch creative writing. We also look for quality literary criticism about mother-centric literature and profiles of mother writers. We publish writing with fresh voices, superior craft, and vivid imagery. Please send submission (copied into e-mail) to appropriate departmental editors. Include a brief cover letter. We tend to like stark revelation (pathos, humor, and joy); clarity; concrete details; strong narrative development; ambiguity; thoughtfulness; delicacy; irreverence; lyricism; sincerity; the elegant. We need the submissions 3 months before the following months: October (Desiring Motherhood); May (Mother's Day Month); and June (Father's Day Month)."

MAISONNEUVE

Maisonneuve Magazine Association, 1051 Boulevard Decarie, P.O. Box 53527, St. Laurent QC H4L 5J9 Canada. **Website:** www.maisonneuve.org. **90% freelance written.** Quarterly magazine covering eclectic curiousity. *Maisonneuve* has been described as a new *New Yorker* for a younger generation, or as *Harper's* meets *Vice*, or as *Vanity Fair* without the vanity—but *Maisonneuve* is its own creature. *Maisonneuve*'s purpose is to keep its readers informed, alert, and entertained, and to dissolve artistic borders between regions, countries, languages, and genres. It does this by providing a diverse range of commentary across the arts, sciences, and daily and social life. The magazine has a balanced perspective and "brings the news" in a wide variety of ways. Estab. 2002. Circ. under 10,000. Byline given. Pays on publication. Offers 25% kill fee. Publishes ms an average of 4-6 months after acceptance. Editorial lead time 4 months. Submit seasonal material 8 months in advance. Accepts simultaneous submissions. Responds in 2 weeks to queries; in 3 months to mss. Sample copy online. Guidelines online.

"*Maisonneuve* considers nonfiction writing of all kinds (reporting, essays, memoir, humour, etc.) and visual art (illustration, photography, comics, etc.). To get a sense of the sort of work we publish, please read some back issues." *Does not accept unsolicited fiction and poetry.*

NONFICTION Needs essays, general interest, historical, humor, interview, personal experience, photo feature. Submit ms via online submissions manager (maisonneuvemagazine.submittable.com) or by mail. Length: 50-5,000 words. **Pays 10¢/word.** Sometimes pays expenses of writers on assignment.

PHOTOS Contact: anna@maisonneuve.org. State availability. Captions, identification of subjects, model releases required. Reviews GIF/JPEG files. Negotiates payment individually.

THE MALAHAT REVIEW

The University of Victoria, P.O. Box 1700, STN CSC, Victoria BC V8W 2Y2 Canada. (250)721-8524. **E-mail:** malahat@uvic.ca (for queries only). **Website:** www.malahatreview.ca. **Contact:** John Barton, editor. **100% freelance written. Eager to work with new/unpublished writers.** Quarterly magazine covering poetry, fiction, creative nonfiction, and reviews. "We try to achieve a balance of views and styles in each issue. We strive for a mix of the best writing by both established and new writers." Estab. 1967. Circ. 2,000. Byline given. Pays on acceptance. No kill fee. Publishes ms an average of 6 months after acceptance. Accepts queries by online submission form. Accepts simultaneous submissions. Responds in 2 weeks to queries; in 3-10 months to mss. Sample copy: $16.95 (US). Guidelines available online.

NONFICTION Submit via online submissions manager: malahatreview.ca/submission_guidelines.html#submittable. Length: 1,000-3,500 words. **Pays $50/magazine page.**

FICTION Needs general fiction and creative nonfiction. **Buys 12-14 mss/year.** Submit via online submissions manager: malahatreview.ca/submission_guidelines.html#submittable. Length: up to 8,000 words. **Pays $50/magazine page.**

POETRY Needs avant-garde, free verse, traditional. Submit 3-5 poems via online submissions manager: malahatreview.ca/submission_guidelines.html#submittable. Buys 100 poems/year. Length: up to 6 pages. **Pays $50/magazine page.**

TIPS "Please do not send more than 1 submission at a time: 3-5 poems, 1 piece of creative nonfiction, or 1 short story (do not mix poetry and prose in the same submission). See *The Malahat Review*'s Open Season Awards for poetry and short fiction, creative nonfiction, long poem, and novella contests in the Awards section of our website."

MANOA

English Dept., University of Hawaii, Honolulu HI 96822. (808)956-3070. **Fax:** (808)956-3083. **E-mail:** mjournal-l@lists.hawaii.edu. **Website:** manoajournal.hawaii.edu. **Contact:** Frank Stewart, editor. Semiannual magazine. *Manoa* is seeking "high-quality literary fiction, poetry, essays, and personal narrative. In general, each issue is devoted to new work from Pacific and Asian nations. Our audience is international. U.S. writing need not be confined to Pacific settings or subjects. Please note that we seldom publish unsolicited work." Estab. 1989. Circ. 1,000 print, 10,000 digital. Byline given. Pays on publication. Editorial lead time 9 months. Accepts simultaneous submissions. Responds in 3 weeks to queries. Sample copy: $15 (U.S.). Guidelines available online.

Manoa has received numerous awards, and work published in the magazine has been selected for prize anthologies. See website for recently published issues.

NONFICTION No Pacific exotica. Query first. Length: 1,000-5,000 words. **Pays $25/printed page.**

FICTION Query first and/or see website. Needs mainstream, contemporary, excerpted novel. No Pacific exotica. **Buys 1-2 in the U.S. (excluding translation) mss/year.** Send complete ms. Length: 1,000-7,500 words. **Pays $100-500 normally ($25/printed page).**

POETRY No light verse. Buys 10-20 poems/year. Submit maximum 5-6 poems. **Pays $25 per poem.**

TIPS "Not accepting unsolicited mss at this time because of commitments to special projects. Please query before sending mss as e-mail attachments."

THE MASSACHUSETTS REVIEW

University of Massachusetts, Photo Lab 309, Amherst MA 01003. (413)545-2689. **E-mail:** massrev@external.umass.edu. **Website:** www.massreview.org. **Contact:** Emily Wojcik, managing editor. Quarterly magazine. Seeks a balance between established writers and promising new ones. Interested in material of variety and vitality relevant to the intellectual and aesthetic questions of our time. Aspire to have a broad appeal. Estab. 1959. Circ. 1,200. Pays on publication. Publishes ms an average of 18 months after acceptance. Accepts queries by mail. Responds in 6 months to mss. Sample copy: $8 for back issue, $10 for current issue. Guidelines available online.

Does not respond to mss without SASE.

NONFICTION No reviews of single books. Articles and essays of breadth and depth are considered, as well as discussions of leading writers; of art, music, and drama; analyses of trends in literature, science, philosophy, and public affairs. Include name and contact information on the first page. Encourages page numbers. Send complete ms or query with SASE Length: up to 6,500 words. **Pays $50.**

FICTION Wants short stories. Accepts 1 short story per submission. Include name and contact information on the first page. Encourages page numbers. Has published work by Ahdaf Soueif, Elizabeth Denton, and Nicholas Montemarano. **Buys 30-40 mss/year.** Send complete ms. Length: up to 30 pages or 8,000 words. **Pays $50.**

POETRY Has published poetry by Catherine Barnett, Billy Collins, and Dara Wier. Include your name and contact on every page. Submit maximum 6 poems. Length: There are no restrictions for length, but generally poems are less than 100 lines. **Pays $50/publication.**

TIPS "No manuscripts are considered May-September. Electronic submission process can be found on website. No fax or e-mail submissions. No simultaneous submissions. Shorter rather than longer stories preferred (up to 28-30 pages)." Looks for works that "stop us in our tracks." Manuscripts that stand out use "unexpected language, idiosyncrasy of outlook, and are the opposite of ordinary."

MICHIGAN QUARTERLY REVIEW

0576 Rackham Bldg., 915 E. Washington, Ann Arbor MI 48109-1070. (734)764-9265. **E-mail:** mqr@umich.edu. **Website:** www.michiganquarterlyreview.com. **Contact:** Jonathan Freedman, editor; Vicki Lawrence, managing editor. **75% freelance written.** Quarterly journal of literature and the humanities publishing literary essays, fiction, poetry, creative nonfiction, memoir, interviews, and book reviews. *MQR* is an eclectic interdisciplinary journal of arts and culture that seeks to combine the best of poetry, fiction, and creative nonfiction with outstanding critical essays on literary, cultural, social, and political matters. The flagship journal of the University of Michigan, *MQR* draws on lively minds here and elsewhere, seeking to present accessible work of all varieties for sophisticated readers from within and without the academy. Estab. 1962. Circ. 1,000. Byline given. Pays on publication. No kill fee. Publishes ms an average of 1 year after acceptance. Accepts queries by mail. Responds in 2 months to queries. Responds in 2 months to mss. Sample copy for $4. Guidelines available online.

The Laurence Goldstein Award is a $500 annual award to the best poem published in *MQR* during the previous year. The Lawrence Foundation Award is a $1,000 annual award to the best short story published in *MQR* during the previous year. The Page Davidson Clayton Award for Emerging Poets is a $500 annual award given to the best poet appearing in *MQR* during the previous year who has not yet published a book.

NONFICTION Needs essays. Special issues: Publishes theme issues. Upcoming themes available in magazine and on website. **Buys 35 mss/year.** Query. Length: 1,500-7,000 words, 5,000 words average. **Pays $10/published page.**

FICTION Contact: Fiction Editor. "No restrictions on subject matter or language. We are very selective. We like stories that are unusual in tone and structure, and innovative in language. No genre fiction written for a market. Would like to see more fiction about social, political, cultural matters, not just centered on a love relationship or dysfunctional family." Receives 300 unsolicited mss/month. Accepts 3-4 mss/issue; 12-16 mss/year. Publishes 1-2 new writers/year. Has published work by Rebecca Makkai, Peter Ho Davies, Laura Kasischke, Gerald Shapiro, and Alan Cheuse. Needs literary. **Buys 10 mss/year.** Send complete ms. Length: 1,500-7,000 words; average length: 5,000 words. **Pays $10/published page.**

POETRY No previously published poems or simultaneous submissions. No e-mail submissions. Cover letter is preferred. "It puts a human face on the ms. A few sentences of biography is all I want, nothing lengthy or defensive." Prefers typed mss. Reviews books of poetry. "All reviews are commissioned." Length: should not exceed 8-12 pages. **Pays $8-12/published page.**

TIPS "Read the journal and assess the range of contents and the level of writing. We have no guidelines to offer or set expectations; every manuscript is judged on its unique qualities. On essays—query with a very thorough description of the argument and a copy of the first page. Watch for announcements of special issues, which are usually expanded issues and draw upon a lot of freelance writing. Be aware that this is a university quarterly that publishes a limited amount of fiction and poetry and that it is directed at an educated audience, one that has done a great deal of reading in all types of literature."

MID-AMERICAN REVIEW

Bowling Green State University, Dept. of English, Bowling Green OH 43403. (419)372-2725. **E-mail:** mar@bgsu.edu. **E-mail:** marsubmissions.bgsu.edu. **Website:** www.bgsu.edu/midamericanreview. **Contact:** Abigail Cloud, editor in chief; Laura Walter, fiction editor. Semiannual magazine of the highest-quality fiction, poetry, and translations of contemporary poetry and fiction. Also publishes creative nonfiction and book reviews of contemporary literature. Reads mss year round. Publishes new and established writers. "We aim to put the best possible work in front of the biggest possible audience. We publish contemporary fiction, poetry, creative nonfiction, translations, and book reviews." Estab. 1981. Circ. 1,500. Byline given. No kill fee. Publishes mss an average of 6 months after acceptance. Accepts queries by online submission form. Responds in 5 months to mss. Sample copy: $9 (current issue), $5 (back issue), $10 (rare back issues). Guidelines available online.

Contests: The Fineline Competition for Prose Poems, Short Shorts, and Everything In Between (June 1 deadline, $10 per 3 pieces, limit 500 words each); The Sherwood Anderson Fiction Award (November 1 deadline, $10 per piece); and the James Wright Poetry Award (November 1 deadline, $10 per 3 pieces).

NONFICTION Needs creative nonfiction, leaning toward lyrical essays; short book reviews (400-500 words). Submit ms by post with SASE or with online submission manager.

FICTION Publishes traditional, character-oriented, literary, experimental, prose poem, and short-short stories. No genre fiction. Submit ms by post with SASE or with online submission manager. Agented fiction 5%. Recently published work by Mollie Ficek and J. David Stevens. Length: 6,000 words maximum.

POETRY Submit by mail with SASE or with online submission manager. Publishes poems with "textured, evocative images, an awareness of how words sound and mean, and a definite sense of voice. Each line should help carry the poem, and an individual vision must be evident." Recently published work by Mary Ann Samyn, G.C. Waldrep, and Daniel Bourne. Submit maximum 6 poems.

TIPS "We are seeking translations of contemporary authors from all languages into English; submissions must include the original and proof of permission to translate. We would also like to see more creative nonfiction."

MISSISSIPPI REVIEW

University of Southern Mississippi, 118 College Dr., #5144, Hattiesburg MS 39406-0001. (601)266-4321. **Fax:** (601)266-5757. **E-mail:** msreview@usm.edu. **Website:** www.usm.edu/mississippi-review. **Contact:** Andrew Malan Milward, editor in chief; Caleb Tankersley and Allison Campbell, associate editors. Semiannual literary magazine. *Mississippi Review* "is one of the most respected literary journals in the country. Raymond Carver, an early contributor to the magazine, once said that *Mississippi Review* 'is one of the most remarkable and indispensable literary journals of our time.' Well-known and established writers have appeared in the pages of the magazine, including Pulitzer and Nobel Prize winners, as well as new and emerging writers who have gone on to publish books and to receive awards." Estab. 1972. Circ. 1,500. No kill fee. Sample copy for $10. "We do not accept unsolicited manuscripts except under the rules and guidelines of the *Mississippi Review* Prize Competition. See website for guidelines."

Publishes 25-30 new writers/year. Annual fiction and poetry competition: $1,000 awarded in each category, plus publication of all winners and finalists. Fiction entries: 8,000 words or less. Poetry entries: 1-5 poems; page limit is 10. $15 entry fee includes copy of prize issue. No limit on number of entries. Deadline December 1. No mss returned.

FICTION Needs experimental, fantasy, humorous, contemporary, avant-garde, art fiction. No juvenile or genre fiction. Length: 30 pages maximum.

THE MISSOURI REVIEW

357 McReynolds Hall, University of Missouri, Columbia MO 65211. (573)882-4474. **Fax:** (573)884-4671. **E-mail:** question@moreview.com. **Website:** www.missourireview.com. **Contact:** Speer Morgan, editor; Michael Nye, managing editor. **90% freelance written.** Quarterly magazine. Publishes contemporary fiction, poetry, interviews, personal essays, cartoons, special features—such as History as Literature series and Found Text series—for the literary and the general reader interested in a wide range of subjects. Estab. 1978. Circ. 6,500. Byline given. Offers signed contract. Editorial lead time 6 months. Accepts queries by mail. Responds in 2 weeks to queries. Responds in 10-12 weeks to mss. Sample copy for $8.95 or online. Guidelines available online.

NONFICTION Contact: Evelyn Somers, associate editor. Needs book excerpts, essays. No literary criticism. **Buys 10 mss/year.** Send complete ms. **Pays $40/printed page.**

FICTION Contact: Speer Morgan, editor. Needs ethnic, humorous, mainstream, novel concepts, literary. No genre or flash fiction. **Buys 25 mss/year.** Send complete ms. Length: 9,000-12,000 words or 2,000 words or less (flash fiction). **Pays $40/printed page. Also, The William Peden Prize of $1,000 is awarded annually to the best piece of fiction to have appeared in the previous volume year. The winner is chosen by an outside judge from stories published in TMR. There is no separate application process.**

POETRY Contact: Chun Ye, poetry editor. *TMR* publishes poetry features only—6-14 pages of poems by each of 3-5 poets per issue. Keep in mind the length of features when submitting poems. Typically, successful submissions include 8-20 pages of unpublished poetry (note: do not send complete mss—published or unpublished—for consideration). **Pays $40/printed page and 3 contributor's copies.**

TIPS "Send your best work."

MODERN HAIKU

P.O. Box 930, Portsmouth RI 02871. **E-mail:** modernhaiku@gmail.com. **Website:** modernhaiku.org. **85% freelance written.** Magazine published 3 times/year in February, June, and October covering haiku poetry. *Modern Haiku* is the foremost international journal of English-language haiku and criticism and publishes high-quality material only. Haiku and related genres, articles on haiku, haiku book reviews, and translations comprise its contents. It has an international circulation; subscribers include many university, school, and public libraries. Estab. 1969. Circ. 650. Byline given. No kill fee. Publishes ms an average of 6 months after acceptance. Editorial lead time 4 months. Accepts queries by mail, e-mail. "Now accepts submissions by e-mail; please review submission guidelines policies on website." Responds in 1 week to queries; in 6-8 weeks to mss. Sample copy: $15 in North America, $16 in Canada, $20 in Mexico, $22 overseas. Subscription: $35 ppd by regular mail in the

U.S. Payment possible by PayPal on the *Modern Haiku* website. Guidelines available for SASE or on website.

Modern Haiku is 140 pages (average), digest-sized, printed on heavy-quality stock, with full-color cover illustrations, 4-page full-color art sections. Receives about 15,000 submissions/year, accepts about 1,000. Press run is 700.

NONFICTION Needs essays, anything related to haiku. Send complete ms. **Pays $5/page.**

COLUMNS/DEPARTMENTS Haiku & Senryu; Haibun; Essays (on haiku and related genres); Reviews (books of haiku or related genres). **Buys 40 mss/year.** Send complete ms. **Pays $5/page.**

POETRY Needs haiku, senryu, haibun, haiga. Postal submissions: "Send 5-15 haiku on 1 or 2 letter-sized sheets. Put name and address at the top of each sheet. Include SASE." E-mail submissions: "May be attachments (recommended) or pasted in body of message. Subject line must read: MH Submission. Adhere to guidelines on the website. No payment for haiku sent/accepted by e-mail." Publishes 750 poems/year. Has published haiku by Roberta Beary, Billy Collins, Lawrence Ferlinghetti, Carolyn Hall, Sharon Olds, Gary Snyder, John Stevenson, George Swede, and Cor van den Heuvel. Does not want "general poetry, tanka, renku, linked-verse forms. No special consideration given to work by children and teens." **No payment.**

TIPS "Study the history of haiku, read books about haiku, learn the aesthetics of haiku and methods of composition. Write about your sense perceptions of the suchness of entities; avoid ego-centered interpretations. Be sure the work you send us conforms to the definitions on our website."

MYTHIC DELIRIUM

3514 Signal Hill Ave. NW, Roanoke VA 24017-5148. **E-mail:** mythicdelirium@gmail.com. **Website:** www.mythicdelirium.com. **Contact:** Mike Allen, editor. "*Mythic Delirium* is an online and e-book venue for fiction and poetry that ranges through science fiction, fantasy, horror, interstitial, and cross-genre territory—we love blurred boundaries and tropes turned on their heads. We are interested in work that demonstrates ambition, that defies traditional approaches to genre, that introduces readers to the legends of other cultures, that re-evaluates the myths of old from a modern perspective, that twists reality in unexpected ways. We are committed to diversity and are open to and encourage submissions from people of every race, gender, nationality, sexual orientation, political affiliation and religious belief. We publish 12 short stories and 24 poems a year. Our quarterly ebooks in PDF, EPUB, and MOBI formats, published in July, October, January, and April, will each contain 3 stories and 6 poems. We will also publish 1 story and 2 poems on our website each month." Reading period: August 1-October 1 annually. Estab. 1998. Responds in 2 months. Accepts electronic submissions only to mythicdelirium@gmail.com.

FICTION "No unsolicited reprints or multiple submissions. Please use the words 'fiction submission' in the e-mail subject line. Stories should be sent in standard manuscript format as .rtf or .doc attachments." Length: up to 4,000 words (firm). **Pays 2¢/word.**

POETRY "No unsolicited reprints. Please use the words 'poetry submission' in the e-mail subject line. Poems may be included in the e-mail as RTF or DOC attachments." Submit maximum 6 poems. Length: open. **Pays $5 flat fee.**

TIPS "*Mythic Delirium* isn't easy to get into, but we publish newcomers in every issue. Show us how ambitious you can be, and don't give up."

N+1

The Editors, 68 Jay St., Suite 405, Brooklyn NY 11201. **E-mail:** editors@nplusonemag.com. **E-mail:** submissions@nplusonemag.com. **Website:** www.nplusonemag.com. **Contact:** Nikil Saval and Dayna Tortorici, editors. A print magazine of literature, culture, and politics published 3 times yearly. The website publishes new, Web-only content 3 times each week. No kill fee. Accepts queries by e-mail. Sample copy and guidelines available online.

NONFICTION Needs essays, exposé, general interest, interview, opinion, sports. Submit queries and finished pieces by e-mail.

FICTION Submit queries or finished pieces by e-mail.

TIPS "Most of the slots available for a given issue will have been filled many months before publication. If you would like to brave the odds, the best submission guidelines are those implied by the magazine itself. Read an issue or two through to get a sense of whether your piece might fit into *n+1*."

THE NATIONAL POETRY REVIEW

P.O. Box 2080, Aptos CA 95001-2080. **E-mail:** editor@nationalpoetryreview.com; nationalpoetryreview@yahoo.com. **Website:** www.nationalpoetryreview.

com. **Contact:** C.J. Sage, editor. *The National Poetry Review* seeks "distinction, innovation, and *joie de vivre*. We agree with Frost about delight and wisdom. We believe in rich sound. We believe in the beautiful—even if that beauty is not in the situation of the poem but simply the sounds of the poem, the images, or (and, ideally) the way the poem stays in the reader's mind long after it's been read." *TNPR* considers both experimental and 'mainstream' work." Does not want "overly self-centered or confessional poetry." Estab. 2003. Time between acceptance and publication is no more than 1 year. "The editor makes all publishing decisions." Sometimes comments on rejected poems. Usually responds in about 1-12 weeks. Guidelines available in magazine or on website.

The National Poetry Review is 80 pages, perfect-bound, with full-color cover. Accepts less than 1% of submissions received. Single copy: $15; subscription: $15/year. Make checks payable to *TNPR* only. Poetry appearing in *The National Poetry Review* has also appeared in *The Pushcart Prize*. Has published poetry by Bob Hicok, Jennifer Michael Hecht, Larissa Szplorluk, Martha Zweig, Nance Van Winkel, William Waltz, and Ted Kooser.

POETRY Submit 3-5 poems at a time by e-mail only to address below; postal submissions will be recycled unread. Considers simultaneous submissions "with notification only. Submit only between December 1 and February 28 unless you are a subscriber or benefactor. Put your name in the subject line of your e-mail and send to tnprsubmissions@yahoo.com." Bio is required. Subscribers and benefactors may submit any time during the year ("please write 'subscriber' or 'benefactor' in the subject line"). See website before submitting. **Pays 1 contributor's copy and small honorarium when funds are available.**

NEON MAGAZINE

UK. **E-mail:** info@neonmagazine.co.uk. **Website:** www.neonmagazine.co.uk. **Contact:** Krishan Coupland. Quarterly website and print magazine covering alternative work of any form of poetry and prose, short stories, flash fiction, artwork and reviews. "Genre work is welcome. Experimentation is encouraged. We like stark poetry and weird prose. We seek work that is beautiful, shocking, intense, and memorable. Darker pieces are generally favored over humorous ones." No kill fee. Accepts queries by e-mail. Responds in 1 month. Query if you have received no reply after 6 weeks. Guidelines available online.

Neon was previously published as *FourVolts Magazine*.

NONFICTION Needs essays, reviews. No word limit.

FICTION Needs experimental, horror, humorous, science fiction, suspense. "No nonsensical prose; we are not appreciative of sentimentality." **Buys 8-12 mss/year.** No word limit. **Pays royalties.**

POETRY "No nonsensical poetry; we are not appreciative of sentimentality. Rhyming poetry is discouraged." Buys 24-30 poems/year. No word limit. **Pays royalties.**

TIPS "Send several poems, 1 or 2 pieces of prose or several images via form e-mail. Include the word 'submission' in your subject line. Include a short biographical note (up to 100 words). Read submission guidelines before submitting your work."

NEW ENGLAND REVIEW

Middlebury College, Middlebury VT 05753. (802)443-5075. **E-mail:** nereview@middlebury.edu. **Website:** www.nereview.com. **Contact:** Carolyn Kuebler, editor. Quarterly literary magazine. *New England Review* is a prestigious, nationally distributed literary journal. Reads September 1-May 31 (postmarked dates). Estab. 1978. Circ. 2,000. Byline given. Pays on publication. No kill fee. Publishes ms an average of 6 months after acceptance. Accepts simultaneous submissions. Responds in 2 weeks to queries; in 3 months to mss. Sometimes comments on rejected mss. Sample copy: $10 (add $5 for overseas). Subscription: $30. Overseas shipping fees add $25 for subscription, $12 for Canada. Guidelines available online.

New England Review is 200+ pages, 7x10, printed on heavy stock, flat-spined, with glossy cover with art. Receives 3,000-4,000 poetry submissions/year, accepts about 70-80 poems/year. Receives 550 unsolicited mss/month, accepts 6 mss/issue, 24 fiction mss/year. Does not accept mss June-August. Agented fiction less than 5%.

NONFICTION Buys 20-25 mss/year. Send complete ms via online submission manager or postal mail (with SASE). No e-mail submissions. Length: up to 7,500 words, though exceptions may be made. **Pays $20/page ($20 minimum) and 2 contributor's copies.**

FICTION Send 1 story at a time, unless it is very short. Serious literary only, novel excerpts. Publishes approximately 10 new writers/year. Has published work by Steve Almond, Christine Sneed, Roy Kesey, Thomas Gough, Norman Lock, Brock Clarke, Carl Phillips, Lucia Perillo, Linda Gregerson, and Natasha Trethewey. Needs literary. **Buys 25 mss/year.** Send complete ms via online submission manager or postal mail (with SASE). No e-mail submissions. "Will consider simultaneous submissions, but must be stated as such and you must notify us immediately if the ms accepted for publication elsewhere." Length: not strict on word count. **Pays $20/page ($20 minimum), and 2 contributor's copies.**

POETRY Submit up to 6 poems at a time. No previously published or simultaneous submissions for poetry. Accepts submissions by postal mail or online submission manager only; accepts questions by e-mail. "Cover letters are useful." Address submissions to "Poetry Editor." Buys 75-90 poems/year. Submit maximum 6 poems. **Pays $20/page ($20 minimum), and 2 contributor's copies.**

TIPS "We consider short fiction, including short shorts, novellas, and self-contained extracts from novels in both traditional and experimental forms. In nonfiction, we consider a variety of general and literary but not narrowly scholarly essays; we also publish long and short poems, screenplays, graphics, translations, critical reassessments, statements by artists working in various media, testimonies, and letters from abroad. We are committed to exploration of all forms of contemporary cultural expression in the U.S. and abroad. With few exceptions, we print only work not published previously elsewhere."

NEW LETTERS

University of Missouri-Kansas City, 5101 Rockhill Rd., Kansas City MO 64110. (816)235-1168. **Fax:** (816)235-2611. **E-mail:** newletters@umkc.edu. **Website:** www.newletters.org. **Contact:** Robert Stewart, editor in chief. **100% freelance written.** Quarterly magazine. "*New Letters* continues to seek the best new writing, whether from established writers or those ready and waiting to be discovered. In addition, it supports those writers, readers, and listeners who want to experience the joy of writing that can both surprise and inspire us all." Estab. 1934. Circ. 5,000. Byline given. Pays on publication. No kill fee. Publishes ms an average of 6 months after acceptance. Editorial lead time 6 months. Submit seasonal material 6 months in advance. Accepts queries by mail. Accepts simultaneous submissions. Responds in 1 month to queries; in 5 months to mss. Sample copy: $10 or sample articles on website. Guidelines available online.

Submissions are not read May 1-October 1.

NONFICTION Needs essays. No self-help, how-to, or nonliterary work. **Buys 8-10 mss/year.** Send complete ms. Length: up to 5,000 words. **Pays $40-100.**

PHOTOS Send photos. Reviews contact sheets, 2x4 transparencies, prints. Pays $10-40/photo.

FICTION Needs ethnic, experimental, humorous, mainstream, contemporary. No genre fiction. **Buys 15-20 mss/year.** Send complete ms. Length: up to 5,000 words. **Pays $30-75.**

POETRY Needs avant-garde, free verse, haiku, traditional. No light verse. Buys 40-50 poems/year. Submit maximum 6 poems. Length: open. **Pays $10-25.**

TIPS "We aren't interested in essays that are footnoted or essays usually described as scholarly or critical. Our preference is for creative nonfiction or personal essays. We prefer shorter stories and essays to longer ones (an average length is 3,500-4,000 words). We have no rigid preferences as to subject, style, or genre, although commercial efforts tend to put us off. Even so, our only fixed requirement is good writing."

NEW OHIO REVIEW

English Department, 360 Ellis Hall, Ohio University, Athens OH 45701. (740)597-1360. **E-mail:** noreditors@ohio.edu. **Website:** www.ohiou.edu/nor. **Contact:** Jill Allyn Rosser, editor. *New Ohio Review*, published biannually in spring and fall, publishes fiction, nonfiction, and poetry. Estab. 2007. Byline given. No kill fee. Accepts queries by mail, online submission form. Accepts simultaneous submissions. Responds in 2-4 months. Single copy: $9. Subscription: $16. Guidelines available on website.

Member CLMP. Reading period is September 15-December 15 and January 15-April 1.

NONFICTION Needs non-academic essays with a personal slant. Submit complete ms. **Pays minimum of $30 in addition to 2 contributor's copies and one-year subscription.**

FICTION Considers literary short fiction; no novel excerpts. Send complete ms. **Pays $30 minimum in addition to 2 contributor's copies and one-year subscription.**

POETRY Needs free verse, formal, experimental; quality is key. "Please do not submit more than once every 6 months." Submit maximum 6 poems.

NEW ORLEANS REVIEW

Box 195, Loyola University, New Orleans LA 70118. (504)865-2295. **E-mail:** noreview@loyno.edu. **Website:** neworleansreview.org. **Contact:** Heidi Braden, managing editor. *New Orleans Review* is a biannual journal of contemporary literature and culture, publishing new poetry, fiction, nonfiction, art, photography, film and book reviews. Estab. 1968. Circ. 1,500. Pays on publication. No kill fee. Accepts queries by online submission form. Accepts simultaneous submissions. Responds in 4 months to mss. Sample copy: $5.

The journal has published an eclectic variety of work by established and emerging writers including Walker Percy, Pablo Neruda, Ellen Gilchrist, Nelson Algren, Hunter S. Thompson, John Kennedy Toole, Richard Brautigan, Barry Spacks, James Sallis, Jack Gilbert, Paul Hoover, Rodney Jones, Annie Dillard, Everette Maddox, Julio Cortazar, Gordon Lish, Robert Walser, Mark Halliday, Jack Butler, Robert Olen Butler, Michael Harper, Angela Ball, Joyce Carol Oates, Diane Wakoski, Dermot Bolger, Roddy Doyle, William Kotzwinkle, Alain Robbe-Grillet, Arnost Lustig, Raymond Queneau, Yusef Komunyakaa, Michael Martone, Tess Gallagher, Matthea Harvey, D. A. Powell, Rikki Ducornet, and Ed Skoog.

FICTION Contact: Christopher Chambers, editor. Needs "good writing, from conventional to experimental." "We are now using an online submission system and require a $3 fee." See website for details. Length: up to 6,500 words. **Pays $25-50 and 2 contributor's copies.**

POETRY Submit maximum 3-6 poems.

TIPS "We're looking for dynamic writing that demonstrates attention to the language and a sense of the medium, writing that engages, surprises, moves us. We're not looking for genre fiction or academic articles. We subscribe to the belief that in order to truly write well, one must first master the rudiments: grammar and syntax, punctuation, the sentence, the paragraph, the line, the stanza. We receive about 3,000 manuscripts a year and publish about 3% of them. Check out a recent issue, send us your best, proofread your work, be patient, be persistent."

THE NEW QUARTERLY

St. Jerome's University, 290 Westmount Rd. N., Waterloo ON N2L 3G3 Canada. (519)884-8111, ext. 28290. **E-mail:** editor@tnq.ca; info@tnq.ca. **Website:** www.tnq.ca. **95% freelance written.** Quarterly book covering Canadian fiction and poetry. "Emphasis on emerging writers and genres, but we publish more traditional work as well if the language and narrative structure are fresh." Estab. 1981. Circ. 1,000. Byline given. Pays on publication. No kill fee. Editorial lead time 6 months. Accepts queries by mail. Accepts simultaneous submissions. Responds in early January to submissions received March 1-August 31; in early June to submissions received September 1-February 28. Sample copy: $16.50 (cover price, plus mailing). Guidelines online.

Open to Canadian writers only. Reading periods: March 1-August 31; September 1-February 28.

NONFICTION Needs essays. Query with a proposal.

FICTION "*Canadian work only.* We are not interested in genre fiction. We are looking for innovative, beautifully crafted, deeply felt literary fiction." Needs literary. **Buys 20-25 mss/year.** Send complete ms. Does not accept submissions by e-mail. Accepts simultaneoues submissions if indicated in cover letter. **Pays $250/story.**

POETRY Needs avant-garde, free verse, traditional. *Canadian work only.* Submit maximum 3 poems. **Pays $40/poem.**

TIPS "Reading us is the best way to get our measure. We don't have preconceived ideas about what we're looking for other than that it must be Canadian work (Canadian writers, not necessarily Canadian content). We want something that's fresh, something that will repay a second reading, something in which the language soars and the feeling is complexly rendered."

NEW WELSH REVIEW

P.O. Box 170, Aberystwyth, Ceredigion Wa SY23 1 WZ United Kingdom. 01970-626230. **E-mail:** editor@newwelshreview.com. **E-mail:** submissions@newwelshreview.com. **Website:** www.newwelshreview.com. **Contact:** Gwen Davies, editor. "*NWR*, a literary quarterly ranked in the top 5 of British literary magazines, publishes stories, poems, and critical essays. The best of Welsh writing in English, past and present, is celebrated, discussed, and debated. We seek poems, short stories, reviews, special features/ articles, and commentary." Quarterly.

FICTION Send hard copy only with SASE or international money order for return. Outside the UK, submission by e-mail only. **Pays "cheque on publication and 1 free copy."**

THE NEW WRITER

1 Vicarage Lane, Stubbington Hampshire PO14 2JU United Kingdom. (44)(158)021-2626. **Website:** newwriteronline.com. "Now under new management and with a new home online, your favourite writing magazine has undergone a rebirth. We're starting with a free weekly e-newsletter delivering the best writing articles from around the Web to your inbox every Friday. Now we're working on turning *The New Writer Online* into a thriving community—a home for writers on the Web." Estab. 1996. Accepts simultaneous submissions.

Currently accepting submissions of flash fiction, which *The New Writer Online* will publish as e-blasts to their online newsletter subscribers.

FICTION Only accepting flash fiction submissions. Submit via online submissions manager. Length: up to 1,000 words.

NORTH AMERICAN REVIEW

University of Northern Iowa, 1222 W. 27th St., Cedar Falls IA 50614. (319)273-6455. **Fax:** (319)273-4326. **E-mail:** nar@uni.edu. **Website:** northamericanreview.wordpress.com. **Contact:** Kim Groninga, nonfiction editor. **90% freelance written.** Published 4 times/year. "The *NAR* is the oldest literary magazine in America and one of the most respected; though we have no prejudices about the subject matter of material sent to us, our first concern is quality." Estab. 1815. Circ. under 5,000. Byline given. No kill fee. Publishes ms an average of 1 year after acceptance. Accepts queries by mail. Responds in 3 months to queries; 4 months to mss. Sample copy: $7. Guidelines available online.

This is the oldest literary magazine in the country and one of the most prestigious. Also one of the most entertaining—and a tough market for the young writer.

NONFICTION Length: open.

FICTION "No flat narrative stories where the inferiority of the character is the paramount concern." Wants to see more "well-crafted literary stories that emphasize family concerns. We'd also like to see more stories engaged with environmental concerns." Reads fiction mss all year. **Publishes 2 new writers/year.** Recently published work by Lee Ann Roripaugh, Dick Allen, Rita Welty Bourke. Accepts submissions by USPS mail only. Send complete ms with SASE.

POETRY No restrictions; highest quality only.

TIPS "We like stories that start quickly and have a strong narrative arc. Poems that are passionate about subject, language, and image are welcome, whether they are traditional or experimental, whether in formal or free verse (closed or open form). Nonfiction should combine art and fact with the finest writing."

NINTH LETTER

Department of English, University of Illinois, 608 S. Wright St., Urbana IL 61801. (217)244-3145. **E-mail:** info@ninthletter.com; editor@ninthletter.com. **Website:** www.ninthletter.com. **Contact:** Jodee Stanley, editor. "*Ninth Letter* accepts submissions of fiction, poetry, and essays from September 1-February 28 (postmark dates). *Ninth Letter* is published semiannually at the University of Illinois, Urbana-Champaign. We are interested in prose and poetry that experiment with form, narrative, and nontraditional subject matter, as well as more traditional literary work." Pays on publication. Accepts queries by mail, online submission form.

NONFICTION Contact: nonfiction@ninthletter.com. "Please send only 1 essay at a time. All mailed submissions must include an SASE for reply." Length: up to 8,000 words. **Pays $25 per printed page and 2 contributor's copies.**

FICTION Contact: fiction@ninthpoetry.com. "Please send only 1 story at a time. All mailed submissions must include an SASE for reply." Length: up to 8,000 words. **Pays $25 per printed page and 2 contributor's copies.**

POETRY Contact: poetry@ninthletter.com. Submit 3-6 poems (no more than 10 pages) at a time. "All mailed submissions must include an SASE for reply." **Pays $25 per printed page and 2 contributor's copies.**

NORTH CAROLINA LITERARY REVIEW

East Carolina University, Mailstop 555 English, Greenville NC 27858-4353. (252)328-1537. **Fax:** (252)328-4889. **E-mail:** nclrsubmissions@ecu.edu. **Website:** www.nclr.ecu.edu. **Contact:** Margaret Bauer. Biannual magazine published online in the winter and in print in the summer covering North Carolina writers, literature, culture, history. "Articles should have a North Carolina slant. Fiction, creative nonfiction, and poetry accepted through yearly contests. First consideration is always for quality of work. Although we treat academic and scholarly subjects, we do not wish to see jargon-laden prose; our readers, we hope, are found as often in bookstores and libraries as in academia. We seek to combine the best elements of a magazine for serious readers with the best of a scholarly journal." Estab. 1992. Circ. 750. Byline given. No kill fee. Publishes ms an average of 1 year after acceptance. Editorial lead time 6 months. Responds in 1 month to queries; in 6 months to mss. Sample copy: $5-25. Guidelines available online.

Accepts submissions through Submittable.

NONFICTION Submit creative nonfiction for Alex Albright Creative Nonfiction Prize competition via Submittable. Length: up to 7,500 words. **Published writers paid in copies of the journal. First-place winners of contests receive a prize of $250.**

PHOTOS State availability. True required. Reviews 5x7 or 8x10 prints; snapshot size or photocopy OK.

FICTION Submit fiction for the Doris Betts Fiction Prize competition via Submittable. Length: up to 6,000 words. **Published writers paid in copies of the journal. First-place winners of contests receive a prize of $250.**

POETRY Submit poetry for the James Applewhite Poetry Prize competition via Submittable. Submit up to 3 poems for $15 entry fee or up to 5 poems for $20 entry fee. **Published writers paid in copies of the journal. First-place winners of contests receive a prize of $250.**

FILLERS Buys 2-5 mss/year. Length: 50-500 words. **$50-100 honorarium, extra copies, back issues or subscription (negotiable)**.

TIPS "By far the easiest way to break in is with special issue sections. We are especially interested in reports on conferences, readings, meetings that involve North Carolina writers, and personal essays or short narratives with a strong sense of place. See back issues for other departments. Interviews are probably the other easiest place to break in; no discussions of poetics/theory, etc., except in reader-friendly (accessible) language. Interviews should be personal, more like conversations, that explore connections between a writer's life and his/her work."

NOTRE DAME REVIEW

University of Notre Dame, B009C McKenna Hall, Notre Dame IN 46556. **Website:** ndreview.nd.edu. "The *Notre Dame Review* is an indepenent, noncommercial magazine of contemporary American and international fiction, poetry, criticism, and art. Especially interested in work that takes on big issues by making the invisible seen, that gives voice to the voiceless. In addition to showcasing celebrated authors like Seamus Heaney and Czelaw Milosz, the *Notre Dame Review* introduces readers to authors they may have never encountered before but who are doing innovative and important work. In conjunction with the *Notre Dame Review*, the online companion to the printed magazine, the *nd[re]view* engages readers as a community centered in literary rather than commercial concerns, a community we reach out to through critique and commentary as well as aesthetic experience." Estab. 1995. Circ. 2,000. Pays on publication. Publishes ms an average of 6 months after acceptance. Accepts simultaneous submissions. Responds in 4 or more months to mss. Sample copy: $6. Guidelines online.

Does not accept e-mail submissions. Only reads hardcopy submissions September-November and January-March.

FICTION "We're eclectic. Upcoming theme issues planned. List of upcoming themes or editorial calendar available for SASE." No genre fiction. **Buys 10 mss/year.** Send complete ms with cover letter. Include 4-sentence bio. Send SASE for response, return of ms, or send a disposable copy of ms. Length: up to 3,000 words. **Pays $5-25.**

POETRY Send complete ms with cover letter. Include 4-sentence bio. Send SASE for response, return of ms, or send a disposable copy of ms. Buys 90 poems/year. Submit maximum 3-5 poems.

TIPS "We're looking for high-quality work that takes on big issues in a literary way. Please read our back issues before submitting."

NOW & THEN: THE APPALACHIAN MAGAZINE

East Tennessee State University, Box 70556, Johnson City TN 37614-1707. (423)439-5348. **Fax:** (423)439-6340. **E-mail:** nowandthen@etsu.edu. **E-mail:** sandersr@etsu.edu. **Website:** www.etsu.edu/cass/nowandthen. **Contact:** Randy Sanders, managing editor; Wayne Winkler, music editor; Charlie War-

CONSUMER MAGAZINES

den, photo editor. Literary magazine published twice/year. "*Now & Then* accepts a variety of writing genres: fiction, poetry, nonfiction, essays, interviews, memoirs, and book reviews. All submissions must relate to Appalachia and to the issue's specific theme. Our readership is educated and interested in the region." Estab. 1984. Circ. 1,000. Responds in 5 months to queries; 5 months to mss. Sample copy: $8 plus $3 shipping. Guidelines and upcoming themes available on website.

Now & Then tells the stories of Appalachia and presents a fresh, revealing picture of life in Appalachia, past and present, with engaging articles, personal essays, fiction, poetry, and photography.

PHOTOS Photos of environmental, landscapes/scenics, architecture, cities/urban, rural, adventure, performing arts, travel, agriculture, political, disasters. Interested in documentary, fine art, historical/vintage. Photographs must relate to theme of issue. Themes are posted on the website. "We publish photo essays based on the magazine's theme." Reviews photos with or without a ms. Model/property release preferred. Photo captions preferred, include where the photos was taken. Require images in digital format sent as e-mail attachments as JPEG or TIFF files at 300 dpi minimum.

FICTION "Absolutely has to relate to Appalachian theme. Can be about adjustment to new environment, themes of leaving and returning, for instance. Nothing unrelated to region." Accepts 1-2 mss/issue. Publishes ms 4 months after acceptance. Publishes some new writers/year. Needs adventure, ethnic/multicultural, experimental, fantasy, historical, humor/satire, literary, mainstream, regional, slice-of-life vignettes, excerpted novel, prose poem. Send complete ms. Accepts submissions by mail, e-mail, with a strong preference for e-mail. Include "information we can use for contributor's note." SASE (or IRC). Rarely accepts simultaneous submissions. Reviews fiction. Length: 1,000-1,500 words. **Pays $50 for each accepted article. Pays on publication.**

POETRY Submit up to 5 poems, with SASE and cover letter including "a few lines about yourself for a contributor's note and whether the work has been published or accepted elsewhere." Will consider simultaneous submissions; occasionally accepts previously published poems. Put name, address, and phone number on every poem. Deadlines: last workday in February (spring/summer issue) and August 31 (fall/winter issues). Publishes theme issues. **Pays $25 for each accepted poem. Pays on publication.**

TIPS "Keep in mind that *Now & Then* only publishes material related to the Appalachian region. Plus we only publish fiction that has some plausible connection to a specific issue's themes. We like to offer first-time publication to promising writers."

ONE STORY

232 3rd St., #A108, Brooklyn NY 11215. **Website:** www.one-story.com. **Contact:** Maribeth Batcha, publisher. **100% freelance written.** Literary magazine covering 1 short story. "*One Story* is a literary magazine that contains, simply, one story. Approximately every 3-4 weeks, subscribers are sent *One Story* in the mail. *One Story* is artfully designed, lightweight, easy to carry, and ready to entertain on buses, in bed, in subways, in cars, in the park, in the bath, in the waiting rooms of doctor's offices, on the couch, or in line at the supermarket. Subscribers also have access to a website where they can learn more about *One Story* authors and hear about *One Story* readings and events. There is always time to read *One Story*." Estab. 2002. Circ. 3,500. Byline given. Pays on publication. Publishes ms an average of 3-6 months after acceptance. Editorial lead time 3-4 months. Accepts simultaneous submissions. Responds in 2-4 months to mss. Sample copy: $2.50 (back issue). Guidelines available online.

Reading period: September 1-May 31.

FICTION Needs short stories. *One Story* only accepts short stories. Do not send excerpts. Do not send more than 1 story at a time. **Buys 18 mss/year.** Send complete ms using online submission form. Length: 3,000-8,000 words. **Pays $500 and 25 contributor's copies.**

TIPS "*One Story* is looking for stories that are strong enough to stand alone. Therefore they must be very good. We want the best you can give."

ORBIS

17 Greenhow Ave., West Kirby Wirral CH48 5EL UK. **E-mail:** carolebaldock@hotmail.com. **Website:** www.orbisjournal.com. **Contact:** Carole Baldock, editor; Noel Williams, reviews editor. *Orbis* covers 84 pages of news, reviews, views, letters, features, prose, and a lot of poetry and cover artwork. Each writer is eligible for the Readers Award: £50 (plus £50 divided between the runners-up). Poems are also submitted to the Forward Prize (UK) and the Pushcart Prize (USA). "*Orbis*

has long been considered one of the top 20 small-press magazines in the UK. We are interested in social inclusion projects and encouraging access to the Arts, young people, Under 20s, and 20-somethings. Subjects for discussion: 'day in the life,' technical, topical." Estab. 1969. No kill fee. Responds in 3 months.

Please see guidelines on website before submitting.

NONFICTION Needs essays, reviews, technical, features. **Pays £50.**

PHOTOS Wants artwork for cover.

FICTION Buys 12 mss/year. Length: 1,000 words max.

POETRY Readers' Award: £50 for piece receiving the most votes in each issue. Four winners selected for submissions to Forward Poetry Prize, Single Poem category. Plus £50 split between 4 or more runners-up. Feature Writer receives £50. NB, work commissioned: 3-4 poems or 1,500 words. Buys 160/year poems/year.

TIPS "Any publication should be read cover to cover because it's the best way to improve your chances of getting published. Enclose SAE with all correspondence. Overseas: 2 IRCs, 3 if work is to be returned."

PALABRA

P.O. Box 86146, Los Angeles CA 90086. **E-mail:** info@palabralitmag.com. **Website:** www.palabralitmag.com. Annual magazine featuring poetry, fiction, short plays, and more. "*PALABRA* is about exploration, risk, and ganas—the myriad intersections of thought, language, story, and art—*el mas alla of letters*, symbols and spaces into meaning." Estab. 2006. Byline given. No kill fee. Accepts queries by mail. Responds in 3-4 months to mss. Guidelines online.

Reading period: September 1-April 30.

NONFICTION Submit complete ms by mail. Include brief cover letter and SASE. **Pays $25-40.**

FICTION Needs experimental/hybrid, mainstream, novel excerpts, flash fiction, short plays. No genre work, i.e., mystery, romance, suspense, science fiction, etc. Send complete ms via postal mail. If submitting in more than one genre submit each one separately. Include brief cover letter and SASE. Length: up to 4,000 words; up to 750 for flash fiction. **Pays $25-$40.**

POETRY Needs avant garde, free verse, traditional. Submit up to 5 poems via postal mail. Include brief cover letter and SASE. **Pays $25-40.**

THE PARIS REVIEW

544 West 27th St., New York NY 10001. (212)343-1333. **E-mail:** queries@theparisreview.org. **Website:** www.theparisreview.org. **Contact:** Lorin Stein, editor; Robyn Creswell, poetry editor. Quarterly magazine. *The Paris Review* publishes "fiction and poetry of superlative quality, whatever the genre, style, or mode. Our contributors include prominent, as well as less well-known and previously unpublished writers. The Writers at Work interview series includes important contemporary writers discussing their own work and the craft of writing." Pays on publication. No kill fee. Accepts queries by mail. Accepts simultaneous submissions. Responds in 4 months to mss. Guidelines available online.

Address submissions to proper department. Do not make submissions via e-mail.

FICTION Study the publication. Annual Plimpton Prize award of $10,000 given to a new voice published in the magazine. Recently published work by Ottessa Moshfegh, John Jeremiah Sullivan, and Lydia Davis. Send complete ms. Length: no limit. **Pays $1,000-3,000.**

POETRY Submit no more than 6 poems at a time. Poetry can be sent to the poetry editor (please include a self-addressed, stamped envelope). **Poets receive $100/poem.**

PARNASSUS: POETRY IN REVIEW

Poetry in Review Foundation, 205 W. 89th St., #8F, New York NY 10024. (212)362-3492. **E-mail:** parnew@aol.com. **Website:** www.parnassusreview.com. **Contact:** Herbert Leibowitz, editor and publisher. Annual magazine covering poetry and criticism. "We now publish 1 double issue/year." *Parnassus: Poetry in Review* provides "a forum where poets, novelists, and critics of all persuasions can gather to review new books of poetry, including translations—international poetries have occupied center stage from our very first issue—with an amplitude and reflectiveness that Sunday book supplements and even the literary quarterlies could not afford. Our editorial philosophy is based on the assumption that reviewing is a complex art. Like a poem or a short story, a review essay requires imagination, scrupulous attention to rhythm, pacing, and supple syntax; space in which to build a persuasive, detailed argument; analytical precision and intuitive gambits; verbal play, wit, and metaphor. We welcome and vigorously seek out voices that break aesthetic molds and disturb xenophobic habits." Estab. 1972. Circ. 1,800. Byline given. Pays on publication. No kill fee. Publishes ms an average of 12-14 months after acceptance. Accepts queries by mail. Responds in 2 months to mss. Sample copy: $15.

NONFICTION Needs essays. **Buys 30 mss/year.** Query with published clips. Length: 1,500-7,500 words. **Pays $200-1,000.**

POETRY Needs avant garde, free verse, traditional. Accepts most types of poetry. Buys 3-4 unsolicited poems/year.

TIPS "Be certain you have read the magazine and are aware of the editor's taste. Blind submissions are a waste of everybody's time. We'd like to see more poems that display intellectual acumen and curiosity about history, science, music, etc., and fewer trivial lyrical poems about the self, or critical prose that's academic and dull. Prose should sing."

THE PEDESTAL MAGAZINE

6815 Honors Court, Charlotte NC 28210. **E-mail:** pedmagazine@carolina.rr.com. **Website:** www.thepedestalmagazine.com. **Contact:** John Amen, editor in chief. Committed to promoting diversity and celebrating the voice of the individual. Estab. 2000. No kill fee. Publishes ms 2-4 weeks after acceptance. Accepts queries by e-mail. Accepts simultaneous submissions. Responds in 1-2 months to mss. Guidelines available online.

See website for reading periods for different forms. Member: CLMP.

NONFICTION Needs essays, reviews, interview. **Pays $40.**

PHOTOS Reviews JPEG, GIF files.

FICTION "We are receptive to all sorts of high-quality literary fiction. Genre fiction is encouraged as long as it crosses or comments upon its genre and is both character-driven and psychologically acute. We encourage submissions of short fiction, no more than 3 flash fiction pieces at a time. There is no need to query prior to submitting; please submit via online submission manager—no e-mail to the editor." Needs adventure, ethnic, experimental, historical, horror, humorous, mainstream, mystery, romance, science fiction, works that don't fit into a specific category. **Buys 10-25 mss/year.** Length: up to 4,000 words; up to 1,000 words for flash fiction. **Pays 3¢/word.**

POETRY Open to a wide variety of poetry, ranging from the highly experimental to the traditionally formal. Submit all poems in 1 form. No need to query before submitting. Submit maximum 5 poems. No length restriction.

TIPS "If you send us your work, please wait for a response to your first submission before you submit again."

PILGRIMAGE MAGAZINE

Colorado State University-Pueblo, Dept. of English, 2200 Bonforte Blvd., Pueblo CO 81001. **E-mail:** info@pilgrimagepress.org. **Website:** www.pilgrimagepress.org. **Contact:** Juan Morales, editor. Biannual magazine welcoming creative prose and poetry. Favors personal writing on themes of place, spirit, peace, and social justice in and beyond the Greater Southwest. Serves an eclectic fellowship of readers, writers, artists, naturalists, contemplatives, activists, seekers, adventurers, and other kindred spirits. Estab. 1976. No kill fee. Accepts simultaneous submissions. Guidelines available online. Submit via online submissions manager (https://pilgrimagemagazine.submittable.com/submit) or snail mail (with SASE for reply only).

FICTION Length: up to 6,000 words. "Shorter works are easier to include, due to space constraints."

POETRY Fit poetry on 1 page.

TIPS "Our interests include wildness in all its forms; inward and outward explorations; home ground, the open road, service, witness, peace, and justice; symbols, story, and myth in contemporary culture; struggle and resilience; insight and transformation; wisdom wherever it is found; and the great mystery of it all. We like good storytellers and a good sense of humor. No e-mail submissions, please."

THE PINCH

English Department, University of Memphis, Memphis TN 38152. (901)678-4591. **E-mail:** editor@pinchjournal.com. **Website:** www.pinchjournal.com. **Contact:** Tim Johnston, editor in chief; Matthew Gallant, managing editor. **100% freelance written.** Semiannual literary magazine. "We publish fiction, creative nonfiction, poetry, and art of literary quality by both established and emerging artists." Estab. 1980. Circ. 2,500. Byline given. Accepts queries by mail, online submission form. Accepts simultaneous submissions. Responds in 3 months to mss. Sample copy: $5. Guidelines available on website.

"The Pinch Literary Awards in Fiction, Poetry, and Nonfiction offer a $1,000 prize and publication. Check our website for details."

NONFICTION Needs essays, personal experience. Special issues: "We do not do themed or special issues." Query by e-mail. "We do NOT accept submissions via e-mail. Submissions sent via e-mail will not receive a response. To submit, see guidelines." Length: up to 5,000 words. **Pays 2 contributor's copies, and 1 work from each genre receives monetary payment.**

FICTION Wants "character-based" fiction with a "fresh use of language." Needs experimental, novel excerpts, literary fiction. No genre fiction. "We do NOT accept submissions via e-mail. Submissions sent via e-mail will not receive a response. To submit, see guidelines." Submit through mail or via online submissions manager. Length: up to 5,000 words.

POETRY "We do not accept submissions via e-mail. Submissions sent via e-mail will not receive a response. To submit, see guidelines." Submit through mail or via online submissions manager. Submit maximum 5 poems.

TIPS "We have a new look and a new edge. We're soliciting work from writers with a national or international reputation as well as strong, interesting work from emerging writers."

PLANET-THE WELSH INTERNATIONALIST

P.O. Box 44, Aberystwyth Ceredigion SY23 3ZZ United Kingdom. **E-mail:** emily.trahair@planetmagazine.org.uk. **Website:** www.planetmagazine.org.uk. **Contact:** Emily Trahair, editor. Bimonthly journal. A literary/cultural/political journal centered on Welsh affairs but with a strong interest in minority cultures in Europe and elsewhere. *Planet: The Welsh Internationalist*, published quarterly, is a cultural magazine "centered on Wales, but with broader interests in arts, sociology, politics, history, and science." Estab. 1970. Circ. 1,400. Publishes ms 4-6 months after acceptance. Accepts queries by mail, e-mail. Responds in 3 months. Single copy: £6.75; subscription: £22 (£40 overseas). Sample copy: £5. Guidelines online.

Planet is 128 pages, A5, professionally printed, perfect-bound, with glossy color card cover. Receives about 500 submissions/year, accepts about 5%. Press run is 1,550 (1,500 subscribers, about 10% libraries, 200 shelf sales).

NONFICTION Needs reviews, articles. Query.

FICTION Would like to see more inventive, imaginative fiction that pays attention to language and experiments with form. No magical realism, horror, science fiction. Submit complete ms via mail or e-mail (with attachment). For postal submissions, no submissions returned unless accompanied by an SASE. Writers submitting from abroad should send at least 3 IRCs for return of typescript; 1 IRC for reply only. Length: 1,500-2,750 words. **Pays £50/1,000 words.**

POETRY Wants "good poetry in a wide variety of styles. No limitations as to subject matter; length can be a problem." Has published poetry by Nigel Jenkins, Anne Stevenson, and Les Murray. Submit 4-6 poems via mail or e-mail (with attachment). For postal submissions, no submissions returned unless accompanied by an SASE. Writers submitting from abroad should send at least 3 IRCs for return of typescript; 1 IRC for reply only. **Pays £30/poem.**

TIPS "We do not look for fiction that necessarily has a 'Welsh' connection, which some writers assume from our title. We try to publish a broad range of fiction, and our main criterion is quality. Try to read copies of any magazine you submit to. Don't write out of the blue to a magazine which might be completely inappropriate for your work. Recognize that you are likely to have a high rejection rate, as magazines tend to favor writers from their own countries."

PLEIADES

Pleiades Press, Department of English, University of Central Missouri, Martin 336, Warrensburg MO 64093. (660)543-8106. **E-mail:** pleiades@ucmo.edu. **Website:** www.ucmo.edu/pleiades. **Contact:** Kevin Prufer, editor-at-large. **100% freelance written.** Semiannual journal. "We publish contemporary fiction, poetry, interviews, literary essays, special-interest personal essays, and reviews for a general and literary audience from authors from around the world." Reads August 15-May 15. Estab. 1991. Circ. 3,000. Byline given. Pays on publication. No kill fee. Publishes ms an average of 9 months after acceptance. Editorial lead time 9 months. Accepts queries by mail. Accepts simultaneous submissions. Responds in 2 months to queries. Responds in 1-4 months to mss. Sample copy for $5 (back issue); $6 (current issue). Guidelines available online.

NONFICTION **Contact:** Phong Nguyen, nonfiction editor. Needs book excerpts, essays, interview, reviews. "Nothing pedantic, slick, or shallow." **Buys 4-6 mss/year.** Send complete ms via online submission manager. Length: 2,000-4,000 words. **Pays $10 and contributor's copies.**

FICTION Contact: Phong Nguyen and Matthew Eck, fiction editors. Reads fiction year-round. Needs ethnic, experimental, humorous, mainstream, novel concepts, Also wants magic realism. No science fiction, fantasy, confession, erotica. **Buys 16-20 mss/year.** Send complete ms via online submission manager. Length: 2,000-6,000 words. **Pays $10 and contributor's copies.**

POETRY Contact: Kathryn Nuernberger, poetry editor. Needs avant-garde, free verse, haiku, light verse, traditional. Submit 3-5 poems at a time via online submission manager. "Nothing didactic, pretentious, or overly sentimental." Buys 40-50 poems/year. Submit maximum 5 poems. **Pays $3/poem, and contributor copies.**

TIPS "Submit only 1 genre at a time to appropriate editors. Show care for your material and your readers—submit quality work in a professional format. Include cover letter with brief bio and list of publications. Include SASE. Cover art is solicited directly from artists. We accept queries for book reviews."

PLOUGHSHARES

Emerson College, 120 Boylston St., Boston MA 02116. (617)824-3757. **E-mail:** pshares@pshares.org. **Website:** www.pshares.org. **Contact:** Ladette Randolph, editor in chief/executive director; Andrea Martucci, managing editor. *Ploughshares*, published 3 times/year, is "a journal of new writing guest-edited by prominent poets and writers to reflect different and contrasting points of view. Translations are welcome if permission has been granted. Our mission is to present dynamic, contrasting views on what is valid and important in contemporary literature and to discover and advance significant literary talent. Each issue is guest-edited by a different writer. We no longer structure issues around preconceived themes." Editors have included Carolyn Forché, Gerald Stern, Rita Dove, Chase Twichell, and Marilyn Hacker. "We do accept electronic submissions—there is a $3 fee per submission, which is waived if you are a subscriber." Estab. 1971. Circ. 6,000. Pays on publication. Publishes ms an average of 6 months after acceptance. Accepts queries by mail, online submission form. Accepts simultaneous submissions. Responds in 3-5 months to mss. Sample copy: $14 current issue, $7 back issue; please inquire for shipping rates. Subscription: $30 domestic, $30 plus shipping (see website) foreign. Guidelines online.

Ploughshares is 200 pages, digest-sized. Receives about 11,000 poetry, fiction, and essay submissions/year. Reads submissions June 1-January 15 (postmark); mss submitted January 16-May 31 will be returned unread.

NONFICTION Needs essays. Submit complete ms via online submissions form or by mail. Length: up to 6,000 words. **Pays $25/printed page ($50 minimum, $250 maximum); 2 contributor's copies; and one-year subscription.**

FICTION Has published work by ZZ Packer, Antonya Nelson, and Stuart Dybek. Needs mainstream, literary. "No genre (science fiction, detective, gothic, adventure, etc.), popular formula or commerical fiction whose purpose is to entertain rather than to illuminate." Submit via online submissions form or by mail. Length: up to 6,000 words **Pays $25/printed page ($50 minimum, $250 maximum); 2 contributor's copies; and one-year subscription.**

POETRY Needs avant-garde, free verse, traditional. Submit up to 5 poems via online submissions form or by mail. Has published poetry by Donald Hall, Li-Young Lee, Robert Pinsky, Brenda Hillman, and Thylias Moss. **Pays $25/printed page ($50 minimum, $250 maximum); 2 contributor's copies; and one-year subscription.**

POETRY

The Poetry Foundation, 61 W. Superior St., Chicago IL 60654. (312)787-7070. **Fax:** (312)787-6650. **E-mail:** editors@poetrymagazine.org. **Website:** www.poetrymagazine.org. Don Share, editor. **Contact:** Don Share, editor. **100% freelance written.** Monthly magazine. *Poetry*, published monthly by The Poetry Foundation (see separate listing in Organizations), "has no special ms needs and no special requirements as to form: We examine in turn all work received and accept that which seems best." Has published poetry by the major voices of our time as well as new talent. Estab. 1912. Circ. 32,500. Byline given. Pays on publication. No kill fee. Publishes ms an average of 9 months after acceptance. Responds in 2 months to mss and queries. Guidelines online.

Poetry's website offers featured poems, letters, reviews, interviews, essays, and web-exclusive features. *Poetry* is elegantly printed, flat-spined. Receives 100,000 submissions/year, accepts about 300-350. Press run is 16,000.

NONFICTION Buys 14 mss/year. Query. No length requirements. **Pays $150/page.**

POETRY Accepts all styles and subject matter. Submit up to 4 poems via online submissions manager. Reviews books of poetry in multibook formats of varying lengths. Does not accept unsolicited reviews. Buys 180-250 poems/year. Length: up to 10 pages total. **Pays $10 line (minimum payment of $300).**

THE PRAIRIE JOURNAL

P.O. Box 68073, 28 Crowfoot Terrace NW, Calgary AB Y3G 3N8 Canada. **E-mail:** editor@prairiejournal.org (queries only); prairiejournal@yahoo.com. **Website:** www.prairiejournal.org. **Contact:** A.E. Burke, literary editor. **100% freelance written.** Semiannual magazine publishing quality poetry, short fiction, drama, literary criticism, reviews, bibliography, interviews, profiles, and artwork. "The audience is literary, university, library, scholarly, and creative readers/writers." Estab. 1983. Circ. 650-750. Byline given. Pays on publication. No kill fee. Publishes ms an average of 4-6 months after acceptance. Editorial lead time 2-6 months. Accepts queries by mail, e-mail. Responds in 2 weeks to queries; 2-6 months to mss. Sample copy: $5. Guidelines available online.

"Use our mailing address for submissions and queries with samples or for clippings."

NONFICTION Needs essays, humor, interview, literary. No inspirational, news, religious, or travel. **Buys 25-40 mss/year.** Query with published clips. Length: 100-3,000 words. **Pays $50-100, plus contributor's copy.**

PHOTOS State availability. Offers additional payment for photos accepted with ms.

COLUMNS/DEPARTMENTS Reviews (books from small presses publishing poetry, short fiction, essays, and criticism), 200-1,000 words. **Buys 5 mss/year.** Query with published clips. **Pays $10-50.**

FICTION Needs mainstream. No genre (romance, horror, western—sagebrush or cowboys), erotic, science fiction, or mystery. **Buys 6 mss/year.** Send complete ms. No e-mail submissions. Length: 100-3,000 words. **Pays $10-75.**

POETRY Needs avant-garde, free verse, haiku. Seeks poetry "of any length; free verse, contemporary themes (feminist, nature, urban, nonpolitical), aesthetic value, a poet's poetry." Does not want to see "most rhymed verse, sentimentality, egotistical ravings. No cowboys or sage brush." Has published poetry by Liliane Welch, Cornelia Hoogland, Sheila Hyland, Zoe Lendale, and Chad Norman. Receives about 1,000 poems/year, accepts 10%. No heroic couplets or greeting card verse. Buys 25-35 poems/year. Submit maximum 6-8 poems. Length: 3-50 lines. **Pays $5-50.**

TIPS "We publish many, many new writers and are always open to unsolicited submissions because we are 100% freelance. Do not send U.S. stamps; always use IRCs. We have poems, interviews, stories, and reviews online (query first)."

PRISM INTERNATIONAL

Dept. of Creative Writing, Buch E462, 1866 Main Mall, University of British Columbia, Vancouver British Columbia V6T 1Z1 Canada. (604)822-2514. **Fax:** (604)822-3616. **E-mail:** prismcirculation@gmail.com. **Website:** www.prismmagazine.ca. **100% freelance written. Works with new/unpublished writers.** A quarterly international journal of contemporary writing—fiction, poetry, drama, creative nonfiction and translation. *PRISM international* is 80 pages, digest-sized, elegantly printed, flat-spined, with original color artwork on a glossy card cover. Readership: public and university libraries, individual subscriptions, bookstores—a world-wide audience concerned with the contemporary in literature. "We have no thematic or stylistic allegiances: Excellence is our main criterion for acceptance of manuscripts." Receives 1,000 submissions/year, accepts about 80. Circulation is for 1,200 subscribers. Subscription: $35/year for Canadian subscriptions, $40/year for US subscriptions, $45/year for international. Sample: $13. Estab. 1959. Circ. 1,200. Pays on publication. No kill fee. Publishes ms an average of 4 months after acceptance. Accepts queries by mail and online. Responds in 4 months to queries. Responds in 3-6 months to mss. Sample copy for $13, more info online. Guidelines available online.

NONFICTION No reviews, tracts, or scholarly essays. **Pays $20/printed page, and 2 copies of issue.**

FICTION For Drama: one-acts/excerpts of no more than 1500 words preferred. Also interested in seeing dramatic monologues. Needs experimental, novel concepts, traditional. "New writing that is contemporary and literary. Short stories and self-contained novel excerpts. Works of translation are eagerly sought and should be accompanied by a copy of the original. Would like to see more translations. No gothic, confession, religious, romance, pornography, or science fiction." **Buys 12-16 mss/year.** Send complete ms. 25

pages maximum **Pays $20/printed page, and 12 copies of issue.**

POETRY Needs avant-garde, traditional. Wants "fresh, distinctive poetry that shows an awareness of traditions old and new. We read everything." Considers poetry by children and teens. "Excellence is the only criterion." Has published poetry by Margaret Avison, Elizabeth Bachinsky, John Pass, Warren Heiti, Don McKay, Bill Bissett, and Stephanie Bolster. Submit maximum up to 6 poems. **Pays $40/printed page, and 2 copies of issue.**

TIPS "We are looking for new and exciting fiction. Excellence is still our No. 1 criterion. As well as poetry, imaginative nonfiction and fiction, we are especially open to translations of all kinds, very short fiction pieces and drama which work well on the page. Translations must come with a copy of the original language work."

A PUBLIC SPACE

323 Dean St., Brooklyn NY 11217. (718)858-8067. **E-mail:** general@apublicspace.org. **Website:** www.apublicspace.org. **Contact:** Brigid Hughes, founding editor; Anne McPeak, managing editor. *A Public Space*, published quarterly, is an independent magazine of literature and culture. "In an era that has relegated literature to the margins, we plan to make fiction and poetry the stars of a new conversation. We believe that stories are how we make sense of our lives and how we learn about other lives. We believe that stories matter." Accepts simultaneous submissions. Single copy: $15; subscription: $36/year or $60/2 years.

Accepts unsolicited submissions from September 15-April 15. Submissions accepted through Submittable or by mail (with SASE).

FICTION Submit 1 complete ms via online submissions manager. No word limit.

POETRY Submit via online submissions manager. No limit on line length.

QUANTUM LEAP

York House, 15 Argyle Terrace, Rothesay, Isle of Bute PA20 0BD Scotland. **Website:** www.qqpress.co.uk. *Quantum Leap*, published quarterly, uses "all kinds of poetry—free verse, rhyming, whatever—as long as it's well written and preferably well punctuated, too. We rarely use haiku." Has published poetry by Pamela Constantine, Ray Stebbing, Leigh Eduardo, Sky Higgins, Norman Bissett, and Gordon Scapens. Estab. 1997. Time between acceptance and publication is usually 3 months "but can be longer now, due to magazine's increasing popularity." Accepts simultaneous submissions. Responds in 3 weeks. Sometimes comments on rejected poems. Single copy: $13; subscription: $40. Sample: $10. Make checks payable to Alan Carter. Guidelines online.

Quantum Leap is 40 pages, digest-sized, desktop-published, saddle-stapled, with card cover. Receives about 2,000 poems/year, accepts about 15%. Press run is 200. "All things being equal in terms of a poem's quality, **I will sometimes favor that of a subscriber (or someone who has at least bought an issue) over a nonsubscriber**, as it is they who keep us solvent."

POETRY Submit 6 poems at a time. Cover letter is required. "Within the U.K., send a SASE; outside it, send IRCs to the return postage value of what has been submitted." Length: 20-40 lines/poem (likes a mix of lengths). **Pays £2 sterling.**

QUARTERLY WEST

University of Utah, 255 S. Central Campus Dr., Room 3500, Salt Lake City UT 84112. **E-mail:** quarterlywest@gmail.com. **Website:** www.quarterlywest.com. **Contact:** Lillian Bertram and Claire Wahmanholm, editors. Triannual magazine. Online only. "We publish fiction, poetry, nonfiction, and new media in long and short formats, and will consider experimental as well as traditional works." Estab. 1976. Circ. 1,900. Publishes ms an average of 6 months after acceptance. Accepts queries by online submission form. Accepts simultaneous submissions. Responds in 3-4 months to mss. Guidelines available online.

Quarterly West was awarded first place for Editorial Content from the American Literary Magazine Awards. Work published in the magazine has been selected for inclusion in the *Pushcart Prize* anthology and *The Best American Short Stories* anthology.

NONFICTION Needs essays, interview, personal experience, travel. Accepts 6-8 mss/year. Send complete ms using online submissions manager only. Length: 10,000 words maximum.

FICTION No preferred lengths; interested in longer, fuller short stories and short shorts. Accepts 6-10 mss/year. Needs ethnic, experimental, humorous, mainstream, novel concepts, slice-of-life vignettes, short shorts, translations. No detective, science fiction, or romance. Send complete ms using online submissions manager only.

POETRY Needs avant-garde, free verse, traditional. Submit 3-5 poems at a time using online submissions manager only. Buys 40-50 poems/year. Submit maximum 5 poems.

TIPS "We publish a special section of short shorts every issue, and we also sponsor an annual novella contest. We are open to experimental work—potential contributors should read the magazine! Don't send more than 1 story per submission. Novella competition guidelines available online. We prefer work with interesting language and detail—plot or narrative are less important. We don't do religious work."

QUEEN'S QUARTERLY

144 Barrie St., Queen's University, Kingston ON K7L 3N6 Canada. (613)533-2667. **Fax:** (613)533-6822. **E-mail:** queens.quarterly@queensu.ca. **Website:** www.queensu.ca/quarterly. **Contact:** Joan Harcourt, literary editor (fiction and poetry); Boris Castel, nonfiction editor (articles, essays and reviews). **95% freelance written.** Quartlery literary magazine. *Queen's Quarterly* is "a general interest intellectual review featuring articles on science, politics, humanities, arts and letters, extensive book reviews, and some poetry and fiction." Estab. 1893. Circ. 3,000. Byline given. Pays on publication. Sends galleys to author. Publishes ms on average 6-12 months after acceptance. Accepts queries by e-mail. Responds in 2-3 months to queries; 1-2 months to ms. Sample: $6.50 U.S. Subscription: $20 Canadian, $25 US for U.S. and foreign subscribers. Guidelines on website.

Has published work by Gail Anderson-Dargatz, Tim Bowling, Emma Donohue, Viktor Carr, Mark Jarman, Rick Bowers, and Dennis Bock.

NONFICTION Send complete ms with SASE and/or IRC. No reply with insufficient postage. Length: up to 3,000 words. **"Payment to new writers will be determined at time of acceptance."**

FICTION Needs historical, literary, mainstream, novel excerpts, short stories, women's. "Special emphasis on work by Canadian writers." Send complete ms with SASE and/or IRC. No reply with insufficient postage. Accepts 2 mss/issue; 8 mss/year. Publishes 5 new writers/year. Length: 2,500-3,000 words. "Submissions over 3,000 words shall not be accepted." **"Payment to new writers will be determined at time of acceptance."**

POETRY Receives about 400 submissions of poetry/year, accepts 40. Submissions can be sent on hard copy with a SASE (no replies/returns for foreign submissions unless accompanied by an IRC) or by e-mail and will be responded to by same. "We are especially interested in poetry by Canadian writers. Shorter poems preferred." Has published poetry by Evelyn Lau, Sue Nevill, and Raymond Souster. Each issue contains about 12 pages of poetry. Buys 25 poems/year. Submit maximum 6 poems. **Usually pays $50 (Canadian)/poem (but it varies), plus 2 copies.**

THE RAG

P.O. Box 17463, Portland OR 97217. **E-mail:** submissions@raglitmag.com. **Website:** raglitmag.com. **Contact:** Seth Porter, editor; Dan Reilly, editor. **90% freelance written.** *The Rag* focuses on the grittier genres that tend to fall by the wayside at more traditional literary magazines. *The Rag*'s ultimate goal is to put the literary magazine back into the entertainment market while rekindling the social and cultural value short fiction once held in North American literature. Estab. 2011. Byline given. Pays prior to publication. Editorial lead time 1-2 months. Accepts queries by e-mail. Accepts simultaneous submissions. Responds in 1 month or less for queries; in 1-2 months for mss.

Fee to submit online ($3) is waived if you subscribe or purchase a single issue.

PHOTOS Reviews GIF/JPEG files. Negotiates payment individually.

FICTION Accepts all styles and themes. Needs humorous, transgressive. **Buys 10 mss/year.** Send complete ms. Length: up to 10,000 words. **Pays 5¢/word, the average being $250/story.**

POETRY Needs Avant-garde, free verse. Accepts all themes and styles. Submit complete ms. Buys 15-20 poems/year. Submit maximum 5 poems. Length: 5 poems or 2,000 words, whichever occurs first. **Pays $20-100+.**

FILLERS Length: 150-1,000 words. **Pays $20-100.**

TIPS "We like gritty material: material that is psychologically believable and that has some humor in it, dark or otherwise. We like subtle themes, original characters, and sharp wit."

RAIN TAXI

Rain Taxi, Inc., P.O. Box 3840, Minneapolis MN 55403. (612)825-1528. **Fax:** (612)825-1528. **E-mail:** info@raintaxi.com. **Website:** www.raintaxi.com. **Contact:** Eric Lorberer, editor. **40% freelance writ-**

ten. Quarterly magazine covering books. "*Rain Taxi* Review of Books, a nonprofit quarterly, is dedicated to covering literature and the arts, including poetry, graphic novels, cultural critique, and quality fiction in all genres. Winner of an Independent Press Award, *Rain Taxi* is a great vehicle for books & authors that may otherwise get lost in the mainstream media." Estab. 1996. Circ. 18,000. Byline given. Payment in issues. No kill fee. Publishes ms an average of 2 months after acceptance. Editorial lead time 2 months. Submit seasonal material 3 months in advance. Accepts queries by mail, e-mail. Responds in 1 week to queries; in 1 month to mss. Sample copy: $5. Guidelines at www.raintaxi.com/submitadvertise/rain-taxi-submission-guidelines.

NONFICTION Needs essays, book reviews, author interviews. Query. Length: 500-2,000 words.

RATTAPALLAX

Rattapallax Press, 217 Thompson St., Suite 353, New York NY 10012. **E-mail:** info@rattapallax.com. **Website:** www.rattapallax.com. **Contact:** Flávia Rocha, editor n chief. **10% freelance written.** Annual literary magazine that focuses on issues dealing with globalization. *Rattapallax*, published semiannually, is named for "Wallace Stevens's word for the sound of thunder. The magazine includes a DVD featuring poetry films and audio files. *Rattapallax* is looking for the extraordinary in modern poetry and prose that reflect the diversity of world cultures. Our goals are to create international dialogue using literature and focus on what is relevant to our society." Estab. 1999. Circ. 3,000. Byline given. Pays on publication. No kill fee. Publishes ms an average of 6 months after acceptance. Editorial lead time 6 months. Submit seasonal material 6 months in advance. Accepts queries by e-mail. Responds in 3 months to queries; in 3 months to mss. Sample copy: $7.95. Make checks payable to *Rattapallax*. Guidelines online.

Rattapallax is 112 pages, magazine-sized, offset-printed, perfect-bound, with 12-pt. CS1 cover; some illustrations; photos. Press run is 2,000 (100 subscribers, 50 libraries, 1,200 shelf sales); 200 distributed free to contributors, reviews, and promos.

FICTION Needs literary. Submit via online submissions manager at rattapallax.submittable.com/submit. Length: up to 2,000 words. **Pays 2 contributor's copies.**

POETRY Needs avant-garde, free verse, traditional. Submit via online submission manager at rattapallax.submittable.com/submit. Often comments on rejected poems. Submit maximum 4 poems. Length: 1 page per poem. **Pays 2 contributor's copies.**

READER'S CARNIVAL

317-7185 Hall Rd., Surrey BC V3W4X5 Canada. **E-mail:** info@readerscarnival.ca; readerscarnival@gmail.com. **Website:** www.readerscarnival.ca. **Contact:** Doug Langille, editor; Anisa Irwin, managing editor. **80% freelance written.** Monthly print and online magazine that covers themed fiction: from homor to horror and everything inbetween. Estab. 2014. Byline given. Kill fee: 15%. Publishes mss 3 months after acceptance. Editorial lead time is 3 months. Submit season material 3 months in advance. Accepts queries by e-mail. Accepts simultaneous submissions. Responds in 2 months to mss. Sample copies available online for $7 CAD. Guidelines available online or via e-mail.

Must be an upgraded member of Writer's Carnival to submit to *Reader's Carnival.* Upgraded members can also enter contests on WC. Contests are every second month with $100 prize.

NONFICTION Needs book excerpts, general interest, historical, how-to, humor, inspirational, interview, nostalgic, photo feature, profile. Special issues: All issues are themed: Western, Tales from the Sea, Empowering Nonfiction, Mayhem and Mysteries, Retro School Days, Beach Theme, Summer Days, Road Trips, Halloween, Movie-Related, Christmas, etc. "We tend to stay away from heavily opinionated, religious, or political pieces." **Buys 5-10 mss/year.** Submit complete ms. Length: 500-2,000 words. **Pays 2¢/word (CAD). Sometimes offers contributor copies.**

FICTION Each issue has a different theme. Needs adventure, ethnic, fantasy, historical, horror, humorous, mainstream, mystery, religious, romance, science fiction, short stories, slice-of-life vignettes, suspense, western. Not interested in erotica, slasher horror (torture, overly gruesome). **Buys 80-100 mss/year.** Submit complete ms. Length: 25-2,000 words. **Pays 2¢/word (CAD). Flash fiction under 250 words is $5 flat.**

POETRY Needs free verse, haiku, light verse, traditional. Buys 35-50 poems/year. Submit maximum 1 poems. Length: 3-16 lines. **Pays $7 (CAD) flat fee.**

FILLERS Seeking anecdotes, facts, gags to be illustrated by a cartoonist, and short humor. **Buys 1-12 mss/year.** Length: 25-250 words. **Pays $5 flat (CAD) fee.**

TIPS "Be open to writing all kinds of fiction. Call us Doug or Anisa, not 'To whom it may concern.' Writing is serious and fun. Edit your work to the best of your ability and write like you love it."

REDACTIONS: POETRY, POETICS, & PROSE

604 N. 31st Ave., Apt. D-2, Hattiesburg MS 39401. **E-mail:** redactionspoetry@yahoo.com (poetry and essays on poetry); redationsprose@yahoo.com (creative prose). **Website:** www.redactions.com. *Redactions*, released every 9 months, covers poems, reviews of new books of poems, translations, manifestos, interviews, essays concerning poetry, poetics, poetry movements, or concerning a specific poet or a group of poets; and anything dealing with poetry. "We now also publish fiction and creative nonfiction." No kill fee. Accepts queries by e-mail. Accepts simultaneous submissions. Responds in 3 months.

NONFICTION Needs essays on poetics, reviews of new books of poems, interviews with poets, art, translation. We are also now accepting creative nonfiction.

REPRINTS "Please mention first publication in *Redactions*."

POETRY "Anything dealing with poetry."

TIPS "We only accept submissions by e-mail. We read submissions throughout the year. E-mail us and attach submission into one Word, Wordpad, Notepad, .rtf, or .txt document, or place in the body of an e-mail. Include brief bio and your snail-mail address. Query after 90 days if you haven't heard from us. See website for full guidelines for each genre, including artwork."

RED WHEELBARROW

De Anza College, 21250 Stevens Creek Blvd., Cupertino CA 95014. **Website:** www.deanza.edu/redwheelbarrow. **98% freelance written.** Estab. 1976 as *Bottomfish*; 2000 as *Red Wheelbarrow*. Circ. 500. Byline given. No kill fee. Publishes ms an average of 2-4 months after acceptance. Accepts queries by mail, e-mail. Accepts simultaneous submissions. Responds in 2 weeks to queries; in 2-4 months to mss. Sample copy: $10 ($2.50 for back issues). Guidelines available online.

"We seek to publish a diverse range of styles and voices from around the country and the world." Publishes a student edition and a national edition.

NONFICTION Needs creative nonfiction, personal experience. **Buys 30-50 mss/year.** Send complete ms by mail (include SASE) or e-mail. Length: up to 4,000 words.

PHOTOS State availability. Reviews 5x7 prints, GIF/JPEG files.

FICTION Send complete ms by mail (include SASE) or e-mail. Length: up to 4,000 words.

POETRY Needs avant-garde, free verse, haiku, traditional. Send up to 5 poems by mail (include SASE) or e-mail. Does not want excessively abstract or excessively sentimental poetry.

TIPS "Write freely, rewrite carefully. Resist clichés and stereotypes. We are not affiliated with Red Wheelbarrow Press or any similarly named publication.

THE RIALTO

P.O. Box 309, Alysham, Norwich NR11 6LN England. **E-mail:** info@therialto.co.uk. **Website:** www.therialto.co.uk. **Contact:** Michael Mackmin, editor. *The Rialto*, published 3 times/year, seeks to publish the best new poems by established and beginning poets. Seeks excellence and originality. Has published poetry by Alice Fulton, Jenny Joseph, Les Murray, George Szirtes, Philip Gross, and Ruth Padel. Estab. 1984. Publishes ms 5 months after acceptance. Responds in 3-4 months.

The Rialto is 64 pages, A4, with full-color cover. Receives about 12,000 poems/year, accepts about 1%. Press run is 1,500. Single copy: £7.50; subscription: £23 (prices listed are for U.S. and Canada). Make checks payable to *The Rialto*. Checks in sterling only. Online payment also available on website.

POETRY Submit up to 6 poems at a time with a SASE. Does not accept e-mail submissions. **Pays £20/poem on publication.**

TIPS "*The Rialto* has recently commenced publishing first collections by poets. Please do not send book-length manuscripts. Query first." Sponsors an annual young poets competition. Details available in magazine and on website. Before submitting, "you will probably have read many poems by many poets, both living and dead. You will probably have put aside each poem you write for at least 3 weeks before considering it afresh. You will have asked yourself, 'Does it work technically?'; checked the rhythm, the rhymes (if used), and checked that each word is fresh and

CONSUMER MAGAZINES

meaningful in its context, not jaded and tired. You will hopefully have read *The Rialto*."
flash, short, and nonfiction; short drama; photography and line art. Guidelines available for SASE, by e-mail, or on website.

RIVER STYX MAGAZINE

Big River Association, 3139A Grand Blvd., Suite 203, St. Louis MO 63118. (314)533-4541. **E-mail:** bigriver@riverstyx.org. **Website:** www.riverstyx.org. **Contact:** Richard Newman, editor. Triannual magazine. "*River Styx* publishes the highest-quality fiction, poetry, interviews, essays, and visual art. We are an internationally distributed multicultural literary magazine. Mss read May-November." Estab. 1975. Byline given. Pays on publication. No kill fee. Publishes ms an average of 6 months after acceptance. Accepts queries by mail. Accepts simultaneous submissions. Responds in 6 months to mss. Sample copy: $9. Guidelines available online.

Work published in *River Styx* has been selected for inclusion in past volumes of *New Stories from the South, The Best American Poetry, Best New Poets, New Poetry from the Midwest*, and *The Pushcart Prize Anthology*.

NONFICTION Needs essays, interview. **Buys 2-5 mss/year.** Send complete ms. **Pays 2 contributor's copies, plus one-year subscription. Cash payment as funds permit.**

PHOTOS Send photos. Reviews 5x7 or 8x10 b&w and color prints and slides. Pays 2 contributor copies, plus one-year subscription. Cash payment as funds permit.

FICTION Recently published work by George Singleton, Philip Graham, Katherine Min, Richard Burgin, Nancy Zafris, Jacob Appel, and Eric Shade. Needs ethnic, experimental, mainstream, short stories, literary. No genre fiction, less thinly veiled autobiography. **Buys 6-9 mss/year.** Send complete ms with SASE. Length: no more than 23-30 manuscript pages. **Pays 2 contributor copies, plus one-year subscription. Cash payment as funds permit.**

POETRY Needs avant-garde, free verse. Wants "excellent poetry—original, energetic, musical, and accessible." Does not want "chopped prose or opaque poetry that isn't about anything." Has published poetry by Jennifer Perrine, Dorianne Laux, Ted Kooser, Louis Simpson, Molly Peacock, Marilyn Hacker, Yusef Komunyakaa, Andrew Hudgins, and Catie Rosemurgy. Include SASE. No religious poetry. Buys 40-50 poems/year. Submit maximum 3-5 poems. **Pays 2 contributor copies, plus one-year subscription. Cash payment as funds permit.**

ROANOKE REVIEW

Roanoke College, 221 College Lane, Salem VA 24153-3794. **E-mail:** review@roanoke.edu. **Website:** http://roanokereview.wordpress.com. **Contact:** Paul Hanstedt, editor. "The *Roanoke Review* is an online literary journal that is dedicated to publishing accessible fiction, nonfiction, and poetry that is smartly written. Humor is encouraged; humility as well." Estab. 1967. Pays on publication for one-time rights. Publishes ms 6-9 months after acceptance. Responds in 1 month to queries; 6 months to mss; 3-6 months to poetry. Sometimes comments on rejected mss. Guidelines available on website.

Has published work by Siobhan Fallon, Jacob M. Appel, and JoeAnn Hart.

FICTION Receives 150 unsolicited mss/month. Accepts 30 mss/year. Does not read mss February 1-September 1. Publishes 1-5 new writers/year. Needs feminist, gay, humor/satire, lesbian, literary, mainstream, regional. Submit via Submittable, or send SASE for return of ms, or send a disposable copy of ms and #10 SASE for reply only. Length: 1,000-5,000 words. Average length: 3,000 words. **Pays $10-50/story (when budget allows).**

POETRY Submit original typed mss; no photocopies. **Pays "cash when budget allows."**

TIPS "Pay attention to sentence-level writing—verbs, metaphors, concrete images. Don't forget, though, that plot and character keep us reading. We're looking for stuff that breaks the MFA story style. Be real. Know rhythm. Concentrate on strong images."

ROOM

P.O. Box 46160, Station D, Vancouver BC V6J 5G5 Canada. **E-mail:** contactus@roommagazine.com. **Website:** www.roommagazine.com. "*Room* is Canada's oldest literary journal by, for, and about women. Published quarterly by a group of volunteers based in Vancouver, *Room* showcases fiction, poetry, reviews, art work, interviews, and profiles about the female experience. Many of our contributors are at the beginning of their writing careers, looking for an opportunity to get published for the first time. Some later go on to great acclaim. *Room* is a space where women can speak, connect, and showcase their creativity. Each quarter we publish original, thought-provoking works that reflect women's strength, sensuality, vulnerability, and wit." Estab. 1975. Circ. 1,000. Byline given. Pays on publication. No kill fee. Accepts queries by online submission form. Responds in 6 months. Sample copy: $13 or online at website.

Room is digest-sized; illustrations, photos. Press run is 1,000 (420 subscribers, 50-100 libraries, 350 shelf sales).

NONFICTION Buys 1-2 mss/year. Submit complete ms via online submissions manager. Length: up to 3,500 words. **Pays $50-120 (Canadian), 2 contributor's copies, and a one-year subscription.**

FICTION Accepts literature that illustrates the female experience—short stories, creative nonfiction, poetry—by, for and about women. Submit complete ms via online submissions manager. **Pays $50-120 (Canadian), 2 contributor's copies, and a one-year subscription.**

POETRY *Room* uses "poetry by and about women, written from a feminist perspective. Nothing simplistic, clichéd. We prefer to receive up to 5 poems at a time, so we can select a pair or group." Submit via online submissions manager. Pays $50-120 (Canadian), 2 contributor's copies, and a one-year subscription.

SALT HILL JOURNAL

Creative Writing Program, Syracuse University, English Deptartment, 401 Hall of Languages, Syracuse University, Syracuse NY 13244. **Website:** salthilljournal.net. **Contact:** Emma DeMilta and Jessica Poli, editors. "*Salt Hill* is published through Syracuse University's Creative Writing MFA program. We strive to publish a mix of the best contemporary and emerging talent in poetry, fiction, and nonfiction. Your work, if accepted, would appear in a long tradition of exceptional contributors, including Steve Almond, Mary Caponegro, Kim Chinquee, Edwidge Danticat, Denise Duhamel, Brian Evenson, B.H. Fairchild, Mary Gaitskill, Terrance Hayes, Bob Hicok, Laura Kasischke, Etgar Keret, Phil Lamarche, Dorianne Laux, Maurice Manning, Karyna McGlynn, Ander Monson, David Ohle, Lucia Perillo, Tomaž Šalamun, Zachary Schomburg, Christine Schutt, David Shields, Charles Simic, Patricia Smith, Dara Wier, and Raúl Zurita among many others." No kill fee. Accepts queries by online submission form. Accepts simultaneous submissions. Guidelines available online.

Only accepts submissions by online submission form; does not accept unsolicited e-mail submissions.

NONFICTION Contact: salthillnonfiction@gmail.com. Needs essays, interview, reviews. Special issues: "We accept a wide-range of creative nonfictions. Currently, we are especially interested in memoir and essay forms." Does not want articles or reports. Submit via online submissions manager; contact nonfiction editor via e-mail for retractions and queries only. Length: up to 30 pages.

PHOTOS Contact: salthillart@gmail.com. "We are interested in unpublished 2D art—drawings, paintings, photography, mixed media, documentation of 3D art, typographic art, diagrams, maps, etc. We are especially interested in b&w work at the moment, but welcome art of all colors, shapes, and stripes. Please e-mail low-res jpegs of your work, or links to specific pieces (not a general website) you would like to submit. Please include a cover letter with a short biography, as well as a title/image list for all work submitted."

FICTION Contact: salthillfiction@gmail.com. Submit via online submissions manager; contact fiction editor via e-mail for retractions and queries only. Length: up to 30 pages.

POETRY Contact: salthillpoetry@gmail.com. Submit up to 5 poems via online submissions manager; contact poetry editor via e-mail for retractions and queries only.

SANTA CLARA REVIEW

Santa Clara Review, Santa Clara University, 500 El Camino Real, Box 3212, Santa Clara CA 95053-3212. (408)554-4484. **E-mail:** santaclarareview@gmail.com. **Website:** www.santaclarareview.com. "*SCR* is one of the oldest literary publications in the West. Entirely student-run by undergraduates at Santa Clara University, the magazine draws upon submissions from SCU affiliates as well as contributors from around the globe. The magazine is published in February and May each year. In addition to publishing the magazine, the Review staff organizes a writing practicum, open mic nights, and retreats for writers and artists, and hosts guest readers. Our printed magazine is also available to view free online. For contacts, queries, and general info, visit our website. *SCR* accepts submissions year round. Estab. 1869. No kill fee. Publishes ms an average of 2 months after acceptance. Accepts queries by online submission form. Guidelines online.

NONFICTION Submit via online submissions manager or mail (include SASE for return of ms). Length: up to 5,000 words.

FICTION Submit via online submissions manager or mail (include SASE for return of ms). Length: up to 5,000 words.

POETRY Submit up to 3 poems via online submissions manager or mail (include SASE for return of ms). Length: up to 10 pages.

THE SAVAGE KICK LITERARY MAGAZINE

Murder Slim Press, 29 Alpha Rd., Gorleston Norfolk NR31 0EQ United Kingdom. **E-mail:** moonshine@murderslim.com. **Website:** www.murderslim.com. **100% freelance written.** Semiannual magazine. "*Savage Kick* primarily deals with viewpoints outside the mainstream: honest emotions told in a raw, simplistic way. It is recommended that you are very familiar with the *SK* style before submitting. Ensure you have a distinctive voice and story to tell." Estab. 2005. Circ. 500+. Byline given. Pays on acceptance. Publishes ms an average of up to 2 months after acceptance. Accepts queries by mail, e-mail. Accepts simultaneous submissions. Responds in 7-10 days to queries. Guidelines free.

NONFICTION Needs interview, personal experience. **Buys 10-20 mss/year.** Send complete ms. Length: 500-3,000 words. **Pays $25-35.**

COLUMNS/DEPARTMENTS Buys up to 4 mss/year. Query. **Pays $25-35.**

FICTION Needs mystery, slice-of-life vignettes, crime. "Real-life stories are preferred, unless the work is distinctively extreme within the crime genre. No poetry of any kind, no mainstream fiction, Oprah-style fiction, Internet/chat language, teen issues, excessive Shakespearean language, surrealism, overworked irony, or genre fiction (horror, fantasy, science fiction, western, erotica, etc.)." **Buys 10-25 mss/year.** Send complete ms. Length: 500-6,000 words. **Pays $35.**

SENECA REVIEW

Hobart and William Smith Colleges, Geneva NY 14456. (315)781-3392. **E-mail:** senecareview@hws.edu. **Website:** www.hws.edu/academics/senecareview/index.aspx. Semiannual magazine publishing mss of poetry, translations, essays on contemporary poetry, and lyric essays (creative nonfiction that borders on poetry). The editors have special interest in translations of contemporary poetry from around the world. Publisher of numerous laureates and award-winning poets, *Seneca Review* also publishes emerging writers and is always open to new, innovative work. Poems from *SR* are regularly honored by inclusion in *The Best American Poetry* and *Pushcart Prize* anthologies. Distributed internationally. No kill fee. Accepts queries by mail or via Submittable. Responds in 3 months. Guidelines available online. E-mail questions to senecareview@hws.edu.

Reading period is September 1-May 1.

NONFICTION Needs essays, translation. Special issues: Past special features include Irish women's poetry; Israeli women's poetry; Polish, Catalan, and Albanian poetry; excerpts from the notebooks of 32 contemporary American poets, an issue of essays devoted to Hayden Carruth; an issue dedicated to editor Deborah Tall; The Lyric Body, Anthology of Poets, Essayists and Artists Intimately Address Difference and Disability. Length: up to 20 pages.

POETRY Submit maximum 3-5 poems.

THE SEWANEE REVIEW

University of the South, 735 University Ave., Sewanee TN 37383-1000. (931)598-1000. **E-mail:** sreview@sewanee.edu. **Website:** review.sewanee.edu. **Contact:** George Core, editor. *The Sewanee Review* is America's oldest continuously published literary quarterly. Publishes original fiction, poetry, essays on literary and related subjects, and book reviews for well-educated readers who appreciate good American and English literature. Only erudite work representing depth of knowledge and skill of expression is published. Estab. 1892. Circ. 2,200. Pays on publication. Responds in 6-8 weeks to mss. Sample copy for $8.50 ($9.50 outside U.S.). Guidelines online.

Does not read mss June 1-August 31.

NONFICTION Submit complete ms by mail; no electronic submissions. Queries accepted but not preferred. Rarely accepts unsolicited reviews. Length: up to 7,500 words. **Pays $10-12/printed page, plus 2 contributor's copies.**

FICTION Needs literary, contemporary. No erotica, science fiction, fantasy, or excessively violent or profane material. **Buys 10-15 mss/year.** Submit complete ms by mail; no electronic submissions. Length: 3,500-7,500 words. No short-short stories. **Pays $10-12/printed page, plus 2 contributor's copies.**

POETRY Submit up to 6 poems by postal mail. Keep in mind that for each poem published in *The Sewanee Review*, approximately 250 poems are considered. Length: up to 40 lines/poem. **Pays $2.50/line, plus 2 contributor's copies (and reduced price for additional copies).**

SHEARSMAN

Shearsman Books Ltd, Shearsman, 50 Westons Hill Drive, Emersons Green, Bristol Bristol BS16 7DF England. **E-mail:** editor@shearsman.com. **Website:** www.shearsman.com/pages/magazine/home.html. Semiannual magazine and website covering contemporary poetry. "We are inclined toward the more exploratory end of the current spectrum. Notwithstanding this, however, quality work of a more conservative kind will always be considered seriously, provided that the work is well written. I always look for some rigour in the work, though I will be more forgiving of failure in this regard if the writer is trying to push out the boundaries." Estab. 1981. No kill fee. Accepts queries by mail, e-mail. Guidelines available online.

POETRY Avoid sending attachments with your e-mails unless they are in PDF format. Include SASE; no IRCs. No sloppy writing of any kind.

TIPS "We no longer read through the year. Our reading window for magazines is March 1-March 31 for the October issue and September 1-September 30 for the April issue; this window is for magazine submissions only. See guidelines online."

SHENANDOAH

Washington and Lee University, Lexington VA 24450. (540)458-8908. **Fax:** (540)458-8461. **E-mail:** shenandoah@wlu.edu. **Website:** shenandoahliterary.org. **Contact:** R.T. Smith, editor. Semiannual digital-only literary journal. For over half a century, *Shenandoah* has been publishing splendid poems, stories, essays, and reviews which display passionate understanding, formal accomplishment, and serious mischief. Estab. 1950. Circ. 2,000. Byline given. Pays on publication. No kill fee. Publishes ms an average of 10 months after acceptance. Responds in 4-6 weeks to mss. Sample copy: $12. Guidelines online.

NONFICTION Needs essays, interview, reviews. **Buys 6 mss/year.** Send complete ms via online submissions manager or postal mail. Query for reviews and interviews. Length: up to 20 pages. **Pays $25/page ($250 maximum), one-year subscription, and 1 contributor's copy.**

FICTION Needs mainstream, novel excerpts. No sloppy, hasty, slight fiction. **Buys 15 mss/year.** Send complete ms via online submissions manager or postal mail. Length: up to 20 pages. **Pays $25/page ($250 maximum), one-year subscription, and 1 contributor's copy.**

POETRY Submit 3-5 poems via online submissions manager or postal mail. No inspirational, confessional poetry. Buys 70 poems/year. Submit maximum 5 poems. **Pays $2.50/line, one-year subscription, and 1 contributor's copy.**

SHORT STUFF

Bowman Publications, 2001 I St., #5, Fairbury NE 68352. (402)587-5003. **E-mail:** shortstf89@aol.com. **98% freelance written.** Bimonthly magazine publishing short fiction that is holiday oriented. "We are perhaps an enigma in that we publish only clean stories in any genre. We'll tackle any subject but don't allow obscene language or pornographic description. Our magazine is for grown-ups, not X-rated 'adult' fare." Estab. 1989. Circ. 5,000. Byline given. Payment and contract upon publication. Editorial lead time 3 months. Submit seasonal material 3 months in advance. Responds in 6 months to mss. Sample copy for 9x12 SAE with 5 first-class (49¢) stamps. Guidelines for #10 SASE.

NONFICTION Needs humor. Special issues: "We are holiday oriented, and each issue reflects the appropriate holidays." Issues are Valentine's (February/March); Easter (April/May); Mom's and Dad's (June/July); Americana (August/September); Halloween (October/November); and Holiday (December/January). **Buys 30 mss/year.** Send complete ms. Include cover letter about the author and synopsis of the story. Length: 500-1,500 words. **Payment varies.**

PHOTOS Send photos. Identification of subjects required. Offers no additional payment for photos accepted with ms.

FICTION Receives 500 unsolicited mss/month. Accepts 9-12 mss/issue; 76 mss/year. Has published work by Bill Hallstead, Dede Hammond, and Skye Gibbons. Needs adventure, historical, humorous, mainstream, mystery, romance, science fiction, (seldom), suspense, western. "We want to see more humor—not essay format—real stories with humor; 1,000-word mysteries, modern lifestyles. The 1,000-word pieces have the best chance of publication. No erotica; nothing morbid or pornographic. **Buys 144 mss/year.** Send complete ms. Length: 500-1,500 words. **Payment varies.**

FILLERS Needs anecdotes, short humor. **Buys 200 mss/year.** Length: 20-500 words. **Filler pays variable amount.**

TIPS "We are holiday oriented; mark on outside of envelope if story is for Easter, Mother's Day, etc. We receive 500 mss each month. This is up about 200%. Because of this, I implore writers to send 1 ms at a time. I would not use stories from the same author more than once an issue, and this means I might keep the others too long. Please don't e-mail your stories! If you have an e-mail address, please include that with the cover letter so we can contact you. If no SASE, we destroy the ms."

SLIPSTREAM

P.O. Box 2071, Dept. W-1, Niagara Falls NY 14301. **E-mail:** editors@slipstreampress.org. **Website:** www.slipstreampress.org/index.html. **Contact:** Dan Sicoli, co-editor. Annual magazine covering poetry only, b&w photos, drawings, and illustrations; a yearly anthology of some of the best poetry and fiction you'll find today in the American small press. Estab. 1980. No kill fee. Accepts queries by mail. Accepts simultaneous submissions. Guidelines available online.

Does not accept e-mail submissions.

PHOTOS It's better to send scans or photocopies of artwork rather than originals.

POETRY Submit poetry via mail or online submission manager, Submittable. Prefers contemporary urban themes—writing from the grit that is not afraid to bark or bite. Shies away from pastoral, religious, and rhyming verse. **Chapbook Contest prize is $1,000 plus 50 professionally printed copies of your chapbook.**

SNOW MONKEY

Ravenna Press, **E-mail:** snowmonkey.editor@comcast.net. **Website:** www.ravennapress.com/snowmonkey/. Online journal covering original unpublished poems and micro-prose 10 times/year. Seeks writing "that's like footprints of the Langur monkeys left at 11,000 feet on Poon Hill, Nepal. Open to most themes." No kill fee. Accepts queries by e-mail. Accepts simultaneous submissions. Responds in 8-10 weeks to mss.

FICTION Up to 10 writers are featured in monthly posting from September through June. Length: up to 500 words. **Does not pay.**

POETRY Submit via e-mail. **Does not pay.**

TIPS "Send submissions as text only in the body of your e-mail. Include your last name in the subject line. We do not currently use bios, but we love to read them."

SNOWY EGRET

The Fair Press, P.O. Box 9265, Terre Haute IN 47808. **Website:** www.snowyegret.net. *Snowy Egret*, published in spring and autumn, specializes in work that is nature-oriented. Features fiction, nonfiction, artwork, and poetry. Estab. 1922. Circ. 400. Pays on publication. Accepts queries by mail. Accepts simultaneous submissions. Responds in 2 months to mss. Sample: $8; subscription: $15/year, $25 for 2 years. Guidelines online.

Snowy Egret is 60 pages, magazine-sized, offset-printed, saddle-stapled.

NONFICTION Needs essays. Special issues: Looking for articles, essays, or stories that celebrate the richness and beauty of nature, encourage a love and respect for the natural world, and examine the variety of ways, both positive and negative, through which human beings interact with the environment. Its readers are typically well-informed, well-educated humanists and naturalists with strong personal affinities to the physical world, natural phenomena, and living things. Send complete ms with SASE. Cover letter optional. **Pays $2/page and 2 contributor's copies.**

FICTION Publishes works which celebrate the abundance and beauty of nature and examine the variety of ways in which human beings interact with landscapes and living things. Wants nature writing from literary, artistic, psychological, philosophical, and historical perspectives. No genre fiction, e.g., horror, western, romance, etc. Send complete ms with SASE. Cover letter optional: do not query. **Pays $2/page and 2 contributor's copies.**

POETRY Wants poetry that celebrates the abundance and beauty of nature or explores the interconnections between nature and the human psyche. Has published poetry by Conrad Hilberry, Lyn Lifshin, Gayle Eleanor, James Armstrong, and Patricia Hooper. Submit poems with SASE. Cover letter optional: do not query. **Pays $4/poem or $4/page and 2 contributor's copies.**

TIPS Looks for "honest, freshly detailed pieces with plenty of description and/or dialogue which will allow the reader to identify with the characters and step into the setting; fiction in which nature affects character development and the outcome of the story."

SOUTHERN HUMANITIES REVIEW

Auburn University, 9088 Haley Center, Auburn University AL 36849. (334)844-9088. **Fax:** (334)844-9027. **E-mail:** shr@auburn.edu. **Website:** www.southernhumanitiesreview.com. **Contact:** Aaron Alford, managing editor. *Southern Humanities Review* publishes fiction, nonfiction, and poetry. Estab. 1967. Circ. approximately 700. Accepts simultaneous submissions. Guidelines online.

THE SOUTHERN REVIEW

338 Johnston Hall, Louisiana State University, Baton Rouge LA 70803. (225)578-5108. **Fax:** (225)578-5098. **E-mail:** southernreview@lsu.edu. **Website:** thesouthernreview.org. **Contact:** Jessica Faust, co-editor and poetry editor; Emily Nemens, co-editor and prose editor. **100% freelance written. Works with a moderate number of new/unpublished writers each year; reads unsolicited mss.** Quarterly magazine with emphasis on contemporary literature in the U.S. and abroad. "*The Southern Review* is one of the nation's premiere literary journals. Hailed by *Time* as 'superior to any other journal in the English language,' we have made literary history since our founding in 1935. We publish a diverse array of fiction, nonfiction, and poetry by the country's—and the world's—most respected contemporary writers." Reading period: September1-December 1. All mss submitted during outside the reading period will be recycled. Estab. 1935. Circ. 2,900. Byline given. Pays on publication. No kill fee. Publishes ms an average of 6 months after acceptance. Accepts queries by mail. Does not accept previously published work.Accepts simultaneous submissions. Responds in 6 months. Sample copy: $12. Guidelines available online.

NONFICTION Needs essays. **Buys 25 mss/year.** Submit ms by mail. Length: up to 8,000 words. **Pays $25/printed page (max $200), 2 contributor's copies, and one-year subscription.**

FICTION Wants short stories of lasting literary merit, with emphasis on style and technique; novel excerpts. "We emphasize style and substantial content. No mystery, fantasy, or religious mss." Submit 1 ms at a time by mail. "We rarely publish work that is longer than 8,000 words. We consider novel excerpts if they stand alone." Length: up to 8,000 words. **Pays $25/printed page (max $200), 2 contributor's copies, and one-year subscription.**

POETRY Submit poems by mail. Submit maximum 5 poems. Length: 1-4 pages. **Pays $25/printed page (max $125); 2 contributor's copies, and one-year subscription.**

TIPS "Careful attention to craftsmanship and technique combined with a developed sense of the creation of story will always make us pay attention."

THE SOW'S EAR POETRY REVIEW

308 Greenfield Ave., Winchester VA 22602. **E-mail:** sowsearpoetry@yahoo.com; rglesman@gmail.com;. **Website:** www.sows-ear.kitenet.net. **Contact:** Kristin Camitta Zimet, editor; Robert G. Lesman, managing editor. **100% freelance written.** Quarterly magazine. *The Sow's Ear* prints fine poetry of all styles and lengths, complemented by b&w art. Also welcomes reviews, interviews, and essays related to poetry. Open to group submissions. "Crossover" section features poetry married to any other art form, including prose, music, and visual media. Estab. 1988. Circ. 700. Publishes ms an average of 1-6 months after acceptance. Editorial lead time 1-6 months. Submit seasonal material 3 months in advance. Accepts queries by mail, e-mail. Accepts simultaneous submissions. Responds in 2 weeks to queries. Responds in 3 months to mss. Sample copy for $8. Guidelines available for SASE, by e-mail, or on website.

NONFICTION Needs essays related to poetry, interviews of poets, reviews of poetry books. Query. Length: 1,000-3,000 words.

PHOTOS Model releases required. Reviews prints, TIFF/JPEG files. Offers no additional payment for photos accepted with ms.

COLUMNS/DEPARTMENTS Review of poetry book published within a year (1,000-3,000 words); interview with a poet; essay related to poetry. Query.

POETRY Needs avant-garde, free verse, haiku, light verse, traditional. Features groups of poets and "Crossovers" combining poetry with another art form. Considers simultaneous submissions "if you tell us promptly when work is accepted elsewhere"; no previously published poems, although will consider poems from chapbooks if they were never published in a magazine. Previously published poems may be included in Crossover if rights are cleared. No e-mail submissions, except for poets outside the US; postal submissions only. Include brief bio and SASE. Pays 2 contributor's copies. Inquire about reviews, interviews, and essays. Contest/Award offerings: *The Sow's*

Ear Poetry Competition and *The Sow's Ear* Chapbook Contest. Open to any style or length. Buys 100 poems/year. Submit maximum 5 poems. No limits on line length.

TIPS "We like work that is carefully crafted, keenly felt, and freshly perceived. We respond to poems with voice, a sense of place, delight in language, and a meaning that unfolds. We look for prose that opens new dimensions to appreciating poetry."

STAND MAGAZINE

Leeds University, School of English, Leeds LS2 9JT United Kingdom. (44)(113)233-4794. **Fax:** (44) (113)233-2791. **E-mail:** stand@leeds.ac.uk. **Website:** www.standmagazine.org. North American submissions: David Latané, Stand Magazine, Dept. of English, Virginia Commonwealth University, Richmond VA 23284. **Contact:** Jon Glover, managing editor. "*Stand Magazine* is concerned with what happens when cultures and literatures meet, with translation in its many guises, with the mechanics of language, with the processes by which the policy receives or disables its cultural makers. *Stand* promotes debate of issues that are of radical concern to the intellectual community worldwide. U.S. submissions can be made through the Virginia office (see separate listing). Estab. 1952. Accepts queries by mail. Guidelines online.

Does not accept e-mail submissions.

FICTION No genre fiction. Length: up to 3,000 words.

POETRY Submit through postal mail only. Include SASE.

THE STORYTELLER

2441 Washington Rd., Maynard AR 72444. (870)647-2137. **E-mail:** storytellermag1@yahoo.com. **Website:** www.thestorytellermagazine.com. **Contact:** Regina Williams, editor. **95% freelance written**. Quarterly magazine featuring short stories, essays, nonfiction, and poetry. Estab. 1996. Circ. 700. Byline given. Publishes ms an average of 1-12 months after acceptance. Editorial lead time 6 months. Submit seasonal material 4 months in advance. Accepts queries by mail, e-mail. Accepts simultaneous submissions. Responds in 1 week to queries; in 2 weeks to mss. Guidelines online.

NONFICTION Needs essays, general interest, historical, how-to, humor, inspirational, opinion, personal experience. Does not want anything graphic, pornographic, or based on *Star Trek* or *Star Wars*. Be original with all your work. "We don't want 'poor me' articles or stories about how life is hard. We all understand that, but give us something at the end where we can see that things are looking up." **Buys 80 mss/year.** Send complete ms with cover letter and SASE.

FICTION Needs adventure, fantasy, historical, horror, humorous, mainstream, mystery, romance, science fiction, slice-of-life vignettes, suspense, western. Does not want pornography, erotica, horror, graphic language or violence, children's stories, or anything deemed racial or biased toward any religion, race, or moral preference. **Buys 180 mss/year.** Send complete ms with cover letter and SASE.

POETRY Needs avant-garde, free verse, haiku, light verse, traditional. Submit up to 3 poems with SASE. Does not want long rambling. Length: up to 40 lines/poem.

TIPS "*The Storyteller* is one of the best places you will find to submit your work, especially new writers. Our best advice, be professional. You have one chance to make a good impression. Don't blow it by being unprofessional."

THE STRAND MAGAZINE

P.O. Box 1418, Birmingham MI 48012-1418. (800)300-6652. **Fax:** (248)874-1046. **E-mail:** strandmag@strandmag.com. **Website:** www.strandmag.com. Quarterly magazine covering mysteries, short stories, essays, book reviews. "After an absence of nearly half a century, the magazine known to millions for bringing Sir Arthur Conan Doyle's ingenious detective, Sherlock Holmes, to the world has once again appeared on the literary scene. First launched in 1891, *The Strand* included in its pages the works of some of the greatest writers of the 20th century: Agatha Christie, Dorothy Sayers, Margery Allingham, W. Somerset Maugham, Graham Greene, P.G. Wodehouse, H.G. Wells, Aldous Huxley, and many others. In 1950, economic difficulties in England caused a drop in circulation which forced the magazine to cease publication." Estab. 1998. Circ. 50,000. Byline given. Pays on acceptance. No kill fee. Publishes ms an average of 4 months after acceptance. Accepts queries by e-mail. Responds in 1 month to queries; in 4-10 months to mss. Sample copy: $10. Guidelines online.

FICTION "We are interested in mysteries, detective stories, tales of terror and the supernatural as well as short stories. Stories can be set in any time or place, provided they are well written, the plots interesting and well thought." Occasionally accepts short shorts and short novellas. Needs horror, humorous, mystery, detective stories, suspense. We are not interested in submissions with any sexual content. Submit complete ms by postal mail. Include SASE. No e-mail submissions. Length: 2,000-6,000 words. **Pays $25-150.**

TIPS "No gratuitous violence, sexual content, or explicit language, please."

$$$ SUBTROPICS

University of Florida, P.O. Box 112075, 4008 Turlington Hall, Gainesville FL 32611-2075. **E-mail:** subtropics@english.ufl.edu. **Website:** www.english.ufl.edu/subtropics. **Contact:** David Leavitt, editor. **100% freelance written.** Magazine published twice/year through the University of Florida's English department. *Subtropics* seeks to publish the best literary fiction, essays, and poetry being written today, both by established and emerging authors. Will consider works of fiction of any length, from short shorts to novellas and self-contained novel excerpts. Gives the same latitude to essays. Appreciates work in translation and, from time to time, republishes important and compelling stories, essays, and poems that have lapsed out of print by writers no longer living. Member: CLMP. Estab. 2005. Circ. 1,500. Byline given. Pays on acceptance for prose; pays on publication of the issue preceding the issue in which the author's work will appear for poetry. Publishes ms an average of 6 months after acceptance. Responds in 1 month to queries and mss. Rarely comments on/critiques rejected mss Sample copy: $12.95. Guidelines online.

Literary magazine/journal: 9x6, 160 pages. Includes photographs. Submissions accepted from September 1-April 15.

NONFICTION Needs essays, literary nonfiction. No book reviews. **Buys 4-5 mss/year.** Send complete ms via online submissions manager. Length: up to 15,000 words. Average length: 5,000 words. **Pays $1,000.**

FICTION Does not read May 1-August 31. Agented fiction 33%. **Publishes 1-2 new writers/year.** Has published John Barth, Ariel Dorfman, Tony D'Souza, Allan Gurganus, Frances Hwang, Kuzhali Manickavel, Eileen Pollack, Padgett Powell, Nancy Reisman, Jarret Rosenblatt, Joanna Scott, and Olga Slavnikova. Needs literary fiction, short shorts. No genre fiction. **Buys 10-12 mss/year.** Submit complete ms via online submissions manager. Length: up to 15,000 words. Average length: 5,000 words. Average length of short shorts: 400 words. **Pays $500 for short shorts; $1,000 for full stories; 2 contributor's copies.**

POETRY Submit up to 4 poems via online submissions manager. Buys 50 poems/year. **Pays $100 per poem.**

TIPS "We publish longer works of fiction, including novellas and excerpts from forthcoming novels. Each issue includes a short-short story of about 250 words on the back cover. We are also interested in publishing works in translation for the magazine's English-speaking audience."

$ TAMPA REVIEW

University of Tampa Press, 401 W. Kennedy Blvd., Tampa FL 33606. (813)253-6266. **Fax:** (813)258-7593. **E-mail:** utpress@ut.edu. **Website:** www.ut.edu/tampareview. **Contact:** Richard Mathews, editor; Elizabeth Winston, nonfiction editor; Yuly Restrepo and Andrew Plattner, fiction editors; Erica Dawson, poetry editor. Semiannual magazine published in hardback format. An international literary journal publishing art and literature from Florida and Tampa Bay as well as new work and translations from throughout the world. Estab. 1988. Circ. 700. Byline given. Pays on publication. No kill fee. Publishes ms an average of 10 months after acceptance. Editorial lead time 18 months. Accepts queries by mail. Responds in 5 months to mss. Sample copy: $7. Guidelines available online.

NONFICTION Needs general interest, interview, personal experience, creative nonfiction. No how-to articles, fads, journalistic reprise, etc. **Buys 6 mss/year.** Send complete ms. Length: 250-7,500 words. **Pays $10/printed page.**

PHOTOS State availability. Captions, identification of subjects required. Reviews contact sheets, negatives, transparencies, prints, digital files. Offers $10/photo.

FICTION Needs ethnic, experimental, fantasy, historical, mainstream, literary. "We are far more interested in quality than in genre. Nothing sentimental as opposed to genuinely moving, nor self-conscious style at the expense of human truth." **Buys 6 mss/year.** Send complete ms. Include brief bio. Length: 200-5,000 words. **Pays $10/printed page.**

POETRY Needs avant-garde, free verse, haiku, light verse, traditional. No greeting card verse, hackneyed, sing-song, rhyme-for-the-sake-of-rhyme. Buys 45 poems/year. Submit maximum 10 poems. Length: 2-225 lines.

TIPS "Send a clear cover letter stating previous experience or background. Our editorial staff considers submissions between September and December for publication in the following year."

THEMA

Thema Literary Society, P.O. Box 8747, Metairie LA 70011-8747. **E-mail:** thema@cox.net. **Website:** http://themaliterarysociety.com. **Contact:** Gail Howard, poetry editor. **100% freelance written.** "*THEMA* is designed to stimulate creative thinking by challenging writers with unusual themes, such as 'The Box Under the Bed' and 'Put It In Your Pocket, Lillian.' Appeals to writers, teachers of creative writing, and general reading audience." Estab. 1988. Byline given. Pays on acceptance. No kill fee. Publishes ms, on average, within 6 months after acceptance. Responds in 1 week to queries. Responds in 5 months to mss. Sample $10 U.S./$15 foreign. Upcoming themes and guidelines available in magazine, for SASE, by e-mail, or on website.

THEMA is 100 pages, digest-sized professionally printed, with glossy card cover. Receives about 400 poems/year, accepts about 8%. Press run is 400 (230 subscribers, 30 libraries). Subscription: $20 U.S./$30 foreign. Has published poetry by Beverly Boyd, Elizabeth Creith, James Penha and Matthew J. Spireng.

FICTION Needs adventure, ethnic, experimental, fantasy, historical, humorous, mainstream, mystery, novel concepts, religious, science fiction, slice-of-life vignettes, suspense, western, contemporary, sports, prose poem. No erotica. Send complete ms with SASE, cover letter; include "name and address, brief introduction, specifying the intended target issue for the mss." SASE. Accepts simultaneous, multiple submissions, and reprints. Does not accept e-mailed submissions. **Pays $10-25.**

POETRY Submit up to 3 poems at a time. Include SASE. "All submissions should be typewritten on standard 812x11 paper. Submissions are accepted all year, but evaluated after specified deadlines." Specify target theme. Editor comments on submissions. "Each issue is based on an unusual premise. Please send SASE for guidelines before submitting poetry to find out the upcoming themes." Does not want "scatologic language, alternate lifestyle, explicit love poetry." **Pays $10/poem and 1 contributor's copy.**

THIRD WEDNESDAY: A LITERARY ARTS MAGAZINE

174 Greenside Up, Ypsilanti MI 48197. (734) 434-2409. **E-mail:** submissions@thirdwednesday.org; LaurenceWT@aol.com. **Website:** http://thirdwednesday.org. **Contact:** Laurence Thomas, editor. "*Third Wednesday* publishes quality (a subjective term at best) poetry, short fiction, and artwork by experienced writers and artists. We welcome work by established writers/artists, as well as those who are not yet well known but headed for prominence." Estab. 2007. Pays on acceptance. Publishes ms 3 months after acceptance. Accepts queries by e-mail. Accepts simultaneous submissions. Responds to mss in 6-8 weeks. Sometimes comments on/critiques rejected mss. Sample copy: $12; includes postage. Subscription: $40. Guidelines available for SASE, or via e-mail. Does not welcome submissions by snail mail.

FICTION Receives 5-10 mss/month. Accepts 3-5 mss/issue. Needs experimental, fantasy, humorous, mainstream, romance, literary, satire. Does not want "purely anecdotal accounts of incidents, sentimentality, pointless conclusions, or stories without some characterization or plot development." Send complete ms with cover letter. Include estimated word count and brief bio. Length: 1,500 words (maximum); average length: 1,000 words. **Pays $3 and 1 contributor's copy.**

POETRY Receives 800 poems/year. Has published poetry by Wanda Coleman, Philip Dacey, Richard Luftig, Simon Perchik, Marge Piercy, Charles Harper Webb. Submit 1-5 poems at a time. Wants "all styles and forms of poetry, from formal to experimental. Emphasis is placed on the ideas conveyed, craft and language, beauty of expression, and the picture that extends beyond the frame of the poem." Does not want "hate-filled diatribes, pornography (though eroticism is acceptable), prose masquerading as poetry, first drafts of anything." **Pays $3 and 1 contributor's copy.**

TIPS "Of course, originality is important, along with skill in writing, deft handling of language, and meaning, which goes hand in hand with beauty—whatever that is. Short fiction is specialized and difficult, so the writer should read extensively in the field."

THE THREEPENNY REVIEW

P.O. Box 9131, Berkeley CA 94709. (510)849-4545. **E-mail:** wlesser@threepennyreview.com. **Website:** www.threepennyreview.com. **Contact:** Wendy Lesser, editor. **100% freelance written. Works with small number of new/unpublished writers each year.** Quarterly tabloid. "We are a general-interest, national literary magazine with coverage of politics, the visual arts, and the performing arts." Reading period: January 1-June 30. Estab. 1980. Circ. 6,000-9,000. Byline given. Pays on acceptance. Publishes ms an average of 1 year after acceptance. Accepts queries by mail, online submission form. Responds in 1 month to queries; in 2 months to mss. Sample copy: $12, or online. Guidelines available online.

NONFICTION Needs essays, expose, historical, personal experience, book, film, theater, dance, music, and art reviews. **Buys 40 mss/year.** Send complete ms. Length: 1,500-4,000 words. **Pays $400.**

FICTION No fragmentary, sentimental fiction. **Buys 10 mss/year.** Send complete ms. Length: 800-4,000 words. **Pays $400.**

POETRY Needs free verse, traditional. No poems without capital letters or poems without a discernible subject. Buys 30 poems/year. Submit maximum 5 poems. Length: up to 100 lines/poem. **Pays $200.**

TIPS Nonfiction (political articles, memoirs, reviews) is most open to freelancers.

TIN HOUSE

McCormack Communications, P.O. Box 10500, Portland OR 97296. (503)219-0622. **E-mail:** info@tinhouse.com. **Website:** www.tinhouse.com. **Contact:** Cheston Knapp, managing editor; Holly MacArthur, founding editor. **90% freelance written.** "We are a general-interest literary quarterly. Our watchword is quality. Our audience includes people interested in literature in all its aspects, from the mundane to the exalted." Estab. 1999. Circ. 11,000. Byline given. Pays on publication. No kill fee. Publishes ms an average of 6 months after acceptance. Editorial lead time 6 months. Submit seasonal material 6 months in advance. Accepts queries by mail, online submission form. Accepts simultaneous submissions. Responds in 6 weeks to queries; in 4 months to mss. Sample copy: $15. Guidelines online.

Reading period: September 1-May 31.

NONFICTION Needs book excerpts, essays, interview, personal experience. Special issues: Check website for upcoming theme issues. Submit via online submissions manager or postal mail. Include cover letter with word count. Length: up to 10,000 words. **Pays $50-800 for assigned articles. Pays $50-500 for unsolicited articles.** Sometimes pays expenses of writers on assignment.

FICTION Needs experimental, literary, mainstream, novel concepts. Submit via online submissions manager or postal mail. Include cover letter with word count. Length up to 10,000 words. **Pays $200-800.**

POETRY Needs avant-garde, free verse, traditional. Submit via online submissions manager or postal mail. Include cover letter. Submit maximum 5 poems. **Pays $50-150.**

TRIQUARTERLY

School of Continuing Studies, Northwestern University, 339 E. Chicago Ave., Chicago IL 60611. **E-mail:** triquarterly@northwestern.edu. **Website:** www.triquarterly.org. **Contact:** Adrienne Gunn, managing editor. *TriQuarterly*, the literary magazine of Northwestern University, welcomes submissions of fiction, creative nonfiction, poetry, short drama, and hybrid work. "We also welcome short-short prose pieces." Reading period: February 16-July 15. Estab. 1964. Accepts queries by online submission form. Accepts simultaneous submissions.

NONFICTION Submit complete ms via online submissions manager. Length: up to 3,500 words. **Pays honoraria.**

FICTION Submit complete ms via online submissions manager. Length: up to 3,500 words. **Pays honoraria.**

POETRY Submit up to 6 poems via online submissions manager. **Pays honoraria.**

TIPS "We are especially interested in work that embraces the world and continues, however subtly, the ongoing global conversation about culture and society that *TriQuarterly* pursued from its beginning in 1964."

U.S. 1 WORKSHEETS

U.S. 1 Poets' Cooperative, U.S. 1 Worksheets, P.O. Box 127, Kingston NJ 08528. **E-mail:** us1poets@gmail.com. **Website:** www.us1poets.com. "Annual journal covering works from U.S. 1 Poets' Cooperative, along with the best poetry we receive. More than half comes from outside the cooperative." "*U.S. 1 Worksheets*, published annually, uses high-quality poetry and prose poems. We prefer complex, well-written work." Estab. 1972. Circ. 500. Accepts simultaneous submissions. Responds in 3-6 months to mss. Guidelines available online.

POETRY Submit up to 5 poems at a time, no more than 7 pages total. Considers simultaneous submissions if indicated; no previously published poems. "We are looking for well-crafted poetry with a focused point of view." Submit maximum 5 poems.

TIPS "Mss are accepted from April 15-June 30 and are read by rotating editors from the cooperative. Send us something unusual, something we haven't read before, but make sure it's poetry. Proofread carefully."

VALLUM: CONTEMPORARY POETRY

5038 Sherbrooke West, P.O. Box 23077, CP Vendome, Montreal Quebec H4A 1T0 Canada. (514)937-8946. **Fax:** (514)937-8946. **E-mail:** info@vallummag.com. **E-mail:** editors@vallummag.com. **Website:** www.vallummag.com. **Contact:** Joshua Auerbach and Eleni Zisimatos, editors. Poetry/fine arts magazine published twice/year. Publishes exciting interplay of poets and artists. Content for magazine is selected according to themes listed on website. Material is not filed but is returned upon request by SASE. E-mail response is preferred. Seeking exciting, unpublished, traditional or avant-garde poetry that reflects contemporary experience. Estab. 2000. Pays on publication. Sample copies available for $10. Guidelines available on website.

Vallum is 100 pages, digest sized (7x8½), digitally printed, perfect-bound, with color images on coated stock cover. Includes ads. Single copy: $12 CDN; subscription: $20/year CDN; $24 U.S. (shipping included). Make checks payable to *Vallum*.

NONFICTION Needs Also publishes reviews, interviews, essays and letters to the editor. Please send queries to editors@vallummag.com before submitting. **Pays $85 for accepted reviews or essays on poetry.**

POETRY Pays honorarium for accepted poems.

VERANDAH LITERARY & ART JOURNAL

Faculty of Arts, Deakin University, 221 Burwood Hwy., Burwood, Victoria 3125 Australia. (61)(3)9251-7134. **E-mail:** verandah@deakin.edu.au. **Website:** www.deakin.edu.au/verandah. *Verandah*, published annually in August, is a high-quality literary journal edited by professional writing students. It aims to give voice to new and innovative writers and artists. Estab. 1985. Sample: $20 AUD. Guidelines available on website.

Submission period: February 1-June 5. Has published work by Christos Tsiolka, Dorothy Porter, Seamus Heaney, Les Murray, Ed Burger, and John Muk Muk Burke. *Verandah* is 120 pages, professionally printed on glossy stock, flat-spined, with full-color glossy card cover.

NONFICTION Submit by mail or e-mail. However, electronic version of work must be available if accepted by *Verandah*. Do not submit work without the required submission form (available for download on website). Reads submissions by June 5 deadline (postmark). Length: 350-2,500 words. **Pays 1 contributor's copy, "with prizes awarded accordingly."**

FICTION Submit by mail or e-mail. However, electronic version of work must be available if accepted by *Verandah*. Do not submit work without the required submission form (available for download on website). Reads submissions by June 5 deadline (postmark). Length: 350-2,500 words. **Pays 1 contributor's copy, "with prizes awarded accordingly."**

POETRY Submit by mail or e-mail. However, electronic version of work must be available if accepted by *Verandah*. Do not submit work without the required submission form (available for download on website). Reads submissions by June 5 deadline (postmark). Length: 100 lines maximum. **Pays 1 contributor's copy, "with prizes awarded accordingly."**

VERSE

English Department, University of Richmond, Richmond VA 23173. **Website:** http://versemag.blogspot.com. **Contact:** Brian Henry, co-editor; Andrew Zawacki, co-editor. *Verse*, published 3 times/year, is an international poetry journal which also publishes interviews with poets, essays on poetry, and book reviews. Wants no specific kind; looks for high-quality, innovative poetry. Focus is not only on American poetry, but on all poetry written in English, as well as translations. Has published poetry by James Tate, John Ashbery, Barbara Guest, Gustaf Sobin, and Rae Armantrout. Estab. 1984. Accepts simultaneous submissions.

Verse is 128-416 pages, digest-sized, professionally printed, perfect-bound, with card cover. Receives about 5,000 poems/year, accepts 10%. Press run is 1,000. Single copy: $10; subscription: $18 for individuals, $39 for institutions. Sample: $6. *Verse* has a $10 reading fee for the print edition. Note that *Verse* will sometimes publish individual pieces on the website if they decide not to publish the entire body of work.

NONFICTION Interested in any nonfiction, plus translations, criticisms, interviews, journals/notebooks, etc. Submissions should be chapbook-length (20-40 pages). **Pays $10/page, $250 minimum.**

FICTION Interested in any genre. Submissions should be chapbook-length (20-40 pages). **Pays $10/page, $250 minimum.**

POETRY Submissions should be chapbook-length (20-40 pages). **Pays $10/page, $250 minimum.**

TIPS "Read widely and deeply. Avoid inundating a magazine with submissions; constant exposure will not increase your chances of getting accepted."

VESTAL REVIEW

127 Kilsyth Road, Apt. 3, Brighton MA 02135. **E-mail:** submissions@vestalreview.net. **Website:** www.vestalreview.org. Semi-annual print magazine specializing in flash fiction. Circ. 1,500. Pays on publication. No kill fee. Publishes ms an average of 6 months after acceptance. Accepts queries by e-mail. Accepts simultaneous submissions. Responds in 1 week to queries; in 6 months to mss. Guidelines online.

Vestal Review's stories have been reprinted in the *Mammoth Book of Miniscule Fiction*, *Flash Writing*, *E2Ink Anthologies*, and in the *WW Norton Anthology Flash Fiction Forward*. **Reading periods:** February-May and August-November.

FICTION Needs ethnic, fantasy, horror, humorous, mainstream. No porn, racial slurs, excessive gore, or obscenity. No children's or preachy stories. Publishes flash fiction. "We accept submissions only through our submission manager." Length: 50-500 words. **Pays 3-10¢/word and 1 contributor's copy; additional copies for $10 (plus postage).**

TIPS "We like literary fiction with a plot that doesn't waste words. Don't send jokes masked as stories."

THE VIRGINIA QUARTERLY REVIEW

P.O. Box 400223, Charlottesville VA 22904. **E-mail:** vqr@vqronline.org. **Website:** www.vqronline.org. **Contact:** W. Ralph Eubanks, editor. "*VQR*'s primary mission has been to sustain and strengthen Jefferson's bulwark, long describing itself as 'A National Journal of Literature and Discussion.' And for good reason. From its inception in prohibition, through depression and war, in prosperity and peace, *The Virginia Quarterly Review* has been a haven—and home—for the best essayists, fiction writers, and poets, seeking contributors from every section of the United States and abroad. It has not limited itself to any special field. No topic has been alien: literary, public affairs, the arts, history, the economy. If it could be approached through essay or discussion, poetry or prose, *VQR* has covered it." Press run is 4,000. Estab. 1925. Accepts queries by online submission form. Responds in 3 months to mss. Guidelines on website.

NONFICTION "We publish literary, art, and cultural criticism; reportage; historical and political analysis; and travel essays. We publish few author interviews or memoirs. In general, we are looking for nonfiction that looks out on the world, rather than within the self." Accepts online submissions only at virginiaquarterlyreview.submittable.com/submit. You can also query via this site. Length: 3,500-10,000 words. **Pays $500 for book reviews; $1,000-3,000 for essays, memoir, criticism, and reportage.**

FICTION "We are generally not interested in genre fiction (such as romance, science fiction, or fantasy)." Accepts online submissions only at virginiaquarterlyreview.submittable.com/submit. Length: 2,000-10,000 words. **Pays $1,000-2,500 for short stories; $1,000-$4,000 for novellas and novel excerpts.**

POETRY *The Virginia Quarterly Review* prints approximately 12 pages of poetry in each issue. No length or subject restrictions. Issues have largely included lyric and narrative free verse, most of which features a strong message or powerful voice. Accepts online submissions only at virginiaquarterlyreview.submittable.com/submit. Submit maximum 5 poems. **Pays $200/poem (up to 50 lines); $300/poem (50-plus lines).**

WEST BRANCH

Stadler Center for Poetry, Bucknell University, Lewisburg PA 17837-2029. (570)577-1853. **Fax:** (570)577-1885. **E-mail:** westbranch@bucknell.edu. **Website:** www.bucknell.edu/westbranch. **Contact:** G.C. Waldrep, editor. Semiannual literary magazine. *West Branch* publishes poetry, fiction, and nonfiction in both traditional and innovative styles. Byline given. Pays on publication. No kill fee. Accepts queries by online submission form. Sample copy for $3. Guidelines available online.

Reading period: August 15-April 1. No more than 3 submissions from a single contributor in a given reading period.

NONFICTION Needs essays, general interest, literary. **Buys 4-5 mss/year.** Send complete ms. Length: no more than 30 pages. **Pays 5¢/word, with a maximum of $100.**

FICTION Needs novel excerpts, short stories. No genre fiction. **Buys 10-12 mss/year.** Send complete ms. Length: no more than 30 pages. **Pays 5¢/word, with a maximum of $100.**

POETRY Needs free and formal verse. Buys 30-40 poems/year. Submit maximum 6 poems. **Pays $50/submission.**

TIPS "All submissions must be sent via our online submission manager. Please see website for guidelines. We recommend that you acquaint yourself with the magazine before submitting."

WESTERLY

University of Wester Australia, The Westerly Centre (M202), Crawley WA 6009 Australia. (61)(8)6488-3403. **Fax:** (61)(8)6488-1030. **E-mail:** westerly@uwa.edu.au. **Website:** westerlymag.com.au. **Contact:** Delys Bird and Tony Hughes-D'Aeth, editors. *Westerly*, published in July and November, prints quality short fiction, poetry, literary criticism, socio-historical articles, and book reviews with special attention given to Australia, Asia, and the Indian Ocean region. "We assume a reasonably well-read, intelligent audience. Past issues of *Westerly* provide the best guides. Not consciously an academic magazine." Estab. 1956. Time between acceptance and publication may be up to 1 year, depending on when work is submitted. "Please wait for a response before forwarding any additional submissions for consideration."

Westerly is about 200 pages, digest-sized, "electronically printed." Press run is 1,200. Subscription information available on website. Deadline for July edition: March 31; deadline for November edition: August 31.

NONFICTION Needs essays, creative nonfiction. Submit complete ms by postal mail, e-mail, or online submissions form. Length: up to 5,000 words for essays; up to 3,500 words for creative nonfiction. **Pays $150 and contributor's copies.**

FICTION Submit complete ms by mail, e-mail, or online submissions form. Length: up to 3,500 words. **Pays $150 and contributor's copies.**

POETRY "We don't dictate to writers on rhyme, style, experimentation, or anything else. We are willing to publish short or long poems." Submit up to 3 poems by mail, e-mail, or online submissions form. **Pays $75 for 1 page or 1 poem, or $100 for 2 or more pages/poems, and contributor's copies.**

WESTERN HUMANITIES REVIEW

University of Utah, English Department, 255 S. Central Campus Dr., Salt Lake City UT 84112-0494. (801)581-6070. **Fax:** (801)585-5167. **E-mail:** whr@mail.hum.utah.edu. **Website:** http://ourworld.info/whrweb/. **Contact:** Barry Weller, editor; Nate Liederbach, managing editor. A tri-annual magazine for educated readers. *Western Humanities Review* is a journal of contemporary literature and culture housed in the University of Utah English Department. Publishes poetry, fiction, nonfiction essays, artwork, and work that resists categorization. Estab. 1947. Circ. 1,000. Pays in contributor copies. Publishes ms an average of 1 year after acceptance. Accepts simultaneous submissions. Responds in 3-5 months. Sample copy for $10. Guidelines available online.

Reading period: September 1-April 15. All submissions must be sent through online submissions manager.

NONFICTION Contact: Stuart Culver, nonfiction editor. **Buys 6-8 unsolicited mss/year.** Send complete ms. **Pays $5/published page.**

FICTION Contact: Michael Mejia, Fiction Editor. Needs experimental, innovative voices. Does not want genre (romance, sci-fi, etc.). **Buys 5-8 mss/year.** Send complete ms. Length: 5,000 words. **Pays $5/published page (when funds available).**

POETRY Contact: Poetry editors: Craig Dworkin, Paisley Rekdal, Tom Stillinger. Considers simultaneous submissions but no more than 5 poems or 25 pages per reading period. No fax or e-mail submissions. Reads submissions October 1-April 1 only. Wants quality poetry of any form, including translations. Has published poetry by Charles Simic, Olena Kalytiak Davis, Ravi Shankar, Karen Volkman, Dan Beachy-Quick, Lucie Brock-Broido, Christine Hume, and Dan Chiasson. Innovative prose poems may be submitted as fiction or non-fiction to the appropriate editor. **Pays 2 contributor's copies.**

TIPS "Because of changes in our editorial staff, we urge familiarity with recent issues of the magazine. We do not publish writer's guidelines because we think that the magazine itself conveys an accurate picture of our requirements. Please, no e-mail submissions."

WILLOW SPRINGS

668 N. Riverpoint Blvd. 2 RPT - #259, Spokane WA 99202. (509)359-7435. **E-mail:** willowspringsewu@gmail.com. **Website:** willowsprings.ewu.edu. **Contact:** Samuel Ligon, editor. **95% freelance written.** *Willow Springs* is a semiannual magazine covering poetry, fiction, literary nonfiction and interviews of notable writers. Published twice a year, in spring and fall. Estab. 1977. Circ. 1,200. Byline given. Publishes ms an average of 3 months after acceptance. Accepts queries by e-mail, online submission form. Accepts simultaneous submissions. Responds in 2 months to mss. Sample copy: $10. Guidelines online.

Reading period: September 1-May 31. Reading fee: $3/submission.

NONFICTION Needs book excerpts, essays, general interest, humor, personal experience. **Buys 2-6 mss/year.** Submit via online submissions manager. **Pays $100 and 2 contributor's copies.**

FICTION "We accept any good piece of literary fiction. Buy a sample copy." Needs adventure, ethnic, experimental, historical, mainstream, mystery, novel concepts, slice-of-life vignettes, suspense, western. Does not want to see genre fiction that does not transcend its subject matter. **Buys 10-15 mss/year.** Submit via online submissions manager. Length: open for short stories; up to 750 words for short shorts. **Pays $100 and 2 contributor's copies for short stories; $40 and 2 contributor's copies for short shorts.**

POETRY Needs avant-garde, free verse, haiku, traditional. "Buy a sample copy to learn our tastes. Our aesthetic is very open." Submit only 3-5 poems at a time. Buys 50-60 poems/year. **Pays $20/poem and 2 contributor's copies.**

TIPS "While we have no specific length restrictions, we generally publish fiction and nonfiction no longer than 10,000 words and poetry no longer than 120 lines, though those are not strict rules. *Willow Springs* values poems and essays that transcend the merely autobiographical and fiction that conveys a concern for language as well as story."

THE WORCESTER REVIEW

1 Ekman St., Worcester MA 01607. (508)797-4770. **E-mail:** twr.diane@gmail.com. **Website:** www.theworcesterreview.org. **Contact:** Diane Mulligan, managing editor. Annual literary journal covering poetry and short fiction. *The Worcester Review*, published annually by the Worcester County Poetry Association, encourages "critical work with a New England connection; no geographic limitation on poetry and fiction." Wants "work that is crafted, intuitively honest and empathetic. We like high-quality, creative poetry, artwork, and fiction. Critical articles should be connected to New England." Estab. 1972. Circ. 500. Publishes ms within 1 year of acceptance. Accepts simultaneous submissions. Responds in 4-8 months to mss. Sometimes comments on rejected mss. Sample copy: $8. Subscription: $30 (includes membership in WCPA). Guidelines available for SASE or on website.

The Worcester Review is 160 pages, digest-sized, professionally printed in dark type on quality stock, perfect-bound, with matte card cover. Press run is 600.

NONFICTION Needs critical essays, literary essays, literary criticism. Send complete ms. Length: 1,000-4,000 words. Average length: 2,000 words. **Pays 2 contributor's copies and honorarium if possible.**

FICTION Accepts about 10% unsolicited mss. Agented fiction less than 10%. Recently published work by Robert Pinsky, Marge Piercy, Wes McNair, and Ed Hirsch. Needs short stories, literary fiction. Send complete ms. "Send only 1 short story—reading editors do not like to read 2 by the same author at the same time. We will use only 1." Length: 1,000-4,000 words. Average length: 2,000 words. **Pays 2 contributor's copies and honorarium if possible.**

POETRY Submit up to 5 poems at a time. Cover letter is optional. Print submissions should be typed on 8.5x11 paper, with poet's name and e-mail address in upper left corner of each page. Include SASE or e-mail for reply. Has published poetry by Kurt Brown, Cleopatra Mathis, and Theodore Deppe. **Pays 2 contributor's copies plus small honorarium.**

TIPS "We generally look for creative work with a blend of craftsmanship, insight, and empathy. This does not exclude humor. We won't print work that is shoddy in any of these areas."

THE WRITING DISORDER

P.O. Box 93613, Los Angeles CA 90093. (323)336-5822. **E-mail:** submit@thewritingdisorder.com. **Website:** www.writingdisorder.com. **Contact:** C.E. Lukather, editor; Paul Garson, managing editor; Julianna Woodhead, poetry editor; Pamela Ramos Langley, fiction editor; C.E. Lukather, nonfiction editor. **90% freelance written.** Quarterly literary magazine featuring new and established writers. "*The Writing Dis-*

order is an online literary magazine devoted to literature, art, and culture. The mission of the magazine is to showcase new and emerging writers—particularly those in writing programs—as well as established ones. The magazine also features original artwork, photography, and comic art. Although we strive to publish original and experimental work, *The Writing Disorder* remains rooted in the classic art of storytelling." Estab. 2009. Circ. 10,000+. Byline, bio, and link given. Pays on publication. No kill fee. Publishes ms an average of 3-6 months after acceptance. Editorial lead time 3 months. Submit seasonal material 6 months in advance. Accepts queries by mail, e-mail. Accepts simultaneous submissions. Responds in 6-12 weeks to queries; 3-6 months to ms. Sample copy online. Guidelines available online.

NONFICTION Needs book excerpts, essays, historical, humor, interview, nostalgic, personal experience, photo feature, profile, travel, comic art. Special issues: "We publish an annual anthology book that showcases the best work from the website during the calendar year." **Buys 1-3 mss/year.** Query. **Pays with a copy of annual anthology for those published within it.**

PHOTOS Reviews GIF/JPEG files. Offers no additional payment for photos accepted with ms.

FICTION Needs ethnic, experimental, fantasy, historical, horror, humorous, mystery, novel excerpts, science fiction, serialized novels, short stories, slice-of-life vignettes, comic art. Does not want to see romance, religious, or fluff. **Buys 1-3 mss/year.** Query. Length: 7,500 words maximum. **Pays contributor's copies.**

POETRY Needs Avant garde, free verse, haiku, light verse, traditional. Query. Annual print anthology of best work published online. **Pays a contributor's copy of anthology to writers whose work has been selected for inclusion.**

TIPS "We are looking for work from new writers, writers in writing programs, and students and faculty of all ages."

$$ THE YALE REVIEW

Yale University, P.O. Box 208243, New Haven CT 06520-8243. (203)432-0499. **Fax:** (203)432-0510. **Website:** www.yale.edu/yalereview. **Contact:** J.D. McClatchy, editor. **20% freelance written.** Quarterly magazine. "Like Yale's schools of music, drama, and architecture, like its libraries and art galleries, *The Yale Review* has helped give the University its leading place in American education. In a land of quick fixes and short view and in a time of increasingly commercial publishing, the journal has an authority that derives from its commitment to bold established writers and promising newcomers, to both challenging literary work and a range of essays and reviews that can explore the connections between academic disciplines and the broader movements in American society, thought, and culture. With independence and boldness, with a concern for issues and ideas, with a respect for the mind's capacity to be surprised by speculation and delighted by elegance, *The Yale Review* proudly continues into its third century." Estab. 1911. Circ. 7,000. Pays prior to publication. No kill fee. Publishes ms an average of 6 months after acceptance. Responds in 1-3 months to mss. Sample copy online. Guidelines online.

NONFICTION Send complete ms with cover letter and SASE. **Pays $400-500.**

FICTION Submit complete ms with SASE. All submissions should be sent to the editorial office. **Pays $400-500.**

POETRY Submit with SASE. All submissions should be sent to the editorial office. **Pays $100-250.**

$ THE YALOBUSHA REVIEW

University of Mississippi, P.O. Box 1848, Dept. of English, University MS 38677. (662)915-3175. **E-mail:** yreditors@gmail.com. **Website:** yr.olemiss.edu. **Contact:** Liam Baranauskas and Marty Cain, senior editors. Annual literary journal seeking quality submissions from around the globe. Estab. 1995. Circ. 500. Accepts queries by online submission form. Accepts simultaneous submissions. Responds in 2-4 months to mss. Sample copy for $5. Guidelines for #10 SASE.

FICTION Needs experimental, historical, humorous, mainstream, novel excerpts, short shorts. **Buys 3-6 mss/year.** Submit 1 short story or up to 3 pieces of flash fiction via online submissions manager. Length: up to 5,000 words for short stories; up to 1,000 words for flash fiction. **Pays honorarium when funding is available.**

POETRY Needs avant-garde, free verse, traditional. Submit 3-5 poems via online submissions manager. **Pays honorarium when funding is available.**

$$$ ZOETROPE: ALL-STORY

Zoetrope: All-Story, The Sentinel Bldg., 916 Kearny St., San Francisco CA 94133. (415)788-7500. **Website:** www.all-story.com. **Contact:** fiction editor. Quarterly magazine specializing in the best of contemporary short fiction. *Zoetrope: All Story* presents a new generation of classic stories. Estab. 1997. Circ. 20,000. Byline given. No kill fee. Publishes ms an average of 5 months after acceptance. Accepts queries by mail. Accepts simultaneous submissions. Responds in 8 months (if SASE included). Sample copy: $8. Guidelines online.

FICTION **Buys 25-35 mss/year.** "Writers should submit only 1 story at a time and no more than 2 stories a year. We do not accept artwork or design submissions. We do not accept unsolicited revisions nor respond to writers who don't include an SASE." Send complete ms by mail. Length: up to 7,000 words. "Excerpts from larger works, screenplays, treatments, and poetry will be returned unread." **Pays up to $1,000.**

TIPS "Before submitting, nonsubscribers should read several issues of the magazine to determine if their works fit with *All-Story*. Electronic versions of the magazine are available to read, in part, at the website, and print versions are available for purchase by single-issue order and subscription."

$ ZYZZYVA

57 Post St., Suite 604, San Francisco CA 94104. (415)757-0465. **E-mail:** editor@zyzzyva.org. **Website:** www.zyzzyva.org. **Contact:** Laura Cogan, editor; Oscar Villalon, managing editor. **100% freelance written. Works with a small number of new/unpublished writers each year.** "Every issue is a vibrant mix of established talents and new voices, providing an elegantly curated overview of contemporary arts and letters with a distinctly San Francisco perspective." Estab. 1985. Circ. 2,500. Byline given. Pays on acceptance. No kill fee. Publishes ms an average of 3 months after acceptance. Accepts queries by mail. Accepts simultaneous submissions. Responds in 1 week to queries; in 1 month to mss. Sample copy: $12. Guidelines online.

Accepts submissions January 1-May 31 and August 1-November 30. Does not accept online submissions.

NONFICTION Needs book excerpts, general interest, historical, humor, personal experience. **Buys 50 mss/year.** Submit by mail. Include SASE and contact information. Length: no limit. **Pays $50.**

PHOTOS Reviews scans only at 300 dpi, 5.5.

FICTION Needs ethnic, experimental, humorous, mainstream. **Buys 60 mss/year.** Send complete ms by mail. Include SASE and contact information. Length: no limit. **Pays $50.**

POETRY Submit by mail. Include SASE and contact information. Buys 20 poems/year. Submit maximum 5 poems. Length: no limit. **Pays $50.**

TIPS "We are not currently seeking work about any particular theme or topic; that said, reading recent issues is perhaps the best way to develop a sense for the length and quality we are looking for in submissions."

MEN'S

GQ

Conde Nast Publications, Inc., 4 Times Square, New York NY 10036. (212)286-2860. **E-mail:** webletters@gq.com. **Website:** www.gq.com. Monthly magazine covering subjects ranging from finance, food, entertainment, technology, celebrity profiles, sports, and fashion. *Gentleman's Quarterly* is devoted to men's personal style and taste, from what he wears to the way he lives his life. Estab. 1957. Circ. 964,264. No kill fee. Accepts queries by e-mail.

Query before submitting.

NONFICTION Needs interview, celebrity. Accepts submissions to Project Upgrade, the GQ City Guides, and the GQ 100. Send e-mail to appropriate department: projectupgrade@gq.com, cityguides@gq.com, gq100@gq.com.

MILITARY

$$ ARMY MAGAZINE

Association of the US Army, 2425 Wilson Blvd., Arlington VA 22201. (800)336-4570. **E-mail:** armymag@ausa.org. **Website:** www.ausa.org/publications/armymagazine. **Contact:** Rick Maze, editor-in-chief. **70% freelance written. Prefers to work with published/established writers.** Monthly magazine emphasizing military interests. Estab. 1950. Circ. 65,000. Byline given. Pays on publication. Publishes ms an average of 5 months after acceptance. Submit seasonal material 3 months in advance. Accepts queries by mail. Sample copy and writer's guidelines for 9x12 SAE with $1 postage or online.

NONFICTION Needs historical, military and original, humor, military feature-length articles and anecdotes, interview, photo feature. Special issues: "We would like to see more pieces about little-known episodes involving interesting military personalities. We especially want material lending itself to heavy, contributor-supplied photographic treatment. The first thing a contributor should recognize is that our readership is very savvy militarily. 'Gee-whiz' personal reminiscences get short shrift, unless they hold their own in a company in which long military service, heroism and unusual experiences are commonplace. At the same time, *ARMY* readers like a well-written story with a fresh slant, whether it is about an experience in a foxhole or the fortunes of a corps in battle." No rehashed history. No unsolicited book reviews. **Buys 40 mss/year.** Submit complete ms (hard copy and disk). Length: 1,000-1,500 words. **Pays 12-18¢/word.**

PHOTOS Send photos. Captions required. Reviews prints and high resolution digital photos. Pays $50-100 for 8x10 b&w glossy prints; $50-350 for 8x10 color glossy prints and 35mm and high resolution (300 dip JPEGs) digital photos.

COLUMNS/DEPARTMENTS Columns: "Front & Center": 750-1,000 words.

$$$$ SOLDIER OF FORTUNE

2135 11th St., Boulder CO 80302. (303)443-0300. **E-mail:** editorsof@aol.com. **Website:** www.sofmag.com. **Contact:** Lt. Col. Robert A. Brown, editor/publisher. **50% freelance written.** Monthly magazine covering military, paramilitary, police, combat subjects, and action/adventure. "We are an action-oriented magazine; we cover combat hot spots around the world. We also provide timely features on state-of-the-art weapons and equipment; elite military and police units; and historical military operations. Readership is primarily active-duty military, veterans, and law enforcement." Estab. 1975. Circ. 60,000. Byline given. Offers 25% kill fee. Responds in 3 weeks to queries. Responds in 1 month to mss. Sample copy for $5. Guidelines with #10 SASE.

NONFICTION Needs expose, general interest, historical, how-to, on weapons and their skilled use, humor, interview, new product, personal experience, photo feature, No. 1 on our list, technical, travel, combat reports, military unit reports, and solid Vietnam and Operation Iraqi Freedom articles. No 'How I won the war' pieces; no op-ed pieces unless they are fully and factually backgrounded; no knife articles (staff assignments only). All submitted articles should have good art; art will sell us on an article. **Buys 75 mss/year.** Query with or without published clips or send complete ms. Send mss to articles editor; queries to managing editor Length: 2,000-3,000 words. **Pays $150-250/page.**

REPRINTS Send disk copy, photocopy of article and information about when and where the material previously appeared. Pays 25% of amount paid for an original article.

PHOTOS Send photos. Captions, identification of subjects required. Reviews contact sheets, transparencies. Pays $500 for cover photo.

FILLERS Contact: Bulletin board editor. Needs newsbreaks, military/paramilitary related has to be documented. Length: 100-250 words. **Pays $50.**

TIPS "Submit a professionally prepared, complete package. All artwork with cutlines, double-spaced typed manuscript with 5.25 or 3.5 IBM-compatible disk, if available, cover letter including synopsis of article, supporting documentation where applicable, etc. Manuscript must be factual; writers have to do their homework and get all their facts straight. One error means rejection. Vietnam features, if carefully researched and art heavy, will always get a careful look. Combat reports, again, with good art, are No. 1 in our book and stand the best chance of being accepted. Military unit reports from around the world are well received, as are law-enforcement articles (units, police in action). If you write for us, be complete and factual; pros read *Soldier of Fortune*, and are very quick to let us know if we (and the author) err."

MUSIC CONSUMER

$$ CHAMBER MUSIC

Chamber Music America, 12 W. 32nd St., 7th Floor, New York NY 10001-3813. (212)242-2022. **Fax:** (212)967-9747. **E-mail:** egoldensohn@chamber-music.org. **E-mail:** Ellen Goldensohn, publications director. **Website:** www.chamber-music.org. Bimonthly magazine covering chamber music. Estab. 1977. Circ. 13,000. Byline given. Pays on publication. Offers kill fee. Publishes ms an average of 5 months after acceptance. Editorial lead time 4 months. Accepts queries by mail, e-mail, phone.

NONFICTION Needs book excerpts, essays, humor, opinion, personal experience, issue-oriented stories of relevance to the chamber music fields written by top music journalists and critics, or music practitioners. No artist profiles or stories about opera or symphonic work. **Buys 35 mss/year.** Query with published clips.

Length: 2,500-3,500 words. **Pays $500 minimum.** Sometimes pays expenses of writers on assignment.
PHOTOS State availability. Offers no payment for photos accepted with ms.

CHURCH MUSIC QUARTERLY

The Royal School of Church Music, 19 The Close, Salisbury Wiltshire SP1 2EB United Kingdom. (44)(1722)424848. **Fax:** (44)(172)242-4849. **E-mail:** cmq@rscm.com; enquiries@rscm.com. **Website:** www.rscm.com. Quarterly publication that offers advice, information, and inspiration to church music enthusiasts around the world. Each issue offers a variety of articles and interviews by distinguished musicians, theologians, and scholars. Circ. 13,500. Pays upon publication. No kill fee. Accepts queries by e-mail. Guidelines by e-mail.

Does not pay for unsolicited articles.

NONFICTION Submit ms, bio. Length: 1,200-1,400 words **Pays £60/page for commissioned articles.**
PHOTOS Reviews prints, 300 dpi digital images.

ROLLING STONE

Wenner Media, 1290 Avenue of the Americas, New York NY 10104. (212)484-1616. **Fax:** (212)484-1664. **E-mail:** rseditors@rollingstone.com. **Website:** www.rollingstone.com. **Contact:** Caryn Ganz, editorial director. Biweekly magazine geared towards young adults interested in news of popular music, entertainment, and the arts; current news events; politics; and American culture. Circ. 1.46 million. No kill fee. Editorial lead time 1 month.

Query before submitting.

$$$ SYMPHONY

League of American Orchestras, 33 W. 60th St., 5th Floor, New York NY 10023. (212)262-5161. **Fax:** (212)262-5198. **E-mail:** clane@americanorchestras.org; jmelick@americanorchestras.org; editor@americanorchestras.org. **Website:** www.symphony.org. **Contact:** Chester Lane, senior editor; Jennifer Melick, managing editor. **50% freelance written.** Quarterly magazine for the orchestra industry and classical music enthusiasts covering classical music, orchestra industry, musicians. *Symphony*, the quarterly magazine of the League of American Orchestras, reports on the critical issues, trends, personalities, and developments of the orchestra world. Every issue includes news, provocative essays, in-depth articles, and cutting-edge research relevant to the entire orchestra field. *Symphony* profiles take readers behind the scenes to meet the people who are making a difference in the orchestra world, while wide-ranging survey articles reveal the strategies and tactics that are helping orchestras meet the challenges of the 21st century. *Symphony* is a matchless source of meaningful information about orchestras and serves as an advocate and connector for the orchestra field. Circ. 18,000. Byline given. Pays on acceptance. No kill fee. Publishes ms an average of 10 weeks after acceptance. Editorial lead time 6 months. Submit seasonal material 8 months in advance. Accepts queries by mail, e-mail. Accepts simultaneous submissions. Guidelines available online.
NONFICTION Needs book excerpts, essays, inspirational, interview, opinion, personal experience, rare, photo feature, trend pieces (by assignment only; pitches welcome). Does not want to see reviews, interviews. **Buys 30 mss/year.** Query with published clips. Length: 1,500-3,500 words. **Pays $500-900.**
PHOTOS Rarely commissions photos or illustrations. State availability of or send photos. Captions, identification of subjects required. Reviews contact sheets, negatives, prints, electronic photos (preferred). Offers no additional payment for photos accepted with ms.
COLUMNS/DEPARTMENTS Repertoire (orchestral music—essays); Comment (personal views and opinions); Currents (electronic media developments); In Print (books); On Record (CD, DVD, video), all 1,000-2,500 words. **Buys 12 mss/year.** Query with published clips.
TIPS "We need writing samples before assigning pieces. We prefer to craft the angle with the writer rather than adapt an existing piece. Pitches and queries should demonstrate a clear relevance to the American orchestra industry and should be timely."

MYSTERY

$ ELLERY QUEEN'S MYSTERY MAGAZINE

Dell Magazines, 267 Broadway, 4th Floor, New York NY 10017. (212)686-7188. **Fax:** (212)686-7414. **E-mail:** elleryqueenmm@dellmagazines.com. **Website:** www.themysteryplace.com/eqmm. **Contact:** Jackie Sherbow, assistant editor. **100% freelance written.** Covers mystery fiction. "*Ellery Queen's Mystery Magazine* welcomes submissions from both new and established writers. We publish every kind of mystery short story: the psychological suspense tale, the deductive puzzle, the private eye case—the gamut of crime and detection from the realistic (including the policeman's lot and stories of police procedure) to the more imaginative (including 'locked rooms' and 'impossible crimes'). We look for strong writing, an original and exciting plot, and professional craftsmanship. We encourage writers whose work meets these general criteria to read an issue of *EQMM* before making a submission." Estab. 1941. Circ. 100,000. Byline given. Pays on acceptance. No kill fee. Publishes ms an average of 6-12 months after acceptance. Accepts queries by online submission form. Accepts simultaneous submissions. Responds in 3 months to mss. Sample copy for $6.50. Guidelines online.

Magazine: 5⅞×8⅝, 112 pages with special 192-page combined March/April and September/October issues.

FICTION "We always need detective stories. Special consideration given to anything timely and original." Publishes ms 6-12 months after acceptance. Agented fiction 50%. **Publishes 10 new writers/year.** Recently published work by Jeffery Deaver, Joyce Carol Oates, and Margaret Maron. Sometimes comments on rejected mss. Needs mystery, suspense. No explicit sex or violence, no gore or horror. Seldom publishes parodies or pastiches. "We do not want true detective or crime stories." **Buys up to 120 mss/year.** "*EQMM* uses an online submission system (eqmm.magazinesubmissions.com) that has been designed to streamline our process and improve communication with authors. We ask that all submissions be made electronically, using this system, rather than on paper. All stories should be in standard manuscript format and submitted in .DOC format. We cannot accept .DOCX, .RTF, or .TXT files at this time. For detailed submission instructions, see eqmm.magazinesubmissions.com or our writers guidelines page (http://www.themysteryplace.com/eqmm/guidelines). Length: 2,500-8,000 words, but occasionally accepts longer and shorter submissions—including minute mysteries of 250 words, stories up to 12,000 words, and novellas of up to 20,000 words from established authors **Pays 5-8¢/word; occasionally higher for established authors.**

POETRY Wants short mystery verses, limericks. *EQMM* uses an online submission system (eqmm.magazinesubmissions.com) that has been designed to streamline our process and improve communication with authors. We ask that all submissions be made electronically, using this system, rather than on paper. All stories should be in standard manuscript format and submitted in .DOC format. We cannot accept .DOCX, .RTF, or .TXT files at this time. For detailed submission instructions, see eqmm.magazinesubmissions.com or our writers guidelines page (www.themysteryplace.com/eqmm/guidelines). Length: up to 1 page, double-spaced.

TIPS "We have a Department of First Stories to encourage writers whose fiction has never before been in print. We publish an average of 10 first stories every year. Mark subject line Attn: Dept. of First Stories."

HARDBOILED

Gryphon Publications, P.O. Box 280209, Brooklyn NY 11228. **E-mail:** gryphonbooks@att.net. **Website:** www.gryphonbooks.com. **Contact:** Gary Lovisi, editor. **100% freelance written.** Semiannual book covering crime/mystery fiction and nonfiction. "Hard-hitting crime fiction and private-eye stories—the newest and most cutting-edge work and classic reprints." Estab. 1988. Circ. 1,000. Byline given. Pays on publication. Offers 100% kill fee. Publishes ms an average of 18 months after acceptance. Editorial lead time 1 year. Submit seasonal material 9 months in advance. Accepts queries by mail, fax. Accepts simultaneous submissions. Responds in 2 weeks to queries; in 1 month to mss. Sample copy: $10. Guidelines for #10 SASE.

Hardboiled, published 1-2 times/year, is 100 pages with color cover.

NONFICTION Needs book excerpts, essays, expose. **Buys 4-6 mss/year.** Query. Length: 500-3,000 words. **Pays 1 contributor's copy.**

REPRINTS Query first.

PHOTOS State availability.

COLUMNS/DEPARTMENTS Occasional review columns/articles on hardboiled writers. **Buys 2-4 mss/year.** Query.

FICTION Needs mystery, private eye, police procedural, noir, hardboiled crime. "No pastiches, violence for the sake of violence." **Buys 40 mss/year.** Query or send complete ms. Length: 500-3,000 words. **Pays $5-50.**

TIPS "Your best bet for breaking in is short hard-crime fiction filled with authenticity and brevity. Try a subscription to *Hardboiled* to get the perfect idea of what we are after."

SUSPENSE MAGAZINE

JRSR Ventures, 26500 W. Agoura Rd., Suite 102-474, Calabasas CA 91302. **Fax:** (310)626-9670. **E-mail:** editor@suspensemagazine.com; john@suspensemagazine.com. **E-mail:** stories@suspensemagazine.com. **Website:** www.suspensemagazine.com. **Contact:** John Raab, publisher/CEO/editor in chief. **100% freelance written.** Monthly consumer magazine covering suspense, mystery, thriller, and horror genres. Estab. 2007. Pays on acceptance. Pays 100% kill fee. Publishes ms 6-9 months after acceptance. Editorial lead time is 6-9 months. Accepts queries by e-mail. Responds in 1-2 weeks to queries; 2-3 months to mss.

NONFICTION Needs true crime. Query. Length: 1,000-3,000 words. **Pays commissions only, by assignment only.** True

COLUMNS/DEPARTMENTS Book Reviews (reviews for newly released fiction); Graphic Novel Reviews (reviews for comic books/graphic novels), 250-1,000 words. **Buys 6-12 mss/year mss/year.** Query. **Pays by assignment only**

FICTION Needs horror, mystery, suspense, thrillers. No explicit scenes. **Buys 15-30 mss/year.** Submit story in body of e-mail. "Attachments will not be opened." Length: 1,500-5,000 words.

TIPS "Unpublished writers are welcome and encouraged to query. Our emphasis is on horror, suspense, thriller, and mystery."

NATURE, CONSERVATION AND ECOLOGY

ALTERNATIVES JOURNAL

200 University Ave., W, Waterloo ON N2L 3G1 Canada. (519)888-4505. **Fax:** (519)746-0292. **E-mail:** editor@alternativesjournal.ca; marcia@alternativesjournal.ca. **Website:** www.alternativesjournal.ca. **Contact:** Laura McDonald, managing editor; Nik Harron, creative director; Marcia Ruby, publisher. **90% freelance written.** Magazine published 6 times/year covering international environmental issues. "*Alternatives Journal*, Canada's national environmental magazine, delivers thoughtful analysis and intelligent debate on Canadian and world environmental issues, the latest news and ideas, as well as profiles of environmental leaders who are making a difference. *A/J* is a bimonthly magazine featuring bright, lively writing by the nation's foremost environmental thinkers and researchers. *A/J* offers a vision of a more sustainable future as well as the tools needed to take us there." Estab. 1971. Circ. 5,000. Byline given. Pays on publication. Offers 50% kill fee. Publishes ms an average of 5 months after acceptance. Editorial lead time 7 months. Submit seasonal material 5 months in advance. Accepts queries by mail, e-mail, fax. Accepts simultaneous submissions. Sample copy free for Canadian writers only. Guidelines available on website.

NONFICTION Needs book excerpts, essays, expose, humor, interview, opinion. **Buys 50 mss/year.** Query with published clips. Length: 800-3,000 words. **Pays $.10/word (Canadian).** Sometimes pays expenses of writers on assignment.

PHOTOS State availability. Identification of subjects required. Offers $35-75/photo.

TIPS "Before responding to this call for submissions, please read several back issues of the magazine so that you understand the nature of our publication. We also suggest you go through our detailed submission procedures to understand the types and lengths of articles we accept. Queries should explain, in less than 300 words, the content and scope of your article, and should convey your intended approach, tone, and style. Please include a list of people you will interview, potential images or sources for images, and the number of words you propose to write. We would also like to receive a very short bio. And if you have not written for *Alternatives* before, please include other examples of your writing. Articles range from about 500 to 4,000 words in length. Keep in mind that our lead time is several months. Articles should not be so time-bound that they will seem dated once published. Alternatives has a limited budget of $.10 per word for several articles. This stipend is available to professional and amateur writers and students only. Please indicate your interest in this funding in your submission."

THE ATLANTIC SALMON JOURNAL

The Atlantic Salmon Federation, P.O. Box 5200, St. Andrews NB E5B 3S8 Canada. (514)457-8737. **Fax:** (506)529-1070. **E-mail:** savesalmon@asf.ca; martinsilverstone@videotron.ca. **Website:** www.asf.ca. **Contact:** Martin Silverstone, editor. **50-68% freelance written.** Quarterly magazine covering conservation efforts for the Atlantic salmon, catering to the dedicated angler and conservationist. Circ. 11,000. Byline given. Pays on publication. No kill fee. Publishes ms an average of 6 months after acceptance. Submit seasonal material 3 months in advance. Accepts simultaneous submissions. Responds in 2 months to queries. Sample copy for 9x12 SAE with $1 (Canadian), or IRC. Guidelines free.

NONFICTION Needs exposé, historical, how-to, humor, interview, new product, opinion, personal experience, photo feature, technical, travel, conservation. **Buys 15-20 mss/year.** Query with published clips. Length: 2,000 words. **Pays $400-800 for articles with photos.** Sometimes pays expenses of writers on assignment.

PHOTOS State availability. Captions, identification of subjects required. Pays $50 minimum; $350-500 for covers; $300 for 2-page spread; $175 for full page photo; $100 for 1/2-page photo.

COLUMNS/DEPARTMENTS Fit To Be Tied (conservation issues and salmon research; the design, construction, and success of specific flies); interesting characters in the sport and opinion pieces by knowledgeable writers, 900 words; Casting Around (short, informative, entertaining reports, book reviews, and quotes from the world of Atlantic salmon angling and conservation). Query. **Pays $50-300.**

TIPS "Articles must reflect informed and up-to-date knowledge of Atlantic salmon. Writers need not be authorities, but research must be impeccable. Clear, concise writing is essential, and submissions must be typed."

$$ THE BEAR DELUXE MAGAZINE

Orlo, 240 N. Broadway, #112, Portland OR 97227. **E-mail:** bear@orlo.org. **Website:** www.orlo.org. **Contact:** Tom Webb, editor in chief; Kristin Rogers Brown, art director. **80% freelance written.** Covers fiction, essay, poetry, other. Do not combine submissions; rather submit poetry, fiction, and essay in separate packages. News essays, on occasion, are assigned if they have a strong element of reporting. Artists contribute to *The Bear Deluxe* in various ways, including: editorial illustration, editorial photography, spot illustration, independent art, cover art, graphic design, and cartoons. "*The Bear Deluxe Magazine* is a national independent environmental arts magazine publishing significant works of reporting, creative nonfiction, literature, visual art, and design. Based in the Pacific Northwest, it reaches across cultural and political divides to engage readers on vital issues effecting the environment. Published twice per year, *The Bear Deluxe* includes a wider array and a higher percentage of visual artwork and design than many other publications. Artwork is included both as editorial support and as standalone or independent art. It has included nationally recognized artists as well as emerging artists. As with any publication, artists are encouraged to review a sample copy for a clearer understanding of the magazine's approach. Unsolicited submissions and samples are accepted and encouraged." Estab. 1993. Circ. 19,000. Byline given. Pays on publication. Offers 25% kill fee. Publishes ms an average of 6 months after acceptance. Editorial lead time 6 months. Submit seasonal material 9 months in advance. Accepts queries by mail, e-mail. Accepts simultaneous submissions. Responds in 3-6 months to mail queries. Only responds to e-mail queries if interested. Sample copy: $5. Guidelines online.

NONFICTION Needs artist profiles, book excerpts, essays, exposé, general interest, interview, new product, opinion, personal experience, photo feature, travel. Special issues: Publishes 1 theme every 2 years. **Buys 40 mss/year.** Query with published clips. Length: 750-4,000 words. **Pays $25-400, depending on piece.** Sometimes pays expenses.

PHOTOS State availability. Identification of subjects, model releases required. Reviews contact sheets, transparencies, 8x10 prints. Offers $30/photo.

COLUMNS/DEPARTMENTS Reviews (almost anything), 100-1,000 words; Front of the Book (mix of short news bits, found writing, quirky tidbits), 300-500 words; Portrait of an Artist (artist profiles), 1,200 words; Back of the Book (creative opinion pieces), 650 words. **Buys 16 mss/year.** Query with published clips. **Pays $25-400, depending on piece.**

FICTION "We are most excited by high-quality writing that furthers the magazine's goal of engaging new and divergent readers. We appreciate strong aspects of storytelling and are open to new formats, though we wouldn't call ourselves publishers of 'experimental fiction.'" Needs adventure, condensed novels, historical, horror, humorous, mystery, novel concepts, western. No traditional sci-fi, horror, romance, or crime/action. **Buys 8 mss/year.** Query or send complete ms. Prefers postal mail submissions. Length: up to 4,000 words. **Pays free subscription to the magazine, contributor's copies, and $25-400, depending on piece; additional copies for postage.**

POETRY Needs avant-garde, free verse, haiku, light verse, traditional. Submit 3-5 poems at a time. Poems are reviewed by a committee of 3-5 people. Publishes 1 theme issue per year. Buys 16-20 poems/year. Length: up to 50 lines/poem. **Pays $20, subscription, and contributor's copies.**

FILLERS Needs facts, newsbreaks, short humor. **Buys 10 mss/year.** Length: 100-750 words.

TIPS "Offer to be a stringer for future ideas. Get a copy of the magazine and guidelines, and query us with specific nonfiction ideas and clips. We're looking for original, magazine-style stories, not fluff or PR. Fiction, essay, and poetry writers should know we have an open and blind review policy and they should keep sending their best work even if rejected once. Be as specific as possible in queries."

BIRD WATCHER'S DIGEST

P.O. Box 110, Marietta OH 45750. (740)373-5285; (800)879-2473. **E-mail:** editor@birdwatchersdigest.com. **E-mail:** submissions@birdwatchersdigest.com. **Website:** www.birdwatchersdigest.com. **Contact:** Bill Thompson III, editor. **60% freelance written.** Bimonthly, digest-sized magazine covering birds, bird watching, travel for birding and natural history. *BWD* is a nontechnical magazine interpreting ornithological material for amateur observers, including the knowledgeable birder, the serious novice and the backyard bird watcher; strives to provide good reading and good ornithology. Works with a small number of new/unpublished writers each year. Estab. 1978. Circ. 42,000. Byline given. Pays after publication. Publishes ms an average of 2 years after acceptance. Submit seasonal material 6 months in advance. Responds within 4 weeks to queries. Sample copy for $4.99 plus shipping or access online. Guidelines available online at www.birdwatchersdigest.com/bwdsite/submissions.

NONFICTION Needs book excerpts, how-to, relating to birds, feeding and attracting, etc., humor, personal experience, travel. No articles on domestic, pet or caged birds, or raising a baby bird. **Buys 30-40 mss/year.** "We gladly accept e-mail queries and ms submissions. When submitting by e-mail, please use the subject line 'Submission—[your topic].' Attach your submission to your e-mail in either MS Word (.doc) or RichText Format (.rtf). Please include full contact information on every page. Decision within 4 months." Length: 600-2,500 words. **Pays up to $300.**

PHOTOS Digital photos only. "Our payment schedule is $75 per image used regardless of size. Images used on our table of contents page or on our website will be paid an additional $25. There is no payment or contract for photos used in 'My Way', or for photos that have been loaned for courtesy use."

TIPS "Obtain a sample copy of *BWD* from us or at your local newsstand, bird store, or bookstore and familiarize yourself with the type of material we regularly publish. We rarely repeat coverage of a topic within a period of 2 to 3 years. We are aimed at an audience ranging from the backyard bird watcher to the very knowledgeable birder; we include in each issue material that will appeal at various levels. We always strive for a good geographical spread, with material from every section of the country. We leave very technical matters to others, but we want facts and accuracy, depth and quality, directed at the veteran bird watcher and at the enthusiastic novice. We stress the joys and pleasures of bird watching, its environmental contribution, and its value for the individual and society."

$$ BIRDWATCHING

Madavor Media, LLC, *BirdWatching* Editorial Dept., 25 Braintree Hill Office Park, Suite 404, Braintree MA 02184. **E-mail:** mail@birdwatchingdaily.com. **Website:** www.birdwatchingdaily.com. Bimonthly magazine for birdwatchers who actively look for wild birds in the field. "*BirdWatching* concentrates on where to find, how to attract, and how to identify wild birds, and on how to understand what they do." Estab. 1987. Circ. 40,000. Byline given. Pays on publication. Accepts queries by mail, e-mail. Guidelines online.

NONFICTION Needs essays, how-to, attracting birds, interview, personal experience, photo feature, bird photography, travel, birding hotspots in North America and beyond, product reviews/comparisons, bird biology, endangered or threatened birds. No poetry, fiction, or puzzles. **Buys 12 mss/year.** Query by mail or e-mail with published clips. Length: 500-2,400 words. **Pays $200-400.**

PHOTOS See photo guidelines online. State availability. Identification of subjects required.

GREEN TEACHER

Green Teacher, 95 Robert St., Toronto ON M2S 2K5 Canada. (416)960-1244. **Fax:** (416)925-3474. **E-mail:** tim@greenteacher.com; info@greenteacher.com. **Website:** www.greenteacher.com. **Contact:** Tim Grant, co-editor; Amy Stubbs, editorial assistant. "We're a nonprofit organization dedicated to helping educators, both inside and outside of schools, promote environmental awareness among young people aged 6-19." Estab. 1991. Circ. 15,000. Pays on acceptance. Publishes ms 8 months after acceptance. Accepts queries by mail, e-mail. Responds to queries in 1 week.

NONFICTION Needs multicultural, nature, environment. Query. Submit one-page summary or outline. Length: 1,500-3,500 words.

$$$$ SIERRA

85 Second St., 2nd Floor, San Francisco CA 94105. **Website:** www.sierraclub.org. Estab. 1893. Accepts queries by e-mail. Responds in 6-8 weeks. Sample copy for $5 and SASE, or on. Guidelines available online.

The bimonthly magazine of the Sierra Club.

NONFICTION Needs "*Sierra* is looking for strong, well-researched, literate nonfiction storytelling about significant environmental and conservation issues, adventure travel, nature, self-propelled sports, and trends in green living. Writers should look for ways to cast new light on well-established issues. We look for stories of national or international significance; local issues, while sometimes useful as examples of broader trends, are seldom of interest in themselves. We are always looking for adventure-travel pieces that weave events, discoveries, and environmental insights into the narrative. We are more interested in showcasing environmental solutions than adding to the list of environmental problems. We publish dramatic investigative stories that have the potential to reach a broad audience. Nonfiction essays on the natural world are welcome too. Features often focus on aspects of the Sierra Club's work, but few subjects are taboo. For more information about the Club's current campaigns, visit sierraclub.org." "We do not want descriptive wildlife articles unless larger conservation issues figure strongly in the story. We are not interested in editorials, general essays about environmentalism, or highly technical writing. We do not publish unsolicited cartoons, poetry, or fiction; please do not submit works in these genres." **Buys 30-36 mss/year.** Well-researched, tightly focused queries should be submitted to **Submissions.Sierra@sierraclub.org.** Phone calls are strongly discouraged. "Please do not send slides, prints, or other artwork. If photos or illustrations are required for your submission, we will request them when your work is accepted for publication." Length: 500-4,000 words. **Features: "Feature lengths range from 500 words to (rarely) 4,000 words or more with payment starting at about 75 cents a word and rising to considerably more for well-known writers with crackerjack credentials." Departments: "Articles are 100 to 1,500 words in length; payment is $50 to $1,000 unless otherwise noted. Payment for all articles is on acceptance, which is contingent on a favorable review of the manuscript by our editorial staff, and by knowledgeable outside reviewers, where appropriate. Kill fees are negotiated when a story is assigned."** Expenses of up to $50 may be paid in some cases.

PHOTOS Publishes photographs pertaining to the natural world and the environment. "We use high-quality, mostly color photographs and prefer digital files. Photographers interested in submitting work to Sierra are encouraged to send a link to their website, along with a stock listing of regions and subjects of specialty for us to review. Please do not send unsolicited transparencies and prints. We review photographers' stock lists (subject matter and locations in photographs) and samples and keep the names of potential contributors on file. Photographers are contacted only when subjects they have in stock are needed. We typically do not post our photo-needs list online or elsewhere. Sierra does not accept responsibility for lost or damaged transparencies sent on spec or for portfolio review. Please e-mail Photo.Submissions@sierraclub.org." Send photos.

TERRAIN.ORG: A JOURNAL OF THE BUILT + NATURAL ENVIROMENTS

Terrain.org, P.O. Box 19161, Tucson AZ 85731-9161. **E-mail:** contact2@terrain.org. **Website:** www.terrain.org. Reviews Editor address: P.O. Box 51332, Irvine CA 92619-1332. **Contact:** Simmons B. Buntin, editor in chief. Covers how environment influences us. Also publishes literary essays, literary criticism, book reviews, poetry, articles, and artwork. *Terrain.org* is based on, and thus welcomes quality submissions from, new and experienced authors and artists alike. Our online journal accepts only the finest poetry, essays, fiction, articles, artwork, and other contributions' material that reaches deep into the earth's fiery core, or humanity's incalculable core, and brings forth new insights and wisdom. *Terrain.org* is searching for that interface—the integration among the built and natural environments, that might be called the soul of place. The works contained within *Terrain.org* ultimately examine the physical realm around us and how those environments influence us and each other physically, mentally, emotionally, and spiritually." Publishes mss 5 weeks-18 months after acceptance. Accepts queries by online submission form. Accepts simultaneous submissions. Responds in 2 weeks to queries; in 2-3 months to mss. Sometimes comments on/critiques rejected mss. Guidelines available online.

NONFICTION Needs essays: creative, photo, personal. Does not want erotica. Accepts submissions online at sub.terrain.org. Include brief bio. Send complete ms with cover letter. Length: 1,500-6,000 words. Average length: 5,000 words.

FICTION Needs adventure, environmental, ethnic, experimental, family saga,fantasy, historical, horror, humorous, literary, mainstream, military/war, mystery, science fiction, suspense, translations, western. Does not want erotica. Accepts submissions online at sub.terrain.org. Include brief bio. Send complete ms with cover letter. Reads September 1-May 30 for regular submissions; contest submissions open year round. Length: up to 6,000 words. Average length: 5,000 words. Publishes short shorts. Average length of short shorts: 750 words.

POETRY Accepts submissions online at sub.terrain.org. Include brief bio. Send complete ms with cover letter. No erotica. Submit maximum 2-6 poems. Length: open.

TIPS "We have 3 primary criteria in reviewing fiction: (1) The story is compelling and well crafted. (2) The story provides some element of surprise; whether in content, form, or delivery we are unexpectedly delighted in what we've read. (3) The story meets an upcoming theme, even if only peripherally. Read fiction in the current issue and perhaps some archived work, and if you like what you read—and our overall enviromental slant—then send us your best work. Make sure you follow our submission guidelines (including cover note with bio), and that your mss is as error-free as possible."

PERSONAL COMPUTERS

WIRED

Condé Nast Publications, 520 Third St., 3rd Floor, San Francisco CA 94107-1815. **E-mail:** submit@wired.com. **Website:** www.wired.com. **Contact:** Joe Brown, executive editor. **95% freelance written.** Monthly magazine covering technology and digital culture. Covers the digital revolution and related advances in computers, communications, and lifestyles. Estab. 1993. Circ. 500,000. Byline given. Pays on publication. Offers 25% kill fee. Publishes ms an average of 3 months after acceptance. Editorial lead time 3 months. Accepts queries by e-mail. Responds in 3 weeks to queries. Sample copy: $4.95. Guidelines by email.

Query before submitting.

NONFICTION Needs essays, interview, opinion. No poetry or trade articles. Query. Pays expenses of writers on assignment.

TIPS "Read the magazine. We get too many inappropriate queries. We need quality writers who understand our audience and who understand how to query."

PHOTOGRAPHY

APOGEE PHOTO MAGAZINE

Jacksonville FL (904)619-2010. **E-mail:** mmeier@apogeephoto.com; general.information@apogeephoto.com. **Website:** apogeephoto.com. **Contact:** Marla Meier, editorial director. "A free online monthly magazine designed to inform, educate and entertain photographers of all ages and levels. Take online photography courses, read photo articles covering a wide range of photo topics and see listings of photo workshops and tours, camera clubs, and books. Submit your articles for publication."

NONFICTION Accepts well-written articles with 600-1,200 words on any photography related subject geared towards the beginner to advanced photographer. Articles must be accompanied by a minimum of 6 high quality photographs.

PHOTOS "*Apogee Photo* is interested in providing an electronic forum for high quality work from photographic writers and photographers. We will accept articles up to 1,200 words on any photographic subject geared towards the beginning to advanced photographer. Articles must have a minimum of 4-6 photographs accompanying them. You must hold the copyright and/or have a copyright release from a 3rd party and you must have signed model releases where applicable for any identifiable person or persons which appear in your photographs." Accepts reviews of new products, 1,000/words max.

TIPS "Please do a search by subject before submitting your article to see if your article covers a new

CONSUMER MAGAZINES

subject or brings a new perspective on a particular subject or theme."

POLITICS AND WORLD AFFAIRS

THE AMERICAN DISSIDENT: A JOURNAL OF LITERATURE, DEMOCRACY & DISSIDENCE

217 Commerce Rd., Barnstable MA 02630. **E-mail:** todslone@hotmail.com. **Website:** www.theamericandissident.org. **Contact:** G. Tod Slone, editor. Journal, published 2 times/year, provides "a forum for, amongst other things, criticism of the academic/literary established order, which clearly discourages vigorous debate, cornerstone of democracy, to the evident detriment of American Literature. The Journal seeks rare poets daring to risk going against that established-order grain." Wants "poetry, reviews, artwork, and short (1,000 words) essays in English, French, or Spanish, written on the edge with a dash of personal risk and stemming from personal experience, conflict with power, and/or involvement." Submissions should be "iconoclastic and parrhesiastic in nature." Estab. 1998. Circ. 200. Publishes ms 2 months after acceptance. Accepts queries by e-mail. Accepts simultaneous submissions. Responds in 1 month. Guidelines available for SASE.

Magazine: 56-64 pages, digest-sized, offset-printed, perfect-bound, with card cover. Press run is 200. Single copy: $9; subscriptions: individuals, $18; institutions $20. Almost always comments on rejected poems.

NONFICTION Needs essays, expose. Length: 1,000 words max.

POETRY Submit 3 poems at a time. E-mail submissions from subscribers only. "Far too many poets submit without even reading the guidelines. Include SASE and cover letter containing not credits, but rather personal dissident information, as well as incidents that provoked you to 'go upright and vital, and speak the rude truth in all ways' (Emerson)." **Pays 1 contributor's copy.**

TIPS "Every poet knows what he or she should not write about to avoid upsetting those in positions of literary, cultural, and/or academic power. *The American Dissident* seeks to publish those poets who now and then will break those taboos and thus raise truth telling above getting published, funded, invited, tenured, nominated, and/or anointed. *The American Dissident* is, by the way, one of the very few literary journals encouraging and publishing in each issue criticism with its regard."

THE AMERICAN SPECTATOR

1611 N. Kent St., Suite 901, Arlington VA 22209. **Website:** www.spectator.org. Monthly conservative magazine covering U.S. politics. "For many years, one ideological viewpoint dominated American print and broadcast journalism. Today, that viewpoint still controls the entertainment and news divisions of the television networks, the mass-circulation news magazines, and the daily newspapers. *The American Spectator* has attempted to balance the Left's domination of the media by debunking its perceived wisdom and advancing alternative ideas through spirited writing, insightful essays, humor, and, most recently, through well-researched investigative articles that have themselves become news." Estab. 1967. Circ. 50,000. No kill fee. Accepts queries by online submission form. Responds only if interested in 3-4 weeks.

NONFICTION Special issues: "Our preference is for reported pieces that provide new information or draw upon rare expertise." No unsolicited poetry, fiction, satire, or crossword puzzles. Reviews unsolicited mss for online publication. Submit via online submission form. Length: 700-1,000 words.

COMMONWEAL

Commonweal Foundation, 475 Riverside Dr., Room 405, New York NY 10115. (212)662-4200. **Fax:** (212)662-4183. **E-mail:** editors@commonwealmagazine.org. **Website:** www.commonwealmagazine.org. **Contact:** Paul Baumann, editor; Tiina Aleman, production editor. Biweekly journal of opinion edited by Catholic lay people, dealing with topical issues of the day on public affairs, religion, literature, and the arts. Estab. 1924. Circ. 20,000. Byline given. Pays on publication. No kill fee. Submit seasonal material 4 months in advance. Responds in 2 months to queries. Sample copy free. Guidelines available online.

NONFICTION Needs essays, general interest, interview, personal experience, religious. **Buys 30 mss/year.** Query with published clips. *Commonweal* welcomes original manuscripts dealing with topical issues of the day on public affairs, religion, literature, and the arts. Looks for articles that are timely, accurate, and well written. Length: 2,000-3,000 words for features. **Pays $200-300 for longer mss; $100-200 for shorter pieces.**

COLUMNS/DEPARTMENTS Upfronts: (750-1,000 words) brief, newsy reportorials, giving facts, information and some interpretation behind the headlines of the day; Last Word: (750 words) usually of a personal nature, on some aspect of the human condition: spiritual, individual, political, or social.

POETRY Needs free verse, traditional. *Commonweal,* published every 2 weeks, is a Catholic general interest magazine for college-educated readers. Does not publish inspirational poems. Buys 20 poems/year. Length: no more than 75 lines. **Pays 75¢/line plus 2 contributor's copies. Acquires all rights. Returns rights when requested by the author.**

TIPS "Articles should be written for a general but well-educated audience. While religious articles are always topical, we are less interested in devotional and churchy pieces than in articles which examine the links between 'worldly' concerns and religious beliefs."

LEFT CURVE

P.O. Box 472, Oakland CA 94604-0472. (510)763-7193. **E-mail:** editor@leftcurve.org. **Website:** www.leftcurve.org. **Contact:** Csaba Polony, editor. "*Left Curve* is an artist-produced journal addressing the problem(s) of cultural forms emerging from the crises of modernity that strive to be independent from the control of dominant institutions, based on the recognition of the destructiveness of commodity (capitalist) systems to all life." Published irregularly. Estab. 1974. Circ. 2,000. Publishes ms 6-12 months after acceptance. Responds in 6 months to mss and poems. Sometimes comments on rejected mss. Sample copy for $12; back copies $10. Guidelines available for SASE, by e-mail, or on website.

Magazine: 8.5×11; 144 pages; 60 lb. paper; 100 pt. C1S gloss layflat lamination cover; illustrations; photos. Receives 50 unsolicited mss/month. Accepts 3-4 mss/issue. Has published work by Mike Standaert, Ilan Pappe, Terrence Cannon, John Gist.

FICTION Needs ethnic/multicultural, experimental, historical, literary, regional, science fiction, translations, contemporary, prose poem, political. "No topical satire, religion-based pieces, melodrama. We publish critical, open, social/political-conscious writing." Send complete ms with cover letter. Include "statement of writer's intent, brief bio, and reason for submitting to *Left Curve.* We accept electronic submissions and hard copy, though for accepted work we request e-mail copy, either in body of text or as attachments. For accepted longer work, we prefer submission of final draft in digital form via disk or e-mail." Length: 500-5,000 words; average length: 2,500 words. Also publishes short shorts. **Pays in contributor's copies.**

POETRY Submit up to 5 poems at a time. Accepts e-mail or postal submissions. Cover letter is required. "Explain why you are submitting." Publishes theme issues. Lines/poem: "Most of our published poetry is 1 page in length, though we have published longer poems of up to 8 pages." **Pays 2-3 contributor's copies.**

TIPS "We look for continuity, adequate descriptive passages, endings that are not simply abandoned (in both meanings). Dig deep; no superficial personalisms, no corny satire. Be honest, realistic, and gouge out the truth you wish to say. Understand yourself and the world. Have writing be a means to achieve or realize what is real."

THE NATION

33 Irving Place, 8th Floor, New York NY 10003. **E-mail:** submissions@thenation.com. **Website:** www.thenation.com. Steven Brower, art director. **Contact:** Roane Carey, managing editory; Ange Mlinko, poetry editor. *The Nation,* published weekly, is a journal of left/liberal opinion, with arts coverage that includes poetry. The only requirement for poetry is excellence. Estab. 1865. Circ. 100,000. Guidelines available online.

Poetry published by *The Nation* has been included in *The Best American Poetry.* Has published poetry by W.S. Merwin, Maxine Kumin, James Merrill, May Swenson, Edward Hirsch, and Charles Simic.

NONFICTION Needs civil liberties, civil rights, labor, economics, environmental, feminist issues, politics, the arts. Queries accepted via e-mail only to online form. Length: 750-2,500 words. **Pays $150-500, depending on length.**

POETRY Submit poems only via mail. Send no more than 8 poems in a calendar year. Include a SASE. Submit maximum 3 poems.

THE NEW VERSE NEWS

Tangerang Indonesia. **E-mail:** nvneditor@gmail.com. **Website:** www.newversenews.com. **Contact:** James

Penha, editor. *The New Verse News*, published online and updated "every day or 2," has "a clear liberal bias but will consider various visions and views." "Normally, poems are published immediately upon acceptance." Submit seasonal poems 1 month in advance. Responds in 1-3 weeks. Does not comment on rejected poems. Guidelines available on website.

POETRY Wants "previously unpublished poems, both serious and satirical, on current events and topical issues; will also consider prose poems." Does not want "work unrelated to the news." Submit 1-5 poems at a time. Accepts only e-mail submissions (pasted into body of message); use "Verse News Submission" as the subject line; no disk or postal submissions. Send brief bio. Reads submissions year round. Poems are circulated to an editorial board. Receives about 1,200 poems/year; accepts about 300. No length restrictions.

PEACE & FREEDOM

Peace & Freedom Press, 17 Farrow Rd., Whaplode Drove, Spalding, Lincs PE12 0TS England. **Website:** http://pandf.booksmusicfilmstv.com/index.htm. Published semiannually; emphasizes social, humanitarian, and environmental issues. Considers submissions from subscribers only. Those new to poetry are welcome. The poetry published is pro-animal rights/welfare, anti-war, environmental; poems reflecting love; erotic, but not obscene; humorous; spiritual, humanitarian; with or without rhyme/meter. Considers poetry by children and teens. Has published poetry by Dorothy Bell-Hall, Freda Moffatt, Andrew Bruce, Bernard Shough, Mona Miller, and Andrew Savage. Estab. 1985. Accepts queries by e-mail (pasted into body of message, no attachments; no fax submissions. Responds to submissions in less than a month usually, with SAE/IRC. Submissions from subscribers only.

Peace & Freedom has a varied format. Subscription: $20 U.S., £10 UK for 6 issues. Sample: $5 U.S., £1.75 UK. Sample copies can be purchased only from the above address. Advisable to buy a sample copy before submitting. Banks charge the equivalent of $5 to cash foreign checks in the UK, so please only send bills, preferably by registered post.

POETRY No previously published poems or simultaneous submissions. Accepts e-mail submissions (pasted into body of message, no attachments; no more than 3 poems/e-mail); no fax submissions. Include bio. Reads submissions year round. Publishes theme issues. Upcoming themes available in magazine, for SAE with IRC, by e-mail, or on website. "Work without correct postage will not be responded to or returned until proper postage is sent." Pays one contributor's copy. Reviews books of poetry. Submit maximum 3 poems/e-mail poems. Lines/poem: 32 max.

TIPS "Too many writers have lost the personal touch that editors generally appreciate. It can make a difference when selecting work of equal merit."

THE PROGRESSIVE

409 E. Main St., Madison WI 53703. (608)257-4626. **Fax:** (608)257-3373. **E-mail:** editorial@progressive.org; mattr@progressive.org. **Website:** www.progressive.org. **Contact:** Matthew Rothschild, editor. **75% freelance written.** Monthly magazine of investigative reporting, political commentary, cultural coverage, activism, interviews, poetry, and humor. It steadfastly stands against militarism, the concentration of power in corporate hands, and the disenfranchisement of the citizenry. It champions peace, social and economic justice, civil rights, civil liberties, human rights, a preserved environment, and a reinvigorated democracy. Its bedrock values are nonviolence and freedom of speech. Estab. 1909. Byline given. Pays on publication. Publishes ms an average of 6 weeks after acceptance. Accepts queries by mail. Responds in 1 month to queries. Sample copy for 9x12 SASE with 4 first-class stamps or sample articles online. Guidelines available online.

NONFICTION Query. Length: 500-4,000 words. **Pays $500-1,300.**

POETRY Publishes 1 original poem a month. "We prefer poems that connect up—in 1 fashion or another, however obliquely—with political concerns." **Pays $150.**

TIPS Sought-after topics include electoral coverage, social movement, foreign policy, activism, and book reviews.

PROGRESSIVE POPULIST

P.O. Box 819, Manchaca TX 78652. (512)828-7245. **E-mail:** populist@usa.net. **Website:** www.populist.com. **90% freelance written.** Biweekly tabloid covering politics and economics. "We cover issues of interest to workers, small businesses, and family farmers and ranchers." Estab. 1995. Circ. 15,000. Byline given. Pays quarterly. No kill fee. Publishes ms an average of 1 month after acceptance. Editorial lead time 3 weeks. Submit seasonal material 1 month in advance.

Accepts queries by mail, e-mail, fax, phone. Accepts simultaneous submissions. Sample copy and writer's guidelines free.

NONFICTION Needs essays, exposé, general interest, historical, humor, interview, opinion. "We are not much interested in 'sound-off' articles about state or national politics, although we accept letters to the editor. We prefer to see more 'journalistic' pieces in which the writer does enough footwork to advance a story beyond the easy realm of opinion." **Buys 400 mss/year.** Query. Length: 600-1,000 words. **Pays $15-50.** Pays writers with contributor copies or other premiums if preferred by writer.

REPRINTS Send photocopy with rights for sale noted and information about when and where the material previously appeared.

PHOTOS State availability. Identification of subjects required. Negotiates payment individually.

TIPS "We do prefer submissions by e-mail. I find it's easier to work with e-mail, and for the writer it probably increases the chances of getting a response."

THEORIA

Berghahn Books, Inc., c/o Turpin North America, 143 West St., New Milford CT 06776. (860)350-0041. **Fax:** (860)350-0039. **E-mail:** theoriasa@gmail.com; editorial@journals.berghahnbooks.com. **Website:** journals.berghahnbooks.com/th. **Contact:** Sherran Clarence, managing editor. **100% freelance written.** Academic journal published 4 times/year. "*Theoria* is an engaged, multidisciplinary, peer-reviewed journal of social and political theory. Its purpose is to address—through scholarly debate—the many challenges posed to intellectual life by the major social, political, and economic forces that shape the contemporary world. Thus, it is principally concerned with questions such as how modern systems of power, processes of globalization, and capitalist economic organization bear on matters such as justice, democracy, and truth." Estab. 1947. Circ. 300. Byline sometimes given. No kill fee. Publishes ms an average of 6 months after acceptance. Editorial lead time 3 months. Submit seasonal material 3 months in advance. Accepts queries by mail, e-mail, fax, phone. Responds in 1 week to queries; in 3-4 months to mss. Sample copy free online. Guidelines online or via e-mail.

NONFICTION Needs book excerpts, essays, expose, general interest, historical, interview, review articles, book reviews, theoretical, philosophical, political. **Buys 1 mss/year.** Send complete ms. "Ms must comply with guidelines." Length: 6,000-9,000 words. "Ms must be ready for blind peer review." **No payment offered.**

PHOTOS State availability. Identification of subjects required. Reviews GIF/JPEG files. Negotiates payment individually.

COLUMNS/DEPARTMENTS Book Reviews, 1,000-1,500 words; Review Articles, 3,000-5,000 words. **Buys 1 mss/year.** Send complete ms.

U.S. NEWS & WORLD REPORT

U.S. News & World Report, Inc., 1050 Thomas Jefferson St. NW, 4th Floor, Washington DC 20007. (202)955-2630. **Fax:** (202)955-2056. **E-mail:** bkelly@usnews.com. **Website:** www.usnews.com. **Contact:** Brian Kelly, editor and chief content officer. Weekly magazine devoted largely to reporting and analyzing national and international affairs, politics, business, health, science, technology, and social trends. Circ. 2,000,000. No kill fee. Editorial lead time 10 days.

Query before submitting.

PSYCHOLOGY & SELF-IMPROVEMENT

THE AWAKENINGS REVIEW

P.O. Box 177, Wheaton IL 60187. **E-mail:** ar@awakeningsproject.org. **Website:** www.awakeningsproject.org. **Contact:** Robert Lundin, editor. *The Awakenings Review* publishes original poetry, short stories, dramatic scenes, essays, photographs, excerpts from larger works, and black-and-white cover art—all created by persons who have had a personal experience with mental illness. *The Awakenings Review* is published by the Awakenings Project. Begun in cooperation with the University of Chicago Center for Psychiatric Rehabilitation in 2000, *The Awakenings Review* has been acclaimed internationally and draws writers from all over the United States and from several other countries including Israel, South Africa, Australia, Finland, Switzerland, the United Kingdom, and Canada. Estab. 1999. Publishes ms 8 months after acceptance. Submit seasonal poems 6 months in advance. Responds in 1 month. Guidelines available in magazine, for SASE, by e-mail, or on website.

FICTION No e-mail submissions. Cover letter is preferred. Include SASE and short bio. Length: 5,000 words max. **Pays 1 contributor's copy, plus discount on additional copies.**

POETRY Submit 5 poems at a time. No e-mail submissions. Cover letter is preferred. Include SASE and short bio. Poems are read by a board of editors. Often comments on rejected poems. Occasionally publishes theme issue. **Pays 1 contributor's copy, plus discount on additional copies.**

$$$$ GRADPSYCH

American Psychological Association, 750 First St. NE, Washington DC 20009. **Fax:** (202)336-6103. **E-mail:** gradpsych@apa.org. **Website:** www.apa.org/gradpsych. **Contact:** Sarah Martin, editor. **50% freelance written.** Quarterly magazine. "We cover issues of interest to psychology graduate students, including career outlook, tips for success in school, profiles of interesting students, and reports on student research. We aim for our articles to be readable, informative, and fun. Grad students have enough dry, technical reading to do at school; we don't want to add to it." Estab. 2003. Circ. 60,000. Byline given. Pays on acceptance. Offers $200 kill fee. Publishes ms an average of 4 months after acceptance. Editorial lead time 3-5 months. Submit seasonal material 4 months in advance. Accepts queries by e-mail. Responds in 2 weeks to queries. Sample copy online.

NONFICTION Needs general interest, how-to, interview, journalism for grad students. **Buys 25 mss/year.** Query with published clips. Length: 300-2,000 words. **Pays $300-2,000 for assigned articles.**

PHOTOS State availability. Identification of subjects, model releases required. Reviews GIF/JPEG files. Negotiates payment individually.

TIPS "Check out our website and pitch a story on a topic we haven't written on before or that gives an old topic a new spin. Also, have quality clips."

SCIENCE OF MIND MAGAZINE

573 Park Point Dr., Golden CO 80401. (720)279-1643. **E-mail:** edit@scienceofmind.com. **Website:** www.scienceofmind.com. Editor: Diane Bishop. **Contact:** Diane Bishop, editor in chief. **30% freelance written.** Monthly magazine featuring articles on spirituality, self-help, and inspiration. "Our publication centers on oneness of all life and spiritual empowerment through the application of *Science of Mind* principles." Byline given. Pays on acceptance. No kill fee. Publishes ms an average of 5 months after acceptance. Submit seasonal material 6 months in advance. Guidelines online.

NONFICTION Needs book excerpts, essays, inspirational, interview, personal experience, spiritual. **Buys 35-45 mss/year.** Length: 750-2,000 words. **Payment varies. Pays in copies for some features written by readers.**

TIPS "We are interested in how to use spiritual principles in worldly situations or other experiences of a spiritual nature having to do with *Science of Mind* principles. Make sure you are familiar with the magazine and its philosophy before submitting."

$ SPOTLIGHT ON RECOVERY MAGAZINE

R. Graham Publishing Company, 9602 Glenwood Road, #140, Brooklyn NY 11236. (347)831-9373. **E-mail:** rgraham_100@msn.com. **Website:** www.spotlightonrecovery.com. **Contact:** Robin Graham, publisher and editor-in-chief. **85% freelance written.** Quarterly magazine covering self-help, recovery, and empowerment. "This is the premiere outreach and resource magazine in New York. Its goal is to be the catalyst for which the human spirit could heal. Everybody knows somebody who has mental illness, substance abuse issues, parenting problems, educational issues, or someone who is homeless, unemployed, physically ill, or the victim of a crime. Many people suffer in silence. *Spotlight on Recovery* will provide a voice to those who suffer in silence and begin the dialogue of recovery." Estab. 2001. Circ. 3,000-6,000. Byline sometimes given. Pays on publication. No kill fee. Publishes ms an average of 6 months after acceptance. Editorial lead time 1 month. Submit seasonal material 1 month in advance. Accepts queries by mail, e-mail. Accepts simultaneous submissions. Responds in 2 weeks to queries; 1 month to mss. Sample copy and guidelines free.

NONFICTION Needs book excerpts, interview, opinion, personal experience. **Buys 30-50 mss/year.** Query with published clips. Length: 150-1,500 words. **Pays 5¢/word or $75-80/article.**

PHOTOS State availability. Identification of subjects required. Reviews GIF/JPEG files. Pays $5-10/photo.

COLUMNS/DEPARTMENTS Buys 4 mss/year. Query with published clips. **Pays 5¢/word or $75-80/column.**

FICTION Needs ethnic, mainstream, slice-of-life vignettes.

FILLERS Needs facts, newsbreaks, short humor. **Buys 2 mss/year. Pays 5¢/word.**

TIPS "Send a query and give a reason why you would choose the subject posted to write about."

REGIONAL

ALABAMA

ALABAMA HERITAGE

University of Alabama, Box 870342, Tuscaloosa AL 35487-0342. (205)348-7467. **Fax:** (205)348-7473. **E-mail:** reyno031@bama.ua.edu. **Website:** www.alabamaheritage.com. **Contact:** Susan Reynolds, associate editor. **90% freelance written.** *Alabama Heritage* is a nonprofit historical quarterly published by the University of Alabama and the Alabama Department of Archives and History for the intelligent lay reader. "We are interested in lively, well-written, and thoroughly researched articles on Alabama/Southern history and culture. Readability and accuracy are essential." Estab. 1986. Byline given. Pays on publication. No kill fee. Accepts queries by mail, e-mail. Guidelines online.

NONFICTION "We do not publish fiction, poetry, articles on current events or living artists, and personal/family reminiscences." Query. Length: 750-4,000 words. **Pays $50-350.**

PHOTOS Identification of subjects required. Reviews contact sheets.

TIPS "Authors need to remember that we regard history as a fascinating subject, not as a dry recounting of dates and facts. Articles that are lively and engaging, in addition to being well researched, will find interested readers among our editors. No term papers, please. All areas are open to freelance writers. Best approach is a written query."

ALABAMA LIVING

Alabama Rural Electric Association, 340 Techna-Center Dr., Montgomery AL 36117. (800)410-2737. **Website:** www.alabamaliving.com. **Contact:** Lenore Vickrey, editor; Michael Cornelison, art director. **80% freelance written.** Monthly magazine covering topics of interest to rural and suburban Alabamians. "Our magazine is an editorially balanced, informational and educational service to members of rural electric cooperatives. Our mix regularly includes Alabama history, Alabama features, gardening, outdoor, and consumer pieces." Estab. 1948. Circ. 400,000. Byline given. Pays on acceptance. No kill fee. Editorial lead time 4 months. Submit seasonal material 4 months in advance. Accepts queries by mail, e-mail. Accepts simultaneous submissions. Responds in 1 month to queries. Sample copy free.

NONFICTION Needs historical, rural-oriented, Alabama slant, Alabama. Special issues: Gardening (March); Travel (April); Home Improvement (May); Holiday Recipes (December). **Buys 20 mss/year.** Send complete ms. Length: 500-750 words. **Pays $250 minimum for assigned articles. Pays $150 minimum for unsolicited articles.**

REPRINTS Send typed manuscript with rights for sale noted. Pays $100.

PHOTOS Buys 1-3 photos from freelancers/issue; 12-36 photos/year. Pays $100 for color cover; $50 for color inside; $60-75 for photo/text package. **Pays on acceptance.** Credit line given. Buys one-time rights for publication and website; negotiable.

TIPS "Preference given to submissions with accompanying art."

MOBILE BAY MONTHLY

PMT Publishing, P.O. Box 66200, Mobile AL 36660. (251)473-6269. **Fax:** (251)479-8822. **E-mail:** mboykin@pmtpublishing.com. **Website:** www.mobilebaymonthly.com. **Contact:** Mallory Boykin, assistant editor. **25% freelance written.** *Mobile Bay Monthly* is a monthly lifestyle magazine for the South Alabama/Gulf Coast region focusing on the people, ideas, issues, arts, homes, food, culture, and businesses that make Mobile Bay an interesting place. Estab. 1990. Circ. 10,000. Byline given. Pays on publication. No kill fee. Publishes ms an average of 4 months after acceptance. Editorial lead time 4 months. Submit seasonal material 6 months in advance. Accepts queries by mail, e-mail, fax.

NONFICTION Needs general interest, historical, how-to, interview, personal experience, photo feature, travel. Query with published clips. Stories must be about something along the Gulf Coast. Length: 1,200-3,000 words.

PHOTOS State availability of images. Identification of subjects required. Negotiates payment individually.

TIPS "We use mostly local writers. Strong familiarity with the Mobile area is a must. No phone calls; please send query letters with writing samples."

ALASKA

$$ ALASKA

301 Arctic Slope Ave., Suite 300, Anchorage AK 99518-3035. **E-mail:** editor@alaskamagazine.com. **Website:** www.alaskamagazine.com. **Contact:** Michelle Theall, editor; Corrynn Cochran, photo editor. **70% freelance written. Eager to work with new/unpublished writers.** Magazine published 10 times/year covering topics uniquely Alaskan. Estab. 1935. Circ. 180,000. Byline given. Pays on publication. No kill fee. Publishes ms an average of 6 months after acceptance. Submit seasonal material 1 year in advance. Accepts queries by mail, e-mail. Responds in 2 months to queries and to mss. Sample copy: $4.99 and 9x12 SASE with 7 first-class stamps. Guidelines online.

NONFICTION Needs historical, humor, interview, personal experience, photo feature, travel, adventure, outdoor recreation (including hunting, fishing), Alaska destination stories. No fiction or poetry. **Buys 40 mss/year.** Query. Length: 700-2,000 words **Pays $100-1,250**

PHOTOS *Alaska* is dedicated to depicting life in Alaska through high-quality images of its people, places, and wildlife. Color photographs from professional freelance photographers are used extensively and selected according to their creative and technical merits. Send photos. Captions, identification of subjects required. Reviews 35mm or larger transparencies, slides labeled with your name. Pays $50 maximum for b&w photos; $75-500 for color photos; $300 maximum/day; $2,000 maximum/complete job; $300 maximum/full page; $500 maximum/cover. Buys limited rights, first North American serial rights, and electronic rights. "Each issue of *Alaska* features a 4-, 6-, and/or 8-page feature. We're looking for themes and photos to show the best of Alaska. We want sharp, artistically composed pictures. Cover photo always relates to stories inside the issue." Photographers on assignment are paid a competitive day rate and reimbursed for approved expenses. All assignments are negotiated in advance.

COLUMNS/DEPARTMENTS Escape (gives readers a reason to get out and explore the Last Frontier); Outdoors (features a variety of Alaska outdoor subjects, including fishing, hunting, hiking, camping, birding, adventure sports, and extreme activities); Alaska History; Alaska Native Culture; all 800-1,000 words. Query.

TIPS "We're looking for top-notch writing—original, well researched, lively. Subjects must be distinctly Alaskan. A story on a mall in Alaska, for example, won't work for us; every state has malls. If you've got a story about a Juneau mall run by someone who is also a bush pilot and part-time trapper, maybe we'd be interested. The point is *Alaska* stories need to be vivid, focused, and unique. Alaska is like nowhere else—we need our stories to be the same way."

ARIZONA

$$ ARIZONA FOOTHILLS MAGAZINE

8132 N. 87th Place, Scottsdale AZ 85258. (480)460-5203. **Fax:** (480)443-1517. **E-mail:** publisher@mediathatdelivers.com. **Website:** www.azfoothillsmag.com. **Contact:** Michael Dee, publisher. **10% freelance written.** Monthly magazine covering Arizona lifestyle. Estab. 1996. Circ. 60,000. Byline given. Pays on publication. No kill fee. Publishes ms an average of 6 months after acceptance. Editorial lead time 6 months. Submit seasonal material at least 4 months in advance. Accepts queries by mail, e-mail. Responds in 1 month to queries. Sample copy for #10 SASE.

NONFICTION Needs general interest, photo feature, travel, fashion, decor, arts, interview. **Buys 10 mss/year.** Query with published clips. Length: 900-2,000 words. **Pays 35-40¢/word for assigned articles.**

PHOTOS Photos may be requested. Captions, identification of subjects, model releases required. Reviews contact sheets, transparencies. Negotiates payment individually.

COLUMNS/DEPARTMENTS Travel, dining, fashion, home decor, design, architecture, wine, shopping, golf, performance & visual arts.

TIPS "We prefer stories that appeal to our affluent audience written with an upbeat, contemporary approach and reader service in mind."

$$$$ ARIZONA HIGHWAYS

2039 W. Lewis Ave., Phoenix AZ 85009-9988. (602)712-2024. **Fax:** (602)254-4505. **E-mail:** kkramer@azdot.gov. **Website:** www.arizonahighways.com. **Contact:** Kelly Kramer, managing editor. **100% freelance written.** Magazine that is state-owned, designed to help attract tourists into and through Arizona. Estab. 1925. Circ. 425,000. Pays on acceptance. No kill fee. Accepts queries by mail, e-mail, fax. Responds in 1 month. Guidelines online.

NONFICTION Buys 50 mss/year. Query with a lead paragraph and brief outline of story. Length: 600-1,800 words. **Pays up to $1/word.**

PHOTOS Contact: Peter Ensenberger, director of photography. For digital requirements, contact the photography department. Pays $125-600.

COLUMNS/DEPARTMENTS Focus on Nature (short feature in first or third person dealing with the unique aspects of a single species of wildlife), 800 words; Along the Way (short essay dealing with life in Arizona, or a personal experience keyed to Arizona), 750 words; Back Road Adventure (personal back-road trips, preferably off the beaten path and outside major metro areas), 1,000 words; Hike of the Month (personal experiences on trails anywhere in Arizona), 500 words. **Pays $50-1,000, depending on department.**

TIPS "Writing must be of professional quality, warm, sincere, in-depth, well peopled, and accurate. Avoid themes that describe first trips to Arizona, the Grand Canyon, the desert, Colorado River running, etc. Emphasis is to be on Arizona adventure and romance as well as flora and fauna, when appropriate, and themes that can be photographed. Double check your manuscript for accuracy. Our typical reader is a 50-something person with the time, the inclination, and the means to travel."

$ PHOENIX MAGAZINE

Cities West Publishing, Inc., 15169 N. Scottsdale Rd., Suite C-310, Scottsdale AZ 85254. (866)481-6970. **Fax:** (602)604-0169. **Website:** www.phoenixmag.com. **70% freelance written.** Monthly magazine covering regional issues, personalities, events, neighborhoods, customs, and history of metro Phoenix. Estab. 1966. Circ. 60,000. Byline given. Pays on publication. No kill fee. Publishes ms an average of 3 months after acceptance. Submit seasonal material 1 year in advance. Accepts queries by mail, e-mail. Responds in 2 months. Sample copy for $3.95 and 9x12 SASE with 5 first-class stamps. Guidelines for #10 SASE.

NONFICTION Needs general interest, interview, investigative, historical, service pieces (where to go and what to do around town). "We do not publish fiction, poetry, personal essays, book reviews, music reviews, or product reviews, and our travel stories are staff written. With the exception of our travel stories, all of the content in *Phoenix* magazine is geographically specific to the Phoenix-metro region. We do not publish any non-travel news or feature stories that are outside the Phoenix area, and we prefer that our freelancers are located in the Phoenix metro area." **Buys 50 mss/year.** Query with published clips via e-mail. "Include a short summary, a list of sources, and an explanation of why you think your idea is right for the magazine and why you're qualified to write it." Length: 150-2,000 words.

TIPS "Stories must appeal to an educated Phoenix audience. We want solidly reported and diligently researched stories on key issues of public concern and the key players involved."

$$ TRENDS MAGAZINE

Trends Publishing, 5685 N. Scottsdale Rd., Suite E160, Scottsdale AZ 85250. (480)990-9007. **Fax:** (480)990-0048. **E-mail:** editor@trendspublishing.com. **Website:** www.trendspublishing.com. **Contact:** Bill Dougherty, publisher. **20% freelance written.** Monthly magazine covering society, affluent lifestyle, luxury goods and services. *Trends Magazine* has a focus on the affluent community, especially in Arizona. Estab. 1982. Circ. 45,000. Byline given. Offers 100% kill fee. Editorial lead time 2-3 months. Submit seasonal material 2-3 months in advance. Accepts queries by mail, e-mail, fax, phone. Accepts simultaneous submissions. Responds in 1 month. Sample copy free. Guidelines by e-mail.

NONFICTION Needs general interest, humor, interview, travel. Does not want technical, religious, or political. Query with published clips. Length: 700-1,200 words. **Pays $350-600.**

TIPS "Just think about subjects that would appeal to affluent readers."

$$ TUCSON LIFESTYLE

Conley Publishing Group, Ltd., Suite 12, 7000 E. Tanque Verde Rd., Tucson AZ 85715-5318. (520)721-2929. **Fax:** (520)721-8665. **E-mail:** scott@tucsonlifestyle.com. **Contact:** Scott Barker, executive editor. **90% freelance written. Prefers to work with published/established writers.** Monthly magazine covering Southern Arizona-related events and topics. Estab. 1982. Circ. 32,000. Byline given. Pays on acceptance. No kill fee. Publishes ms an average of 6 months after acceptance. Submit seasonal material 1 year in advance. Accepts queries by mail, e-mail. Responds in 2 months to queries; in 3 months to mss. Sample copy: $3.99, plus $3 postage. Guidelines free.

NONFICTION "Avoid obvious tourist attractions and information that most residents of the Southwest are likely to know. No anecdotes masquerading as articles. Not interested in fish-out-of-water, Easterner-visiting-the-Old-West pieces." **Buys 20 mss/year. Pays $50-500.**

PHOTOS Query about photos before submitting anything.

TIPS "Read the magazine before submitting anything."

CALIFORNIA

CARLSBAD MAGAZINE

Wheelhouse Media, P.O. Box 2089, Carlsbad CA 92018. (760)729-9099. **Fax:** (760)729-9011. **E-mail:** tim@wheelhousemedia.com. **Website:** www.clickoncarlsbad.com. **Contact:** Tim Wrisley. **80% freelance written.** Bimonthly magazine covering people, places, events, arts in Carlsbad, California. "We are a regional magazine highlighting all things pertaining specifically to Carlsbad. We focus on history, events, people, and places that make Carlsbad interesting and unique. Our audience is both Carlsbad residents and visitors or anyone interested in learning more about Carlsbad. We favor a conversational tone that still adheres to standard rules of writing." Estab. 2004. Circ. 35,000. Byline given. Pays on publication. Publishes ms an average of 6 months after acceptance. Editorial lead time 4 months. Submit seasonal material 6-12 months in advance. Accepts queries by mail, e-mail. Accepts simultaneous submissions. Responds in 2 months to queries and mss. Sample copy: $2.31. Guidelines by e-mail.

NONFICTION Needs historical, interview, photo feature, home, garden, arts, events. Does not want self-promoting articles for individuals or businesses, real estate how-tos, advertorials. **Buys 3 mss/year.** Query with published clips. Length: 300-2,700 words. **Pays 20-30¢/word for assigned articles. Pays 20¢/word for unsolicited articles.** Sometimes pays expenses of writers on assignment.

PHOTOS State availability. Reviews GIF/JPEG files. Offers $15-400/photo.

COLUMNS/DEPARTMENTS Carlsbad Arts (people, places, or things related to cultural arts in Carlsbad); Happenings (events that take place in Carlsbad); Carlsbad Character (unique Carlsbad residents who have contributed to Carlsbad's character); Commerce (Carlsbad business profiles); Surf Scene (subjects pertaining to the beach/surf in Carlsbad), all 500-700 words. Garden (Carlsbad garden feature); Home (Carlsbad home feature), both 700-1,200 words. **Buys 60 mss/year.** Query with published clips. **Pays $50 flat fee or 20¢/word.**

TIPS "The main thing to remember is that any pitches need to be subjects directly related to Carlsbad. If the subjects focus on surrounding towns, they aren't going to make the cut. We are looking for well-written feature magazine-style articles. E-mail is the preferred method for queries; you will get a response."

THE EAST BAY MONTHLY

The Berkeley Monthly, Inc., 1305 Franklin St., Suite 501, Oakland CA 94612. (510)238-9101. **Fax:** (510)238-9163. **Website:** www.themonthly.com. **95% freelance written.** Monthly general interest tabloid covering the San Francisco Bay Area. "We feature distinctive, intelligent articles of interest to *East Bay* readers." Estab. 1970. Circ. 62,000. Byline given. Pays on publication. No kill fee. Editorial lead time 2+ months. Submit seasonal material 3 months in advance. Accepts queries by mail, e-mail. Accepts simultaneous submissions. Responds in 1 month to queries. Responds in 1 month to mss. Sample copy for $3. Writer's guidelines for #10 SASE or by e-mail.

NONFICTION No fiction or poetry. Query with published clips. Length: 1,000-3,000 words. **Pays $100-500.**

REPRINTS Send tearsheet and information about when and where the material previously appeared.

PHOTOS State availability. Identification of subjects required. Negotiates payment individually.

COLUMNS/DEPARTMENTS First Person, 2,000 words. Query with published clips.

NOB HILL GAZETTE

Nob Hill Gazette, Inc., 950 Mason St., Mezzanine Level, San Francisco CA 94108. (415)227-0190. **E-mail:** email@nobhillgazette.com. **E-mail:** fred@nobhillgazette.com. **Website:** www.nobhillgazette.com. **Contact:** Fred Albert, editor. **95% freelance written.** Monthly magazine covering upscale lifestyles in the Bay Area. "The *Gazette* caters to an audience upscale in taste and lifestyle. Our main purpose is to publicize events that raise millions of dollars for local cultural programs and charities, and to recognize the dedicated volunteers who work behind the scenes. With publisher Lois Lehrman at the helm, each trendsetting issue of our monthly magazine includes about 200 photos and 15 or more local interest stories. Our features, often 'tongue-in-chic,' cover art, beauty, books, entertainment, fashion, health, history, interiors, profiles, travels, and much, much more." Estab. 1978. Circ. 75,000. Byline given. Pays on 15th of month following publication. Offers $50 kill fee. Publishes ms an average of 2-3 months after acceptance. Editorial lead time 1-2 months. Submit seasonal material 1-2 months in advance. Accepts queries by e-mail. Responds in 2 weeks to queries; 2 months to mss. Sample copy online. Guidelines free.

NONFICTION Needs general interest, historical, interview, opinion, photo feature, trends, lifestyles, fashion, health, fitness, entertaining, decor, real estate, charity and philanthropy, culture and the arts. Does not want first-person articles, anything commercial (from a business or with a product to sell), profiles of people not active in the community, anything technical, anything on people or events not in the Bay Area. **Buys 75 mss/year.** Query with published clips. Length: 800-1,000 words. **Pays $150.**

PHOTOS State availability. Captions, identification of subjects required. Reviews GIF/JPEG files. Offers no additional payment for photos accepted with ms.

COLUMNS/DEPARTMENTS "All our columnists are freelancers, but they write for us regularly, so we don't take other submissions relating to their topics."

TIPS "Before a submission, a writer should look at our publication and read the articles to get some idea of our style and range of subjects."

$$ ORANGE COAST MAGAZINE

Orange Coast Kommunications, Inc., 3701 Birch St., Suite 100, Newport Beach CA 92660. (949)862-1133. **Fax:** (949)862-0133. **E-mail:** editorial@orangecoast.com. **Website:** www.orangecoast.com. **Contact:** Martin J. Smith, editor-in-chief. **90% freelance written.** Monthly magazine designed to inform and enlighten the educated, upscale residents of Orange County, California; highly graphic and well researched. Estab. 1974. Circ. 52,000. Byline given. Pays on publication. Offers 20% kill fee. Publishes ms an average of 4 months after acceptance. Editorial lead time 5 months. Submit seasonal material 6 months in advance. Accepts queries by mail, e-mail. Accepts simultaneous submissions. Responds in 3 months to queries; 3 months to mss. Guidelines online.

NONFICTION Needs general interest, with Orange County focus, inspirational, interview, prominent Orange County citizens, personal experience, celebrity profiles, guides to activities and services. Special issues: Health, Beauty, and Fitness (January); Dining (March and August); International Travel (April); Home Design (June); Arts (September); Local Travel (October). We do not accept stories that do not have specific Orange County angles. We want profiles on local people, stories on issues going on in our community, informational stories using Orange County-based sources. We cannot emphasize the local angle enough. **Buys up to 65 mss/year.** Query with published clips. Length: 1,000-2,000 words. **Negotiates payment individually.**

PHOTOS State availability. Captions, identification of subjects required. Negotiates payment individually.

COLUMNS/DEPARTMENTS Short Cuts (stories for the front of the book that focus on Orange County issues, people, and places), 150-250 words. **Buys up to 25 mss/year.** Query with published clips. **Negotiates payment individually.**

TIPS We're looking for more local personality profiles, analysis of current local issues, local takes on national issues. Most features are assigned to writers we've worked with before. Don't try to sell us 'generic' journalism. *Orange Coast* prefers articles with specific and unusual angles focused on Orange County. A lot of freelance writers ignore our Orange County focus. We get far too many generalized manuscripts.

$$ PALM SPRINGS LIFE

Desert Publications, Inc., 303 N. Indian Canyon, Palm Springs CA 92262. (760)325-2333. **Fax:** (760)325-7008. **Website:** www.palmspringslife.com. **Contact:** Olga Reyes, managing editor. **80% freelance written.** Monthly magazine covering affluent Palm Springs-area desert resort communities. *Palm Springs Life* celebrates the good life. Estab. 1958. Circ. 20,000. Byline given. Pays on publication. Offers negotiable kill fee. Publishes ms an average of 3 months after acceptance. Submit seasonal material 6 months in advance. Responds in 4-6 weeks to queries. Guidelines online.

Increased focus on desert style, home, fashion, art, culture, personalities, celebrities.

NONFICTION Needs book excerpts, essays, interview, feature stories, celebrity, fashion, spa, epicurean. Query with published clips. Length: 500-2,500 words. **Pays $100-500.**

PHOTOS State availability. Captions, identification of subjects, model releases required. Reviews contact sheets. Pays $75-350/photo.

COLUMNS/DEPARTMENTS The Good Life (art, fashion, fine dining, philanthropy, entertainment, luxury living, luxury auto, architecture), 250-750 words. **Buys 12 mss/year.** Query with or without published clips. **Pays $200-350.**

$$$ SACRAMENTO MAGAZINE

Sacramento Magazines Corp., 231 Lathrop Way, Suite A, Sacramento CA 95815. (916)426-1720. **Website:** www.sacmag.com. Publisher: Joe Chiodo. **80% freelance written. Works with a small number of new/unpublished writers each year.** Monthly magazine with a strictly local angle on local issues, human interest and consumer items for readers in the middle to high income brackets. Prefers to work with writers local to Sacramento area. Estab. 1975. Circ. 50,000. Pays on publication. No kill fee. Publishes ms an average of 3 months after acceptance. Accepts queries by mail. Responds in 3 months.

NONFICTION Buys 5 unsolicited feature mss/year. Query. 1,500-3,000 words, depending on author, subject matter and treatment. **Pays $400 and up.**

PHOTOS Send photos. Captions, identification of subjects required. Payment varies depending on photographer, subject matter and treatment.

COLUMNS/DEPARTMENTS Business, home and garden, first person essays, regional travel, gourmet, profile, sports, city arts, health, home and garden, profiles of local people (1,000-1,800 words); UpFront (250-300 words). **Pays $600-800.**

$$ SAN DIEGO MAGAZINE

San Diego Magazine Publishing Co., 707 Broadway, Suite 1100, San Diego CA 92101-7901. (619)230-9292. **Fax:** (619)230-0490. **E-mail:** erin@sandiegomagazine.com. **Website:** www.sandiegomagazine.com. **Contact:** Erin Chambers Smith, editor. **30% freelance written.** Monthly magazine covering San Diego. "We produce informative and entertaining features and investigative reports about politics; community and neighborhood issues; lifestyle; sports; design; dining; arts; and other facets of life in San Diego." Estab. 1948. Circ. 55,000. Byline given. Pays on publication. Offers 25% kill fee. Publishes ms an average of 2 months after acceptance. Editorial lead time 2 months. Submit seasonal material 4 months in advance. Accepts simultaneous submissions.

NONFICTION Needs expose, general interest, historical, how-to, interview, travel, lifestyle. **Buys 12-24 mss/year.** Send complete ms. Length: 1,000-3,000 words. **Pays $250-750.**

PHOTOS State availability. Offers no additional payment for photos accepted with ms.

$$$$ SAN FRANCISCO

243 Vallejo St., San Francisco CA 94111. (415)398-2800. **E-mail:** preulbach@modernluxury.com. **Website:** modernluxury.com/san-francisco. **Contact:** Paul Reulbach. **50% freelance written. Prefers to work with published/established writers.** Monthly city/regional magazine. Estab. 1968. Circ. 180,000. Byline given. Pays on publication. Offers 25% kill fee. Publishes ms an average of 2 months after acceptance. Submit seasonal material 5 months in advance. Responds in 2 months.

NONFICTION Needs arts, exposé, interview, travel. Query with published clips. Length: 200-4,000 words. **Pays $100-2,000 and some expenses.**

SONG OF THE SAN JOAQUIN

P.O. Box 1161, Modesto CA 95353. **E-mail:** cleor36@yahoo.com. **Website:** www.chaparralpoets.org/SSJ.html. **Contact:** Cleo Griffith, editor. *Song of the San Joaquin*, published quarterly, features "subjects about or pertinent to the San Joaquin Valley of Central California. This is defined geographically as the region from Fresno to Stockton, and from the foothills on the west to those on the east." Estab. 2003. Publishes ms 3-6 months after acceptance. Submit seasonal poems at least 3 months in advance. Responds in up to 3 months. Guidelines available for SASE or by e-mail.

Reads submissions "periodically throughout the year." Considers poetry by children and teens.

POETRY Needs Wants all forms and styles of poetry. "Keep subject in mind." Does not want "pornographic, demeaning, vague, or trite approaches." This is a quarterly; please keep in mind the seasons of the year. E-mail submissions are preferred; no disk submissions. Cover letter is preferred. "SASE required. All submissions must be typed on 1 side of the page only. Proofread submissions carefully. Name, address, phone number, and e-mail address should appear on all pages. Cover letter should include any awards, honors, and previous publications for each poem and a biographical sketch of 75 words or less." Has published poetry by Robert Cooperman, Taylor Graham, Dan

Williams, Jennifer Fenn, and Charles Rammelkamp. Submit maximum 3 poems. Length: up to 40 lines. **Pays 1 contributor's copy.**

CANADA/INTERNATIONAL

ALBERTA VIEWS

Alberta Views, Ltd., Suite 208, 320 23rd Ave. SW, Calgary AB T2S 0J2 Canada. (403)243-5334; (877)212-5334. **Fax:** (403)243-8599. **E-mail:** queries@albertaviews.ab.ca. **Website:** www.albertaviews.ab.ca. **Contact:** Evan Osenton, editor. **50% freelance written.** Bimonthly magazine covering Alberta culture: politics, economy, social issues, and art. "We are a regional magazine providing thoughtful commentary and background information on issues of concern to Albertans. Most of our writers are Albertans." Estab. 1997. Circ. 30,000. Byline given. Pays on publication. Offers 50% kill fee. Publishes ms an average of 3 months after acceptance. Editorial lead time 4 months. Submit seasonal material 3 months in advance. Accepts queries by e-mail. Responds in 6 weeks to queries; 2 months to mss. Sample copy free. "If you are a writer, illustrator, or photographer interested in contributing to *Alberta Views*, please see our contributor's guidelines online."

No phone queries.

NONFICTION Needs essays. **Buys 18 mss/year.** "Query with written proposal of 300–500 words outlining your intended contribution to *Alberta Views*, why you are qualified to write about your subject, and what sources you intend to use; a résumé outlining your experience and education; recent examples of your published work (tear sheets)." Length: 3,000-5,000 words. **Pays $1,000-1,500 for assigned articles; $350-750 for unsolicited articles.**

PHOTOS State availability. Negotiates payment individually.

FICTION Only fiction by Alberta writers via the annual *Alberta Views* fiction contest. **Buys 6 mss/year.** Send complete ms. Length: 2,500-4,000 words. **Pays up to $1,000.**

POETRY Accepts unsolicited poetry. Submit complete ms.

HAMILTON MAGAZINE

Town Media, a division of Sun Media, 1074 Cooke Blvd., Burlington ON L7T 4A8 Canada. (905)634-8003. **Fax:** (905)634-7661. **E-mail:** marc.skulnick@sunmedia.ca; tm.info@sunmedia.ca. **Website:** www.hamiltonmagazine.com. **Contact:** Marc Skulnick, editor; Kate Sharrow, art director. **50% freelance written.** Quarterly magazine devoted to the Greater Hamilton and Golden Horseshoe area (Ontario, Canada). "Our mandate: to entertain and inform by spotlighting the best of what our city and region has to offer. We invite readers to take part in a vibrant community by supplying them with authoritative and dynamic coverage of local culture, food, fashion, and design. Each story strives to expand your view of the area, every issue an essential resource for exploring, understanding and unlocking the region. Packed with insight, intrigue and suspense, *Hamilton Magazine* delivers the city to your doorstep." Estab. 1978. Byline given. Pays on publication. Offers 50% kill fee. Editorial lead time 2-3 months. Submit seasonal material 2-3 months in advance. Accepts queries by e-mail. Responds in 1 week to queries and to mss. Sample copy with #10 SASE. Guidelines by e-mail.

NONFICTION Needs book excerpts, essays, expose, historical, how-to, humor, inspirational, interview, personal experience, photo feature, religious, travel. Does not want generic articles that could appear in any mass-market publication. Send complete ms. Length: 800-2,000 words. **Pays $200-1,600 for assigned articles; $100-800 for unsolicited articles.** Sometimes pays expenses of writers on assignment.

PHOTOS State availability of or send photos. Identification of subjects required. Reviews 8×10 prints, JPEG files (8×10 at 300dpi). Negotiates payment individually.

COLUMNS/DEPARTMENTS A&E Art, 1,200-2,000 words; A&E Music, 1,200-2,000 words; A&E Books, 1,200-1,400 words. **Buys Buys 12 columns/yr. mss/year.** Send complete ms. **Pays $200-400.**

TIPS "Unique local voices are key and a thorough knowledge of the area's history, politics, and culture is invaluable."

MONDAY MAGAZINE

Black Press Ltd., 818 Broughton St., Victoria BC V8W 1E4 Canada. (250)382-6188. **Website:** www.mondaymag.com. **Contact:** Kyle Slovin, editor. **10% freelance written.** Weekly tabloid covering local news. "*Monday Magazine* is Victoria's only alternative newsweekly. For more than 35 years, we have published fresh, informative, and alternative perspectives on local events. We prefer lively, concise writing with a sense of humor and insight." Estab. 1975. Circ. 20,000. Byline given. **Currently not accepting freelance articles requiring payment.** Pays 1 month after publication. No kill fee. Publishes ms an average of 1 month after acceptance. Editorial lead time 1-2 months. Submit seasonal material 2 months in advance. Accepts queries by e-mail. Responds in 6-8 weeks to queries; 3 months to mss. Guidelines online.

NONFICTION Needs expose, general interest, humor, interview, personal experience. Special issues: Body, Mind, Spirit (October); Student Survival Guide (August). Does not want fiction, poetry, or conspiracy theories. Send complete ms. Length: 300-1,000 words. **Pays $25-50. Currently not accepting freelance articles requiring payment.**

PHOTOS Send photos. Captions, identification of subjects required. Reviews GIF/JPEG files (300 dpi at 4x6). Offers no additional payment for photos accepted with ms.

TIPS "Local writers tend to have an advantage, as they are familiar with the issues and concerns of interest to a Victoria audience."

TORONTO LIFE

St. Joseph Media Corp., Queen Richmond Centre, Toronto ON M5C 1S2 Canada. (416)364-3333. **Fax:** (416)861-1169. **E-mail:** editorial@torontolife.com; pitch@torontolife.com. **Website:** www.torontolife.com. **Contact:** Sarah Fulford, editor. **95% freelance written. Prefers to work with published/established writers.** Monthly magazine emphasizing local issues and social trends, short humor/satire, and service features for upper income, well-educated and, for the most part, young Torontonians. Circ. 92,039. Byline given. Pays on acceptance. Offers kill fee. Pays 50% kill fee for commissioned articles only. Publishes ms an average of 4 months after acceptance. Responds in 3 weeks to queries.

NONFICTION Query with published clips and SASE. Length: 1,000-6,000 words. **Pays $500-5,000.**

COLUMNS/DEPARTMENTS "We run about 5 columns an issue. They are all freelanced, though most are from regular contributors. They are mostly local in concern and cover politics, business, performing arts, media, design, and food." Length: 2,000 words. Query with published clips and SASE. **Pays $2,000.**

TIPS "Submissions should have strong Toronto orientation."

COLORADO

STEAMBOAT MAGAZINE

Ski Town Publications, Inc., 1120 S. Lincoln Ave., Suite F, Steamboat Springs CO 80487. (970)871-9413. **Fax:** (970)871-1922. **Website:** www.steamboatmagazine.com. **Contact:** Deborah Olsen, president/publisher; Suzi Mitchell, editor. **80% freelance written.** "Quarterly magazine showcasing the history, people, lifestyles, and interests of Northwest Colorado. Our readers are generally well-educated, well-traveled, upscale, active people visiting our region to ski in winter and recreate in summer. They come from all 50 states and many foreign countries. Writing should be fresh, entertaining, and informative." Estab. 1978. Circ. 20,000. Byline given. Pays 50% on acceptance, 50% on publication. No kill fee. Submit seasonal material 1 year in advance. Accepts queries by mail, e-mail, fax, phone. Responds in 3 months to queries. Guidelines free.

NONFICTION Needs book excerpts, essays, general interest, historical, humor, interview, photo feature, travel. **Buys 10-15 mss/year.** Query with published clips. Length: 150-1,500 words. **Pays $50-300 for assigned articles.**

PHOTOS Prefers to review viewing platforms, JPEGs, and dupes. Will request original transparencies when needed. State availability. Captions, identification of subjects required. Pays $50-250/photo.

TIPS "Stories must be about Steamboat Springs and the Yampa Valley to be considered. We're looking for new angles on ski/snowboard stories in the winter and activity-related stories all year round. Please query first with ideas to make sure subjects are fresh and appropriate. We try to make subjects and treatments 'timeless' in nature because our magazine is a 'keeper' with a multiyear shelf life."

TELLURIDE MAGAZINE

Big Earth Publishing, Inc., P.O. Box 3488, Telluride CO 81435. (970)728-4245. **Fax:** (866)936-8406. **E-mail:** deb@telluridemagazine.com. **Website:** www.telluridemagazine.com. **Contact:** Deb Dion Kees, editor in chief. **75% freelance written.** Telluride: community, events, recreation, ski resort, surrounding region, San Juan Mountains, history, tourism, mountain living. "*Telluride Magazine* speaks specifically to Telluride and the surrounding mountain environment. Telluride is a resort town supported by the ski industry in winter, festivals in summer, outdoor recreation year round, and the unique lifestyle all of that affords. As a National Historic Landmark District with a colorful mining history, it weaves a tale that readers seek out. The local/visitor interaction is key to Telluride's success in making profiles an important part of the content. Telluriders are an environmentally minded and progressive bunch who appreciate efforts toward sustainability and protecting the natural landscape and wilderness that are the region's number one draw." Estab. 1982. Circ. 70,000. Byline given. Pays 60 days from publication. Editorial lead time and advance on seasonal submissions is 6 months. Accepts queries by e-mail. Responds in 2 weeks to queries; in 2 months to mss. Sample copy online at website. Guidelines by e-mail.

NONFICTION Needs historical, humor, lifestyle, nostalgic, personal experience, photo feature, recreation, travel. No articles about places or adventures other than Telluride. **Buys 10 mss/year.** Query with published clips. Length: 1,000-2,000 words. **Pays $200-700 for assigned articles; $100-700 for unsolicited articles.**

PHOTOS Send no more than 20 jpeg comps (low-res) via e-mail, or send CD/DVD with submission. Reviews JPEG/TIFF files. Offers $35-300 per photo; negotiates payment individually.

COLUMNS/DEPARTMENTS Telluride Turns (news and current topics); Mountain Health (health issues related to mountain sports and living at altitude); Nature Notes (explores the flora, fauna, geology, and climate of San Juan Mountains); Green Bytes (sustainable and environmentally sound ideas and products for home building), all 500 words. **Buys 40 mss/year.** Query. **Pays $50-200.**

FICTION "Please contact us; we are very specific about what we will accept." Needs adventure, historical, humorous, recreation in the mountains, slice-of-life vignettes, western. **Buys 2 mss/year.** Query with published clips. Length: 800-1,200 words.

POETRY Needs Any poetry must reflect mountains or mountain living. Buys 1 poems/year. Length: 3 lines minimum. **Pays up to to $100.**

FILLERS Wants anecdotes, facts, short humor. Seldom buys fillers. Length: 300-1,000 words. **Pays up to $500.**

CONNECTICUT

$$$ CONNECTICUT MAGAZINE

Journal Register Co., 200 Gando Dr., New Haven CT 06513. (203)789-5226. **Fax:** (203)789-5255. **E-mail:** rbendici@connecticutmag.com. **E-mail:** dclement@connecticutmag.com. **Website:** www.connecticutmag.com. **Contact:** Doug Clement, verticals editor; Ray Bendici, content manager. **75% freelance written. "Prefers to work with published/established writers who know the state and live/have lived here.** Monthly magazine for an affluent, sophisticated, suburban audience. "We want only articles that pertain to living in Connecticut." Estab. 1971. Circ. 93,000. Byline given. Pays on publication. Offers 20% kill fee. Publishes ms an average of 4 months after acceptance. Submit seasonal material 4 months in advance. Accepts queries by mail, e-mail, fax. Responds in 6 weeks to queries.

NONFICTION Needs book excerpts, expose, general interest, interview, topics of service to Connecticut readers. Special issues: Dining/entertainment, northeast/travel, home/garden and Connecticut bride twice/year. Also, business (January) and healthcare 4-6/year. No personal essays. **Buys 50 mss/year.** Query with published clips. Length: 3,000 words maximum. **Pays $600-1,200.**

PHOTOS Send photos. Identification of subjects, model releases required. Reviews contact sheets, transparencies. Pays $50 minimum/photo.

COLUMNS/DEPARTMENTS Business, Health, Politics, Connecticut Calendar, Arts, Dining Out, Gardening, Environment, Education, People, Sports, Media, From the Field (quirky, interesting regional stories with broad appeal). Length: 1,500-2,500 words. **Buys 50 mss/year.** Query with published clips. **Pays $400-700.**

FILLERS Short pieces about Connecticut trends, curiosities, interesting short subjects, etc. Length: 150-400 words. **Pays $75-150.**

TIPS "Make certain your idea has not been covered to death by the local press and can withstand a time lag of a few months. Again, we don't want something that has already received a lot of press."

DELAWARE

$$ DELAWARE TODAY

3301 Lancaster Pike, Suite 5C, Wilmington DE 19805. (302)656-1809. **Fax:** (302)656-5843. **Website:** www.delawaretoday.com. Managing Editor: Drew Ostroski. **50% freelance written.** Monthly magazine geared toward Delaware people, places and issues. All stories must have Delaware slant. No pitches such as Delawareans will be interested in a national topic. Estab. 1962. Circ. 25,000. Byline given. Pays on publication. Offers 50% kill fee. Publishes ms an average of 4 months after acceptance. Editorial lead time 3 months. Submit seasonal material 6 months in advance. Responds in 2 months to queries.

NONFICTION Needs historical, interview, photo feature, lifestyles, issues. Special issues: Newcomer's Guide to Delaware. **Buys 40 mss/year.** Query with published clips. Length: 100-3,000 words. **Pays $50-750.** Sometimes pays expenses of writers on assignment.

PHOTOS State availability. Identification of subjects required. Negotiates payment individually.

COLUMNS/DEPARTMENTS Business, Health, History, People, all 1,500 words. **Buys 24 mss/year.** Query with published clips. **Pays $150-250.**

FILLERS Needs anecdotes, newsbreaks, short humor. **Buys 10 mss/year.** Length: 100-200 words. **Pays $50-75.**

TIPS "No story ideas that we would know about, i.e., a profile of the governor. Best bets are profiles of quirky/unique Delawareans that we'd never know about or think of."

DISTRICT OF COLUMBIA

$$$ THE WASHINGTONIAN

1828 L St. NW, Suite 200, Washington DC 20036. (202)296-3600. **E-mail:** editorial@washingtonian.com. **Website:** www.washingtonian.com. **20-25% freelance written**. Monthly magazine. "Writers should keep in mind that we are a general interest city-and-regional magazine. Nearly all our articles have a hard Washington connection. And, please, no political satire." Estab. 1965. Circ. 160,000. Byline given. Pays on publication. No kill fee. Publishes ms an average of 3 months after acceptance. Editorial lead time 10 weeks. Accepts queries by mail, fax. Guidelines online.

NONFICTION Needs book excerpts, expose, general interest, historical, with specific Washington, D.C. focus, interview, personal experience, photo feature, travel. **Buys 15-30 mss/year.** Query with published clips. **Pays 50¢/word.**

COLUMNS/DEPARTMENTS First Person (personal experience that somehow illuminates life in Washington area), 650-700 words. **Buys 9-12 mss/year.** Query. **Pays $325.**

TIPS "The types of articles we publish include service pieces; profiles of people; investigative articles; rating pieces; institutional profiles; first-person articles; stories that cut across the grain of conventional thinking; articles that tell the reader how Washington got to be the way it is; light or satirical pieces (send the complete ms, not the idea, because in this case execution is everything)."

FLORIDA

$$$$ BOCA RATON MAGAZINE

JES Publishing, 1000 Clint Moore Road, Suite 103, Boca Raton FL 33487. (561)997-8683. **Fax:** (561)997-8909. **E-mail:** kevin@bocamag.com. **Website:** www.bocamag.com. **Contact:** Kevin Kaminski, editor. **30% freelance written.** Lifestyle and city/regional magazine devoted to the residents of South Florida, featuring fashion, interior design, food, people, places, and community issues that shape the affluent South Florida market. Estab. 1981. Circ. 25,000. Byline given. Pays 45 days after acceptance. No kill fee. Publishes ms an average of 3 months after acceptance. Submit seasonal material 7 months in advance. Accepts simultaneous submissions. Responds in 1 month to queries. Does not accept unsolicited queries. Guidelines for #10 SASE.

NONFICTION Needs general interest, historical, humor, interview, photo feature, travel. Send complete ms. Length: 800-2,500 words. **Pays $350-1,200.**

REPRINTS Send tearsheet. Payment varies.

PHOTOS Send photos.

COLUMNS/DEPARTMENTS Body & Soul (health, fitness and beauty column, general interest); Hitting Home (family and social interactions); History or Arts (relevant to South Florida); all 1,000 words. Query with published clips, or send complete ms. **Pays $350-400.**

TIPS "We prefer shorter ms, highly localized articles, and excellent art/photography."

$ FT. MYERS MAGAZINE

15880 Summerlin Rd., Suite 189, Fort Myers FL 33908. (516)652-6072. **E-mail:** ftmyers@optonline.net. **Website:** www.ftmyersmagazine.com. **90% freelance written.** Bimonthly magazine covering regional arts and living for educated, active, successful and creative residents of Lee & Collier counties (FL) and guests at resorts and hotels in Lee County. "Content: Arts, entertainment, media, travel, sports, health, home, garden, environmental issues." Estab. 2001. Circ. 20,000. Byline given. 30 days after publication. No kill fee. Publishes ms an average of 2-6 months after acceptance. Editorial lead time 2-4 months. Submit seasonal material 2-4 months in advance. Accepts queries by e-mail. Accepts simultaneous submissions. Responds in 3 months to queries and to mss. Guidelines available online.

NONFICTION Needs essays, general interest, historical, how-to, humor, interview, personal experience, reviews, previews, news, informational. **Buys 10-25 mss/year.** Send complete ms. Length: 750-1,500 words. **Pays $50-150 or approximately 10¢/word.** Sometimes pays expenses of writers on assignment.

PHOTOS State availability of or send photos. Captions, identification of subjects required. Negotiates payment individually; generally offers $25-100/photo or art.

COLUMNS/DEPARTMENTS Media: books, music, video, film, theater, Internet, software (news, previews, reviews, interviews, profiles), 750-1,500 words. Lifestyles: art & design, science & technology, house & garden, health & wellness, sports & recreation, travel & leisure, food & drink (news, interviews, previews, reviews, profiles, advice), 750-1,500 words. **Buys 60 mss/year. mss/year.** Query with or without published clips or send complete ms. **Pays $50-150.**

$$$ GULFSHORE LIFE

Open Sky Media, 1421 Pine Ridge Rd., Suite 100, Naples FL 34109. (239)449-4111. **Fax:** (239)431-8420. **E-mail:** dsendler@gulfshorelifemag.com. **Website:** www.gulfshorelife.com. Editor-in-Chief: David Sendler. **75% freelance written.** Magazine published 10 times/year for southwest Florida, the workings of its natural systems, its history, personalities, culture and lifestyle. Estab. 1970. Circ. 35,000. Byline given. Pays on publication. Publishes ms an average of 4 months after acceptance. Submit seasonal material 8 months in advance. Accepts queries by mail, e-mail, fax. Accepts simultaneous submissions.

NONFICTION Needs historical, interview. **Buys 100 mss/year.** Query with published clips. Length: 500-3,000 words. **Pays $100-1,000.**

PHOTOS Send photos. Identification of subjects, model releases required. Pays $50-100.

TIPS "We buy superbly written stories that illuminate southwest Florida personalities, places and issues. Surprise us!"

$$ JACKSONVILLE

White Publishing Co., 1261 King St., Jacksonville FL 32204. (904)389-3622. **Fax:** (904)389-3628. **E-mail:** joe@jacksonvillemag.com. **Website:** www.jacksonvillemag.com. **Contact:** Joseph White, publisher/editor. **50% freelance written.** Monthly magazine covering life and business in northeast Florida for upwardly mobile residents of Jacksonville and the Beaches, Orange Park, St. Augustine and Amelia Island, Florida. Estab. 1985. Circ. 25,000. Byline given. Pays on publication. Offers kill fee. Offers 25-33% kill fee to writers on assignment. Editorial lead time 3 months. Submit seasonal material 4 months in advance. Responds in 6 weeks to queries; 1 month to mss. Sample copy for $5 (includes postage). Guidelines online.

NONFICTION Needs book excerpts, expose, general interest, historical, how-to, service articles, humor, interview, personal experience, photo feature, travel, commentary. **Buys 50 mss/year.** Query with published clips. Length: 1,200-3,000 words. **Pays $50-500 for feature length pieces.**

REPRINTS Send photocopy. Payment varies.

PHOTOS State availability. Captions, model releases required. Negotiates payment individually.

COLUMNS/DEPARTMENTS Business (trends, success stories, personalities), 1,000-1,200 words; Health (trends, emphasis on people, hopeful outlooks), 1,000-1,200 words; Money (practical personal financial advice using local people, anecdotes and examples), 1,000-1,200 words; Real Estate/Home (service, trends, home photo features), 1,000-1,200 words; Travel (weekends; daytrips; excursions locally and regionally), 1,000-1,200 words; occasional departments and columns covering local history, sports, family issues, etc. **Buys 40 mss/year. Pays $150-250.**

TIPS "We are a writer's magazine and demand writing that tells a story with flair."

PENSACOLA MAGAZINE

Ballinger Publishing, 41 N. Jefferson St., Suite 402, Pensacola FL 32502. **E-mail:** kelly@ballingerpublishing.com. **Website:** www.ballingerpublishing.com. Executive Editor: Kelly Oden. **75% freelance written.** Monthly magazine. *Pensacola Magazine*'s articles are written in a casual, conversational tone. We cover a broad range of topics that citizens of Pensacola relate to. Most of our freelance work is assigned, so it is best to send a resume, cover letter and 3 clips to the above e-mail address. Estab. 1987. Circ. 10,000. Byline given. Pays at end of shelf life. Offers 20% kill fee. Editorial lead time 1 month. Submit seasonal material 6 months in advance. Accepts queries by e-mail. Accepts simultaneous submissions. Responds in 2 weeks to queries. Sample copy for $1, SASE and 1 First-Class stamp... Guidelines available online.

NONFICTION Special issues: Wedding (February); Home & Garden (May). Query with published clips. Length: 700-2,100 words. **Pays 10-15¢/word.** Sometimes pays expenses of writers on assignment.

PHOTOS State availability of or send photos. Captions, identification of subjects, model releases required. Reviews GIF/JPEG files. Offers $7/photo.

TIPS We accept submissions for *Pensacola Magazine*, *Northwest Florida's Business Climate*, and *Coming of Age*. Please query by topic via e-mail to shannon@ballingerpublishing.com. If you do not have a specific query topic, please send a resume and three clips via e-mail, and you will be given story assignments if your writing style is appropriate. You do not have to be locally or regionally located to write for us.

TALLAHASSEE MAGAZINE

Rowland Publishing, Inc., 1932 Miccosukee Rd., Tallahassee FL 32308. **Website:** www.tallahasseemagazine.com. **20% freelance written.** Bimonthly magazine covering life in Florida's Capital Region. All content has a Tallahassee, Florida connection. Estab. 1978. Circ. 18,000. Byline given. Pays on acceptance. No kill fee. Publishes ms an average of 2 months after acceptance. Editorial lead time 4 months. Submit seasonal material 6 months in advance. Accepts queries by mail, e-mail. Accepts simultaneous submissions. Responds in 3 months to queries & mss. Sample copy for $4. Guidelines by e-mail.

NONFICTION Needs book excerpts, essays, historical, inspirational, interview, new product, personal experience, photo feature, travel, sports, business, Calendar items. No fiction, poetry, or travel. No general interest. **Buys 15 mss/year.** Query with published clips. Length: 500-2,500 words. **Pays $100-350.**

PHOTOS Send photos. Captions, identification of subjects, model releases required. Reviews prints, GIF/JPEG files. Negotiates payment individually.

TIPS "We're looking for fresh ideas and new slants that are related to Florida's Capital Region. Because we work so far in advance, it is difficult to be timely, so be sure to give us ideas that aren't too time specific."

THE THIRTY-A REVIEW

227 Sandy Springs Place, Suite D-297, Sandy Springs GA 30328. (404)560-3677. **E-mail:** miles@thirtyareview.com; mneiman@piedmontreview. **Website:** thirtyareview.com. Monthly magazine focusing on 30-A and the surrounding areas. "We tell the human-interest stories that make 30-A's entrepreneurs, developers and artists tick, making the magazine appealing to both tourists and locals alike." Accepts queries by e-mail.

NONFICTION Needs general interest, interview. Query with published clips.

WHERE (WHERE GUESTBOOK, WHERE MAP, WHERE NEWSLETTER)

Morris Visitor Publications, 699 Broad St., Suite 500, Augusta GA 30901. **Fax:** (305)892-2991. **E-mail:** editorial@wheretraveler.com. **Website:** www.wheretraveler.com. **Contact:** Geoff Kohl, chief travel editor. **40% freelance written.** Monthly magazine covering tourism in U.S. cities, certain European cities, and Singapore. Estab. 1936. Circ. 30,000. Byline for features only, but all writers listed on masthead. Pays on publication. Editorial lead time 3 months. Submit seasonal material 3 months in advance. Accepts queries by mail, e-mail. Responds in 1 week to queries Sample copy available online. Guidelines by e-mail.

Query before submitting.

NONFICTION Needs new product, photo feature, travel. Query. Length: 500 words.

PHOTOS Send photos. Captions, identification of subjects, model releases required. Reviews GIF/JPEG files. Negotiates payment individually.

COLUMNS/DEPARTMENTS Columns (all 50 words): Dining; Entertainment; Museums & Attractions; Art Galleries; Shops & Services. Queries for writer clips only per page of 1 blurbs per page.

TIPS "We look for a new slant on a 'where to go' or 'what to do' in each location."

GENERAL REGIONAL

$$ BLUE RIDGE COUNTRY

Leisure Media360, 3424 Brambleton Ave., Roanoke VA 24018. (540)989-6138. **Fax:** (540)989-7603. **E-mail:** krheinheimer@leisuremedia360.com. **Website:** www.blueridgecountry.com. **Contact:** Kurt Rheinheimer, editor. **90% freelance written.** Bimonthly, full-color magazine covering the Blue Ridge region. "The magazine is designed to celebrate the history, heritage and beauty of the Blue Ridge region. It is aimed at adult, upscale readers who enjoy living or traveling in the mountain regions of Virginia, North Carolina, West Virginia, Maryland, Kentucky, Tennessee, South Carolina, Alabama, and Georgia." Estab. 1988. Circ. 425,000. Byline given. Pays on publication. Offers kill fee. Offers $50 kill fee for commissioned pieces only. Publishes ms an average of 8 months after acceptance. Submit seasonal material 6 months in advance. Accepts queries by mail, e-mail, fax; prefer e-mail. Responds in 3-4 months to queries. Responds in 2 months to mss. Sample copy with 9x12 SASE with 6 first-class stamps. Guidelines available online.

NONFICTION Needs essays, general interest, historical, personal experience, photo feature, travel. Special issues: "The photo essay will continue to be part of each issue, but for the foreseeable future will be a combination of book and gallery/museum exhibit previews, and also essays of work by talented individual photographers—though we cannot pay, this is a good option for those who are interested in editorial coverage of their work. Those essays will include short profile, web link and contact information, with the idea of getting them, their work and their business directly in front of 425,000 readers' eyes." **Buys 25-30 mss/year.** Send complete ms. Length: 200-1,500 words. **Pays $50-250.**

PHOTOS Photos must be shot in region. Outline of region can be found online. Send photos. Identification of subjects required. Reviews transparencies. Pays $40-150 for color inside photo; pays $150 for color cover. Pays on publication. Credit line given.

COLUMNS/DEPARTMENTS Inns and Getaways (reviews of inns); Mountain Delicacies (cookbooks and recipes); Country Roads (shorts on regional news, people, destinations, events, history, antiques, books); Inns and Getaways (reviews of inns); On the Mountainside (first-person outdoor recreation pieces excluding hikes). **Buys 30-42 mss/year.** Query. **Pays $25-125.**

TIPS "Would like to see more pieces dealing with contemporary history (1940s-70s). Freelancers needed for regional departmental shorts and macro issues affecting whole region. Need field reporters from all areas of Blue Ridge region, especially more from Kentucky, Maryland and South Carolina. We are also looking for updates on the Blue Ridge Parkway, Appalachian Trail, national forests, ecological issues, preservation movements, affordable travel, and interesting short profiles of regional people."

$$$$ COWBOYS & INDIANS MAGAZINE

USFR Media Group, 6688 N. Central Expressway, Suite 650, Dallas TX 75206. (214)750-8222. **E-mail:** queries@cowboysindians.com. **Website:** www.cowboysindians.com. **60% freelance written**. Magazine published 8 times/year covering people and places of the American West. The Premier Magazine of the West, *Cowboys & Indians* captures the romance, drama, and grandeur of the American frontier—both past and present—like no other publication. Undeniably exclusive, the magazine covers a broad range of lifestyle topics: art, home interiors, travel, fashion, Western film, and Southwestern cuisine. Estab. 1993. Circ. 101,000. Byline given. Pays on publication. Offers 20% kill fee. Publishes ms an average of 2 months after acceptance. Editorial lead time 4 months. Submit seasonal material 6 months in advance. Accepts queries by mail, e-mail, fax. Sample copy for $5. Guidelines by email.

NONFICTION Needs book excerpts, expose, general interest, historical, interview, photo feature, travel, art. No essays, humor, poetry, or opinion. **Buys 40-50 mss/year.** Query. Length: 500-3,000 words. **Pays $250-5,000 for assigned articles. Pays $250-1,000 for unsolicited articles.**

PHOTOS State availability. Captions, identification of subjects required. Reviews contact sheets, 21/4x21/4 transparencies. Negotiates payment individually.

COLUMNS/DEPARTMENTS Art; Travel; Music; Home Interiors; all 200-1,000 words. **Buys 50 mss/year.** Query. **Pays $200-1,500.**

TIPS "Our readers are educated, intelligent, and well-read Western enthusiasts, many of whom collect Western Americana, read other Western publications, attend shows and have discerning tastes. Therefore, articles should assume a certain level of prior knowledge of Western subjects on the part of the reader. Articles should be readable and interesting to the novice and general interest reader as well. Please keep your style lively, above all things, and fast-moving, with snappy beginnings and endings. Wit and humor are always welcome."

MIDWEST LIVING

Meredith Corp., 1716 Locust St., Des Moines IA 50309. **E-mail:** midwestliving@meredith.com. **Website:** www.midwestliving.com. **Contact:** Query Editor. Bimonthly magazine covering Midwestern families. Regional service magazine that celebrates the interest, values, and lifestyles of Midwestern families. Estab. 1987. Circ. 925,000. Pays 2-3 weeks after acceptance. No kill fee. Editorial lead time 1 year. Accepts queries by mail. Sample copy: $3.95. Guidelines by email.

Query before submitting.

NONFICTION Needs general interest, good eating, festivals and fairs, historical, interesting slices of Midwestern history, customs, traditions and the people who preserve them, interview, towns, neighborhoods, families, people whose stories exemplify the Midwest spirit and values, travel, Midwestern destinations with emphasis on the fun and affordable. Does not want personal essays, stories about vacations, humor, nostalgia/reminiscent pieces, celebrity profiles, routine pieces on familiar destinations such as the dells, the Black Hills, or Navy Pier. Query by mail.

PHOTOS State availability.

TIPS "As a general rule of thumb, we're looking for stories that are useful to the reader with information of ideas they can act on in their own lives. Most important, we want stories that have direct relevance to our Midwest audience."

THE OXFORD AMERICAN

P.O. BOX 3235, Little Rock AR 72205. (501)374-0000. **Fax:** (501)374-0001. **E-mail:** editors@oxfordamerican.org. **Website:** www.oxfordamerican.org. **Contact:** Roger D. Hodge, editor; Eliza Bornè, managing editor. Quarterly literary magazine from the South with a national audience. Circ. 55,000. Pays on publication. Accepts queries by mail. Responds in 2-3 months or sooner to mss. Guidelines available at www.oxfordamerican.org/about/submission-guidelines.

"*The Oxford American* will consider only unpublished mss that are from and/or about the South. Especially interested in nonfiction from diverse perspectives. Considers excerpts from forthcoming books."

NONFICTION Needs short and long essays (500 to 3,000 words), general interest, how-to, humor, personal experience, travel, reporting, business. Query with SASE or send complete ms.

PHOTOS Uses photos for the cover and throughout issue. Also uses illustration, original art, and comics. Send photos. Reviews contact sheets, GIF/JPEG files, slides.

COLUMNS/DEPARTMENTS Odes, Travel, Politics, Business, Writing on Writing, Southerner Abroad, Reports, Literature.

FICTION Stories should be from or about the South. Send complete ms.

POETRY Poems should be from or about the South. Submit maximum 3-5 poems.

SOUTHERN LIVING

Time Inc. Lifestyle Group, 2100 Lakeshore Dr., Birmingham AL 35209. (205)445-6000. **Fax:** (205)445-6700. **E-mail:** sl_online@timeinc.com; southernliving@customersvc.com. **Website:** www.southernliving.com. **Contact:** Claire Machamer, online editor. Monthly magazine covering southern lifestyle. Publication addressing the tastes and interest of contemporary southerners. Estab. 1966. Circ. 2.54 million. No kill fee. Editorial lead time 3 months. Accepts queries by mail. NoSample copy for $4.99 at newsstands. Guidelines by e-mail.

Accepts submissions for their Southern Journal column. Article must be southern, commenting on life in this region. "Make it personal, contemporary in the author's point of view; original, not published."

NONFICTION Needs essays. Send ms (typed, double-spaced) by postal mail. Southern Living column: Above all, it must be southern. Need comments on life in this region, written from the standpoint of a person who is intimately familiar with this part of the world. It's personal, almost always involving something that happened to the writer or someone he or she knows very well. Takes special note of stories that are contemporary in their point of view. Length: 500-600 words.

TIPS "The easiest way to break into the magazine for writers new to us is to propose short items."

YANKEE

Yankee Publishing, Inc., P.O. Box 520, Dublin NH 03444-0520. (603)563-8111. **Fax:** (603)563-8298. **E-mail:** editors@yankeepub.com. **Website:** www.yankeemagazine.com. **Contact:** Joe Bills, editor; Heather Marcus, photo editor. **60% freelance written.** Monthly magazine covering the New England states of Connecticut, Massachusetts, Maine, New Hampshire, Rhode Island, and Vermont. "Our feature articles, as well as the departments of Home, Food, and Travel, reflect what is happening currently in these New England states. Our mission is to express and perhaps, indirectly, preserve the New England culture—and to do so in an entertaining way. Our audience is national and has one thing in common—it loves New England." Estab. 1935. Circ. 317,000. Byline given. Pays on acceptance. Offers kill fee. Editorial lead time 12 months. Submit seasonal material 1 year in advance. Accepts queries by mail, but email queries and submission preferred. Accepts simultaneous submissions. Responds in 2 months to queries. Guidelines online.

NONFICTION Needs essays, general interest, interview. Does not want "good old days" pieces or dialect, humor, or anything outside New England. **Buys 30 mss/year.** Query or submit complete ms with published clips and SASE. Length: up to 2,500 words. **Pays per assignment.** Pays expenses of writers on assignment when appropriate.

PHOTOS All photos and art are assigned to experienced professionals. If interested, send a portfolio with 35mm, 2.25, or 4x5 color transparencies. Do not send any unsolicited original photos or artwork.

TIPS "Submit lots of ideas. Don't censor yourself—let us decide whether an idea is good or bad. We might surprise you. Remember that we've been publishing since 1935, so chances are we've already done every 'classic' New England subject. Try to surprise us—it isn't easy. Study the ones we publish—the format should be apparent. It is to your advantage to read several issues of the magazine before sending us a query or a ms. *Yankee* does not publish fiction, poetry, humor, history, memoir, or cartoons as a routine format, nor do we solicit submissions."

GEORGIA

ATHENS MAGAZINE

One Press Place, Athens GA 30603. (706)208-2331. **Fax:** (706)208-2339. **Website:** www.athensmagazine.com. **70% freelance written.** Quarterly magazine focused on Athens, GA community and surrounding area (does not include Atlanta metro). Estab. 1989. Circ. 5,000. Byline given. Pays on publication. Offers 20% kill fee. Publishes ms an average of 6 months after acceptance. Editorial lead time 6-9 months. Submit seasonal material 12 months in advance. Accepts queries by mail, e-mail. Responds in 6-8 weeks to queries. Sample copy free. Guidelines online.

PHOTOS State availability. Captions, identification of subjects required. Reviews GIF/JPEG files. Negotiates payment individually.

FILLERS Needs anecdotes, facts, short humor. Length: 25-150 words. **Pays $20-150.**

TIPS "I need freelancers who are well-acquainted with Athens area who can write to its unique audience of students, retirees, etc."

FLAGPOLE MAGAZINE

P.O. Box 1027, Athens GA 30603. (706)549-9523. **Fax:** (706)548-8981. **E-mail:** editor@flagpole.com. **Website:** www.flagpole.com. **Contact:** Pete McCommons, editor and publisher. **75% freelance written.** Local alternative weekly with a special emphasis on popular (and unpopular) music. Will consider stories on national, international musicians, authors, politicians, etc., even if they don't have a local or regional news peg. However, those stories should be original and irreverent enough to justify inclusion. Of course, local/Southern news/feature stories are best. We like reporting and storytelling more than opinion pieces. Estab. 1987. Circ. 16,000. Byline given. Pays on publication. No kill fee. Publishes ms an average of 1 month after acceptance. Editorial lead time 2 months. Submit seasonal material 2 months in advance. Responds in 2 weeks to queries. Responds in 1 month to mss. Sample copy online.

NONFICTION Needs book excerpts, essays, expose, interview, new product, personal experience. **Buys 50 mss/year.** Query by e-mail Length: 600-2,000 words.

REPRINTS Send tearsheet, photocopy or typed ms with rights for sale noted and information about when and where the material previously appeared.

PHOTOS State availability. Captions required. Reviews prints. Negotiates payment individually.

TIPS "Read our publication online before querying, but don't feel limited by what you see. We can't afford to pay much, so we're open to young/inexperienced writer-journalists looking for clips. Fresh, funny/insightful voices make us happiest, as does reportage over opinion. If you've ever succumbed to the temptation to call a pop record 'ethereal' we probably won't bother with your music journalism. No faxed submissions, please."

$$ GEORGIA MAGAZINE

Georgia Electric Membership Corp., P.O. Box 1707, Tucker GA 30085. (770)270-6500. **Fax:** (770)270-6995. **E-mail:** ann.orowski@georgiaemc.com. **Website:** www.georgiamagazine.org. **Contact:** Ann Orowski, editor. **50% freelance written.** We are a monthly magazine for and about Georgians, with a friendly, conversational tone and human interest topics. Estab. 1945. Circ. 516,000. Byline given. Pays on acceptance. No kill fee. Publishes ms an average of 6 months after acceptance. Editorial lead time 2 months. Submit seasonal material 6 months in advance. Accepts simultaneous submissions. Responds in 1 month to subjects of interest. Sample copy for $2. Guidelines for #10 SASE, or by e-mail.

NONFICTION Needs general interest, Georgia-focused, historical, how-to, in the home and garden, humor, inspirational, interview, photo feature, travel. Query with published clips. Length: 1,000-1,200 words; 800 words for smaller features and departments. **Pays $350-500.**

PHOTOS State availability. Identification of subjects, model releases required. Reviews digital images, websites and prints. Negotiates payment individually.

$$ KNOWATLANTA MAGAZINE

New South Publishing, Inc., 9040 Roswell Rd., Suite 210, Atlanta GA 30350. (770)650-1102. **Fax:** (770)650-2848. **E-mail:** lindsay@knowatlanta.com. **Website:** www.knowatlanta.com. Editor: Lindsay Field. **Contact:** Lindsay Field, editor. **80% freelance written.** Quarterly magazine covering the Atlanta area. *KNOWAtlanta* is metro Atlanta's premier relocation guide. The magazine provides valuable information to people relocating to the area with articles on homes, healthcare, jobs, finances, temporary housing, apartments, education, county-by-county guides and so much more. *KNOWAtlanta* puts Atlanta at its readers' fingertips. The magazine is used by executives relocating their companies, Realtors working with future Atlantans and individuals moving to the "capital of the Southeast." Estab. 1986. Circ. 192,000. Byline given. Pays on publication. Offers 100% kill fee. Editorial lead time 2 months. Submit seasonal material 2 months in advance. Accepts queries by mail, e-mail, fax. Sample copy free.

NONFICTION Needs general interest, how-to, relocate, interview, personal experience, photo feature. No fiction. **Buys 20 mss/year.** Query with clips. Length: 800-1,500 words. **Pays $100-500 for assigned articles. Pays $100-300 for unsolicited articles.** Sometimes pays expenses of writers on assignment.

$$ SAVANNAH MAGAZINE

Morris Publishing Group, P.O. Box 1088, Savannah GA 31402. **Fax:** (912)525-0611. **E-mail:** editor@savannahmagazine.com. **Website:** www.savannahmagazine.com. **Contact:** Annabelle Carr, editor; Amy Paige Condon, associate and digital editor. **95% freelance written.** Bimonthly magazine focusing on homes and entertaining covering coastal lifestyle of Savannah and South Carolina area. "*Savannah Magazine* publishes articles about people, places, and events of interest to the residents of the greater Savannah areas, as well as coastal Georgia and the South Carolina low country. We strive to provide our readers with information that is both useful and entertaining—written in a lively, readable style." Estab. 1990. Circ. 16,000. Byline given. Pays on publication. Offers 20% kill fee. Publishes ms an average of 2 months after acceptance. Editorial lead time 2 months. Submit seasonal material 4 months in advance. Accepts queries by mail, e-mail, fax. Accepts simultaneous submissions. Responds in 4 weeks to queries; 6 weeks to mss. Sample copy free. Guidelines by e-mail.

NONFICTION Needs general interest, historical, humor, interview, travel. Does not want fiction or poetry. Query with published clips. Length: 500-750 words. **Pays $250-450.**

PHOTOS State availability. Reviews GIF/JPEG files. Negotiates payment individually. Offers no additional payment for photos accepted with ms.

HAWAII

$$$ HONOLULU MAGAZINE

PacificBasin Communications, 1000 Bishop St., Suite 405, Honolulu HI 96813. (808)537-9500. **Fax:** (808)537-6455. **E-mail:** kristinl@honolulumagazine.com. **Website:** www.honolulumagazine.com. **Contact:** Kristin Lipman, senior art director. **Prefers to work with published/established writers.** Monthly magazine covering general interest topics relating to Hawaii residents. Estab. 1888. Circ. 30,000. Byline given. Pays about 30 days after publication. Where appropriate, kill fee of half of assignment fee. Accepts queries by mail, e-mail. Guidelines available online.

NONFICTION Needs historical, interview, sports, politics, lifestyle trends, all Hawaii-related. "We write for Hawaii residents, so travel articles about Hawaii are not appropriate." Send complete ms. determined when assignments discussed. **Pays $250-1,200.** Sometimes pays expenses of writers on assignment.

PHOTOS State availability. Pays $100 for stock, $200 for assigned shot. Package rates also negotiated.

COLUMNS/DEPARTMENTS Length determined when assignments discussed. Query with published clips or send complete ms. **Pays $100-300.**

IDAHO

$$ SUN VALLEY MAGAZINE

Valley Publishing, LLC, 111 First Ave. N. #1M, Meriwether Bldg., Hailey ID 83333. (208)788-0770. **Fax:** (208)788-3881. **E-mail:** adam@sunvalleymag.com; julie@sunvalleymag.com. **Website:** www.sunvalleymag.com. **Contact:** Adam Tanous, editor; Julie Molema, art director. **95% freelance written.** Quarterly magazine covering the lifestyle of the Sun Valley area. *Sun Valley Magazine* presents the lifestyle of the Sun Valley area and the Wood River Valley, including recreation, culture, profiles, history and the arts. Estab. 1973. Circ. 17,000. Byline given. Pays on publication. No kill fee. Publishes ms an average of 5 months after acceptance. Editorial lead time 1 year. Submit seasonal material 14 months in advance. Accepts queries by mail. Accepts simultaneous submissions. Responds in 5 weeks to queries. Responds in 2 months to mss. Sample copy for $4.95 and $3 postage. Guidelines for #10 SASE.

NONFICTION Needs historical, interview, photo feature, travel. Special issues: Sun Valley home design and architecture (spring); Sun Valley weddings/wedding planner (summer). Query with published clips. **Pays $40-500.** Sometimes pays expenses of writers on assignment.

REPRINTS Only occasionally purchases reprints.

PHOTOS State availability. Identification of subjects, model releases required. Reviews transparencies. Offers $60-275/photo.

COLUMNS/DEPARTMENTS Conservation issues, winter/summer sports, health and wellness, mountain-related activities and subjects, home (interior design), garden. All columns must have a local slant. Query with published clips. **Pays $40-300.**

TIPS "Most of our writers are locally based. Also, we rarely take submissions that are not specifically assigned, with the exception of fiction. However, we always appreciate queries."

ILLINOIS

$$$$ CHICAGO MAGAZINE

435 N. Michigan Ave., Suite 1100, Chicago IL 60611. (312)222-8999. **E-mail:** bfenner@chicagomag.com; tnoland@chicagomag.com. **Website:** www.chicagomag.com. **Contact:** Elizabeth Fenner, editor-in-chief; Terrance Noland, executive editor. **50% freelance written. Prefers to work with published/established writers.** Monthly magazine for an audience which is 95% from Chicago area; 90% college educated; upper income, overriding interests in the arts, politics, dining, good life in the city and suburbs. Most are in 25-50 age bracket, well-read and articulate. "Produced by the city's best magazine editors and writers, Chicago Magazine is the definitive voice on top dining, entertainment, shopping and real estate in the region. It also offers provocative narrative stories and topical features that have won numerous awards. Chicago Magazine reaches 1.5 million readers and is published by Tribune Company." Estab. 1968. Circ. 182,000. Pays on acceptance. No kill fee. Publishes ms an average of 3 months after acceptance. Submit seasonal material 4 months in advance. Accepts queries by mail, e-mail. Responds in 1 month to queries. For sample copy, send $3 to Circulation Department. Guidelines for #10 SASE.

NONFICTION Needs expose, humor, personal experience, think pieces, profiles, spot news, historical articles. Does not want anything about events outside the city or profiles on people who no longer live in the city. **Buys 100 mss/year.** Query; indicate specifics, knowledge of city and market, and demonstrable access to sources. Length: 200-6,000 words. **Pays $100-3,000 and up.** Pays expenses of writers on assignment.

PHOTOS Usually assigned separately, not acquired from writers. Reviews 35mm transparencies, color and b&w glossy prints.

TIPS "Submit detailed queries, be business-like, and avoid cliche ideas."

$$$$ CHICAGO READER

Sun-Times Media, LLC, 350 N. Orleans St., Chicago IL 60654. (312)321-9613. **E-mail:** mail@chicagoreader.com; letters@chicagoreader.com. **Website:** www.chicagoreader.com. **Contact:** Mara Shalhoup, editor; Jake Malooley, managing editor. **50% freelance written.** Weekly alternative tabloid for Chicago. "The *Chicago Reader* is primarily a staff-written publication, but occasionally we'll run a great feature, insightful criticism, timely blog post, or expertly composed video that comes to us from a freelancer." Estab. 1971. Circ. 120,000. Byline given. Pays on publication. Occasional kill fee. Publishes ms an average of 2 weeks after acceptance. Editorial lead time up to 6 months. Accepts queries by mail, e-mail. Accepts simultaneous submissions. Responds if interested. Sample copy free. Guidelines available online.

NONFICTION **Buys 500 mss/year.** Send complete ms. Length: Features: 1,500 words and longer; Music and culture reviews: 600-1,200 words. **Pays $100-3,000.** Sometimes pays expenses of writers on assignment.

COLUMNS/DEPARTMENTS Local color, 500-2,500 words; arts and entertainment reviews, up to 1,200 words.

TIPS "Our greatest need is for full-length magazine-style feature stories on Chicago topics. We're *not* looking for: hard news (What the Mayor Said About the Schools Yesterday); commentary and opinion (What I Think About What the Mayor Said About the Schools Yesterday); or poetry. We are not particularly interested in stories of national (as opposed to local) scope, or in celebrity for celebrity's sake (a la *Rolling Stone*, *Interview*, etc.). More than half the articles published in the *Reader* each week come from freelancers, and once or twice a month we publish 1 that's come in 'over the transom'—from a writer we've never heard of and may never hear from again. We think that keeping the *Reader* open to the greatest possible number of contributors makes a fresher, less predictable, more interesting paper. We not only publish unsolicited freelance writing, we depend on it. Our last issue in December is dedicated to original fiction."

$ ILLINOIS ENTERTAINER

4223 W. Lake St., Suite 420, Chicago IL 60624. (773)717-5665. **Fax:** (773)717-5666. **E-mail:** service@illinoisentertainer.com. **Website:** www.illinoisentertainer.com. **80% freelance written.** Monthly free magazine covering popular and alternative music, as well as other entertainment (film, media) in Illinois. Estab. 1974. Circ. 55,000. Byline given. Pays on publication. Offers 50% kill fee. Publishes ms an average of 2 months after acceptance. Editorial lead time 2 months. Submit seasonal material 2 months in advance. Accepts queries by mail. Accepts simultaneous submissions. Responds in 2 months to queries. Sample copy for $5.

NONFICTION Needs expose, how-to, humor, interview, new product, reviews. No personal, confessional, or inspirational articles. **Buys 75 mss/year.** Query with published clips. Length: 600-2,600 words. **Pays $15-160.** Sometimes pays expenses of writers on assignment.

REPRINTS Send typed ms with rights for sale noted and information about when and where the material previously appeared. Pays 100% of amount paid for an original article.

PHOTOS Send photos. Captions, identification of subjects, model releases required. Reviews contact sheets, transparencies, 5x7 prints. Offers $20-200/photo.

COLUMNS/DEPARTMENTS Spins (LP reviews), 100-400 words. **Buys 200-300 mss/year.** Query with published clips. **Pays $8-25.**

TIPS "Send clips, résumé, etc. and be patient. Also, sending queries that show you've seen our magazine and have a feel for it greatly increases your publication chances. Don't send unsolicited material. No e-mail solicitations or queries of any kind."

$$ NORTHWEST QUARTERLY MAGAZINE

Hughes Media Corp., 728 N. Prospect St., Rockford IL 61107. **Fax:** (815)316-2301. **E-mail:** clinden@northwestquarterly.com. **Website:** www.northwestquarterly.com. **20% freelance written.** Quarterly magazine covering regional lifestyle of Northern Illinois and Southern Wisconsin, and also Kane and McHenry counties (Chicago collar counties), highlighting strengths of living and doing business in the area. Estab. 2004. Circ. 42,000. Byline given. Pays on publication. Publishes ms an average of 4-6 months after acceptance. Editorial lead time 6 months. Submit seasonal material 6 months in advance. Accepts queries by mail, e-mail. Responds in 2 weeks to queries; in 2 months to mss. Sample copy and guidelines by e-mail.

NONFICTION Needs historical, interview, photo feature, regional features. Does not want opinion, fiction, or "anything unrelated to our geographic region." **Buys 150 mss/year.** Query. Length: 700-2,500 words. **Pays $25-500.** Sometimes pays expenses of writers on assignment.

PHOTOS State availability. Captions required. Reviews GIF/JPEG files. Negotiates payment individually.

COLUMNS/DEPARTMENTS Health & Fitness, 1,000-2,000 words; Home & Garden, 1,500 words; Destinations & Recreation, 1,000-2,000 words; Environment & Nature, 2,000-3,000 words. **Buys 120 mss/year.** Query. **Pays $100-500.**

FILLERS Needs short humor. **Buys 24 mss/year.** Length: 100-200 words. **Pays $30-50.**

TIPS "Any interesting, well-documented feature relating to the 15-county area we cover may be considered. Nature, history, geography, culture, and destinations are favorite themes."

INDIANA

$$$ INDIANAPOLIS MONTHLY

Emmis Communications, 1 Emmis Plaza, 40 Monument Circle, Suite 100, Indianapolis IN 46204. (317)237-9288. **Fax:** (317)684-2080. **Website:** www.indianapolismonthly.com. **Contact:** Amanda Heckert, editor-in-chief. **30% freelance written. Prefers to work with published/established writers.** *Indianapolis Monthly* attracts and enlightens its upscale, well-educated readership with bright, lively editorial on subjects ranging from personalities to social issues, fashion to food. Its diverse content and attention to service make it the ultimate source by which the Indianapolis area lives. Estab. 1977. Circ. 50,000. Byline given. Pays on publication. Offers kill fee. Offers negotiable kill fee. Publishes ms an average of 2 months after acceptance. Editorial lead time 3 months. Submit seasonal material 3 months in advance. Accepts queries by mail, e-mail. Responds in 6 weeks to queries. Sample copy for $6.10.

This magazine is using more first-person essays, but they must have a strong Indianapolis or Indiana tie. It will consider nonfiction book excerpts of material relevant to its readers.

NONFICTION Needs book excerpts by Indiana authors or with strong Indiana ties, essays, expose, general interest, interview, photo feature. "No poetry, fiction, or domestic humor; no 'How Indy Has Changed Since I Left Town', 'An Outsider's View of the 500', or generic material with no or little tie to Indianapolis/Indiana." **Buys 35 mss/year.** Query by mail with published clips. Length: 200-3,000 words. **Pays $50-1,000.**

TIPS "Our standards are simultaneously broad and narrow: Broad in that we're a general interest magazine spanning a wide spectrum of topics, narrow in that we buy only stories with a heavy emphasis on Indianapolis (and, to a lesser extent, Indiana). Simply inserting an Indy-oriented paragraph into a generic national article won't get it: All stories must pertain primarily to things Hoosier. Once you've cleared that hurdle, however, it's a wide-open field. We've done features on national celebrities—Indianapolis native David Letterman and *Mir* astronaut David Wolf of Indianapolis, to name 2—and we've published 2-paragraph items on such quirky topics as an Indiana gardening supply house that sells insects by mail. Query with clips showing lively writing and solid reporting."

IOWA

$$ THE IOWAN

Pioneer Communications, Inc., 300 Walnut St., Suite 6, Des Moines IA 50309. (515)246-0402. **Fax:** (515)282-0125. **E-mail:** editor@iowan.com. **Website:** www.iowan.com. **Contact:** Dan Weeks, editor. **75% freelance written.** Bimonthly magazine covering the state of Iowa. *The Iowan* is a bimonthly magazine exploring everything Iowa has to offer. Each issue travels into diverse pockets of the state to discover the sights, meet the people, learn the history, taste the cuisine, and experience the culture. Estab. 1952. Circ. 20,000. Byline given. Pays on acceptance. Offers $100 kill fee. Publishes ms an average of 3 months after acceptance. Editorial lead time 9-10 months. Submit seasonal material 6-12 months in advance. Accepts queries by mail, e-mail. Responds to queries received twice/year. Sample copy for $4.95, plus s&h. Guidelines available at www.iowan.com/about/contributors.

NONFICTION Needs essays, general interest, historical, interview, photo feature, travel. **Buys 30 mss/year.** Query with published clips, an overview of the proposed story idea, an explanation of where, when, and why it fits, and suggested image possibilities. Each issue offers readers a colleciton of "shorts" that cover timely issues, current trends, interesting people, noteworthy work, enticing food, historical and historic

CONSUMER MAGAZINES

moments, captivating arts and culture, beckoning recreational opportunities, and more. Features cover every topic imaginable with only 2 primary rules: 1) solid storytelling and 2) great photography potential. Length: 500-750 words for "shorts"; 1,000-1,500 words for features. **Pays $150-450.** Sometimes pays expenses of writers on assignment. ; pre-approved only

PHOTOS Send photos. Captions, identification of subjects, model releases required. Reviews contact sheets, GIF/JPEG files (8x10 at 300 dpi min). Negotiates payment individually, according to space rates.

COLUMNS/DEPARTMENTS Last Word (essay), 800 words. **Buys 6 mss/year.** Query with published clips. **Pays $100.**

TIPS "Must have submissions in writing, either via e-mail or snail mail. Submitting published clips is preferred."

KANSAS

KANSAS!

1020 S. Kansas Ave, Suite 200, Topeka KS 66612-1354. (785)296-8478. **Fax:** (785)296-6988. **E-mail:** ksmagazine@sunflowerpub.com. **Website:** www.travelks.com/ks-mag/. **Contact:** Andrea Etzel. **90% freelance written.** Quarterly magazine emphasizing Kansas travel attractions and events. Estab. 1945. Circ. 45,000. Byline and courtesy bylines are given to all content. Pays on acceptance. No kill fee. Purchased content will publish an average of 1 year after acceptance. Submit seasonal material 8 months in advance. Accepts queries by mail. Responds in 2 months to queries. Guidelines available on website.

NONFICTION Needs general interest, photo feature, travel. Query by mail. Length: 750-1,250 words. **Pays $200-350.** Mileage reimbursement is available for writers on assignment in the state of Kansas; TBD by assignment editor.

PHOTOS "We are a full-color photograph/manuscript publication. Send digital photos (original transparencies only or CD with images available in high resolution) with query." Captions and location of the image (county and city) are required. Pays $25-75 for gallery images, $150 for cover. Assignments also available, welcome queries.

TIPS "History and nostalgia or essay stories do not fit into our format because they can't be illustrated well with color photos. Submit a query letter describing one appropriate idea with outline for possible article and suggestions for photos. Do not send unsolicited mss."

KENTUCKY

KENTUCKY LIVING

Kentucky Association of Electric Co-Ops, P.O. Box 32170, Louisville KY 40232. (800)595-4846. **Fax:** (502)459-1611. **E-mail:** e-mail@kentuckyliving.com. **Website:** www.kentuckyliving.com. **Contact:** Paul Wesslund, editor; Anita Travis Richter, managing editor. **Mostly freelance written. Prefers to work with published/established writers.** Monthly feature magazine primarily for Kentucky residents. Estab. 1948. Circ. 500,000. Byline given. Pays on acceptance. No kill fee. Publishes ms an average of 12 months after acceptance. Submit seasonal material at least 6 months in advance. Accepts simultaneous submissions. Responds in 1 month to queries. Sample copy with SASE (9x12 envelope and 4 first-class stamps). Guidelines available online.

NONFICTION Buys 18-24 mss/year. Prefers queries rather than submissions. Send complete ms. Stories of interest include: Kentucky-related profiles (people, places, or events), business and social trends, history, biography, recreation, travel, leisure or lifestyle articles or book excerpts; articles on contemporary subjects of general public interest, and general consumer-related features. Send queries by mid-June; editorial calendar and assignments finalized in July. Length: 500-1,500 words. **Pays $75-935** Sometimes pays expenses of writers on assignment.

PHOTOS State availability of or send photos. Identification of subjects required. Reviews photo efiles at online link or sent on CD. Payment for photos included in payment for ms.

COLUMNS/DEPARTMENTS Accepts queries for Worth the Trip column. Other columns have established columnists.

TIPS "The quality of writing and reporting (factual, objective, thorough) is considered in setting payment price. We prefer general interest pieces filled with quotes and anecdotes. Avoid boosterism. Well-researched, well-written feature articles are preferred. All articles must have a strong Kentucky connection."

KENTUCKY MONTHLY

P.O. Box 559, Frankfort KY 40602-0559. (502)227-0053; (888)329-0053. **Fax:** (502)227-5009. **E-mail:**

kymonthly@kentuckymonthly.com; steve@kentuckymonthly.com. **Website:** www.kentuckymonthly.com. **Contact:** Stephen Vest, editor. **50% freelance written.** Monthly magazine. "We publish stories about Kentucky and by Kentuckians, including stories written by those who live elsewhere." Estab. 1998. Circ. 40,000. Byline given. Pays within 3 months of publication. No kill fee. Publishes ms an average of 3 months after acceptance. Editorial lead time 4-12 months. Submit seasonal material 4-10 months in advance. Accepts queries by e-mail. Accepts simultaneous submissions. Responds in 1-3 months to queries; in 1 month to mss. Sample copy and writer's guidelines online.

NONFICTION Needs book excerpts, general interest, historical, how-to, humor, interview, photo feature, religious, travel, All pieces should have a Kentucky angle. **Buys 50 mss/year.** Query. Length: 300-2,000 words. **Pays $45-300 for assigned articles. Pays $50-200 for unsolicited articles.**

PHOTOS State availability. Captions required. Reviews negatives.

FICTION We publish stories about Kentucky and by Kentuckians, including stories written by those who live elsewhere." Needs adventure, historical, mainstream, novel concepts, Wants Kentucky-related stories. **Buys 30 mss/year.** Query with published clips. Accepts submissions by e-mail. Length: 1,000-5,000 words. **Pays $50-100.**

TIPS "Please read the magazine to get the flavor of what we're publishing each month. We accept articles via e-mail. Approximately 70% of articles are assigned."

LOUISIANA

$$ PRESERVATION IN PRINT

Preservation Resource Center of New Orleans, 923 Tchoupitoulos St., New Orleans LA 70130. (504)581-7032. **Fax:** (504)636-3073. **E-mail:** prc@prcno.org. **Website:** www.prcno.org. **Contact:** Danielle Del Sol, editor and director of publications. **30% freelance written.** Monthly magazine covering preservation. Looking for articles about interest in the historic architecture of New Orleans. Estab. 1975. Circ. 10,000. Byline given. Pays on acceptance. No kill fee. Publishes ms an average of 1 month after acceptance. Editorial lead time 1 month. Submit seasonal material 1-2 months in advance. Accepts queries by mail, e-mail, fax, phone. Accepts simultaneous submissions. Sample copy available online. Guidelines free.

NONFICTION Needs essays, historical, interview, photo feature, technical. **Buys 30 mss/year.** Query. Length: 700-1,000 words. **Pays $100-200 for assigned articles.** Sometimes pays expenses of writers on assignment.

MAINE

$ DISCOVER MAINE MAGAZINE

10 Exchange St., Suite 208, Portland ME 04101. (207)874-7720. **Fax:** (207)874-7721. **E-mail:** info@discovermainemagazine.com. **Website:** www.discovermainemagazine.com. **Contact:** Jim Burch, editor and publisher. **100% freelance written.** Monthly magazine covering Maine history and nostalgia. Sports and hunting/fishing topics are also included. "Discover Maine Magazine is dedicated to bringing the amazing history of the great state of Maine to readers in every corner of the state and to those from away who love the rich heritage and traditions of Maine. From the history of Maine's mill towns, to the traditions of family farming and coastal fishing, nine times a year Discover Maine's stories tell of life in the cities and towns across Maine as it was years ago." Estab. 1992. Circ. 12,000. Byline given. Pays on publication. No kill fee. Publishes ms an average of 2-3 months after acceptance. Editorial lead time 3 months. Submit seasonal material 3 months in advance. Accepts queries by mail, fax, phone. Accepts simultaneous submissions. Responds in 2 weeks to queries; 1 month to mss.

NONFICTION Needs historical. Does not want to receive poetry. **Buys 200 mss/year.** Send complete ms. Length: 500-2,000 words. **Pays $20-30**

PHOTOS Send photos. Negotiates payment individually.

TIPS Call first and talk with the publisher.

MARYLAND

$$ BALTIMORE MAGAZINE

1000 Lancaster St., Suite 400, Baltimore MD 21202. (443)873-3900. **E-mail:** wmax@baltimoremagazine.net. **E-mail:** wmax@baltimoremagazine.net; mjane@baltimoremagazine.net; ghilary@balimoremagazine.net; iken@baltimoremagazine.net; cron@baltimoremagazine.net; wlydia@baltimoremagazine.net. **Website:** www.baltimoremagazine.net. **Con-**

tact: Send correspondence to the appropriate editor: Max Weiss (lifestyle, film, pop culture, general inquiries); Jane Marion (food, travel); Hilary Geisbert (style, home, beauty, wellness); Ken Iglehart (business, special editions); Ron Cassie (politics, environment, health, sports); Lydia Woolever (calendar, events, party pages). **50-60% freelance written.** Monthly city magazine featuring news, profiles, and service articles. "Pieces must address an educated, active, affluent reader and must have a very strong Baltimore angle." Estab. 1907. Circ. 70,000. Byline given. Pays within 1 month of publication. Offers kill fee in some cases. Submit seasonal material 4 months in advance. Accepts queries by mail, e-mail (preferred). Sample copy: $4.99. Guidelines online.

NONFICTION Needs book excerpts, Baltimore subject or author, essays, exposé, general interest, historical, humor, interview with a Baltimorean, new product, personal experience, photo feature, travel, local and regional to Maryland. Does not want anything "that lacks a strong Baltimore focus or angle. Unsolicited personal essays are almost never accepted. We've printed only 2 over the past few years; the last was by a 19-year veteran city judge reminiscing on his time on the bench and the odd stories and situations he encountered there. Unsolicited food and restaurant reviews, whether positive or negative, are likewise never accepted." Query appropriate subject editor by e-mail (preferred) or mail with published clips or send complete ms. Length: 1,600-2,500 words. **Pays 30-40¢/word.** Sometimes pays expenses.

PHOTOS No answer.

COLUMNS/DEPARTMENTS "The shorter pieces are the best places to break into the magazine." Up Front, 300-700 words; Hot Shots and Cameo, 800-2,000 words. Query with published clips.

TIPS "Too many writers send us newspaper-style articles. We are seeking: (1) *Human interest features*—strong, even dramatic profiles of Baltimoreans of interest to our readers. (2) *First-person accounts* of experience in Baltimore or experiences of a Baltimore resident. (3) *Consumer*—according to our editorial needs and with Baltimore sources. Writers should read/familiarize themselves with the style of *Baltimore Magazine* before submitting. You're most likely to impress us with writing that demonstrates how well you handle character, dramatic narrative, and factual analysis. We also admire inspired reporting and a clear, surprising style. We strongly prefer receiving queries via e-mail. If you use standard U.S. mail, your query should fit on one page."

MASSACHUSETTS

⊘ BOSTON MAGAZINE

300 Massachusetts Ave., Boston MA 02115. (617)262-9700. **Fax:** (617)267-4925. **E-mail:** editor@bostonmagazine.com. **Website:** www.bostonmagazine.com. **Contact:** Carly Carioli, editor. **10% freelance written.** Monthly magazine covering the city of Boston. Estab. 1962. Circ. 125,000. Byline given. Pays on publication. Offers 20% kill fee. Publishes ms an average of 3 months after acceptance. Editorial lead time 2 months. Submit seasonal material 4 months in advance. Accepts queries by mail, e-mail, fax.

NONFICTION Needs book excerpts, expose, general interest, interview, politics. **Buys 20 mss/year.** Query. *No unsolicited mss.* Length: 1,200-12,000 words. Pays expenses of writers on assignment.

PHOTOS State availability. Negotiates payment individually.

COLUMNS/DEPARTMENTS Query.

TIPS "Read *Boston*, and pay attention to the types of stories we use. Suggest which column/department your story might best fit, and keep your focus on the city and its environs. We like a strong narrative style, with a slightly 'edgy' feel—we rarely do 'remember when' stories. Think *city* magazine."

$$ CAPE COD MAGAZINE

Lighthouse Media Solutions, 396 Main St., Suite 15, Hyannis MA 02601. (508)534-9291. **Fax:** (508)534-9774. **E-mail:** editor@capecodmagazine.com. **Website:** www.capecodmagazine.com. **80% freelance written.** Magazine published 9 times/year covering Cape Cod lifestyle. *Cape Cod Magazine* showcases the people, architecture, history, arts and entertainment that makes living and visiting Cape Cod a rich and rewarding experience. *Cape Cod Magazine* and capecodmagazine.com deliver readers the best dining experiences, most beautiful homes, enriching arts and cultural experiences daily in a multi-platform experience that brings Cape Cod to life. Estab. 1996. Circ. 16,000. Byline given. Pays 30 days after publication. Offers 25% kill fee. Publishes ms an average of 3 months after acceptance. Editorial lead time 6 months. Submit seasonal material 1 year in advance. Accepts queries by mail, e-mail. Responds in 3 weeks to queries. Responds in 2 months to mss. Sample copy for $5. Guidelines by e-mail.

NONFICTION Needs book excerpts, essays, general interest, historical, humor, interview, personal experience. Does not want clichéd pieces, interviews, and puff features. **Buys 3 mss/year.** Send complete ms. Length: 800-2,500 words. **Pays $300-500 for assigned articles. Pays $100-300 for unsolicited articles.** Sometimes pays expenses of writers on assignment.

COLUMNS/DEPARTMENTS Last Word (personal observations in typical back page format), 700 words. **Buys 4 mss/year.** Query with or without published clips or send complete ms. **Pays $150-300.**

TIPS "Read good magazines. We strive to offer readers the quality they find in good national magazines, so the more informed they are of what good writing is, the better the chance they'll get published in our magazine."

MICHIGAN

$$$ ANN ARBOR OBSERVER

Ann Arbor Observer Co., 2390 Winewood, Ann Arbor MI 48103. **Fax:** (734)769-3375. **E-mail:** hilton@aaobserver.com. **Website:** www.annarborobserver.com. **50% freelance written.** Monthly magazine. "We depend heavily on freelancers, and we're always glad to talk to new ones. We look for the intelligence and judgment to fully explore complex people and situations, and the ability to convey what makes them interesting." Estab. 1976. Circ. 60,000. Byline given in some sections. Pays on publication. No kill fee. Publishes ms an average of 2 months after acceptance. Accepts queries by mail, e-mail, fax, phone. Responds in 3 weeks to queries; several months to mss. Sample copy for 12.5 x 15 SAE with $3 postage. Guidelines for #10 SASE.

NONFICTION Buys 75 mss/year. Length: 100-2,500 words. **Pays up to $1,000.** Sometimes pays expenses of writers on assignment.

COLUMNS/DEPARTMENTS Up Front (short, interesting tidbits), 150 words. **Pays $100.** Inside Ann Arbor (concise stories), 300-500 words. **Pays $200.** Around Town (unusual, compelling ancedotes), 750-1,500 words. **Pays $150-200.**

TIPS "If you have an idea for a story, write a 100- to 200-word description telling us why the story is interesting. We are open most to intelligent, insightful features about interesting aspects of life in Ann Arbor."

MINNESOTA

$$ LAKE SUPERIOR MAGAZINE

Lake Superior Port Cities, Inc., P.O. Box 16417, Duluth MN 55816-0417. (218)722-5002. **Fax:** (218)722-4096. **E-mail:** edit@lakesuperior.com. **Website:** www.lakesuperior.com. **Contact:** Konnie LeMay, editor. **40% freelance written. Works with a small number of new/unpublished writers each year. Please include phone number and address with e-mail queries.** Bimonthly magazine covering contemporary and historic people, places, and current events around Lake Superior. Estab. 1979. Circ. 20,000. Byline given. Pays on publication. No kill fee. Publishes ms an average of 10 months after acceptance. Submit seasonal material 1 year in advance. Accepts queries by mail, e-mail. Responds in 3 months to queries. Sample copy: $4.95 plus 6 first-class stamps. Guidelines available online.

NONFICTION Needs book excerpts, general interest, historical, humor, interview, local, personal experience, photo feature, local, travel, local, city profiles, regional business, some investigative. **Buys 15 mss/year.** Prefers mss, but accepts short queries via mail or e-mail. Length: 1,600-2,000 words for features. **Pays $200-400.** Sometimes pays expenses of writers on assignment. , with assignments.

PHOTOS Quality photography is our hallmark. Send photos. Captions, identification of subjects, model releases required. Reviews contact sheets, 2x2 and larger transparencies, 4x5 prints. Offers $50/image; $150 for covers.

COLUMNS/DEPARTMENTS Shorter articles on specific topics of interest: Homes, Health & Wellness, Lake Superior Journal, Wild Superior, Heritage, Destinations, Profile, all 800-1,200 words. **Buys 20 mss/year.** Query with published clips. **Pays $75-200.**

FICTION Must be targeted regionally. Needs historical, humorous, mainstream, novel excerpts, slice-of-life vignettes, ghost stories. Wants stories that are Lake Superior related. Rarely uses fiction stories. **Buys 2-3 mss/year.** Query with published clips. Length: 300-2,500 words. **Pays $50-125.**

TIPS "Well-researched queries are attended to. We actively seek queries from writers in Lake Superior communities. We prefer manuscripts to queries. Provide enough information on why the subject is important to the region and our readers, or why and how something is unique. We want details. The writer must have a thorough knowledge of the subject and how it relates to our region. We prefer a fresh, unused approach to the subject which provides the reader with an emotional involvement. Almost all of our articles feature quality photography, color or b&w. It is a prerequisite of all nonfiction. All submissions should include a *short* biography of author/photographer; mug shot sometimes used. Blanket submissions need not apply."

$$$ MPLS. ST. PAUL MAGAZINE

MSP Communications, 220 S. 6th St., Suite 500, Minneapolis MN 55402. **E-mail:** edit@mspmag.com. **Website:** www.mspmag.com. **Contact:** Kelly Ryan Kegans, executive editor. Monthly magazine covering the Minneapolis-St. Paul area. *Mpls. St. Paul Magazine* is a city magazine serving upscale readers in the Minneapolis-St. Paul metro area. Circ. 80,000. Pays on publication. Editorial lead time 3 months. Accepts queries by mail, e-mail. Sample copy: $10.

NONFICTION Needs book excerpts, essays, general interest, historical, interview, personal experience, photo feature, travel. **Buys 150 mss/year.** Query with published clips. Length: 500-4,000 words. **Pays 50-75¢/word for assigned articles.**

MISSISSIPPI

$$ MISSISSIPPI MAGAZINE

Downhome Publications, 5 Lakeland Circle, Jackson MS 39216. (601)982-8418. **Fax:** (601)982-8447. **E-mail:** editor@mismag.com. **Website:** www.mississippimagazine.com. **Contact:** Melanie M. Ward, editor. **90% freelance written.** Bimonthly magazine covering Mississippi—the state and its lifestyles. "We are interested in positive stories reflecting Mississippi's rich traditions and heritage and focusing on the contributions the state and its natives have made to the arts, literature, and culture. In each issue we showcase homes and gardens, in-state travel, food, design, art, and more." Estab. 1982. Circ. 40,000. Byline given. Pays on publication. Offers 25% kill fee. Publishes ms an average of 6 months after acceptance. Editorial lead time 6 months. Submit seasonal material 1 year in advance. Accepts queries by mail, fax. Responds in 2 months to queries. Guidelines for #10 SASE or online.

NONFICTION Needs general interest, historical, how-to, home decor, interview, personal experience, travel, in-state. No opinion, political, sports, expose. **Buys 15 mss/year.** Query. Length: 100-1,200 words. **Pays $25-350.**

PHOTOS Send photos with query. Captions, identification of subjects, model releases required. Reviews transparencies, prints, digital images on CD. Negotiates payment individually.

COLUMNS/DEPARTMENTS Southern Scrapbook (see recent issues for example), 100-600 words; Gardening (short informative article on a specific plant or gardening technique), 800-1,200 words; Culture Center (story about an event or person relating to Mississippi's art, music, theatre, or literature), 800-1,200 words; On Being Southern (personal essay about life in Mississippi; only ms submissions accepted), 750 words. **Buys 6 mss/year.** Query. **Pays $150-225.**

MISSOURI

$$ 417 MAGAZINE

Whitaker Publishing, 2111 S. Eastgate Ave., Springfield MO 65809. (417)883-7417. **Fax:** (417)889-7417. **E-mail:** editor@417mag.com. **Website:** www.417mag.com. **Contact:** Katie Pollock Estes, editor. **50% freelance written.** Monthly magazine. "*417 Magazine* is a regional title serving southwest Missouri. Our editorial mix includes service journalism and lifestyle content on home, fashion and the arts; as well as narrative and issues pieces. The audience is affluent, educated, mostly female." Estab. 1998. Circ. 20,000. Byline given. Pays on acceptance. Publishes ms an average of 2-3 months after acceptance. Editorial lead time 6 months. Accepts queries by e-mail. Responds in 1-2 months to queries. Sample copy by e-mail. Guidelines online.

NONFICTION Needs essays, expose, general interest, how-to, humor, inspirational, interview, new product, personal experience, photo feature, travel, local book reviews. "We are a local magazine, so anything not reflecting our local focus is something we have to pass on." **Buys 175 mss/year.** Query with published clips. Length: 300-3,500 words. **Pays $30-500, sometimes more.** Sometimes pays expenses of writers on assignment.

TIPS "Read the magazine before contacting us. Send specific ideas with your queries. Submit story ideas of local interest. Send published clips. Be a curious reporter, and ask probing questions."

KC MAGAZINE

Anthem Publishing, 4303 W. 119th St., Leawood KS 66209. (913)894-6923. **Website:** www.kcmag.com.

75% freelance written. Monthly magazine covering life in Kansas City, Kansas. "Our mission is to celebrate living in Kansas City. We are a consumer lifestyle/general-interest magazine focused on Kansas City, its people, and places." Estab. 1994. Circ. 31,000. Byline given. Pays on acceptance. Offers 10% kill fee. Publishes ms an average of 3 months after acceptance. Editorial lead time 4 months. Submit seasonal material 6 months in advance. Accepts queries by mail, e-mail. Accepts simultaneous submissions. Sample copy for 8.5x11 SAE or online.

NONFICTION Needs exposé, general interest, interview, photo feature. **Buys 15-20 mss/year.** Query with published clips. Length: 250-3,000 words.

PHOTOS Negotiates payment individually.

COLUMNS/DEPARTMENTS Entertainment (Kansas City only), 1,000 words; Food (Kansas City food and restaurants only), 1,000 words. **Buys 12 mss/year.** Query with published clips.

MISSOURI LIFE

501 High St., Suite A, Boonville MO 65233. (660)882-9898. **Fax:** (660)882-9899. **E-mail:** dcawthon@missourilife.com. **Website:** www.missourilife.com. **Contact:** David Cawthon, associate editor. **85% freelance written.** Bimonthly magazine covering the state of Missouri. "*Missouri Life*'s readers are mostly college-educated people with a wide range of travel and lifestyle interests. Our magazine discovers the people, places, and events—both past and present—that make Missouri a great place to live and/or visit." Estab. 1973. Circ. 96,800. Byline given. Pays on publication. Editorial lead time 6 months. Submit seasonal material 6 months in advance. Accepts queries by mail, e-mail, fax. Responds in approximately 2 months to queries. Sample copy available for $4.95 and SASE with $2.44 first-class postage (or a digital version can be purchased online). Guidelines available online.

NONFICTION Needs general interest, historical, travel, all Missouri related. Length: 300-2,000 words. **No set amount per word.**

PHOTOS Contact: Sarah Herrera, associate art director. E-mail: sarah@missourilife.com. (Also contact for art/illustration.). State availability in query; buys all rights nonexclusive. Captions, identification of subjects, model releases required. Offers $50-150/photo.

COLUMNS/DEPARTMENTS "All Around Missouri (people and places, past and present, written in an almanac style); Missouri Artist (features a Missouri artist), 500 words; Made in Missouri (products and businesses native to Missouri), 500 words. Contact assistant manager for restaurant review queries.

RELOCATING TO THE LAKE OF THE OZARKS

Showcase Publishing, 2820 Bagnell Dam Blvd., #1B, Lake Ozark MO 65049. (573)365-2323, ext. 301. **Fax:** (573)365-2351. **E-mail:** spublishingco@msn.com. **Website:** www.relocatingtothelakeoftheozarks.com. **Contact:** Dave Leathers, publisher. Semi-annual relocation guide; free for people moving to the area. Circ. 12,000. Byline given. Pays on publication. No kill fee. Publishes ms an average of 6 months after acceptance. Accepts queries by e-mail. Sample copy for $8.95.

NONFICTION Needs historical, travel, local issues. Length: 600-1,000 words.

PHOTOS Purchases images portraying recreational activities, tourism, nature, business development, cultural events, historical sites, and the people of the lake area. Send color positive film in 35mm or larger format, or send high-resoultion digital images. State availability of or send photos. Identification of subjects required. Pays $20-300, depending on size.

TIPS "Read the magazine and understand our audience."

RURAL MISSOURI MAGAZINE

Association of Missouri Electric Cooperatives, P.O. Box 1645, Jefferson City MO 65102. **E-mail:** hberry@ruralmissouri.coop. **Website:** www.ruralmissouri.coop. **5% freelance written.** Monthly magazine covering rural interests in Missouri; people, places, and sights in Missouri. "Our audience is comprised of rural electric cooperative members in Missouri. We describe our magazine as 'being devoted to the rural way of life.'" Estab. 1948. Circ. 555,000. Byline given. Pays on acceptance. Publishes ms an average of 6 months after acceptance. Editorial lead time 6 months. Submit seasonal material 6 months in advance. Accepts queries by mail, e-mail. Responds in 6-8 weeks to queries and to mss. Sample copy available online. Guidelines available online.

NONFICTION Needs general interest, historical. Does not want personal experiences or nostalgia pieces. Send complete ms. Length: 1,000-1,100 words. **Pays variable amount for each piece.**

TIPS "We look for tight, well-written history pieces. Remember: History doesn't mean boring. Bring it to life for us; attribute quotes. Make us feel what you're describing to us."

MONTANA

$$ MONTANA MAGAZINE

Lee Enterprises, P.O. Box 8689, Missoula MT 59807. **E-mail:** editor@montanamagazine.com. **Website:** www.montanamagazine.com. **90% freelance written.** Bimonthly magazine. Strictly Montana-oriented magazine that features community profiles, contemporary issues, wildlife and natural history, travel pieces. Estab. 1970. Circ. 20,000. Byline given. No kill fee. Publishes ms an average of 1 year after acceptance. Submit seasonal material 1 year in advance. Accepts queries by e-mail. Accepts simultaneous submissions. Responds in 6 months to queries. Sample copy for $5 or online. Guidelines available online.

NONFICTION Needs essays, general interest, interview, photo feature, travel. Special issues: Special features on summer and winter destination points. No 'me and Joe' hiking and hunting tales; no blood-and-guts hunting stories; no poetry; no fiction; no sentimental essays. **Buys 30 mss/year.** Query with samples and SASE. Length: 800-1,000 words. **Pays 20¢/word.** Sometimes pays expenses of writers on assignment.

REPRINTS Send photocopy of article with rights for sale and information about when and where the material previously appeared. Pays 50% of amount paid for an original article.

PHOTOS Send photos. Captions, identification of subjects. model releases required. Photos must be sent digitally in high-res format with cutline information included in file information. Offers additional payment for photos accepted with ms.

COLUMNS/DEPARTMENTS Memories (reminisces of early-day Montana life), 800-1,000 words; Outdoor Recreation, 1,500-2,000 words; Community Festivals, 500 words, plus b&w or color photo; Montana-Specific Humor, 800-1,000 words. Query with samples and SASE.

TIPS "We avoid commonly known topics so Montanans won't ho-hum through more of what they already know. If it's time to revisit a topic, we look for a unique slant."

NEVADA

$$ NEVADA MAGAZINE

401 N. Carson St., Carson City NV 89701. (775)687-0610. **Fax:** (775)687-6159. **E-mail:** editor@nevadamagazine.com. **Website:** www.nevadamagazine.com. **25% freelance written. Works with a small number of new/unpublished writers each year.** Bimonthly magazine published by the state of Nevada to promote tourism. Estab. 1936. Circ. 20,000. Byline given. Pays on publication. No kill fee. Publishes ms an average of 6 months after acceptance. Submit seasonal material 6 months in advance. Accepts queries by e-mail (preferred). Responds in 1 month to queries. Sample copy available by request. Guidelines available online.

NONFICTION Prefers a well-written query or outline with specific story elements before receiving the actual story. Write, e-mail, or call if you have a story that might work. Length: 500-1,500 words. **Pays flat rate of $250 or less. For web stories, pays $100 or $200 depending on the assignment.**

PHOTOS Contact: Query art director Sean Nebeker (snebeker@nevadamagazine.com). Reviews digital images. Pays $25-250; cover, $250.

COLUMNS/DEPARTMENTS Columns include: Up Front (the latest Nevada news), Visions (emphasizes outstanding photography with extended captions), City Limits (features destination stories for Nevada's larger cities), Wide Open (features destination stories for Nevada's rural towns and regions), Cravings (stories centered on food and drink), Travels (people traveling Nevada, sharing their adventures), History, and Events & Shows.

TIPS "Keep in mind the magazine's purpose is to promote Nevada tourism."

NEW JERSEY

$$$$ NEW JERSEY MONTHLY

55 Park Place, P.O. Box 920, Morristown NJ 07963-0920. (973)539-8230. **Fax:** (973)538-2953. **E-mail:** dcarter@njmonthly.com. **Website:** www.njmonthly.com. **Contact:** Deborah Carter, managing editor. **75-80% freelance written.** Monthly magazine covering just about anything to do with New Jersey, from news, politics, and sports to decorating trends and lifestyle issues. Our readership is well-educated, affluent, and on average our readers have lived in New Jersey 20

years or more. Estab. 1976. Circ. 92,000. Byline given. Pays on completion of fact-checking. Offers 20% kill fee. Publishes ms an average of 3 months after acceptance. Editorial lead time 3 months. Submit seasonal material 6 months in advance. Accepts queries by mail, e-mail, fax, phone. Accepts simultaneous submissions. Responds in 2-3 months to queries. Guidelines online.

This magazine continues to look for strong investigative reporters with novelistic style and solid knowledge of New Jersey issues.

NONFICTION Needs book excerpts, essays, expose, general interest, historical, humor, interview, personal experience, photo feature, travel, within New Jersey, arts, sports, politics. No experience pieces from people who used to live in New Jersey or general pieces that have no New Jersey angle. **Buys 90-100 mss/year.** Query with published magazine clips and SASE. Length: 250-3,000 words. **Pays $750-2,500.** Pays reasonable expenses of writers on assignment with prior approval.

COLUMNS/DEPARTMENTS Exit Ramp (back page essay usually originating from personal experience but written in a way that tells a broader story of statewide interest), 1,200 words. **Buys 12 mss/year.** Query with published clips. **Pays $400.**

FILLERS Needs anecdotes, for front-of-book. **Buys 12-15 mss/year.** Length: 200-250 words. **$100.**

TIPS "The best approach: Do your homework! Read the past year's issues to get an understanding of our well-written, well-researched articles that tell a tale from a well-established point of view."

NEW MEXICO

NEW MEXICO MAGAZINE

Lew Wallace Bldg., 495 Old Santa Fe Trail, Santa Fe NM 87501-2750. (505)827-7447. **E-mail:** artdirector@nmmagazine.com. **Website:** www.nmmagazine.com. **70% freelance written.** Covers areas throughout the state. "We want to publish a lively editorial mix, covering both the down-home (like a diner in Tucumcari) and the upscale (a new bistro in world-class Santa Fe)." Explore the gamut of the Old West and the New Age. "Our magazine is about the power of place—in particular more than 120,000 square miles of mountains, desert, grasslands, and forest inhabited by a culturally rich mix of individuals. It is an enterprise of the New Mexico Tourism Department, which strives to make potential visitors aware of our state's multicultural heritage, climate, environment, and uniqueness." Estab. 1923. Circ. 100,000. Pays on acceptance. 20% kill fee. Publishes ms an average of 3 months after acceptance. Submit seasonal material 1 year in advance. Accepts queries by mail, e-mail (preferred). Does not accept previously published submissions.Responds to queries if interested. Sample copy for $5. Guidelines available online.

No unsolicited mss. Does not return unsolicited material.

NONFICTION Submit story idea along with a working head and subhead and a paragraph synopsis. Include published clips and a short sum-up about your strengths as a writer. Considers proposal as well as writer's potential to write the conceptualized stories.

REPRINTS Rarely publishes reprints, but sometimes publishes excerpts from novels and nonfiction books.

PHOTOS "Purchased as portfolio or on assignment. Photographers interested in photo assignments should reference submission guidelines on the contributors' page of our website."

NEW YORK

CITY LIMITS

Community Service Society of New York, 31 E. 32nd St., 3rd Floor, New York NY 10016. (212)481-8484, ext. 313. **E-mail:** editor@citylimits.org. **Website:** www.citylimits.org. **Contact:** Jarrett Murphy, executive editor and publisher. **50% freelance written.** Monthly magazine covering urban politics and policy in New York City. *City Limits* is a nonprofit online magazine focusing on issues facing New York City and its neighborhoods, particularly low-income communities. The magazine is strongly committed to investigative journalism, in-depth policy analysis, hard-hitting profiles, and investigation of pressing civic issues in New York City. Driven by a mission to inform public discourse, the magazine provides the factual reporting, human faces, data, history, and breadth of knowledge necessary to understanding the nuances, complexities, and hard truths of the city, its politics, and its people. Estab. 1976. Byline given. Pays on publication. Offers 50% kill fee. Publishes ms an average of 3 months after acceptance. Editorial lead time 2 months. Accepts queries by mail, e-mail, fax. Accepts simultaneous submissions. Responds in 1 month. Sample copy for $2.95. Guidelines free.

NONFICTION Needs book excerpts, exposè, humor, interview, opinion, photo feature. No essays, polemics. **Buys 25 mss/year.** Query with published clips. Length: 400-3,500 words. **Pays $150-2,000 for assigned articles. Pays $100-800 for unsolicited articles.** Pays expenses of writers on assignment.

PHOTOS State availability. Model release required for children. Reviews contact sheets, negatives, transparencies. Buys 20 photos from freelancers/issue; 200 photos/year. Pays $100 for color cover; $50-100 for b&w inside. Pays on publication. Credit line given. Buys rights for use in *City Limits* in print and online; higher rate given for online use.

COLUMNS/DEPARTMENTS Making Change (nonprofit business), Big Idea (policy news), Book Review—all 800 words; Urban Legend (profile), First Hand (Q&A)—both 350 words. **Buys 15 mss/year.** Query with published clips.

TIPS "Our specialty is covering low-income communities. We want to report untold stories about news affecting neighborhoods at the grassroots. We're looking for stories about housing, health care, criminal justice, child welfare, education, economic development, welfare reform, politics, and government. We need good photojournalists who can capture the emotion of a scene. We offer huge pay for great photos."

$$$$ NEW YORK MAGAZINE

New York Media, Editorial Submissions, 75 Varick St., New York NY 10013. **E-mail:** editorialsubmissions@nymag.com. **Website:** www.newyorkmag.com. **25% freelance written.** Weekly magazine focusing on current events in the New York metropolitan area. Circ. 405,149. Pays on acceptance. Offers 25% kill fee. Submit seasonal material 2 months in advance. Responds in 1 month to queries. Sample copy: $6.99 or on website.

Does not accept unsolicited mss. Query first.

NONFICTION Query by e-mail or mail. **Pays $1/word.** Pays expenses of writers on assignment.

NORTH CAROLINA

$$ AAA CAROLINAS GO MAGAZINE

6600 AAA Dr., Charlotte NC 28212. **Fax:** (704)569-7815. **Website:** www.aaacarolinas.com. **20% freelance written.** Member publication for the Carolina affiliate of American Automobile Association covering travel and auto-related issues. Estab. 1922. Circ. 1.1 million. Byline given. Pays on publication. No kill fee. Editorial lead time 2 months. Accepts queries by mail. Responds in 4-6 weeks. Sample copy and writer's guidelines for #10 SASE.

The online magazine carries original content not found in the print edition.

NONFICTION Needs travel, auto safety. Length: 750-1,000 words. **Pays $150.**

PHOTOS Send photos. Identification of subjects required. Reviews slides. Offers no additional payment for photos accepted with ms.

TIPS "Submit regional stories that focus on travel and auto safety in North and South Carolina and surrounding states."

$$ FIFTEEN 501

Weiss and Hughes Publishing, 189 Wind Chime Court, Suite 104, Raleigh NC 27615. (919)870-1722. **Fax:** (919)719-5260. **E-mail:** djackson@whmags.com. **Website:** www.fifteen501.com. **Contact:** Danielle Jackson, editor. **50% freelance written.** Quarterly magazine covering lifestyle issues relevant to residents in the U.S. 15/501 corridor of Durham, Orange, and Chatham counties in North Carolina. "We cover issues important to residents of Durham, Orange and Chatham counties. We're committed to improving our readers' overall quality of life and keeping them informed of the lifestyle amenities there." Estab. 2006. Circ. 30,000. Byline given. Pays within 30 days of publication. Offers 25% kill fee. Publishes ms an average of 2 months after acceptance. Editorial lead time 2-3 months. Submit seasonal material 6 months in advance. Accepts queries by mail, e-mail. Accepts simultaneous submissions. Responds in 2-4 weeks to queries. Sample copy available online. Guidelines by e-mail.

NONFICTION Needs general interest, historical, how-to, home interiors, landscaping, gardening, technology, inspirational, interview, personal experience, photo feature, technical, travel. Does not want opinion pieces or political or religious topics. Query. Length: 600-1,200 words. **Pays 35¢/word.** Sometimes pays expenses of writers on assignment.

PHOTOS State availability. Captions, identification of subjects required. Reviews transparencies, GIF/JPEG files. Offers no additional payment for photos accepted with ms.

COLUMNS/DEPARTMENTS Around Town (local lifestyle topics), 1,000 words; Hometown Stories, 600 words; Travel (around North Carolina), 1,000 words;

Home Interiors/Landscaping (varies), 1,000 words; Restaurants (local, fine dining), 600-1,000 words. **Buys 20-25 mss/year.** Query. **Pays 35¢/word.**

TIPS "All queries must be focused on the issues that make Durham, Chapel Hill, Carrboro, Hillsborough, and Pittsboro unique and wonderful places to live."

NORTH DAKOTA

$$ NORTH DAKOTA LIVING MAGAZINE

North Dakota Association of Rural Electric Cooperatives, 3201 Nygren Dr. NW, P.O. Box 727, Mandan ND 58554. (701)663-6501. **Fax:** (701)663-3745. **E-mail:** dhill@ndarec.com. **Website:** www.ndliving.com. **Contact:** Dennis Hill, editor in chief. **20% freelance written.** Monthly magazine covering information of interest to memberships of electric cooperatives and telephone cooperatives. "We publish a general-interest magazine for North Dakotans. We treat subjects pertaining to living and working in the northern Great Plains. We provide progress reporting on electric cooperatives and telephone cooperatives." Estab. 1954. Circ. 70,000. Byline given. Pays on acceptance. No kill fee. Publishes ms an average of 6 months after acceptance. Editorial lead time 6 months. Submit seasonal material 6 months in advance. Accepts queries by mail, e-mail. Accepts simultaneous submissions.

NONFICTION Needs general interest, historical, how-to, humor, interview, new product, travel. **Buys 20 mss/year.** Query with published clips. Length: 1,500-2,000 words. **Pays $100-500 minimum for assigned articles. Pays $300-600 for unsolicited articles.** Sometimes pays expenses of writers on assignment.

PHOTOS State availability. Identification of subjects required. Reviews contact sheets. Negotiates payment individually.

COLUMNS/DEPARTMENTS Energy Use and Financial Planning, both 750 words. **Buys 6 mss/year.** Query with published clips. **Pays $100-300.**

FICTION Needs historical, humorous, slice-of-life vignettes, western. **Buys 1 mss/year.** Query with published clips. Length: 1,000-2,500 words. **Pays $100-400.**

TIPS "Deal with what's real: real data, real people, real experiences, real history, etc."

OHIO

$$$ CINCINNATI MAGAZINE

Emmis Publishing Corp., 441 Vine St., Suite 200, Cincinnati OH 45202-2039. (513)421-4300. **Fax:** (513)562-2746. **Website:** www.cincinnatimagazine.com. **Contact:** Jay Stowe, editor; Amanda Boyd Walters, deputy editor. Monthly magazine emphasizing Cincinnati living. Circ. 38,000. Byline given. Pays on publication. No kill fee. Accepts queries by mail, e-mail. Send SASE for writer's guidelines; view content on magazine website.

NONFICTION Buys 12 mss/year. Query. Length: 2,500-3,500 words. **Pays $500-1,000.**

COLUMNS/DEPARTMENTS Topics are Cincinnati media, arts and entertainment, people, politics, sports, business, regional. Length: 1,000-1,500 words. **Buys 10-15 mss/year.** Query. **Pays $200-400.**

TIPS "It's most helpful on us if you query in writing, with clips. All articles have a local focus. No generics, please. Also: No movie, book, theater reviews, poetry, or fiction. For special advertising sections, query special sections editor Marnie Hayutin; for *Cincinnati Wedding*, query custom publishing editor Kara Renee Hagerman."

$$$ CLEVELAND MAGAZINE

City Magazines, Inc., 1422 Euclid Ave., Suite 730, Cleveland OH 44115. (216)771-2833. **Fax:** (216)781-6318. **E-mail:** gleydura@clevelandmagazine.com; miller@clevelandmagazine.com. **Website:** www.clevelandmagazine.com. **Contact:** Kristen Miller, design director; Steve Gleydura, editor. **60% freelance written. Mostly by assignment.** Monthly magazine with a strong Cleveland/Northeast Ohio angle. Estab. 1972. Circ. 50,000. Byline given. Pays on publication. No kill fee. Publishes ms an average of 3 months after acceptance. Editorial lead time 6 months. Submit seasonal material 8 months in advance. Accepts queries by mail, e-mail, fax. Accepts simultaneous submissions. Responds in 2 months to queries.

NONFICTION Needs general interest, historical, humor, interview, travel, home and garden. Query with published clips. Length: 800-4,000 words. **Pays $250-1,200.**

PHOTOS Buys an average of 50 photos from freelancers/issue; 600 photos/year. Model release required for portraits; property release required for individual homes. Photo captions required; include names, date, location, event, phone. Pays on publication. Credit line given. Buys one-time publication, electronic and promotional rights.

COLUMNS/DEPARTMENTS Talking Points (opinion or observation-driven essay), approximately 1,000 words. Query with published clips. **Pays $300.**

HYDE PARK LIVING

Community Publications, Inc., 179 Fairfield Ave., Bellevue KY 41073. (859)291-1412. **E-mail:** hydepark@livingmagazines.com. **Website:** www.livingmagazines.com. **Contact:** Grace DeGregorio. Monthly magazine covering Hyde Park community. Estab. 1983. Circ. 6,800. Byline given. Pays on publication. Editorial lead time 2 months. Submit seasonal material 3 months in advance. Accepts queries by mail, e-mail, fax. Guidelines by e-mail.

NONFICTION Needs essays, general interest, historical, humor, inspirational, interview, new product, personal experience, photo feature feature, travel. "Does not want anything unrelated to Hyde Park, Ohio." Query.

PHOTOS State availability. Captions, identification of subjects, model releases required. Reviews contact sheets, negatives, transparencies, prints, GIF/JPEG files. Negotiates payment individually.

COLUMNS/DEPARTMENTS Financial; Artistic (reviews, etc.); Historic; Food. Query.

POETRY Needs free verse, light verse, traditional. Please query.

FILLERS Needs anecdotes, short humor. Please query.

$$$ OHIO MAGAZINE

Great Lakes Publishing Co., 1422 Euclid Ave., Suite 730, Cleveland OH 44115. (216)771-2833. **E-mail:** vpospisil@ohiomagazine.com. **Website:** www.ohiomagazine.com. **Contact:** Vivian Pospisil, executive editor. **50% freelance written.** "*Ohio Magazine* serves energetic and involved Ohioans by providing award-winning stories and pictures of Ohio's most interesting people, arts, entertainment, history, homes, dining, family life, festivals, and regional travel. We capture the beauty, the adventure, and the fun of life in the Buckeye State." Estab. 1978. Circ. 40,000. Byline given. Pays on publication. 20% kill fee. Publishes ms an average of 6 months after acceptance. Submit seasonal material 6 months in advance. Accepts queries by mail, e-mail. Responds in 3 months to queries; in 3 months to mss. Sample copy: $3.95 and 9x12 SAE or online. Guidelines online.

NONFICTION Query with résumé and at least 3 published clips. Length: 1,000-3,000 words. **Pays $300-1,200.** Sometimes pays expenses of writers on assignment.

REPRINTS Contact Emily Vanuch, advertising coordinator. Pays 50% of amount paid for an original article.

PHOTOS Contact: Lesley Blake, art director (lblake@ohiomagazine.com). Rate negotiable.

COLUMNS/DEPARTMENTS Buys 5 unsolicited mss/year. Pays $100-600.

TIPS "Freelancers should send all queries in writing (either by mail or e-mail), not by telephone. Successful queries demonstrate an intimate knowledge of the publication. We are looking to increase our circle of writers who can write about the state in an informative and upbeat style. Strong reporting skills are highly valued."

OKLAHOMA

$$ OKLAHOMA TODAY

P.O. Box 1468, Oklahoma City OK 73101-1468. (405)230-8450. **Fax:** (405)230-8650. **E-mail:** megan.rossman@travelok.com. **Website:** www.oklahomatoday.com. Managing Editor: Nathan Gunter. **Contact:** Megan Rossman, photography editor. **80% freelance written. Works with approximately 25 new/unpublished writers each year.** Bimonthly magazine covering people, places, and things ofOklahoma. "We are interested in showing off the best Oklahoma has to offer; we're pretty serious about our travel slant but regularly run history, nature, and personality profiles." Estab. 1956. Circ. 45,000. Byline given. Pays on publication. No kill fee. Publishes ms an average of 6 months after acceptance. Submit seasonal material 1 year in advance. Accepts queries by mail, e-mail. Responds in 4 months to queries. Sample copy for $4.95 and 9x12 SASE or online. Guidelines available on website.

NONFICTION Needs book excerpts, on Oklahoma topics, historical, Oklahoma only, interview, Oklahomans only, photo feature, in Oklahoma, travel, in Oklahoma. No phone queries. **Buys 20-40 mss/year.** Query with published clips. Length: 250-3,000 words. **Pays $25-750.**

PHOTOS "We are especially interested in developing contacts with photographers who live in Oklahoma or have shot here. Send samples. Photo guidelines with

SASE." No answer. Captions, identification of subjects required.

TIPS "The best way to become a regular contributor to *Oklahoma Today* is to query us with 1 or more story ideas, each developed to give us an idea of your proposed slant. We're looking for lively, concise, well-researched and reported stories, stories that don't need to be heavily edited and are not newspaper style. We have a 3-person full-time editorial staff, and freelancers who can write and have done their homework get called again and again."

PENNSYLVANIA

$$ BERKS COUNTY LIVING

201 Washington St., Suite 525, GoggleWorks Center for the Arts, Reading PA 19601. (610)763-7500. **Fax:** (610)898-1933. **E-mail:** nmurry@berkscountyliving.com. **Website:** www.berkscountyliving.com. **Contact:** Nikki M. Murry, editor in chief. **90% freelance written.** Bimonthly magazine covering topics of interest to people living in Berks County, Pennsylvania. Estab. 2000. Circ. 36,000. Byline given. Pays on publication. Offers 25% kill fee. Publishes ms an average of 4 months after acceptance. Editorial lead time 3 months. Submit seasonal material 4 months in advance. Accepts queries by mail, e-mail. Accepts simultaneous submissions. Responds in 1 week to queries. Responds in 1 month to mss.

NONFICTION Needs exposé, general interest, historical, how-to, humor, inspirational, interview, new product, photo feature, travel, food, health. **Buys 25 mss/year.** Query. Length: 750-2,000 words. **Pays $150-400.** Sometimes pays expenses of writers on assignment.

PHOTOS State availability. Captions, identification of subjects, model releases required. Reviews 35mm or greater transparencies, any size prints. Negotiates payment individually.

$$ PENNSYLVANIA

Pennsylvania Magazine Co., P.O. Box 755, Camp Hill PA 17001-0755. (717)697-4660. **E-mail:** editor@pa-mag.com. **Website:** www.pa-mag.com. **Contact:** Matt Holliday, editor. **90% freelance written.** Bimonthly magazine covering people, places, events, and history in Pennsylvania. Estab. 1981. Circ. 33,000. Byline given. Pays on acceptance except for articles (by authors unknown to us) sent on speculation. Offers 25% kill fee for assigned articles. Publishes ms an average of 9 months after acceptance. Submit seasonal material 9 months in advance. Accepts queries by mail, e-mail. Responds in 4-6 weeks to queries. Sample copy free. Guidelines for #10 SASE or by e-mail.

NONFICTION Nothing on Amish topics, hunting, or skiing. **Buys 75-120 mss/year.** Query. Length: 750-2,500 words. **Pays 15¢/word.**

REPRINTS For reprints, send photocopy with rights for sale noted and information about when and where the material previously appeared. Pays 5¢/word.

PHOTOS "Contact editor via e-mail for photography instructions. We work primarily with digital images and prefer raw when possible." Photography Essay (highlights annual photo essay contest entries and showcases individual photographers). Captions required. Digital photos (send printouts and CD or DVD or contact to upload to Dropbox folder. Pays $25-35 for inside photos; $150 for covers.

COLUMNS/DEPARTMENTS Round Up (short items about people, unusual events, museums, historical topics/events, family and individually owned consumer-related businesses), 250-1,300 words; Town and Country (items about people or events illustrated with photos or commissioned art), 500 words. Include SASE. Query. **Pays 15¢/word.**

TIPS "Our publication depends on freelance work—send queries. Remember that a subject isn't an idea. Send the topic and your approach when you query. Answer the question: Would this be interesting to someone across the state? Find things that interest you enough that you'd travel 30-50 miles in a car to see/do/explore it, and send a query on that."

$$ PENNSYLVANIA HERITAGE

The Pennsylvania Heritage Foundation, Commonwealth Keystone Bldg., Plaza Level, 400 North St., Harrisburg PA 17120. (717)787-2407. **Fax:** (717)346-9099. **Website:** www.paheritage.org. **Contact:** Kyle Weaver, editor. **75% freelance written. Prefers to work with published/established writers.** Quarterly magazine covering history and culture in Pennsylvania. *Pennsylvania Heritage* introduces readers to Pennsylvania's rich culture and historic legacy; educates and sensitizes them to the value of preserving that heritage; and entertains and involves them in such a way as to ensure that Pennsylvania's past has a future. The magazine is intended for intelligent lay readers. Estab. 1974. Circ. 10,000. Byline given. Pays on publication. Publishes ms an average of 1 year after acceptance. Accepts queries by mail, e-mail. Responds in 10 weeks to queries. Responds in 8 months to mss. Sample copy for $5 and 9x12 SAE or online. Guidelines for #10 SASE.

NONFICTION No articles which do not relate to Pennsylvania history or culture. **Buys 20-24 mss/year.** Prefers to see mss with suggested illustrations. Considers freelance submissions that are shorter in length; pictorial/photographic essays; biographies of famous (and not-so-famous) Pennsylvanians; and interviews with individuals who have helped shape, make, and preserve the Keystone State's history and heritage. Length: 2,000-3,500 words. **Pays $100-500.**

PHOTOS State availability of or send photos. Captions, identification of subjects required. Pays $25-200 for transparencies; $5-75 for b&w photos.

TIPS "We are looking for well-written, interesting material that pertains to any aspect of Pennsylvania history or culture. Potential contributors should realize that, although our articles are popularly styled, they are not light, puffy, or breezy; in fact they demand strident documentation and substantiation (sans footnotes). The most frequent mistake made by writers in completing articles for us is making them either too scholarly or too sentimental or nostalgic. We want material which educates, but also entertains. Authors should make history readable and enjoyable. Our goal is to make the Keystone State's history come to life in a meaningful, memorable way."

$$$$ PITTSBURGH MAGAZINE

WiesnerMedia, Washington's Landing, 600 Waterfront Dr., Suite 100, Pittsburgh PA 15222-4795. (412)304-0900. **Fax:** (412)304-0938. **E-mail:** editors@pittsburghmagazine.com. **Website:** www.pittsburghmag.com. **Contact:** Cindi Lash, editor in chief; Betsy Benson, publisher and vice president. **70% freelance written.** Monthly magazine covering the Pittsburgh metropolitan area. *Pittsburgh* presents issues, analyzes problems, and strives to encourage a better understanding of the community. Region is Western Pennsylvania, Eastern Ohio, Northern West Virginia, and Western Maryland. Estab. 1970. Circ. 75,000. Byline given. Pays on publication. Offers kill fee. Publishes ms an average of 2 months after acceptance. Submit seasonal material 6 months in advance. Accepts queries by mail. Responds in 2 months to queries. Sample copy: $2 (old back issues). Guidelines online at www.pittsburghmagazine.com/Pittsburgh-Magazine/Writers-Guidelines, or via SASE.

NONFICTION Needs exposé, sports, informational, service, business, medical, profile, food, and lifestyle. "We do not publish fiction, poetry, advocacy, or personal reminiscence pieces." Query in writing with outline and clips. Length: 1,200-4,000 words. **Pays $300-1,500+.**

PHOTOS Query. Model releases required. Pays pre-negotiated expenses of writer on assignment.

TIPS "Best bet to break in is through a fresh take on news, sparkling writing, and a pitch with regional import or interest; also seeking fresh ideas for service pieces or profiles with a regional interest. We *never* consider any story without a strong regional focus or demonstrable relevance to our region."

SOUTH CAROLINA

CHARLESTON MAGAZINE

P.O. Box 1794, Mt. Pleasant SC 29465. (843)971-9811 or (888)242-7624. **E-mail:** dshankland@charlestonmag.com; anna@charlestonmag.com; jed@charlestonmag.com. **Website:** www.charlestonmag.com. **Contact:** Darcy Shankland, editor-in-chief; Anna Evans, managing editor; Jed Drew, publisher. **80% freelance written.** Bimonthly magazine covering current issues, events, arts and culture, leisure pursuits, travel, and personalities, as they pertain to the city of Charleston and surrounding areas. Estab. 1972. Circ. 25,000. Byline given. Pays 1 month after publication. No kill fee. Submit seasonal material 4 months in advance. Accepts queries by mail, e-mail, fax. Sample copies may be ordered at cover price from office. Guidelines for #10 SASE.

NONFICTION Needs general interest, humor, interview, opinion, photo feature, travel, food, architecture, sports, current events/issues, art. Not interested in "Southern nostalgia" articles or gratuitous history pieces. **Buys 40 mss/year.** Query with published clips and SASE. Length: 150-1,500 words. **Payment negotiated.** Sometimes pays expenses of writers on assignment.

REPRINTS Send photocopy and information about when and where the material previously appeared. Payment negotiable.

PHOTOS Send photos. Identification of subjects required. Reviews contact sheets, transparencies, slides.

COLUMNS/DEPARTMENTS Channel Markers (general local interest), 50-400 words; Local Seen (profile of local interest), 500 words; In Good Taste (restaurants and culinary trends in the city), 1,000-1,200 words, plus recipes; Chef at Home (profile of local chefs), 1,200 words, plus recipes; On the Road (travel opportunities near Charleston), 1,000-1,200 words; Southern View (personal experience about Charleston life), 750 words; Doing Business (profiles of exceptional local businesses and entrepreneurs), 1,000-1,200 words; Native Talent (local profiles), 1,000-1,200 words; Top of the Shelf (reviews of books with Southern content or by a Southern author), 750 words.

TIPS "Charleston, although a city with a 300-year history, is a vibrant, modern community with a tremendous dedication to the arts and no shortage of newsworthy subjects. We're looking for the freshest stories about Charleston—and those don't always come from insiders, but also outsiders who are keenly observant."

$$ HILTON HEAD MONTHLY

P.O. Box 5926, Hilton Head Island SC 29938. (843)842-6988, ext. 230. **E-mail:** lance@hiltonheadmonthly.com. **Website:** www.hiltonheadmonthly.com. **Contact:** Lance Hanlin, editor in chief. **75% freelance written.** Monthly magazine covering the people, business, community, environment, and lifestyle of Hilton Head, SC, and the surrounding Lowcountry. "Our mission is to offer lively, fresh writing about Hilton Head Island, an upscale, environmentally conscious, and intensely proactive resort community on the coast of South Carolina." Circ. 35,000. Byline given. Pays on publication. Offers 50% kill fee. Publishes ms an average of 6 months after acceptance. Editorial lead time 3 months. Submit seasonal material 4 months in advance. Accepts queries by mail, e-mail. Accepts simultaneous submissions. Responds in 1 week to queries; in 4 months to mss. Sample copy: $3.

NONFICTION Needs general interest, historical (Hilton Head Island history only), how-to, home related, humor, interview (Hilton Head residents only), opinion, general humor or Hilton Head Island community affairs, personal experience, travel. "Everything is local, local, local, so we're especially interested in profiles of notable residents (or those with Lowcountry ties) and original takes on home design/maintenance, environmental issues, entrepreneurship, health, sports, arts and entertainment, humor, travel, and volunteerism. We like to see how national trends/issues play out on a local level." **Buys 225-250 mss/year.** Query with published clips.

PHOTOS State availability. Reviews contact sheets, prints, digital samples. Negotiates payment individually.

COLUMNS/DEPARTMENTS News; Business; Lifestyles (hobbies, health, sports, etc.); Home; Around Town (local events, charities, and personalities); People (profiles, weddings, etc.). Query with synopsis. **Pays 20¢/word.**

TIPS "Sure, Hilton Head is known primarily as an affluent resort island, but there's plenty more going on than just golf and tennis; this is a lively community with a strong sense of identity and decades-long tradition of community, volunteerism, and environmental preservation. We don't need any more tales of why you chose to retire here or how you fell in love with the beaches, herons, or salt marshes. Seek out lively, surprising characters—there are plenty—and offer fresh (but not trendy) takes on local personalities, Southern living, and green issues."

TENNESSEE

$$ MEMPHIS

Contemporary Media, 460 Tennessee St., Suite 200, Memphis TN 38103. (901)521-9000. **Fax:** (901)521-0129. **E-mail:** murtaugh@memphismagazine.com. **Website:** www.memphismagazine.com. **Contact:** Frank Murtaugh, managing editor. **30% freelance written. Works with a small number of new/unpublished writers.** Monthly magazine covering Memphis and the local region. Our mission is to provide Memphis with a colorful and informative look at the people, places, lifestyles and businesses that make the Bluff City unique. Estab. 1976. Circ. 24,000. No byline given. Pays on publication. Submit seasonal material 3 months in advance. Accepts queries by mail, e-mail, fax.

NONFICTION Needs essays, general interest, historical, interview, photo feature, travel, Interiors/exteriors, local issues and events. Special issues: Restaurant Guide and City Guide. **Buys 20 mss/year.** Query with published clips. Length: 500-3,000 words. **Pays 10-30¢/word.** Sometimes pays expenses of writers on assignment.

PHOTOS State availability. Reviews contact sheets, transparencies.

FICTION One story published annually as part of contest. Open only to those within 150 miles of Memphis. See website for details.

TEXAS

$$$$ TEXAS MONTHLY

Emmis Publishing LP, P.O. Box 1569, Austin TX 78767. (512)320-6900. **Fax:** (512)476-9007. **E-mail:** lbaldwin@texasmonthly.com. **Website:** www.texasmonthly.com. **Contact:** Brian D. Sweany, editor; Leslie Baldwin, photo editor; Andi Beierman, deputy art director. **10% freelance written.** Monthly magazine covering Texas. Estab. 1973. Circ. 300,000. Byline given. Pays on acceptance, $1/word and writer's expenses. Publishes ms an average of 1-3 months after acceptance. Editorial lead time 2 months. Submit seasonal material 3 months in advance. Accepts queries by mail, e-mail, fax. Responds in 6-8 weeks to queries and mss. Guidelines available online.

NONFICTION Contact: John Broders, associate editor (jbroders@texasmonthly.com). Needs book excerpts, essays, expose, general interest, interview, personal experience, photo feature, travel. Does not want articles without a Texas connection. Query. Length: 2,000-5,000 words.

PHOTOS Contact: Leslie Baldwin (lbaldwin@texasmonthly.com).

TIPS "Stories must appeal to an educated Texas audience. *Texas Monthly* covers the state's politics, sports, business, culture and changing lifestyles. We like solidly researched reporting that uncovers issues of public concern, reveals offbeat and previously unreported topics, or uses a novel approach to familiar topics. It contains lengthly features, interviews, essays, book excerpts, and reviews of books and movies. Does not want articles without a Texas connection. Any issue of the magazine would be a helpful guide; sample copy for $7."

$$ TEXAS PARKS & WILDLIFE

4200 Smith School Rd., Bldg. D, Austin TX 78744. (800)937-9393. **Fax:** (512)389-8397. **E-mail:** magazine@tpwd.texas.gov. **Website:** www.tpwmagazine.com. **20% freelance written.** Monthly magazine featuring articles about "Texas hunting, fishing, birding, outdoor recreation, game and nongame wildlife, state parks, environmental issues." All articles must be about Texas. Estab. 1942. Circ. 150,000. Byline given. Pays on acceptance. Offers kill fee. Negotiable. Publishes ms an average of 4 months after acceptance. Accepts queries by e-mail. Responds in 1 month to queries; 3 months to mss. Sample copy and guidelines available online.

Texas Parks & Wildlife needs more short items for front-of-the-book scout section and wildlife articles written from a natural history perspective (not for hunters).

NONFICTION Needs general interest (Texas only), how-to, outdoor activities, photo feature, travel, state parks, and small towns. **Buys 20 mss/year.** Query with published clips; follow up by e-mail 1 month after submitting query. Length: 500-2,500 words. **Pays per article content.** Sometimes pays expenses of writers on assignment. , but must be approved in advance.

PHOTOS Send photos to photo editor. Captions, identification of subjects required. Reviews transparencies. Offers $65-500/photo.

TIPS "Queries with a strong seasonal peg are preferred. Our planning progress begins 7-8 months (or longer) before the date of publication. That means you have to think ahead: *What will Texas outdoor enthusiasts want to read about 7-12 months from today?*"

VERMONT

$$ VERMONT LIFE MAGAZINE

One National Life Dr., 6th Floor, Montpelier VT 05620. (802)828-3241. **Fax:** (802)828-3366. **E-mail:** editors@vtlife.com. **Website:** www.vermontlife.com. **Contact:** Bill Anderson, managing editor. **90% freelance written. Prefers to work with published/established writers.** Quarterly magazine. "We read all story ideas submitted, but we cannot reply individually to each one. If we want to pursue a given manuscript or idea, we will contact you within 30 days of receiving it. Please bear in mind that *Vermont Life* produces pages as much as 6 months in advance of publication and may require photographs to be taken a year ahead of publication. We seek stories that have to do with contemporary Vermont culture and the Vermont way of life. As the state magazine, we are most interested in ideas that present positive aspects of life in Vermont. However, while we are nonpartisan, we have no rules about avoiding controversy when the presentation of the subject can illustrate some aspect of Vermont's unique character. We prefer reporting and journalism built around original ideas and insights, emerging trends, and thought-provoking connections in a Vermont context." Estab. 1946. Circ. 53,000. Byline given. Publishes ms an average of 9 months after acceptance. Submit seasonal material 1 year in advance. Accepts queries by e-mail only; no phone queries. Responds in 1 month to queries. "Read online guidelines before submitting: http://www.vermontlife.com/guidelines-for-contributors."

PHOTOS Buys seasonal photographs. Gives assignments but only with experienced photographers. Query via e-mail only. Original digital photos from cameras of at least 6 megapixels. Photographs should be current (taken within the last 3 years). Metadata for each image must include captions; photographer's name, the location from which the photo was taken, especially the town; identification of subjects and important landmarks; date; model releases required. Pays $75-200 inside color; $500 for cover.

TIPS "Review online guidelines before submitting queries or photography."

VIRGINIA

$$ ALBEMARLE

Carden Jennings Publishing, 375 Greenbrier Dr., Suite 100, Charlottesville VA 22901. (434)817-2010. **Fax:** (434)817-2020. **E-mail:** info@albemarlemagazine.com. **E-mail:** editorial@albemarlemagazine.com. **Website:** www.albemarlemagazine.com. **80% freelance written.** Bimonthly magazine covering lifestyle for central Virginia. "*albemarle* is a lifestyle magazine originating from the birthplace of Thomas Jefferson. We are committed to Jeffersonian ideals: intellectual depth, love for the land, historic and cultural significance, humor, and celebration of life. Much of the content is regional and seeks to enlighten, educate, and entertain readers who are long-time residents, newcomers, and visitors to Charlottesville and Albemarle County." Estab. 1987. Circ. 10,000. Byline given. Pays on publication. Offers 30% kill fee. Publishes ms an average of 4 months after acceptance. Editorial lead time 6-8 months. Submit seasonal material 6 months in advance. Accepts queries by e-mail. Accepts simultaneous submissions. Responds in 1 month to queries; in 2 months to mss. Sample copy for $6; e-mail eden@cjp.com. Guidelines online.

NONFICTION Needs essays, historical, interview, photo feature, travel. No fiction, poetry, or anything without a direct tie to central Virginia. **Buys 30-35 mss/year.** Query with published clips. Length: 900-3,500 words. **Payment varies based on type of article.** Sometimes pays expenses of writers on assignment.

PHOTOS State availability. Captions, identification of subjects, model releases required. Reviews transparencies. Negotiates payment individually.

COLUMNS/DEPARTMENTS Etcetera (personal essay), 900-1,200 words; Leisure (travel, sports), 3,000 words. **Buys 20 mss/year.** Query with published clips. **Pays $75-150.**

TIPS "Be familiar with the central Virginia area and lifestyle. We prefer a regional slant, which should include a focus on someone or something located in the region, or a focus on someone or something from the region making an impact in other parts of the world. Quality writing is a must. Story ideas that lend themselves to multiple sources will give you a leg up on the competition."

$$ VIRGINIA LIVING

Cape Fear Publishing, 109 E. Cary St., Richmond VA 23219. **E-mail:** erinparkhurst@capefear.com. **Website:** www.virginialiving.com. **Contact:** Erin Parkhurst, editor. **80% freelance written.** Bimonthly magazine covering life and lifestyle in Virginia. "We are a large-format (10x13) glossy magazine covering life in Virginia, from food, architecture, and gardening to issues, profiles, and travel." Estab. 2002. Circ. 70,000. Byline given. Pays on publication. Publishes ms an average of 4-6 months after acceptance. Editorial lead time 2-6 months. Submit seasonal material 1 year in advance. Accepts queries by mail. Accepts simultaneous submissions. Responds in 1-3 month to queries. Sample copy: $5.95.

NONFICTION Needs book excerpts, essays, exposé, general interest, historical, interview, new product, personal experience, photo feature, travel, architecture, design. No fiction, poetry, previously published articles, or stories with a firm grasp of the obvious. **Buys 180 mss/year.** Query with published clips or send complete ms. Length: 300-3,000 words. **Pays 50¢/word.**

PHOTOS **Contact:** Sonda Andersson Pappan, art director. Captions, identification of subjects, model releases required. Reviews contact sheets, 6x7 transparencies, 8x10 prints, GIF/JPEG files. Negotiates payment individually.

COLUMNS/DEPARTMENTS Beauty; Travel; Books; Events; Sports (all with a unique Virginia slant), all

1,000-1,500 words. **Buys 50 mss/year.** Send complete ms. **Pays $120-200.**

TIPS "Queries should be about fresh subjects in Virginia. Avoid stories about Williamsburg, Chincoteague ponies, Monticello, the Civil War, and other press release-type topics. We prefer to introduce new subjects, faces, and ideas, and get beyond the many clichés of Virginia. Freelancers would also do well to think about what time of the year they are pitching stories for, as well as art possibilities. We are a large-format magazine, so photography is a key component to our stories."

WASHINGTON

$$$ SEATTLE WEEKLY

307 Third Ave. S., 2nd Floor, Seattle WA 98104. (206)623-0500. **Fax:** (206)467-4338. **E-mail:** editorial@seattleweekly.com. **E-mail:** mbaumgarten@seattleweekly.com. **Website:** www.seattleweekly.com. **Contact:** Matt Baumgarten, editor-in-chief. **20% freelance written.** Weekly tabloid covering arts, politics, food, business and books with local and regional emphasis. The *Seattle Weekly* publishes stories on Northwest politics and art, usually written by regional and local writers, for a mostly upscale, urban audience; writing is high-quality magazine style. Estab. 1976. Circ. 105,000. Byline given. Pays on publication. Offers variable kill fee. Publishes ms an average of 1 month after acceptance. Submit seasonal material 2 months in advance. Responds in 1 month to queries. Sample copy for $3.

NONFICTION Needs book excerpts, expose, general interest, historical, Northwest, humor, interview, opinion. **Buys 6-8 mss/year.** Query with cover letter, résumé, published clips, and SASE. Length: 300-4,000 words. **Pays $50-800.** Sometimes pays expenses of writers on assignment.

REPRINTS Send tearsheet. Payment varies.

WISCONSIN

$$ MADISON MAGAZINE

Morgan Murphy Media, 7025 Raymond Rd., Madison WI 53719. (608)270-3600. **Fax:** (608)270-3636. **E-mail:** bnardi@madisonmagazine.com. **Website:** www.madisonmagazine.com. **Contact:** Brennan Nardi, editor; Katie Vaughn, managing editor. **75% freelance written.** Monthly magazine covering life in the greater Madison, Wisconsin, area. Estab. 1978. Byline given. Pays on publication. Offers 33% kill fee. Publishes ms an average of 2 months after acceptance. Editorial lead time 3 months. Submit seasonal material 3-4 months in advance. Accepts queries by mail, e-mail. Accepts simultaneous submissions. Responds in 3 weeks to queries. Responds in 3 weeks to mss. Sample copy free. Guidelines available via e-mail.

NONFICTION Needs book excerpts, essays, expose, general interest, historical, how-to, humor, inspirational, interview, new product, opinion, personal experience, photo feature, religious, technical, travel.

PHOTOS State availability. Reviews contact sheets. Negotiates payment individually.

COLUMNS/DEPARTMENTS Columns: Your Town (local events) and OverTones (local arts/entertainment), both 300 words; Habitat (local house/garden) and Business (local business), both 800 words. **Buys 120 mss/year.** Query with published clips. **Pays variable amount.**

FILLERS Needs anecdotes, facts, gags, newsbreaks, short humor. Length: 100 words. **Pays 20-30¢/word.**

TIPS "Our magazine is local, so only articles pertaining to Madison, Wisconsin, are considered. Specific queries are heavily appreciated. We like fresh, new content taken in a local perspective. Show us what you're like to write for us."

$$$$ MILWAUKEE MAGAZINE

126 N. Jefferson St., Milwaukee WI 53202. (414)273-1101. **Fax:** (414)273-0016. **Website:** www.milwaukeemag.com. **Contact:** E-mail appropriate editor (see website). **40% freelance written.** Monthly magazine covering the people, issues, and places of theMilwaukee, Wisconsin, area. "We publish stories about Milwaukee, of service to Milwaukee-area residents and exploring the area's changing lifestyle, business, arts, politics, and dining. Our goal has always been to create an informative, literate and entertaining magazine that will challenge Milwaukeeans with in-depth reporting and analysis of issues of the day, provide useful service features, and enlighten readers with thoughtful stories, essays and columns. Underlying this mission is the desire to discover what is unique about Wisconsin and its people, to challenge conventional wisdom when necessary, criticize when warranted, heap praise when deserved, and season all with affection and concern for the place we call home." Circ. 40,000. Byline given. Pays on publication. Offers

20% kill fee. Publishes ms an average of 2 months after acceptance. Submit seasonal material 6 months in advance. Accepts queries by e-mail. Responds in 6 weeks to queries. Sample copy for $6. Guidelines online.

NONFICTION Needs essays, expose, general interest, historical, interview, photo feature, travel, food and dining, and other services. No articles without a strong Milwaukee or Wisconsin angle. **Buys 30-50 mss/year.** Query with published clips. Length: 2,500-5,000 words for full-length features; 800 words for 2-page breaker features (short on copy, long on visuals). **Pays $700-2,000 for full-length articles.** Sometimes pays expenses of writers on assignment.

COLUMNS/DEPARTMENTS Insider (inside information on Milwaukee, exposé, slice-of-life, unconventional angles on current scene), up to 500 words; Mini Reviews for Insider, 125 words. Query with published clips.

TIPS "Pitch something for the Insider, or suggest a compelling profile we haven't already done. Submit clips that prove you can do the job. The department most open is Insider. Think short, lively, offbeat, fresh, people-oriented. We are actively seeking freelance writers who can deliver lively, readable copy that helps our readers make the most out of the Milwaukee area. Because we're only human, we'd like writers who can deliver copy on deadline that fits the specifications of our assignment. If you fit this description, we'd love to work with you."

WISCONSIN NATURAL RESOURCES

Wisconsin Department of Natural Resources, P.O. Box 7921, Madison WI 53707-7921. (608)266-1510. **Fax:** (608)264-6293. **E-mail:** natasha.kassulke@wisconsin.gov. **E-mail:** Natasha Kassulke. **Website:** www.wnrmag.com. **30% freelance written.** Bimonthly magazine covering environment, natural resource management, and outdoor skills. "We cover current issues in Wisconsin aimed to educate and advocate for resource conservation, outdoor recreation, and wise land use." Estab. 1931. Circ. 88,000. Byline given. Publishes ms an average of 8 months after acceptance. Editorial lead time 6 months. Submit seasonal material 1 year in advance. Accepts queries by mail, e-mail. Accepts simultaneous submissions. Responds in 3 weeks to queries; in 6 months to mss. Sample copy free. Guidelines available online.

NONFICTION Needs essays, how-to, photo feature, features on current outdoor issues and environmental issues. Does not want animal rights pieces, poetry, or fiction. Query. Length: 1,500-2,700 words.

PHOTOS Also seeks photos of pets at state properties like wildlife areas, campsites, and trails. Send photos. Identification of subjects required. Reviews transparencies, JPEG files. Offers no additional payment for photos accepted with ms.

TIPS "Provide images that match the copy."

$$ WISCONSIN TRAILS

333 W. State St., Milwaukee WI 53201. **Fax:** (414)647-4723. **E-mail:** clewis@jrn.com. **Website:** www.wisconsintrails.com. **Contact:** Chelsey Lewis, assistant editor. **40% freelance written.** Bimonthly magazine for readers interested in Wisconsin and its contemporary issues, personalities, recreation, history, natural beauty, and arts. Estab. 1960. Circ. 55,000. Byline given. Pays 1 month from publication. Kill fee 20%, up to $75. Publishes ms an average of 6 months after acceptance. Submit seasonal material 1 year in advance. Accepts queries by mail, e-mail, fax. Responds in 2-3 months to queries. Sample copy for $4.95. Guidelines for #10 SASE or online.

NONFICTION Does not accept unsolicited mss. Query or send a story idea via e-mail. Length: 250-1,500 words. **Pays 25¢/word.** Sometimes pays expenses of writers on assignment.

PHOTOS "Because *Wisconsin Trails* works primarily with professional photographers, we do not pay writers for accompanying images nor do we reimburse for any related expenses. Photos will be credited and the photographer retains all rights." Contact editor. Pays $75-250.

TIPS "When querying, submit well-thought-out ideas about stories specific to people, places, events, arts, outdoor adventures, etc., in Wisconsin. Include published clips with queries. Do some research—many queries we receive are pitching ideas for stories we recently have published. Know the tone, content, and audience of the magazine. Refer to our writer's guidelines, or request them, if necessary."

WYOMING

$ WYOMING RURAL ELECTRIC NEWS (WREN)

2710 Thomas Ave., Cheyenne WY 82001. (307)772-1986. **Fax:** (307)634-0728. **E-mail:** wren@wyomingrea.org. **Website:** www.wyomingrea.org/community/wren-magazine.php. **40% freelance written.**

CONSUMER MAGAZINES

Monthly magazine (except in January) for audience of small town residents, vacation-home owners, farmers, and ranchers. Estab. 1954. Circ. 39,100. Byline given. Pays on acceptance. No kill fee. Publishes ms an average of 2 months after acceptance. Submit seasonal material 2 months in advance. Accepts queries by mail, e-mail. Responds in 1 month to queries. Sample copy for $2.50 and 9x12 SASE. Guidelines for #10 SASE.

NONFICTION No nostalgia, sarcasm, or tongue-in-cheek. **Buys 4-10 mss/year.** Send complete ms. Length: 600-800 words. **Pays up to $150, plus 3 copies.**

REPRINTS Send tearsheet or photocopy and information about when and where the material previously appeared.

PHOTOS Color only.

TIPS "Always looking for fresh, new writers. Submit entire ms. Don't submit a regionally set story from some other part of the country. Photos and illustrations (if appropriate) are always welcomed. We want factual articles that are blunt, to the point, accurate."

RELIGIOUS

ALIVE NOW

1908 Grand Ave., P.O. Box 340004, Nashville TN 37203. (615)340-7254. **E-mail:** alivenow@upperroom.org. **Website:** www.alivenow.org; alivenow.upperroom.org. **Contact:** Beth A. Richardson, editor. *Alive Now,* published bimonthly, is a devotional magazine that invites readers to enter an ever-deepening relationship with God. "*Alive Now* seeks to nourish people who are hungry for a sacred way of living. Submissions should invite readers to see God in the midst of daily life by exploring how contemporary issues impact their faith lives. Each word must be vivid and dynamic and contribute to the whole. We make selections based on a list of upcoming themes. Manuscripts which do not fit a theme will be returned." Estab. 1971. Circ. 70,000. Pays on acceptance. Accepts queries by mail, e-mail. Subscription: $17.95/year (6 issues); $26.95 for 2 years (12 issues). Additional subscription information, including foreign rates, available on website. Guidelines online at website. Submissions should invite readers to seek God in the midst of daily life by exploring how contemporary issues impact their faith lives. If ms does not fit a theme, it will not be considered. Themes can be found on website. Prefers electronic submissions attached as Word document. Postal submissions should include SASE. Include name, address, theme on each sheet. Payment will be made at the time of acceptance for publication.

FICTION Needs religious. **Pays $35 or more on acceptance.**

POETRY Pays $35 or more on acceptance.

ANCIENT PATHS

E-mail: skylarburris@yahoo.com. **Website:** www.editorskylar.com/magazine/table.html. **Contact:** Skylar H. Burris, Editor. *Ancient Paths* provides "a forum for quality Christian poetry and flash fiction. All works should have a spiritual theme. The theme may be explicitly Christian or broadly religious. Works published in *Ancient Paths* explore themes such as redemption, sin, forgiveness, doubt, faith, gratitude for the ordinary blessings of life, spiritual struggle, and spiritual growth. Please, no overly didactic works. Subtlety is preferred." Estab. 1998. Responds in 4-6 weeks "if rejected; longer if being seriously considered." Single past printed sample copy: $9. Make checks payable to Skylar Burris. Guidelines available on website.

New issues of *Ancient Paths* are no longer being produced in print. *Ancient Paths* online is published as a regularly updated Facebook page.

FICTION E-mail submissions only. Paste flash fiction directly in e-mail message. Use the subject heading "AP Online Submission (title of your work)." Include name and e-mail address at top of e-mail. Previously published works accepted, provided they are not currently available online. Please indicate if your work has been published elsewhere." Needs flash fiction. Length: no more than 900 words. **Pays $1.25 per work published. Published authors also receive discount code for $3 off 2 past printed issues.**

POETRY E-mail all submissions. Paste poems in e-mail message. Use the subject heading "AP Online Submission (title of your work)." Include your name and e-mail address at the top of your e-mail. Poems may be rhymed, unrhymed, free verse, or formal. Does not want "preachy" poetry, inconsistent meter, or forced rhyme; no stream of conscious or avant-garde work; no esoteric academic poetry. Length: no more than 60 lines. **Pays $1.25 per poem. Published poets also receive discount code for $3 off 2 past printed issues.**

TIPS "Read the great religious poets: John Donne, George Herbert, T.S. Eliot, Lord Tennyson. Remember not to preach. This is a literary magazine, not a pulpit. This does not mean you do not communicate morals or celebrate God. It means you are not overbearing or simplistic when you do so."

BIBLE ADVOCATE

Bible Advocate, Church of God (Seventh Day), P.O. Box 33677, Denver CO 80233. (303)452-7973. **E-mail:** bibleadvocate@cog7.org. **Website:** baonline.org. **Contact:** Sherri Langton, associate editor. **25% freelance written.** Religious magazine published 6 times/year. "Our purpose is to advocate the Bible and represent the Church of God (Seventh Day) to a Christian audience." Estab. 1863. Circ. 13,500. Byline given. Pays on publication. No kill fee. Publishes ms an average of 9 months after acceptance. Editorial lead time 3 months. Submit seasonal material 6 months in advance. Accepts queries by mail, e-mail. Accepts simultaneous submissions. Responds in 2 months to queries. Sample copy for SAE with 9x12 envelope and 3 first-class stamps. Guidelines online.

NONFICTION Needs inspirational, personal experience, religious, Biblical studies. No articles on Christmas or Easter. **Buys 5-10 mss/year.** Send complete ms and SASE. Length: 1,000-1,200 words. **Pays $25-55.**

REPRINTS E-mail ms with rights for sale noted.

POETRY Needs free verse, traditional, Christian/Bible themes. Prefers e-mail submissions. Cover letter is preferred. "No handwritten submissions, please. I read them first and reject those that won't work for us. I send good ones to editor for approval." Seldom comments on rejected poems. No avant-garde. Buys 10-12 poems/year. Submit maximum 5 poems. Length: 5-20 lines. **Pays $20 and 2 contributor's copies.**

TIPS "Be fresh, not preachy! Articles must be in keeping with the doctrinal understanding of the Church of God (Seventh Day). Therefore, the writer should become familiar with what the Church generally accepts as truth as set forth in its doctrinal beliefs. We reserve the right to edit mss to fit our space requirements, doctrinal stands, and church terminology. Significant changes are referred to writers for approval. No fax or handwritten submissions, please."

THE BREAKTHROUGH INTERCESSOR

Breakthrough, Inc., P.O. Box 121, Lincoln VA 20160. **Fax:** (540)338-1934. **E-mail:** breakthrough@intercessors.org. **Website:** intercessors.org. *The Breakthrough Intercessor*, published quarterly, focuses on "encouraging people in prayer and faith; preparing and equipping those who pray." Accepts multiple articles per issue: 300- to 1,000-word true stories on prayer, or poems on prayer. Estab. 1980. Time between acceptance and publication varies. Subscription: $18. Make checks payable to Breakthrough, Inc. Guidelines available on website.

The Breakthrough Intercessor is 36 pages, magazine-sized, professionally printed, saddle-stapled with self-cover, includes art/graphics. Press run is 4,000.

NONFICTION Needs essays, memoir. Send complete ms, along with article name, author's name, address, phone number, and e-mail. Considers previously published articles. Accepts fax, e-mail (pasted into body of message or attachment), and mailed hard copy. Articles are circulated to an editorial board. Length: approximately 1,000 words.

POETRY Send poem, along with title, author's name, address, phone number, and e-mail. Accepts fax, e-mail (pasted into body of message or attachment), and mailed hard copy. Length: 12 lines/poem minimum.

CATHOLIC DIGEST

P.O. Box 6015, New London CT 06320. (800)321-0411. **Fax:** (860)457-3013. **E-mail:** queries@catholicdigest.com. **Website:** www.catholicdigest.com. **12% freelance written.** Magazine published 9 times/year on Catholic lifestyle and faith. Publishes features and advice on topics ranging from health, psychology, humor, adventure, and family to ethics, spirituality, and Catholics, from modern-day heroes to saints through the ages. Helpful and relevant reading culled from secular and religious periodicals. Estab. 1936. Circ. 275,000. Byline given. Pays on publication. No kill fee. Editorial lead time 3 months. Submit seasonal material 4-5 months in advance. Accepts queries by mail, e-mail. Responds in 2 months to mss. Sample copy free. Guidelines available on website.

NONFICTION Needs book excerpts, essays, general interest, historical, how-to, humor, inspirational, interview, personal experience, religious, travel. Special issues: Accepts features on the following topics: Marriage, Practical Spirituality, Parish/Work, Parenting, Grandparenting, Homemaking, Relationships, Good Looks. Does not accept unsolicited submissions. Query with 1-2 relevant writing samples. Length: 350-1,500 words. **Pays $500.**

REPRINTS For reprints, send tearsheet or typed ms with rights for sale noted and information about when and where the material previously appeared. Pays $100.

PHOTOS State availability. "If your query is accepted and you have photos that may be used to accompany your submission, please attach them as JPEG files. Photos must be at least 300 dpi to be used in the magazine. Appropriate credit lines and captions should also accompany the photos." Reviews contact sheets, transparencies, prints. Negotiates payment individually.

FILLERS Open Door (statements of true incidents through which people are brought into the Catholic faith, or recover the Catholic faith they had lost), 350-600 words, send to opendoor@catholicdigest.com; Last Word (back page, personal, inspirational, reflective essay), 550-700 words, send to queries@catholicdigest.com. Query with 1-2 relevant writing samples. **Pays $500 for Last Word, $100 for Open Door.**

TIPS "Spiritual, self-help, and all wellness is a good bet for us. We would also like to see material with an innovative approach to daily living, articles that show new ways of looking at old ideas, problems. You've got to dig beneath the surface."

CHRISTIAN HOME & SCHOOL

Christian Schools International, 3350 E. Paris Ave. SE, Grand Rapids MI 49512. (616)957-1070, ext. 240. **Fax:** (616)957-5022. **E-mail:** rheyboer@csionline.org. **Website:** www.csionline.org/christian_home_and_school. **30% freelance written. Works with a small number of new/unpublished writers each year.** Magazine published 2 times/year during the school year covering family life and Christian education. In addition, a special high school issue is published each spring. *Christian Home & School* is designed for parents in the U.S. and Canada who send their children to Christian schools and are concerned about the challenges facing Christian families today. These readers expect a mature, Biblical perspective in the articles, not just a Bible verse tacked onto the end. Estab. 1922. Circ. 66,000. Byline given. Pays on publication. No kill fee. Publishes ms an average of 4 months after acceptance. Submit material 4 months in advance. Accepts queries by mail, e-mail. Responds in 1 month to queries. Sample copy for 9x12 SAE with 4 first-class stamps. Guidelines only for #10 SASE or online. For article topics, refer to the editorial calendar on website.

The editor reports an interest in seeing articles on how to experience and express forgiveness in your home, help your child make good choices, and raise kids who are opposites, and promote good educational practices in Christian schools and current education issues. Please visit website to view editorial calendar and specific topics for each issue.

NONFICTION Needs book excerpts, interview, opinion, personal experience, articles on parenting and school life. **Buys 30 mss/year.** Send complete ms as a Word document. Length: 1,000-2,000 words. **Pays $175-250.**

TIPS "Features are the area most open to freelancers. We are publishing articles that deal with contemporary issues that affect parents. Use an informal, easy-to-read style rather than a philosophical, academic tone. Try to incorporate vivid imagery and concrete, practical examples from real life. We look for mss with a mature Christian perspective."

COLUMBIA

1 Columbus Plaza, New Haven CT 06510. (203)752-4398. **Fax:** (203)752-4109. **E-mail:** columbia@kofc.org. **Website:** www.kofc.org/columbia. **Contact:** Alton Pelowski, editor. *Columbia* is a monthly magazine for Catholic families that caters primarily to members of the Knights of Columbus. Estab. 1921. Circ. 1,500,000. Pays on acceptance. No kill fee. Accepts queries by mail, e-mail. Sample copy and writer's guidelines on website.

NONFICTION No reprints, poetry, cartoons, puzzles, short stories/fiction. Query with SASE or by e-mail. Length: 750-1,500 words. **Payment varies.**

DAVEY AND GOLIATH'S DEVOTIONS

Evangelical Lutheran Church in America, ELCA Churchwide Ministries, 8765 W. Higgins Rd., Chicago IL 60631. **E-mail:** daveyandgoliath@elca.org. **E-mail:** cllsub@augsburgfortress.org. **Website:** www.daveyandgoliath.org. "*Davey and Goliath's Devotions* is a magazine with concrete ideas that families can use to build Biblical literacy and share faith and serve others. It includes Bible stories, family activities, crafts, games, and a section of puzzles and mazes." Pays on acceptance.

A booklet of interactive conversations and activities related to weekly devotional material. Used primarily by Lutheran families with elementary school-age children.

NONFICTION Needs religious. Special issues: "Each quarter of *Davey and Goliath's Devotions* will have 2 writers. One writer will create 4 pages of content for each week, and 1 writer will create 13 puzzles, mazes, and other fun games for kids." If you are interested in writing weekly content or puzzles or games, query with samples. Follow Weekly Content or Puzzles and Games Content guidelines, available online. Length: 350-400 words for Weekly Content.

TIPS "Pay attention to details in the sample devotional. Follow the process laid out in the information for prospective writers. Ability to interpret Bible texts appropriately for children is required. Content must be doable and fun for families on the go."

$$ EFCA TODAY

Evangelical Free Church of America, 418 Fourth St., NE, Charlottesville VA 22902. **E-mail:** editor@efca.org. **Website:** efcatoday.org. **Contact:** Diane J. McDougall, editor. **30% freelance written.** Quarterly digital magazine. "*EFCA Today*'s purpose is to unify church leaders around the overall mission of the EFCA by bringing its stories and vision to life, and to sharpen those leaders by generating conversations over topics pertinent to faith and life in the 21st century." Estab. 1931. Byline given. Pays on acceptance. Offers 50% kill fee. Publishes ms an average of 3 months after acceptance. Editorial lead time 5 months. Submit seasonal material 6 months in advance. Accepts queries by e-mail. Rarely accepts previously published material.Responds in 6 weeks. Sample available online. Guidelines online.

NONFICTION Needs articles related to *EFCA* themes, book reviews, blog posts. Special issues: "Each *EFCA Today* is devoted to a topic designed to stimulate thoughtful dialogue and leadership growth, and to highlight how EFCA leaders are already involved in living out that theme. Examples of themes are: new paradigms for 'doing church,' church planting, and rural/small-town churches. These articles focus on an issue rather than on an individual, although individuals indeed illustrate each theme." Query. Length: 500-2,000 words for articles. **Pays 23¢/word.**

REPRINTS Reprint payment varies.

$ EUROPEAN JUDAISM

LBC, The Sternberg Centre, 80 East End Rd., London N3 2SY England. **E-mail:** european.judaism@lbc.ac.uk. **Website:** www.journals.berghahnbooks.com/ej. **Contact:** managing editor. "For over 40 years, *European Judaism* has provided a voice for the postwar Jewish world in Europe. It has reflected the different realities of each country and helped to rebuild Jewish consciousness after the Holocaust. It is a peer-reviewed journal with emphasis on European Jewish theology, philosophy, literature, and history. Each issue includes a poetry and book reviews section." Estab. 1966. *European Judaism* is available online. Individual Rate (Online Only): $34.95/£21.95/€24.95. Student Rate (Online Only): $19.95/ £12.95/ €14.95. Please visit the website for institutional pricing. Guidelines available online.

NONFICTION The Board of Editors welcomes articles, letters, and comments for publication. Submit by e-mail, accompanied by 1 double-spaced copy and a brief biographical note on the author. Please visit the website for further details.

POETRY Submit by e-mail, accompanied by 1 double-spaced copy and a brief biographical note on the author. Please visit the website for further details.

EVANGEL

Light and Life Communications, 770 N. High School Rd., Indianapolis IN 46214. (317)244-3660. **Contact:** Julie Innes, editor. *Evangel*, published quarterly, is an adult Sunday School paper. "Devotional in nature, it lifts up Christ as the source of salvation and hope. The mission of *Evangel* is to increase the reader's understanding of the nature and character of God and the nature of a life lived for Christ. Material fitting this mission and not longer than 1,200 words will be considered." Press run is less than 10,000. Estab. 1897 by Free Methodist denomination. Pays on publication. Publishes ms 18-36 months after acceptance. Submit seasonal poems 1 year in advance. Accepts simultaneous submissions. Responds in 6-10 weeks to submissions. Seldom comments on rejected poems. Sample copy and writer's guidelines for #10 SASE. Subscription: $2.69/quarter (13 weeks). "Write 'guidelines request' on your envelope to separate it from the submissions."

FICTION Fiction involves people coping with everyday crises, making decisions that show spiritual growth. Accepts 3-4 mss/issue; 156-200 mss/year. Needs true religious/inspirational. "No fiction without any semblance of Christian message or where the message clobbers the reader. Looking for devotional-style short pieces, 500 words or less." Send complete ms. Accepts multiple submissions. **Pays 5¢/word and 2 contributor's copies.**

POETRY Submit no more than 5 poems at a time. Cover letter is preferred. "Poetry must be typed on 8.5x11 white paper. In the upper left corner of each page, include your name, address, and phone number. In the upper right corner of cover page, specify what rights you are offering. One-eighth of the way down the page, give the title. All subsequent material must be double-spaced with 1-inch margins." Accepts about 5% of poetry received. Rarely uses rhyming work. **Pays $10/poem plus 2 contributor's copies.**

TIPS Desires concise, tight writing that supports a solid thesis and fits the mission expressed in the guidelines.

EVANGELICAL MISSIONS QUARTERLY

Billy Graham Center/Wheaton College, P.O. Box 794, Wheaton IL 60187. (630)752-7158. **Fax:** (630)752-7155. **E-mail:** emq@wheaton.edu. **Website:** www.emqonline.com. **Contact:** Laurie Fortunak Nichols, managing editor; A. Scott Moreau, editor. **67% freelance written.** Quarterly magazine covering evangelical missions. *Evangelical Missions Quarterly* is a professional journal serving the worldwide missions community. *EMQ* articles reflect missionary life, thought, and practice. Each issue includes articles, book reviews, editorials, and letters. Subjects are related to worldwide mission and evangelism efforts and include: successful ministries, practical ideas, new tactics and strategies, trends in world evangelization, church planting and discipleship, health and medicine, literature and media, education and training, relief and development, missionary family life, and much more. Estab. 1964. Circ. 7,000. Byline given. Pays on publication. Offers negotiable kill fee. Publishes ms an average of 18 months after acceptance. Editorial lead time 1 year. Accepts queries by e-mail. Responds in 2 weeks to queries. Sample copy free. Guidelines available online.

NONFICTION Needs book reviews, essays, interview, opinion, personal experience, religious. No sermons, poetry, or straight news. **Buys 24 mss/year.** Query. Length: 3,000 words. **Pays $25-100.**

PHOTOS Send photos. Identification of subjects required. Offers no additional payment for photos accepted with ms.

COLUMNS/DEPARTMENTS In the Workshop (practical how to's), 800-2,000 words; Perspectives (opinion), 800 words. **Buys 8 mss/year.** Query. **Pays $50-100.**

TIPS "We prefer articles about deeds done, showing the why and the how, claiming not only success but also admitting failure. Principles drawn from one example must be applicable to missions more generally. *EMQ* does not include articles which have been previously published in journals, books, websites, etc."

FAITH TODAY

Evangelical Fellowship of Canada, P.O. Box 5885, West Beaver Creek Post Office, Richmond Hill ON L4B 0B8 Canada. (905)479-5885. **Fax:** (905)479-4742. **Website:** www.faithtoday.ca. Bimonthly magazine. "*Faith Today* is the magazine of an association of more than 40 evangelical denominations but serves evangelicals in all denominations. It focuses on church issues, social issues, and personal faith as they are tied to the Canadian context. Writing should explicitly acknowledge that Canadian evangelical context." Estab. 1983. Circ. 20,000. Byline given. Pays on publication. Offers 30-50% kill fee. Publishes ms an average of 4 months after acceptance. Editorial lead time 4 months. Accepts queries by mail, e-mail, fax. Responds in 6 weeks to queries. Sample copy for SASE in Canadian postage. Guidelines available online at www.faithtoday.ca/writers. "View complete back issues at www.faithtoday.ca/digital. Or download 1 of our free apps from www.faithtoday.ca/mobile."

NONFICTION Needs book excerpts, Canadian authors only, essays, Canadian authors only, interview, Canadian subjects only, opinion, religious, news feature. **Buys 75 mss/year.** Query. Length: 400-2,000 words. **Pays $100-500 Canadian.** Sometimes pays expenses of writers on assignment.

REPRINTS Send photocopy. Rarely used. Pays 50% of amount paid for an original article.

PHOTOS State availability. True required. Reviews contact sheets.

TIPS "Query should include brief outline and names of the sources you plan to interview in your research. Use Canadian postage on SASE."

FCA MAGAZINE

Fellowship of Christian Athletes, 8701 Leeds Rd., Kansas City MO 64129. (816)921-0909; (800)289-0909. **Fax:** (816)921-8755. **E-mail:** mag@fca.org. **Website:** www.fca.org/mag. **Contact:** Clay Meyer, editor; Matheau Casner, creative director. **50% freelance written. Prefers to work with published/established**

writers, but works with a growing number of new/unpublished writers each year. Published 6 times/year. *FCA Magazine*'s mission is to serve as a ministry tool of the Fellowship of Christian Athletes by informing, inspiring and involving coaches, athletes and all whom they influence, that they may make an impact for Jesus Christ. Estab. 1959. Circ. 75,000. Byline given. Pays on publication. No kill fee. Publishes ms an average of 4 months after acceptance. Submit seasonal material 6 months in advance. Responds to queries/mss in 3 months. Sample copy for $2 and 9x12 SASE with 3 first-class stamps. Guidelines available at www.fca.org/mag/media-kit.

NONFICTION Needs inspirational, interview (with name athletes and coaches solid in their faith), personal experience, photo feature. **Buys 5-20 mss/year.** Articles should be accompanied by at least 3 quality photos. Query and submit via e-mail. Length: 1,000-2,000 words. **Pays $150-400 for assigned and unsolicited articles.**

PHOTOS State availability. Reviews contact sheets. Payment based on size of photo.

TIPS "Profiles and interviews of particular interest to coed athlete, primarily high school and college age. Our graphics and editorial content appeal to youth. The area most open to freelancers is profiles on or interviews with well-known athletes or coaches (male, female, minorities) who have been or are involved in some capacity with FCA."

THE FRIEND

The Friend Publications Ltd, 173 Euston Rd., London England NW1 2BJ United Kingdom. (44)(207)663-1010. **Fax:** (44)(207)663-1182. **E-mail:** editorial@thefriend.org. **Website:** www.thefriend.org. **Contact:** Ian Kirk Smith. Weekly magazine. Completely independent, *The Friend* brings readers news and views from a Quaker perspective, as well as from a wide range of authors whose writings are of interest to Quakers and non-Quakers alike. There are articles on issues such as peace, spirituality, Quaker belief, and ecumenism, as well as news of Friends from Britain and abroad. Circ. 3,250. Byline given. No kill fee. Accepts queries by mail, e-mail, phone. Guidelines available online.

Prefers queries, but sometimes accepts unsolicited mss.

NONFICTION Query. Length: 550 words/full page; 1,100 words/double page spread.

PHOTOS Accepts illustrations (photos or drawings). Reviews color or b&w prints. Covers costs if photographs are commissioned.

COLUMNS/DEPARTMENTS Art reviews (new books, plays, videos, exhibitions), 550 words.

POETRY There are no rules regarding poetry, but doesn't want particularly long poems.

GUIDE

Pacific Press Publishing Association, P.O. Box 5353, Nampa ID 83653. (301)393-4037. **Fax:** (301)393-4055. **E-mail:** guide@pacificpress.com. **Website:** www.guidemagazine.org. **Contact:** Randy Fishell, editor; Brandon Reese, designer. *Guide* is a Christian story magazine for young people ages 10-14. The 32-page, 4-color publication is published weekly by the Pacific Press. Their mission is to show readers, through stories that illustrate Bible truth, how to walk with God now and forever. Estab. 1953. Byline given. Pays on acceptance. Accepts queries by mail, e-mail. Responds in 6 weeks to mss. Sample copy free with 6x9 SAE and 2 first-class stamps. Guidelines available on website.

NONFICTION Send complete ms. "Each issue includes 3-4 true stories. *Guide* does not publish fiction, poetry, or articles (devotionals, how-to, profiles, etc.). However, we sometimes accept quizzes and other unique nonstory formats. Each piece should include a clear spiritual element." Looking for pieces on adventure, personal growth, Christian humor, inspiration, biography, story series, and nature. Length: 1,000-1,200 words. **Pays 7-10¢/word.**

TIPS "Children's magazines want mystery, action, discovery, suspense, and humor—no matter what the topic. For us, truth is stronger than fiction."

HIGHWAY NEWS

Transport For Christ, P.O. Box 117, 1525 River Rd., Marietta PA 17547. (717)426-9977. **Fax:** (717)426-9980. **E-mail:** editor@transportforchrist.org. **Website:** www.transportforchrist.org. **Contact:** Inge Koenig. **50% freelance written.** Monthly magazine covering trucking and Christianity. "We publish human interest stories, testimonials, and teachings that have a foundation in Biblical/Christian values. Since truck drivers and their families are our primary readers, we publish works that they will find edifying and helpful." Estab. 1957. Circ. 20,000. Byline given. Publishes ms an average of 1 year after acceptance. Submit seasonal material 1 year in advance. Accepts queries by mail, e-mail, fax. Yes, if permission is granted by the publisherAccepts simultaneous submissions. Only responds to unsolicited submissions when they are due for publishing. Sample copy free. Writer's guidelines by e-mail.

Does not pay writers. Only accepts trucking-related articles at this time.

NONFICTION Needs trucking-related essays, general interest, humor, inspirational, interview, personal experience, photo feature, religious, trucking. Nothing of political nature. Send complete ms. Length: 600-800 words.

PHOTOS Send photos of trucking-related subjects only. Captions, identification of subjects, model releases required. Reviews prints, GIF/JPEG files. Does not pay for photos.

COLUMNS/DEPARTMENTS From the Road (stories by truckers on the road), 600 words. Send complete ms.

TIPS "We are especially interested in human interest stories about truck drivers. Find a trucker doing something unusual or good, and write a story about him or her. Be sure to send pictures."

HOLINESS TODAY

Nazarene Global Ministry Center, 17001 Prairie Star Pkwy., Lenexa KS 66220. (913)577-0500. **E-mail:** holinesstoday@nazarene.org. **Website:** www.holinesstoday.org. **Contact:** Carmen J. Ringhiser, managing editor; Frank M. Moore, editor in chief. *Holiness Today,* published bimonthly online and in print, is the primary print voice of the Church of the Nazarene, with articles geared to enhance holiness living by connecting Nazarenes with our heritage, vision, and mission through real-life stories of God at work in the world. *Holiness Today* (print) is 40 pages. Circ. 20,000. Subscription: $12/year U.S.

$ HORIZONS

100 Witherspoon St., Louisville KY 40202-1396. (844)797-2872. **E-mail:** yvonne.hileman@pcusa.org. **Website:** www.pcusa.org/horizons. **Contact:** Yvonne Hileman, assistant editor. Bimonthly. *Horizons* magazine provides information, inspiration, and education from the perspectives of women who are committed to Christ, the church and faithful discipleship. *Horizons* brings current issues dealing with family life, the mission of the church and the challenges of culture and society to its readers. Interviews, feature articles, Bible study resources, and departments offer help and insight for up-to-date, day-to-day concerns of the church and individual Christians. Estab. 1988. Circ. 20,000. Pays on publication. No kill fee. Publishes ms an average of 4 months after acceptance. Accepts queries by mail, e-mail, fax. Sample copy for $4 and 9x12 SAE. Guidelines for writers are on the *Horizons* website.

NONFICTION Needs essays. Accepts nonfiction articles and essays only, on theme. Send complete ms by mail, e-mail, or fax. Include contact information. Length: 600-1,800 words. **Pays an honorarium of no less than $50 per page printed in the magazine—amount will vary depending on time and research required for writing the article.**

FICTION Submit queries and/or complete ms by mail, e-mail, or fax. Include contact information. Length: 600-1,800 words. **Pays an honorarium of no less than $50 per page printed in the magazine—amount will vary depending on time and research required for writing the article.**

POETRY Accepts poems of varying themes and topics.

$$ LIGHT & LIFE MAGAZINE [LLM]

Free Methodist Church-USA, 770 N. High School Rd., Indianapolis IN 46214. (317)616-4776. **Fax:** (317)244-1247. **E-mail:** jeff.finley@fmcusa.org. **Website:** http://llcomm.org; http://fmcusa.org. **Contact:** Jeff Finley, managing editor. **20% freelance written.** "*Light & Life Magazine* [LLM] is a monthly magazine by Light & Life Communications, the publishing arm of the Free Methodist Church–USA. Each issue focuses on a specific theme with a cohesive approach in which the articles complement each other." Estab. 1868. Circ. 53,000 (English); 6,000 (Spanish). Byline given. Pays on publication. No kill fee. Accepts queries by e-mail. Responds in 2 months. Guidelines available at http://llcom.org/writersguidelines.

NONFICTION Query. Length: 2,100 words for a feature article, 800 words for a print discipleship article, and 500-1,000 words for an online discipleship article; 500-1,000 words for online articles not published in the magazine. **Pays $100/article, $200/feature, $50/discipleship article.**

$$ LIGUORIAN

One Liguori Dr., Liguori MO 63057. (636)223-1538. **Fax:** (636)223-1595. **E-mail:** liguorianeditor@liguori.org. **Website:** www.liguorian.org. **Contact:** Elizabeth Herzing, managing editor. **25% freelance written. Prefers to work with published/established writers.**

Magazine published 10 times/year for Catholics. "Our purpose is to lead our readers to a fuller Christian life by helping them better understand the teachings of the gospel and the church and by illustrating how these teachings apply to life and the problems confronting them as members of families, the church, and society." Estab. 1913. Circ. 60,000. Pays on acceptance. Submit seasonal material 8 months in advance. Accepts queries by mail, e-mail, fax. Responds in 3 months to mss. Sample copy for 9x12 SAE with 3 first-class stamps or online. Guidelines for #10 SASE and on website.

NONFICTION "No travelogue approach or unresearched ventures into controversial areas. Also, no material found in secular publications—fad subjects that already get enough press, pop psychology, or negative articles. *Liguorian* does not consider *retold* Bible stories." **Buys 30-40 unsolicited mss/year.** Length: 400-2,200 words. **Pays 12-15¢/word and 5 contributor's copies.**

PHOTOS Photographs on assignment only unless submitted with and specific to article.

FICTION Needs religious, inspirational, senior citizen/retirement. Send complete ms. Length: 1,500-2,200 words. **Pays 12-15¢/word and 5 contributor's copies.**

TIPS "First read several issues containing short stories. We look for originality and creative input in each story we read. Consideration requires the author studies the target market and presents a carefully polished manuscript. We publish 1 fiction story per issue. Compare this with the 25 or more we receive over the transom each month. We believe fiction is a highly effective mode for transmitting the Christian message; however, many fiction pieces are written without a specific goal or thrust—an interesting incident that goes nowhere is not a story."

$$ LIVE

Gospel Publishing House, 1445 N. Boonville Ave., Springfield MO 65802-1894. (417)862-1447. **Fax:** (417)862-0416. **E-mail:** rl-live@gph.org. **Website:** www.gospelpublishing.com. **100% freelance written.** Weekly magazine for weekly distribution covering practical Christian living. "*LIVE* is a take-home paper distributed weekly in young adult and adult Sunday school classes. We seek to encourage Christians in living for God through fiction and true stories which apply Biblical principles to everyday problems." Estab. 1928. Circ. 35,000. Byline given. Pays on acceptance. No kill fee. Publishes ms an average of 18 months after acceptance. Editorial lead time 12 months. Submit seasonal material 18 months in advance. Accepts queries by mail, e-mail. Accepts simultaneous submissions. Responds in 2 weeks to queries; in 6 weeks to mss. Sample copy for #10 SASE. Guidelines for #10 SASE or on website: www.gospelpublishing.com/store/startcat.cfm?cat=tWRITGUID.

NONFICTION Needs inspirational, religious. No preachy articles or stories that refer to religious myths (e.g., Santa Claus, Easter Bunny, etc.). **Buys 50-100 mss/year.** Send complete ms. Length: 450-1,100 words. **Pays 7-10¢/word.**

REPRINTS Send tearsheet, photocopy, or typed ms with rights for sale noted and information about when and where the material previously appeared. Pays 7¢/word.

PHOTOS Send photos. Identification of subjects required. Reviews 35mm transparencies and 3x4 prints or larger. Higher resolution digital files also accepted. Offers $35-60/photo.

FICTION Contact: Wade Quick, editor. Needs religious, inspirational, prose poem. No preachy fiction, fiction about Bible characters, or stories that refer to religious myths (e.g., Santa Claus, Easter Bunny, etc.). No science or Bible fiction. No controversial stories about such subjects as feminism, war, or capital punishment. **Buys 20-50 mss/year.** Send complete ms. Length: 800-1,200 words. **Pays 7-10¢/word.**

POETRY Needs free verse, haiku, light verse, traditional. Buys 15-24 poems/year. Submit maximum 3 poems. Length: 12-25 lines. **Pays $35-60.**

TIPS "Don't moralize or be preachy. Provide human interest articles with Biblical life application. Stories should consist of action, not just thought-life, interaction, not just insight. Heroes and heroines should rise above failures, take risks for God, prove that scriptural principles meet their needs. Conflict and suspense should increase to a climax! Avoid pious conclusions. Characters should be interesting, believable, and realistic. Avoid stereotypes. Characters should be active, not just pawns to move the plot along. They should confront conflict and change in believable ways. Describe the character's looks and reveal his personality through his actions to such an extent that the reader feels he has met that person. Readers should care about the character enough to finish the story. Feature racial, ethnic, and regional characters in rural and urban settings."

LIVE WIRE

8805 Governor's Hill Dr., Suite 400, Cincinnati OH 45249. (513)931-4050. **Fax:** (877)867-5751. **E-mail:** lnickelson@standardpub.com. **Website:** www.standardpub.com. **Contact:** Lu Ann Nickelson, editor. Estab. 1949.

Live Wire has decided to reuse much of the material that was a part of the first publication cycle. They will not be sending out theme lists, sample copies, or writers guidelines or accepting any unsolicited material because of this policy.

THE LIVING CHURCH

Living Church Foundation, P.O. Box 510705, Milwaukee WI 53203-0121. (414)276-5420. **Fax:** (414)276-7483. **E-mail:** jschuessler@livingchurch.org. **E-mail:** tlc@livingchurch.org. **Website:** www.livingchurch.org. **Contact:** John Schuessler, managing editor; Douglas LeBlanc, associate editor. **50% freelance written.** Magazine covering news or articles of interest to members of the Episcopal Church. Weekly magazine that presents news and views of the Episcopal Church and the wider Anglican Communion, along with articles on spirituality, Anglican heritage, and the application of Christianity in daily life. There are commentaries on scripture, book reviews, editorials, letters to the editor, and special thematic issues. Estab. 1878. Circ. 9,500. Byline given. Does not pay unless article is requested. No kill fee. Publishes ms an average of 3 months after acceptance. Editorial lead time 3 weeks. Submit seasonal material 2 months in advance. Accepts queries by mail, e-mail, fax. Responds in 2 weeks to queries. Responds in 1 month to mss. Sample copy free.

NONFICTION Needs opinion, personal experience, photo feature, religious. **Buys 10 mss/year.** Send complete ms. Length: 1,000 words. **Pays $25-100.** Sometimes pays expenses of writers on assignment.

PHOTOS Send photos. Reviews any size prints. Offers $15-50/photo.

COLUMNS/DEPARTMENTS Benediction (devotional), 250 words; Viewpoint (opinion), under 1,000 words. Send complete ms. **Pays $50 maximum.**

POETRY Needs light verse, traditional.

THE LOOKOUT

Standard Publishing, 8805 Governor's Hill Dr., Suite 400, Cincinnati OH 45249. (513)931-4050. **Fax:** (513)931-0950. **E-mail:** lookout@standardpub.com. **Website:** www.lookoutmag.com. **Contact:** Kelly Carr, editor. **50% freelance written.** Weekly magazine for Christian adults, with emphasis on spiritual growth, family life, and topical issues. "Our purpose is to provide Christian adults with practical, Biblical teaching and current information that will help them mature as believers." Estab. 1894. Circ. 35,000. Byline given. Pays on acceptance. Offers 33% kill fee. Publishes ms an average of 1 year after acceptance. Editorial lead time 9 months. Submit seasonal material 1 year in advance. Accepts queries by mail, e-mail. No previously published materialAccepts simultaneous submissions. Responds in 10 weeks to queries and mss. Sample copy for $1. Guidelines by e-mail or online.

Audience is mainly conservative Christians. Manuscripts only on request.

NONFICTION Needs inspirational, interview, opinion, personal experience, religious. No fiction or poetry. **Buys 100 mss/year.** Send complete ms. Length: 1,200-1,400 words. **Pays 11-17¢/word.**

PHOTOS State availability. Identification of subjects required. Offers no additional payment for photos accepted with ms.

TIPS "*The Lookout* publishes from a theologically conservative, nondenominational, and noncharismatic perspective. We aim primarily for those aged 30-55. Most readers are married and have elementary to young adult children. Our emphasis is on the needs of ordinary Christians who want to grow in their faith. We value well-informed articles that offer lively and clear writing as well as strong application. We often address tough issues and seek to explore fresh ideas or recent developments affecting today's Christians."

THE LUTHERAN DIGEST

The Lutheran Digest, Inc., 6160 Carmen Ave., Inver Grove Heights MN 55076. (952)933-2820. **Fax:** (952)933-5708. **E-mail:** editor@lutherandigest.com. **Website:** www.lutherandigest.com. **Contact:** Lori Rosenkvist, editor. **95% freelance written.** Quarterly magazine covering Christianity from a Lutheran perspective. Publishes articles, humor, and poetry. Articles frequently reflect a Lutheran Christian perspective but are not intended to be sermonettes. Popular stories show how God has intervened in a person's life to help solve a problem. Estab. 1953. Circ. 50,000. Byline given. Pays on publication. No kill fee. Publishes ms an average of 6 months after acceptance. Editorial lead time 9 months. Submit seasonal material 9 months in advance. "No queries, please." Accepts queries by e-mail mss only as Microsoft Word or Rich Text attachments. Accepts simultaneous submissions. Responds in 1 month to queries; in 4 months to mss. No response to e-mailed mss unless selected for publication. Sample copy: $3.50. Subscription: $16/year, $22/2 years. Guidelines available online.

The Lutheran Digest is 64 pages, digest-sized, offset-printed, saddle-stapled, with 4-color paper cover, includes local ads. Receives about 200 poems/year, accepts 10-20%. Press run is 60,000-65,000; most distributed free to Lutheran churches.

NONFICTION Needs general interest, historical, how-to, personal or spiritual growth, humor, inspirational, personal experience, religious, nature and science. Does not want to see personal tributes to deceased relatives or friends. These are seldom used unless the subject of the article is well known. Avoids articles about the moment a person finds Christ as his or her personal savior. **Buys 50-60 mss/year.** Send complete ms. Length: up to 1,500 words. **Pays $35-50.**

REPRINTS Accepts previously published submissions. "We prefer this as we are a digest and 70-80% of our articles are reprints."

PHOTOS "We never print photos from outside sources."

POETRY Submit up to 3 poems at a time. Prefers e-mail submissions but also accepts mailed submissions. Cover letter is preferred. Include SASE only if return is desired. Poems are selected by editor and reviewed by publication panel. Length: up to 25 lines/poem. **Pays 1 contributor's copy.**

TIPS "Reading our writers' guidelines and sample articles online is encouraged and is the best way to get a feel for the type of material we publish."

THE MENNONITE

718 N. Main St., Newton KS 67114-1703. (866)866-2872 ext. 34398. **Fax:** (316)283-0454. **E-mail:** gordonh@themennonite.org. **Website:** www.themennonite.org. **Contact:** Gordon Houser, associate editor. *The Mennonite*, published monthly, seeks "to help readers glorify God, grow in faith, and become agents of healing and hope in the world. Our readers are primarily people in Mennonite churches." Estab. 1998. Circ. 6,700. Publishes ms up to 1 year after acceptance. Responds in 2 weeks. Single copy: $4; subscription: $46 U.S. Guidelines online.

NONFICTION Needs general interest, religious, Bible study, prayer, environment, aging, death/dying, Christmas, Easter, children, parenting, marriage, singleness, racism, peace and justice, worship, health issues, arts, personal stories of Mennonites exercising their faith. Query via e-mail (preferred). Include name, address, phone number, one-sentence summary of the article and "3 catchy, creative titles. Illustrations, charts, graphs, and photos (in color) to go with the article are welcome." If sending by regular mail, also include an SASE. Length: 1,200-1,500 words for feature articles. **Payment varies. We only pay for solicited articles.**

TIPS "Writing should be concise, accessible to the general reader, and with strong lead paragraphs. This last point cannot be overemphasized. The lead paragraph is the foundation of a good article. It should provide a summary of the article. We are especially interested in personal stories of Mennonites exercising their faith."

$$ ONE

Catholic Near East Welfare Association, 1011 First Ave., New York NY 10022-4195. (212)826-1480. **Fax:** (212)838-1344. **E-mail:** cnewa@cnewa.org. **Website:** www.cnewa.org. **Contact:** Deacon Greg Kandra, executive editor. **75% freelance written.** Bimonthly magazine for a Catholic audience with interest in the Near East, particularly its current religious, cultural, and political aspects. Estab. 1974. Circ. 100,000. Byline given. Pays on publication. No kill fee. Publishes ms an average of 6 months after acceptance. Accepts queries by mail, fax. Responds in 1 month to queries. Sample copy and writer's guidelines for 7.5x10.5 SAE with 2 first-class stamps.

NONFICTION Query. Length: 1,200-1,800 words. **Pays 20¢/edited word.**

PHOTOS "Photographs to accompany ms are welcome; they should illustrate the people, places, ceremonies, etc. which are described in the article. We prefer color transparencies but occasionally use b&w." Pay varies depending on use—scale from $50-300.

TIPS "We are interested in current events in the Near East as they affect the cultural, political, and religious lives of the people."

OUTREACH MAGAZINE

5550 Tech Center Dr., Colorado Springs CA 80919. (800)991-6011, ext. 3315. **E-mail:** tellus@outreachmagazine.com. **Website:** www.outreachmagazine.com. **80% freelance written.** Bimonthly magazine covering outreach in Christianity. *Outreach* magazine is the gathering place of ideas, insights and stories for Christian churches focused on reaching out to their community—locally and globally—with the love of Christ. Primary readers are senior pastors and church leadership, as well as laity who are passionate about outreach. Circ. 30,000. Byline given. Pays on publication. Offers 10% kill fee. Publishes ms an average of 2-4 months after acceptance. Editorial lead time 6 months. Submit seasonal material 6 months in advance. Accepts queries by mail, e-mail. Accepts simultaneous submissions. Responds in 2 months to queries. Responds in 8 months to mss. Sample copy free. Guidelines available online.

NONFICTION Needs book excerpts, how-to, humor, inspirational, interview, personal experience, photo feature, religious. Special issues: Vacation Bible School (January); Church Growth—America's Fastest-Growing Churches (Special Issue). Does not want fiction, poetry, non-outreach-related articles. **Buys 30 mss/year.** Query with published clips. Length: 1,500-2,500 words. **Pays $375-600 for assigned articles; $375-500 for unsolicited articles.** Sometimes pays expenses of writers on assignment.

PHOTOS Send photos. Identification of subjects required. Reviews GIF/JPEG files. Negotiates payment individually.

COLUMNS/DEPARTMENTS Pulse (short stories about outreach-oriented churches and ministries), 250-350 words; Ideas (a profile of a church that is using a transferable idea or concept for outreach), 300 words, plus sidebar; Soulfires (short interviews with known voices about the stories and people that have informed their worldview and faith perspective), 600 words. **Buys Buys 6 mss/year. mss/year.** Query with published clips. **Pays $100-375.**

FILLERS Needs facts, gags. **Buys Buys 6 mss/year. mss/year.** Length: 25-100 words. **Pays negotiated fee.**

TIPS "Study our magazine and writer's guidelines. Send published clips that showcase tight, bright writing as well as your ability to interview; research; and organize numerous sources into an article; and write a 100-word piece as well as a 1,600-word piece."

THE PINK CHAMELEON

E-mail: dpfreda@juno.com. **Website:** www.thepinkchameleon.com. **Contact:** Dorothy Paula Freda, editor/publisher. *The Pink Chameleon*, published annually online, contains "family-oriented, upbeat poetry, stories, essays, and articles, any genre in good taste that gives hope for the future." Estab. 2000. Time between acceptance and publication is up to 1 year, depending on date of acceptance. Responds in 1 month to ms. Sometimes comments on rejected mss. Sample copy and writer's guidelines online.

Reading period is January 1-April 30 and September 1-October 31.

NONFICTION Needs nonfiction short stories, articles. Send complete ms in the body of the e-mail. No attachments. Length: 500-2,500 words; average length: 2,000 words. **No payment.**

FICTION Needs short stories, adventure, family saga, fantasy, humor/satire, literary, mainstream, mystery/suspense, religious/inspirational, romance, science fiction, western, young adult/teen, psychic/supernatural. "No violence for the sake of violence." No novels or novel excerpts. Send complete ms in the body of the e-mail. No attachments. Accepts reprints. Has published work by Deanne F. Purcell, Martin Green, Albert J. Manachino, James W. Collins, Ron Arnold, Sally Kosmalski, Susan Marie Davniero, and Glenn D. Hayes. Length: 500-2,500 words; average length: 2,000 words. **No payment.**

POETRY Needs Wants "poems about nature, loved ones, rare moments in time." Also considers poetry by children and teens. Submit 1-4 poems at a time. Accepts e-mail submissions only (pasted into body of message; no attachments.) Use plain text and include a brief bio. Often comments on rejected poems. Receives about 50 poems/year, accepts about 50%. Does not want "pornography, cursing, swearing; nothing evoking despair." Submit maximum 4 poems. Length: 6-24 lines. **No payment.**

TIPS Wants "simple, honest, evocative emotion; upbeat fiction and nonfiction submissions that give hope for the future; well-paced plots; stories, poetry, articles, essays that speak from the heart. Read guidelines carefully. Use a good, but not ostentatious, opening hook. Stories should have a beginning, middle, and end that make the reader feel the story was worth his or her time. This also applies to articles and essays. In the latter 2, wrap your comments and conclusions in a neatly packaged final paragraph. Turnoffs include violence and bad language. Simple, genuine, and sensitive work does not need to shock with vulgarity to be interesting and enjoyable."

POINT

Converge Worldwide (Baptist General Conference), Mail Code 200, 11002 Lake Hart Dr., Orlando FL 32832. **Fax:** (866)990-8980. **E-mail:** bob.putman@convergeww.org. **Website:** www.convergeworldwide.org. **15% freelance written.** Nonprofit, religious, evangelical Christian magazine published 4 times/year covering Converge Worldwide. *Point* is the official magazine of Converge Worldwide (BCG). Almost exclusively uses articles related to Converge, their churches, or by/about Converge people. Circ. 45,000. Byline given. Pays on publication. Offers 50% kill fee. Editorial lead time 6 months. Submit seasonal material 6 months in advance. Accepts queries by e-mail. Responds in 1 month to queries; in 3 months to mss. Sample copy for #10 SASE. Guidelines available free.

NONFICTION Buys 6-8 mss/year. Query with published clips. Wants "articles about our people, churches, missions. View online at: www.convergeworldwide.org. before sending anything." Length: 300-1,500 words. **Pays $60-280.** Sometimes pays expenses of writers on assignment.

PHOTOS State availability. Captions, identification of subjects, model releases required. Reviews prints, some high-resolution digital. Offers $15-60/photo.

COLUMNS/DEPARTMENTS Converge Connection (blurbs of news happening in Converge Worldwide), 50-150 words. Send complete ms and photos. **Pays $30.**

TIPS "Please study the magazine and the denomination. We will send sample copies to interested freelancers and give further information about our publication needs upon request. Freelancers from our churches who are interested in working on assignment are especially welcome."

PRAIRIE MESSENGER

Benedictine Monks of St. Peter's Abbey, P.O. Box 190, Muenster Saskatchewan S0K 2Y0 Canada. (306)682-1772. **Fax:** (306)682-5285. **E-mail:** pm.canadian@stpeterspress.ca. **Website:** www.prairiemessenger.ca. **Contact:** Maureen Weber, associate editor. **10% Freelance written.** Weekly Catholic publication published by the Benedictine Monks of St. Peter's Abbey. Has a strong focus on ecumenism, social justice, interfaith relations, aboriginal issues, arts and culture. Estab. 1904. Circ. 5,000. Byline given. Pays on publication. No kill fee. Publishes ms an average of 4 months after acceptance. Submit seasonal material 3 months in advance. Accepts queries by mail, e-mail, fax, phone. Accepts simultaneous submissions. Responds only if interested; send nonreturnable samples. Sample copy for 9x12 SASE with $1 Canadian postage or IRCs. Guidelines available online. "Because of government subsidy regulations, we are no longer able to accept non-Canadian freelance material."

NONFICTION Needs interview, opinion, religious. **Buys 15 mss/year.** Send complete ms. Length: 500-800 words. **Pays $60/article.** Sometimes pays expenses of writers on assignment.

PHOTOS Send photos. Captions required. Reviews 3x5 prints. Offers $25/photo.

PRESBYTERIANS TODAY

Presbyterian Church (U.S.A.), 100 Witherspoon St., Louisville KY 40202-1396. (502)569-5627. **Fax:** (502)569-8887. **E-mail:** editor@pcusa.org. **Website:** www.pcusa.org/today. **Contact:** Patrick David Heery, editor. **25% freelance written. Prefers to work with published/established writers.** Denominational magazine published 8 times/year covering religion, denominational activities, and public issues for members of the Presbyterian Church (U.S.A.). "The magazine's purpose is to increase understanding and appreciation of what the church and its members are doing to live out their Christian faith." Estab. 1867. Circ. 40,000. Byline given. Pays on acceptance. Offers 50% kill fee. Publishes ms an average of 6 months after acceptance. Editorial lead time 3 months. Submit seasonal material 3 months in advance. Accepts queries by e-mail. Responds in 2 weeks to queries. Sample copy free. Guidelines available online.

NONFICTION Needs how-to, inspirational, Presbyterian programs, everyday Christian issues. **Buys 20 mss/year.** Send complete ms. Length: 1,000-1,800 words. **Pays $300 maximum for assigned articles; $75-300 for unsolicited articles.**

PHOTOS State availability. Identification of subjects required. Reviews contact sheets, transparencies, color prints, digital images. Negotiates payment individually.

PURPOSE

718 N. Main St., Newton KS 67114. (316)281-4412. **Fax:** (316)283-0454. **E-mail:** CarolD@MennoMedia.org; info@MennoMedia.org. **Website:** www.faithan-

dliferesources.org. **Contact:** Carol Duerksen, contract editor. **75% freelance written.** Magazine focuses on Christian discipleship—how to be a faithful Christian in the midst of everyday life situations. Uses personal story form to present models and examples to encourage Christians in living a life of faithful discipleship. *Purpose*, published monthly by Mennomedia, an imprint of the Mennonite Publishing Network (the official publisher for the Mennonite Church in the US and Canada), is a "religious young adult/adult monthly." Focuses on "action-oriented, discipleship living." Estab. 1968. Circ. 8,500. Pays upon publication. No kill fee. Publishes ms an average of 18 months after acceptance. Submit seasonal material 1 year in advance. Accepts queries by e-mail. Accepts simultaneous submissions. Responds in 3 months to queries, responds in 6 months to mss. Sample (with guidelines): $2 and 9x12 SAE. Guidelines available online: www.faithandliferesources.org/periodicals/purpose.

Purpose is digest-sized with 4-color printing throughout. Receives about 2,000 poems/year, accepts 150.

NONFICTION Special issues: Needs short, personal true anecdotal stories. Must meet monthly themes (see website). **Buys 140 mss/year.** E-mail submissions preferred. Length: 350-600 words. **Pays $25-50.**

PHOTOS Photos purchased with ms must be sharp enough for reproduction; requires prints in all cases. Captions required.

POETRY Needs free verse, light verse, traditional. Prefers e-mail submissions. Postal submissions should be double-spaced, typed on 1 side of sheet only. Buys 140 poems/year. Length: 12 lines maximum. **Pays $10-20/poem depending on length and quality, plus 2 contributor's copies.**

FILLERS 6¢/word maximum.

TIPS "Many stories are situational, how to respond to dilemmas. Looking for first-person storylines. The story form is an excellent literary device to help readers explore discipleship issues. The first 2 paragraphs are crucial in establishing the mood/issue to be resolved in the story. Work hard on the development of these."

QUAKER LIFE

Friends United Meeting, 101 Quaker Hill Dr., Richmond IN 47374. (765)962-7573. **Fax:** (765)966-1293. **E-mail:** quakerlife@fum.org; annieg@fum.org. **Website:** www.fum.org. **Contact:** Annie Glen, communications editor. **50% freelance written.** A Christian Quaker magazine published 6 times/year that covers news, inspirational, devotional, peace, equality, and justice issues. Estab. 1960. Circ. 3,000. Byline given. No kill fee. Publishes ms an average of 3-6 months after acceptance. Editorial lead time 2-3 months. Submit seasonal material 4-6 months in advance. Accepts queries by mail, e-mail. Accepts simultaneous submissions. Responds in 1 week to queries; in 1-3 months to mss. Sample copy and writer's guidelines free.

NONFICTION Needs book excerpts, general interest, humor, inspirational, interview, personal experience, photo feature, religious, travel, Bible study. No poetry or fiction. Query. Length: 400-1,500 words. **Pays 3 contributor's copies.**

PHOTOS Reviews b&w or color prints and JPEG files. Occasionally, line drawings and b&w cartoons are used. Send photos. Does not pay for photos.

COLUMNS/DEPARTMENTS News Brief (newsworthy events among Quakers), 75-200 words; Devotional/Inspirational (personal insights or spiritual turning points), 750 words; Ideas That Work (ideas from meetings that could be used by others), 750 words; Book/Media Reviews, 75-300 words.

RADIX MAGAZINE

Radix Magazine, Inc., P.O. Box 4307, Berkeley CA 94704. (510)548-5329. **E-mail:** radixmag@aol.com. **Website:** www.radixmagazine.com. **Contact:** Sharon Gallagher, editor. **10% freelance written.** *Radix Magazine*, published quarterly, is named for the Latin word for "root" and "has its roots both in the 'real world' and in the truth of Christ's teachings." Wants poems that reflect a Christian world-view, but aren't preachy. Has published poetry by John Leax, Czeslaw Milosz, Madeleine L'Engle, and Luci Shaw. Estab. 1979. Circ. 3,000. Byline given. No kill fee. Publishes ms 3 months to 3 years after acceptance. Editorial lead time 6 months. Submit seasonal material 6 months in advance. Accepts queries by e-mail. Responds in 2 months to queries and to mss. Sample copy for $5. Guidelines by e-mail.

Radix is 32 pages, magazine-sized, offset-printed, saddle-stapled, with 60-lb. self cover. Receives about 120 poems/year, accepts about 10%. Press run varies. Subscription: $15. Sample: $5. Make checks payable to *Radix Magazine*."

NONFICTION Contact: Sharon Gallagher, editor. Needs essays, religious. Query. Length: 500-2,000 words.

POETRY Needs avant-garde, free verse, haiku. Submit 1-4 poems at a time. Buys 8 poems/year. Submit maximum 4 poems. Length: 4-20 lines. **Pays 2 contributor copies.**

TIPS "We accept very few unsolicited manuscripts. We do not accept fiction. All articles and poems should be based on a Christian world view. Freelancers should have some sense of the magazine's tone and purpose."

ST. ANTHONY MESSENGER

Franciscan Media, 28 W. Liberty St., Cincinnati OH 45202-6498. (513)241-5615. **Fax:** (513)241-0399. **E-mail:** magazineeditors@franciscanmedia.org. **Website:** www.stanthonymessenger.org. **Contact:** John Feister, editor-in-chief. **55% freelance written.** Monthly general-interest magazine for a national readership of Catholic families, most of which have children or grandchildren in grade school, high school, or college. *St. Anthony Messenger* is a Catholic family magazine which aims to help its readers lead more fully human and Christian lives. "We publish articles that report on a changing church and world, opinion pieces written from the perspective of Christian faith and values, personality profiles, and fiction which entertains and informs." Estab. 1893. Circ. 105,000. Byline given. Pays on acceptance. No kill fee. Publishes ms within an average of 1 year after acceptance. Submit seasonal material 6 months in advance. Accepts queries by mail, e-mail, fax. Responds in 3 weeks to queries. Responds in 2 months to mss. Sample copy for 9x12 SAE with 4 first-class stamps. Please study writers' guidelines at StAnthonyMessenger.org.

NONFICTION Needs how-to, on psychological and spiritual growth, problems of parenting/better parenting, marriage problems/marriage enrichment, humor, inspirational, interview, opinion, limited use; writer must have special qualifications for topic, personal experience, if pertinent to our purpose, photo feature, informational, social issues. **Buys 35-50 mss/year.** Query with published clips. Length: 2,000-2,500 words. **Pays 20¢/word.** Sometimes pays expenses of writers on assignment.

FICTION Needs mainstream, religious, senior citizen/retirement. "We do not want mawkishly sentimental or preachy fiction. Stories are most often rejected for poor plotting and characterization, bad dialogue (listen to how people talk), and inadequate motivation. Many stories say nothing, are 'happenings' rather than stories. No fetal journals, no rewritten Bible stories." **Buys 12 mss/year.** Send complete ms. Length: 2,000-2,500 words. **Pays 20¢/word maximum and 2 contributor's copies; $1 charge for extras.**

POETRY Contact: Poetry Editor. Submit a few poems at a time. "Please include your phone number and a SASE with your submission. Do not send us your entire collection of poetry. Poems must be original." Submit seasonal poems several months in advance. "Our poetry needs are very limited." Submit maximum 4-5 poems. Length: up to 20-25 lines; "the shorter, the better." **Pays $2/line; $20 minimum.**

TIPS "The freelancer should consider why his or her proposed article would be appropriate for us, rather than for *Redbook* or *Saturday Review*. We treat human problems of all kinds, but from a religious perspective. Articles should reflect Catholic theology, spirituality, and employ a Catholic terminology and vocabulary. We need more articles on prayer, scripture, Catholic worship. Get authoritative information (not merely library research); we want interviews with experts. Write in popular style; use lots of examples, stories, and personal quotes. Word length is an important consideration."

THE SECRET PLACE

P.O. Box 851, Valley Forge PA 19482. (610)768-2434. **E-mail:** thesecretplace@abc-usa.org. **Website:** www.judsonpress.com/catalog_secretplace.cfm. **100% freelance written.** Quarterly devotional covering Christian daily devotions. Estab. 1937. Circ. 250,000. Byline given. Pays on acceptance. No kill fee. Editorial lead time 1 year. Submit seasonal material 9 months in advance. Guidelines online.

NONFICTION Needs inspirational. **Buys about 400 mss/year.** Send complete ms. Length: 100-200 words. **Pays $20.**

POETRY Needs avant-garde, free verse, light verse, traditional. Submit up to 6 poems by mail or e-mail. Buys 12-15 poems/year. Submit maximum 6 poems. Length: 4-30 lines/poem. **Pays $20.**

TIPS "Prefers submissions via e-mail."

SEEK

8805 Governor's Hill Dr., Suite 400, Cincinnati OH 45239. (513)931-4050, ext. 351. **E-mail:** seek@standardpub.com. **Website:** www.standardpub.com. "Inspirational stories of faith-in-action for Christian adults; a Sunday School take-home paper." Quarterly. Estab. 1970. Circ. 27,000. Byline given. Pays on acceptance. No kill fee. Acceptance to publishing time is 1 year. Accepts queries by e-mail. Writer's guidelines online.

Magazine: 5.5×8.5; 8 pages; newsprint paper; art and photo in each issue.

NONFICTION Send complete ms. **Pays 7¢/word for first rights; 5¢/word for reprint rights.**

FICTION List of upcoming themes available online. Accepts 150 mss/year. Send complete ms. Prefers submissions by e-mail. "*SEEK* corresponds to the topics of Standard Publishing's adult curriculum line and is designed to further apply these topics to everyday life." Unsolicited mss must be written to a theme list. Needs religious/inspirational, religious fiction and religiously slanted historical and humorous fiction. Does not want poetry. Send complete ms. Prefers submissions by e-mail. **Pays 7¢/word.**

TIPS "Write a credible story with a Christian slant—no preachments; avoid overworked themes such as joy in suffering, generation gaps, etc. Most mss are rejected by us because of irrelevant topic or message, unrealistic story, or poor character and/or plot development. We use fiction stories that are believable."

SOCIAL JUSTICE REVIEW

3835 Westminster Place, St. Louis MO 63108. (314)371-1653. **Fax:** (314)371-0889. **Website:** www.socialjusticereview.org. **25% freelance written. Works with a small number of new/unpublished writers each year.** Bimonthly magazine "to promote a true Christian humanism with respect for the dignity and rights of all human beings." Estab. 1908. No kill fee. Publishes ms an average of 1 year after acceptance. Accepts queries by mail. Sample copy for SAE with 9x12 envelope and 3 first-class stamps.

NONFICTION Query by mail only with SASE. Length: 2,500-3,000 words. **Pays about 2¢/word.**

REPRINTS Send typed ms with rights for sale noted and information about when and where the material previously appeared. Pays about 2¢/word.

TIPS "Write moderate essays completely compatible with papal teaching and readable to the average person."

SUCCESS STORIES

Franklin Publishing Company, 2723 Steamboat Circle, Arlington TX 76006. (817)548-1124. **E-mail:** ludwigotto@sbcglobal.net. **Website:** www.franklinpublishing.net; www.londonpress.us. **Contact:** Dr. Ludwig Otto. **59% freelance written.** Monthly journal covering positive responses to the problems in life. Estab. 1983. Circ. 1,000. Byline given. Does not pay, but offers 15% discount on issues purchased and one-year free membership in the International Association of Professionals. No kill fee. Publishes ms an average of 1 month after acceptance. Editorial lead time 1 month. Submit seasonal material 3 months in advance. Accepts queries by mail, e-mail. Accepts simultaneous submissions. Responds in 1 week to queries and mss. Guidelines available online.

NONFICTION Needs book excerpts, essays, general interest, historical, how-to, humor, inspirational, interview, new product, opinion, personal experience, religious, technical, travel. Send complete ms. Length: 750-6,000 words.

FICTION Needs adventure, condensed novels, ethnic, horror, humorous, mainstream, mystery, novel concepts, religious, science fiction, slice-of-life vignettes of life, suspense, western. Send complete ms.

POETRY Needs avant-garde, free verse, haiku, light verse, traditional.

FILLERS Needs anecdotes, facts, gags.

SUNSTONE

343 N. Third W., Salt Lake City UT 84103-1215. (801)355-5926. **E-mail:** info@sunstonemagazine.com. **Website:** www.sunstonemagazine.com. *Sunstone*, published 6 times/year, prints scholarly articles of interest to an open, Mormon audience; personal essays; fiction (selected only through contests), and poetry. Has published poetry by Susan Howe, Anita Tanner, Robert Parham, Ryan G. Van Cleave, Robert Rees, and Virgil Suárez. Estab. 1974. Publishes ms 2 years after acceptance. Responds in 3 months. Sample copy: $10 postpaid. Subscription: $45 for 6 issues. Guidelines online.

Sunstone is 64 pages, magazine-sized, professionally printed, saddle-stapled, with semi-glossy paper cover. Receives more than 500 poems/year, accepts 40-50. Press run is 3,000.

NONFICTION Interested in feature- and column-length articles and essays relevant to Mormonism from a variety of perspectives, news stories about Mormons and the LDS Church, and short reflections and commentary. Length: up to 8,000 words.

POETRY Wants both lyric and narrative poetry that engages the reader with fresh, strong images; skillful use of language; and a strong sense of voice and/or place. Short poems, including haiku, limericks, couplets, and one liners, are welcome. Does not want didactic poetry, sing-song rhymes, or in-process work. Submit by mail or e-mail. Include name, address, and e-mail on each poem. Seldom comments on rejected poems. Length: up to 40 lines/poem. **Pays 5 contributor's copies.**

TRICYCLE

89 5th Ave., Suite 301, New York NY 10013. (212)929-0320. **E-mail:** editorial@tricycle.com. **Website:** www.tricycle.com. **Contact:** Emma Varvaloucas, managing editor. **80% freelance written.** Quarterly magazine providing a unique and independent public forum for exploring Buddhist teachings and practices, establishing a dialogue between Buddhism and the broader culture, and introducing Buddhist thinking to Western disciplines. "*Tricycle* readers tend to be well educated and open minded." Estab. 1991. Circ. 50,000. Byline given. Pays on publication. Offers 25% kill fee. Editorial lead time 3 months. Accepts queries by mail, e-mail (preferable). Accepts simultaneous submissions. Responds in 1-2 months to queries. Sample copy: $7.95 or online at website. Guidelines online.

NONFICTION Needs book excerpts, essays, general interest, historical, humor, inspirational, interview, personal experience, photo feature, religious, travel. **Buys 4-6 mss/year.** Query. Include name, address, date, and word count. Length: up to 4,000 words.

PHOTOS State availability. Captions, identification of subjects required. Reviews contact sheets. Negotiates payment individually.

TIPS "For your submission to be considered, we ask that you first send us a one-page query outlining your idea, relevant information about your writing background and any Buddhist background, your familiarity with the subject of your proposal, and so on. If you have clips or writing samples, please send these along with your proposal."

THE UNITED CHURCH OBSERVER

478 Huron St., Toronto ON M5R 2R3 Canada. (416)960-8500. **Fax:** (416)960-8477. **E-mail:** dnwilson@ucobserver.org. **Website:** www.ucobserver.org. **50% freelance written. Prefers to work with published/established writers.** Monthly general interest magazine for people associated with The United Church of Canada and non-churchgoers interested in issues of faith, justice, and ethical living. Deals primarily with events, trends, and policies having religious significance. Most coverage is Canadian, but reports on international or world concerns will be considered. Byline usually given. Pays on publication. No kill fee. Publishes ms an average of 4 months after acceptance. Accepts queries by mail, e-mail, fax.

NONFICTION No poetry. Queries preferred. **Rates depend on subject, author, and work involved.** Pays expenses of writers on assignment as negotiated.

REPRINTS Send tearsheet or photocopy and information about when and where the material previously appeared. Payment negotiated.

PHOTOS Buys color photographs with mss. Send via e-mail. Payment varies.

TIPS "The writer has a better chance of breaking in at our publication with short articles. Include samples of previous magazine writing with query."

U.S. CATHOLIC

Claretian Publications, 205 W. Monroe St., Chicago IL 60606. (312)236-7782. **Fax:** (312)236-8207. **E-mail:** editors@uscatholic.org. **E-mail:** submissions@uscatholic.org. **Website:** www.uscatholic.org. **Mostly freelance written.** Monthly magazine covering contemporary issues from a Catholic perspective. "*U.S. Catholic* puts faith in the context of everyday life. With a strong focus on social justice, we offer a fresh and balanced take on the issues that matter most in our world, adding a faith perspective to such challenges as poverty, education, family life, the environment, and even pop culture." Estab. 1935. Circ. 25,000. Byline given. Pays on acceptance. No kill fee. Publishes ms an average of 6 months after acceptance. Editorial lead time 8 months. Submit seasonal material 6 months in advance. Accepts queries by mail, e-mail. Responds in 1 month to queries; in 2 months to mss. Guidelines on website.

Please include SASE with written ms.

NONFICTION Needs essays, inspirational, opinion, personal experience, religious. **Buys 100 mss/year.** Send complete ms. Length: 700-1,400 words. **Pays minimum $200.**

PHOTOS State availability.

FICTION Accepts short stories. "Topics vary, but unpublished fiction should be no longer than 1,500 words and should include strong characters and cause readers to stop for a moment and consider their relationships with others, the world, and/or God. Specifically religious themes are not required; subject matter is not restricted. E-mail submissions@uscatholic.org." Needs ethnic, mainstream, religious, slice-of-life vignettes. **Buys 4-6 mss/year.** Send complete ms. Length: 700-1,500 words. **Pays minimum $200.**

POETRY Needs free verse. Submit 3-5 poems at a time. Accepts e-mail submissions (pasted into body of message or as attachments). Cover letter is preferred. No light verse. Buys 12 poems/year. Length: up to 50 lines/poem. **Pays $75.**

$$ THE WAR CRY

The Salvation Army, 615 Slaters Lane, Alexandria VA 22314. (703)684-4128. **Fax:** (703)684-5539. **E-mail:** war_cry@usn.salvationarmy.org. **Website:** publications.salvationarmyusa.org. **10% freelance written.** "Inspirational magazine with evangelical emphasis and portrayals that express the mission of the Salvation Army. Fourteen issues published per year, including special Easter and Christmas issues." Estab. 1881. Circ. 200,000 monthly; 1.7 million Christmas; 1.1 million Easter. Byline given. Pays on publication. No kill fee. Publishes ms an average of 2 months to 1 year after acceptance. Editorial lead time 2 months before issue date; Christmas and Easter issues: 6 months before issue date. Submit seasonal material 6 months in advance. Accepts simultaneous submissions. Responds in 3-4 weeks to mss. Sample copy, theme list, and writer's guidelines free with #10 SASE or online.

NONFICTION Needs "*The War Cry* represents The Salvation Army's mission through features, news, profiles, commentaries, and stories. It seeks to bring people to Christ, help believers grow in faith and character, and promote redemptive cultural practices from the perspective of The Salvation Army programs, minisitries, and doctrines." No missionary stories, confessions. **Buys 30 mss/year.** Complete mss and reprints accepted through website at publications.salvationarmyusa.org/writers-submissions. Submissions strengthened when photos included where appropriate. **Pays 25¢/word.**

REPRINTS Considers reprints.

PHOTOS Accepts submissions for the "In the Moment" feature appearing in each issue. High-resolution photos (600 dpi) with captions. Identification of subjects required. Pays $50.

POETRY Purchases limited poetry.

FILLERS Needs anecdotes. **Buys 10-20 mss/year.** Length: 50-350 words. **Pays 25¢/word.**

$ WESLEYAN LIFE

The Wesleyan Publishing House, P.O. Box 50434, Indianapolis IN 46250. (317)774-7909. **Fax:** (317)774-3924. **E-mail:** communications@wesleyan.org; macbethw@wesleyan.org; rifet@wesleyan.org. **Website:** www.wesleyanlifeonline.com. **Contact:** Wayne MacBeth, executive editor; Kerry Kind, editor; Tricia Rife, assistant editor. Quarterly magazine of The Wesleyan Church. Estab. 1842. Circ. 40,000+ print plus digital (ePub). Byline given. No honoraria or expenses paid. Accepts simultaneous submissions.

"No unsolicited mss are needed for the quarterly magazine. Additional stories and articles are continuously published on our website and in social media and circulated through WesLife, an e-mailed newsletter with 24 issues per year with circulation of 14,000+. We do accept unsolicited stories and articles for these channels of publication, with items about or of interest to The Wesleyan Church."

NONFICTION Needs inspirational, religious. Length: 250-1,000 words.

RETIREMENT

$$$$ AARP THE MAGAZINE

AARP, c/o Editorial Submissions, 601 E. St. NW, Washington DC 20049. **E-mail:** aarpmagazine@aarp.org. **Website:** www.aarp.org/magazine. **50% freelance written. Prefers to work with published/established writers.** Bimonthly magazine covering issues that affect people over the age of 50. *AARP The Magazine* is devoted to the varied needs and active life interests of AARP members, age 50 and over, covering such topics as financial planning, travel, health, careers, retirement, relationships, and social and cultural change. Its editorial content serves the mission of AARP seeking through education, advocacy, and service to enhance the quality of life for all by promoting independence, dignity, and purpose. Circ. 22,721,661. Byline given. Pays on acceptance. Offers 25% kill fee. Publishes ms an average of 6 months after acceptance. Submit seasonal material 6 months in advance. Accepts queries by mail, e-mail only. Responds in 3 months to queries. Sample copy free. Guidelines available online.

NONFICTION No previously published articles. Query with published clips. Explain the idea of the piece, tell how you would approach it as a writer, give some sense of your writing style, and mention the section of the magazine for which the piece is intended. *No unsolicited mss.* Only personal essays should be submitted in full. Features and departments cover the following categories: money, health and fitness, food and nutrition, travel, consumerism, general interest, relationships, and personal essay. Length: Up to 2,000 words. **Pays $1/word.** Sometimes pays expenses of writers on assignment.

PHOTOS Photos purchased with or without accompanying mss. Pays $250 and up for color; $150 and up for b&w.

TIPS "The most frequent mistake made by writers in completing an article for us is poor follow-through with basic research. The outline is often more interesting than the finished piece. We do not accept unsolicited mss."

$ CHRISTIAN LIVING IN THE MATURE YEARS

The United Methodist Publishing House, 2222 Rosa L. Parks Blvd., P.O. Box 17890, Nashville TN 37228-7890. (615)749-6474. **Fax:** (615)749-6512. **E-mail:** matureyears@umpublishing.org. **80% freelance written. Prefers to work with published/established writers.** Quarterly magazine designed to help persons in and nearing the retirement years understand and appropriate the resources of the Christian faith in dealing with specific problems and opportunities related to aging. Estab. 1954. Circ. 55,000. Pays on acceptance. No kill fee. Publishes ms an average of 1 year after acceptance. Submit seasonal material 14 months in advance. Responds in 6-7 months to mss. Sample copy: $6, plus 9x12 SAE. Writer's guidelines for #10 SASE or by e-mail.

NONFICTION Needs how-to, hobbies, inspirational, religious, travel, special guidelines, older adult health, finance issues. **Buys 75-80 mss/year.** Send complete ms; e-mail submissions preferred. Length: 900-2,000 words. **Pays $45-125.** Sometimes pays expenses of writers on assignment.

REPRINTS Send tearsheet, photocopy, or typed ms with rights for sale noted and information about when and where the material previously appeared. Pays at same rate as for previously unpublished material.

PHOTOS Send high-resolution photos. Captions, model releases required. Negotiates pay individually.

COLUMNS/DEPARTMENTS Health Hints (retirement, health), 900-1,500 words; Going Places (travel, pilgrimage), 1,000-1,500 words; Fragments of Life (personal inspiration), 250-600 words; Modern Revelations (religious/inspirational), 900-1,500 words; Money Matters (personal finance), 1,200-1,800 words; Merry-Go-Round (cartoons, jokes, 4-6 line humorous verse); Puzzle Time (religious puzzles, crosswords). **Buys 4 mss/year.** Send complete ms. **Pays $25-45.**

POETRY Needs free verse, haiku, light verse, traditional. Submit seasonal and nature poems for spring from December through February; for summer from March through May; for fall from June through August; and for winter from September through November. Accepts fax and e-mail submissions (e-mail preferred). Buys 24 poems/year. Submit maximum 6 poems. Length: 3-16 lines of up to 50 characters maximum. **Pays $5-20.**

TIPS "Practice writing dialogue! Listen to people talk; take notes; master dialogue writing! Not easy but well worth it! Most inquiry letters are far too long. If you can't sell me an idea in a brief paragraph, you're not going to sell the reader on reading your finished article or story."

$ MATURE LIVING

Lifeway Christian Resources, 1 Lifeway Plaza, Nashville TN 37234. (615)251-2000. **E-mail:** matureliving@lifeway.com. **Website:** www.lifeway.com. **Contact:** Rene Holt. **90% freelance written.** "Monthly leisure reading magazine for senior adults 55 and older. *Mature Living* is Christian in content, and the material required is what would appeal to the 55-and-over age group: inspirational, informational, nostalgic, humorous. Our magazine is distributed mainly through churches (especially Southern Baptist churches) that buy the magazine in bulk and distribute it to members in this age group." Estab. 1977. Circ. 320,000. Byline given. Pays on acceptance. No kill fee. Publishes ms an average of 7-8 weeks after acceptance. Submit seasonal material 1 year in advance. Responds in 3 months to mss. Sample copy: $4. Guidelines for #10 sase.

NONFICTION Needs crafts, general interest, historical, how-to, humor, inspirational, interview, personal experience, travel. No pornography, profanity, occult, liquor, dancing, drugs, gambling. **Buys 100 mss/year.** Query. Length: 600-1,200 words. **Pays $85-115**

PHOTOS State availability. Offers $10-25/photo. Pays on publication.

COLUMNS/DEPARTMENTS Cracker Barrel (brief, humorous, original quips and verses), **pays $15**; Grandparents' Brag Board (something humorous or insightful said or done by your grandchild or great-grandchild), **pays $15**; Inspirational (devotional items), **pays $25**; Food (introduction and 4-6 recipes), **pays $50**; Over the Garden Fence (vegetable or flower gardening), **pays $40**; Crafts (step-by-step procedures), **pays $40**; Game Page (crossword or word-search puzzles and quizzes), **pays $40**.

RURAL

$$ BACKWOODS HOME MAGAZINE

P.O. Box 712, Gold Beach OR 97444. (541)247-8900. **Fax:** (541)247-8600. **E-mail:** editor@backwoodshome.com; lisa@backwoodshome.com. **E-mail:** article-submission@backwoodshome.com. **Website:** www.backwoodshome.com. **Contact:** Lisa Nourse, editorial coordinator; Dave Duffy, editor and publisher; Jessie Denning, managing editor. **90% freelance written.** Bimonthly magazine covering self-reliance. *Backwoods Home Magazine* is written for people who have a desire to pursue personal independence, self-sufficiency, and their dreams. Offers how-to articles on self-reliance. Estab. 1989. Circ. 38,000. Byline given. Pays on acceptance. Editorial lead time 4-6 months. Submit seasonal material 4-6 months in advance. Accepts queries by mail, e-mail. Sample copy for 9x10 SAE and 6 first-class stamps. Guidelines available online.

NONFICTION Needs general interest, how-to, humor, personal experience, technical. **Buys 120 mss/year.** Send complete ms via e-mail; no attachments. Looking for straightforward, clear writing similar to what you would find in a good newspaper. Length: 500 words. **Pays $40-200.**

PHOTOS Send photos. Captions, identification of subjects, model releases required. Offers no additional payment for photos accepted with ms.

$$ FARM & RANCH LIVING

Reiman Media Group, 1610 N. 2nd St., Suite 102, Milwaukee WI 53212-3906. (414)423-0100. **Fax:** (414)423-8463. **E-mail:** submissions@farmandranchliving.com. **Website:** www.farmandranchliving.com. **30% freelance written. Eager to work with new/unpublished writers.** Bimonthly magazine aimed at families that farm or ranch full time. *F&RL* is *not* a 'how-to' magazine—it focuses on people rather than products and profits. Estab. 1978. Circ. 400,000. Byline given. Pays on publication. No kill fee. Publishes ms an average of 6 months after acceptance. Submit seasonal material 6 months in advance. "We are unable to respond to queries." To purchase a single copy, contact customercare@farmandranchliving.com.

NONFICTION Needs humor, rural only, inspirational, interview, personal experience, farm/ranch related, photo feature, nostalgia, prettiest place in the country (photo/text tour of ranch or farm). No issue-oriented stories (pollution, animal rights, etc.). **Buys 30 mss/year.** Send complete ms. Length: 600-1,200 words. **Pays up to $300 for text/photo package. Payment for Prettiest Place negotiable.**

REPRINTS Send photocopy with rights for sale noted. Payment negotiable.

PHOTOS "We no longer accept slides. We look for photos of farm animals, people, and rural scenery." State availability. Pays $75-200.

TIPS "Our readers enjoy stories and features that are upbeat and positive. A freelancer must see *F&RL* to fully appreciate how different it is from other farm publications—ordering a sample is strongly advised (not available on newsstands). Photo features (about interesting farm or ranch families) and personality profiles are most open to freelancers."

MONADNOCK TABLE: THE GUIDE TO OUR REGION'S FOOD, FARMS, & COMMUNITY

60 West Street, Keene NH 03431. (603)369-2525. **E-mail:** marcia@monadnocktable.com; info@monadnocktable.com. **Website:** www.monadnocktable.com. **Contact:** Marcia Passos Duffy, editor. Quarterly magazine for local food/farms in the Monadnock Region of New Hampshire. Estab. 2010. Circ. 10,000. Byline given. Pays on publication. 25% kill fee. Publishes ms 3 months after acceptance. Editorial lead time 3 months. Submit seasonal material 3 months in advance. Accepts queries by e-mail. Responds in 1 month to queries and mss. Sample copy available online. Guidelines are available on website.

"Must be about trends, profiles, etc., of local food and farms in the Monadnock Region of New Hampshire."

NONFICTION Needs book excerpts, essays, how-to, interview, opinion, personal experience. Length:

500-1,000 words. **Pays $75 for profile stories up to 600 words and $125 for features up to 1,200 words.** Sometimes pays expenses of writers on assignment. (limit agreed upon in advance)

PHOTOS Freelancers should state of photos with submission. Captions required. Reviews GIF/JPEG files. Offers no additional payment for photos accepted with ms.

COLUMNS/DEPARTMENTS Local Farmer (profile of local farmer in Monadnock Region), up to 600 words; Local Eats (profile of local chef and/or restaurant using local food), up to 600 words; Feature (how-to or "think" piece about local foods), up 1,000; Books/Opinion/Commentary (review of books, book excerpt, commentary, opinion pieces about local food), up to 500 words. **Buys 10 mss/year.** Query.

TIPS "Please query first with your qualifications. Please read magazine first for style (magazines available online). Must have a local (Monadnock Region, New Hampshire) angle."

$$ RANGE

Purple Coyote Corp., 106 E. Adams St., Suite 201, Carson City NV 89706. (775)884-2200. **Fax:** (775)884-2213. **E-mail:** edit@rangemagazine.com. **Website:** www.rangemagazine.com. **Contact:** C.J. Hadley, editor/publisher. **70% freelance written.** *RANGE* covers ranching, farming, and the issues that affect agriculture. *RANGE* magazine is devoted to the issues that threaten the West, its people, lifestyles, lands, and wildlife. No stranger to controversy, *RANGE* is the leading forum for opposing viewpoints in the search for solutions that will halt the depletion of a national resource, the American rancher. Estab. 1991. Pays on publication. Publishes ms an average of 3-6 months after acceptance. Accepts queries by e-mail. Responds in 1-2 months to queries; in 1-4 months to mss. Sample copy: $2. Guidelines available online.

NONFICTION Needs major ranch features in American West, issues that affect ranchers, profiles, short nonfiction book excerpts that suit range, humor, photo essays. No sports or events. No book reviews. Writer must be familiar with *RANGE*. Query. Length: 500-2,000 words. **Pays $50-500.**

PHOTOS State availability of photography. Captions, photo credit, and contact information must be included with all photos. Reviews high-res digitals (JPEGS or TIFFS) on disk or flash drive with contact sheets. FTP site available. Slides and prints also reviewed. Pays $25-75, $100 for cover.

$$ RURALITE

5605 N.E. Elam Young Pkwy., Hillsboro OR 97124. (503)357-2105. **E-mail:** editor@ruralite.org. **E-mail:** curtisc@ruralite.org. **Website:** www.ruralite.org. **Contact:** Curtis Condon, editor. **80% freelance written. Works with new, unpublished writers.** Monthly magazine aimed at members of consumer-owned electric utilities throughout 7 western states. General-interest publication used by 48 rural electric cooperatives and PUDs. Readers are predominantly rural and small-town residents interested in stories about people and issues that affect Northwest lifestyles. Estab. 1954. Circ. 330,000. Byline given. Pays on acceptance. No kill fee. Accepts queries by mail. Responds in 2 months to queries. Sample copy for 9x12 SAE with $1.61 of postage affixed. Guidelines available online.

NONFICTION Buys 50-60 mss/year. Query. Length: 100-2,000 words. **Pays $50-500.**

REPRINTS Send typed ms with rights for sale noted and information about when and where the material previously appeared.

PHOTOS Illustrated stories are the key to a sale. Stories without art rarely make it. Color prints/negatives, color slides, all formats accepted. No b&w. Inside color is $25-100; cover photo is $250-350.

TIPS "Study recent issues. Follow directions when given an assignment. Be able to deliver a complete package (story and photos). We're looking for regular contributors to whom we can assign topics from our story list after they've proven their ability to deliver quality mss."

SCIENCE

$$ AD ASTRA

National Space Society, 1155 15th St. NW, Suite 500, Washington DC 20005. (202)429-1600. **Fax:** (202)530-0659. **E-mail:** adastra@nss.org. **Website:** www.nss.org/adastra. **Contact:** Gary Barnhard, editor-in-chief. **90% freelance written.** *Ad Astra* ("to the stars") is the award-winning magazine of the National Space Society, featuring the latest news in space exploration and stunning full-color photography. Published quarterly. "We publish non-technical, lively articles about all aspects of international space programs, from shuttle missions to planetary probes to plans for the future and commercial space." Estab. 1989. Circ. 25,000. Byline given. Pays on publication. No kill fee. Responds only when interested. Sample copy for 9x12 SASE.

NONFICTION Needs book excerpts, essays, exposè, general interest, interview, opinion, photo feature, technical. No science fiction or UFO stories. Query with published clips. Length: 1,000-4,000 words with 2-8 full-size (8.5x11) color images at 300 dpi; 100-600 words for sidebars; 600-750 words for book reviews. **Pays 25¢/word.**

PHOTOS State availability. Identification of subjects required. Reviews color prints, digital, JPEG-IS, GISS. Negotiates pay.

TIPS "We require mss to be in Word or text file formats. Know the field of space technology, programs, and policy. Know the players. Look for fresh angles. And, please, know how to write!"

$$$$ AMERICAN ARCHAEOLOGY

The Archaeological Conservancy, 1717 Girard Blvd., NE, Albuquerque NM 87106. (505)266-9668. **Fax:** (505)266-0311. **E-mail:** tacmag@nm.net. **Website:** www.americanarchaeology.org. **Contact:** Michael Bawaya, editor; Vicki Singer, art director. **60% freelance written.** Quarterly magazine. "We're a popular archaeology magazine. Our readers are very interested in this science. Our features cover important digs, prominent archaeologists, and most any aspect of the science. We only cover North America." Estab. 1997. Circ. 35,000. Byline given. Pays on acceptance. Offers 20% kill fee. Publishes ms an average of 3 months after acceptance. Editorial lead time 3 months. Accepts queries by mail, e-mail, fax. Responds in 3 weeks to queries. Responds in 1 month to mss

NONFICTION No fiction, poetry, humor. **Buys 15 mss/year.** Query with published clips. Length: 1,500-3,000 words. **Pays $1,000-2,000.** Pays expenses of writers on assignment.

PHOTOS State availability. Identification of subjects required. Reviews transparencies, prints. Pays $50 and up for occasional stock images; assigns work by project (pay varies); negotiable. **Pays on acceptance.** Credit line given. Buys one-time rights. Offers $400-600/photo shoot. Negotiates payment individually.

TIPS "Read the magazine. Features must have a considerable amount of archaeological detail."

$$$ CHEMICAL HERITAGE

Chemical Heritage Foundation (CHF), 315 Chestnut St., Philadelphia PA 19106. (215)925-2222. **E-mail:** editor@chemheritage.org. **Website:** www.chemheritage.org. **40% freelance written.** Published 3 times/year. *Chemical Heritage* reports on the history of the chemical and molecular sciences and industries, on Chemical Heritage Foundation activities, and on other activities of interest to our readers. Estab. 1982. Circ. 17,000. Byline given. Pays on acceptance. Publishes ms an average of 6-12 months after acceptance. Editorial lead time 4 months. Accepts queries by e-mail. Responds in 1 month to queries and mss. Sample copy free.

NONFICTION Needs book excerpts, essays, historical, interview. "No exposés or excessively technical material. Many of our readers are highly educated professionals, but they may not be familiar with, for example, specific chemical processes." **Buys 3-5 mss/year.** Query. Length: 1,000-3,500 words. **Pays 50¢-$1/word.**

PHOTOS State availability. Captions required. Offers no additional payment for photos accepted with ms.

COLUMNS/DEPARTMENTS Book reviews: 200 or 750 words; CHF collections: 300-500 words; policy: 1,000 words; personal remembrances: 750 words; profiles of CHF awardees and oral history subjects: 600-900 words: buys 3-5 mms/year. **Buys 10 mss/year.** Query.

TIPS "CHF attends exhibits at many scientific trade shows and scholarly conferences. Our representatives are always happy to speak to potential authors genuinely interested in the past, present, and future of chemistry. We are a good venue for scholars who want to reach a broader audience or for science writers who want to bolster their scholarly credentials."

CHEMMATTERS

1155 16th St., NW, Washington DC 20036. (202)872-6164. **Fax:** (202)833-7732. **E-mail:** chemmatters@acs.org. **Website:** www.acs.org/chemmatters. **Contact:** Patrice Pages, editor; Cornithia Harris, art director. Covers content covered in a standard high school chemistry textbook. *ChemMatters*, published 4 times/year, is a magazine that helps high school students find connections between chemistry and the world around them. Estab. 1983. Pays on acceptance. Publishes ms 6 months after acceptance. Accepts queries by mail, e-mail. Accepts simultaneous submissions. Responds to queries/mss in 4 weeks. Sample copies free for 10x13 SASE and 3 first-class stamps. Writer's guidelines free for SASE (available as e-mail attachment upon request).

NONFICTION Query with published clips. **Pays $500-1,000 for article. Additional payment for mss/illustration packages and for photos accompanying articles.**

TIPS "Be aware of the content covered in a standard high school chemistry textbook. Choose themes and topics that are timely, interesting, fun, *and* that relate to the content and concepts of the first-year chemistry course. Articles should describe real people involved with real science. Best articles feature young people making a difference or solving a problem."

$$$$ INVENTORS DIGEST

Inventors Digest, LLC, 520 Elliot St., Suite 200, Charlotte NC 28202. (704)369-7312. **Fax:** (704)333-5115. **E-mail:** info@inventorsdigest.com. **Website:** www.inventorsdigest.com. **50% freelance written.** Monthly magazine covering inventions, technology, engineering, intellectual property issues. *Inventors Digest* is committed to educating and inspiring entry- and enterprise-level inventors and professional innovators. As the leading print and online publication for the innovation culture, *Inventors Digest* delivers useful, entertaining and cutting-edge information to help its readers succeed. Estab. 1983. Circ. 40,000. Byline given. Pays on publication. Offers 40% kill fee. Publishes ms an average of 2 months after acceptance. Editorial lead time 2 months. Submit seasonal material 4 months in advance. Accepts queries by mail, e-mail. Responds in 3 weeks to queries; 1 month to mss. Sample copy available online. Guidelines free.

NONFICTION Needs book excerpts, historical, how-to, secure a patent, find a licensing manufacturer, avoid scams, inspirational, interview, new product, opinion, (does not mean letters to the editor), personal experience, technical. Special issues: Editorial calendar available online. "We don't want poetry. No stories that talk about readers—stay away from 'one should do X' construction. Nothing that duplicates what you can read elsewhere." **Buys 4 mss/year mss/year.** Query. Length: Varies. For any piece more than 2,000 words, send a 300-word synopsis first. **Payment varies, usually at least $50 for both requested and unsolicited articles.**

PHOTOS Contact: Mike Drummond. State availability. Identification of subjects required. Reviews GIF/JPEG files. Negotiates payment individually.

COLUMNS/DEPARTMENTS Cover (the most important package-puts a key topic in compelling context), 2,000-3,000 words; Radar (news/product snippets), 1,200; Bookshelf (book reviews), 700; Pro Bono (legal issues), 850; Profile (human interest stories on inventors and innovators), BrainChild (celebration of young inventors and innovators), FirstPerson (inventors show how they've overcome hurdles), 1,000; MeetingRoom (learn secrets to success of best inventor groups in the country), 900; TalkBack (Q&A with manufacturers, retailers, etc. in the innovation industry), Five Questions With...(a conversation with some of the brightest and most controversial minds in Technology, manufacturing, academia and other fields), 800. **Buys 4 mss/year mss/year.** Query. **Pays $20.**

TIPS "We prefer e-mail. If it's a long piece (more than 2,000 words), send a synopsis, captivating us in 300 words. Put 'Article Query' in the subject line. A great story should have conflict or obstacles to overcome. Show us something surprising and why we should care, and put it in context. Sweep, color, scene and strong character anecdotes are important. If there's no conflict-moral, institutional, cultural, obstacles to overcome-there's no story. If you send it in analog form, write to: *Inventors Digest*, Article Query, P.O. Box 36761, Charlotte, NC 28236."

SCIENCE WEEKLY

P.O. Box 70638, Chevy Chase MD 20813. (301)680-8804. **E-mail:** info@scienceweekly.com. **Website:** www.scienceweekly.com. **Contact:** Dr. Claude Mayberry, publisher. *Science Weekly* uses freelance writers to develop and write an entire issue on a single science topic. Send résumé only, not submissions. Authors preferred within the greater D.C./Virginia/Maryland area. *Science Weekly* works on assignment only. Estab. 1984. Circ. 200,000. Pays on publication. Sample copy free online.

Submit résumé only.

NONFICTION Needs young readers, middle readers (K-6th grade): science/math education, education, problem-solving.

SCIENCE EDITOR

Council of Science Editors, 10200 W. 44th Ave., Suite 304, Wheat Ridge CO 80033. (720)881-6046. **Fax:** (303)422-8894. **E-mail:** pkbaskin@gmail.com; cse@councilscienceeditors.org. **Website:** www.councilscienceeditors.org. **Contact:** Patty K. Baskin, editor in chief. *Science Editor*, published 3 times/year, is a forum for the exchange of information and ideas among professionals concerned with publishing in the sciences. Estab. 2000. Circ. 1,500. Publishes ms 3-6 months after acceptance. Submit seasonal material 9 months in advance. Accepts queries by e-mail. Responds in 3-6 weeks. Guidelines by e-mail.

NONFICTION Welcomes contributions on research on peer review, editorial processes, publication technology, publication ethics, and other items of interest to the journal's readers. Submit complete ms by e-mail; include phone number. Must be in the style recommended by *Scientific Style and Format*, with references in order of citation.

SKY & TELESCOPE

F+W, A Content and Ecommerce Company, 90 Sherman St., Cambridge MA 02140. (617)864-7360. **Fax:** (617)864-6117. **E-mail:** editors@skyandtelescope.com. **Website:** skyandtelescope.com. **Contact:** Peter Tyson, editor in chief. **15% freelance written.** Monthly magazine covering astronomy. "*Sky & Telescope* is the magazine of record for astronomy. We cover amateur activities, research news, equipment, book, and software reviews. Our audience is the amateur astronomer who wants to learn more about the night sky." Estab. 1941. Circ. 65,000. Byline given. Pays on publication. 20% kill fee. Publishes ms an average of 6 months after acceptance. Editorial lead time 4 months. Submit seasonal material 1 year in advance. Accepts queries by mail, e-mail, fax. Responds in 3 weeks to queries; in 1 month to mss. Sample copy: $6.99. Guidelines available online.

NONFICTION Needs essays, historical, how-to, opinion, personal experience, photo feature, technical. No poetry, crosswords, New Age, or alternative cosmologies. **Buys 10 mss/year.** Query. Length: 1,500-2,500 words. **Pays at least 25¢/word.** Sometimes pays expenses of writers on assignment.

PHOTOS Send photos. Identification of subjects required. Reviews contact sheets. Negotiates payment individually.

COLUMNS/DEPARTMENTS Focal Point (opinion), 550 words. **Buys 12 mss/year.** Query. **Pays 25¢/word.**

TIPS "We're written exclusively by astronomy professionals, hobbyists, and insiders. Good artwork is key. Keep the text lively, and provide captions."

SCIENCE FICTION, FANTASY AND HORROR

ANALOG SCIENCE FICTION & FACT

Dell Magazines, 44 Wall St., Suite 904, New York NY 10005-2401. **E-mail:** analog@dellmagazines.com. **Website:** www.analogsf.com. **Contact:** Trevor Quachri, editor. **100% freelance written. Eager to work with new/unpublished writers.** *Analog* seeks "solidly entertaining stories exploring solidly thought-out speculative ideas. But the ideas, and consequently the stories, are always new. Real science and technology have always been important in *ASF*, not only as the foundation of its fiction but as the subject of articles about real research with big implications for the future." Estab. 1930. Circ. 50,000. Byline given. Pays on acceptance. No kill fee. Publishes ms an average of 10 months after acceptance. Accepts queries by mail, online submission form. Responds in 2-3 months to mss. Sample copy: $5 and SASE. Guidelines online.

Fiction published in *Analog* has won numerous Nebula and Hugo Awards.

NONFICTION Needs fact articles. Special issues: Articles should deal with subjects of not only current but future interest, i.e., with topics at the present frontiers of research whose likely future developments have implications of wide interest. **Buys 11 mss/year.** Send complete ms via online submissions manager (preferred) or postal mail. Does not accept e-mail submissions. Length: up to 4,000 words. **Pays 9¢/word.**

FICTION "Basically, we publish science fiction stories. That is, stories in which some aspect of future science or technology is so integral to the plot that, if that aspect were removed, the story would collapse. The science can be physical, sociological, psychological. The technology can be anything from electronic engineering to biogenetic engineering. But the stories must be strong and realistic, with believable people (who needn't be human) doing believable things—no matter how fantastic the background might be." Needs science fiction, hard science/technological, soft/sociological, novellas, serials. No fantasy or stories in which the scientific background is implausible or plays no essential role. Send complete ms via online submissions manager (preferred) or postal mail. Does not accept e-mail submissions. Length: 2,000-7,000 words for short stories, 10,000-20,000 words for novelettes and novellas, and 40,000-80,000 for serials. **Analog pays 8-10¢/word for short stories up to 7,500 words, 8-8.5¢ for longer material, 6¢/word for serials.**

POETRY Send poems via online submissions manager (preferred) or postal mail. Does not accept e-mail submissions. Length: up to 40 lines/poem. **Pays $1/line.**

TIPS "I'm looking for irresistibly entertaining stories that make me think about things in ways I've never done before. Read several issues to get a broad feel for our tastes, but don't try to imitate what you read."

APEX MAGAZINE

Apex Publications, LLC, P.O. Box 24323, Lexington KY 40524. (859)312-3974. **E-mail:** jason@apexbookcompany.com. **Website:** www.apexbookcompany.com. **Contact:** Lesley Conner, managing editor. **100% freelance written.** Monthly e-zine publishing dark speculative fiction. "An elite repository for new and seasoned authors with an other-worldly interest in the unquestioned and slightly bizarre parts of the universe." Estab. 2004. Circ. 28,000 unique visits per month. Byline given. Pays on publication. Offers 30% kill fee. Publishes mss an average of 6 months after acceptance. Editorial lead time 2 weeks. Submit seasonal material 6 months in advance. Accepts queries by e-mail. Responds in 20-30 days to queries and to mss. Sample copy available online. Guidelines available online.

"We want science fiction, fantasy, horror, and mash-ups of all three of the dark, weird stuff down at the bottom of your little literary heart." Monthly e-zine publishing dark speculative fiction.

NONFICTION Buys 36 mss/year. Send complete ms. Length: 100-7,500 words. **Pays 6¢/word.**

FICTION Needs fantasy, horror, science fiction. **Buys 36 mss/year.** Send complete ms. Length: 100-7,500 words. **Pays 6¢/word.**

POETRY Submit up to 5 poems. Length: up to 200 lines/poem. **Pays 25¢/line.**

ASCENT ASPIRATIONS

1560 Arbutus Dr., Nanoose Bay BC C9P 9C8 Canada. **E-mail:** ascentaspirations@shaw.ca. **Website:** www.ascentaspirations.ca. **Contact:** David Fraser, editor. E-zine specializing in short fiction (all genres) and poetry, spoken work videos, essays, visual art. "*Ascent Aspirations* magazine publishes monthly online and once in print. The print issues are operated as contests. Please refer to current guidelines before submitting. *Ascent Aspirations* is a quality electronic publication dedicated to the promotion and encouragement of aspiring writers of any genre. The focus, however, is toward interesting experimental writing in dark mainstream, literary, science fiction, fantasy, and horror. Poetry can be on any theme. Essays need to be unique, current, and have social, philosophical commentary." Estab. 1997. Accepts simultaneous submissions. Responds in 1 week to queries; 3 months to mss. Sometimes comments on rejected mss. Guidelines by e-mail or on website. Accepts multiple submissions and reprints.

Magazine: 40 electronic pages; illustrations; photos. Receives 100-200 unsolicited mss/month. Accepts 40 mss/issue; 240 mss/year. Publishes ms 3 months after acceptance. Publishes 10-50 new writers/year. Has published work by Taylor Graham, Janet Buck, Jim Manton, Steve Cartwright, Don Stockard, Penn Kemp, Sam Vargo, Vernon Waring, Margaret Karmazin, Bill Hughes, and recently spoken-word artists Sheri-D Wilson, Missy Peters, Ian Ferrier, Cathy Petch, and Bob Holdman.

NONFICTION Needs literary essays, literary criticism. Query by e-mail with Word attachment. Include estimated word count, brief bio, and list of publications. "If you have to submit by mail because it is your only avenue, provide a SASE with either International Coupons or Canadian stamps only." Length: up to 1,000 words **"No payment at this time."**

FICTION Needs erotica, experimental, fantasy (space fantasy), feminist, horror (dark fantasy, futuristic, psychological, supernatural), literary, mainstream, mystery/suspense, New Age, psychic/supernatural/occult, science fiction (hard science/technological, soft/sociological). Query by e-mail with Word attachment. Include estimated word count, brief bio, and list of publications. "If you have to submit by mail because it is your only avenue, provide a SASE with either International Coupons or Canadian stamps only." Length: up to 1,000 words. Publishes short shorts. **"No payment at this time."**

POETRY Submit 1-5 poems at a time. Prefers e-mail submissions (pasted into body of message or as attachment in Word); no disk submissions. "If you must submit by postal mail because it is your only avenue, provide a SASE with IRCs or Canadian stamps." Reads submissions on a regular basis year round.

"We accept all forms of poetry on any theme. Poetry needs to be unique and touch the reader emotionally with relevant human, social, and philosophical imagery." Considers poetry by children and teens. Does not want poetry "that focuses on mainstream, overtly religious verse." **"No payment at this time."**

TIPS "Short fiction should first of all tell a good story, take the reader to new and interesting imaginary or real places. Short fiction should use language lyrically and effectively, be experimental in either form or content, and take the reader into realms where they can analyze and think about the human condition. Write with passion for your material, be concise and economical, and let the reader work to unravel your story. In terms of editing, always proofread to the point where what you submit is the best it possibly can be. Never be discouraged if your work is not accepted; it may just not be the right fit for a current publication."

ASIMOV'S SCIENCE FICTION

Dell Magazines, 44 Wall St., Suite 904, New York NY 10005. **E-mail:** asimovs@dellmagazines.com. **Website:** www.asimovs.com. **Contact:** Sheila Williams, editor; Victoria Green, senior art director. **98% freelance written. Works with a small number of new/unpublished writers each year.** *Asimov's*, published 10 times/year, including 2 double issues, is 5.875x8.625 (trim size); 112 pages; 30 lb. newspaper; 70 lb. to 8 pt. C1S cover stock; illustrations; rarely has photos. "Magazine consists of science fiction and fantasy stories for adults and young adults. Publishes the best short science fiction available." Estab. 1977. Circ. 50,000. Pays on acceptance. No kill fee. Publishes ms an average of 6-12 months after acceptance. Accepts queries by mail. Responds in 2 months to queries; in 3 months to mss. Sample copy: $5. Guidelines online or for #10 SASE.

Named for a science fiction "legend," *Asimov's* regularly receives Hugo and Nebula Awards.

FICTION Wants "science fiction primarily. Some fantasy and humor. It is best to read a great deal of material in the genre to avoid the use of some very old ideas." Submit ms via online submissions manager or postal mail; no e-mail submissions. Needs fantasy, science fiction, hard science, soft sociological. No horror or psychic/supernatural, sword and sorcery, explicit sex or violence that isn't integral to the story. Would like to see more hard science fiction. Length: 750-15,000 words. **Pays 8-10¢/word for short stories up to 7,500 words; 8-8.5¢/word for longer material. Works between 7,500-10,000 words by authors who make more than 8¢/word for short stories will receive a flat rate that will be no less than the payment would be for a shorter story.**

TIPS "In general, we're looking for 'character-oriented' stories, those in which the characters, rather than the science, provide the main focus for the reader's interest. Serious, thoughtful, yet accessible fiction will constitute the majority of our purchases, but there's always room for the humorous as well."

BEYOND CENTAURI

White Cat Publications, LLC, 33080 Industrial Rd., Suite 101, Livonia MI 48150. **E-mail:** beyondcentauri@whitecatpublications.com. **Website:** www.whitecatpublications.com/guidelines/beyond-centauri. *Beyond Centauri*, published quarterly, contains fantasy, science fiction, sword and sorcery, very mild horror short stories, poetry, and illustrations for readers ages 10 and up. Estab. 2003. Publishes ms 1-2 months after acceptance. Responds in 2-3 months. Single copy: $7.

Beyond Centauri is 44 pages, magazine-sized, offset printed, perfect-bound, with paper cover for color art, includes ads. Receives about 200 poems/year, accepts about 50 (25%). Press run is 100; 5 distributed free to reviewers.

NONFICTION Considers short articles about space exploration, science, and technology; opinion pieces; and movie and book reviews. Send in the body of an e-mail, or as an RTF attachment. Length: up to 1,500 words. **Pays $7/piece, plus a contributor's copy.**

FICTION Looks for themes of science fiction or fantasy. "Science fiction and especially stories that take place in outer space will find great favor with us." Submit in the body of an e-mail, or as an RTF attachment. Length: up to 2,500 words. **Pays $6/story, $3/reprints, and $2/flash fiction (under 1,000 words), plus 1 contributor's copy.**

POETRY Wants fantasy, science fiction, spooky horror, and speculative poetry for younger readers. Considers poetry by children and teens. Has published poetry by Bruce Boston, Bobbi Sinha-Morey, Debbie Feo, Dorothy Imm, Cythera, and Terrie Leigh Relf. Looks for themes of science fiction and fantasy. Poetry should be submitted in the body of an e-mail, or as an RTF attachment. Does not want horror with excessive blood and gore. Length: up to 50 lines/poem. **Pays $2/**

original poem, $1/reprints, $1/scifaiku and related form, plus 1 contributor's copy.

THE FIFTH DI...

P.O. Box 782, Cedar Rapids IO 52406-0782. **E-mail:** thefifthdi@yahoo.com. **Website:** www.nomadicdeliriumpress.com/fifth.htm. *The Fifth Di...*, published quarterly online, features fiction from the science fiction and fantasy genres. Estab. 1994. Publishes ms 3 months after acceptance. Responds in 2 months to mss. Guidelines online.

FICTION Open to most forms, but all submissions must be science fiction or fantasy. Does not want horror, or anything that is not science fiction or fantasy. Submit by e-mail with .RTF attachment only; no .DOC or .DOCX submissions. Include the word "Submission" in subject line. Length: up to 7,500 words. **Pays $10 per story.**

LEADING EDGE

4087 JKB, Provo UT 84602. **E-mail:** editor@leadingedgemagazine.com; fiction@leadingedgemagazine.com; art@leadingedgemagazine.com. **Website:** www.leadingedgemagazine.com. **Contact:** Kenna Blaylock, editor in chief. **90% freelance written.** Semiannual magazine covering science fiction and fantasy. "*Leading Edge* is a magazine dedicated to new and upcoming talent in the fields of science fiction and fantasy. We strive to encourage developing and established talent and provide high-quality speculative fiction to our readers." Does not accept mss with sex, excessive violence, or profanity. Estab. 1981. Circ. 200. Byline given. Pays on publication. No kill fee. Publishes ms an average of 2-4 months after acceptance. Responds in 2-4 months to mss. Single copy: $5.95. "We no longer provide subscriptions, but *Leading Edge* is now available on Amazon Kindle, as well as print-on-demand." Guidelines available online at website.

Accepts unsolicited submissions.

FICTION Needs fantasy, science fiction. **Buys 14-16 mss/year.** Send complete ms with cover letter and SASE. Include estimated word count. Length: 15,000 words maximum. **Pays 1¢/word; $10 minimum.**

POETRY Needs avant-garde, haiku, light verse, traditional. "Publishes 2-4 poems per issue. Poetry should reflect both literary value and popular appeal and should deal with science fiction- or fantasy-related themes." Submit 1 or more poems at a time. No e-mail submissions. Cover letter is preferred. Include name, address, phone number, length of poem, title, and type of poem at the top of each page. Please include SASE with every submission." Submit maximum 10 poems. Pays $10 for first 4 pages; $1.50/each subsequent page.

TIPS "Buy a sample issue to know what is currently selling in our magazine. Also, make sure to follow the writer's guidelines when submitting."

THE MAGAZINE OF FANTASY & SCIENCE FICTION

P.O. Box 3447, Hoboken NJ 07030. (201) 876-2551. **E-mail:** fandsf@aol.com. **Website:** www.fandsf.com. **Contact:** C.C. Finlay, editor. **100% freelance written.** "*The Magazine of Fantasy and Science Fiction* publishes various types of science fiction and fantasy short stories and novellas, making up about 80% of each issue. The balance of each issue is devoted to articles about science fiction, a science column, book and film reviews, cartoons, and competitions." Bimonthly. Estab. 1949. Circ. 40,000. Byline given. Pays on acceptance. No kill fee. Publishes ms an average of 9-12 months after acceptance. Submit seasonal material 8 months in advance. Responds in 2 months to queries. Sample copy: $6. Guidelines for SASE, by e-mail, or on website.

The *Magazine of Fantasy and Science Fiction* won a Nebula Award for Best Novelet for *What We Found* by Geoff Ryman in 2012. Also won the 2012 World Fantasy Award for Best Short Story for *The Paper Menagerie* by Ken Liu.

COLUMNS/DEPARTMENTS Curiosities (reviews of odd and obscure books), up to 270 words. Accepts 6 mss/year. Query. **Pays $-$50.**

FICTION "Prefers character-oriented stories. We receive a lot of fantasy fiction but never enough science fiction." Needs adventure, fantasy, horror, space fantasy, sword & sorcery, dark fantasy, futuristic, psychological, supernatural, science fiction, hard science/technological, soft/sociological. **Buys 60-90 mss/year.** No electronic submissions. Send complete ms. Length: up to 25,000 words. **Pays 7-10¢/word.**

POETRY Wants only poetry that deals with the fantastic or the science fictional. Has published poetry by Rebecca Kavaler, Elizabeth Bear, Sophie M. White, and Robert Frazier. **Pays $50/poem and 2 contributor's copies.**

TIPS "Good storytelling makes a submission stand out. Regarding manuscripts, a well-prepared manuscript (i.e., one that follows the traditional format, like that describted here: www.sfwa.org/writing/vonda/vonda.htm) stands out more than any gimmicks. Read an issue of the magazine before submitting. New writers should keep their submissions under 15,000 words—we rarely publish novellas by new writers."

MINAS TIRITH EVENING-STAR: JOURNAL OF THE AMERICAN TOLKIEN SOCIETY

American Tolkien Society, P.O. Box 97, Highland MI 48357-0097. **E-mail:** editor@americantolkiensociety.org; americantolkiensociety@yahoo.com. **Website:** www.americantolkiensociety.org. **Contact:** Amalie A. Helms, editor. *Minas Tirith Evening-Star: Journal of the American Tolkien Society*, published quarterly, publishes poetry, book reviews, essays, and fan fition. *Minas Tirith Evening-Star* is digest-sized, offset-printed from typescript, with cartoon-like b&w graphics. Press run is 400. Single copy: $3.50; subscription: $12.50. Sample: $3. Make checks payable to American Tolkien Society. Estab. 1967. Responds in 2 weeks. Guidelines for SASE or by e-mail.

NONFICTION Needs scholary essays, material rooted in and consistent with published works of J.R.R. Tolkien. Submit complet ms by mail or e-mail. **Pays 1 contributor's copy.**

FICTION Needs fan fiction. Submit complete ms by mail or e-mail. **Pays 1 contributor's copy.**

POETRY Uses poetry of fantasy about Middle-earth and Tolkien. Considers poetry by children and teens. Has published poetry by Thomas M. Egan, Anne Etkin, Nancy Pope, and Martha Benedict. Submit by mail or e-mail. Reviews related books of poetry; length depends on the volume ("a sentence to several pages"). Send materials for review consideration. **Pays 1 contributor's copy.**

MORPHEUS TALES

E-mail: morpheustales@blueyonder.co.uk. **Website:** www.morpheustales.com. **Contact:** Adam Bradley, publisher. **100% freelance written.** Quarterly magazine covering horror, science fiction, and fantasy. "We publish the best in horror, science fiction, and fantasy—both fiction and nonfiction." Estab. 2008. Circ. 1,000. No kill fee. Publishes ms an average of 18 months after acceptance. Editorial lead time 3 months. Submit seasonal material 6 months in advance. Accepts queries by e-mail. Responds in 1 week to queries; in 1 month to mss. Sample copy: $7. Guidelines available online.

NONFICTION Needs book excerpts, essays, general interest, how-to, inspirational, interview, new product, opinion, photo feature, letters to the editor. "All material must be based on horror, science fiction, or fantasy genre." **Buys 6 mss/year.** Query. Length: 1,000-3,000 words. Sometimes pays expenses of writers on assignment.

PHOTOS Model and property release are required.

FICTION Needs experimental, fantasy, horror, mystery, novel concepts, science fiction, serialized, suspense. **Buys 20 mss/year.** Send complete ms. Length: 800-3,000 words.

ON SPEC

P.O. Box 4727, Station South, Edmonton AB T6E 5G6 Canada. (780)628-7121. **E-mail:** onspec@onspec.ca. **Website:** www.onspec.ca. **95% freelance written.** Quarterly magazine covering Canadian science fiction, fantasy, and horror. "We publish speculative fiction and poetry by new and established writers, with a strong preference for Canadian-authored works." Estab. 1989. Circ. 2,000. Byline given. Pays on acceptance. No kill fee. Publishes ms an average of 6-18 months after acceptance. Editorial lead time 6 months. Accepts queries by mail. Accepts simultaneous submissions. Responds in 2 weeks to queries; in 6 months after deadline to mss. Sample copy: $8. Guidelines on website.

See website guidelines for submission announcements. "Please refer to website for information regarding submissions, as we are not open year round."

FICTION Needs fantasy, horror, science fiction, magic realism, ghost stories, fairy stories. No media tie-in or shaggy-alien stories. No condensed or excerpted novels, religious/inspirational stories, fairy tales. **Buys 50 mss/year.** Send complete ms. Electronic submissions preferred. Length: 1,000-6,000 words.

POETRY Needs avant-garde, free verse. No rhyming or religious material. Buys 6 poems/year. Submit maximum 10 poems. Length: 4-100 lines. **Pays $50 and 1 contributor's copy.**

TIPS "We want to see stories with plausible characters, a well-constructed, consistent, and vividly described setting, a strong plot, and believable emotions; characters must show us (not tell us) their emotional responses to each other and to the situation and/or challenge they face. Also: Don't send us stories written for television. We don't like media tie-ins, so don't watch TV for inspiration! Read instead! Strong preference given to submissions by Canadians."

PENNY DREADFUL: TALES & POEMS OF FANTASTIC TERROR

P.O. Box 719, Radio City Station, Hell's Kitchen NY 10101-0719. **E-mail:** mmpendragon@aol.com. **Website:** www.mpendragon.com. *Penny Dreadful: Tales & Poems of Fanastic Terror*, published irregularly (about once a year), features goth-romantic poetry and prose. Publishes poetry, short stories, essays, letters, listings, reviews, and b&w artwork "which celebrate the darker aspects of Man, the World, and their Creator." Wants "literary horror in the tradition of Poe, M.R. James, Shelley, M.P. Shiel, and LeFanu—dark, disquieting tales and verses designed to challenge the reader's perception of human nature, morality, and man's place within the Darkness. Stories and poems should be set prior to 1910 and/or possess a timeless quality." Does not want "references to 20th- and 21st-century personages/events, graphic sex, strong language, excessive gore and shock elements." Estab. 1996. Accepts queries by mail, e-mail. Accepts simultaneous submissions. Sample: $10. Subscription: $25/3 issues. Make checks payable to Michael Pendragon. Guidelines online.

"Works appearing in *Penny Dreadful* have been reprinted in *The Year's Best Fantasy and Horror*." *Penny Dreadful* nominates best tales and poems for Pushcart Prizes. *Penny Dreadful* is over 100 pages, digest-sized, desktop-published, perfect-bound. Press run is 200.

NONFICTION Submit complete ms. "Mss should be submitted in the standard, professional format: typed, double-spaced, name and address on the first page, name and title of work on all subsequent pages, etc. Include SASE for reply. Also include brief cover letter with a brief bio and publication history." Length: up to 5,000 words. **Pays 1 contributor's copy.**

FICTION Submit complete ms by mail or e-mail. "Mss should be submitted in the standard, professional format: typed, double-spaced, name and address on the first page, name and title of work on all subsequent pages, etc. Include SASE for reply. Also include brief cover letter with a brief bio and publication history." Length: up to 5,000 words. **Pays 1 contributor's copy.**

POETRY Submit by mail or e-mail. Rhymed, metered verse preferred. Has published poetry by Nancy Bennett, Michael R. Burch, Lee Clark, Louise Webster, K.S. Hardy, and Kevin N. Roberts. Length: up to 5 pages. **Pays 1 contributor's copy.**

SCARY MONSTERS MAGAZINE

Dennis Druktenis Publishing and Mail Order, Inc., 348 Jocelyn Place, Highwood IL 60040. **E-mail:** scaremail@aol.com. **Website:** www.scarymonstersmagazine.com. Horror magazine specializing in scary monsters.

NONFICTION Query first.

SCIFAIKUEST

P.O. Box 782, Cedar Rapids IA 52406. **E-mail:** gatrix65@yahoo.com. **Website:** albanlake.com/scifaikuest. **Contact:** Tyree Campbell, managing editor; Teri Santitoro, editor. *Scifaikuest*, published quarterly both online and in print, features "science fiction/fantasy/horror minimalist poetry, especially scifaiku, and related forms. We also publish articles about various poetic forms and reviews of poetry collections. The online and print versions of *Scifaikuest* are different." Estab. 2003. Time between acceptance and publication is 1-2 months. Submit seasonal poems 6 months in advance. Responds in 6-8 weeks. Single copy: $7; subscription: $20/year, $37 for 2 years. Make checks payable to Tyree Campbell/Alban Lake Publishing. Guidelines available on website.

Scifaikuest (print edition) is 32 pages, digest-sized, offset-printed, perfect-bound, with color cardstock cover, includes ads. Receives about 500 poems/year, accepts about 160 (32%). Press run is 100/issue; 5 distributed free to reviewers. Member: The Speculative Literature Foundation. *Scifaikuest* was voted #1 poetry magazine in the 2004 Preditors & Editors poll.

POETRY Wants "artwork, scifaiku, and speculative minimalist forms such as tanka, haibun, ghazals, senryu. Submit 5 poems at a time. Accepts e-mail submissions (pasted into body of message). No disk submissions; artwork as e-mail attachment or inserted body of e-mail. "Submission should include snail-mail address and a short (1-2 lines) bio." Reads submissions year round. "Editor Teri Santitoro makes all decisions regarding acceptances." Often comments on rejected poems. Has published poetry by Tom Brinck, Oino Sakai, Deborah P. Kolodji, Aurelio Rico Lopez III, Joanne Morcom, and John Dunphy. "No 'traditional' poetry." Length: varies, depending on poem type. **Pays $1/poem, $4/review or article, and 1 contributor's copy.**

SPACE AND TIME

458 Elizabeth Ave., Somerset NJ 08873. **Website:** www.spaceandtimemagazine.com. **Contact:** Hildy Silverman, editor-in-chief. "We love stories that blend elements—horror and science fiction, fantasy with SF elements, etc. We challenge writers to try something new and send us their unclassifiable works-—what other publications reject because the work doesn't fit in their 'pigeonholes.'" Estab. 1966. Circ. 2,000. Pays on publication. Publishes ms 3-6 months after acceptance. Accepts queries by e-mail. Sample copy available for $6. Guidelines available only on website.

FICTION "We are looking for creative blends of science fiction, fantasy, and/or horror." Needs fantasy, horror, science fiction, short stories, romance, futuristic, supernatural. "Do not send children's stories." Submit electronically as a Word doc or .rtf attachment. Length: 1,000-10,000/words. Average length: 6,500 words. Average length of short shorts: 1,000. **Pays 1¢/word.**

POETRY Needs speculative nature—science fiction, fantasy, horror. "Multiple submissions are okay within reason (don't send an envelope stuffed with 10 poems). Submit embedded in an e-mail or as a Word doc or .rtf attacment." **Pays $5/poem.**

SEX

EXOTIC MAGAZINE

X Publishing Inc., 818 SW 3rd Ave., Suite 1324, Portland OR 97204. (503)241-4317. **Fax:** (503)914-0439. **E-mail:** editorial@xmag.com; info@xmag.com. **Website:** www.xmag.com. **Contact:** John R. Voge, editor. Monthly magazine covering adult entertainment and sexuality. "*Exotic* is pro-sex, informative, amusing, mature, and intelligent. Our readers rent and/or buy adult videos, visit strip clubs, and are interested in topics related to the adult entertainment industry and sexuality/culture. Don't talk down to them or fire too far over their heads. Many readers are computer literate and well-traveled. We're also interested in insightful fetish material. We are not a 'hard core' publication." Estab. 1993. Circ. 75,000. Byline given. Pays 30 days after publication. No kill fee. Accepts queries by fax. Accepts simultaneous submissions. Responds in 2 weeks to queries. Responds in 2 months to mss. Sample copy for SAE with 9x12 envelope and 5 first-class stamps. Guidelines for #10 SASE.

NONFICTION Needs expose, general interest, historical, how-to, humor, interview, travel, news. No men writing as women, articles about being a "horny guy," or opinion pieces pretending to be fact pieces. **Buys 36 mss/year.** Send complete ms. Length: 1,000-1,800 words. **Pays 10¢/word, up to $150.**

REPRINTS Send typed ms with rights for sale noted and information about when and where the material previously appeared. Pays 100% of amount paid for an original article.

PHOTOS Rarely buys photos. Most provided by staff. Model releases required. Reviews prints. Negotiates payment individually.

FICTION "We are currently overwhelmed with fiction submissions. Please only send fiction if it's really amazing." Needs erotica, slice-of-life vignettes, must present either erotic element or some vice of modern culture, such as gambling, music, dancing. Send complete ms. Length: 1,000-1,800 words. **Pays 10¢/word, up to $150.**

TIPS "Read adult publications, spend time in the clubs doing more than just tipping and drinking. Look for new insights in adult topics. For the industry to continue to improve, those who cover it must also be educated consumers and affiliates. Please type, spell-check and be realistic about how much time the editor can take 'fixing' your ms."

M.I.P. COMPANY

P.O. Box 27484, Minneapolis MN 55427. (763)544-5915. **Website:** www.mipco.com. **Contact:** Michael Peltsman, editor. Specializes in Russian erotic poetry. The publisher of controversial Russian literature (erotic poetry). Estab. 1984. Accepts simultaneous submissions. Responds to queries in 1 month. Seldom comments on rejected poems.

POETRY Considers simultaneous submissions; no previously published poems.

PLAYBOY MAGAZINE

9346 Civic Center Dr., #200, Beverly Hills CA 90210. (310)264-6600. **Fax:** (310)786-7440. **Website:** www.playboy.com. Monthly magazine. The preeminent entertainment magazine for the sophisticated urban male. This legendary brand continues to produce top-tier literature and journalism while maintaining its legacy as the industry's most artful and provocative image maker. Estab. 1953.

Query before submitting.

VANILLEROTICA LITERARY EZINE

Cleveland OH 44102. (216)799-9775. **E-mail:** talentdripseroticpublishing@yahoo.com. **Website:** eroticatalentdrips.wordpress.com. **Contact:** Kimberly Steele, founder. *Vanillerotica*, published monthly online, focuses solely on showcasing new erotic fiction. Estab. 2007. Time between acceptance and publication is 2 months. Accepts queries by e-mail. Accepts previously published material and poetryAccepts simultaneous submissions. Responds to general and submission queries within a week. Guidelines on website.

FICTION Needs erotic short stories. Submit short stories by e-mail to talentdripseroticpublishing@yahoo.com. Stories should be pasted into body of message. Reads submissions during publication months only. Length: 5,000-10,000 words. **Pays $15 for each accepted short story.**

POETRY Needs erotic. Submit by e-mail to talentdripseroticpublishing@yahoo.com. Accepts e-mail pasted into body of message. Reads submissions during publication months only. Submit maximum 2-3 poems. Length: up to 30 lines/poem. **Pays $10 for each accepted poem.**

TIPS "Please read our take on the difference between *erotica* and *pornography*; it's on the website. *Vanillerotica* does not accept pornography. And please keep poetry 30 lines or less."

SPORTS

ARCHERY AND BOWHUNTING

$$ BOW & ARROW HUNTING

Beckett Media LLC, 22840 Savi Ranch Pkwy., Suite 200, Yorba Linda CA 92887. (714)200-1900. **Fax:** (800)249-7761. **E-mail:** JBell@Beckett.com; editorial@bowandarrowhunting.com. **Website:** www.bowandarrowhunting.com. **Contact:** Joe Bell, editor. **70% freelance written.** Magazine published 9 times/year covering bowhunting. Dedicated to serve the serious bowhunting enthusiast. Writers must be willing to share their secrets so readers can become better bowhunters. Estab. 1962. Circ. 90,000. Byline given. Pays on publication. No kill fee. Publishes ms an average of 2 months after acceptance. Submit seasonal material 6 months in advance. Accepts queries by mail, e-mail. Accepts simultaneous submissions. Responds in 1 month to queries; 6 weeks to mss. Sample copy and writer's guidelines free.

NONFICTION Needs how-to, humor, interview, opinion, personal experience, technical. **Buys 60 mss/year.** Send complete ms. Length: 1,700-3,000 words. **Pays $200-450.**

PHOTOS Send photos. Captions required. Reviews contact sheets, digital images only; no slides or prints accepted. Offers no additional payment for photos accepted with ms.

FILLERS Needs facts, newsbreaks. **Buys 12 mss/year.** Length: 500 words. **Pays $20-100.**

TIPS "Inform readers how they can become better at the sport, but don't forget to keep it fun! Sidebars are recommended with every submission."

$$ BOWHUNTER

InterMedia Outdoors, 6385 Flank Dr., Suite 800, Harrisburg PA 17112. (717)695-8085. **Fax:** (717)545-2527. **E-mail:** curt.wells@imoutdoors.com. **Website:** www.bowhunter.com. Mark Olszewski, art director; Jeff Waring, publisher. **Contact:** Curt Wells, editor. **50% freelance written.** Bimonthly magazine covering hunting big and small game with bow and arrow. "We are a special-interest publication, produced by bowhunters for bowhunters, covering all aspects of the sport. Material included in each issue is designed to entertain and inform readers, making them better bowhunters." Estab. 1971. Circ. 126,480. Byline given. Pays on acceptance. No kill fee. Submit seasonal material 8 months in advance. Accepts queries by mail, e-mail, fax. Responds in 1 month to queries. Responds in 2 months to mss. Sample copy for $2 and 8 1/2x11 SASE with appropriate postage. Guidelines for #10 SASE or on website.

NONFICTION Needs general interest, how-to, interview, opinion, personal experience, photo feature. **Buys 60-plus mss/year.** Query. Length: 250-2,000 words. **Pays $500 maximum for assigned articles. Pays $100-400 for unsolicited articles.** Sometimes pays expenses of writers on assignment.

PHOTOS Send photos. Captions required. Reviews high-res digital images. Reviews photos with or without a manuscript. Offers $50-300/photo. Pays $50-125 for b&w inside; $75-300 for color inside; $600 for cover, "occasionally more if photo warrants it." **Pays on acceptance**. Credit line given. Buys one-time publication rights.

TIPS "A writer must know bowhunting and be willing to share that knowledge. Writers should anticipate *all* questions a reader might ask, then answer them in the article itself or in an appropriate sidebar. Articles should be written with the reader foremost in mind; we won't be impressed by writers seeking to prove how good they are—either as writers or bowhunters. We care about the reader and don't need writers with 'I' trouble. Features are a good bet because most of our material comes from freelancers. The best advice is: Be yourself. Tell your story the same as if sharing the experience around a campfire. Don't try to write like you think a writer writes."

BASEBALL

$ JUNIOR BASEBALL

JSAN Publishing LLC, Wilton CT 06897. (203)210-5726. **E-mail:** publisher@juniorbaseball.com. **Website:** www.juniorbaseball.com. **Contact:** Jim Beecher, publisher. **25% freelance written.** Bimonthly magazine focused on youth baseball players ages 7-17 (including high school) and their parents/coaches. Edited to various reading levels, depending upon age/skill level of feature. Estab. 1996. Circ. 20,000. Byline given. Pays on publication. No kill fee. Publishes ms an average of 4 months after acceptance. Editorial lead time 3 months. Submit seasonal material 4 months in advance. Accepts simultaneous submissions. Responds in 2 weeks to queries; 1 month to mss. Sample copy: $5 or free online.

NONFICTION Needs skills, tips, features, how to play better baseball, etc., interview with major league players (only on assignment), personal experience from coaches' or parents' perspective. No trite first-person articles about your kid. No fiction or poetry. **Buys 8-12 mss/year.** Query. Length: 500-1,000 words. **Pays $50-100.**

PHOTOS Photos can be e-mailed in 300 dpi JPEGs. State availability. Captions, identification of subjects required. Reviews 35mm transparencies, 3x5 prints. Offers $10-100/photo; negotiates payment individually.

COLUMNS/DEPARTMENTS Freelance columns: When I Was a Kid (a current Major League Baseball player profile); Parents Feature (topics of interest to parents of youth ball players); all 1,000-1,500 words. In the Spotlight (news, events, new products), 50-100 words; Hot Prospect (written for the 14 and older competitive player. High school baseball is included, and the focus is on improving the finer points of the game to make the high school team, earn a college scholarship, or attract scouts, written to an adult level), 500-1,000 words. **Buys 8-12 mss/year. Pays $50-100.**

TIPS "Must be well-versed in baseball! Have a child who is very involved in the sport, or have extensive hands-on experience in coaching baseball, at the youth, high school, or higher level. We can always use accurate, authoritative skills information, and good photos to accompany is a big advantage! This magazine is read by experts. No fiction, poems, games, puzzles, etc." Does not want first-person articles about your child.

BICYCLING

$$$ ADVENTURE CYCLIST

Adventure Cycling Association, Box 8308, Missoula MT 59807. (406)721-1776, ext. 222. **Fax:** (406)721-8754. **E-mail:** magazine@adventurecycling.org. **Website:** www.adventurecycling.org/adventure-cyclist. **Contact:** Greg Siple, art director; Michael Deme, editor. **75% freelance written.** Published 9 times/year for Adventure Cycling Association members, emphasizing bicycle tourism and travel. Estab. 1975. Circ. 45,500. Byline given. Pays on publication. Kill fee 25%. Submit seasonal material 12 months in advance. Sample copy and guidelines for 9x12 SAE with 4 first-class stamps. Info available at www.adventurecycling.org/adventure-cyclist/adventure-cyclist-submissions.

NONFICTION Needs first-person bike-travel accounts (U.S. and worldwide), essays, how-to, profiles, photo feature, technical, U.S. or foreign tour accounts. **Buys 20-25 mss/year.** Send complete ms. Length: 1,400-3,500 words. **Inquiries requested prior to complete manuscripts. Pays sliding scale per word.**

PHOTOS State availability.

AUSTRALIAN MOUNTAIN BIKE

Next Media, Level 6, Building A, 207 Pacific Hwy., St. Leonards NSW 2065 Australia. **E-mail:** amb@nextmedia.com.au; mblewitt@nextmedia.com.au. **Website:** ambmag.com.au. **Contact:** Mike Blewitt, editor. Covers off-road cycling for all levels of riders. "*Australian Mountain Bike* (*AMB*) is the no. 1 mountain biking magazine in Australia. *AMB* delivers to a passionate community of mountain biker's expert views, reviews, bike and equipment tests, tracks and trail guides, interviews, and event coverage. *AMB* is a trusted authority for advice for the reader whether novice or pro, weekend warriors, cross country racers, downhill demons or dirt jumpers." Circ. 20,000.

NONFICTION Needs general interest, how-to, new product, personal experience. Query.

$$ BIKE MAGAZINE

Source Interlink Media, P.O. Box 1028, Dana Point CA 92629. (949)325-6200. **Fax:** (949)325-6196. **E-mail:** bikemag@sorc.com. **Website:** www.bikemag.com. **Contact:** Brice Minnigh, editor. **35% freelance written.** Magazine publishes 8 times/year covering mountain biking. Estab. 1993. Circ. 170,000. Byline given. Pays on publication. Offers 25% kill fee. Publishes ms an average of 2 months after acceptance. Editorial lead time 4 months. Submit seasonal material 6 months in advance. Accepts queries by mail, e-mail. Responds in 2 months to queries. Sample copy: $5.99.

"*Bike Magazine* showcases the sport of mountain biking like no other publication. It captures the sport's personalities, trends, and issues with a style all its own. Using insightful feature articles and the sport's best photography, *Bike* is sure to make you want to get outside and ride."

NONFICTION Needs humor, interview, personal experience, photo feature, travel. **Buys 20 mss/year.** Query. Length: 1,000-2,500 words. **Pays 50¢/word.** Sometimes pays expenses: $500 maximum.

PHOTOS **Contact:** David Reddick, photo editor. Send photos. Captions, identification of subjects required. Reviews color transparencies, b&w prints. Negotiates payment individually.

COLUMNS/DEPARTMENTS Splatter (news), 300 words; Urb (details a great ride within 1 hour of a major metropolitan area), 600-700 words. **Buys 20 mss/year.** Query. **Pays 50¢/word.**

TIPS "Remember that we focus on hardcore mountain biking, not beginners. We're looking for ideas that deliver the excitement and passion of the sport in ways that aren't common or predictable. Ideas should be vivid, unbiased, irreverent, probing, fun, humorous, funky, quirky, smart, good. Great feature ideas are always welcome, especially features on cultural matters or issues in the sport. However, you're much more likely to get published in *Bike* if you send us great ideas for short articles. In particular we need stories for our Splatter, a front-of-the-book section devoted to news, funny anecdotes, quotes, and odds and ends. We also need personality profiles of 600 words or so for our People Who Ride section. Racers are OK, but we're more interested in grassroots people with interesting personalities—it doesn't matter if they're Mother Theresas or scumbags, so long as they make mountain biking a little more interesting. Short descriptions of great rides are very welcome for our Urb column."

$$ CYCLE CALIFORNIA! MAGAZINE

1702-L Meridian Ave. #289, San Jose CA 95125. (408)924-0270. **Fax:** (408)292-3005. **E-mail:** tcorral@cyclecalifornia.com; BMack@cyclecalifornia.com. **Website:** www.cyclecalifornia.com. **Contact:** Tracy L. Corral; Bob Mack, publisher. **75% freelance written.** Magazine published 11 times/year covering Northern California bicycling events, races, people. Issues (topics) covered include bicycle commuting, bicycle politics, touring, racing, nostalgia, history—anything at all to do with riding a bike. Estab. 1995. Circ. 32,000 print; 88,000 digital. Byline given. Pays on publication. No kill fee. Publishes ms an average of 3 months after acceptance. Editorial lead time 6 weeks. Submit seasonal material 8 weeks in advance. Accepts queries by e-mail. Accepts simultaneous submissions. Responds in 1 month to queries. Sample copy with 9x12 SASE and $1.39 first-class postage. Guidelines with #10 SASE.

NONFICTION Needs historical, how-to, interview, opinion, personal experience, technical, travel. Special issues: Bicycle Tour & Travel (January/February). No articles about any sport that doesn't relate to bicycling. No product reviews. **Buys 36 mss/year.** Query. Length: 500-1,500 words. **Pays 10-15¢/word.**

PHOTOS Send photos. Identification of subjectspreferred. Negotiates payment individually.

COLUMNS/DEPARTMENTS **Buys 2-3 mss/year.** Query with published clips. **Pays 10-15¢/word.**

TIPS "E-mail us with good ideas. While we don't exclude writers from other parts of the country, articles really should reflect a Northern California slant, or be of general interest to bicyclists. We prefer stories written by people who like and use their bikes."

BOATING

$$$ CANOE & KAYAK

GrindMedia, LLC, 236 Avenida Fabricante, Suite 201, San Clemente CA 92672. (425)827-6363. **E-mail:**

aaron@canoekayak.com. **Website:** www.canoekayak.com. **Contact:** Aaron Schmidt. **75% freelance written.** Bimonthly magazine covering paddlesports. "*Canoe & Kayak* is North America's No. 1 paddlesports resource. Our readers include flatwater and whitewater canoeists and kayakers of all skill levels. We provide comprehensive information on destinations, technique and equipment. Beyond that, we cover canoe and kayak camping, safety, the environment, and the history of boats and sport." Estab. 1972. Circ. 70,000. Byline given. Pays on publication. No kill fee. Publishes ms an average of 6 months after acceptance. Editorial lead time 6 months. Submit seasonal material 8 months in advance. Accepts queries by mail, e-mail. Responds in 2 months to queries. Sample copy and writer's guidelines for 9x12 SAE with 7 first-class stamps.

NONFICTION Needs historical, how-to, canoe, kayak camp, load boats, paddle whitewater, etc., personal experience, photo feature, technical, travel. Special issues: Whitewater Paddling; Beginner's Guide; Kayak Touring; Canoe Journal. No cartoons, poems, stories in which bad judgement is portrayed or 'Me and Molly' articles. **Buys 25 mss/year.** Send complete ms. Length: 400-2,500 words. **Pays $100-800 for assigned articles. Pays $100-500 for unsolicited articles.**

PHOTOS "Some activities we cover are canoeing, kayaking, canoe fishing, camping, canoe sailing or poling, backpacking (when compatible with the main activity) and occasionally inflatable boats. We are not interested in groups of people in rafts, photos showing disregard for the environment or personal safety, gasoline-powered engines unless appropriate to the discussion, or unskilled persons taking extraordinary risks." State availability. Captions, identification of subjects, model releases required. Reviews 35mm transparencies, 4x6 prints. Offers $75-500/photo.

COLUMNS/DEPARTMENTS Put In (environment, conservation, events), 500 words; Destinations (canoe and kayak destinations in US, Canada), 1,500 words; Essays, 750 words. **Buys 40 mss/year.** Send complete ms. **Pays $100-350.**

FILLERS Needs anecdotes, facts, newsbreaks. **Buys 20 mss/year.** Length: 200-500 words. **Pays $25-50.**

TIPS "Start with Put-In articles (short featurettes) or short, unique equipment reviews. Or give us the best, most exciting article we've ever seen—with great photos. Read the magazine before submitting."

COAST&KAYAK MAGAZINE

Wild Coast Publishing, P.O. Box 24 Stn. A, Nanaimo BC V9R 5K4 Canada. (360)406-4708; (866)984-6437. **Fax:** (866)654-1937. **E-mail:** editor@coastandkayak.com; kayak@coastandkayak.com. **Website:** www.coastandkayak.com. **Contact:** John Kimantas, editor. **75% freelance written.** Quarterly magazine with a major focus on paddling the Pacific coast. "We promote safe paddling, guide paddlers to useful products and services, and explore coastal environmental issues." Estab. 1991. Circ. 65,000 print and electronic readers. Byline given. Pays on publication. Publishes ms an average of 4 months after acceptance. Editorial lead time 4 months. Submit seasonal material 4 months in advance. Accepts queries by mail, e-mail. Sample copy and guidelines available online.

NONFICTION Needs how-to, paddle, travel, humor, new product, personal experience, technical, travel, trips. **Buys 25 mss/year.** Query. Length: 1,000-1,500 words. **Pays $50-75.**

PHOTOS State availability. Captions, identification of subjects required. Reviews low-res JPEGs. Offers $25-50/photo.

TIPS "You must know paddling—though novice paddlers are welcome. A strong environmental or wilderness appreciation component is advisable. We are willing to help refine work with flexible people. E-mail queries preferred. Check out our editorial calendar for our upcoming features."

CRUISING WORLD

The Sailing Co., 55 Hammarlund Way, Middletown RI 02842. (401)845-5100. **Fax:** (401)845-5180. **E-mail:** cw.manuscripts@gmail.com; elaine.lembo@cruisingworld.com. **Website:** www.cruisingworld.com. **Contact:** Elaine Lembo, deputy editor. **60% freelance written.** Monthly magazine covering sailing, cruising/adventuring, do-it-yourself boat improvements. "*Cruising World* is a publication by and for sailboat owners who spend time in home waters as well as voyaging the world. Its readership is extremely loyal, savvy, and driven by independent thinking." Estab. 1974. Circ. 91,244. Byline given. **Pays on acceptance for articles;** on publication for photography. No kill fee. Publishes ms an average of 18 months after acceptance. Editorial lead time 3 months. Submit seasonal material 1 year in advance. Accepts queries by mail. Responds in 2 months to queries. Responds in

4 months to mss. Sample copy free. Guidelines available online.

NONFICTION Needs book excerpts, essays, expose, general interest, historical, how-to, humor, interview, new product, opinion, personal experience, photo feature, technical, travel. No travel articles that have nothing to do with cruising aboard sailboats from 20-50 feet in length. **Buys dozens mss/year.** Send complete ms. **Pays $50-1,500 for assigned articles. Pays $50-1,000 for unsolicited articles.** Sometimes pays expenses of writers on assignment.

PHOTOS Send high-res (minimum 300 DPI) images on CD. Send photos. Captions required. Payment upon publication. Also buys stand-alone photos.

COLUMNS/DEPARTMENTS Underway Shoreline (sailing news, people, and short features; contact Elaine Lembo), 300 words maximum; Hands-on Sailor (refit, voyaging, seamanship, how-to), 1,000-1,500 words. **Buys dozens mss/year.** Query with or without published clips or send complete ms.

TIPS "*Cruising World's* readers know exactly what they want to read, so our best advice to freelancers is to carefully read the magazine and envision which exact section or department would be the appropriate place for proposed submissions."

GOOD OLD BOAT

Partnership for Excellence, Inc., 7340 Niagara Lane N., Maple Grove MN 55311-2655. (701)952-9433. **Fax:** (701)952-9434. **E-mail:** karen@goodoldboat.com. **Website:** www.goodoldboat.com. **Contact:** Karen Larson, editor. **90% freelance written.** Bimonthly magazine covering sailing. *Good Old Boat* magazine focuses on maintaining, upgrading, and loving fiberglass cruising sailboats from the 1960s and well into the 2000s. Readers see themselves as part of a community of sailors who share similar maintenance and replacement concerns not generally addressed in the other sailing publications. Readers do much of the writing about projects they have done on their boats and the joy they receive from sailing them. Estab. 1998. Circ. 30,000. Pays 2 months in advance of publication. No kill fee. Publishes ms an average of 12-18 months after acceptance. Editorial lead time 4 months. Submit seasonal material 12-15 months in advance. Accepts queries by mail, e-mail. Accepts simultaneous submissions. Responds in 1-2 weeks to queries. Responds in 2-6 months to mss. Downloadable sample copy free. Guidelines available online.

NONFICTION Needs general interest, historical, how-to, interview, personal experience, photo feature, technical. "Articles written by non-sailors serve no purpose for us." **Buys 150 mss/year.** Query or send complete ms. Length: Up to 5,000 words. **Payment varies.**

PHOTOS State availability of or send photos. "We do not pay additional fees for photos except when they run as covers, or are specifically requested to support an article."

TIPS "Our shorter pieces are the best way to break into our magazine. We publish many Simple Solutions and Quick & Easy pieces. These are how-to tips that have worked for sailors on their boats. In addition, our readers send lists of projects which they've done on their boats and which they could write for publication. We respond to these queries with a thumbs up or down by project. Articles are submitted on speculation, but they have a better chance of being accepted once we have approved of the suggested topic."

$$ HEARTLAND BOATING

The Waterways Journal, Inc., 319 N. Fourth St., Suite 650, St. Louis MO 63102. (314)241-4310. **Fax:** (314)241-4207. **E-mail:** brad@heartlandboating.com. **Website:** www.heartlandboating.com. **Contact:** Brad Kovach, editor. **75% freelance written.** Magazine published 5 times/year covering recreational boating on the inland waterways of mid-America, from the Great Lakes south to the Gulf of Mexico. "Our writers must have experience with, and a great interest in, boating in mid-America. *Heartland Boating*'s content is both informative and inspirational—describing boating life as the heartland boater knows it. The content reflects the challenge, joy, and excitement of our way of life. We are devoted to both power and sailboating enthusiasts throughout America's inland waterways. Estab. 1989. Circ. 10,000. Byline given. Pays on publication. No kill fee. Editorial lead time 3 months. Accepts queries by mail. Responds only if interested. Sample copy upon request. Guidelines for #10 SASE.

NONFICTION Needs how-to, articles about navigation, maintenance, upkeep, or making time spent aboard easier and more comfortable, humor, personal experience, technical, Great Loop legs, trips along waterways and on-land stops. Special issues: Annual houseboat issue in March looks at what is coming out on the houseboat market for the coming year. **Buys**

100 mss/year. Send complete ms. Length: 850-1,500 words. **Pays $150-250.**

REPRINTS Send tearsheet, photocopy or typed ms and information about when and where the material previously appeared.

PHOTOS Magazine published 5 times/year covering recreational boating on the inland waterways of mid-America, from the Great Lakes south to the Gulf of Mexico and over to the east. Send photos. Model release is required, property release is preferred, photo captions are required. Include names and locations. Reviews prints, digital images. Offers no additional payment for photos accepted with ms.

COLUMNS/DEPARTMENTS Books Aboard (assigned book reviews), 400 words. Buys 8-10 mss/year. Pays $40. Handy Hints (boat improvement or safety projects), 1,000 words. Buys 8 mss/year. Pays $180. Heartland Haunts (waterside restaurants, bars or B&Bs), 1,000 words. Buys 16 mss/year. Pays $160. Query with published clips or send complete ms.

TIPS "We begin planning the next year's schedule starting in August. So submitting material between August 1 and October 15 is the best way to proceed."

HOUSEBOAT MAGAZINE

Harris Publishing, Inc., 360 B St., Idaho Falls ID 83402. (208)524-7000. **Fax:** (208)522-5241. **E-mail:** blk@houseboatmagazine.com. **Website:** www.houseboatmagazine.com. **Contact:** Brady L. Kay, executive editor. **35% freelance written.** Quarterly magazine for houseboaters who enjoy reading everything that reflects the unique houseboating lifestyle. If it is not a houseboat-specific article, please do not query. Estab. 1990. Circ. 25,000. Byline given. Pays on acceptance. Offers 25% kill fee. Publishes ms an average of 3 months after acceptance. Editorial lead time 6 months. Submit seasonal material 6 months in advance. Accepts simultaneous submissions. Responds in 1 month to queries. Sample copy for $5. Guidelines by e-mail.

No unsolicited mss. Accepts queries by mail and fax, but e-mail strongly preferred.

NONFICTION Needs how-to, interview, new product, personal experience, travel. **Buys 36 mss/year.** Query before submitting. Length: 1,500-2,200 words. **Pays $200-500.**

PHOTOS Often required as part of submission package. Color prints discouraged. Digital prints are unacceptable. Seldom purchases photos without ms, but occasionally buys cover photos. Captions, model releases required. Reviews transparencies, high-resolution electronic images. Offers no additional payment for photos accepted with ms.

COLUMNS/DEPARTMENTS Pays $150-300.

TIPS "As a general rule, how-to articles are always in demand. So are stories on unique houseboats or houseboaters. You are less likely to break in with a travel piece that does not revolve around specific people or groups. Personality profile pieces with excellent supporting photography are your best bet."

NORTHERN BREEZES, SAILING MAGAZINE

Northern Breezes, Inc., 3949 Winnetka Ave. N, Minneapolis MN 55427. (763)542-9707. **Fax:** (763)542-8998. **E-mail:** info@sailingbreezes.com. **Website:** www.sailingbreezes.com. **70% freelance written.** Magazine published 8 times/year for the Great Lakes and Midwest sailing community. Focusing on regional cruising, racing, and day sailing. Digital publication only. Estab. 1989. Circ. 22,300. Byline given. Does not offer payment. No kill fee. Editorial lead time 1 months. Submit seasonal material 3 months in advance. Accepts queries by mail, e-mail, fax. Responds in 1 month to queries. Responds in 2 months to mss. Sample copy free.

NONFICTION Needs book excerpts, how-to, sailing topics, humor, inspirational, interview, new product, personal experience, photo feature, technical, travel. No boating reviews. **Buys 24 mss/year.** Query with published clips. Length: 300-3,500 words.

PHOTOS Send photos. Captions required. Reviews negatives, 35mm slides, 3x5 or 4x6 prints. "Digital submission preferred." Offers no payment for photos accepted with ms.

COLUMNS/DEPARTMENTS This Old Boat (sailboat), 500-1,000 words; Surveyor's Notebook, 500-800 words. **Buys 8 mss/year.** Query with published clips.

TIPS "Query with a regional connection already in mind."

PACIFIC YACHTING

OP Publishing, Ltd., 1166 Alberni St., Suite 802, Vancouver British Columbia V6E 3Z3 Canada. (604)428-0259. **Fax:** (604)620-0425. **E-mail:** editor@pacificyachting.com; ayates@oppublishing.com. **Website:** www.pacificyachting.com. **Contact:** Dale Miller, editor; Arran Yates, art director. **90% freelance written.**

Monthly magazine covering all aspects of recreational boating in the Pacific Northwest. "The bulk of our writers and photographers not only come from the local boating community, many of them were long-time *PY* readers before coming aboard as a contributor. The *PY* reader buys the magazine to read about new destinations or changes to old haunts on the British Columbia coast and the Pacific Northwest and to learn the latest about boats and gear." Estab. 1968. Circ. 19,000. Byline given. Pays on publication. No kill fee. Publishes ms an average of 6 months after acceptance. Editorial lead time 4 months. Submit seasonal material 6 months in advance. Accepts queries by mail, e-mail, fax. Sample copy for $6.95, plus postage charged to credit card. Guidelines available online.

NONFICTION Needs historical, British Columbia coast only, how-to, humor, interview, personal experience, technical, boating related, travel, cruising, and destination on the British Columbia coast. "No articles from writers who are obviously not boaters!" Query. Length: 800-2,000 words. **Pays $150-500. Pays some expenses of writers on assignment for unsolicited articles.** Pays expenses of writers on assignment.

PHOTOS Send photos. Identification of subjects required. Reviews digital photos transparencies, 4 x 6 prints, and slides. Offers no additional payment for photos accepted with ms. Offers $25-400 for photos accepted alone.

COLUMNS/DEPARTMENTS Currents (current events, trade and people news, boat gatherings, and festivities), 50-250 words. Reflections; Cruising, both 800-1,000 words. Query. **Pay varies.**

TIPS "Our reader wants you to balance important navigation details with first-person observations, blending the practical with the romantic. Write tight, write short, write with the reader in mind, write to inform, write to entertain. Be specific, accurate, and historic."

$$ PONTOON & DECK BOAT

Harris Publishing, Inc., 360 B. St., Idaho Falls ID 83402. (208)524-7000. **Fax:** (208)522-5241. **E-mail:** blk@pdbmagazine.com. **Website:** www.pdbmagazine.com. **Contact:** Brady L. Kay, editor. **15% freelance written.** Magazine published 11 times/year covering boating. A boating niche publication geared toward the pontoon and deck boating lifestyle and consumer market. Audience is comprised of people who utilize these boats for varied family activities and fishing. Magazine is promotional of the PDB industry and its major players. Seeks to give the reader a twofold reason to read publication: to celebrate the lifestyle, and to do it aboard a first-class craft. Estab. 1995. Circ. 84,000. Byline given. Pays on publication. No kill fee. Editorial lead time 2 months. Submit seasonal material 3 months in advance. Accepts simultaneous submissions. Responds in 6 weeks to queries; in 3 months to mss. Sample copy and writer's guidelines free.

NONFICTION Needs how-to, personal experience, technical, remodeling, rebuilding. "We are saturated with travel pieces; no general boating, humor, fiction, or poetry." **Buys 15 mss/year.** Send complete ms. Length: 600-2,000 words. **Pays $50-300.** Sometimes pays expenses of writers on assignment.

PHOTOS State availability. Captions, model releases required. Reviews transparencies.

COLUMNS/DEPARTMENTS No Wake Zone (short, fun quips); Better Boater (how-to). **Buys 6-12 mss/year.** Query with published clips. **Pays $50-150.**

TIPS "Be specific to pontoon and deck boats. Any general boating material goes to the slush pile. The more you can tie together the lifestyle, attitudes, and the PDB industry, the more interest we'll take in what you send us."

$$$ SAILING MAGAZINE

125 E. Main St., P.O. Box 249, Port Washington WI 53074. (262)284-3494. **Fax:** (262)284-7764. **E-mail:** editorial@sailingmagazine.net. **Website:** www.sailingmagazine.net. **Contact:** Greta Schanen, managing editor. Monthly magazine for the experienced sailor. Covers all aspects of sailing, from learning how to sail in a dinghy to crossing the ocean on a large cruiser to racing around the buoys against the best sailors in the world. Typically focuses on sailing in places that are realistic destinations for readers, but will occasionally feature an outstanding and unique sailing destination. Estab. 1966. Circ. 45,000. Pays after publication. No kill fee. Accepts queries by mail, e-mail. Responds in 3 months to unsolicited submission.

NONFICTION Needs book excerpts, how-to, tech pieces on boats and gear, interview, personal experience, travel by sail. **Buys 15-20 mss/year.** Send complete ms in Word as an attachment, or send via mail. Length: 1,000-3,000 words. **Pays $50-500.**

PHOTOS Captions required. Reviews color transparencies. Pays $50-400.

COLUMNS/DEPARTMENTS Splashes, short news stories (100-500 words).

$$ SAILING WORLD

Bonnier Corporation, 55 Hammarlund Way, Middletown RI 02842. (401)845-5100. **Fax:** (401)845-5180. **E-mail:** editor@sailingworld.com. **E-mail:** dave.reed@sailingworld.com. **Website:** www.sailingworld.com. **Contact:** Dave Reed, editor. **40% freelance written.** Magazine published 8 times/year covering performance sailing. Estab. 1962. Circ. 65,000. Byline given. Pays on publication. No kill fee. Publishes ms an average of 4 months after acceptance. Accepts queries by e-mail. Responds in 1 month to queries. Sample copy: $7. Guidelines online.

NONFICTION Needs how-to for racing and performance-oriented sailors, interview, photo feature, regatta sports and charter. Special issues: "The emphasis here is on performance sailing: Keep in mind that the *Sailing World* readership is relatively educated about the sport. Unless you are dealing with a totally new aspect of sailing, you can and should discuss ideas on an advanced technical level; however, extensive formulae and graphs don't play well to our audience. When in doubt as to the suitability of an article or idea, submit a written query before time and energy are misdirected." No travelogs. **Buys 5-10 unsolicited mss/year.** Query unsolicited articles to dave.reed@sailingworld.com. No phone queries. Length: up to 2,000 words. **Pays $400 for up to 2,000 words.** Does not pay expenses of writers on assignment unless preapproved.

PHOTOS Reviews color slides, prints, digital.

TIPS "Prospective contributors should study recent issues of the magazine to determine appropriate subject matter."

SEA MAGAZINE

17782 Cowan, Suite C, Irvine CA 92614. (949)660-6150. **Fax:** (949)660-6172. **Website:** www.seamag.com. Monthly magazine covering West Coast power boating. Estab. 1908. Circ. 55,000. Byline given. Pays on publication. Publishes ms an average of 6 months after acceptance. Editorial lead time 3 months. Submit seasonal material 6 months in advance. Accepts simultaneous submissions. Responds in 3 months to queries.

NONFICTION Needs how-to, new product, personal experience, technical, travel. **Buys 36 mss/year.** Send complete ms. Length: 1,000-1,500 words. **Payment varies.** Pays expenses of writers on assignment.

PHOTOS State availability of photos. Captions, identification of subjects, model releases required. Reviews transparencies, high-res digital. Offers $50-250/photo.

$$ SOUTHERN BOATING

Southern Boating & Yachting, Inc., 330 N. Andrews Ave., Ft. Lauderdale FL 33301. (954)522-5515. **Fax:** (954)522-2260. **E-mail:** liz@southernboating.com; john@southernboating.com. **Website:** www.southernboating.com. **Contact:** Liz Pasch, editorial director; John Lambert, art director. **50% freelance written.** Monthly boating magazine. Upscale monthly yachting magazine focusing on the Southeast US, Bahamas, Caribbean, and Gulf of Mexico. Estab. 1972. Circ. 40,000. Byline given. Pays within 30 days of publication. Publishes ms an average of 3 months after acceptance. Editorial lead time 3 months. Submit seasonal material 3 months in advance. Accepts queries by e-mail.

NONFICTION Needs how-to, boat maintenance, travel, boating related, destination pieces. **Buys 50 mss/year.** Query. Length: 900-1,200 words. **Pays $500-600 with art.**

PHOTOS State availability of or send photos. Captions, identification of subjects, model releases required. Reviews digital files.

COLUMNS/DEPARTMENTS Weekend Workshop (how-to/maintenance), 900 words; What's New in Electronics (electronics), 900 words; Engine Room (new developments), 900 words. **Buys 24 mss/year.** Query first; see media kit for special issue focus.

$ WATERFRONT TIMES

Storyboard Media Inc., 2787 E. Oakland Park Blvd., Suite 205, Ft. Lauderdale FL 33306. (954)524-9450. **Fax:** (954)524-9464. **E-mail:** editor@waterfronttimes.com. **Website:** www.waterfronttimes.com. **Contact:** Jennifer Heit, editor. **20% freelance written.** Monthly tabloid covering marine and boating topics for the Greater Ft. Lauderdale waterfront community. Estab. 1984. Circ. 20,000. Byline given. Pays on publication. No kill fee. Publishes ms an average of 2 months after acceptance. Submit seasonal material 3 months in advance. Responds in 1 month to queries. Sample copy for SAE with 9x12 envelope and 4 first-class stamps.

NONFICTION Needs interview of people important in boating, i.e., racers, boat builders, designers, etc.

from south Florida; regional articles on south Florida's waterfront issues; marine communities; travel pieces of interest to boaters, including docking information. Length: 500-1,000 words. **Pays $100-125 for assigned articles.**

PHOTOS Send photos. Reviews JPEG/TIFF files.

TIPS "No fiction. Keep it under 1,000 words. Photos or illustrations help. Send for a sample copy of *Waterfront Times* so you can acquaint yourself with our publication and our unique audience. Although we're not necessarily looking for technical articles, it helps if the writer has sailing or powerboating experience. Writers should be familiar with the region and be specific when dealing with local topics."

WATERWAYS WORLD

Waterways World, Ltd, 151 Station St., Burton-on-Trent Staffordshire DE14 1BG United Kingdom. 01283 742950. **E-mail:** editorial@waterwaysworld.com. **Website:** www.waterwaysworld.com. **Contact:** Bobby Cowling, editor. Monthly magazine publishing news, photographs, and illustrated articles on all aspects of inland waterways in Britain, and on limited aspects of waterways abroad. Estab. 1972. Pays on publication. No kill fee. Editorial lead time 2 months. Accepts queries by mail, e-mail. NoGuidelines by e-mail.

NONFICTION Does not want poetry or fiction. Submit query letter or complete ms with SAE.

PHOTOS Captions required. Reviews transparencies, gloss prints, 300 dpi digital images, maps/diagrams.

GOLF

AFRICAN AMERICAN GOLFER'S DIGEST

80 Wall St., Suite 720, New York NY 10005. (212)571-6559. **E-mail:** debertcook@aol.com. **Website:** www.africanamericangolfersdigest.com. **Contact:** Debert Cook, managing editor. **100% freelance written.** Quarterly. Covering golf lifestyle, health, travel destinations and reviews, golf equipment, golfer profiles. "Editorial should focus on interests of our market demographic of African Americans with historical, artistic, musical, educational (higher learning), automotive, sports, fashion, entertainment, and other categories of high interest to them." Estab. 2003. Circ. 20,000. Byline given. No kill fee. Publishes ms an average of 3 months after acceptance. Editorial lead time 3-6 months. Submit seasonal material 3-6 months in advance. Accepts queries by e-mail. Accepts simultaneous submissions. Responds in 3 weeks to queries. Responds in 3 months to mss. Sample copy for $6. Guidelines by e-mail.

NONFICTION Needs how-to, interview, new product, personal experience, photo feature, technical, travel., golf-related. **Buys 3 mss/year.** Query. Length: 250-1,500 words. **Pays 10-50¢/word.**

PHOTOS State availability. Captions, identification of subjects, model releases required. Reviews GIF/JPEG files (300 dpi or higher at 4x6). Negotiates payment individually. Credit line given.

COLUMNS/DEPARTMENTS Profiles (celebrities, national leaders, entertainers, corporate leaders, etc., who golf); Travel (destination/golf course reviews); Golf Fashion (jewelry, clothing, accessories). **Buys 3 mss/year.** Query. **Pays 10-50¢/word.**

FILLERS Needs anecdotes, facts, gags, newsbreaks, short humor. **Buys 3 mss/year. mss/year.** Length: 20-125 words. **Pays 10-50¢/word.**

TIPS "Emphasize golf and African American appeal."

AZ GOLF INSIDER

Arizona Golf Association, 7600 E. Redfield Rd., Suite 130, Scottsdale AZ 85260. (602)944-3035. **Fax:** (602)944-3228. **Website:** www.azgolf.org. **Contact:** Brian Foster, director of marketing and communications. **50% freelance written.** Quarterly magazine covering golf in Arizona, the official publication of the Arizona Golf Association. Estab. 1999. Circ. 45,000. Byline given. Pays on acceptance. No kill fee. Editorial lead time 6 months. Submit seasonal material 3 months in advance. Accepts queries by mail. Accepts simultaneous submissions. Sample copy and writer's guidelines free.

NONFICTION Needs book excerpts, essays, historical, how-to, golf, humor, inspirational, interview, new product, opinion, personal experience, photo feature, travel, destinations. **Buys 5-10 mss/year.** Query. Length: 500-2,000 words. **Pays $50-500.** Sometimes pays expenses of writers on assignment.

PHOTOS State availability. Captions, identification of subjects required. Reviews contact sheets. Negotiates payment individually.

COLUMNS/DEPARTMENTS Short Strokes (golf news and notes); Improving Your Game (golf tips); Out of Bounds (guest editorial), 800 words. Query.

VIRGINIA GOLFER

Touchpoint Publishing, Inc., 600 Founders Bridge Blvd., Midlothian VA 23113. (804)378-2300, ext. 12.

Fax: (804)378-2369. **E-mail:** ablair@vsga.org. **Website:** www.vsga.org. **Contact:** Andrew Blair, editor. **65% freelance written.** Bimonthly magazine covering golf in Virginia, the official publication of the Virginia State Golf Association. Estab. 1983. Circ. 45,000. Byline given. Pays on publication. No kill fee. Editorial lead time 6 months. Submit seasonal material 3 months in advance. Accepts queries by mail, e-mail. Accepts simultaneous submissions. Sample copy and writer's guidelines free.

NONFICTION Needs book excerpts, essays, historical, how-to, golf, humor, inspirational, interview, personal experience, photo feature, technical, golf equipment, where to play, golf business. **Buys 30-40 mss/year.** Send complete ms. Length: 500-2,500 words. **Pays $50-200.** Sometimes pays expenses of writers on assignment.

PHOTOS State availability. Captions, identification of subjects required. Reviews contact sheets. Negotiates payment individually.

COLUMNS/DEPARTMENTS Chip ins & Three Putts (news notes), Rules Corner (golf rules explanations and discussion), Your Game, Golf Travel (where to play), Great Holes, Q&A, Golf Business (what's happening?), Fashion. Query.

GUNS

$$ MUZZLE BLASTS

P.O. Box 67, Friendship IN 47021. (812)667-5131. **Fax:** (812)667-5136. **E-mail:** ttrowbridge@nmlra.org. **Website:** www.nmlra.org. **65% freelance written.** Monthly magazine. "Articles must relate to muzzleloading or the muzzleloading era of American history." Estab. 1939. Circ. 17,500. Byline given. Pays on publication. Offers $50 kill fee. Publishes ms an average of 6 months after acceptance. Editorial lead time 4 months. Submit seasonal material 6 months in advance. Responds in 1 month to mss. Sample copy and writer's guidelines free.

NONFICTION Needs Muzzle Loading Hunting, book excerpts, general interest, historical, how-to, humor, interview, new product, personal experience, photo feature, technical, travel. No subjects that do not pertain to muzzleloading. **Buys 80 mss/year.** Query. Length: 2,000-2,500 words. **Pays $150 minimum for assigned articles. Pays $50 minimum for unsolicited articles.**

PHOTOS Send photos. Captions, model releases required. Reviews prints and digital images. Negotiates payment individually.

COLUMNS/DEPARTMENTS Buys 96 mss/year. Query. **Pays $50-200.**

FICTION Must pertain to muzzleloading. Needs adventure, historical, humorous. **Buys 6 mss/year.** Query. Length: 2,500 words. **Pays $50-300.**

FILLERS Needs facts. **Pays $50.**

$$ SHOTGUN SPORTS MAGAZINE

P.O. Box 6810, Auburn CA 95604. (530)889-2220. **Fax:** (530)889-9106. **E-mail:** shotgun@shotgunsportsmagazine.com. **Website:** www.shotgunsportsmagazine.com. **Contact:** Johnny Cantu, editor in chief. **50% freelance written. Welcomes new writers.** Monthly magazine covering all the shotgun sports and shotgun hunting—sporting clays, trap, skeet, hunting, gunsmithing, shotshell patterning, shotsell reloading, mental training for the shotgun sports, shotgun tests, anything shotgun. Pays on publication. No kill fee. Publishes ms an average of 1-6 months after acceptance. Responds within 3 weeks. Sample copy and writer's guidelines available on the website. Subscription: $32.95 (U.S.); $49.95 (Canada); $79.95 (foreign).

NONFICTION Needs Currently needs anything with a "shotgun" subject. Think pieces, roundups, historical, interviews, etc. No articles promoting a specific club or sponsored hunting trip, etc. Submit complete ms with photos by mail with SASE. Can submit by e-mail. Length: 1,500-3,000 words. **Pays $50-150.**

REPRINTS Photo

PHOTOS 5x7 or 8x10 b&w or 4-color with appropriate captions. On disk or e-mailed at least 5 inches and 300 dpi (contact Graphics Artist for details). Reviews transparencies (35 mm or larger), b&w, or 4-color. Send photos.

TIPS "Do not fax manuscript. Send good photos. Take a fresh approach. Create a professional yet friendly article. Send diagrams, maps, and photos of unique details, if needed. For interviews, more interested in 'words of wisdom' than a list of accomplishments. Reloading articles must include source information and backup data. Check your facts and data! If you can't think of a fresh approach, don't bother. If it's not about shotguns or shotgunners, don't send it. Never say, 'You don't need to check my data; I never make mistakes.'"

HOCKEY

$$ MINNESOTA HOCKEY JOURNAL

Touchpoint Sports, 505 N. Hwy 169, Ste. 465, Minneapolis MN 55441. (763)595-0808. **Fax:** (763)595-0016. **E-mail:** contactus@minnesotahockeyjournal.com. **E-mail:** aaron@touchpointmedia.com. **Website:** www.minnesotahockeyjournal.com. **Contact:** Aaron Paitich, editor. **50% freelance written.** Journal published 4 times/year covering Minnesota hockey. Estab. 2000. Circ. 40,000. Byline given. Pays on publication. No kill fee. Editorial lead time 6 months. Submit seasonal material 4 months in advance. Accepts simultaneous submissions. Sample copy and writer's guidelines free.

NONFICTION Needs essays, general interest, historical, how-to, play hockey, humor, inspirational, interview, new product, opinion, personal experience, photo feature, travel, hockey camps, pro hockey, juniors, college, Olympics, youth. **Buys 3-5 mss/year.** Query. Length: 500-1,500 words. **Pays $100-300.**

PHOTOS State availability. Captions, identification of subjects required. Reviews contact sheets. Negotiates payment individually.

HORSE RACING

$$ HOOF BEATS

6130 S. Sunbury Rd., Westerville OH 43081-9309. **E-mail:** hoofbeats@ustrotting.com. **Website:** www.hoofbeatsmagazine.com. **60% freelance written.** Monthly magazine covering harness racing and standardbred horses. "Articles and photos must relate to harness racing or standardbreds. We do not accept any topics that do not touch on these subjects." Estab. 1933. Circ. 10,000. Byline given. Pays on publication. Offers 25% kill fee. Publishes ms an average of 2-4 months after acceptance. Editorial lead time 6 months. Submit seasonal material 6 months in advance. Accepts queries by mail, e-mail, fax. Accepts simultaneous submissions. Responds in 2 weeks to queries. Responds in 1 month to mss. Sample copy available online. Guidelines free.

NONFICTION Needs general interest, how-to, interview, personal experience, photo feature, technical. "We do not want any fiction or poetry." **Buys 48-72 mss/year.** Query. Length: 750-3,000 words. **Pays $100-500. Pays $100-500 for unsolicited articles.**

PHOTOS State availability. Identification of subjects required. Reviews contact sheets. We offer $25-100 per photo.

COLUMNS/DEPARTMENTS Equine Clinic (standardbreds who overcame major health issues), 900-1,200 words; Profiles (short profiles on people or horses in harness racing), 600-1,000 words; Industry Trends (issues impacting standardbreds & harness racing), 1,000-2,000 words. **Buys 60 mss/year mss/year.** Query. **Pays $100-500.**

TIPS "We welcome new writers who know about harness racing or are willing to learn about it. Make sure to read *Hoof Beats* before querying to see our slant & style. We look for informative/promotional stories on harness racing—not exposés on the sport."

HUNTING AND FISHING

$$ ALABAMA GAME & FISH

Game & Fish, 3330 Chastain Meadows Pkwy. N.W., Suite 200, Kennesaw GA 30144. (770)953-9222. **Fax:** (678)279-7512. **E-mail:** ken.dunwoody@imoutdoors.com. **Website:** www.alabamagameandfish.com. **Contact:** Ken Dunwoody, editorial director; Paul Rackley, editor. Covers fishing and hunting opportunities in Alabama. See listing for *Game & Fish* for more information.

$$ AMERICAN ANGLER

735 Broad St., Augusta GA 30904. (706)828-3971. **E-mail:** benjaminromans@gmail.com; wayne.knight@morris.com. **Website:** www.americanangler.com. **Contact:** Ben Romans, editor; Wayne Knight, art director. **95% freelance written.** Bimonthly magazine covering fly fishing. "*American Angler* is devoted exclusively to fly fishing. We focus mainly on coldwater fly fishing for trout, steelhead, and salmon, but we also run articles about warmwater and saltwater fly fishing. Our mission is to supply our readers with well-written, accurate articles on every aspect of the sport—angling techniques and methods, reading water, finding fish, selecting flies, tying flies, fish behavior, places to fish, casting, managing line, rigging, tackle, accessories, entomology, and any other relevant topics. Each submission should present specific, useful information that will increase our readers' enjoyment of the sport and help them catch more fish." Estab. 1976. Circ. 32,000. Byline given. Pays on publication. No kill fee. Publishes ms an average of 6 months after acceptance. Editorial lead time 3 months. Submit seasonal materi-

CONSUMER MAGAZINES

al 5 months in advance. Accepts queries by e-mail. Accepts simultaneous submissions. Responds in 6 weeks to queries. Responds in 2 months to mss.

NONFICTION Needs how-to, most important, personal experience, photo feature, seldom, technical. No superficial, broad-brush coverage of subjects. **Buys 45-60 mss/year.** Query with published clips. Length: 800-2,200 words. **Pays $200-600.**

REPRINTS Send information about when and where the material previously appeared. Pay negotiable.

PHOTOS "How-to pieces—those that deal with tactics, rigging, fly tying, and the like—must be accompanied by appropriate photography or rough sketches for our illustrator. Naturally, where-to stories must be illustrated with shots of scenery, people fishing, anglers holding fish, and other pictures that help flesh out the story and paint the local color. Do not bother sending sub-par photographs. We only accept photos that are well lit, tack sharp, and correctly framed. A fly-tying submission should always include samples of flies to send to our staff photographer, even if photos of the flies are included." Send photos. Captions, identification of subjects required. Digital photos only. Offers no additional payment for photos accepted with ms. Pays $600-700 for color cover; $30-350 for color inside. Pays on publication. Credit line given. Buys one-time rights, first rights for covers. "Payment is made just prior to publication. "We don't pay by the word, and length is only one of the variables considered. The quality and completeness of a submission may be more important than its length in determining rates, and articles that include good photography are usually worth more. As a guideline, the following rates generally apply: Feature articles pay $450 (and perhaps a bit more if we're impressed), while short features pay $200 to $400. Generally, these rates assume that useful photos, drawings, or sketches accompany the words.

COLUMNS/DEPARTMENTS One-page shorts (problem solvers), 350-750 words. Query with published clips. **Pays $100-300.**

TIPS "If you are submitting for the first time, please submit complete queries."

$$$ AMERICAN HUNTER

National Rifle Association of America, 11250 Waples Mill Rd., Fairfax VA 22030-9400. (800)672-3888. **E-mail:** publications@nrahq.org. **E-mail:** americanhunter@nrahq.org. **Website:** www.americanhunter.org. **Contact:** Editor in Chief. Monthly magazine for hunters who are members of the National Rifle Association (NRA). *American Hunter*, the official journal of the National Rifle Association, contains articles dealing with various sport hunting and related activities both at home and abroad. With the encouragement of the sport as a prime game management tool, emphasis is on technique, sportsmanship, and safety. In each issue, hunting equipment and firearms are evaluated, legislative happenings affecting the sport are reported, lore and legend are retold, and the business of the Association is recorded in the Official Journal section. Circ. 1,000,000. Byline given. Pays on publication. No kill fee. Accepts queries by mail, e-mail. Responds in 6 months to queries. Guidelines online at www.professionaloutdoormedia.org/sites/all/downloads/American%20Hunter%20Writer%27s%20Guidelines.pdf.

NONFICTION Special issues: Special issues: pheasants, whitetail tactics, black bear feed areas, mule deer, duck hunters' transport by land and sea, tech topics to be decided, rut strategies, muzzleloader moose and elk, fall turkeys, staying warm, goose talk, long-range muzzleloading. Not interested in material on fishing, camping, or firearms knowledge. Query (preferred) or submit complete ms by mail or e-mail. Length: 2,000-3,000 words. **Pays up to $1,500 for full-length features with complete photo packages.**

REPRINTS Copies for author will be provided upon publication. No reprints possible.

PHOTOS Captions preferred. Accepts images in digital format only, no slides. Model release required "for every recognizable human face in a photo." Pays $125-600/image; $1,000 for color cover; $400-1,400 for text/photo package. Pays on publication. Credit line given. No additional payment made for photos used with ms. Photos purchased with or without accompanying mss.

COLUMNS/DEPARTMENTS Build Your Skills (technical how-to column on hunting-related procedure); Hardware (covers new firearms, ammunition, and optics used for hunting), 800-1,200 words. **Pays $500-1,000.**

TIPS "Although unsolicited mss are accepted, detailed query letters outlining the proposed topic and approach are appreciated and will save both writers and editors a considerable amount of time. If we like your story idea, you will be contacted by mail or phone and given direction on how we'd like the topic covered."

ARKANSAS SPORTSMAN

Game & Fish, 3330 Chastain Meadows Pkwy. N.W., Suite 200, Kennesaw GA 30144. (770)953-9222. **Fax:** (678)279-7512. **E-mail:** ken.dunwoody@imoutdoors.com. **Website:** www.arkansassportsmanmag.com. **Contact:** Ken Dunwoody, editorial director; Nick Gilmore, editor. Covers fishing and hunting opportunities in Arkansas. See listing for *Game & Fish* for more information.

BC OUTDOORS HUNTING AND SHOOTING

Outdoor Group Media, 201a-7261 River Place, Mission British Columbia V4S 0A2 Canada. (604)820-3400. **Fax:** (604)820-3477. **E-mail:** info@outdoorgroupmedia.com; mmitchell@outdoorgroupmedia.com; production@outdoorgroupmedia.com. **Website:** www.bcoutdoorsmagazine.com. **Contact:** Mike Mitchell, editor. **80% freelance written.** Biannual magazine covering hunting, shooting, camping, and backroads in British Columbia, Canada. *BC Outdoors Magazine* publishes 7 sport fishing issues a year with 2 hunting and shooting supplement issues each summer and fall. "Our magazine is about the best outdoor experiences in BC. Whether you're camping on an ocean shore, hiking into your favorite lake, or learning how to fly-fish on your favourite river, we want to showcase what our province has to offer to sport fishing and outdoor enthusiasts. *BC Outdoors Hunting and Shooting* provides trusted editorial for trapping, deer hunting, big buck, bowhunting, bag limits, baitling, decoys, calling, camouflage, tracking, trophy hunting, pheasant hunting, goose hunting, hunting regulations, duck hunting, whitetail hunting, hunting regulations, hunting trips, and mule deer hunting." Estab. 1945. Circ. 30,000. Byline given. Pays on publication. Offers kill fee. Publishes ms an average of 3 months after acceptance. Accepts queries by e-mail. Guidelines for 8x10 SASE with 7 Canadian first-class stamps.

NONFICTION Needs how-to, new or innovative articles on hunting subjects, personal experience, outdoor adventure, outdoor topics specific to British Columbia. **Buys 50 mss/year.** Query the publication before submitting. Do not send unsolicited mss or photos. Submit no more than 100-words outlining exactly what your story will be. "You should be able to encapsulate the essence of your story and show us why our readers would be interested in reading or knowing what you are writing about. Queries need to be clear, succinct and straight to the point. Show us why we should publish your article in 150 words or less." Length: 1,700-2,000 words. **Pays $300-500.**

PHOTOS Biannual magazine emphasizing hunting, RV camping, canoeing, wildlife and management issues in British Columbia only. Sample copy available for $4.95 Canadian. Family oriented. "By far, most photos accompany manuscripts. We are always on the lookout for good covers—wildlife, recreational activities, people in the outdoors—of British Columbia, vertical and square format. Photos with manuscripts must, of course, illustrate the story. There should, as far as possible, be something happening. Photos generally dominate lead spread of each story. They are used in everything from double-page bleeds to thumbnails." State availability. Model/property release preferred. Photo captions or at least full identification required.

COLUMNS/DEPARTMENTS Column needs basically supplied in-house.

TIPS "Send us material on fishing and hunting. We generally just send back nonrelated work. We want in-depth information and professional writing only. Emphasis on environmental issues. Those pieces with a conservation component have a better chance of being published. Subject must be specific to British Columbia. We receive many mss written by people who obviously do not know the magazine or market. The writer has a better chance of breaking in with short, lesser-paying articles and fillers, because we have a stable of regular writers who produce most main features."

CALIFORNIA GAME & FISH

Game & Fish, 3330 Chastain Meadows Pkwy. N.W., Suite 200, Kennesaw GA 30144. (770)953-9222. **Fax:** (678)279-7512. **E-mail:** ken.dunwoody@imoutdoors.com. **Website:** www.californiagameandfish.com. Covers fishing and hunting opportunities in California. See listing for *Game & Fish* for more information.

DEER & DEER HUNTING

F+W Media, Inc., 700 E. State St., Iola WI 54990. (715)445-2214. **E-mail:** Outdoorsfw@gmail.com. **Website:** www.deeranddeerhunting.com. **Contact:** Dan Schmidt, editor-in-chief. **95% freelance written.** Magazine published 10 times/year covering white-tailed deer. "Readers include a cross section of the deer hunting population—individuals who hunt with bow, gun, or camera. The editorial content of the magazine focuses on white-tailed deer biology and behavior, management principle and practices, habitat requirements, natural history of deer, hunting techniques, and hunting ethics. We also publish a wide range of how-to articles designed to help hunters locate and get close to deer at all times of the year. The majority of our readership consists of 2-season hunters (bow & gun) and approximately one-third camera hunt." Estab. 1977. Circ. 200,000. Byline given. Pays on acceptance. No kill fee. Publishes ms an average of 18 months after acceptance. Editorial lead time 6 months. Submit seasonal material 12 months in advance. Accepts queries by mail, e-mail. Responds in 1 month to queries. Responds in 2 months to mss. Sample copy for 9x12 SASE. Guidelines available on website.

NONFICTION Needs general interest, historical, how-to, photo feature, technical. No "Joe and me" articles. **Buys 100 mss/year.** Send complete ms. Length: 1,000-2,000 words. **Pays $150-600 for assigned articles. Pays $150-400 for unsolicited articles.** Sometimes pays expenses of writers on assignment.

PHOTOS Send photos. Captions required. Reviews transparencies. Offers $25-200/photo; $500 for cover photos.

COLUMNS/DEPARTMENTS Columns: Deer Browse (odd occurrences), 200-500 words. **Buys 10 mss/year.** Query. **Pays $25-250.**

FICTION Mood deer hunting pieces. **Buys 9 mss/year.** Send complete ms.

FILLERS Needs facts, newsbreaks. **Buys 40-50 mss/year.** Length: 100-500 words. **Pays $15-150.**

TIPS "Feature articles dealing with deer biology or behavior should be documented by scientific research (the author's or that of others) as opposed to a limited number of personal observations."

$$ FLORIDA GAME & FISH

Game & Fish, 3330 Chastain Meadows Pkwy. N.W., Suite 200, Kennesaw GA 30144. (770)953-9222. **Fax:** (678)279-7512. **E-mail:** ken.dunwoody@imoutdoors.com. **Website:** www.floridagameandfish.com. **Contact:** Ken Dunwoody, editorial director; Paul Rackley, editor. Covers fishing and hunting opportunities in Florida. See listing for *Game & Fish* for more information.

$$ FLORIDA SPORTSMAN

Wickstrom Communications, Intermedia Outdoors, 2700 S. Kanner Hwy., Stuart FL 34994. (772)219-7400. **Fax:** (772)219-6900. **E-mail:** editor@floridasportsman.com. **Website:** www.floridasportsman.com. **Contact:** Jeff Weakley, executive editor. **30% freelance written.** Monthly magazine covering fishing, boating, hunting, and related sports—Florida and Caribbean only. Edited for the boat owner and offshore, coastal, and fresh water fisherman. It provides a how, when, and where approach in its articles, which also includes occasional camping, diving, and hunting stories—plus ecology (in-depth articles and editorials attempting to protect Florida's wilderness, wetlands, and natural beauty). Circ. 115,000. Byline given. Pays on acceptance. No kill fee. Publishes ms an average of 6 months after acceptance. Submit seasonal material 6 months in advance. Accepts queries by mail, e-mail. Responds in 1 month to queries. Sample copy free. E-mail editor for submission guidelines.

NONFICTION Needs essays on environment or nature, how-to (fishing, hunting, boating), humor (outdoors angle), personal experience in fishing, etc., technical (boats, tackle, etc.) as particularly suitable for Florida specialties. **Buys 20-40 mss/year.** Query. Length: 1,500-2,500 words. **Pays $475.**

PHOTOS High-res digital images on CD preferred. Reviews 35mm transparencies, 4×5 and larger prints. Offers no additional payment for photos accepted with ms. Pays up to $750 for cover photos.

TIPS "Feature articles are sometimes open to freelancers; however there is little chance of acceptance unless contributor is an accomplished and avid outdoorsman *and* a competent writer-photographer with considerable experience in Florida."

$$ GEORGIA SPORTSMAN

Game & Fish, 3330 Chastain Meadows Pkwy. N.W., Suite 200, Kennesaw GA 30144. (770)953-9222. **Fax:** (678)279-7512. **E-mail:** ken.dunwoody@imoutdoors.com. **Website:** www.georgiasportsmanmag.com. **Contact:** Ken Dunwoody, editorial director; Paul Rackley, editor. Covers fishing and hunting opportunities in Georgia. See listing for *Game & Fish* for more information.

$$ ILLINOIS GAME & FISH

Game & Fish, 3330 Chastain Meadows Pkwy. N.W., Suite 200, Kennesaw GA 30144. (770)953-9222. **Fax:** (678)279-7512. **E-mail:** ken.dunwoody@imoutdoors.com. **Website:** www.illinoisgameandfish.com. **Contact:** Ken Dunwoody, editorial director; Shaun Epperson, editor. Covers fishing and hunting opportunities in Illinois. See listing for *Game & Fish* for more information.

$$ IOWA GAME & FISH

Game & Fish, 3330 Chastain Meadows Pkwy. N.W., Suite 200, Kennesaw GA 30144. (770)953-9222. **Fax:** (678)279-7512. **E-mail:** ken.dunwoody@imoutdoors.com. **Website:** www.iowagameandfish.com. **Contact:** Ken Dunwoody, editorial director; Shaun Epperson, editor. Covers fishing and hunting opportunities in Iowa. See listing for *Game & Fish* for more information.

$$ KENTUCKY GAME & FISH

Game & Fish, 3330 Chastain Meadows Pkwy. N.W., Suite 200, Kennesaw GA 30144. (770)953-9222. **Fax:** (678)279-7512. **E-mail:** ken.dunwoody@imoutdoors.com. **Website:** www.kentuckygameandfish.com. **Contact:** Ken Dunwoody, editorial director; Paul Rackley, editor. Covers fishing and hunting opportunities in Kentucky. See listing for *Game & Fish* for more information.

$$ MICHIGAN SPORTSMAN

Game & Fish, 3330 Chastain Meadows Pkwy. N.W., Suite 200, Kennesaw GA 30144. (770)953-9222. **Fax:** (678)279-7512. **E-mail:** ken.dunwoody@imoutdoors.com. **Website:** www.michigansportsmanmag.com. **Contact:** Ken Dunwoody, editorial director; Nick Gilmore, editor. Covers fishing and hunting opportunities in Michigan. See listing for *Game & Fish* for more information.

$ MIDWEST OUTDOORS

MidWest Outdoors, Ltd., 111 Shore Dr., Burr Ridge IL 60527. (630)887-7722. **Fax:** (630)887-1958. **Website:** www.midwestoutdoors.com. **100% freelance written.** Monthly tabloid emphasizing fishing, hunting, camping, and boating. Estab. 1967. Byline given. Pays on publication. No kill fee. Publishes ms an average of 3 months after acceptance. Submit seasonal material 2 months in advance. Accepts simultaneous submissions. Responds in 3 weeks to queries. Sample copy for $1 or online. Guidelines for #10 SASE.

NONFICTION Needs how-to, fishing, hunting, camping in the Midwest, where-to-go (fishing, hunting, camping within 500 miles of Chicago). "We do not want to see any articles on 'my first fishing, hunting, or camping experiences,' 'cleaning my tackle box,' 'tackle tune-up,' 'making fishing fun for kids,' or 'catch and release.'" **Buys 1,800 unsolicited mss/year.** Send complete ms. Submissions should be e-mailed to info@midwestoutdoors.com (Microsoft Word format preferred). Length: 1,000-1,500 words. **Pays $15-30.**

PHOTOS Captions required. Reviews slides and b&w prints. Offers no additional payment for photos accompanying ms.

COLUMNS/DEPARTMENTS Fishing; Hunting. Send complete ms. **Pays $30.**

TIPS "Break in with a great unknown fishing hole or new technique within 500 miles of Chicago. Where, how, when, and why. Know the type of publication you are sending material to."

$$ MINNESOTA SPORTSMAN

Game & Fish, 3330 Chastain Meadows Pkwy. N.W., Suite 200, Kennesaw GA 30144. (770)953-9222. **Fax:** (678)279-7512. **E-mail:** ken.dunwoody@imoutdoors.com. **Website:** www.minnesotasportsmanmag.com. **Contact:** Ken Dunwoody, editorial director; Nick Gilmore, editor. Covers fishing and hunting opportunities in Minnesota. See listing for *Game & Fish* for more information. Pays a kill fee.

$$ MISSISSIPPI/LOUISIANA GAME & FISH

Game & Fish, 3330 Chastain Meadows Pkwy. N.W., Suite 200, Kennesaw GA 30144. (770)953-9222. **Fax:** (678)279-7512. **E-mail:** ken.dunwoody@imoutdoors.com. **Website:** www.mississippigameandfish.com; www.lagameandfish.com. Jimmy Jacobs, editor. **Contact:** Ken Dunwoody, editorial director. Covers fishing and hunting opportunities in Mississippi and Louisiana. See listing for *Game & Fish* for more information.

$$ MUSKY HUNTER MAGAZINE

P.O. Box 340, 7978 Hwy. 70 E., St. Germain WI 54558. (715)477-2178. **Fax:** (715)477-8858. **E-mail:** editor@muskyhunter.com. **Website:** www.muskyhunter.com. **Contact:** Jim Saric, editor. **90% freelance written.** Bimonthly magazine on musky fishing. Serves the vertical market of musky fishing enthusiasts. "We're interested in how-to, where-to articles." Estab. 1988. Circ. 37,000. Byline given. Pays on publication. No kill fee. Publishes ms an average of 4 months after acceptance. Submit seasonal material 4 months in advance. Responds in 2 months to queries. Sample copy for 9x12 SASE and $2.79 postage. Guidelines for #10 SASE.

NONFICTION Needs historical, related only to musky fishing, how-to, catch muskies, modify lures, boats, and tackle for musky fishing, personal experience (must be musky fishing experience), technical, fishing equipment, travel, to lakes and areas for musky fishing. **Buys 50 mss/year.** Send complete ms. Length: 1,000-2,500 words. **Pays $100-300 for assigned articles. Pays $50-300 for unsolicited articles.**

PHOTOS Send photos. Identification of subjects required. Reviews 35mm transparencies, 3x5 prints, high-res digital images preferred. Offers no additional payment for photos accepted with ms.

$$ NEW ENGLAND GAME & FISH

Game & Fish, 3330 Chastain Meadows Pkwy. N.W., Suite 200, Kennesaw GA 30144. (770)953-9222. **Fax:** (678)279-7512. **E-mail:** ken.dunwoody@imoutdoors.com. **Website:** www.newenglandgameandfish.com. **Contact:** Ken Dunwoody, editorial director; David Johnson, editor. Covers fishing and hunting opportunities in New England region (Connecticut, Maine, Massachusetts, New Hampshire, Rhode Island, and Vermont). See listing for *Game & Fish* for more information.

$$ NEW YORK GAME & FISH

Game & Fish, 3330 Chastain Meadows Pkwy. N.W., Suite 200, Kennesaw GA 30144. (770)953-9222. **Fax:** (678)279-7512. **E-mail:** ken.dunwoody@imoutdoors.com. **Website:** www.newyorkgameandfish.com. **Contact:** Ken Dunwoody, editorial director; David Johnson, editor. Covers fishing and hunting opportunities in New York. See listing for *Game & Fish* for more information.

$$ NORTH CAROLINA GAME & FISH

Game & Fish, 3330 Chastain Meadows Pkwy. N.W., Suite 200, Kennesaw GA 30144. (770)953-9222. **Fax:** (678)279-7512. **E-mail:** ken.dunwoody@imoutdoors.com. **Website:** www.ncgameandfish.com. **Contact:** Ken Dunwoody, editorial director; David Johnson, editor. Covers fishing and hunting opportunities in North Carolina. See listing for *Game & Fish* for more information.

$$ OHIO GAME & FISH

Game & Fish, 3330 Chastain Meadows Pkwy. N.W., Suite 200, Kennesaw GA 30144. (770)953-9222. **Fax:** (678)279-7512. **E-mail:** ken.dunwoody@imoutdoors.com. **Website:** www.ohiogameandfish.com. **Contact:** Ken Dunwoody, editorial director; David Johnson, editor. Covers fishing and hunting opportunities in Ohio. See listing for *Game & Fish* for more information.

$$ OKLAHOMA GAME & FISH

Game & Fish, 3330 Chastain Meadows Pkwy. N.W., Suite 200, Kennesaw GA 30144. (770)953-9222. **Fax:** (678)279-7512. **E-mail:** ken.dunwoody@imoutdoors.com. **Website:** www.oklahomagameandfish.com. **Contact:** Ken Dunwoody, editorial director; Nick Gilmore, editor. Covers fishing and hunting opportunities in Oklahoma. See listing for *Game & Fish* for more information.

$$ PENNSYLVANIA GAME & FISH

Game & Fish, 3330 Chastain Meadows Pkwy. N.W., Suite 200, Kennesaw GA 30144. (770)953-9222. **Fax:** (678)279-7512. **E-mail:** ken.dunwoody@imoutdoors.com. **Website:** www.pagameandfish.com. **Contact:** Ken Dunwoody, editorial director; David Johnson, editor. Covers fishing and hunting opportunities in Pennsylvania. See listing for *Game & Fish* for more information.

$$ RACK MAGAZINE

Buckmasters, Ltd., 10350 U.S. Hwy. 80 E., Montgomery AL 36117. (800)240-3337. **Fax:** (334)215-3535. **E-mail:** loconnor@buckmasters.com. **Website:** www.buckmasters.com. **50% freelance written.** Monthly (July-December) magazine covering big game hunting. "All features are either first- or third-person narratives detailing the successful hunts for world-class, big game animals—mostly white-tailed deer and other North American species." Estab. 1998. Circ. 75,000. Byline given. Pays on publication. No kill fee. Publishes ms an average of 9 months after acceptance. Editorial lead time 9-12 months. Submit seasonal material 9 months in advance. Accepts queries by e-mail. Accepts simultaneous submissions. Responds in 1 month to queries; in 2 months to mss.

NONFICTION Needs personal experience. "We're interested only in articles chronicling successful hunts." **Buys 40-50 mss/year.** Query. Length: 1,000 words. **Pays $100-325 for assigned and unsolicited articles.**

PHOTOS Send photos. Captions, identification of subjects required. Reviews transparencies, prints, GIF/JPEG files.

$$ ROCKY MOUNTAIN GAME & FISH

Game & Fish, 3330 Chastain Meadows Pkwy. N.W., Suite 200, Kennesaw GA 30144. (770)935-9222. **Fax:** (678)279-7512. **E-mail:** ken.dunwoody@imoutdoors.com. **Website:** www.rmgameandfish.com. **Contact:** Ken Dunwoody, editorial director; Shaun Epperson, editor. Covers fishing and hunting opportunities in Rocky Mountain region (Montana, Idaho, Wyoming, Nevada, Utah, Colorado, New Mexico, and Arizona). See listing for *Game & Fish* for more information.

SALT WATER SPORTSMAN

Bonnier Corporation, 460 N. Orlando Ave., Suite 200, Winter Park FL 32789. (407)628-4802. **E-mail:** editor@saltwatersportsman.com. **Website:** www.saltwatersportsman.com. **Contact:** Glenn Law, editor. **85% freelance written.** Monthly magazine covering saltwater sport fishing. *Salt Water Sportsman* is edited for serious marine sport fishermen whose lifestyle includes the pursuit of game fish in U.S. waters and around the world. It provides information on fishing trends, techniques, and destinations, both local and international. Each issue reviews offshore and inshore fishing boats, high-tech electronics, innovative tackle, engines, and other new products. Coverage also focuses on sound fisheries management and conservation. Circ. 170,000. Byline given. Pays on acceptance. Offers kill fee. Publishes ms an average of 5 months after acceptance. Submit seasonal material 8 months in advance. Accepts queries by mail, e-mail. Responds in 1 month to queries. Guidelines available by request.

NONFICTION Needs how-to, personal experience, technical, travel, to fishing areas. **Buys 100 mss/year.** Query. Length: 900-1,200 words. **Pay for feature/photo package starts at $750.**

PHOTOS Captions required. Reviews low-res digital files, requires RAW files for publication. Pays $1,500 minimum for cover.

COLUMNS/DEPARTMENTS Sportsman's Tips (short, how-to tips and techniques on salt water fishing; emphasis is on building, repairing, or reconditioning specific items or gear). Send complete ms.

TIPS "There are a lot of knowledgeable fishermen/budding writers out there who could be valuable to us with a little coaching. Many don't think they can write a story for us, but they'd be surprised. We work with writers. Shorter articles that get to the point and are accompanied by good, sharp photos are hard for us to turn down. Having to delete unnecessary wordage—conversation, clichés, etc.—that writers feel is mandatory is annoying. Often they don't devote enough attention to specific, repeatable fishing information."

SOUTH CAROLINA GAME & FISH

Game & Fish, 3330 Chastain Meadows Pkwy. N.W., Suite 200, Kennesaw GA 30144. (770)953-9222. **Fax:** (678)279-7512. **E-mail:** ken.dunwoody@imoutdoors.com. **Website:** www.scgameandfish.com. **Contact:** Ken Dunwoody, editorial director; David Johnson, editor. Covers fishing and hunting opportunities in South Carolina. See listing for *Game & Fish* for more information.

TENNESSEE SPORTSMAN

Game & Fish, 3330 Chastain Meadows Pkwy. N.W., Suite 200, Kennesaw GA 30144. (770)953-9222. **Fax:** (678)279-7512. **E-mail:** ken.dunwoody@imoutdoors.com. **Website:** www.tennesseesportsmanmag.com. **Contact:** Ken Dunwoody, editorial director; Paul Rackley, editor. Covers fishing and hunting opportunities in Tennessee. See listing for *Game & Fish* for more information.

TEXAS SPORTSMAN

Game & Fish, 3330 Chastain Meadows Pkwy. N.W., Suite 200, Kennesaw GA 30144. (770)953-9222. **Fax:** (678)279-7512. **E-mail:** ken.dunwoody@imoutdoors.com. **Website:** www.texassportsmanmag.com. **Contact:** Ken Dunwoody, editorial director; Nick Gilmore, editor. Covers fishing and hunting opportunities in Texas. See listing for *Game & Fish* for more information.

TRAPPER & PREDATOR CALLER

F+W, A Content + Ecommerce Company, 700 E. State St., Iola WI 54990. (715)445-2214. **E-mail:** jared.blohm@fwcommunity.com. **Website:** www.trapperpredatorcaller.com. **75% freelance written.** Tabloid published 10 times/year covering trapping and predator calling, fur trade. "Our editorial goal is to inform, educate, and entertain our readers with articles, photographs, and illustrations that promote trapping and predator calling." Must have mid-level to advanced knowledge because *T&PC* is heavily how-to focused. Estab. 1975. Circ. 34,000. Byline given. Pays within 45 days of publication. No kill fee. Publishes ms an average of 6 months after acceptance. Editorial lead time 1 year. Submit seasonal material 1 year in advance. Accepts queries by e-mail.

NONFICTION Needs how-to, interview, personal experience, travel. **Buys 100 mss/year.** Query or send complete ms via e-mail. Length: 1,500-2,500 words. **Pays $250 for assigned articles.**

PHOTOS Send photos. Reviews high-resolution digital photos, slides, prints. Digital photos should be saved as TIFF or JPEG files. Minimum 300 dpi.

TIPS "Check your facts. An error in fact reduces the credibility of the magazine and hurts your relationship with us. Please double-check spelling, dates, proper names, etc."

$$ TURKEY COUNTRY

National Wild Turkey Federation, P.O. Box 530, Edgefield SC 29824-0530. (803)637-3106. **E-mail:** info@nwtf.net. **E-mail:** klee@nwtf.net. **Website:** www.turkeycountrymagazine.com. **Contact:** Karen Lee, editor; Matt Lindler, photo editor. **50-60% freelance written.** Bimonthly educational magazine for members of the National Wild Turkey Federation. Topics covered include hunting, history, restoration, management, biology, and distribution of wild turkey. Estab. 1973. Circ. 180,000. Byline given. Pays on acceptance. No kill fee. Publishes ms an average of 6 months after acceptance. Editorial lead time 1 year. Accepts queries by mail, e-mail. Responds in 2 months to queries Sample copy: $5 and 9x12 SAE. Guidelines online.

Submit queries by June 1 of each year.

NONFICTION Query (preferred) or send complete ms. Length: 1,000-1,200 words. **Pays $350-550.**

PHOTOS "We want quality photos submitted with features. Illustrations also acceptable. We are using more and more inside color illustrations. No typical hunter-holding-dead-turkey photos or setups using mounted birds or domestic turkeys. Photos with how-to stories must make the techniques clear (i.e., how to make a turkey call; how to sculpt or carve a bird in wood)." Identification of subjects, model releases required. Reviews transparencies, high-resolution digital images. Pays $150 for half-page, $200 for full page, $300 for two-page spread, $250 for contents pages, and $800 for cover.

COLUMNS/DEPARTMENTS Acquires for various departments, all 500-1,000 words. Query. **Pays $250-350.**

TIPS "The writer should simply keep in mind that the audience is 'expert' on wild turkey management, hunting, life history, and restoration/conservation history. Know the subject."

$$ WEST VIRGINIA GAME & FISH

Game & Fish, 3330 Chastain Meadows Pkwy. N.W., Suite 200, Kennesaw GA 30144. (770)953-9222. **Fax:** (678)279-7512. **Website:** www.wvgameandfish.com. **Contact:** Ken Dunwoody, editorial director; Paul Rackley, editor. Covers fishing and hunting opportunities in West Virginia. See listing for *Game & Fish* for more information.

$$ WISCONSIN SPORTSMAN

Game & Fish, 3330 Chastain Meadows Pkwy. N.W., Suite 200, Kennesaw GA 30144. (770)953-9222. **Fax:** (678)279-7512. **E-mail:** ken.dunwoody@imoutdoors.com. **Website:** www.wisconsinsportsmanmag.com. **Contact:** Ken Dunwoody, editorial director; Nick Gilmore, editor. Covers fishing and hunting opportunities in Wisconsin. See listing for *Game & Fish* for more information.

MISCELLANEOUS SPORTS

$$ AMERICAN CHEERLEADER

Macfadden Performing Arts Media LLC, 110 William St., 23rd Floor, New York NY 10038. (646)459-4800. **Fax:** (646)459-4900. **E-mail:** editors@americancheerleader.com. **Website:** www.americancheerleader.com. **Contact:** Marisa Walker, editor-in-chief. **30% freelance written.** Bimonthly magazine covering high school, college, and competitive cheerleading. "We try to keep a young, informative voice for all articles—'for cheerleaders, by cheerleaders.'" Estab. 1995. Circ. 200,000. Byline given. Pays on publication. Offers 25% kill fee. Publishes ms an average of 4 months after acceptance. Editorial lead time 3 months. Submit seasonal material 4 months in advance. Accepts queries by mail, e-mail, online submission form. Responds in 4 weeks to queries. Responds in 2 months to mss. Sample copy for $2.95. Guidelines free.

NONFICTION Needs young adults: biography, interview/profile (sports personalities), careers, fashion, beauty, health, how-to (cheering techniques, routines, pep songs, etc.), problem-solving, sports, cheerleading-specific material. Special issues: Special issues: Tryouts (April); Camp Basics (June); College (October); Competition (December). No professional cheerleading stories, i.e., no Dallas Cowboy cheerleaders. **Buys 20 mss/year.** Query by e-mail; provide résumé, business card, and tearsheets to be kept on file. "We're looking for authors who know cheerleading." Length: 750-2,000 words. **Pays $100-250 for assigned articles; $100 maximum for unsolicited articles.** Sometimes pays expenses of writers on assignment.

PHOTOS State availability. Model releases required. Reviews transparencies, 5x7 prints. Offers $50/photo.

COLUMNS/DEPARTMENTS Freelance columns: Gameday Beauty (skin care, celeb how-tos), 600 words; Health & Fitness (teen athletes), 1,000 words; Profiles (winning squads), 1,000 words. **Buys 12 mss/year.** Query with published clips. **Pays $100-250.**

TIPS "We invite proposals from freelance writers who are involved in or have been involved in cheerleading—i.e., coaches, sponsors, or cheerleaders. Our writing style is upbeat and 'sporty' to catch and hold the attention of our teenaged readers. Articles should be broken down into lots of sidebars, bulleted lists, Q&As, etc."

ESPN THE MAGAZINE

ESPN Inc. (The Walt Disney Company/Hearst Corporation), 19 E. 34th St., New York NY 10016. **E-mail:** post@espnmag.com. **Website:** www.espn.go.com/magazine. **Contact:** Craig Winston, managing editor. Bi-weekly sports magazine published by ESPN. *ESPN The Magazine* covers Major League Baseball, National Basketball Association, National Football League, National Hockey League, college basketball, and college football. The magazine typically takes a more lighthearted and humorous approach to sporting news. Estab. 1998. Circ. 2.1 million.

Query before submitting. Difficult market to break into.

LACROSSE MAGAZINE

113 W. University Pkwy., Baltimore MD 21210. (410)235-6882. **Fax:** (410)366-6735. **E-mail:** feedback@laxmagazine.com; mdasilva@uslacrosse.org. **Website:** www.laxmagazine.com; www.uslacrosse.org. **Contact:** Matt DaSilva, editor; Gabriella O'Brien, art director. **60% freelance written.** Monthly magazine covering the sport of lacrosse. "*Lacrosse* is the only national feature publication devoted to the sport of lacrosse. It is a benefit of membership in U.S. Lacrosse, a nonprofit organization devoted to promoting the growth of lacrosse and preserving its history. U.S. Lacrosse maintains *Lacrosse Magazine Online* (*LMO*) at www.laxmagazine.com. *LMO* features daily lacrosse news and scores directly from lacrosse-playing colleges. *LMO* also includes originally produced features and news briefs covering all levels of play. Occasional feature articles printed in *Lacrosse* are republished at *LMO*, and vice versa. The online component of *Lacrosse* does things that a printed publication can't—provide news, scores, and information in a timely manner." Estab. 1978. Circ. 235,000. Byline given. Pays on publication. No kill fee. Publishes ms an average of 2 months after acceptance. Editorial lead time 2 months. Submit seasonal material 2 months in advance. Sample copy free.

NONFICTION Needs book excerpts, general interest, historical, how-to, drills, conditioning, x's and o's, etc., interview, new product, opinion, personal experience, photo feature, technical. **Buys 30-40 mss/year.** Length: 500-1,750 words. **Payment negotiable.** Sometimes pays expenses of writers on assignment.

PHOTOS State availability. Captions, identification of subjects required. Reviews contact sheets, 4x6 prints. Negotiates payment individually.

COLUMNS/DEPARTMENTS First Person (personal experience), 1,000 words; Fitness (conditioning/strength/exercise), 500-1,000 words; How-to, 500-1,000 words. **Buys 10-15 mss/year. Payment negotiable.**

TIPS "As the national development center of lacrosse, we are particularly interested in stories about the growth of the sport in nontraditional areas of the U.S. and abroad, written for an audience already knowledgeable about the game."

MUSHING MAGAZINE

P.O. Box 1195, Willow AK 99688. (907)495-2468. **E-mail:** editor@mushing.com. **Website:** www.mushing.com. **Contact:** Greg Sellentin, publisher and executive editor. Bimonthly magazine covering "all aspects of the growing sports of dogsledding, skijoring, carting, dog packing, and weight pulling. *Mushing* promotes responsible dog care through feature articles and updates on working animal health care, safety, nutrition, and training." Estab. 1987. Circ. 10,000. Byline given. Pays within 3 months of publication. No kill fee. Publishes ms an average of 4 months after acceptance. Submit seasonal material 4 months in advance. Accepts queries by mail, e-mail, fax, phone. Responds in 8 months to queries. Sample copy: $5 ($6 U.S. to Canada). Guidelines online.

NONFICTION Needs historical, how-to. Special issues: Iditarod (January/February); Skijor/Sprint/Peak of Season (March/April); Health and Nutrition (May/June); Meet the Mushers/Tour Business Directory (July/August); Equipment (September/October); Races and Places/Sled Dog Events Calendar (November/December). See website for current editorial calendar. Query with or without published clips. "We prefer detailed queries but also consider unsolicited mss. Please make proposals informative yet to the point. Spell out your qualifications for handling the topic. We like to see clips of previously published material but are eager to work with new and unpublished authors, too." Considers complete ms by postal mail (with SASE) or e-mail (as attachment or part of message). Also accepts disk submissions. Length: 1,000-2,500 words. **Pays $50-250.** Sometimes pays expenses of writers on assignment.

PHOTOS "We look for good-quality color for covers and specials." Send photos. Captions, identification of subjects. Reviews digital images only. Pays $20-165/photo.

COLUMNS/DEPARTMENTS Query with or without published clips or send complete ms. Length: 150-500 words.

FILLERS Needs anecdotes, facts, newsbreaks, short humor, cartoons, puzzles. Length: 100-250 words. **Pays $20-35.**

TIPS "Read our magazine. Know something about dog-driven, dog-powered sports."

POLO PLAYERS' EDITION

6008 Reynolds Rd., Lake Worth FL 33449. (561)968-5208. **Fax:** (561)968-5209. **E-mail:** gwen@poloplayersedition.com; info@poloplayersedition.com. **Website:** www.poloplayersedition.com. **Contact:** Gwen Rizzo, editor/publisher. Monthly magazine on the sport and lifestyle polo. "Our readers are affluent, well educated, well read, and highly sophisticated." Circ. 6,150. Pays on acceptance. Offers kill fee; varies. Publishes ms an average of 2 months after acceptance. Submit seasonal material 3 months in advance. Accepts queries by mail, e-mail. Accepts simultaneous submissions. Responds in 3 months to queries. Guidelines for #10 SAE with 2 stamps.

NONFICTION Needs historical, interview, personal experience, photo feature, technical, travel. Special issues: Annual Art Issue/Gift Buying Guide; Winter Preview/Florida Supplement. **Buys 20 mss/year.** Send complete ms. Length: 800-3,000 words. **Pays $150-400 for assigned articles. Pays $100-300 for unsolicited articles.** Sometimes pays expenses of writers on assignment.

REPRINTS Send tearsheet or typed ms with rights for sale noted and information about when and where the material previously appeared. Pays 50% of amount paid for an original article.

PHOTOS State availability of or send photos. Captions required. Reviews contact sheets, transparencies, prints. Offers $20-150/photo.

COLUMNS/DEPARTMENTS Yesteryears (historical pieces), 500 words; Profiles (clubs and players), 800-1,000 words. **Buys 15 mss/year.** Query with published clips. **Pays $100-300.**

TIPS "Query us on a personality or club profile or historic piece or, if you know the game, state availability to cover a tournament. Keep in mind that ours is a sophisticated, well-educated audience."

TRANSWORLD SKATEBOARDING

2052 Corte del Nogal, Suite 100, Carlsbad CA 92011. (760)722-7777. **E-mail:** lauren.machen@transworld.net. **Website:** www.skateboarding.transworld.net. **Contact:** Kevin Duffel, editor; Joey Shigeo-Mueliner, managing editor; Monica Campana, publisher; Oliver Barton, director of video and photo; Sam Muller, senior photographer. Monthly magazine for skateboarding enthusiasts. *TransWorld SKATEboarding* has been the largest, most progressive and most respected skateboarding magazine in the world for nearly 25 years. Delivering the most innovative photography and cutting-edge editorial content, it offers readers an inside look at skate culture through news, product reviews and in-depth profiles of the world's top skateboarders. It covers the American and global skateboard scenes from street and vert-ramp skating to international competition, and it features in-depth interviews with the top pros and up-and-coming riders. Designed to spread the culture of skateboarding in its purest form, the magazine provides bold, inside coverage of events, personalities, equipment and techniques. A market leader in skateboarding video production and events, *TransWorld SKATEboarding* founded the TransWorld SKATEboarding Awards, the first and largest professional skateboarding awards ceremony in the world, and has produced more than 25 feature films, by far the most within the skateboarding industry. Circ. 243,000. No kill fee. Editorial lead time 3 months.

Query before submitting.

MOTOR SPORTS

$ DIRT RIDER

Bonnier Corp., 15215 Alton Pkwy., Suite 100, Irvine CA 92618. (760)707-0100. **E-mail:** drmail@bonniercorp.com. **Website:** www.dirtrider.com. Monthly magazine devoted to the sport of off-road motorcycle riding that showcases the many ways enthusiasts can enjoy dirt bikes. Circ. 200,000. No kill fee.

NONFICTION Query before submitting.

$$ SAND SPORTS MAGAZINE

Wright Publishing Co., Inc., 3176 Pullman, Suite 107, Costa Mesa CA 92626. (714)979-2560, ext. 107. **E-mail:** info@sandsports.net. **Website:** www.sandsports.net. **Contact:** Michael Sommer, editor. **20% freelance written.** Bimonthly magazine covering vehicles for off-road and sand dunes. Estab. 1995. Circ. 35,000. Byline given. Pays on publication. Editorial lead time 3 months. Submit seasonal material 6 months in advance. Accepts queries by mail. Sample copy and writer's guidelines free.

NONFICTION Needs how-to, technical-mechanical, photo feature, technical. **Buys 20 mss/year.** Query. Length: 1,500 words minimum. **Pays $175/page.** Sometimes pays expenses of writers on assignment.

PHOTOS Send photos. Captions, identification of subjects, model releases required. Reviews color slides or high-res digital images. Negotiates payment individually.

RUNNING

$$$$ RUNNER'S WORLD

Rodale, 400 S. Tenth St., Emmaus PA 18098-0099. (610)967-8441. **Fax:** (610)967-8883. **E-mail:** rwedit@rodale.com. **Website:** www.runnersworld.com. **Contact:** David Willey, editor-in-chief; Suzanne Perrault, managing editor; Benjamen Purvis, design director. **5% freelance written.** Monthly magazine on running—mainly long-distance running. *Runner's World* is the magazine for and about distance running, training, health and fitness, nutrition, motivation, injury prevention, race coverage, and personalities of the sport. Estab. 1966. Circ. 500,000. Byline given. Pays on publication. No kill fee. Publishes ms an average of 6 months after acceptance. Submit seasonal material 6 months in advance. Accepts queries by mail. Responds in 2 months to queries. Guidelines available online.

NONFICTION Needs how-to, train, prevent injuries, interview, personal experience. No "my first marathon" stories. No poetry. **Buys 5-7 mss/year.** Query. **Pays $1,500-2,000.** Pays expenses of writers on assignment.

PHOTOS State availability. Identification of subjects required.

COLUMNS/DEPARTMENTS Finish Line (back-of-the-magazine essay, personal experience, humor). **Buys 24 mss/year.** Send complete ms. **Pays $300.**

TIPS "We are always looking for 'Adventure Runs' from readers—runs in wild, remote, beautiful, and interesting places. These are rarely race stories but more like backtracking/running adventures. Great color slides are crucial; 2,000 words maximum."

$$ RUNNING TIMES

Rodale, Inc., 400 S. 10th St., Emmaus PA 18098-0099. (610)967-5171. **Fax:** (610)967-8964. **E-mail:** editor@runningtimes.com. **Website:** www.runningtimes.com. **Contact:** Jonathan Beverly, editor-in-chief. **40% freelance written.** Magazine published 10 times/year covering distance running and racing. "*Running Times* is the national magazine for the experienced running participant and fan. Our audience is knowledgeable about the sport and active in running and racing. All editorial relates specifically to running: improving performance, enhancing enjoyment, or exploring events, places, and people in the sport." Estab. 1977. Circ. 125,000. Byline given. Pays on publication. No kill fee. Publishes ms an average of 3 months after acceptance. Editorial lead time 4-6 months. Submit seasonal material 6 months in advance. Accepts queries by mail, e-mail. Responds in 1 month to queries. Responds in 2 months to mss. Sample copy for $8. Guidelines available online.

NONFICTION Needs book excerpts, essays, historical, how-to, training, humor, inspirational, interview, new product, opinion, personal experience, with theme, purpose, evidence of additional research and/or special expertise, photo feature, news, reports. No basic, beginner how-to, generic fitness/nutrition, or generic first-person accounts. **Buys 35 mss/year.** Query. Length: 1,500-3,000 words. **Pays $600-2,500 for assigned articles. Pays $500-2,000 for unsolicited articles.** Sometimes pays expenses of writers on assignment.

PHOTOS State availability. Identification of subjects required. Negotiates payment individually.

COLUMNS/DEPARTMENTS Training (short topics related to enhancing performance), 1,000 words; Sports-Med (application of medical knowledge to running), 1,000 words; Nutrition (application of nutritional principles to running performance), 1,000 words. **Buys 10 mss/year.** Query. **Pays $200-400.**

FICTION Any genre, with running-related theme or characters. Buys 1 ms/year. Send complete ms. Length: 1,500-3,000 words. **Pays $100-500.**

TIPS "Thoroughly get to know runners and the running culture, both at the participant level and the professional, elite level."

SKIING AND SNOW SPORTS

$ SKATING

United States Figure Skating Association, 20 First St., Colorado Springs CO 80906. (719)635-5200. **Fax:** (719)635-9548. **E-mail:** info@usfigureskating.org. **Website:** www.usfsa.org. "*Skating* magazine is the official publication of U.S. Figure Skating, and thus we cover skating at both the championship and grass roots level." Published 10 times/year. Estab. 1923. Circ. 42,000. Byline given. Pays on publication. No kill fee. Publishes ms an average of 3 months after acceptance. Accepts queries by mail, e-mail, fax. Sample copy online.

NONFICTION Needs general interest, historical, how-to, interview, background and interests of skaters, volunteers, or other U.S. Figure Skating members, photo feature, technical and competition reports, figure skating issues and trends, sports medicine. **Buys 10 mss/year.** Query. Length: 500-2,500 words. **Payment varies.**

PHOTOS Photos purchased with or without accompanying ms. Query. Pays $10 for 8x10 or 5x7 b&w glossy prints, and $25 for color prints or transparencies.

COLUMNS/DEPARTMENTS Ice Breaker (news briefs); Foreign Competition Reports; Health and Fitness; In Synch (synchronized skating news); Takeoff (up-and-coming athletes), all 500-2,000 words.

TIPS "We want writing by experienced persons knowledgeable in the technical and artistic aspects of figure skating with a new outlook on the development of the sport. Knowledge and background in technical aspects of figure skating is helpful but not necessary to the quality of writing expected. We would like to see articles and short features on U.S. Figure Skating volunteers, skaters, and other U.S. Figure Skating members who normally wouldn't get recognized, as opposed to features on championship-level athletes, which are usually assigned to regular contributors. Good-quality color photos are a must with submissions. Also would be interested in seeing figure skating 'issues and trends' articles, instead of just profiles. No professional skater material. Synchronized skating and adult skating are the 2 fastest growing aspects of U.S. Figure Skating. We would like to see more stories dealing with these unique athletes."

$$$$ SKIING

Bonnier Corporation, 5720 Flatiron Pkwy., Boulder CO 80301. (303)253-6300. **E-mail:** editor@skiingmag.com. **Website:** www.skinet.com. **Contact:** Sam Bass, editor-in-chief. Magazine published 7 times/year for skiers who "deeply love winter, and who live for travel, adventure, instruction, gear, and news." *Skiing* is the user's guide to winter adventure. It is equal parts jaw-dropping inspiration and practical information, action and utility, attitude, and advice. It relates the lifestyles of dedicated skiers and captures their spirit of daring and exploration. Dramatic photography transports readers to spine-tingling mountains with breathtaking immediacy. Reading *Skiing* is almost as much fun as being there. Estab. 1948. Circ. 400,000. Byline given. Offers 40% kill fee. No

NONFICTION **Buys 10-15 (feature) and 12-24 (short) mss/year.** Query. Length: 1,500-2,000 words (feature); 100-500 words (short). **Pays $1,000-2,500/feature; $100-500/short piece.**

COLUMNS/DEPARTMENTS Length: 200-1,000 words. **Buys 2-3 mss/year.** Query. **Pays $150-1,000.**

TIPS "Consider less obvious subjects: smaller ski areas, specific local ski cultures, unknown aspects of popular resorts. Be expressive, not merely descriptive."

WATER SPORTS

$$ ROWING NEWS

The Independent Rowing News, Inc., Rivermill Suite 440, 85 Mechanic St., Lebanon NH 03766. (603)448-5090. **Website:** www.rowingnews.com. **Contact:** Ed Winchester, editor. **75% freelance written.** Monthly magazine covering rowing (the Olympic sport). "We write for a North American readership, serving the rowing community with features, how-to, and dispatches from the rowing world at large." Estab. 1994. Circ. 20,000. Byline given. Pays on publication. No kill fee. Publishes ms an average of 1-2 months after acceptance. Editorial lead time 1-12 months. Submit seasonal material 1-2 months in advance. Responds in 6 weeks to queries. Sample copy online.

NONFICTION Needs essays, how-to, rowing only, interview, new product, personal experience, rowing, travel. **Buys 12 mss/year.** Query with published clips. "Everything must be directedly related to rowing." Length: 1,500-5,000 words. Sometimes pays expenses of writers on assignment.

PHOTOS Reviews JPEG/TIFF. Negotiates payment individually.

TIPS "Make sure you are familiar with the magazine."

$ THE WATER SKIER

1251 Holy Cow Rd., Polk City FL 33868. (863)324-4341. **Fax:** (863)325-8259. **E-mail:** satkinson@usawaterski.org. **Website:** www.usawaterski.org. **Contact:** Scott Atkinson, editor. **10-20% freelance written.** Magazine published 6 times/year. *The Water Skier* is the membership magazine of USA Water Ski, the national governing body for organized water skiing in the United States. The magazine has a controlled circulation and is available only to USA Water Ski's membership, which is made up of 17,000 active competitive water skiers. The editorial content of the magazine features distinctive and informative writing about the sport of water skiing and wakeboarding. Estab. 1951. Circ. 20,000. Byline given. Editorial lead time 4 months. Submit seasonal material 6 months in advance. Responds in 2 weeks to queries. Sample copy for $3.50. Guidelines with #10 SASE.

NONFICTION Buys 10-15 mss/year. Query. Length: 1,500-3,000 words. **Pays $100-150.**

REPRINTS Send photocopy. Payment negotiable.

PHOTOS State availability. Captions, identification of subjects required. Reviews contact sheets. Negotiates payment individually.

COLUMNS/DEPARTMENTS The Water Skier News (small news items about people and events in the sport), 400-500 words. Other topics include safety, training (3-event, barefoot, disabled, show ski, ski race, kneeboard, and wakeboard); champions on their way; new products. Query. **Pays $50-100.**

TIPS "Contact the editor through a query letter (please, no phone calls) with an idea. Avoid instruction, these articles are written by professionals. Concentrate on articles about the people of the sport. We are always looking for interesting stories about people in the sport."

TEEN AND YOUNG ADULT

$$ CICADA MAGAZINE

Cricket Magazine Group, 70 E. Lake St., Suite 800, Chicago IL 60601. **E-mail:** cicada@cicadamag.com. **Website:** www.cricketmag.com/cicada. **Contact:** submissions editor. "*Cicada* is a YA lit/comics magazine fascinated with the lyric and strange and committed to work that speaks to teens' truths. We publish poetry, realistic and genre fiction, essay, and comics by adults and teens. (We are also inordinately fond of Viking jokes.) Our readers are smart and curious; submissions are invited but not required to engage young adult themes." Bimonthly literary magazine for ages 14 and up. Publishes 6 issues/year. Estab. 1998. Circ. 6,000. Pays after publication. Accepts simultaneous submissions. Responds in 3-6 months to mss. Guidelines available online at submittable.cricketmag.com or www.cricketmag.com/submissions.

NONFICTION Needs narrative nonfiction (especially teen-written), essays on literature, culture, and the arts. Prefers online submissions (submittable.cricketmag.com; www.cricketmag.com/submissions). Length: up to 5,000 words. **Pays up to 25¢/word.**

FICTION Needs realism, science fiction, fantasy, historical fiction. Wants everything from flash fiction to novellas. Length: up to 9,000 words. **Pays up to 25¢/word.**

POETRY Needs free verse, light verse, traditional. Reviews serious, humorous, free verse, rhyming. Length: up to 25 lines/poem. **Pays up to $3/line ($25 minimum).**

TIPS "Favorite writers, YA and otherwise: Bennett Madison, Sarah McCarry, Leopoldine Core, J. Hope Stein, José Olivarez, Sofia Samatar, Erica Lorraine Scheidt, David Levithan, Sherman Alexie, Hilary Smith, Nnedi Okorafor, Teju Cole, Anne Boyer, Mallory Ortberg. @cicadamagazine; cicadamagazine.tumblr.com."

FACES MAGAZINE

Cobblestone Publishing, Editorial Dept., 30 Grove St., Peterborough NH 03458. (603)924-7209. **E-mail:** ecarpentiere@caruspub.com. **Website:** www.cricketmag.com. **Contact:** Elizabeth Crooker, Carpentiere. *FACES Magazine*, published 9 times/year, features cultures from around the globe for children ages 9-14.

"Readers learn how other kids live around the world and about the important inventions and ideas that a particular culture has given to the world. All material must relate to the theme of a specific upcoming issue in order to be considered." Wants "clear, objective imagery. Serious and light verse considered. Must relate to theme." Responds to queries in "several months." Does not respond for unused queries. Sample copy: $6.95, plus $2 s&h.

Publishes theme issues; visit website for details.

NONFICTION Needs features, supplemental, activities, puzzles and games. Special issues: Wants feature articles ("in-depth nonfiction highlighting an aspect of the featured culture, interviews, and personal accounts"); supplemental nonfiction ("subjects directly or indirectly related to the theme; editors like little-known information but encourage writers not to overlook the obvious"); activities ("crafts, games, recipes, projects, etc., which children can do either alone or with adult supervision; should be accompanied by sketches and description of how activity relates to theme."); puzzles and games ("word puzzles [but not crossword puzzles] using the vocabulary of the edition's theme; mazes and picture puzzles that relate to the theme"). Query with cover letter stating subject and word length of proposed article. Provide detailed one-page outline explaining information to be presented and bibliography of materials intended for use in preparing the article (if appropriate). Length: up to 800 words for feature articles; 300-600 for supplemental nonfiction.

PHOTOS *FACES Magazine*, published 9 times/year, features cultures from around the globe for children ages 9-14. "Readers learn how other kids live around the world and about the important inventions and ideas that a particular culture has given to the world. All material must relate to the theme of a specific upcoming issue in order to be considered." Wants "clear, objective imagery. Serious and light verse considered. Must relate to theme." Pays $15-100 for b&w, $25-100 for color. Cover fees are set on an individual basis.

FICTION Query with cover letter stating subject and word length of proposed article. Provide detailed one-page outline explaining information to be presented and bibliography of materials intended for use in preparing the article (if appropriate). Wants "retold legends, folktales, stories, and original plays from around the world, etc., relating to the theme." Length: up to 800 words.

INSIGHT

Pacific Press Publishing Association, P.O. Box 5353, Nampa ID 83653. (208)465-2579. **E-mail:** insight@rhpa.org. **E-mail:** insight@pacificpress.com. **Website:** www.insightmagazine.org. **80% freelance written.** Weekly 16-page magazine covering spiritual life of teenagers. *Insight* publishes true dramatic stories, interviews, and community and mission service features that relate directly to the lives of Christian teenagers, particularly those with a Seventh-day Adventist background. Estab. 1970. Circ. 8,000. Byline given. Pays on publication. No kill fee. Publishes ms an average of 4 months after acceptance. Editorial lead time 6 months. Submit seasonal material 6 months in advance. Accepts queries by mail, e-mail, fax. Responds in 1 month to mss. Sample copy for $2 and #10 SASE. Guidelines available online.

NONFICTION Needs how-to, teen relationships and experiences, humor, interview, personal experience, photo feature, religious. **Buys 120 mss/year.** Send complete ms. Articles should address topics of interest to today's teenagers from a Christian perspective. An article should begin with a story or several anecdotes to introduce the topic. The story or anecdotes should be true and involve teenagers. Length: 500-1,000 words. **Pays $25-150 for assigned articles. Pays $25-125 for unsolicited articles.**

REPRINTS Send typed ms with rights for sale noted and information about when and where the material previously appeared. Pays $50.

PHOTOS State availability. Model releases required. Reviews contact sheets, negatives, transparencies, prints. Negotiates payment individually.

COLUMNS/DEPARTMENTS Columns: Big Deal (topic of importance to teens) 800-1,000 words; Interviews (Christian culture figures, especially musicians), 1,000 words; It Happened to Me (first-person teen experiences containing spiritual insights), 1,000 words; On the Edge (dramatic true stories about Christians), 800-1,000 words; So I Said...(true short stories in the first person of common, everyday events and experiences that taught the writer something), 300-500 words. Send complete ms. **Pays $25-125.**

TIPS "Skim 2 months of *Insight.* Write about your teen experiences. Use informed, contemporary style and vocabulary. Follow Jesus' life and example."

SEVENTEEN MAGAZINE

300 W. 57th St., 17th Floor, New York NY 10019. (917)934-6500. **Fax:** (917)934-6574. **E-mail:** mail@seventeen.com. **Website:** www.seventeen.com. **Contact:** Consult masthead to contact appropriate editor. Monthly magazine covering topics geared toward young adult American women. "We reach 14.5 million girls each month. Over the past 6 decades, *Seventeen* has helped shape teenage life in America. We represent an important rite of passage, helping to define, socialize, and empower young women. We create notions of beauty and style, proclaim what's hot in popular culture, and identify social issues." Estab. 1944. Circ. 2,000,000. Byline sometimes given. Pays on publication. Accepts queries by mail. Writer's guidelines for SASE.

Seventeen no longer accepts fiction submissions.

NONFICTION Needs young adults: careers, cooking, hobbies, how-to, humorous, interview/profile, multicultural, social issues. **Buys 7-12 mss/year.** Query by mail. Consult masthead to pitch appropriate editor. Length: 200-2,000 words.

TIPS "Send for guidelines before submitting."

TEEN VOGUE

Condè Nast Publications, 4 Times Square, 10th Floor, New York NY 10036. (212)286-2860. **Fax:** (212)286-2378. **Website:** www.teenvogue.com. Magazine published 10 times/year. Written for sophisticated teenage girls age 12-17 years old. Circ. 450,000. No kill fee. Editorial lead time 2 months.

Query before submitting.

YOUNG SALVATIONIST

The Salvation Army, P.O. Box 269, Alexandria VA 22313-0269. (703)684-5500. **Fax:** (703)684-5539. **E-mail:** ys@usn.salvationarmy.org. **Website:** www.youngsalvationist.org. **Contact:** Captain Pamela Maynor, editor. **10% freelance written.** Monthly magazine for teens and early college youth. "*Young Salvationist* provides young people with biblically based inspiration and resources to develop their spirituality within the context of the Salvation Army." Circ. 40,000. Byline given. Pays on publication. No kill fee. Publishes ms an average of 6 months after acceptance. Submit seasonal material 6 months in advance. Responds in 2 months to mss. Sample copy and theme list free with #10 SASE or online.

"Works with a small number of new/unpublished writers each year."

NONFICTION Needs how-to, humor, inspirational, interview, personal experience, photo feature, religious. **Buys 10 mss/year.** Send complete ms through website at publications.salvationarmyusa.org/writers-submissions. Length: 700-900 words. **Pays 25¢/word.**

REPRINTS Considers reprints.

TIPS "Study magazine, familiarize yourself with the unique 'Salvationist' perspective of *Young Salvationist*; learn a little about the Salvation Army; media, sports, sex, and dating are strongest appeal."

TRAVEL, CAMPING AND TRAILER

AAA GOING PLACES

AAA Auto Club South, 1515 N. Westshore Blvd., Tampa FL 33607. (813)289-5923. **Fax:** (813)288-7935. **Website:** www.aaagoingplaces.com. **50% freelance written.** Bimonthly magazine on auto tips, cruise travel, tours. Estab. 1982. Circ. 2,500,000. Byline given. Pays on publication. No kill fee. Publishes ms an average of 6 months after acceptance. Submit seasonal material 9 months in advance. Accepts simultaneous submissions. Responds in 2 months to mss. Writer's guidelines for SAE.

NONFICTION Needs historical, how-to, humor, interview, personal experience, photo feature, travel. **Buys 15 mss/year.** Send complete ms. Length: 500-1,200 words. **Pays $50/printed page.**

PHOTOS State availability. Captions required. Reviews 2â—Š2 transparencies, 300 dpi digital images. Offers no additional payment for photos accepted with ms.

COLUMNS/DEPARTMENTS What's Happening (local attractions in Florida, Georgia, or Tennessee).

TIPS We prefer lively, upbeat stories that appeal to a well-traveled, sophisticated audience, bearing in mind that AAA is a conservative company.

AAA MIDWEST TRAVELER

AAA Auto Club of Missouri, 12901 N. 40 Dr., St. Louis MO 63141. (314)523-7350, ext. 6301. **Fax:** (314)523-6982. **E-mail:** dreinhardt@aaamissouri.com. **Website:** www.aaa.com/traveler. **Contact:** Deborah Reinhardt, managing editor. **80% freelance written.** Bimonthly magazine covering travel and automotive safety. "We provide members with useful information on travel, auto safety and related topics." Estab. 1901. Circ. 500,000. Byline given. Pays on acceptance. Offers $50 kill fee. Editorial lead time 1 year. Submit seasonal material 6 months in advance. Accepts queries by mail, e-mail, fax. Accepts simultaneous submissions. Responds in 1 month to queries. Responds in 1 month to mss. Sample copy with 10x13 SASE and 4 First-Class stamps. Guidelines with #10 SASE.

NONFICTION Needs travel. No humor, fiction, poetry or cartoons. **Buys 20-30 mss/year.** Query; query with published clips the first time. Length: 800-1,200 words. **Pays $400.**

PHOTOS State availability. Captions required. Reviews transparencies, prints. Offers no additional payment for photos accepted with ms.

TIPS "Send queries between December and February, as we plan our calendar for the following year. Request a copy. Serious writers ask for media kit to help them target their piece. Send a SASE or download online. Travel destinations and tips are most open to freelancers; all departments and auto-related news handled by staff. We see too many `Here's a recount of our family vacation' manuscripts. Go easy on first-person accounts."

BACKROADS

P.O. Box 317, Branchville NJ 07826. (973)948-4176. **Fax:** (973)948-0823. **E-mail:** editor@backroadsusa.com. **Website:** www.backroadsusa.com. **50% freelance written.** Monthly tabloid covering motorcycle touring. "*Backroads* is a motorcycle tour magazine geared toward getting motorcyclists on the road and traveling. We provide interesting destinations, unique roadside attractions and eateries, plus Rip & Ride Route Sheets. We cater to all brands. Although *Backroads* is geared towards the motorcycling population, it is not by any means limited to just motorcycle riders. Non-motorcyclists enjoy great destinations, too. As time has gone by, *Backroads* has developed more and more into a cutting-edge touring publication. We like to see submissions that give the reader the distinct impression of being part of the ride they're reading. Words describing the feelings and emotions brought on by partaking in this great and exciting lifestyle are encouraged." Estab. 1995. Circ. 50,000. Byline given. Pays 1 month after publication. Editorial lead time 1 month. Submit seasonal material 3 months in advance. Accepts queries by mail, e-mail. Responds in 1 month. Sample copy: $4. Guidelines available online at website.

NONFICTION "What *Backroads* does not want is any 'us vs. them' submissions. We are decidedly non-political and secular. *Backroads* is about getting out and riding, not getting down on any particular group, nor do we feel this paper should be a pulpit for a writer's beliefs ... be they religious, political, or personal." Query. Needs travel features: "This type of story offers a good opportunity for prospective contributors. They MUST feature spectacular photography, color preferably, and may be used as a cover story, if of acceptable quality. **All submissions must be accompanied by images**, with an SASE of adequate size (10x13) to return all material sent, as well as a copy of the issue in which they were published, and a hard copy printout of the article, including your name, address, and phone number. If none is enclosed, the materials will not be returned. Text submissions are accepted via U.S. mail or e-mail. We can usually convert most file types, although it is easier to submit in plain text format, sometimes called ASCII." **Pays $75 and up; varies.**

PHOTOS Digital photos may be sent via U.S. mail on CD or via e-mail if they are in a stuffed file. All images must be no smaller then 300 dpi and at least 4x6. If you are sending images at 72 dpi, they MUST BE NO SMALLER THAN 20x30 FOR PROPER RESIZING. We do not accept photographs, slides, or negatives. Send photos. Offers no additional payment for photos accepted with ms.

COLUMNS/DEPARTMENTS We're Outta Here (weekend destinations), 500-750 words; Great All-American Diner Run (good eateries with great location), 500-750 words; Thoughts from the Road (personal opinion/insights), 400-600 words; Mysterious America (unique and obscure sights), 500-750 words; Big City Getaway (day trips), 500-750 words. **Buys 20-24 mss/year.** Query. **Pays $75/article.**

$ CAMPING TODAY

Family Campers and RVers, 4804 Transit Rd., Bldg. 2, Depew NY 14043. (716)668-6242; (800)245-9755. **E-mail:** d_johnston01@msn.com. **Website:** www.fcrv.org/news/camping-today. **Contact:** DeWayne Johnston, editor. *Camping Today* is the member magazine for Family Campers & RVers, a nonprofit camping and RV organization with over 4,000 families in the U.S. and Canada. Many of the members are retired.

Some take grandchildren camping. Working families with kids travel and camp when time permits. FCRV has local clubs or chapters in almost every state and province. Seventy percent of the magazine's content is member activities, including promotion for FCRV's 2 biggest annual events, the National Campvention (rally) in July, which moves to a different location each year, and the Retiree Rally in March in the sun belt. Estab. 1983. Byline given. Pays on publication. Submit seasonal material 3 months in advance. Accepts simultaneous submissions. Responds in 2 months. Sample copy for 3 first-class stamps. E-mail editor for guidelines.

"We can only use about 12 freelance articles/year on interesting places for RVers to visit, camping-related humor, tips for campers, etc. Monthly maintenance column is already in place."

NONFICTION Needs humor, camping or travel related, interview, interesting campers, new product, technical, RVs related, travel, interesting places to visit by RV, camping. Query by mail or e-mail or send complete ms with photos. E-mail photos separate from text, or mail copy and prints with SASE. Length: 700-2,000 words. **Pays $50-150.**

REPRINTS Send typed ms with rights for sale noted and information about when and where the material previously appeared. Pays 35-50% of amount paid for original article.

PHOTOS Needs b&w or sharp color prints. Send photos. Captions required.

TIPS "Freelance material on RV travel, RV maintenance/safety, and items of general camping interest throughout the U.S. and Canada will receive special attention. Good photos increase your chances. See website."

ESCAPEES

Sharing the RV Lifestyle, Roving Press, 100 Rainbow Dr., Livingston TX 77351. (888)757-2582. **Fax:** (409)327-4388. **E-mail:** editor@escapees.com. **Website:** escapees.com. **Contact:** Megan Swander, editorial assistant. *Escapees* magazine's contributors are RVers interested in sharing the RV lifestyle. Audience includes full-time RVers, snowbirds, and those looking forward to traveling extensively. *Escapees* members have varying levels of experience; therefore, the magazine looks for a wide variety of material, beyond what is found in conventional RV magazines, and welcomes submissions on all phases of RV life, especially relevant mechanical/technical information. About 85% of the club members are retired, over 98% travel without children, and about 50% live in their motorhomes, fifth-wheels, or travel trailers on a full-time basis. A bimonthly magazine that provides a total support network to RVers and shares the RV lifestyle. Estab. 1979. Circ. 25,000. Byline given. Pays on publication. Publishes ms an average of 3-6 months after acceptance. Editorial lead time 3 months. Submit season material 6 months in advance. Accepts simultaneous submissions. Responds in 2 weeks to queries; in 3 months to ms. Sample copy available for free online. Guidelines available online and by e-mail at departmentseditor@escapees.com. Editor does not accept articles based on queries alone. Decisions for use of material are based on the full article with any accompanying photos, graphics, or diagrams. Only complete articles will be considered.

NONFICTION Needs general interest, historical, how-to, humor, inspirational, interview, nostalgic, personal experience, photo feature, profile, technical, travel. Do not send anything religious, political, or unrelated to RVs. Submit complete ms. When submitting an article via email as an attachment, please include the text in the body of the email. Length: 300-1,400 words. Please include word count on first page of article. **Pays $50-150 for unsolicited articles.** Publication sometimes "pays" writers with contributor copies rather than a cash payment, often in exchange for company bio/company product-themed photos.

PHOTOS **Contact:** Cole Carter, graphic artist. Freelancers should send photos with submissions. Captions, model releases, and identification of subjects all required. Reviews GIF/JPEG files. Negotiates payment individually.

COLUMNS/DEPARTMENTS **Contact:** Megan Swander, editorial assistant. SKP Stops (short blurbs with photos on unique travel destination stops for RVers), 300-500 words. **Buys 10-15 mss/year.** Submit complete ms. **Pays $25-75 for columns.**

TIPS "Use an engaging, conversational tone. Well-placed humor is refreshing. Eliminate any fluff and verbosity. Avoid colloquialisms."

FAMILY MOTOR COACHING

8291 Clough Pike, Cincinnati OH 45244. (513)474-3622; (800)543-3622. **Fax:** (513)388-5286. **E-mail:** rgould@fmca.com; magazine@fmca.com. **Website:**

www.fmca.com. **Contact:** Robbin Gould, editor. **80% freelance written. We prefer that writers be experienced RVers.** Monthly magazine emphasizing travel by motorhome, motorhome mechanics, maintenance, and other technical information. "*Family Motor Coaching* magazine is edited for the members and prospective members of the Family Motor Coach Association who own or are about to purchase self-contained, motorized recreational vehicles known as motorhomes. Featured are articles on travel and recreation, association news and activities, plus articles on new products and motorhome maintenance and repair. Approximately 1/3 of editorial content is devoted to travel and entertainment, 1/3 to association news, and 1/3 to new products, industry news, and motorhome maintenance." Estab. 1963. Circ. 140,000. Byline given. Pays on acceptance. Publishes ms an average of 8 months after acceptance. Submit seasonal material 4 months in advance. Accepts queries by mail, e-mail, fax. Responds in 3 months to queries. Sample copy for $3.99; $5 if paying by credit card. Guidelines with #10 SASE or request PDF by e-mail.

NONFICTION Needs how-to, do-it-yourself motorhome projects and modifications, humor, interview, new product, technical, motorhome travel (various areas of North America accessible by motorhome), bus conversions, nostalgia. **Buys 50-75 mss/year.** Query with published clips. Length: 1,000-2,000 words. **Pays $100-500, depending on article category.**

PHOTOS State availability. Captions, model releases, True required. Offers no additional payment for b&w contact sheets, 35mm 21/4x21/4 color transparencies, or high-res electronic images (300 dpi and at least 4x6 in size).

TIPS "The greatest number of contributions we receive are travel; therefore, that area is the most competitive. However, it also represents the easiest way to break into our publication. Articles should be written for those traveling by self-contained motorhome. The destinations must be accessible to motorhome travelers and any peculiar road conditions should be mentioned."

$$ HIGHROADS

AAA Arizona, 2375 E. Camelback Rd., Suite 500, Phoenix AZ 85016. (602)650-2732. **Fax:** (602)241-2917. **E-mail:** highroads@arizona.aaa.com. **Website:** www.aaa.com. **50% freelance written.** *Highroads*, the AAA Arizona member magazine, offers inspiring travel articles about destinations throughout Arizona and around the world, automotive news and reviews, and educational resources on insurance and finance. The print edition is published bimonthly, and has been honored for writing and design with Communicator Awards, Davey Awards, and Maggie Awards. Byline given. Pays on publication. Offers 30% kill fee. Editorial lead time 6 months. Submit seasonal material 6 months in advance. Accepts queries by mail, e-mail, fax. Accepts simultaneous submissions. Sample copy for #10 SASE. Guidelines by e-mail and online.

NONFICTION Needs travel, auto-related. Does not want articles unrelated to travel, automotive, or Arizona living. **Buys 21 mss/year.** Query with published clips. Length: 1,600 words for features. **Pays $0.35/word for assigned articles; $0.35/word for unsolicited articles.**

PHOTOS Identification of subjects required. Offers $75-500 per photo.

COLUMNS/DEPARTMENTS As with most publications, the best place to start for new writers is in departments, which include the travel sections "Weekender," 400 words about a short getaway you can travel to from Arizona; "Road Trip," 800 words with driving directions about attractions along a specific stretch of road reachable from Arizona; and "Talk of the Town," 400 words about an Arizona town with a unique hidden attraction. **Buys 10 mss/year. Pays $0-35.**

$$ HIGHWAYS

Affinity Group, Inc., 2575 Vista Del Mar Dr., Ventura CA 93001. (805)667-4100. **E-mail:** highways@goodsamclub.com. **Website:** www.goodsamclub.com/highways. Monthly magazine covering recreational vehicle lifestyle. "All of our readers own some type of RV—a motorhome, trailer, pop-up, tent—so our stories need to include places that you can go with large vehicles, and campgrounds in and around the area where they can spend the night." Estab. 1966. Circ. 975,000. Byline given. Pays on acceptance. Offers 50% kill fee. Publishes ms an average of 6 months after acceptance. Accepts queries by e-mail. Responds in 2 weeks to queries. Sample copy and writer's guidelines free or online.

NONFICTION Needs how-to, repair/replace something on an RV, humor, technical, travel, all RV related. **Buys 15-20 mss/year.** Query. Length: 800-1,100 words.

PHOTOS Do not send or e-mail unless approved by staff. No answer.

COLUMNS/DEPARTMENTS On the Road (issue related); RV Insight (for people new to the RV lifestyle); Action Line (consumer help); Tech Topics (tech Q&A); Camp Cuisine (cooking in an RV); Product Previews (new products). No plans on adding new columns/departments.

TIPS "Know something about RVing. People who drive motorhomes or pull trailers have unique needs that have to be incorporated into our stories. We're looking for well-written, first-person stories that convey the fun of this lifestyle and way to travel."

INNS MAGAZINE

Harworth Publishing Inc., 521 Woolwich St., Guelph ON N1H 3X9 Canada. (519)767-6059. **Fax:** (519)821-0479. **E-mail:** info@harworthpublishing.com. **Website:** www.innsmagazine.com. **Contact:** Mary Hughes, editor. *Inns* is a national publication for travel, dining, and pastimes. It focuses on inns, beds and breakfasts, resorts, and travel in North America. The magazine is targeted to travelers looking for exquisite getaways. Accepts queries by e-mail. Guidelines by e-mail.

NONFICTION Needs general interest, interview, new product, opinion, personal experience, travel. Query. Length: 300-600 words. **Pays $175-250 (Canadian).**

FILLERS Short quips or nominations at 75 words are $25 each. All stories submitted have to accompany photos. E-mail photos to designer@harworthpublishing.com.

ISLANDS

Bonnier Corp., 460 N. Orlando Ave., Suite 200, Winter Park FL 32789. (407)628-4802. **E-mail:** editor@islands.com. **Website:** www.islands.com. **80% freelance written.** Magazine published 8 times/year. "We cover accessible and once-in-a-lifetime islands from many different perspectives: travel, culture, lifestyle. We ask our authors to give us the essence of the island and do it with literary flair." Estab. 1981. Circ. 250,000. Byline given. Pays on publication. Offers 25% kill fee. Publishes ms an average of 8 months after acceptance. Accepts queries by e-mail. Responds in 2 months to queries. Responds in 6 weeks to mss. Sample copy for $6. "E-mail us for writer's guidelines."

NONFICTION Needs book excerpts, essays, general interest, interview, photo feature, travel, service shorts, island-related material. **Buys 25 feature mss/year.** Send complete ms. Length: 2,000-4,000 words. **Pays $750-2,500.** Sometimes pays expenses of writers on assignment.

PHOTOS "Fine color photography is a special attraction of *Islands*, and we look for superb composition, technical quality, and editorial applicability. Will not accept or be responsible for unsolicited images or artwork."

COLUMNS/DEPARTMENTS Discovers section (island related news), 100-250 words; Taste (island cuisine), 900-1,000 words; Travel Tales (personal essay), 900-1,100 words; Live the Life (island expat Q&A). Query with published clips. **Pays $25-1,000.**

JOURNEY MAGAZINE

AAA, 1745 114th Ave., SE, Bellevue WA 98004. (800)562-2582. **E-mail:** sueboylan@aaawin.com; robbhatt@aaawin.com. **Website:** www.aaajourney.com/magazine. **Contact:** Rob Bhatt, editor. Bimonthly magazine. "For members of AAA Washington; reaches readers in Washington and northern Idaho. Our goal is to present readers with lively and informative stories on lifestyle, travel, and automotive topics that encourage them to discover and explore the Northwest and beyond." Circ. 550,000. Pays on acceptance. Responds within 3 months with SASE.

NONFICTION "We assign stories based on writers' proposals and rarely accept completed manuscripts. We look for writers who combine sound research and reporting skills with a strong voice and excellent storytelling ability. We adhere to AP style. A solid knowledge of the Pacific Northwest is also required. We create our editorial calendar in the spring for the following calendar year. We encourage you to read several issues of *Journey* to familiarize yourself with our publication before you submit article ideas. Some stories run alternatively in our Western and Puget Sound editions and may also be published on the website. We run all articles with high-quality photographs and illustrations. If you are a published photographer, let us know but please do not submit any photos unless requested. To be considered for an assignment, mail a query along with 3 samples of published work." Length: 500-1,800 words. **Pays up to $1/word.**

RECREATION NEWS

Official Publication of the RecGov.org, 1607 Sailaway Circle, Baltimore MD 21221. (410)638-6901. **Fax:** (410)638-6902. **E-mail:** editor@recreationnews.com. **Website:** www.recreationnews.com. **Contact:** Marvin Bond, editor. **75% freelance written.** Monthly guide to leisure-time activities for federal and private industry workers covering Mid-Atlantic travel destinations, outdoor recreation, and cultural activities. Estab. 1982. Circ. 115,000. Byline given. Pays on publication. No kill fee. Publishes ms an average of 6 months after acceptance. Submit seasonal material 10 months in advance. Accepts queries by mail, e-mail, phone. Accepts simultaneous submissions. Responds in 2 months to queries. See sample copy and writer's guidelines online.

NONFICTION Needs Mid-Atlantic travel destinations, outdoor recreation. Query with published clips or links. Length: 600-1,000 words. **Pays $50-300.**

REPRINTS Send tearsheet or typed ms with rights for sale noted and information about when and where the material previously appeared. Pays $50.

TIPS "Our articles are lively and conversational and deal with specific travel destinations in the Mid-Atlantic. We do not buy international or Caribbean stories. Outdoor recreation of all kinds is good, but avoid first-person narrative. Stories need to include info on nearby places of interest, places to eat, and places to stay. Keep contact information in separate box at end of story."

TIMES OF THE ISLANDS

Times Publications, Ltd., P.O. Box 234, Lucille Lightbourne Bldg., #7, Providenciales Turks & Caicos Islands British West Indies. (649)946-4788. **Fax:** (649)946-4788. **E-mail:** timespub@tciway.tc. **Website:** www.timespub.tc. **60% freelance written.** Quarterly magazine covering the Turks & Caicos Islands. "*Times of the Islands* is used by the public and private sector to inform visitors and potential investors/developers about the Islands. It goes beyond a superficial overview of tourist attractions with in-depth articles about natural history, island heritage, local personalities, new development, offshore finance, sporting activities, visitors' experiences, and Caribbean fiction." Estab. 1988. Circ. 10,000. Byline given. Pays on publication. No kill fee. Publishes ms an average of 6 months after acceptance. Editorial lead time 4 months. Submit seasonal material at least 4 months in advance. Accepts queries by e-mail. Accepts simultaneous submissions. Responds in 6 weeks to queries. Responds in 2 months to mss. Sample copy for $6. Guidelines available online.

NONFICTION Needs book excerpts, essays, general interest, Caribbean art, culture, cooking, crafts, historical, humor, interview, locals, personal experience, trips to the Islands, photo feature, technical, island businesses, travel, book reviews, nature, ecology, business (offshore finance), watersports. **Buys 20 mss/year.** Query. Length: 500-3,000 words. **Pays $150-500.**

REPRINTS Send photocopy and information about when and where the material previously appeared. Payment varies

PHOTOS Send photos. Identification of subjects required. Reviews digital photos. Pays $15-150/photo.

COLUMNS/DEPARTMENTS On Holiday (unique experiences of visitors to Turks & Caicos), 500-1,500 words. **Buys 4 mss/year. mss/year.** Query. **Pays $150.**

FICTION Needs adventure, sailing, diving, ethnic, Caribbean, historical, Caribbean, humorous, travel-related, mystery, novel concepts. **Buys 2-3 mss/year.** Query. Length: 1,000-3,000 words. **Pays $250-400.**

TIPS "Make sure that the query/article specifically relates to the Turks and Caicos Islands. The theme can be general (ecotourism, for instance), but the manuscript should contain specific and current references to the Islands. We're a high-quality magazine, with a small budget and staff, and are very open-minded to ideas (and manuscripts). Writers who have visited the Islands at least once would probably have a better perspective from which to write."

TRAILER LIFE

GS Media & Events, 2750 Park View Ct, Suite 240, Oxnard CA 93036. **Fax:** (805)667-4484. **E-mail:** info@trailerlife.com. **Website:** www.trailerlife.com. **Contact:** Tom Kaiser, managing editor. **40% freelance written.** Monthly magazine covering RV traveling. "*Trailer Life* magazine is written specifically for active people whose overall lifestyle is based on travel and recreation in their RV. Every issue includes product tests, travel articles, and other features—ranging from lifestyle to vehicle maintenance." Estab. 1941. Circ. 270,000. Byline given. Pays on acceptance. Offers kill fee. Offers 30% kill fee for assigned articles that are not acceptable. Publishes ms an average of 6 months after acceptance. Editorial lead time 4 months. Submit seasonal material 6 months in advance. Accepts queries by mail. Responds in 2 months to queries. Responds in 2 months to mss. Sample copy free. Guidelines available online.

NONFICTION Needs historical, how-to, technical, humor, new product, opinion, personal experience, travel. "No vehicle tests, product evaluations or road tests; tech material is strictly assigned. No diaries or trip logs, no non-RV trips; nothing without an RV-hook." **Buys 75 mss/year.** Query. Length: Travel Features: 1,500-1,800 words; Personality Profiles: 1,200 words; Technical Features: 1,000-2,000 words; Do-It-Yourself Features: 1,200 words. **Pays $100-700.** Sometimes pays expenses of writers on assignment.

PHOTOS Send photos. Identification of subjects, model releases required. Reviews transparencies, b&w contact sheets . Offers no additional payment for photos accepted with ms, does pay for supplemental photos.

COLUMNS/DEPARTMENTS Around the Bend (news, trends of interest to RVers), 75-100 words; "10-Minute Tech" (50-200 words). **Buys 70 mss/year.** Query or send complete ms **Pays $75-250.**

TIPS "Prerequisite: Must have RV focus, and photos must be magazine quality. These are the 2 biggest reasons why mss are rejected. Our readers are travel enthusiasts who own all types of RVs (travel trailers, truck campers, van conversions, motorhomes, tent trailers, fifth-wheels) in which they explore North America and beyond, embrace the great outdoors in national, state and private parks. They're very active and very adventurous."

$ TRAVEL NATURALLY

Internaturally, Inc., P.O. Box 317, Newfoundland NJ 07435-0317. (973)697-3552. **Fax:** (973)697-8313. **E-mail:** naturally@internaturally.com. **Website:** www.internaturally.com. **90% freelance written.** Quarterly magazine covering wholesome family nude recreation and travel locations. "*Travel Naturally* looks at why millions of people believe that removing clothes in public is a good idea, and at places specifically created for that purpose—with good humor, but also in earnest. *Travel Naturally* takes you to places where your personal freedom is the only agenda and to places where textile-free living is a serious commitment." Estab. 1981. Circ. 35,000. Byline given. Pays on publication. No kill fee. Editorial lead time 4 months. Submit seasonal material 4 months in advance. Accepts queries by mail, e-mail, fax. Accepts simultaneous submissions. Sample copy: $9.95 (back issue).

Travel Naturally is 72 pages, magazine-sized, printed on glossy paper, saddle-stapled.

NONFICTION Needs general interest, interview, personal experience, photo feature, travel. **Buys 12 mss/year.** Send complete ms. Length: 2 pages. **Pays $80/published page, including photos.**

REPRINTS Pays 50% of original rate.

PHOTOS Send photos. Reviews contact sheets, negatives, transparencies, prints, high-resolution digital images.

POETRY Wants poetry about the naturalness of the human body and nature; any length. Considers previously published poems and simultaneous submissions. Accepts e-mail and fax submissions. "Name and address must be submitted with e-mail."

FILLERS Needs anecdotes, facts, gags, newsbreaks, short humor, poems, artwork. **Payment is pro-rated based on length.**

TIPS "*Travel Naturally* invokes the philosophies of naturism and nudism, but also activities and beliefs in the mainstream that express themselves, barely: spiritual awareness, New Age customs, pagan and religious rites, alternative and fringe-lifestyle beliefs, artistic expressions, and many individual nude interests. Our higher purpose is simply to help restore our sense of self. Although the term 'nude recreation' may, for some, conjure up visions of sexual frivolities inappropriate for youngsters—because that can also be technically true—these topics are outside the scope of *Travel Naturally*. Here the emphasis is on the many varieties of human beings, of all ages and backgrounds, recreating in their most natural state, at extraordinary places, their reasons for doing so, and the benefits they derive. We incorporate a travel department to advise and book vacations in locations reviewed in travel articles."

WOMEN'S

ALLURE

Conde Nast Publications, 4 Times Square, 10th Floor, New York NY 10036. (212)286-2860. **Fax:** (212)286-4654. **Website:** www.allure.com. **Contact:** Linda Wells, editor in chief. Monthly magazine covering fashion, beauty, fitness, etc. Geared toward the professional, modern woman, *Allure* offers the most comprehensive understanding of trends, science, and service information, as well as the most valued product recommendations in the field. Circ. 1,139,932.

Query before submitting.

$$$ BRIDAL GUIDE

RFP, LLC, 228 E. 45th St., 11th Floor, New York NY 10017. (212)838-7733; (800)472-7744. **Fax:** (212)308-

7165. **E-mail:** editorial@bridalguide.com. **Website:** www.bridalguide.com. **20% freelance written.** Bimonthly magazine covering relationships, sexuality, fitness, wedding planning, psychology, finance, and travel. Only works with experienced/published writers. Pays on acceptance. No kill fee. Accepts queries by mail. Responds in 3 months to queries and mss. Sample copy for $5 and SAE with 4 first-class stamps. Guidelines available.

NONFICTION "Please do not send queries concerning beauty, fashion, or home design stories since we produce them in-house. We do not accept personal wedding essays, fiction, or poetry. Address travel queries to travel editor. All correspondence accompanied by an SASE will be answered." **Buys 100 mss/year.** Query with published clips from national consumer magazines. Length: 1,000-2,000 words. **Pays 50¢/word.**

PHOTOS Photography and illustration submissions should be sent to the art department.

TIPS "We are looking for service-oriented, well-researched pieces that are journalistically written. Writers we work with use at least 3 top expert sources, such as physicians, book authors, and business people in the appropriate field. Our tone is conversational, yet authoritative. Features are also generally filled with real-life anecdotes. We also do features that are completely real-person based—such as roundtables of bridesmaids discussing their experiences, or grooms-to-be talking about their feelings about getting married. In queries, we are looking for a well-thought-out idea, the specific angle of focus the writer intends to take, and the sources he or she intends to use. Queries should be brief and snappy—and titles should be supplied to give the editor an even better idea of the direction the writer is going in."

CHATELAINE

One Mount Pleasant Rd., 8th Floor, Toronto ON M4Y 2Y5 Canada. (416)764-2000. **Fax:** (416)764-1888. **E-mail:** storyideas@chatelaine.rogers.com. **Website:** www.chatelaine.com. Monthly magazine covering Canadian women's lifestyles. "*Chatelaine* is edited for Canadian women ages 25-49, their changing attitudes and lifestyles. Key editorial ingredients include health, finance, social issues, and trends, as well as fashion, beauty, food, and home décor. Regular departments include Health pages, Entertainment, Money, Home, Humour, and How-to." Byline given. Pays on acceptance. Offers 25-50% kill fee. Accepts queries by mail, e-mail (preferred). Responds in 2 months to queries. Guidelines online.

Does not accept unsolicited mss. Submit story ideas online.

NONFICTION Query. **Pays $1/word.**

ESSENCE

135 W. 50th St., 4th Floor, New York NY 10020. **Website:** www.essence.com. Monthly magazine. *Essence* is the magazine for today's black women. Edited for career-minded, sophisticated and independent achievers, *Essence*'s editorial is dedicated to helping its readers attain their maximum potential in various lifestyles and roles. The editorial content includes career and educational opportunities; fashion and beauty; investing and money management; health and fitness; parenting; information on home decorating and food; travel; cultural reviews; fiction; and profiles of achievers and celebrities. Estab. 1970. Circ. 1 million. Byline given. Pays on acceptance. Offers 25% kill fee. Editorial lead time 6 months. Submit seasonal material 6 months in advance. Accepts queries by mail, fax. Responds in 2 months to queries. Responds in 2 months to mss. Sample copy for $3.25. Guidelines available online.

NONFICTION Needs book excerpts, novel excerpts. **Buys 200 mss/year.** Query with a letter that explains story concept, proposed story length, possible experts, and why this idea would appeal to the *Essence* reader. Query letters should be no longer than 1 page and should address a specific editor. Departments include: Arts and Entertainment (Cori Murray), Books and Poetry (Patrik Henry Bass), Beauty (Corynne Corbett), Health, Relationships, and Food (Sharon Boone), Personal Essays (Rosemarie Robotham), News (Wendy Wilson), Work and Wealth (Tanisha Sykes), and Feature Articles/Personal Growth (Teresa Wiltz and Rosemarie Robotham). Length will be given upon assignment. **Pays by the word.**

REPRINTS Send tearsheet and information about when and where the material previously appeared. Pays 50% of the amount paid for the original article.

PHOTOS Would like to see photographs for our travel section that feature Black travelers. State availability. Model releases required. Pays from $200 up depending on the size of the image.

TIPS Please note that *Essence* no longer accepts unsolicited mss for fiction or nonfiction, except for the

Brothers, Where There's a Will, Making Love Work, Our World, Back Talk and Interiors columns. So please only send query letters for nonfiction story ideas.

FIRST FOR WOMEN

Bauer Media Group, 270 Sylvan Ave., Englewood Cliffs NJ 07632. (201)569-6699. **E-mail:** contactus@firstforwomen.com. **Website:** www.firstforwomen.com. *First for Women*, published 17 times/year, covers everything from beauty, health, nutrition, cooking, decor, and fun. Every issue also includes a 24-page cookbook that pulls out from the center of the magazine. Magazine is visual with a lot of quick tips. Estab. 1989. Circ. 1.3 million.

Query before submitting. Difficult market to break into.

$$$$ GOOD HOUSEKEEPING

Hearst Corp., 300 W. 57th St., 28th Floor, New York NY 10019. (212)649-2200. **Website:** www.goodhousekeeping.com. Monthly magazine covering women's interests. *Good Housekeeping* is edited for the new traditionalist. Articles which focus on food, fitness, beauty, and childcare draw upon the resources of the Good Housekeeping Institute. Editorial includes human interest stories, articles that focus on social issues, money management, health news, and travel. Circ. 4,000,000. Byline given. Pays on acceptance. Offers 25% kill fee. Submit seasonal material 6 months in advance. Responds in 2-3 months to queries and mss. Call for a sample copy. Guidelines online.

NONFICTION **Buys 4-6 mss/year.** Query by mail with published clips. Include SASE. Length: 500 words. Pays expenses of writers on assignment.

PHOTOS Photos purchased mostly on assignment. State availability. Model releases required. Pays $100-350 for b&w; $200-400 for color photos.

COLUMNS/DEPARTMENTS Blessings (about a person or event that proved to be a blessing), 500 words. Query by mail with published clips. Include SASE. **Pays $1/word.**

TIPS "Always send an SASE and clips. We prefer to see a query first. Do not send material on subjects already covered in-house by the Good Housekeeping Institute—these include food, beauty, needlework, and crafts."

$$ GRACE ORMONDE WEDDING STYLE

Elegant Publishing, Inc., P.O. Box 89, Barrington RI 02806. (401)245-9726. **Fax:** (401)245-5371. **E-mail:** contact@weddingstylemagazine.com. **Website:** www.weddingstylemagazine.com. **Contact:** Human Resources. **90% freelance written.** Monthly digital and print magazine covering weddings for the affluent bride. Estab. 1997. Circ. 400,000. Pays on publication. No kill fee. Publishes ms an average of 4 months after acceptance. Editorial lead time 6 months. Guidelines by e-mail.

Does not accept queries.

PHOTOS State availability. Reviews transparencies. Negotiates payment individually.

TIPS E-mail resume and 5 clips/samples in any area of writing.

$$$$ HARPER'S BAZAAR

The Hearst Corp., 300 W. 57th St., New York NY 10019. (212)903-5000. **E-mail:** editors@harpersbazaar.com. **Website:** www.harpersbazaar.com. **Contact:** Joyann King, editor. *Harper's Bazaar* is a specialist magazine published 10 times/year for women who enjoy fashion and beauty. It is edited for sophisticated women with exceptional taste. *Harper's Bazaar* offers ideas in fashion and beauty, and reports on issues and interests relevant to the lives of modern women. Estab. 1867. Circ. 734,504. Byline given. Pays on publication. Offers 25% kill fee. Responds in 2 months to queries.

NONFICTION **Buys 36 mss/year.** Query with published clips. Length: 2,000-3,000 words. **Payment negotiable.**

COLUMNS/DEPARTMENTS Length: 500-700 words. **Payment negotiable.**

$$$$ LADIES' HOME JOURNAL

Meredith Corp., 375 Lexington Ave., 9th Floor, New York NY 10017. (212)557-6600. **E-mail:** lhj@mdp.com. **Website:** www.divinecaroline.com/ladies-home-journal. **50% freelance written.** Monthly magazine focusing on issues of concern to women 30-45. *Ladies' Home Journal* is for active, empowered women who are evolving in new directions. It addresses informational needs with highly focused features and articles on a variety of topics: self, style, family, home, world, health, and food. Estab. 1882. Circ. 4.1 million. Pays on acceptance. Offers 25% kill fee. Publishes ms an average of 4-12 months after acceptance. Editorial lead time 4 months. Accepts queries by mail, e-mail. Accepts simultaneous submissions. Responds in 3 months to queries. Guidelines available online.

NONFICTION Send 1-2 page query, SASE, résumé, and clips via mail or e-mail (preferred). Length: 2,000-3,000 words. **Pays $2,000-4,000.** Pays expenses of writers on assignment.

PHOTOS *LHJ* arranges for its own photography almost all the time. State availability. Captions, identification of subjects, model releases required. Offers variable payment for photos accepted with ms.

FICTION Only short stories and novels submitted by an agent or publisher will be considered. No poetry of any kind. **Buys 12 mss/year.** Send complete ms. Length: 2,000-2,500 words.

MORE

Meredith Corp., 125 Park Ave., New York NY 10017. **E-mail:** more@meredith.com. **Website:** www.more.com. **Contact:** Ila Stanger, managing editor. Magazine published 10 times/year. *More* celebrates women of style and substance. The magazine is the leading voice for the woman who lives in a constant state of possibility. Estab. 1998. Circ. 1.8 million. Byline given. Editorial lead time 4 months. Accepts queries by mail. Guidelines online.

Query before submitting.

NONFICTION *More* only accepts queries, before submissions. Keep query brief (1-2 pages), citing lead and describing how you will research and develop story. Be specific, and direct query to the appropriate editor, as listed on the masthead of the magazine. Send published clips, credits, and a résumé. Does not respond unless a SASE is enclosed. Word length is discussed upon assignment. Average story length is 2,000 words. **Payment is discussed upon assignment.**

$$$$ MS. MAGAZINE

433 S. Beverly Dr., Beverly Hills CA 90212. (310)556-2515. **Fax:** (310)556-2514. **E-mail:** mkort@msmagazine.com. **Website:** www.msmagazine.com. **Contact:** Michele Kort, senior editor. **80-90% freelance written.** Quarterly magazine on women's issues and news. Estab. 1972. Circ. 150,000. Byline given. Offers 25% kill fee. Responds in 3 months to queries. Responds in 3 months to mss. Sample copy for $9. Guidelines available online.

NONFICTION Needs international and national women's news, investigative reporting, personal narratives of prize-winning journalists and feminist thinkers. Does not consider articles on fashion, beauty, fitness, travel, food, or of a "self-help" variety. **Buys 4-5 feature (2,000-3,000 words) and 4-5 short (500 words) mss/year.** Query with published clips and a brief bio. *Ms.* is looking for pieces that use a feminist lens: considers articles on politics, social commentary, popular culture, law, education, art, and the environment. Length: 300-3,500 words. **Pays $1/word; 50¢/word for news stories and book reviews.**

COLUMNS/DEPARTMENTS **Buys 6-10 mss/year. Pays $1/word.**

FICTION "*Ms.* welcomes the highest-quality original fiction and poetry, but is publishing these infrequently as of late."

$$ NA'AMAT WOMAN

505 Eighth Ave., Suite 1204, New York NY 10018. (212)563-5222. **E-mail:** naamat@naamat.org; judith@naamat.org. **Website:** www.naamat.org. **Contact:** Judith Sokoloff, editor. **80% freelance written.** Quarterly magazine covering Jewish issues/subjects. "Magazine covering a wide variety of subjects of interest to the Jewish community— including political and social issues, arts, profiles; many articles about Israel and women's issues. Fiction must have a Jewish theme. Readers are the American Jewish community." Estab. 1926. Circ. 12,000. Byline given. Pays on publication. No kill fee. Publishes ms an average of 6 months after acceptance. Submit seasonal material 6 months in advance. Accepts queries by e-mail. Accepts simultaneous submissions. Responds in 4 weeks to queries. Responds in 3 months to mss. Sample copy for $2. Guidelines by e-mail.

NONFICTION Needs book excerpts, essays, historical, interview, personal experience, photo feature, travel, Jewish topics & issues, political & social issues & women's issues. **Buys 16-20 mss/year.** Send complete ms. **Pays 10-20¢/word for assigned and unsolicited articles.** Some

PHOTOS State availability. Reviews GIF/JPEG files. Negotiates payment individually.

FICTION "We want serious fiction, with insight, reflection and consciousness." Needs novel excerpts, literary with Jewish content. "We do not want fiction that is mostly dialogue. No corny Jewish humor. No Holocaust fiction." **Buys 1-2 mss/year. mss/year.** Query with published clips or send complete ms. Length: 2,000-3,000 words. **Pays 10-20¢/word for assigned articles and for unsolicited articles.**

TIPS "No maudlin nostalgia or romance; no hackneyed Jewish humor."

$$$ REDBOOK MAGAZINE

Hearst Corp., Articles Department, Redbook, 300 W. 57th St., 22nd Floor, New York NY 10019. **Website:** www.redbookmag.com. Monthly magazine covering women's issues. *Redbook* is targeted to women between the ages of 25-45 who define themselves as smart, capable, and happy with their lives. Many, but not all, readers are going through 1 of 2 key life transitions: single to married, and married to mom. Each issue is a provocative mix of features geared to entertain and inform them, including: news stories on contemporary issues that are relevant to the reader's life and experience and that explore the emotional ramifications of cultural and social changes; first-person essays about dramatic pivotal moments in a woman's life; marriage articles with an emphasis on strengthening the relationship; short parenting features on how to deal with universal health and behavioral issues; reporting on exciting trends in women's lives. Estab. 1903. Circ. 2,200,000. Pays on acceptance. No kill fee. Publishes ms an average of 6 months after acceptance. Responds in 3 months to queries and mss. Guidelines online.

NONFICTION Query with published clips and SASE. Length: 2,500-3,000 words for features; 1,000-1,500 words for short articles.

TIPS "Most *Redbook* articles require solid research, well-developed anecdotes from on-the-record sources, and fresh, insightful quotes from established experts in a field that pass our 'reality check' test. Articles must apply to women in our demographics. Writers are advised to read at least the last 6 issues of the magazine (available in most libraries) to get a better understanding of appropriate subject matter and treatment. We prefer to see detailed queries rather than completed mss, and suggest that you provide us with some ideas for sources/experts. Please enclose 2 or more samples of your writing, as well as a SASE."

$$ SKIRT!

Morris Communications, 1 Henrietta St., First Floor, Charleston SC 29403. (843)958-0027. **Fax:** (843)958-0029. **E-mail:** submissions@skirt.com; digitalmedia@skirt.com. **Website:** www.skirt.com. **Contact:** Nikki Hardin, publisher. **50% freelance written.** Monthly magazine covering women's interest. *Skirt!* is all about women—their work, play, families, creativity, style, health, wealth, bodies, and souls. The magazine's attitude is spirited, independent, outspoken, serious, playful, irreverent, sometimes controversial, and always passionate. Estab. 1994. Circ. 285,000. Byline given. Pays on publication. No kill fee. Publishes ms an average of 2 months after acceptance. Editorial lead time 2-3 months. Submit seasonal material 2-3 months in advance. Accepts queries by e-mail (preferred). Accepts simultaneous submissions. Responds in 6-8 weeks to queries. Responds in 1-2 months to mss. Guidelines on website.

NONFICTION Needs essays, humor, personal experience. "Do not send feature articles. We only accept submissions of completed personal essays that will work with our monthly themes available online." **Buys 100+ mss/year.** Send complete ms (preferably as a Rich Text Format attachment) via e-mail. Publishes 5-6 personal essays every month on topics related to women and women's interests. Length: 800-1,100 words. **Pays $150-200.**

TIPS "Surprise and charm us. We look for fearless essays that take chances with content and subject. *Skirt!* is not your average women's magazine. We push the envelope and select content that makes our readers think. Please review guidelines and themes online before submitting."

$$$ THAT'S LIFE!

H Bauer Publishing, Freepost LON12043, London England NW1 1YU United Kingdom. (44)(207)241-8000. **E-mail:** stories@thatslife.co.uk. **Website:** www.thatslife.co.uk. **Contact:** Sophie Hearsey, editor. "*that's life!* is packed with the most amazing true-life stories and fab puzzles offering big-money prizes including family sunshine holidays and even a car! We also have bright, up-to-date fashion, health, and beauty pages with top tips and readers' letters. And just to make sure we get you smiling too, there's our rib-tickling rude jokes and 'aren't men daft' tales." Estab. 1995. Circ. 550,000. No kill fee. Submit seasonal material 3 months in advance. Accepts queries by mail, online submission form. Responds in 6 weeks to mss. Guidelines by e-mail.

NONFICTION Needs true-life stories, humor, health. Special issues: "Have you got a story to tell? It can be sexy, saucy, wicked or sad." Submit via online submissions form. **Pay varies.**

TIPS "Study the magazine for a few weeks to get an idea of our style and flavor."

TODAY'S BRIDE

Family Communications, 65 The East Mall, Toronto ON M8Z SW3 Canada. (416)537-2604. **Fax:** (416)538-1794. **E-mail:** erind@canadianbride.com. **Website:** www.todaysbride.ca; www.canadianbride.com. **20% freelance written.** Semiannual magazine on wedding planning. Magazine provides information to engaged couples on all aspects of wedding planning, including tips, fashion advice, etc. Also contains beauty, home, groom, and honeymoon travel sections. Estab. 1979. Circ. 102,000. Byline given. Pays on acceptance. No kill fee. Editorial lead time 6 months. Accepts queries by mail, e-mail. Accepts simultaneous submissions. Responds in 2 weeks-1 month.

NONFICTION Needs humor, opinion, personal experience. No travel pieces. Send complete ms. Length: 800-1,400 words. **Pays $250-300.**

PHOTOS Send photos. Identification of subjects required. Reviews transparencies, prints. Negotiates payment individually.

TIPS "Send us tight writing about topics relevant to all brides and grooms. Stories for grooms, especially those written by/about grooms, are also encouraged."

TRUE CONFESSIONS

105 E. 34th St., Box 141, New York NY 10016. **E-mail:** shazell@truerenditionsllc.com. **Contact:** Samantha Hazell, editor. "*True Confessions* is a women's magazine featuring true-to-life stories about working-class women and their families. The stories must be in first-person and generally deal with family problems, relationship issues, romances, single moms, abuse, and any other realistic issue women face in our society. The stories we look for are true or at least believable. We look for stories that evoke some sort of emotion, be it happiness or sadness, but in the end there needs to be some sort of moral or lesson learned." Pays on last week of the month after publication. Editorial lead time 3 months. Submit seasonal material 6 months in advance. Guidelines online.

NONFICTION E-mail submissions preferred (trueswriters@yahoo.com). Include contact information and brief synopsis of story. To submit by postal mail, include disk saved in Word, a hard copy, and SASE for return of materials. Length: 3,000-7,000 words. **Pays 3¢/word.**

COLUMNS/DEPARTMENTS My Man! (about a special man in your life); That's Incredible! (about an experience in your life that reaffirms your faith); The Life I Live (about an inspirational time in your life); My Moment with God (thoughts during a meditative moment, quiet reflection, or prayer); Phenomenal Woman (about a special woman in your life). E-mail submissions preferred (trueswriters@yahoo.com). Include contact information and brief synopsis of story. To submit by postal mail, include disk saved in Word, a hard copy, and SASE for return of materials. **Pays $65-100.**

FICTION "Stories should be written in first person and past tense. We generally look for more serious stories. The underlying theme is overcoming adversities in life. These are supposed to be 'true' stories—or at least stories that could be true!" E-mail submissions preferred (trueswriters@yahoo.com). Include contact information and brief synopsis of story. To submit by postal mail, include disk saved in Word, a hard copy, and SASE for return of materials. Length: 3,000-7,000 words. **Pays 3¢/word.**

WOMAN'S WORLD

Bauer Publishing, 270 Sylvan Ave., Englewood Cliffs NJ 07632. (201)569-6699. **Fax:** (201)569-3584. **E-mail:** dearww@womansworldmag.com. **Website:** www.womansworldmag.com. Weekly magazine covering human interest and service pieces of interest to family-oriented women across the nation. *Woman's World* is a women's service magazine. It offers a blend of fashion, food, parenting, beauty, and relationship features coupled with the true-life human interest stories. Publishes short romances and mini-mysteries for all women, ages 18-68. Estab. 1980. Circ. 1.6 million. Pays on acceptance. No kill fee. Publishes ms an average of 4 months after acceptance. Submit seasonal material 4 months in advance. Accepts queries by mail. Responds in 2 months to mss. Guidelines for #10 SASE.

Woman's World is not looking for freelancers to take assigments generated by the staff, but it will assign stories to writers who have made a successful pitch.

NONFICTION Query.

FICTION Contact: Johnene Granger, fiction editor. Wants romance and mainstream short stories of 800 words and mini-mysteries of 1,000 words. Each of story should have a light romantic theme and can be written from either a masculine or feminine point of view. Women characters may be single, married, or divorced. Plots must be fast moving with vivid dialogue and action. The problems and dilemmas inherent in them should be contemporary and realistic, handled with warmth and feeling. The stories must have a positive resolution. Specify Fiction on envelope. Always enclose SASE. Mini-mysteries may revolve around anything from a theft to murder. Not interested in sordid or grotesque crimes. Emphasis should be on intricacies of plot rather than gratuitous violence. The story must include a resolution that clearly states the villain is getting his or her come-uppance. Submit complete mss. Specify Mini-Mystery on envelope. Needs mystery, romance, contemporary. Not interested in science fiction, fantasy, historical romance, or foreign locales. No explicit sex, graphic language, or steamy settings. Send complete ms. Romances: 800 words; mysteries: 1,000 words. **Pays $1,000.**

TIPS The whole story should be sent when submitting fiction. Stories slanted for a particular holiday should be sent at least 6 months in advance. "Familiarize yourself totally with our format and style. Read at least a year's worth of *Woman's World* fiction. Analyze and dissect it. Regarding romances, scrutinize them not only for content but tone, mood, and sensibility."

ZINK

304 Park Ave. S., 11th Floor, New York NY 10010. (212)260-9725. **E-mail:** jennifer.stevens@zinkmediagroup.com. **Website:** www.zinkmagazine.com. **Contact:** Jennifer Stevens, fashion/managing editor. *Zink* is a monthly fashion magazine catering to a savvy, well-cultured, and upscale audience. Accepts queries by e-mail.

NONFICTION Query first.

TRADE JOURNALS

Many writers who pick up *Writer's Market* for the first time do so with the hope of selling an article to one of the popular, high-profile consumer magazines found on newsstands and in bookstores. Many of those writers are surprised to find an entire world of magazine publishing exists outside the realm of commercial magazines—trade journals. Writers who *have* discovered trade journals have found a market that offers the chance to publish regularly in subject areas they find interesting, editors who are typically more accessible than their commercial counterparts, and pay rates that rival those of the big-name magazines.

Trade journal is the general term for any publication focusing on a particular occupation or industry. Other terms used to describe the different types of trade publications are business, technical, and professional journals. They are read by truck drivers, bricklayers, farmers, fishermen, heart surgeons, and just about everyone else working in a trade or profession. Trade periodicals are sharply angled to the specifics of the professions on which they report. They offer business-related news, features, and service articles that will foster their readers' professional development.

Writers for trade journals have to either possess knowledge about the field in question or be able to report it accurately from interviews with those who do. Writers who have or can develop a good grasp of a specialized body of knowledge will find trade magazine editors who are eager to hear from them.

An ideal way to begin your foray into trade journals is to write for those that report on your present profession. If you don't have experience in a profession but can demonstrate an ability to understand (and write about) the intricacies and issues of a particular trade that interests you, editors will still be willing to hear from you.

ADVERTISING, MARKETING AND PR

$$$ BRAND PACKAGING

BNP Media, 2401 W. Big Beaver Rd., Suite 700, Troy MI 48084. (248)205-6869. **E-mail:** zielinskil@bnpmedia.com. **Website:** www.brandpackaging.com. **Contact:** Laura Zielinski, editor-in-chief. **15% freelance written.** Magazine published 10 times/year covering how packaging can be a marketing tool. Publishes strategies and tactics to make products stand out on the shelf. Market is brand managers who are marketers but need to know something about packaging. Estab. 1997. Circ. 33,000. Byline given. Pays on acceptance. Publishes ms an average of 2 months after acceptance. Editorial lead time 3 months. Submit seasonal material 3 months in advance. Accepts queries by mail, fax. Sample copy free.

NONFICTION Needs how-to, interview, new product. **Buys 10 mss/year.** Send complete ms. Length: 600-2,400 words. **Pays 40-50¢/word.**

COLUMNS/DEPARTMENTS Emerging Technology (new packaging technology), 600 words. **Buys 10 mss/year.** Query. **Pays $150-300.**

$ DECA DIRECT

1908 Association Dr., Reston VA 20191. (703)860-5000. **E-mail:** publications@deca.org; communications@deca.org. **E-mail:** christopher_young@deca.org. **Website:** www.decadirect.org. **Contact:** Christopher Young, editor in chief. **30% freelance written.** Quarterly magazine covering marketing, professional development, business, career training during school year (no issues published May-August). *DECA Direct* is the membership magazine for DECA—The Association of Marketing Students, primarily ages 15-19 in all 50 states, the U.S. territories, Germany, and Canada. The magazine is delivered through the classroom. Students are interested in developing professional, leadership, and career skills. Estab. 1947. Circ. 160,000. Byline given. Pays on publication. No kill fee. Editorial lead time 3 months. Submit seasonal material 4 months in advance. Accepts queries by mail, e-mail, fax, phone. Accepts simultaneous submissions. Sample copy free online.

NONFICTION Needs essays, general interest, how-to, get jobs, start business, plan for college, etc., interview, business leads, personal experience, working, leadership development. **Buys 10 mss/year.** Submit a paragraph description of your article by e-mail. Length: 500-1,000 words. **Pays $125 for assigned articles. Pays $100 for unsolicited articles.**

COLUMNS/DEPARTMENTS Professional Development; Leadership, 500-1,000 words. **Buys 6 mss/year.** Send complete ms. **Pays $75-100.**

$$ O'DWYER'S PR REPORT

271 Madison Ave., #600, New York NY 10016. (212)679-2471; (866)395-7710. **Fax:** (212)683-2750. **E-mail:** john@odwyerpr.com. **Website:** www.odwyerpr.com. **Contact:** John O'Dwyer, associate publisher/editor. Monthly magazine providing PR articles. *O'Dwyer's* has been covering public relations, marketing communications, and related fields for over 40 years. The company provides the latest news and information about PR firms and professionals, the media, corporations, legal issues, jobs, technology, and much more through its website, weekly newsletter, monthly magazine, directories, and guides. Many of the contributors are PR people publicizing themselves while analyzing something. Byline given.

NONFICTION Needs opinion. Query. **Pays $250.**

$$$ PROMO MAGAZINE

Access Intelligence, (203)899-8442. **E-mail:** podell@accessintel.com. **Website:** www.chiefmarketer.com/promotional-marketing. **Contact:** Patricia Odell, executive editor. **5% freelance written.** Monthly magazine covering promotion marketing. *Promo* serves marketers, and stories must be informative, well written, and familiar with the subject matter. Estab. 1987. Circ. 25,000. Byline given. Pays on publication. Offers 25% kill fee. Publishes ms an average of 2 months after acceptance. Editorial lead time 3 months. Submit seasonal material 3 months in advance. Responds in 1 month to queries. Sample copy for $5.

NONFICTION Needs exposè, general interest, how-to, marketing programs, interview, new product, promotion. No general marketing stories not heavily involved in promotions. Generally does not accept unsolicited mss; query first. **Buys 6-10 mss/year.** Query with published clips. **Pays $1,000 maximum for assigned articles. Pays $500 maximum for unsolicited articles.** Sometimes pays expenses of writers on assignment.

$$ SIGN BUILDER ILLUSTRATED

Simmons-Boardman Publishing Corp., 55 Broad St., 26th Floor, New York NY 10004. (252)355-5806.

E-mail: jwooten@sbpub.com; abray@sbpub.com. **Website:** www.signshop.com. **Contact:** Jeff Wooten, editor; Ashley Bray, associate editor. **40% freelance written.** Monthly magazine covering sign and graphic industry. *Sign Builder Illustrated* targets sign professionals where they work: on the shop floor. Topics cover the broadest spectrum of the sign industry, from design to fabrication, installation, maintenance, and repair. Readers own a similarly wide range of shops, including commercial, vinyl, sign erection and maintenance, electrical and neon, architectural, and awnings. Estab. 1987. Circ. 14,500. Byline given. Pays on acceptance. Offers 10% kill fee. Publishes ms an average of 3 months after acceptance. Editorial lead time 3 months. Submit seasonal material 4 months in advance. Accepts queries by mail, e-mail, fax, phone. Accepts simultaneous submissions. Responds in 1 month to queries. Sample copy and writer's guidelines free.

NONFICTION Needs historical, how-to, humor, interview, photo feature, technical. **Buys 50-60 mss/year.** Query. Length: 1,000-1,500 words. **Pays $250-550 for assigned articles.**

$$ SIGNCRAFT

SignCraft Publishing Co., Inc., P.O. Box 60031, Fort Myers FL 33906. (239)939-4644. **Fax:** (239)939-0607. **E-mail:** signcraft@signcraft.com. **Website:** www.signcraft.com. **10% freelance written.** Bimonthly magazine covering the sign industry. Estab. 1980. Circ. 14,000. Byline given. Pays on publication. Offers negotiable kill fee. Publishes ms an average of 6 months after acceptance. Accepts queries by mail, e-mail, fax. Responds in 1 month to queries. Sample copy and writer's guidelines for $3.

NONFICTION Needs interview. **Buys 10 mss/year.** Query. Length: 500-2,000 words.

$$$ SOCAL MEETINGS + EVENTS MAGAZINE

Tiger Oak Publications, One Tiger Oak Plaza, 900 S. Third St., Minneapolis MN 55415. **Fax:** (612)338-0532. **E-mail:** bobby.hart@tigeroak.com. **Website:** http://meetingsmags.com. **Contact:** Bobby Hart, managing editor. **80% freelance written.** Meetings + Events Media Group, including Minnesota Meetings + Events, Illinois Meetings + Events, Colorado Meetings & Events, Michigan Meetings + Events, California Meetings + Events, Texas Meetings + Events, Northwest Meetings + Events, Mountain Meetings, Pennsylvania Meetings + Evens and New Jersey Meetings + Events is a group of premier quarterly trade magazines for meetings planners and hospitality service providers throughout the US. Thesemagazines aim to report on and promote businesses involved in the meetings and events industry, covering current and emerging trends, people and venues in the meetings and events industry in their respective regions. Estab. 1993. Circ. approximately 20,000 per title. Byline given. Pays on acceptance. Offers 20% kill fee. Publishes ms an average of 4 months after acceptance. Editorial lead time 4-6 months. Submit seasonal material 6 months in advance. Accepts queries by mail. Accepts simultaneous submissions. Responds in 1-2 weeks to queries.

NONFICTION Needs general interest, historical, interview, new product, opinion, personal experience, photo feature, technical, travel. **Buys 30 mss/year.** "Each query should tell us: What the story will be about; how you will tell the story (what sources you will use, how you will conduct research, etc.); why is the story pertinent to the market audience. Please also attach PDFs of 3 published magazine articles." Length: 600-1,500 words. **The average department length story (4-700 words) pays about $2-300 and the average feature length story (1,000-1,200 words) pays up to $800, depending on the story. These rates are not guaranteed and vary.**

COLUMNS/DEPARTMENTS Meet + Eat (restaurant reviews); Facility Focus (venue reviews); Regional Spotlight (city review), 1,000 words. **Buys 30 mss/year.** Query with published clips. **Pays $400-600.**

$$$ TEXAS MEETINGS + EVENTS

Tiger Oak Publications, One Tiger Oak Plaza, 900 S. 3rd St., Minneapolis MN 55401. (612)548-3180. **Fax:** (612)548-3181. **E-mail:** bobby.hart@tigeroak.com. **Website:** http://tx.meetingsmags.com. **Contact:** Bobby Hart, managing editor. **80% freelance written.** Quarterly magazine covering meetings and events industry. *Texas Meetings & Events* magazine is the premier trade publication for meetings planners and hospitality service providers in the state. This magazine aims to report on and promote businesses involved in the meetings and events industry. The magazine covers current and emerging trends, people and venues in the meetings and events industry in the state. Estab. 1993. Circ. 20,000. Byline given. Pays on acceptance. Offers 20% kill fee. Publishes ms an average of 4 months after acceptance. Editorial lead time 4-6 months. Submit seasonal material 6 months in advance. Accepts queries by mail. Accepts simultaneous submissions. Responds in 1-2 weeks to queries. Guidelines available online.

NONFICTION Needs general interest, historical, interview, new product, opinion, personal experience, photo feature, technical, travel. **Buys 30 mss/year.** Query with published clips of 3 magazine articles. Length: 600-1,500 words. **Pays $400-800.**

COLUMNS/DEPARTMENTS Meet + Eat (restaurant reviews); Facility Focus (venue reviews); Regional Spotlight (city review), 1,000 words. **Buys 30 mss/year.** Query with published clips. **Pays $400-600.**

ART, DESIGN & COLLECTIBLES

$$ AIRBRUSH ACTION MAGAZINE

Action, Inc., P.O. Box 438, Allenwood NJ 08720. (732)223-7878; (800)876-2472. **Fax:** (732)223-2855. **E-mail:** ceo@airbrushaction.com. **Website:** www.airbrushaction.com. **Contact:** Cliff Stieglitz, publisher. **80% freelance written.** Bimonthly magazine covering the spectrum of airbrush applications: automotive and custom paint applications, illustration, T-shirt airbrushing, fine art, automotive and sign painting, hobby/craft applications, wall murals, fingernails, temporary tattoos, artist profiles, reviews, and more. Estab. 1985. Circ. 35,000. Byline given. Pays 1 month after publication. Publishes ms an average of 6 months after acceptance. Editorial lead time 6 months. Submit seasonal material 6 months in advance. Accepts queries by mail, e-mail, fax. Accepts simultaneous submissions.

NONFICTION Needs how-to, humor, inspirational, interview, new product, personal experience, technical. Doesn't want anything unrelated to airbrush. Query with published clips. **Pays 15¢/word.** Sometimes pays expenses of writers on assignment.

COLUMNS/DEPARTMENTS Query with published clips.

$$ ANTIQUEWEEK

MidCountry Media, 27 N. Jefferson St., P.O. Box 90, Knightstown IN 46148. (800)876-5133. **Fax:** (800)345-3398. **E-mail:** davidb@antiqueweek.com; tony@antiqueweek.com. **Website:** www.antiqueweek.com. **Contact:** David Blower, Jr., senior editor; Tony Gregory, publisher. **80% freelance written.** Weekly tabloid covering antiques and collectibles with 3 editions: Eastern, Central, and National, plus the monthly *AntiqueWest*. *AntiqueWeek* has a wide range of readership from dealers and auctioneers to collectors, both advanced and novice. Readers demand accurate information presented in an entertaining style. Estab. 1968. Circ. 50,000. Byline given. Pays on publication. Offers 10% kill fee or $25. Submit seasonal material 1 month in advance. Accepts queries by mail, e-mail. Sample copy free. Guidelines by e-mail.

NONFICTION Needs historical, how-to, interview, opinion, personal experience, antique show and auction reports, feature articles on particular types of antiques and collectibles. **Buys 400-500 mss/year.** Query. Length: 1,000-2,000 words. **Pays $50-250.**

$ THE APPRAISERS STANDARD

New England Appraisers Association, 6973 Crestridge Dr., Memphis TN 38119. (901)758-2659. **E-mail:** ETuten551@aol.com. **Website:** www.newenglandappraisers.org. **Contact:** Edward Tuten, editor. **50% freelance written. Works with a small number of new/unpublished writers each year.** Quarterly publication covering the appraisals of antiques, art, collectibles, jewelry, coins, stamps, and real estate. Estab. 1980. Circ. 1,000. Short bio and byline given. Pays on publication. No kill fee. Publishes ms an average of 1 year after acceptance. Submit seasonal material 2 months in advance. Accepts queries by mail, e-mail. Accepts simultaneous submissions. Responds in 1 month to queries. Responds in 2 months to mss.

NONFICTION Needs interview, personal experience, technical, travel. Send complete ms. Length: 700 words. **Pays $60.**

$$ ART MATERIALS RETAILER

Fahy-Williams Publishing, Inc., 171 Reed St., P.O. Box 1080, Geneva NY 14456. (315)789-0458. **Fax:** (315)789-4263. **E-mail:** tmanzer@fwpi.com. **Website:** www.artmaterialsretailer.com. J. Kevin Fahy, publisher (kfahy@fwpi.com). **Contact:** Tina Manzer, editorial director. **10% freelance written.** Quarterly magazine covering retail stores that sell art materials. Offers book reviews, retailer-recommended products, and profiles of stores from around the country. Estab. 1998. Byline given. Pays on publication. No kill fee. Editorial lead time 2 months. Submit seasonal material 3 months in advance. Accepts simultaneous submissions. Responds in 3 weeks to queries. Responds in 3 months to mss. Sample copy and writer's guidelines free.

NONFICTION Needs book excerpts, how-to, interview, personal experience. **Buys 2 mss/year.** Send complete ms. Length: 1,500-3,000 words. **Pays $50-250.** Sometimes pays expenses of writers on assignment.

FILLERS Needs anecdotes, facts, newsbreaks. **Buys 5 mss/year.** Length: 500-1,500 words. **Pays $50-125.**

$$ FAITH + FORM

47 Grandview Terrace, Essex CT 06426. (860)575-4702. **E-mail:** mcrosbie@faithandform.com. **Website:** www.faithandform.com. **Contact:** Michael J. Crosbie, editor-in-chief. **50% freelance written.** Quarterly magazine covering relgious buildings and art. *Faith + Form*, devoted to religious art and architecture, is read by artists, designers, architects, clergy, congregations, and all who care about environments for worship. Writers must be knowledgeable about environments for worship, or able to explain them. Estab. 1967. Circ. 4,500. Byline given. Publishes ms an average of 6 months after acceptance. Editorial lead time 6 months. Submit seasonal material 6 months in advance. Accepts queries by online submission form. Accepts simultaneous submissions. Responds in 2 weeks to queries; 1 month to mss. Sample copy online. Guidelines available.

NONFICTION Needs book excerpts, essays, how-to, inspirational, interview, opinion, personal experience, photo feature, religious, technical. **Buys 6 mss/year.** Query. Submit via online submission form, in Microsoft Word or Rich Text format. Length: 500-2,500 words.

COLUMNS/DEPARTMENTS News, 250-750 words; Book Reviews, 250-500 words. **Buys 3 mss/year.** Query.

$$$ HOW

F+W Media, Inc., 10151 Carver Rd., Suite 200, Blue Ash OH 45242. (513)531-2690. **Fax:** (513)531-2902. **E-mail:** editorial@howdesign.com. **Website:** www.howdesign.com. **75% freelance written.** Bi-monthly magazine covering graphic design profession. *HOW: Design Ideas at Work* strives to serve the business, technological and creative needs of graphic-design professionals. The magazine provides a practical mix of essential business information, up-to-date technological tips, the creative whys and hows behind noteworthy projects, and profiles of professionals who are impacting design. The ultimate goal of *HOW* is to help designers, whether they work for a design firm or for an inhouse design department, run successful, creative, profitable studios. Estab. 1985. Circ. 40,000. Byline given. Pays on acceptance. No kill fee. Responds in 6 weeks to queries.

NONFICTION Special issues: Self-Promotion Annual (September/October); Business Annual (November/December); In-House Design Annual (January/February); International Annual of Design (March/April); Creativity/Paper/Stock Photography (May/June); Digital Design Annual (July/August). No how-to articles for beginning artists or fine-art-oriented articles. **Buys 40 mss/year.** Query with published clips and samples of subject's work, artwork, or design. Length: 1,500-2,000 words. **Pays $700-900.** Sometimes pays expenses of writers on assignment.

COLUMNS/DEPARTMENTS Creativity (focuses on creative exercises and inspiration) 1,200-1,500 words. In-House Issues (focuses on business and creativity issues for corporate design groups), 1,200-1,500 words. Business (focuses on business issue for design firm owners), 1,200-1, 500 words. **Buys Number of columns: 35. mss/year.** Query with published clips. **Pays $250-400.**

$$ PASTEL JOURNAL

F+W, 10151 Carver Rd., Suite #200, Cincinnati OH 45242. (513)531-2690. **Fax:** (513)891-7153. **E-mail:** pjedit@fwmedia.com. **Website:** www.pasteljournal.com. **Contact:** Anne Hevener, editor; Jessica Canterbury, managing editor. Bimonthly magazine covering pastel art. *Pastel Journal* is the only national magazine devoted to the medium of pastel. Addressing the working professional as well as passionate amateurs, *Pastel Journal* offers inspiration, information, and instruction to our readers. Estab. 1999. Circ. 22,000. Byline given. Pays on acceptance. Offers 25% kill fee. Publishes ms an average of 3-6 months after acceptance. Editorial lead time 6 months. Submit seasonal material 6 months in advance. Accepts queries by mail. Accepts simultaneous submissions. Responds in 4-6 weeks to queries. Guidelines online.

NONFICTION Needs how-to, interview, new product, profile. Does not want articles that aren't art-related. Review magazine before submitting. Query with or without published clips. Length: 500-2,000 words. **Payment does not exceed $600.**

$$$ PRINT

F+W Media, Inc., 10151 Carver Rd., Suite 200, Blue Ash OH 45242. (513)531-2690. **E-mail:** info@printmag.com. **Website:** www.printmag.com. **75% freelance written.** Bimonthly magazine covering graphic design and visual culture. *PRINT*'s articles, written by design specialists and cultural critics, focus on the social, political, and historical context of graphic design, and on the places where consumer culture and popular culture meet. Aims to produce a general interest magazine for professionals with engagingly written text and lavish illustrations. By covering a broad spectrum of topics, both international and local, *Print* tries to demonstrate the significance of design in the world at large. Estab. 1940. Circ. 45,000. Byline given. Pays on acceptance. Offers 25% kill fee. Publishes ms an average of 3 months after acceptance. Editorial lead time 3 months. Submit seasonal material 3 months in advance. Accepts queries by e-mail. Responds in 2 weeks to queries. Responds in 1 month to mss.

NONFICTION Needs essays, interview, opinion. **Buys 35-40 mss/year.** Query with published clips. Length: 1,000-2,500 words. **Pays $1,250.** Sometimes pays expenses of writers on assignment.

COLUMNS/DEPARTMENTS Query with published clips. **Pays $800.**

$$ PROFESSIONAL ARTIST

Turnstile Media Group, 1500 Park Center Dr., Orlando FL 32835. (407)563-7000. **Fax:** (407)563-7099. **E-mail:** info@professionalartistmag.com. **Website:** www.professionalartistmag.com. **Contact:** Jenny Andreasson, assistant editor. **75% freelance written.** Monthly magazine. *Professional Artist* is dedicated to providing independent visual artists from all backgrounds with the insights, encouragement and business strategies they need to make a living with their artwork. Estab. 1986. Circ. 20,000. Pays on publication. No kill fee. YesSample print copy for $5. Guidelines online.

NONFICTION Needs essays, the psychology of creativity, how-to, interview, successful artists with a focus on what made them successful, networking articles, marketing topics, technical articles (new equipment, new media, computer software, Internet marketing.), cartoons, art law, including pending legislation that affects artists (copyright law, Internet regulations, etc.). Does not run reviews or art historical pieces, nor writing characterized by "criticspeak," philosophical hyperbole, psychological arrogance, politics, or New Age religion. Also, does not condone a get-rich-quick attitude. Send complete ms. **Pays $150-350.**

COLUMNS/DEPARTMENTS "If an artist or freelancer sends us good articles regularly, and based on results we feel that he is able to produce a column at least 3 times per year, we will invite him to be a contributing writer. If a gifted artist-writer can commit to producing an article on a monthly basis, we will offer him a regular column and the title contributing editor." Send complete ms.

$ TEXAS ARCHITECT

Texas Society of Architects, 500 Chicon St., Austin TX 78702. (512)478-7386. **Fax:** (512)478-0528. **Website:** www.texasarchitect.org. **Contact:** Catherine Gavin, editor. **30% freelance written. Mostly written by unpaid members of the professional society.** Bimonthly journal covering architecture and architects of Texas. *Texas Architect* is a highly visually-oriented look at Texas architecture, design, and urban planning. Articles cover varied subtopics within architecture. Readers are mostly architects and related building professionals. Estab. 1951. Circ. 12,500. Byline given. Pays on publication. No kill fee. Publishes ms an average of 3 months after acceptance. Submit seasonal material 4 months in advance. Accepts queries by mail, e-mail. Responds in 6 weeks to queries. Guidelines available online.

NONFICTION Needs interview, photo feature, technical, book reviews. Query with published clips. Length: 100-2,000 words. **Pays $50-100 for assigned articles.**

COLUMNS/DEPARTMENTS News (timely reports on architectural issues, projects, and people), 100-500 words. **Buys 10 articles/year mss/year.** Query with published clips. **Pays $50-100.**

$$ WATERCOLOR ARTIST

F+W, a Content + eCommerce Company, 10151 Carver Rd., Suite 200, Blue Ash OH 45242. (513)531-2690. **Fax:** (513)891-7153. **Website:** www.watercolorartistmagazine.com. **Contact:** Jennifer Hoffman, art director; Kelly Kane, editor. Bimonthly magazine covering water media arts. Estab. 1984. Circ. 44,000. Byline given. Pays on acceptance. Publishes ms an average of 3-6 months after acceptance. Editorial lead time 6 months. Submit seasonal material 6 months in advance. Accepts queries by mail. Accepts simultaneous submissions. Writer's guidelines available at http://www.artistsnetwork.com/contactus.

NONFICTION Needs book excerpts, essays, how-to, inspirational, interview, new product, personal experience. Does not want articles that aren't art-related. Review magazine before submitting. **Buys 36 mss/year.** Send query letter with images. Length: 350-2,500 words. **Pays $150-600.**

AUTO AND TRUCK

$$ AUTOINC.

Automotive Service Association, 8209 Mid Cities Blvd., North Richland Hills TX 76182. (817)514-2900, ext. 119. Direct line: (817)514-2919. **Fax:** (817)514-0770. **E-mail:** editor@asashop.org. **Website:** www.autoinc.org. **10% freelance written.** The mission of *AutoInc.*, ASA's official publication, is to be the informational authority for ASA and industry members nationwide. Its purpose is to enhance the professionalism of these members through management, technical and legislative articles, researched and written with the highest regard for accuracy, quality, and integrity. Estab. 1952. Circ. 14,000. Byline given. Pays on publication. No kill fee. Publishes ms an average of 3 months after acceptance. Editorial lead time 2 months. Accepts queries by mail, e-mail, fax. Accepts simultaneous submissions. Responds in 6 weeks to queries and in 2 months to mss. Sample copy for $5 or online. Guidelines available online.

NONFICTION Needs how-to, automotive repair, technical. No coverage of staff moves or financial reports. **Buys 6 mss/year.** Query with published clips. Length: 1,200 words. **Pays $300.** Sometimes pays phone expenses of writers on assignment.

$$ BUSINESS FLEET

Bobit Publishing, 3520 Challenger St., Torrance CA 90501. (310)533-2400. **E-mail:** chris.brown@bobit.com. **Website:** www.businessfleet.com. **Contact:** Chris Brown, executive editor. **10% freelance written.** Bimonthly magazine covering businesses which operate 10-50 company vehicles. Estab. 2000. Circ. 100,000. Byline given. Pays on publication. Offers 25% kill fee. Publishes ms an average of 3 months after acceptance. Editorial lead time 2 months. Submit seasonal material 2 months in advance. Accepts queries by mail, e-mail, fax. Responds in 3 weeks to queries. Responds in 2 months to mss. Sample copy and writer's guidelines free.

NONFICTION Needs how-to, interview, new product, personal experience, photo feature, technical. **Buys 16 mss/year.** Query with published clips. Length: 500-2,000 words. **Pays $100-400.** Sometimes pays expenses of writers on assignment.

$$ FENDERBENDER

DeWitt Publishing, 1043 Grand Ave. #372, St. Paul MN 55105. (651)224-6207. **Fax:** (651)224-6212. **E-mail:** news@fenderbender.com; jweyer@fenderbender.com. **Website:** www.fenderbender.com. **Contact:** Jake Weyer, editor. **50% freelance written.** Monthly magazine covering automotive collision repair. Estab. 1999. Circ. 58,000. Byline given. Pays on publication. Offers 20% kill fee. Publishes ms an average of 2 months after acceptance. Editorial lead time 3 months. Submit seasonal material 6 months in advance. Accepts queries by e-mail. Accepts simultaneous submissions. Responds in 1-2 months to queries. Responds in 2-3 months to mss. Sample copy for SAE with 10x13 envelope and 6 first-class stamps. Guidelines available online.

NONFICTION Needs exposè, how-to, inspirational, interview, technical. Does not want personal narratives or any other first-person stories. No poems or creative writing mss. Query with published clips. Length: 1,800-2,500 words. **Pays 25-60¢/word.** Sometimes pays expenses of writers on assignment.

COLUMNS/DEPARTMENTS Q&A, 600 words; Shakes, Rattles & Rollovers; Rearview Mirror. Query with published clips. **Pays 25-35¢/word.**

$$ FLEETSOLUTIONS

NAFA Fleet Management Association, 125 Village Blvd., Suite 200, Princeton NJ 08540. (609)986-1053; (609)720-0882. **Fax:** (609)720-0881; (609)452-8004. **E-mail:** publications@nafa.org; info@nafa.org. **Website:** www.nafa.org. **10% freelance written.** Magazine published 6 times/year covering automotive fleet management. Generally focuses on car, van, and light-duty truck management in US and Canadian corporations, government agencies, and utilities. Editorial emphasis is on general automotive issues; improving jobs skills, productivity, and professionalism; legislation and regulation; alternative fuels; safety; interviews with prominent industry personalities; technology; association news; public service fleet management; and light-duty truck fleet management. Estab.

1957. Circ. 4,000. Bylines provided. Pays on publication. No kill fee. Publishes ms an average of 4 months after acceptance. Editorial lead time 2 months. Accepts queries by mail. Accepts simultaneous submissions. Responds in 1 month to queries. Sample copy available online. Guidelines free.

NONFICTION Needs interview, technical. **Buys 24 mss/year.** Query with published clips. Length: 500-3,000 words. **Pays $500 maximum.**

OVERDRIVE

Randall-Reilly Publishing, 3200 Rice Mine Rd. NE, Tuscaloosa AL 35406. (205)349-2990. **Fax:** (205)750-8070. **E-mail:** mheine@rrpub.com; jcrissey@rrpub.com. **Website:** www.etrucker.com. **Contact:** Max Heine, editorial director; Jeff Crissey, editor. **5% freelance written.** Monthly magazine for independent truckers. Estab. 1961. Circ. 100,000. Byline given. Pays on publication. Offers 10% kill fee. Publishes ms an average of 2 months after acceptance. Responds in 2 months to queries. Sample copy for 9x12 SASE. Digital copy available online.

NONFICTION Needs essays, exposè, how-to, truck maintenance and operation, interview, successful independent truckers, personal experience, photo feature, technical. Send complete ms. Length: 500-2,500 words. **Pays $300-1,500 for assigned articles.**

TIRE NEWS

Rousseau Automotive Communication, 455, Notre-Dame East, Suite 311, Montreal QC H2Y 1C9 Canada. (514)289-0888; 1-877-989-0888. **Fax:** (514)289-5151. **E-mail:** administration@autosphere.ca. **Website:** www.autosphere.ca. **Contact:** Luc Champagne, editor-in-chief. Bimonthly magazine covering the Canadian tire industry. *Tire News* focuses on education/training, industry image, management, new tires, new techniques, marketing, HR, etc. Estab. 2004. Circ. 18,725. Byline given. Pays on publication. Publishes ms an average of 2 months after acceptance. Editorial lead time 2 months. Submit seasonal material 2 months in advance. Accepts simultaneous submissions. Responds in 2 weeks to queries. Responds in 2 months to mss. Guidelines by e-mail.

NONFICTION Needs general interest, how-to, inspirational, interview, new product, technical. Does not want opinion pieces. **Buys 5 mss/year.** Query with published clips. Length: 550-610 words. **Pays up to $200 (Canadian).**

FILLERS Needs facts. **Buys 2 mss/year.** Length: 550-610 words. **Pays $0-200.**

TOWING & RECOVERY FOOTNOTES

Dominion Enterprises, 2484 Windy Pines Bend, Virginia Beach VA 23456. (757)351-8633. **Fax:** (757)233-7047. **E-mail:** david@trfootnotes.com; heidi@trfootnotes.com. **Website:** www.trfootnotes.com. **100% freelance written.** Monthly trade newspaper and marketplace for the nation's towing and recovery industry. Estab. 1991. Circ. 25,000. Byline given. Pays within 2-3 weeks of acceptance. No kill fee. Publishes ms an average of 2-3 months after acceptance. Editorial lead time 2 months. Submit seasonal material 2 months in advance. Accepts queries by mail, e-mail, phone. Responds in 2 weeks to queries. Responds in 1 month to mss. Sample copy free. Guidelines free.

NONFICTION Needs historical, how-to, humor, interview, new product, opinion, personal experience, photo feature, technical. **Buys 500 mss/year.** Query with published clips. Length: 800-2,000 words. **Pays $200-$600 for assigned articles.**

COLUMNS/DEPARTMENTS Columns vary from issue to issue; no regular departments available to freelancers; columns are given names appropriate to topic, and often repeat no matter who the author is. **Buys 250 mss/year.** Query with published clips.

WESTERN CANADA HIGHWAY NEWS

Craig Kelman & Associates, 2020 Portage Ave., 3rd Floor, Winnipeg MB R3J 0K4 Canada. (204)985-9785. **Fax:** (204)985-9795. **E-mail:** terry@kelman.ca. **Website:** http://highwaynews.ca. **Contact:** Terry Ross, editor. **30% freelance written.** Quarterly magazine covering trucking. The official magazine of the Alberta, Saskatchewan, and Manitoba trucking associations. As the official magazine of the trucking associations in Alberta, Saskatchewan and Manitoba, *Western Canada Highway News* is committed to providing leading edge, timely information on business practices, technology, trends, new products/services, legal and legislative issues that affect professionals in Western Canada's trucking industry. Estab. 1995. Circ. 4,500. Byline given. Pays on publication. No kill fee. Publishes ms an average of 2 months after acceptance. Editorial lead time 3 months. Submit seasonal material 3 months in advance. Accepts simultaneous submissions. Responds in 1 month to queries and mss.

Sample copy for 10x13 SAE with 1 IRC. Guidelines for #10 SASE.

NONFICTION Needs essays, general interest, how-to, run a trucking business, interview, new product, opinion, personal experience, photo feature, technical, profiles in excellence (bios of trucking or associate firms enjoying success). **Buys 8-10 mss/year.** Query. Length: 500-3,000 words. **Pays 18-25¢/word.** Sometimes pays expenses of writers on assignment.

COLUMNS/DEPARTMENTS Safety (new safety innovation/products), 500 words; Trade Talk (new products), 300 words. Query. **Pays 18-25¢/word.**

AVIATION AND SPACE

$$ AEROSAFETY WORLD MAGAZINE

Flight Safety Foundation, 801 N. Fairfax St., Suite 400, Alexandria VA 22314-1774. (703)739-6700. **Fax:** (703)739-6708. **E-mail:** jackman@flightsafety.org. **Website:** www.flightsafety.org. **Contact:** Frank Jackman, director of publications. Monthly newsletter covering safety aspects of airport operations. Full-color monthly magazine offers in-depth analysis of important safety issues facing the industry, with emphasis on timely news coverage in a convenient format and eye-catching contemporary design. Estab. 1974. Pays on publication. Accepts queries by mail, e-mail. "Generally, the ms must be unpublished and must not be under consideration for publication elsewhere. In some circumstances, the Foundation may consider a previously published ms if it has been rewritten and adapted for Foundation readers. If your ms has been copyrighted, a copyright transfer may be required before your ms will be published by the Foundation."Catalog available on website. Guidelines available on website.

NONFICTION Needs technical. Query. **Pays $300-1,500.**

$$ AIRCRAFT MAINTENANCE TECHNOLOGY

Cygnus Business Media, 1233 Janesville Ave., Fort Atkinson WI 53538. (920)563-6388. **Fax:** (920)569-4603. **E-mail:** barb.zuehlke@AviationPros.com. **Website:** www.amtonline.com. **Contact:** Barb Zuehlke, senior editor. **10% freelance written.** Magazine published 10 times/year covering aircraft maintenance. *Aircraft Maintenance Technology* provides aircraft maintenance professionals worldwide with a curriculum of technical, professional, and managerial development information that enables them to more efficiently and effectively perform their jobs. Estab. 1989. Circ. 41,500 worldwide. Byline given. Pays on publication. No kill fee. Publishes ms an average of 2 months after acceptance. Editorial lead time 3 months. Submit seasonal material 6 months in advance. Accepts queries by online submission form. Accepts simultaneous submissions. Responds in 2 weeks to queries. Responds in 1 month to mss. Sample copy free. Guidelines for #10 SASE or by e-mail.

NONFICTION Needs how-to, technical, safety. Special issues: Aviation career issue (August). No travel/pilot-oriented pieces. **Buys 10-12 mss/year.** Query with published clips. Please use the online form to contact us. 600-1,500 words, technical articles 2,000 words **Pays $200.**

COLUMNS/DEPARTMENTS Professionalism, 1,000-1,500 words; Safety Matters, 600-1,000 words; Human Factors, 600-1,000 words. **Buys 10-12 mss/year.** Query with published clips. **Pays $200**

$$ AVIATION INTERNATIONAL NEWS

The Convention News Co., 214 Franklin Ave., Midland Park NJ 07432. (201)444-5075. **Fax:** (201)444-4647. **E-mail:** nmoll@ainonline.com; editor@ainonline.com; ayannaco@ainonline.com. **Website:** www.ainonline.com. **Contact:** Nigel Moll, editor; Annmarie Yannaco, managing editor. **30-40% freelance written.** Monthly magazine, with daily onsite issues published at 3 conventions and 2 international air shows each year, and twice-weekly AINalerts via e-mail covering business and commercial aviation with news features, special reports, aircraft evaluations, and surveys on business aviation worldwide, written for business pilots and industry professionals. "While the heartbeat of *AIN* is driven by the news it carries, the human touch is not neglected. We pride ourselves on our people stories about the industry's 'movers and shakers' and others in aviation who make a difference." Estab. 1972. Circ. 40,000. Byline given. Pays on acceptance and upon receipt of writer's invoice. Offers variable kill fee. Publishes ms an average of 2 months after acceptance. Editorial lead time 2 months. Submit seasonal material 3 months in advance. Accepts queries by mail, e-mail, fax. Responds in 6 weeks to queries. Responds in 2 months to mss. Sample copy for $10.

NONFICTION Needs how-to, aviation, interview, new product, opinion, personal experience, photo feature, technical. Does not puff pieces. "Our readers expect serious, real news. We don't pull any punches. *AIN* is not a 'good news' publication; it tells the story, both good and bad." **Buys 150-200 mss/year.** Query with published clips. Do not send mss by e-mail unless requested. Length: 200-3,000 words. **Pays 40¢/word to first timers, higher rates to proven *AIN* freelancers.** Pays expenses of writers on assignment.

$$ GROUND SUPPORT WORLDWIDE MAGAZINE

Cygnus Business Media, 1233 Janesville Ave., Fort Atkinson WI 53538. (920)563-1644. **Fax:** (920)563-1699. **E-mail:** steve.smith@AviationPros.com. **Website:** www.aviationpros.com/magazine/gsm. **Contact:** Steve Smith, editor. **20% freelance written.** Magazine published 10 times/year. Readers are those aviation professionals who are involved in ground support: the equipment manufacturers, the suppliers, the ramp operators, ground handlers, and airport and airline managers. Covesr issues of interest to this community: deicing, ramp safety, equipment technology, pollution, etc. Estab. 1993. Circ. 15,000+. Pays on publication. No kill fee. Publishes ms an average of 2 months after acceptance. Editorial lead time 2 months. Accepts queries by mail, e-mail, fax. Responds in 3 weeks to queries; 3 months to mss. Sample copy for SAE with 9x11 envelope and 5 first-class stamps.

NONFICTION Needs how-to, use or maintain certain equipment, interview, new product, opinion, photo feature, technical aspects of ground support and issues, industry events, meetings, new rules and regulations. **Buys 12-20 mss/year.** Send complete ms. Length: 500-2,000 words. **Pays $100-300.**

$$$ PROFESSIONAL PILOT

Queensmith Communications Corp., 30 S. Quaker Lane, Suite 300, Alexandria VA 22314. (703)370-0606. **Fax:** (703)370-7082. **E-mail:** editor@propilotmag.com; jcohen@propilotmag.com; editorial@propilotmag.com. **Website:** www.propilotmag.com. **Contact:** Murray Smith, editor/publisher; Jessica Cohen, associate editor. **75% freelance written.** Monthly magazine covering corporate, noncombat government, law enforcement, and various other types of professional aviation. The typical reader of *Professional Pilot* has a sophisticated grasp of piloting/aviation knowledge and is interested in articles that help him/her do the job better or more efficiently. Estab. 1967. Circ. 40,000. Byline given. Pays on publication. Offers kill fee. Kill fee negotiable. Publishes ms an average of 2-3 months after acceptance. Accepts queries by mail, e-mail.

NONFICTION Buys 40 mss/year. Query. Length: 750-2,500 words. **Pays $200-1,000, depending on length. A fee for the article will be established at the time of assignment.** Sometimes pays expenses of writers on assignment.

BEAUTY AND SALON

$$ BEAUTY STORE BUSINESS

Creative Age Communications, 7628 Densmore Ave., Van Nuys CA 91406. (818)782-7328, ext. 353; (800)442-5667. **Fax:** (818)782-7450. **E-mail:** mbatist@creativeage.com; mbirenbaum@creativeage.com; skelly@creativeage.com. **Website:** www.beautystorebusiness.com. Shelley Moench-Kelly, managing editor. **Contact:** Manyesha Batist, editor/online editor. **50% freelance written.** Monthly magazine covering beauty store business management, news, and beauty products. The primary readers of the publication are owners, managers, and buyers at open-to-the-public beauty stores, including general-market and multicultural market-oriented ones with or without salon services. Secondary readers are those at beauty stores only open to salon industry professionals. Also goes to beauty distributors. Estab. 1994. Circ. 15,000. Byline given. Pays on acceptance. Offers kill fee. Offers negotiable kill fee. Publishes ms an average of 3 months after acceptance. Editorial lead time 3 months. Submit seasonal material 4 months in advance. Accepts queries by mail, e-mail, fax. Responds in 1 week to queries. Responds in 2 weeks, if interested. Sample copy free.

NONFICTION Needs how-to, business management, merchandising, e-commerce, retailing, interview, industry leaders/beauty store owners. **Buys 20-30 mss/year.** Query. Length: 1,800-2,200 words. **Pays $250-525 for assigned articles.** Sometimes pays expenses of writers on assignment.

○$$ COSMETICS

Rogers Publishing Limited, One Mount Pleasant Rd., 8th Floor, Toronto ON M4Y 2Y5 Canada. (416)764-1680. **Fax:** (416)764-1704. **E-mail:** kristen.vinakmens@cosmetics.rogers.com. **Website:** www.cosmeticsmag.com. **Contact:** Kristen Vinakmens, editor-in-chief. **10% freelance written.** Bimonthly magazine covering cosmetics for industry professionals. Estab. 1972. Circ. 13,000. Byline given. Pays on acceptance. Offers 50% kill fee. Publishes ms an average of 3 months after acceptance. Editorial lead time 4 months. Submit seasonal material 4 months in advance. Accepts queries by mail. Responds in 1 month to queries. Sample copy for $6 (Canadian) and 8% GST.

NONFICTION Needs general interest, interview, photo feature. **Buys 1 mss/year.** Query. Length: 250-1,200 words. **Pays 25¢/word.** Sometimes pays expenses of writers on assignment.

COLUMNS/DEPARTMENTS "All articles assigned on a regular basis from correspondents and columnists that we know personally from the industry."

$$ DAYSPA

Creative Age Publications, 7628 Densmore Ave., Van Nuys CA 91406. (818)782-7328, ext. 301. **Fax:** (818)782-7450. **Website:** www.dayspamagazine.com. **Contact:** Linda Kossoff, executive editor. **50% freelance written.** Monthly magazine covering the business of day spas, multi-service/skincare salons, and resort/hotel spas. *Dayspa* includes only well-targeted business and trend articles directed at the owners and managers. It serves to enrich, enlighten, and empower spa/salon professionals. Estab. 1996. Circ. 31,000. Byline given. Pays on acceptance. No kill fee. Publishes ms an average of 4 months after acceptance. Editorial lead time 4 months. Submit seasonal material 4 months in advance. Accepts queries by mail, e-mail, fax, phone, online submission form. Responds in 2 months to queries. Sample copy for $5.

NONFICTION Buys 40 mss/year. Query. Length: 1,500-1,800 words. **Pays $150-500.**

COLUMNS/DEPARTMENTS Legal Pad (legal issues affecting salons/spas); Money Matters (financial issues); Management Workshop (spa management issues); Health Wise (wellness trends), all 1,200-1,500 words. **Buys 20 mss/year.** Query. **Pays $150-400.**

$$ MASSAGE MAGAZINE

5150 Palm Valley Rd., Suite 103, Ponte Vedra Beach FL 32082. (904)285-6020. **Fax:** (904)285-9944. **E-mail:** kmenehan@massagemag.com. **Website:** www.massagemag.com. **60% freelance written.** Magazine about massage and other touch therapies published 10-12 times/year. Readers are professional therapists who have been in practice for several years. About 80% are self-employed; 95% live in the United States. The vast majority of readers have completed formal training in massage therapy. The techniques they practice include Swedish, sports and geriatric massage, energy work and myotherapy, among many others. Readers work in settings ranging from home-based studios to spas to integrated clinics. Estab. 1985. Circ. 50,000. Byline given. Pays on publication. Publishes ms an average of 2 months-24 months after acceptance. Accepts queries by e-mail. Responds in 2 months to queries. Responds in 3 months to mss. Sample copy for $6.95. Guidelines available online.

NONFICTION Needs book excerpts, essays, general interest, how-to, interview, personal experience, photo feature, technical, experiential. No multiple submissions. Length: 1,500-3,000 words. **Pays $50-400.**

COLUMNS/DEPARTMENTS Profiles; News and Current Events; Practice Building (business); Technique; Mind/Body/Spirit. Length: anywhere from 200-2,500 words. See website for details. **Pays $75-300 for assigned articles.**

FILLERS Needs facts, newsbreaks. Length: 100-800 words. **Pays $125 maximum.**

$$ NAILPRO

Creative Age Publications, 7628 Densmore Ave., Van Nuys CA 91406. (800)442-5667; (818)782-7328. **Fax:** (818)782-7450. **E-mail:** nailpro@creativeage.com. **Website:** www.nailpro.com. **Contact:** Stephanie Yaggy, executive editor. **75% freelance written.** Monthly magazine written for manicurists and nail technicians working in a full-service salon or nails-only salons. Estab. 1989. Circ. 65,000. Byline given. Pays on acceptance. No kill fee. Publishes ms an average of 6 months after acceptance. Editorial lead time 3 months. Submit seasonal material 3 months in advance. Accepts queries by mail, e-mail, fax. Accepts simultaneous submissions. Responds in 6 weeks to queries. Sample copy for $2 and 9x12 SASE.

NONFICTION Needs book excerpts, how-to, humor, inspirational, interview, personal experience, photo feature, technical. No general interest articles or business articles not geared to the nail-care industry. **Buys 50 mss/year.** Query. Length: 1,000-3,000 words. **Pays $150-450.**

COLUMNS/DEPARTMENTS All Business (articles on building salon business, marketing and advertising, dealing with employees), 1,500-2,000 words; Attitudes (aspects of operating a nail salon and trends in the nail industry), 1,200-2,000 words. **Buys 50 mss/year.** Query. **Pays $250-350.**

Ø$$ NAILS

Bobit Business Media, 3520 Challenger St., Torrance CA 90503. (310)533-2457. **Fax:** (310)533-2507. **E-mail:**

judy.lessin@bobit.com. **Website:** www.nailsmag.com. **Contact:** Judy Lessin, features editor. **10% freelance written.** Monthly magazine. *NAILS* seeks to educate its readers on new techniques and products, nail anatomy and health, customer relations, working safely with chemicals, salon sanitation, and the business aspects of running a salon. Estab. 1983. Circ. 55,000. Byline given. Pays on acceptance. No kill fee. Submit seasonal material 4 months in advance. Accepts queries by mail, e-mail. Responds in 1 month to queries. Visit website to view past issues.

NONFICTION Needs historical, how-to, inspirational, interview, personal experience, photo feature, technical. No articles on 1 particular product, company profiles, or articles slanted toward a particular company or manufacturer. **Buys 20 mss/year.** Query with published clips. Length: 1,200-2,000 words. **Pays $200-400.** Sometimes pays expenses of writers on assignment.

$$ PULSE MAGAZINE

HOST Communications Inc., 2365 Harrodsburg Rd., Suite A325, Lexington KY 40504. (859)226-4326. **Fax:** (859)226-4445. **E-mail:** mae.manacap-johnson@ispastaff.com. **Website:** www.experienceispa.com/media/pulse-magazine. **Contact:** Mae Manacap-Johnson, editor. **20% freelance written.** Magazine published 10 times/year covering spa industry. *Pulse* is the magazine for the spa professional. As the official publication of the International SPA Association, its purpose is to advance the business of the spa professionals by informing them of the latest trends and practices and promoting the wellness aspects of spa. *Pulse* connects people, nurtures their personal and professional growth, and enhances their ability to network and succeed in the spa industry. Estab. 1991. Circ. 5,300. Byline given. Pays on publication. Publishes ms an average of 1 month after acceptance. Editorial lead time 3 months. Submit seasonal material 4 months in advance. Accepts queries by e-mail. Sample copy for #10 SASE. Guidelines by e-mail.

NONFICTION Needs general interest, how-to, interview, new product. Does not want articles focused on spas that are not members of ISPA, consumer-focused articles (market is the spa industry professional), or features on hot tubs ("not *that* spa industry"). **Buys 8-10 mss/year.** Query with published clips. Length: 800-2,000 words. **Pays $250-500.** Sometimes pays expenses of writers on assignment.

$$ SKIN DEEP

Associated Skin Care Professionals, 25188 Genesee Trail Rd., Suite 200, Golden CO 80401. (800)789-0411. **E-mail:** editor@ascpskincare.com; getconnected@ascpskincare.com. **Website:** www.ascpskincare.com. **Contact:** Carrie Patrick, editor. **80% freelance written.** Bimonthly magazine covering technical, educational, and business information for estheticians with an emphasis on solo practitioners and spa/salon employees or independent contractors. Audience is the U.S. individual skin care practitioner who may work on her own and/or in a spa or salon setting. Magazine keeps her up to date on skin care trends and techniques and ways to earn more income doing waxing, facials, peels, microdermabrasion, body wraps and other skin treatments. Product-neutral stories may include novel spa treatments within the esthetician scope of practice. Does not cover mass-market retail products, hair care, nail care, makeup, physician only treatments/products, cosmetic surgery, or invasive treatments like colonics or ear candling. Successful stories have included how-tos on paraffin facials, aromatherapy body wraps, waxing tips, how to read ingredient labels, how to improve word-of-mouth advertising, and how to choose an online scheduling software package. Estab. 2003. Circ. 12,000+. Byline given. Pays on acceptance. No kill fee. Publishes ms an average of 4-6 months after acceptance. Editorial lead time 4-5 months. Submit seasonal material 7 months in advance. Accepts queries by e-mail. Responds in 2 weeks to queries.

NONFICTION "We don't run general consumer beauty material or products that are very rarely run a new product that is available through retail outlets. 'New' products means introduced in the last 12 months. We do not run industry personnel announcements or stories on individual spas/salons or getaways. We don't cover hair or nails." **Buys 12 mss/year.** Query. Length: 1,200-1,600 words. **Pays $75-300 for assigned articles.**

$$ SKIN INC. MAGAZINE

Allured Business Media, 336 Gundersen Dr., Suite A, Carol Stream IL 60188. (630)653-2155. **Fax:** (630)653-2192. **E-mail:** kwegrzyn@allured.com. **Website:** www.skininc.com. **Contact:** Kristen Wegrzyn, assistant editor. **30% freelance written.** Magazine published 12 times/year as an educational resource for skin care professionals interested in business solutions, treatment techniques, and skin science. Estab. 1988. Circ. 30,000. Byline given. Pays on publication. No kill fee. Publishes ms an average of 6 months after acceptance. Editorial lead time 6 months. Submit seasonal material 1 year in advance. Accepts queries by mail, e-mail, fax, phone. Responds in 3 weeks to queries. Responds in 1 month to mss. Sample copy and writer's guidelines free.

NONFICTION Needs general interest, how-to, interview, personal experience, technical. **Buys 6 mss/year.** Query with published clips. Length: 2,000 words. **Pays $100-300 for assigned articles. Pays $50-200 for unsolicited articles.**

COLUMNS/DEPARTMENTS Finance (tips and solutions for managing money), 2,000-2,500 words; Personnel (managing personnel), 2,000-2,500 words; Marketing (marketing tips for salon owners), 2,000-2,500 words; Retail (retailing products and services in the salon environment), 2,000-2,500 words. Query with published clips. **Pays $50-200.**

FILLERS Needs facts, newsbreaks. **Buys Buys 6 mss/year. mss/year.** Length: 250-500 words. **Pays $50-100.**

BEVERAGES AND BOTTLING

BAR & BEVERAGE BUSINESS MAGAZINE

Mercury Publications, 1740 Wellington Ave., Winnipeg MB R3H 0E8 Canada. (204)954-2085. **Fax:** (204)954-2057. **E-mail:** edufault@mercurypublications.ca; editorial@mercurypublications.ca. **Website:** www.barandbeverage.com. **Contact:** Elaine Dufault, associate publisher and national account manager. **33% freelance written.** Bimonthly magazine providing information on the latest trends, happenings, buying-selling of beverages and product merchandising. Estab. 1998. Circ. 16,077. Byline given. Pays 30-45 days from receipt of invoice. Offers 33% kill fee. Submit seasonal material 3 months in advance. Accepts simultaneous submissions. Sample copy and writer's guidelines free or by e-mail.

NONFICTION Needs how-to, making a good drink, training staff, etc., interview. Industry reports, profiles on companies. Query with published clips. Length: 500-9,000 words. **Pays 25-35¢/word.** Sometimes pays expenses of writers on assignment.

COLUMNS/DEPARTMENTS Out There (bar and beverage news in various parts of the country), 100-500 words. Query. **Pays $0-100.**

MICHIGAN HOSPITALITY REVIEW

Michigan Licensed Beverage Association, 920 N. Fairview, Lansing MI 48912. (800)292-2896. **Fax:** (517)374-1165. **E-mail:** editor@mlba.org; info@mlba.org. **Website:** www.mlba.org. **Contact:** Nicole Jones, editor. **40-50% freelance written.** Monthly trade magazine devoted to the beer, wine, and spirits industry in Michigan. It is dedicated to serving those who make their living serving the public and the state through the orderly and responsible sale of beverages. Estab. 1983. Circ. 4,200. Pays on publication. No kill fee. Editorial lead time 3 months. Submit seasonal material 3 months in advance. Accepts queries by mail, e-mail. Responds in 2 weeks to queries. Responds in 1 month to mss. Sample copy for $5 or online.

NONFICTION Needs essays, general interest, historical, how-to, make a drink, human resources, tips, etc., humor, interview, new product, opinion, personal experience, photo feature, technical. **Buys 24 mss/year.** Send complete ms. Length: 1,000 words. **Pays $20-200.**

COLUMNS/DEPARTMENTS Open to essay content ideas. Interviews (legislators, others), 750-1,000 words; personal experience (waitstaff, customer, bartenders), 500 words. **Buys 12 mss/year.** Send complete ms. **Pays $25-100.**

VINEYARD & WINERY MANAGEMENT

P.O. Box 14459, Santa Rosa CA 95402-6459. (707)577-7700. **Fax:** (707)577-7705. **E-mail:** tcaputo@vwm-media.com. **Website:** www.vwmmedia.com. **Contact:** Tina Caputo, editor-in-chief. **80% freelance written.** Bimonthly magazine of professional importance to grape growers, winemakers, and winery sales and business people. Headquartered in Sonoma County, California, *Vineyard & Winery Management* proudly remains a leading independent wine trade magazine serving all of North America. Estab. 1975. Circ. 6,500. Byline given. Pays on publication. 20% kill fee. Accepts queries by e-mail. Responds in 3 weeks to queries. Responds in 1 month to mss. Sample copy free. Guidelines for by e-mail.

NONFICTION Needs how-to, interview, new product, technical. **Buys 30 mss/year.** Query. Length: 1,500-2,000 words. **Pays approximately $500/feature.** Sometimes pays expenses of writers on assignment.

WINES & VINES

Wine Communications Group, 65 Mitchell Blvd., Suite A, San Rafael CA 94903. (415)453-9700; (866)453-9701. **Fax:** (415)453-2517. **E-mail:** edit@winesandvines.com; info@winesandvines.com. **Website:** www.winesandvines.com. **Contact:** Jim Gordon, editor; Kate Lavin, managing editor. **50% freelance written.** Monthly magazine covering the North American winegrape and winemaking industry. "Since 1919, *Wines & Vines Magazine* has been the authoritative voice of the wine and grape industry—from prohibition to phylloxera, we have covered it all. Our paid circulation reaches all 50 states and many foreign countries. Because we are intended for the trade—including growers, winemakers, winery owners, wholesalers, restauranteurs, and serious amateurs—we accept more technical, informative articles. We do not accept wine reviews, wine country tours, or anything of a wine consumer nature." Estab. 1919. Circ. 5,000. Byline given. Pays 30 days after acceptance. No kill fee. Publishes ms an average of 3 months after acceptance. Editorial lead time 2 months. Submit seasonal material 4 months in advance. Accepts queries by e-mail. Responds in 2-3 weeks to queries. Sample copy for $5. Guidelines free.

NONFICTION Needs interview, new product, technical. "No wine reviews, wine country travelogues, 'lifestyle' pieces, or anything aimed at wine consumers. Our readers are professionals in the field." **Buys 60 mss/year.** Query with published clips. Length: 1,000-2,000 words. **Pays flat fee of $500 for assigned articles.**

BOOK AND BOOKSTORE

THE BLOOMSBURY REVIEW

1245 E. Colfax, Suite 304, Denver CO 80218. (303)455-3123. **Fax:** (303)455-7039. **E-mail:** info@bloomsburyreview.com. **E-mail:** editors@bloomsburyreview.com. **Website:** www.bloomsburyreview.com. **Contact:** Marilyn Auer, editor-in-chief/publisher. **75% freelance written.** Quarterly tabloid covering books and book-related matters. Publishes book reviews, interviews with writers and poets, literary essays, and original poetry. Audience consists of educated, literate, general readers. Estab. 1980. Circ. 35,000. Byline given. Pays on publication. No kill fee. Publishes ms an average of 4-6 months after acceptance. Accepts queries by mail. Responds in 4 months to queries. Sample copy for $5 and 9x12 SASE. Guidelines for #10 SASE or online.

NONFICTION Needs essays, interview, book reviews. **Buys 60 mss/year.** Send complete ms. Length: 100-1,000 words. **Pays $10-20. Sometimes pays writers with contributor copies or other premiums if writer agrees.**

COLUMNS/DEPARTMENTS Book reviews and essays, 500-1,500 words. **Buys 6 mss/year.** Query with published clips or send complete ms. **Pays $10-20.**

POETRY Contact: Ray Gonzalez, poetry editor. Needs Needs avant-garde, free verse, haiku, traditional. Buys 20 poems/year. Submit maximum 5 poems. **Pays $5-10.**

FOREWORD REVIEWS

425 Boardman Ave., Suite B, Traverse City MI 49684. (231)933-3699. **Fax:** (231)933-3899. **E-mail:** howard@forewordreviews.com; victoria@forewordreviews.com. **Website:** www.forewordreviews.com. **Contact:** Howard Lovy, book review editor; Victoria Sutherland, publisher. **95% freelance written.** Bimonthly magazine covering reviews of good books independently published. In each issue of the magazine, there are 3 to 4 feature *ForeSight* articles focusing on trends in popular categories. These are in addition to the 75 or more critical reviews of forthcoming titles from independent presses in the *Review* section. Look online for review submission guidelines or view editorial calendar. Estab. 1998. Circ. 16,000 (about 80% librarians, 10% bookstores, 10% publishing professionals). Byline given. Pays 2 months after publication. No kill fee. Publishes ms an average of 2-3 months after acceptance. Editorial lead time 3-4 months. Submit seasonal material 5 months in advance. Accepts queries by mail, e-mail. Responds in 1 month. Sample copy for $10 and 8 ½ x11 SASE with $1.50 postage.

NONFICTION Query with published clips. All review submissions should be sent to the book review editor. Submissions should include a fact sheet or press release. Length: 400-1,500 words. **Pays $25-200 for assigned articles.**

BRICK, GLASS AND CERAMICS

STAINED GLASS

Stained Glass Association of America, 9313 East 63rd St., Raytown MO 64133. (800)438-9581. **Fax:**

(816)737-2801. **E-mail:** stainedglassquarterly@gmail.com. **Website:** www.stainedglassquarterly.com. **Contact:** Richard Gross, editor and media director. **70% freelance written.** Quarterly magazine. *Stained Glass* is the official voice of the Stained Glass Association of America. As the oldest, most respected stained glass publication in North America, *Stained Glass* preserves the techniques of the past as well as illustrates the trends of the future. This vital information, of significant value to the professional stained glass studio, is also of interest to those for whom stained glass is an avocation or hobby. Estab. 1906. Circ. 8,000. Byline given. Pays on publication. No kill fee. Publishes ms an average of 1 year after acceptance. Editorial lead time 6 months. Submit seasonal material 8 months in advance. Accepts queries by mail, e-mail, fax. Responds in 3 months to queries. Sample copy free. Guidelines on website.

NONFICTION Needs how-to, humor, interview, new product, opinion, photo feature, technical. **Buys 9 mss/year.** Query or send complete ms, but must include photos or slides—very heavy on photos. Length: 2,500-3,500 words. **Pays $125/illustrated article; $75/nonillustrated.**

COLUMNS/DEPARTMENTS Columns must be illustrated. Teknixs (technical, how-to, stained and glass art), word length varies by subject. **Buys 4 mss/year.** Query or send complete ms, but must be illustrated.

$$ US GLASS, METAL & GLAZING

Key Communications, Inc., P.O. Box 569, Garrisonville VA 22463. (540)720-5584, ext.114. **Fax:** (540)720-5687. **E-mail:** info@glass.com; erogers@glass.com. **Website:** www.usglassmag.com. **Contact:** Ellen Rogers, editor. **25% freelance written.** Monthly magazine for companies involved in the flat glass trades. Estab. 1966. Circ. 27,000. Byline given. Pays on publication. No kill fee. Publishes ms an average of 3 months after acceptance. Editorial lead time 3 months. Submit seasonal material 2 months in advance. Accepts queries by mail, e-mail. Accepts simultaneous submissions. Responds in 1 month to queries. Responds in 2 months to mss. Sample copy online.

NONFICTION **Buys 12 mss/year.** Query with published clips. **Pays $300-600 for assigned articles.** Sometimes pays expenses of writers on assignment.

BUILDING INTERIORS

$$ FABRICS + FURNISHINGS INTERNATIONAL

SIPCO Publications + Events, 3 Island Ave., Suite 6i, Miami Beach FL 33139. **E-mail:** eric@sipco.net. **Website:** www.fandfi.com. **Contact:** Eric Schneider, editor/publisher. **10% freelance written.** Bimonthly magazine covering commercial, hospitality interior design, and manufacturing. *F+FI* covers news from vendors who supply the hospitality interiors industry. Estab. 1990. Circ. 11,000+. Byline given. Pays on publication. Offers $100 kill fee. Editorial lead time 3 months. Submit seasonal material 3 months in advance. Accepts queries by e-mail. Accepts simultaneous submissions. Sample copy available online.

NONFICTION Needs interview, technical. Does not want opinion or consumer pieces. Readers must learn something from our stories. Query with published clips. Length: 500-1,000 words. **Pays $250-350.**

$$ KITCHEN & BATH DESIGN NEWS

Cygnus Business Media, 3 Huntington Quadrangle, Suite 301N, Melville NY 11747. **Fax:** (631)845-7218. **E-mail:** janice.costa@cygnuspub.com. **Website:** www.forresidentialpros.com. **15% freelance written.** Monthly tabloid for kitchen and bath dealers and design professionals, offering design, business and marketing advice to help our readers be more successful. It is not a consumer publication about design, a book for do-it-yourselfers, or a magazine created to showcase pretty pictures of kitchens and baths. Rather, the magazine covers the professional kitchen and bath design industry in depth, looking at the specific challenges facing these professionals, and how they address these challenges. Estab. 1983. Circ. 51,000. Byline given. Pays on publication. Publishes ms an average of 2-3 months after acceptance. Editorial lead time 2 months. Accepts queries by mail, e-mail, fax. Responds in 2-4 weeks to queries. Sample copy available online. Guidelines by e-mail.

NONFICTION Needs how-to, interview. Does not want consumer stories, generic business stories, or "I remodeled my kitchen and it's so beautiful" stories. This is a magazine for trade professionals, so stories need to be both slanted for these professionals, as well as sophisticated enough so that people who have been working in the field 30 years can still learn something from them. **Buys 16 mss/year.** Query with published clips. Length: 1,100-3,000 words. **Pays $200-650.** Sometimes pays expenses of writers on assignment.

$$ QUALIFIED REMODELER

Cygnus Business Media, 1233 Janesville Ave., Fort Atkinson WI 53538. **E-mail:** Rob.Heselbarth@cygnus.com. **Website:** www.forresidentialpros.com. **Contact:** Rob Heselbarth, editorial director. **5% freelance written.** Monthly magazine covering residential remodeling. Estab. 1975. Circ. 83,500. Byline given. Pays on acceptance. No kill fee. Publishes ms an average of 1 month after acceptance. Editorial lead time 3 months. Submit seasonal material 2 months in advance. Accepts queries by mail, e-mail, fax, phone. Sample copy available online.

NONFICTION Needs how-to, business management, new product, photo feature, best practices articles, innovative design. **Buys 12 mss/year.** Query with published clips. Length: 1,200-2,500 words. **Pays $300-600 for assigned articles. Pays $200-400 for unsolicited articles.** Sometimes pays expenses of writers on assignment.

$$$$ REMODELING

HanleyWood, LLC, One Thomas Circle NW, Suite 600, Washington DC 20005. (202)452-0800. **Fax:** (202)785-1974. **E-mail:** salfano@hanleywood.com; ibush@hanleywood.com; sbell@hanleywood.com. **Website:** www.remodelingmagazine.com. **Contact:** Sal Alfano, editorial director; Ingrid Bush, managing editor; Sarah Bell, art director. **10% freelance written.** Monthly magazine covering residential and light commercial remodeling. "We cover the best new ideas in remodeling design, business, construction and products." Estab. 1985. Circ. 80,000. Byline given. Pays on publication. Offers 5¢/word kill fee. Publishes ms an average of 3 months after acceptance. Accepts queries by mail, e-mail, fax. Sample copy free.

NONFICTION Needs interview, new product, technical, small business trends. **Buys 6 mss/year.** Query with published clips. Length: 250-1,000 words. **Pays $1/word.** Sometimes pays expenses of writers on assignment.

$$ WALLS & CEILINGS

2401 W. Big Beaver Rd., Suite 700, Troy MI 48084. (313)894-7380. **Fax:** (248)362-5103. **E-mail:** wyattj@bnpmedia.com; mark@wwcca.org. **Website:** www.wconline.com. **Contact:** John Wyatt, editor; Mark Fowler, editorial director. **20% freelance written.** Monthly magazine for contractors involved in lathing and plastering, drywall, acoustics, fireproofing, curtain walls, and movable partitions, together with manufacturers, dealers, and architects. Estab. 1938. Circ. 30,000. Byline given. Pays on publication. No kill fee. Publishes ms an average of 6 months after acceptance. Submit seasonal material 4 months in advance. Accepts queries by mail, e-mail. Accepts simultaneous submissions. Responds in 6 months to queries. Sample copy for 9x12 SAE with $2 postage. Guidelines for #10 SASE.

NONFICTION Needs how-to, drywall and plaster construction and business management, technical. **Buys 20 mss/year.** Query or send complete ms. Length: 1,000-1,500 words. **Pays $50-500.**

BUSINESS MANAGEMENT

$$$$$ BEDTIMES

International Sleep Products Association, 501 Wythe St., Alexandria VA 22314. (703)683-8371. **E-mail:** jkitchen@sleepproducts.org. **Website:** www.bedtimesmagazine.com; www.sleepproducts.org. **Contact:** Jane Kitchen, editor-in-chief. **20-40% freelance written.** Monthly magazine covering the mattress manufacturing industry. Estab. 1917. Circ. 3,800. Byline given. Pays on acceptance. No kill fee. Publishes ms an average of 3 months after acceptance. Editorial lead time 2 months. Accepts queries by e-mail. Accepts simultaneous submissions. Responds in 1 month to queries. Sample copy for $4. Guidelines by e-mail.

NONFICTION No pieces that do not relate to business in general or mattress industry in particular. **Buys 15-25/year mss/year.** Query with published clips. Length: 500-2,500 words. **Pays 50-$1/word for short features; $2,000 for cover story.**

$$$ BUSINESS TRAVEL EXECUTIVE

5768 Remington Dr., Winston-Salem NC 27104. (336)766-1961. **E-mail:** dbooth@askbte.com. **Website:** www.askbte.com. **Contact:** Dan Booth, managing editor. **90% freelance written.** Monthly magazine covering corporate procurement of travel services. Byline given. Pays on publication. No kill fee. Publishes ms an average of 2 months after acceptance. Editorial lead time 0-3 months. Accepts queries by e-mail.

NONFICTION Needs how-to, technical. **Buys 48 mss/year.** Please send unsolicited submissions, at your own risk. Please enclose a SASE for return of

TRADE JOURNALS

material. Submission of letters implies the right to edit and publish all or in part. Length: 800-2,000 words. **Pays $200-800.**

COLUMNS/DEPARTMENTS Meeting Place (meeting planning and management); Hotel Pulse (hotel negotiations, contracting and compliance); Security Watch (travel safety); all 1,000 words. **Buys 24 mss/year.** Query. **Pays $200-400.**

TIPS "We are not a travel magazine. We publish articles designed to help corporate purchasers of travel negotiate contracts, enforce policy, select automated services, track business travelers, and account for their safety and expenditures, understand changes in the various industries associated with travel. Do not submit mss without an assignment. Look at the website for an idea of what we publish."

$$ CBA RETAILERS + RESOURCES

CBA, the Association for Christian Retail, 9240 Explorer Dr., Suite 200, Colorado Springs CO 80920. **Fax:** (719)272-3510. **E-mail:** cellis@cbaonline.org; info@cbaonline.org. **Website:** www.cbaonline.org. **30% freelance written.** Monthly magazine covering the Christian retail industry. Writers must have knowledge of and direct experience in the Christian retail industry. Subject matter must specifically pertain to the Christian retail audience. Estab. 1968. Byline given. Pays on publication. No kill fee. Publishes ms an average of 3 months after acceptance. Editorial lead time 3 months. Submit seasonal material 6 months in advance. Accepts queries by e-mail. Responds in 2 months to queries.

NONFICTION Buys 24 mss/year. Query. Length: 750-1,500 words. **Pays 25¢/word upon publication.**

$$ CONTRACTING PROFITS

Trade Press Publishing, 2100 W. Florist Ave., Milwaukee WI 53209. (414)228-7701; (800)727-7995. **Fax:** (414)228-1134. **E-mail:** dan.weltin@tradepress.com. **Website:** www.cleanlink.com/cp. **Contact:** Dan Weltin, editor-in-chief. **40% freelance written.** Magazine published 10 times/year covering building service contracting and business management advice. The pocket MBA for this industry—focusing not only on cleaning-specific topics, but also discussing how to run businesses better and increase profits through a variety of management articles. Estab. 1995. Circ. 32,000. Byline given. Pays within 30 days of acceptance. No kill fee. Editorial lead time 2 months. Submit seasonal material 3 months in advance. Accepts queries by mail, e-mail. Responds in weeks to queries. Sample copy available online. Guidelines free.

NONFICTION Needs expose, how-to, interview, technical. No product-related reviews or testimonials. **Buys 30 mss/year.** Query with published clips. Length: 1,000-1,500 words. **Pays $100-500.** Sometimes pays expenses of writers on assignment.

$$ CONTRACT MANAGEMENT

National Contract Management Association, 21740 Beaumeade Circle, Suite 125, Ashburn VA 20147. (571)382-0082. **Fax:** (703)448-0939. **E-mail:** khansen@ncmahq.org. **Website:** www.ncmahq.org. **Contact:** Kerry McKinnon Hansen, director of publications and editor-in-chief. **10% freelance written.** Monthly magazine covering contract and business management. Most of the articles published in *Contract Management (CM)* are written by NCMA members, although one does not have to be an NCMA member to be published in the magazine. Articles should concern some aspect of the contract management profession, whether at the level of a beginner or that of the advanced practitioner. Estab. 1960. Circ. 23,000. Byline given. Pays on publication. No kill fee. Publishes ms an average of 3 months after acceptance. Editorial lead time 10 weeks. Submit seasonal material 3 months in advance. Accepts queries by mail, e-mail, fax, phone. Accepts simultaneous submissions. Responds in 2 weeks to queries. Responds in 1 month to mss. Sample copy and writer's guidelines available online.

NONFICTION Needs essays, general interest, how-to, humor, inspirational, new product, opinion, technical. No company or CEO profiles. Read a copy of publication before submitting. **Buys 6-10 mss/year.** Query with published clips. Send an inquiry including a brief summary (150 words) of the proposed article to the managing editor before writing the article. Length: 1,800-4,000 words. **Pays $300.**

COLUMNS/DEPARTMENTS Professional Development (self-improvement in business), 1,000-1,500 words; Back to Basics (basic how-tos and discussions), 1,500-2,000 words. **Buys 2 mss/year.** Query with published clips. **Pays $300.**

$$ EXPANSION MANAGEMENT

Penton Media, Inc., 1300 E. 9th St., Cleveland OH 44114. (216)931-9252. **E-mail:** aselko@industryweek.com. **Website:** www.industryweek.com/expansion-management. **Contact:** Adrienne Selko, senior editor.

50% freelance written. Monthly magazine covering economic development. Estab. 1986. Circ. 45,000. Byline given. Pays on acceptance. No kill fee. Publishes ms an average of 1 month after acceptance. Editorial lead time 2 months.

NONFICTION Buys 120 mss/year. Query with published clips. Length: 800-1,200 words. **Pays $200-400 for assigned articles.** Sometimes pays expenses of writers on assignment.

$$$ EXPO

Red 7 Media, 10 Norden Place, Norwalk CT 06855. (203)899-8428. **E-mail:** mrondon@accessintel.com; mhart@accessintel.com. **E-mail:** tsilber@accessintel.com. **Website:** www.expoweb.com. **Contact:** Tony Silber, general manager; Michael Rondon, associate editor; Michael Hart, editor. **80% freelance written.** Magazine covering expositions. *EXPO* is published 10 times a year. It includes sales- and marketing-focused features about destinations, case studies and revenue-generating ideas, as well as coverage of new products and services for its audience—show organizers and their managers. Byline given. Pays on publication. Offers 50% kill fee. Editorial lead time 3 months. Accepts queries by mail, e-mail, fax. Responds in 3 weeks to queries. Sample copy and guidelines free.

NONFICTION Needs how-to, interview. Query with published clips. Length: 600-2,400 words. **Pays 50¢/word.** Pays expenses of writers on assignment.

$$ INTENTS

Industrial Fabrics Association International, 1801 County Rd. B W, Roseville MN 55113. (651)225-2508; (800)-225-4324. **Fax:** (651)631-9334. **E-mail:** editorial@ifai.com; srniemi@ifai.com; jclafferty@ifai.com. **Website:** www.ifai.com/publications/intents; http://intentsmag.com. **Contact:** Susan R. Niemi, publisher; Jill C. Lafferty, editor. **50% freelance written.** Bimonthly magazine covering tent-rental and special-event industries. *InTents* is the official publication of IFAI's Tent Rental Division, delivering "the total tent experience." *InTents* offers focused, credible information needed to stage and host safe, successful tented events. Issues of the magazine include news, trends and behind-the-scenes coverage of the latest events in tents. Estab. 1995. Circ. 12,000. Byline given. Pays on acceptance. No kill fee. Publishes ms an average of 2 months after acceptance. Editorial lead time 3 months. Accepts queries by mail, e-mail, fax.

NONFICTION Needs how-to, interview, new product, photo feature, technical. **Buys 12-18 mss/year.** Query. Length: 800-2,000 words. **Pays $300-500.** Sometimes pays expenses of writers on assignment.

$$ MAINEBIZ

Mainebiz Publications, Inc., 48 Free St., Portland ME 04101. (207)761-8379. **Fax:** (207)761-0732. **E-mail:** pvanallen@mainebiz.biz; editorial@mainebiz.biz. **Website:** www.mainebiz.biz. **Contact:** Peter Van Allen, editor. **25% freelance written.** Biweekly tabloid covering business in Maine. *Mainebiz* is read by business decision makers across the state. Readerslook to the publication for business news and analysis. Estab. 1994. Circ. 13,000. Byline given. Pays on publication. Offers 10% kill fee. Publishes ms an average of 1 month after acceptance. Editorial lead time 1 month. Submit seasonal material 2 months in advance. Accepts queries by mail, e-mail. Responds in 3 weeks to queries. Sample copy online.

NONFICTION Needs essays, expose, interview, business trends. Special issues: See website for editorial calendar. **Buys 50+ mss/year.** Query with published clips. Length: 500-2,500 words. **Pays $75-350.** True

$$$$ NATIONAL BLACK MBA MAGAZINE

1 E. Wacker, Suite 3500, Chicago IL 60601. (312)236-2622. **Fax:** (312)236-0390. **E-mail:** elaine@naylor.com. **Website:** www.nbmbaa.org. **80% freelance written.** Online magazine covering business career strategy, economic development, and financial management. Estab. 1997. Circ. 45,000. Byline given. Pays after publication. Offers 10-20% or $500 kill fee. Publishes ms an average of 1 month after acceptance. Editorial lead time 2-3 months. Submit seasonal material 3-4 months in advance. Accepts queries by mail, e-mail, fax. No

COLUMNS/DEPARTMENTS Management Strategies (leadership development), 1,200-1,700 words; Features (business management, entreprenuerial finance); Finance; Technology. Send complete ms. **Pays $500-1,000.**

$$ RETAIL INFO SYSTEMS NEWS

Edgell Communications, 4 Middlebury Blvd., Randolph NJ 07869. (973)607-1300. **Fax:** (973)607-1395. **E-mail:** ablair@edgellmail.com; jskorupa@edgellmail.com. **Website:** www.risnews.com. **Contact:** Adam Blair, editor; Joe Skorupa, group editor-in-chief. **65% freelance written.** Monthly magazine covering retail technology. Estab. 1988. Circ. 22,000. Byline sometimes given. Pays on publication. No kill fee. Publishes ms an average of 2 months after acceptance. Editorial lead time 3 months. Submit seasonal material 3 months in advance. Accepts queries by mail. Sample copy available online.

NONFICTION Needs essays, exposè, how-to, humor, interview, technical. **Buys 80 mss/year.** Query with published clips. Length: 700-1,900 words. **Pays $600-1,200 for assigned articles.** Sometimes pays expenses of writers on assignment.

COLUMNS/DEPARTMENTS News/trends (analysis of current events), 150-300 words. **Buys 4 articles/year mss/year.** Query with published clips. **Pays $100-300.**

$$ RTOHQ: THE MAGAZINE

1504 Robin Hood Trail, Austin TX 78703. (800)204-2776. **Fax:** (512)794-0097. **E-mail:** nferguson@rtohq.org; bkeese@rtohq.org. **Website:** www.rtohq.org. **Contact:** Neil Ferguson, art director; Bill Keese, executive editor. **50% freelance written.** Bimonthly magazine covering the rent-to-own industry. *RTOHQ: The Magazine* is the only publication representing the rent-to-own industry and members of APRO. The magazine covers timely news and features affecting the industry, association activities, and member profiles. Awarded best 4-color magazine by the American Society of Association Executives in 1999. Estab. 1980. Circ. 5,500. Byline given. Pays on acceptance. Offers 25% kill fee. Publishes ms an average of 2 months after acceptance. Editorial lead time 2 months. Submit seasonal material 4 months in advance. Accepts queries by mail, e-mail, fax, phone, online submission form. Accepts simultaneous submissions. Responds in 1 month to queries. Responds in 2 months to mss. Sample copy free.

NONFICTION Needs expose, general interest, how-to, inspirational, interview, technical, industry features. **Buys 12 mss/year.** Query with published clips. Length: 1,200-2,500 words. **Pays $150-700.** Sometimes pays expenses of writers on assignment.

$$ SECURITY DEALER & INTEGRATOR

Cygnus Business Media, 12735 Morris Rd., Bldg. 200, Suite 180, Alpharetta GA 30004. (800)547-7377, ext 2226. **E-mail:** paul.rothman@cygnus.com. **Website:** www.securityinfowatch.com/magazine. **Contact:** Paul Rothman, editor-in-chief. **25% freelance written.** Circ. 25,000. Byline sometimes given. Pays 3 weeks after publication. No kill fee. Publishes ms an average of 3 months after acceptance. Accepts queries by e-mail. Accepts simultaneous submissions.

NONFICTION Needs how-to, interview, technical. No consumer pieces. Query by e-mail. Length: 1,000-3,000 words. **Pays $300 for assigned articles; $100-200 for unsolicited articles.** Sometimes pays expenses of writers on assignment.

COLUMNS/DEPARTMENTS Closed Circuit TV, Access Control (both on application, installation, new products), 500-1,000 words. **Buys 25 mss/year.** Query by mail only. **Pays $100-150.**

$$ SMART BUSINESS

Smart Business Network, Inc., 835 Sharon Dr., Suite 200, Cleveland OH 44145. (440)250-7000. **Fax:** (440)250-7001. **E-mail:** tshryock@sbnonline.com. **Website:** www.sbnonline.com. **Contact:** Todd Shryock, managing editor. **5% freelance written.** Monthly business magazine with an audience made up of business owners and top decision makers. *Smart Business* is one of the fastest growing national chains of regional management journals for corporate executives. Every issue delves into the minds of the most innovative executives in each of our regions to report on how market leaders got to the top and what strategies they use to stay there. Estab. 1989. Byline given. Pays on publication. Offers 50% kill fee. Publishes ms an average of 2 months after acceptance. Editorial lead time 3 months. Submit seasonal material 3 months in advance. Accepts queries by mail, e-mail. Responds in 2 weeks to queries. Responds in 1 month to mss. Sample copy available online. Guidelines by e-mail.

NONFICTION Needs how-to, interview. No breaking news or news features. **Buys 10-12 mss/year.** Query with published clips. Length: 1,150-2,000 words. **Pays $200-500.** Sometimes pays expenses of writers on assignment.

$$ STAMATS MEETINGS MEDIA

655 Montgomery St., Suite 900, San Francisco CA 94111. **Fax:** (415)788-1358. **E-mail:** tyler.davidson@meetingsfocus.com. **Website:** www.meetingsfocus.com. **Contact:** Tyler Davidson, chief content director. **75% freelance written.** Monthly tabloid covering meeting, event, and conference planning. Estab. 1986. Circ. *Meetings East* and *Meetings South* 22,000; *Meetings West* 26,000. Byline given. Pays 1 month after publication. No kill fee. Publishes ms an average of 1 month after acceptance. Editorial lead time

3 months. Submit seasonal material 3 months in advance. Accepts queries by mail, e-mail, fax. Responds in 3 weeks to queries. Sample copy for DSR with 9x13 envelope and 5 first-class stamps.

NONFICTION Needs how-to, travel, as it pertains to meetings and conventions. "No first-person fluff—this is a business magazine." **Buys 150 mss/year.** Query with published clips. Length: 1,200-2,000 words. **Pays $500 flat rate/package.**

$ THE STATE JOURNAL

WorldNow, P.O. Box 11848, Charleston WV 25339. (304)395-1313. **E-mail:** aali@wowktv.com. **Website:** www.statejournal.com. **Contact:** Ann Ali, managing editor. **30% freelance written.** Weekly journal dedicated to providing stories of interest to the business community in West Virginia. Estab. 1984. Circ. 10,000. Byline given. Pays on publication. No kill fee. Publishes ms an average of 3 weeks after acceptance. Submit seasonal material 4 months in advance. Accepts queries by mail, e-mail, fax. Sample copy and writer's guidelines for #10 SASE.

NONFICTION Needs general interest, interview, new product, (all business related). **Buys 400 mss/year.** Query. Length: 250-1,500 words. **Pays $50.** Sometimes pays expenses of writers on assignment.

$$$ VENECONOMY/VENECONOMA

VenEconomia, Edificio Gran Sabana, Piso 1, Ave. Abraham Lincoln, No. 174, Blvd. de Sabana Grande, Caracas Venezuela. (58)(212)761-8121. **Fax:** (58)(212)762-8160. **E-mail:** mercadeo@veneconomia.com. **Website:** www.veneconomia.com; www.veneconomy.com. **70% freelance written.** Monthly business magazine covering business, political, and social issues in Venezuela. *VenEconomy*'s subscribers are mostly business people, both Venezuelans and foreigners doing business in Venezuela. Some academics and diplomats also read our magazine. The magazine is published monthly both in English and Spanish. Freelancers may query in either language. Slant is decidedly pro-business, but not dogmatically conservative. Development, human rights, political, and environmental issues are covered from a business-friendly angle. Estab. 1983. Byline given. Pays on publication. Offers 50% kill fee. Publishes ms an average of 1 month after acceptance. Editorial lead time 1-2 months. Submit seasonal material 1 month in advance. Accepts queries by e-mail. Accepts simultaneous submissions. Responds in 2 weeks to queries. Responds in 4 months to mss. Sample copy by e-mail.

NONFICTION Contact: Francisco Toro, political editor. Needs essays, expose, interview, new product, opinion. No first-person stories or travel articles. **Buys 50 mss/year.** Query. Length: 1,100-3,200 words. **Pays 10-15¢/word for assigned articles.** Sometimes pays expenses of writers on assignment.

$$$ WORLD TRADE

2401 W. Big Beaver Rd., Suite 700, Troy MI 48084. (216)280-4467. **Fax:** (248)502-1060. **E-mail:** toscanoc@bnpmedia.com. **Website:** www.worldtradewt100.com. **Contact:** Cristina Toscano. **50% freelance written.** Monthly magazine covering international business. Estab. 1988. Circ. 75,000. Byline given. Pays on publication. No kill fee. Publishes ms an average of 1 month after acceptance. Editorial lead time 3 months. Accepts queries by mail, fax.

NONFICTION Needs interview, technical, market reports, finance, logistics. **Buys 40-50 mss/year.** Query with published clips. Length: 450-1,500 words. **Pays 50¢/word.**

COLUMNS/DEPARTMENTS International Business Services, 800 words; Shipping, Supply Chain Management, Logistics, 800 words; Software & Technology, 800 words; Economic Development (US, International), 800 words. **Buys 40-50 mss/year. Pays 50¢/word.**

CHURCH ADMINISTRATION AND MINISTRY

$ CHRISTIAN COMMUNICATOR

9118 W. Elmwood Dr., Suite 1G, Niles IL 60714-5820. (847)296-3964. **Fax:** (847)296-0754. **E-mail:** ljohnson@wordprocommunications.com. **Website:** acwriters.com. **Contact:** Lin Johnson, managing editor; Sally Miller, poetry editor (sallymiller@ameritech.net). **50% freelance written.** Monthly magazine covering Christian writing and speaking. Circ. 2,000. Byline given. Pays on publication. No kill fee. Publishes ms an average of 6-12 months after acceptance. Editorial lead time 3 months. Submit seasonal material 9 months in advance. Accepts queries by e-mail. Responds in 6-8 weeks to queries; in 8-12 weeks to mss. Sample copy for SAE and 5 first-class stamps. Writer's guidelines by e-mail or on website.

NONFICTION Needs how-to, interview, "Articles on writing nonfiction, research, creativity." **Buys 60**

mss/year. Query or send complete ms only by e-mail. Length: 700-1,000 words. **Pays $10. $5 for reviews. ACW CD for anecdotes.**

POETRY Needs free verse, light verse, traditional. Buys Publishes 22 poems/year. poems/year. Submit maximum 3 poems. Length: 4-20 lines. **Pays $5.**

FILLERS Needs anecdotes, short humor. **Buys 10-30 mss/year.** Length: 75-300 words. **Pays CD.**

$ CREATOR MAGAZINE

P.O. Box 3538, Pismo Beach CA 93448. (800)777-6713. **E-mail:** customerservice@creatormagazine.com. **Website:** www.creatormagazine.com. **Contact:** Bob Burroughs, editor. **35% freelance written.** Bimonthly magazine. Most readers are church music directors and worship leaders. Content focuses on the spectrum of worship styles from praise and worship to traditional to liturgical. All denominations subscribe. Articles on worship, choir rehearsal, handbells, children's/youth choirs, technique, relationships, etc. Estab. 1978. Circ. 6,000. Byline given. Pays on publication. No kill fee. Publishes ms an average of 3 months after acceptance. Editorial lead time 3 months. Submit seasonal material 4 months in advance. Accepts queries by mail. Accepts simultaneous submissions. Sample copy for SAE with 9x12 envelope and 5 first-class stamps. Guidelines free.

NONFICTION Needs essays, how-to, be a better church musician, choir director, rehearsal technician, etc., humor, short personal perspectives, inspirational, interview, call first, new product, call first, opinion, personal experience, photo feature, religious, technical, choral technique. Special issues: July/August is directed toward adult choir members, rather than directors. **Buys 20 mss/year.** Query or send complete ms. Length: 1,000-10,000 words. **Pays $30-75 for assigned articles. Pays $30-60 for unsolicited articles.**

$$ GROUP MAGAZINE

Simply Youth Ministry, 1515 Cascade Ave., Loveland CO 80538. (970)669-3836. **E-mail:** sfirestone@group.com. **Website:** www.youthministry.com/group-magazine. **Contact:** Scott Firestone IV, associate editor. **50% freelance written.** Bimonthly magazine for Christian youth workers. *Group* is the interdenominational magazine for leaders of Christian youth groups. *Group*'s purpose is to supply ideas, practical help, inspiration, and training for youth leaders. Estab. 1974. Circ. 55,000. Byline sometimes given. Pays on acceptance. No kill fee. Editorial lead time 4 months. Submit seasonal material 5 months in advance. Accepts queries by mail, e-mail, fax. Responds in 8-10 weeks to queries. Responds in 2 months to mss. Sample copy for $2, plus 10x12 SAE and 3 first-class stamps.

NONFICTION Needs inspirational, personal experience, religious. No fiction, prose, or poetry. **Buys 30 mss/year.** Query. Submit online, through website. Length: 200-2,000 words. **Pays $50-250.** Sometimes pays expenses of writers on assignment.

COLUMNS/DEPARTMENTS "Try This One" section needs short ideas (100-250 words) for youth group use. These include games, fundraisers, crowd-breakers, Bible studies, helpful hints, outreach ideas, and discussion starters. "Hands-on Help" section needs mini-articles (100-350 words) that feature practical tips for youth leaders on working with students, adult leaders, and parents. **Pays $50.**

$$ THE JOURNAL OF ADVENTIST EDUCATION

General Conference of SDA, 12501 Old Columbia Pike, Silver Spring MD 20904. (301)680-5069. **Fax:** (301)622-9627. **E-mail:** mcgarrellf@gc.adventist.org; goffc@gc.adventist.org. **Website:** jae.adventist.org. **Contact:** Faith-Ann McGarrell, editor; Chandra Goff. Bimonthly (except skips issue in summer) professional journal covering teachers and administrators in Seventh Day Adventist school systems. Published 5 times/year in English, 2 times/year in French, Spanish, and Portuguese. Emphasizes procedures, philosophy and subject matter of Christian education. Estab. 1939. Circ. 14,000 in English; 13,000 in other languages. Byline given. Pays on publication. No kill fee. Publishes ms an average of 1 year after acceptance. Editorial lead time 1 year. Accepts queries by mail, e-mail, fax, phone. Responds in 6 weeks to queries; 4 months to mss. Sample copy for sae with 10x12 envelope and 5 first-class stamps. Guidelines online.

NONFICTION Needs book excerpts, essays, how-to, education-related, personal experience, photo feature, religious, education. "No brief first-person stories about Sunday Schools." Query. All articles must be submitted in electronic format. Store in Word or .rtf format. If you submit a CD, include a printed copy of the article with the CD. Articles should be 6-8 pages long, with a max of 10 pages, including references. Two-part articles will be considered. Length: 1,000-1,500 words. **Pays $25-300.**

LEADERSHIP JOURNAL

Christianity Today International, 465 Gundersen Dr., Carol Stream IL 60188. (630)260-6200. **Fax:** (630)260-0114. **E-mail:** ljeditor@leadershipjournal.net. **Website:** www.christianitytoday.com/le. Skye Jethani, managing editor. **Contact:** Marshall Shelley, editor-in-chief. **75% freelance written. Works with a small number of new/unpublished writers each year**. Quarterly magazine. Writers must have a knowledge of and sympathy for the unique expectations placed on pastors and local church leaders. Each article must support points by illustrating from real life experiences in local churches. Estab. 1980. Circ. 48,000. Byline given. Pays on acceptance. Offers 33% kill fee. Publishes ms an average of 6 months after acceptance. Editorial lead time 6 months. Submit seasonal material 6 months in advance. Accepts queries by mail, e-mail, fax. Responds in 2 weeks to queries. Responds in 2 months to mss.

NONFICTION Needs how-to, humor, interview, personal experience, sermon illustrations. No articles from writers who have never read our journal. No unsolicited ms. **Buys 60 mss/year.** Query with proposal. Send a brief query letter describing your idea and how you plan to develop it. Length: 300-3,000 words. **Pays $35-400.** Sometimes pays expenses of writers on assignment.

COLUMNS/DEPARTMENTS **Contact:** Skye Jethanis, managing editor. Toolkit (book/software reviews), 500 words. **Buys 8 mss/year. mss/year.** Query.

MOMENTUM

National Catholic Educational Association, 1005 N. Glebe Rd., Suite 525, Arlington VA 22201. (800)711-6232. **Fax:** (703)243-0025. **E-mail:** momentum@ncea.org. **Website:** www.ncea.org/publications/momentum. **Contact:** Gabrielle Gallagher, editor. **65% freelance written.** Quarterly educational journal covering educational issues in Catholic schools and parishes. *Momentum* is a membership journal of the National Catholic Educational Association. The audience is educators and administrators in Catholic schools K-12, and parish programs. Estab. 1970. Circ. 19,000. Byline given. Pays on publication. No kill fee. Publishes ms an average of 3 months after acceptance. Accepts queries by e-mail. Sample copy for $5 SASE and 8 first-class stamps. Guidelines online.

NONFICTION No articles unrelated to educational and catechesis issues. **Buys 40-60 mss/year.** Query and send complete ms. Length: 1,500 words for feature articles; 700-1,000 words for columns, "From the Field," and opinion pieces or essays; 500-750 words for book reviews. **Pays $75 maximum.**

THE PRIEST

Our Sunday Visitor, Inc., 200 Noll Plaza, Huntington IN 46750. (800)348-2440. **Fax:** (260)359-9117. **E-mail:** tpriest@osv.com. **Website:** www.osv.com. **Contact:** Editorial Department. **40% freelance written.** Monthly magazine that publishes articles to aid priests in their day-to-day parish ministry. Includes items on spirituality, counseling, administration, theology, personalities, the saints, etc. Byline given. Pays on acceptance. No kill fee. Editorial lead time 3 months. Submit seasonal material 4 months in advance. Accepts queries by mail, e-mail, fax, phone. Responds in 5 weeks to queries; 3 months to mss. Sample copy free. Guidelines online.

NONFICTION Needs essays, historical/nostalgic, humor, inspirational, interview/profile, opinion, personal experience, photo feature, religious. **Buys 96 mss/year.** Send complete ms. Length: 1,500 words maximum. **Pays $200 minimum for assigned articles; $50 minimum for unsolicited articles.**

RTJ'S CREATIVE CATECHIST

Twenty-Third Publications, P.O. Box 6015, New London CT 06320. (800)321-0411, ext. 188. **Fax:** (860)437-6246. **E-mail:** creativesubs@rtjscreativecatechist.com; editor@rtjscreativecatechist.com. **Website:** www.rtjscreativecatechist.com. **Contact:** Robyn Lee, editor. Monthly magazine for Catholic catechists and religion teachers. The mission of *RTJ's Creative Catechist* is to encourage and assist Catholic DREs and catechists in their vocation to proclaim the gospel message and lead others to the joy of following Jesus Christ. *RTJ* provides professional support, theological content, age appropriate methodology, and teaching tools. Estab. 1966. Circ. 30,000. Byline given. Pays on acceptance. Publishes ms an average of 3-20 months after acceptance. Editorial lead time 4 months. Submit seasonal material 6 months in advance. Accepts queries by mail, e-mail. Accepts simultaneous submissions. Responds in 1-2 weeks to queries. Responds in 1-2 months to mss. Sample copy for SAE with 9x12 envelope and 3 first-class stamps. Guidelines free.

NONFICTION Needs how-to, inspirational, personal experience, religious, articles on celebrating church seasons, sacraments, on morality, on prayer, on saints. Special issues: Sacraments; Prayer; Advent/Christmas; Lent/Easter. All should be written by people who have experience in religious education, or a good background in Catholic faith. Does not want fiction, poems, plays, articles written for Catholic school teachers (i.e., math, English, etc.), or articles that are academic rather than catechetical in nature. **Buys 35-40 mss/year.** Send complete ms. Length: 600-1,300 words. **Pays $100-125 for assigned articles. Pays $75-125 for unsolicited articles.**

COLUMNS/DEPARTMENTS Catechist to Catechist (brief articles on crafts, games, etc., for religion lessons); Faith and Fun (full-page religious word games, puzzles, mazes, etc., for children). **Buys 30 mss/year.** Send complete ms. **Pays $20-125.**

$$ TODAY'S CATHOLIC TEACHER

Peter Li Education Group, 2621 Dryden Rd., Suite 300, Dayton OH 45439. (937)293-1415; (800)523-4625, x1139. **Fax:** (937)293-1310. **E-mail:** bshepard@peterli.com. **E-mail:** bshepard@peterli.com. **Website:** www.catholicteacher.com. **Contact:** Elizabeth Shepard, editor. **60% freelance written.** Magazine published 6 times/year during school year covering Catholic education for grades K-12. Looks for topics of interest and practical help to teachers in Catholic elementary schools in all curriculum areas including religion technology, discipline, and motivation. Estab. 1972. Circ. 50,000. Byline given. Pays on publication. No kill fee. Publishes ms an average of 2 months after acceptance. Editorial lead time 3 months. Submit seasonal material 6 months in advance. Accepts queries by mail, e-mail, fax. Accepts simultaneous submissions. Responds in 1 month to queries. Responds in 3 months to mss. Sample copy for $3 or on website. Guidelines available online.

NONFICTION Needs essays, how-to, humor, interview, personal experience. No articles pertaining to public education. **Buys 15 mss/year.** Query or send complete ms. Query letters are encouraged. E-mail, write, call, or fax the editor for editorial calendar. Articles may be submitted as hard copy; submission by e-mail with accompanying hard copy is appreciated. Length: 600-1,500 words. **Pays $100-250.** Sometimes pays expenses of writers on assignment.

$$$ WORSHIP LEADER MAGAZINE

32234 Paseo Adelanto, Suite A, San Juan Capistrano CA 92675. (949)240-9339. **Fax:** (949)240-0038. **Website:** www.worshipleader.com. **Contact:** Jeremy Armstrong, managing editor. **80% freelance written.** Bimonthly magazine covering all aspects of Christian worship. *Worship Leader Magazine* exists to challenge, serve, equip, and train those involved in leading the 21st century church in worship. The intended readership is the worship team (all those who plan and lead) of the local church. Estab. 1990. Circ. 40,000. Byline given. Pays on publication. Offers 50% kill fee. Editorial lead time 3 months. Submit seasonal material 6 months in advance. Accepts queries by online submission form. Responds in 6 weeks to queries. Responds in 3 months to mss. Sample copy for $5.

NONFICTION Needs general interest, how-to, related to purpose/audience, inspirational, interview, opinion. **Buys 15-30 mss/year.** Unsolicited articles are only accepted for the web and should be between 700 and 900 words. Web articles are published on a gratis basis and are often the first step in creating a relationship with *Worship Leader Magazine* and its readers, which could lead to more involvement as a writer. Length: 700-900 words. **Pays $200-800 for assigned articles. Pays $200-500 for unsolicited articles.** Sometimes pays expenses of writers on assignment.

$$ YOUTHWORKER JOURNAL

Salem Publishing/CCM Communications, 402 BNA Dr., Suite 400, Nashville TN 37217-2509. **E-mail:** articles@youthworker.com. **E-mail:** ALee@SalemPublishing.com. **Website:** www.youthworker.com. **Contact:** Steve Rabey, editor; Amy L. Lee, managing editor. **100% freelance written.** Website and bimonthly magazine covering professional youth ministry in the church and parachurch. Estab. 1984. Circ. 20,000. Byline given. Pays on publication. No kill fee. Publishes ms an average of 3 months after acceptance for print; immediately online. Editorial lead time 6 months for print; immediately online. Submit seasonal material 6 months in advance for print. Accepts queries by e-mail, online submission form. Responds within 6 weeks to queries. Sample copy for $5. Guidelines available online.

NONFICTION Needs essays, new product, youth ministry books only, personal experience, photo feature, religious. Special issues: See website for themes in upcoming issues. Query. Length: 250-3,000 words. **Pays $15-200.**

CLOTHING

$$$ FOOTWEAR PLUS

9 Threads, 36 Cooper Square, 4th Floor, New York NY 10003. (646)278-1550. **Fax:** (646)278-1553. **E-mail:** editorialrequests@9threads.com. **Website:** www.footwearplusmagazine.com. **Contact:** Brittany Leitner, assistant editor. **20% freelance written.** Monthly magazine covering footwear fashion and business. A business-to-business publication targeted at footwear retailers. Covers all categories of footwear and age ranges with a focus on new trends, brands and consumer buying habits, as well as retailer advice on operating the store more effectively. Estab. 1990. Circ. 18,000. Byline given. Pays on publication. No kill fee. Publishes ms an average of 1-2 months after acceptance. Editorial lead time 1-2 months. Sample copy for $5.

NONFICTION Needs interview, new product, technical. Does not want pieces unrelated to footwear/fashion industry. **Buys 10-20 mss/year.** Query. Length: 500-2,500 words. **Pays $1,000 maximum.** Sometimes pays expenses of writers on assignment.

$$ MADE TO MEASURE

The Uniform Magazine, UniformMartket LLC, 633 Skokie Blvd., Suite 490, Northbrook IL 60062. (224)406-8840. **Fax:** (224)406-8850. **E-mail:** news@uniformmarket.com. **Website:** www.madetomeasuremag.com; www.uniformmarketnews.com. **Contact:** Rick Levine, editor. **50% freelance written.** Semi-annual magazine covering uniforms and career apparel. A semi-annual magazine/buyers' reference containing leading sources of supply, equipment, and services of every description related to the Uniform, Career Apparel, and allied trades, throughout the entire US. Estab. 1930. Circ. 25,000. Byline given. Pays on acceptance. No kill fee. Publishes ms an average of 2 months after acceptance. Editorial lead time 4 months. Submit seasonal material 4 months in advance. Accepts queries by mail, e-mail. Accepts simultaneous submissions. Responds in 3 weeks to queries.

NONFICTION Needs interview, new product, personal experience, photo feature, technical. **Buys 6-8 mss/year.** Query with published clips. Length: 1,000-3,000 words.

$$ TEXTILE WORLD

Billian Publishing Co., 2100 RiverEdge Pkwy., Suite 1200, Atlanta GA 30328. (770)955-5656. **Fax:** (770)952-0669. **E-mail:** editor@textileworld.com. **Website:** www.textileworld.com. **Contact:** James Borneman, editor-in-chief. **5% freelance written.** Bimonthly magazine covering the business of textile, apparel, and fiber industries with considerable technical focus on products and processes. Estab. 1868. Byline given. Pays on publication. No kill fee.

NONFICTION Needs business, technical. No puff pieces pushing a particular product. **Buys 10 mss/year.** Query. Length: 500 words minimum. **Pays $200/published page.**

CONSTRUCTION AND CONTRACTING

$$ AUTOMATED BUILDER

CMN Associates, Inc., 2401 Grapevine Dr., Oxnard CA 93036. (805)351-5931. **Fax:** (805)351-5755. **E-mail:** cms03@pacbell.net. **Website:** www.automatedbuilder.com. **Contact:** Don O. Carlson, editor/publisher. **5% freelance written.** "*Automated Builder* covers management, production and marketing information on all 7 segments of home, apartment and commercial construction. Home and commercial buyers will see the latest in homes and commercial structures." Estab. 1964. Circ. 75,000 when printed. Byline given if desired. Pays on acceptance. Publishes ms an average of 2 months after acceptance. Editorial lead time 2 months. Accepts queries by mail, e-mail, fax. Responds in 2 weeks to queries.

NONFICTION "No fiction and no planned 'dreams.' Housing projects must be built or under construction. Same for commercial structures" **Buys 6-8 mss/year.** Phone queries OK. Length: 500-750 words. **Pays $250 for stories including photos.**

$$$ THE CONCRETE PRODUCER

Hanley-Wood, LLC, 8725 W. Higgins Rd., Suite 600, Chicago IL 60631. (773)824-2400; (773)824-2496. **E-mail:** tbagsarian@hanleywood.com; ryelton@hanleywood.com; TCPeditor@hanleywood.com. **Website:** www.theconcreteproducer.com. **Contact:** Tom Bagsarian group managing ditor; Richard Yelton, editor-at-large. **25% freelance written.** Monthly magazine covering concrete production. Audience consists of producers who have succeeded in making concrete the preferred building material through management, operating, quality control, use of the latest technology, or use of superior materials. Estab. 1982. Circ.

TRADE JOURNALS

18,000. Byline given. Pays on acceptance. No kill fee. Publishes ms an average of 2 months after acceptance. Editorial lead time 4 months. Accepts queries by mail, e-mail, fax, phone. Responds in 1 week to queries. Responds in 2 months to mss. Sample copy for $4. Guidelines free.

NONFICTION Needs how-to, promote concrete, new product, technical. **Buys 10 mss/year.** Send complete ms. Length: 500-2,000 words. **Pays $200-1,000.** Sometimes pays expenses of writers on assignment.

$ HARD HAT NEWS

Lee Publications, Inc., P.O. Box 121, Palatine Bridge NY 13428. (518)673-3763; (800)218-5586. **Fax:** (518)673-2381. **E-mail:** jcasey@leepub.com. **Website:** www.hardhat.com. **Contact:** Jon Casey, editor. **50% freelance written.** Biweekly tabloid covering heavy construction, equipment, road, and bridge work. "Our readers are contractors and heavy construction workers involved in excavation, highways, bridges, utility construction, and underground construction." Estab. 1980. Circ. 15,000. Byline given. No kill fee. Editorial lead time 2 weeks. Submit seasonal material 2 weeks in advance. Accepts queries by mail, e-mail, fax, phone. Sample copy and writer's guidelines free.

NONFICTION Needs interview, new product, opinion, photo feature, technical. Send complete ms. Length: 800-2,000 words. **Pays $2.50/inch.** Sometimes pays expenses of writers on assignment.

COLUMNS/DEPARTMENTS Association News; Parts and Repairs; Attachments; Trucks and Trailers; People on the Move.

$$ HOME ENERGY MAGAZINE

1250 Addison St., Suite 211B, Berkeley CA 94702. (510)524-5405. **Fax:** (510)981-1406. **E-mail:** contact@homeenergy.org; jpgunshinan@homeenergy.org. **Website:** www.homeenergy.org. **Contact:** Jim Gunshinan, managing editor. **10% freelance written.** Bimonthly magazine covering green home building and renovation. Readers are building contractors, energy auditors, and weatherization professionals. They expect technical detail, accuracy, and brevity. Estab. 1984. Circ. 5,000. Byline given. Pays on publication. Offers 10% kill fee. Publishes ms an average of 4 months after acceptance. Editorial lead time 4 months. Accepts queries by e-mail. Responds in 2 weeks to queries; 2 months to mss. Guidelines online.

NONFICTION Needs interview, technical. Does not want articles for consumers/general public. **Buys 6 mss/year.** Query with published clips. Submit article via e-mail. Length: 400-2,500 words. **Pays 20¢/word; $400 maximum for both assigned and unsolicited articles.**

COLUMNS/DEPARTMENTS "Trends" are short stories explaining a single advance or research result (400-1,500 words). "Features" are longer pieces that provide more in-depth information (1,500-2,500 words). "Field Notes" provide readers with first-person testimonials (1,500-2,500 words). "Columns" provide readers with direct answers to their specific questions (400-1,500 words). Submit columns via e-mail. Accepts Word, RTF documents, Text documents, and other common formats.

$$$ INTERIOR CONSTRUCTION

Ceilings & Interior Systems Construction Association, 1010 Jorie Blvd., Suite 30, Oak Brook IL 60523. (630)584-1919. **Fax:** (866)560-8537. **E-mail:** rmgi@comcast.net; cisca@cisca.org. **Website:** www.cisca.org. **Contact:** Rick Reuland, managing editor. Quarterly magazine on acoustics and commercial specialty ceiling construction. The resource for the Ceilings & Interior Systems Construction Industry. Features examine leading industry issues and trends like specialty ceilings, LEED, acoustics, and more. Each issue features industry news, new products, columns from industry experts, and CISCA news and initiatives. Estab. 1950. Circ. 3,000. Byline given. Pays on publication. No kill fee. Publishes ms an average of 1 1/2 months after acceptance. Editorial lead time 2-3 months. Accepts queries by e-mail. Sample copy by e-mail. Guidelines available.

NONFICTION Needs new product, technical. Query with published clips. Publishes 1-2 features per issue. Length: 700-1,700 words. **Pays $400 minimum, $800 maximum for assigned articles.**

$$ KEYSTONE BUILDER MAGAZINE

Pennsylvania Builders Association, 600 N. 12th St., Lemoyne PA 17043. (717)730-4380; 800-692-7339. **Fax:** (717)730-4396. **E-mail:** admin@pabuilders.org; metshied@pabuilders.org. **Website:** www.pabuilders.org. **10% freelance written.** Bimonthly trade publication for builders, remodelers, subcontractors, and other affiliates of the home building industry in Pennsylvania. Estab. 1988. Circ. 9,300. Byline given. Pays on publication. No kill fee. Publishes ms an average of 1 year after acceptance. Editorial lead time 3 months. Submit seasonal material 9 months in advance. Accepts queries by mail, e-mail. Accepts simultaneous submissions. Responds in 2 weeks to queries. Responds in 3 months to mss. Guidelines by e-mail.

NONFICTION Needs general interest, how-to, new product, technical. No personnel or company profiles. **Buys 1-2 mss/year.** Send complete ms. Length: 200-500 words. **Pays $200.**

METAL ROOFING MAGAZINE

a Division of F+W Media, Inc., 700 E. Iola St., Iola WI 54990-0001. (715)445-4612. **Fax:** (715)445-4087. **Website:** www.constructionmagnet.com/metal-roofing. **10% freelance written.** Bimonthly magazine covering roofing. *Metal Roofing Magazine* offers contractors, designers, suppliers, architects, and others in the construction industry a wealth of information on metal roofing—a growing segment of the roofing trade. Estab. 2000. Circ. 26,000. Byline given. Pays on publication. Publishes ms an average of 3 months after acceptance. Editorial lead time 3 months. Submit seasonal material 3 months in advance. Accepts queries by mail. Accepts simultaneous submissions. Sample copy free.

NONFICTION Needs book excerpts, historical, how-to, interview, new product, opinion, photo feature, technical. No advertorials. **Buys 15 mss/year.** Query with published clips. Length: 750 words minimum. **Pays $100-500 for assigned articles.**

COLUMNS/DEPARTMENTS Gutter Opportunities; Stay Cool; Metal Roofing Details; Spec It. **Buys 15 mss/year.** Send complete ms. **Pays $0-500.**

NETCOMPOSITES

4a Broom Business Park, Bridge Way Chesterfield S41 9QG UK. **E-mail:** info@netcomposites.com. **Website:** www.netcomposites.com. **1% freelance written.** Bimonthly newsletter covering advanced materials and fiber-reinforced polymer composites, plus a weekly electronic version called *Composite eNews. Advanced Materials & Composites News* covers markets, applications, materials, processes, and organizations for all sectors of the global hi-tech materials world. Audience is management, academics, researchers, government, suppliers, and fabricators. Focus on news about growth opportunities. Estab. 1978. Circ. 15,000+. Byline sometimes given. Pays on publication. No kill fee. Publishes ms an average of 1 month after acceptance. Editorial lead time 2 weeks. Submit seasonal material 1 month in advance. Accepts queries by e-mail. Responds in 1 week to queries. Responds in 1 month to mss. Sample copy for #10 SASE.

NONFICTION Needs new product, technical, industry information. **Buys 4-6 mss/year.** Query. 300 words. **Pays $200/final printed page.**

POB MAGAZINE

BNP Media, 2401 W. Big Beaver Rd., Suite 700, Troy MI 48084. (248)362-3700. **E-mail:** mehtab@bnpmedia.com. **Website:** www.pobonline.com. **Contact:** Benita Mehta, managing editor. **5% freelance written,.** Monthly magazine covering surveying, mapping, and geomatics. Estab. 1975. Circ. 39,000. Byline given. Pays on publication. Publishes ms an average of 3 months after acceptance. Editorial lead time 3 months. Accepts queries by e-mail, phone. Sample copy and guidelines available online.

NONFICTION Query. Document should be saved in Microsoft Word or text-only format. Also include an author byline and biography. Length: 1,700-2,200 words, with 2 graphics included. **Pays $400.**

PRECAST INC./MC MAGAZINE

National Precast Concrete Association, 1320 City Center Dr., Suite 200, Carmel IN 46032. (317)571-9500. **Fax:** (317)571-0041. **E-mail:** rhyink@precast.org. **Website:** www.precast.org. **Contact:** Ron Hyink, managing editor. **75% freelance written.** Bimonthly magazine covering manufactured concrete products. *Precast Inc.* is a publication for owners and managers of factory-produced concrete products used in construction. Publishes business articles, technical articles, company profiles, safety articles, and project profiles, with the intent of educating our readers in order to increase the quality and use of precast concrete. Estab. 1995. Circ. 8,500. Byline given. Pays on acceptance. No kill fee. Publishes ms an average of 6 months after acceptance. Editorial lead time 3 months. Accepts queries by mail, e-mail, fax. Accepts simultaneous submissions. Responds in 1 month to queries. Responds in 2 months to mss. Sample copy available online. Guidelines available online.

NONFICTION Needs how-to, business, interview, technical, concrete manufacturing. No humor, essays, fiction, or fillers. **Buys 8-14 mss/year.** Query or send complete ms. Length: 1,500-2,500 words. **Pays $250-750.** Sometimes pays expenses of writers on assignment.

RURAL BUILDER

a Division of F+W Media, Inc., 700 E. State St., Iola WI 54990-0001. (715)445-4612, ext. 13644. **Fax:** (715)445-

4087. **E-mail:** sharon.thatcher@fwcommunity.com. **Website:** www.ruralbuilder.com. **10% freelance written**. Magazine published 8 times/year covering rural building. "*Rural Builder* serves diversified town and country builders, offering them help managing their businesses through editorial and advertising material about metal, wood, post-frame, and masonry construction." Estab. 1967. Circ. 29,000. Byline given. Pays on publication. Publishes ms an average of 3 months after acceptance. Editorial lead time 3 months. Submit seasonal material 3 months in advance. Accepts queries by mail, e-mail. Accepts simultaneous submissions. Sample copy free.

NONFICTION Needs how-to, photo feature, technical. No advertorials. **Buys 10 mss/year.** Query with published clips. Length: 750 words minimum. **Pays $100-300.**

COLUMNS/DEPARTMENTS Money Talk (taxes for business); Tech Talk (computers for builders); Tool Talk (tools); Management Insights (business management); all 1,000 words. **Buys 10 mss/year.** Send complete ms. **Pays $0-250.**

$$ UNDERGROUND CONSTRUCTION

Oildom Publishing Company of Texas, Inc., P.O. Box 941669, Houston TX 77094-8669. (281)558-6930, ext. 220. **Fax:** (281)558-7029. **E-mail:** rcarpenter@oildom.com; efitzpatrick@oildom.com. **Website:** www.undergroundconstructionmagazine.com. **Contact:** Robert Carpenter, editor-in-chief; Oliver Klinger, publisher; Elizabeth Fitzpatrick, art director. **35% freelance written.** Monthly magazine covering underground oil and gas pipeline, water and sewer pipeline, cable construction for contractors, and owning companies. Circ. 40,000. No kill fee. Publishes ms an average of 6 months after acceptance. Accepts queries by mail, e-mail, fax, phone. Responds in 1 month to mss.

NONFICTION Needs how-to, job stories and industry issues. Query with published clips. Length: 1,000-2,000 words. **Pays $500.**

DECORATIVE APPAREL AND IMPRINTED INDUSTRY

$$ IMPRESSIONS

Nielsen Business Media, 1145 Sanctuary Pkwy., Suite 355, Alpharetta GA 30009-4772. (800)241-9034. **Fax:** (770)777-8733. **E-mail:** mderryberry@impressionsmag.com; jlaster@impressionsmag.com; michelle.havich@emeraldexpo.com. **Website:** www.impressionsmag.com. **Contact:** Marcia Derryberry, editor-in-chief; Jamar Laster, senior editor; Michelle Havich, managing editor. **30% freelance written.** Magazine, published 13 times/year, covering computerized embroidery and digitizing design. Authoritative, up-to-date information on screen printing, embroidery, heat-applied graphics and inkjet-to-garment printing. Readable, practical business and/or technical articles that show readers how to succeed in their profession. Estab. 1994. Circ. 20,000. Byline given. Pays on publication. No kill fee. Publishes ms an average of 3 months after acceptance. Editorial lead time 3 months. Submit seasonal material 6 months in advance. Accepts queries by mail, e-mail. Accepts simultaneous submissions. Sample copy for $10.

NONFICTION Needs how-to, embroidery, sales, marketing, design, general business info, interview, new product, photo feature, technical, computerized embroidery. **Buys 40 mss/year.** Query. Length: 800-2,000 words. **Pays $200 and up for assigned articles.**

DRUGS, HEALTH CARE AND MEDICAL PRODUCTS

$$$$⊘ ACP INTERNIST/ACP HOSPITALIST

American College of Physicians, 191 N. Independence Mall W., Philadelphia PA 19106-1572. (215)351-2400. **E-mail:** acpinternist@acponline.org; acphospitalist@acponline.org. **Website:** www.acpinternist.org; www.acphospitalist.org. **Contact:** Jennifer Kearney-Strouse, editor of *ACP Internist*; Jessica Berthold, editor of *ACP Hospitalist*. **40% freelance written.** Monthly magazine covering internal medicine/hospital medicine. Writes for specialists in internal medicine, not a consumer audience. Topics include clinical medicine, practice management, health information technology, and Medicare issues. Estab. 1981. Circ. 85,000 (*Internist*), 24,000 (*Hospitalist*). Byline given. Offers kill fee. Negotiable. Publishes ms an average of 2 months after acceptance. Editorial lead time 4 months. Submit seasonal material 6 months in advance. Accepts queries by e-mail. Guidelines free.

NONFICTION Needs interview. Query with published clips. Length: 700-2,000 words. **Pays $500-2,000 for assigned articles.** Pays expenses of writers on assignment.

$$ LABTALK

P.O. Box 593, Big Bear City CA 92314. (909)547-2234. **E-mail:** cwalker@jobson.com. **Website:** www.LabTalkOnline.com. **Contact:** Christie Walker, editor. **20% freelance written.** Magazine published 6 times/year for the eye wear industry. Estab. 1970. Accepts simultaneous submissions.

$$$ VALIDATION TIMES

Washington Information Source Co., 19-B Wirt St. SW, Leesburg VA 20175. (703)779-8777. **Fax:** (703)779-2508. **E-mail:** rmashaw@fdainfo.com. **Website:** www.fdainfo.com. **Contact:** Rebecca Masahw, managing editor. Monthly newsletters covering regulation of pharmaceutical and medical devices. Writes to executives who have to keep up on changing FDA policies and regulations, and on what their competitors are doing at the agency. Estab. 1999. Byline given. Pays on publication. No kill fee. Publishes ms an average of 1 month after acceptance. Editorial lead time 1 month. Submit seasonal material 1 month in advance. Accepts queries by mail. Responds in 1 month to queries. Sample copy and writer's guidelines free.

NONFICTION Needs how-to, technical, regulatory. No lay interest pieces. **Buys 50-100 mss/year.** Query. Length: 600-1,500 words. **Pays $100/half day; $200 full day to cover meetings and same rate for writing.** Sometimes pays expenses of writers on assignment.

EDUCATION AND COUNSELING

$ ARTS & ACTIVITIES

Publishers' Development Corp., 12345 World Trade Dr., San Diego CA 92128. (858)605-0242. **Fax:** (858)605-0247. **E-mail:** ed@artsandactivities.com. **Website:** www.artsandactivities.com. **Contact:** Maryellen Bridge, editor-in-chief. **95% freelance written. Eager to work with new/unpublished writers.** Monthly (except July and August) magazine covering art education at levels from preschool through college for educators and therapists engaged in arts and crafts education and training. Estab. 1932. Circ. 20,000. Byline given. Pays on publication. No kill fee. Publishes ms 6 months to 3 years after acceptance. Submit seasonal material 6 months in advance. Accepts queries by mail, e-mail. Responds in 3 months to queries. Sample copy for SAE with 9x12 envelope and 8 first-class stamps. Guidelines available on website.

NONFICTION Needs historical, arts, activities, history, how-to, classroom art experiences, artists' techniques, interviews of artists, opinion on arts activities curriculum, ideas of how-to do things better, philosophy of art education, personal experience (ties in with the how-to) articles of exceptional art programs. **Buys 80-100 mss/year.** Length: 500-1,500 words. **Pays $35-150.**

TIPS "Frequently in unsolicited mss, writers obviously have not studied the magazine to see what style of articles we publish. Send for a sample copy to familiarize yourself with our style and needs. The best way to find out if his/her writing style suits our needs is for the author to submit a ms on speculation. We prefer an anecdotal style of writing so that readers will feel as though they are there in the art room as the lesson/project is taking place. Also, good quality photographs of student artwork are important. We are a visual art magazine!"

$ THE ATA MAGAZINE

11010 142nd St. NW, Edmonton AB T5N 2R1 Canada. (780)447-9400. **Fax:** (780)455-6481. **E-mail:** government@teachers.ab.ca. **Website:** www.teachers.ab.ca. Quarterly magazine covering education. Estab. 1920. Circ. 42,100. Byline given. Pays on publication. No kill fee. Publishes ms an average of 4 months after acceptance. Editorial lead time 2 months. Submit seasonal material 2 months in advance. Accepts queries by mail, e-mail, fax, phone. Accepts simultaneous submissions. Responds in 2 months to queries. Previous articles available for viewing online. Guidelines available online.

NONFICTION Query with published clips. Length: 500-1,500 words. **Pays $100 (Canadian).**

$ THE FORENSIC TEACHER MAGAZINE

Wide Open Minds Educational Services, P.O. Box 5263, Wilmington DE 19808. **E-mail:** admin@theforensicteacher.com. **Website:** www.theforensicteacher.com. **Contact:** Dr. Mark R. Feil, editor. **70% freelance written.** Quarterly magazine covering forensic education. Readers are middle, high and post-secondary teachers who are looking for better, easier and more engaging ways to teach forensics as well as law enforcement and scientific forensic experts. Writers understand this and are writing from a forensic or educational background, or both. Prefers a first-person writing style. Estab. 2006. Circ. 30,000. Byline given. Pays 60 days after publication. No kill fee. Publishes ms an average of 6 months after acceptance. Editorial lead time 6 months. Submit seasonal material 6 months in advance. Accepts queries by e-mail. Accepts simultaneous submissions. Responds in 2 weeks to queries; 2 months to mss. Sample copy available at website. Guidelines available online.

NONFICTION Needs how-to, personal experience, photo feature, technical, lesson plans. Does not want poetry, fiction or anything unrelated to medicine, law, forensics or teaching. **Buys 18 mss/year.** Send complete ms. Length: 400-2,000 words. **Pays 2¢/word.**

COLUMNS/DEPARTMENTS Needs lesson experiences or ideas, personal or professional experiences with a branch of forensics. "If you've done it in your classroom please share it with us. Also, if you're a professional, please tell our readers how they can duplicate the lesson/demo/experiment in their classrooms. Please share what you know."

FILLERS Needs : facts, newsbreaks. **Buys 15 fillers/year. mss/year.** Length: 50-200 words. **Pays 2¢/word.**

$$ THE HISPANIC OUTLOOK IN HIGHER EDUCATION

220 Kinderkamack Rd., Westwood NJ 07675. (800)549-8280. **Fax:** (201)587-9105. **Website:** www.hispanicoutlook.com. **50% freelance written.** Biweekly magazine (except during the summer) covering higher education of Hispanics. Looking for higher education story articles, with a focus on Hispanics and the advancements made by and for Hispanics in higher education. Circ. 28,000. Byline given. Pays on publication. No kill fee. Publishes ms an average of 2 months after acceptance. Editorial lead time 2 months. Submit seasonal material 3 months in advance. Accepts queries by mail, e-mail, fax. Accepts simultaneous submissions. Sample copy free.

NONFICTION Needs historical, interview of academic or scholar, opinion on higher education, personal experience egarding higher education only. **Buys 20-25 mss/year.** Query with published clips. Length: 1,800-2,200 words. **Pays $400 minimum for print articles, and $300 for online articles when accepted.** Pays expenses of writers on assignment.

$$ PTO TODAY

PTO Today, Inc., 100 Stonewall Blvd., Suite 3, Wrentham MA 02093. (800)644-3561. **Fax:** (508)384-6108. **E-mail:** editor@ptotoday.com. **Website:** www.ptotoday.com. **Contact:** Craig Bystrynski, editor-in-chief. **50% freelance written.** Magazine published 6 times during the school year covering the work of school parent-teacher groups. Celebrates the work of school parent volunteers and provide resources to help them do that work more effectively. Estab. 1999. Circ. 80,000. Byline given. Pays on acceptance. Offers 30% kill fee. Publishes ms an average of 4-6 months after acceptance. Editorial lead time 4 months. Submit seasonal material 4 months in advance. Accepts queries by e-mail. Guidelines by e-mail.

NONFICTION Needs general interest, how-to, interview, personal experience. **Buys 20 mss/year.** Query. "We review but do not encourage unsolicited submissions." Features are roughly 1,200-2,200 words. Average assignment is 1,200 words. Department pieces are 600-1,200 words. **Payment depends on the difficulty of the topic and the experience of the writer. "We pay by the assignment, not by the word; our pay scale ranges from $200 to $700 for features and $150 to $400 for departments. We occasionally pay more for high-impact stories and highly experienced writers. We buy all rights, and we pay on acceptance (within 30 days of invoice)."**

$$ TEACHING THEATRE

Educational Theatre Association, 2343 Auburn Ave., Cincinnati OH 45219-2815. (513)421-3900. **E-mail:** jpalmarini@schooltheatre.org. **Website:** www.schooltheatre.org. **Contact:** James Palmarini, editor. **65% freelance written.** Quarterly magazine covering education theater K-12; primary emphasis on middle and secondary level education. Estab. 1989. Circ. 5,000. Byline given. Pays on acceptance. No kill fee. Publishes ms an average of 3 months after acceptance. Editorial lead time 2 months. Accepts queries by mail, e-mail. Accepts simultaneous submissions. Responds in 4-6 weeks to queries. Responds in 3 months to mss. Sample copy available online. Guidelines available by request.

NONFICTION Needs book excerpts, essays, how-to, interview, opinion, technical theater. **Buys 12-15 mss/year.** Query. A typical issue might include: an article on theatre curriculum development; a profile of an exemplary theatre education program; a how-to teach piece on acting, directing, or playwriting; and a news story or 2 about pertinent educational theatre issues and events. Once articles are accepted, authors are asked to supply their work electronically via e-mail. Length: 750-4,000 words **Pays $50-350.**

$$$$ TEACHING TOLERANCE

A Project of The Southern Poverty Law Center, 400 Washington Ave., Montgomery AL 36104. (334)956-8374. **Fax:** (334)956-8488. **E-mail:** editor@teachingtolerance.org. **Website:** www.teachingtolerance.org. **30% freelance written.** Semiannual magazine. Estab. 1991. Circ. 400,000. Byline given. Pays on acceptance. No kill fee. Editorial lead time 6 months. Submit seasonal material 6 months in advance. Accepts queries by mail, fax, online submission form. Sample copy avialble online. Guidelines availabel online.

NONFICTION Needs essays, how-to, classroom techniques, personal experience, classroom, photo feature. No jargon, rhetoric or academic analysis. No theoretical discussions on the pros/cons of multicultural education. **Buys 2-4 mss/year.** Submit outlines or complete mss. Length: 400-1,600 words. **Pays $1/word.** Pays expenses of writers on assignment.

COLUMNS/DEPARTMENTS Features (stories and issues related to anti-bias education), 800-1,600 words; Why I Teach (personal reflections about life in the classroom), 600 words or less; Story Corner (designed to be read by or to students and must cover topics that are appealing to children), 600 words; Activity Exchange (brief descriptions of classroom lesson plans, special projects or other school activities that can be used by others to promote tolerance), 400 words. **Buys 8-12 mss/year.** Query with published clips. Does not accept unsolicited mss. **Pays $1/ word or $250/submission, pending.**

$ TECH DIRECTIONS

Prakken Publications, Inc., P.O. Box 8623, P, Ann Arbor MI 48107-8623. (734)975-2800. **Fax:** (734)975-2787. **E-mail:** susanne@techdirections.com. **Website:** www.techdirections.com. **Contact:** Susanne Peckham, managing editor. **100% freelance written. Eager to work with new/unpublished writers.** Monthly (except June and July) magazine covering issues, trends, and activities of interest to science, technical, and technology educators at the elementary through post-secondary school levels. Estab. 1934. Circ. 40,000. Byline given. Pays on publication. No kill fee. Publishes ms an average of 1 year after acceptance. Responds in 1 month to queries. Sample copy for $5. Guidelines available online.

NONFICTION Needs general interest, how-to, personal experience, technical, think pieces. **Buys 50 unsolicited mss/year.** Length: 2,000-3,000 words. **Pays $50-150.**

COLUMNS/DEPARTMENTS Direct from Washington (education news from Washington, DC); Technology Today (new products under development); Technologies Past (profiles the inventors of last century); Mastering Computers, Technology Concepts (project orientation).

ELECTRONICS AND COMMUNICATION

$$ THE ACUTA JOURNAL

Information Communications Technology in Higher Education, ACUTA, 152 W. Zandale Dr., Suite 200, Lexington KY 40503. (859)278-3338. **Fax:** (859)278-3268. **E-mail:** aburton@acuta.org; pscott@acuta.org. **Website:** www.acuta.org. **Contact:** Amy Burton, director of strategic relationships; Patricia Scott, director of communications. **20% freelance written.** Quarterly professional association journal covering information communications technology (ICT) in higher education. Audience includes, primarily, middle to upper management in the IT/telecommunications department on college/university campuses. They are highly skilled, technology-oriented professionals who provide data, voice, and video communications services for residential and academic purposes. Estab. 1997. Circ. 2,200. Byline given. Pays on publication. No kill fee. Publishes ms an average of 6 months after acceptance. Editorial lead time 6 months. Accepts queries by mail, e-mail, fax, phone. Responds in 1 month to queries. Responds in 2 months to mss. Sample copy for SAE with 9x12 envelope and 6 first-class stamps. Guidelines free.

NONFICTION Needs how-to, ICT, technical, technology, case study, college/university application of technology. **Buys 6-8 mss/year.** Query. Length: 1,200-4,000 words. **Pays 8-10¢/word.** Sometimes pays expenses of writers on assignment.

$$ DIGITAL OUTPUT

Rockport Custom Publishing, LLC, 100 Cummings Center, Suite 321E, Beverly MA 01915. (978)921-7850, ext. 13. **E-mail:** mdonovan@rdigitaloutput.net; edit@rockportpubs.com. **Website:** www.digitaloutput.net. **Contact:** Melissa Donovan, editor. **70% freelance written.** Monthly magazine covering electronic prepress, desktop publishing, and digital imaging, with articles ranging from digital capture and design to electronic prepress and digital printing. *Digital Output* is a national business publication for electronic publishers and digital imagers, providing monthly articles which examine the latest technologies and digital methods and discuss how to profit from them. Readers include service bureaus, prepress and reprographic houses, designers, commercial printers, wide-format printers, ad agencies, corporate communications, sign shops, and others. Estab. 1994. Circ. 25,000. Byline given. Pays on publication. Offers 10-20% kill fee. Publishes ms an average of 2 months after acceptance. Editorial lead time 3 months. Submit seasonal material 3 months in advance. Accepts queries by mail, e-mail. Responds in 3 weeks to queries. Responds in 1 month to mss. Sample copy online.

NONFICTION Needs how-to, interview, technical, case studies. **Buys 36 mss/year.** Query with published clips or hyperlinks to posted clips. Length: 1,500-4,000 words. **Pays $250-600.**

$$$ SOUND & VIDEO CONTRACTOR

NewBay Media, LLC, 28 E. 28th St., 12th Floor, New York NY 10016. (818)236-3667. **Fax:** (913)514-3683. **E-mail:** cwisehart@nbmedia.com; jgutierrez@nbmedia.com. **Website:** www.svconline.com. Cynthia Wisehart, editor. **Contact:** Cynthia Wisehart, editor; Jessaca Gutierrez, managing and online editor. **60% freelance written.** Monthly magazine covering professional audio, video, security, acoustical design, sales, and marketing. Estab. 1983. Circ. 24,000. Byline given. Pays on acceptance. No kill fee. Publishes ms an average of 3 months after acceptance. Editorial lead time 3 months. Accepts queries by mail, e-mail, fax, phone. Accepts simultaneous submissions. Responds ASAP to queries. Sample copy and writer's guidelines free.

NONFICTION Needs historical, how-to, photo feature, technical, professional audio/video applications, installations, product reviews. No opinion pieces, advertorial, interview/profile, expose/gossip. **Buys 60 mss/year.** Query. Length: 1,000-2,500 words. **Pays $200-1,200 for assigned articles. Pays $200-650 for unsolicited articles.**

COLUMNS/DEPARTMENTS Security Technology Review (technical install information); Sales & Marketing (techniques for installation industry); Video Happenings (Pro video/projection/storage technical info), all 1,500 words. **Buys 30 mss/year.** Query. **Pays $200-350.**

$$ SQL SERVER MAGAZINE

Penton Media, 221 E. 29th St., Loveland CO 80538. (970)663-4700. **Fax:** (970)667-2321. **E-mail:** articles@sqlmag.com. **Website:** www.sqlmag.com. **Contact:** Lavon Peters, managing editor. **35% freelance written.** Monthly magazine covering Microsoft SQL Server. *SQL Server Magazine* is the only magazine completely devoted to helping developers and DBAs master new and emerging SQL Server technologies and issues. It provides practical advice and lots of code examples for SQL Server developers and administrators, and includes how-to articles, tips, tricks, and programming techniques offered by SQL Server experts. Estab. 1999. Circ. 20,000. Byline given. "Penton Media pays for articles upon publication. Payment rates are based on the author's writing experience and the quality of the article submitted. We will discuss the payment rate for your article when we notify you of its acceptance." Offers $100 kill fee. Publishes ms an average of 6 months after acceptance. Editorial lead time 4+ months. Accepts queries by mail, e-mail. Responds in 6 weeks to queries. Responds in 2-3 months to mss. Sample copy available online. Guidelines available online.

NONFICTION Needs how-to, technical, SQL Server administration and programming. Nothing promoting third-party products or companies. **Buys 25-35 mss/year.** Send complete ms. Length: 1,800-2,500 words. **Pays $200 for feature articles; $500 for Focus articles.**

COLUMNS/DEPARTMENTS **Contact:** R2R Editor. Reader to Reader (helpful SQL Server hints and tips from readers), 200-400 words. **Buys 6-12 mss/year.** Send complete ms. **Pays $50**

ENERGY AND UTILITIES

$$ ELECTRICAL APPARATUS

Barks Publications, Inc., Suite 901, 500 N. Michigan Ave., Chicago IL 60611. (312)321-9440. **Fax:** (312)321-1288. **E-mail:** eamagazine@barks.com. **Website:** www.barks.com/eacurr.html. **Contact:** Elizabeth Van Ness, publisher; Kevin N. Jones, senior editor. Monthly magazine for persons working in electrical and electronic maintenance, in industrial plants and service and sales centers, who install and service electric motors, transformers, generators, controls, and related equipment. Contact staff members by telephone for their preferred e-mail addresses. Estab. 1967. Circ.

16,000. Byline given. Pays on publication. No kill fee. Publishes ms an average of 1 month after acceptance. Accepts queries by mail, e-mail, fax. Responds in 1 week to queries sent by US mail.

NONFICTION Needs technical. Length: 1,500-2,500 words. **Pays $250-500 for assigned articles.**

TIPS "We welcome queries re: technical columns on electro-mehanical subjects as pump repari, automation, drives, etc. All feature articles are assigned to staff and contributing editors and correspondents. Professionals interested in appointments as contributing editors and correspondents should submit résumé and article outlines, including illustration suggestions. Writers should be competent with a camera, which should be described in résumé. Technical expertise is absolutely necessary, preferably an E.E. degree, or practical experience. We are also book publishers and some of the material in *EA* is now in book form, bringing the authors royalties. Also publishes an annual directory, subtitled *ElectroMechanical Bench Reference.*"

ELECTRICAL BUSINESS

CLB Media, Inc., 222 Edward St., Aurora ON L4G 1W6 Canada. (905)727-0077; (905)713-4391. **Fax:** (905)727-0017. **E-mail:** acapkun@annexweb.com. **Website:** www.ebmag.com. **Contact:** Anthony Capkun, editor. **35% freelance written.** Tabloid published 10 times/year covering the Canadian electrical industry. *Electrical Business* targets electrical contractors and electricians. It provides practical information readers can use right away in their work and for running their business and assets. Estab. 1964. Circ. 18,097. Byline given. Pays on acceptance. Offers 50% kill fee. Publishes ms an average of 1-2 months after acceptance. Editorial lead time 3 months. Submit seasonal material 6 months in advance. Accepts queries by e-mail, phone. Accepts simultaneous submissions. Responds in 1 month to queries. Responds in 1 month to mss. Sample copy available online. Guidelines free.

NONFICTION Needs how-to, technical. Special issues: Summer Blockbuster issue (June/July); Special Homebuilders' issue (November/December). **Buys 15 mss/year.** Query. Length: 800-1,200 words. **Pays 40¢/word.** Sometimes pays expenses of writers on assignment.

COLUMNS/DEPARTMENTS Atlantic Focus (stories from Atlantic Canada); Western Focus (stories from Western Canada, including Manitoba); Trucks for the Trade (articles pertaining to the vehicles used by electrical contractors); Tools for the Trade (articles pertaining to tools used by contractors); all 800 words. **Buys 6 mss/year.** Query. **Pays 40¢/word.**

PUBLIC POWER

2451 Crystal Dr., Suite 1000, Arlington VA 22202-4804. (202)467-2900. **Fax:** (202)467-2910. **E-mail:** news@publicpower.org; ldalessandro@publicpower.org; rthomas@publicpower.org. **Website:** www.publicpower.org. **Contact:** Laura D'Alessandro, editor; Robert Thomas, art director. **60% freelance written. Prefers to work with published/established writers.** Publication of the American Public Power Association, published 6 times a year. Emphasizes electric power provided by cities, towns, and utility districts. Estab. 1942. Byline given. Pays on acceptance. No kill fee. Publishes ms an average of 3 months after acceptance. Accepts queries by mail, e-mail, fax. Responds in 6 months to queries. Sample copy and writer's guidelines free.

NONFICTION Pays $500 and up.

SOLAR INDUSTRY

Zackin Publications, Inc., P.O. Box 2180, Waterbury CT 06722. (800)325-6745. **Fax:** (203)262-4680. **E-mail:** mputtre@solarindustrymag.com. **Website:** www.solarindustrymag.com. **Contact:** Michael Puttrè, editor. **5% freelance written. Prefers to work with published/established writers.** *Solar Industry* magazine is a monthly trade publication serving professionals in the solar energy industry. Estab. 1980. Circ. 10,000. Pays on publication. No kill fee. Publishes ms an average of 2 months after acceptance. Submit seasonal material 4 months in advance. Accepts queries by mail, e-mail, fax, phone. Responds in 2 weeks to queries. Sample copies available online. Guidelines available online.

NONFICTION Needs how-to, improve retail profits and business know-how, interview, of successful retailers in this field. No general business articles not adapted to this industry. **Buys 10 mss/year.** Query. Length: 1,500-2,000 words. **Pay varies.**

TEXAS CO-OP POWER

Texas Electric Cooperatives, Inc., 1122 Colorado St., 24th Floor, Austin TX 78701. (512)486-6242. **E-mail:** editor@texas-ec.org. **Website:** www.texascooppower.com. **60% freelance written.** Monthly magazine covering rural and suburban Texas life, people, and places. *Texas Co-op Power* provides more than 1 million households and businesses educational and technical information about electric cooperatives in a high-quality and entertaining format to promote the general welfare of cooperatives, their member-owners, and the areas in which they serve. *Texas Co-op Power* is published by your electric cooperative to enhance the quality of life of its member-customers in an educational and entertaining format. Estab. 1948. Circ. 1.3 million. Byline given. Pays after any necessary rewrites. No kill fee. Publishes ms an average of 6 months after acceptance. Editorial lead time 4-5 months. Submit seasonal material 6 months in advance. Accepts queries by mail, e-mail, fax, online submission form. Accepts simultaneous submissions. Responds in 1 month to queries. Responds in 3 months to mss. Sample copy available online. Guidelines for #10 SASE.

NONFICTION Needs general interest, historical, interview, photo feature, travel. **Buys 30 mss/year.** Query with published clips. Length: 800-1,200 words. **Pays $500-1,200.** Sometimes pays expenses of writers on assignment.

ENGINEERING AND TECHNOLOGY

✪$$$ CANADIAN CONSULTING ENGINEER

Business Information Group, 80 Valleybrook Dr., Toronto ON M3B 2S9 Canada. (416)510-5119. **Fax:** (416)510-5134. **E-mail:** bparsons@ccemag.com. **Website:** www.canadianconsultingengineer.com. **Contact:** Bronwen Parsons, editor. **20%% freelance written. Freelancers must sign a copyright agreement.** Bimonthly magazine covering consulting engineering in private practice. Estab. 1958. Circ. 8,900. Byline given depending on length of story. Pays on publication. Offers 50% kill fee. Publishes ms an average of 4 months after acceptance. Editorial lead time 6 months. Responds in 3 months to mss. Sample copy free.

NONFICTION Needs historical, new product, technical, engineering/construction projects, environmental/construction issues. **Buys 8-10 mss/year.** Length: 300-1,500 words. **Pays $200-1,000 (Canadian).** Sometimes pays expenses of writers on assignment.

COLUMNS/DEPARTMENTS Export (selling consulting engineering services abroad); Management (managing consulting engineering businesses); On-Line (trends in CAD systems); Employment; Business; Construction and Environmental Law (Canada); all 800 words. **Buys 4 mss/year.** Query with published clips. **Pays $250-400.**

$$ COMPOSITES MANUFACTURING MAGAZINE

American Composites Manufacturers Association, 3033 Wilson Blvd., Suite 420, Arlington VA 22201. (703)525-0511. **E-mail:** communications@acmanet.org; info@acmanet.org. **Website:** www.acmanet.org. Monthly magazine covering any industry that uses reinforced composites: marine, aerospace, infrastructure, automotive, transportation, corrosion, architecture, tub and shower, sports, and recreation. Primarily publishes educational pieces, the how-to of the shop environment. Also publishes marketing, business trends, and economic forecasts relevant to the composites industry. Estab. 1979. Circ. 12,000. Byline given. Pays on acceptance. No kill fee. Publishes ms an average of 2-3 months after acceptance. Editorial lead time 2 months. Accepts queries by e-mail. Accepts simultaneous submissions. Responds in 1 week to queries. Responds in 1 month to mss.

NONFICTION Needs how-to, composites manufacturing, new product, technical, marketing, related business trends and forecasts. Special issues: "Each January we publish a World Market Report where we cover all niche markets and all geographic areas relevant to the composites industry. Freelance material will be considered strongly for this issue." No need to query company or personal profiles unless there is an extremely unique or novel angle. **Buys 5-10 mss/year.** Query. *Composites Manufacturing* invites freelance feature submissions, all of which should be sent via e-mail as a Microsoft Word attachment. A query letter is required. Length: 1,500-2,000 words. **Pays 20-40¢/word (negotiable).** Sometimes pays expenses of writers on assignment.

COLUMNS/DEPARTMENTS "We publish columns on HR, relevant government legislation, industry lessons learned, regulatory affairs, and technology. Average word length for columns is 500 words. We would entertain any new column idea that hits hard on industry matters." Query. **Pays $300-350.**

✪$$$ CONNECTIONS+

The Magazine for ICT Professionals, Business Information Group, 80 Valleybrook Dr., Toronto ON M3B

2S9 Canada. (416)510-6752. **Fax:** (416)510-5134. **E-mail:** pbarker@connectionsplus.ca. **Website:** www.connectionsplus.ca. **Contact:** Paul Barker, editor. **50% freelance written.** Magazine published 6 times/year covering the structured cabling/telecommunications industry. Estab. 1998. Circ. 15,000 print; 45,000 electronic. Byline given. Pays on publication. No kill fee. Publishes ms an average of 1 month after acceptance. Editorial lead time 3 months. Submit seasonal material 1 month in advance. Accepts queries by mail, e-mail, phone. Accepts simultaneous submissions. Sample copy available online. Guidelines free.

NONFICTION Needs technical, case studies, features. No reprints or previously written articles. All articles are assigned by editor based on query or need of publication. **Buys 12 mss/year.** Query with published clips. Length: 1,500-2,500 words. **Pays 40-50¢/word.** Sometimes pays expenses of writers on assignment.

COLUMNS/DEPARTMENTS Focus on Engineering/Design; Focus on Installation; Focus on Maintenance/Testing; all 1,500 words. **Buys 7 mss/year.** Query with published clips. **Pays 40-50¢/word.**

$$$ ENTERPRISE MINNESOTA MAGAZINE

Enterprise Minnesota, Inc., 310 4th Ave. S., Suite 7050, Minneapolis MN 55415. (612)373-2900; (800)325-3073. **Fax:** (612)373-2901. **E-mail:** editor@enterpriseminnesota.org. **Website:** www.enterpriseminnesota.org. **Contact:** Tom Mason, editor. **90% freelance written.** Magazine published 5 times/year. *Minnesota Technology* is for the owners and top management of Minnesota's technology and manufacturing companies. The magazine covers technology trends and issues, global trade, management techniques, and finance. Profile new and growing companies, new products, and the innovators and entrepreneurs of Minnesota's technology sector. Estab. 1991. Circ. 16,000. Byline given. Pays on publication. Offers 10% kill fee. Publishes ms an average of 3 months after acceptance. Editorial lead time 1 month. Submit seasonal material 1 year in advance. Accepts queries by mail, e-mail. Guidelines free.

NONFICTION Needs general interest, how-to, interview. **Buys 60 mss/year.** Query with published clips. **Pays $150-1,000.**

COLUMNS/DEPARTMENTS Feature Well (Q&A format, provocative ideas from Minnesota business and industry leaders), 2,000 words; Up Front (mini profiles, anecdotal news items), 250-500 words. Query with published clips.

$$ LD+A

Illuminating Engineering Society of North America, 120 Wall St., 17th Floor, New York NY 10005-4001. (212)248-5000, ext. 108. **Fax:** (212)248-5017. **E-mail:** ptarricone@ies.org; ies@ies.org. **Website:** www.ies.org. **Contact:** Paul Tarricone, editor/associate publisher. **10% freelance written.** Monthly magazine. *LD+A* is geared to professionals in lighting design and the lighting field in architecture, retail, entertainment, etc. Estab. 1971. Circ. 10,000. Byline given. Pays on acceptance. No kill fee. Publishes ms an average of 4 months after acceptance. Editorial lead time 2 months. Submit seasonal material 4 months in advance. Accepts queries by mail, e-mail, fax, phone. Accepts simultaneous submissions. Responds in 2 weeks to queries. Sample copy free. Guidelines available on website.

NONFICTION Needs historical, how-to, opinion, personal experience, photo feature, technical. No articles blatantly promoting a product, company, or individual. **Buys 6-10 mss/year.** Query. Length: 1,500-2,000 words.

COLUMNS/DEPARTMENTS Essay by Invitation (industry trends), 1,200 words. Query. **Does not pay for columns.**

$$ MFRTECH EJOURNAL

Manufacturers Group Inc., P.O. Box 4310, Lexington KY 40544. **E-mail:** editor@mfrtech.com. **Website:** www.mfrtech.com. **40% freelance written.** Magazine published daily online covering manufacturing and technology from news throughout the U.S. Editorial includes anufacturing news, expansions, acquisition white papers, case histories, new product announcements, feature submissions, book synopsis. Estab. 1976 (print). Circ. 60,000+ weekly subscribers (e-mail); 750,000 monthly online visitors. Byline given. Pays 30 days following publication. Offers 25% kill fee. Publishes ms 3-4 days after acceptance. Editorial lead time 2 weeks. Submit seasonal material 2 weeks in advance. Sample copy online. Guidelines by e-mail.

NONFICTION Needs new product, opinion, technical. Does not want general interest, inspirational, personal, travel, book excerpts. Length: 750-1,500 words; byline: 75 words. **Pays $0.20/word published (prior to approval from editor).**

COLUMNS/DEPARTMENTS New Plant Announcement, Acquisitions, Expansions, New Technology, Federal, Case Histories, Human Resources, Marketing. Query. **Pays $0.20/word (prior to approval from editor).**

$$ MINORITY ENGINEER

Equal Opportunity Publications, Inc., 445 Broad Hollow Rd., Suite 425, Melville NY 11747. (631)421-9421. **Fax:** (516)421-0359. **E-mail:** jschneider@eop.com; info@eop.com. **Website:** www.eop.com. **Contact:** James Schneider, director, editorial and production. **60% freelance written. Prefers to work with published/established writers.** Triannual magazine covering career guidance for minority engineering students and minority professional engineers. Estab. 1969. Circ. 15,000. Byline given. Pays on publication. No kill fee. Publishes ms an average of 3 months after acceptance. Editorial lead time 3 months. Accepts queries by mail, e-mail, fax, phone. Accepts simultaneous submissions. Responds in 2 weeks to queries. Responds in 2 months to mss. Sample copy and writer's guidelines for 9x12 SAE with 5 first-class stamps. Guidelines free.

NONFICTION Needs book excerpts, general interest, on specific minority engineering concerns, how-to, land a job, keep a job, etc., interview, minority engineer role models, opinion, problems of ethnic minorities, personal experience, student and career experiences, technical, on career fields offering opportunities for minority engineers, articles on job search techniques, role models. No general information. Query. Length: 1,500-2,500 words. **Pays $350 for assigned articles.** Sometimes pays expenses of writers on assignment.

$$$$ RAILWAY TRACK AND STRUCTURES

Simmons-Boardman Publishing, 55 Broad St., 26th Floor, New York NY 10004. (212)620-7200. **Fax:** (212)633-1165. **E-mail:** Mischa@sbpub-chicago.com; Jnunez@sbpub-chicago.com. **Website:** www.rtands.com. **Contact:** Mischa Wanek-Libman, editor; Jennifer Nunez, assistant editor. **1% freelance written.** Monthly magazine covering railroad civil engineering. *RT&S* is a nuts-and-bolts journal to help railroad civil engineers do their jobs better. Estab. 1904. Circ. 9,500. Byline given. Pays on publication. Offers 90% kill fee. Publishes ms an average of 1 month after acceptance. Editorial lead time 2 months. Submit seasonal material 3 months in advance. Accepts queries by mail, fax, phone. Accepts simultaneous submissions. Responds in 1 month to queries and to mss. Sample copy available online.

NONFICTION Needs how-to, new product, technical. Does not want nostalgia or "railroadiana." **Buys 1 mss/year.** Query. Length: 900-2,000 words. **Pays $500-1,000.** Sometimes pays expenses of writers on assignment.

$$ WOMAN ENGINEER

Equal Opportunity Publications, Inc., 445 Broad Hollow Rd., Suite 425, Melville NY 11747. (631)421-9421. **Fax:** (631)421-1352. **E-mail:** info@eop.com; jschneider@eop.com. **Website:** www.eop.com. **Contact:** James Schneider, editor. **60% freelance written. Works with a small number of new/unpublished writers each year.** Triannual magazine aimed at advancing the careers of women engineering students and professional women engineers. Estab. 1968. Circ. 16,000. Byline given. Pays on publication. No kill fee. Publishes ms an average of 3 months after acceptance. Editorial lead time 3 months. Accepts queries by mail, e-mail, fax, phone. Responds in 2 weeks to queries. Responds in 2 months to mss. Sample copy and writer's guidelines free.

NONFICTION Needs how-to, find jobs, interview, personal experience. Query. Length: 1,500-2,500 words. **Pays $350 for assigned articles.**

ENTERTAINMENT AND THE ARTS

$$$ AMERICAN CINEMATOGRAPHER

American Society of Cinematographers, 1782 N. Orange Dr., Hollywood CA 90028. (800)448-0145; outside US: (323)969-4333. **Fax:** (323)876-4973. **E-mail:** stephen@ascmag.com. **Website:** www.theasc.com. **Contact:** Stephen Pizzello, editor-in-chief and publisher; Jon Witmer, managing editor. **90% freelance written.** Monthly magazine covering cinematography (motion picture, TV, music video, commercial). "*American Cinematographer* is a trade publication devoted to the art and craft of cinematography. Our readers are predominantly film industry professionals." Estab. 1919. Circ. 45,000. Byline given. Pays on publication. Offers 50% kill fee. Publishes ms an average of 2-3 months after acceptance. Editorial lead time 2 months. Submit seasonal material 3 months in advance. Accepts queries by mail, e-mail, phone. Responds in 2 weeks to queries; 2 months to mss. Sample copy and guidelines free.

NONFICTION Needs interview, new product, technical. No reviews or opinion pieces. **Buys 20-25 mss/year.** Query with published clips. Length: 1,000-4,000 words. **Pays $400-1,500.**

AMERICAN THEATRE

Theatre Communications Group, 520 8th Ave., 24th Floor, New York NY 10018. (212)609-5900. **E-mail:** jim@tcg.org. **Website:** www.tcg.org. **Contact:** Jim O'Quinn, editor-in-chief. **60% freelance written.** Monthly magazine covering theatre. Focus is on American regional nonprofit theatre. *American Theatre* typically publishes 2 or 3 features and 4-6 back-of-the-book articles covering trends and events in all types of theatre, as well as economic and legislative developments affecting the arts. *American Theatre* covers trends and events in all types of theatre, as well as economic and legislative developments affecting the arts. *American Theatre* rarely publishes articles about commercial, amateur or university theatre, nor about works that would widely be classified as dance or opera, except at the editors' discretion. While significant productions may be highlighted in the Critic's Notebook section, *American Theatre* does not review productions (but does review theatre-related books). Estab. 1982. Circ. 100,000. Byline given. Pays on publication. Editorial lead time 2 months. Submit seasonal material 3 months in advance. Accepts queries by mail, e-mail, online submission form. Accepts simultaneous submissions. Responds in 2 months to queries. Sample copy and guidelines available online.

NONFICTION Needs book excerpts, essays, exposè, general interest, historical, how-to, humor, inspirational, interview, opinion, personal experience, photo feature, travel. Special issues: Training (January); International (May/June); Season Preview (October). No unsolicited submissions (rarely accepted). No reviews. Query with outlined proposal and published clips. Include brief rèsumè and SASE. Length: 200-2,000 words. **"While fees are negotiated per ms, we pay an average of $350 for full-length (2,500-3,500 words) features, and less for shorter pieces."**

BOXOFFICE MAGAZINE

Boxoffice Media, LLC, 9107 Wilshire Blvd., Suite. 450, Beverly Hills CA 90210. (310) 876-9090. **E-mail:** ken@boxoffice.com. **Website:** www.BoxOffice.com. **15% freelance written.** Providing news and numbers to the film industry since 1920. Magazine about the motion picture industry for executives and managers working in the film business, including movie theater owners and operators, Hollywood studio personnel and leaders in allied industries. Estab. 1920. Circ. 6,000. Byline given. Pays on publication. No kill fee. Publishes ms an average of 3 months after acceptance. Submit seasonal material 5 months in advance. Accepts queries by mail, e-mail, fax. Sample copy for $5 in US; $10 outside U.S.

NONFICTION Needs book excerpts, essays, interview, new product, personal experience, photo feature, technical, investigative all regarding movie theatre business. Query with published clips. Length: 800-2,500 words. **Pays 10¢/word.**

DANCE TEACHER

McFadden Performing Arts Media, 333 Seventh Ave., 11th Floor, New York NY 10001. **Fax:** (646)459-4000. **E-mail:** khildebrand@dancemedia.com. **Website:** www.dance-teacher.com. **Contact:** Karen Hildebrand, editor-in-chief; Joe Sullivan, managing editor. **60% freelance written.** Monthly magazine. Estab. 1979. Circ. 25,000. Byline given. Pays on publication. No kill fee. Publishes ms an average of 3 months after acceptance. Submit seasonal material 6 months in advance. Accepts queries by mail, e-mail, fax, phone, online submission form. Responds in 3 months to mss. Sample copy for SAE with 9x12 envelope and 6 first-class stamps. Guidelines available for free.

NONFICTION Needs how-to, teach, health, business, legal. Special issues: Summer Programs (January); Music & More (May); Costumes and Production Preview (November); College/Training Schools (December). No PR or puff pieces. All articles must be well researched. **Buys 50 mss/year.** Query. Length: 700-2,000 words. **Pays $100-300.**

EMMY MAGAZINE

Academy of Television Arts & Sciences, 5220 Lankershim Blvd., North Hollywood CA 91601. **E-mail:** emmymag@emmys.org. **Website:** www.emmymagazine.com; www.emmys.tv/emmy-magazine. **Contact:** Juan Morales, editor-in-chief; Gail Polevoi, editor. **90% freelance written. Prefers to work with published/established writers.** Bimonthly magazine on television for TV professionals. Circ. 14,000. Byline given. Pays on publication or within 6 months. Offers 25% kill fee. Publishes ms an average of 4 months after acceptance. Accepts queries by mail. Responds in 1 month to queries. Sample copy for sae with 9x12 envelope and 6 first-class stamps. Guidelines available online.

NONFICTION Query with published clips. Length: 1,500-2,000 words. **Pays $1,000-1,200.**

COLUMNS/DEPARTMENTS Mostly written by regular contributors, but newcomers can break in with filler items with In the Mix or short profiles in Labors of Love. Length: 250-500 words, depending on department. Query with published clips. **Pays $250-500.**

$$ MAKE-UP ARTIST MAGAZINE

12808 NE 95th St., Vancouver WA 98682. (360)882-3488. **E-mail:** heatherw@kpgmedia.com. **Website:** www.makeupmag.com; www.makeup411.com; www.imats.net. **Contact:** Heather Wisner, managing editor; Michael Key, publisher/editor-in-chief. **90% freelance written.** Bimonthly magazine covering all types of professional make-up artistry. Audience is a mixture of high-level make-up artists, make-up students, and movie buffs. Writers should be comfortable with technical writing, and should have substantial knowledge of at least 1 area of makeup, such as effects or fashion. This is an entertainment-industry magazine, so writing should have an element of fun and storytelling. Good interview skills required. Estab. 1996. Circ. 16,000. Byline given. Pays within 30 days of publication. No kill fee. Editorial lead time 6 weeks. Submit seasonal material 2 months in advance. Accepts queries by e-mail. Accepts simultaneous submissions. Sample copy for $7. Guidelines available via e-mail.

NONFICTION Needs features, how-to, new products, photo features, profile. "Does not want fluff pieces about consumer beauty products." **Buys 20+ mss/year.** Query with published clips. Length: 500-3,000 words. **Pays 20-50¢/word.** Sometimes pays expenses of writers on assignment.

COLUMNS/DEPARTMENTS Cameo (short yet thorough look at a make-up artist not covered in a feature story), 800 words (15 photos); Lab Tech (how-to advice for effects artists, usually written by a current make-up artist working in a lab), 800 words (3 photos); Backstage (analysis, interview, tips, and behind the scenes info on a theatrical production's make-up), 800 words (3 photos). **Buys Buys 30 columns/year. mss/year.** Query with published clips. **Pays $100.**

FARM

AGRICULTURAL EQUIPMENT

$ AG WEEKLY

Lee Agri-Media, P.O. Box 918, Bismarck ND 58501. (701)255-4905. **Fax:** (701)255-2312. **E-mail:** mark.conlon@lee.net. **Website:** www.agweekly.com. **Contact:** Mark Conlon, editor. **40% freelance written.** *Ag Weekly* is an agricultural publication covering production, markets, regulation, politics. Writers need to be familiar with Idaho agricultural commodities. No printed component; website with 6,000 monthly unique visitors; weekly email newsletter with 3,000 subscribers. Byline given. Pays on publication. Publishes ms an average of 1 month after acceptance. Editorial lead time 1 month. Accepts queries by e-mail. Accepts simultaneous submissions. Responds in 2 weeks to queries. Responds in 1 month to mss.

NONFICTION Needs interview, new product, opinion, travel, ag-related. Does not want anything other than local/regional ag-related articles. No cowboy poetry. **Buys 100 mss/year.** Query. Length: 250-700 words. **Pays $40-70.**

$$ IMPLEMENT & TRACTOR

Farm Journal, 222 S. Jefferson St., Mexico MO 65265. (573)581-9641. **E-mail:** meckelkamp@farmjournal.com; editors@agweb.com. **Website:** www.implementandtractor.com. **Contact:** Margy Eckelkamp. **10% freelance written.** Bimonthly magazine covering the agricultural equipment industry. *Implement & Tractor* offers equipment reviews and business news for agricultural equipment dealers, ag equipment manufacturers, distributors, and aftermarket suppliers. Estab. 1895. Circ. 5,000. Byline given. Pays on publication. No kill fee. Publishes ms an average of 3-4 months after acceptance. Editorial lead time 2 months. Accepts queries by mail, e-mail. Responds in 2 months to queries. Sample copy for $6.

CROPS AND SOIL MANAGEMENT

$$ AMERICAN/WESTERN GROWER

Meister Media Worldwide, 37733 Euclid Ave., Willoughby OH 44094. (440)942-2000. **E-mail:** bdsparks@meistermedia.com; deddy@meistermedia.com. **Website:** www.fruitgrower.com. **Contact:**

Brian Sparks, editor; David Eddy, editor. **3% freelance written.** Annual magazines covering commercial fruit growing. Estab. 1880. Circ. 44,000. Byline given. Pays on publication. No kill fee. Publishes ms an average of 4 months after acceptance. Editorial lead time 2 months. Submit seasonal material 4 months in advance. Accepts queries by mail, e-mail, fax, phone. Responds in 2 weeks to queries. Responds in 2 months to mss. Sample copy and writer's guidelines free.

NONFICTION Needs how-to, better grow fruit crops. **Buys 6-10 mss/year.** Send complete ms. Length: 800-1,200 words. **Pays $200-250.** Sometimes pays expenses of writers on assignment.

$$ COTTON GROWER MAGAZINE

Meister Media Worldwide, Cotton Media Group, 8000 Centerview Pkwy., Suite 114, Cordova TN 38018-4246. (901)756-8822. **E-mail:** mccue@meistermedia.com. **Website:** www.cotton247.com. **Contact:** Mike McCue, editor. **5% freelance written.** Monthly magazine covering cotton production, cotton markets, and related subjects. Circ. 43,000. Byline given. Pays on acceptance. No kill fee. Publishes ms an average of 2 months after acceptance. Editorial lead time 2 months. Submit seasonal material 2 months in advance. Accepts queries by mail, e-mail, fax, phone.

NONFICTION Needs interview, new product, photo feature, technical. No fiction or humorous pieces. **Buys 5-10 mss/year.** Query with published clips. Length: 500-800 words. **Pays $200-400.** Sometimes pays expenses of writers on assignment.

$ FRUIT GROWERS NEWS

Great American Publishing, P.O. Box 128, Sparta MI 49345. (616)887-9008. **Fax:** (616)887-2666. **E-mail:** fgnedit@fruitgrowersnews.com. **Website:** www.fruitgrowersnews.com. **Contact:** Matt Milkovich, managing editor; Lee Dean, editorial director. **10% freelance written.** Monthly tabloid covering agriculture. "Our objective is to provide commercial fruit growers of all sizes with information to help them succeed." Estab. 1961. Circ. 16,429. Pays on publication. No kill fee. Publishes ms an average of 2 months after acceptance. Editorial lead time 1-2 months. Submit seasonal material 3 months in advance. Accepts queries by mail, e-mail, fax. Accepts simultaneous submissions. Responds in 2 weeks to queries. Responds in 1 month to mss. Sample copy free.

NONFICTION Needs general interest, interview, new product. No advertorials or other puff pieces. **Buys 25 mss/year.** Query with published clips and résumé. Length: 600-1,000 words. **Pays $150-250.** Sometimes pays expenses of writers on assignment.

$$ GOOD FRUIT GROWER

Washington State Fruit Commission, 105 S. 18th St., #217, Yakima WA 98901. (509)575-2315. **E-mail:** casey.corr@goodfruit.com. **Website:** www.goodfruit.com. **Contact:** O. Casey Corr, managing editor. **10% freelance written.** Semi-monthly magazine covering tree fruit/grape growing. Estab. 1946. Circ. 11,000. Byline given. Pays on acceptance. Publishes ms an average of 2 months after acceptance. Accepts queries by mail, e-mail. Accepts simultaneous submissions. Responds in 1 week to queries. Responds in 1 month to mss. Sample copy free. Guidelines free.

NONFICTION Buys 20 mss/year. Query. Length: 500-1,500 words. **Pays 40-50¢/word.** Sometimes pays expenses of writers on assignment.

$ GRAIN JOURNAL

Country Journal Publishing Co., 3065 Pershing Court, Decatur IL 62526. (800)728-7511. **E-mail:** ed@grainnet.com. **Website:** www.grainnet.com. **Contact:** Ed Zdrojewski, editor. **5% freelance written.** Bimonthly magazine covering grain handling and merchandising. *Grain Journal* serves the North American grain industry, from the smallest country grain elevators and feed mills to major export terminals. Estab. 1972. Circ. 12,000. Byline sometimes given. Pays on publication. No kill fee. Publishes ms an average of 2 months after acceptance. Editorial lead time 2 months. Submit seasonal material 2 months in advance. Accepts simultaneous submissions. Sample copy free.

NONFICTION Needs how-to, interview, new product, technical. Query. 750 words maximum. **Pays $100.**

$ ONION WORLD

Columbia Publishing, 8405 Ahtanum Rd., Yakima WA 98903. (509)949-0550. **Fax:** (509)248-4056. **E-mail:** dkeller@columbiapublications.com. **Website:** www.onionworld.net. **Contact:** Denise Keller, editor. **25% freelance written.** Monthly magazine covering the world of onion production and marketing for onion growers and shippers. Estab. 1985. Circ. 5,500. Byline given. Pays on publication. No kill fee. Publishes ms an average of 1 month after acceptance. Submit seasonal material 1 month in advance. Accepts queries by e-mail or phone. Accepts simultaneous submissions. Responds in 1 month to queries. Sample copy for SAE with 9x12 envelope and 5 first-class stamps.

NONFICTION Needs general interest, historical, interview. Special issues: Editorial calendar available online. **Buys 30 mss/year.** Query. Length: 1,200-1,250 words. **Pays $100-250 per article, depending upon length. Mileage paid, but query first.**

$ SPUDMAN

Great American Publishing, P.O. Box 128, Sparta MI 49345. (616)887-9008. **Fax:** (616)887-2666. **E-mail:** bills@spudman.com; spudedit@spudman.com. **Website:** www.spudman.com. **Contact:** Bill Schaefer, managing editor. **10% freelance written.** Monthly magazine covering potato industry's growing, packing, processing, and chipping. Estab. 1964. Circ. 10,000. Byline given. Pays on publication. Offers $75 kill fee. Publishes ms an average of 2 months after acceptance. Editorial lead time 2 months. Submit seasonal material 4 months in advance. Accepts queries by mail, e-mail. Responds in 2-3 weeks to queries. Sample copy for SAE with 8½ x 11 envelope and 3 first-class stamps. Guidelines for #10 SASE.

$ THE VEGETABLE GROWERS NEWS

Great American Publishing, P.O. Box 128, Sparta MI 49345. (616)887-9008, ext. 102. **Fax:** (616)887-2666. **E-mail:** vgnedit@vegetablegrowersnews.com. **Website:** www.vegetablegrowersnews.com. **Contact:** Matt Milkovich, managing editor. **10% freelance written.** Monthly tabloid covering agriculture. Estab. 1970. Circ. 16,000. Pays on publication. No kill fee. Publishes ms an average of 2 months after acceptance. Editorial lead time 1-2 months. Submit seasonal material 3 months in advance. Accepts queries by mail, e-mail, fax. Accepts simultaneous submissions. Responds in 2 weeks to queries. Responds in 1 month to mss. Sample copy free.

NONFICTION Needs general interest, interview, new product. No advertorials, other puff pieces. **Buys 25 mss/year.** Query with published clips and résumé. Length: 800-1,200 words. **Pays $100-125.** Sometimes pays expenses of writers on assignment.

LIVESTOCK

$$ ANGUS BEEF BULLETIN

Angus Productions, Inc., 3201 Frederick Ave., St. Joseph MO 64506-2997. (816)383-5270. **E-mail:** journal@angusjournal.com; shermel@angusjournal.com. **Website:** www.angusbeefbulletin.com. **Contact:** Shauna Rose Hermel, editor. **45% freelance written.** Tabloid published 5 times/year covering commercial cattle industry. The *Bulletin* is mailed free to commercial cattlemen who have purchased an Angus bull and had the registration transferred to them, and to others who sign a request card. Estab. 1985. Circ. 65,000-70,000. Byline given. Pays on publication. No kill fee. Publishes ms an average of 3 months after acceptance. Editorial lead time 3 months. Submit seasonal material 3 months in advance. Accepts queries by mail, e-mail. Accepts simultaneous submissions. Responds in 3 weeks to queries; in 3 months to mss. Sample copy: $5. Guidelines for #10 SASE.

NONFICTION Needs how-to, cattle production, interview, technical, cattle production. **Buys 10 mss/year.** Query with published clips. Length: 800-2,500 words. **Pays $50-600.** Pays expenses of writers on assignment.

$$$ ANGUS JOURNAL

Angus Productions, Inc., 3201 Frederick Ave., St. Joseph MO 64506-2997. (816)383-5270. **E-mail:** shermel@angusjournal.com. **Website:** www.angusjournal.com. **40% freelance written.** Monthly magazine covering Angus cattle. The *Angus Journal* is the official magazine of the American Angus Association. Its primary function as such is to report to the membership association activities and information pertinent to raising Angus cattle. Estab. 1919. Circ. 13,500. Byline given. Pays on publication. No kill fee. Publishes ms an average of 3 months after acceptance. Editorial lead time 2 months. Submit seasonal material 3 months in advance. Accepts queries by mail, e-mail. Accepts simultaneous submissions. Responds in 3 weeks to queries; in 2 months to mss. Sample copy: $5. Guidelines with #10 SASE.

NONFICTION Needs how-to, cattle production, interview, technical, related to cattle. **Buys 20-30 mss/year.** Query with published clips. Length: 800-3,500 words. **Pays $50-1,000.** Pays expenses of writers on assignment.

$$ THE BRAHMAN JOURNAL

Carl and Victoria Lambert, 915 12th St., Hempstead TX 77445. (979)826-4347. **Fax:** (979)826-2007. **E-mail:** info@brahmanjournal.com; vlambert@brahmanjournal.com. **Website:** www.brahmanjournal.com. **Contact:** Victoria Lambert, editor. **10% free-**

lance written. Monthly magazine promoting, supporting, and informing the owners and admirers of American Brahman Cattle through honest and forthright journalism. *The Brahman Journal* provides timely and useful information about one of the largest and most dynamic breeds of beef cattle in the world. In each issue, *The Brahman Journal* reports on Brahman shows, events, and sales as well as technical articles and the latest research as it pertains to the Brahman Breed. Estab. 1971. Circ. 4,000. Byline given. Pays on publication. No kill fee. Publishes ms an average of 2 months after acceptance. Submit seasonal material 3 months in advance. Sample copy for SAE with 9x12 envelope and 5 first-class stamps.

NONFICTION Needs general interest, historical, interview. Special issues: See the Calendar online for special issues. **Buys 3-4 mss/year.** Query with published clips. Length: 1,200-3,000 words. **Pays $100-250.**

$$ THE CATTLEMAN

Texas and Southwestern Cattle Raisers Association, 1301 W. Seventh St., Suite 201, Fort Worth TX 76102. **E-mail:** ehbrisendine@tscra.org. **Website:** www.thecattlemanmagazine.com. **Contact:** Ellen H. Brisendine, editor. **25% freelance written.** Monthly magazine covering the Texas/Oklahoma beef cattle industry. Specializes in in-depth, management-type articles related to range and pasture, beef cattle production, animal health, nutrition, and marketing. Wants "how-to" articles. Estab. 1914. Circ. 15,000. Byline given. Pays on acceptance. No kill fee. Publishes ms an average of 2 months after acceptance. Editorial lead time 2 months. Submit seasonal material 6 months in advance. Accepts queries by mail, e-mail. Sample copy free. Guidelines online.

NONFICTION Needs how-to, interview, new product, personal experience, technical, ag research. Does not want to see anything not specifically related to beef production in the Southwest. **Buys 20 mss/year.** Query with published clips. Length: 1,500-2,000 words. **Pays $350-500 for assigned articles. Pays $100-350 for unsolicited articles.**

$$ FEED LOT MAGAZINE

Feed Lot Magazine, Inc., P.O. Box 850, Dighton KS 67839. (620)397-2838. **Fax:** (620)397-2839. **E-mail:** feedlot@st-tel.net. **Website:** www.feedlotmagazine.com. **60% freelance written.** Bimonthly magazine that provides readers with the most up-to-date information on the beef industry in concise, easy-to-read articles designed to increase overall awareness among the feedlot community. "The editorial information content fits a dual role: large feedlots and their related cow/calf operations, and large 500pl cow/calf, 100pl stocker operations. The information covers all phases of production from breeding, genetics, animal health, nutrition, equipment design, research through finishing fat cattle. *Feed Lot* publishes a mix of new information and timely articles which directly affect the cattle industry." Estab. 1992. Circ. 12,000. Byline given. Pays on publication. Offers 50% kill fee. Publishes ms an average of 2 months after acceptance. Editorial lead time 2 months. Submit seasonal material 6 months in advance. Accepts queries by mail, e-mail, fax. Responds in 1 month to queries. Sample copy and writer's guidelines e-mailed.

NONFICTION Needs interview, new product, cattle-related, photo feature. Send complete ms; original material only. Length: 100-700 words. **Pays 30¢/word.**

TIPS "Know what you are writing about—have a good knowledge of the subject."

$ SHEEP! MAGAZINE

Countryside Publications, Ltd., 145 Industrial Dr., Medford WI 54451. (715)785-7979; (800)551-5691. **Fax:** (715)785-7414. **E-mail:** sheepmag@tds.net; singersol@countrysidemag.com. **Website:** www.sheepmagazine.com. **Contact:** Nathan Griffith, editor. **35% freelance written. Prefers to work with published/established writers.** Bimonthly magazine published in north-central Wisconsin. Estab. 1980. Circ. 11,000. Byline given. Pays on publication. Offers $30 kill fee. Submit seasonal material 3 months in advance.

NONFICTION Needs book excerpts, how-to, on innovative lamb and wool marketing and promotion techniques, efficient record-keeping systems, or specific aspects of health and husbandry, interview, on experienced sheep producers who detail the economics and management of their operation, new product, of value to sheep producers; should be written by someone who has used them, technical, on genetics health and nutrition. **Buys 80 mss/year.** Send complete ms. Length: 750-2,500 words. **Pays $45-150.**

MANAGEMENT

$ AG JOURNAL

Arkansas Valley Publishing, 422 Colorado Ave., (P.O. Box 500), La Junta CO 81050. (719)384-1453. **E-mail:**

TRADE JOURNALS

publisher@ljtdmail.com; bcd@ljtdmail.com. **Website:** www.agjournalonline.com. **Contact:** Candi Hill, publisher/editor; Jennifer Justice, assistant editor. **20% freelance written.** Weekly journal covering agriculture. Estab. 1949. Circ. 11,000. Byline given. Pays on publication. No kill fee. Publishes ms an average of 2 weeks after acceptance. Editorial lead time 1 month. Submit seasonal material 1 month in advance. Accepts queries by e-mail. Responds in 2 weeks to queries. Sample copy and writer's guidelines free.

NONFICTION Needs how-to, interview, new product, opinion, photo feature, technical. Query by e-mail only. **Pays 4¢/word.** Sometimes pays expenses of writers on assignment.

NEW HOLLAND NEWS AND ACRES MAGAZINE

P.O. Box 1895, New Holland PA 17557-0903. (610)621-2253. **E-mail:** contact@newhollandmediakit.com. **Website:** www.newholland.com/na; agriculture.newholland.com. **Contact:** Gary Martin, editor. **75% freelance written. Works with a small number of new/unpublished writers each year.** Each magazine published 4 times/year covering agriculture and nonfarm country living; designed to entertain and inform farm families and rural homeowners and provide ideas for small acreage outdoor projects. Estab. 1960. Byline given. Pays on acceptance. Offers negotiable kill fee. Publishes ms an average of 8 months after acceptance. Submit seasonal material 8 months in advance. Accepts queries by mail. Responds in 2 months to queries. Sample copy and writer's guidelines for 9x12 SAE with 2 first-class stamps.

NONFICTION **Buys 40 mss/year.** Query. **Pays $700-900.** Pays expenses of writers on assignment.

SMALLHOLDER MAGAZINE

Newsquest Media Group, 3 Falmouth Business Park, Bickland Water Rd., Falmouth Cornwall TR11 4SZ United Kingdom. (01)326-213338. **Fax:** (01)326-212084. **E-mail:** editorial@smallholder.co.uk. **Website:** www.smallholder.co.uk. **Contact:** Graham Smith. Smallholder magazine is the leading monthly publication for the small producer and self-reliant household and has a publishing history spanning more than 100 years. The magazine has a reputation for quality and informed editorial content, and back issues are highly collectable. It is available nationally, through newsagent sales, specialist retail outlets and by subscription. No kill fee. Accepts queries by e-mail. Sample copy available online. Guidelines by e-mail.

NONFICTION Length: 700-1,400 words. **Pays 4£/word.**

MISCELLANEOUS FARM

ACRES U.S.A.

P.O. Box 301209, Austin TX 78703. (512)892-4400. **Fax:** (512)892-4448. **E-mail:** editor@acresusa.com. **Website:** www.acresusa.com. "Monthly trade journal written by people who have a sincere interest in the principles of organic and sustainable agriculture." Estab. 1970. Circ. 20,000. Byline given. Pays on publication. No kill fee. Editorial lead time 3 months. Submit seasonal material 6 months in advance. Accepts queries by mail, e-mail, fax. Accepts simultaneous submissions. Sample copy and writer's guidelines free.

NONFICTION Needs expose, how-to, personal experience. Special issues: Seeds (January), Poultry (March), Certified Organic (May), Livestock (June), Homesteading (August), Soil Fertility & Testing (October). Does not want poetry, fillers, product profiles, or anything with a promotional tone. **Buys about 50 mss/year.** Send complete ms. Length: 1,000-2,500 words. **Pays 10¢/word**

BEE CULTURE

P.O. Box 706, Medina OH 44256-0706. (330)725-6677; (800)289-7668. **Fax:** (330)725-5624. **E-mail:** kim@beeculture.com. **Website:** www.beeculture.com. **Contact:** Mr. Kim Flottum, editor. **50% freelance written.** Covers the natural science of honey bees. "Monthly magazine for beekeepers and those interested in the natural science of honey bees, with environmentally-oriented articles relating to honey bees or pollination." Estab. 1873. Pays on publication. No kill fee. Publishes ms an average of 4 months after acceptance. Accepts queries by mail, e-mail, fax, phone. Responds in 1 month to mss. Sample copy with 9x12 SASE and 5 first-class stamps. Guidelines and sample copy available online.

NONFICTION Needs interview, personal experience, photo feature. No "How I Began Beekeeping" articles. Highly advanced, technical, and scientific abstracts accepted for review for quarterly Refered section. Length: 2,000 words average. **Pays $200-250.**

$$$ PRODUCE BUSINESS

Phoenix Media Network Inc., P.O. Box 810425, Boca Raton FL 33481. (561)994-1118. **E-mail:** kwhitacre@phoenixmedianet.com; info@producebusiness.com. **Website:** www.producebusiness.com. **Contact:** Ken Whitacre, publisher/editorial director. **90% freelance written.** Monthly magazine covering produce and floral marketing. Addresses the buying end of the produce/floral industry, concentrating on supermarkets, chain restaurants, etc. Estab. 1985. Circ. 16,000. Byline given. Pays 30 days after publication. Offers $50 kill fee. Editorial lead time 2 months. Accepts queries by e-mail. NoSample copy and guidelines free.

NONFICTION Does not want unsolicited articles. **Buys 150 mss/year.** Query with published clips. Length: 1,200-10,000 words. **Pays $240-1,200.** Pays expenses of writers on assignment.

REGIONAL FARM

$$ AMERICAN AGRICULTURIST

5227 Baltimore Pike, Littlestown PA 17340. (717)359-0150. **Fax:** (717)359-0250. **E-mail:** jvogel@farmprogress.com. **Website:** www.farmprogress.com. **20% freelance written.** Monthly magazine covering cutting-edge technology and news to help farmers improve their operations. Publishes cutting-edge technology with ready on-farm application. Estab. 1842. Circ. 32,000. Pays on publication. No kill fee. Publishes ms an average of 3 months after acceptance. Editorial lead time 3 months. Submit seasonal material 3 months in advance. Accepts queries by e-mail, fax. Responds in 2 weeks to queries. Responds in 1 month to mss. Guidelines for #10 SASE.

NONFICTION Needs how-to, humor, inspirational, interview, new product, technical, No stories without a strong tie to Mid-Atlantic farming. **Buys 20 mss/year.** Query. Length: 500-1,000 words. **Pays $250-500.** Sometimes pays expenses of writers on assignment.

COLUMNS/DEPARTMENTS Country Air (humor, nostalgia, inspirational), 300-400 words. **Buys Buys 12 mss/year mss/year.** Send complete ms. **Pays $100.**

$$ FLORIDA GROWER

Meister Media Worldwide, 37733 Euclid Ave., Willoughby OH 44094. (440)942-2000. **E-mail:** fgiles@meistermedia.com; pprusnak@meistermedia.com. **Website:** www.growingproduce.com/floridagrower; www.meistermedia.com/publications/florida-grower. **Contact:** Frank Giles, editor; Paul Rusnak, managing editor. **10% freelance written.** Monthly magazine edited for the Florida farmer with commercial production interest primarily in citrus, vegetables, and other ag endeavors. Goal is to provide articles that update and inform on such areas as production, ag financing, farm labor relations, technology, safety, education, and regulation. Estab. 1907. Circ. 12,200. Byline given. Pays on publication. No kill fee. Editorial lead time 2 months. Submit seasonal material 3 months in advance. Accepts queries by mail, e-mail, fax, phone. Responds in 1 month to queries. Sample copy for SAE with 9x12 envelope and 5 First-Class stamps. Guidelines free.

NONFICTION Needs interview, photo feature, technical. Query with published clips. Length: 700-1,000 words. **Pays $150-250.**

$$ MAINE ORGANIC FARMER & GARDENER

Maine Organic Farmers & Gardeners Association, 662 Slab City Rd., Lincolnville ME 04849. (207)763-3043. **E-mail:** jenglish@tidewater.ne. **Website:** www.mofga.org. **40% freelance written. Prefers to work with published/established local writers.** Quarterly newspaper. "The *MOF&G* promotes and encourages sustainable agriculture and environmentally sound living. Our primary focus is organic farming, gardening, and forestry, but we also deal with local, national, and international agriculture, food, and environmental issues." Estab. 1976. Circ. 10,000. Byline and bio offered. Pays on publication. No kill fee. Publishes ms an average of 8 months after acceptance. Submit seasonal material 1 year in advance. Accepts queries by mail, e-mail. Accepts simultaneous submissions. Responds in 2 months to queries. Sample copy for $2 and SAE with 7 first-class stamps; from MOFGA, P.O. Box 170, Unity ME 04988. Guidelines available at www.mofga.org.

NONFICTION Buys 30 mss/year. Send complete ms. Length: 250-3,000 words. **Pays $25-300.**

FINANCE

✪$$$ ADVISOR'S EDGE

Rogers Media, Inc., 333 Bloor St. E., 6th Floor, Toronto ON M4W 1G6 Canada. **E-mail:** philip.porado@rci.rogers.com. **Website:** www.advisor.ca. **Contact:** Philip Porado, executive editor. Monthly magazine covering the financial industry (financial advisors and investment advisors). *Advisor's Edge* focuses on sales and marketing opportunities for the financial advisor (how they can build their business and improve relationships with clients). Estab. 1998. Circ. 36,000. Byline given. Pays on publication. Offers 25% kill fee. Publishes ms an average of 3 months after acceptance. Editorial lead time 3 months. Accepts queries by e-mail. Sample copy available online.

NONFICTION Needs how-to, interview. No articles that aren't relevant to how a financial advisor does his/her job. **Buys 12 mss/year.** Query with published clips. Length: 1,500-2,000 words. **Pays $900 (Canadian).**

AFP EXCHANGE

Association for Financial Professionals, 4520 East-West Hwy., Suite 750, Bethesda MD 20814. (301)907-2862. **E-mail:** exchange@afponline.org. **Website:** www.afponline.org/exchange. **20% freelance written.** Monthly magazine covering corporate treasury, corporate finance, B2B payments issues, corporate risk management, accounting and regulatory issues from the perspective of corporations. Welcomes interviews with CFOs and senior level practitioners. Best practices and practical information for corporate CFOs and treasurers. Tone is professional, intended to appeal to financial professionals on the job. Most accepted articles are written by professional journalists and editors, many featuring high-level AFP members in profile and case studies. Estab. 1979. Circ. 25,000. Byline given. Pays on publication. Offers kill fee. Pays negotiable kill fee in advance. Editorial lead time 2 months. Submit seasonal material 3 months in advance. Accepts queries by e-mail. Responds in 1 week to queries. Responds in 1 month to mss.

NONFICTION Needs book excerpts, how-to, interview, personal experience, technical. No PR-type articles pointing to any type of product or solution. **Buys 3-4 mss/year.** Query. Length: 1,100-1,800 words. **Pays 75¢-$1 for assigned articles.**

COLUMNS/DEPARTMENTS Cash Flow Forecasting (practical tips for treasurers, CFOs); Financial Reporting (insight, practical tips); Risk Management (practical tips for treasurers, CFOs); Corporate Payments (practical tips for treasurers), all 1,000-1,300 words; Professional Development (success stories, career related, about high level financial professionals), 1,100 words. **Buys 10 mss/year.** Query. **Pays 75¢-$1/word.**

FILLERS Needs anecdotes. Length: 400-700 words. **Pays 75¢/word.**

COLLECTIONS & CREDIT RISK

SourceMedia, One State St. Plaza, 27th Floor, New York NY 10004. (212)803-8200. **Fax:** (212)843-9600. **E-mail:** darren.waggoner@sourcemedia.com. **Website:** www.collectionscreditrisk.com. **Contact:** Darren Waggoner, chief editor. **33% freelance written.** Monthly journal covering debt collections and credit risk management. *Collections & Credit Risk* is the only magazine that brings news and trends of strategic and competitive importance to collections and credit-policy executives who are driving the collections industry's growth and diversification in both commercial and consumer credit. These executives work for financial institutions, insurance companies, collections agencies, law firms and attorney networks, health-care providers, retailers, telecoms and utility companies, manufacturers, wholesalers, and government agencies. Estab. 1996. Circ. 30,000. Byline given. Pays on acceptance. Offers kill fee. Kill fee determined case by case. Publishes ms an average of 3 months after acceptance. Editorial lead time 3 months. Accepts queries by mail. Sample copy free or online.

NONFICTION Needs interview, technical, business news and analysis. No unsolicited submissions accepted—freelancers work on assignment only. **Buys 30-40 mss/year.** Query with published clips. Length: 1,000-2,500 words. **Pays $800-1,000.** Sometimes pays expenses of writers on assignment.

CREDIT TODAY

P.O. Box 720, Roanoke VA 24004. (540)343-7500. **E-mail:** robl@credittoday.net; editor@credittoday.net. **Website:** www.credittoday.net. **Contact:** Rob Lawson, publisher. **10% freelance written.** Web-based publication covering business or trade credit. Estab. 1997. No byline given. Pays on acceptance. Publishes ms an average of 1 week after acceptance. Editorial lead time 1-2 months. Accepts queries by e-mail. NoSample copy free. Guidelines free.

NONFICTION Needs how-to, interview, technical. Does not want "puff" pieces promoting a particular product or vendor. **Buys 20 mss/year.** Send complete ms. Length: 700-1,800 words. **Pays $200-1,400.**

CREDIT UNION MANAGEMENT

Credit Union Executives Society, 5510 Research Park Dr., Madison WI 53711. (608)271-2664. **E-mail:** lisa@cues.org; cues@cues.org. **Website:** www.cumanagement.org. **Contact:** Lisa Hochgraf, editor. **44% freelance written.** Monthly magazine covering credit union, banking trends, management, HR, and marketing issues. "Our philosophy mirrors the credit union industry of cooperative financial services." Estab. 1978. Circ. 7,413. Pays on acceptance. No kill fee. Publishes ms an average of 2 months after acceptance. Editorial lead time 3 months. Submit seasonal material 4 months in advance. Accepts queries by mail. Accepts simultaneous submissions. Responds in 2 weeks to queries; 1 month to mss. Sample copy and writer's guidelines free.

NONFICTION Needs book excerpts, how-to, be a good mentor/leader, recruit, etc., interview, technical. **Buys 74 mss/year.** Query with published clips. Length: 700-2,400 words. **$250-350 for assigned features.** Phone expenses only

COLUMNS/DEPARTMENTS Management Network (book/Web reviews, briefs), 300 words; e-marketing, 700 words; Point of Law, 700 words; Best Practices (new technology/operations trends), 700 words. Query with published clips.

$$$ THE FEDERAL CREDIT UNION

National Association of Federal Credit Unions, 3138 10th St. N., Arlington VA 22201. (703)522-4770; (800)336-4644. **Fax:** (703)524-1082. **E-mail:** msc@nafcu.org; sbroaddus@nafcu.org. **Website:** www.nafcu.org/tfcuonline. **Contact:** Susan Broaddus, managing editor. **30% freelance written.** Published bimonthly, *The Federal Credit Union* is the official publication of the National Association of Federal Credit Unions. The magazine is dedicated to providing credit union management, staff, and volunteers with in-depth information (HR, technology, security, board management, etc.) they can use to fulfill their duties and better serve their members. The editorial focus includes coverage of management issues, operations, and technology as well as volunteer-related issues. Looking for writers with financial, banking, or credit union experience, but will work with inexperienced (unpublished) writers based on writing skill. Estab. 1967. Circ. 8,000. Byline given. Pays on publication. No kill fee. Publishes ms an average of 3 months after acceptance. Submit seasonal material 5 months in advance. Accepts queries by mail, e-mail, fax. Accepts simultaneous submissions. Responds in 2 months to queries.

NONFICTION Needs humor, inspirational, interview. Query with published clips and SASE. Length: 1,200-2,000 words. **Pays $400-1,000.**

$$ SERVICING MANAGEMENT

Zackin Publications, P.O. Box 2180, Waterbury CT 06722. (800)325-6745. **Fax:** (203)262-4680. **E-mail:** pbarnard@sm-online.com. **Website:** www.sm-online.com. **Contact:** Patrick Barnard, editor. **15% freelance written.** Monthly magazine covering residential mortgage servicing. Estab. 1989. Circ. 20,000. Byline given. Pays on acceptance. No kill fee. Publishes ms an average of 2 months after acceptance. Accepts queries by mail, e-mail, fax, phone. Responds in 2 weeks to queries. Sample copy free. Guidelines available online.

NONFICTION Needs how-to, interview, new product, technical. **Buys 10 mss/year.** Query. Length: 1,500-2,500 words.

COLUMNS/DEPARTMENTS Buys 5 mss/year. Query. **Pays $200.**

$$$$ USAA MAGAZINE

USAA, 9800 Fredericksburg Rd., San Antonio TX 78288. **E-mail:** usaamagazine@usaa.com. **Website:** www.usaa.com/maglinks. **80% freelance written.** Quarterly magazine covering financial security for USAA members. Conservative, common-sense approach to personal finance issues. Especially interested in how-to articles and pieces with actionable tips. Estab. 1970. Circ. 5.1 million. Byline given. Pays on acceptance. Offers 25% kill fee. Publishes ms an average of 4 months after acceptance. Editorial lead time 6 months. Submit seasonal material 6 months in advance. Accepts queries by e-mail. Responds in 6-8 weeks to queries. No mss accepted. Sample copy available online. Guidelines by e-mail.

NONFICTION Needs general interest, (finance), historical, (military), how-to, (personal finance), interview, (military/financial), personal experience, (finance). No poetry, photos, lifestyle unrelated to military or personal finance. **Buys 20 mss/year.** Submit a detailed query letter explaining story idea and listing possible sources. Does not accept unsolicited mss. Length: 600-1,500 words. **Pays $750-1,500 for assigned articles.** Sometimes pays expenses of writers on assignment.

FLORIST, NURSERIES AND LANDSCAPERS

$$ DIGGER

Oregon Association of Nurseries, 29751 S.W. Town Center Loop W., Wilsonville OR 97070. (503)682-

5089; (800) 342-6401. **Fax:** (503)682-5099. **E-mail:** ckipp@oan.org; info@oan.org. **Website:** www.oan.org. **Contact:** Curt Kipp, publications manager. **50% freelance written.** Monthly magazine covering nursery and greenhouse industry. *Digger* is a monthly magazine that focuses on industry trends, regulations, research, marketing, and membership activities. In August the magazine becomes *Digger Farwest Edition*, with all the features of *Digger* plus a complete guide to the annual Farwest Show, one of North America's top-attended nursery industry trade shows. Circ. 8,000. Byline given. Pays on receipt of copy. Offers 100% kill fee. Publishes ms an average of 2 months after acceptance. Editorial lead time 6 weeks. Submit seasonal material 2 months in advance. Accepts queries by mail, e-mail, fax, phone. Sample copy and writer's guidelines free.

NONFICTION Needs general interest, how-to, propagation techniques, other crop-growing tips, interview, personal experience, technical. Special issues: Farwest Edition (August): this is a triple-size issue that runs in tandem with our annual trade show (14,500 circulation for this issue). No articles not related or pertinent to nursery and greenhouse industry. **Buys 20-30 mss/year.** Query. Length: 800-2,000 words. **Pays $125-400 for assigned articles. Pays $100-300 for unsolicited articles.** Sometimes pays expenses of writers on assignment.

$ GROWERTALKS

Ball Publishing, 622 Town Rd., P.O. Box 1660, West Chicago IL 60186. (630)231-3675; (630)588-3401. **Fax:** (630)231-5254. **E-mail:** info@ballpublishing.com; jzurko@ballpublishing.com; cbeytes@growertalks.com. **Website:** www.growertalks.com. **Contact:** Jen Zurko, managing editor; Chris Beytes, editor. **50% freelance written.** Monthly magazine covering horticulture. *GrowerTalks* serves the commercial greenhouse grower. Editorial emphasis is on floricultural crops: bedding plants, potted floral crops, foliage, and fresh cut flowers. Readers are growers, managers, and owners. Looking for writers who've had experience in the greenhouse industry. Estab. 1937. Circ. 9,500. Byline given. Pays on publication. No kill fee. Publishes ms an average of 3 months after acceptance. Editorial lead time 4 months. Submit seasonal material 3 months in advance. Accepts queries by mail, e-mail, fax. Responds in 1 month to queries. Sample copy and writer's guidelines free.

NONFICTION Needs how-to, time- or money-saving projects for professional flower/plant growers, interview, ornamental horticulture growers, personal experience, of a grower, technical, about growing process in greenhouse setting. No articles that promote only 1 product. **Buys 36 mss/year.** Query. Length: 1,200-1,600 words. **Pays $125 minimum for assigned articles. Pays $75 minimum for unsolicited articles.**

$$ TREE CARE INDUSTRY MAGAZINE

Tree Care Industry Association, 136 Harvey Rd., Suite 101, Londonderry NH 03053. (800)733-2622 or (603)314-5380. **Fax:** (603)314-5386. **E-mail:** editor@tcia.org. **Website:** www.tcia.org. **Contact:** Don Staruk, editor. **50% freelance written.** Monthly magazine covering tree care and landscape maintenance. Estab. 1990. Circ. 24,000. Byline given. Pays within 1 month of publication. No kill fee. Publishes ms an average of 3 months after acceptance. Editorial lead time 10 weeks. Submit seasonal material 3 months in advance. Accepts queries by e-mail. Responds within 2 days to queries; 2 months to mss. Sample copies online. Guidelines free.

NONFICTION Needs book excerpts, historical, interview, new product, technical. **Buys 60 mss/year.** Query with published clips. Length: 900-3,500 words. **Pays negotiable rate.**

COLUMNS/DEPARTMENTS Buys 40 mss/year. Send complete ms. **Pays $100 and up.**

GOVERNMENT AND PUBLIC SERVICE

$$ AMERICAN CITY & COUNTY

Penton Media, 6151 Powers Ferry Rd. NW, Suite 200, Atlanta GA 30339. (770)618-0199. **Fax:** (770)618-0349. **E-mail:** bill.wolpin@penton.com; erin.greer@penton.com. **Website:** www.americancityandcounty.com. **Contact:** Bill Wolpin, editorial director; Erin Greer, managing editor. **40% freelance written.** Monthly magazine covering local and state government in the U.S. Estab. 1909. Circ. 65,000. Byline given. Pays on publication. Offers 25% kill fee. Publishes ms an average of 2 months after acceptance. Editorial lead time 3 months. Accepts queries by e-mail. Accepts simultaneous submissions. Sample copy available online. Guidelines by e-mail.

NONFICTION Needs new product, local and state government news analysis. **Buys 36 mss/year.** Query.

Length: 600-2,000 words. **Pays 30¢/published word.** Sometimes pays expenses of writers on assignment.

COLUMNS/DEPARTMENTS Issues & Trends (local and state government news analysis), 500-700 words. **Buys Buys 24 mss/year.** Query. **Pays $150-250.**

$$ COUNTY

Texas Association of Counties, 1210 San Antonio St., Austin TX 78701. (512)478-8753. **Fax:** (512)481-1240. **E-mail:** marias@county.org. **Website:** www.county.org. **Contact:** Maria Sprow, managing editor. **15% freelance written.** Bimonthly magazine covering county and state government in Texas. Provides elected and appointed county officials with insights and information that help them do their jobs and enhances communications among the independent office-holders in the courthouse. Estab. 1988. Circ. 5,500. Byline given. Pays on acceptance. No kill fee. Publishes ms an average of 2 months after acceptance. Editorial lead time 2 months. Submit seasonal material 4 months in advance. Accepts queries by mail, e-mail, phone. Responds in 2 weeks to queries. Responds in 1 month to mss. Sample copy and writer's guidelines for 8x10 SAE with 3 first-class stamps.

NONFICTION Needs historical, photo feature, government innovations. **Buys 5 mss/year.** Query with published clips. Length: 1,000-3,000 words. **Pays $500-700.** Sometimes pays expenses of writers on assignment.

COLUMNS/DEPARTMENTS Safety; Human Resources; Risk Management (all directed toward education of Texas county officials), maximum length 1,000 words. **Buys 2 mss/year.** Query with published clips. **Pays $500.**

$$ FIRE CHIEF

Primedia Business, 330 N. Wabash Ave., Suite 2300, Chicago IL 60611. (312)595-1080. **Fax:** (312)595-0295. **E-mail:** lisa@firechief.com; sundee@firechief.com. **Website:** www.firechief.com. **Contact:** Lisa Allegretti, editor; Sundee Koffarnus; art director. **60% freelance written.** Monthly magazine covering the fire chief occupation. "*Fire Chief* is the management magazine of the fire service, addressing the administrative, personnel, training, prevention/education, professional development, and operational issues faced by chiefs and other fire officers, whether in paid, volunteer, or combination departments. We're potentially interested in any article that can help them do their jobs better, whether that's as incident commanders, financial managers, supervisors, leaders, trainers, planners, or ambassadors to municipal officials or the public." Estab. 1956. Circ. 53,000. Byline given. Pays on publication. Offers kill fee. Kill fee negotiable. Publishes ms an average of 6 months after acceptance. Editorial lead time 2 months. Submit seasonal material 4 months in advance. Accepts queries by mail, e-mail, fax. Responds in 1 month to queries. Responds in 2 months to mss. Sample copy and submission guidelines free.

NONFICTION Needs how-to, technical. "We do not publish fiction, poetry, or historical articles. We also aren't interested in straightforward accounts of fires or other incidents, unless there are one or more specific lessons to be drawn from a particular incident, especially lessons that are applicable to a large number of departments." **Buys 50-60 mss/year.** Query first with published clips. Length: 1,000-10,000 words. **Pays $50-400.** Sometimes pays expenses of writers on assignment.

COLUMNS/DEPARTMENTS Training Perspectives; EMS Viewpoints; Sound Off; Volunteer Voice; all 1,000-1,800 words.

$$ FIREHOUSE MAGAZINE

Cygnus Business Media, 1233 Janesville Ave., Fort Atkinson WI 53538. (800)547-7377. **E-mail:** lizfn@cygnuspub.com. **Website:** www.firehouse.com. **Contact:** Elizabeth Friszell-Nerouslas, managing editor. **85% freelance written. Works with a small number of new/unpublished writers each year.** Monthly magazine. *Firehouse* covers major fires nationwide, controversial issues and trends in the fire service, the latest firefighting equipment and methods of firefighting, historical fires, firefighting history and memorabilia. Fire-related books, fire safety education, hazardous-materials incidents, and the emergency medical services are also covered. Estab. 1976. Circ. 83,538 (print). Byline given. Pays on publication. No kill fee. Accepts queries by mail, e-mail, fax, online submission form. Sample copy for SAE with 9x12 envelope and 8 first-class stamps.

NONFICTION Needs book excerpts, of recent books on fire, EMS, and hazardous materials, historical, great fires in history, fire collectibles, the fire service of yesteryear, how-to, fight certain kinds of fires, buy and maintain equipment, run a fire department, technical on almost any phase of firefighting, techniques, equipment, training, administration, trends in the fire service. No profiles of people or departments that are not unusual or innovative, reports of nonmajor fires, articles not slanted toward firefighters' interests. No poetry. **Buys 100 mss/year.** Query. "If you have any story ideas, questions, hints, tips, etc., please do not hesitate to call." Length: 500-3,000 words. The average length of each article is between 2-3 pages, including visuals. **Pays $50-400 for assigned articles.**

COLUMNS/DEPARTMENTS Training (effective methods); Book Reviews; Fire Safety (how departments teach fire safety to the public); Communicating (PR, dispatching); Arson (efforts to combat it). Length: 750-1,000 words. **Buys 50 mss/year.** Query or send complete ms. **Pays $100-300.**

$$ LAW ENFORCEMENT TECHNOLOGY MAGAZINE

Cygnus Business Media, 1233 Janesville Ave., Fort Atkinson WI 53538. (800)547-7377. **E-mail:** sara.scullin@cygnus.com. **Website:** www.officer.com. **Contact:** Sara Scullin, editor. **40% freelance written.** Monthly magazine covering police management and technology. Estab. 1974. Circ. 30,000. Byline given. Pays on publication. No kill fee. Publishes ms an average of 4 months after acceptance. Editorial lead time 6 months. Responds in 1 month to queries; 2 months to mss. Guidelines free.

NONFICTION Needs how-to, interview, photo feature, police management and training. **Buys 30 mss/year.** Query. Length: 1,200-2,000 words. **Pays $75-400 for assigned articles.**

$$ PLANNING

American Planning Association, 205 N. Michigan Ave., Suite 1200, Chicago IL 60601. (312)431-9100. **Fax:** (312)786-6700. **E-mail:** slewis@planning.org. **Website:** www.planning.org. **Contact:** Sylvia Lewis, editor; Joan Cairney, art director. **30% freelance written.** Monthly magazine emphasizing urban planning for adult, college-educated readers who are regional and urban planners in city, state, or federal agencies or in private business, or university faculty or students. Estab. 1972. Circ. 44,000. Byline given. Pays on publication. No kill fee. Publishes ms an average of 2 months after acceptance. Accepts queries by mail, e-mail, fax. Responds in 5 weeks to queries. Guidelines available online.

NONFICTION Special issues: Transportation Issue. Also needs news stories up to 500 words. **Buys 44 features and 33 news story mss/year.** Length: 500-3,000 words. **Pays $150-1,500.**

$$ POLICE AND SECURITY NEWS

DAYS Communications, Inc., 1208 Juniper St., Quakertown PA 18951-1520. (215)538-1240. **Fax:** (215)538-1208. **E-mail:** dyaw@policeandsecuritynews.com. **Website:** www.policeandsecuritynews.com. **Contact:** David Yaw, publisher. **40% freelance written.** Bimonthly periodical on public law enforcement and Homeland Security. "Our publication is designed to provide educational and entertaining information directed toward management level. Technical information written for the expert in a manner the nonexpert can understand." Estab. 1984. Circ. 24,000. Byline given. Pays on publication. No kill fee. Publishes ms an average of 2 months after acceptance. Accepts queries by mail, e-mail, fax, phone, online submission form. Accepts simultaneous submissions. Sample copy and writer's guidelines with 10x13 SASE with $2.53 postage.

NONFICTION Contact: Al Menear, articles editor. Needs exposè, historical, how-to, humor, interview, opinion, personal experience, photo feature, technical. **Buys 12 mss/year.** Query. Length: 200-2,500 words. **Pays 10¢/word. Sometimes pays in trade-out of services.**

FILLERS Needs facts, newsbreaks, short humor. **Buys 6 mss/year.** Length: 200-2,000 words. **10¢/word.**

$$$$ YOUTH TODAY

Kennesaw State University, 1000 Chastain Rd., MD 2212, Bldg. 22, Kennesaw GA 30144. (678)797-2899. **E-mail:** jfleming@youthtoday.org. **Website:** www.youthtoday.org. **Contact:** John Fleming, editor. **50% freelance written.** Bi-monthly newspaper covering businesses that provide services to youth. Audience is people who run youth programs—mostly nonprofits and government agencies—who want help in providing services and getting funding. Estab. 1994. Circ. 9,000. Byline given. Pays on publication. Offers $200 kill fee for features. Editorial lead time 2 months. Accepts queries by mail, e-mail, or disk. Accepts simultaneous submissions. Responds in 2 weeks to queries. Responds in 1 month to mss. Sample copy for $5. Guidelines available on website.

NONFICTION Needs exposè, general interest, technical. "No feel-good stories about do-gooders. We examine the business of youth work." **Buys 5 mss/year.** Query. Send rèsumè, short cover letter, clips. Length:

600-2,500 words. **Pays $150-2,000 for assigned articles.** Pays expenses of writers on assignment.

COLUMNS/DEPARTMENTS "*Youth Today* also publishes 750-word guest columns, called Viewpoints. These pieces can be based on the writer's own experiences or based on research, but they must deal with an issue of interest to our readership and must soundly argue an opinion, or advocate for a change in thinking or action within the youth field."

GROCERIES AND FOOD PRODUCTS

$$$ CONVENIENCE DISTRIBUTION

American Wholesale Marketers Association, 2750 Prosperity Ave., Suite 530, Fairfax VA 22031. (703)208-3358. **Fax:** (703)573-5738. **E-mail:** info@awmanet.org; joanf@awmanet.org. **Website:** www.awmanet.org. **Contact:** Joan Fay, associate publisher and editor. **70% freelance written.** Magazine published 10 times/year. See website for editorial calendar. Covers trends in candy, tobacco, groceries, beverages, snacks, and other product categories found in convenience stores, grocery stores, and drugstores, plus distribution topics. Contributors should have prior experience writing about the food, retail, and/or distribution industries. Editorial includes a mix of columns, departments, and features (2-6 pages). Also covers AWMA programs. Estab. 1948. Circ. 11,000. Byline given. Pays on acceptance. No kill fee. Publishes ms an average of 2 months after acceptance. Editorial lead time 3-4 months. Accepts queries by e-mail only. Guidelines available online.

NONFICTION Needs how-to, technical, industry trends, also profiles of distribution firms. No comics, jokes, poems, or other fillers. **Buys 40 mss/year.** Query with published clips. Length: 1,200-3,600 words. **Pays 50¢/word.** Pays expenses of writers on assignment.

$$$$ FOOD PRODUCT DESIGN MAGAZINE

P.O. Box 3439, Northbrook IL 60065-3439. (480)990-1101 ext. 1241; (800)581-1811. **E-mail:** lkuntz@vpico.com. **Website:** www.foodproductdesign.com. **Contact:** Lynn A. Kuntz, editor-in-chief. **50% freelance written.** Monthly magazine covering food processing industry. Written for food technologists by food technologists. No food service/restaurant, consumer, or recipe development. Official media for SupplySide, *Food Product Design* delivers practical, use-it-now, take-it-to-the-bench editorial for product development professionals, as well as market intelligence and analysis of industry news for the executive-level reader. *Food Product Design* is the industry's leading product development content and information source. Estab. 1991. Circ. 30,000. Byline given. Pays on acceptance. Publishes ms an average of 2 months after acceptance. Editorial lead time 4 months. Sample copy for SAE with 9x12 envelope and 5 first-class stamps.

NONFICTION Needs technical. **Buys 30 mss/year.** Length: 1,500-7,000 words. **Pays $100-1,500.** Sometimes pays expenses of writers on assignment.

$$ THE PRODUCE NEWS

800 Kinderkamack Rd., Suite 100, Oradell NJ 07649. (201)986-7990. **Fax:** (201)986-7996. **E-mail:** groh@theproducenews.com. **Website:** www.theproducenews.com. **Contact:** John Groh, editor/publisher. **10% freelance written. Works with a small number of new/unpublished writers each year.** Weekly magazine for commercial growers and shippers, receivers, and distributors of fresh fruits and vegetables, including chain store produce buyers and merchandisers. Estab. 1897. Pays on publication. No kill fee. Publishes ms an average of 2 weeks after acceptance. Accepts queries by mail, e-mail. Responds in 1 month to queries. Sample copy and writer's guidelines for 10x13 SAE and 4 first-class stamps.

NONFICTION Query. **Pays $1/column inch minimum.** Sometimes pays expenses of writers on assignment.

$$ PRODUCE RETAILER

Vance Publishing Corp., 10901 West 84th Ter., Suite 200, Lenexa KS 66214. (913)438-0603; (512)906-0733. **E-mail:** pamelar@produceretailer.com; treyes@produceretailer.com. **Website:** produceretailer.com. **Contact:** Pamela Riemenschneider, editor; Tony Reyes, art director. **10% freelance written.** Monthly magazine. "*Produce Merchandising* is the only monthly journal on the market that is dedicated solely to produce merchandising information for retailers. Our purpose is to provide information about promotions, merchandising, and operations in the form of ideas and examples." Estab. 1988. Circ. 12,000. Byline given. Pays on acceptance. No kill fee. Publishes ms an average of 3 months after acceptance. Editorial lead time 3 months. Accepts queries by mail. Responds in 2 weeks to queries. Sample copy free.

NONFICTION Needs how-to, interview, new product, photo feature, technical, contact the editor for a specific assignment. **Buys 48 mss/year.** Query with published clips. Length: 1,000-1,500 words. **Pays $200-600.** Pays expenses.

WESTERN GROCER MAGAZINE

Mercury Publications Ltd., 1740 Wellington Ave., Winnipeg MB R3H 0E8 Canada. (204)954-2085, ext. 291; (800)337-6372. **Fax:** (204)954-2057. **E-mail:** rbradley@mercurypublications.ca. **Website:** www.westerngrocer.com. **Contact:** Robin Bradley, associate publisher and national account manager. **75% freelance written.** Bimonthly magazine covering the grocery industry. Reports for the Western Canadian grocery, allied non-food and institutional industries. Each issue features a selection of relevant trade news and event coverage from the West and around the world. Feature reports offer market analysis, trend views, and insightful interviews from a wide variety of industry leaders. *The Western Grocer* target audience is independent retail food stores, supermarkets, manufacturers and food brokers, distributors and wholesalers of food, and allied non-food products, as well as bakers, specialty and health food stores, and convenience outlets. Estab. 1916. Circ. 15,500. Byline given. Pays 30-45 days from receipt of invoice. Offers 33% kill fee. Submit seasonal material 3 months in advance. Sample copy and writer's guidelines free.

NONFICTION Needs how-to, interview. Does not want industry reports and profiles on companies. Query with published clips. Length: 500-9,000 words. **Pays 25-35¢/word.** Sometimes pays expenses of writers on assignment.

HOME FURNISHINGS AND HOUSEHOLD GOODS

HOME FURNISHINGS RETAILER

National Home Furnishings Association (NHFA), 3910 Tinsley Dr., Suite 101, High Point NC 27265-3610. (336)801-6156. **Fax:** (336)801-6102. **E-mail:** wynnryan@rcn.com. **Website:** www.nhfa.org. **Contact:** Mary Wynn Ryan, editor-in-chief. **75% freelance written.** Monthly magazine published by NHFA covering the home furnishings industry. "We hope home furnishings retailers view our magazine as a profitability tool. We want each issue to help them make or save money." Estab. 1927. Circ. 15,000. Byline given. Pays on acceptance. No kill fee. Publishes ms an average of 6 weeks after acceptance. Editorial lead time 3 months. Accepts queries by mail, e-mail. Responds in 1 month to queries. Sample copy available with proper postage.

NONFICTION Query. "When submitting a query or requesting a writing assignment, include a résumé, writing samples, and credentials. When articles are assigned, *Home Furnishings Retailer* will provide general direction along with suggestions for appropriate artwork. The author is responsible for obtaining photographs or other illustrative material. Assigned articles should be submitted via e-mail or on disc along with a list of sources with telephone numbers, fax numbers, and e-mail addresses." Length: 3,000-5,000 words (features). **Pays $350-500.**

HOSPITALS, NURSING AND NURSING HOMES

CURRENT NURSING IN GERIATRIC CARE

Freiberg Press Inc., P.O. Box 612, Cedar Falls IA 50613. (319)553-0642; (800)354-3371. **Fax:** (319)553-0644. **E-mail:** bfreiberg@cfu.net. **Website:** www.care4elders.com. **Contact:** Bill Freiberg. **25% freelance written.** Bimonthly trade journal covering medical information and new developments in research for geriatric nurses and other practitioners. Estab. 2006. Byline sometimes given. Pays on acceptance. No kill fee. Accepts queries by e-mail. Sample copy free; send e-mail to Kathy Freiderg at kfreiberg@cfu.net.

NONFICTION Query. Length: 500-1,500 words. **Pays 15¢/word for assigned articles.**

HOSPITALS & HEALTH NETWORKS

Health Forum Inc., 155 N. Wacker Dr., Suite 400, Chicago IL 60606. (312)893-6800. **Fax:** (312)422-4500. **E-mail:** rhill@healthforum.com; bsantamour@healthforum.com. **Website:** www.hhnmag.com. **Contact:** Richard Hill, editor; Bill Santamour, managing editor. **25% freelance written.** Monthly magazine covering hospitals. Online business publication for hospital and health system executives. Uses only writers who are thoroughly familiar with the hospital field. Potential articles should focus on a critical aspect of health care leadership and, if possible, should address the future of health care. Estab. 1926. Circ. 88,000. Byline given. Pays on acceptance. Offers variable kill fee. Publishes ms an average of 3 months after acceptance. Editorial lead time 6-7 months. Accepts queries by e-mail. Responds in 2-4 months to queries. Guidelines available online.

NONFICTION Needs interview, technical. Query editor with a working title, a 50-100 word abstract, and a short biographical sketch. Length: 800-1,200 words.

$$$ NURSEWEEK

Gannett Healthcare Group, 1721 Moon Lake Blvd., Suite 540, Hoffman Estates IL 60169. **E-mail:** editor@nurse.com. **Website:** www.nurse.com. **Contact:** Nick Hut, editor. **98% freelance written.** Biweekly magazine covering nursing news. Covers nursing news about people, practice, and the profession. Review several issues for content and style. Also consider e-mailing your idea to the editorial director in your region (see list online). The editorial director can help you with the story's focus or angle, along with the organization and development of ideas. Estab. 1999. Circ. 155,000. Byline given. Pays on publication. Offers $200 kill fee. Publishes ms an average of 2 months after acceptance. Editorial lead time 2-3 months. Submit seasonal material 4 months in advance. Accepts queries by e-mail. Accepts simultaneous submissions. Sample copy free. Guidelines on website.

NONFICTION Needs interview, personal experience, articles on innovative approaches to clinical care and evidence-based nursing practice, health-related legislation and regulation, community health programs, healthcare delivery systems, and professional development and management, advances in nursing specialties such as critical care, geriatrics, perioperative care, women's health, home care, long-term care, emergency care, med/surg, pediatrics, advanced practice, education, and staff development. **Buys 20 mss/year mss/year.** Query with a 50-word summary of story and a list of RN experts you plan to interview. Length: 900 words. **Pays $200-800 for assigned or unsolicited articles.**

$ SCHOOL NURSE NEWS

Franklin Communications, Inc., 71 Redner Rd., Morristown NJ 07960. (973)644-4003. **Fax:** (973)644-4062. **E-mail:** editor@schoolnursenews.org. **Website:** www.schoolnursenews.org. **Contact:** Deb Ilardi. **10% freelance written.** Magazine published 5 times/year covering school nursing. *School Nurse News* focuses on topics related to the health issues of school-aged children and adolescents (grades K-12), as well as the health and professional issues that concern school nurses. This is an excellent opportunity for both new and experienced writers. *School Nurse News* publishes feature articles as well as news articles and regular departments, such as Asthma & Allergy Watch, Career & Salary Survey, Oral Health, Nursing Currents, and Sights & Sounds. Estab. 1982. Circ. 7,500. Byline given. Pays on publication. Publishes ms an average of 3-6 months after acceptance. Editorial lead time 3-6 months. Submit seasonal material 6 months in advance. Accepts queries by e-mail, fax, phone. Sample copy free. Guidelines available on website.

NONFICTION Needs how-to, interview, new product, personal experience. **Buys 1-2 mss/year.** Query. Send via e-mail or forward ms with disk. Mss can include case histories, scenarios of health office situations, updates on diseases, reporting of research, and discussion of procedures and techniques, among others. The author is responsible for the accuracy of content. References should be complete, accurate, and in APA format. Tables, charts and photographs are welcome. Authors are responsible for obtaining permission to reproduce any material that has a pre-existing copyright. The feature article, references, tables, and charts should total 8-10 typewritten pages, double-spaced. The author's name should be included only on the top sheet. The top sheet should also include the title of the article, the author's credentials, current position, address, and phone. **Pays $100.**

HOTELS, MOTELS, CLUBS AND RESTAURANTS

$$ BARTENDER MAGAZINE

Foley Publishing, P.O. Box 158, Liberty Corner NJ 07938. (908)766-6006. **Fax:** (908)766-6607. **E-mail:** barmag@aol.com. **Website:** www.bartender.com. **Contact:** Jackie Foley, editor. **100% freelance written. Prefers to work with published/established writers; eager to work with new/unpublished writers.** Quarterly magazine emphasizing liquor and bartending for bartenders, tavern owners, and owners of restaurants with full-service liquor licenses. Estab. 1979. Circ. 150,000. Byline given. Pays on publication. No kill fee. Publishes ms an average of 3 months after acceptance. Submit seasonal material 3 months in advance. Accepts simultaneous submissions. Responds in 2 months to mss. Sample copy with 9x12 SAE and 4 first-class stamps.

NONFICTION Needs general interest, historical, how-to, humor, interview with famous bartenders or ex-bartenders, new product, opinion, personal experience, photo feature, travel, nostalgia, unique bars, new techniques, new drinking trends, bar sports, bar magic tricks. Special issues: Special issues: Annual Calendar and Daily Cocktail Recipe Guide. Send complete ms and SASE. Length: 100-1,000 words.

COLUMNS/DEPARTMENTS Bar of the Month; Bartender of the Month; Creative Cocktails; Bar Sports; Quiz; Bar Art; Wine Cellar; Tips from the Top (from prominent figures in the liquor industry); One For the Road (travel); Collectors (bar or liquor-related items); Photo Essays. Length: 200-1,000 words. Query by mail only with SASE. **Pays $50-200.**

FILLERS Needs anecdotes, newsbreaks, short humor, clippings, jokes, gags. Length: 25-100 words. **Pays $5-25.**

$$ EL RESTAURANTE (FORMERLY EL RESTAURANTE MEXICANO)

P.O. Box 2249, Oak Park IL 60303-2249. (708)267-0023. **E-mail:** kfurore@comcast.net. **Website:** www.restmex.com. **Contact:** Kathleen Furore, editor. Bimonthly magazine covering Mexican and other Latin cuisines. "*el Restaurante* offers features and business-related articles that are geared specifically to owners and operators of Mexican, Tex-Mex, Southwestern, and Latin cuisine restaurants and other foodservice establishments that want to add that type of cuisine." Estab. 1997. Circ. 25,000. Byline given. Pays on publication. No kill fee. Publishes ms an average of 3 months after acceptance. Responds in 2 months to queries. Sample copy free.

NONFICTION "No specific knowledge of food or restaurants is needed; the key qualification is to be a good reporter who knows how to slant a story toward the Mexican restaurant operator." **Buys 2-4 mss/year.** Query with published clips. Length: 800-1,200 words. **Pays $250-300.**

Ø$$$$ HOSPITALITY TECHNOLOGY

Edgell Communications, 4 Middlebury Blvd., Randolph NJ 07869. (973)607-1300. **E-mail:** alorden@edgellmail.com; dcreamer@edgellmail.com. **Website:** www.htmagazine.com. **Contact:** Abigail Lorden, editor-in-chief; Dorothy Creamer, managing editor. **70% freelance written.** Magazine published 9 times/year covering restaurant and lodging executives who manage hotels, casinos, cruise lines, quick service restaurants, etc. Covers the technology used in foodservice and lodging. Readers are the operators, who have significant IT responsibilities. Estab. 1996. Circ. 16,000. Byline given. Pays on acceptance. No kill fee. Publishes ms an average of 1 month after acceptance. Editorial lead time 2 months. Accepts queries by mail, e-mail. Responds in 2 weeks to queries.

NONFICTION Needs how-to, interview, new product, technical. Special issues: Publishes 2 studies each year: the Restaurant Industry Technology Study and the Lodging Industry Technology Study. No unsolicited mss. **Buys 40 mss/year.** Query with published clips. Length: 800-1,200 words. **Pays $1/word.** Sometimes pays expenses of writers on assignment.

✪$$ HOTELIER

Kostuch Media Ltd., 101-23 Lesmill Rd., Toronto ON M3B 3P6 Canada. (416)447-0888. **Fax:** (416)447-5333. **E-mail:** rcaira@foodservice.ca. **Website:** www.hoteliermagazine.com. **Contact:** Rosanna Caira, editor & publisher. **40% freelance written.** Magazine published 8 times/year covering the Canadian hotel industry. Canada's leading hotel publication. Provides comprehensive and insightful content focusing on business developments, trend analysis, and profiles of the industry's movers and shakers. Estab. 1989. Circ. 9,000. Byline given. Pays on publication. No kill fee. Editorial lead time 3 months. Submit seasonal material 2 months in advance. Accepts queries by mail, fax. Query for free sample copy. Query for free guidelines.

NONFICTION Needs how-to, new product. No case studies. **Buys 30-50 mss/year.** Query. Length: 700-1,500 words. **Pays 35¢/word (Canadian) for assigned articles.** Sometimes pays expenses of writers on assignment.

$$ INSITE

Christian Camp and Conference Association, P.O. Box 62189, Colorado Springs CO 80962-2189. (719)260-9400. **Fax:** (719)260-6398. **E-mail:** editor@ccca.org; info@ccca.org. **Website:** www.ccca.org. **75% freelance written. Prefers to work with published/established writers.** Bimonthly magazine emphasizing the broad scope of organized camping with emphasis on Christian camps and conference centers. All who work in youth camps and adult conferences read *InSite* for inspiration and to get practical help in ways to serve in their operations. Estab. 1963.

Circ. 8,500. Byline given. Pays on publication. No kill fee. Publishes ms an average of 4 months after acceptance. Accepts queries by mail, e-mail. Responds in 1 month to queries. Sample copy for $4.99 plus 9x12 SASE. Guidelines available on website.

NONFICTION Needs general interest, trends in organized camping in general (Christian camping in particular), how-to, anything involved with organized camping (including motivating staff, programming, healthcare, maintenance, and camper follow-up), inspirational, profiles and practical applications of Scriptural principles to everyday situations in camping, interviews with movers and shakers in Christian camping. **Buys 15-20 mss/year.** Query required. Length: Features: 1,200-1,500 words; How-To: 1,000-1,200 words; Sidebars: 250-500 words. **Pays 20¢/word.**

$$$ PIZZA TODAY

Macfadden Protech, LLC, 908 S. 8th St., Suite 200, Louisville KY 40203. (502)736-9500. **Fax:** (502)736-9502. **E-mail:** jwhite@pizzatoday.com. **Website:** www.pizzatoday.com. **Contact:** Jeremy White, editor-in-chief. **30% freelance written. Works with published/established writers; occasionally works with new writers.** Monthly magazine for the pizza industry, covering trends, features of successful pizza operators, business and management advice, etc. Estab. 1984. Circ. 44,000. Byline given. Pays on acceptance. No kill fee. Publishes ms an average of 2 months after acceptance. Submit seasonal material 3 months in advance. Accepts queries by mail, e-mail, fax. Responds in 2 months to queries. Responds in 3 weeks to mss. Sample copy for sae with 10x13 envelope and 6 first-class stamps. Guidelines for #10 SASE and online.

NONFICTION Needs interview, entrepreneurial slants, pizza production and delivery, employee training, hiring, marketing, and business management. No fillers, humor, or poetry. **Buys 85 mss/year.** Length: 1,000 words. **Pays 50¢/word, occasionally more.** Sometimes pays expenses of writers on assignment.

$$$ SANTÉ MAGAZINE

On-Premise Communications, 160 Benmont Ave., Suite 92, Third Floor, West Wing, Bennington VT 05201. (802)442-6771. **Fax:** (802)442-6859. **E-mail:** mvaughan@santemagazine.com. **Website:** www.isantemagazine.com. **Contact:** Mark Vaughan, editor. **75% freelance written.** Four-issues-per-year magazine covering food, wine, spirits, and management topics for restaurant professionals. Information and specific advice for restaurant professionals on operating a profitable food and beverage program. Writers should "speak" to readers on a professional-to-professional basis. Estab. 1996. Circ. 45,000. Byline given. Pays on publication. Offers 50% kill fee. Publishes ms an average of 2 months after acceptance. Editorial lead time 3 months. Submit seasonal material 6 months in advance. Accepts queries by e-mail. Responds in 2 weeks to queries. Does not accept mss. Sample copy available. Guidelines by email.

NONFICTION Needs interview, restaurant business news. Does not want consumer-focused pieces. **Buys 20 mss/year.** Query with published clips. Length: 650-1,800 words. Sometimes pays expenses of writers on assignment.

COLUMNS/DEPARTMENTS Due to a Redesign, 650 words; Bar Tab (focuses on 1 bar's unique strategy for success), 1,000 words; Restaurant Profile (a business-related look at what qualities make 1 restaurant successful), 1,000 words; Maximizing Profits (covers 1 great profit-maximizing strategy per issue from several sources), Signature Dish (highlights 1 chef's background and favorite dish with recipe), Sommeliers Choice (6 top wine managers recommend favorite wines; with brief profiles of each manager), Distillations (6 bar professionals offer their favorite drink for a particular type of spirit; with brief profiles of each manager), 1,500 words; Provisions (like The Goods only longer; an in-depth look at a special ingredient), 1,500 words. **Buys 20 mss/year.** Query with published clips. **Pays $300-800.**

○$$ WESTERN HOTELIER MAGAZINE

Mercury Publications, Ltd., 1740 Wellington Ave., Winnipeg MB R3H 0E8 Canada. (204)954-2085. **Fax:** (204)954-2057. **E-mail:** dbastable@mercurypublications.ca. **Website:** www.westernhotelier.com. **Contact:** David Bastable, associate publisher and national accounts manager. **33% freelance written.** Quarterly magazine covering the hotel industry. *Western Hotelier* is dedicated to the accommodation industry in Western Canada and U.S. western border states. *WH* offers the West's best mix of news and feature reports geared to hotel management. Feature reports are written on a sector basis and are created to help generate enhanced profitability and better understanding. Circ. 4,342. Byline given. Pays 30-45 days from receipt of invoice. Offers 33% kill fee. Submit seasonal material

3 months in advance. Accepts queries by mail, fax. Accepts simultaneous submissions. Responds in 2 weeks to queries. Sample copy and writer's guidelines free.

NONFICTION Needs how-to, train staff, interview. Industry reports and profiles on companies. Query with published clips. Length: 500-9,000 words. **Pays 25-35¢/word.** Sometimes pays expenses of writers on assignment.

WESTERN RESTAURANT NEWS

Mercury Publications, Ltd., 1740 Wellington Ave., Winnipeg MB R3H 0E8 Canada. (204)954-2085. **Fax:** (204)954-2057. **E-mail:** editorial@mercury.mb.ca. **Website:** www.westernrestaurantnews.com; www.mercury.mb.ca. **Contact:** Nicole Sherwood, editorial coordinator. **20% freelance written.** Bimonthly magazine covering the restaurant trade in Western Canada. Reports profiles and industry reports on associations, regional business developments, etc. *Western Restaurant News* is the authoritative voice of the foodservice industry in Western Canada. Offering a total package to readers, *WRN* delivers concise news articles, new product news, and coverage of the leading trade events in the West, across the country, and around the world. Estab. 1994. Circ. 14,532. Byline given. Pays 30-45 days from receipt of invoice. Offers 33% kill fee. Submit seasonal material 3 months in advance. Accepts queries by mail, fax. Accepts simultaneous submissions. Sample copy and writer's guidelines free.

NONFICTION Needs how-to, interview. Industry reports and profiles on companies. Query with published clips. "E-mail, fax, or mail a query outlining your experience, interests, and pay expectations. Include clippings." Length: 500-9,000 words. **Pays 25-35¢/word.** Sometimes pays expenses of writers on assignment.

INDUSTRIAL OPERATIONS

COMMERCE & INDUSTRY

Mercury Publications, Ltd., 1740 Wellington Ave., Winnipeg MB R3H 0E8 Canada. (204)954-2085. **Fax:** (204)954-2057. **E-mail:** editorial@mercury.mb.ca. **Website:** www.commerceindustry.ca. **Contact:** Nicole Sherwood, editorial coordinator. **75% freelance written.** Bimonthly magazine covering the business and industrial sectors. Offers new product news, industry event coverage, and breaking trade specific business stories. Industry reports and company profiles provide readers with an in-depth insight into key areas of interest in their profession. Estab. 1948. Circ. 18,876. Byline given. Pays 30-45 days from receipt of invoice. Offers 33% kill fee. Submit seasonal material 3 months in advance. Accepts queries by mail, e-mail, fax. Accepts simultaneous submissions. Responds in 2 weeks to queries. Sample copy and writer's guidelines free or by e-mail.

NONFICTION Needs how-to, interview. Industry reports and profiles on companies. Query with published clips. Length: 500-9,000 words. **Pays 25-35¢/word.** Sometimes pays expenses of writers on assignment.

INDUSTRIAL WEIGH & MEASURE

WAM Publishing Co., P.O. Box 2247, Hendersonville TN 37077. (615)239-8087. **E-mail:** dave.mathieu@comcast.net. **Website:** www.weighproducts.com. **Contact:** David M. Mathieu, publisher. Bimonthly magazine for users of industrial scales; covers material handling and logistics industries. Estab. 1914. Circ. 13,900. Byline given. Pays on acceptance. Offers 20% kill fee. Accepts queries by mail, e-mail, phone. Responds in 2 weeks to queries. Sample copy available online.

NONFICTION Needs interview with presidents of companies, personal experience, guest editorials on government involvement in business, technical, profilse (about users of weighing and measurement equipment). **Buys 15 mss/year.** Query on technical articles; submit complete ms for general interest material. Length: 1,000-2,500 words. **Pays $175-300.**

MODERN MATERIALS HANDLING

Peerless Media, 111 Speen St., Suite 200, Framingham MA 01701. (508)663-1500. **E-mail:** mlevans@ehpub.com; robert.trebilcock@myfairpoint.net. **Website:** www.mmh.com. **Contact:** Michael Levans, editorial director. **40% freelance written.** Magazine published 13 times/year covering warehousing, distribution centers, and inventory. *Modern Materials Handling* is a national magazine read by managers of warehouses and distribution centers. Focuses on lively, well-written articles telling readers how they can achieve maximum facility productivity and efficiency. Covers technology, too. Estab. 1945. Circ. 81,000. Byline given. Pays on acceptance (allow 4-6 weeks for invoice processing). No kill fee. Publishes ms an average of 1 month after acceptance. Editorial lead time 3 months.

Accepts queries by mail, e-mail, fax. Sample copy and guidelines free.

NONFICTION Needs how-to, new product, technical. Special issues: State-of-the-Industry Report, Peak Performer, Salary and Wage survey, Warehouse of the Year. Doesn't want anything that doesn't deal with the topic of warehousing. No general-interest profiles or interviews. **Buys 25 mss/year.** Query with published clips. **Pays $300-650.**

PEM PLANT ENGINEERING & MAINTENANCE

CLB Media, Inc., 222 Edward St., Aurora ON L4G 1W6 Canada. (905)727-0077. **Fax:** (905)727-0017. **E-mail:** rbegg@annexweb.com. **Website:** www.pem-mag.com. **Contact:** Rehana Begg, editor. **30% freelance written.** Bimonthly magazine looking for informative articles on issues that affect plant floor operations and maintenance. Estab. 1977. Circ. 18,500. Byline given. Pays on publication. No kill fee. Publishes ms an average of 3 months after acceptance. Editorial lead time 4 months. Submit seasonal material 4 months in advance. Accepts simultaneous submissions. Responds in 3 weeks to queries. Responds in 1 month to mss. Sample copy free. Guidelines available.

NONFICTION Needs how-to, keep production downtime to a minimum, better operate an industrial operation, new product, technical. **Buys 6 mss/year.** Query with published clips. Length: 750-4,000 words. **Pays $500-1,400 (Canadian).** Sometimes pays expenses of writers on assignment.

INFORMATION SYSTEMS

DESKTOP ENGINEERING

Level 5 Communications, Inc., 1283 Main St., P.O. Box 1039, Dublin NH 03444. (603)563-1631. **Fax:** (603)563-8192. **E-mail:** jgooch@deskeng.com. **E-mail:** de-editors@deskeng.com. **Website:** www.deskeng.com. **Contact:** Jamie Gooch, managing editor. **90% freelance written.** Monthly magazine covering computer hardware/software for hands-on design and mechanical engineers, analysis engineers, and engineering management. Ten special supplements/year. Estab. 1995. Circ. 63,000. Byline given. Pays in month of publication. Kill fee for assigned story. Publishes ms an average of 2 months after acceptance. Editorial lead time 3 months. Accepts queries by mail, e-mail, phone. Responds in 2 weeks to queries; 1 month to mss. Sample copy for free with 8x10 SASE. Guidelines available on website.

NONFICTION Needs how-to, new product, reviews, technical, design. No fluff. **Buys 50-70 mss/year.** Query. Submit outline before you write an article. Length: 800-1,200 word articles (plus artwork) presenting tutorials, application stories, product reviews or other features; 500-700 word guest commentaries for almost any topic related to desktop engineering. **Pays per project. Pay negotiable for unsolicited articles.** Sometimes pays expenses of writers on assignment.

COLUMNS/DEPARTMENTS Product Briefs, 50-100 words; Reviews, 500-1,500 words.

SYSTEM INEWS

Penton Technology Media, 748 Whalers Way, Fort Collins CO 80525. (970)663-4700; (800)621-1544. **E-mail:** editors@iprodeveloper.com. **Website:** www.iseriesnetwork.com. **40% freelance written.** Magazine, published 12 times/year, focused on programming, networking, IS management, and technology for users of IBM AS/400, iSERIES, SYSTEM i, AND IBM i platform. Estab. 1982. Circ. 30,000 (international). Byline given. Pays on publication. Offers 50% kill fee. Publishes ms an average of 3 months after acceptance. Editorial lead time 4 months. Submit seasonal material 4 months in advance. Accepts queries by e-mail. Responds in 3 weeks to queries. Responds in 5 weeks to mss. Guidelines available online.

NONFICTION Needs technical. Query. Length: 1,500-2,500 words. **Pays $300-500 flat fee for assigned articles, depending on quality and technical depth.**

TECHNOLOGY REVIEW

MIT, One Main St., 13th Floor, Cambridge MA 02142. (617)475-8000. **Fax:** (617)475-8042. **E-mail:** jason.pontin@technologyreview.com; david.rotman@technologyreview.com. **Website:** www.technologyreview.com. **Contact:** Jason Pontin, editor-in-chief; David Rotman, editor. Magazine published 10 times/year covering information technology, biotech, material science, and nanotechnology. *Technology Review* promotes the understanding of emerging technologies and their impact. Estab. 1899. Circ. 310,000. Pays on acceptance. Accepts queries by mail, e-mail.

NONFICTION Query with a pitch via online contact form. Length: 2,000-4,000 words. **Pays $1-3/word.**

FILLERS Short tidbits that relate laboratory prototypes on their way to market in 1-5 years. Length: 150-250 words. **Pays $1-3/word.**

INSURANCE

$$$$ ADVISOR TODAY

NAIFA, 2901 Telestar Court, Falls Church VA 22042. (703)770-8204. **E-mail:** amseka@naifa.org. **Website:** www.advisortoday.com. **Contact:** Ayo Mseka, editor-in-chief. **25% freelance written.** Monthly magazine covering life insurance and financial planning. Writers must demonstrate an understanding at what insurance agents and financial advisors do to earn business and serve their clients. Estab. 1906. Circ. 110,000. Pays on acceptance or publication (by mutual agreement with editor). No kill fee. Publishes ms an average of 3 months after acceptance. Editorial lead time: 3 months. Submit seasonal material 6 months in advance. Accepts queries by mail, e-mail, fax, phone. Accepts simultaneous submissions. Sample copy free. Guidelines available online.

NONFICTION Buys 8 mss/year. "We prefer e-mail submissions in Microsoft Word format. For other formats and submission methods, please query first. For all articles and queries, contact Ayo Mseka. Web articles should cover the same subject matter covered in the magazine. The articles can be between 300-800 words and should be submitted to Ayo Mseka. Please indicate where a story has been previously published articles have been accepted." Length: 2,300 words for cover articles; 1,000 words for feature articles; 650-700 words for columns and speciality articles; 300-800 words for web articles. **Pays $800-2,000.**

JEWELRY

$$ THE ENGRAVERS JOURNAL

P.O. Box 318, Brighton MI 48116. (810)229-5725. **Fax:** (810)229-8320. **E-mail:** editor@engraversjournal.com. **Website:** www.engraversjournal.com. **Contact:** Managing editor. **70% freelance written.** Monthly magazine covering the recognition and identification industry (engraving, marking devices, awards, jewelry, and signage). "We provide practical information for the education and advancement of our readers, mainly retail business owners." Estab. 1975. Byline given. Pays on acceptance. No kill fee. Publishes ms an average of 3-9 months after acceptance. Accepts queries by mail, e-mail, fax. Responds in 2 weeks to mss. Sample copy free. Guidelines free.

NONFICTION Needs general interest, industry related, how-to, small business subjects, increase sales, develop new markets, use new sales techniques, etc., technical. No general overviews of the industry. Length: 1,000-5,000 words. **Pays $200 and up.**

JOURNALISM AND WRITING

$$$$ AMERICAN JOURNALISM REVIEW

University of Maryland Foundation, Knight Hall, University of Maryland, College Park MD 20742. (301)405-8805. **Fax:** (301)405-8323. **E-mail:** editor@ajr.umd.edu. **Website:** www.ajr.org. **Contact:** Lucy Dalglish, dean and publisher. **80% freelance written.** Bimonthly magazine covering print, broadcast, and online journalism. American Journalism Review covers ethical issues, trends in the industry, and coverage that falls short. Circ. 25,000. Byline given. Pays within 1 month after publication. Offers 25% kill fee. Publishes ms an average of 2 months after acceptance. Editorial lead time 1 month. Accepts queries by mail, e-mail. Responds in 1 month to queries and unsolicited mss. Guidelines available online.

NONFICTION Needs expose, personal experience, ethical issues. **Buys many mss/year.** Send complete ms. Length: 2,000-4,000 words. **Pays $1,500-2,000.** Pays expenses of writers on assignment.

FILLERS Needs anecdotes, facts, short humor, short pieces. Length: 150-1,000 words. **Pays $100-250.**

✪$$ CANADIAN SCREENWRITER

Writers Guild of Canada, 366 Adelaide St. W., Suite 401, Toronto ON M5V 1R9 Canada. (416)979-7907. **Fax:** (416)979-9273. **E-mail:** info@wgc.ca; m.parker@wgc.ca. **Website:** www.wgc.ca. **Contact:** Maureen Parker, executive director. **80% freelance written.** Magazine published 3 times/year covering Canadian screenwriting for television, film, radio, and digital media. *Canadian Screenwriter* profiles Canadian screenwriters, provides industry news, and offers practical writing tips for screenwriters. Estab. 1998. Circ. 4,000. Byline given. Pays on acceptance. Offers 50% kill fee. Publishes ms an average of 1 month after acceptance. Editorial lead time 2 months. Submit seasonal material 2 months in advance. Accepts queries by e-mail. Responds in 1 week to queries. Responds in 1 month to mss. Sample copy free. Guidelines by e-mail.

NONFICTION Needs how-to, humor, interview. Does not want writing on foreign screenwriters; the focus is on Canadian-resident screenwriters. **Buys 12 mss/year.** Query with published clips. Length: 750-2,200 words. **Pays 50¢/word.** Sometimes pays expenses of writers on assignment.

$$$ ECONTENT MAGAZINE

Information Today, Inc., 143 Old Marlton Pike, Medford NJ 08055. (609)654-6266. **Fax:** (609)654-4309. **E-mail:** theresa.cramer@infotoday.com. **Website:** www.econtentmag.com. **Contact:** Theresa Cramer, editor. **90% freelance written.** Monthly magazine covering digital content trends, strategies, etc. *EContent* is a business publication. Readers need to stay on top of industry trends and developments. Estab. 1979. Circ. 12,000. Byline given. Pays within 1 month of publication. Accepts queries by email. Responds in 3 weeks to queries. Responds in 1 month to mss. Sample copy and writer's guidelines online.

NONFICTION Needs expose, how-to, interview, new product, opinion, technical, news features, strategic and solution-oriented features. No academic or straight Q&A. **Buys 48 mss/year.** Query with published clips. Submit electronically as e-mail attachment. Length: 1,000 words. **Pays 40-50¢/word.** Sometimes pays expenses of writers on assignment.

COLUMNS/DEPARTMENTS Profiles (short profile of unique company, person or product), 1,200 words; New Features (breaking news of content-related topics), 500 words maximum. **Buys 40 mss/year.** Query with published clips. **Pays 30-40¢/word.**

$$ FREELANCE WRITER'S REPORT

CNW Publishing, Inc., 45 Main St., P.O. Box A, North Stratford NH 03590-0167. (603)922-8338. **E-mail:** fwrwm@writers-editors.com. **Website:** www.writers-editors.com. **25% freelance written.** Monthly newsletter covering the business of freelance writing. *FWR* covers the marketing and business/office management aspects of running a freelance writing business. Articles must be of value to the established freelancer; nothing basic. Estab. 1982. Byline given. Pays on publication. No kill fee. Publishes ms an average of 12 months after acceptance. Editorial lead time 2 months. Submit seasonal material 2 months in advance. Accepts simultaneous submissions. Responds in 1 week to queries. Responds in 2 weeks to mss. Sample copy for 6x9 SAE with 2 first-class stamps (for back copy); $4 for current copy. Guidelines and sample copy available online.

NONFICTION Needs book excerpts, how-to (market, increase income or profits). Does not want articles about the basics of freelancing. **Buys 15 mss/year.** Send complete ms by e-mail. Length: up to 900 words. **Pays 10¢/word.**

$$ NOVEL & SHORT STORY WRITER'S MARKET

F+W Media, Inc., 10151 Carver Rd., Suite 200, Blue Ash OH 45242. (513)531-2690. **Fax:** (513)531-2686. **E-mail:** marketbookupdates@fwmedia.com. **Website:** www.writersmarket.com. **Contact:** Rachel Randall, managing editor. **85% freelance written.** Annual resource book covering the fiction market. In addition to thousands of listings for places to get fiction published, *NSSWM*'s feature articles on the craft and business of fiction writing, as well as interviews with successful fiction writers, editors, and agents. Articles are unique in that they always offer an actionable takeaway. In other words, readers must learn something immediately useful about the creation or marketing of fiction. Estab. 1981. Byline given. Pays on acceptance plus 45 days. Offers 25% kill fee. Accepts queries by e-mail only. Include "NSSWM Query" in the subject line. Responds in 4 weeks to queries.

NONFICTION Needs how-to, write, sell and promote fiction; find an agent; etc., interview, personal experience. **Buys 12-15 mss/year.** Length: 1,500-2,500 words. **Pays $400-700.**

$$ POETS & WRITERS MAGAZINE

90 Broad St., Suite 2100, New York NY 10004. (212)226-3586. **E-mail:** editor@pw.org. **Website:** www.pw.org/magazine. **Contact:** Kevin Larimer, editor. **95% freelance written.** Bimonthly professional trade journal for poets and fiction writers and creative nonfiction writers. Estab. 1987. Circ. 60,000. Byline given. Pays on publication. Offers 25% kill fee. Publishes ms an average of 4 months after acceptance. Submit seasonal material 4 months in advance. Accepts queries by mail, e-mail. Responds in 2 months to mss. Sample copy for $5.95. Guidelines available online.

NONFICTION Needs how-to, craft of poetry, fiction or creative nonfiction writing, interviews, with poets or writers of fiction and creative nonfiction, personal essays about literature, regional reports of literary activity, reports on small presses, service pieces about publishing trends. **Buys 35 mss/year.** Send complete ms. Length: 700-3,000 (depending on topic) words.

COLUMNS/DEPARTMENTS Literary and Publishing News, 700-1,000 words; Profiles of Emerging and Established Poets, Fiction Writers and Creative Nonfiction Writers, 2,000-3,000 words; Craft Essays and Publishing Advice, 2,000-2,500 words. Query with published clips or send complete ms. **Pays $225-500.**

$$ QUILL & SCROLL MAGAZINE

Quill and Scroll International Honorary Society for High School Journalists, University of Iowa, School of Journalism and Mass Communication, 100 Adler Journalism Bldg., Iowa City IA 52242. (319)335-3457. **Fax:** (319)335-3989. **E-mail:** quill-scroll@uiowa.edu. **Website:** www.quillandscroll.org. **Contact:** Vanessa Shelton, executive director. **20% freelance written.** Fall and spring issues covering scholastic journalism-related topics during school year. Primary audience is high school journalism students working on and studying topics related to newspapers, yearbooks, radio, television, and online media; secondary audience is their teachers and others interested in this topic. Invites journalism students and advisers to submit mss about important lessons learned or obstacles overcome. Estab. 1926. Circ. 10,000. Byline given. Pays on acceptance and publication. No kill fee. Publishes ms an average of 4 months after acceptance. Editorial lead time 2 months. Accepts queries by mail, e-mail. Accepts simultaneous submissions. Responds in 2 weeks to queries. Guidelines available.

NONFICTION Needs essays, how-to, humor, interview, new product, opinion, personal experience, photo feature, technical, travel, types on topic. Does not want articles not pertinent to high school student journalists. Query with your submission. Length: 600-1,000 words. **Pays $100-500 for assigned articles. Pays complementary copy and $200 maximum for unsolicited articles.** Sometimes pays expenses of writers on assignment.

$$$ QUILL MAGAZINE

Society of Professional Journalists, 3909 N. Meridian St., Indianapolis IN 46208. **Fax:** (317)920-4789. **E-mail:** sleadingham@spj.org; quill@spj.org. **Website:** www.spj.org/quill.asp. **Contact:** Scott Leadingham, editor. **75% freelance written.** Monthly magazine covering journalism and the media industry. *Quill* is a how-to magazine written by journalists. Focuses on the industry's biggest issues while providing tips on how to become better journalists. Estab. 1912. Circ. 10,000. Byline given. Pays on acceptance. Offers 25% kill fee. Publishes ms an average of 2 months after acceptance. Editorial lead time 2-3 months. Submit seasonal material 2-3 months in advance. Accepts queries by e-mail. Accepts simultaneous submissions. Sample copy available online.

NONFICTION Needs general interest, how-to, technical. Does not want personality profiles and straight research pieces. **Buys 12 mss/year.** Query. Length: 800-2,500 words. **Pays $150-800.**

$$ THE WRITER'S CHRONICLE

Association of Writers & Writing Programs (AWP), Carty House MS 1E3, George Mason University, Fairfax VA 22030-4444. (703)993-4301. **Fax:** (703)993-4302. **E-mail:** chronicle@awpwriter.org. **Website:** www.awpwriter.org. **90% freelance written.** Published 6 times during the academic year; 3 times a semester. Magazine covering the art and craft of writing. "*Writer's Chronicle* strives to: present the best essays on the craft and art of writing poetry, fiction and nonfiction; help overcome the over-specialization of the literary arts by presenting a public forum for the appreciation, debate, and analysis of contemporary literature; present the diversity of accomplishments and points of view within contemporary literature; provide serious and committed writers and students of writing the best advice on how to manage their professional lives; provide writers who teach with new pedagogical approaches for their classrooms; provide the members and subscribers with a literary community as a compensation for a devotion to a difficult and lonely art; provide information on publishing opportunities, grants, and awards; and promote the good works of AWP, its programs, and its individual members." Estab. 1967. Circ. 35,000. Byline given. Pays on publication. No kill fee. Editorial lead time 3 months. Accepts queries by Electronic queries OK but send submissions by postal mail. Accepts simultaneous submissions. Responds in 2 weeks to queries. Sample copy free. Guidelines online. Reading period: February 1-August 31.

NONFICTION Needs essays, interview, opinion, (does not mean letters to the editor). No personal essays. **Buys 15-20 mss/year.** Send complete ms. Length: 2,500-7,000 words. **Pays $14 per 100 words for assigned articles.**

$$$ WRITER'S DIGEST

F+W Media, Inc., 10151 Carver Rd., Suite #200, Blue Ash OH 45242. (513)531-2690. **E-mail:** wdsubmissions@fwmedia.com. **Website:** www.writersdigest.com. **75% freelance written.** Magazine for those who want to write better, get published, and participate in the vibrant culture of writers. Readers look for specific ideas and tips that will help them succeed, whether success means getting into print, finding personal fulfillment through writing, or building and maintaining a thriving writing career and network. *Writer's Digest*, the No. 1 magazine for writers, celebrates the writing life and what it means to be a writer in today's publishing environment. Estab. 1920. Byline given. Pays on acceptance. Offers 25% kill fee. Publishes ms an average of 4 months after acceptance. Accepts queries by e-mail only. Responds in 1-4 months to queries and mss. Guidelines and editorial calendar available online (writersdigest.com/submission-guidelines).

NONFICTION Needs , essays; short front-of-book pieces; how-to (writing craft, business of publishing, etc.); humor; inspirational; interviews/profiles (rarely, as those are typically handled in house). Does not accept phone, snail mail, or fax queries, and queries of this nature will receive no response. Does not buy newspaper clippings or reprints of articles previously published in other mainstream media, whether in print or online. Product reviews are handled in-house. **Buys 80 mss/year.** A query should include a thorough outline that introduces your article proposal and highlights each of the points you intend to make. Your query should discuss how the article will benefit readers, why the topic is timely, and why you're the appropriate writer to discuss the topic. Please include your publishing credential related to your topic with your submission. Do not send attachments. Length: 800-2,400 words. **Pays 30-50¢/word.**

$$$$ WRITTEN BY

7000 W. Third St., Los Angeles CA 90048. (323)782-4699. **Fax:** (323)782-4800. **Website:** www.wga.org/writtenby/writtenby.aspx. **40% freelance written.** Magazine published 9 times/year. *Written By* is the premier magazine written by and for America's screen and TV writers. Focuses on the craft of screenwriting and covers all aspects of the entertainment industry from the perspective of the writer. Audience is screenwriters and most entertainment executives. Estab. 1987. Circ. 12,000. Byline given. Pays on acceptance. Offers 10% kill fee. Publishes ms an average of 2 months after acceptance. Editorial lead time 4 months. Submit seasonal material 4 months in advance. Accepts queries by mail, e-mail, fax, phone, online submission form. Guidelines for #10 SASE.

NONFICTION Needs book excerpts, essays, historical, humor, interview, opinion, personal experience, photo feature, technical, software. No beginner pieces on how to break into Hollywood, or how to write scripts. **Buys 20 mss/year.** Query with published clips. Length: 500-3,500 words. **Pays $500-3,500 for assigned articles.** Sometimes pays expenses of writers on assignment.

LAW

$$$$ ABA JOURNAL

American Bar Association, 321 N. Clark St., 20th Floor, Chicago IL 60654. (312)988-6018. **Fax:** (312)988-6014. **E-mail:** releases@americanbar.org. **Website:** www.abajournal.com. **Contact:** Allen Pusey, editor and publisher. **10% freelance written.** Monthly magazine covering the trends, people and finances of the legal profession from Wall Street to Main Street to Pennsylvania Avenue. The *ABA Journal* is an independent, thoughtful, and inquiring observer of the law and the legal profession. The magazine is edited for members of the American Bar Association. Circ. 380,000. Byline given. Pays on acceptance. No kill fee. Accepts queries by e-mail, fax. Sample copy free. Guidelines available online.

NONFICTION "We don't want anything that does not have a legal theme. No poetry or fiction." **Buys 5 mss/year.** "We use freelancers with experience reporting for legal or consumer publications; most have law degrees. If you are interested in freelancing for the *Journal*, we urge you to include your résumé and published clips when you contact us with story ideas." Length: 500-3,500 words. **Pays $300-2,000 for assigned articles.**

COLUMNS/DEPARTMENTS The National Pulse/Ideas from the Front (reports on legal news and trends), 650 words; eReport (reports on legal news and trends), 500-1,500 words. "The *ABA Journal eReport* is our weekly online newsletter sent out to members." **Buys 25 mss/year.** Query with published clips. **Pays $300, regardless of story length.**

$$$ BENCH & BAR OF MINNESOTA

Minnesota State Bar Association, 600 Nicollet Mall #380, Minneapolis MN 55402. (612)333-1183; 800-882-6722. **Fax:** (612)333-4927. **E-mail:** jhaverkamp@mnbar.org. **Website:** www.mnbar.org. **Contact:** Judson Haverkamp, editor. **5% freelance written.** Magazine published 11 times/year. *Bench & Bar* seeks reportage, analysis, and commentary on changes in the law, trends and issues in the law and the legal profession, especially in Minnesota. Preference to items of practical/professional human interest to lawyers and judges. Audience is mostly Minnesota lawyers. Estab. 1931. Circ. 17,000. Byline given. Pays on acceptance. No kill fee. Publishes ms an average of 3 months after acceptance. Responds in 1 month to queries. Guidelines for free online or by mail.

NONFICTION Needs analysis and exposition of current trends, developments and issues in law, legal profession, especially in Minnesota. Balanced commentary and "how-to" considered. Does not want one-sided opinion pieces or advertorial. **Buys 2-3 mss/year.** Send query or complete ms. Length: 1,000-3,500 words. **Pays $500-1,500.** Some expenses of writers on assignment.

$$$$ CALIFORNIA LAWYER

Daily Journal Corp., 44 Montgomery St., Suite 250, San Francisco CA 94104. (415)296-2400. **Fax:** (415)296-2440. **E-mail:** bo_links@dailyjournal.com. **Website:** www.callawyer.com. **Contact:** Bo Links, legal editor. **30% freelance written.** Monthly magazine of law-related articles and general-interest subjects of appeal to lawyers and judges. Primary mission is to cover the news of the world as it affects the law and lawyers, helping readers better comprehend the issues of the day and to cover changes and trends in the legal profession. Readers are all California lawyers, plus judges, legislators, and corporate executives. Although the magazine focuses on California and the West, they have subscribers in every state. *California Lawyer* is a general interest magazine for people interested in law. Estab. 1981. Circ. 140,000. Byline given. Pays on acceptance. Offers 25% kill fee. Publishes ms an average of 3 months after acceptance. Editorial lead time 3 months. Accepts queries by e-mail. No previously published articles.Sample copy and writer's guidelines for #10 SASE.

NONFICTION Needs essays, general interest, interview, news and feature articles on law-related topics. **Buys 12 mss/year.** Send complete ms. "We are interested in concise, well-written and well-researched articles on issues of current concern, as well as well-told feature narratives with a legal focus. We would like to see a description or outline of your proposed idea, including a list of possible sources." Length: 500-5,000 words. **Pays $50-2,000.** Pays expenses of writers on assignment.

COLUMNS/DEPARTMENTS California Esq. (current legal trends), 300 words. **Buys 6 mss/year.** Query with or without published clips. **Pays $50-250.**

$$$$ INSIDECOUNSEL

222 S. Riverside Plaza, Suite 620, Chicago IL 60606. (312)654-3500. **E-mail:** rsteeves@insidecounsel.com. **Website:** www.insidecounsel.com. **Contact:** Rich Steeves, managing editor. **50% freelance written.** Monthly tabloid covering legal information for attorneys. *InsideCounsel* is a monthly national magazine that gives general counsel and inhouse attorneys information on legal and business issues to help them better manage corporate law departments. It routinely addresses changes and trends in law departments, litigation management, legal technology, corporate governance and inhouse careers. Law areas covered monthly include: intellectual property, international, technology, project finance, e-commerce, and litigation. All articles need to be geared toward the inhouse attorney's perspective. Estab. 1991. Circ. 45,000. Byline given. Pays on publication. No kill fee. Publishes ms an average of 3 months after acceptance. Editorial lead time 3 months. Submit seasonal material 3 months in advance. Accepts queries by mail, e-mail. Responds in 3 weeks to queries. Sample copy for $17. Guidelines available online.

NONFICTION Needs interview, news about legal aspects of business issues and events. **Buys 12-25 mss/year.** Query with published clips. Length: 500-3,000 words. **Pays $500-2,000.**

$$$ JCR

National Court Reporters Association, 8224 Old Courthouse Rd., Vienna VA 22180. (800)272-6272, ext. 164. **E-mail:** jschmidt@ncra.org. **Website:** www.theJCR.com. **Contact:** Jacqueline Schmidt, editor. **10% freelance written.** Monthly, except bimonthly November/December, magazine covering court reporting, captioning, and CART provision. "The *JCR* has 2 complementary purposes: to communicate the activities, goals, and mission of its publisher, the National Court Reporters Association; and, simultaneously, to seek out and publish diverse information and views on matters significantly related to the court reporting and captioning professions." Estab. 1899. Circ. 18,000. Byline sometimes given. Pays on acceptance. No kill fee. Publishes ms an average of 4-5 months after acceptance. Editorial lead time 4 months. Submit seasonal material 4 months in advance. Accepts queries by mail, e-mail. Sample copy free. Ms guidelines are available on www.NCRA.org under "Submit content."

NONFICTION Needs book excerpts, how-to, interview, technical, legal issues. **Buys 6-10 mss/year.** Query. Length: 1,200-2,500 words. **Pays $1,000 maximum for assigned articles. Pays $100 maximum for unsolicited articles.** Sometimes pays expenses of writers on assignment.

COLUMNS/DEPARTMENTS Language (proper punctuation, grammar, dealing with verbatim materials); Technical (new technologies, using mobile technology, using technology for work); Book excerpts (language, crime, legal issues)—all 1,000 words.

$$$ JOURNAL OF COURT REPORTING

National Court Reporters Association, 8224 Old Courthouse Rd., Vienna VA 22180. (800)272-6272, ext. 164. **E-mail:** jschmidt@ncrahq.org. **Website:** www.ncraonline.org. **Contact:** Jacqueline Schmidt, editor. **10% freelance written.** Monthly (bimonthly July/August and November/December) magazine. The *Journal of Court Reporting* has 2 complementary purposes: to communicate the activities, goals and mission of its publisher, the National Court Reporters Association; and, simultaneously, to seek out and publish diverse information and views on matters significantly related to the court reporting and captioning professions. Estab. 1899. Circ. 20,000. Byline sometimes given. Pays on acceptance. No kill fee. Publishes ms an average of 4-5 months after acceptance. Editorial lead time 4 months. Submit seasonal material 4 months in advance. Accepts queries by mail, e-mail. Accepts simultaneous submissions. Sample copy free. Guidelines available online.

NONFICTION Needs book excerpts, how-to, interview, technical, legal issues. **Buys 10 mss/year.** Query. Length: no more than 1,000 words. Sometimes pays expenses of writers on assignment.

COLUMNS/DEPARTMENTS Language (proper punctuation, grammar, dealing with verbatim materials); Technical (new technologies, using mobile technology, using technology for work); Book excerpts (language, crime, legal issues), all 1,000 words; Puzzles (any, but especially word-related games). **Pays $100.**

$$$$$ NATIONAL

The Canadian Bar Association, 500-865 Carling Ave., Ottawa ON K1S 5S8 Canada. (613)237-2925. **Fax:** (613)237-0185. **E-mail:** beverleys@cba.org; national@cba.org. **Website:** www.nationalmagazine.ca. **Contact:** Beverley Spencer editor-in-chief. **90% freelance written.** Magazine published 8 times/year covering practice trends and business developments in the law, with a focus on technology, innovation, practice management, and client relations. Estab. 1993. Circ. 37,000. Byline given. Pays on acceptance. Offers 50% kill fee. Publishes ms an average of 2 months after acceptance. Editorial lead time 2 months. Accepts queries by e-mail. Sample copy free.

NONFICTION Buys 25 mss/year. Query with published clips. Length: 1,000-2,500 words. **Pays $1/word.** Sometimes pays expenses of writers on assignment.

$$ THE NATIONAL JURIST AND PRE LAW

Cypress Magazines, 7670 Opportunity Rd #105, San Diego CA 92111. (858)300-3201; (800)296-9656. **Fax:** (858)503-7588. **E-mail:** jack@cypressmagazines.com; callahan@cypressmagazines.com. **Website:** www.nationaljurist.com. **Contact:** Jack Crittenden, editor-in-chief. **25% freelance written.** Bimonthly magazine covering law students and issues of interest to law students. Estab. 1991. Circ. 145,000. Pays on publication. No kill fee. Accepts queries by mail, e-mail.

NONFICTION Needs general interest, how-to, humor, interview. **Buys 4 mss/year.** Query. Length: 750-3,000 words. **Pays $100-500.**

COLUMNS/DEPARTMENTS Pays $100-500.

$ PARALEGAL TODAY

Conexion International Media, Inc., 6030 Marshalee Dr., Elkridge MD 21075-5935. (443)445-3057. **Fax:** (443)445-3257. **E-mail:** pinfanti@connexionmedia.com. **Website:** www.paralegaltoday.com. **Contact:** Patricia E. Infanti, editor-in-chief; Charles Buckwalter, publisher. Quarterly magazine geared toward all legal assistants/paralegals throughout the U.S. and Canada, regardless of specialty (litigation, corporate, bankruptcy, environmental law, etc.). How-to articles to help paralegals perform their jobs more effectively are most in demand, as are career and salary information, technolgoy tips, and trends pieces. Estab. 1983. Circ. 8,000. Byline given. Pays on publication. Offers kill fee ($25-50 standard rate). Editorial lead time is 10 weeks. Submit seasonal material 3 months in advance. Accepts queries by mail, e-mail, fax, online submission form. Accepts simultaneous submissions. Responds in 2 months to mss. Sample copy available online. Guidelines available online.

NONFICTION Needs interview, unique and interesting paralegals in unique and particular work-related situations, news (brief, hard news topics regarding paralegals), features (present information to help paralegals advance their careers). Send query letter first; if electronic, send submission as attachment. **Pays $75-300.**

$$ THE PENNSYLVANIA LAWYER

Pennsylvania Bar Association, 100 South St., P.O. Box 186, Harrisburg PA 17108. **E-mail:** editor@pabar.org; palawyer@editorialenterprises.com. **Website:** www.pabar.org. **Contact:** Donald C. Sarvey, editorial director. **25% freelance written. Prefers to work with published/established writers.** Bimonthly magazine published as a service to the legal profession and the members of the Pennsylvania Bar Association. Estab. 1979. Circ. 30,000. Byline given. Pays on acceptance. No kill fee. Publishes ms an average of 6 months after acceptance. Submit seasonal material 6 months in advance. Accepts queries by mail, e-mail, online submission form. Responds in 2 months to queries and mss. Sample copy for $2. Writer's guidelines for #10 SASE or by e-mail.

NONFICTION Needs how-to, interview, law-practice management, technology. **Buys 8-10 mss/year.** Query. Length: 1,200-1,500 words. **Pays $50 for book reviews; $75-400 for assigned articles; $150 for unsolicited articles.** Sometimes pays expenses of writers on assignment.

$$$$ SUPER LAWYERS

Thomson Reuters, 610 Opperman Dr., Eagan MN 55123. (877)787-5290. **Website:** www.superlawyers.com. **Contact:** Erik Lundegaard, editor. **100% freelance written.** Monthly magazine covering law and politics. Publishes glossy magazines in every region of the country; all serve a legal audience and have a storytelling sensibility. Writes profiles of interesting attorneys exclusively. Estab. 1990. Byline given. Pays on acceptance. Offers 25% kill fee. Publishes ms an average of 1 month after acceptance. Editorial lead time 6 months. Submit seasonal material 6 months in advance. Accepts queries by phone, online submission form. Accepts simultaneous submissions. Sample copy free. Guidelines free.

NONFICTION Needs general interest, historical. Query. Length: 500-2,000 words. **Pays 50¢-$1.50/word.**

LUMBER

$$ PALLET ENTERPRISE

Industrial Reporting, Inc., 10244 Timber Ridge Dr., Ashland VA 23005. (804)550-0323. **Fax:** (804)550-2181. **E-mail:** edb@ireporting.com; chaille@ireporting.com. **Website:** www.palletenterprise.com. **Contact:** Edward C. Brindley, Jr., Ph.D., publisher; Chaille Brindley, assistant publisher. **40% freelance written.** Monthly magazine covering lumber and pallet operations. The *Pallet Enterprise* is a monthly trade magazine for the sawmill, pallet, remanufacturing, and wood processing industries. Articles should offer technical, solution-oriented information. Anti-forest articles are not accepted. Articles should focus on machinery and unique ways to improve profitability/make money. Estab. 1981. Circ. 14,500. Pays on publication. Editorial lead time 2 months. Submit seasonal material 2 months in advance. Accepts queries by mail, e-mail, fax, phone. Accepts simultaneous submissions. Sample copy available online.

NONFICTION Needs interview, new product, opinion, technical, industry news, environmental, forests operation/plant features. No lifestyle, humor, general news, etc. **Buys 20 mss/year.** Query with published clips. Length: 1,000-3,000 words. **Pays $200-400 for assigned articles. Pays $100-400 for unsolicited articles.** Sometimes pays expenses of writers on assignment.

COLUMNS/DEPARTMENTS Green Watch (environmental news/opinion affecting US forests), 1,500 words. **Buys 12 mss/year.** Query with published clips. **Pays $200-400.**

TIPS "Provide unique environmental or industry-oriented articles. Many of our freelance articles are company features of sawmills, pallet manufacturers, pallet recyclers, and wood waste processors."

$$ TIMBERLINE

Industrial Reporting, Inc., 10244 Timber Ridge Dr., Ashland VA 23005. (804)550-0323. **Fax:** (804)550-

2181. **E-mail:** chaille@ireporting.com. **Website:** www.timberlinemag.com. **Contact:** Chaille Brindley, assistant publisher. **50% freelance written.** Monthly tabloid covering the forest products industry. Estab. 1994. Circ. 30,000. Byline given. Pays on publication. Editorial lead time 2 months. Submit seasonal material 2 months in advance. Accepts queries by mail, e-mail, fax. Accepts simultaneous submissions. Sample copy available online. Guidelines free.

NONFICTION Contact: Tim Cox, editor. Needs historical, interview, new product, opinion, technical, industry news, environmental operation/plant features. No lifestyles, humor, general news, etc. **Buys 25 mss/year.** Query with published clips. Length: 1,000-3,000 words. **Pays $200-400 for assigned articles. Pays $100-400 for unsolicited articles.** Sometimes pays expenses of writers on assignment.

COLUMNS/DEPARTMENTS Contact: Tim Cox, editor. From the Hill (legislative news impacting the forest products industry), 1,800 words; Green Watch (environmental news/opinion affecting U.S. forests), 1,500 words. **Buys 12 mss/year.** Query with published clips. **Pays $200-400.**

$$ TIMBERWEST

TimberWest Publications, LLC, P.O. Box 610, Edmonds WA 98020. (425)778-3388. **Fax:** (425)771-3623. **E-mail:** timberwest@forestnet.com; diane@forestnet.com. **Website:** www.forestnet.com. **Contact:** Diane Mettler, managing editor. **75% freelance written.** Monthly magazine covering logging and lumber segment of the forestry industry in the Northwest. Publishes primarily profiles on loggers and their operations—with an emphasis on the machinery—in Washington, Oregon, Idaho, Montana, Northern California, and Alaska. Some timber issues are highly controversial, and although the magazine will report on the issues, this is a pro-logging publication. Does not publish articles with a negative slant on the timber industry. Estab. 1975. Circ. 10,000. Byline given. Pays on acceptance. No kill fee. Editorial lead time 3 months. Accepts queries by mail, fax. Responds in 3 weeks to queries. Sample copy for $2. Guidelines for #10 sase.

NONFICTION Needs historical, interview, new product. No articles that put the timber industry in a bad light, such as environmental articles against logging. **Buys 50 mss/year.** Query with published clips. Length: 1,100-1,500 words. **Pays $350.** True

FILLERS Needs facts, newsbreaks. **Buys 10 mss/year.** Length: 400-800 words. **Pays $100-250.**

MACHINERY AND METAL

$$$ AMERICANMACHINIST.COM

Penton Media, 1300 E. 9th St., Cleveland OH 44114. (216)931-9464. **Fax:** (913)514-6386. **E-mail:** robert.brooks@penton.com. **Website:** www.americanmachinist.com. **Contact:** Robert Brooks, editor-in-chief. **10% freelance written.** Monthly online website covering all forms of metalworking covering all forms of metalworking. Accepts contributed features and articles. *American Machinist* is an essential online source dedicated to metalworking in the United States. Readers are the owners and managers of metalworking shops. Publishes articles that provide the managers and owners of job shops, contract shops, and captive shops the information they need to make their operations more efficient, more productive, and more profitable. Articles are technical in nature and must be focused on technology that will help these shops to become more competitive on a global basis. Readers are skilled machinists. This is not the place for lightweight items about manufacturing. Not interested in articles on management theories. Estab. 1877. Circ. 80,000. Byline sometimes given. Offers 20% kill fee. Publishes ms an average of 1-2 months after acceptance. Editorial lead time 3-6 months. Submit seasonal material 4-6 months in advance. Accepts queries by mail, e-mail, phone. Responds in 1-2 weeks to queries. Responds in 1 month to mss. Sample copy available online.

NONFICTION Needs general interest, how-to, new product, opinion, personal experience, photo feature, technical. Query with published clips. Length: 600-2,400 words. **Pays $300-1,200.** Sometimes pays expenses of writers on assignment.

FILLERS Needs anecdotes, facts, gags, newsbreaks, short humor. **Buys 12-18 mss/year. mss/year.** Length: 50-200 words. **Pays $25-100.**

$$$ CUTTING TOOL ENGINEERING

CTE Publications, Inc., 1 Northfield Plaza, Suite 240, Northfield IL 60093. (847)714-0175. **Fax:** (847)559-4444. **E-mail:** alanr@jwr.com. **Website:** www.ctemag.com. **Contact:** Alan Richter, editor. **40% freelance written.** Monthly magazine covering industrial metal cutting tools and metal cutting operations. *Cutting Tool Engineering* serves owners, managers, and engineers who work in manufacturing, specifically manufacturing that involves cutting or grinding metal or other materials. Writing should be geared toward improving manufacturing processes. Circ. 48,000. Byline given. Pays on publication. Offers 50% kill fee. Publishes ms an average of 2 months after acceptance. Editorial lead time 2 months. Accepts queries by mail, fax. Responds in 2 months to mss. Sample copy and writers guidelines free.

NONFICTION Needs how-to, opinion, personal experience, technical. Does not want fiction or articles that don't relate to manufacturing. **Buys 10 mss/year.** Length: 1,500-3,000 words. **Pays $750-1,500.** Pays expenses of writers on assignment.

❍$$ EQUIPMENT JOURNAL

Pace Publishing, 5160 Explorer Dr., Unit 6, Mississauga ON L4W 4T7 Canada. (416)459-5163. **E-mail:** editor@equipmentjournal.com. **Website:** www.equipmentjournal.com. Canada's national heavy equipment newspaper. Focuses on the construction, material handling, mining, forestry and on-highway transportation industries." Estab. 1964. Circ. 23,000 subscriber. Byline given. Pays on publication. No kill fee. Publishes ms an average of 1-2 months after acceptance. Editorial lead time 2-3 months. Accepts queries by mail. Accepts simultaneous submissions. Sample copy and guidelines free.

NONFICTION Needs how-to, interview, new product, photo feature, technical. No material that falls outside of *EJ*'s mandate—the Canadian equipment industry. **Buys 15 mss/year.** Send complete ms. "We prefer electronic submissions. We do not accept unsolicited freelance submissions." Length: 500-1,500 words. **$250-400 for assigned and unsolicited articles.** Sometimes pays expenses of writers on assignment.

$$$ THE FABRICATOR

833 Featherstone Rd., Rockford IL 61107. (815)399-8700. **Fax:** (815)381-1370. **E-mail:** timh@thefabricator.com. **Website:** www.thefabricator.com; www.fmacommunications.com. **Contact:** Dan Davis, editor-in-chief; Tim Heston, senior editor. **15% freelance written.** Monthly magazine covering metal forming and fabricating. Purpose is to disseminate information about modern metal forming and fabricating techniques, machinery, tooling, and management concepts for the metal fabricator. Estab. 1971. Circ. 58,000. Byline given. Pays on publication. No kill fee. Editorial lead time 6 months. Accepts queries by mail, e-mail. Responds in 2 weeks to queries; 1 month to mss. Sample copy free.

NONFICTION Needs how-to, technical, company profile. Query with published clips. Length: 1,200-2,000 words.

$$ SPRINGS

Spring Manufacturers Institute, 2001 Midwest Rd., Suite 106, Oak Brook IL 60523-1335. (630)495-8588. **Fax:** (630)495-8595. **E-mail:** lynne@smihq.org. **Website:** www.smihq.org. **Contact:** Lynne Carr, general manager. **10% freelance written.** Quarterly magazine covering precision mechanical spring manufacture. Articles should be aimed at spring manufacturers. Estab. 1962. Circ. 10,800. Byline given. Pays on publication. No kill fee. Publishes ms an average of 3-6 months after acceptance. Editorial lead time 4 months. Accepts simultaneous submissions. Sample copy free. Guidelines available online.

NONFICTION Needs general interest, how-to, interview, opinion, personal experience, technical. **Buys 4-6 mss/year.** Length: 2,000-10,000 words. **Pays $100-600 for assigned articles.**

$$$ STAMPING JOURNAL

Fabricators & Manufacturers Association (FMA), 833 Featherstone Rd., Rockford IL 61107. (815)399-8700. **Fax:** (815)381-1370. **E-mail:** dand@thefabricator.com; timh@thefabricator.com. **Website:** www.thefabricator.com. **Contact:** Dan Davis, editor-in-chief; Tim Heston, senior editor. **15% freelance written.** Bimonthly magazine covering metal stamping. Looks for how-to and educational articles. Estab. 1989. Circ. 35,000. Byline given. Pays on publication. No kill fee. Editorial lead time 6 months. Accepts queries by mail, e-mail, phone. Responds in 2 weeks to queries.

NONFICTION Pays 40-80¢/word. Sometimes pays expenses of writers on assignment.

$$$$ TODAY'S MACHINING WORLD

Screw Machine World, Inc., 4235 W. 166th St., Oak Forest IL 60452. (708)535-2237. **Fax:** (708)850-1334. **E-mail:** emily@todaysmachiningworld.com; noah@todaysmachiningworld.com. **Website:** www.todaysmachiningworld.com. **Contact:** Emily Halgrimson, managing editor; Noah Graff, writer/website editor. **40% freelance written.** Online magazine covering metal turned parts manufacturing in the US and worldwide. Hire writers to tell a success story or challenge regarding our industry. Estab. 2001. Byline given. Pays on publication. Publishes ms an average of 2 months after acceptance. Editorial lead time 2-4 months. Submit seasonal material 2 months in advance. Responds in 1 month to mss. Guidelines free.

NONFICTION Needs general interest, how-to. **Buys 12-15 mss/year.** Query. Do not send unsolicited mss. Length: 1,500-2,500 words.

COLUMNS/DEPARTMENTS Shop Doc (manufacturing problem/solution), 500 words. Query.

MAINTENANCE AND SAFETY

$$ AMERICAN WINDOW CLEANER MAGAZINE

12 Publishing Corp., 750-B NW Broad St., Southern Pines NC 28387. (910)693-2644. **Fax:** (910)246-1681. **E-mail:** info@awcmag.com; karen@awcmag.com. **Website:** www.awcmag.com. **Contact:** Karen Grinter, creative director. **20% freelance written.** Bimonthly magazine on window cleaning. Produces articles to help window cleaners become more profitable, safe, professional, and feel good about what they do. Estab. 1986. Circ. 8,000. Byline given. Pays on acceptance. Offers 33% kill fee. Publishes ms an average of 4-8 months after acceptance. Editorial lead time 2 months. Submit seasonal material 3 months in advance. Responds in 2 weeks to queries. Responds in 1 month to mss. Sample copy free.

NONFICTION Needs how-to, humor, inspirational, interview, personal experience, photo feature, technical, add-on business. "We do not want PR-driven pieces. We want to educate—not push a particular product." **Buys 20 mss/year.** Query. Length: 500-5,000 words. **Pays $50-250.**

COLUMNS/DEPARTMENTS Window Cleaning Tips (tricks of the trade); 1,000-2,000 words; Humor-anecdotes-feel good-abouts (window cleaning industry); Computer High-Tech (tips on new technology), all 1,000 words **Buys 12 mss/year.** Query. **Pays $50-100.**

$$ EXECUTIVE HOUSEKEEPING TODAY

The International Executive Housekeepers Association, 1001 Eastwind Dr., Suite 301, Westerville OH 43081-3361. (614)895-7166. **Fax:** (614)895-1248. **E-mail:** ldriscoll@ieha.org; excel@ieha.org. **Website:** www.ieha.org. **Contact:** Leah Driscoll, editor. **50% freelance written.** Monthly magazine for nearly 5,000 decision makers responsible for housekeeping management (cleaning, grounds maintenance, laundry, linen, pest control, waste management, regulatory compliance, training) for a variety of institutions: hospitality, healthcare, education, retail, government. Estab. 1930. Circ. 5,500. Byline given. No kill fee. Publishes ms an average of 6 months after acceptance. Editorial lead time 2 months. Submit seasonal material 3 months in advance. Accepts queries by mail, e-mail, fax, phone.

NONFICTION Needs general interest, interview, new product, related to magazine's scope, personal experience, in housekeeping profession, technical. **Buys 30 mss/year.** Query with published clips. Length: 1,500-2,000 words.

COLUMNS/DEPARTMENTS Federal Report (OSHA/EPA requirements), 1,000 words; Industry News; Management Perspectives (industry specific), 1,500-2,000 words. Query with published clips.

MANAGEMENT AND SUPERVISION

$$$ HUMAN RESOURCE EXECUTIVE

LRP Publications Magazine Group, P.O. Box 980, Horsham PA 19044-0980. (215)784-0910. **Fax:** (215)784-0275. **E-mail:** kfrasch@lrp.com. **E-mail:** tgarrison@lrp.com. **Website:** www.hronline.com. **Contact:** Kristen B. Frasch, managing editor; Terri Garrison, editorial assistant. **30% freelance written.** Magazine published 16 times/year serving the information needs of chief human resource professionals/executives in companies, government agencies, and nonprofit institutions with 500 or more employees. Estab. 1987. Circ. 75,000. Byline given. Pays on acceptance. Offers kill fee. Pays 50% kill fee on assigned stories. Publishes ms an average of 2 months after acceptance. Accepts queries by mail, e-mail, fax. Responds in 1 month to mss. Guidelines available online.

NONFICTION Needs book excerpts, interview. **Buys 16 mss/year.** Query with published clips. Length: 1,800 words. **Pays $200-1,000.** Sometimes pays expenses of writers on assignment.

$$ INCENTIVE

Northstar Travel Media LLC, 100 Lighting Way, Secaucus NJ 07094. (201)902-2000; (201)902-1975. **E-mail:** lcioffi@ntmllc.com; dting@ntmllc.com. **Website:** www.incentivemag.com. **Contact:** Lori Cioffi, editorial director; Deanna Ting, managing editor.

Monthly magazine covering sales promotion and employee motivation: managing and marketing through motivation. Estab. 1905. Circ. 41,000. Byline given. Pays on acceptance. No kill fee. Publishes ms an average of 3 months after acceptance. Accepts queries by mail, e-mail, fax. Responds in 1 month to queries. Responds in 2 months to mss. Sample copy for SAE with 9x12 envelope.

NONFICTION Needs general interest, motivation, demographics, how-to, types of sales promotion, buying product categories, using destinations, interview, sales promotion executives, travel, incentive-oriented, corporate case studies. **Buys 48 mss/year.** Query with published clips. Length: 1,000-2,000 words. **Pays $250-700 for assigned articles. Does not pay for unsolicited articles.** Pays expenses of writers on assignment.

$$ PLAYGROUND MAGAZINE

Harris Publishing, 360 B St., Idaho Falls ID 83402. (208)652-3683. **Fax:** (208)652-7856. **Website:** www.playgroundmag.com. **25% freelance written.** Magazine published quarterly covering playgrounds, play-related issues, equipment, and industry trends. *Playground Magazine* targets park and recreation management, elementary school teachers and administrators, child care facilities, and parent-group leader readership. Articles should focus on play and the playground market as a whole, including aquatic play and surfacing. Estab. 2000. Circ. 35,000. Byline given. Pays on publication. No kill fee. Publishes ms an average of 6 months after acceptance. Editorial lead time 2 months. Submit seasonal material 1 year in advance. Accepts queries by mail, e-mail. Accepts simultaneous submissions. Responds in 1 month to queries. Responds in 2 months to mss. Sample copy for $5. Guidelines for #10 SASE.

NONFICTION Needs how-to, interview, new product, opinion, personal experience, photo feature, technical, travel. *Playground Magazine* does not publish any articles that do not directly relate to play and the playground industry. **Buys 4-6 mss/year.** Query. Length: 800-1,500 words. **Pays $50-300 for assigned articles.** Sometimes pays expenses of writers on assignment.

MARINE AND MARITIME INDUSTRIES

$$ CURRENTS

Marine Technology Society, 1100 H St. NW, Suite LL-100, Washington DC 20005. (202)717-8705. **Fax:** (202)347-4302. **E-mail:** publications@mtsociety.org. **Website:** www.mtsociety.org. **Contact:** Mary Beth Loutinsky, communications manager. Bimonthly newsletter covering commercial, academic, scientific marine technology. Readers are engineers and technologists who design, develop ,and maintain the equipment and instruments used to understand and explore the oceans. The newsletter covers society news, industry news, science and technology news, and similar news. Estab. 1963. Circ. 3,200. Byline given. Pays on acceptance. No kill fee. Editorial lead time 1-2 months. Accepts queries by e-mail.

NONFICTION Needs interview, technical. **Buys 1-6 mss/year.** Query. Length: 250-500 words. **Pays $100-500 for assigned articles.** Sometimes pays expenses of writers on assignment.

$$ PROFESSIONAL MARINER

Navigator Publishing, P.O. Box 569, Portland ME 04112. (207)772-2466. **Fax:** (207)772-2879. **E-mail:** dyanchunas@professionalmariner.com. **Website:** www.professionalmariner.com. **Contact:** Dom Yanchunas, editor. **75% freelance written.** Bimonthly magazine covering professional seamanship and maritime industry news. Estab. 1993. Circ. 29,000. Byline given. Pays on publication. No kill fee. Editorial lead time 3 months. Accepts queries by mail, e-mail. Accepts simultaneous submissions.

NONFICTION Buys 15 mss/year. Query. Length: varies; short clips to long profiles/features. **Pays 25¢/word.** Sometimes pays expenses of writers on assignment.

MEDICAL

$$$ AHIP COVERAGE

America's Health Insurance Plans, 601 Pennsylvania Ave. NW, South Bldg., Suite 500, Washington DC 20004. (202)778-8493. **Fax:** (202)331-7487. **E-mail:** ahip@ahip.org. **Website:** www.ahip.org. **75% freelance written.** Bimonthly magazine geared toward administrators in America's health insurance companies. Articles should inform and generate interest and discussion about topics on anything from patient care to regulatory issues. Estab. 1990. Circ. 12,000. Byline given. Pays within 30 days of acceptance of article in final form. Offers 30% kill fee. Publishes ms an average of 2 months after acceptance. Editorial lead time 2 months. Submit seasonal material 4 months in advance. Accepts queries by mail, e-mail, fax. Accepts simultaneous submissions. Sample copy free.

NONFICTION Needs book excerpts, how-to, how industry professionals can better operate their health plans, opinion. "We do not accept stories that promote products." Send complete ms. Length: 1,800-2,500 words. **Pays 65¢/word minimum.** Pays phone expenses of writers on assignment.

$$ JEMS

PennWell Corporation, 525 B St., Suite 1800, San Diego CA 92101. (800)266-5367. **E-mail:** rkelley@pennwell.com. **Website:** www.jems.com. **Contact:** Ryan Kelley, senior editor. **95% freelance written.** Monthly magazine directed to personnel who serve the prehospital emergency medicine industry: paramedics, EMTs, emergency physicians and nurses, administrators, EMS consultants, etc. Estab. 1980. Circ. 45,000. Byline given. Pays on publication. No kill fee. Publishes ms an average of 6 months after acceptance. Submit seasonal material 6 months in advance. Accepts queries by e-mail. Responds in 2-3 months to queries. Sample copy free. Guidelines available at www.jems.com/about/author-guidelines.

NONFICTION Needs essays, expose, general interest, how-to, humor, interview, new product, opinion, personal experience, photo feature, technical; continuing education. **Buys 50 mss/year.** Query Ryan Kelley with contact information, suggested title, ms document (can be an outline), a summary, a general ms classification, and photos or figures to be considered with the ms. **Pays $100-350.**

COLUMNS/DEPARTMENTS Length: 850 words maximum. Query with or without published clips. **Pays $50-250.**

$$$ MANAGED CARE

780 Township Line Rd., Yardley PA 19067. (267)685-2788. **Fax:** (267)685-2966. **E-mail:** jmarcille@managedcaremag.com. **Website:** www.managedcaremag.com. **Contact:** John Marcille, editor. **75% freelance written.** Monthly magazine that delivers high-interest, full-length articles and shorter features on clinical and business aspects of the health care industry. Emphasizes practical, usable information that helps HMO medical directors and pharmacy directors cope with the options, challenges, and hazards in the rapidly changing health care industry. Estab. 1992. Circ. 44,000. Byline given. Pays on acceptance. Offers 20% kill fee. Publishes ms an average of 6 weeks after acceptance. Editorial lead time 3 months. Submit seasonal material 4 months in advance. Accepts queries by mail, e-mail, fax. Responds in 3 weeks to queries. Responds in 2 months to mss. Sample copy free. Guidelines available online.

NONFICTION Needs book excerpts, general interest, trends in health-care delivery and financing, quality of care, and employee concerns, how-to, deal with requisites of managed care, such as contracts with health plans, affiliation arrangements, accredidation, computer needs, etc., original research and review articles that examine the relationship between health care delivery and financing. Also considered occasionally are personal experience, opinion, interview/profile, and humor pieces, but these must have a strong managed care angle and draw upon the insights of (if they are not written by) a knowledgeable managed care professional. **Buys 40 mss/year.** Query with published clips. Length: 1,000-3,000 words. **Pays 75¢/word.** Pays expenses of writers on assignment.

○$$ OPTICAL PRISM

250 The East Mall, Suite 1113, Toronto ON M9B 6L3 Canada. (416)233-2487. **Fax:** (416)233-1746. **E-mail:** info@opticalprism.ca. **Website:** www.opticalprism.ca. **30% freelance written.** Magazine published 10 times/year. Covers the health, fashion, and business aspects of the optical industry in Canada. Estab. 1982. Circ. 10,000. Byline given. Pays on publication. Publishes ms an average of 2 months after acceptance. Editorial lead time 3 months. Submit seasonal material 3 months in advance. Accepts queries by mail, e-mail. Accepts simultaneous submissions. Digital copy available online.

NONFICTION Needs interview, related to optical industry. Special issues: Editorial themes and feature topics available online in media kit. Query. Length: 1,000-1,600 words. **Pays 40¢/word (Canadian).** Sometimes pays expenses of writers on assignment.

COLUMNS/DEPARTMENTS Insight (profiles on people in the eyewear industry—also sometimes schools and businesses), 700-1,000 words. **Buys 5 mss/year.** Query. **Pays 40¢/word.**

$$ PHYSICIAN MAGAZINE

Physicians News Network, 707 Wilshire Blvd., Suite 3800, Los Angeles CA 90017. (760)805-5040. **E-mail:**

sheri@physiciansnetwork.com; editors@physiciansnewsnetwork.com. **Website:** www.physiciansnewsnetwork.com. **Contact:** Sheri Carr, COO/editor. **25% freelance written.** Monthly magazine covering non-technical articles of relevance to physicians. Estab. 1908. Circ. 18,000. Byline given. Pays on acceptance. Offers 10% kill fee. Publishes ms an average of 2-3 months after acceptance. Editorial lead time 2-3 months. Accepts queries by e-mail. Accepts simultaneous submissions. Responds in 4 weeks to queries. Responds in 2 months to mss.

NONFICTION Needs general interest. **Buys 12-24 mss/year.** Query with published clips. Length: 600-3,000 words. **Pays $200-600 for assigned articles.**

PLASTIC SURGERY NEWS

American Society of Plastic Surgeons, 444 E. Algonquin Rd., Arlington Heights IL 60005. **Fax:** (847)981-5458. **E-mail:** mss@plasticsurgery.org. **Website:** www.plasticsurgery.org. **Contact:** Mike Stokes, managing editor. **15% freelance written.** Monthly tabloid covering plastic surgery. *Plastic Surgery News* readership is comprised primarily of plastic surgeons and those involved with the specialty (nurses, techs, industry). The magazine is distributed via subscription and to all members of the American Society of Plastic Surgeons. The magazine covers a variety of specialty-specific news and features, including trends, legislation, and clinical information. Estab. 1960. Circ. 6,000. Byline given. Pays on acceptance. Offers 25% kill fee. Publishes ms an average of 1-2 months after acceptance. Editorial lead time 1-3 months. Accepts queries by e-mail. Accepts simultaneous submissions. Responds in 2 weeks to queries. Responds in 3 months to mss. Sample copy for 10 first-class stamps. Guidelines by e-mail.

NONFICTION Needs expose, how-to, new product, technical. Does not want celebrity or entertainment based pieces. **Buys 20 mss/year.** Query with published clips. Length: 1,000-3,500 words. **Pays 20-40¢/word.** Sometimes pays expenses of writers on assignment.

COLUMNS/DEPARTMENTS Digital Plastic Surgeon (technology), 1,500-1,700 words.

PRIMARY CARE OPTOMETRY NEWS

SLACK Inc., 6900 Grove Rd., Thorofare NJ 08086-9447. (856)848-1000. **Fax:** (856)848-5991. **E-mail:** editor@healio.com; optometry@healio.com. **Website:** www.healio.com/optometry. **Contact:** Michael D. DePaolis, editor. **5% freelance written.** Monthly tabloid covering optometry. *Primary Care Optometry News* strives to be the optometric professional's definitive information source by delivering timely, accurate, authoritative and balanced reports on clinical issues, socioeconomic and legislative affairs, ophthalmic industry, and research developments, as well as updates on diagnostic and thereapeutic regimens and techniques to enhance the quality of patient care. Estab. 1996. Circ. 39,000. Byline given. Pays on publication. Offers 50% kill fee. Publishes ms an average of 2 months after acceptance. Editorial lead time 2 months. Accepts queries by mail, e-mail, fax, phone. Responds in 2 weeks to queries.

NONFICTION Needs how-to, interview, new product, opinion, technical. **Buys 20 mss/year.** Query. Length: 800-1,000 words. **Pays $350-500.** Sometimes pays expenses of writers on assignment.

COLUMNS/DEPARTMENTS What's Your Diagnosis (case presentation), 800 words. **Buys 40 mss/year.** Query. **Pays $100-500.**

STRATEGIC HEALTH CARE MARKETING

Health Care Communications, 11 Heritage Ln., P.O. Box 594, Rye NY 10580. (914)967-6741. **Fax:** (914)967-3054. **E-mail:** mhumphrey@plainenglishmedia.com. **Website:** www.strategichealthcare.com. **Contact:** Matt Humphrey, publisher. **90% freelance written.** Monthly newsletter covering health care marketing and management in a wide range of settings, including hospitals, medical group practices, home health services, and managed care organizations. Emphasis is on strategies and techniques employed within the health care field and relevant applications from other service industries. Works with published/established writers only. *Strategic Health Care Marketing* is specifically seeking writers with expertise/contacts in managed care, patient satisfaction, and e-health. Estab. 1984. Byline given. Pays on publication. Offers 25% kill fee. Publishes ms an average of 2 months after acceptance. Accepts queries by mail, e-mail. Responds in 1 month to queries. Sample copy for SAE with 9x12 envelope and 3 first-class stamps. Guidelines sent with sample copy only.

NONFICTION Needs how-to, interview, new product, technical. **Buys 50 mss/year.** Query. Length: 1,000-1,800 words. **Pays $100-500.** Sometimes pays expenses of writers on assignment with prior authorization.

MUSIC TRADE

CLASSICAL SINGER MAGAZINE

Classical Publications, Inc., P.O. Box 1710, Draper UT 84020. (801)254-1025, ext. 14. **Fax:** (801)254-3139. **E-mail:** editorial@classicalsinger.com. **Website:** www.classicalsinger.com. **Contact:** Sara Thomas. Monthly magazine covering classical singers. Estab. 1988. Circ. 7,000. Byline given, plus bio and contact info. Pays on publication. No kill fee. Publishes ms an average of 3 months after acceptance. Editorial lead time 3 months. Submit seasonal material 3 months in advance. Accepts queries by e-mail. Responds in 1 month to queries. Potential writers will be given password to website version of magazine and writer's guidelines online.

NONFICTION Needs book excerpts, expose, carefully done, how-to, humor, interview, new product, personal experience, photo feature, religious, technical, travel, , crossword puzzles on opera theme. Does not want reviews unless they are assigned. Query with published clips. Length: 500-3,000 words. **Pays 5¢/word ($50 minimum). Writers also receive 10 contributor's copies.** Pays telephone expenses of writers with assignments when Xerox copy of bill submitted.

INTERNATIONAL BLUEGRASS

International Bluegrass Music Association, 608 W. Iris Dr., Nashville TN 37204. (615)256-3222. **Fax:** (615)256-0450. **E-mail:** info@ibma.org. **Website:** www.ibma.org. **10% freelance written.** Bimonthly newsletter of the International Bluegrass Music Association. *International Bluegrass* is the business publication for the bluegrass music industry. Interested in hard news and features concerning how to reach that potential and how to conduct business more effectively. Estab. 1985. Circ. 4,500. Byline given. Pays on publication. No kill fee. Publishes ms an average of 2 months after acceptance. Submit seasonal material 4 months in advance. Accepts queries by mail, e-mail, phone. Accepts simultaneous submissions. Responds in 1 month to queries. Sample copy for SAE with 6x9 envelope and 2 first-class stamps.

NONFICTION Needs book excerpts, essays, how-to, conduct business effectively within bluegrass music, new product, opinion. No interview/profiles/feature stories of performers (rare exceptions) or fans. **Buys 6 mss/year.** Query. Length: 1,000-1,200 words. **Pays up to $150/article for assigned articles.**

THE MUSIC & SOUND RETAILER

Testa Communications, 25 Willowdale Ave., Port Washington NY 11050. (516)767-2500. **E-mail:** dferrisi@testa.com. **Website:** www.msretailer.com. **Contact:** Dan Ferrisi, editor. **10% freelance written.** Monthly magazine covering business to business publication for music instrument products. *The Music & Sound Retailer* covers the music instrument industry and is sent to all dealers of these products, including Guitar Center, Sam Ash, and all small independent stores. Estab. 1983. Circ. 11,700. Byline given. Pays on publication. Offers $100 kill fee. Editorial lead time 1 month. Submit seasonal material 2 months in advance. Accepts queries by e-mail. Accepts simultaneous submissions. Responds in 2 weeks to queries. Responds in 1 month to mss.

NONFICTION Needs how-to, new product, opinion, (does not mean letters to the editor), personal experience. Concert and CD reviews are never published; neiter are interviews with musicians. **Buys 25 mss/year.** Query with published clips. Length: 1,000-2,000 words. **Pays $300-400 for assigned and unsolicited articles.** Sometimes pays expenses of writers on assignment.

OPERA NEWS

Metropolitan Opera Guild, Inc., 70 Lincoln Center Plaza, 6th Floor, New York NY 10023. **E-mail:** info@operanews.com. **Website:** www.operanews.com. **Contact:** Kitty March. **75% freelance written.** Monthly magazine for people interested in opera—the opera professional as well as the opera audience. Estab. 1936. Circ. 105,000. Byline given. Pays on publication. No kill fee. Publishes ms an average of 4 months after acceptance. Editorial lead time 4 months. Accepts queries by e-mail. Sample copy for $5.

NONFICTION Needs historical, interview, informational, think pieces, opera, and CD, DVD and book reviews. Does not accept works of fiction or personal remembrances. Send unsolicited mss, article proposals and queries, along with several published clips. Length: 1,500-2,800 words. **Pays $450-1,200.** Sometimes pays expenses of writers on assignment.

COLUMNS/DEPARTMENTS Buys 24 mss/year.

$ OVERTONES

Handbell Musicians of America, P.O. Box 1765, Findlay OH 45839-1765. **E-mail:** jrsmith@handbellmusicians.org. **Website:** http://handbellmusicians.org/music-resources/overtones. **Contact:** J.R. Smith, publications director. **80% freelance written.** Bimonthly magazine covering English handbell ringing and conducting. *Overtones* is a 48-page magazine with extensive educational articles, photos, advertisements, and graphic work. Handbell Musicians of America is dedicated to advancing the musical art of handbell/handchime ringing through education, community, and communication. The purpose of *Overtones* is to provide a printed resource to support that mission. Offers how-to articles, inspirational stories, and interviews with well-known people and unique ensembles. Estab. 1954. Circ. 8,000. Byline given. Pays on publication. No kill fee. Publishes ms an average of 4 months after acceptance. Editorial lead time 4 months. Submit seasonal material 4 months in advance. Accepts queries by mail, e-mail. Responds in 1 month to queries and to mss. Sample copy available by e-mail. Guidelines available online. Style guideline should follow *The Chicago Manual of Style*.

NONFICTION Needs essays, general interest, historical, how-to, inspirational, interview, religious, technical. Does not want product news or promotional material. **Buys 8-12 mss/year.** Send complete ms via e-mail, CD, DVD, or hard copy. Length: 1,200-2,000 words. **Pays $120.** Sometimes pays expenses of writers on assignment.

COLUMNS/DEPARTMENTS Handbells in Education (topics covering the use of handbells in school setting, teaching techniques, etc.); Handbells in Worship (topics and ideas for using handbells in a church setting); Tips & Tools (variety of topics from ringing and conducting techniques to score study to maintenance); Community Connections (topics covering issues relating to the operation/administration/techniques for community groups); Music Reviews (recommendations and descriptions of music following particular themes, i.e., youth music, difficult music, seasonal, etc.). Length should be 800-1,200 words. Query. **Pays $80.**

$$ VENUES TODAY

18350 Mt. Langley, Suite 201, Fountain Valley CA 92708. (714)378-5400. **Fax:** (714)378-0040. **E-mail:** linda@venuestoday.com; dave@venuestoday.com. **Website:** www.venuestoday.com. **Contact:** Linda Deckard, publisher and editor-in-chief; Dave Broks, senior writer and assignment editor. **70% freelance written.** Weekly magazine covering the live entertainment industry and the buildings that host shows and sports. Needs writers who can cover an exciting industry from the business side, not the consumer side. Readers are venue managers, concert promoters, those in the concert and sports business, not the audience for concerts and sports. Need business journalists who can cover the latest news and trends in the market. Estab. 2002. Byline given. Pays on publication. Publishes ms an average of 1 month after acceptance. Editorial lead time 1-2 months. Submit seasonal material 1-2 months in advance. Accepts queries by mail, e-mail, fax. Accepts simultaneous submissions. Responds in 1 week to queries.

NONFICTION Needs interview, photo feature, technical, travel. Does not want customer slant, marketing pieces. Query with published clips. Length: 500-1,500 words. **Pays $100-250.** Pays expenses of writers on assignment.

COLUMNS/DEPARTMENTS Venue News (new buildings, trend features, etc.); Bookings (show tours, business side); Marketing (of shows, sports, convention centers); Concessions (food, drink, merchandise). Length: 500-1,200 words. **Buys 250 mss/year. mss/year.** Query with published clips. **Pays $100-250.**

FILLERS Needs gags. **Buys 6 mss/year. Pays $100-300.**

PAPER

$$ THE PAPER STOCK REPORT

McEntee Media Corp., 9815 Hazelwood Ave., Strongsville OH 44149. (440)238-6603. **Fax:** (440)238-6712. **E-mail:** ken@recycle.cc; psr@recycle.cc. **Website:** www.recycle.cc/psrpage.htm. **Contact:** Ken McEntee, editor/publisher. Bimonthly newsletter covering market trends and news in the paper recycling industry. Audience is interested in new innovative markets, applications for recovered scrap paper, as well as new laws and regulations impacting recycling. Estab. 1990. Circ. 2,000. Byline given. Pays on publication. No kill fee. Publishes ms an average of 1 month after acceptance. Editorial lead time 2 months. Submit seasonal material 2 months in advance. Accepts queries by mail, e-mail, fax, phone. Accepts simultaneous submissions. Responds in 1 month to queries. Sample copy for #10 SAE with 55¢ postage.

NONFICTION Needs book excerpts, essays, expose, general interest, historical, interview, new product, opinion, photo feature, technical, all related to paper recycling. **Buys 0-13 mss/year.** Send complete ms. Length: 250-1,000 words. **Pays $50-250 for assigned articles. Pays $25-250 for unsolicited articles.** Pays expenses of writers on assignment.

RECYCLED PAPER NEWS

McEntee Media Corp., 9815 Hazelwood Ave., Strongsville OH 44149. (440)238-6603. **Fax:** (440)238-6712. **E-mail:** ken@recycle.cc. **Website:** www.recycle.cc. **Contact:** Ken McEntee, owner. **10% freelance written.** Monthly newsletter covering the recycling and composting industries. Interested in any news impacting the paper recycling industry, as well as other environmental issues in the paper industry, i.e., water/air pollution, chlorine-free paper, forest conservation, etc., with special emphasis on new laws and regulations. Estab. 1990. Pays on publication. No kill fee. Publishes ms an average of 2 months after acceptance. Editorial lead time 1 month. Submit seasonal material 1 month in advance. Accepts queries by mail, e-mail, fax, phone. Accepts simultaneous submissions. Responds in 2 months to queries. Sample copy for 9x12 SAE and 55¢ postage. Guidelines for #10 SASE.

NONFICTION Needs book excerpts, essays, how-to, interview, new product, opinion, personal experience, photo feature, technical, new business, legislation, regulation, business expansion. **Buys 0-5 mss/year.** Query with published clips. **Pays $10-500.**

COLUMNS/DEPARTMENTS Query with published clips. **Pays $10-500.**

PETS

PET AGE

Journal Multimedia, 220 Davidson Ave., Suite 302, Somerset NJ 08873. (732)246-5722. **Website:** www.petage.com. **Contact:** Michelle Maskaly, editor-in-chief. **90% freelance written.** Monthly magazine for pet/pet supplies retailers, covering the complete pet industry. Estab. 1971. Circ. 23,022. Byline given. Pays on acceptance. No kill fee. Publishes ms an average of 3 months after acceptance. Sample copy and writer's guidelines available.

NONFICTION No profiles of industry members and/or retail establishments or consumer-oriented pet articles. **Buys 80 mss/year.** Query with published clips. Length: 1,500-2,200 words. **Pays 15¢/word for assigned articles.** Pays documented telephone expenses.

PET PRODUCT NEWS INTERNATIONAL

I-5 Publishing, LLC, P.O. Box 6050, Mission Viejo CA 92690. (949)855-8822. **Fax:** (949)855-3045. **E-mail:** ppneditor@i5publishing.com; erothrock@i5publishing.com. **Website:** www.petproductnews.com. **Contact:** Ellyce Rothrock, editor. **70% freelance written.** Monthly magazine. *Pet Product News* covers business/legal and economic issues of importance to pet product retailers, suppliers, and distributors, as well as product information and animal care issues. Looking for straightforward articles on the proper care of dogs, cats, birds, fish, and exotics (reptiles, hamsters, etc.) as information the retailers can pass on to new pet owners. Estab. 1947. Circ. 26,000. Byline given. Pays on publication. Offers $50 kill fee. Editorial lead time 3 months. Submit seasonal material 4 months in advance. Accepts queries by mail, fax. Responds in 2 weeks to queries. Sample copy for $5.50. Guidelines for #10 SASE.

NONFICTION Needs general interest, interview, new product, photo feature, technical. No "cute" animal stories or those directed at the pet owner. **Buys 150 mss/year.** Query. Length: 500-1,500 words. **Pays $175-350.**

COLUMNS/DEPARTMENTS The Pet Dealer News™ (timely news stories about business issues affecting pet retailers), 800-1,000 words; Industry News (news articles representing coverage of pet product suppliers, manufacturers, distributors, and associations), 800-1,000 words; Pet Health News™ (pet health and articles relevant to pet retailers); Dog & Cat (products and care of), 1,000-1,500 words; Fish & Bird (products and care of), 1,000-1,500 words; Small Mammals (products and care of), 1,000-1,500 words; Pond/Water Garden (products and care of), 1,000-1,500 words. **Buys 120 mss/year.** Query. **Pays $150-300.**

PLUMBING, HEATING, A/C AND REFRIGERATION

HPAC: HEATING PLUMBING AIR CONDITIONING

80 Valleybrook Dr., Toronto ON M3B 2S9 Canada. (416)510-5218. **Fax:** (416)510-5140. **E-mail:** sma-

cisaac@hpacmag.com; kturner@hpacmag.com. **E-mail:** smacisaac@hpacmag.com. **Website:** www.hpacmag.com. **Contact:** Sandy MacIsaac, art director; Kerry Turner, editor. **20% freelance written.** Monthly magazine. Estab. 1923. Circ. 19,500. Pays on publication. No kill fee. Publishes an average of 3 months after acceptance. Accepts queries by mail, e-mail. Responds in 2 months to queries.

NONFICTION Needs how-to, technical. Length: 1,000-1,500 words. **Pays 50¢/word.**

$$ SNIPS MAGAZINE

BNP Media, 2401 W. Big Beaver Rd., Suite 700, Troy MI 48084. (248)244-6416. **Fax:** (248)362-0317. **E-mail:** mcconnellm@bnpmedia.com. **Website:** www.snipsmag.com. **Contact:** Michael McConnell. **2% freelance written.** Monthly magazine for sheet metal, heating, ventilation, air conditioning, and metal roofing contractors. Estab. 1932. No kill fee. Publishes ms an average of 3 months after acceptance. Accepts queries by mail, e-mail, fax, phone. Call for writer's guidelines.

NONFICTION Length: under 1,000 words unless on special assignment. **Pays $200-300.**

PRINTING

$$ THE BIG PICTURE

ST Media Group International, 11262 Cornell Park Dr., Cincinnati OH 45242. (513)421-2050. **E-mail:** gregory.sharpless@stmediagroup.com. **Website:** http://bigpicture.net. **Contact:** Gregory Sharpless, editor-in-chief. **20% freelance written.** Magazine published 9 times/year covering wide-format digital printing. *The Big Picture* covers wide-format printing as well as digital workflow, finishing, display, capture, and other related topics. Readers include digital print providers, sign shops, commercial printers, in-house print operations, and other print providers across the country. Primarily interested in the technology and work processes behind wide-format printing, but also run trend features on segments of the industry (innovations in point-of-purchase displays, floor graphics, fine-art printing, vehicle wrapping, textile printing, etc.). Estab. 1996. Circ. 21,500 controlled. Byline given. Pays on publication. Offers 20% kill fee. Publishes ms an average of 2 months after acceptance. Editorial lead time 2 months. Accepts queries by e-mail. Accepts simultaneous submissions. Responds in 2 weeks to queries. Responds in 1 month to mss. Sample copy available online. Guidelines available.

NONFICTION Needs how-to, interview, new product, technical. Does not want broad consumer-oriented pieces that do not speak to the business and technical aspects of producing print for pay. **Buys 15-20 mss/year.** Query with published clips. Length: 1,500-2,500 words. **Pays $500-700 for assigned articles.**

$$ IN-PLANT GRAPHICS

North American Publishing Co., 1500 Spring Garden St., 12th Floor, Philadelphia PA 19130. (215)238-5321. **Fax:** (215)238-5457. **E-mail:** bobneubauer@napco.com. **Website:** www.ipgonline.com. **Contact:** Bob Neubauer, editor. **40% freelance written.** *In-Plant Graphics* features articles designed to help in-house printing departments increase productivity, save money, and stay competitive. *IPG* features advances in graphic arts technology and shows in-plants how to put this technology to use. Audience consists of print shop managers working for (nonprint related) corporations (i.e., hospitals, insurance companies, publishers, nonprofits), universities, and government departments. They often oversee graphic design, prepress, printing, bindery, and mailing departments. Estab. 1951. Circ. 23,100. Byline given. Pays on publication. No kill fee. Publishes ms an average of 3 months after acceptance. Editorial lead time 2 months. Submit seasonal material 3 months in advance. Accepts queries by mail, e-mail, fax. Guidelines available online.

NONFICTION Needs new product, graphic arts, technical, graphic arts/printing/prepress. No articles on desktop publishing software or design software. No Internet publishing articles. **Buys 5 mss/year.** Query with published clips. Length: 800-1,500 words. **Pays $350-500.**

$$ SCREEN PRINTING

ST Media Group International, 11262 Cornell Park Dr., Cincinnati OH 45242. (513)421-2050, ext. 331. **Fax:** (513)421-5144. **E-mail:** gregory.sharpless@stmediagroup.com. **Website:** www.screenweb.com. **Contact:** Gregory Sharpless. **30% freelance written.** Monthly magazine for the screen printing industry, including screen printers (commercial, industrial, and captive shops), suppliers and manufacturers, ad agencies, and allied profession. Estab. 1953. Circ. 17,500. Byline given. Pays on publication. No kill fee. Publishes ms an average of 3 months after acceptance. Accepts queries by mail, e-mail, fax. Sample copy available. Guidelines for #10 SASE.

NONFICTION Buys 10-15 mss/year. Query. Unsolicited mss not returned. **Pays $400 minimum for major features.**

PROFESSIONAL PHOTOGRAPHY

$$ NEWS PHOTOGRAPHER

National Press Photographers Association, Inc., 6677 Whitemarsh Valley Walk, Austin TX 78746-6367. **E-mail:** magazine@nppa.org; info@nppa.org. **Website:** www.nppa.org. **Contact:** Donald R. Winslow, editor. Magazine on photojournalism published 10 times/year. *News Photographer* magazine is dedicated to the advancement of still and television news photography. The magazine presents articles, interviews, profiles, history, new products, electronic imaging, and news related to the practice of photojournalism. Estab. 1946. Circ. 11,000. Byline given. Pays on acceptance. Offers 100% kill fee. Publishes ms an average of 4 months after acceptance. Editorial lead time 2 months. Submit seasonal material 2 months in advance. Accepts queries by mail, e-mail, fax, phone. Accepts simultaneous submissions. Responds in 1 month to queries. Sample copy for SAE with 9x12 envelope and 3 first-class stamps. Guidelines free.

NONFICTION Needs historical, how-to, interview, new product, opinion, personal experience, photo feature, technical. **Buys 10 mss/year.** Query. Length: 1,500 words. **Pays $300.** Pays expenses of writers on assignment.

$$ THE PHOTO REVIEW

140 E. Richardson Ave., Suite 301, Langhorne PA 19047. (215)891-0214. **Fax:** (215)891-9358. **E-mail:** info@photoreview.org. **Website:** www.photoreview.org. **50% freelance written**. Quarterly magazine covering art photography and criticism. "*The Photo Review* publishes critical reviews of photography exhibitions and books, critical essays, and interviews. We do not publish how-to or technical articles." Estab. 1976. Circ. 2,000. Byline given. Pays on publication. No kill fee. Publishes ms an average of 9-12 months after acceptance. Editorial lead time 3 months. Submit seasonal material 6 months in advance. Accepts queries by mail. Accepts simultaneous submissions. Responds in 2 months to queries. Responds in 3 months to mss. Sample copy for $7. Email for guidelines.

NONFICTION Needs interview, photography essay, critical review. No how-to articles. **Buys 20 mss/year.** Send complete ms. 2-20 typed pages by email **Pays $10-250.**

REAL ESTATE

$$ AREA DEVELOPMENT ONLINE

Halcyon Business Publications, Inc., 400 Post Ave., Westbury NY 11590. (516)338-0900, ext. 211. **Fax:** (516)338-0100. **E-mail:** gerri@areadevelopment.com. **Website:** www.areadevelopment.com. **Contact:** Geraldine Gambale, editor. **80% freelance written. Prefers to work with published/established writers.** Quarterly magazine covering corporate facility planning and site selection for industrial chief executives worldwide. Estab. 1965. Circ. 60,000. Byline given. Pays on publication. No kill fee. Publishes ms an average of 2 months after acceptance. Accepts queries by mail, e-mail, fax. Responds in 3 months to queries. Sample copy free. Guidelines for #10 sase.

NONFICTION Needs historical, if it deals with corporate facility planning, how-to, experiences in site selection and all other aspects of corporate facility planning, interview, corporate executives and industrial developers. **Buys 75 mss/year.** Query. Length: 1,500-2,000 words. **Pays 40¢/word.** Sometimes pays expenses of writers on assignment.

$$ THE COOPERATOR

Yale Robbins, Inc., 102 Madison Ave., 5th Floor, New York NY 10016. (212)683-5700. **Fax:** (212)545-0764. **E-mail:** editorial@cooperator.com. **Website:** www.cooperator.com. **70% freelance written.** Monthly tabloid covering real estate in the New York City metro area. *The Cooperator* covers condominium and cooperative issues in New York and beyond. It is read by condo unit owners and co-op shareholders, real estate professionals, board members and managing agents, and other service professionals. Estab. 1980. Circ. 40,000. Byline given. Pays on publication. No kill fee. Publishes ms an average of 3 months after acceptance. Submit seasonal material 3 months in advance. Accepts queries by mail, e-mail, fax. Responds in 1 month to queries. Sample copy and writer's guidelines free.

NONFICTION Needs interview, new product, personal experience. No submissions without queries.

Query with published clips. Length: 1,500-2,000 words. **Pays $325-425.** Sometimes pays expenses of writers on assignment.

FLORIDA REALTOR MAGAZINE

Florida Association of Realtors, 7025 Augusta National Dr., Orlando FL 32822. (407)438-1400. **Fax:** (407)438-1411. **E-mail:** flrealtor@floridarealtors.org. **Website:** www.floridarealtormagazine.com. **Contact:** Doug Damerst, editor-in-chief. **70% freelance written.** Journal published 10 times/year covering the Florida real estate profession. "As the official publication of the Florida Association of Realtors, we provide helpful articles for our 125,000 members. We report new practices that lead to successful real estate careers and stay up on the trends and issues that affect business in Florida's real estate market." Estab. 1925. Circ. 114,592. Byline given. Pays on publication. No kill fee. Publishes ms an average of 2 months after acceptance. Editorial lead time 3 months. Accepts queries by mail, e-mail, fax. Sample copy available online.

NONFICTION No fiction or poetry. **Buys varying number of mss/year.** Query with published clips. Length: 800-1,500 words. **Pays $500-700.** Sometimes pays expenses of writers on assignment.

COLUMNS/DEPARTMENTS Some written inhouse: Law & Ethics, 900 words; Market It, 600 words; Technology & You, 800 words; ManageIt, 600 words. **Buys varying number of mss/year. Payment varies.**

OFFICE BUILDINGS MAGAZINE

Yale Robbins, Inc., 102 Madison Ave., New York NY 10016. (212)683-5700. **Fax:** (212)497-0017. **E-mail:** mrosupport@mrofficespace.com. **Website:** http://marketing.yrpubs.com/officebuildings. **15% freelance written.** Annual magazine published in 12 separate editions covering market statistics, trends, and thinking of area professionals on the current and future state of the real estate market. Estab. 1987. Circ. 10,500. Byline sometimes given. Pays 1 month after publication. Offers kill fee. Editorial lead time 2 months. Accepts queries by mail, e-mail. Sample copy and writer's guidelines free.

NONFICTION Buys 15-20 mss/year. Query with published clips. Length: 1,500-2,000 words. **Pays $600-700.** Sometimes pays expenses of writers on assignment.

PROPERTIES MAGAZINE

Properties Magazine, Inc., 3826 W. 158th St., Cleveland OH 44111. (216)251-2655. **Fax:** (216)251-0064. **E-mail:** mwatt@propertiesmag.com. **Website:** www.propertiesmag.com. **Contact:** Mark Watt, managing editor/art director. **25% freelance written.** Monthly magazine covering real estate, residential, commerical construction. *Properties Magazine* is published for executives in the real estate, building, banking, design, architectural, property management, tax, and law community—busy people who need the facts presented in an interesting and informative format. Estab. 1946. Circ. over 10,000. Byline given. Pays on publication. No kill fee. Publishes ms an average of 2 months after acceptance. Editorial lead time 2 months. Submit seasonal material 2 months in advance. Accepts queries by mail, fax. Responds in 3 weeks to queries. Sample copy for $3.95.

NONFICTION Needs general interest, how-to, humor, new product. Special issues: Environmental issues (September); Security/Fire Protection (October); Tax Issues (November); Computers In Real Estate (December). **Buys 30 mss/year.** Send complete ms. Length: 500-2,000 words. **Pays 50¢/column line.** Sometimes pays expenses of writers on assignment.

ZONING PRACTICE

American Planning Association, 205 N. Michigan Ave., Suite 1200, Chicago IL 60601. (312)431-9100. **Fax:** (312)786-6700. **E-mail:** zoningpractice@planning.org. **Website:** www.planning.org/zoningpractice/index.htm. **90% freelance written.** Monthly newsletter covering land-use regulations including zoning. Publication is aimed at practicing urban planners and those involved in land-use decisions, such as zoning administrators and officials, planning commissioners, zoning boards of adjustment, land-use attorneys, developers, and others interested in this field. The material published comes from writers knowledgeable about zoning and subdivision regulations, preferably with practical experience in the field. Anything published needs to be of practical value to our audience in their everyday work. Estab. 1984. Circ. 2,000. Byline given. Pays on publication. Offers 50% kill fee. Publishes ms an average of 3 months after acceptance. Editorial lead time 6 months. Accepts queries by mail, e-mail, fax, phone. Responds in 2 weeks to queries. Responds in 1 month to mss. Sample copy free. Guidelines available atwww.planning.org/zoningpractice/contribguidelines.htm.

NONFICTION Needs technical. See description. We do not need general or consumer-interest articles about zoning because this publication is aimed at practitioners. **Buys 12 mss/year.** Query. Length: 3,000-5,000 words. **Pays $300 minimum for assigned articles.** Sometimes pays expenses of writers on assignment.

RESOURCES AND WASTE REDUCTION

$$ COMPOSTING NEWS

McEntee Media Corp., 9815 Hazelwood Ave., Strongsville OH 44149. (440)238-6603. **Fax:** (440)238-6712. **E-mail:** ken@recycle.cc. **Website:** www.compostingnews.com. **Contact:** Ken McEntee, editor. **5% freelance written.** Monthly newsletter about the composting industry. *Composting News* features the latest news and vital issues of concern to the producers, marketers, and end-users of compost, mulch and other organic waste-based products. Estab. 1992. Circ. 1,000. Pays on publication. No kill fee. Publishes ms an average of 1 month after acceptance. Editorial lead time 1 month. Submit seasonal material 1 month in advance. Accepts queries by mail, e-mail, fax, phone. Accepts simultaneous submissions. Responds in 2 months to queries. Sample copy for 9x12 SAE and 55¢ postage. Guidelines for #10 SASE.

NONFICTION Needs book excerpts, essays, general interest, how-to, interview, new product, opinion, personal experience, photo feature, technical, new business, legislation, regulation, business expansion. **Buys 0-5 mss/year.** Query with published clips. Length: 100-5,000 words. **Pays $10-500.**

$$$ EROSION CONTROL

Forester Media Inc., 2946 De La Vina St., Santa Barbara CA 93105. (805)682-1300. **Fax:** (805)682-0200. **E-mail:** eceditor@forester.net. **Website:** www.erosioncontrol.com. **Contact:** Janice Kaspersen, editor. **60% freelance written.** Magazine published 7 times/year covering all aspects of erosion prevention and sediment control. *Erosion Control* is a practical, hands-on, how-to professional journal. Readers are civil engineers, landscape architects, builders, developers, public works officials, road and highway construction officials and engineers, soils specialists, farmers, landscape contractors, and others involved with any activity that disturbs significant areas of surface vegetation. Estab. 1994. Circ. 23,000. Byline given. Pays 1 month after acceptance. No kill fee. Publishes ms an average of 3 months after acceptance. Editorial lead time 4 months. Submit seasonal material 4 months in advance. Accepts queries by mail, e-mail, fax, phone. Responds in 3 weeks to queries. Sample copy and writer's guidelines free.

NONFICTION Needs photo feature, technical. **Buys 15 mss/year.** Query with published clips. Length: 3,000-4,000 words. **Pays $700-850.** Sometimes pays expenses of writers on assignment.

$$ MSW MANAGEMENT

Forester Media Inc., P.O. Box 3100, Santa Barbara CA 93130. (805)682-1300. **Fax:** (805)682-0200. **E-mail:** jtrotti@forester.net. **Website:** www.mswmanagement.com. **Contact:** John Trotti, group editor. **70% freelance written.** Bimonthly magazine. *MSW Management* is written for public sector solid waste professionals—the people working for the local counties, cities, towns, boroughs, and provinces. They run the landfills, recycling programs, composting, and incineration. They are responsible for all aspects of garbage collection and disposal; buying and maintaining the associated equipment; and designing, engineering, and building the waste processing facilities, transfer stations, and landfills. Estab. 1991. Circ. 25,000. Byline given. Pays 30 days after acceptance. No kill fee. Editorial lead time 4 months. Submit seasonal material 4 months in advance. Accepts queries by mail, e-mail, fax, phone. Accepts simultaneous submissions. Responds in 6 weeks to queries. Responds in 2 months to mss. Sample copy and writer's guidelines free.

NONFICTION Needs photo feature, technical. No rudimentary, basic articles written for the average person on the street. Readers are experienced professionals with years of practical, in-the-field experience. Any material submitted that is too fundamental will be rejected. **Buys 15 mss/year.** Query. Length: 3,000-4,000 words. **Pays $350-750.** Sometimes pays expenses of writers on assignment.

$$$ STORMWATER

Forester Media Inc., 2946 De La Vina St., Santa Barbara CA 93105. (805)682-1300. **Fax:** (805)682-0200.

E-mail: sweditor@forester.net. **Website:** www.stormh2o.com. **Contact:** Janice Kaspersen, editor. **10% freelance written.** Magazine published 8 times/year covering stormwater issues. *Stormwater* is a practical business journal for professionals involved with surface water quality issues, protection, projects, and programs. Readers are municipal employees, regulators, engineers, and consultants concerned with stormwater management. Estab. 2000. Circ. 20,000. Byline given. Pays 1 month after acceptance. No kill fee. Publishes ms an average of 3 months after acceptance. Editorial lead time 4 months. Submit seasonal material 4 months in advance. Accepts queries by mail, e-mail. Responds in 3 weeks to queries. Guidelines free.

NONFICTION Needs technical. **Buys 8-10 mss/year.** Query with published clips. Length: 3,000-4,000 words. **Pays $500-900.** Sometimes pays expenses of writers on assignment.

$$ WATER WELL JOURNAL

National Ground Water Association, 601 Dempsey Rd., Westerville OH 43081. **Fax:** (614)898-7786. **E-mail:** tplumley@ngwa.org. **Website:** www.waterwelljournal.org. **Contact:** Thad Plumley, director of publications; Mike Price, associate editor. Each month the *Water Well Journal* covers the topics of drilling, rigs and heavy equipment, pumping systems, water quality, business management, water supply, on-site waste water treatment, and diversification opportunities, including geothermal installations, environmental remediation, irrigation, dewatering, and foundation installation. It also offers updates on regulatory issues that impact the ground water industry. Circ. 24,000. Byline given. Pays on publication. Publishes ms an average of 3 months after acceptance. Editorial lead time 6 weeks. Submit seasonal material 3 months in advance. Accepts queries by mail. Responds in 2 weeks to queries. Responds in 1 month to mss. Guidelines free.

NONFICTION Needs essays, sometimes, historical, sometimes, how-to, recent examples include how-to chlorinate a well; how-to buy a used rig; how-to do bill collections, interview, new product, personal experience, photo feature, technical, business management. No company profiles or extended product releases. **Buys up to 30 mss/year.** Query with published clips. Length: 1,000-3,000 words. **Pays $150-400.**

SELLING AND MERCHANDISING

$$ BALLOONS & PARTIES MAGAZINE

PartiLife Publications, 65 Sussex St., Hackensack NJ 07601. (201)441-4224. **Fax:** (201)342-8118. **E-mail:** mark@balloonsandparties.com. **Website:** www.balloonsandparties.com. **Contact:** Mark Zettler, publisher. **10% freelance written.** International trade journal published bi-monthly for professional party decorators and gift delivery businesses. *BALLOONS & Parties Magazine* is published 6 times a year by PartiLife Publications, L.L.C., for the balloon, party and event fields. New product data, letters, mss, and photographs should be sent as "Attention: Editor" and should include sender's full name, address, and telephone number. SASE required on all editorial submissions. All submissions considered for publication unless otherwise noted. Unsolicited materials are submitted at sender's risk and *BALLOONS & Parties*/PartiLife Publications, L.L.C., assumes no responsibility for unsolicited materials. Estab. 1986. Circ. 7,000. Byline given. Pays on publication. No kill fee. Publishes ms an average of 3 months after acceptance. Submit seasonal material 6 months in advance. Accepts queries by mail, e-mail, fax, phone. Responds in 6 weeks to queries. Sample copy for SAE with 9x12 envelope.

NONFICTION Needs essays, how-to, interview, new product, personal experience, photo feature, technical, craft. **Buys 12 mss/year.** Send complete ms. Length: 500-1,500 words. **Pays $100-300 for assigned articles. Pays $50-200 for unsolicited articles.** Sometimes pays expenses of writers on assignment.

$$ CASUAL LIVING MAGAZINE

Progresive Business Media/Today Group, 7025 Albert Pick Rd., Suite 200, Greensboro NC 27409. (336)605-1122. **Fax:** (336)605-1143. **E-mail:** cingram@casualliving.com. **Website:** www.casualliving.com. **Contact:** Cinde Ingram, editor-in-chief. **10% freelance written.** Monthly magazine covering outdoor furniture and accessories, barbecue grills, spas, and more. *Casual Living* is a trade only publication for the casual furnishings and related industries, published monthly. Writes about new products, trends, and casual furniture retailers, plus industry news. Estab. 1958. Circ. 10,000. Pays on publication. Publishes ms an average of 1-2 months after acceptance. Editorial lead time 1-2 months. Submit seasonal material 2 months in advance. Accepts queries by mail, e-mail. Responds in 2 weeks to queries. Sample copy available online.

NONFICTION Needs how-to, interview. **Buys 20 mss/year.** Query with published clips. Length: 300-1,000 words. **Pays $300-700.** Sometimes pays expenses of writers on assignment.

$$$$ CONSUMER GOODS TECHNOLOGY

Edgell Communications, 4 Middlebury Blvd., Randolph NJ 07869. (973)607-1300. **Fax:** (973)607-1395. **E-mail:** aackerman@edgellmail.com. **Website:** www.consumergoods.edgl.com. **Contact:** Alliston Ackerman, editor. **40% freelance written.** Monthly tabloid benchmarking business technology performance. Estab. 1987. Circ. 25,000. Byline given. Pays on publication. No kill fee. Publishes ms an average of 2 months after acceptance. Editorial lead time 3 months. Accepts queries by e-mail. Sample copy available online. Guidelines by e-mail.

NONFICTION Needs essays, expose, interview. **Buys 60 mss/year.** Query with published clips. Length: 700-1,900 words. **Pays $600-1,200.** Sometimes pays expenses of writers on assignment.

COLUMNS/DEPARTMENTS Columns 400-750 words—featured columnists. **Buys 4 mss/year.** Query with published clips. **Pays 75¢-$1/word.**

$$ NICHE

The Rosen Group, 3000 Chestnut Ave., Suite 300, Baltimore MD 21211. (410)889-3093, ext. 231. **Fax:** (410)243-7089. **E-mail:** hoped@rosengrp.com. **Website:** www.nichemagazine.com. **Contact:** Hope Daniels, editorial director. **80% freelance written.** Quarterly trade magazine for the progressive craft gallery retailer. Each issue includes retail gallery profiles, store design trends, management techniques, financial information, and merchandising strategies for small business owners, as well as articles about craft artists and craft mediums. Estab. 1988. Circ. 25,000. Byline given. Pays on publication. No kill fee. Publishes ms an average of 6-9 months after acceptance. Editorial lead time 9 months. Submit queries for seasonal material 1 year in advance. Accepts queries by e-mail. Responds in 4-6 weeks to queries. Responds in 3 months to mss. Sample copy for $3.

NONFICTION Needs interview, photo feature, articles targeted to independent retailers and small business owners. **Buys 15-20 mss/year.** Query with published clips. **Pays $300-700.** Sometimes pays expenses of writers on assignment.

COLUMNS/DEPARTMENTS Retail Details (short items at the front of the book, general retail information); Artist Profiles (short biographies of American Craft Artists); Retail Resources (including book/video/seminar reviews and educational opportunities pertaining to retailers). Query with published clips. **Pays $25-100 per item.**

$$ SMART RETAILER

Emmis Communications, P.O. Box 5000, N7528 Aanstad Rd., Iola WI 54945. (800)331-0038. **Fax:** (715)445-4053. **E-mail:** jonespublishingeditor@yahoo.com; carief@smart-retailer.com. **Website:** www.smart-retailer.com. **Contact:** Carie Ferg, publisher. **50% freelance written.** Magazine published 7 times/year covering independent retail, gift, and home decor. *Smart Retailer* is a trade publication for independent retailers of gifts and home accents. Estab. 1993. Circ. 32,000. Byline given. Pays 1 month after acceptance of final ms. Offers $50 kill fee. Publishes ms an average of 4-6 months after acceptance. Editorial lead time 4-6 months. Submit seasonal material 8-10 months in advance. Accepts queries by mail, e-mail, fax. Accepts simultaneous submissions. Usually responds in 4-6 weeks (only if accepted). Sample articles are available on website. Guidelines by e-mail.

NONFICTION Needs how-to, pertaining to retail, interview, new product, finance, legal, marketing, small business. No fiction, poetry, fillers, photos, artwork, or profiles of businesses, unless queried and first assigned. **Buys 20 mss/year.** Send complete ms, with résumé and published clips to: Writers Query, *Smart Retailer*. Length: 1,000-2,500 words. **Pays $275-500 for assigned articles. Pays $200-350 for unsolicited articles.** Sometimes pays expenses of writers on assignment. Limit agreed upon in advance.

$$ TRAVEL GOODS SHOWCASE

Travel Goods Association, 301 North Harrison St., #412, Princeton NJ 08540. (877)842-1938. **Fax:** (877)842-1938. **E-mail:** info@travel-goods.org; cathy@travel-goods.org. **Website:** www.travel-goods.org. **Contact:** Cathy Hays. **5-10% freelance written.** Magazine published quarterly. *Travel Goods Showcase*, the largest trade magazine devoted to travel products, contains articles for retailers, dealers, manufacturers, and suppliers about luggage, business cases, personal leather goods, handbags, and accessories. Special articles report on trends in fashion, promotions, selling and marketing techniques, industry statistics, and other educational and promotional improvements and advancements. Estab. 1975. Circ. 21,000. Byline given. Pays on acceptance. Offers $50 kill fee. Publishes ms an average of 2 months after acceptance. Editorial lead time 3 months. Submit seasonal material 2 months in advance. Accepts queries by mail, e-mail. Responds in 2 weeks to queries. Responds in 1 month to mss. Sample copy and writer's guidelines free.

NONFICTION Needs interview, new product, technical, travel, retailer profiles with photos. No manufacturer profiles. **Buys 3 mss/year.** Query with published clips. Length: 1,200-1,600 words. **Pays $200-400.**

$$$ VERTICAL SYSTEMS RESELLER

Edgell Communications, Inc., 4 Middlebury Blvd., Randolph NJ 07869. (973)607-1300. **Fax:** (973)607-1395. **E-mail:** gkoroneos@edgellmail.com. **Website:** www.vsr.edgl.com. **Contact:** George L. Koroneos, editor-in-chief. **60% freelance written.** Monthly journal covering channel strategies that build business. Estab. 1992. Circ. 30,000. Byline given. Pays on acceptance. No kill fee. Publishes ms an average of 2 months after acceptance. Editorial lead time 3 months. Accepts queries by mail, e-mail, fax. Accepts simultaneous submissions. Responds in 2 weeks to queries. Responds in 2 months to mss.

NONFICTION Needs interview, opinion, technical, technology/channel issues. **Buys 36 mss/year.** Query with published clips. Editorial calendar available online with lead-generation opportunities. Length: 1,000-1,700 words. **Pays $200-800 for assigned articles.** Sometimes pays expenses of writers on assignment.

SPORT TRADE

$$ AQUATICS INTERNATIONAL

Hanley Wood, LLC, 6222 Wilshire Blvd., Suite 600, Los Angeles CA 90048. **Fax:** (323)801-4972. **E-mail:** etaylor@hanleywood.com. **Website:** www.aquaticsintl.com. **Contact:** Erika Taylor, editor. Magazine published 10 times/year covering public swimming pools and waterparks. Devoted to the commercial and public swimming pool industries. The magazine provides detailed information on designing, building, maintaining, promoting, managing, programming, and outfitting aquatics facilities. Estab. 1989. Circ. 30,000. Byline given. Pays on publication. No kill fee. Publishes ms an average of 3 months after acceptance. Editorial lead time 3 months. Responds in 1 month to queries. Sample copy for $10.50.

NONFICTION Needs how-to, interview, technical. **Buys 6 mss/year.** Send query letter with published clips/samples. Length: 1,500-2,500 words. **Pays $525 for assigned articles.**

COLUMNS/DEPARTMENTS Pays $250.

$$ ARROWTRADE MAGAZINE

Arrow Trade Publishing Corp., 3479 409th Ave. NW, Braham MN 55006. (320)396-3473. **Fax:** (320)396-3206. **E-mail:** timdehn@arrowtrademag.com. **Website:** www.arrowtrademag.com. **80% freelance written.** Bimonthly magazine covering the archery industry. Readers are interested in articles that help them operate their businesses better. They are primarily owners or managers of sporting goods stores and archery pro shops. Estab. 1996. Circ. 13,000. Byline given. Pays on publication. No kill fee. Publishes ms an average of 2 months after acceptance. Editorial lead time 2 months. Accepts queries by mail, e-mail, fax. Responds in 2 weeks to queries.

NONFICTION Needs interview, new product. "Generic business articles won't work for our highly specialized audience." **Buys 24 mss/year.** Query with published clips. Length: 3,400-4,800 words. **Pays $350-550.** Sometimes pays expenses of writers on assignment.

$$ BOATING INDUSTRY

EPG Media, 3300 Fernbrook Lane N., Suite 200, Plymouth MN 55447. (763)383-4400. **E-mail:** jonathan.sweet@boatingindustry.com. **Website:** www.boatingindustry.com. **Contact:** Jonathan Sweet, editor-in-chief. **Less than 10% freelance written.** Bimonthly magazine covering recreational marine industry management. "We write for those in the industry—not the consumer. Our subject is the business of boating. All of our articles must be analytical and predictive, telling our readers where the industry is going, rather than where it's been." Estab. 1929. Circ. 23,000. Byline given. Pays on publication. Offers 50% kill fee. Publishes ms an average of 2 months after acceptance. Editorial lead time 2 months. Submit seasonal material 2 months in advance. Accepts queries by mail, e-mail. Responds in 1 month to queries.

NONFICTION Needs technical, business. **Buys 30 mss/year.** Query with published clips. Length: 250-

2,500 words. **Pays $25-250.** Sometimes pays expenses of writers on assignment.

BOWLING CENTER MANAGEMENT

Luby Publishing, 122 S. Michigan Ave., Suite 1806, Chicago IL 60603. (312)341-1110. **Fax:** (312)341-1180. **E-mail:** mikem@lubypublishing.com. **Website:** www.bcmmag.com. **Contact:** Michael Mazek, editor. **50% freelance written.** Monthly magazine covering bowling centers, family entertainment. *Bowling Center Management* is the industry's leading business publication and offical trade magazien of the Bowling Proprietor's Association of America. Readers are looking for novel ways to draw more customers. Accordingly, the magazine looks for articles that effectively present such ideas. Estab. 1995. Circ. 12,000. Byline given. Pays on acceptance. Publishes ms an average of 3 months after acceptance. Editorial lead time 3 months. Submit seasonal material 6 months in advance. Accepts queries by e-mail. Accepts simultaneous submissions. Responds in 2-3 weeks to queries. Sample copy for $10.

NONFICTION Needs how-to, interview. **Buys 10-20 mss/year.** Query. Length: 750-1,500 words. **Pays $150-350.**

GOLF COURSE MANAGEMENT

Golf Course Superintendents Association of America, 1421 Research Park Dr., Lawrence KS 66049. (800)472-7878. **Fax:** (785)832-3643. **E-mail:** shollister@gcsaa.org; bsmith@gcsaa.org; tcarson@gcsaa.org. **Website:** www.gcsaa.org. **Contact:** Scott Hollister, editor-in-chief; Bunny Smith, senior managing editor; Teresa Carson, senior science editor. **50% freelance written.** Monthly magazine covering the golf course superintendent. *GCM* helps the golf course superintendent become more efficient in all aspects of their job. Estab. 1924. Circ. 40,000. Byline given. Pays on acceptance. No kill fee. Publishes ms an average of 6 months after acceptance. Editorial lead time 6 months. Submit seasonal material 6 months in advance. Accepts simultaneous submissions. Responds in 3 weeks to queries. Responds in 1 month to mss.

NONFICTION Needs how-to, interview. No articles about playing golf. **Buys 40 mss/year.** Query for either feature, research, or superintendent article. Submit electronically, preferably as e-mail attachment. Send 1-page synopsis or query for feature article to Scott Hollister. For research articles, submit to Teresa Carson. If you are a superintendent, contact Bunny Smith. Length: 1,500-2,000 words. **Pays $400-600.** Sometimes pays expenses of writers on assignment.

INTERNATIONAL BOWLING INDUSTRY

B2B Media, Inc., 12655 Ventura Blvd., Studio City CA 91604. (818)789-2695. **Fax:** (818)789-2812. **E-mail:** info@bowlingindustry.com. **Website:** www.bowlingindustry.com. **40% freelance written.** Online monthly magazine covering ownership and management of bowling centers (alleys) and pro shops. *IBI* publishes articles in all phases of bowling center and bowling pro shop ownership and management, among them finance, promotion, customer service, relevant technology, architecture, and capital improvement. The magazine also covers the operational areas of bowling centers and pro shops such as human resources, food and beverage, corporate and birthday parties, ancillary attractions (go-karts, gaming and the like), and retailing. Articles must have strong how-to emphasis. They must be written specifically in terms of the bowling industry, although content may be applicable more widely. Estab. 1993. Circ. 10,200. Byline given. Pays on acceptance. Offers $50 kill fee. Publishes ms an average of 3 months after acceptance. Submit seasonal material 3 months in advance. Accepts queries by mail, e-mail, fax. Accepts simultaneous submissions. Responds in 2 weeks to queries. Responds in 1 month to mss. Sample copy for #10 SASE. Guidelines free.

NONFICTION Needs how-to, interview, new product, technical. **Buys 40 mss/year.** Send complete ms. Length: 1,100-1,400 words. **Pays $250.** Sometimes pays expenses of writers on assignment.

NSGA RETAIL FOCUS

National Sporting Goods Association, 1601 Feehanville Dr., Suite 300, Mt. Prospect IL 60056-6035. (847)296-6742. **Fax:** (847)391-9827. **E-mail:** info@nsga.org. **Website:** www.nsga.org. **Contact:** Bruce Hammond. **20% freelance written. Works with a small number of new/unpublished writers each year.** Bimonthly magazine. *NSGA Retail Focus* serves as a bimonthly trade journal for sporting goods retailers who are members of the association. Estab. 1948. Circ. 2,000. Byline given. Pays on publication. Offers kill fee. Publishes ms an average of 1 month after acceptance. Submit seasonal material 6 months in advance. Accepts queries by e-mail. Sample copy for sae with 9x12 envelope and 5 first-class stamps.

NONFICTION Needs interview, photo feature. No articles written without sporting goods retail business people in mind as the audience. In other words, no generic articles sent to several industries. **Buys 12 mss/year.** Query with published clips. **Pays $150-300.** Sometimes pays expenses of writers on assignment.

$$ POOL & SPA NEWS

Hanley Wood, LLC, 6222 Wilshire Blvd., Suite 600, Los Angeles CA 90048. (323)801-4972. **Fax:** (323)801-4986. **E-mail:** etaylor@hanleywood.com; jmcclain@hanleywood.com. **Website:** http://poolspanews.com. **Contact:** Erika Taylor, editorial director; Joanne McClain, managing editor. **15% freelance written.** Semimonthly magazine covering the swimming pool and spa industry for builders, retail stores, and service firms. Estab. 1960. Circ. 16,300. Pays on publication. No kill fee. Publishes ms an average of 2 months after acceptance. Accepts queries by mail, e-mail. Responds in 1 month to queries. Sample copy for $5 and 9x12 SAE and 11 first-class stamps.

NONFICTION Needs interview, technical. Send résumé with published clips. Length: 500-2,000 words. **Pays $150-550.** Pays expenses of writers on assignment.

$$ SKI AREA MANAGEMENT

Beardsley Publications, 84 Cross Brook Rd., P.O. Box 644, Woodbury CT 06798. (203)263-0888. **Fax:** (203)266-0452. **E-mail:** donna@saminfo.com; jenn@saminfo.com. **Website:** www.saminfo.com. **Contact:** Donna Jacobs. **85% freelance written.** Bimonthly magazine covering everything involving the management and development of ski resorts. Report on new ideas, developments, marketing, and regulations with regard to ski and snowboard resorts. Estab. 1962. Circ. 4,500. Byline given. Pays on publication. Offers kill fee. Offers kill fee. Editorial lead time 2 months. Submit seasonal material 3 months in advance. Accepts queries by mail, e-mail. Responds in 2 weeks to queries. Sample copy for 9x12 SAE with $3 postage or online. Guidelines for #10 SASE.

NONFICTION Needs historical, how-to, interview, new product, opinion, personal experience, technical. Does not want anything that does not specifically pertain to resort operations, management, or financing. **Buys 25-40 mss/year.** Query. Length: 500-2,500 words. **Pays $50-400.**

$$ REFEREE

Referee Enterprises, Inc., 2017 Lathrop Ave., Racine WI 53405. (800)733-6100. **Fax:** (262)632-5460. **E-mail:** submissions@referee.com. **Website:** www.referee.com. **Contact:** Julie Sternberg, managing editor. **75% freelance written.** Monthly magazine covering sports officiating. *Referee* is a magazine for and read by sports officials of all kinds with a focus on baseball, basketball, football, softball, and soccer officiating. Estab. 1976. Circ. 40,000. Byline given. Pays on acceptance. Offers kill fee. Kill fee negotiable. Publishes ms an average of 6 months after acceptance. Editorial lead time 6 months. Accepts queries by mail, e-mail. Responds in 2 weeks to queries; 1 month to mss. Sample copy with #10 SASE. Guidelines online.

NONFICTION Needs book excerpts, essays, historical, how-to, sports officiating related, humor, interview, opinion, photo feature, technical, as it relates to sports officiating. "We don't want to see articles with themes not relating to sport officiating. General sports articles, although of interest to us, will not be published." **Buys 40 mss/year.** Query with published clips. Length: 500-3,500 words. **Pays $50-400.**

STONE, QUARRY AND MINING

$$ CANADIAN MINING JOURNAL

Business Information Group, 80 Valleybrook Dr., Toronto ON M3B 2S9 Canada. (416)510-6742. **Fax:** (416)510-5138. **E-mail:** rnoble@canadianminingjournal.com. **Website:** www.canadianminingjournal.com. **Contact:** Russell Noble, editor. **5% freelance written.** Magazine covering mining and mineral exploration by Canadian companies. *Canadian Mining Journal* provides articles and information of practical use to those who work in the technical, administrative, and supervisory aspects of exploration, mining, and processing in the Canadian mineral exploration and mining industry. Estab. 1882. Circ. 11,000. Byline given. Pays on publication. No kill fee. Publishes ms an average of 3 months after acceptance. Submit seasonal material 3 months in advance. Accepts queries by mail, e-mail, fax, phone. Responds in 1 week to queries. Responds in 1 month to mss.

NONFICTION Needs opinion, technical, operation descriptions. **Buys 6 mss/year.** Query with published clips. Length: 500-1,400 words. **Pays $100-600.** Pays expenses of writers on assignment.

$$ PIT & QUARRY

Questex Media Group, 1360 E. Ninth St., Suite 1070, Cleveland OH 44114. (216)706-3711; (216)706-3747. **Fax:** (216)706-3710. **E-mail:** info@pitandquarry.com; kyanik@northcoastmedia.net. **Website:** www.pitandquarry.com. **Contact:** Kevin Yanik, managing editor. **10-20% freelance written.** Monthly magazine covering nonmetallic minerals, mining, and crushed stone. Audience has knowledge of construction-related markets, mining, minerals processing, etc. Estab. 1916. Circ. 23,000. Byline given. Pays on acceptance. No kill fee. Publishes ms an average of 2 months after acceptance. Editorial lead time 2 months. Accepts queries by e-mail. Accepts simultaneous submissions. Responds in 1 month to queries. Responds in 4 months to mss.

NONFICTION Needs how-to, interview, new product, technical. No humor or inspirational articles. **Buys 3-4 mss/year.** Query. Length: 2,000-2,500 words. **Pays $250-500 for assigned articles. Does not pay for unsolicited articles.** Sometimes pays expenses of writers on assignment.

$ STONE WORLD

BNP Media, 2401 W. Big Beaver Rd., Suite 700, Troy MI 48084. (201)291-9001. **Fax:** (201)291-9002. **E-mail:** jennifer@stoneworld.com. **Website:** www.stoneworld.com. **Contact:** Jennifer Adams, editor. Monthly magazine on natural building stone for producers and users of granite, marble, limestone, slate, sandstone, onyx, and other natural stone products. Estab. 1984. Circ. 21,000. Byline given. Pays on publication. No kill fee. Publishes ms an average of 4 months after acceptance. Submit seasonal material 6 months in advance. Responds in 2 months to queries. Sample copy for $10.

NONFICTION Needs how-to, fabricate and/or install natural building stone, interview, photo feature, technical, architectural design, artistic stone uses, statistics, factory profile, equipment profile, trade show review. **Buys 10 mss/year.** Send complete ms. Length: 600-3,000 words. **Pays $6/column inch.** Pays expenses of writers on assignment.

TOY, NOVELTY AND HOBBY

$$ MODEL RETAILER

Kalmbach Publishing Co., 21027 Crossroads Circle, Waukesha WI 53187. (262)796-8776. **E-mail:** jreich@kalmbach.com. **E-mail:** editor@modelretailer.com. **Website:** www.modelretailer.com. **Contact:** Jeff Reich, editor. **30% freelance written.** Monthly magazine. *Model Retailer* covers the business of hobby retailing, from financial and store management issues to product and industry trends. Goal is to provide owners and managers with the tools and information they need to be successful retailers. Estab. 1987. Circ. 6,000. Byline given. Pays on acceptance. Kill fee: 25%. Publishes ms an average of 2 months after acceptance. Editorial lead time 3 months. Submit seasonal material 6 months in advance. Accepts queries by e-mail. Sample copy free. Guidelines online.

NONFICTION Needs how-to, business, new product. No articles that do not have a strong hobby or small retail component. **Buys 30-40 mss/year.** Query with published clips. "We welcome queries for feature articles and columns and the submission of articles sent on speculation. Queries and submissions accepted by e-mail only." Length: 800-1,600 words. **Pays $100-450.**

TRANSPORTATION

$$ METRO MAGAZINE (CALIFORNIA)

Bobit Business Media, 3520 Challenger St., Torrance CA 90503. (310)533-2400. **Fax:** (310)533-2502. **E-mail:** info@metro-magazine.com. **E-mail:** alex.roman@bobit.com. **Website:** www.metro-magazine.com. **Contact:** Alex Roman, managing editor. **10% freelance written.** Magazine published 10 times/year covering transit bus, passenger rail, and motorcoach operations. METRO's coverage includes both public transit systems and private bus operators, addressing topics such as funding mechanisms, procurement, rolling stock maintenance, privatization, risk management, and sustainability. *Metro Magazine* delivers business, government policy, and technology developments that are *industry specific* to public transportation. Estab. 1904. Circ. 20,500. Byline given. Pays on acceptance. Offers 10% kill fee. Publishes ms an average of 2 months after acceptance. Editorial lead time 3 months. Submit seasonal material 3 months in advance. Accepts queries by e-mail. Responds in 2 weeks to queries. Responds in 1 month to mss. Sample copy for $8. Guidelines by e-mail.

NONFICTION Needs how-to, interview, of industry figures, new product, related to transit—bus and rail—private bus, technical. **Buys 6-10 mss/year.** Query. Length: 400-1,500 words. **Pays $80-400.**

COLUMNS/DEPARTMENTS Query. **Pays 20¢/word.**

$$⊘ SCHOOL BUS FLEET

Bobit Business Media, 3520 Challenger St., Torrance CA 90503. (310)533-2400. **Fax:** (310)533-2512. **E-mail:** sbf@bobit.com. **Website:** www.schoolbusfleet.com. Magazine covering school transportation of K-12 population. Most readers are school bus operators, public and private. Estab. 1956. Circ. 28,000. Byline given. Pays on acceptance. Offers 25% kill fee or $50. Publishes ms an average of 3 months after acceptance. Editorial lead time 3 months. Submit seasonal material 3 months in advance. Accepts queries by mail, e-mail, fax. Responds in 1 month to queries. Sample copy free. *Not currently accepting submissions.* Query first.

TRAVEL TRADE

$$ CRUISE INDUSTRY NEWS

441 Lexington Ave., Suite 809, New York NY 10017. (212)986-1025. **Fax:** (212)986-1033. **E-mail:** oivind@cruiseindustrynews.com. **Website:** www.cruiseindustrynews.com. **Contact:** Oivind Mathisen, editor. **20% freelance written.** Quarterly magazine covering cruise shipping. Magazine about the business of cruise shipping for the industry, including cruise lines, shipyards, financial analysts, etc. Estab. 1991. Circ. 10,000. Byline given. Pays on acceptance or on publication. Offers 25% kill fee. Publishes ms an average of 4 months after acceptance. Editorial lead time 3 months. Accepts queries by mail. Reponse time varies. Sample copy for $15. Guidelines for #10 SASE.

NONFICTION Needs interview, new product, photo feature, business. No travel stories. **Buys more than 20 mss/year.** Query with published clips. Length: 500-1,500 words. **Pays $.50/word published.** Sometimes pays expenses of writers on assignment.

$$ LEISURE GROUP TRAVEL

Premier Tourism Marketing, 621 Plainfield Rd., Suite 406, Willowbrook IL 60527. (630)794-0696. **Fax:** (630)794-0652. **E-mail:** randy@ptmgroups.com. **E-mail:** editor@ptmgroups.com. **Website:** www.leisuregrouptravel.com. **Contact:** Randy Mink, managing editor. **35% freelance written.** Bimonthly magazine covering group travel. Covers destinations and editorial relevant to the group travel market. Estab. 1994. Circ. 15,012. Byline given. Pays on publication. No kill fee. Editorial lead time 6 months. Submit seasonal material 6 months in advance. Accepts queries by mail, e-mail. Sample copy available online.

NONFICTION Needs travel. **Buys 75 mss/year.** Query with published clips. Length: 1,200-3,000 words. **Pays $0-1,000.**

$$ MIDWEST MEETINGS®

Hennen Publishing, 302 Sixth St. W, Brookings SD 57006. (605)692-9559. **Fax:** (605)692-9031. **E-mail:** info@midwestmeetings.com; editor@midwestmeetings.com. **Website:** www.midwestmeetings.com. **Contact:** Randy Hennen. **20% freelance written.** Quarterly magazine covering meetings/conventions industry. We provide information and resources to meeting/convention planners with a Midwest focus. Estab. 1996. Circ. 28,500. Byline given. Pays on acceptance. Publishes ms an average of 5 months after acceptance. Editorial lead time 3 months. Submit seasonal material 3 months in advance. Accepts queries by e-mail. Sample copy free. Guidelines by e-mail.

NONFICTION Needs essays, general interest, historical, how-to, humor, interview, personal experience, travel. Does not want marketing pieces related to specific hotels/meeting facilities. **Buys 15-20 mss/year.** Send complete ms. Length: 500-1,000 words. **Pays 5-50¢/word.**

$$ SCHOOL TRANSPORTATION NEWS

STN Media Co., P.O. Box 789, Redondo Beach CA 90277. (310)792-2226. **Fax:** (310)792-2231. **E-mail:** ryan@stnonline.com; sylvia@stonline.com. **Website:** www.stnonline.com. **Contact:** Ryan Gray, editor-in-chief; Sylvia Arroyo, managing editor. **20% freelance written.** Monthly magazine covering school bus and pupil transportation industries in North America. Contributors to *School Transportation News* must have a basic understanding of K-12 education and automotive fleets and specifically of school buses. Articles cover such topics as manufacturing, operations, maintenance and routing software, GPS, security and legislative affairs. A familiarity with these principles is preferred. Additional industry information is available on website. New writers must perform some research of the industry or exhibit core competencies in the subject matter. Estab. 1991. Circ. 24,000. Byline given. Pays on publication. No kill fee. Editorial lead time 1-2 months. Submit seasonal material 3 months in advance. Accepts queries by e-mail. Accepts simultaneous submissions. Sample copy free. Guidelines free.

NONFICTION Needs book excerpts, general interest, historical, humor, inspirational, interview, new product, personal experience, photo feature, technical. Does not want strictly localized editorial. Wants articles that put into perspective the issues of the day. Query with published clips. Length: 600-1,200 words. **Pays $150-300.** Sometimes pays expenses of writers on assignment.

$$ SPECIALTY TRAVEL INDEX

Alpine Hansen, P.O. Box 458, San Anselmo CA 94979. (415)455-1643. **E-mail:** info@specialtytravel.com. **Website:** www.specialtytravel.com. **90% freelance written.** Semiannual magazine covering adventure and special interest travel. Estab. 1980. Circ. 35,000. Byline given. Pays on receipt and acceptance of all materials. No kill fee. Editorial lead time 3 month. Submit seasonal material 3 months in advance. Accepts queries by mail, e-mail. Writer's guidelines on request.
NONFICTION Needs how-to, personal experience, photo feature, travel. **Buys 15 mss/year.** Query. Length: 1,250 words. **Pays $300 minimum.**

VETERINARY

$$ VETERINARY ECONOMICS

8033 Flint St., Lenexa KS 66214. (800)255-6864. **Fax:** (913)871-3808. **E-mail:** ve@advanstar.com. **Website:** http://veterinarybusiness.dvm360.com. **20% freelance written.** Monthly magazine covering veterinary practice management. "We address the business concerns and management needs of practicing veterinarians." Estab. 1960. Circ. 54,000. Byline given. Pays on publication. No kill fee. Publishes ms an average of 6 months after acceptance. Editorial lead time 3 months. Submit seasonal material 3 months in advance. Accepts queries by mail, e-mail. Accepts simultaneous submissions. Responds in 3 months to queries.
NONFICTION Needs how-to, interview, personal experience. **Buys 24 mss/year.** Send complete ms. Length: 1,000-2,000 words. **Pays $40-350.**
COLUMNS/DEPARTMENTS Practice Tips (easy, unique business tips), 250 words or fewer. Send complete ms. **Pays $40.**

CONTESTS & AWARDS

The contests and awards listed in this section are arranged by subject. Nonfiction writers can turn immediately to nonfiction awards listed alphabetically by the name of the contest or award. The same is true for fiction writers, poets, playwrights and screenwriters, journalists, children's writers, and translators. You'll also find general book awards, fellowships offered by arts councils and foundations, and multiple category contests.

New contests and awards are announced in various writer's publications nearly every day. However, many lose their funding or fold, and sponsoring magazines go out of business just as often. **Contact names, entry fees,** and **deadlines** have been highlighted and set in bold type for your convenience.

To make sure you have all the information you need about a particular contest, always send a SASE to the contact person in the listing before entering a contest or check their website. The listings in this section are brief, and many contests have lengthy, specific rules and requirements that we could not include in our limited space. Often a specific entry form must accompany your submission.

When you receive a set of guidelines, you'll see some contests are not applicable to all writers. The writer's age, previous publication, geographic location, and length of the work are common matters of eligibility. Read the requirements to ensure you don't enter a contest for which you're not qualified.

Winning a contest or award can launch a successful writing career. Take a professional approach by doing a little extra research. Find out who the previous winner of the award was by investing in a sample copy of the magazine in which the prize-winning article, poem, or short story appeared. Attend the staged reading of an award-winning play. Your extra effort will be to your advantage in competing with writers who simply submit blindly.

PLAYWRITING & SCRIPTWRITING

10 MINUTE PLAY CONTEST & FESTIVAL

Weathervane Playhouse, 1301 Weathervane Lane, Akron OH 44313. (330)836-2626. **E-mail:** 10minuteplay@weathervaneplayhouse.com. **Website:** www.weathervaneplayhouse.com. **Contact:** Eileen Moushey. Annual 8x10 TheatreFest. Must be US citizen 18 years or older. All rights remain with writers. Maximum running time is 10 minutes. Less is fine. Each year there is a special prop that must be incorporated into that year's plays. See website for details. All entries must be sent electronically, as attachments. Printed plays will not be considered. Guidelines available on website. The mission of the Weathervane Playhouse 8x10 TheatreFest is to promote the art of play writing, present new works, and introduce area audiences to the short play form. The competition will provide Weathervane with recognition for quality and innovative theatre. Deadline: May 15. Submission period begins December 1. Prize: Each of 8 finalists receive full productions of their plays during the Festival, held in mid-July. 1st Place: $350; 2nd Place: $250; 3rd Place: $150; 5 runners-up: $50 each. First round judges include individuals with experience in every area of stagecraft, including tech designers, actors, directors, stage managers, and playwrights.

THE ACADEMY NICHOLL FELLOWSHIP IN SCREENWRITING

1313 Vine St., Hollywood CA 90028-8107. (310)247-3010. **E-mail:** nicholl@oscars.org. **Website:** www.oscars.org/nicholl. An entrant's total earnings for motion picture and television writing may not exceed $25,000 before the end of the competition. This limit applies to compensation for motion picture and television writing services as well as for the sale of (or sale of an option on) screenplays, teleplays, stage plays, books, treatments, stories, premises and any other source material. Members and employees of the Academy of Motion Picture Arts and Sciences and their immediate families are not eligible, nor are competition judges and their immediate families. Deadline: April 10. The first and quarterfinal rounds are judged by industry professionals who are not members of the Academy. The semifinal round is judged by Academy members drawn from across the spectrum of the motion picture industry. The finalist scripts are judged by the Academy Nicholl Committee.

ACCLAIM FILM AND TV SCRIPT CONTESTS

Acclaim Scripts, 300 Central Ave, Suite 501, St. Petersburg FL 33701. **E-mail:** info@acclaimscripts.com. **Website:** www.acclaimscripts.com. Annual contest for TV and film scripts. Open to all writers worldwide. Work must be original material of the author(s). Must not be sold or optioned at time of submission. Multiple entries may be submitted (include separate entry form for each submission). Two categories for TV: comedy and drama. Deadline: February 7 (early); March 7 (regular); April 11 (late). Contests are ongoing and deadlines chance; visit website to check for updated deadlines. Prize: TV: Winner of each category receives $500. Film: 1st Place: $1,000. All winners and finalists may receive consideration by established production companies and agencies.

ACCOLADE COMPETITION

8837 Villa La Jolla Dr., #13131, La Jolla CA 92039. (858)454-9868. **E-mail:** info@accoladecompetition.org. **Website:** www.accoladecompetition.org. The Accolade Global Film Competition is unique in the industry. Attracting both powerhouse companies as well as talented new filmmakers it is an exceptional, truly international awards competition, not a traditional film festival—which allows filmmakers from around the world to enter their films in this prestigious competition. Currently in its 10th year, Accolade Global Film Competition is an avant-garde worldwide competition that strives to give talented directors, producers, actors, creative teams and new media creators the positive exposure they deserve. It discovers and honors the achievements of filmmakers who produce high quality shorts and new media. The Accolade promotes award winners through press releases to over 40,000 filmmakers, industry contacts and additional media/distribution outlets. We are currently creating a filmmaker representative program to assist with the distribution of award winning films. Submissions in other than English must be subtitled or include transcript. Multiple entries are allowed and each entry may be entered in multiple categories. Submit on DVD in NTSC or PAL format. Entries will not be returned. Deadline: March 7. Deadline changes, check website for up-to-date information. Prize: Awards include: Annual Humanitarian Award, Fast Focus Short Film Award, $4,800

Post-Production Award, and $1,500 Studio Award. See website for details on these awards. Also recognizes: Best of Show, Awards of Excellence, & Award of Merit. Best of Show honors are granted only if worthy productions are discovered. No more than 15% of entries are granted Awards of Excellence. Notable artistic and technical productions are recognized at the Award Of Merit award level. Judged by in-house staff.

ANNUAL AUSTIN FILM FESTIVAL SCREENPLAY & TELEPLAY COMPETITION

Austin Film Festival, 1801 Salina St., Austin TX 78702. (512)478-4795. **Fax:** (512)478-6205. **E-mail:** screenplaydirector@austinfilmfestival.com; info@austinfilmfestival.com. **Website:** www.austinfilmfestival.com. **Contact:** Matt Dy, screenplay competition director. The Austin Film Festival, held annually in late October, is looking for quality screenplays and teleplays which will be read by industry professionals. AFF provides 'Readers' notes' to all Second Rounders (top 10%) and higher for no charge. Two main categories: Drama Category and Comedy Category. Two optional Award Categories (additional entry of $20 per category); Latitude Productions Award and Dark Hero Studios Sci-Fi Award. Teleplay Competition: The teleplay competition is now open to pilots as well as spec scripts. Two main categories: Half-hour Sitcom and One-Hour Drama/Comedy. Deadline: Screenplay: April 30. Late Screenplay: May 31. Teleplay: April 30. Prize: $5,000 in Comedy and Drama; $2,500 for Sponsored Award and Sci-Fi Award.

ANNUAL NATIONAL PLAYWRITING COMPETITION

Wichita State University, School of Performing Arts, 1845 Fairmount, Box 153, Wichita KS 67260. (316)978-3646. **Fax:** (316)978-3202. **E-mail:** bret.jones@wichita.edu. **Contact:** Bret Jones, director of theatre. The contest will be open to all undergraduate and graduate students enrolled at any college or university in the United States. Please indicate school affiliation. All submissions must be original, unpublished and unproduced. Both full-length and one-act plays may be submitted. Full-length plays in 1 or more acts should be a minimum of 90 minutes playing time. Two or 3 short plays on related themes by the same author will be judged as 1 entry. The total playing time should be a minimum of 90 minutes. One-act plays should be a minimum of 30 minutes playing time to a maximum of 60 minutes playing time. Musicals should be a minimum of 90 minutes playing time and must include a CD of the accompanying music. Scripts should contain no more than 4-6 characters and setting must be suitable for an 85-seat Black box theatre. Eligible playwrights may submit up to 2 entries per contest year. One typewritten, bound copy should be submitted. Scripts must be typed and arranged in professional play script format. See information provided in *The Dramatist's Sourcebook* or the following website (www.pubinfo.vcu.edu/artweb/playwriting/format.html) for instruction on use of professional format. Two title pages must be included: 1 bound and the other unbound. The unbound title page should display the author's name, address, telephone number, and e-mail address if applicable. The bound title page should only display the name of the script; do not include any personal identifying information on the bound title page. Scripts may be submitted via e-mail. Submit in PDF format. Include all information requested for mail in scripts with electronic submission. Deadline: January 16. Prize: Production by the Wichita State University Theatre. Winner will be announced after March 15. No entry may be withdrawn after March 1. Judged by a panel of 3 or more selected from the school faculty. May also include up to 3 experienced, faculty approved WSU School of Performing Arts students.

BLUECAT SCREENPLAY COMPETITION

P.O. Box 2635, Hollywood CA 90028. **E-mail:** info@bluecatscreenplay.com. **Website:** www.bluecatscreenplay.com/. Since 1998, the BlueCat Screenplay Competition has developed and discovered thousands of writers through our commitment to providing written feedback to all entrants and substantial cash awards to their best screenplays. Scripts must be between 75-125 pages. Deadline: November 15. Prize: Feature winner receives $15,000. Four finalists receive $2,500. Short screenplay winner receives $10,000. Three finalists receive $1,500. Every writer recevies a written script analysis of their screenplay.

TIPS A list of past winners and their coverage is available online.

CALIFORNIA YOUNG PLAYWRIGHTS CONTEST

Playwrights Project, 3675 Ruffin Rd., Suite 330, San Diego CA 92123-1870. (858)384-2970. **Fax:** (858)384-2974. **E-mail:** write@playwrightsproject.org. **Website:** www.playwrightsproject.org. **Contact:** Cecelia Kouma, executive director. Annual contest open to Californians under age 19. Annual contest. "Our organization and the contest is designed to nurture promising young writers. We hope to develop playwrights and audiences for live theater. We also teach playwriting." Submissions are required to be unpublished and not produced professionally. Submissions made by the author. SASE for contest rules and entry form. Scripts must be a minimum of 10 standard typewritten pages; send 2 copies. Scripts will *not* be returned. If requested, entrants receive detailed evaluation letter. Guidelines available online. Deadline: June 1. Prize: Scripts will be produced in spring at a professional theatre in San Diego. Writers submitting scripts of 10 or more pages receive a detailed script evaluation letter upon request. Judged by professionals in the theater community, a committee of 5-7; changes somewhat each year.

CREATIVE WORLD AWARDS (CWA) INTERNATIONAL SCREENWRITING COMPETITION

4712 Admiralty Way #268, Marina del Rey CA 90292. **E-mail:** info@creativeworldawards.com. **Website:** www.creativeworldawards.com. **Contact:** Marlene Neubauer/Heather Waters. CWA's professionalism, industry innovation, and exclusive company list make this competition a leader in the industry. CWA offers the grand prize winner a production opportunity and has helped many past entrants get optioned and representation. CWA accepts all genres of features, shorts, and television. Check out the website for more details. All screenplays must be in English and in standard spec screenplay format. See website's FAQ page for more detailed information. Deadline: See website. Prize: Over $30,000 in cash and prizes awarded in 10 categories.

DRURY UNIVERSITY ONE-ACT PLAY CONTEST

Drury University, 900 N. Benton Ave., Springfield MO 65802-3344. **E-mail:** msokol@drury.edu. **Contact:** Mick Sokol. Offered in even-numbered years for unpublished and professionally unproduced plays. One play per playwright. Guidelines for SASE or by e-mail. Deadline: December 1. Prize: 1st Place: $300; Honorable Mention: $150.

ESSENTIAL THEATRE PLAYWRITING AWARD

The Essential Theatre, 1414 Foxhall Ln., #10, Atlanta GA 30316. (404) 212-0815. **E-mail:** pmhardy@aol.com. **Website:** www.essentialtheatre.com. **Contact:** Peter Hardy. Offered annually for unproduced, full-length plays by Georgia resident writers. No limitations as to style or subject matter. Submissions can be e-mailed in PDF or Word Documents, or sent by postal mail. See website for full guidelines. Deadline: April 23. Prize: $600 and full production.

SHUBERT FENDRICH MEMORIAL PLAYWRITING CONTEST

Pioneer Drama Service, Inc., P.O. Box 4267, Englewood CO 80155. (303)779-4035. **Fax:** (303)779-4315. **E-mail:** editors@pioneerdrama.com. **E-mail:** submissions@pioneerdrama.com. **Website:** www.pioneerdrama.com. **Contact:** Lori Conary, submissions editor. Annual competition that encourages the development of quality theatrical material for educational, community and children's theatre markets. Previously unpublished submissions only. Only considers mss with a running time between 20-90 minutes. Open to all writers not currently published by Pioneer Drama Service. Guidelines available online. No entry fee. Cover letter, SASE for return of ms, and proof of production or staged reading must accompany all submissions. Deadline: Ongoing contest; a winner is selected by June 1 each year from all submissions received the previous year. Prize: $1,000 royalty advance in addition to publication. Judged by editors.

GARDEN STATE FILM FESTIVAL SCREENPLAY COMPETITION

3101 Boardwalk, Tower Two, Suite 1405, Atlantic City NJ 08401. **E-mail:** info@gsff.org. **Website:** www.gsff.org. **Contact:** Diane Raver, executive director. This contest is designed to introduce audiences to the cinematic arts and assist in the revitalization of Asbury Park by filling a cultural void. Entered screenplays must not have been previously optioned, sold, or produced. All screenplays should be registered with the WGA and/or a Library of Congress copyright. Screenplays must be the original work of the writer. If based on another person's life story, a statement attesting to the rights obtained must be attached. No adaptations of other written work will be accepted. Multiple entries are accepted. A separate entry form and fee must accompany each script. Screenplays containing multiple writers are also accepted. Include two cover pages with each screenplay. One that only contains the screenplay's title. A second one that contains all contact information (name, address, phone, and email and Withoutabox tracking number). The writer's name must not appear any where inside the body of the screenplay. All screenplays must abide by proper industry format. All screenplays must be in English, with numbered, plain-write pages. All screenplays MUST be uploaded as a PDF via withoutbox.com. No substitutions of new drafts, or corrected pages, for any screenplay, for any reason, will be accepted after the initial submission. Please enter the draft you are most confident about. No individual feedback or coverage will be made available pertaining to submitted screenplays. Deadline: November 1. Submissions are accepted beginning June 1 each year. Prize: The winner receives a live staged reading with a professional director and professional actors in a seated venue during the festival.

THE MARILYN HALL AWARDS FOR YOUTH THEATRE

P.O. Box 148, Beverly Hills CA 90213. **Website:** www.beverlyhillstheatreguild.com. **Contact:** Candace Coster, competition coordinator. The Marilyn Hall Awards consist of 2 monetary prizes for plays suitable for grades 6-8 (middle school) or for plays suitable for grades 9-12 (high school). The 2 prizes will be awarded on the merits of the play scripts, which includes its suitability for the intended audience. The plays should be approximately 45-75 minutes in length. There is no production connected to any of the prizes, though a staged reading is optional at the discretion of the BHTG. Unpublished submissions only. Authors must be U.S. citizens or legal residents and must sign entry form personally. Deadline: The last day of February. Submission period begins January 15. Prize: 1st Prize: $700; 2nd Prize: $300.

HENRICO THEATRE COMPANY ONE-ACT PLAYWRITING COMPETITION

P.O. Box 90775, Henrico VA 23273. (804)501-5138. **Fax:** (804)501-5284. **E-mail:** per22@co.henrico.va.us. **Contact:** Amy A. Perdue, theatre arts specialist. Offered annually for previously unpublished or unproduced plays or musicals to produce new dramatic works in one-act form. Scripts with small casts and simpler sets given preference. Controversial themes and excessive language should be avoided. Only one-act plays or musicals will be considered. The manuscript should be a one-act original (not an adaptation), unpublished, and unproduced, free of royalty and copyright restrictions. Scripts with smaller casts and simpler sets may be given preference. Controversial themes and excessive language should be avoided. Standard play script form should be used. All plays will be judged anonymously; therefore, there should be two title pages; the first must contain the play's title and the author's complete address and telephone number. The second title page must contain only the play's title. The playwright must submit two excellent quality copies. Receipt of all scripts will be acknowledged by mail. Scripts will be returned if SASE is included. No scripts will be returned until after the winner is announced. The HTC does not assume responsibility for loss, damage or return of scripts. All reasonable care will be taken. Deadline: July 1. Prize: $300 prize. $200 to runner-up. Winning entries may be produced; DVD sent to author.

HRC SHOWCASE THEATRE PLAYWRITING CONTEST

P.O. Box 940, Hudson NY 12534. (518)851-7244. **E-mail:** hrcshowcaseplaycontest@gmail.com. **Website:** www.hrc-showcasetheatre.com. **Contact:** Jesse Waldinger, chair. HRC Showcase Theatre invites submissions of full-length plays to its annual contest from new, aspiring, or established playwrights. Each submitted play should be previously unpublished, run no more than 90 minutes, require no more than 6 actors, and be suitable for presentated as a staged reading by Equity actors. Deadline: March 1. Prize: $500. Four runner-ups will receive $100 each.

THE KILLER NASHVILLE SILVER FALCHION AWARD

Killer Nashville, P.O. Box 680759, Franklin TN 37068-0750. (615)599-4032. **E-mail:** awards@killernashville.com. **Website:** www.killernashville.com. **Contact:** Clay Stafford. Any fiction or nonfiction book-length work published for the first time in the previous calendar year, in which a crime drives the storyline, may be nominated by either the publisher or author of the book. Four copies of the work being nominated must be submitted with entry forms to be considered. Deadline: March 1. Entries will be evaluated by judges, who will choose five finalists from the following categories: Best Novel, Best First Novel, Best Paperback, Best e-Book Original, Best Nonfiction, Best Juvenile, Best Young Adult, and Best Anthology. Winners chosen by the Killer Nashville Writers' Conference attendees.

MCKNIGHT ADVANCEMENT FELLOWSHIP

The Playwrights' Center, 2301 Franklin Ave. E., Minneapolis MN 55406-1099. (612)332-7481. **Fax:** (612)332-6037. **Website:** www.pwcenter.org. **Contact:** Amanda Robbins-Butcher, artistic administrator. The Playwrights' Center today serves more playwrights in more ways than any other organization in the country. Applications are screened for eligibility by the Playwrights' Center and evaluated by an initial select panel of professional theater artists; finalists are then evaluated by a second panel of national theater artists. Selection is based on artistic excellence and professional achievement, and is guided by the Playwrights' Center's mission statement. The McKnight Advancement Fellowships recognize playwrights whose work demonstrates exceptional artistic merit and excellence in the field, and whose primary residence is in the state of Minnesota. Deadline: January 10. Prize: 2 fellowships of $25,000 each will be awarded. Additional funds of $2,500 can be used to support a play development workshop and other professional expenses.

MCLAREN MEMORIAL COMEDY PLAY WRITING COMPETITION

2000 W. Wadley, Midland TX 79705. (432)682-2544. **Fax:** (432)682-6136. **Website:** www.mctmidland.org. The McLaren Memorial Comedy Play Writing Competition was established to honor long-time MCT volunteer Mike McLaren who loved a good comedy, whether he was on stage or in the front row. Open to students. Annual contest. Unpublished submissions only. Submissions made by author. Rights to winning material acquired or purchased. First right of production or refusal is acquired by MCT. The contest is open to any playwright, but the play submitted must be unpublished and never produced in a for-profit setting. One previous production in a nonprofit theatre is acceptable. "Readings" do not count as productions. Deadline: February 28. Prize: $400. Judged by the audience present at the McLaren festival when the staged readings are performed.

NATIONAL ONE-ACT PLAYWRITING COMPETITION (CANADA)

Ottawa Little Theatre, 400 King Edward Ave., Ottawa ON K1N 7M7 Canada. (613)233-8948. **Fax:** (613)233-8027. **Website:** www.ottawalittletheatre.com. **Contact:** Lynn McGuigan, executive director. Encourages literary and dramatic talent in Canada. Guidelines available online. Deadline: October 15. Prize: 1st Place: $1,000; 2nd Place: $750; 3rd Place: $500; Sybil Cooke Award for a Play Written for Children or Young People: $500. All winning plays will receive a public reading in April, and the winning playwrights will have a one-on-one meeting with a resident dramaturg.

ONE-ACT PLAY CONTEST

Tennessee Williams/New Orleans Literary Festival, 938 Lafayette St., Suite 514, New Orleans LA 70113. (504)581-1144. **E-mail:** info@tennesseewilliams.net. **Website:** www.tennesseewilliams.net/contests. **Contact:** Paul J. Willis. Annual contest for an unpublished play. Plays should run no more than one hour in length. Unlimited entries per person. Production criteria include scripts requiring minimal technical support for a 100-seat theater. Cast of characters must be small. See website for additional guidelines and entry form. "The One-Act Play Competition is an opportunity for playwrights to see their work fully produced before a large audience during one of the largest literary festivals in the nation, and for the festival to showcase undiscovered talent." Deadline: November 1. Prize: $1,500, staged read at the next festival, full production at the festival the following year, VIP All-Access Festival pass for two years ($1,000 value), and publication in Bayou. Judged by an anonymous expert panel.

THE PAGE INTERNATIONAL SCREENWRITING AWARDS

The PAGE Awards Committee, 7510 Sunset Blvd., #610, Hollywood CA 90046-3408. **E-mail:** info@PAGEawards.com. **Website:** www.PAGEawards.com. **Contact:** Zoe Simmons, contest coordinator. Annual competition to discover the most talented new screenwriters from across the country and around the world. Each year, awards are presented to 31 screenwriters in 10 different genre categories: action/adventure, comedy, drama, family film, historical film, science fiction, thriller/horror, short film script, TV drama pilot, and TV comedy pilot. Guidelines and entry forms are online. The contest is open to all writers 18 years of age and older who have not previously earned more than $25,000 writing for film and/or television. Please visit contest website for a complete list of rules and regulations. Deadline: January 15 (early); February 15 (regular); March 15 (late); April 15 (last minute). Prize: Over $50,000 in cash and prizes, including a $25,000 grand prize, plus gold, silver, and bronze prizes in all 10 categories. Most importantly, the award-winning writers receive extensive publicity and industry exposure. Judging is done entirely by Hollywood professionals, including industry script readers, consultants, agents, managers, producers, and development executives.

SCRIPTAPALOOZA TELEVISION WRITING COMPETITION

7775 Sunset Blvd., Suite #200, Hollywood CA 90046. (310)801-5366. **E-mail:** info@scriptapalooza.com. **Website:** www.scriptapaloozatv.com. Biannual competition accepting entries in 4 categories: Reality shows, sitcoms, original pilots, and 1-hour dramas. There are more than 30producers, agents, and managers reading the winning scripts. Two past winners won Emmys because of Scriptapalooza and 1 past entrant now writes for Comedy Central. Winners announced February 15 and August 30. For contest results, visit website. Length: Standard television format whether 1 hour, 1-half hour, or pilot. Open to any writer 18 or older. Guidelines available on website. Accepts inquiries by e-mail or phone. Deadline: October 1 and April 15. Prize: 1st Place: $500; 2nd Place: $200; 3rd Place: $100 (in each category); production company consideration.

TIPS Pilots should be fresh, new, and easy to visualize. Spec scripts should stay current with the shows, up-to-date story lines, characters, etc.

SCRIPT PIPELINE SCREENWRITING COMPETITION

2900 Airport Ave., Unit F, Santa Monica CA 90405. (323)424-4243. **E-mail:** entry@scriptpipeline.com. **Website:** scriptpipeline.com. **Contact:** Matt Misetich, director of development. The Annual Script Pipeline Screenwriting Contest continues a long tradition of discovering up-and-coming creative talent and connecting them with top producers, agencies, and managers across both studio and independent markets. This process has proven enormously successful, with numerous screenwriting contest alumni worldwide finding elite representation and gaining crucial introductions to otherwise impossible-to-reach industry executives. This is an international competition open to all original feature film screenplays that have yet to be produced, optioned, or sold. Open to writers 18 years and older. All genres, styles, and formats accepted. Over 200 companies review the finalists, and numerous contest alumni have caught the attention of major agencies, including WME, Paradigm, and CAA. The result: $5 million in specs sold from Pipeline competition finalists and "Recommend" writers since 2003. Last season, close to 5,000 scripts were entered in the Screenwriting and TV Writing contests combined, making Script Pipeline one of the leading companies reviewing spec material. Early deadline: March 1. Regular deadline: May 1. Prize: $20,000 in cash for the winner and $1,000 in cash to the runner0up.

SOUTHERN PLAYWRIGHTS COMPETITION

Jacksonville State University, Department of English, 700 Pelham Rd. N., Jacksonville AL 36265-1602. (256)782-5498. **Fax:** (256)782-5441. **E-mail:** smoersch@jsu.edu. **E-mail:** swhitton@jsu.edu. **Website:** www.jsu.edu/depart/english/southpla.htm. **Contact:** Sarah Moersch. Competition for playwrights native to or a resident of Alabama, Arkansas, Florida, Georgia, Kentucky, Louisiana, Mississippi, North Carolina, South Carolina, Tennessee, Texas, Virginia, or West Virginia. Plays must deal with the Southern experience. Entries must be original, full-length plays. No musicals or adaptations will be accepted. The playwright may submit only one play. All entries must be typed, securely bound, and clearly identified. Synopsis of script must be included. No electronic entries accepted. Legal clearance of all materials not in the public domain will be the responsibility of the playwright. The Southern Playwrights Competition seeks to identify and encourage the best of Southern playwriting. Deadline: January 15. Prize: $1,000 and production of the play.

SOUTHWEST WRITERS ANNUAL WRITING CONTEST

3200 Carlisle Blvd., NE Suite #114, Albuquerque NM 87110. (505)830-6034. **E-mail:** swwriters@juno.com. **Website:** www.southwestwriters.com. The SouthWest Writers Writing Contest encourages and honors excellence in writing. In addition to competing for cash prizes, contest entrants may receive an optional written critique of their entry from a qualified contest critiquer. Non-profit organization dedicated to helping members of all levels in their writing. Members enjoy perks such as networking with professional and aspiring writers; substantial discounts on mini-conferences, workshops, writing classes, and annual and quarterly SWW writing contest; monthly newsletter; two writing programs per month; critique groups, critique service (also for nonmembers); discounts at bookstores and other businesses; and website linking. Deadline: May 1 (up to May 15 with a late fee). Submissions begin February 1. Prize: A 1st, 2nd, and 3rd place winner will be judged in each of the categories. 1st place: $300; 2nd place: $200; 3rd place: $150. Judged by a panel; the top 10 in each category will be sent to appropriate editors or literary agents to determine the final top 3 places.

TELEVISION OUTREACH PROGRAM (TOP)

The Scriptwriters Network (SWN), P.O. Box 642806, Los Angeles CA 90064. **E-mail:** info@scriptwritersnetwork.org. **E-mail:** top@scriptwritersnetwork.org. **Website:** www.scriptwritersnetwork.org. **Contact:** Hoda Shoukry and Mark Litton, co-directors. The Television Outreach Program (TOP) is a Scriptwriters Network program to support undiscovered television writing talent. The program's objective is to help writers improve their craft so that they may achieve their goals of obtaining representation, script development, mentoring and career counseling services, landing writing assignments, and/or selling their work.

THEATRE CONSPIRACY ANNUAL NEW PLAY CONTEST

Theatre Conspiracy, 10091 McGregor Blvd., Ft. Myers FL 33919. (239)936-3239. **E-mail:** info@theatreconspiracy.org. **Website:** theatreconspiracy.org. **Contact:** Bill Taylor, producing artistic director. Offered annually for full-length plays that are unproduced. Work submitted to the contest must be a full length play with 7 actors or less and have simple to moderate technical demands. Plays having up to three previous productions are welcome. No musicals. Deadline: March 30. Prize: $700 and full production. Judged by a panel of qualified theatre teachers, directors, and performers.

JACKIE WHITE MEMORIAL NATIONAL CHILDREN'S PLAY WRITING CONTEST

1800 Nelwood, Columbia MO 65202-1447. (573)874-5628. **E-mail:** bybetsy@yahoo.com. **Website:** www.cectheatre.org. **Contact:** Betsy Phillips, contest director. Annual contest that encourages playwrights to write quality plays for family audiences Previously unpublished submissions only. Submissions made by author. Play may be performed during the following season. All submissions will be read by at least 3 readers. Author will receive a written evaluation of the script. Guidelines available online. Send materials to: Betsy Phillips, Jackie White Memorial National Children's Playwriting Contest, 309 Parkade Blvd., Columbia, MO 65202-1447. Deadline: June 1. Prize: $500 with production possible. Judging by current and past board members of CEC and by non-board members who direct plays at CEC.

WRITE NOW

Indiana Repertory Theatre, 140 W. Washington St., Indianapolis IN 46204. 480-921-5770. **E-mail:** info@writenow.co. **Website:** www.writenow.co. The purpose of this biennial workshop is to encourage writers to create strikingly original scripts for young audiences. It provides a forum through which each playwright receives constructive criticism and the support of a development team consisting of a professional director and dramaturg. Finalists will spend approximately one week in workshop with their development team. At the end of the week, each play will be read as a part of the Write Now convening. Guidelines available online. Deadline: July 31.

YOUNG PLAYWRIGHTS FESTIVAL NATIONAL PLAYWRITING COMPETITION

Young Playwrights, Inc., P.O. Box 5134, New York NY 10185. (212)594-5440. **Fax:** (212)594-5441. **E-mail:** literary@youngplaywrights.org. **Website:** youngplaywrights.org. **Contact:** Literary Manager. The Young Playwrights Inc. Festival National Playwriting Competition is offered annually to identify talented American playwrights aged 18 or younger. Please include your address, phone number, email address, and date of birth on the title page. Open to US residents only. Deadline: January 2 (postmarked). Prize: Winners receive an invitation to New York City for the annual Young Playwrights, Inc. Writers Conference and a professionally staged reading of their play. Entrants retain all rights to their work.

YOUNG PLAYWRIGHTS INC. WRITE A PLAY! NYC COMPETITION

Young Playwrights, Inc., Young Playwrights Inc. NYC, P.O. Box 5134, New York NY 10185. (212)594-5440.

Fax: (212)684-4902. **E-mail:** literary@youngplaywrights.org. **Website:** www.youngplaywrights.org. **Contact:** Literary Manager. Offered annually for stage plays of any length (no musicals, screenplays, or adaptations) by NYC elementary, middle, and high school students only. Play must be submitted by students, not teachers. There are no restrictions on length, style, or subject, but collaborations of more than 3 writers will not be accepted. Screenplays and musicals are not eligible, nor are adaptations. Scripts should be typed and stapled, and pages must be numbered. Scripts must have a cover page with title of play, playwright's name, home address (with apartment number and zip code), phone number, school, grade, and date of birth. Submit a copy of your play and keep the original; scripts will not be returned. Deadline: postmarked on or before March 2. Prize: Prize varies.

ANNA ZORNIO MEMORIAL CHILDREN'S THEATRE PLAYWRITING COMPETITION

University of New Hampshire, Department of Theatre and Dance, PCAC, 30 Academic Way, Durham NH 03824. (603)862-3038. **Fax:** (603)862-0298. **E-mail:** mike.wood@unh.edu. **Website:** http://cola.unh.edu/theatre-dance/resource/zornio. **Contact:** Michael Wood. Offered every 4 years for unpublished well-written plays or musicals appropriate for young audiences with a maximum length of 60 minutes. May submit more than 1 play, but not more than 3. Honors the late Anna Zornio, an alumna of The University of New Hampshire, for dedication to and inspiration of playwriting for young people, K-12th grade. Deadline: March of 2017. Prize: $500.

ARTS COUNCILS & FELLOWSHIPS

$50,000 GIFT OF FREEDOM

A Room of Her Own Foundation, P.O. Box 778, Placitas NM 87043. **E-mail:** awards@aroho.org. **Website:** www.aroomofherownfoundation.org. **Contact:** Tracey Cravens-Gras, associate director. The publicly funded award provides very practical help—both materially and in professional guidance and moral support with mentors and advisory council—to assist women in making their creative contribution to the world. The Gift of Freedom competition will determine superior finalists from each of 3 genres: Creative nonfiction, fiction, and poetry. Open to female residents of the US. Award application cycle dates are yet to be determined. Visit website at www.aroho.org for more information about the next application window. Deadline: November 2. Prize: One genre finalist will be awarded the $50,000 Gift of Freedom grant, distributed over 2 years in support of the completion of a particular creative project. The 2 remaining genre finalists will each receive a $5,000 prize.

ADVANCED ARTIST AWARD

Government of Yukon, P.O. Box 2703, (L-3), Whitehorse YT Y1A 2C6 Canada. (867)667-8789. **Fax:** (867)393-6456. **E-mail:** artsfund@gov.yk.ca. **Website:** www.tc.gov.yk.ca/aaa.html. The Advanced Artist Award (AAA) assists individual Yukon visual, literary and performing artists practicing at a senior level with innovative projects, travel, or educational pursuits that contribute to their personal artistic development and to their community. The intended results and outcomes of the Advanced Artist Award are to encourage artistic creativity, to enable artists to develop their skills, and to improve the ability of artists to promote their works or talents. Guidelines and application available online. Deadlines: April 1 and October 1. Prize: Level A artists: up to $10,000; Level B artists: up to $5,000. Judged by peer assessment (made up of senior Yukon artists representing the various disciplines seen in applicants for that round).

GEORGE BENNETT FELLOWSHIP

Phillips Exeter Academy, 20 Main St., Exeter NH 03833. **E-mail:** teaching_opportunities@exeter.edu. **Website:** www.exeter.edu/bennettfellowship. Annual award for fellow and family to provide time and freedom from material considerations to a person seriously contemplating or pursuing a career as a writer. Applicants should have a manuscript in progress which they intend to complete during the fellowship period. Manuscript should be fiction, nonfiction, novel, short stories, or poetry. Duties: To be in residency at the Academy for the academic year; to make oneself available informally to students interested in writing. Committee favors writers who have not yet published a book with a major publisher. Deadline for application: November 30. A choice will be made, and all entrants notified in mid-April. Prize: Cash stipend (currently $14,933), room and board. Judged by committee of the English department.

CHLA RESEARCH GRANTS

Children's Literature Association, 1301 W. 22nd Street, Suite 202, Oak Brook IL 60523. (630)571-

4520. **Fax:** (708)876-5598. **E-mail:** info@childlitassn.org. **Website:** www.childlitassn.org. **Contact:** ChLA Grants Chair. Offered annually. Three types of grants are available: Faculty Research Grants, Beiter Graduate Student Research Grants, and Diversity Research Grant. The grants are awarded for proposals dealing with criticism or original scholarship with the expectation that the undertaking will lead to publication (or a conference presentation for student awards) and make a significant contribution to the field of children's literature in the area of scholarship or criticism. Funds are not intended for work leading to the completion of a professional degree. Guidelines available online. Deadline: February 1. Prize: $500-1,500. Judged by the ChLA Grants Committee and Diversity Committee, respectively.

DOBIE PAISANO WRITER'S FELLOWSHIP

The Graduate School, The University of Texas at Austin, Attn: Dobie Paisano Program, 110 Inner Campus Drive Stop G0400, Austin TX 78712-0531. (512)232-3609. **Fax:** (512)471-7620. **E-mail:** gbarton@austin.utexas.edu. **Website:** www.utexas.edu/ogs/Paisano. **Contact:** Gwen Barton. Sponsored by the Graduate School at The University of Texas at Austin and the Texas Institute of Letters, the Dobie Paisano Fellowship Program provides solitude, time, and a comfortable place for Texas writers or writers who have written significantly about Texas through fiction, nonfiction, poetry, plays, or other mediums. The Dobie Paisano Ranch is a very rural and rustic setting, and applicants should read the guidelines closely to insure their ability to reside in this secluded environment. At the time of the application, the applicant must meet one of the following requirements: (1) be a native Texan, (2) have resided in Texas at least three years at some time, or (3) have published significant work with a Texas subject. Those who meet requirement 1 or 2 do not have to meet the Texas subject matter restriction. Deadline: January 15. Prize: The Ralph A. Johnston memorial Fellowship is for a period of 4 months with a stipend of $6,250 per month. It is aimed at writers who have already demonstrated some publishing and critical success. The Jesse H. Jones Writing Fellowship is for a period of approximately 6 months with a stipend of $3,000 per month. It is aimed at, but not limited to, writers who are early in their careers.

TIPS "Three sets of each complete application must be submitted. Electronic submissions are not allowed. Guidelines and application forms are on the website (http://www.utexas.edu/ogs/Paisano/info.html) or may be requested by sending a SASE (3-ounce postage) to the above address, attention of 'Dobie Paisano Fellowship Project.'"

FELLOWSHIPS FOR CREATIVE AND PERFORMING ARTISTS AND WRITERS

American Antiquarian Society, 185 Salisbury St., Worcester MA 01609-1634. (508)755-5221. **Fax:** (508)753-3311. **Website:** www.americanantiquarian.org. **Contact:** James David Moran. Annual fellowship for creative and performing artists, writers, filmmakers, journalists, and other persons whose goals are to produce imaginative, non-formulaic works dealing with pre-20th century American history. Application instructions available online. Website also lists potential fellowship projects. Deadline: October 5. Prize: The stipend will be $1,350 for fellows residing on campus (rent-free) in the society's scholars' housing, located next to the main library building. The stipend will be $1,850 for fellows residing off campus. Fellows will not be paid a travel allowance. Judged by AAS staff and outside reviewers.

TIPS "Successful applicants are those whose work is for the general public rather than for academic or educational audiences."

THE HODDER FELLOWSHIP

Lewis Center for the Arts, 185 Nassau St., Princeton NJ 08544. (609)258-6926. **E-mail:** ysabelg@princeton.edu. **Website:** arts.princeton.edu. **Contact:** Ysabel Gonzalez, fellowships assistant. The Hodder Fellowship will be given to writers of exceptional promise to pursue independent projects at Princeton University during the current academic year. Typically the fellows are poets, playwrights, novelists, creative nonfiction writers and translators who have published one highly acclaimed work and are undertaking a significant new project that might not be possible without the "studious leisure" afforded by the fellowship. Preference is given to applicants outside academia. Candidates for the Ph.D. are not eligible. Submit a resume, sample of previous work (10 pages maximum, not returnable), and a project proposal of 2-3 pages. Guidelines available on website. Princeton University is an equal opportunity employer and complies with applicable EEO and affirmative action regulations. Apply online. Deadline: October 1. Open to applications in July. Prize: $75,000 stipend.

MARILYN HOLINSHEAD VISITING SCHOLARS FELLOWSHIP

University of Minnesota, 113 Anderson Library, 222 21st Ave. South, Minneapolis MN 55455. **Website:** http://www.lib.umn.edu/clrc/awards-grants-and-fellowships. Marilyn Hollinshead Visiting Scholars Fund for Travel to the Kerlan Collection is available for research study. Applicants may request up to $1,500. Send a letter with the proposed purpose and plan to use specific research materials (manuscripts and art), dates, and budget (including airfare and per diem). Travel and a written report on the project must be completed and submitted in the previous year. Deadline: January 30.

INDIVIDUAL EXCELLENCE AWARDS

Ohio Arts Council, 30 E. Broad St., 33rd Floor, Columbus OH 43215-2613. (614)466-2613. **E-mail:** olgahelpdesk@oac.state.oh.us. **Website:** www.oac.state.oh.us. The Individual Excellence Awards program recognizes outstanding accomplishments by artists in a variety of disciplines. The awards give the artists who receive them the time and resources to experiment, explore and reflect as they develop their skills and advance their art form. They also provide affirmation and acknowledgment of the excellent work of Ohio artists. In odd-numbered years, applications will be accepted in: choreography, criticism, fiction/nonfiction, music composition, playwriting/screenplays, and poetry. In even-numbered years, applications will be accepted in: crafts, design arts/illustration, interdisciplinary/performance art, media arts, photography, and visual arts. Applicants must be an Ohio resident for 1 year prior to the deadline and cannot be a student enrolled in any degree- or certificate-granting program. Length: 20-30 pages fiction/nonfiction, 10-15 pages poetry, 30-50 pages criticism, 1 play or 2 short 1-act plays. Cover letter should include name, address, title of work. None of this information should appear on the actual manuscript. Writers may submit own work. Deadline: September 1. Prize: $5,000. Judged by 3-person panel of out-of-state panelists, anonymous review.

TIPS "Submit concise bodies of work or sections, not a sampling of styles."

MINNESOTA STATE ARTS BOARD ARTIST INITIATIVE GRANT

Minnesota State Arts Board, Park Square Court, Suite 200, 400 Sibley St., St. Paul MN 55101-1928. (651)215-1600 or (800)866-2787. **Fax:** (651)215-1602. **E-mail:** kathee.foran@arts.state.mn.us. **Website:** www.arts.state.mn.us. **Contact:** Kathee Foran, program officer. The Artist Initiative Grant Program is designed to support and assist professional Minnesota artists at various stages in their careers by encouraging artistic development, nurturing artistic creativity, and recognizing the contributions of individual artists to the creative environment of the state of Minnesota. Literary categories include prose, poetry, playwriting, and screenwriting. Open to Minnesota residents. Prize: Grant amounts of $2,000-10,000

OREGON LITERARY FELLOWSHIPS

925 S.W. Washington, Portland OR 97205. (503)227-2583. **E-mail:** susan@literary-arts.org. **Website:** www.literary-arts.org. **Contact:** Susan Denning, director of programs and events. Oregon Literary Fellowships are intended to help Oregon writers initiate, develop or complete literary projects in poetry, fiction, literary nonfiction, drama and young readers literature. Writers in the early stages of their career are encouraged to apply. The awards are merit-based. Guidelines available in February for SASE. Accepts inquiries by e-mail, phone. Oregon residents only. Recipients announced in January. Deadline: Last Friday in June. Prize: $2,500 minimum award, for approximately 10 writers and 2 publishers. Judged by out-of-state writers

TENNESSEE ARTS COMMISSION LITERARY FELLOWSHIP

Tennessee Arts Commission, 401 Charlotte Ave., Nashville TN 37243-0780. **Fax:** (615)741-8559. **E-mail:** lee.baird@state.tn.us. **Website:** tn.gov/arts. **Contact:** Lee Baird, director of literary programs. Awarded annually in recognition of professional Tennessee artists, i.e., individuals who have received financial compensation for their work as professional writers. Applicants must have a publication history other than vanity press. Three fellowships awarded annually to outstanding literary artists who live and work in Tennessee. Categories are in fiction, creative nonfiction, and poetry. Deadline: January 26. Prize: $5,000. Judged by an out-of-state adjudicator.

VERMONT ARTS COUNCIL

136 State St., Montpelier VT 05633-6001. (802)828-3293. **Fax:** (802)828-3363. **E-mail:** zeastes@vermontartscouncil.org. **Website:** www.vermontartscouncil.org. **Contact:** Sonia Rae, (802)828-4325 or by e-mail at

srae@vermontartscouncil.org. Annual grants awarded once per year for specific projects. Creation Grants (awards of $3,000) for artists working in any medium including writers, visual artists and performing artists. Three-year Arts Partnership Grants of up to $7,000 and annual Project Grants of up to $3,000 for not-for-profit organizations (including writing programs and not-for-profit presses). Rolling grants are available in the following categories: Artist Development Grants of up to $1,000 providing professional development funds for individual artists and Technical Assistance Grants of up to $1,500 providing grants for organizational development to non-profit arts organizations. Open to Vermont residents only.

FICTION

24-HOUR SHORT STORY CONTEST

WritersWeekly.com, 5726 Cortez Rd. W., #349, Bradenton FL 34210. **E-mail:** writersweekly@writersweekly.com. **Website:** www.writersweekly.com/misc/contest.php. **Contact:** Angela Hoy. Quarterly contest in which registered entrants receive a topic at start time (usually noon Central Time) and have 24 hours to write a story on that topic. All submissions must be returned via e-mail. Each contest is limited to 500 people. Upon entry, entrant will receive guidelines and details on competition, including submission process. Deadline: Quarterly—see website for dates. Prize: 1st Place: $300; 2nd Place: $250; 3rd Place: $200. There are also 20 honorable mentions and 60 door prizes (randomly drawn from all participants). The top 3 winners' entries are posted on WritersWeekly.com (non-exclusive electronic rights only) and receive a Freelance Income Kit. Writers retain all rights to their work. See website for full details on prizes. Judged by Angela Hoy (publisher of WritersWeekly.com and Booklocker.com).

AEON AWARD

Albedo One/Aeon Press, Aeon Award, Albedo One, 2 Post Road, Lusk, Dublin Ireland. +353 1 8730177. **E-mail:** fraslaw@yahoo.co.uk. **Website:** www.albedo1.com. **Contact:** Frank Ludlow, event coordinator. Prestigious fiction writing competition for short stories in any speculative fiction genre, such as fantasy, science fiction, horror, or anything in-between or unclassifiable. Submit your story (which must be less than 10,000 words in length and previously unpublished) in the body of an e-mail with contact details and "Aeon Award Submission" as the subject. Deadline: November 30. Contest begins January 1. Prize: Grand Prize: €1,000; 2nd Prize: €200;, and 3rd Prize: €100. The top three stories are guaranteed publication in *Albedo One*. Judged by Ian Watson, Eileen Gunn, Todd McCaffrey, and Michael Carroll.

AHWA FLASH & SHORT STORY COMPETITION

AHWA (Australian Horror Writers Association), **E-mail:** ahwacomps@australianhorror.com; ahwa@australianhorror.com. **E-mail:** ctrost@hotmail.com. **Website:** www.australianhorror.com. **Contact:** David Carroll, competitions officer. Competition/award for short stories and flash fiction. There are 2 categories: short stories (1,001 to 5,000 words) and flash fiction (less than 1,000 words). Writers may submit to one or both categories, but entry is limited to 1 story per author per category. Please send submission as an attached rtf or doc. Mail submissions only accepted as a last resort. No previously published entries will be accepted—all tales must be an original work by the author. Stories can be as violent or as bloody as the storyline dictates, but those containing gratuitous sex or violence will not be considered. Please check entries for spelling and grammar mistakes and follow standard submission guidelines (eg, 12 point font, Ariel, Times New Roman, or Courier New, one and a half spacing between lines, with title and page number on each page). Looking for horror stories, tales that frighten, yarns that unsettle readers in their comfortable homes. All themes in this genre will be accepted, from the well-used (zombies, vampires, ghosts etc) to the highly original, so long as the story is professional and well written. Deadline: May 31. Prize: The authors of the winning Flash Fiction and Short Story entries will each receive paid publication in *Midnight Echo*, The Magazine of the AHWA and an engraved plaque.

AMERICAN MARKETS NEWSLETTER SHORT STORY COMPETITION

1974 46th Ave., San Francisco CA 94116. **E-mail:** sheila.oconnor@juno.com. Award is to give short story writers more exposure. Contest offered biannually. Open to any writer. All kinds of fiction are considered. Especially looking for women's pieces—romance, with a twist in the tale—but all will be considered. Results announced within 3 months of deadlines. Winners notified by mail if they include SASE. Accepts fiction and nonfiction up to 2,000 words. Entries are eligible for cash prizes, and all entries are eligible for worldwide syndication whether they win or not. For guidelines, send SASE, fax or e-mail. Published and unpublished stories are actively encouraged. Add a note of where and when previously published. Send double-spaced mss with your story/article title, byline, word count, and address on the first page above your article/story's first paragraph (no need for separate cover page). There is no limit to the number of entries you may send. Deadline: June 30 and December 31. Prize: 1st Place: $300; 2nd Place: $100; 3rd Place: $50. Judged by a panel of independent judges.

THE SHERWOOD ANDERSON FOUNDATION FICTION AWARD

12330 Ashton Mill Terrace, Glen Allen VA 23059. **E-mail:** sherwoodandersonfoundation@gmail.com. **Website:** www.sherwoodandersonfoundation.org. **Contact:** Anna McKean, foundation president. Contest is to honor, preserve and celebrate the memory and literary work of Sherwood Anderson, American realist for the first half of the 20th century. Annual award supports developing writers of short stories and novels. Entrants must have published at least one book of fiction or have had several short stories published in major literary and/or commercial publication. Self-published stories do not qualify. Send a detailed résumé that includes a bibliography of your publications. Include a cover letter that provides a history of your writing experience and your plans for writing projects. Also, submit 2 or 3 examples of what you consider to be your best work. Do not send manuscripts by e-mail. Only mss in English will be accepted. Open to any writer who meets the qualifications listed above. Accepts inquiries by e-mail. Mail your application to the above address. No mss or publications will be returned. Deadline: April 1. Prize: $20,000 grant award.

SHERWOOD ANDERSON SHORT FICTION AWARD

Mid-American Review, Mid-American Review, Dept. of English, Box WM, BGSU, Bowling Green OH 43403. (419)372-2725. **Fax:** (419)372-4642. **E-mail:** mar@bgsu.edu. **Website:** www.bgsu.edu/midamericanreview. **Contact:** Abigail Cloud, editor-in-chief. Offered annually for unpublished mss (6,000 word limit). Contest is open to all writers not associated with a judge or *Mid-American Review*. Guidelines available online or for SASE. Deadline: November 1. Prize: $1,000, plus publication in the spring issue of *Mid-American Review*. Four Finalists: Notation, possible publication. Judged by editors and a well-known writer, i.e., Aimee Bender or Anthony Doerr.

AUTUMN HOUSE FICTION PRIZE

Autumn House Press, 87 ½ Westwood St., Pittsburgh PA 15211. **E-mail:** info@autumnhouse.org. **Website:** http://autumnhouse.org. Fiction submissions should be approximately 200-300 pages. All fiction sub-genres (short stories, short-shorts, novellas, or novels), or any combination of sub-genres, are eligible. All finalists will be considered for publication. Include SASE for results. Autumn House Press assumes no responsibility for lost or damaged manuscripts. All entries must be clearly marked "Fiction Prize" on the outside envelope. Thirty dollar handling fee (check or money order) must be enclosed. Send manuscript and fee to: Autumn House Press: P.O. Box 60100, Pittsburgh, PA 15211. Deadline: June 30. Prize: Winners will receive book publication, $1,000 advance against royalties, and a $1,500 travel grant to participate in the Autumn House Master Authors Series in Pittsburgh. Final judge is Sharon Dilworth.

BALCONES FICTION PRIZE

Austin Commmunity College, Department of Creative Writing, 1212 Rio Grande St., Austin TX 78701. (512)584-5045. **E-mail:** joconne@austincc.edu. **Website:** http://www.austincc.edu/crw/html/balconescenter.html. **Contact:** Joe O'Connell. Awarded to the best book of literary fiction published the previous year. Books of prose may be submitted by publisher or author. Send three copies. Deadline: January 31. Prize: $1,500, winner is flown to Austin for a campus reading.

THE BALTIMORE REVIEW CONTESTS

The Baltimore Review, 6514 Maplewood Rd., Baltimore MD 21212. **Website:** www.baltimorereview.org. **Contact:** Barbara Westwood Diehl, senior editor. Each summer and winter issue includes a contest theme (see submissions guidelines for theme). Prizes are awarded for first, second, and third place among all categories—poetry, short stories, and creative nonfiction. All entries are considered for publication. Open to all writers. Only unpublished work will be considered. Asks only for the right to publish the work for the first time. Deadline: May 31 and November 30. Prize: 1st Place: $500; 2nd Place: $200; 3rd Place: $100. All entries are considered for publication.

Judged by the editors of *The Baltimore Review* and a guest, final judge.

BARD FICTION PRIZE

Bard College, P.O. Box 5000, Annandale-on-Hudson NY 12504-5000. (845)758-7087. **E-mail:** bfp@bard.edu. **Website:** www.bard.edu/bfp. **Contact:** Irene Zedlacher. The Bard Fiction Prize is awarded to a promising, emerging writer who is an American citizen aged 39 years or younger at the time of application. Cover letter should include name, address, phone, e-mail and name of publisher where book was previously published. Entries must be previously published. Open to U.S. citizens aged 39 and below. Guidelines available by SASE, fax, phone, e-mail, or on website. Results announced by October 15. Winners notified by phone. For contest results, e-mail, or visit website. The Bard Fiction Prize is intended to encourage and support young writers of fiction to pursue their creative goals and to provide an opportunity to work in a fertile and intellectual environment. Deadline: June 15. Prize: $30,000 and appointment as writer-in-residence at Bard College for 1 semester.

BELLEVUE LITERARY REVIEW GOLDENBERG PRIZE FOR FICTION

Bellevue Literary Review, NYU Dept of Medicine, 550 First Ave., OBV-A612, New York NY 10016. (212)263-3973. **E-mail:** info@blreview.org; stacy@blreview.org. **Website:** www.blreview.org. **Contact:** Stacy Bodziak, managing editor. The BLR prizes award outstanding writing related to themes of health, healing, illness, the mind and the body. Annual competition/award for short stories. Receives about 200-300 entries per category. Send credit card information or make checks payable to Bellevue Literary Review. Guidelines available in February. Accepts inquiries by e-mail, phone, mail. Submissions open in February. Results announced in December and made available to entrants with SASE, by e-mail, on website. Winners notified by mail, by e-mail. Entries should be unpublished. Anyone may enter contest. Length: No minimum; maximum of 5,000 words. Writers may submit own work. Deadline: July 1. Prize: $1,000 and publication in *The Bellevue Literary Review*. BLR editors select semi-finalists to be read by an independent judge who chooses the winner. Previous judges include Nathan Englander, Jane Smiley, Francine Prose, and Andre Dubus III.

BINGHAMTON UNIVERSITY JOHN GARDNER FICTION BOOK AWARD

Creative Writing Program, Binghamton University, Binghamton University, Department of English, General Literature, and Rhetoric, Library North Room 1149, P.O. Box 6000, Binghamton NY 13902-6000. (607)777-2713. **E-mail:** cwpro@binghamton.edu. **Website:** http://binghamton.edu/english/creative-writing/. **Contact:** Maria Mazziotti Gillan, director. Contest offered annually for a novel or collection of fiction published in previous year in a press run of 500 copies or more. Each book submitted must be accompanied by an application form. Publisher may submit more than 1 book for prize consideration. Send 3 copies of each book. Guidelines available on website. Author or publisher may submit. Deadline: March 1. Prize: $1,000. Judged by a professional writer not on Binghamton University faculty.

BOULEVARD SHORT FICTION CONTEST FOR EMERGING WRITERS

Boulevard Magazine, 6614 Clayton Rd., PMB #325, Richmond Heights MO 63117. (314)862-2643. **Website:** www.richardburgin.net/boulevard. **Contact:** Jessica Rogen, managing editor. Offered annually for unpublished short fiction to a writer who has not yet published a book of fiction, poetry, or creative nonfiction with a nationally distributed press. Holds first North American rights on anything not previously published. Open to any writer with no previous publication by a nationally known press. Guidelines for SASE or on website. Accepts works up to 8,000 words. Simultaneous submissions are allowed, but previously accepted or published work is ineligible. Entries will be judged by the editors of *Boulevard Magazine*. Submit online or via postal mail. Deadline: December 31. Prize: $1,500, and publication in 1 of the next year's issues.

THE CAINE PRIZE FOR AFRICAN WRITING

51 Southwark St., London SE1 1RU United Kingdom. **E-mail:** info@caineprize.com. **Website:** www.caineprize.com. **Contact:** Lizzy Attree. Entries must have appeared for the first time in the 5 years prior to the closing date for submissions, which is January 31 each year. Publishers should submit 6 copies of the published original with a brief cover note (no pro forma application). "Please indicate nationality or passport held." Submissions should be made by publishers

only. Only one story per author will be considered in any one year. Only fiction work is eligible. Indicative length is between 3,000 and 10,000 words. See website for more details and rules. The Caine Prize is open to writers from anywhere in Africa for work published in English. Its focus is on the short story, reflecting the contemporary development of the African storytelling tradition. Deadline: January 31. Prize: £10,000.

JOHN W. CAMPBELL MEMORIAL AWARD FOR BEST SCIENCE FICTION NOVEL OF THE YEAR

English Department, University of Kansas, Lawrence KS 66045. (785)864-3380. **Fax:** (785)864-1159. **E-mail:** cmckit@ku.edu. **Website:** www.sfcenter.ku.edu/campbell.htm. **Contact:** Chris McKitterick. Honors the best science fiction novel of the year. Entries must be previously published. Open to any writer. Accepts inquiries by e-mail and fax. "Ordinarily publishers should submit work, but authors have done so when publishers would not. Send for list of jurors." Results announced in July. For contest results, send SASE. Deadline: Check website. Prize: Campbell Award trophy. Winners receive an expense-paid trip to the university to receive their award. Their names are also engraved on a permanent trophy. Judged by a jury.

CANADIAN AUTHORS ASSOCIATION AWARD FOR FICTION

6 West St. N., Suite 203, Orilla ON L3X 5B8 Canada. **Website:** www.canadianauthors.org. **Contact:** Anita Purcell, executive director. Award for full-length, English language literature for adults by a Canadian author. Deadline: January 15. Prize: $2,000 and a silver medal. Judging: Each year a trustee for each award appointed by the Canadian Authors Association selects up to 3 judges. Identities of the trustee and judges are confidential.

CANADIAN SHORT STORY COMPETITION

Red Tuque Books, Unit #6, 477 Martin St., Penticton BC V2A 5L2 Canada. (778)476-5750. **Fax:** (778)476-5750. **E-mail:** dave@redtuquebooks.ca. **Website:** www.redtuquebooks.ca. **Contact:** David Korinetz, contest director. Offered annually for unpublished works. Purpose of award is to promote Canada and Canadian publishing. Stories require a Canadian element. There are three ways to qualify. They can be written by a Canadian, written about Canadians, or take place somewhere in Canada. Deadline: December 31. Prize: 1st Place: $500; 2nd Place: $150; 3rd Place: $100; and 10 prizes of $25 will be given to honorable mentions. All 13 winners will be published in an anthology. They will each receive a complimentary copy. Judged by Canadian authors in the fantasy/sci-fi/horror field. Acquires first print rights. Contest open to anyone.

THE ALEXANDER CAPPON PRIZE FOR FICTION

New Letters, University of Missouri-Kansas City, *New Letters* Awards for Writers, UMKC, University House, 5101 Rockhill Rd., Kansas City MO 64110-2499. (816)235-1168. **Fax:** (816)235-2611. **E-mail:** newletters@umkc.edu. **Website:** www.newletters.org. Offered annually for the best short story to discover and reward new and upcoming writers. Buys first North American serial rights. Open to any writer. Short story should not exceed 8,000 words. Deadline: May 18. Prize: 1st Place: $1,500 and publication in a volume of *New Letters*. All entries will be given consideration for publication in future issues of *New Letters*.

CASCADE WRITING CONTEST & AWARDS

Oregon Christian Writers, 1075 Willow Lake Road N., Keizer Oregon 97303. **E-mail:** cascade@oregonchristianwriters.org. **Website:** http://oregonchristianwriters.org/. **Contact:** Marilyn Rhoads and Julie McDonald Zander. The Cascade Awards are presented at the annual Oregon Christian Writers Summer Conference (held at the Red Lion on the River in Portland, Oregon each August) attended by national editors, agents, and professional authors. The contest is open for both published and unpublished works in the following categories: contemporary fiction book, historical fiction book, speculative fiction book, nonfiction book, memoir book, young adult/middle grade fiction book, young adult/middle grade nonfiction book, children's chapter book and picture book (fiction and nonfiction), poetry, devotional, article, column, story, or blog post. Two additional special Cascade Awards are presented each year, the Trailblazer Award to a writer who has distinguished him/herself in the field of Christian writing and a Writer of Promise Award for a writer who demonstrates unusual promise in the field of Christian writing. For a full list of categories, entry rules, and scoring elements, visit website. Guidelines and rules available on the website. Entry forms will be available on the first day for entry. Annual multi-genre competition to encourage both published and emerging writers in the field of Christian writing. Deadline: March 31. Submissions period begins February 14. Prize: Award certificate presented at the Cascade Awards ceremony during the Oregon Christian Writers Annual Summer Conference. Finalists are listed in the conference notebook and winners are listed online. Cascade Trophies are awarded to the recipients of the Trailblazer and Writer of Promise Awards. Judged by published authors, editors, librarians, and retail book store owners and employees. Final judging by editors, agents, and published authors from the Christian publishing industry.

KAY CATTARULLA AWARD FOR BEST SHORT STORY

Texas Institute of Letters, P.O. Box 609, Round Rock TX 78680. **E-mail:** tilsecretary@yahoo.com. **Website:** www.texasinstituteofletters.org. Offered annually for work published January 1-December 31 of previous year to recognize the best short story. The story submitted must have appeared in print for the first time to be eligible. Writers must have been born in Texas, must have lived in Texas for at least 2 consecutive years, or the subject matter of the work must be associated with Texas. See website for guidelines. See website for details and instructions on entering the competition. Deadline: January 10. Prize: $1,000.

G. S. SHARAT CHANDRA PRIZE FOR SHORT FICTION

BkMk Press, BkMk Press, University of Missouri-Kansas City, 5100 Rockhill Rd., Kansas City MO 64110-2499. (816)235-2558. **Fax:** (816)235-2611. **E-mail:** bkmk@umkc.edu; newletters@umkc.edu. **Website:** www.newletters.org. Offered annually for the best book-length ms collection (unpublished) of short fiction in English by a living author. Translations are not eligible. Initial judging is done by a network of published writers. Final judging is done by a writer of national reputation. Guidelines for SASE, by e-mail, or on website. Short fiction collections should be approximately 125 pages minimum, 300 pages maximum, double spaced. Deadline: January 15. Prize: $1,000, plus book publication by BkMk Press.

PEGGY CHAPMAN-ANDREWS FIRST NOVEL AWARD

P.O. Box 6910, Dorset DT6 9QB United Kingdom. **E-mail:** info@bridportprize.org.uk. **Website:** www.bridportprize.org.uk. **Contact:** Frances Everitt, administrator. Award to promote literary excellence and new writers. Enter first chapters of novel, up to 8,000 words (minimum 5,000 words) plus 300 word synopsis. Send SASE for entry form or enter online. Deadline: May 31. Prize: 1st Place: £1,000 plus mentoring & possible publication; Runner-Up: £500. Judged by The Literary Consultancy & A.M. Heath Literary Agents.

THE CHARITON REVIEW SHORT FICTION PRIZE

Truman State University Press, 100 East Normal Ave., Kirksville MO 63501-4221. **Website:** http://tsup.truman.edu. An annual award for the best unpublished short fiction on any theme up to 5,000 words in English. Mss must be double-spaced on standard paper and bound only with a clip. Electronic submissions are not allowed. Include 2 title pages: 1 with the ms title and the author's contact information (name, address, phone, e-mail), and the other with only the ms title. (The author's name must not appear on or within the ms.) Enclose a SASE for notification when your ms is received. Mss will not be returned. Current Truman State University faculty, staff, or students are not eligible to compete. Deadline: September 30. Prize: $500 and publication in *The Chariton Review* for the winner. Two or three finalists will also be published and receive $200 each. The final judge will be announced after the finalists have been selected in January.

COPTALES CONTEST

Sponsored by Oak Tree Press, 140 E. Palmer St., Taylorville IL 62568. **E-mail:** publisher@oaktreebooks.com. **E-mail:** CT-ContestAdmin@oaktreebooks.com. **Website:** www.oaktreebooks.com. **Contact:** Billie Johnson, publisher. Open to novels and true stories that feature a law enforcement main character. Word count should range from 60,000-80,000 words. Text must be typed in a clean, readable word document and double-spaced. Ms cover page must list author e-mail address and estimated word count. Guidelines and entry forms are available for SASE or online. The goal of the CopTales Contest is to discover and publish new authors, or authors shifting to a new genre. This annual contest is open to writers who have not published in the mystery genre in the past three years, as well as completely unpublished authors. Deadline: September 1. Prize: Publishing contract, book published in trade paperback and e-book formats with a professionally designed, four-color cover. See website for details. Judged by a select panel of editors and professional crime writers.

THE DANAHY FICTION PRIZE

University of Tampa, 401 W. Kennedy Blvd., Tampa FL 33606. **E-mail:** utpress@ut.edu. **Website:** www.utpress.ut.edu. Annual award for the best previously unpublished short fiction. Deadline: November 30. Prize: $1,000, plus publication in *The Tampa Review*.

DARK OAK MYSTERY CONTEST

Oak Tree Press, 140 E. Palmer St., Taylorville IL 62568. (217)824-6500. **E-mail:** oaktreepub@aol.com. **E-mail:** DO-ContestAdmin@oaktreebooks.com. **Website:** www.oaktreebooks.com. Offered annually for an unpublished mystery manuscript (between 60,00-80,000 words) of any sort from police procedurals to amateur sleuth novels. Acquires first North American, audio and film rights to winning entry. Open to authors not published in the past 3 years. Deadline: September 1. Prize: Publishing Agreement, and launch of the title. Judged by a select panel of editors and professional mystery writers.

DEAD OF WINTER

E-mail: editors@toasted-cheese.com. **Website:** www.toasted-cheese.com. **Contact:** Stephanie Lenz, editor. The contest is a winter-themed horror fiction contest with a new topic each year. Topic and word limit announced October 1. The topic is usually geared toward a supernatural theme. Entries must be unpublished. Accepts inquiries by e-mail. Cover letter should include name, address, e-mail, word count, and title. Word limit varies each year. Open to any writer. Guidelines available in October on website. Deadline: December 21. Results announced January 31. Winners notified by e-mail. List of winners on website. Prize: Amazon gift certificates and publication in *Toasted Cheese*. Also offers honorable mention. Judged by 2 *Toasted Cheese* editors who blind judge each contest. Each judge uses her own criteria to rate entries.

TIPS "Follow online submission guidelines."

JACK DYER FICTION PRIZE

Crab Orchard Review, Department of English, Mail Code 4503, Faner Hall 2380, Southern Illinois University at Carbondale, 1000 Faner Drive, Carbondale IL 62901. **E-mail:** jtribble@siu.edu. **Website:** www.craborchardreview.siu.edu. **Contact:** Jon C. Tribble, managing editor. Offered annually for unpublished short fiction. *Crab Orchard Review* acquires first North American serial rights to all submitted work. One winner and at least 2 finalists will be chosen. Entries must be unpublished. Length: 6,000 words maximum. Please note that no stories will be returned. Results announced by end of August. Guidelines available on website. Deadline: April 21. Submissions period begins February 21. Prize: $2,000, publication and 1-year subscription to *Crab Orchard Review*. Finalists are offered $500 and publication. Judged by editorial staff (pre-screening); winner chosen by genre editor.

TIPS "Carefully read directions for entering and follow them exactly. Send us your best work. Note that simultaneous submissions are accepted for this prize, but the winning entry must NOT be accepted elsewhere. No electronic submissions."

MARY KENNEDY EASTHAM FLASH FICTION PRIZE

Category in the Soul-Making Keats Literary Competition, The Webhallow House, 1544 Sweetwood Dr., Broadmoor Village CA 94015-2029. **E-mail:** SoulKeats@gmail.com. **Website:** www.soulmakingcontest.us. **Contact:** Eileen Malone. Keep each story under 500 words. Three stories per entry. One story per page, typed, double-spaced, and unidentified. Deadline: November 30. Prize: 1st Place: $100; 2nd Place: $50; 3rd Place: $25.

TIPS "Send me your best stuff but more than that make my heart beat faster. Surprise me. Read great writing daily and WRITE. WRITE. WRITE. To be successful you need to do your best every day for a very long time."

THE EMILY CONTEST

18207 Heaton Dr., Houston TX 77084. **E-mail:** emily.contest@whrwa.com. **Website:** www.whrwa.com. Annual award to promote publication of previously unpublished writers of romance. Open to any writer who has not published in a given category within the past 3 years. Send up to first 5,600 words and end on a hook. Contest is open to published and unpublished writers. Unpublished authors may enter in any category not contracted in (book-length) by the deadline. Published authors may enter in a category not published (book-length) in the past three years. (Book-length: 40,000+ words.) See website for specific details. The mission of The Emily is to professionally support writers and guide them toward a path to publication. Deadline: October 7. Submission period begins September 1. Prize: $100. Final judging done by an editor and an agent.

AURA ESTRADA SHORT STORY CONTEST

Boston Review, Short Story Contest, Boston Review, P.O. Box 425786, Cambridge MA 02142. (617)324-1360. **Website:** bostonreview.net. Stories should not exceed 5,000 words and must be previously unpublished. Mailed mss should be double-spaced and submitted with a cover note listing the author's name, address, and phone number. No cover note is necessary for online submissions. Enter using online contest entry manager at website. Aura Estrada (1977-2007), was a promising young Mexican writer and student, and the wife of Francisco Goldman. This prize is meant to honor her memory by supporting other burgeoning writers. Deadline: October 1. Prize: $1,500 and publication in the July/August issue of *Boston Review*. Runners up may also be published.

FABLERS MONTHLY CONTEST

818 Los Arboles Lane, Santa Fe NM 87501. **Website:** www.fablers.net. **Contact:** W.B. Scott. Monthly contest for previously unpublished writers to help develop amateur writers. Guidelines posted online. No entry fee. Open to any writer. Deadline: 14th of each month. Prize: $100. Judged by members of website.

THE FAR HORIZONS AWARD FOR SHORT FICTION

The Malahat Review, University of Victoria, P.O. Box 1700, Stn CSC, Victoria BC V8W 2Y2 Canada. (250)721-8524. **Fax:** (250)472-5051. **E-mail:** malahat@uvic.ca. **E-mail:** horizons@uvic.ca. **Website:** www.malahatreview.ca. **Contact:** John Barton, editor. Submissions must be unpublished. No simultaneous submissions. Submit 1 piece of short fiction, 3,500 words maximum; no restrictions on subject matter or aesthetic approach. Include separate page with author's name, address, e-mail, and title; no identifying information on mss pages. E-mail submissions are accepted. Do not include SASE for results; mss will not be returned. Guidelines available on website. Winner and finalists contacted by e-mail. Open to "emerging short fiction writers from Canada, the US, and elsewhere" who have not yet published their fiction in a full-length book (48 pages or more). 2011 winner: Zoey Peterson; 2013 winner: Kerry-Lee Powell. Deadline: May 1 (odd-numbered years). Prize: $1,000 CAD, publication in fall issue of *The Malahat Review* (see separate listing in Magazines/Journals). Announced in fall on website, Facebook page, and in quarterly e-newsletter, *Malahat Lite*.

FAW CHRISTINA STEAD AWARD

Fellowship of Australian Writers, 6-8 Davies St., Brunswick VIC 3095 Australia. **E-mail:** secretary@writers.asn.au; treasurer@writers.asn.au. **Website:** www.writers.asn.au. **Contact:** Awards Co-ordinator. Annual award for a work of fiction published since November 30 the previous year by an Australian writer. Guidelines for SASE or online. Closing date: November 30. Opens on September 1. Prize: $500.

FIRSTWRITER.COM INTERNATIONAL SHORT STORY CONTEST

firstwriter.com, United Kingdom. **Website:** www.firstwriter.com. **Contact:** J. Paul Dyson, managing editor. Accepts short stories up to 3,000 words on any subject and in any style. Deadline: April 1. Prize: Totals about $300. Ten special commendations will also be awarded and all the winners will be published in *firstwriter* magazine and receive a $36 subscription voucher, allowing an annual subscription to be taken out for free. All submissions are automatically considered for publication in *firstwriter* magazine and may be published there online. Judged by *firstwriter* magazine editors.

FISH PUBLISHING FLASH FICTION COMPETITION

Durrus, Bantry, County Cork Ireland. **E-mail:** info@fishpublishing.com. **Website:** www.fishpublishing.com. Annual prize awarding flash fiction. Max length: 300 words. You may enter as many times as you wish. See website for details and rules. "This is an opportunity to attempt what is one of the most difficult and rewarding tasks—to create, in a tiny fragment, a completely resolved and compelling story in 300 words or less." Deadline: February 28. Prize: First Prize: $1,200. The 10 published authors will receive 5 copies of the Anthology and will be invited to read at the launch during the West Cork Literary Festival in July.

FISH SHORT STORY PRIZE

Durrus, Bantry Co. Cork Ireland. **E-mail:** info@fishpublishing.com. **Website:** www.fishpublishing.com. Annual worldwide competition to recognize the best short stories. Entries must not have been published before. Enter online or by post. See website for full details of competitions, and information on the Fish Editorial and Critique Services, and the Fish Online Writing Courses. Deadline: November 30. Prize:

Overall prize fund: $6,000. 1st prize: $3,750. 2nd Prize: 1 week at Anam Cara Writers Retreat in West Cork and $350. 3rd Prize: $350. Closing date 30th November. The best 10 will be published in the Fish Anthology, launched in July at the West Cork Literary Festival. Winners announced March 17.

FLASHCARD FLASH FICTION CONTEST

Sycamore Review, Department of English, 500 Oval Dr., Purdue University, West Lafayette IN 47907. **E-mail:** sycamore@purdue.edu; sycamorefiction@purdue.edu. **Website:** www.sycamorereview.com/contest/. **Contact:** Kara Krewer, editor-in-chief. Annual contest for unpublished flash fiction. For each submission, send a piece of flash fiction of no more than 500 words. Ms pages should be numbered and should include the title of the piece. See website for more guidelines. Submit via online submissions manager. Deadline: February 1.Submissions period begins January 1. Prize: $100, publication online, and publication on a flashcard to be distributed with *Sycamore Review* at AWP.

H.E. FRANCIS SHORT STORY COMPETITION

Ruth Hindman Foundation, University of Alabama in Huntsville, Department of English, Morton Hall Room 222, Huntsville AL 35899. **Website:** www.hefranciscompetition.com. Offered annually for unpublished work, not to exceed 5,000 words. Acquires first-time publication rights. Using the electronic submission system or by mail, submit a story of up to 5,000 words. If submitting by mail, include three copies of the story. Send an SASE or visit the website for complete guidelines. Deadline: January 15. Prize: $2,000, publication as an Amazon Kindle Single, an announcement in Poets and Writers, and publication on the website. Judged by a panel of nationally recognized, award-winning authors, directors of creative writing programs, and editors of literary journals.

THE GHOST STORY SUPERNATURAL FICTION AWARD

The Ghost Story, P.O. Box 601, Union ME 04862. **E-mail:** editor@theghoststory.com. **Website:** www.theghoststory.com. **Contact:** Paul Guernsey. Biannual contest for unpublished fiction. "Ghost stories are welcome, of course—but submissions may involve *any* paranormal or supernatural theme, as well as magic realism. What we're looking for is fine writing, fresh perspectives, and maybe a few surprises in the field of supernatural fiction." Guidelines available online. Length: 1,000-10,000 words. Deadline: April 30 and September 30. Prize: $1,000 and publication in *The Ghost Story*. A second writer will receive an Honorable Mention that includes publication and $100. Judged by the editors of *The Ghost Story*.

GIVAL PRESS NOVEL AWARD

Gival Press, LLC, P.O. Box 3812, Arlington VA 22203. (703)351-0079. **E-mail:** givalpress@yahoo.com. **Website:** www.givalpress.com. **Contact:** Robert L. Giron. Offered annually for a previously unpublished original novel (not a translation). Guidelines by phone, on website, via e-mail, or by mail with SASE. Results announced late fall of same year. Winners notified by phone. Results made available to entrants with SASE, by e-mail, on website. Open to any author who writes original work in English. Length: 30,000-100,000 words. Cover letter should include name, address, phone, e-mail, word count, novel title; include a short bio and short synopsis. Only the title and word count should appear on the actual ms. Writers may submit own work. Purpose is to award the best literary novel. Deadline: May 30. Prize: $3,000, plus publication of book with a standard contract and author's copies. Final judge is announced after winner is chosen. Entries read anonymously.

TIPS "Review the types of mss Gival Press has published. We stress literary works."

GIVAL PRESS SHORT STORY AWARD

Gival Press, P.O. Box 3812, Arlington VA 22203. (703)351-0079. **E-mail:** givalpress@yahoo.com. **Website:** www.givalpress.com. **Contact:** Robert L. Giron, publisher. Annual literary, short story contest. Entries must be unpublished. Open to anyone who writes original short stories, which are not a chapter of a novel, in English. Receives about 100-150 entries per category. Guidelines available online, via e-mail, or by mail. Results announced in the fall of the same year. Winners notified by phone. Results available with SASE, by e-mail, and on website. Length: 5,000-15,000 words. Include name, address, phone, e-mail, word count, title on cover letter; include short bio. Only the title and word count should be found on ms. Writers may submit their own ficiton. Recognizes the best literary short story. Deadline: August 8. Prize: $1,000 and publication on website. Judged anonymously.

GLIMMER TRAIN'S FAMILY MATTERS CONTEST

Glimmer Train, 4763 SW Maplewood Rd., P.O. Box 80430, Portland OR 97280. (503)221-0836. **Fax:** (503)221-0837. **E-mail:** eds@glimmertrain.org. **Website:** www.glimmertrain.org. **Contact:** Susan Burmeister-Brown. This contest is now held twice a year, during the months of May and September. Winners are contacted 2 months after the close of each contest, and results officially announced one week later. Submit online at www.glimmertrain.org. The word count for this contest generaly ranges from 1,500 to 5,000 words, though up 12,000 words is fine. See complete guidelines online. Deadline: May 31 and September 30. Prize: 1st Place: $1,500, publication in *Glimmer Train Stories*, and 20 copies of that issue; 2nd Place: $500 and consideration for publication; 3rd Place: $300 and consideration for publication.

TIPS "We are looking for stories about families of all configurations. It's fine to draw heavily on real life experiences, but the work must read like fiction and all stories accepted for publication will be presented as fiction."

GLIMMER TRAIN'S FICTION OPEN

Glimmer Train, Inc., Glimmer Train Press, Inc., 4763 SW Maplewood Rd., P.O. Box 80430, Portland OR 97280. (503)221-0836. **Fax:** (503)221-0837. **E-mail:** eds@glimmertrain.org. **Website:** www.glimmertrain.org. **Contact:** Linda Swanson-Davies. Submissions to this category generally range from 2,000-8,000 words, but up to 20,000 is fine. Held twice a year. Submit online at www.glimmertrain.org. Winners will be called 2 months after the close of the contest. Deadline: June 30 and December 31. Prize: 1st Place $2,500, publication in *Glimmer Train Stories*, and 20 copies of that issue; 2nd Place $1,000 and consideration for publication; 3rd Place: $600 and consideration for publication.

GLIMMER TRAIN'S SHORT-STORY AWARD FOR NEW WRITERS

Glimmer Train Press, Inc., 4763 SW Maplewood Rd., P.O. Box 80430, Portland OR 97280. (503)221-0836. **Fax:** (503)221-0837. **E-mail:** eds@glimmertrain.org. **Website:** www.glimmertrain.org. **Contact:** Linda Swanson-Davies. Offered for any writer whose fiction hasn't appeared in a nationally distributed print publication with a circulation over 5,000. Submissions to this category generally range from 1,500-6,000 words, but up to 12,000 is fine. Held quarterly. Submit online at www.glimmertrain.org. Winners will be called 2 months after the close of the contest. Deadline: February 28, May 31, August 31, and November 30. Prize: 1st Place: $1,500, publication in *Glimmer Train Stories*, and 20 copies of that issue; 2nd Place: $500 and consideration for publication; 3rd Place: $300 and consideration for publication.

TIPS "This contest is now held quarterly. In a recent edition of *Best American Short Stories*, of the top '100 Distinguished Short Stories,' 10 appeared in *Glimmer Train Stories*, more than any other publication in the country, including *The New Yorker*. Of those 10, 3 were those authors' first stories accepted for publication."

GLIMMER TRAIN'S VERY SHORT FICTION CONTEST

Glimmer Train Press, Inc., 4763 SW Maplewood Rd., P.O. Box 80430, Portland OR 97280. (503)221-0836. **Fax:** (503)221-0837. **E-mail:** eds@glimmertrain.org. **Website:** www.glimmertrain.org. **Contact:** Susan Burmeister-Brown. Offered to encourage the art of the very short story. Word count: 3,000 maximum. Held quarterly. Submit online at www.glimmertrain.org. Results announced 2 months after the close of the contest. Deadline: January 31, April 30, July 31, and October 31. Prize: 1st Place: $1,500, publication in *Glimmer Train Stories*, and 20 copies of that issue; 2nd Place: $500 and consideration for publication; 3rd Place: $300 and consideration for publication.

TIPS "There is no minimum word count, though it is rare for a piece under 500 words to read as a full story."

THE GOVER PRIZE

Best New Writing, P.O. Box 11, Titusville NJ 08530. **Fax:** (609)968-1718. **E-mail:** submissions@bestnewwriting.com. **Website:** http://www.bestnewwriting.com/BNWgover.html. **Contact:** Christopher Klim, senior editor. The Gover Prize, named after groundbreaking author Robert Gover, awards an annual prize and publication in *Best New Writing* for the best short fiction and creative nonfiction. Open to all writers. Submissions must be previously unpublished. Guidelines available on website. Entries limited to 500 words or less. Deadline: September 15-January 10. Prize: $250 grand prize; publication in *Best New Writing* for finalists (approximately 12), holds 6-month world exclusive rights. Judged by *Best New Writing* editorial staff.

LYNDALL HADOW/DONALD STUART SHORT STORY COMPETITION

Fellowship of Australian Writers (WA), P.O. Box 6180, Swanbourne WA 6910 Australia. (61)(8)9384-4771. **Fax:** (61)(8)9384-4854. **E-mail:** fellowshipaustralianwriterswa@gmail.com. **Website:** www.fawwa.org. Annual contest for unpublished short stories (maximum 3,000 words). Reserves the right to publish entries in a FAWWA publication or on website. Guidelines online or for SASE. Deadline: June 1. Submissions period begins April 1. Prize: 1st Place: $400; 2nd Place; $100; Highly Commended: $50.

WILDA HEARNE FLASH FICTION CONTEST

Big Muddy: A Journal of the Mississippi River Valley, WHFF Contest, Southeast Missouri State University Press, One University Plaza, MS 2650, Cape Girardeau MO 63701. **E-mail:** sswartwout@semo.edu. **Website:** www6.semo.edu. **Contact:** Susan Swartwout, publisher. Annual competition for flash fiction, held by Southeast Missouri State University Press. Work must not be previously published. Send maximum of 500 words, double-spaced, with no identifying name on the pages, and a separate cover sheet with story title, author's name, address, and phone number. Send SASE for notification of results; all manuscripts will be recycled. Entries should be sent via postal mail. Deadline: October 1. Prize: $500 and publication in *Big Muddy: A Journal of the Mississippi River Valley.* Semi-finalists will be chosen by a regional team of published writers. The final manuscript will be chosen by Susan Swartwout, publisher of the Southeast Missouri State University Press.

DRUE HEINZ LITERATURE PRIZE

University of Pittsburgh Press, 7500 Thomas Blvd., Pittsburgh PA 15260. (412)383-2492. **Fax:** (412)383-2466. **Website:** www.upress.pitt.edu. Offered annually to writers who have published a book-length collection of fiction or a minimum of 3 short stories or novellas in commercial magazines or literary journals of national distribution. Does not return mss. Deadline: Submit May 1- June 30 only. Prize: $15,000. Judged by anonymous nationally known writers such as Robert Penn Warren, Joyce Carol Oates, and Margaret Atwood.

LORIAN HEMINGWAY SHORT STORY COMPETITION

Hemingway Days Festival, P.O. Box 993, Key West FL 33041. **E-mail:** shortstorykeywest@hushmail.com. **Website:** www.shortstorycompetition.com. **Contact:** Eva Eliot, editorial assistant. Offered annually for unpublished short stories up to 3,500 words. Guidelines available via mail, e-mail, or online. Accepts inquiries by SASE, e-mail, or visit website. Entries must be unpublished. Open to all writers whose work has not appeared in a nationally distributed publication with a circulation of 5,000 or more. Looking for excellence, pure and simple—no genre restrictions, no theme restrictions. We seek a writer's voice that cannot be ignored. All entrants will receive a letter from Lorian Hemingway and a list of winners, via mail or e-mail, by October 1. Results announced at the end of July during Hemingway Days festival. Winners notified by phone prior to announcement. Award to encourage literary excellence and the efforts of writers whose voices have yet to be heard. Deadline: May 15. Prize: 1st Place: $1,500, plus publication of his or her winning story in *Cutthroat: A Journal of the Arts*; 2nd-3rd Place: $500; honorable mentions will also be awarded. Judged by a panel of writers, editors, and literary scholars selected by author Lorian Hemingway. (Lorian Hemingway is the competition's final judge.)

TONY HILLERMAN PRIZE

Wordharvest, 1063 Willow Way, Santa Fe NM 87507. (505)471-1565. **E-mail:** wordharvest@wordharvest.com. **Website:** www.wordharvest.com. **Contact:** Anne Hillerman and Jean Schaumberg, co-organizers. Awarded annually, and sponsored by St. Martin's Press, for the best first mystery set in the Southwest. Murder or another serious crime or crimes must be at the heart of the story, with the emphasis on the solution rather than the details of the crime. Multiple entries accepted. Accepts inquiries by e-mail, phone. Entries should be unpublished; self-published work is generally accepted. Length: no less than 220 type written pages, or approximately 60,000 words. Cover letter should include name, address, phone, e-mail, list of publishing credits. Please include SASE for response. Writers may submit their own work. Entries should be mailed to St. Martin's Press: St. Martin's Minotaur/THWC Competition, St. Martin's Minotaur, 175 Fifth Ave., New York, NY 10010. Honors the contributions made by Tony Hillerman to the art and craft of the mystery. Deadline: June 1. Prize: $10,000 advance and publication by St. Martin's Press. Nominees will be selected by judges chosen by the editorial staff of St. Martin's Press, with the assistance of independent judges selected by organizers of the Tony Hillerman Writers Conference (Wordharvest), and the winner will be chosen by St. Martin's editors.

TOM HOWARD/JOHN H. REID FICTION & ESSAY CONTEST

c/o Winning Writers, 351 Pleasant St., PMB 222, Northampton MA 01060-3961. (866)946-9748. **Fax:** (413)280-0539. **E-mail:** adam@winningwriters.com. **Website:** www.winningwriters.com. **Contact:** Adam Cohen, President. Now in its 23rd year. Open to all writers. Submit any type of short story, essay or other work of prose. Both published and unpublished works are welcome. In the case of published work, the contestant must own the online publication rights. Contest sponsored by Winning Writers. Nonexclusive rights to publish submissions online, in e-mail newsletters, in e-books, and in press releases. See website for guidelines and to submit your poem. Prefers inquiries by e-mail. Length: 6,000 words max per entry. Writers may submit own work. Winners notifed by e-mail. Results made available to entrants on website. Deadline: April 30. Prize: Two 1st prizes of $1,000 will be awarded, plus 10 honorable mentions of $100 each. Judged by Arthur Powers.

L. RON HUBBARD'S WRITERS OF THE FUTURE CONTEST

P.O. Box 1630, Los Angeles CA 90078. (323)466-3310. **Fax:** (323)466-6474. **E-mail:** contests@authorservicesinc.com. **Website:** www.writersofthefuture.com. **Contact:** Joni Labaqui, contest director. Foremost competition for new and amateur writers of unpublished science fiction or fantasy short stories or novelettes. Offered to find, reward and publicize new speculative fiction writers so they may more easily attain professional writing careers. Open to writers who have not professionally published a novel or short novel, more than 1 novelette, or more than 3 short stories. Entries must be unpublished. Limit 1 entry per quarter. Open to any writer. Results announced quarterly in e-newsletter. Winners notified by phone. Contest has 4 quarters. There shall be 3 cash prizes in each quarter. In addition, at the end of the year, the 4 first-place, quarterly winners will have their entries rejudged, and a grand prize winner shall be determined. Eligible entries are previously unpublished short stories or novelettes (under 17,000 words) of science fiction or fantasy. Guidelines for SASE or on website. Accepts inquiries by fax, e-mail, phone. Mss: White paper, black ink; double-spaced; typed; each page appropriately numbered with title, no author name. Include cover page with author's name, address, phone number, e-mail address (if available), as well as estimated word count and the title of the work. Online submissions are accepted. Hard copy submissions will not be returned. Deadline: December 31, March 31, June 30, September 30. Prize: Prize (awards quarterly): 1st Place: $1,000; 2nd Place: $750; and 3rd Place: $500. Annual grand prize: $5,000. Judged by Dave Wolverton (initial judge), then by a panel of 4 professional authors.

INDIANA REVIEW FICTION CONTEST

Ballantine Hall 465, Indiana University, 1020 E. Kirkwood Ave., Bloomington IN 47405-7103. (812)855-3439. **Fax:** (812)855-4253. **E-mail:** inreview@indiana.edu. **Website:** http://indianareview.org. **Contact:** Katie Moulton, editor. Contest for fiction in any style and on any subject. Open to any writer. Mss will not be returned. No works forthcoming elsewhere, are eligible. Simultaneous submissions accepted, but in the event of entrant withdrawal, contest fee will not be refunded. Maximum length: 8,000 words. Deadline: October 31. Submission period begins September 1. Prize: $1,000, publication in the *Indiana Review* and contributor's copies. Judged by guest judges.

TIPS "We look for a command of language and structure, as well as a facility with compelling and unusual subject matter. It's a good idea to obtain copies of issues featuring past winners to get a more concrete idea of what we are looking for."

INK & INSIGHTS WRITING CONTEST

2408 W. 8th, Amarillo TX 79106. **E-mail:** contest@critiquemynovel.com. **Website:** http://critiquemynovel.com/ink_insights_2015. **Contact:** Catherine York, contest/award director. This contest is for new and seasoned writers who need to gauge their work in addition to competing for prizes. The focus is on the feedback writers are given for their work, as well as competin for prizes and a guaranteed read with feedback from several literary agents. Three categories: Novels (new writers), Novels (ready to publish), and nonfiction. Send the first 10,000 words of your manuscript (unpublished, self-published, or published through a vanity/independent press). Include a cover sheet that contains the following information: novel title, genre, word count of full ms, e-mail address. Do not put name on submission. See website for full details and guidelines. Deadline: March 1-April 30 (regular entry), May 1-June 30 (late entry). Prize: Prizes vary depending on category. Every novel receives personal feedback from 4 judges. Judges listed on website, including the agents who will be helping choose the top winners this year.

INTERNATIONAL 3-DAY NOVEL CONTEST

210-111 West Hastings Street, Vancouver BC V6B 1H4 Canada. **E-mail:** info@3daynovel.com. **Website:** www.3daynovel.com. **Contact:** Brittany Huddart, managing editor. "Can you produce a masterwork of fiction in three short days? The 3-Day Novel Contest is your chance to find out. Each Labour Day weekend, fueled by adrenaline and the desire for literary nirvana, hundreds of writers step up to the challenge. It's a thrill, a grind, a 72-hour kick in the pants and an awesome creative experience. How many crazed plotlines, coffee-stained pages, pangs of doubt and moments of genius will next year's contest bring forth? And what will you think up under pressure?" Entrants write in whatever setting they wish, in whatever genre they wish, anywhere in the world. Entrants may start writing as of midnight on Friday night, and must stop by midnight on Monday night. Then they print entry and mail it in to the contest for judging. Deadline: Friday before Labor Day weekend. Prize: 1st place receives publication; 2nd place receives $500; 3rd place receives $100.

THE IOWA SHORT FICTION AWARD & JOHN SIMMONS SHORT FICTION AWARD

Iowa Writers' Workshop, 507 N. Clinton St., 102 Dey House, Iowa City IA 52242-1000. **Website:** www.uiowapress.org. **Contact:** James McCoy, director. Annual award to give exposure to promising writers who have not yet published a book of prose. Open to any writer. Current University of Iowa students are not eligible. No application forms are necessary. Announcement of winners made early in year following competition. Winners notified by phone. No application forms are necessary. Do not send original ms. Include SASE for return of ms. Entries must be unpublished, but stories previously published in periodicals are eligible for inclusion. The ms must be a collection of short stories of at least 150 word-processed, double-spaced pages. Deadline: September 30. Submission period begins August 1. Prize: Publication by University of Iowa Press Judged by senior Iowa Writers' Workshop members who screen mss; published fiction author of note makes final selections.

JERRY JAZZ MUSICIAN SHORT FICTION AWARD

Jerry Jazz Musician, 2207 NE Broadway, Portland OR 97232. **E-mail:** jm@jerryjazz.com. **Website:** www.jerryjazzmusician.com. Three times a year, *Jerry Jazz Musician* awards a writer who submits the best original, previously unpublished work of approximately 1,000-5,000 words. The winner will be announced via a mailing of the *Jerry Jazz* newsletter. Publishers, artists, musicians, and interested readers are among those who subscribe to the newsletter. Additionally, the work will be published on the home page of *Jerry Jazz Musician* and featured there for at least 4 weeks. The *Jerry Jazz Musician* reader tends to have interests in music, history, literature, art, film, and theater—particularly that of the counter-culture of mid-20th century America. Guidelines available online. Deadline: September, January, and May. See website for specific dates. Prize: $100. Judged by the editors of *Jerry Jazz Musician*.

JESSE H. JONES AWARD FOR BEST WORK OF FICTION

P.O. Box 609, Round Rock TX 78680. **E-mail:** tilsecretary@yahoo.com. **Website:** http://texasinstituteofletters.org. Offered annually by Texas Institute of Letters for work published January 1-December 31 of year before award is given to recognize the writer of the best book of fiction entered in the competition. Writers must have been born in Texas, have lived in the state for at least 2 consecutive years at some time, or the subject matter of the work should be associated with the state. See website for details and information on submitting. Deadline: January 10. Prize: $6,000.

JAMES JONES FIRST NOVEL FELLOWSHIP

Wilkes University, Creative Writing Department, Wilkes University, 84 West South Street, Wilkes-Barre PA 18766. (570)408-4547. **Fax:** (570)408-3333. **E-mail:** jamesjonesfirstnovel@wilkes.edu. **Website:** www.wilkes.edu/. Offered annually for unpublished novels and novellas (must be works-in-progress). This competition is open to all American writers who have not previously published novels. Submit a 2-page (maximum) outline of the entire novel and the first 50 pages of the novel-in-progress are to be submitted. The ms must be typed and double-spaced; outline may be single-spaced. Entrants submitting via snail mail should include their name, address, telephone number and e-mail address (if available) on the title page, but nowhere else on the manuscript. For those entrants submitting online, name, address, telephone number and e-mail address should not appear anywhere on the manuscript. Pages should be numbered. The award is intended to honor the spirit of unblinking honesty, determination, and insight into modern culture exemplified by the late James Jones. Deadline: March 15. Submission period begins October 1. Prize: $10,000; 2 runners-up get $1,000 honorarium.

E.M. KOEPPEL SHORT FICTION AWARD

P.O. Box 140310, Gainesville FL 32614-0310. **Website:** www.writecorner.com. **Contact:** Mary Sue Koeppel, editor. Annual awards for unpublished fiction in any style and any theme. Maximum length: 3,000 words. Stories must be unpublished. Send 2 title pages: One with title only and one with title, name, address, phone, e-mail, short bio. Place no other identification of the author on the ms that will be used in the judging. Guidelines available for SASE or on website. Accepts inquiries by e-mail and phone. Winning stories published on website. Winners notified by mail, phone in July (or earlier). For results, send SASE or see website. Deadline: April 30. Submission period begins October 1. Prize: 1st Place: $1,100. Editors' Choice: $100 each. $500 scholarship, in addition, if winner is a student. Judged by award-winning fiction writers.

THE LAWRENCE FOUNDATION AWARD

Prairie Schooner, 123 Andrews Hall, University of Nebraska-Lincoln, Lincoln NE 68588-0334. (402)472-0911. **Fax:** (402)472-9771. **E-mail:** prairieschooner@unl.edu. **Website:** www.prairieschooner.unl.edu. Offered annually for the best short story published in Prairie Schooner in the previous year. Only work published in *Prairie Schooner* in the previous year is considered. Work is nominated by editorial staff. Results announced in the Spring issue. Winners notified by mail in February or March. Prize: $1,000. Judged by editorial staff of *Praire Schooner*.

LAWRENCE FOUNDATION PRIZE

Michigan Quarterly Review, 0576 Rackham Bldg., 915 E. Washington Street, Ann Arbor MI 48109-1070. (734)764-9265. **E-mail:** mqr@umich.edu. **Website:** www.michiganquarterlyreview.com. **Contact:** Vicki Lawrence, managing editor. This annual prize is awarded by the *Michigan Quarterly Review* editorial board to the author of the best short story published in *MQR* that year. The prize is sponsored by University of Michigan alumnus and fiction writer Leonard S. Bernstein, a trustee of the Lawrence Foundation of New York. Approximately 20 short stories are published in *MQR* each year. Guidelines available under submission guidelines on website. Prize: $1,000. Judged by editorial board.

LITERAL LATTÉ FICTION AWARD

Literal Latté, 200 E. 10th St., Suite 240, New York NY 10003. (212)260-5532. **E-mail:** litlatte@aol.com. **Website:** www.literal-latte.com. **Contact:** Edward Estlin, contributing editor. Award to provide talented writers with 3 essential tools for continued success: money, publication, and recognition. Offered annually for unpublished fiction (maximum 10,000 words). Guidelines online. Open to any writer. Winners notified by phone. Winners announced in April. All winners published in *Literal Latté*. Deadline: January 15. Prize: 1st Place: $1,000 and publication in *Literal Latté*; 2nd Place: $300; 3rd Place: $200; also up to 7 honorable mentions.

LITERAL LATTE SHORT SHORTS CONTEST

Literal Latté, 200 E. 10th St., Suite 240, New York NY 10003. (212)260-5532. **E-mail:** litlatte@aol.com. **Website:** www.literal-latte.com. **Contact:** Jenine Gordon Bockman, editor. Annual contest. Send unpublished shorts. 2,000 words max. All styles welcome. Name, address, phone number, email address (optional) on cover page only. Include SASE or email address for reply. All entries considered for publication. Deadline: June 30. Prize: $500. Judged by the editors.

LITERARY FICTION CONTEST

The Writers' Workshop of Asheville, NC, Literary Fiction Contest, 387 Beaucatcher Rd., Asheville NC 28805. **Website:** www.twwoa.org. Submit a short story or chapter of a novel of 5,000 words or less. Multiple entries are accepted. All work must be unpublished. Pages should be paper clipped, with your name, address, phone and title of work on a cover sheet. Double-space and use 12-point font. Deadline: November 30. Prize: 1st Place: Your choice of a 2 night stay at the Mountain Muse B&B in Asheville, 3 free online workshops, or 50pages line-edited and revised by editorial staff; 2nd Place: 2 free workshops or 35pages line-edited; 3rd Place: 1 free workshop or 25 pages line-edited; 10 Honorable Mentions.

THE MARY MACKEY SHORT STORY PRIZE CATEGORY

Soul-Making Keats Literary Competition, The Webhallow House, 1544 Sweetwood Dr., Broadmoor Village CA 94015. **E-mail:** SoulKeats@mail.com. **Website:** www.soulmakingcontest.us. **Contact:** Eileen Malone. Open annually to any writer. One story/entry, up to 5,000 words. All prose works must be typed, page numbered, and double-spaced. Identify only with 3x5 card. Deadline: November 30. Prize: Cash prizes.

THE MALAHAT REVIEW NOVELLA PRIZE

The Malahat Review, University of Victoria, P.O. Box 1700 STN CSC, Victoria BC V8W 2Y2 Canada. (250)721-8524. **E-mail:** malahat@uvic.ca. **E-mail:** novella@uvic.ca. **Website:** malahatreview.ca. **Contact:** John Barton, editor. Held in alternate years with the Long Poem Prize. Submit novellas between 10,000 and 20,000 words in length. Include separate page with author's name, address, e-mail, and novella title; no identifying information on mss. pages. E-mail submissions are now accepted. Do not include SASE for results; mss will not be returned. Guidelines available on website. Winner and finalists contacted by e-mail. Offered to promote unpublished novellas. Obtains first world rights. After publication rights revert to the author. Open to any writer. Deadline: February 1 (even years). Prize: $1,500 CAD and one year's subscription. Winner published in summer issue of *The Malahat Review* and announced on website, Facebook page, and in quarterly e-newsletter, *Malahat Lite*.

MARY MCCARTHY PRIZE IN SHORT FICTION

Sarabande Books, 2234 Dundee Rd., Suite 200, Louisville KY 40205. (502)458-4028. **Fax:** (502)458-4065. **E-mail:** info@sarabandebooks.org. **Website:** www.sarabandebooks.org. **Contact:** Kirby Gann, managing editor. Annual competition to honor a collection of short stories, novellas, or a short novel. All mss should be between 150 and 250 pages. All finalists considered for publicaiton. Guidelines available online. Deadline: February 15. Submission period begins January 1. Prize: $2,000 and publication (standard royalty contract).

MARJORIE GRABER MCINNIS SHORT STORY AWARD

ACT Writers Centre, Gorman House Arts Centre, Ainslie Ave., Braddon ACT 2612 Australia. (61)(2)6262-9191. **Fax:** (61)(2)6262-9191. **E-mail:** admin@actwriters.org.au. **Website:** www.actwriters.org.au. Open theme for a short story with 1,500-3,000 words. Guidelines available on website. Open only to unpublished emerging writers residing within the ACT or region. Deadline: September 25. Submissions period begins in early September. Prize: $600 and publication. Five runners-up receive book prizes. All winners may be published in the ACT Writers Centre newsletter and on the ACT Writers Centre website.

MEMPHIS MAGAZINE FICTION CONTEST

Memphis Magazine, co-sponsored by booksellers of Laurelwood and Burke's Book Store, Fiction Contest, c/o *Memphis* magazine, P.O. Box 1738, Memphis TN 38101. (901)521-9000, ext. 451. **Fax:** (901)521-0129. **E-mail:** sadler@memphismagazine.com. **Website:** www.memphismagazine.com. **Contact:** Marilyn Sadler. Annual award for authors of short fiction living within 150 miles of Memphis. Each story should be between 3,000 and 4,500 words long. See website for guidelines and rules. Deadline: February 15. Prize: $1,000 grand prize, along with being published in the annual Cultural Issue; two honorable-mention awards of $500 each will be given if the quality of entries warrants.

DAVID NATHAN MEYERSON PRIZE FOR FICTION

Southwest Review, P.O. Box 750374, Dallas TX 75275-0374. (214)768-1037. **Fax:** (214)768-1408. **E-mail:** swr@smu.edu. **Website:** www.smu.edu/southwestreview. **Contact:** Jennifer Cranfill, senior editor. Annual award given to a writer who has not published a first book of fiction, either a novel or collection of stories. All contest entrants will receive a copy of the issue in which the winning piece appears. Submissions must be no longer than 8,000 words. Work should be printed without the author's name. Name and address should appear only on the cover letter. Submissions will not be returned. Deadline: May 1 (postmarked). Prize: $1,000 and publication in the *Southwest Review*.

TIPS "A cover letter with name, address, and other relevant information may accompany the piece which must be printed without any identifying information. Get guidelines for SASE or online."

MILKWEED NATIONAL FICTION PRIZE

1011 Washington Ave. S., Suite 300, Minneapolis MN 55415. (612)332-3192. **Fax:** (612)215-2550. **E-mail:** editor@milkweed.org. **Website:** www.milkweed.org. **Contact:** Patrick Thoman, editor and program manager. Annual award for unpublished works. Mss should be one of the following: a novel, a collection of short stories, one or more novellas, or a combination of short stories and one or more novellas. Mss should be of high literary quality and between 150-400 pages in length. Work previously published as a book in the US is not eligible, but individual stories or novellas previously published in magazines or anthologies are eligible. Guidelines available online. Deadline: Rolling submissions. Check website for details of when they're accepting mss. Prize: Publication by Milkweed Editions and a cash advance of $5,000 against royalties, agreed upon in the contractual arrangement negotiated at the time of acceptance. Judged by the editors.

MILKWEED PRIZE FOR CHILDREN'S LITERATURE

Milkweed Editions, 1011 Washington Ave. S., Suite 300, Minneapolis MN 55415. (612)332-3192. **Fax:** (612)215-2550. **E-mail:** editor@milkweed.org. **Website:** www.milkweed.org. Milkweed Editions will award the Milkweed Prize for Children's Literature to the best mss for young readers that Milkweed accepts for publication during the calendar year by a writer not previously published by Milkweed. All mss for young readers submitted for publication by Milkweed are automatically entered into the competition. Seeking full-length fiction between 90-200 pages. Does not consider picture books or poetry collections for young readers. Recognizes an outstanding literary novel for readers ages 8-13 and encourage writers to turn their attention to readers in this age group. Prize: $10,000 cash prize in addition to a publishing contract negotiated at the time of acceptance. Judged by the editors of Milkweed Editions.

MONTANA PRIZE IN FICTION

Cutbank Literary Magazine, *CutBank*, University of Montana, English Dept., LA 133, Missoula MT 59812. **E-mail:** editor.cutbank@gmail.com. **Website:** www.cutbankonline.org. **Contact:** Allison Linville, editor-in-chief. The Montana Prize in Fiction seeks to highlight work that showcases an authentic voice, a boldness of form, and a rejection of functional fixedness. Accepts online submissions only. Send a single work, no more than 35 pages. Guidelines available online. Deadline: January 15. Submissions period begins November 1. Prize: $500 and featured in the magazine. Judged by a guest judge each year.

THE HOWARD FRANK MOSHER SHORT FICTION PRIZE

Vermont College, 36 College St., Montpelier VT 05602. (802)828-8517. **E-mail:** hungermtn@vcfa.edu. **Website:** www.hungermtn.org. **Contact:** Miciah Bay Gault, editor. The Howard Frank Mosher Short Fiction Prize is an annual contest for short fiction. Enter one original, unpublished story under 10,000 words. Do not put name or address on the story; entries are judged blind. Accepts submissions online or via postal mail. Deadline: June 30. Prize: One first place winner receives $1,000 and publication. Two honorable mentions receive $100 each, and are considered for publication.

NATIONAL WRITERS ASSOCIATION NOVEL WRITING CONTEST

The National Writers Association, 10940 S. Parker Rd. #508, Parker CO 80134. (303)841-0246. **E-mail:** natlwritersassn@hotmail.com. **Website:** www.nationalwriters.com. **Contact:** Sandy Whelchel, director. Open to any genre or category. Contest begins December 1. Open to any writer. Entries must be unpublished. Length: 20,000-100,000 words. Contest forms are available on the NWA website or an attachment will be sent upon request via e-mail or with an SASE. Annual contest to help develop creative skills, to recognize and reward outstanding ability, and to increase the opportunity for the marketing and subsequent publication of novel mss. Deadline: April 1. Prize: 1st Place: $500; 2nd Place: $250; 3rd Place: $150. Judged by editors and agents.

NATIONAL WRITERS ASSOCIATION SHORT STORY CONTEST

10940 S. Parker Rd., #508, Parker CO 80134. (303)841-0246. **E-mail:** natlwritersassn@hotmail.com. **Website:** www.nationalwriters.com. Opens April 1. Any genre of short story manuscript may be entered. All entries must be postmarked by July 1. Only unpublished works may be submitted. All manuscripts must be typed, double-spaced, in the English language. Maximum length is 5,000 words. Those unsure of proper manuscript format should request Research Report #35. The entry must be accompanied by an entry form (photocopies are acceptable) and return SASE if you wish the material and rating sheets returned. Submissions will be destroyed, otherwise. Receipt of entry will not be acknowledged without a return postcard. Author's name and address must appear on the first page. Entries remain the property of the author and may be submitted during the contest as long as they are not published before the final notification of winners. Final prizes will be awarded in June. The purpose of the National Writers Assn. Short Story Contest is to encourage the development of creative skills, recognize and reward outstanding ability in the area of short story writing. Prize: 1st Prize: $250; 2nd Prize: $100; 3rd Prize: $50; 4th-10th places will receive a book. 1st-3rd place winners may be asked to grant one-time rights for publication in *Authorship* magazine. Honorable Mentions receive a certificate. Judging will be based on originality, marketability, research, and reader interest. Copies of the judges evaluation sheets will be sent to entrants furnishing an SASE with their entry.

THE NELLIGAN PRIZE FOR SHORT FICTION

Colorado Review/Center for Literary Publishing, 9105 Campus Delivery, Dept. of English, Colorado State University, Ft. Collins CO 80523-9105. (970)491-5449. **E-mail:** creview@colostate.edu. **Website:** http://nelliganprize.colostate.edu. **Contact:** Stephanie G'Schwind, editor. Annual competition/award for short stories. Receives approximately 900 stories. All entries are read blind by Colorado Review's editorial staff. 10-15 entries are selected to be sent on to a final judge. Stories must be unpublished and under 50 pages. "The Nelligan Prize for Short Fiction was established in memory of Liza Nelligan, a writer, editor, and friend of many in Colorado State University's English Department, where she received her master's degree in literature in 1992. By giving an award to the author of an outstanding short story each year, we hope to honor Liza Nelligan's life, her passion for writing, and her love of fiction." Deadline: March 14. Prize: $2,000 and publication of story in *Colorado Review.*

THE FLANNERY O'CONNOR AWARD FOR SHORT FICTION

The University of Georgia Press, Main Library, 3rd Floor, 320 S. Jackson St., Athens GA 30602. (706)369-6130. **Fax:** (706)369-6131. **Website:** www.ugapress.org. This competition welcomes short story or novella collections. Stories may have been published singly, but should not have appeared in a book-length collection of the author's own work. Length: 40,000-75,000 words. Accepts electronic submissions via website. Accepts multiple submissions, and simultaneous submissions, if identified. Title, author's name, and contact information should appear on a top cover sheet only. Include a table of contents. All submissions and announcement of winners and finalists will be confirmed via e-mail. Deadline: April 1-May 31. Prize: 2 winners receive $1,000 and book contracts from the University of Georgia Press.

SEAN O'FAOLAIN SHORT STORY COMPETITION

The Munster Literature Centre, Frank O'Connor House, 84 Douglas Street, Cork Ireland. +353-0214319255. **E-mail:** munsterlit@eircom.net. **Website:** www.munsterlit.ie. **Contact:** Patrick Cotter, artistic director. Entries should be unpublished. Anyone may enter contest. Length: 3,000 words max. Cover letter should include name, address, phone, e-mail, word count, novel/story title. Purpose is to reward writers of outstanding short stories. Deadline: July 31. Prize: 1st prize €1500 (approx US $2,200); 2nd prize €500 (approx $730). Four runners-up prizes of €100 (approx $146). All six stories to be published in *Southword Literary Journal*. First-Prize Winner offered week's residency in Anam Cara Artist's Retreat in Ireland.

ON THE PREMISES CONTEST

On The Premises, LLC, 4323 Gingham Court, Alexandria VA 22310. **E-mail:** questions@onthepremises.com. **Website:** www.onthepremises.com. **Contact:** Tarl Roger Kudrick or Bethany Granger, co-publishers. *On the Premises* aims to promote newer and/or relatively unknown writers who can write creative, compelling stories told in effective, uncluttered and evocative prose. Each contest challenges writers to produce a great story based on a broad premise that the editors supply as part of the contest. Submissions are accepted only through web-based submissions system. Entries should be unpublished. Length: minimum 1,000 words; maximum 5,000. No name or contact info should be in ms. Writers may submit own work. Check website for details on the specific premise that writers should incorporate into their story. Results announced within 2 weeks of contest deadline. Winners notified via e-mail and with publication of

On the Premises. Results made available to entrants on website and in publication. Deadline: Short story contests held twice a year; smaller mini-contests held four times a year; check website for exact dates. Prize: 1st Prize: $210; 2nd Prize: $160; 3rd Prize: $110; Honorable Mentions recieve $60. All prize winners are published in *On the Premises* magazine in HTML and PDF format. Judged by a panel of judges with professional editing and writing experience.

TIPS "Write something compelling, creative, and well-crafted. Above all, clearly use the contest premise."

KENNETH PATCHEN AWARD FOR THE INNOVATIVE NOVEL

Eckhard Gerdes Publishing, 12 Simpson Street, Apt. D, Geneva IL 60134. **E-mail:** egerdes@experimentalfiction.com. **Website:** www.experimentalfiction.com. **Contact:** Eckhard Gerdes. This award will honor the most innovative novel submitted during the previous calendar year. Kenneth Patchen is celebrated for being among the greatest innovators of American fiction, incorporating strategies of concretism, asemic writing, digression, and verbal juxtaposition into his writing long before such strategies were popularized during the height of American postmodernist experimentation in the 1970s. See guidelines and application form online at website. Deadline: All submissions must be postmarked between January 1 and July 31. Prize: $1,000 and 20 complimentary copies. Judged by novelist James Chapman.

THE PATERSON FICTION PRIZE

The Poetry Center at Passaic Community College, One College Blvd., Paterson NJ 07505. (973)684-6555. **Fax:** (973)523-6085. **E-mail:** mgillan@pccc.edu. **Website:** www.pccc.edu/poetry. **Contact:** Maria Mazziotti Gillan, executive director. Offered annually for a novel or collection of short fiction published the previous calendar year. For more information, visit the website or send SASE. Deadline: April 1. Prize: $1,000.

EDGAR ALLAN POE AWARD

1140 Broadway, Suite 1507, New York NY 10001. (212)888-8171. **Fax:** (212)888-8107. **E-mail:** mwa@mysterywriters.org. **Website:** www.mysterywriters.org. Mystery Writers of America is the leading association for professional crime writers in the United States. Members of MWA include most major writers of crime fiction and non-fiction, as well as screenwriters, dramatists, editors, publishers, and other professionals in the field. Categories include: Best Novel, Best Frist Novel by an American Author, Best Paperback/E-Book Original, Best Fact Crime, Best Critical/Biographical, Best Short Story, Best Juvenile Mystery, Best Young Adult Myster, Best Television Series Episode Teleplay, and Mary Higgins Clark Award. Purpose of the award: Honor authors of distinguished works in the mystery field. Previously published submissions only. Submissions made by the author, author's agent; "normally by the publisher." Work must be published/produced the year of the contest. Deadline: November 30. Prize: Awards ceramic bust of "Edgar" for winner; scrolls for all nominees. Judged by professional members of Mystery Writers of America (writers).

THE KATHERINE ANNE PORTER PRIZE FOR FICTION

Nimrod International Journal, The University of Tulsa, 800 S. Tucker Dr., Tulsa OK 74104. (918)631-3080. **Fax:** (918)631-3033. **E-mail:** nimrod@utulsa.edu. **Website:** www.utulsa.edu/nimrod. **Contact:** Eilis O'Neal. Submissions must be unpublished. Work must be in English or translated by original author. Author's name must not appear on ms. Include cover sheet with title, author's name, address, phone number, and e-mail address (author must have a US address by October of contest year to enter). Mark "Contest Entry" on submission envelop and cover sheet. Include SASE for results only; mss will not be returned. Guidelines available for #10 SASE or on website. 7,500-word maximum for short stories. Deadline: April 30. Prize: 1st Place: $2,000 and publication; 2nd Place: $1,000 and publication. Judged by the *Nimrod* editors, who select the finalists and a recognized author, who selects the winners.

PRESS 53 AWARD FOR SHORT FICTION

Press 53, 560 N. Trade St., Suite 193, Winston-Salem NC 27101. **E-mail:** kevin@press53.com. **Website:** www.press53.com. **Contact:** Kevin Morgan Watson, publisher. Awarded to an outstanding, unpublished collection of short stories. Details and guidelines available online. Deadline: December 31. Submission period begins September 1. Finalists announced March 1. Winner announced on May 3. Publication in October. Prize: Publication of winning short story collection, $1,000 cash advance, travel expenses and lodging for a special reading and book signing in Winston-Salem, NC, attendance as special guest to the Press 53/*Prime Number Magazine* Gathering of Writers, and 10 copies of the book. Judged by publisher Kevin Morgan Watson and fiction editor Christine Norris.

PRISM INTERNATIONAL ANNUAL SHORT FICTION CONTEST

Creative Writing Program, UBC, Buch. E462 - 1866 Main Mall, Vancouver BC V6T 1Z1 Canada. (604)822-2514. **Fax:** (604)822-3616. **Website:** http://prismmagazine.ca/contests. **Contact:** Clara Kumagai, executive editor, promotions. Offered annually for unpublished work to award the best in contemporary fiction. Works of translation are eligible. Guidelines by SASE, by e-mail, or on website. Acquires first North American serial rights upon publication, and rights to publish online for promotional or archival purposes. Open to any writer except students and faculty in the Creative Writing Department at UBC, or people who have taken a creative writing course at UBC with the 2 years prior to the contest deadline. Deadline: January 23. Prize: 1st Place: $2,000; 1st Runner-up: $300; 2nd Runner-up: $200; winner is published.

THE ROGERS WRITERS' TRUST FICTION PRIZE

The Writers' Trust of Canada, 460 Richmond St. W., Suite 600, Toronto ON M5V 1Y1 Canada. (416)504-8222. **Fax:** (416)504-9090. **E-mail:** info@writerstrust.com. **Website:** www.writerstrust.com. **Contact:** Amanda Hopkins. Awarded annually to the best novel or short story collection published within the previous year. Presented at the Writers' Trust Awards event held in Toronto each fall. Open to Canadian citizens and permanent residents only. Deadline: August. Prize: $25,000 and $2,500 to 4 finalists.

JOANNA CATHERINE SCOTT NOVEL EXCERPT PRIZE CATEGORY

Soul-Making Keats Literary Competition Category, The Webhallow House, 1544 Sweetwood Dr., Broadmoor Village CA 94015-2029. **E-mail:** soulkeats@mail.com. **Website:** www.soulmakingcontest.us. **Contact:** Eileen Malone. Open annually to any writer. Send first chapter or the first 20 pages, whichever comes first. Include a 1-page synopsis indicating category at top of page. Identify with 3x5 card only. Deadline: November 30. Prize: 1st Place: $100; 2nd Place: $50; 3rd Place: $25.

SCREAMINMAMAS MAGICAL FICTION CONTEST

1911 Cleveland St., Hollywood FL 33020. **E-mail:** screaminmamas@gmail.com. **Website:** www.screaminmamas.com/contests. **Contact:** Darlene Pistocchi, editor/managing director. This contest celebrates moms and the magical spirit of the holidays. If you had an opportunity to be anything you wanted to be, what would you be? Transport yourself! Become that character and write a short story around that character. Can be any genre. Length: 800-3,000 words. Open only to moms. Deadline: June 30. Prize: complementary subscription to magazine, plus publication.

SHEEHAN YA BOOK PRIZE

P.O. Box 172873, Tampa FL 33672. **E-mail:** elephantrockbooksya@gmail.com. **Website:** elephantrockbooks.com/ya.html. **Contact:** Jotham Burrello and Amanda Hurley. Guidelines are available on the website: http://www.elephantrockbooks.com/about.html#submissions. "Elephant Rock Books' teen imprint is looking for a great story to follow our critically acclaimed novel, *The Carnival at Bray*. We're after quality stories with heart, guts, and a clear voice. We're especially interested in the quirky, the hopeful, and the real. We are not particularly interested in genre fiction and prefer standalone novels, unless you've got the next *Hunger Games*. We seek writers who believe in the transformative power of a great story, so show us what you've got." Deadline: July 1. Prize: $1,000 as an advance

STORYSOUTH MILLION WRITERS AWARD

E-mail: terry@storysouth.com. **Website:** www.storysouth.com. **Contact:** Terry Kennedy, editor. Annual award to honor and promote the best fiction published in online literary journals and magazines during the previous year. Anyone may nominate one story for the award. To be eligible for nomination, a story must be longer than 1,000 words. See website for details on how to nominate someone. Most literary prizes for short fiction have traditionally ignored web-published fiction. This award aims to show that world-class fiction is being published online and to promote to the larger reading and literary community. Deadline: August 15. Nominations of stories begins on March 15. Prize: Prize amounts subject to donation. Check website for details.

THREE CHEERS AND A TIGER

E-mail: editors@toasted-cheese.com. **Website:** www.toasted-cheese.com. **Contact:** Stephanie Lenz, editor. Contestants are to write a short story (following a specific theme) within 48 hours. Contests are held first weekend in spring (mystery) and first weekend in fall (sf/f). Word limit announced at the start of the contest. Contest-specific information is announced 48 hours before the contest submission deadline. Results announced in April and October. Winners notified by e-mail. List of winners on website. Entries must be unpublished. Open to any writer. Accepts inquiries by e-mail. Cover letter should include name, address, e-mail, word count and title. Information should be in the body of the e-mail. It will be removed before the judging begins. Prize: Amazon gift certificates and publication. Blind-judged by 2 *Toasted Cheese* editors. Each judge uses his or her own criteria to choose entries.

TIMELESS LOVE/ROMANCE CONTEST

Sponsored by Oak Tree Press, 140 E. Palmer St., Taylorville IL 62568. **E-mail:** tl-contestadmin@oaktreebooks.com. **Website:** www.oaktreebooks.com. Annual contest for unpublished authors or authors shifting to a new genre. Accepts novels of all romance genres, from sweet to supernatural. Guidelines and entry forms are available for SASE. Deadline: July 31. Prize: Publication in both paper and e-book editions. Judged by publishing industry professionals who prescreen entries; publisher makes final selection.

STEVEN TURNER AWARD FOR BEST FIRST WORK OF FICTION

6335 W. Northwest Hwy., #618, Dallas TX 75225. **Website:** www.texasinstituteofletters.org. Offered annually for work published January 1-December 31 for the best first book of fiction. Writers must have been born in Texas, have lived in the state for at least 2 consecutive years at some time, or the subject matter of the work should be associated with the state. Guidelines online. Deadline: normally first week in January; see website for specific date. Prize: $1,000.

WAASNODE SHORT FICTION PRIZE

Passages North, Department of English, Northern Michigan University, 1401 Presque Isle Ave., Marquette MI 49855. (906)227-1203. **Fax:** (906)227-1096. **E-mail:** passages@nmu.edu. **Website:** www.passagesnorth.com. **Contact:** Jennifer Howard. Offered every 2 years to publish new voices in literary fiction (maximum 10,000 words). Guidelines for SASE or online. Submissions accepted online. Deadline: March 15. Submission period begins January 15. Prize: $1,000 and publication for winner; 2 honorable mentions also published; all entrants receive copy of *Passages North.*

WABASH PRIZE FOR FICTION

Sycamore Review, Department of English, 500 Oval Dr., Purdue University, West Lafayette IN 47907. **E-mail:** sycamore@purdue.edu; sycamorefiction@purdue.edu. **Website:** www.sycamorereview.com/contest/. **Contact:** Kara Krewer, editor-in-chief. Annual contest for unpublished fiction. For each submission, send one story (limit 7,500 words). Ms pages should be numbered and should include the title of the piece. All stories must be previously unpublished. See website for more guidelines. Submit via online submissions manager. Deadline: April 1. Submissions period begins March 1. Prize: $1,000 and publication.

THE WASHINGTON WRITERS' PUBLISHING HOUSE FICTION PRIZE

Washington Writers' Publishing House, P.O. Box 15271, Washington DC 20003. **E-mail:** wwphpress@gmail.com. **Website:** www.washingtonwriters.org. Fiction writers living within 75 miles of the Capitol are invited to submit a ms of either a novel or a collection of short stories (no more than 350 pages, double-spaced). Author's name should not appear on the manuscript. The title page of each copy should contain the title only. Provide name, address, telephone number, e-mail address, and title on a separate cover sheet accompanying the submission. A separate page for acknowledgments may be included for stories or excerpts previously published in journals and anthologies. Send electronic copies to wwphpress@gmail.com or mail paper copies and/or reading fee (check to WWPH) with SASE to: Washington Writers' Publishing House Fiction Prize, c/o Elisavietta Ritchie, P.O. Box 298, Broomes Island, MD 20615. Deadline: November 1. Submission period begins July 1. Prize: $1,000 and 50 copies of the book.

THOMAS WOLFE FICTION PRIZE

North Carolina Writers' Network, Thomas Wolfe Fiction Prize, Great Smokies Writing Program, Attn: Nancy Williams, CPO #1860, UNC, Asheville NC 28805. **Website:** www.ncwriters.org. The Thomas Wolfe Fiction Prize honors internationally celebrated North Carolina novelist Thomas Wolfe. The prize is administered by Tommy Hays and the Great Smokies Writing Program at the University of North Carolina at Asheville. Competition is open to all writers, regardless of geographical location or prior publication. Submit 2 copies of an unpublished fiction ms (short story or self-contained novel excerpt) not to exceed 12 double-spaced, single-sided pages. Deadline: January 30. Submissions period begins December 1. Prize: $1,000 and potential publication in *The Thomas Wolfe Review.*

TOBIAS WOLFF AWARD FOR FICTION

Bellingham Review, Mail Stop 9053, Western Washington University, Bellingham WA 98225. (360)650-4863. **E-mail:** bellingham.review@wwu.edu. **Website:** www.bhreview.org. **Contact:** Brenda Miller, editor-in-chief; Kaitlyn Teer, managing editor. Offered annually for unpublished work. Guidelines available on website; online submissions only. Categories: novel exceprts and short stories. Entries must be unpublished. Length: 6,000 words or less per story or chapter. Open to any writer. Electronic submissions only. Enter submissions through Submittable, a link to which is available on the website. Winner announced in August and notified by e-mail. Deadline: March 15. Submissions period begins December 1. Prize: $1,000, plus publication and subscription.

WORLD FANTASY AWARDS

P.O. Box 43, Mukilteo WA 98275. **E-mail:** sfexecsec@gmail.com. **Website:** www.worldfantasy.org. **Contact:** Peter Dennis Pautz, president. Offered annually for previously published work in several categories, including life achievement, novel, novella, short story, anthology, collection, artist, special award-pro and special award-nonpro. Works are recommended by attendees of current and previous 2 years' conventions and a panel of judges. Entries must be previously published. Published submissions from previous calendar year. Word length: 10,000-40,000 for novella, 10,000 for short story. All fantasy is eligible, from supernatural horror to Tolkien-esque to sword and sorcery to the occult, and beyond. Cover letter should include name, address, phone, e-mail, word count, title, and publications where submission was previously published, submitted to the address above and the panel of judges when they appear on the website. Results announced November 1 at annual convention. For contest results, visit website. Guidelines available in December for SASE or on website. Awards to recognize excellence in fantasy literature worldwide. Deadline: June 1. Prize: Bust of H.P. Lovecraft. Judged by panel.

WOW! WOMEN ON WRITING QUARTERLY FLASH FICTION CONTEST

WOW! Women on Writing, P.O. Box 41104, Long Beach CA 90853. **E-mail:** contestinfo@wow-womenonwriting.com. **Website:** www.wow-womenonwriting.com/contest.php. **Contact:** Angela Mackintosh, editor. Contest offered quarterly. "We are open to all themes and genres, although we do encourage writers to take a close look at our literary agent guest judge for the season if you are serious about winning." Entries must be 250-750 words. Deadline: August 31, November 30, February 28, May 31. Prize: 1st place: $350 cash prize, $25 Amazon gift certificate, book from sponsor, story published on WOW! Women On Writing, interview on blog; 2nd place: $250 cash prize, $25 Amazon gift certificate, book our sponsor, story published on WOW! Women On Writing, interview on blog; 3rd place: $150 cash prize, $25 Amazon gift certificate, book from sponsor, story published on WOW! Women On Writing, interview on blog; 7 runners up: $25 Amazon gift certificate, book from sponsor, story published on WOW! Women on Writing, interview on blog; 10 honorable mentions: $20 gift certificate from Amazon, book our sponsor, story title and name published on WOW!Women On Writing.

WRITER'S DIGEST SHORT SHORT STORY COMPETITION

Writer's Digest, 10151 Carver Road, Suite 200, Blue Ash OH 45242. (715)445-4612; ext. 13430. **E-mail:** WritersDigestShortShortStoryCompetition@fwmedia.com. **Website:** www.writersdigest.com. **Contact:** Nicole Howard. Looking for fiction that's bold, brilliant, and brief. Send your best in 1,500 words or fewer. All entries must be original, unpublished, and not submitted elsewhere at the time of submission. *Writer's Digest* reserves one-time publication rights to the 1st-25th winning entries. Winners will be notified by Feb. 28. Early bird deadline: November 17. Final deadline: December 15. Prize: 1st Place: $3,000 and a trip to the Writer's Digest Conference; 2nd Place: $1,500; 3rd Place: $500; 4th-10th Place: $100; 11th-25th Place: $50 gift certificate for writersdigestshop.com.

ZOETROPE SHORT STORY CONTEST

Zoetrope: All Story, Zoetrope: All-Story, Attn: Fiction Editor, 916 Kearny St., San Francisco CA 94133. (415)788-7500. **E-mail:** contests@all-story.com. **Web-**

site: www.all-story.com. Annual short fiction contest. Considers submissions of short stories and one-act plays no longer than 7,000 words. Excerpts from larger works, screenplays, treatments, and poetry will be returned unread. For details, visit the website during the summer. Deadline: October 1. Submissions period begins July 1. Prize: 1st place: $1,000 and publication on website; 2nd place: $500; 3rd place: $250.

ZONE 3 FICTION AWARD

Zone 3, Austin Peay State University, P.O. Box 4565, Clarksville TN 37044. (931)221-7031. **Fax:** (931)221-7149. **E-mail:** wallacess@apsu.edu. **Website:** www.apsu.edu/zone3/contests. **Contact:** Susan Wallace, Managing Editor. Annual contest for unpublished fiction. Open to any fiction writer. Accepts entries online and via postal mail. Deadline: April 1. Prize: $250 and publication.

NONFICTION

AMERICA & ME ESSAY CONTEST

Farm Bureau Insurance, P.O. Box 30400, Lansing MI 48909. **E-mail:** lfedewa@fbinsmi.com. **Website:** www.farmbureauinsurance-mi.com. Focuses on encouraging students to write about their personal Michigan heroes: someone they know personally who has encouraged them and inspired them to want to live better and achieve more. Open to Michigan eighth graders. Contest rules and entry form available on website. Encourages Michigan youth to explore their roles in America's future. Deadline: November 18. Prize: $1,000, plaque, and medallion for top 10 winners.

ANNUAL MEMOIRS COMPETITION

The Writers' Workshop of Asheville, NC, Memoirs Contest, 387 Beaucatcher Rd., Asheville NC 28805. **Website:** www.twwoa.org. Submit a memoir of 5,000 words or less. Multiple entries are accepted. All work must be unpublished. Pages should be paper claipped, with your name, address, phone and title of work on a cover sheet. Double-space and use 12-point font. Deadline: November 30. Prize: 1st Place: A 2 night stay at the Mountain Muse B&B and 50 pages line-edited and revised by editorial staff; 2nd Place: A 2 night stay at the B&B and 50 pages line-edited; 3rd Place: 25 pages line-edited. Up to 10 Honorable Mentions.

ANTHEM ESSAY CONTEST

The Ayn Rand Institute, P.O. Box 57044, Irvine CA 92619-7044. (949)222-6550. **Fax:** (949)222-6558. **E-mail:** info@aynrandnovels.com. **Website:** www.essaycontest.aynrandnovels.org. Offered annually to encourage analytical thinking and excellence in writing (600-1,200 word essay), and to expose students to the philosophic ideas of Ayn Rand. "For information contact your English teacher or guidance counselor or visit our website." Open to 8th, 9th and 10th graders. See website for topics. Deadline: March 20. Prize: 1st Place: $2,000; 2nd Place (5): $500; 3rd Place (10): $200; Finalist (45): $50; Semifinalist (175): $30.

ATLAS SHRUGGED ESSAY CONTEST

The Ayn Rand Institute, P.O. Box 57044, Irvine CA 92619-7044. (949)222-6550, ext. 247. **Fax:** (949)222-6558. **E-mail:** info@aynrandnovels.com. **Website:** http://essaycontest.aynrandnovels.org. Offered annually to encourage analytical thinking and excellence in writing, and to expose students to the philosophic ideas of Ayn Rand. Open to 12th graders, college undergraduates, and graduate students. Essay length: 800-1,600 words. Essays are judged both on style and content. Guidelines and topics available on the website. The winning applicant will be judged on both style and content. Judges will look for writing that is clear, articulate and logically organized. Winning essays must demonstrate an outstanding grasp of the philosophic meaning of *Atlas Shrugged*. Essay submissions are evaluated in a fair and unbiased four-round judging process. Judges are individually selected by the Ayn Rand Institute based on a demonstrated knowledge and understanding of Ayn Rand's works. Deadline: October 24. Prize: 1st Place: $10,000; 2nd Place (3 awards): $2,000; 3rd Place (5 awards): $1,000; Finalists (25 awards): $100; Semifinalists (50 awards): $50.

BANCROFT PRIZE

Columbia University, c/o Office of the University Librarian, 517 Butter Library, Mail Code 1101, 535 W. 114th St., New York NY 10027. (212)854-7309. **Fax:** (212)854-9099. **Website:** http://library.columbia.edu/about/awards/bancroft.html. **Contact:** Bancroft Prize Committee. The Bancroft Prizes are awarded annually by Columbia University in the City of New York. Two annual prizes are awarded to the authors of distinguished works in either or both of the following categories: American History (including biography) and Diplomacy. Awards are for books published in the previous year. Send 4 copies, 3 for the members of the jury on the award and 1 for the Libraries of Columbia University. Deadline: November 1. Prize: $10,000 for the winning entry in each category.

BRITISH CZECH AND SLOVAK ASSOCIATION WRITING COMPETITION

24 Ferndale, Tunbridge Wells Kent TN2 3NS England. **E-mail:** prize@bcsa.co.uk. **Website:** www.bcsa.co.uk/specials.html. Annual contest for original writing (entries should not exceed 2,000 words) in English on the links between Britain and the Czech/Slovak Republics, or describing society in transition in the Republics since 1989. Entries can be fact or fiction. Topics can include history, politics, the sciences, economics, the arts, or literature. Deadline: June 30. Winners announced in November. Prize: 1st Place: £300; 2nd Place: £100.

CANADIAN LIBRARY ASSOCIATION STUDENT ARTICLE CONTEST

Canadian Library Association, 1150 Morrison Dr., Suite 400, Ottawa ON K2H 8S9 Canada. (613)232-9625, ext. 322. **Fax:** (613)563-9895. **E-mail:** info@cla.ca. **Website:** www.cla.ca. **Contact:** Marketing and Communications Manager. Offered annually to unpublished articles discussing, analyzing, or evaluating timely issues in librarianship or information science. Open to all students registered in or recently graduated from a Canadian library school, a library techniques program, or faculty of education library program. Submissions may be in English or French. Deadline: March 31. Prize: $200 and the winning article will be published in *Feliciter*, the magazine of the Canadian Library Association.

THE DOROTHY CAPPON PRIZE FOR THE BEST ESSAY

New Letters, University of Missouri-Kansas City, *New Letters* Awards for Writers, UMKC, University House, 5101 Rockhill Rd., Kansas City MO 64110-2499. (816)235-1168. **Fax:** (816)235-2611. **E-mail:** newletters@umkc.edu. **Website:** www.newletters.org. **Contact:** Ashley Kaine. Contest is offered annually for unpublished work to discover and reward emerging writers and to give experienced writers a place to try new genres. Acquires first North American serial rights. Open to any writer. Guidelines by SASE or online. Entries should not exceed 8,000 words. Deadline: May 18. Prize: 1st Place: $1,500 and publication in a volume of *New Letters*; runner-up will receive a copy of a recent book of poetry or fiction courtesy of BkMk Press. All entries will receive consideration for publication in future editions of *New Letters*.

MORTON N. COHEN AWARD

Modern Language Association of America, 26 Broadway, 3rd Floor, New York NY 10004-1789. (646)576-5141. **Fax:** (646)458-0030. **E-mail:** awards@mla.org. **Website:** www.mla.org. **Contact:** Coordinator of Book Prizes. Awarded in odd-numbered years for a distinguished collection of letters. At least 1 volume of the edition must have been published during the previous 2 years. Editors need not be members of the MLA. Under the terms of the award, the winning collection will be one that provides readers with a clear, accurate, and readable text; necessary background information; and succinct and eloquent introductory material and annotations. The edited collection should be in itself a work of literature. Deadline: May 1. Prize: A cash award and a certificate to be presented at the Modern Language Association's annual convention in January.

THE SHAUGHNESSY COHEN PRIZE FOR POLITICAL WRITING

The Writers' Trust of Canada, 460 Richmond St. W., Suite 600, Toronto ON M5V 1Y1 Canada. (416)504-8222. **Fax:** (416)504-9090. **E-mail:** info@writerstrust.com. **Website:** www.writerstrust.com. **Contact:** Amanda Hopkins. Awarded annually for a nonfiction book of outstanding literary merit that enlarges understanding of contemporary Canadian political and social issues. Presented at the Politics & the Pen event each spring in Ottawa. Open to Canadian citizens and permanent residents only. Prize: $25,000 and $2,500 to 4 finalists.

CARR P. COLLINS AWARD FOR NONFICTION

The Texas Institute of Letters, P.O. Box 609, Round Rock TX 78680. **E-mail:** tilsecretary@yahoo.com. **Website:** http://texasinstituteofletters.org/. Offered annually for work published January 1-December 31 of the previous year to recognize the best nonfiction book by a writer who was born in Texas, who has lived in the state for at least 2 consecutive years at one point, or a writer whose work has some notable connection with Texas. See website for guidelines and instructions on submitting. Deadline: January 10. Prize: $5,000.

THE LELA COMMON AWARD FOR CANADIAN HISTORY

6 West St. N, Suite 203, Orillia ON L3V 5B8 Canada. (705)325-3926. **E-mail:** admin@canadianauthors.org. **Website:** www.canadianauthors.org. **Contact:** Anita Purcell, executive director. Offered annually for a work of historical nonfiction on a Canadian topic by a Canadian author. Entry form required. Obtain entry form from contact name or download from website. Deadline: January 15. Prize: $2,000 and a silver medal. The CAA Awards Chair appoints a trustee for this award. That trustee selects two judges. The identities of the trustee and judges are confidential throughout the judging process. Decisions of the trustee and judges are final, and they may choose not to award a prize. A shortlist of the best three entries in each category is announced in June. The winners are announced at the gala awards banquet during the annual CanWrite! conference in June.

CONNELL GUIDES ESSAY PRIZE

0207-633-3791. **Website:** www.connellguides.com. Essay competition. Write about which novel, play, or poem has made an impact on you, and why you find it interesting and enjoyable. Essay should combine insight, originality, and clarity. Address chosen subject with argumentative energy, showing why it has made an impact on you. Essays need to show logic in the way they are structured and precision in their choice of words. Take an original point of view, make intelligent use of evidence found in and around chose text(s). Where appropriate, reference the history and culture surrounding the text(s) to support points. Essays should be between 1,200-1,500 words. Deadline: January 26. Winners announced on March 2. Prize: £500. Two runners up will receive a complete set of Connell Guides. Judged by Philip Pullman in 2014.

CREATIVE NONFICTION BOOK AWARD

Zone 3, Austin Peay State University, Austin Peay State University, PO Box 4565, Clarksville TN 37044. (931)221-7031. **Fax:** (931)221-7149. **E-mail:** wrighta@apsu.edu@aspu.edu; wallacess@apsu.edu. **Website:** www.apsu.edu/zone3/contests. **Contact:** Amy Wright, acquisitions editor; Susan Wallace, managing editor. This competition is open to all authors writing original works in English. Mss that embrace creative nonfiction's potential by combining lyric exposition, researched reflection, travel dialogues, or creative criticism are encouraged. Memoir, personal narrative, essay collections, and literary nonfiction are also invited. Submit one copy of your ms, 150-300 pages. Accepts entries via postal mail or online. Separate instructions for both, see website for guidelines and details. Deadline: April 1. Prize: $1,000 and publication.

CREATIVE NONFICTION CONTEST

PRISM International, Creative Writing Program, UBC, Buch E462--1866 Main Mall, Vancouver BC V6T 1Z1 Canada. **E-mail:** promotions@prismmagazine.ca. **Website:** www.prismmagazine.ca. Offered annually for published and unpublished writers to promote and reward excellence in literary creative nonfiction. *PRISM* buys first North American serial rights upon publication. Also buys limited web rights for pieces selected for the website. Open to anyone except students and faculty of the Creative Writing Program at UBC or people who have taken a creative writing course at UBC in the 2 years prior to contest deadline. All entrants receive a 1-year subscription to *PRISM*. Entries are accepted via Submittable at http://prisminternational.submittable.com/submit or by mail. Deadline: November 21. Prize: $2,000 grand prize, $300 runner-up, and $200 second runner-up.

DIAGRAM ESSAY CONTEST

Department of English, University of Arizona, P.O. Box 210067, Tucson AZ 85721-0067. **E-mail:** nmp@thediagram.com; editor@thediagram.com. **Website:** www.thediagram.com/contest.html. **Contact:** Ander Monson, editor. Contest for essays up to 10,000 words. Deadline: End of November. Check website for more details. Prize: $1,000 and publication. Finalist essay also published. Judged by editors Ander Monson and Nicole Walker.

ANNIE DILLARD AWARD FOR CREATIVE NONFICTION

Bellingham Review, Mail Stop 9053, 516 High St., Western Washington University, Bellingham WA 98225. (360)650-4863. **E-mail:** bellingham.review@wwu.edu. **Website:** www.bhreview.org. **Contact:** Brenda Miller, editor-in-chief; Kaitlyn Teer, managing editor. Offered annually for unpublished essays on any subject and in any style. Guidelines available online. Deadline: March 15. Submission period begins December 1. Prize: $1,000, plus publication and copies. All finalists considered for publication. All entrants receive subscription.

TIPS "The *Bellingham Review* seeks literature of palpable quality: poems, stories, and essays so beguiling they invite us to come closer, look deeper, touch, sniff and taste their essence. We hunger for a kind of writing that nudges the limits of form or executes traditional forms exquisitely."

GORDON W. DILLON/RICHARD C. PETERSON MEMORIAL ESSAY PRIZE

American Orchid Society, Inc., American Orchid Society at Fairchild Tropical Botanic Garden, 10901 Old Cutler Rd., Coral Gables FL 33156. (305)740-2010. **Fax:** (305)740-2011. **E-mail:** theaos@aos.org. **E-mail:** rmchatton@aos.org. **Website:** www.aos.org. **Contact:** Ron McHatton. The Gordon W. Dillon\Richard C. Peterson Memorial Essay Prize is an annual writing competition. Open to amateur and professional writers. The theme is announced each May in *Orchids* magazine. All themes deal with an aspect of orchids. Acquires one-time rights. The essay must be an original, unpublished article. Submissions must be no more than 5,000 words in length. Submissions will be judged without knowledge of the identity of the author. Established to honor the memory of two former editors of the *AOS Bulletin* (now *Orchids*). Deadline: November 30. Prize: Cash prize and a certificate. Winning entry usually published in the June issue of *Orchids* magazine.

THE DONNER PRIZE

The Award for Best Book on Public Policy by a Canadian, The Donner Canadian Foundation, 400 Logan Ave., Toronto ON M4M 2N9 Canada. (416)368-8253. **E-mail:** sherry@naylorandassociates.com. **Website:** www.donnerbookprize.com. **Contact:** Sherry Naylor. Annual award that rewards excellence and innovation in public policy writing by Canadians. Deadline: November 30. Prize: Winning book receives $50,000; shortlisted titles get $7,500 each.

EDUCATOR'S AWARD

The Delta Kappa Gamma Society International, P.O. Box 1589, Austin TX 78767-1589. (888)762-4685. **Fax:** (512)478-3961. **Website:** www.dkg.org. **Contact:** Carolyn Pittman, chair. Offered annually for quality research and nonfiction published January-December of previous year. This award recognizes educational research and writings of female authors whose work may influence the direction of thought and action necessary to meet the needs of today's complex society. The book must be written by 1 or 2 women who are citizens of any country in which The Delta Kappa Gamma Society International is organized: Canada, Costa Rica, Denmark, Estonia, Finland, Germany, Great Britain, Guatemala, Iceland, Mexico, The Netherlands, Norway, Puerto Rico, Sweden, US, Panama. Guidelines (required) for SASE. The Educators Award Committee is charged with the responsibility of selecting an appropriate book as winner of the annual Educator's Award. Committee members read and evaluate books submitted by publishers that meet the criteria of having been written by women and whose content may influence the direction of thought and action necessary to meet the needs of today's complex society; furthermore, the content must be of more than local interest with relationship, direct or implied, to education everywhere. Deadline: February 1. Prize: $2,500. Judged by Educators Award Committee.

EVANS BIOGRAPHY & HANDCART AWARDS

Mountain West Center for Regional Studies, Room 339, Old Main, 0735 Old Main Hill, Utah State University, Logan UT 84322-0735. (435)797-0299. **Fax:** (435)797-1092. **E-mail:** mwc@usu.edu. **Website:** http://mountainwest.usu.edu/evans.aspx. **Contact:** Patricia Lambert, director. The Evans Biography and Handcart Awards encourage the best in research and writing about the Interior West through the giving of two annual prizes for excellence in biography. The Evans Biography Award is given to the best biography of a person who lived a significant portion of his or her life in the Interior West, or, in the words of the awards' founders, "Mormon Country"—that region historically influenced by Mormon institutions and social practices. The Evans Handcart Award is given to a biography addressing similar subjects as the Evans Biography Award, but often by an emerging author or written as a family history. Send 6 copies of the book and one copy of the author's resume. See website for details. Deadline: January 1 for books published in the previous calendar year. Prize: $10,000 for the Evans Biography Award; and $2,500 for the Evans Handcart Award. Judged by a local jury of five scholars and book experts.

EVENT CREATIVE NONFICTION CONTEST

EVENT, Poetry and Prose., P.O. Box 2503, New Westminster BC V3L 5B2 Canada. (604)527-5293. **Fax:** (604)527-5095. **E-mail:** event@douglascollege.ca. **Website:** www.eventmagazine.ca. Offered annually for unpublished creative nonfiction. Maximum length: 5,000 words. Acquires first North American serial print rights and limited non-exclusive digital rights for the winning entries. Open to any writer, except Douglas College employees and students. Previously published material, including that which has appeared online or has been accepted for publication elsewhere, cannot be considered. No simultaneous submissions. The writer should not be identified on the entry. Include separate cover sheet with name, address, phone number/email, and title(s). Enter online or send to address above. Multiple entries are allowed; however, each entry must be accompanied by its own entry fee. Pay online or make check or international money order payable to EVENT. Deadline: April 15. Prize: $1,500 in prizes, plus publication in *EVENT*. Judges reserve the right to award 2 or 3 prizes: 3 at $500 or 2 at $750, plus publication payment.

THE IRA DINA FEITELSON RESEARCH AWARD

International Reading Association, Division of Research & Policy, P.O. Box 8139, Newark DE 19714-8139. (302)731-1600, ext. 423. **Fax:** (302)731-1057. **E-mail:** research@reading.org. **Website:** www.reading.org. **Contact:** Marcella Moore. This is an award for an exemplary work published in English in a refereed journal that reports on an empirical study investigating aspects of literacy acquisition, such as phonemic awareness, the alphabetic principle, bilingualism, or cross-cultural studies of beginning reading. Articles may be submitted for consideration by researchers, authors, et al. Copies of the applications and guidelines can be downloaded in PDF format from the website. Deadline: September 1. Prize: $500 award and recognition at the International Reading Association's annual convention.

JOHN GUYON LITERARY NONFICTION PRIZE

Crab Orchard Review, Department of English, Faner Hall 2380 - Mail Code 4503, 1000 Faner Drive, Carbondale IL 62901. **E-mail:** jtribble@siu.edu. **Website:** www.craborchardreview.siu.edu. **Contact:** Jon C. Tribble, managing editor. Offered annually for excellence in the writing of creative nonfiction. Not a prize for academic essays. *Crab Orchard Review* acquires first North American serial rights to submitted works. Open to US citizens only. See website for guidelines and details. Deadline: April 21. Submission period begins February 21. Prize: $2,000 and publication. Finalists are each offered $500 and publication.

ALBERT J. HARRIS AWARD

International Reading Association, P.O. Box 8139, Newark DE 19714-8139. (302)731-1600, ext. 423; (800)336-7323. **Fax:** (302)731-1057. **E-mail:** research@reading.org. **Website:** www.reading.org. **Contact:** Marcella Moore. The IRA Albert J. Harris Award is given for a recently published journal article or monograph that makes an outstanding contribution to our understanding of prevention or assessment of reading or learning disabilities. Publications may be submitted by the author or anyone else. Copies may be duplicated from the actual publication; reprints are also acceptable. Nomination for the IRA Albert J. Harris Award is open to all literacy professionals. Deadline: September 1. Prize: Monetary award and recognition at the International Reading Association's annual convention.

HENDRICKS AWARD

The New Netherland Institute, Cultural Education Center, Room 10D45, 222 Madison Ave., Albany NY 12230. **Fax:** (518)473-0472. **E-mail:** nyslfnn@nysed.gov. **Website:** www.newnetherlandinstitute.org. Given annually to the best book or book-length ms relating to any aspect of New Netherland and its legacy. Two categories of submissions will be considered in alternate years: (1) recently completed dissertations and unpublished book-length manuscripts, and (2) recently published books. If there is no suitable winner in the designated category in any particular year, submissions from the alternate category will be considered. In addition, submissions from previous years will be reconsidered for the Award. Entries must be based on research completed or published within three years prior to the deadline for submission. Entries may deal with any aspect of New Netherland and its legacy. Biographies of individuals whose careers illuminate aspects of the history of New Netherland and its legacy are eligible, as are manuscripts dealing with literature and the arts, provided that the methodology is historical. Deadline: February 1. Prize: $5,000 and a framed print of a painting by L.F. Tantillo. Judged by a 5-member panel of scholars.

THOMAS J. HRUSKA MEMORIAL PRIZE IN NONFICTION

Passages North, Department of English, Northern Michigan University, 1401 Presque Isle Ave., Marquette MI 49855. (906) 227-1203. **Fax:** (906) 227-1096. **Website:** www.passagesnorth.com. **Contact:** Kate Myers Hanson, acquisitions. Contest for nonfiction, held biennially. *Passages North* also offers poetry and fiction contests. Send SASE for announcement of winners. Author's name may appear anywhere on ms or cover letter. Manuscripts will not be returned. All entrants receive a contest issue. Honorable mentions will also be chosen for each contest and may or may not be published according to the needs of the editors. Deadline: February 15. Prize: $1,000 1st Place prize and publication.

THE HUNGER MOUNTAIN CREATIVE NONFICTION PRIZE

Vermont College, 36 College St., Montpelier VT 05602. (802)828-8517. **E-mail:** hungermtn@vcfa.edu. **Website:** www.hungermtn.org. **Contact:** Miciah Bay Gault, editor. Annual contest for the best writing in creative nonfiction. Submit essays under 10,000 words. Guidelines available on website. Accepts entries online or via mail. Deadline: September 10. Prize: $1,000 and publication. Two honorable mentions receive $100 each.

IRA OUTSTANDING DISSERTATION OF THE YEAR AWARD

International Reading Association, 800 Barksdale Rd., P.O. Box 8139, Newark DE 19714-8139. (302)731-1600. **Fax:** (302)731-1057. **E-mail:** research@reading.org. **Website:** www.reading.org. **Contact:** Marcella Moore, project manager. Dissertations in reading or related fields are eligible for the competition. Studies using any research approach (ethnographic, experimental, historical, survey, etc.) are encouraged. Each study is assessed in the light of this approach, the scholarly qualification of its report, and its significant contributions to knowledge within the reading field. The application process is open to those who have completed dissertations in any aspect of the field of reading or literacy between May 15 and May 14 of the calendar year. A routine check is made with the home university of the applicant to protect all applicants, their universities, and the International Reading Association from false claims. Studies may use any research approach (ethnographic, experimental, historical, survey, etc.). Each study will be assessed in light of its approach, its scholarship, and its significant contributions to knowledge within the reading/literacy field. Deadline: January 15. Prize: $1,000.

TILIA KLEBENOV JACOBS RELIGIOUS ESSAY PRIZE CATEGORY

Soul Making Keats Literary Competition, The Webhallow House, 1544 Sweetwood Dr., Broadmoor Village CA 94015-2029. **E-mail:** SoulKeats@mail.com. **Website:** www.soulmakingcontest.us. **Contact:** Eileen Malone. Call for thoughtful writings of up to 3,000 words. "No preaching, no proselytizing." Open annually to any writer. Previously published material is accepted. Indicate category on cover page and on identifying 3x5 card. Up to 3,000 words, double-spaced. See website for more details. Deadline: November 30. Prize: 1st Place: $100; 2nd Place $50; 3rd Place $25.

KATHERINE SINGER KOVACS PRIZE

Modern Language Association of America, 26 Broadway, 3rd Floor, New York NY 10004-1789. (646)576-5141. **Fax:** (646)458-0030. **E-mail:** awards@mla.org. **Website:** www.mla.org. **Contact:** Coordinator of Book Prizes. Offered annually for an outstanding book published in English or Spanish in the field of Latin American and Spanish literatures and cultures. Competing books should be broadly interpretive works that enhance understanding of the interrelations among literature, the other arts, and society. Books must have been published in the previous year. Authors need not be members of the MLA. Must send 6 copies of book. Deadline: May 1. Prize: A cash award and a certificate to be presented at the Modern Language Association's annual convention in January.

KATHERYN KROTZER LABORDE CREATIVE NONFICTION PRIZE CATEGORY

Soul-Making Keats Literary Competition, The Webhallow House, 1544 Sweetwood Dr., Broadmoor Village CA 94015-2029. **E-mail:** SoulKeats@mail.com. **Website:** www.soulmakingcontest.us. **Contact:** Eileen Malone. Creative nonfiction is the child of fiction and journalism. Unlike fiction, the characters and events are real, not imagined. Unlike journalism, the writer is part of the story she tells, if not as a participant then as a thoughtful observer. Must be typed, page numbered, and double-spaced. Each entry up to 3,000 words. Identify only with 3x5 card. Open annually to any writer. Deadline: November 30. Prize: First Place: $100; Second Place: $50; Third Place: $25.

TIPS "Looking for a strong voice, a solid sense of the story, and a clear sense of one's writing style. One last note: think about the STORY you are trying to tell and don't be a slave to the truth, the whole truth, and nothing but. This is art, not sworn testimony!"

THE GILDER LEHRMAN LINCOLN PRIZE

Gettysburg College and Gilder Lehrman Institute of American History, 300 N. Washington St., Campus Box 435, Gettysburg PA 17325. (717)337-8255. **Fax:** (717)337-6596. **E-mail:** lincolnprize@gettysburg.edu. **Website:** www.gilderlehrman.org. The Gilder Lehrman Lincoln Prize, sponsored by the Gilder Lehrman Institute and Gettysburg College, is awarded annually for the finest scholarly work in English on Abraham Lincoln or the American Civil War era. Send 7 copies of the nominated work. Deadline: November 1. Prize: $50,000.

TIPS "This contest is for adults writers only."

LITERAL LATTÉ ESSAY AWARD

Literal Latté, 200 E. 10th St., Suite 240, New York NY 10003. (212)260-5532. **E-mail:** litlatte@aol.com. **Website:** www.literal-latte.com. **Contact:** Jenine Gordon Bockman. Open to any writer. Send previously unpublished personal essays, 10,000 words max. All topics accepted. Include email address for reply. Acquires first rights. Visit website for guidelines and tastes. Deadline: September 30. Prize: 1st Place: $1,000; 2nd Place: $300; 3rd Place: $200. Judged by the editors.

JAMES RUSSELL LOWELL PRIZE

Modern Language Association of America, 26 Broadway, 3rd Floor, New York NY 10004-1789. (646)576-5141. **Fax:** (646)458-0030. **E-mail:** awards@mla.org. **Website:** www.mla.org. **Contact:** Coordinator of Book Prizes. For an outstanding literary or linguistic study, a critical edition of an important work, or a critical biography. Open to studies dealing with literary theory, media, cultural history, or interdisciplinary topics. Books must be published in the previous year. Authors must be current members of the MLA. Send 6 copies of the book. Deadline: March 1. Prize: A cash award and a certificate to be presented at the Modern Language Association's annual convention in January.

RICHARD J. MARGOLIS AWARD

c/o Margolis & Bloom, LLP, 535 Boylston St., 8th Floor, Boston MA 02116. (617)267-9700, ext. 517. **Fax:** (617)267-3166. **E-mail:** hsm@margolis.com. **E-mail:** award@margolis.com. **Website:** www.margolis.com/award. **Contact:** Harry S. Margolis. Sponsored by the Blue Mountain Center, this annual award is given to a promising new journalist or essayist whose work combines warmth, humor, wisdom, and concern with social justice. Applicants should be aware that this award is for nonfiction reporting and commentary, not for creative nonfiction, fiction, or poetry. Applications should include at least 2 examples of your work (published or unpublished, 30 pages maximum) and a short biographical note including a description of your current and anticipated work. Also please indicate what you will work on while attending the Blue Mountain residency. Please send to award@margolis.com. Deadline: July 1. Prize: $5,000, plus a one0month residency at the Blue Mountain Center.

HOWARD R. MARRARO PRIZE

Modern Language Association of America, 26 Broadway, 3rd Floor, New York NY 10004-1789. (646)576-5141. **Fax:** (646)458-0030. **E-mail:** awards@mla.org. **Website:** www.mla.org. **Contact:** Coordinator of Book Prizes. Offered in even-numbered years for an outstanding scholarly work on any phase of Italian literature or comparative literature involving Italian. Books must have been published in the previous year. Authors must be members of the MLA. Requires 4 copies of the book. Deadline: May 1. Prize: A cash award and a certificate to be presented at the Modern Language Association's annual convention in January.

KENNETH W. MILDENBERGER PRIZE

Modern Language Association of America, 26 Broadway, 3rd Floor, New York NY 10004-1789. (646)576-5141. **Fax:** (646)458-0030. **E-mail:** awards@mla.org. **Website:** www.mla.org. **Contact:** Coordinator of Book Prizes. Offered in odd-numbered years for a publication from the previous year in the field of language, culture, literacy, or literature with a strong application to the teaching of languages other than English. Author need not be a member of the MLA. Books must have been published in the previous 2 years. Requires 4 copies of the book. Deadline: May 1. Prize: A cash award, and a certificate, to be presented at the Modern Language Association's annual convention in January, and a year's membership in the MLA.

C. WRIGHT MILLS AWARD

The Society for the Study of Social Problems, 901 McClung Tower, University of Tennessee, Knoxville TN 37996-0490. (865)689-1531. **Fax:** (865)689-1534. **E-mail:** mkoontz3@utk.edu. **Website:** www.sssp1.org. **Contact:** Michele Smith Koontz, Administrative Officer and Meeting Manager. Offered annually for a book published the previous year that most effectively critically addresses an issue of contemporary public importance; brings to the topic a fresh, imaginative perspective; advances social scientific understanding of the topic; displays a theoretically informed view and empirical orientation; evinces quality in style of writing; and explicitly or implicitly contains implications for courses of action. Self-nominations are acceptable. Edited volumes, textbooks, fiction, and self-published works are not eligible. Deadline: December 15. Prize: $500 stipend.

MLA PRIZE FOR A BIBLIOGRAPHY, ARCHIVE, OR DIGITAL PROJECT

Modern Language Association of America, 26 Broadway, 3rd Floor, New York NY 10004-1789. (646)576-5141. **Fax:** (646)458-0030. **E-mail:** awards@mla.org. **Website:** www.mla.org. **Contact:** Coordinator of Book Prizes. Offered in even-numbered years for an outstanding enumerative or descriptive bibliography, archive, or digital project. Open to any writer or publisher. At least 1 volume must have been published in the previous 2 years. Editors need not be members of the MLA. Criteria for determining excellence include evidence of analytical rigor, meticulous scholarship, intellectual creativity, and subject range and depth. Deadline: May 1. Prize: A cash prize and a certificate to be presented at the Modern Language Association's annual convention in January.

MLA PRIZE FOR A FIRST BOOK

Modern Language Association of America, 26 Broadway, 3rd Floor, New York NY 10004-1789. (646)576-5141. **Fax:** (646)458-0030. **E-mail:** awards@mla.org. **Website:** www.mla.org. **Contact:** Coordinator of Book Prizes. Offered annually for the first book-length scholarly publication by a current member of the association. To qualify, a book must be a literary or linguistic study, a critical edition of an important work, or a critical biography. Studies dealing with literary theory, media, cultural history, and interdisciplinary topics are eligible; books that are primarily translations will not be considered. See listing for James Russell Lowe Prize—prize offered for same criteria. Deadline: April 1. Prize: A cash award and a certificate to be presented at the Modern Language Association's annual convention in January.

MLA PRIZE FOR A SCHOLARLY EDITION

Modern Language Association of America, 26 Broadway, 3rd Floor, New York NY 10004. (646)576-5141. **Fax:** (646)458-0030. **E-mail:** awards@mla.org. **Website:** www.mla.org. Offered in odd-numbered years for an outstanding scholarly edition. Editions may be in single or multiple volumes. At least one volume must have been published in the 2 years prior to the award deadline. Editors need not be members of the MLA. To qualify for the award, an edition should be based on an examination of all available relevant textual sources; the source texts and the edited text's deviations from them should be fully described; the edition should employ editorial principles appropriate to the materials edited, and those principles should be clearly articulated in the volume; the text should be accompanied by appropriate textual and other historical contextual information; the edition should exhibit the highest standards of accuracy in the presentation of its text and apparatus; and the text and apparatus should be presented as accessibly and elegantly as possible. Deadline: May 1. Prize: A cash award and a certificate to be presented at the Modern Language Association's annual convention in January.

MLA PRIZE FOR INDEPENDENT SCHOLARS

Modern Language Association of America, 26 Broadway, 3rd Floor, New York NY 10004. (646)576-5141. **Fax:** (646)458-0030. **E-mail:** awards@mla.org. **Website:** www.mla.org. Offered in even-numbered years for a scholarly book in the field of English or other modern languages and literatures. Book must have been published within the 2 years prior to prize deadline. At the time of publication of the book, author must not be enrolled in a program leading to an academic degree or hold a tenured, tenure-accruing, or tenure-track position in postsecondary education. Authors need not be members of the MLA. Requires 6 copies of the book and a completed application. Deadline: May 1. Prize: A cash award, a certificate, and a year's membership in the MLA.

MONTANA PRIZE IN CREATIVE NONFICTION

CutBank Literary Magazine, *CutBank*, University of Montana, English Dept., LA 133, Missoula MT 59812. **E-mail:** editor.cutbank@gmail.com. **Website:** www.cutbankonline.org. **Contact:** Allison Linville, editor-in-chief. The Montana Prize in Creative Nonfiction seeks to highlight work that showcases an authentic voice, a boldness of form, and a rejection of functional fixedness. Accepts online submissions only. Send a single work, no more than 35 pages. Guidelines available online. Deadline: January 15. Submissions period begins November 1. Prize: $500 and featured in the magazine. Judged by a guest judge each year.

LINDA JOY MYERS MEMOIR VIGNETTE PRIZE CATEGORY

Soul-Making Keats Literary Competition, Webhallow House, 1544 Sweetwood Dr., Broadmoor Village CA 94015-2029. **E-mail:** soulkeats@mail.com. **Website:** www.soulmakingcontest.us. **Contact:** Eileen Malone. Open annually to any writer. One memoir/entry, up to 1,500 words, double spaced. Previously published material is acceptable. Indicate category on first page. Identify only with 3x5 card. Deadline: November 30. Prize: 1st Place: $100; 2nd Place: $50; 3rd Place: $25.

NATIONAL WRITERS ASSOCIATION NONFICTION CONTEST

The National Writers Association, 10940 S. Parker Rd., #508, Parker CO 80134. (303)841-0246. **E-mail:** natlwritersassn@hotmail.com. **Website:** www.nationalwriters.com. Only unpublished works may be submitted. Judging of entries will not begin until the contest ends. Nonfiction in the following areas will be accepted: articles—submission should include query letter, 1st page of manuscript, separate sheet citing 5 possible markets; essay—the complete essay and 5 possible markets on separate sheet; nonfiction book proposal including query letter, chapter by chapter outline, first chapter, bio and market analysis. Those unsure of proper manuscript format should request Research Report #35. The purpose of the National Writers Association Nonfiction Contest is to encourage the writing of nonfiction and recognize those who excel in this field. Deadline: December 31. Prize: 1st-5th place awards. Other winners will be notified by March 31st. 1st Prize: $200 and Clearinghouse representation if winner is book proposal; 2nd Prize: $100; 3rd Prize: $50; 4th-10th places will receive a book. Honorable Mentions receive a certificate. Judging will be based on originality, marketability, research, and reader interest. Copies of the judges evaluation sheets will be sent to entrants furnishing an SASE with their entry.

THE PHI BETA KAPPA AWARD IN SCIENCE

The Phi Beta Kappa Society, 1606 New Hampshire Ave. NW, Washington DC 20009. (202)265-3808. **Fax:** (202)986-1601. **E-mail:** awards@pbk.org. **Website:** www.pbk.org/bookawards. **Contact:** Awards Coordinator. Offered annually for outstanding contributions by scientists to the literature of science. To be eligible, biographies of scientists must have a substantial critical emphasis on their scientific research. Entries must have been published in the previous calendar year. Entries must be submitted by the publisher and be preceded by a letter certifying that the book(s) conforms to all the conditions of eligibility and stating the publication date of each entry. Two copies of the book must be sent with the nomination form. Books will not be entered officially in the competition until all copies and the letter of certification have been received. Open only to original works in English and authors of US residency and publication. The intent of the award is to encourage literate and scholarly interpretations of the physical and biological sciences and mathematics; monographs and compendiums are not eligible. Deadline: January 15. Prize: $10,000.

PRESERVATION FOUNDATION CONTESTS

The Preservation Foundation, Inc., 2313 Pennington Bend, Nashville TN 37214. **E-mail:** preserve@storyhouse.org. **Website:** www.storyhouse.org. **Contact:** Richard Loller, publisher. Three contests offered annually for unpublished nonfiction. Biography/Autobiography (1,500-10,000 words)—a true story of an individual personally known to the author. Or a true story from the author's life, the whole or an episode. General nonfiction (1,500-10,000 words)—any appropriate nonfiction topic. Travel nonfiction (1,500-10,000 words)—must be the true story of trip by author or someone known personally by author. Open to any previously unpublished writer. Defined as having earned no more than $750 by creative writing in any previous year. Stories must be submitted by e-mail or as electronic files by regular mail. No paper mss can be considered. No story may be entered in more than one contest. See website for contest details. Deadline: August 31. Prize: 1st Place: $100 in each category; certificates for finalists.

ALDO AND JEANNE SCAGLIONE PRIZE FOR COMPARATIVE LITERARY STUDIES

Modern Language Association of America, 26 Broadway, 3rd Floor, New York NY 10004-1789. (646)576-5141. **Fax:** (646)458-0030. **E-mail:** awards@mla.org. **Website:** www.mla.org. **Contact:** Coordinator of Book Prizes. Offered annually for outstanding scholarly work in comparative literary studies involving at least 2 literatures. Works of literary history, literary criticism, philology, and literary theory are eligible, as are works dealing with literature and other arts and disciplines, including cinema; books that are primarily translations will not be considered. Books must have been published in the past calendar year. Authors must be current members of the MLA. Requires 4 copies of the book. Deadline: May 1. Prize: A cash award and a certificate to be presented at the Modern Language Association's annual convention in January.

ALDO AND JEANNE SCAGLIONE PRIZE FOR FRENCH AND FRANCOPHONE STUDIES

Modern Language Association of America, 26 Broadway, 3rd Floor, New York NY 10004. (646)576-5141. **Fax:** (646)458-0030. **E-mail:** awards@mla.org. **Website:** www.mla.org. Offered annually for an outstanding scholarly work in French or francophone linguistics or literary studies. Works of literary history, literary criticism, philology, and literary theory are eligible for consideration; books that are primarily translations will not be considered. Books must have been published in the previous year. Authors must be current members of the MLA. Requires 4 copies of the book. Deadline: May 1. Prize: A cash award and a certificate to be presented at the Modern Language Association's annual convention in January.

ALDO AND JEANNE SCAGLIONE PRIZE FOR ITALIAN STUDIES

Modern Language Association of America, 26 Broadway, 3rd Floor, New York NY 10004-1789. (646)576-5141. **Fax:** (646)458-0030. **E-mail:** awards@mla.org. **Website:** www.mla.org. **Contact:** Coordinator of Book Prizes. Offered in odd-number years for an outstanding scholarly work on any phase of Italian literature or culture or comparative literature involving Italian. This shall include works that study literary or cultural theory, science, history, art, music, society, politics, cinema, and linguistics, preferably but not necessarily relating other disciplines to literature. Books must have been published in the previous year. Authors must be members of the MLA. Requires 4 copies of the book. Deadline: May 1. Prize: A cash award and a certificate to be presented at the Modern Language Association's annual convention in January.

ALDO AND JEANNE SCAGLIONE PRIZE FOR STUDIES IN GERMANIC LANGUAGES & LITERATURE

Modern Language Association of America, 26 Broadway, 3rd Floor, New York NY 10004. (646)576-5141. **Fax:** (646)458-0030. **E-mail:** awards@mla.org. **Website:** www.mla.org. Offered in even-numbered years for an outstanding scholarly work on the linguistics or literatures of any of the Germanic languages (Danish, Dutch, German, Norwegian, Swedish, Yiddish). Works of literary history, literary criticism, philology, and literary theory are eligible for consideration; books that are primarily translations will not be considered. Books must have been published in the previous 2 years. Authors must be members of the MLA. Requires 4 copies of the book. Deadline: May 1. Prize: A cash award, and a certificate to be presented at the Modern Language Association's annual convention in January.

ALDO AND JEANNE SCAGLIONE PUBLICATION AWARD FOR A MANUSCRIPT IN ITALIAN LITERARY STUDIES

Modern Language Association, 26 Broadway, 3rd Floor, New York NY 10004-1789. (646)576-5141. **Fax:** (646)458-0030. **E-mail:** awards@mla.org. **Website:** www.mla.org. **Contact:** Coordinator of Book Prizes. Offerred annualy for an outstanding ms dealing with any aspect of the languages and literatures of Italy, including medieval Latin and comparative studies or intellectual history if the work's main thrust is clearly related to the humanities. Materials from ancient Rome are eligible if related to postclassical developments. Also eligible are translations of classical works of prose and poetry produced in Italy prior to 1900 in any language (e.g., neo-Latin, Greek) or in a dialect of Italian (e.g., Neapolitan, Roman, Sicilian). Eligible are book manuscripts in English or Italian that are ready for submission or already submitted to a press. Mss must be approved or ready for publication before award deadline. Authors must be current members of the MLA, residing in the United States or Canada. Requires 4 copies, plus contact and biographical information. Deadline: June 1. Prize: A cash award and a certificate to be presented at the Modern Language Association's annual convention in January.

WILLIAM SANDERS SCARBOROUGH PRIZE

Modern Language Association of America, 26 Broadway, 3rd Floor, New York NY 10004-1789. (646)576-5141. **Fax:** (646)458-0030. **E-mail:** awards@mla.org. **Website:** www.mla.org. **Contact:** Coordinator of book prizes. Offered annually for an outstanding study of black American literature or culture. Books must have been published in the previous year. Authors need not be members of the MLA. Requires 4 copies of the book. Deadline: May 1. Prize: A cash award, and a certificate to be presented at the Modern Language Association's annual convention in January.

MINA P. SHAUGHNESSY PRIZE

Modern Language Association of America, 26 Broadway, 3rd Floor, New York NY 10004-1789. (646)576-5141. **Fax:** (646)458-0030. **E-mail:** awards@mla.org. **Website:** www.mla.org. **Contact:** Coordinator of Book Prizes. Offered in even-numbered years for a work in the fields of language, culture, literacy, or literature with strong application to the teaching of English. Books must have been published in the previous 2 years. Authors need not be members of the MLA. Requires 4 copies of the book. Deadline: May 1. Prize: A cash prize, a certificate, to be presented at the Modern Language Association's annual convention in January, and a 1-year membership in the MLA.

STAGE OF LIFE ESSAY WRITING CONTESTS

StageofLife.com, P.O. Box 580950, Minneapolis MN 55458-0950. **Fax:** (717)650-3855. **E-mail:** contact@stageoflife.com. **Website:** www.stageoflife.com. Monthly writing contests for teens, college students, brides, grooms, married couples, homeowners, parents, and grandparents using a nonfiction, memoir, blogging, essay-style format. Submitted essays must be 500 words or less. Style, grammar, point of view, and authentic voice are all important aspects in the submissions. Press for the StageofLife.com writing contest has appeared on Time.com, ABC TV'S "Mary Talks Money", *The Wall Street Journal*'s MarketWatch, Socialtimes.com, and other media outlets. Deadline: 12am PST the last day of the month. Prize: Offers $25-50 cash prize or equivalent gift card from current contest sponsor, "Featured Writer" status on StageofLife.com, and mention in the site's monthly press release. Editorial staff headed by Eric Thiegs, CEO; Rebecca Thiegs, senior editor; Michelle Pease, essay editor; and a panel of 12 freelance editors judge monthly contests.

VFW VOICE OF DEMOCRACY

Veterans of Foreign Wars of the U.S., National Headquarters, 406 W. 34th St., Kansas City MO 64111. (816)968-1117. **E-mail:** kharmer@vfw.org. **Website:** http://www.vfw.org/Community/Voice-of-Democracy/. The Voice of Democracy Program is open to students in grades 9-12 (on the Nov. 1 deadline), who are enrolled in a public, private or parochial high school or home study program in the United States and its territories. Contact your local VFW Post to enter (entry must not be mailed to the VFW National Headquarters, only to a local, participating VFW Post. Purpose is to give high school students the opportunity to voice their opinions about their responsibility to our country and to convey those opinions via the broadcast media to all of America. Deadline: November 1. Prize: Winners receive awards ranging from $1,000-30,000.

WABASH PRIZE FOR NONFICTION

Sycamore Review, Department of English, 500 Oval Dr., Purdue University, West Lafayette IN 47907. **E-mail:** sycamore@purdue.edu; sycamorenf@purdue.edu. **Website:** www.sycamorereview.com/contest/. **Contact:** Kara Krewer, editor-in-chief. Annual contest for unpublished nonfiction. For each submission, send one nonfiction piece (limit 7,500 words). Ms pages should be numbered and should include the title of the piece. All stories must be previously unpublished. See website for more guidelines. Submit via online submissions manager. Deadline: December 1. Prize: $1,000 and publication.

WESTERN WRITERS OF AMERICA

271CR 219, Encampment WY 82325. (307)329-8942. **Fax:** (307)327-5465 (call first). **E-mail:** wwa.moulton@gmail.com. **Website:** www.westernwriters.org. **Contact:** Candy Moulton, executive director. 17 Spur Award categories in various aspects of the American West. Send entry form with your published work. Accepts multiple submissions, each with its own entry form. The nonprofit Western Writers of America has promoted and honored the best in Western literature with the annual Spur Awards, selected by panels of judges. Awards, for material published last year, are given for works whose inspirations, image and literary excellence best represent the reality and spirit of the American West.

THE HILARY WESTON WRITERS' TRUST PRIZE FOR NONFICTION

The Writers' Trust of Canada, 460 Richmond St. W., Suite 600, Toronto ON M5V 1Y1 Canada. (416)504-8222. **Fax:** (416)504-9090. **E-mail:** info@writerstrust.com. **Website:** www.writerstrust.com. **Contact:** Amanda Hopkins. Offered annually for a work of nonfiction published in the previous year. Award presented at a a gala event held in Toronto each fall. Open to Canadian citizens and permanent residents only. Deadline: August. Prize: $60,000 and $5,000 to 4 finalists.

WRITING CONFERENCE WRITING CONTESTS

P.O. Box 664, Ottawa KS 66067-0664. (785)242-2947. **Fax:** (785)242-2473. **E-mail:** jbushman@writingconference.com. **E-mail:** support@studentq.com. **Website:** www.writingconference.com. **Contact:** John H. Bushman, contest director. Unpublished submissions only. Submissions made by the author or teacher. Purpose of contest: To further writing by students with awards for narration, exposition and poetry at the elementary, middle school, and high school levels. Deadline: January 8. Prize: Awards plaque and publication of winning entry in The Writers' Slate online, April issue. Judged by a panel of teachers.

YEARBOOK EXCELLENCE CONTEST

100 Adler Journalism Building, Iowa City IA 52242-2004. (319)335-3457. **Fax:** (319)335-3989. **E-mail:** quill-scroll@uiowa.edu. **Website:** www.quillandscroll.org. **Contact:** Vanessa Shelton, executive director. High school students who are contributors to or staff members of a student yearbook at any public or private high school are invited to enter the competition. Awards will be made in each of the 18 divisions. There are two enrollment categories: Class A: more than 750 students; Class B: 749 or less. Winners will receive Quill and Scroll's National Award Gold Key and, if seniors, are eligible to apply for one of the Edward J. Nell Memorial or George and Ophelia Gallup scholarships. Open to students whose schools have Quill and Scroll charters. Previously published submissions only. Submissions made by the author or school yearbook adviser. Must be published in the 12-month span prior to contest deadline. Visit website for list of current and previous winners. Purpose is to recognize and reward student journalists for their work in yearbooks and to provide student winners an opportunity to apply for a scholarship to be used freshman year in college for students planning to major in journalism. Deadline: November 1.

ZONE 3 NONFICTION AWARD

Zone 3, Austin Peay State University, P.O. Box 4565, Clarksville TN 37044. (931)221-7031. **Fax:** (931)221-7149. **E-mail:** wallacess@apsu.edu. **Website:** www.apsu.edu/zone3/contests. **Contact:** Susan Wallace, Managing Editor. Annual contest for unpublished nonfiction. Open to any writer. Accepts entries online and via postal mail. Deadline: April 1. Prize: $250 and publication.

WRITING FOR CHILDREN & YOUNG ADULTS

AMERICAN ASSOCIATION OF UNIVERSITY WOMEN AWARD IN JUVENILE LITERATURE

4610 Mail Service Center, Raleigh NC 27699-4610. (919)807-7290. **E-mail:** michael.hill@ncdcr.gov. **Website:** www.ncdcr.gov. **Contact:** Michael Hill, awards coordinator. Annual award. Book must be published during the year ending June 30. Submissions made by author, author's agent or publisher. SASE for contest rules. Author must have maintained either legal residence or actual physical residence, or a combination of both, in the state of North Carolina for 3 years immediately preceding the close of the contest period. Only published work (books) eligible. Recognizes the year's best work of juvenile literature by a North Carolina resident. Deadline: July 15. Prize: Awards a cup to the winner and winner's name inscribed on a plaque displayed within the North Carolina Office of Archives and History. Judged by three-judge panel.

HANS CHRISTIAN ANDERSEN AWARD

Nonnenweg 12, Postfach Basel CH-4003 Switzerland. **E-mail:** liz.page@ibby.org. **E-mail:** ibby@ibby.org. **Website:** www.ibby.org. **Contact:** Liz Page, director. The Hans Christian Andersen Award, awarded every two years by the International Board on Books for Young People (IBBY), is the highest international recognition given to an author and an illustrator of children's books. The Author's Award has been given since 1956, the Illustrator's Award since 1966. Her Majesty Queen Margrethe II of Denmark is the Patron of the Hans Christian Andersen Awards. The awards are presented at the biennial congresses of IBBY. Awarded to an author and to an illustrator, living at the time of the nomination, who by the outstanding value of their work are judged to have made a lasting contribution to literature for children and young people. The complete works of the author and of the illustrator will be taken into consideration in awarding the medal, which will be accompanied by a diploma. Candidates are nominated by National Sections of IBBY in good standing. Prize: Awards medals according to literary and artistic criteria. Judged by the Hans Christian Andersen Jury.

MARILYN BAILLIE PICTURE BOOK AWARD

The Canadian Children's Book Centre, 40 Orchard View Blvd., Suite 217, Toronto ON M4R 1B9 Canada. (416)975-0010, ext. 222. **Fax:** (416)975-8970. **E-mail:** meghan@bookcentre.ca. **Website:** www.bookcentre.ca. **Contact:** Meghan Howe. The Marilyn Baillie Picture Book Award honors excellence in the illustrated picture book format. To be eligible, the book must be an original work in English, aimed at children ages 3-8, written and illustrated by Canadians and first published in Canada. Eligible genres include fiction, non-fiction and poetry. Books must be published between Jan. 1 and Dec. 31 of the previous calendar year. New editions or re-issues of previously published books are not eligible for submission. Send 5 copies of title along with a completed submission form. Deadline: December 17. Prize: $20,000.

TIPS "Please visit website for submission guidelines and eligibility criteria."

MILDRED L. BATCHELDER AWARD

50 E. Huron St., Chicago IL 60611-2795. **Website:** http://www.ala.org/alsc/awardsgrants/bookmedia/batchelderaward. The Batchelder Award is given to the most outstanding children's book originally published in a language other than English in a country other than the United States, and subsequently translated into English for publication in the US. Visit website for terms and criteria of award. The purpose of the award, a citation to an American publisher, is to encourage international exchange of quality children's books by recognizing US publishers of such books in translation. Deadline: December 31.

JOHN AND PATRICIA BEATTY AWARD

2471 Flores St., San Mateo CA 94403. (650)376-0886. **Fax:** (650)539-2341. **E-mail:** bartlett@scfl.lib.ca.us. **Website:** www.cla-net.org. **Contact:** Diane Bartlett, award chair. The California Library Association's John and Patricia Beatty Award, sponsored by Baker & Taylor, honors the author of a distinguished book for children or young adults that best promotes an awareness of California and its people. Must be a children's or young adult books published in the previous year, set in California, and highlight California's cultural heritage or future. Send title suggestiosn to the committee members. Deadline: January 31. Prize: $500 and an engraved plaque. Judged by a committee of CLA members, who select the winning title from books published in the United States during the preceding year.

THE GEOFFREY BILSON AWARD FOR HISTORICAL FICTION FOR YOUNG PEOPLE

The Canadian Children's Book Centre, 40 Orchard View Blvd., Suite 217, Toronto ON M4R 1B9 Canada. (416)975-0010, ext. 222. **Fax:** (416)975-8970. **Website:** www.bookcentre.ca. **Contact:** Meghan Howe. Awarded annually to reward excellence in the writing of an outstanding work of historical fiction for young readers, by a Canadian author, published in the previous calendar year. Open to Canadian citizens and residents of Canada for at least 2 years. Books must be published between January 1 and December 31 of the previous year. Books must be first foreign or first Canadian editions. Autobiographies are not eligible. Jury members will consider the following: historical setting and accuracy, strong character and plot development, well-told, original story, and stability of book for its intended age group. Send 5 copies of the title along with a completed submission form. Deadline: December 17. Prize: $5,000.

THE IRMA S. AND JAMES H. BLACK AWARD

Bank Street College of Education, 610 W. 112th St., New York NY 10025-1898. (212)875-4458. **Fax:** (212)875-4558. **E-mail:** kfreda@bankstreet.edu. **Website:** http://bankstreet.edu/center-childrens-literature/irma-black-award/. **Contact:** Kristin Freda. Award give to an outstanding book for young children—a book in which text and illustrations are inseparable, each enhancing and enlarging on the other to produce a singular whole. Entries must have been published during the previous calendar year. Publishers submit books. Submit only one copy of each book. Does not accept unpublished mss. Deadline: mid-December. Prize: A scroll with the recipient's name and a gold seal designed by Maurice Sendak. Judged by a committee of older children and children's literature professionals. Final judges are first-, second-, and third-grade classes at a number of cooperating schools.

BOSTON GLOBE-HORN BOOK AWARDS

The Boston Globe, Horn Book, Inc., 300 The Fenway, Palace Road Building, Suite P-311, Boston MA 02115. (617)628-0225. **Fax:** (617)628-0882. **E-mail:** info@hbook.com; khedeen@hbook.com. **Website:** hbook.com/bghb/. **Contact:** Katrina Hedeen. Offered annually for excellence in literature for children and young adults (published June 1-May 31). Categories: picture book, fiction and poetry, nonfiction. Judges may also name up to 2 honor books in each category. Books must be published in the US, but may be written or illustrated by citizens of any country. The Horn Book Magazine publishes speeches given at awards ceremonies. Guidelines for SASE or online. Submit a book directly to each of the judges. See website for details on submitting, as well as contest guidelines. Deadline: May 15. Prize: $500 and an engraved silver bowl; honor book recipients receive an engraved silver plate. Judged by a panel of 3 judges selected each year.

ANN CONNOR BRIMER BOOK AWARD

The Ann Connor Brimer Award, P.O. Box 36036, Halifax NS B3J 3S9 Canada. (902)490-2742. **Website:** www.atlanticbookawards.ca/. **Contact:** Laura Carter, Atlantic Book Awards Festival Coordinator. In 1990, the Nova Scotia Library Association established the Ann Connor Brimer Award for writers residing in Atlantic Canada who have made an outstanding contribution to writing for Atlantic Candian young people. Author must be alive and residing in Atlantic Canada at time of nomination. Book intended for youth up to the age of 15. Book in print and readily available. Fiction or non-fiction (except textbooks). Book must have been published within the previous year. Prize: $2,000.

CHILDREN'S AFRICANA BOOK AWARD

Outreach Council of the African Studies Association, c/o Rutgers University, 132 George St., New Brunswick NJ 08901. (732)932-8173; (301)585-9136. **Fax:** (732)932-3394. **E-mail:** africaaccess@aol.com. **E-mail:** harrietmcguire@earthlink.net. **Website:** www.africaaccessreview.org. **Contact:** Brenda Randolph, chairperson. The Children's Africana Book Awards are presented annually to the authors and illustrators of the best books on Africa for children and young people published or republished in the U.S. The awards were created by the Outreach Council of the African Studies Association (ASA) to dispel stereotypes and encourage the publication and use of accurate, balanced children's materials about Africa. The awards are presented in 2 categories: Young Children and Older Readers. Entries must have been published in the calendar year previous to the award. Work submitted for awards must be suitable for children ages 4-18; a significant portion of books' content must be about Africa; must by copyrighted in the calendar year prior to award year; must be published or republished in the US. Books should be suitable for children and young adults, ages 4-18. A significant portion of the book's content should be about Africa. Books must be copyrighted the previous year to be eligible for the awards. Judged by African Studies and Children's Literature scholars. Nominated titles are read by committee members and reviewed by external African Studies scholars with specialized academic training.

CHILDREN'S BOOK GUILD AWARD FOR NONFICTION

E-mail: theguild@childrensbookguild.org. **Website:** www.childrensbookguild.org. Annual award. "One doesn't enter. One is selected. Our jury annually selects one author for the award." Honors an author or illustrator whose total work has contributed significantly to the quality of nonfiction for children. Prize: Cash and an engraved crystal paperweight. Judged by a jury of Children's Book Guild specialists, authors, and illustrators.

CLA YOUNG ADULT BOOK AWARD

1150 Morrison Dr., Suite 400, Ottawa ON K2H 8S9 Canada. (613)232-9625. **Fax:** (613)563-9895. **E-mail:** svollick@shaw.ca. **Website:** www.cla.ca. **Contact:** Stephanie Vollick, chair. This award recognizes an author of an outstanding English language Canadian book which appeals to young adults between the ages of 13 and 18. To be eligible for consideration, the following must apply: it must be a work of fiction (novel, collection of short stories, or graphic novel), the title must be a Canadian publication in either hardcover or paperback, and the author must be a Canadian citizen or landed immigrant. The award is given annually, when merited, at the Canadian Library Association's annual conference. Deadline: December 31. Prize: $1,000.

MARGARET A. EDWARDS AWARD

50 East Huron St., Chicago IL 60611-2795. (312)280-4390 or (800)545-2433. **Fax:** (312)280-5276. **E-mail:** yalsa@ala.org. **Website:** www.ala.org/yalsa/edwards. **Contact:** Nichole O'Connor. Annual award administered by the Young Adult Library Services Association (YALSA) of the American Library Association (ALA) and sponsored by *School Library Journal* magazine. Awarded to an author whose book or books, over a period of time, have been accepted by young adults as an authentic voice that continues to illuminate

their experiences and emotions, giving insight into their lives. The book or books should enable them to understand themselves, the world in which they live, and their relationship with others and with society. The book or books must be in print at the time of the nomination. Submissions must be previously published no less than 5years prior to the first meeting of the current Margaret A. Edwards Award Committee at Midwinter Meeting. Nomination form is available on the YALSA website. Deadline: December 1. Prize: $2,000. Judged by members of the Young Adult Library Services Association.

DOROTHY CANFIELD FISHER CHILDREN'S BOOK AWARD

Midstate Library Service Center, 578 Paine Tpke. N., Berlin VT 05602. (802)828-6954. **E-mail:** grace.greene@state.vt.us. **Website:** www.dcfaward.org. **Contact:** Mary Linney, chair. Annual award to encourage Vermont children to become enthusiastic and discriminating readers by providing them with books of good quality by living American or Canadian authors published in the current year. E-mail for entry rules. Titles must be original work, published in the U.S., and be appropriate to children in grades 4-8. The book must be copyrighted in the current year. It must be written by an American author living in the U.S. or Canada, or a Canadian author living in Canada or the U.S. Deadline: December of year book was published. Prize: Awards a scroll presented to the winning author at an award ceremony. Judged by children, grades 4-8, who vote for their favorite book.

THE NORMA FLECK AWARD FOR CANADIAN CHILDREN'S NONFICTION

The Canadian Children's Book Centre, 40 Orchard View Blvd., Suite 217, Toronto ON M4R 1B9 Canada. (416)975-0010 ext. 222. **Fax:** (416)975-8970. **E-mail:** meghan@bookcentre.ca. **Website:** www.bookcentre.ca. **Contact:** Meghan Howe. The Norma Fleck Award was established by the Fleck Family Foundation to recognize and raise the profile of exceptional nonfiction books for children. Offered annually for books published between January 1 and December 31 of the previous calendar year. Open to Canadian citizens or landed immigrants. Books must be first foreign or first Canadian editions. Nonfiction books in the following categories are eligible: culture and the arts, science, biography, history, geography, reference, sports, activities, and pastimes. Deadline: December 17. Prize: $10,000. The award will go to the author unless 40% or more of the text area is composed of original illustrations, in which case the award will be divided equally between author and illustrator.

FLICKER TALE CHILDREN'S BOOK AWARD

Morton Mandan Public Library, 609 W. Main St., Mandan ND 58554. **E-mail:** laustin@cdln.info. **Website:** www.ndla.info/ftaward.htm. **Contact:** Linda Austin. Award gives children across the state of North Dakota a chance to vote for their book of choice from a nominated list of 20: 4 in the picture book category; 4 in the intermediate category; 4 in the juvenile category (for more advanced readers); 4 in the upper grade level nonfiction category. Also promotes awareness of quality literature for children. Previously published submissions only. Submissions nominated by librarians and teachers across the state of North Dakota. Deadline: April 1. Prize: A plaque from North Dakota Library Association and banquet dinner. Judged by children in North Dakota.

THEODOR SEUSS GEISEL AWARD

Association for Library Service to Children, Division of the American Library Association, 50 E. Huron, Chicago IL 60611. (800)545-2433. **E-mail:** alscawards@ala.org. **Website:** www.ala.org. The Theodor Seuss Geisel Awar is given annually to the author(s) and illustrator(s) of the most distinguished American book for beginning readers published in English in the United States during the preceding year. The award is to recognize the author(s) and illustrator(s) who demonstrate great creativity and imagination in his/her/their literary and artistic achievements to engage children in reading. Terms and criteria for the award are listed on the website. Entry will not be returned. Deadline: December 31. Prize: Medal, given at awards ceremony during the ALA Annual Conference.

GOLDEN KITE AWARDS

Society of Children's Book Writers and Illustrators (SCBWI), SCBWI Golden Kite Awards, 8271 Beverly Blvd., Los Angeles CA 90048-4515. (323)782-1010. **Fax:** (323)782-1892. **E-mail:** sararutenberg@scbwi.org. **Website:** www.scbwi.org. Given annually to recognize excellence in children's literature in 4 categories: fiction, nonfiction, picture book text, and picture book illustration. Books submitted must be published in the previous calendar year. Both individuals and publishers may submit. Submit 4 copies of book. Submit to one category only, except in the case of picture books. Must be a current member of the SCBWI. Deadline: December 1. Submission period begins July 1. Prize: One Golden Kite Award Winner and one Honor Book will be chosen per category. Winners and Honorees will receive a commemorative poster also sent to publishers, bookstores, libraries, and schools; a press release; an announcement on the SCBWI website; and on SCBWI Social Networks.

CAROL OTIS HURST CHILDREN'S BOOK PRIZE

Westfield Athenaeum, 6 Elm St., Westfield MA 01085. (413)568-7833. **Website:** www.westath.org. The Carol Otis Hurst Children's Book Prize honors outstanding works of fiction and nonfiction, including biography and memoir, written for children and young adults through the age of eighteen that exemplify the highest standards of research, analysis, and authorship in their portrayal of the New England Experience. The prize will be presented annually to an author whose book treats the region's history as broadly conceived to encompass one or more of the following elements: political experience, social development, fine and performing artistic expression, domestic life and arts, transportation and communication, changing technology, military experience at home and abroad, schooling, business and manufacturing, workers and the labor movement, agriculture and its transformation, racial and ethnic diversity, religious life and institutions, immigration and adjustment, sports at all levels, and the evolution of popular entertainment. The public presentation of the prize will be accompanied by a reading and/or talk by the recipient at a mutually agreed upon time during the spring immediately following the publication year. Books must have been copyrighted in their original format during the calendar year, January 1 to December 31, of the year preceding the year in which the prize is awarded. Any individual, publisher, or organization may nominate a book. See website for details and guidelines. Prize: $500.

INTERNATIONAL READING ASSOCIATION CHILDREN'S AND YOUNG ADULTS BOOK AWARDS

P.O. Box 8139, 800 Barksdale Rd., Newark DE 19714-8139. (302)731-1600, ext. 221. **E-mail:** kbaughman@reading.org. **E-mail:** committees@reading.org. **Website:** www.reading.org. **Contact:** Kathy Baughman. The IRA Children's and Young Adults Book Awards are intended for newly published authors who show unusual promise in the children's and young adults' book field. Awards are given for fiction and nonfiction in each of three categories: primary, intermediate, and young adult. Books from all countries and published in English for the first time during the previous calendar year will be considered. See website for eligibility and criteria information. Entry should be the author's first or second book. Deadline: October 31. Prize: $1,000.

THE IODE JEAN THROOP BOOK AWARD

The Lillian H. Smith Children's Library, 239 College St., Toronto ON M5T 1R5 Canada. (905)522-9537. **E-mail:** mcscott@torontopubliclibrary.ca; iodeontario@bellnet.ca. **Website:** www.iodeontario.ca. **Contact:** Martha Scott. Each year, the Municipal Chapter of Toronto IODE presents an award intended to encourage the publication of books for children between the ages of 6-12 years. The award-winner must be a Canadian citizen, resident in Toronto or the surrounding area, and the book must be published in Canada. Deadline: January 31. Prize: Award and cash prize of $2,000. Judged by a selected committee.

IRA SHORT STORY AWARD

International Reading Association, International Reading Association, 800 Barksdale Rd., PO Box 8139, Newark DE 19714-8139. (302)731-1600. **Fax:** (302)731-1057. **E-mail:** committees@reading.org. **Website:** www.reading.org. Offered to reward author of an original short story published for the first time in a periodical for children. (Periodicals should generally be aimed at readers around age 12.) Write for guidelines or download from website. Award is non-monetary. Both fiction and nonfiction stories are eligible; each will be rated according to the characteristics that are appropriate for the genre. The story should: create a believable world for the readers, be truthful and authentic in its presentation of information, serve as a reading and literary standard by which readers can measure other writing, and encourage young readers by providing them with an enjoyable reading experience. Deadline: November 15.

JEFFERSON CUP AWARD

P.O. Box 56312, Virginia Beach VA 23456. (757)689-0594. **E-mail:** catlettsm@gmail.com. **Website:** www.vla.org. **Contact:** Susan M. Catlett, current chairperson. The Jefferson Cup honors a distinguished biography, historical fiction, or American history book for young people. The Jefferson Cup Committee's goal is to promote reading about America's past; to encourage the quality writing of United States history, biography, and historical fiction for young people; and to recognize authors in these disciplines. Deadline: January 31.

EZRA JACK KEATS/KERLAN MEMORIAL FELLOWSHIP

University of Minnesota Libraries, 499 Wilson Library, 309 19th Ave. S, Minneapolis MN 55455. **E-mail:** asc-clrc@umn.edu. **Website:** https://www.lib.umn.edu/clrc/awards-grants-and-fellowships. This fellowship from the Ezra Jack Keats Foundation will provide $1,500 to a talented writer and/or illustrator of children's books who wishes to use the Kerlan Collection for the furtherance of his or her artistic development. Special consideration will be given to someone who would find it difficult to finance a visit to the Kerlan Collection. The Ezra Jack Keats Fellowship recipient will receive transportation costs and a per diem allotment. See website for application deadline and for digital application materials. Winner will be notified in February. Study and written report must be completed within the calendar year. Deadline: January 30.

KENTUCKY BLUEGRASS AWARD

Northern Kentucky University, 405 Steely Library, Nunn Drive, Highland Heights KY 41099. (859)572-6620. **E-mail:** smithjen@nku.edu. **Website:** kba.nku.edu. The Kentucky Bluegrass Award is a student choice program. The KBA promotes and encourages Kentucky students in kindergarten through grade 12 to read a variety of quality literature. Each year, a KBA committee for each grade category chooses the books for the four Master Lists (K-2, 3-5, 6-8 and 9-12). All Kentucky public and private schools, as well as public libraries, are welcome to participate in the program. To nominate a book, see the website for form and details. Deadline: March 1. Judged by students who read books and choose their favorite.

CORETTA SCOTT KING BOOK AWARDS

50 E. Huron St., Chicago IL 60611-2795. (800)545-2433. **Website:** www.ala.org/emiert/cskbookawards. The Coretta Scott King Book Awards are given annually to outstanding African American authors and illustrators of books for children and young adults that demonstrate an appreciation of African American culture and universal human values. This award commemorates the life and work of Dr. Martin Luther King, Jr., and honors his wife, Mrs. Coretta Scott King, for her courage and determination to continue the work for peace and world brotherhood. Must be written for a youth audience in one of three categories: preschool-4th grade; 5th-8th grade; or 9th-12th grade. Book must be published in the year preceding the year the award is given, evidenced by the copyright date in the book. See website for full details, criteria, and eligibility concerns. Deadline: December 1.

THE VICKY METCALF AWARD FOR LITERATURE FOR YOUNG PEOPLE

The Writers' Trust of Canada, 460 Richmond St. W., Suite 600, Toronto ON M5V 1Y1 Canada. (416)504-8222. **E-mail:** info@writerstrust.com. **Website:** www.writerstrust.com. **Contact:** Amanda Hopkins. The Vicky Metcalf Award is presented to a Canadian writer for a body of work in children's literature at The Writers' Trust Awards event held in Toronto each Fall. Open to Canadian citizens and permanent residents only.

JOHN NEWBERY MEDAL

Association for Library Service to Children, Division of the American Library Association, 50 E. Huron, Chicago IL 60611. (800)545-2433, ext. 2153. **Fax:** (312)280-5271. **E-mail:** alscawards@ala.org. **Website:** www.ala.org. The Newbery Medal is awarded annually by the American Library Association for the most distinguished contribution to American literature for children. Previously published submissions only; must be published prior to year award is given. SASE for award rules. Entries not returned. Medal awarded at Caldecott/Newbery banquet during ALA annual conference. Deadline: December 31. Judged by Newbery Award Selection Committee.

NEW ENGLAND BOOK AWARDS

1955 Massachusetts Ave., #2, Cambridge MA 02140. (617)547-3642. **Fax:** (617)547-3759. **E-mail:** nan@neba.org. **Website:** http://www.newenglandbooks.org/BookAwards. **Contact:** Nan Sorenson, administrative coordinator. Annual award. Previously published submissions only. Submissions made by New England booksellers; publishers. Submit written nominations only; actual books should not be sent. Member bookstores receive materials to display winners' books. Award is given to a specific title, fiction, nonfiction, children's. The titles must be either about New England, set in New England or by an author residing in the New England. The titles must be hardcover, paperback orginal or reissue that was published between September 1 and August 31. Entries must be still in print and available. Deadline: June 13. Prize: Winners will receive $250 for literacy to a charity of their choice. Judged by NEIBA membership.

OKLAHOMA BOOK AWARDS

200 NE 18th St., Oklahoma City OK 73105. (405)521-2502. **Fax:** (405)525-7804. **E-mail:** connie.armstrong@libraries.ok.gov. **Website:** www.odl.state.ok.us/ocb. **Contact:** Connie Armstrong, executive director. This award honors Oklahoma writers and books about Oklahoma. Awards are presented to best books in fiction, nonfiction, children's, design and illustration, and poetry books about Oklahoma or books written by an author who was born, is living or has lived in Oklahoma. SASE for award rules and entry forms. Winner will be announced at banquet in Oklahoma City. The Arrell Gibson Lifetime Achievement Award is also presented each year for a body of work. Previously published submissions only. Submissions made by the author, author's agent, or entered by a person or group of people, including the publisher. Must be published during the calendar year preceding the award. Deadline: January 10. Prize: Awards a medal. Judging by a panel of 5 people for each category, generally a librarian, a working writer in the genre, booksellers, editors, etc.

ONCE UPON A WORLD CHILDREN'S BOOK AWARD

Museum of Tolerance, 1399 S. Roxbury Dr., Los Angeles CA 90035-4709. (310)772-7605. **Fax:** (310)772-7628. **E-mail:** bookaward@wiesenthal.com. **Website:** www.museumoftolerance.com. **Contact:** Adaire J. Klein, award director. The Simon Wiesenthal Center/Museum of Tolerance welcomes submissions for the Once Upon a World Children's Book Award. Book publishers and members of the public are invited to nominate children's books that meet the following criteria: young readers' books for ages 6-8 that promote the themes of tolerance, diversity, and social justice; older readers' books for ages 9-12 that promote the themes of tolerance, diversity, respect, and social justice. Books may be a picture book, fiction, nonfiction, or poetry. Deadline: February 28. Prize: $1,000 award in each category.

ORBIS PICTUS AWARD FOR OUTSTANDING NONFICTION FOR CHILDREN

1111 W. Kenyon Rd., Urbana IL 61801-1096. (217)328-3870. **Fax:** (217)328-0977. **E-mail:** elementary@ncte.org. **Website:** www.ncte.org/awards/orbispictus. The NCTE Orbis Pictus Award promotes and recognizes excellence in the writing of nonfiction for children. Orbis Pictus commemorates the work of Johannes Amos Comenius, *Orbis Pictus—The World in Pictures* (1657), considered to be the first book actually planned for children. Submissions should be made by an author, the author's agent, or by a person or group of people. Must be published in the calendar year of the competition. Deadline: December 31. Prize: A plaque given at the NCTE Elementary Section Luncheon at the NCTE Annual Convention in November. Up to 5 honor books awarded. Judged by members of the Orbis Pictus Committee.

HELEN KEATING OTT AWARD FOR OUTSTANDING CONTRIBUTION TO CHILDREN'S LITERATURE

CSLA, 10157 SW Barbur Blvd. #102C, Portland OR 97219. (503)244-6919. **Fax:** (503)977-3734. **E-mail:** sharperl@kent.edu. **Website:** www.cslainfo.org. **Contact:** S. Meghan Harper, awards chair. Annual award given to a person or organization that has made a significant contribution to promoting high moral and ethical values through children's literature. Recipient is honored in July during the conference. Awards certificate of recognition, the awards banquet, and one-night's stay in the hotel. A nomination for an award may be made by anyone. An application form is available online. Elements of creativity and innovation will be given high priority by the judges.

PATERSON PRIZE FOR BOOKS FOR YOUNG PEOPLE

The Poetry Center at Passaic County Community College, One College Blvd., Paterson NJ 07505. (973)684-6555. **Fax:** (973)523-6085. **E-mail:** mgillan@pccc.edu. **Website:** www.pccc.edu/poetry. **Contact:** Maria Mazziotti Gillan, executive director. Award for a book published in the previous year in each age category (Pre-K-Grade 3, Grades 4-6, Grades 7-12). Deadline: March 15. Prize: $500.

THE KATHERINE PATERSON PRIZE FOR YOUNG ADULT AND CHILDREN'S WRITING

Hunger Mountain, Vermont College of Fine Arts, 36 College St., Montpelier VT 05602. (802)828-8517. E-

mail: hungermtn@vcfa.edu. **Website:** www.hungermtn.org. **Contact:** Miciah Bay Gault, editor. The annual Katherine Paterson Prize for Young Adult and Children's Writing honors the best in young adult and children's literature. Submit young adult or middle grade mss, and writing for younger children, short stories, picture books, or novel excerpts, under 10,000 words. Guidelines available on website. Deadline: June 30. Prize: $1,000 and publication for the first place winner; $100 each and publication for the three category winners. Judged by a guest judge every year. The 2014 judge is Katherine Applegate, the Newbery Award-winning author of *The One and Only Ivan*.

PENNSYLVANIA YOUNG READERS' CHOICE AWARDS PROGRAM

148 S. Bethelehem Pike, Ambler PA 19002-5822. **Website:** www.psla.org. **Contact:** Alice L. Cyphers, coordinator. Submissions nominated by a person or group. Must be published within 5 years of the award—for example, books published in 2010 to present are eligible for the 2014-2015 award. Check the Program wiki at pyrca.wikispaces.com for submission information. View information at the Pennsylvania School Librarians' website or the Program wiki. Must be currently living in North America. The purpose of the Pennsylvania Young Reader's Choice Awards Program is to promote the reading of quality books by young people in the Commonwealth of Pennsylvania, to encourage teacher and librarian collaboration and involvement in children's literature, and to honor authors whose works have been recognized by the students of Pennsylvania. Deadline: October 15. Prize: Framed certificate to winning authors. Four awards are given, one for each of the following grade level divisions: K-3, 3-6, 6-8, YA. Judged by children of Pennsylvania (they vote).

PEN/PHYLLIS NAYLOR WORKING WRITER FELLOWSHIP

PEN American Center, 588 Broadway, Suite 303, New York NY 10012. **E-mail:** awards@pen.org. **Website:** www.pen.org. **Contact:** Arielle Anema, literary awards coordinator. Offered annually to an author of children's or young-adult fiction. The Fellowship has been developed to help writers whose work is of high literary caliber but who have not yet attracted a broad readership. The Fellowship is designed to assist a writer at a crucial moment in his or her career to complete a book-length work-in-progress. Candidates have published at least two novels for children or young adults which have been received warmly by literary critics, but have not generated suficient income to support the author. Writers must be nominated by an editor or fellow author. See website for eligibility and nomination guidelines. Deadline: December 19. Submission period begins September 1. Prize: $5,000.

PLEASE TOUCH MUSEUM BOOK AWARD

Memorial Hall in Fairmount Park, 4231 Avenue of the Republic, Philadelphia PA 19131. (215)578-5153. **Fax:** (215)578-5171. **E-mail:** hboyd@pleasetouchmuseum.org. **Website:** www.pleasetouchmuseum.org. **Contact:** Heather Boyd. This prestigious award has recognized and encouraged the publication of high quality books. The award was exclusively created to recognize and encourage the writing of publications that help young children enjoy the process of learning through books, while reflecting PTM's philosophy of learning through play. The awards to to books that are imaginative, exceptionally illustrated, and help foster a child's life-long love of reading. To be eligible for consideration, a book must be distinguished in text, illustration, and ability to explore and clarify an idea for young children (ages 7 and under). Deadline: October 1. Books for each cycle must be published within previous calendar year (September-August). Judged by a panel of volunteer educators, artists, booksellers, children's authors, and librarians in conjunction with museum staff.

POCKETS FICTION-WRITING CONTEST

P.O. Box 340004, Nashville TN 37203-0004. (615)340-7333. **Fax:** (615)340-7267. **E-mail:** pockets@upperroom.org. **Website:** www.pockets.upperroom.org. **Contact:** Lynn W. Gilliam, senior editor. Designed for 6- to 12-year-olds, *Pockets* magazine offers wholesome devotional readings that teach about God's love and presence in life. The content includes fiction, scripture stories, puzzles and games, poems, recipes, colorful pictures, activities, and scripture readings. Freelance submissions of stories, poems, recipes, puzzles and games, and activities are welcome. Stories should be 750-1,000 words. Multiple submissions are permitted. Past winners are ineligible. The primary purpose of *Pockets* is to help children grow in their relationship with God and to claim the good news of the gospel of Jesus Christ by applying it to their daily lives. *Pockets* espouses respect for all human beings and for God's creation. It regards a child's faith journey as an integral part of all of life and sees prayer as undergirding that journey. Deadline: August 15. Submission period begins March 15. Prize: $500 and publication in magazine.

MICHAEL L. PRINTZ AWARD

Young Adult Library Services Association, Division of the American Library Association, 50 E. Huron, Chicago IL 60611. (800)545-2433. **Fax:** (312)280-5276. **E-mail:** yalsa@ala.org; ala@ala.org. **Website:** www.ala.org/yalsa/printz. **Contact:** Nichole O'Connor, program officer for events and conferences. The Michael L. Printz Award annually honors the best book written for teens, based entirely on its literary merit, each year. In addition, the Printz Committee names up to 4 honor books, which also represent the best writing in young adult literature. The award-winning book can be fiction, nonfiction, poetry or an anthology, and can be a work of joint authorship or editorship. The books must be published between January 1 and December 31 of the preceding year and be designated by its publisher as being either a young adult book or one published for the age range that YALSA defines as young adult, e.g. ages 12 through 18. Deadline: December 1. Judged by an award committee.

PURPLE DRAGONFLY BOOK AWARDS

4696 W. Tyson St., Chandler AZ 85226-2903. (480)940-8182. **Fax:** (480)940-8787. **E-mail:** cristy@fivestarpublications.com; fivestarpublications@gmail.com. **Website:** www.purpledragonflybookawards.com; www.fivestarpublications.com; www.fivestarbookawards.com. **Contact:** Cristy Bertini, contest coordinator. Five Star Publications presents the Purple Dragonfly Book Awards, which were conceived and designed with children in mind. "Not only do we want to recognize and honor accomplished authors in the field of children's literature, but we also want to highlight and reward up-and-coming, newly published authors and younger published writers." The Purple Dragonfly Book Awards are divided into 3 distinct subject categories, ranging from books on the environment and cooking to sports and family issues. (Click on the "Categories" tab on the website for a complete list.) The Purple Dragonfly Book Awards are geared toward stories that appeal to children of all ages. Looking for stories that inspire, inform, teach or entertain. "A Purple Dragonfly seal on your book's cover tells parents, grandparents, educators and caregivers they are giving children the very best in reading excellence." Being honored with a Purple Dragonfly Award confers credibility upon the winner, as well as provides positive publicity to further their success. The goal of these awards is to give published authors the recognition they deserve and provide a helping hand to further their careers. The awards are open to books published in any calendar year and in any country that are available for purchase. Books entered must be printed in English. Traditionally published, partnership published and self-published books are permitted, as long as they fit the above criteria. Submit materials to: Cristy Bertini, Attn: Five Star Book Awards, 1271 Turkey St., Ware, MA 01082. Deadline: May 1 (postmarked). Submissions postmarked March 1 or earlier that meet all submission requirements are eligible for the Early Bird reward: A free copy of *The Economical Guide to Self-Publishing* or *Promote Like a Pro: Small Budget, Big Show.* Prize: Grand Prize winner will receive a $300 cash prize, 100 foil award seals (more can be ordered for an extra charge), 1 hour of marketing consultation from Five Star Publications, and $100 worth of Five Star Publications' titles, as well as publicity on Five Star Publications' websites and inclusion in a winners' news release sent to a comprehensive list of media outlets. The Grand Prize winner will also be placed in the Five Star Dragonfly Book Awards virtual bookstore with a thumbnail of the book's cover, price, 1-sentence description and link to Amazon.com for purchasing purposes, if applicable. 1st Place: All first-place winners of categories will be put into a drawing for a $100 prize. In addition, each first-place winner in each category receives a certificate commemorating their accomplishment, 25 foil award seals (more can be ordered for an extra charge) and mention on Five Star Publications' websites.

QUILL AND SCROLL INTERNATIONAL WRITING AND PHOTO CONTEST, AND BLOGGING COMPETITION

School of Journalism, Univ. of Iowa, 100 Adler Journalism Bldg., Iowa City IA 52242-2004. (319)335-3457. **Fax:** (319)335-3989. **E-mail:** quill-scroll@uiowa.edu. **E-mail:** vanessa-shelton@uiowa.edu. **Website:** quillandscroll.org. **Contact:** Vanessa Shelton, contest director. Entries must have been published in a high school or profesional newspaper or website during the previous year, and must be the work of a currently enrolled high school student, when published. Open to students. Annual contest. Previously published submissions only. Submissions made by the author or school media adviser. Deadline: February 5. Prize: Winners will receive *Quill and Scroll*'s National Award Gold Key and, if seniors, are eligible to apply for one of the scholarships offered by *Quill and Scroll*. All winning entries are automatically eligible for the International Writing and Photo Sweepstakes Awards. Engraved plaque awarded to sweepstakes winners.

THE RED HOUSE CHILDREN'S BOOK AWARD

Red House Children's Book Award, 123 Frederick Road, Cheam, Sutton, Surrey SM1 2HT United Kingdom. **E-mail:** info@rhcba.co.uk. **Website:** www.redhousechildrensbookaward.co.uk. **Contact:** Sinead Kromer, national coordinator. The Red House Children's Book Award is the only national book award that is entirely voted for by children. A shortlist is drawn up from children's nominations and any child can then vote for the winner of the three categories: Books for Younger Children, Books for Younger Readers and Books for Older Readers. The book with the most votes is then crowned the winner of the Red House Children's Book Award. Deadline: December 31.

TOMÁS RIVERA MEXICAN AMERICAN CHILDREN'S BOOK AWARD

Dr. Jesse Gainer, Texas State University, 601 University Drive, San Marcos TX 78666-4613. (512)245-2357. **E-mail:** riverabookaward@txstate.edu. **Website:** www.riverabookaward.org. **Contact:** Dr. Jesse Gainer, award director. Texas State University College of Education developed the Tomas Rivera Mexican American Children's Book Award to honor authors and illustrators who create literature that depicts the Mexican American experience. The award was established in 1995 and was named in honor of Dr. Tomas Rivera, a distinguished alumnus of Texas State University. The book will be written for younger children, ages pre-K to 5th grade (awarded in even years), or older children, ages 6th grade to 12 grade (awarded in odd years). The text and illustrations will be of highest quality. The portrayal/representations of Mexican Americans will be accurate and engaging, avoid stereotypes, and reflect rich characterization. The book may be fiction or non- fiction. See website for more details and directions. Deadline: November 1.

ROCKY MOUNTAIN BOOK AWARD: ALBERTA CHILDREN'S CHOICE BOOK AWARD

Box 42, Lethbridge AB T1J 3Y3 Canada. (403)381-0855. **Website:** http://www.rmba.info. **Contact:** Michelle Dimnik, contest director. Annual contest open to Alberta students. No entry fee. Awards: Gold medal and author tour of selected Alberta schools. Judging by students. Canadian authors and/or illustrators only. Submit entries to Richard Chase. Previously unpublished submissions only. Submissions made by author's agent or nominated by a person or group. Must be published within the 3 years prior to that year's award. Register before January 20th to take part in the Rocky Mountain Book Award. SASE for contest rules and entry forms. Purpose of contest: "Reading motivation for students, promotion of Canadian authors, illustrators and publishers."

SCBWI MAGAZINE MERIT AWARDS

8271 Beverly Blvd., Los Angeles CA 90048. (323)782-1010. **Fax:** (323)782-1892. **E-mail:** grants@scbwi.org. **Website:** www.scbwi.org. **Contact:** Stephanie Gordon, award coordinator. The SCBWI is a professional organization of writers and illustrators and others interested in children's literature. Membership is open to the general public at large. All magazine work for young people by an SCBWI member—writer, artist or photographer—is eligible during the year of original publication. In the case of co-authored work, both authors must be SCBWI members. Members must submit their own work. Requirements for entrants: 4 copies each of the published work and proof of publication (may be contents page) showing the name of the magazine and the date of issue.Previously published submissions only. For rules and procedures see website. Must be a SCBWI member. Recognizes outstanding original magazine work for young people published during that year, and having been written or illustrated by members of SCBWI. Deadline: December 15 of the year of publication. Submission period begins January 1. Prize: Awards plaques and honor certificates for each of 4 categories (fiction, nonfiction, illustration and poetry). Judged by a magazine editor and two "full" SCBWI members.

SCBWI WORK-IN-PROGRESS GRANTS

8271 Beverly Blvd., Los Angeles CA 90048. (323)782-1010. **Fax:** (323)782-1892. **E-mail:** grants@scbwi.org. **E-mail:** wipgrant@scbwi.org. **Website:** www.scbwi.

org. The SCBWI Work-in-Progress Grants have been established to assist children's book writers in the completion of a specific project. Five categories: Picture Book Text, Chapter Books/Early Readers, Middle Grade, Young Adult Fiction, Nonfiction, and Multi-Cultural Fiction or Nonfiction. SASE for applications for grants. The grants are available to both full and associate members of the SCBWI. They are not available for projects on which there are already contracts. Previous recipients not eligible to apply. Deadline: March 31. Submission period begins March 1.

SKIPPING STONES BOOK AWARDS

Skipping Stones, P.O. Box 3939, Eugene OR 97403-0939. **Website:** www.skippingstones.org. Open to published books, publications/magazines, educational videos, and DVDs. Annual awards. Submissions made by the author or publishers and/or producers. Send request for contest rules and entry forms or visit website. Many educational publications announce the winners of our book awards. The winning books and educational videos/DVDs are announced in the July-September issue of *Skipping Stones* and also on the website. In addition to announcements on social media pages, the reviews of winning titles are posted on website. *Skipping Stones* multicultural magazine has been published for over 25 years. Recognizes exceptional, literary and artistic contributions to juvenile/children's literature, as well as teaching resources and educational audio/video resources in the areas of multicultural awareness, nature and ecology, social issues, peace, and nonviolence. Deadline: February 1. Prize: Winners receive gold honor award seals, attractive honor certificates and publicity via multiple outlets. Judged by a multicultural selection committee of editors, students, parents, teachers, and librarians.

SKIPPING STONES YOUTH AWARDS

P.O. Box 3939, Eugene OR 97403-0939. (541)342-4956. **Fax:** (541)342-4956. **E-mail:** editor@skippingstones.org. **Website:** www.skippingstones.org. **Contact:** Arun N. Toké. Annual awards to promote creativity as well as multicultural and nature awareness in youth. Cover letter should include name, address, phone, and e-mail. Entries must be unpublished. Length: 1,000 words maximum; 30 lines maximum for poems. Open to any writer between 7 and 17 years old. Guidelines available by SASE, e-mail, or on website. Accepts inquiries by e-mail or phone. Results announced in the October-December issue of *Skipping Stones*. Winners notified by mail. For contest results, visit website. Everyone who enters receives the issue which features the award winners. Deadline: June 25. Prize: Publication in the autumn issue of *Skipping Stones*, honor certificate, subscription to magazine, plus 5 multicultural and/or nature books.

SYDNEY TAYLOR BOOK AWARD

Association of Jewish Libraries, P.O. Box 1118, Teaneck NJ 07666. (212)725-5359. **E-mail:** chair@sydneytaylorbookaward.org; mls4bug@sbcglobal.net. **Website:** www.sydneytaylorbookaward.org. **Contact:** Diane Rauchwerger, chair. The Sydney Taylor Book Award is presented annually to outstanding books for children and teens that authentically portray the Jewish experience. Deadline: December 31, "but we cannot guarantee that books received after November 30 will be considered.". Prize: Gold medals are presented in 3 categories: younger readers, older readers, and teen readers. Honor books are awarded in silver medals, and notable books are named in each category.

SYDNEY TAYLOR MANUSCRIPT COMPETITION

Association of Jewish Libraries, Sydney Taylor Manuscript Award Competition, 204 Park St., Montclair NJ 07042-2903. **E-mail:** stmacajl@aol.com. **Website:** www.jewishlibraries.org/main/Awards/SydneyTaylorManuscriptAward.aspx. **Contact:** Aileen Grossberg. This competition is for unpublished writers of fiction. Material should be for readers ages 8-13, with universal appeal that will serve to deepen the understanding of Judaism for all children, revealing positive aspects of Jewish life. Download rules and forms from website. Must be an unpublished fiction writer or a student; also, books must range from 64-200 pages in length. "AJL assumes no responsibility for publication, but hopes this cash incentive will serve to encourage new writers of children's stories with Jewish themes for all children." Deadline: September 30. Prize: $1,000. Judging by qualified judges from within the Association of Jewish Libraries.

TD CANADIAN CHILDREN'S LITERATURE AWARD

The Canadian Children's Book Centre, 40 Orchard View Blvd., Suite 217, Toronto ON M4R 1B9 Canada. (416)975-0010, ext. 222. **Fax:** (416)975-8970. **Website:** www.bookcentre.ca. **Contact:** Meghan Howe. The TD Canadian Children's Literature Award is for the most distinguished book of the year. All books, in any genre, written and illustrated by Canadians and for children ages 1-12 are eligible. Only books first published in Canada are eligible for submission. Books must be published between January 1 and December 31 of the previous calendar year. Open to Canadian citizens and/or permanent residents of Canada. Submission deadline: December 17. Prize: Two prizes of $30,000, 1 for English, 1 for French. $20,000 will be divided among the Honour Book English titles and Honour Book French titles, to a maximum of 4; $2,500 shall go to each of the publishers of the English and French grand-prize winning books for promotion and publicity.

TIPS "Please visit website for submission guidelines and eligibility criteria, as well as specific submission deadline."

VEGETARIAN ESSAY CONTEST

The Vegetarian Resource Group, P.O. Box 1463, Baltimore MD 21203. (410)366-VEGE. **Fax:** (410)366-8804. **E-mail:** vrg@vrg.org. **Website:** www.vrg.org. Write a 2-3 page essay on any aspect of vegetarianism. Entrants should base their paper on interviewing, research, and/or personal opinon. You need not be a vegetarian to enter. Three different entry categories: age 14-18; age 9-13; and age 8 and under. Prize: $50.

RITA WILLIAMS YOUNG ADULT PROSE PRIZE CATEGORY

Soul-Making Keats Literary Competition, The Webhallow House, 1544 Sweetwood Drive, Broadmoor Village CA 94015-2029. **E-mail:** SoulKeats@mail.com. **Website:** www.soulmakingcontest.us. **Contact:** Eileen Malone. For writers in grades 9-12 or equivalent age. Up to 3,000 words in prose form of choice. Complete rules and guidelines available online. Deadline: November 30 (postmarked). Prize: $100 for first place; $50 for second place; $25 for third place. Judged (and sponsored) by Rita Wiliams, an Emmy-award winning investigative reporter with KTVU-TV in Oakland, California.

YOUNG READER'S CHOICE AWARD

Paxson Elementary School, 101 Evans, Missoula MT 59801. **E-mail:** hbray@missoula.lib.mt.us. **Website:** www.pnla.org. **Contact:** Honore Bray, president. The Pacific Northwest Library Association's Young Reader's Choice Award is the oldest children's choice award in the U.S. and Canada. Nominations are taken only from children, teachers, parents and librarians in the Pacific Northwest: Alaska, Alberta, British Columbia, Idaho, Montana and Washington. Nominations will not be accepted from publishers. Nominations may include fiction, nonfiction, graphic novels, animae, and manga. Nominated titles are those published 3 years prior to the award year. Deadline: February 1. Books will be judged on popularity with readers. Age appropriateness will be considered when choosing which of the three divisions a book is placed. Other considerations may include reading enjoyment; reading level; interest level; genre representation; gender representation; racial diversity; diversity of social, political, economic, or religions viewpoints; regional consideration; effectiveness of expression; and imagination. The Pacific Northwest Library Association is committed to intellectual freedom and diversity of ideas. No title will be excluded because of race, nationality, religion, gender, sexual orientation, political or social view of either the author or the material.

GENERAL

AUSTRALIAN CHRISTIAN BOOK OF THE YEAR AWARD

SparkLit, P.O. Box 198, Forest Hill Victoria 3131 Australia. **E-mail:** admin@sparklit.org. **Website:** www.sparklit.org. **Contact:** The Awards Coordinator. The Australian Christian Book of the Year Award is given annually to an original book written by an Australian citizen normally resident in Australia and published by an Australian publisher. The award recognizes and encourages excellence in Australian Christian writing. Entries must be published after April 1 of the year prior to the competition. Deadline: March 31. Prize: $2,500 (AUD) and a framed certificate.

JAMIE CAT CALLAN HUMOR PRIZE

Category in the Soul-Making Keats Literary Competition, The Webhallow House, 1544 Sweetwood Dr., Broadmoor Village CA 94015-2029. **E-mail:** SoulKeats@mail.com. **Website:** www.soulmakingcontest.us. **Contact:** Eileen Malone. Any form, 2,500 words or less. One piece per entry. Previously published material is accepted. Open annually to any writer. Deadline: November 30. Prize: First Place: $100; Second Place: $50; Third Place: $25. Judged by Jamie Cat Callan.

J.W. DAFOE BOOK PRIZE

J.W. Dafoe Foundation, 351 University College, University of Manitoba, Winnipeg MB R3T 2M8 Canada. **E-mail:** james.fergusson@ad.umanitoba.ca. **Website:** www.dafoefoundation.ca. **Contact:** Dr. James Fergusson. The Dafoe Book Prize was established to honor John Dafoe, editor of the *Winnipeg Free Press* from 1900 to 1944, and is awarded each year for distinguished writing by Canadians or authors in resident in Canada that contributes to the understanding of Canada, Canadians, and/or Canada's place in the world. Books must be published January-December of previous publishing year. Co-authored books are eligible, but not edited books consisting of chapters from many different authors. Submit 4 copies of book. Deadline: December 6. Prize: $10,000. Judged by board members and academics.

THE DEBUT DAGGER

Crime Writers' Association, New Writing Competition, P.O. Box 3408, Norwich NR3 3WE England. **E-mail:** director@thecwa.co.uk. **Website:** www.thecwa.co.uk. **Contact:** Mary Andrea Clarke. Annual competition for unpublished crime writers. Submit the opening 3,000 words of a crime novel, plus a 500-1,000 word synopsis of its continuance. Open to any writer who has not had a novel commercially published in any genre. Only accepts entries in Microsoft Word Document or PDF form. Submissions should not include entrant's name anywhere on the documents. See website for details on guidelines and submitting. Deadline: January 31. Submission period begins November 1. Prize: 1st Prize: £700. All shortlisted entrants will receive a professional assessment of their entries. Judged by a panel of top crime editors and agents, and the shortlisted entries are sent to publishers and agents.

THE FOUNTAINHEAD ESSAY CONTEST

The Ayn Rand Institute, P.O. Box 57044, Irvine CA 92619-7044. **E-mail:** info@aynrandnovels.com. **Website:** www.aynrand.org/contests. Offered annually to encourage analytical thinking and excellence in writing, and to expose students to the philosophic ideas of Ayn Rand. "For information contact your English teacher or guidance counselor, or visit our website." Length: 800-1,600 words. Open to 11th and 12th graders. Deadline: April 26. Prize: 1st Place: $10,000; 2nd Place (5): $2,000; 3rd Place (10): $1,000; Finalist (45): $100; Semifinalist (175): $50.

THE GLENNA LUSCHEI PRAIRIE SCHOONER AWARDS

Prairie Schooner, 123 Andrews Hall, P.O. Box 880334, Lincoln NE 68588-0334. (402)472-0911. **Fax:** (402)472-1817. **E-mail:** prairieschooner@unl.edu; psbookprize@unl.edu. **Website:** http://prairieschooner.unl.edu/. **Contact:** Kwame Dawes. Annual awards for work published in *Prairie Schooner* in the previous year. Offers one large prize and 10 smaller awards. See website for more details. Contact *Prairie Schooner* for further information. Prize: One award of $1,500 and 10 awards of $250 each.

INDEPENDENT PUBLISHER BOOK AWARDS

Jenkins Group/Independent Publisher Online, 1129 Woodmere Ave., Ste. B, Traverse City MI 49686. (231)933-0445. **Fax:** (231)933-0448. **E-mail:** jimb@bookpublishing.com. **Website:** www.independentpublisher.com. **Contact:** Jim Barnes. Honors the year's best independently published titles from around the world. The IPPY Awards reward those who exhibit the courage, innovation, and creativity to bring about change in the world of publishing. Independent spirit and expertise comes from publishers of all areas and budgets, and they judge books with that in mind. Entries will be accepted in over 75 categories, visit website to see details. Open to any published writer. Accepts books published within the past 2 years. See website for guidelines and details. Deadline: March 16. Price of submission rises after January 25. Prize: Gold, silver and bronze medals for each category; foil seals available to all. Judged by a panel of experts representing the fields of design, writing, bookselling, library, and reviewing.

DOROTHEA LANGE—PAUL TAYLOR PRIZE

Center for Documentary Studies, 1317 W. Pettigrew St., Duke University, Durham NC 27705. (919)660-3662. **Fax:** (919)681-7600. **E-mail:** alexad@duke.edu; docstudies@duke.edu. **Website:** http://documentarystudies.duke.edu/awards/dorothea-lange-paul-taylor-prize. **Contact:** Alexa Dilworth. Award from the Center for Documentary Studies at Duke University, supporting documentary artists, working alone or in teams, who are involved in extended, on-going fieldwork projects that rely on and exploit the interplay of words and images. More information available on website. First announced a year after the Center for Documentary Studies' founding at Duke University, the prize was created to encourage a collaboration between documentary writers and photographers in the tradition of the acclaimed photographer Dorothea Lange and writer and social scientist Paul Taylor. Deadline: May 7. Submissions accepted starting in February.

MLA PRIZE IN UNITED STATES LATINA & LATINO AND CHICANA & CHICANO LITERARY AND CULTURAL STUDIES

Modern Language Association of America, 26 Broadway, 3rd Floor, New York NY 10004-1789. (646)576-5141. **Fax:** (646)458-0030. **E-mail:** awards@mla.org. **Website:** www.mla.org. **Contact:** Coordinator of Book Prizes. Offered in odd-numbered years for an outstanding scholarly study in any language of United States Latina and Latino or Chicana and Chicano literature or culture. Books must have been published in the two previous years before the award. Authors must be current members of the MLA. Requires 4 copies of the book. Deadline: May 1. Prize: A cash award, and a certificate to be presented at the Modern Language Association's annual convention in January.

PUSHCART PRIZE

Pushcart Press, P.O. Box 380, Wainscott NY 11975. (631)324-9300. **Website:** www.pushcartprize.com. **Contact:** Bill Henderson. Published every year since 1976, The Pushcart Prize - Best of the Small Presses series "is the most honored literary project in America. Hundreds of presses and thousands of writers of short stories, poetry and essays have been represented in the pages of our annual collections." Little magazine and small book press editors (print or online) may make up to six nominations from their year's publicatoins by the deadline. The nominations may be any combination of poetry, short fiction, essays or literary whatnot. Editors may nominate self-contained portions of books — for instance, a chapter from a novel. Deadline: December 1.

DAVID RAFFELOCK AWARD FOR PUBLISHING EXCELLENCE

National Writers Association, 10940 S. Parker Rd., #508, Parker CO 80134. (303)841-0246. **E-mail:** natlwritersassn@hotmail.com. **Website:** www.nationalwriters.com. **Contact:** Sandy Whelchel. Contest is offered annually for books published the previous year. Published works only. Open to any writer. Guidelines for SASE, by e-mail or on website. Winners will be notified by mail or phone. List of winners available for SASE or visit website. Purpose is to assist published authors in marketing their works and to reward outstanding published works. Deadline: May 15. Prize: Publicity tour, including airfare, valued at $5,000.

TEXAS INSTITUTE OF LETTERS AWARD FOR MOST SIGNIFICANT SCHOLARLY BOOK

The Texas Institute of Letters, P.O. Box 609, Round Rock TX 78680. **E-mail:** tilsecretary@yahoo.com. **Website:** http://texasinstituteofletters.org. Offered annually for submissions published January 1-December 31 of previous year to recognize the writer of the book making the most important contribution to knowledge. Writer must have been born in Texas, have lived in the state at least 2 consecutive years at some time, or the subject matter of the book should be associated with the state. See website for guidelines. Deadline: Visit website for exact date. Prize: $2,500.

FRED WHITEHEAD AWARD FOR DESIGN OF A TRADE BOOK

Texas Institute of Letters, P.O. Box 609, Round Rock TX 78680. **E-mail:** tilsecretary@yahoo.com. **Website:** www.texasinstituteofletters.org. Offered annually for the best design for a trade book. Open to Texas residents or those who have lived in Texas for 2 consecutive years. See website for guidelines. Deadline: early Janaury; see website for exact date. Prize: $750.

THE WRITERS' TRUST ENGEL/FINDLEY AWARD

The Writers' Trust of Canada, 460 Richmond St. W., Suite 600, Toronto ON M5V 1Y1 Canada. (416)504-8222. **Fax:** (416)504-9090. **E-mail:** info@writerstrust.com. **Website:** www.writerstrust.com. **Contact:** Amanda Hopkins. The Writers' Trust Engel/Findley Award is presented annually at The Writers' Trust Awards Event, held in Toronto each fall, to a Canadian writer for a body of work in hope of continued contribution to the richness of Canadian literature. Open to Canadian citizens and permanent residents only. Prize: $25,000.

JOURNALISM

AAAS KAVLI SCIENCE JOURNALISM AWARDS

American Association for the Advancement of Science, Office of News and Information, 1200 New York Ave. NW, Washington DC 20005. **E-mail:** sja@aaas.org. **Website:** www.aaas.org/SJAwards. **Contact:** Awards Coordinator. The AAAS Kavli Science Journalism Awards represent the pinnacle of achievement for professional journalists in the science writing field. The awards recognize outstanding reporting for a general audience and honor individuals (rather than institutions, publishers or employers) for their coverage of the sciences, engineering and mathematics. Entries are submitted online, only. Enter e-mail address in online contact form to be alerted when entry forms are available. See website for guidelines and details. Deadline: August 1. Prize: $3,000 and a trip to AAAS Annual Meeting (travel and hotel expenses will be reimbursed). Judged by committees of reporters and editors.

AMY WRITING AWARDS

The Amy Foundation, P.O. Box 16091, Lansing MI 48901. (517)323-6233. **Fax:** (517)321-2572. **E-mail:** amyawards@wng.org. **Website:** www.amyfound.org; www.worldmag.com/amyawards. The Amy Foundation Writing Awards program is designed to recognize creative, skillful writing that applies in a sensitive, thought-provoking manner the biblical principles to issues affecting the world today, with an emphasis on discipling. Submitted articles must be published in a secular, non-religious publication (either printed or online) and must be reinforced with at least one passage of scripture. The article must have been published between January 1 and December 31 of the current calendar year. Deadline: January 31. Prize: 1st Prize: $10,000; 2nd Prize: $5,000; 3rd Prize: $4,000; 4th Prize: $3,000; 5th Prize: $2,000; and 10 prizes of $1,000.

FRANK LUTHER MOTT-KAPPA TAU ALPHA RESEARCH AWARD IN JOURNALISM

University of Missouri School of Journalism, 76 Gannett Hall, Columbia MO 65211-1200. (573)882-7685. **E-mail:** umcjourkta@missouri.edu. **Website:** www.kappataualpha.org. **Contact:** Dr. Keith Sanders, exec. dir., Kappa Tau Alpha. Offered annually for best researched book in mass communication. Submit 6 copies; no forms required. Deadline: December 9. Prize: $1,000. Judged by a panel of university professors of journalism and mass communication and national officers of Kappa Tau Alpha.

INVESTIGATIVE JOURNALISM GRANT

Fund For Investigative Journalism, Fund for Investigative Journalism, 529 14th Street NW, 13th Floor, Washington DC 20045. (202)662-7564. **E-mail:** fundfij@gmail.com. **Website:** www.fij.org. **Contact:** Sandy Bergo, executive director. Offered 3 times/year for original investigative print, online, radio, and TV stories and books. Guidelines online. See website for details on applying for a grant. Deadlines: Vary. Check website. Prize: Grants of $500-10,000. (TypicalGrant: $5,000.)

LIVINGSTON AWARDS FOR YOUNG JOURNALISTS

University of Michigan, Wallace House, 620 Oxford, Ann Arbor MI 48104. (734)998-7575. **Fax:** (734)998-7979. **E-mail:** livawards@umich.edu. **Website:** www.livawards.org. **Contact:** Charles Eisendrath. Offered annually for journalism published in the previous year to recognize and further develop the abilities of young journalists. Includes print, online, and broadcast. Guidelines available online. Open to journalists who are 34 years or younger as of December 31 of previous year and whose work appears in US-controlled media. Deadline: February 1. Prize: $10,000 each for local reporting, national reporting, and international reporting.

NATIONAL MAGAZINE AWARDS

National Magazine Awards Foundation, 2300 Yonge St., Suite 1600, Toronto ON M4P 1E4 Canada. (416)939-6200. **E-mail:** staff@magazine-awards.com. **Website:** www.magazine-awards.com. Offered annually for work by Canadian citizens or landed immigrants published in a Canadian magazine during the previous calendar year. Awards presented for writers, art directors, illustrators and photographers in written and visual categories. Open to Canadian residents only. Deadline: January 19. Prize: Monetary rewards.

SCIENCE IN SOCIETY AWARDS

National Association of Science Writers, Inc., P.O. Box 7905, Berkeley CA 94707. (510)647-9500. **E-mail:** director@nasw.org. **Website:** www.nasw.org. **Contact:** Tinsley Davis. Offered annually for investigative or interpretive reporting about the sciences and their impact on society. Categories: books, commentary and opinions, science reporting, longform science reporting, and science reporting for a local or regional market. Material may be a single article or broadcast, or a series. Works must have been first published or broadcast in North America between January 1 and December 31 of the previous year. Deadline: February 1. Prize: $2,500, and a certificate of recognition in each category.

SOVEREIGN AWARD

The Jockey Club of Canada, P.O. Box 66, Station B, Etobicoke ON M9W 5K9 Canada. (416)675-7756. **Fax:** (416)675-6378. **E-mail:** jockeyclub@bellnet.ca. **Website:** www.jockeyclubcanada.com. **Contact:** Stacie Roberts, exec. dir. The Jockey Club of Canada was founded in 1973 by E.P. Taylor to serve as the international representative of the Canadian Thoroughbred industry and to promote improvements to Thoroughbred racing and breeding, both in Canada and internationally. Submissions for these media awards must be of Canadian Thoroughbred racing or breeding content. They must have appeared in a media outlet recognized by The Jockey Club of Canada. See website for eligibility details and guidelines. Deadline: December 31.

TRANSLATION

AMERICAN-SCANDINAVIAN FOUNDATION TRANSLATION PRIZE

The American-Scandinavian Foundation, 58 Park Ave., New York NY 10016. (212)779-3587. **E-mail:** grants@amscan.org; info@amscan.org. **Website:** www.amscan.org. **Contact:** Matthew Walters, director of fellowships & grants. The annual ASF translation competition is awarded for the most outstanding translations of poetry, fiction, drama, or literary prose written by a Scandinavian author born after 1800. Accepts inquiries by e-mail, or through online application. Instructions an application available online. Entries must be unpublished. Length: No more than 50 pages for drama and fiction; no more than 25 pages for poetry. Open to any writer. Results announced in November. Winners notified by e-mail. Results available on the ASF website. Guidelines available online. Deadline: June 1. Prize: The Nadia Christensen Prize includes a $2,500 award, publication of an excerpt in *Scandinavian Review*, and a commemorative bronze medallion; The Leif and Inger Sjöberg Award, given to an individual whose literature translations have not previously been published, includes a $2,000 award, publication of an excerpt in *Scandinavian Review*, and a commemorative bronze medallion.

DER-HOVANESSIAN PRIZE

New England Poetry Club, 376 School St., Watertown MA 02472. **E-mail:** contests@nepoetryclub.org. **Website:** www.nepoetryclub.org. **Contact:** Audrey Kalajin. For a translation from any language into English. Send a copy of the original. Funded by John Mahtesian. Contest open to members and nonmembers. Poems should be typed and submitted in duplicate with author's name, address, phone, and e-mail address of writer on only 1 copy. Label poems with contest name. Entries should be sent by regular mail only. Entries should be original, unpublished poems in English. No poem should be entered in more than 1 contest, nor have won a previous contest. Deadline: May 31. Prize: $200. Judges are well-known poets and sometimes winners of previous NEPC contests.

SOEURETTE DIEHL FRASER AWARD FOR BEST TRANSLATION OF A BOOK

P.O. Box 609, Round Rock TX 78680. **E-mail:** tilsecretary@yahoo.com. **Website:** http://texasinstituteofletters.org. Offered every 2 years to recognize the best translation of a literary book into English. Translator must have been born in Texas or have lived in the state for at least 2 consecutive years at some time. Check website for guidelines and instructions on submitting. Deadline: January 10. Prize: $1,000.

THE FRENCH-AMERICAN AND THE FLORENCE GOULD FOUNDATIONS TRANSLATION PRIZES

28 W. 44th St., Suite 1420, New York NY 10036. (646)588-6781. **E-mail:** tchareton@frenchamerican.org. **Website:** www.frenchamerican.org. **Contact:** Thibault Chareton. Annual contest to promote French literature in the United States by extending its reach beyond the first language and giving translators and their craft greater visibility among publishers and readers alike. The prize also seeks to increase the visibility of the publishers who bring these important French works of literature, in translation of exceptional quality, to the American market by publicizing the titles and giving more visibility to the books they publish. Entries must have been published for the first time in the United States between January 1 and December 31, of the previous year. Submissions must

be completed online and are usually submitted by the publisher. Deadline: January 15. Prize: $10,000 award.

JOHN GLASSCO TRANSLATION PRIZE

Literary Translators' Association of Canada, 615-01 Concordia University, 1455 boul. de Maisonneuve Ouest, Montréal QC H3G 1M8 Canada. (514)848-2424, ext. 8702. **E-mail:** info@attlc-ltac.org. **Website:** http://attlc-ltac.org/john-glassco-translation-prize. **Contact:** Glassco Prize Committee. Offered annually for a translator's first book-length literary translation into French or English, published in Canada during the previous calendar year. The translator must be a Canadian citizen or permanent resident. Eligible genres include fiction, creative nonfiction, poetry, and children's books. Deadline: July 31. Prize: $1,000.

THE HAROLD MORTON LANDON TRANSLATION AWARD

Academy of American Poets, 75 Maiden Lane, Suite 901, New York NY 10038. (212)274-0343. **Fax:** (212)274-9427. **E-mail:** awards@poets.org. **Website:** www.poets.org. **Contact:** Awards Coordinator. Offered annually to recognize a published translation of poetry from any language into English. Open to living US citizens. Deadline: February 15. Prize: $1,000.

FENIA AND YAAKOV LEVIANT MEMORIAL PRIZE IN YIDDISH STUDIES

Modern Language Association of America, 26 Broadway, 3rd Floor, New York NY 10004-1789. (646)576-5141. **Fax:** (646)458-0030. **E-mail:** awards@mla.org. **Website:** www.mla.org. **Contact:** Coordinator of book prizes. Offered in even-numbered years for an outstanding English translation of a Yiddish literary work or the publication of a scholarly work. Cultural studies, critical biographies, or edited works in the field of Yiddish folklore or linguistic studies are eligible to compete. See website for details on which they are accepting. Books must have been published within the past 4 years. Authors need not be members of the MLA. Requires 4 copies of the book. Deadline: May 1. Prize: A cash prize, and a certificate, to be presented at the Modern Language Association's annual convention in January.

MARSH AWARD FOR CHILDREN'S LITERATURE IN TRANSLATION

The English-Speaking Union, Dartmouth House, 37 Charles St., London En W1J 5ED United Kingdom. 020 7529 1591. **E-mail:** melanie.aplin@esu.org. **Website:** www.marshcristiantrust.org; www.esu.org. **Contact:** Melanie Aplin, senior education officer. The Marsh Award for Children's Literature in Translation, awarded biennially, was founded to celebrate the best translation of a children's book from a foreign language into English and published in the UK. It aims to spotlight the high quality and diversity of translated fiction for young readers. The Award is administered by the ESU on behalf of the Marsh Christian Trust. Submissions will be accepted from publishers for books produced for readers from 5 to 16 years of age. Guidelines and eligibility criteria available online.

PEN AWARD FOR POETRY IN TRANSLATION

PEN American Center, 588 Broadway, Suite 303, New York NY 10012. (212)334-1660, ext. 108. **E-mail:** awards@pen.org. **Website:** www.pen.org. **Contact:** Arielle Anema. This award recognizes book-length translations of poetry from any language into English, published during the current calendar year. All books must have been published in the US. Translators may be of any nationality. US residency/citizenship not required. Submissions must be made publishers or literary agents. Self-published books are not eligible. Books with more than 2 translators are not eligible. Re-translations are ineligible, unless the work can be said to provide a significant revision of the original translation. Deadline: November 15. Prize: $3,000. Judged by a single translator of poetry appointed by the PEN Translation Committee.

PEN TRANSLATION PRIZE

PEN American Center, 588 Broadway, Suite 303, New York NY 10012. (212)334-1660, ext. 108. **Fax:** (212)334-2181. **E-mail:** awards@pen.org. **Contact:** Arielle Anema. Offered for book-length translations from any language into English, published during the current calendar year. No technical, scientific, or bibliographic translations. PEN will only accept submissions from publishers or literary agents. Self-published books are not eligible. Although all eligible books must have been published in the United States, translators may be of any nationality; US residency or citizenship is not required. Deadline: November 15. Prize: $3,000.

LOIS ROTH AWARD

Modern Language Association, 26 Broadway, 3rd Floor, New York NY 10004. (646)576-5141. **Fax:** (646)458-0030. **E-mail:** awards@mla.org. **Website:**

www.mla.org. Offered in odd-numbered years for an outstanding translation into English of a book-length literary work. Translators need not be members of the MLA. Translations must have been published in the previous calendar year. Requires 6 copies, plus 12-15 pages of text in the original language. Deadline: April 1. Prize: A cash award and a certificate to be presented at the Modern Language Association's annual convention in January.

ALDO AND JEANNE SCAGLIONE PRIZE FOR A TRANSLATION OF A LITERARY WORK

Modern Language Association, 26 Broadway, 3rd Floor, New York NY 10004-1789. (646)576-5141. **Fax:** (646)458-0030. **E-mail:** awards@mla.org. **Website:** www.mla.org. **Contact:** Coordinator of Book Prizes. Offered in even-numbered years for an outstanding translation into English of a book-length literary work. Translations must have been published in the previous calendar year. Translators need not be members of the MLA. Requires 6 copies of the book, plus 12-15 pages of text in the original language. Deadline: April 1. Prize: A cash award and a certificate to be presented at the Modern Language Association's annual convention in January.

ALDO AND JEANNE SCAGLIONE PRIZE FOR A TRANSLATION OF A SCHOLARLY STUDY OF LITERATURE

Modern Language Association of America, 26 Broadway, 3rd Floor, New York NY 10004-1789. (646)576-5141. **Fax:** (646)458-0030. **E-mail:** awards@mla.org. **Website:** www.mla.org. **Contact:** Coordinator of Book Prizes. Offered in odd-numbered years for an outstanding translation into English of a book-length work of literary history, literary criticism, philology, or literary theory. Translators need not be members of the MLA. Books must have been published in the previous 2 years. Requires 4 copies of the book. Deadline: May 1. Prize: A cash award and a certificate to be presented at the Modern Language Association's annual convention in January.

ALDO AND JEANNE SCAGLIONE PRIZE FOR STUDIES IN SLAVIC LANGUAGES AND LITERATURES

Modern Language Association of America, 26 Broadway, 3rd Floor, New York NY 10004-1789. (646)576-5141. **Fax:** (646)458-0030. **E-mail:** awards@mla.org. **Website:** www.mla.org. **Contact:** Coordinator of Book Prizes. Offered in odd-numbered years for an outstanding work on the linguistics or literatures of the Slavic languages. Books must have been published in the previous 2 years. Requires 4 copies of the book. Authors need not be members of the MLA. Deadline: May 1. Prize: A cash award and a certificate to be presented at the Modern Language Association's annual convention in January.

POETRY

49TH PARALLEL AWARD FOR POETRY

Western Washington University, Mail Stop 9053, Bellingham WA 98225. (360)650-4863. **E-mail:** bellingham.review@wwu.edu. **Website:** www.bhreview.org. **Contact:** Brenda Miller, editor-in-chief; Kaitlyn Teer, managing editor. Annual poetry contest, supported by the *Bellingham Review*, given for a poem or group of poems of any style or length. Upload entries via Submittable online. Up to 3 poems per entry. Deadline: March 15. Submissions period begins December 1. Prize: $1,000.

J.M. ABRAHAM POETRY PRIZE

Writers' Federation of Nova Scotia, 1113 Marginal Rd., Halifax NS B3H 4P7 Canada. (902)423-8116. **Fax:** (902)422-0881. **E-mail:** director@writers.ns.ca. **Website:** www.writers.ns.ca. The J.M. Abraham Poetry Prize is an annual award designed to honor the best book of poetry by a resident of Atlantic Canada. Formerly known as the Atlantic Poetry Prize. Detailed guidelines and eligibility criteria available online. Deadline: First Friday in December. Prize: Valued at $2,000 for the winning title.

ACORN-PLANTOS AWARD FOR PEOPLES POETRY

Acorn-Plantos Award Committee, 36 Sunset Ave., Hamilton ON L8R 1V6 Canada. **E-mail:** jeffhamiltonjeff@gmail.com. **Contact:** Jeff Seffinga. Annual contest for work that appeared in print in the previous calender year. This award is given to the Canadian poet who best (through the publication of a book of poems) exemplifies populist or peoples poetry in the tradition of Milton Acorn, Ted Plantos, et al. Work may be entered by the poet or the publisher; the award goes to the poet. Entrants must submit 5 copies of each title. Poet must be a citizen of Canada or a landed immigrant. Publisher need not be Canadian. Deadline: June 30. Prize: $500 (CDN) and a medal. Judged by a panel of poets in the tradition who are not entered in the current year.

AKRON POETRY PRIZE

The University of Akron Press, 120 E. Mill St., Suite 415, Akron OH 44308. **E-mail:** uapress@uakron.edu. **Website:** www.uakron.edu/uapress/akron-poetry-prize/. **Contact:** Mary Biddinger, editor/award director. Submissions must be unpublished. Considers simultaneous submissions (with notification of acceptance elsewhere). Submit 48 or more pages, typed, single-spaced; optional self-addressed postcard for confirmation. Mss will not be returned. Do not send mss bound or enclosed in covers. See website for complete guidelines. Competition receives 500+ entries. 2014 winner was John Repp for *Pictures at an Exhibition*. Winner posted on website by September 30. Intimate friends, relatives, current and former students of the final judge (students in an academic, degree-conferring program or its equivalent) and current faculty, staff, students, and alumni of the University of Akron or the Northeast Ohio MFA Program (NEOMFA) are not eligible to enter the Akron Poetry Prize competition. Deadline: April 15-June 15. Prize: $1,500, plus publication of a book-length ms.

THE AMERICAN POETRY JOURNAL BOOK PRIZE

P.O. Box 2080, Aptos CA 95001-2080. **E-mail:** dreamhorsepress@yahoo.com. **Website:** www.dreamhorsepress.com. Both free and formal verse styles are welcome. Multiple submissions are acceptable. Submit 50-65 paginated pages of poetry, table of contents, acknowledgments, bio, and e-mail address (for results). No SASE required; mss will be recycled. Guidelines available on website. Deadline: February 28 for snail mail postmarks, five days later for electronic submissions. Prize: $1,000, publication and 20 copies. All entries will be considered for publication.

ANABIOSIS PRESS CHAPBOOK CONTEST

2 South New St., Bradford MA 01835. (978)469-7085. **E-mail:** rsmyth@anabiosispress.org. **Website:** www.anabiosispress.org. **Contact:** Richard Smyth, editor. Submit 16-20 pages of poetry on any subject. Include separate pages with a biography, table of contents, and acknowledgments for any previous publications. Include SASE with correct postage for return of ms or notification of winner. All entrants receive a copy of the winning chapbook). Winners announced by September 30. The 2014 winner was Danielle Beazer Dubrasky's *Ruin and Light*. Deadline: June 30 (postmarked). Prize: $100, plus publication of the winning chapbook, and 100 copies of the first run.

THE ANHINGA PRESS-ROBERT DANA PRIZE FOR POETRY

Anhinga Press, P.O. Box 3665, Tallahassee FL 32315. **E-mail:** info@anhinga.org. **Website:** www.anhinga.org. **Contact:** Kristine Snodgrass, poetry editor. Offered annually for a book-length collection of poetry by an author writing in English. Guidelines on website. Past winners include Frank X. Gaspar, Earl S. Braggs, Julia Levine, Keith Ratzlaff, Lynn Aarti Chandhok, and Rhett Iseman Trull. Mss must be 48-80 pages, excluding front matter. Deadline: Submissions will be accepted from February 15-May 15. Prize: $2,000, a reading tour of selected Florida colleges and universities, and the winning ms will be published. Past judges include Jan Beatty, Richard Blaco, Denise Duhamel, Donald Hall, Joy Harjo, Robert Dana, Mark Jarman, and Tony Hoagland.

ANNUAL GIVAL PRESS OSCAR WILDE AWARD

Gival Press, LLC, P.O. Box 3812, Arlington VA 22203. (703)351-0079. **E-mail:** givalpress@yahoo.com. **Website:** www.givalpress.com. **Contact:** Robert L. Giron. Award given to the best previously unpublished original poem—written in English of any length, in any style, typed, double-spaced on 1 side only—which best relates gay/lesbian/bisexual/transgendered life, by a poet who is 18 years or older. Entrants are asked to submit their poems without any kind of identification (with the exception of titles) and with a separate cover page with the following information: name, address (street, city, and state with zip code), telephone number, e-mail address (if available), and a list of poems by title. Checks drawn on American banks should be made out to Gival Press, LLC. Deadline: June 27 (postmarked). Prize: $100 and the poem, along with information about the poet, will be published on the Gival Press website.

ANNUAL VENTURA COUNTY WRITERS CLUB POETRY CONTEST IN HONOR OF JOYCE LA MERS

Ventura County Writers Club Poetry Contest, P.O. Box 3373, Thousand Oaks CA 91362. **E-mail:** poetrycontest@venturacountywriters.com. **Website:** www.venturacountywriters.com. **Contact:** Poetry Contest Chair. Annual poetry contest for youth and adult poets. Youth division for poets under 18: Division A is open to entrants ages 13-18; and, Division B is open to poets ages 12 and under. Adult division for poets 18 and older. Club mebership not required to enter and entries accepted worldwide as long as fees are paid and the poem is in English. Enter through website. Deadline: February 15. Entries accepted beginning January 1. Prize: The adult winners will be awarded $100 for first place, $75 for second and $50 for third place. The two youth categories will receive $50 for first place, $35 for second and $25 for third place.

⊘ ANNUAL WORLD HAIKU COMPETITION & ANNUAL WORLD TANKA CONTEST

P.O. Box 17331, Arlington VA 22216. **E-mail:** LPEzineSubmissions@gmail.com. **Website:** http://lyricalpassionpoetry.yolasite.com. **Contact:** Raquel D. Bailey. Contest is open to all writers. Requires first rights for all previously unpublished works. Only e-mail entries accepted for contests. Promotes Japanese short form poetry. Deadline: See website for details. Prize: Monetary compensation and publication. Judged by experienced editors and award-winning writers from the contemporary writing community.

ART AFFAIR POETRY CONTEST

P.O. Box 54302, Oklahoma City OK 73154. **E-mail:** okpoets@aol.com. **Website:** www.shadetreecreations.com. **Contact:** Barbara Shepherd, contest chair. The annual Art Affair Poetry Contest is open to any poet. Multiple entries accepted with entry fee for each and may be mailed in the same packet. Guidelines available on website. Winners' list will be published on the Art Affair website in December. Poems must be unpublished. Submit original poems on any subject, in any style, no more than 60 lines (put line count in the upper right-hand corner of first page). Include cover page with poet's name, address, phone number, and title of poem. Do not include SASE; poems will not be returned. Deadline: October 1. Prize: 1st Prize: $40 and certificate; 2nd Prize: $25 and certificate; and 3rd Prize: $15 and certificate. Honorable Mention certificates will be awarded at the discretion of the judges.

ATLANTIS AWARD

The Poet's Billow, 245 N. Collingwood, Syracuse NY 13206. **E-mail:** thepoetsbillow@gmail.com. **Website:** http://thepoetsbillow.org. **Contact:** Robert Evory. Annual award open to any writer to recognize one outstanding poem from its entries. Finalists with strong work will also be published. Submissions must be previously unpublished. Deadline: October 1. Submissions open July 1. Prize: $100 and winning poet will be featured in an interview on The Poet's Billow website. Poem will be published and displayed in The Poet's Billow Literary Art Gallery and nominated for a Pushcart Prize. If the poet qualifies, the poem will also be submitted to The Best New Poets anthology. Judged by the editors, and, occasionally, a guest judge.

BARROW STREET PRESS BOOK CONTEST

P.O. Box 1558, Kingston RI 02881. **E-mail:** submissions@barrowstreet.org. **Website:** www.barrowstreet.org. The Barrow Street Press Book Contest award will be given for the best previously unpublished ms of poetry in English. Submit a 50-70 page unpublished ms of original poetry in English. Please number the pages of your ms and include a table of contents and an acknowledgments page for any previously published poems. Include two title pages. The author's name, address, and telephone number should appear on the first title page only and should not appear anywhere else in the ms. The second title page should contain only the ms title. Deadline: June 30. Prize: $1,000. Judged by Denise Duhamel.

ELINOR BENEDICT POETRY PRIZE

Passages North, Northern Michigan University, 1401 Presque Isle Ave., Marquette MI 49855. **E-mail:** passages@nmu.edu. **Website:** passagesnorth.com/contests/. **Contact:** Jennifer A. Howard, Editor-in-Chief. Prize given biennially for a poem or a group of poems. Check website to see if award is currently being offered this year. Deadline: March 22. Submission period begins January 15. Prize: $1,000 and publication for winner; 2 honorable mentions are also published; all entrants receive a copy of *Passages North*.

BERMUDA TRIANGLE PRIZE

The Poet's Billow, 245 N. Collingwood, Syracuse NY 13206. **E-mail:** thepoetsbillow@gmail.com. **Website:** http://thepoetsbillow.org. **Contact:** Robert Evory. Annual award open to any writer to recognize three poems that address a theme set by the editors. Finalists with strong work will also be published. Submissions must be previously unpublished. Please submit online. Deadline: March 15. Submission period begins November 15. Prize: $50 each to three poems. The winning poems will be published and displayed in The Poet's Billow Literary Art Gallery and nominated for a Pushcart Prize. If the poet qualifies, the poem will also be submitted to The Best New Poets anthology. Judged by the editors, and, occasionally, a guest judge.

THE PATRICIA BIBBY FIRST BOOK AWARD

Patricia Bibby Award, Tebot Bach, P.O. Box 7887, Huntington Beach CA 92615-7887. **E-mail:** mifanwy@tebotbach.org; info@tebotbach.org. **Website:** www.tebotbach.org. **Contact:** Mifanwy Kaiser. Annual competition open to all poets writing in English who have not committed to publishing collections of poetry of 36 poems or more in editions of over 400 copies. Offers award and publication of a book-length poetry ms by Tebot Bach. Complete guidelines available by e-mail or on website. Deadline: October 31. Prize: $500 and book publication. Judges for each year's competition announced online.

BINGHAMTON UNIVERSITY MILT KESSLER POETRY BOOK AWARD

Binghamton University Creative Writing Program, Department of English, General Literature, and Rhetoric, Library North Room 1149, Vestal Parkway East, P.O. Box 6000, Binghamton NY 13902-6000. (607)777-2713. **Fax:** (607)777-2408. **E-mail:** cwpro@binghamton.edu. **Website:** www2.binghamton.edu/english/creative-writing/binghamton-center-for-writers. **Contact:** Maria Mazziotti Gillan, creative writing program director. Annual award for a book of poems written in English, 48 pages or more in length, selected by judges as the strongest collection of poems published in that year. Print on demand is acceptable but no self-published or vanity press work will be considered. Each book submitted must be accompanied by an application form available online. Poet or publisher may submit more than 1 book for prize consideration. Send 2 copies of each book. Deadline: March 1. Prize: $1,000.

THE BITTER OLEANDER PRESS LIBRARY OF POETRY AWARD

The Bitter Oleander Press, 4983 Tall Oaks Dr., Fayetteville NY 13066-9776. (315)637-3047. **Fax:** (315)637-5056. **E-mail:** info@bitteroleander.com. **Website:** www.bitteroleander.com. **Contact:** Paul B. Roth. The Bitter Oleander Press Library of Poetry Book Award replaces the 15-year long run of the Frances Locke Memorial Poetry Award. Guidelines available on website. Entrants must have had at least 1 standard edition of poetry published previously, not self-published, not a chapbook. Mss must be 48-80 pages of poetry in length, legibly typed or computer generated, with 2 cover sheets: 1 with title and author's contact information; the other having the title only. No e-mail submissions will be allowed. Winning ms to be published the following year. Deadline: June 15 (postmarked). Open to submissions on May 1. Early or late entries will be disqualified. Prize: $1,000, plus book publication of the winning ms.

BLUE MOUNTAIN ARTS/SPS STUDIOS POETRY CARD CONTEST

P.O. Box 1007, Boulder CO 80306. (303)449-0536. **Fax:** (303)447-0939. **E-mail:** poetrycontest@sps.com; editorial@sps.com. **Website:** www.sps.com. Biannual poetry card contest. All entries must be the original creation of the submitting author. Looking for original poetry that is rhyming or non-rhyming, although non-rhyming poetry reads better. Poems may also be considered for possible publication on greeting cards or in book anthologies. Guidelines available online. Deadline: December 31 and June 30. Prize: 1st Place: $300; 2nd Place: $150; 3rd Place: $50. Judged by the Blue Mountain Arts editorial staff.

TIPS "We suggest that you write about real emotions and feelings and that you have some special person or occasion in mind as you write."

THE FREDERICK BOCK PRIZE

Poetry, 61 W. Superior St., Chicago IL 60654. (312)787-7070. **Fax:** (312)787-6650. **E-mail:** editors@poetrymagazine.org. **Website:** www.poetryfoundation.org. Several prizes are awarded annually for the best work printed in *Poetry* during the preceding year. Only poems already published in the magazine are eligible for consideration, and no formal application is necessary. The winners are announced in the November issue. Upon acceptance, *Poetry* licenses exclusive worldwide first serial rights, including electronic rights, for publication, as well as non-exclusive rights to reprint, reuse, and archive the work, in any format, in perpetuity. Copyright reverts to author upon first publication. Any writer may submit poems to *Poetry*. Prize: $500.

THE BOSTON REVIEW ANNUAL POETRY CONTEST

Poetry Contest, Boston Review, P.O. Box 425786, Cambridge MA 02142. (617)324-1360. **Fax:** (617)452-3356. **E-mail:** review@bostonreview.net. **Website:** www.bostonreview.net. Offers $1,500 and publication in *Boston Review* (see separate listing in Magazines/Journals). Any poet writing in English is eligible, unless he or she is a current student, former student, or close personal friend of the judge. Submissions must be unpublished. Submit up to 5 poems, no more than 10 pages total, via online contest entry manager. Include cover sheet with poet's name, address, and phone number; no identifying information on the poems themselves. No cover note is necessary for online submissions. No mss will be returned. Guidelines available for SASE or on website. Deadline: June 1. Winner announced in early November on website. Prize: $1,500 and publication.

BOULEVARD POETRY CONTEST FOR EMERGING POETS

PMB 325, 6614 Clayton Rd., Richmond Heights MO 63117. **E-mail:** richardburgin@att.net; jessicarogen@boulevardmagazine.org. **Website:** www.boulevard-magazine.org. **Contact:** Jessica Rogen, managing editor. Annual Emerging Poets Contest offers $1,000 and publication in *Boulevard* (see separate listing in Magazines/Journals) for the best group of 3 poems by a poet who has not yet published a book of poetry with a nationally distributed press. All entries will be considered for publication and payment at regular rates. Submissions must be unpublished. Considers simultaneous submissions. Submit 3 poems, typed; may be a sequence or unrelated. On page one of first poem type poet's name, address, phone number, and titles of the 3 poems. Deadline: June 1. Prize: $1,000 and publication.

BP NICHOL CHAPBOOK AWARD

113 Bond St., St. John's NL A1C 1T6 Canada. (416)964-7919. **Fax:** (416)964-6941. **E-mail:** meetthepresses@gmail.com. **Website:** meetthepresses.wordpress.com. **Contact:** Beth Follett. Offered annually to a chapbook (10-48 pages) of poetry in English, published in Canada in the previous year. Open to any Canadian writer. Author or publisher may make submissions. Send 3 copies (non-returnable), plus a short author CV. Deadline: April 30. Prize: $4,000 (Canadian) to author and $500 (Canadian) to publisher.

BARBARA BRADLEY PRIZE

New England Poetry Club, 376 School St., Watertown MA 02472 . **E-mail:** contests@nepoetryclub.org. **Website:** www.nepoetryclub.org. **Contact:** Audrey Kalajin. For a lyric poem under 20 lines, written by a woman. Contest open to members and nonmembers. Poems should be typed and submitted in duplicate with author's name, address, phone, and e-mail address of writer on only 1 copy. (Judges receive copies without names.) Copy only. Label poems with contest name. Entries should be sent by regular mail only. Special delivery or signature required mail will be returned by the post office. Entries should be original, unpublished poems in English. No poem should be entered in more than 1 contest, nor have won a previous contest. No entries will be returned. NEPC will not engage in correspondence regarding poems or contest decisions. Deadline: May 31. Prize: $200. Judged by well-known poets and sometimes winners of previous NEPC contests.

BRICK ROAD POETRY BOOK CONTEST

Brick Road Poetry Press, Inc., P.O. Box 751, Columbus GA 31902. (706)649-3080. **Fax:** (706)649-3094. **E-mail:** editor@brickroadpoetrypress.com. **Website:** www.brickroadpoetrypress.com. **Contact:** Ron Self and Keith Badowski, co-editors/founders. Annual competition for an original collection of 50-100 pages of poetery. Book-length poetry mss only. Simultaneous submissions accepted. Single sideded, single spaced only. No more than one poem per page. Electronic submissions are accepted, see website for details. Include a cover letter with poetry publication/recognition highlights. Deadline: November 1. Submission period begins August 1. Prize: $1,000, publication in both print and e-book formats, and 25 copies of the book. May also offer publication contracts to the top finalists.

BRIGHT HILL PRESS POETRY CHAPBOOK COMPETITION

Bright Press Hill & Literary Center, 94 Church St., Treadwell NY 13846. (607)829-5055. **E-mail:** brighthillpress@stny.rr.com; wordthur@stny.rr.com. **Website:** www.brighthillpress.org. The annual Bright Hill Press Chapbook Award recognizes an outstanding collection of poetry. Guidelines available for SASE, by e-mail, or on website. Collection of original poetry, 48-64 pages, single spaced, one poem to a page (no name) with table of contents. Ms must be submitted in Times New Roman, 12 pt. type only. No illustrations, no cover suggestions. Bio and acknowledgments of poems that have been previously published should be included in a separate document, or in comments box if submitting online. See website for more details, and information on submitting a hard copy. Deadline: December 15. Submission period begins October 25. Prize: A publication contract with Bright Hill Press and $1,000, publication in print format, and 30 copies of the printed book. Judged by a nationally-known poet.

BRITTINGHAM PRIZE IN POETRY

University of Wisconsin Press, 1930 Monroe St., 3rd Floor, Madison WI 5311-2059. (608)263-1110. **Fax:** (608)263-1132. **E-mail:** rwallace@wisc.edu. **E-mail:** uwiscpress@uwpress.wisc.edu. **Website:** www.wisc.edu/wisconsinpress/poetryguide.html. **Contact:** Ronald Wallace, contest director. The annual Brittingham Prize in Poetry is 1 of 2 prizes awarded by The University of Wisconsin Press (see separate listing for the Felix Pollak Prize in Poetry in this section). Submissions must be unpublished as a collection, but individual poems may have been published elsewhere (publication must be acknowledged). Considers simultaneous submissions if notified of selection elsewhere. Submit 60-90 unbound ms pages, typed single-spaced (with double spaces between stanzas). Clean photocopies are acceptable. Include 1 title page with poet's name, address, and telephone number and 1 with title only. No translations. Strongly encourages electronic submissions via web page. SASE required for postal submissions. Will return results only; mss will not be returned. Guidelines online. The Brittingham Prize in Poetry awarded annually to best book-length ms of original poetry submitted in an open competition. The award is administered by the University of Wisconsin–Madison English Department, and the winner is chosen by a nationally recognized poet. The resulting book is published by the University of Wisconsin Press. Deadline: Submit August 15-September 15. Prize: Offers $1,000, plus publication. Judged by a distinguished poet who will remain anonymous until the winners are announced in mid-February.

BOB BUSH MEMORIAL AWARD FOR FIRST BOOK OF POETRY

Texas Institute of Letters, P.O. Box 609, Round Rock TX 78680. **Website:** www.texasinstituteofletters.org. Offered annually for best first book of poetry published in previous year. Writer must have been born in Texas, have lived in the state at least 2 consecutive years at some time, or the subject matter should be associated with the state. Deadline: See website for exact date. Prize: $1,000.

GERALD CABLE BOOK AWARD

Silverfish Review Press, P.O. Box 3541, Eugene OR 97403. (541)344-5060. **E-mail:** sfrpress@earthlink.net. **Website:** www.silverfishreviewpress.com. **Contact:** Rodger Moody, editor. Awarded annually to a book-length ms of original poetry by an author who has not yet published a full-length collection. There are no restrictions on the kind of poetry or subject matter; translations are not acceptable. Mss should be at least 48 pages in length. Clean photo copies are acceptable. The poet's name should not appear on the ms. Include a separate title page with name, address, and phone number. Poems may have appeared in periodicals, chapbooks, or anthologies, but should not be acknowledged. Simultaneous submissions are accepted. Accepts e-mail submissions. See website for more details and guidelines. Deadline: October 15. Prize: $1,000, publication, and 25 copies of the book. The winner will be announced in March.

CAKETRAIN COMPETITION

P.O. Box 82588, Pittsburgh PA 15218. **E-mail:** editors@caketrain.org. **Website:** www.caketrain.org. **Contact:** Amanda Raczkowski, editor; Joseph Reed, editor. Annual contest for full length works of fiction and poetry chapbooks sponsored by *Caketrain* literary journal. Can submit by mail with SASE or by e-mail. See website for guidelines. Deadline: October 1. Prize: $250 cash and 25 copies of their book.

CANADIAN AUTHORS ASSOCIATION AWARD FOR POETRY

6 West St. N, Suite 203, Orillia ON L3V 5B8 Canada. (705)325-3926. **E-mail:** admin@canadianauthors.org. **Website:** www.canadianauthors.org. **Contact:** Anita Purcell, executive director. Offered annually for a full-length English-language book of poems for adults, by a Canadian writer. Deadline: January 15. Prize: $2,000 and a silver medal. Judging: Each year a trustee for each award appointed by the Canadian Authors Association selects up to 3 judges. Identities of the trustee and judges are confidential.

CAROLINA WREN PRESS POETRY SERIES CONTEST

120 Morris St., Durham NC 27701. (919)560-2738. **Fax:** (919)560-2759. **E-mail:** carolinawrenpress@earthlink.net. **Website:** www.carolinawrenpress.org. **Contact:** Ravi Shankar, founding editor. Carolina Wren Press is a nonprofit organization whose mission is to publish quality writing, especially by writers historically neglected by mainstream publishing, and to develop diverse and vital audiences through publishing, outreach, and educational programs. Submit a copy of a 48-72 page manuscript. Manuscript

should be single-spaced and paginated. Please include a table of contents. Title page should not include author information–no name, or address etc. Within the manuscript, do include a page acknowledging individual poems that have been previously published. Open only to poets who have had no more than one full-lenth book published. Deadline: March 31. Prize: $1,000 and publication.

THE CENTER FOR BOOK ARTS POETRY CHAPBOOK COMPETITION

The Center for Book Arts, 28 W. 27th St., 3rd Floor, New York NY 10001. (212)481-0295. **Fax:** (866)708-8994. **E-mail:** info@centerforbookarts.org. **Website:** www.centerforbookarts.org. Annual competition for unpublished collections of poetry. Individual poems may have been previously published. Collection must not exceed 500 lines or 24 pages (does not include cover page, title pages, table of contents, or acknowledgements pages). Copies of winning chapbooks available through website. The cover page should contain, on a single detachable page, the ms title and author's name, along with address, phone number, and e-mail. The author's name should not appear anywhere else. A second title page should be provided without the author's name or other identification. Please provide a table of contents and a separate acknowledgements page containing prior magazine or anthology publication of individual poems. Mss should be bound with a simple spring clip. Poems may have appeared in journals or anthologies but not as part of a book-length collection. Competition is open to all poets writing in English who have published no more than 2 full-length books. Poets may not have studied with either judge in a degree-granting program for the last 5 years. Deadline: December 15. Prize: $500 award, $500 honorarium for a reading, publication, and 10 copies of chapbook.

CHAPBOOK COMPETITION FOR OHIO POETS

Wick Poetry Center, Kent State University, 301 Satterfield Hall, Kent State University, P.O. Box 5190, Kent OH 44242-0001. (330)672-2067. **Fax:** (330)672-3333. **Website:** www2.kent.edu/wick/competitions. **Contact:** David Hassler, director. The Chapbook Competition for Ohio Poets is open to all current residents of Ohio, including students in an Ohio college or university. Does not accept postal submissions. Mss should be 16-30 pages of poetry, with no more than one poem per page. Deadline: October 31. Submissions period begins August 31. Prize: Publication and a reading at Kent State University.

JOHN CIARDI PRIZE FOR POETRY

BkMk Press, University of Missouri-Kansas City, 5100 Rockhill Rd., Kansas City MO 02903-1803. (816)235-2558. **E-mail:** bkmk@umkc.edu. **Website:** www.newletters.org. Offered annually for the best book-length collection (unpublished) of poetry in English by a living author. Translations are not eligible. Guidelines for SASE, by e-mail, or on website. Poetry mss should be approximately 50-110 pages, single-spaced. Deadline: January 15. Prize: $1,000, plus book publication by BkMk Press. Judged by a network of published writers. Final judging is done by a writer of national reputation.

CIDER PRESS REVIEW BOOK AWARD

P.O. Box 33384, San Diego CA 92163. **E-mail:** editor@ciderpressreview.com. **Website:** http://ciderpressreview.com/. Annual award from *Cider Press Review*. Submissions must be unpublished as a collection, but individual poems may have been previously published elsewhere. Submit book-length ms of 48-80 pages. Submissions can be made online using the submission form on the website or by mail. If sending by mail, include 2 cover sheets—1 with title, author's name, and complete contact information; and 1 with title only, all bound with a spring clip. Does not require SASE; notification via e-mail and on the website, only. Mss cannot be returned. Online submissions must be in Word for PC or PDF format, and should not include title page with author's name. The editors strongly urge contestants to use online delivery if possible. Review the complete submission guidelines and learn more online at website. Deadline: November 30. Open to submissions on September 1. Prize: $1,500, publication, and 25 author's copies of a book length collection of poetry. Author receives a standard publishing contract. Initial print run is not less than 1,000 copies. CPR acquires first publication rights. Judged by Jeffrey Harrison in 2014. Previous judge was Charles Harper Webb.

CLEVELAND STATE UNIVERSITY POETRY CENTER PRIZES

Cleveland State University Poetry Center, Cleveland State University Poetry Center, 2121 Euclid Avenue, Rhodes Tower, Room 1841, Cleveland OH 44115-2214. (216)687-3986. **Fax:** (216)687-6943. **E-mail:** poetrycenter@csuohio.edu. **Website:** www.csuohio.edu/poetrycenter. **Contact:** Frank Giampietro. Manuscript should contain a minimum of 48 and a maximum of 100 pages of poetry. See website for specific details and rules. Offered annually to identify, reward, and publish the best unpublished book-length poetry ms (minimum 48 pages) in 2 categories: First Book Award and Open Competition (for poets who have published at least one collection with a press run of 500). Deadline: March 31. Submissions open on January 1. Prize: First Book and Open Book Competitions awards publication and a $1,000 advance against royalties for an original manuscript of poetry in each category

CLOCKWISE CHAPBOOK COMPETITION

Tebot Bach, Tebot Bach, Clockwise, P.O. Box 7887, Huntington Beach CA 92615. (714)968-0905. **Fax:** (714)968-4677. **E-mail:** mifanwy@tebotbach.org. **Website:** www.tebotbach.org/clockwise.html. Annual competition for a collection of poetry. Submit 24-32 pages of original poetry in English. Must be previously unpublished poetry for the full collection; individual poems may have been published. Full guidelines, including submission info, available online. Deadline: April 15. Prize: $500 and a book publication in Perfect Bound Editions. Winner announced in September with publication the following April. Judged by Gail Wronsky.

CLOUDBANK CONTEST

P.O. Box 610, Corvallis OR 97339. **E-mail:** michael@cloudbankbooks.com. **Website:** www.cloudbankbooks.com. **Contact:** Michael Malan. For contest submissions, the writer's name, address, e-mail, and the titles of the poems/flash fiction pieces being submitted should be typed on a cover sheet only, not on the pages of poems or flash fiction. No electronic submissions. Send no more than 5 poems or flash fiction pieces (500 words or less) for the contest or for regular submissions. Prize: $200 and publication, plus an extra copy of the issue in which the winning poem appears. Two contributors' copies will be sent to writers whose work appears in the magazine. Judged by Michael Malan and Peter Sears.

TOM COLLINS POETRY PRIZE

Fellowship of Australian Writers (WA), P.O. Box 6180, Swanbourne WA 6910 Australia. (61)(8)9384-4771. **Fax:** (61)(8)9384-4854. **E-mail:** fellowshipaustralianwriterswa@gmail.com. **Website:** www.fawwa.org. Annual contest for unpublished poems, maximum 60 lines. Reserves the right to publish entries in a FAWWA publication or on its website. Guidelines online or for SASE. See website for details, guidelines, and entry form. Deadline: December 15. Submission period begins September 1. Prize: 1st Place: $1,000; 2nd Place; $400; 4 Highly Commended: $150 each.

THE COLORADO PRIZE FOR POETRY

Colorado Review/Center for Literary Publishing, Department of English, Colorado State University, 9105 Campus Delivery, Ft. Collins CO 80523. (970)491-5449. **E-mail:** creview@colostate.edu. **Website:** http://coloradoprize.colostate.edu. **Contact:** Stephanie G'Schwind, editor; Donald Revell, poetry editor. Submission must be unpublished as a collection, but individual poems may have been published elsewhere. Submit mss of 48-100 pages of poetry on any subject, in any form, double- or single-spaced. Include 2 titles pages: 1 with ms title only, the other with ms title and poet's name, address, and phone number. Enclose SASP for notification of receipt and SASE for results; mss will not be returned. Guidelines available for SASE or by e-mail. Guidelines available for SASE or online at website. Poets can also submit online via our online submission manager through our website. Deadline: Early January. Check website for exact deadline. Prize: $2,000 and publication of a book-length ms.

CONCRETE WOLF POETRY CHAPBOOK CONTEST

P.O. Box 1808, Kingston WA 98346. **E-mail:** concretewolf@yahoo.com. **Website:** http://concretewolf.com. Prefers chapbooks that have a theme, either obvious (i.e., chapbook about a divorce) or understated (i.e., all the poems mention the color blue). Likes a collection that feels more like a whole than a sampling of work. No preference as to formal or free verse. Slightly favors lyric and narrative poetry to language and concrete, but excellent examples of any style will grab their attention. Considers simultaneous submissions if notified of acceptance elsewhere. Submit up to 26 pages of poetry, paginated. Include table of contents and acknowledgments page. Include 2 cover sheets: 1 with ms title, poet's name, address, phone number, and e-mail; 1 without poet's identification. Include SASE for results; mss will not be returned. Send 10x12 envelope stamped with $3.50 for copy of winning chapbook. Guidelines available on website.

Deadline: November 30. Prize: Publication and 100 author copies of a perfectly-bound chapbook.

THE CONNECTICUT RIVER REVIEW POETRY CONTEST

P.O. Box 270554, W. Hartford CT 06127. **Website:** ct-poetry.net. Send up to 3 unpublished poems, any form, 80-line limit. Include 2 copies of each poem: 1 with complete contact informatoin and 1 with no contact information. Include a SASE. Deadline: September 30. Prize: 1st Place: $400; 2nd Place: $100; 3rd Place: $50.

CPR EDITOR'S PRIZE FIRST OR SECOND BOOK AWARD

P.O. Box 33384, San Diego CA 92163. **E-mail:** editor@ciderpressreview.com. **Website:** http://ciderpressreview.com/bookaward. Annual award from *Cider Press Review*. Submissions must be unpublished as a collection, but individual poems may have been previously published elsewhere. Submit book-length ms of 48-80 pages of original poetry. Submissions can be made online using the submission form on the website or by mail. If sending by mail, include 2 cover sheets—1 with title, author's name, and complete contact information; and 1 with title only, all bound with a spring clip. Check website for change of address coming in the future. Include SASE for results only if no email address included; notification via email and on the website; manuscripts cannot be returned. Online submissions must be in Word for PC or PDF format, and should not include title page with author's name. The editors strongly urge contestants to use online delivery if possible. Review the complete submission guidelines and learn more online at website. Deadline: submit between April 1-June 30. Prize: $1,000, publication, and 25 author's copies of a book length collection of poetry. Author receives a standard publishing contract. Initial print run is not less than 1,000 copies. CPR acquires first publication rights. Judged by *Cider Press Review* editors.

CRAB ORCHARD SERIES IN POETRY FIRST BOOK AWARD

First Book Award, Dept. of English, Mail Code 4503, Southern Illinois University Carbondale, 1000 Faner Drive, Carbondale IL 62901. (618)453-6833. **E-mail:** jtribble@siu.edu. **Website:** www.craborchardreview.siu.edu. **Contact:** Jon Tribble, series editor. Annual award that selects a first book of poems for publication from an open competition of manuscripts, in English, by a U.S. citizen or permanent resident who has neither published, nor committed to publish, a volume of poetry 48 pages or more in length in an edition of over 500 copies (individual poems may have been previously published; for the purposes of the Crab Orchard Series in Poetry, a ms which was in whole or in part submitted as a thesis or dissertation as a requirement for the completion of a degree is considered unpublished and is eligible). See website for complete formatting instructions. Guidelines available for SASE or on website. Accepts submissions only through Submittable, online. Mss are recommended to be a minimum of 50 pages to a recommended maximum of 75 pages of original poetry. Deadline: July 8. Submission period begins May 15. Prize: Offers $4,000 and a publication contract.

CRAB ORCHARD SERIES IN POETRY OPEN COMPETITION AWARDS

Department of English, Mail Code 4503, Faner Hall 2380, Southern Illinois University at Carbondale, Carbondale IL 62901. **E-mail:** jtribble@siu.edu. **Website:** www.craborchardreview.siu.edu. **Contact:** Jon Tribble, series editor. Annual competition to award unpublished, original collections of poems written in English by United States citizens and permanent residents (individual poems may have been previously published). Two volumes of poems will be selected from the open competition of mss. Considers simultaneous submissions, but series editor must be informed immediately upon acceptance. Mss should be typewritten or computer-generated (letter quality only; no dot matrix), single-spaced; clean photocopy is recommended as mss are not returned. See guidelines for complete formatting instructions. Guidelines available for SASE or on website. Deadline: December 5. Submission period begins October 1. Prize: Both winners will be awarded a $2500 prize and $1500 as an honorarium for a reading at Southern Illinois University Carbondale. Both readings will follow the publication of the poets' collections by Southern Illinois University Press.

THE CRAZYHORSE PRIZE IN POETRY

Crazyhorse, Department of English, College of Charleston, 66 George St., Charleston SC 29424. (843)953-4470. **E-mail:** crazyhorse@cofc.edu. **Website:** http://crazyhorse.cofc.edu. **Contact:** Prize Director. The *Crazyhorse* Prize in Poetry is for a single poem. All entries will be considered for publication. Submissions must be unpublished. Submit online or by mail up to 3 original poems (no more than 10 pages). Include cover page (placed on top of ms) with poet's name, address, e-mail, and telephone number; no identifying information on mss (blind judging). Accepts multiple submissions with separate fee for each. Include SASP for notification of receipt of ms and SASE for results only; mss will not be returned. Guidelines available for SASE or on website. Deadline: January 31. Submissions period begins January 1. Prize: $2,000 and publication in *Crazyhorse*. Judged by genre judges for first round, guest judge for second round. Judges change on a yearly basis.

DANCING POETRY CONTEST

AEI Contest Chair, Judy Cheung, 704 Brigham Ave., Santa Rosa CA 95404-5245. (707)528-0912. **E-mail:** jhcheung@comcast.net. **Website:** www.dancingpoetry.com. **Contact:** Judy Cheung, contest chair. Line Limit: 40 lines maximum each poem. No limit on number of entries. Send 2 typed, clear copies of each entry. Show name, address, telephone number, e-mail and how you heard about the contest on one copy only. Poems must be in English or include English translation Deadline: May 15. Prize: Three Grand Prizes will receive $100 each plus the poems will be danced and videotaped at this year's Dancing Poetry Festival; six First Prizes will receive $50 each; twelve Second Prizes will receive $25 each; and thirty Third Prizes will receive $10 each.

TIPS "We always look for something new and different including new twists to old themes, different looks at common situations, inovative concepts for dynamic, thought provoking entertainment."

DREAM HORSE PRESS NATIONAL POETRY CHAPBOOK PRIZE

P.O. Box 2080, Aptos CA 95001-2080. **E-mail:** dreamhorsepress@yahoo.com. **Website:** www.dreamhorsepress.com. **Contact:** J.P. Dancing Bear, Editor/Publisher. All entries will be considered for publication. Submissions may be previously published in magazines/journals but not in books or chapbooks. Considers simultaneous submissions with notification. Submit 20-28 pages of poetry in a readable font with table of contents, acknowledgments, bio, e-mail address for results, and entry fee. Poet's name should not appear anywhere on the manuscript. Accepts multiple submissions (with separate fee for each entry). Manuscripts will be recycled after judging. Guidelines available on website. Make checks/money orders made payable to Dream Horse Press. Recent previous winners include M.R.B. Chelko, Cynthia Arrieu-King, and Ariana-Sophia Kartsonis. Deadline: June 30. Prize: $500, publication, and 25 copies of a handsomely printed chapbook. Judged by C.J. Sage.

T.S. ELIOT PRIZE FOR POETRY

Truman State University Press, 100 E. Normal Ave., Kirksville MO 63501. (660)785-7336. **Fax:** (660)785-4480. **E-mail:** tsup@truman.edu. **Website:** tsup.truman.edu. The ms may include individual poems previously published in journals or anthologies, but may not include a significant number of poems from a published chapbook or self-published book. Submit 60-100 pages. Include 2 title pages: 1 with poet's name, address, e-mail address, phone number, and ms title; the other with ms title only. Include SASE for acknowledgment of ms receipt only; mss will not be returned. Guidelines available for SASE or on website. Deadline: October 31. Prize: $2,000 and publication. Judge announced after close of competition.

FAR HORIZONS AWARD FOR POETRY

The Malahat Review, University of Victoria, P.O. Box 1700, Stn CSC, Victoria BC V8W 2Y2 Canada. (250)721-8524. **Fax:** (250)472-5051. **E-mail:** malahat@uvic.ca. **Website:** www.malahatreview.ca. **Contact:** John Barton, editor. The biennial Far Horizons Award for Poetry offers $1,000 CAD and publication in *The Malahat Review*. Winner and finalists contacted by e-mail. Winner published in fall in *The Malahat Review* and announced on website, Facebook page, and in quarterly e-newsletter, *Malahat lite*. Submissions must be unpublished. No simultaneous submissions. Submit up to 3 poems per entry, each poem not to exceed 60 lines; no restrictions on subject matter or aesthetic approach. Include separate page with poet's name, address, e-mail, and poem title(s); no identifying information on mss pages. E-mail submissions are acceptable: please send to horizons@uvic.ca. Do not include SASE for results; mss will not be returned. Full guidelines available on website. Open to "emerging poets from Canada, the United States, and elsewhere" who have not yet published a full-length book (48 pages or more). Deadline: May 1 of even-numbered years. Prize: $1,000.

JANICE FARRELL POETRY PRIZE CATEGORY

Soul-Making Keats Literary Competition, The Webhallow House, 1544 Sweetwood Dr., Broadmoor Village CA 94015. **E-mail:** SoulKeats@mail.com. **Website:** www.soulmakingcontest.us. **Contact:** Eileen Malone. Previously published okay. Poetry may be double- or single-spaced. One-page poems only, and only 1 poem/page. All poems must be titled. Three poems/entry. Identify with 3x5 card only. Open to all writers. Deadline: November 30. Prize: Cash prizes. Judged by a local San Francisco successfully published poet.

THE JEAN FELDMAN POETRY PRIZE

Washington Writers' Publishing House, P.O. Box 15271, Washington DC 20003. **E-mail:** wwphpress@gmail.com. **Website:** www.washingtonwriters.org. Poets living within 75 miles of the Capitol are invited to submit a ms of either a novel or a collection of short stories. Ms should be 50-70 pages, single spaced. Author's name should not appear on the manuscript. The title page of each copy should contain the title only. Provide name, address, telephone number, e-mail address, and title on a separate cover sheet accompanying the submission. A separate page for acknowledgments may be included for stories or excerpts previously published in journals and anthologies. E-mail electronic copies to wwphpress@gmail.com or mail paper copies and/or reading fee (check to WWPH) with SASE to: The Jean Feldman Poetry Prize, WWPH, c/o Holly Karapetkova, 4640 23rd Rd. N., Arlington, VA 22207 Deadline: November 1. Submission period begins July 1. Prize: $1,000 and 50 copies of the book.

FIELD POETRY PRIZE

Oberlin College Press/FIELD, 50 N. Professor St., Oberlin OH 44074-1095. (440)775-8408. **Fax:** (440)775-8124. **E-mail:** oc.press@oberlin.edu. **Website:** www.oberlin.edu/ocpress/prize.htm. **Contact:** Marco Wilkinson, managing editor. Offered annually for an unpublished book-length collection of poetry (mss of 50-80 pages). Contest seeks to encourage the finest in contemporary poetry writing. Open to any writer. Deadline: Submit in May only. Prize: $1,000 and a standard royalty contract.

FIRST BOOK AWARD FOR POETRY

Zone 3, Austin Peay State University, Austin Peay State University, PO Box 4565, Clarksville TN 37044. (931)221-7031. **Fax:** (931)221-7149. **E-mail:** spofforda@aspu.edu; wallacess@apsu.edu. **Website:** www.apsu.edu/zone3/. **Contact:** Andrea Spofford, poetry editor; Susan Wallace, managing editor. Annual poetry award for anyone who has not published a full-length collection of poems (48 pages or more). Accepts entries via postal mail or online. Separate instructions for both, see website for guidelines and details. Deadline: April 1. Prize: $1,000 and publication.

FISH POETRY PRIZE

Durrus, Bantry Co. Cork Ireland. **E-mail:** info@fishpublishing.com. **Website:** www.fishpublishing.com. For poems up to 300 words. Age Range: Adult. The best 10 will be published in the Fish Anthology, launched in July at the West Cork Literary Festival. Entries must not have been published before. Enter online or by post. See website for full details of competitions, and information on the Fish Editorial and Critique Services, and the Fish Online Writing Courses. Do not put your name or address or any other details on the poem, use a separate sheet. Receipt of entry will be acknowleged by e-mail. Poems will not be returned. Word count: 200 max for each poem. You may enter as many as you wish, provided there is an entry fee for each one. Full details and rules are online. Entry is deemed to be acceptance of these rules. Publishing rights of the 10 winning poems are held by Fish Publishing for one year after the publication of the Anthology. The aim of the competition is to discover and publish new writers. Deadline: March 30. Prize: $1,200. Results announced April 30.

FIVE POINTS JAMES DICKEY PRIZE FOR POETRY

Five Points, Georgia State University, P.O. Box 3999, Atlanta GA 30302-3999. (404)413-5812. **Website:** www.fivepoints.gsu.edu. Offered annually for unpublished poetry. Enter on website or send 3 unpublished poems, no longer than 50 lines each, name and address on each poem, SASE for receipt and notification of winner. Winner announced in Spring issue. Deadline: December 1. Prize: $1,000, plus publication.

FOOD VERSE CONTEST

Literal Latte, 200 East 10th St., Suite 240, New York NY 10003. (212)260-5532. **E-mail:** litlatte@aol.com. **Website:** www.literal-latte.com. **Contact:** Jenine Gordon Bockman, editor. Open to any writer. Poems should have food as an ingredient. Submissions required to be unpublished. Guidelines online at website. Literal Latté acquires first rights. Annual contest to give support and exposure to great writing. Deadline: March 15. Prize: $500. Judged by the editors.

THE LEVIS POETRY PRIZE

Four Way Books, Box 535, Village Station, New York NY 10014. (212)334-5430. **Fax:** (212)334-5435. **E-mail:** editors@fourwaybooks.com. **Website:** www.fourwaybooks.com. **Contact:** Martha Rhodes, director. The Levis Poetry Prize, offered biennially in odd-numbered years, offers publication by Four Way Books (see separate listing in Book Publishers), honorarium, and a reading at one or more participating series. Open to any poet writing in English. Entry form and guidelines available on website. Deadline: March 31 (postmark or online submission). Winner announced by e-mail and on website. Prize: Publication and $1,000. Copies of winning books available through Four Way Books online and at bookstores (to the trade through University Press of New England).

GERTRUDE PRESS POETRY CHAPBOOK CONTEST

P.O. Box 28281, Portland OR 97228. **E-mail:** editor@gertrudepress.org; poetry@gertrudepress.org. **Website:** www.gertrudepress.org. Annual chapbook contest for 25-30 pages of poetry. Individual poems may have been previously published; unpublished poems are welcome. Poetry may be of any subject matter, and writers from all backgrounds are encouraged to submit. Include list of acknowledgments and cover letter indicating how poet learned of the contest. Include 1 title page with identifying information and 1 without. Guidelines available in *Gertrude* (see separate listing in Magazines/Journals), for SASE, by e-mail, or on website. Deadline: May 15. Submission period begins September 15. Prize: $250, publication, 50 complimentary copies of the chapbook, and 2 e-book files.

ALLEN GINSBERG POETRY AWARDS

The Poetry Center at Passaic County Community College, One College Blvd., Paterson NJ 07505. (973)684-6555. **Fax:** (973)523-6085. **E-mail:** mgillan@pccc.edu. **Website:** www.pccc.edu/poetry. **Contact:** Maria Mazziotti Gillan, executive director. All winning poems, honorable mentions, and editor's choice poems will be published in *The Paterson Literary Review*. Winners will be asked to participate in a reading that will be held in the Paterson Historic District. Submissions must be unpublished. Submit up to 5 poems (no poem more than 2 pages long). Send 4 copies of each poem entered. Include cover sheet with poet's name, address, phone number, e-mail address and poem titles. Poet's name should not appear on poems. Include SASE for results only; poems will not be returned. Guidelines available for SASE or on website. Deadline: April 1 (postmark). Prize: 1st Prize: $1,000; 2nd Prize: $200; 3rd Prize: $100.

GIVAL PRESS POETRY AWARD

Gival Press, LLC, P.O. Box 3812, Arlington VA 22203. (703)351-0079. **E-mail:** givalpress@yahoo.com. **Website:** www.givalpress.com. **Contact:** Robert L. Giron, editor. Offered annually for a previously unpublished poetry collection as a complete ms, which may include previously published poems; previously published poems must be acknowledged, and poet must hold rights. Guidelines for SASE, by e-mail, or online. Open to any writer, as long as the work is original, not a translation, and is written in English. The copyright remains in the author's name; certain rights fall to the publisher per the contract. Must be at least 45 typed pages of poetry, on one side only. Entrants are asked to submit their poems without any kind of identification (with the exception of the titles) and with a separate cover page with the following information: Name, address (street, city, state, and zip code), telephone number, e-mail address (if available), short bio, and a list of the poems by title. Checks drawn on American banks should be made out to Gival Press, LLC. The competition seeks to award well-written, origional poetry in English on any topic, in any style. Deadline: December 15 (postmarked). Prize: $1,000, publication, and 20 copies of the publication. The editor narrows entries to the top 10; previous winner selects top 5 and chooses the winner—all done anonymously.

PATRICIA GOEDICKE PRIZE IN POETRY

CutBank Literary Magazine, *CutBank*, University of Montana, English Dept., LA 133, Missoula MT 59812. **E-mail:** editor.cutbank@gmail.com. **Website:** www.cutbankonline.org. **Contact:** Allison Linville, editor-in-chief. The Patricia Goedicke Prize in Poetry seeks to highlight work that showcases an authentic voice, a boldness of form, and a rejection of functional fixedness. Accepts online submissions only. Submit up to 5 poems. Guidelines available online. Deadline: January 15. Submissions period begins November 1. Prize: $500 and featured in the magazine. Judged by a guest judge each year.

GOLDEN ROSE AWARD

New England Poetry Club, 654 Green St., No. 2, Cambridge MA 02139. **Website:** www.nepoetryclub.org. **Contact:** NEPC contest coordinator. Given annually to the poet, who by their poetry and inspiration to and encouragement of other writers, has made a significant mark on American poetry. Traditionally given to a poet with some ties to New England so that a public reading may take place. Contest open to members and nonmembers. Poems should be typed and submitted in duplicate with author's name, address, phone, and e-mail address of writer on only 1 copy. (Judges receive copies without names.) Copy only. Label poems with contest name. Entries should be sent by regular mail only. Special delivery or signature required mail will be returned by the post office. Entries should be original, unpublished poems in English. No poem should be entered in more than 1 contest, nor have won a previous contest. No entries will be returned. NEPC will not engage in correspondence regarding poems or contest decisions. Deadline: May 31. Judged by well-known poets and sometimes winners of previous NEPC contests.

THE GREEN ROSE PRIZE IN POETRY

New Issues Poetry & Prose, Deptartment of English, Western Michigan University, 1903 W. Michigan Ave., Kalamazoo MI 49008-5331. (269)387-8185. **Fax:** (269)387-2562. **Website:** www.wmich.edu/newissues. Offered annually for unpublished poetry. The university will publish a book of poems by a poet writing in English who has published 1 or more full-length collections of poetry. *New Issues* may publish as many as 3 additional mss from this competition. Guidelines for SASE or online. *New Issues Poetry & Prose* obtains rights for first publication. Book is copyrighted in the author's name. Considers simultaneous submissions, but *New Issues* must be notified of acceptance elsewhere. Submit a ms of at least 48 pages, typed; single-spaced preferred. Clean photocopies acceptable. Do not bind; use manila folder or metal clasp. Include cover page with poet's name, address, phone number, and title of the ms. Also include brief bio, table of contents, and acknowledgments page. Submissions are also welcome through the online submission manager www.newissuespoetryprose.submittable.com. For hardcopy manuscripts only, you may include SASP for notification of receipt of ms and SASE for results only; mss will be recycled. Guidelines available for SASE, by fax, e-mail, or on website. Winner is announced in January or February on website. The winning manuscript will be published in spring of following year. 2014 winner was Kathleen Halme (*My Multiverse*). Deadline: Submit May 1-September 30. Winner is announced in January or February on website. Prize: $2,000 and publication of a book of poems.

THE GRIFFIN POETRY PRIZE

The Griffin Trust for Excellence in Poetry, 363 Parkridge Crescent, Oakville ON L6M 1A8 Canada. (905)618-0420. **E-mail:** info@griffinpoetryprize.com. **Website:** www.griffinpoetryprize.com. **Contact:** Ruth Smith. The Griffin Poetry Prize is one of the world's most generous poetry awards. The awards go to one Canadian and one international poet for a first collection written in, or translated into, English. Submissions must come from publishers. A book of poetry must be a first-edition collection. Books should have been published in the previous calendar year. Deadline: December 31. Prize: Two $65,000 (CAD) prizes. An additional $10,000 (CAD) goes to each shortlisted poet for their participation in the Shortlist Readings.

GREG GRUMMER POETRY AWARD

Phoebe, MSN 2C5, George Mason University, 4400 University Dr., Fairfax VA 22030. **E-mail:** phoebeliterature@gmail.com. **Website:** www.phoebejournal.com. **Contact:** Elizabeth Deanna Morris Lakes, poetry editor. Offered annually for unpublished work. Submit up to 4 poems, no more than 10 pages total. Guidelines online. Requests first serial rights, if work is to be published. The purpose of the award is to recognize new and exciting poetry. Deadline: February 15. Prize: $800 and publication in the *Phoebe*.

THE BESS HOKIN PRIZE

Poetry, 61 W. Superior St., Chicago IL 60654. (312)787-7070. **Fax:** (312)787-6650. **E-mail:** editors@poetrymagazine.org. **Website:** www.poetrymagazine.org. Offered annually for poems published in *Poetry* during the preceding year (October-September). Upon acceptance, *Poetry* licenses exclusive worldwide first serial rights, including electronic rights, for publication, as well as non-exclusive rights to reprint, reuse, and archive the work, in any format, in perpetuity. Copyright reverts to author upon first publication. "Established in 1947 through the generosity of our late friend and guarantor, Mrs. David Hokin, and is given annually in her memory." Prize: $1,000.

FIRMAN HOUGHTON PRIZE

New England Poetry Club, 376 School St., Watertown MA 02472. **E-mail:** contests@nepoetryclug.org. **Website:** www.nepoetryclub.org. **Contact:** Audrey Kalajin.

For a lyric poem in honor of the former president of NEPC. Contest guidelines available on website. Deadline: May 31. Prize: $250. Judged by well-known poets and sometimes winners of previous NEPC contests.

TOM HOWARD/MARGARET REID POETRY CONTEST

Sponsored by Winning Writers, Winning Writers, 351 Pleasant St., PMB 222, Northampton MA 01060-3961. **E-mail:** adam@winningwriters.com. **Website:** www.winningwriters.com. **Contact:** Adam Cohen. Offers annual awards of Tom Howard Prize, for a poem in any style or genre, and Margaret Reid Prize, for a poem that rhymes or has a traditional style. See website for guidelines and to submit your poem. Nonexclusive right to publish submissions online, in e-mail newsletters, in e-books, and in press releases. All entries that win cash prizes will be published on the Winning Writers website. Submissions maybe published or unpublished, may have won prizes elsewhere, and may be entered in other contests. Length limit: 250 lines per poem. Deadline: September 30. Submission period begins April 15. Prize: Each prize is $1,500, with 10 Honorable Mentions of $100 each (any style).

⊘ ILLINOIS STATE POETRY SOCIETY ANNUAL CONTEST

Illinois State Poetry Society, 543 E. Squirrel Trail Dr., Tucson AZ 85704. **Website:** www.illinoispoets.org. **Contact:** Alan Harris. Annual contest to encourage the crafting of excellent poetry. Guidelines and entry forms available for SASE. Deadline: September 30. Prize: Cash prizes of $50, $30, and $10. Three Honorable Mentions. Poet retains all rights. Judged by out-of-state professionals.

INDIANA REVIEW POETRY PRIZE

Indiana Review, Poetry Prize, Indiana Review, Ballantine Hall 465, 1020 E. Kirkwood Ave., Bloomington IN 47405-7103. (812)855-3439. **Fax:** (812)855-9535. **E-mail:** inreview@indiana.edu. **Website:** www.indianareview.org. **Contact:** Michael Mlekoday, Poetry Editor. Offered annually for unpublished work. Open to any writer. Guidelines available on website. All entries are considered for publication. Send no more than 3 poems per entry, 8 pages maximum. Each fee entitles entrant to a 1-year subscription. Does not accept postal submissions. Deadline: March 15. Submission period begins February 1. Prize: $1,000 and publication. Judged by Edward C. Corral in 2015. Different judge every year.

IOWA POETRY PRIZE

University of Iowa Press, 119 West Park Rd., 100 Kuhl House, Iowa City IA 52242. (319)335-2000. **Fax:** (319)335-2055. **E-mail:** uipress@uiowa.edu. **Website:** www.uiowapress.org. Offered annually to encourage poets and their work. Submissions must be postmarked during the month of April; put name on title page only. This page will be removed before ms is judged. Open to writers of English (US citizens or not). Mss will not be returned. Previous winners are not eligible. Mss should be 50-150 pages in length. Poems included in the collection may have appeared in journals or anthologies; poems from a poet's previous collections may be included only in manuscripts of new and selected poems. Deadline: April 30. Prize: Publication under standard royalty agreement.

ALICE JAMES AWARD

Alice James Books, University of Maine at Farmington, 114 Prescott St., Farmington ME 04938. (207)778-7071. **Fax:** (207)778-7766. **E-mail:** ajb@alicejamesbooks.org; info@alice jamesbooks.org. **Website:** www.alicejamesbooks.org. **Contact:** Alyssa Neptune, managing editor. Offered annually for unpublished, full-length poetry collections. Emerging and established poets are welcome. Submit 48-80 pages of poetry. Guidelines for submissions available online. Deadline: November 1. Prize: $2,000, publication, and distribution through Consortium.

RANDALL JARRELL POETRY COMPETITION

North Carolina Writers' Network, Terry L. Kennedy, MFA Writing Program, 3302 MHRA Building, UNC Greensboro, Greensboro NC 27402-6170. **E-mail:** tlkenned@uncg.edu. **Website:** www.ncwriters.org. **Contact:** Terry L. Kennedy, associate director. Offered annually for unpublished work to honor Randall Jarrell and his life at UNC Greensboro, by recognizing the best poetry submitted. The competition is open to any writer who is a legal resident of North Carolina or a member of the North Carolina Writers' Network. Submissions should be one poem only (40-line limit). Poem must be typed (single-spaced) and stapled in the left-hand corner. Author's name should not appear on the poem. Instead, include a separate cover sheet with author's name, address, e-mail address, phone number, and poem title. Poem will not be returned. Include a self-addressed stamped envelope for a list of winner and finalists. The winner and finalists will be announced in May. Deadline: March 1. Prize: $200 and publication at *storySouth* (www.storysouth.com).

JUNIPER PRIZE FOR POETRY

University of Massachusetts Press, East Experiment Station, 671 North Pleasant St., Amherst MA 01003. (413)545-2217. **Fax:** (413)545-1226. **E-mail:** info@umpress.umass.edu; kfisk@umpress.umass.edu; poetry@umpress.umass.edu. **Website:** www.umass.edu/umpress. **Contact:** Karen Fisk, competition coordinator. The University of Massachusetts Press offers the annual Juniper Prize for Poetry, awarded in alternate years for the first and subsequent books. Considers simultaneous submissions. Mss by more than 1 author, entries of more than 1 mss simultaneously or within the same year, and translations are not eligible. Submit paginated ms of 50-70 pages of poetry, with paginated contents page, credits page, and information on previously published books. Include 2 cover sheets: 1 with contract information, 1 without. Mss will not be returned. Guidelilnes online. Deadline: September 30. Submissions period begins August 1. Winners announced online in April on the press website. Prize: Publication and $1,500 in addition to royalties.

BARBARA MANDIGO KELLY PEACE POETRY AWARDS

Nuclear Age Peace Foundation, PMB 121, 1187 Coast Village Rd., Suite 1, Santa Barbara CA 93108-2794. (805)965-3443. **Fax:** (805)568-0466. **E-mail:** wagingpeace@napf.org; cwarner@napf.org. **Website:** www.wagingpeace.org; www.peacecontests.org. **Contact:** Carol Warner, poetry award coordinator. The Barbara Mandigo Kelly Peace Poetry Contest was created to encourage poets to explore and illuminate positive visions of peace and the human spirit. The annual contest honors the late Barbara Kelly, a Santa Barbara poet and longtime supporter of peace issues. Awards are given in 3 categories: adult (over 18 years), youth between 12 and 18 years, and youth under 12. All submitted poems should be unpublished. Deadline: July 1 (postmarked). Prize: Adult: $1,000; Youth (13-18): $200; Youth (12 and under): $200. Honorable Mentions may also be awarded. Judged by a committee of poets selected by the Nuclear Age Peace Foundation. The foundation reserves the right to publish and distribute the award-winning poems, including honorable mentions.

THE LEAGUE OF MINNESOTA POETS CONTEST

2029 103rd Ave. NW, Coon Rapids MN 55433. **E-mail:** pwilliamstein@yahoo.com; schambersmediator@yahoo.com. **Website:** www.mnpoets.com. **Contact:** Peter Stein; Sue Chambers. Annual contest offers 22 different categories, with 3 prizes in each category. See guidelines for poem lengths, forms, and subjects. Guidelines available for #10 SASE, by e-mail, or on website. Additional information regarding LOMP membership available on website. Must be original work of the contestant. Entrant must not have won a *money* award in any contest. Deadline: July 31. Submissions period begins May 1. Prize: See specific categories. Prize amounts vary from $10 up to $125, depending on category and place. Judged by nationally known, non-Minnesota judges. Winners will be announced at the October LOMP Conference and by mail.

LEVIS READING PRIZE

Virginia Commonwealth University, Department of English, Levis Reading Prize, VCU Department of English, 900 Park Avenue, Hibbs Hall, Room 306, P.O. Box 842005, Richmond VA 23284-2005. (804)828-1329. **Fax:** (804)828-8684. **E-mail:** detischc@mymail.vcu.edu. **Website:** www.english.vcu.edu/mfa/levis. **Contact:** Christian Detisch, Levis Fellow. Offered annually for books of poetry published in the previous year to encourage poets early in their careers. The entry must be the writer's first or second published book of poetry. Previously published books in other genres, or previously published chapbooks or self-published material, do not count as books for this purpose. Entries may be submitted by either author or publisher, and must include three copies of the book (48 pages or more), a cover letter, and a brief biography of the author including previous publications. (Entries from vanity presses are not eligible.) The book must have been published in the previous calendar year. Entrants wishing acknowledgment of receipt must include a self-addressed stamped postcard. Deadline: February 1. Prize: $2,000 and an expense-paid trip to Richmond to present a public reading.

THE RUTH LILLY POETRY PRIZE

Poetry, 61 W. Superior St., Chicago IL 60654. (312)787-7070. **Fax:** (312)787-6650. **E-mail:** editors@poetrymagazine.org. **Website:** www.poetrymagazine.org. Awarded annually, the $100,000 Ruth Lilly Poetry

Prize honors a living U.S. poet whose lifetime accomplishments warrant extraordinary recognition. Established in 1986 by Ruth Lilly, the Prize is one of the most prestigious awards given to American poets and is one of the largest literary honors for work in the English language. Deadline: No submissions or nominations considered. Prize: $100,000.

LITERAL LATTÉ POETRY AWARD

Literal Latté, 200 E. 10th St., Suite 240, New York NY 10003. (212)260-5532. **E-mail:** LitLatte@aol.com. **Website:** www.literal-latte.com. **Contact:** Jenine Gordon Bockman, editor. Offered annually to any writer for unpublished poetry (maximum 2,000 words per poem). All styles welcome. Winners published in *Literal Latté*. Acquires first rights. Deadline: Postmark by July 15. Prize: 1st Place: $1,000; 2nd Place: $300; 3rd Place: $200. Judged by the editors.

LUMINA POETRY CONTEST

Sarah Lawrence College, 1 Mead Way, Bronxville NY 10708. **E-mail:** lumina@gm.slc.edu. **Website:** www.luminajournal.com/contests. *Lumina* is the literary magazine of the graduate writing program of Sarah Lawrence College. This contest provides a place for the publication of some of the best original poetry written in English. Include a 100-word bio at the bottom of cover letter. Submit up to 3 poems, 60 lines maximum per poem. Submit work in a single document. Do not include name or personal information in the body of submission. Previously published works will not be considered. Submit online. Deadline: October 15. Prize: 1st Place: $500 and publication; 2nd Place: $250 and publication: 3rd Place: $100 and publication online. Judged by Patricia Lockwood in 2014.

THE MACGUFFIN NATIONAL POET HUNT CONTEST

The MacGuffin, The MacGuffin, Schoolcraft College, 18600 Haggerty Rd., Livonia MI 48152. (734)462-4400, ext. 5327. **Fax:** (734)462-4679. **E-mail:** macguffin@schoolcraft.edu. **Website:** www.schoolcraft.edu/a-z-index/the-macguffin. **Contact:** Gordon Krupsky, managing editor. *The MacGuffin* is a national literary magazine from Schoolcraft College in Livonia, Michigan. An entry consists of three poems. Poems must not be previously published, and must be the original work of the contestant. See website for additional details. The mission of *The MacGuffin* is to encourage, support, and enhance the literary arts in the Schoolcraft College community, the region, the state, and the nation. Deadline: June 3. Submissions period begins April 1. Prize: $500. Judged by Carl Dennis.

NAOMI LONG MADGETT POETRY AWARD

Lotus Press, Inc., 8300 East Jefferson Ave., #504, Detroit MI 48214. (313)736-5338. **E-mail:** broadsidelotus@gmail.com. **Website:** www.lotuspress.org. **Contact:** Gloria House. Offered annually to recognize an unpublished book-length poetry ms by an African American. Guidelines available online. Poems in the ms should total *approximately* 60-90 pages, exclusive of a table of contents or other optional introductory material. Poems that have been published individually in periodicals or anthologies are acceptable. Will not consider an entire collection that has been previously published. Deadline: March 1. Submission period begins January 2. Prize: $500 and publication by Lotus Press.

MAIN STREET RAG'S ANNUAL POETRY BOOK AWARD

P.O. Box 690100, Charlotte NC 28227. (704)573-2516. **E-mail:** editor@mainstreetrag.com. **Website:** www.MainStreetRag.com. **Contact:** M. Scott Douglass, editor/publisher. Submit 48-84 pages of poetry, no more than 1 poem/page (individual poems may be longer than 1 page). Guidelines available on website. Deadline: January 31. Prize: 1st Place: $1,200 and 50 copies of book; runners-up are also be offered publication.

THE MALAHAT REVIEW LONG POEM PRIZE

The Malahat Review, Box 1700 STN CSC, Victoria BC V8W 2Y2 Canada. **E-mail:** malahat@uvic.ca. **Website:** www.malahatreview.ca. **Contact:** John Barton, editor. Long Poem Prize offered in alternate years with the Novella Contest. Open to any writer. Offers 2 awards of $1,000 CAD each for a long poem or cycle (10-20 printed pages). Includes publication in *The Malahat Review* and a 1-year subscription. Open to entries from Canadian, American, and overseas authors. Obtains first world rights. Publication rights after revert to the author. Submissions must be unpublished. No simultaneous submissions. Submit a single poem or cycle of poems, 10-20 published pages (a published page equals 32 lines or less, including breaks between stanzas); no restrictions on subject matter or aesthetic approach. Include separate page with poet's name, address, e-mail, and title; no identifying information on mss pages. Do not include SASE for results; mss will not be returned. Guidelines available on website. Deadline: February 1 (odd-numbered years). Prize: Two $1,000 prizes. Winners published in the summer issue of *The Malahat Review*, announced in summer on website, Facebook page, and in quarterly e-newsletter *Malahat lite*. Judged by 3 recognized poets. Preliminary readings by editorial board.

THE MORTON MARR POETRY PRIZE

Southwest Review, Southern Methodist University, P.O. Box 750374, Dallas TX 75275. (214)768-1037. **Fax:** (214)768-1408. **E-mail:** swr@mail.smu.edu. **Website:** www.smu.edu/southwestreview. **Contact:** Prize coordinator. Annual award for poem(s) by a writer who has not yet published a book of poetry. Submit no more than 6 poems in a "traditional" form (e.g., sonnet, sestine, villanelle, rhymed stanzas, blank verse, et al.). Submissions will not be returned. All entrants will receive a copy of the issue in which the winning poems appear. Deadline: September 30. Prize: $1,000 for 1st place; $500 for 2nd place; plus publication in the Southwest Review.

MARSH HAWK PRESS POETRY PRIZE

P.O. Box 206, East Rockaway NY 11518-0206. **E-mail:** marshhawkpress1@aol.com. **Website:** www.MarshHawkPress.org. **Contact:** prize director. The Marsh Hawk Press Poetry Prize offers $1,000, plus publication of a book-length ms. Additionally, The Robert Creeley Poetry Prize and The Rochelle Ratner Poetry Award go to the runners-up. Submissions must be unpublished as a collection, but individual poems may have been previously published elsewhere. Submit 48-70 pages of original poetry in any style in English, typed single-spaced, and paginated. (Longer mss will be considered if the press is queried before submission.) Contest mss may be submitted by electronic upload. See website for more information. If submitting via Post Office mail, the ms must be bound with a spring clip. Include 2 title pages: 1 with ms title, poet's name, and contact information only; 1 with ms title only (poet's name must not appear anywhere in the ms). Also include table of contents and acknowledgments page. Include SASE for results only; ms will not be returned. Guidelines available on website. Deadline: April 30.

KATHLEEN MCCLUNG SONNET PRIZE CATEGORY

Soul-Making Keats Literary Competition, The Webhallow House, 1544 Sweetwood Dr., Broadmoor Village CA 94015-2029. **E-mail:** soulkeats@mail.com. **Website:** www.soulmakingcontest.us. **Contact:** Eileen Malone. Call for Shakespearean and Petrarchan sonnets on the theme of the "beloved." Previously published material is accepted. Indicate category on cover page and on identifying 3x5 card. Open annually to any writer. Deadline: November 30. Prize: Prize:1st Place: $100; 2nd Place: $50; 3rd Place: $25.

VASSAR MILLER PRIZE IN POETRY

University of North Texas Press, 1155 Union Circle, #311336, Denton TX 76203. (940)565-2142. **Fax:** (940)565-4590. **Website:** http://untpress.unt.edu. **Contact:** John Poch. Annual prize awarded to a collection of poetry. No limitations to entrants. In years when the judge is announced, it is asked that students of the judge not enter to avoid a perceived conflict. All entries should contain identifying material only on the one cover sheet. Entries are read anonymously. Deadline: Mss may be submitted between 9 A.M. on September 1 and 5 P.M. on October 31, through online submissions manager only. Prize: $1,000 and publication by University of North Texas Press. Judged by a different eminent writer selected each year. Some prefer to remain anonymous until the end of the contest.

THE KATHRYN A. MORTON PRIZE IN POETRY

Sarabande Books, Inc., 2234 Dundee Rd., Suite 200, Louisville KY 40205. (502)458-4028. **E-mail:** info@sarabandebooks.org. **Website:** www.sarabandebooks.org. **Contact:** Sarah Gorham, editor-in-chief. The Kathryn A. Morton Prize in Poetry is awarded annually to a book-length ms (at least 48 pages). All finalists are considered for publication. Competition receives approximately 1,400 entries. Guidelines available online. Mss can be submitted online or via postal mail. Deadline: February 15. Submissions period begins January 1. Prize: $2,000, publication, and a standard royalty contract.

SHEILA MARGARET MOTTON PRIZE

New England Poetry Club, 2 Farrar St., Cambridge MA 02138. (617)744-6034. **E-mail:** info@nepoetryclub.org. **Website:** www.nepoetryclub.org. **Contact:** Audrey Kalajin. Awarded for a book of poems published in the last 2 years. Send 2 copies of book. Deadline: May 31. Prize: $500. Judged by well-known poets and sometimes winners of previous NEPC contests.

ERIKA MUMFORD PRIZE

New England Poetry Club, 376 School St., Watertown MA 02472. **E-mail:** contests@nepoetryclub.org. **Website:** www.nepoetryclub.org/contests.htm. **Contact:** Audrey Kalajin. Offered annually for a poem in any form about foreign culture or travel. Funded by Erika Mumford's family and friends. Contest open to members and nonmembers. Deadline: May 31. Prize: $250. Judged by well-known poets and sometimes winners of previous NEPC contests.

NATIONAL WRITERS ASSOCIATION POETRY CONTEST

The National Writers Association, 10940 S. Parker Rd. #508, Parker CO 80134. (303)841-0246. **E-mail:** natlwritersassn@hotmail.com. **Website:** www.nationalwriters.com. **Contact:** Sandy Whelchel, director. Annual contest to encourage the writing of poetry, an important form of individual expression but with a limited commercial market. Deadline: October 1. Prize: 1st Place: $100; 2nd Place: $50; 3rd Place: $25.

THE PABLO NERUDA PRIZE FOR POETRY

Nimrod International Journal, 800 S. Tucker Dr., Tulsa OK 74104. (918)631-3080. **Fax:** (918)631-3033. **E-mail:** nimrod@utulsa.edu. **Website:** www.utulsa.edu/nimrod. **Contact:** Eilis O'Neal. Annual award to discover new writers of vigor and talent. Open to US residents only. Submissions must be unpublished. Work must be in English or translated by original author. Submit 3-10 pages of poetry (1 long poem or several short poems). Poet's name must not appear on ms. Include cover sheet with poem title(s), poet's name, address, phone and fax numbers, and e-mail address (poet must have a US address by October of contest year to enter). Mark "Contest Entry" on submission envelope and cover sheet. Include SASE for results only; mss will not be returned. Guidelines available for #10 SASE or on website. Deadline: April 30. Prize: 1st Place: $2,000 and publication; 2nd Place: $1,000 and publication. Judged by the *Nimrod* editors (finalists). A recognized author selects the winners.

THE NEW ISSUES POETRY PRIZE

New Issues Poetry & Prose, New Issues Poetry & Prose, Department of English, Western Michigan University, 1903 W. Michigan Ave., Kalamazoo MI 49008-5331. (269)387-8185. **Fax:** (269)387-2562. **E-mail:** new-issues@wmich.edu. **Website:** www.wmich.edu/newissues. Offered annually for publication of a first book of poems by a poet writing in English who has not previously published a full-length collection of poems in an edition of 500 or more copies. *New Issues Poetry & Prose* obtains rights for first publication. Book is copyrighted in author's name. Guidelines for SASE or online. Additional mss will be considered from those submitted to the competition for publication. Considers simultaneous submissions, but *New Issues* must be notified of acceptance elsewhere. Submit ms of at least 48 pages, typed, single-spaced preferred. Clean photocopies acceptable. Do not bind; use manila folder or metal clasp. Include cover page with poet's name, address, phone number, and title of the ms. Also include brief bio and acknowledgments page. Submissions are also welcome through the online submission manager www.newissuespoetryprose.submittable.com. For hardcopy submissions only, you may include SASP for notification of receipt of ms and SASE for results only; no mss will be returned. Winning manuscript will be named in May and published in the next spring. Deadline: November 30. Prize: $2,000, plus publication of a book-length ms. A national judge selects the prize winner and recommends other manuscripts. The editors decide on the other books considering the judge's recommendation, but are not bound by it. 2015 judge: Major Jackson.

NEW LETTERS PRIZE FOR POETRY

New Letters Awards for Writers, UMKC, University House, 5101 Rockhill Rd., Kansas City MO 64110-2499. **E-mail:** newletters@umkc.edu. **Website:** www.newletters.org. The annual New Letters Poetry Prize awards $1,500 and publication in *New Letters* (see separate listing in Magazines/Journals) to the best group of 3-6 poems. All entries will be considered for publication in *New Letters*. Submissions must be unpublished. Considers simultaneous submissions with notification upon acceptance elsewhere. Accepts multiple entries with separate fee for each. Submit up to 6 poems (need not be related). Include 2 cover sheets: 1 with poet's name, address, e-mail, phone number, prize category (poetry), and poem title(s); the second with category and poem title(s) only. No identifying information on ms pages. Accepts electronic submissions. Include SASE for notification of receipt of ms and entry number, and SASE for results only (send only 1 envelope if submitting multiple entries); mss will not be returned. Guidelines available by SASE or on website. Current students and employees of the University of Missouri-Kansas City, and current volunteer members of the *New Letters* and BkMk Press staffs, are not eligible. Deadline: May 18 (postmarked). Prize: $1,500 and publication.

PANGAEA PRIZE

The Poet's Billow, 245 N. Collingwood, Syracuse NY 13206. **E-mail:** thepoetsbillow@gmail.com. **Website:** http://thepoetsbillow.org. **Contact:** Robert Evory. Annual award open to any writer to recognize the best series of poems, ranging between two and up to seven poems in a group. Finalists with strong work will also be published. Submissions must be previously unpublished. Please submit online. Deadline: May 1. Prize: $100. The winning poem will be published and displayed in The Poet's Billow Literary Art Gallery and nominated for a Pushcart Prize. If the poet qualifies, the poem will also be submitted to The Best New Poets anthology. Judged by the editors, and, occasionally, a guest judge.

THE PATERSON POETRY PRIZE

The Poetry Center at Passaic County Community College, One College Blvd., Paterson NJ 07505. (973)684-6555. **Fax:** (973)523-6085. **E-mail:** mgillan@pccc.edu. **Website:** www.pccc.edu/poetry. **Contact:** Maria Mazziotti Gillan, executive director. The Paterson Poetry Prize offers an annual award for the strongest book of poems (48 or more pages) published in the previous year. The winner will be asked to participate in an awards ceremony and to give a reading at The Poetry Center. Minimum press run: 500 copies. Publishers may submit more than 1 title for prize consideration; 3 copies of each book must be submitted. Include SASE for results; books will not be returned (all entries will be donated to The Poetry Center Library). Guidelines and application form (required) available for SASE or on website. Deadline: February 1. Prize: $1,000.

PAVEMENT SAW PRESS CHAPBOOK AWARD

321 Empire St., Montpelier OH 43543-1301. **E-mail:** info@pavementsaw.org. **E-mail:** editor@pavementsaw.org. **Website:** www.pavementsaw.org. **Contact:** David Baratier, editor. Pavement Saw Press has been publishing steadily since the fall of 1993. Each year since 1999, they have published at least 4 full-length paperback poetry collections, with some printed in library edition hard covers, 1 chapbook, and a yearly literary journal anthology. Theyspecialize in finding authors who have been widely published in literary journals but have not published a chapbook or full-length book. Submit up to 32 pages of poetry. Include signed cover letter with poet's name, address, phone number, e-mail, publication credits, a brief biography, and ms title. Also include 2 cover sheets: 1 with poet's contact information and ms title, 1 with the ms title only. Do not put name on mss pages except for first title page. No mss will be returned. Deadline: December 31 (postmark). Prize: Chapbook Award offers $500, publication, and 50 author copies.

JEAN PEDRICK PRIZE

New England Poetry Club, 2 Farrar St., Cambridge MA 02138. **E-mail:** contests@nepoetryclub.org. **Website:** www.nepoetryclub.org. **Contact:** Audrey Kalajin. Prize for a chapbook of poems published in the last two years. Send 2 copies of the chapbook. Deadline: May 31. Prize: $100. Judged by well-known poets and sometimes winners of previous NEPC contests.

PEN/JOYCE OSTERWEIL AWARD FOR POETRY

PEN American Center, 588 Broadway, Suite 303, New York NY 10012. (212)334-1660, ext. 126. **E-mail:** awards@pen.org. **Website:** www.pen.org. **Contact:** Arielle Anema. *Candidates may only be nominated by members of PEN.* This award recognizes the high literary character of the published work to date of a new and emerging American poet of any age, and the promise of further literary achievement. Nominated writer may not have published more than 1 book of poetry. Offered in odd-numbered years and alternates with the PEN/Voelcker Award for Poetry. Send letters of nomination to PEN American Center. See website for details. Deadline: November 15. Prize: $5,000. Judged by a panel of 3 judges selected by the PEN Awards Committee.

⊘ POETS & PATRONS ANNUAL CHICAGOLAND POETRY CONTEST

Sponsored by Poets & Patrons of Chicago, 416 Gierz St., Downers Grove IL 60515. **E-mail:** eatonb1016@aol.com. **Website:** www.poetsandpatrons.net. **Contact:** Barbara Eaton, director. Annual contest for unpublished poetry. Guidelines available for self-addressed, stamped envelope. The purpose of the contest is to encourage the crafting of poetry. Deadline: September 1. Prize: 1st Place: $45; 2nd Place: $20; 3rd Place: $10 cash. Poet retains rights. Judged by out-of-state professionals.

FELIX POLLAK PRIZE IN POETRY

University of Wisconsin Press, 1930 Monroe St., 3rd Floor, Madison WI 53711. (608)263-1110. **Fax:** (608)263-1120. **E-mail:** uwiscpress@wisc.edu. **Website:** uwpress.wisc.edu. The Felix Pollak Prize in Poetry is awarded annually to the best book-length ms of original poetry submitted in an open competition. The award is administered by the University of Wisconsin–Madison English department, and the winner is chosen by a nationally recognized poet. The resulting book is published by the University of Wisconsin Press. Submissions must be unpublished as a collection, but individual poems may have been published elsewhere (publication must be acknowledged). Considers simultaneous submissions if notified of selection elsewhere. Submit 50-80 unbound ms pages, typed single-spaced (with double spaces between stanzas). Clean photocopies are acceptable. Include 1 title page with poet's name, address, and telephone number; 1 title page with title only. No translations. Complete guidelines available online. Deadline: September 15. Prize: $1,000 cash prize, plus publication.

A. POULIN, JR. POETRY PRIZE

BOA Editions, Ltd., P.O. Box 30971, Rochester NY 14603. **E-mail:** fisher@boaeditions.org. **Website:** www.boaeditions.org. The A. Poulin, Jr. Poetry Prize is awarded to honor a poet's first book, while also honoring the late founder of BOA Editions, Ltd., a not-for-profit publishing house of poetry, poetry in translation, and short fiction. Published books in other genres do not disqualify contestants from entering this contest. Send by first class or priority mail (recommended). Entrants must be a citizen or legal resident of the US. Poets who are at least 18 years of age, and who have yet to publish a full-length book collection of poetry, are eligible. Translations are not eligible. Individual poems may have been previously published in magazines, journals, anthologies, chapbooks of 32 pages or less, or self-published books of 46 pages or less, but must be submitted in ms form. Submit 48-100 pages of poetry, paginated consecutively, typed or computer-generated in 11 point font. Bind with spring clip (no paperclips). Include cover/title page with poet's name, address, telephone number, and e-mail address. Also include the table of contents, list of acknowledgments, and entry form (available for download on website). Multiple entries accepted with separate entry fee for each. No e-mail submissions. Deadline: Submit between August 1-Nov. 30. Prize: Awards $1,500 honorarium and book publication in the A. Poulin, Jr. New Poets of America Series.

PRESS 53 AWARD FOR POETRY

Press 53, 560 N. Trade St., Suite 103, Winston-Salem NC 27101. **E-mail:** kevin@press53.com. **Website:** www.press53.com. **Contact:** Kevin Morgan Watson, publisher. Awarded to an outstanding, unpublished collection of poetry. Details and guidelines available online. Deadline: July 31. Submission period begins April 1. Finalists announced October 1. Winner announced on December 1. Publication in April. Prize: Publication of winning poetry collection as a Tom Lombardo Poetry Selection, $1,000 cash advance, travel expenses and lodging for a special reading and book signing in Winston-Salem, NC, attendance as special guest to the Press 53/Jacar Press Gathering of Writers, and 10 copies of the book. Judged by Press 53 poetry series editor Tom Lombardo.

RATTLE POETRY PRIZE

RATTLE, 12411 Ventura Blvd., Studio City CA 91604. (818) 505-6777. **E-mail:** tim@rattle.com. **E-mail:** prize@rattle.com. **Website:** www.rattle.com. **Contact:** Timothy Green, editor. *Rattle*'s mission is to promote the practice of poetry. To enter, purchase a one-year subscription to *Rattle* at the regular $20 rate. Open to writers, worldwide; poems must be written in English. No previously published works, or works accepted for publication elsewhere. No simultaneous submissions are allowed. Send up to 4 poems per entry. "More than anything, our goal is to promote a community of active poets." Deadline: July 15. Prize: One $10,000 winner and ten $200 finalists will be selected in a blind review by the editors of *Rattle* and printed in the Winter issue; one $1,000 Readers' Choice Award will then be chosen from among the Finalists by subscriber and entrant vote. Judged by the editors of *Rattle*.

RHINO FOUNDERS' PRIZE

RHINO, The Poetry Forum, P.O. Box 591, Evanston IL 60204. **E-mail:** editors@rhinopoetry.org. **Website:** rhinopoetry.org. **Contact:** Editors. Send best, unpublished poetry, translations, and flash fiction (750 words max). Visit website for previous winners and more information. Submit online or by mail. Include a cover letter listing your name, address, e-mail, and/or telephone number, titles of poems, how you learned about RHINO, and fee. Mss will not be returned. Deadline: September 1-October 31. Prize: $300, publication, featured on website, and nominated for a Pushcart Prize. Two runners-ups will receive $50, publication, and will be featured on website. Occasionally nominates runner-up for a Pushcart Prize. **TIPS** "RHINO values original voice, musicality, fresh language, and respect for the reader."

ROANOKE-CHOWAN POETRY AWARD

The North Carolina Literary & Historical Assoc., 4610 Mail Service Center, Raleigh NC 27699-4610. (919)807-7290. **Fax:** (919)733-8807. **E-mail:** michael.hill@ncdcr.gov. **Website:** www.history.ncdcr.gov/affiliates/lit-hist/awards/awards.htm. **Contact:** Michael Hill, awards coordinator. Offers annual award for an original volume of poetry published during the 12 months ending June 30 of the year for which the award is given. Open to authors who have maintained legal or physical residence, or a combination of both, in North Carolina for the 3 years preceding the close of the contest period. Submit 3 copies of each entry. Guidelines available for SASE or by fax or e-mail. Winner announced October 15. Deadline: July 15.

BENJAMIN SALTMAN POETRY AWARD

Red Hen Press, P.O. Box 40820, Pasadena CA 91114. (818)831-0649. **Fax:** (818)831-6659. **E-mail:** productioncoordinator@redhen.org. **Website:** www.redhen.org. **Contact:** Alisa Trager, production coordinator. Offered annually for unpublished work to publish a winning book of poetry. Open to any writer. Name on cover sheet only, 48 page minimum. Send SASE for notification. Deadline: August 31. Prize: $3,000 and publication.

SCREAMINMAMAS MOTHER'S DAY POETRY CONTEST

1911 Cleveland St., Hollywood FL 33020. **E-mail:** screaminmamas@gmail.com. **Website:** www.screaminmamas.com/contests. **Contact:** Darlene Pistocchi, editor/managing director. "What does it mean to be a mom? There is so much to being a mom—get deep, get creative! We challenge you to explore different types of poetry: descriptive, reflective, narrative, lyric, sonnet, ballad, limerick... you can even go epic!" Open only to moms. Deadline: December 31. Prize: complementary subscription to magazine, publication.

SHORT GRAIN CONTEST

Box 67, Saskatoon SK S7K 3K1 Canada. (306)244-2828. **E-mail:** grainmag@skwriter.com. **Website:** www.grainmagazine.ca/short-grain-contest. **Contact:** Jordan Morris, business administrator (inquiries only). The annual Short Grain Contest includes a category for poetry of any style up to 100 lines and fiction of any style up to 2,500 words, offering 3 prizes. Each entry must be original, unpublished, not submitted elsewhere for publication or broadcast, nor accepted elsewhere for publication or broadcast, nor entered simultaneously in any other contest or competition for which it is also eligible to win a prize. Entries must be typed on 8½x11 paper. It must be legible. No simultaneous submissions. A separate covering page must be attached to the text of your entry, and must provide the following information: Author's name, complete mailing address, telephone number, e-mail address, entry title, category name, and line count. Online submissions are accepted, see website for details. An absolutely accurate word or line count is required. No identifying information on the text pages. Entries will not be returned. Names of the winners and titles of the winning entries will be posted on the *Grain Magazine* website in August; only the winners will be notified. Deadline: April 1. Prize: $1,000, plus publication in *Grain Magazine*.

SLIPSTREAM ANNUAL POETRY CHAPBOOK CONTEST

Slipstream, Slipstream Poetry Contest, Dept. W-1, P.O. Box 2071, Niagara Falls NY 14301. **E-mail:** editors@slipstreampress.org. **Website:** www.slipstreampress.org. **Contact:** Dan Sicoli, co-editor. Slipstream Magazine is a yearly anthology of some of the best poetry you'll find today in the American small press. Send up to 40 pages of poetry: any style, format, or theme (or no theme). Send only copies of your poems, not originals. Manuscripts will no longer be returned. See website for specific details. Offered annually to help promote a poet whose work is often overlooked or ignored. Open to any writer. Deadline: December 1. Prize: $1,000 plus 50 professionally-printed copies of your book.

HELEN C. SMITH MEMORIAL AWARD FOR BEST BOOK OF POETRY

The Texas Institute of Letters, P.O. Box 609, Round Rock TX 78680. **E-mail:** tilsecretary@yahoo.com. **Website:** http://texasinstituteofletters.org/. Offered annually for the best book of poems published January 1-December 31 of previous year. Poet must have been born in Texas, have lived in the state at some time for at least 2 consecutive years, or the subject matter must be associated with the state. See website for submission details and information. Deadline: January 10. Prize: $1,200.

THE RICHARD SNYDER MEMORIAL PUBLICATION PRIZE

Ashland Poetry Press, 401 College Ave., Ashland University, Ashland OH 44805. **E-mail:** app@ashland.edu. **Website:** www.ashlandpoetrypress.com. **Contact:** Wendy Hall, managing editor. Offers annual award of $1,000 plus book publication. Submissions must be unpublished in book form. Considers simultaneous submissions. Submit 50-96 pages of poetry. Competition receives 400+ entries/year. Winners will be announced in *Writer's Chronicle* and *Poets & Writers*. Copies of winning books available from Small Press Distribution and directly from the Ashland University Bookstore online. The Ashland Poetry Press publishes 2-4 books of poetry/year. Deadline: April 30. Judged by David St. John in 2015.

THE SOW'S EAR POETRY COMPETITION

The Sow's Ear Poetry Review, P.O. Box 127, Millwood VA 22646. **E-mail:** rglesman@gmail.com. **Website:** www.sows-ear.kitenet.net. **Contact:** Robert G. Lesman, managing editor. Open to adults. Send unpublished poems to the address above. Please do not put your name on poems. Include a separate sheet with poem titles, name, address, phone, and e-mail address if available, or a SASE for notification of results. No length limit on poems. Simultaneous submission acceptable (checks with finalists before sending to final judge). Send poems in September or October. Deadline: November 1. Prize: $1,000, publication, and the option of publication for approximately 20 finalists.

THE RUTH STONE POETRY PRIZE

Vermont College, 36 College St., Montpelier VT 05602. (802)828-8517. **E-mail:** hungermtn@vcfa.edu. **Website:** www.hungermtn.org. **Contact:** Miciah Bay Gault, editor. The Ruth Stone Poetry Prize is an annual poetry contest. Enter up to 3 original, unpublished poems. Do not include name or address on submissions; entries are read blind. Accepts submissions online or via postal mail. Deadline: December 10. Prize: One first place winner receives $1,000 and publication on Hunger Mountain online. Two honorable mentions receive $100 and publication on Hunger Mountain online.

THE ELIZABETH MATCHETT STOVER MEMORIAL AWARD

Southwest Review, Southern Methodist University, P.O. Box 750374, Dallas TX 75275-0374. (214)768-1037. **Fax:** (214)768-1408. **E-mail:** swr@mail.smu.edu. **Website:** www.smu.edu/southwestreview. **Contact:** Jennifer Cranfill, senior editor, and Willard Spiegelman, editor-in-chief. Offered annually to the best works of poetry that have appeared in the magazine in the previous year. Please note that mss are submitted for publication, not for the prizes themselves. Guidelines for SASE and online. Prize: $300. Judged by Jennifer Cranfill and Willard Spiegelman.

TIPS "Not an open contest. Annual prize in which winners are chosen from published pieces during the preceding year."

THE TAMPA REVIEW PRIZE FOR POETRY

University of Tampa, 401 W. Kennedy Blvd., Tampa FL 33606. **E-mail:** utpress@ut.edu. **Website:** www.utpress.ut.edu. Annual award for the best previously unpublished collection of poetry (at least 48 pages, though preferably 60-100). Deadline: December 31. Prize: $2,000, plus publication.

THE TENTH GATE PRIZE

c/o Leslie McGrath, Series Editor, The Tenth Gate Prize, English Department, Central CT State University, 1615 Stanley St., New Britain CT 06050. **E-mail:** editor@wordworksbooks.org. **Website:** www.wordworksbooks.org. Publication and cash prize awarded annually by The Word Works to a full-length ms by a poet who has already published at least 2 full-length collections. Submit 48-80 pages. Include 2 title pages, one with and one without identifying information, and a cover letter including a brief bio that includes previous book publications, dates, and publishers. Submissions accepted online or via mail. See website for guidelines. Deadline: July 15. Open to submissions on June 1. Prize: $1,000 and publication.

THE HILARY THAM CAPITAL COLLECTION

The Word Works, Nancy White, c/o SUNY Adiorndack, 640 Bay Rd., Queensbury NY 12804. **E-mail:** editor@wordworksbooks.org. **Website:** www.wordworksbooks.org. **Contact:** Nancy White, editor. The Hilary Tham Capital Collection publishes only poets who volunteer for literary nonprofits. Every nominated poet is invited to submit; authors have until May 1 to send their ms via online submissions at website, or to Nancy White. Details available online. Deadline: April 15 to send nomination.

TOR HOUSE PRIZE FOR POETRY

Robinson Jeffers Tor House Foundation, Poetry Prize Coordinator, Tor House Foundation, Box 223240, Carmel CA 93922. (831)624-1813. **Fax:** (831)624-3696. **E-mail:** thf@torhouse.org. **Website:** www.torhouse.org. **Contact:** Eliot Ruchowitz-Roberts, Poetry Prize Coordinator. The annual Prize for Poetry is a living memorial to American poet Robinson Jeffers (1887-1962). Open to well-crafted poetry in all styles, ranging from experimental work to traditional forms, including short narrative poems. Poems must be original and unpublished. Each poem should be typed on 8 1/2" by 11" paper, and no longer than three pages. On a cover sheet only, include: name, mailing address, telephone number and email; titles of poems; bio optional. Multiple and simultaneous submissions welcome. Deadline: March 14. Prize: $1,000 honorarium for award-winning poem; $200 Honorable Mention.

TRANSCONTINENTAL POETRY AWARD

Pavement Saw Press, 321 Empire St., Montpelier OH 43543. (419)485-0524. **E-mail:** info@pavementsaw.org. **Website:** pavementsaw.org. **Contact:** David Baratier, editor. Offered annually for a first or second book of poetry. Each year, Pavement Saw Press will seek to publish at least 1 book of poetry and/or prose poems from manuscripts received during this competition, which is open to anyone who has not previously published a volume of poetry or prose. Poets who have not published a book, who have published 1 collection, or who have published a second collection of fewer than 40 pages, or who have published a second full-length collection with a print run of no more than 500 copies are eligible. More than 1 prize may be awarded. Submit 48-70 pages of poetry (1 poem/page), paginated and bound with a single clip. Include 2 cover sheets: 1 with ms title, poet's name, address, phone number, and e-mail; if available, the second with ms title only (this sheet should be clipped to ms). Also include 1-page cover letter (a brief biography, ms title, poet's name, address, and telephone number, e-mail, and poet's signature) and acknowledgments page (journal, anthology, chapbook, etc., and poem published). Include SASP for acknowledgment of receipt; SASE unnecessary as result will be sent with free book and no mss will be returned. Guidelines available for SASE or on website. Deadline: Reads submissions in June, July, and until August 15 (must have August 15 or earlier postmark). Prize: $1,000, publication, and a percentage of the print run for a first or second book. Judged by the editor and a guest judge.

TUFTS POETRY AWARDS

Kingsley & Kate Tufts Poetry Awards, Claremont Graduate University, 160 E. Tenth St., Harper East B7, Claremont CA 91711-6165. (909)621-8974. **E-mail:** tufts@cgu.edu. **Website:** www.cgu.edu/tufts. Unlike many literary awards, which are coronations for a successful career or body of work, the Kingsley Tufts Poetry Award was created to both honor the poet and provide the resources that allow artists to continue working towards the pinnacle of their craft. "Any poet will tell you that the only thing more rare than meaningful recognition is a meaningful payday. For two outstanding poets each year, the Kingsley and Kate Tufts awards represent both." Deadline: September 1. Submissions period begins June 30. Prize: $100,000 for the Kingsley Tufts Poetry Award and $10,000 for the Kate Tufts Discovery Award.

UTMOST CHRISTIAN POETRY CONTEST

Utmost Christian Writers Foundation, 121 Morin Maze, Edmonton Alberta T6K 1V1 Canada. (780)265-4650. **E-mail:** nnharms@telusplanet.net. **Website:** www.utmostchristianwriters.com. **Contact:** Nathan Harms, executive director. Utmost is founded on—and supported by—the dreams, interests and aspirates of individual people. Contest is only open to Christians. Poems may be rhymed or free verse, up to 60 lines, but must not have been published previously or have won any prize in any previous competition of any kind. Submit up to 5 poems. Deadline: February 28. Prize: 1st Place: $1,000; 2nd Place: $500; 10 prizes of $100 are offered for honorable mention; $300 for best rhyming poem and $200 for an honorable mention rhyming poem. Judged by a committee of the Directors of Utmost Christian Writers Foundation (who work under the direction of Barbara Mitchell, chief judge).

TIPS "Besides providing numerous resources for Christian writers and poets, Utmost also provides a marketplace where Christian writers and poets can sell their work. Please follow our guidelines. We receive numerous unsuitable submissions from writers. We encourage writers to submit suitable material. The best way to do this is to read the guidelines specific to your project—poetry, book reviews, articles—and then take time to look at the material we have already published in that area. The final step is to evaluate your proposed submission in comparison to the material we have used previously. If you complete these steps and strongly feel that your material is appropriate for us, we encourage you to submit it."

DANIEL VAROUJAN AWARD

New England Poetry Club, 376 School St., Watertown MA 02472. **E-mail:** contests@nepoetryclub.org. **Website:** www.nepoetryclub.org. **Contact:** Audrey Kalajin. For an unpublished poem (not a translation) worthy of Daniel Varoujan, a poet killed by the Turks in the genocide which destroyed three-fourths of the Armenian population. Previous winners may not enter again. Send entry in duplicate, one without name and address of writer. Deadline: May 31. Prize: $1,000. Judged by well-known poets and sometimes winners of previous NEPC contests.

MARICA AND JAN VILCEK PRIZE FOR POETRY

Bellevue Literary Review, New York University School of Medicine, OBV-A612, 550 First Ave., New York NY 10016. (212)263-3973. **E-mail:** info@BLReview.org. **Website:** www.BLReview.org. **Contact:** Stacy Bodziak. The annual Marica and Jan Vilcek Prize for Poetry recognizes outstanding writing related to themes of health, healing, illness, the mind, and the body. All entries will be considered for publication. No previously published poems (including Internet publication). Submit up to 3 poems (5 pages maximum). Electronic (online) submissions only; combine all poems into 1 document and use first poem as document title. See guidelines for additional submission details. Guidelines available for SASE or on website. Deadline: July 1. Prize: $1,000 for best poem and publication in *Bellevue Literary Review*. Previous judges include Mark Doty, Cornelius Eady, Naomi Shihab Nye, and Tony Hoagland.

WABASH PRIZE FOR POETRY

Sycamore Review, Department of English, 500 Oval Dr., Purdue University, West Lafayette IN 47907. **E-mail:** sycamore@purdue.edu; sycamorepoetry@purdue.edu. **Website:** www.sycamorereview.com/contest/. **Contact:** Kara Krewer, editor-in-chief. Annual contest for unpublished poetry. For each submission, send up to 3 poems (no more than 6 total pages). Ms pages should be numbered and should include the title of each poem. See website for more guidelines. Submit via online submissions manager. Deadline: December 1. Prize: $1,000 and publication.

THE WASHINGTON PRIZE

Dearlove Hall, SUNY Adirondack, 640 Bay Rd., Queensbury NY 12804. **E-mail:** editor@wordworksbooks.org. **Website:** www.wordworksdc.com. **Contact:** Rebecca Kutzer-Rice, Washington Prize administrator. Sponsors an ongoing poetry reading series, educational programs, and and three additional imprints: The Tenth Gate, International Editions, and the Hilary Tham Capital Collection. Sponsors The Washington Prize, one of the older manuscript publishing prizes, and The Jacklyn Potter Young Poets Competition. Additional information available on website. Winners announced in August. Book publication planned for January of the following year. Submit a poetry ms of 48-80 pages. Submit online, or if on paper, include 2 title pages, 1 with and 1 without author information, an acknowledgments page, a table of contents and a cover letter containing a brief bio. Electronic submissions are accepted at www.wordworksbooks.org. Deadline: Submit January 15-March 15 (postmark). Prize: $1,500 and publication of a book-length ms of original poetry in English by a living American poet (US or Canadian citizen).

WERGLE FLOMP HUMOR POETRY CONTEST

Winning Writers, 351 Pleasant St., PMB 222, Northampton MA 01060. (866)946-9748. **Fax:** (413)280-0539. **E-mail:** adam@winningwriters.com. **Website:** www.winningwriters.com. **Contact:** Adam Cohen. This annual contest seeks today's best humor poems. One poem of any length should be submitted. Poem may be published or unpublished. The poem should be in English. Inspired gibberish is also accepted. See website for guidelines, examples, and to submit your poem. Nonexclusive right to publish submissions on WinningWriters.com, in e-mail newsletters, in e-books, and in press releases. Submit one humor poem online. No length limit. Deadline: April 1. Prize: 1st prize of $1,000, plus 10 honorable mentions of $100 each. Judged by Jendi Reiter (final).

WHITE PINE PRESS POETRY PRIZE

White Pine Press, P.O. Box 236, Buffalo NY 14201. **E-mail:** wpine@whitepine.org. **Website:** www.whitepine.org. **Contact:** Dennis Maloney, editor. Offered annually for previously published or unpublished poets. Manuscript: Up to 80 pages of original work;

translations are not eligible. Poems may have appeared in magazines or limited-edition chapbooks. Open to any US citizen. Deadline: November 30 (postmarked). Prize: $1,000 and publication. Final judge is a poet of national reputation. All entries are screened by the editorial staff of White Pine Press.

STAN AND TOM WICK POETRY PRIZE

301 Satterfield Hall, Kent State University, P.O. Box 5190, Kent OH 44242-0001. (330)672-2067. **E-mail:** dhassle1@kent.edu. **Website:** www2.kent.edu/wick/competitions. **Contact:** David Hassler, director. Offered annually to a poet who has not previously published a full-length collection of poetry (a volume of 50 or more pages published in an edition of 500 or more copies). Submissions must consist of 50-70 pages of poetry, typed on one side only, with no more than one poem included on a single page. Also accepts submissions online through Submittable. See website for details and guidelines. Deadline: May 1. Submissions period begins February 1. Prize: $2,500 and publication of full-length book of poetry by Kent State University Press.

MILLER WILLIAMS POETRY PRIZE

University of Arkansas Press, McIlroy House, 105 N. McIlroy Avenue, Fayetteville AR 72701. (479)575-7258. **Fax:** (479)575-6044. **E-mail:** info@uapress.com; mbieker@uark.edu. **Website:** www.uapress.com. **Contact:** Billy Collins, judge and series editor; Mike Bieker, director. Each year, the University of Arkansas Press accepts submissions for the Miller Williams Poetry Series and from the books selected awards the Miller Williams Poetry Prize in the following summer. Mss should be between 60-90 pages. Individual poems may have been published in chapbooks, journals, and anthologies. Guidelines available online. Submit online. Deadline: September 30. Accepts submissions all year long. Prize: $5,000, publication, and featured reading at the University of Arkansas. Judged by Billy Collins, series editor.

THE J. HOWARD AND BARBARA M.J. WOOD PRIZE

Poetry, 61 W. Superior St., Chicago IL 60654. (312)787-7070. **Fax:** (312)787-6650. **E-mail:** editors@poetrymagazine.org. **Website:** www.poetrymagazine.org. Offered annually for poems published in *Poetry* during the preceding year (October-September). Upon acceptance, *Poetry* licenses exclusive worldwide first serial rights, including electronic rights, for publication, as well as non-exclusive rights to reprint, reuse, and archive the work, in any format, in perpetuity. Copyright reverts to author upon first publication. Prize: $5,000.

WORKING PEOPLE'S POETRY COMPETITION

Blue Collar Review, P.O. Box 11417, Norfolk VA 23517. **E-mail:** red-ink@earthlink.net. **Website:** www.partisanpress.org. Poetry should be typed as you would like to see it published, with your name and address on each page. Include cover letter with entry. Guidelines available on website. Deadline: May 15. Prize: $100, 1-year subscription to *Blue Collar Review* (see separate listing in Magazines/Journals) and 1-year posting of winning poem to website.

JAMES WRIGHT POETRY AWARD

Mid-American Review, Dept. of English, Bowling Green State University, Bowling Green OH 43403. (419)372-2725. **Fax:** (419)372-4642. **E-mail:** clouda@bgsu.edu. **Website:** www.bgsu.edu/midamericanreview. **Contact:** Abigail Cloud, editor. Offered annually for unpublished poetry. Open to all writers not associated with *Mid-American Review* or judge. Guidelines available online or for SASE. Deadline: November 1. Prize: $1,000 and publication in spring issue of *Mid-American Review*. Judged by editors and a well known writer, i.e., Kathy Fagan, Bob Hicok, Michelle Boisseau.

THE YALE SERIES OF YOUNGER POETS

Yale University Press, P.O. Box 209040, New Haven CT 06520-9040. **Website:** www.youngerpoets.org; yalepress.yale.edu/yupbooks/youngerpoets.asp. The Yale Series of Younger Poets champions the most promising new American poets. The Yale Younger Poets prize is the oldest annual literary award in the United States. Open to U.S. citizens under age 40 at the time of entry who have not published a volume of poetry; poets may have published a limited edition chapbook of 300 copies or less. Poems may have been previously published in newspapers and periodicals and used in the book ms if so identified. No translations. Submit 48-64 pages of poetry, paginated, with each new poem starting on a new page. Accepts hard copy and electronic submissions. Deadline: November 15. Submissions period begins October 1.

ZONE 3 POETRY AWARD

Zone 3, Austin Peay State University, Austin Peay State University, PO Box 4565, Clarksville TN 37044. (931)221-7031. **Fax:** (931)221-7149. **E-mail:** spofforda@aspu.edu; wallacess@apsu.edu. **Website:** www.apsu.edu/zone3/. **Contact:** Andrea Spofford, poetry editor; Susan Wallace, managing editor. Offered annually for unpublished poetry. Submit up to 3 poems via online submissions manager. Deadline: April 1. Prize: $250 and publication.

MULTIPLE WRITING AREAS

ADELAIDE FESTIVAL AWARDS FOR LITERATURE

Arts SA, GPO Box 2308, Adelaide SA 5001 Australia. (61)(8)8463-5444. **Fax:** (61)(8)8463-5420. **E-mail:** artssa@dpc.sa.gov.au. **Website:** www.arts.sa.gov.au. The Adelaide Festival Awards for Literature are presented in even-numbered years during Adelaide Writer's week as part of the Adelaide Festival. Introduced by the South Australia Government, the awards celebrate Australia's writing culture by offering national and State-based literary prizes, as well as fellowships for South Australian writers. Award categories: Premier's Award, Children's Literature, Fiction, John Bray Poetry, Non-Fiction, Young Adult Fiction, Jill Blewett Playwright's and Wakefield Press Unpublished Manuscript. Deadline: June 26. Nominations open on February 27. Prize: $10,000-25,000 for each award.

AESTHETICA ART PRIZE

P.O. Box 371, York YO23 1WL United Kingdom. **E-mail:** info@aestheticamagazine.com. **E-mail:** artprize@aestheticamagazine.com. **Website:** www.aestheticamagazine.com. The Aesthetica Art Prize is a celebration of excellence in art from across the world and offers artists the opportunity to showcase their work to wider audiences and further their involvement in the international art world. There are 4 categories: Photograpic & Digital Art, Three Dimensional Design & Sculpture, Painting & Drawing, Video Installation & Performance. See guidelines at Artwork & Photography, Fiction, and Poetry. See guidelines at www.aestheticamagazine.com. The Aesthetica Art Prize is a celebration of excellence in art from across the world and offers artists the opportunity to showcase their work to wider audiences and further their involvement in the international art world. There are 4 categories: Photograpic & Digital Art, Three Dimensional Design & Sculpture, Painting & Drawing, Video Installation & Performance. See guidelines at Artwork & Photography, Fiction, and Poetry. See guidelines at www.aestheticamagazine.com. The Aesthetica Art Prize is a celebration of excellence in art from across the world and offers artists the opportunity to showcase their work to wider audiences and further their involvement in the international art world. There are 4 categories: Photograpic & Digital Art, Three Dimensional Design & Sculpture, Painting & Drawing, Video Installation & Performance. See guidelines at Artwork & Photography, Fiction, and Poetry. See guidelines at www.aestheticamagazine.com. Works should be completed in English Deadline: 31 August. Prize: Prizes include: £5,000 main prize courtesy of Hiscox, £1,000 Student Prize courtesy of Hiscox, group exhibition and publication in the Aesthetica Art Prize Anthology. Entry is £15 and permits submission of two works in one category.

MARIE ALEXANDER POETRY SERIES

English Department, 2801 S. University Ave., Little Rock AR 72204. **E-mail:** editor@mariealexanderseries.com. **Website:** mariealexanderseries.com. **Contact:** Nickole Brown. Annual contest for a collection of previously unpublished prose poems or flash fiction by a U.S. writer. Deadline: July 1-31. Prize: $1,000, plus publication.

AMERICAN LITERARY REVIEW CONTESTS

American Literary Review, P.O. Box 311307, University of North Texas, Denton TX 76203-1307. (940)565-2755. **E-mail:** americanliteraryreview@gmail.com. **Website:** www.americanliteraryreview.com. Contest to award excellence in short fiction, creative nonfiction, and poetry. Multiple entries are acceptable, but each entry must be accompanied with a reading fee. Do not put any identifying information in the file itself; include the author's name, title(s), address, e-mail address, and phone number in the boxes provided in the online submissions manager. Short fiction: Limit 8,000 words per work. Creative nonfiction: Limit 6,500 words per work. Deadline: October 1. Submission period begins June 1. Prize: $1,000 prize for each category, along with publication in the Spring online issue of the *American Literary Review*.

AMERICAS AWARD

Consortium of Latin American Studies Program, University of Wisconsin-Milwaukee, P.O. Box 413,

Milwaukee WI 53201. **Website:** http://claspprograms.org/americasaward. **Contact:** Claire Gonzalez. The Américas Award encourages and commends authors, illustrators, and publishers who produce quality children's and young adult books that portray Latin America, the Caribbean, or Latinos in the United States. Up to 2 awards (for primary and secondary reading levels) are given in recognition of US published works of fiction, poetry, folklore, or selected nonfiction (from picture books to works for young adults). The award winners and commended titles are selected for their (1) distinctive literary quality; (2) cultural contextualization; (3) exceptional integration of text, illustration and design; and (4) potential for classroom use. To nominate a copyright title from the previous year, publishers are invited to submit review copies to the committee members listed on the website. Publishers should send 8 copies of the nominated book. Deadline: January 18. Prize: $500, plaque and a formal presentation at the Library of Congress, Washington DC.

A MIDSUMMER TALE

E-mail: editors@toasted-cheese.com. **Website:** www.toasted-cheese.com. **Contact:** Theryn Fleming, editor. A Midsummer Tale is open to non-genre fiction and creative nonfiction. There is a different theme each year. Entries must be unpublished. Accepts inquiries by e-mail. Cover letter should include name, address, e-mail, word count, and title. Length: 1,000-5,000 words. Open to any writer. Guidelines available in April on website. Deadline: June 21. Results announced on July 31. Winners notified by e-mail. List of winners on website. Prize: Amazon gift certificates and publication in Toasted Cheese. Entries are blind-judged.

ARIZONA LITERARY CONTEST & BOOK AWARDS

6145 W. Echo Lane, Glendale AZ 85302. (623)847-9343. **E-mail:** info@azauthors.com. **Website:** www.azauthors.com. Arizona Authors Association sponsors annual literary contest in poetry, short story, essay, unpublished novels, and published books (fiction, nonfiction, and children's literature). Awards publication in *Arizona Literary Magazine*, and prizes by Five Star Publications, Inc. Poetry, short story, and essay submissions must be unpublished. Work must have been published in the last calendar year. Considers simultaneous submissions. Entry form and guidelines available on website or for SASE. Deadline: July 1. Begins reading submissions on January 1. Prize: Grand Prize, Arizona Book of the Year Award: $500. All categories: 1st Prize: $150 and publication; 2nd Prize: $75 and publication; 3rd Prize: $30 and publication. Features in *Arizona Literary Magazine* can be taken instead of money and publication. 1st Prize Published Fiction and Nonfiction: Listing on AuthorsandExperts.com. 1st Prize Chilren's Literature: Listing on SchoolBookings.com. 1st and 2nd Prize winners in Poetry, Essay, Short Story: Nomination for the Pushcart Prize. Judged by Arizona authors, editors, and reviewers. Winners announced at an award banquet by November 8.

THE ATHENAEUM LITERARY AWARD

The Athenaeum of Philadelphia, 219 S. 6th St., Philadelphia PA 19106-3794. (215)925-2688. **Fax:** (215)925-3755. **E-mail:** jilly@PhilaAthenaeum.org. **Website:** www.PhilaAthenaeum.org. **Contact:** Jill Lee, Circulation Librarian. The Athenaeum Literary Award was established to recognize and encourage literary achievement among authors who are bona fide residents of Philadelphia or Pennsylvania living within a radius of 30 miles of City Hall at the time their book was written or published. Any volume of general literature is eligible; technical, scientific, and juvenile books are not included. Nominated works are reviewed on the basis of their significance and importance to the general public as well as for literary excellence. Deadline: December 31.

ATLANTIC WRITING COMPETITION FOR UNPUBLISHED MANUSCRIPTS

Writers' Federation of Nova Scotia, 1113 Marginal Rd., Halifax NS B3H 4P7. (902)423-8116. **Fax:** (902)422-0881. **E-mail:** programs@writers.ns.ca. **Website:** www.writers.ns.ca. **Contact:** Robin Spittal, communications and development officer. Annual program designed to honor work by unpublished writers in all 4 Atlantic Provinces. Entry is open to writers unpublished in the category of writing they wish to enter. Prizes are presented in the fall of each year. Categories include: novel, writing for children, poetry, short story, juvenile/young adult novel, creative non-fiction, and play. Judges return written comments when competition is concluded. Page lengths and rules vary based on categories. See website for details. Anyone resident in the Atlantic Provinces since September 1st immediately prior to the deadline date is eligible to enter. Only one entry per category is allowed. Each entry requires its own entry form and registration fee. Deadline: February 2. Prize: Prizes vary based on categories. See website for details.

AUTUMN HOUSE POETRY, FICTION, AND NONFICTION PRIZES

P.O. Box 60100, Pittsburgh PA 15211. (412)381-4261. **E-mail:** gcerto@autumhouse.org; info@autumnhouse.org. **E-mail:** autumnh420@gmail.com. **Website:** http://autumnhouse.org. **Contact:** Giuliana Certo, managing editor. Offers annual prize and publication of book-length ms with national promotion. Submission must be unpublished as a collection, but individual poems, stories, and essays may have been previously published elsewhere. Considers simultaneous submissions. "Autumn House is a nonprofit corporation with the mission of publishing and promoting poetry and other fine literature. We have published books by Gerald Stern, Ruth L. Schwartz, Ed Ochester, Andrea Hollander Budy, George Bilgere, Jo McDougall, and others." Submit 50-80 pages of poetry or 200-300 pages of prose (include 2 cover sheets requested). Guidelines available for SASE, by e-mail, or on website. Competition receives 1,500 entries/year. Winners announced through mailings, website, and ads in *Poets & Writers, American Poetry Review*, and *Writer's Chronicle* (extensive publicity for winner). Copies of winning books available from Amazon.com, Barnes & Noble, and other retailers. Deadline: June 30. Prize: The winner (in each of three categories) will receive book publication, $1,000 advance against royalties, and a $1,500 travel/publicity grant to promote his or her book. Judged by Dorianne Laux (poetry), Sharon Dilworth (fiction), and Dinty W. Moore (nonfiction).

TIPS "Include only your best work."

AWP AWARD SERIES

Association of Writers & Writing Programs, George Mason University, 4400 University Drive, MSN 1E3, Fairfax VA 22030. **E-mail:** supriya@awpwriter.org. **Website:** www.awpwriter.org. **Contact:** Supriya Bhatnagar, director of publications. AWP sponsors the Award Series, an annual competition for the publication of excellent new book-length works. The competition is open to all authors writing in English regardless of nationality or residence, and is available to published and unpublished authors alike. Guidelines on website. Entries must be unpublished. Open to any writer. Entries are not accepted via postal mail. Offered annually to foster new literary talent. Deadline: Postmarked between January 1 and February 28. Prize: AWP Prize for the Novel: $2,500 and publication by New Issues Press; Donald Hall Prize for Poetry: $5,500 and publication by the University of Pittsburgh Press; Grace Paley Prize in Short Fiction: $5,500 and publication by the University of Massachusetts Press; and AWP Prize for Creative Nonfiction: $2,500 and publication by the University of Georgia Press.

AWP INTRO JOURNALS PROJECT

The Association of Writers & Writing Programs, Dept. of English, Bluffton University, 1 University Dr., Bluffton OH 45817-2104. **E-mail:** awp@awpwriter.org. **Website:** www.awpwriter.org. **Contact:** Susan Streeter Carpenter. This is a prize for students in AWP member-university creative writing programs only. Authors are nominated by the head of the Creative Writing Department. Each school may nominate no more than 1 work of nonfiction, 1 work of short fiction, and 3 poems. Open to students in AWP member-university creative writing programs only. Deadline: December 1. Prize: $100, plus publication in participating journal. Judged by AWP.

THE BASKERVILLE PUBLISHERS POETRY AWARD & THE BETSY COLQUITT POETRY AWARD

descant, Texas Christian University's literary journal, TCU, Box 297270, Fort Worth TX 76129. (817)257-5907. **Fax:** (817)257-6239. **E-mail:** descant@tcu.edu. **Website:** www.descant.tcu.edu. **Contact:** Alex Lemon, poetry editor. Annual award for an outstanding poem published in an issue of *descant*. Deadline: September-April. Prize: $250 for Baskerville Award; $500 for Betsy Colquitt Award. Publication retains copyright, but will transfer it to the author upon request.

JAMES TAIT BLACK MEMORIAL PRIZES

University of Edinburgh, School of Literatures, Languages, and Cultures, 50 George Square, Edinburgh EH8 9JH Scotland. **Website:** www.ed.ac.uk/news/events/tait-black/introduction. Open to any writer. Entries must be previously published. Winners notified by phone, via publisher. Contact department of English Literature for list of winners or check website. Accepts inquiries by e-mail or phone. Eligible works must be written in English and first published or co-published in Britain in the year of the award. Works should be submitted by publishers. Deadline: December 1. Prize: Two prizes each of £10,000 are awarded: one for the best work of fiction, one for the best biography or work of that nature, published during the calendar year January 1 to December 31. Judged by professors of English Literature with the assistance of teams of postgraduate readers.

THE BLACK RIVER CHAPBOOK COMPETITION

Black Lawrence Press, 326 Bingham St., Pittsburgh PA 15211. **E-mail:** editors@blacklawrencepress.com. **Website:** www.blacklawrencepress.com. Twice each year, Black Lawrence Press runs the Black River Chapbook Competition for an unpublished chapbook of poems or short fiction between 18-36 pages in length. Submit through Submittable. Spring deadline: May 31. Fall deadline: October 31. Prize: $500, publication, and 10 copies. Judged by a revolving panel of judges, in addition to the Chapbook Editor and other members of the BLP editorial staff.

THE BOARDMAN TASKER PRIZE FOR MOUNTAIN LITERATURE

The Boardman Tasker Charitable Trust, 8 Bank View Rd., Darley Abbey Derby DE22 1EJ UK. 01332 342246. **E-mail:** steve@people-matter.co.uk. **Website:** www.boardmantasker.com. **Contact:** Steve Dean. Offered annually to reward a work with a mountain theme, whether fiction, nonfiction, drama, or poetry, written in the English language (initially or in translation). Subject must be concerned with a mountain environment. Previous winners have been books on expeditions, climbing experiences, a biography of a mountaineer, novels. Guidelines available in January by e-mail or on website. Entries must be previously published. Open to any writer. Writers may obtain information, but entry is by publishers only (includes self-publishing). Awarded for a work published or distributed for the first time in the United Kingdom during the previous year. Not an anthology. The award is to honor Peter Boardman and Joe Tasker, who disappeared on Everest in 1982. Deadline: August 1. Prize: £3,000 Judged by a panel of 3 judges elected by trustees.

BOROONDARA LITERARY AWARDS

City of Boroondara, 340 Camberwell Rd., Camberwell VIC 3124 Australia. **E-mail:** bla@boroondara.vic.gov.au. **Website:** www.boroondara.vic.gov.au/literary-awards. Contest for unpublished work in 2 categories: Young Writers: 5th-6th grade (Junior), 7th-9th grade (Middle), and 10th-12th grade (Senior), prose and poetry on any theme; and Open Short Story (1,500-3,000 words). Deadline: 5pm on August 28. Prize: Young Writers, Junior: 1st Place: $150; 2nd Place: $100; 3rd Place: $50. Young Writers, Middle and Senior: 1st Place: $600; 2nd Place: $400; 3rd Place: $200. Open Short Story: 1st Place: $1,500; 2ndPlace: $1000; 3rd Place $500.

THE BRIAR CLIFF REVIEW FICTION, POETRY, AND CREATIVE NONFICTION COMPETITION

The Briar Cliff Review, Briar Cliff University, 3303 Rebecca St., Sioux City IA 51104-0100. **E-mail:** tricia.currans-sheehan@briarcliff.edu (editor); jeanne.emmons@briarcliff.edu (poetry). **Website:** www.bcreview.org. **Contact:** Tricia Currans-Sheehan, editor. *The Briar Cliff Review* sponsors an annual contest offering $1,000 and publication to each 1st Prize winner in fiction, poetry, and creative nonfiction. Previous year's winner and former students of editors ineligible. Winning pieces accepted for publication on the basis of first-time rights. Considers simultaneous submissions, "but notify us immediately upon acceptance elsewhere. We guarantee a considerate reading." No mss returned. Word limit for short story/creative nonfiction is 5,000. For poetry, no more than one poem per page. Award to reward good writers and showcase quality writing. Deadline: November 1. Prize: $1,000 and publication to each 1st Prize winner in fiction, poetry, and creative nonfiction.

THE BRIDPORT PRIZE

P.O. Box 6910, Dorset DT6 9QB United Kingdom. **E-mail:** info@bridportprize.org.uk; kate@bridportprize.org.uk. **Website:** www.bridportprize.org.uk. **Contact:** Kate Wilson, Bridport Prize administrator. Award to promote literary excellence, discover new talent. Categories: Short stories, poetry, flash fiction. Entries must be unpublished. Length: 5,000 maximum for short stories; 42 lines for poetry, and 250 words for flash fiction. Deadline: May 31. Open for submissions starting November 15. Prize: £5,000 ; £1,000 ; £500 ; various runners-up prizes and publication of approximately 13 best stories and 13 best poems in anthology; plus 6 best flash fiction stories. £1,000 1st Prize for the best short, short story of under 250 words. Judged by 1 judge for short stories (in 2014, Andrew Miller), 1 judge for poetry (in 2014, Liz Lochhead) and 1 judge for flash fiction (in 2014, Tania Hershman).

BURNABY WRITERS' SOCIETY CONTEST

E-mail: info@bws.ca. **Website:** www.bws.ca; www.burnabywritersnews.blogspot.com. **Contact:** Contest Committee. Offered annually for unpublished work. Open to all residents of British Columbia. Categories vary from year to year. Send SASE for current rules. For complete guidelines see website or burnabywritersnews.blogspot.com. Purpose is to encourage talented writers in all genres. Deadline: May 31. Prize: 1st Place: $200; 2nd Place: $100; 3rd Place: $50; and public reading.

CALIFORNIA BOOK AWARDS

Commonwealth Club of California, 595 Market St., San Francisco CA 94105. (415)597-6700. **Fax:** (415)597-6729. **E-mail:** bookawards@commonwealthclub.org. **Website:** www.commonwealthclub.org/. Offered annually to recognize California's best writers and illuminate the wealth and diversity of California-based literature. Award is for published submissions appearing in print during the previous calendar year. Can be nominated by publisher or author. Open to California residents (or residents at time of publication). Submit at least 3 copies of each book entered with an official entry form. Open to books, published during the year prior to the contest, whose author must have been a legal resident of California at the time the manuscript was submitted for publication. Entry form and guidelines available for SASE or on website. Deadline: December 31. Prize: Medals and cash prizes to be awarded at publicized event. Judged by 12-15 California professionals with a diverse range of views, backgrounds, and literary experience.

CANADIAN AUTHORS ASSOCIATION AWARDS PROGRAM

6 West St. N, Suite 203, Orillia ON L3V 5B8 Canada. (705)325-3926. **E-mail:** admin@canadianauthors.org. **Website:** www.canadianauthors.org. **Contact:** Anita Purcell. Offered annually for fiction, poetry, and Canadian history. Entrants must be Canadians by birth, naturalized Canadians, or landed immigrants. Entry form required for all awards. Obtain entry form from contact name or download from website. Deadline: January15. Prize: Cash and a silver medal.

CANADIAN AUTHORS ASSOCIATION EMERGING WRITER AWARD

6 West St. N., Suite 203, Orilla ON L3X 5B8 Canada. **Website:** www.canadianauthors.org. **Contact:** Anita Purcell, executive director. Annual award for a writer under 30 years of age deemed to show exceptional promise in the field of literary creation. Deadline: January 15. Prize: $500. Judging: Each year a trustee for each award appointed by the Canadian Authors Association selects up to 3 judges. Identities of the trustee and judges are confidential.

CBC LITERARY PRIZES/PRIX LITTÉRAIRES RADIO-CANADA

CBC Radio/Radio Canada, Canada Council for the Arts, *enRoute* magazine, P.O. Box 6000, Montreal QC H3C 3A8 Canada. (877)888-6788. **E-mail:** canadawrites@cbc.ca. **Website:** www.cbc.ca/canadawrites. **Contact:** Christopher DiRaddo, coordinator. The CBC Literary Prizes Competitions are the only literary competitions that celebrate original, unpublished works in Canada's 2 official languages. There are 3 categories: short story, poetry, and creative nonfiction. Submissions to the short story and creative nonfiction must be 1,200-1,500 words; poetry submissions must be 400-600 words. Poetry submissions can take the form of a long narrative poem, a sequence of connected poems, or a group of unconnected poems. Canadian citizens, living in Canada or abroad, and permanent residents of Canada are eligible to enter. Deadline: November 1 for short story; March 1 for creative nonfiction; June 1 for poetry. See website for when each competition is accepting entries. Prize: For each category, in both English and French: 1st Prize: $6,000; 2nd Prize: $1,000. In addition, winning entries are published in Air Canada's *enRoute* magazine and broadcast on CBC radio. Winning authors also get a 2-weeks residency at the Banff Centre. First publication rights are granted by winners to *enRoute* magazine and broadcast rights are given to CBC radio. Submissions are judged blind by a jury of qualified writers and editors from around the country. Each category has 3 jurors.

CHAUTAUQUA LITERARY JOURNAL ANNUAL EDITORS PRIZES

Chautauqua Literary Journal, P.O. Box 2039, York Beach ME 03910 (for contest entries only). **E-mail:** clj@uncw.edu. **Website:** www.ciweb.org/literary-arts/literary-journal. **Contact:** Jill and Philip Gerard, co-editors. Annual award for work that best captures the spirit of Chautauqua Institution and the theme. Offered for unpublished work in the categories of poetry and prose (short stories, flash, and/or creative nonfiction). First place winner automatically nominated for the Pushcart Prize. All submissions must be submitted through Submittable. Guidelines available online at http://ciwebdev.squarespace.com/submission-guidelines/. Deadline: Reading periods are August 15-November 15 and February 15-April 15. Prize: 1st Place: $500; 2nd Place: $250; 3rd Place: $100.

CHRISTIAN BOOK AWARDS

Evangelical Christian Publishers Association, 9633 S. 48th St., Suite 140, Phoenix AZ 85044. (480)966-3998. **Fax:** (480)966-1944. **E-mail:** info@ecpa.org; mkuyper@ecpa.org. **Website:** www.ecpa.org. **Contact:** Mark W. Kuyper, president and CEO. The Evangelical Christian Publishers Association recognizes quality and encourages excellence by presenting the ECPA Christian Book Awards (formerly known as Gold Medallion) each year. Categories include children, fiction, nonfiction, Bibles, Bible reference, inspiration, and new author. All entries must be evangelical in nature and submitted through an ECPA member publisher. Books must have been published in the calendar year prior to the award. Publishing companies submitting entries must be ECPA members in good standing. See website for details. The Christian Book Awards recognize the highest quality in Christian books and is among the oldest and most prestigious awards program in Christian publishing. Deadline: September 30. Submission period begins September 1.

THE CITY OF VANCOUVER BOOK AWARD

Cultural Services Dept., Woodward's Heritage Building, 111 W. Hastings St., Suite 501, Vancouver BC V6B 1H4 Canada. (604) 829-2007. **Fax:** (604)871-6005. **E-mail:** marnie.rice@vancouver.ca; culture@vancouver.ca. **Website:** https://vancouver.ca/people-programs/city-of-vancouver-book-award.aspx. The annual City of Vancouver Book Award recognizes authors of excellence of any genre who contribute to the appreciation and understanding of Vancouver's history, unique character, or the achievements of its residents. The book must exhibit excellence in one or more of the following areas: content, illustration, design, format. The book must not be copyrighted prior to the previous year. Submit four copies of book. See website for details and guidelines. Deadline: May 14. Prize: $3,000. Judged by an independent jury.

COLORADO BOOK AWARDS

Colorado Humanities & Center for the Book, 7935 E. Prentice Ave., Suite 450, Greenwood Village CO 80111. (303)894-7951, ext. 19. **Fax:** (303)864-9361. **E-mail:** stephanie@coloradohumanities.org. **Website:** www.coloradohumanities.org. **Contact:** Stephanie March. An annual program that celebrates the accomplishments of Colorado's outstanding authors, editors, illustrators, and photographers. Awards are presented in at least ten categories including anthology/collection, biography, children's, creative nonfiction, fiction, history, nonfiction, pictorial, poetry, and young adult. To be eligible for a Colorado Book Award, a primary contributor to the book must be a Colorado writer, editor, illustrator, or photographer. Current Colorado residents are eligible, as are individuals engaged in ongoing literary work in the state and authors whose personal history, identity, or literary work reflect a strong Colorado influence. Authors not currently Colorado residents who feel their work is inspired by or connected to Colorado should submit a letter with his/her entry describing the connection. Submissions should have been published in the previous year. Deadline: January 2.

THE CRUCIBLE POETRY AND FICTION COMPETITION

Crucible, Barton College, College Station, Wilson NC 27893. (800)345-4973 x6450. **E-mail:** crucible@barton.edu. **Website:** www.barton.edu. **Contact:** Terrence L. Grimes, editor. Open annually to all writers. Entries must be completely original, never published, and in ms form. Does not accept simultaneous submissions. Fiction is limited to 8,000 words; poetry is limited to 5 poems. Guidelines online or by email or for SASE. All submissions should be electronic. Deadline: May 1. Prize: 1st Place: $150; 2nd Place: $100 (for both poetry and fiction). Winners are also published in *Crucible*. Judged by in-house editorial board.

THE CUTBANK CHAPBOOK CONTEST

CutBank Literary Magazine, *CutBank*, University of Montana, English Dept., LA 133, Missoula MT 59812. **E-mail:** editor.cutbank@gmail.com. **Website:** www.cutbankonline.org. **Contact:** Allison Linville, editor-in-chief. This competition is open to original English language mss in the genres of poetry, fiction, and creative nonfiction. While previously published stand-alone pieces or excerpts may be included in a ms, the ms as a whole must be an unpublished work. Looking for startling, compelling, and beautiful original work. "We're looking for a fresh, powerful manuscript. Maybe it will overtake us quietly; gracefully defy genres; satisfyingly subvert our expectations; punch us in the mouth page in and page out. We're interested in both prose and poetry—and particularly work that straddles the lines between genres." Accepts online submissions only. Submit up to 25-40 pages of poetry or prose. Guidelines available online. Deadline: January 15. Submissions period begins November 1. Prize: $1,000 and 25 contributor copies. Judged by a guest judge each year.

CWW ANNUAL WISCONSIN WRITERS AWARDS

Council for Wisconsin Writers, 6973 Heron Way, De Forest WI 53532. **E-mail:** karlahuston@gmail.com. **Website:** www.wiswriters.org. **Contact:** Geoff Gilpin, president and annual awards co-chair; Karla Huston, secretary and annual awards co-chair; Marilyn L. Taylor, annual awards chair; Alice D'Allesio, annual awards co-chair. Offered annually for work published by Wisconsin writers during the previous calendar year. Nine awards: Major Achievement (presented in alternate years); short fiction; short nonfiction; nonfiction book; poetry book; fiction book; children's literature; Lorine Niedecker Poetry Award; Christopher Latham Sholes Award for Outstanding Service to Wisconsin Writers p(resented in alternate years); Essay Award for Young Writers. Open to Wisconsin residents. Entries may be submitted via postal mail or e-mail, based on category. See website for guidelines and entry forms. Deadline: January 31. Submissions open on November 1. Prize: First place prizes: $500. Honorable mentions: $50.

DANA AWARDS IN THE NOVEL, SHORT FICTION, AND POETRY

200 Fosseway Dr., Greensboro NC 27445. (336)644-8028. **E-mail:** danaawards@gmail.com. **Website:** www.danaawards.com. **Contact:** Mary Elizabeth Parker, chair. Three awards offered annually for unpublished work written in English. Works previously published online are not eligible. Categories: Novel: For the first 40 pages of a novel completed or in progress; Fiction: Short fiction (no memoirs) up to 10,000 words; Poetry: For best group of 5 poems based on excellence of all 5 (no light verse, no single poem over 100 lines). Purpose is monetary award for work that has not been previously published or received monetary award, but will accept work published simply for friends and family. Deadline: October 31 (postmarked). Prize: $1,000 for each of the 3 awards.

DIAGRAM/NEW MICHIGAN PRESS CHAPBOOK CONTEST

New Michigan Press, P.O. Box 210067, English, ML 424, University of Arizona, Tucson AZ 85721. **E-mail:** nmp@thediagram.com. **Website:** www.thediagram.com. **Contact:** Ander Monson, editor. The annual *DIAGRAM*/New Michigan Press Chapbook Contest offers $1,000, plus publication and author's copies, with discount on additional copies. Submit 18-44 pages of poetry, fiction, mixed-genre, or genre-bending work. Do not send originals of anything. Include SASE. Guidelines available on website. Deadline: April 27. Prize: $1,000, plus publication. Finalist chapbooks also considered for publication.

EATON LITERARY AGENCY'S ANNUAL AWARDS PROGRAM

Eaton Literary Agency, P.O. Box 49795, Sarasota FL 34230-6795. (941)366-6589. **Fax:** (941)365-4679. **E-mail:** eatonlit@aol.com. **Website:** www.eatonliterary.com. **Contact:** Richard Lawrence, V.P. Offered biannually for unpublished mss. Entries must be unpublished. Open to any writer. Guidelines available for SASE, by fax, e-mail, or on website. Accepts inquiries by fax, phone and e-mail. Results announced in April and September. Winners notified by mail. For contest results, send SASE, fax, e-mail, or visit website. Deadline: March 31 (short story); August 31 (book-length). Prize: $2,500 (book-length); $500 (short story). Judged by an independent agency in conjunction with some members of Eaton's staff.

THE VIRGINIA FAULKNER AWARD FOR EXCELLENCE IN WRITING

Prairie Schooner, 123 Andrews Hall, University of Nebraska-Lincoln, Lincoln NE 68588-0334. (402)472-0911. **Fax:** (402)472-1817. **E-mail:** PrairieSchooner@unl.edu. **Website:** www.prairieschooner.unl.edu. **Contact:** Kwame Dawes. Offered annually for work published in *Prairie Schooner* in the previous year. Categories: short stories, essays, novel excerpts and translations. Accepts inquiries by fax and e-mail. Reads unsolicited mss between May 1 and September 1. Winning entry must have been published in *Prairie*

Schooner in the year preceeding the award. Results announced in the Spring issue. Winners notified by mail in February or March. Prize: $1,000. Judged by Editorial Board.

FINELINE COMPETITION FOR PROSE POEMS, SHORT SHORTS, AND ANYTHING IN BETWEEN

Mid-American Review, Dept. of English, Bowling Green State University, Bowling Green OH 43403. (419)372-2725. **E-mail:** mar@bgsu.edu. **Website:** www.bgsu.edu/midamericanreview. **Contact:** Abigail Cloud, editor-in-chief. Offered annually for previously unpublished submissions. Contest open to all writers not associated with current judge or *Mid-American Review*. Deadline: June 1. Prize: $1,000, plus publication in fall issue of *Mid-American Review*; 10 finalists receive notation plus possible publication. 2015 judge: Michael Czyzniejewski.

FIRST NOVEL CONTEST

Harrington & Harrington Press, 3400 Yosemite, San Diego CA 92109. **E-mail:** press@harringtonandharrington.com. **Website:** www.harringtonandharrington.com. **Contact:** Laurie Champion, contest/award director. Annual contest for any writer who has not previously published a novel. Entries may be self-published. Accepts full-length works in literary fiction, creative nonfiction, memoir, genre fiction, and short story collections. No poetry. Guidelines available online. Harrington & Harrington Press aims to support writers, and the First Novel Contest will provide many ways to promote authors through networks and connections with writers, artists, and those involved in the technical production of art. Deadline: August 15. Prize: $500 advance royalty and publication by Harrington & Harrington Press. Judged by the Harrington & Harrington staff for the preliminary round. A respected author with numerous publications will act as the final judge.

FISH SHORT MEMOIR PRIZE

Fish Publishing, Durrus, Bantry Co. Cork Ireland. **E-mail:** info@fishpublishing.com. **Website:** www.fishpublishing.com. Annual worldwide contest to recognize the best memoirs submitted to Fish Publishing. Submissions must not have been previously published. Enter online or via postal mail. See website for full details. Word limit: 4,000. Deadline: January 31. Prize: 1st Prize: $1,200. The 10 best memoirs will be published in the Fish Anthology, launched in July at the West Cork Literary Festival.

THE FLORIDA REVIEW EDITOR'S PRIZE

Dept. of English, P.O. Box 161346, University of Central Florida, P.O. Box 161346, Orlando FL 32816. **E-mail:** flreview@mail.ucf.edu. **Website:** http://floridareview.cah.ucf.edu/. Annual awards for the best unpublished fiction, poetry, and creative nonfiction. Deadline: March 17. Prize: $1,000 (in each genre) and publication in *The Florida Review*. Judged by the editors in each genre. Judging is blind, so names should not appear on mss.

FOREWORD'S INDIEFAB AWARDS

ForeWord Magazine, 425 Boardman Ave., Traverse City MI 49684. (231)933-3699. **Fax:** (231)933-3899. **Website:** www.forewordreviews.com. Awards offered annually. In order to be eligible, books must have a current year copyright. *ForeWord*'s Book of the Year Award was established to bring increased attention from librarians and booksellers to the literary achievements of independent publishers and their authors. Deadline: January 15. Prize: $1,500 cash will be awarded to a Best Fiction and Best Nonfiction choice, as determined by the editors of *ForeWord Magazine*. Judged by a jury of librarians, booksellers, and reviewers who are selected to judge the categories for entry and select winners and finalists in 62 categories based on editorial excellence and professional production as well as the originality of the narrative and the value the book adds to its genre.

TIPS "The best ideas have always come from independent thinkers, and we believe that maxim holds true for written ideas as well."

FREEFALL SHORT PROSE AND POETRY CONTEST

Freefall Literary Society of Calgary, 922 9th Ave. SE, Calgary AB T2G 0S4 Canada. **E-mail:** editors@freefallmagazine.ca. **Website:** www.freefallmagazine.ca. **Contact:** Ryan Stromquist, managing editor. Offered annually for unpublished work in the categories of poetry (5 poems/entry) and prose (3,000 words or less). Recognizes writers and offers publication credits in a literary magazine format. Contest rules and entry form online. Acquires first Canadian serial rights; ownership reverts to author after one-time publication. Deadline: December 31. Prize: 1st Place: $500 (CAD); 2nd Place: $250 (CAD); 3rd Place: $75; Honorable Mention: $25. All prizes include publica-

CONTESTS & AWARDS

tion in the spring edition of *FreeFall Magazine*. Winners will also be invited to read at the launch of that issue, if such a launch takes place. Honorable mentions in each category will be published and may be asked to read. Travel expenses not included. Judged by current guest editor for issue (who are also published authors in Canada).

GOVERNOR GENERAL'S LITERARY AWARDS

Canada Council for the Arts, 150 Elgin St., P.O. Box 1047, Ottawa ON K1P 5V8 Canada. (613)566-4414, ext. 5573. **Website:** www.canadacouncil.ca. Established by Parliament, the Canada Council for the Arts provides a wide range of grants and services to professional Canadian artists and art organizations in dance, media arts, music, theater, writing, publishing, and the visual arts. Books must be first edition trade books written, translated, or illustrated by Canadian citizens or permanent residents of Canada and published in Canada or abroad in the previous year. Collections of poetry must be at least 48 pages long, and at least half the book must contain work not published previously in book form. In the case of translation, the original work must also be a Canadian-authored title. Books must be submitted by publishers with a Publisher's Registration Form, which is available by request from the Writing and Publishing Section of the Canada Council for the Arts. Guidelines and current deadlines are available on our website, by mail, telephone, fax, or e-mail. The Governor General's Literary Awards are given annually for the best English-language and French-language work in each of 7 categories, including fiction, nonfiction, poetry, drama, children's literature (text), children's literature (illustration), and translation. Deadline: Depends on the book's publication date. See website for details. Prize: Each GG winner receives $25,000. Non-winning finalists receive $1,000. Judged by fellow authors, translators, and illustrators. For each category, a jury makes the final selection.

GRANDMOTHER EARTH NATIONAL AWARD

Grandmother Earth Creations, P.O. Box 2018, Cordova TN 38088. (901)309-3692. **E-mail:** gmoearth@gmail.com. **Website:** www.grandmotherearth.org. **Contact:** Frances Cowden, Award Director. Annual national award open to anyone. Submissions may be published or unpublished. Considers simultaneous submissions. Submit at least 3 poems, any subject, in any form. See website for changes in the rules. Include SASE for winners list. Guidelines available for SASE or on website. Winners will be announced in October at the Life Press Writers Conference in August in Cordova, TN. Copies of winning poems or books available from Grandmother Earth Creations. Deadline: July 7. Prize: Offers annual award of $1,250 with varying distributions each year; separate contest for students ages 2-12; $1,250 minimum in awards for poetry and prose; $100 first, etc., plus publication in anthology; non-winning finalists considered for anthology if permission is given.

GREAT LAKES COLLEGES ASSOCIATION NEW WRITERS AWARD

535 W. William, Suite 301, Ann Arbor MI 48103. (734)661-2350. **Fax:** (734)661-2349. **E-mail:** wegner@glca.org. **Website:** www.glca.org. **Contact:** Gregory R. Wegner. Annual award for a first published volume of poetry, fiction, and creative nonfiction. Nominations should be made by the publisher and should emphasize literary excellence. Deadline: July 25. Prize: Honorarium of at least $500. Each award winner has the opportunity to tour the 13 colleges giving readings, meetings students and faculty, and leading discussions or classes. Judged by professors of literature and writers in residence at GLCA colleges.

THE GRUB STREET NATIONAL BOOK PRIZE

Grub Street, 162 Boylston Street, 5th Floor, Boston MA 02116. (617) 695-0075. **Fax:** (617) 695-0075. **E-mail:** info@grubstreet.org; chris@grubstreet.org. **Website:** http://grubstreet.org. **Contact:** Christopher Castellani, artistic director. The Grub Street National Book Prize is awarded once annually to an American writer outside New England publishing his or her second, third, fourth (or beyond...) book. First books are not eligible. Writers whose primary residence is Massachusetts, Vermont, Maine, New Hampshire, Connecticut or Rhode Island are also not eligible. Genre of the prize rotates from year to year, between fiction, nonfiction, and poetry. Submissions should include: 2 copies of the author's most recent or upcoming book, in bound galleys or final form; a Curriculum vitae; and a 500-word synposis of the proposed craft class. See website for details on current prize and genre requirements. Deadline: October 1. Prize: $5,000.

HACKNEY LITERARY AWARDS

1305 2nd Ave. N, #103, Birmingham AL 35203. (205)226-4921. **E-mail:** info@hackneyliteraryawards.org. **Website:** www.hackneyliteraryawards.org. **Contact:** Myra Crawford, PhD, executive director. Offered annually for unpublished novels, short stories (maximum 5,000 words), and poetry (50 line limit). Guidelines on website. Deadline: September 30 (novels), November 30 (short stories and poetry). Prize: $5,000 in annual prizes for poetry and short fiction ($2,500 national and $2,500 state level). 1st Place: $600; 2nd Place: $400; 3rd Place: $250); plus $5,000 for an unpublished novel. Competition winners will be announced on the website each March.

HAMMETT PRIZE

International Association of Crime Writers, North American Branch, 243 Fifth Avenue, #537, New York NY 10016. **E-mail:** mfrisque@igc.org. **Website:** www.crimewritersna.org. **Contact:** Mary A. Frisque, executive director, North American Branch. Award for crime novels, story collections, nonfiction by one author. "Our reading committee seeks suggestions from publishers and they also ask the membership for recommendations." Nominations announced in January; winners announced in fall. Winners notified by e-mail or mail and recognized at awards ceremony. For contest results, send SASE or e-mail. For guidelines, send SASE or e-mail. Accepts inquiries by e-mail. Entries must be previously published. To be eligible, the book must have been published in the US or Canada during the calendar year. The author must be a US or Canadian citizen or permanent resident. Award established to honor a work of literary excellence in the field of crime writing by a US or Canadian author. Deadline: December 15. Prize: Trophy. Judged by a committee of members of the organization. The committee chooses 5 nominated books, which are then sent to 3 outside judges for a final selection. Judges are outside the crime writing field.

ERIC HOFFER AWARD

Hopewell Publications, LLC, P.O. Box 11, Titusville NJ 08560-0011. **Fax:** (609)964-1718. **E-mail:** info@hopepubs.com. **Website:** www.hofferaward.com. **Contact:** Christopher Klim, chair. Annual contest for previously published books. Recognizes excellence in independent publishing in many unique categories: Art (titles capture the experience, execution, or demonstration of the arts); Poetry (all styles); General Fiction (nongenre-specific fiction); Commercial Fiction (genre-specific fiction); Children (titles for young children); Young Adult (titles aimed at the juvenile and teen markets); Culture (titles demonstrating the human or world experience); Memoir (titles relating to personal experience); Business (titles with application to today's business environment and emerging trends); Reference (titles from traditional and emerging reference areas); Home (titles with practical applications to home or home-related issues, including family); Health (titles promoting physical, mental, and emotional well-being); Self-help (titles involving new and emerging topics in self-help); Spiritual (titles involving the mind and spirit, including relgion); Legacy (titles over 2 years of age that hold particular relevance to any subject matter or form). Open to any writer of published work within the last 2 years, including categores for older books. This contest recognizes excellence in independent publishing in many unique categories. Also awards the Montaigne Medal for most though-provoking book, the Da Vinci Eye for best cover, and the First Horizon Award for best new authors. Results published in the US Review of Books.

INDIANA REVIEW ½ K PRIZE

Indiana Review, Ballantine Hall 465, 1020 E. Kirkwood Ave., Indiana University, Bloomington IN 47405-7103. (812)855-3439. **Fax:** (812)855-9535. **E-mail:** inreview@indiana.edu. **Website:** http://indianareview.org. **Contact:** Katie Moulton, consulting editor. Offered annually for unpublished work. Maximum story/poem length is 500 words. Guidelines available in March for SASE, by phone, e-mail, on website, or in publication. Open to any writer. Cover letter should include name, address, phone, e-mail, word count and title. No identifying information on ms. "We look for command of language and form." Results announced in August. Winners notified by mail. For contest results, send SASE or visit website. Deadline: May 31. Submission period begins August 1. Prize: $1,000, plus publication, contributor's copies, and a year's subscription to *Indiana Review*.

INSIGHT WRITING CONTEST

Insight Magazine, 55 W. Oak Ridge Dr., Hagerstown MD 21740-7390. **Fax:** (301)393-4055. **E-mail:** insight@rhpa.org. **Website:** www.insightmagazine.org. **Contact:** Omar Miranda, editor. Annual contest for writers in the categories of student short story, general short story, and student poetry. Unpublished submissions only. General category is open to all writers; student categories must be age 22 and younger. Deadline: July 31. Prize: Student Short and General Short Story: 1st Prize: $250; 2nd Prize: $200; 3rd Prize: $150. Student Poetry: 1st Prize: $100; 2nd Prize: $75; 3rd Prize: $50.

TIPS "Your entry must be a true, unpublished work by you, with a strong spiritual message. We appreciate the use of Bible texts."

THE IOWA REVIEW AWARD IN POETRY, FICTION, AND NONFICTION

308 EPB, University of Iowa, Iowa City IA 52242. **E-mail:** iowa-review@uiowa.edu. **Website:** www.iowareview.org. *The Iowa Review* Award in Poetry, Fiction, and Nonfiction presents $1,500 to each winner in each genre, $750 to runners-up. Winners and runners-up published in *The Iowa Review.* Submissions must be unpublished. Considers simultaneous submissions (with notification of acceptance elsewhere). Submit up to 25 pages of prose, (double-spaced) or 10 pages of poetry (1 poem or several, but no more than 1 poem per page). Submit online. Include cover page with writer's name, address, e-mail and/or phone number, and title of each work submitted. Personal identification must not appear on ms pages. Guidelines available on website. Deadline: Submit January 1-31. Judged by Srikanth Reddy, Kevin Brockmeier, and Wayne Koestenbaum in 2015.

LEAGUE OF UTAH WRITERS CONTEST

The League of Utah Writers, The League of Utah Writers, P.O. Box 64, Lewiston UT 84320. (435)755-7609. **E-mail:** luwcontest@gmail.com. **Website:** www.luwriters.org. Open to any writer, the LUW Contest provides authors an opportunity to get their work read and critiqued. Multiple categories are offered; see website for details. Entries must be the original and unpublished work of the author. Winners are announced at the Annual Writers Round-Up in September. Those not present will be notified by e-mail. Deadline: June 15. Submissions period begins March 15. Prize: Cash prizes are awarded. Judged by professional authors and editors from outside the League.

LES FIGUES PRESS NOS BOOK CONTEST

P.O. Box 7736, Los Angeles CA 90007. (323)734-4732. **E-mail:** info@lesfigues.com. **Website:** www.lesfigues.com. **Contact:** Teresa Carmody and Vanessa Place, co-directors. Les Figues Press creates aesthetic conversations between writers/artists and readers, especially those interested in innovative/experimental/avant-garde work. The Press intends in the most premeditated fashion to champion the trinity of Beauty, Belief, and Bawdry. Submit a 64-250 page unpublished manuscript through electronic submissions manager. Eligible submissions include: poetry, novellas, innovative novels, anti-novels, short story collections, lyric essays, hybrids, and all forms *not otherwise specificed.* Guidelines available online. Deadline: September 15. Prize: $1,000, plus publication by Les Figues Press. Each entry receives LFP book.

LET'S WRITE LITERARY CONTEST

The Gulf Coast Writers Association, P.O. Box 952, Long Beach MS 39560. **E-mail:** writerpllevin@gmail.com. **Website:** www.gcwriters.org. **Contact:** Philip Levin. The Gulf Coast Writers Association sponsors this nationally recognized contest, which accepts unpublished poems and short stories from authors all around the US. This is an annual event which has been held for over 20 years. Deadline: April 10. Prize: 1st Prize: $100; 2nd Prize: $60; 3rd Prize: $25.

THE HUGH J. LUKE AWARD

Prairie Schooner, 123 Andrews Hall, University of Nebraska-Lincoln, Lincoln NE 68588-0334. (402)472-0911. **Fax:** (402)472-1817. **E-mail:** prairieschooner@unl.edu. **Website:** www.prairieschooner.unl.edu. **Contact:** Kwame Dawes. Offered annually for work published in *Prairie Schooner* in the previous year. Results announced in the Spring issue. Winners notified by mail in February or March. Prize: $250. Judged by editorial staff of *Prairie Schooner.*

MANITOBA BOOK AWARDS

c/o Manitoba Writers' Guild, 218-100 Arthur St., Winnipeg MB R3B 1H3 Canada. (204)944-8013. **E-mail:** events@mbwriter.mb.ca. **Website:** www.manitobabookawards.com. **Contact:** Anita Daher. Offered annually: The McNally Robinson Book of Year Award (adult); The McNally Robinson Book for Young People Awards (8 and under and 9 and older); The John Hirsch Award for Most Promising Manitoba Writer; The Mary Scorer Award for Best Book by a Manitoba Publisher; The Carol Shields Winnipeg Book Award; The Eileen McTavish Sykes Award for Best First Book; The Margaret Laurence Award for Fiction; The Alexander Kennedy Isbister Award for Nonfiction; The Manuela Dias Book Design of the Year Award; The Best Illustrated Book of the Year Award; the biennial Le Prix Littéraire Rue-Deschambault; The Beatrice

Mosionier Aboriginal Writer of the Year Award; and The Chris Johnson Award for Best Play by a Manitoba Playwright. Guidelines and submission forms available online. Open to Manitoba writers only. Deadline: October 31 and December 31. See website for specific details on book eligibility at deadlines. Prize: Several prizes up to $5,000 (Canadian).

⊘ THE MCGINNIS-RITCHIE MEMORIAL AWARD

Southwest Review, P.O. Box 750374, Dallas TX 75275-0374. (214)768-1037. **Fax:** (214)768-1408. **E-mail:** swr@mail.smu.edu. **Website:** www.smu.edu/southwestreview. **Contact:** Jennifer Cranfill, senior editor, and Willard Spiegelman, editor-in-chief. The McGinnis-Ritchie Memorial Award is given annually to the best works of fiction and nonfiction that appeared in the magazine in the previous year. Mss are submitted for publication, not for the prizes themselves. Guidelines for SASE or online. Prize: $500. Judged by Jennifer Cranfill and Willard Spiegelman.

TIPS "Not an open contest. Annual prize in which winners are chosen from published pieces during the preceding year."

MINNESOTA BOOK AWARDS

325 Cedar Street, Suite 555, St. Paul MN 55101. **E-mail:** mnbookawards@thefriends.org; friends@thefriends.org; info@thefriends.org. **Website:** www.thefriends.org. A year-round program celebrating and honoring Minnesota's best books, culminating in an annual awards gala. Recognizes and honors achievement by members of Minnesota's book community. All books must be the work of a Minnesota author or primary artistic creator (current Minnesota resident who maintains a year-round residence in Minnesota). All books must be published within the calendar year of the competition.

MISSISSIPPI REVIEW PRIZE

Mississippi Review, 118 College Dr., #5144, Hattiesburg MS 39406-0001. (601)266-4321. **Fax:** (601)266-5757. **E-mail:** msreview@usm.edu. **Website:** www.mississippireview.com. Annual contest starting August 1 and running until January 1. Winners and finalists will make up next winter's print issue of the national literary magazine *Mississippi Review.* Each entrant will receive a copy of the prize issue. Contest is open to all writers in English except current or former students or employees of The University of Southern Mississippi. Fiction entries should be 1,000-8,000 words, poetry entries should be 3-5poems totaling 10 pages or less. There is no limit on the number of entries you may submit. Online submissions must be submitted through Submittable site: mississippireview.submittable.com/submit. No manuscripts will be returned. Previously published work is ineligible. Winners will be announced in March and publication is scheduled for Junenext year. Entries should have 'MR Prize,' author name, address, phone, e-mail and title of work on page 1. Deadline: January1. Prize: $1,000 in fiction and poetry.

NATIONAL BOOK AWARDS

The National Book Foundation, 90 Broad St., Suite 604, New York NY 10004. (212)685-0261. **E-mail:** nationalbook@nationalbook.org; agall@nationalbook.org. **Website:** www.nationalbook.org. **Contact:** Amy Gall. The National Book Foundation and the National Book Awards celebrate the best of American literature, expand its audience, and enhance the cultural value of great writing in America. The contest offers prizes in 4 categories: fiction, nonfiction, poetry, and young people's literature. Books should be published between December 1 and November 30 of the past year. Submissions must be previously published and must be entered by the publisher. General guidelines available on website. Interested publishes should phone or e-mail the Foundation. Deadline: Entry form and payment by May 15; a copy of the book by July 1. Prize: $10,000 in each category. Finalists will each receive a prize of $1,000. Judged by a category specific panel of 5 judges for each category.

NATIONAL OUTDOOR BOOK AWARDS

921 S. 8th Ave., Stop 8128, Pocatello ID 83209. (208)282-3912. **E-mail:** wattron@isu.edu. **Website:** www.noba-web.org. **Contact:** Ron Watters. Nine categories: History/biography, outdoor literature, instructional texts, outdoor adventure guides, nature guides, children's books, design/artistic merit, natural history literature, and nature and the environment. Additionally, a special award, the Outdoor Classic Award, is given annually to books which, over a period of time, have proven to be exceptionally valuable works in the outdoor field. Application forms and eligibilty requirements are available online. Applications for the Awards program become available in early June. Deadline: September 1. Prize: Winning books are promoted nationally and are entitled to display the National Outdoor Book Award (NOBA) medallion.

THE NEUTRINO SHORT-SHORT CONTEST

Passages North, Dept. of English, Northern Michigan University, 1401 Presque Isle Ave., Marquette MI 49855. (906)227-1203. **Fax:** (906)227-1096. **E-mail:** passages@nmu.edu. **Website:** www.passagesnorth.com. **Contact:** Jennifer Howard. Offered every 2 years to publish new voices in literary fiction, nonfiction, hybrid-essays and prose poems (maximum 1,000 words). Guidelines available for SASE or online. Deadline: March 15. Submission period begins January 15. Prize: $1,000, and publication for the winner; 2 honorable mentions also published; all entrants receive a copy of *Passages North*. Judged by Connie Voisine in 2014.

NEW LETTERS LITERARY AWARDS

New Letters, UMKC, University House, Room 105, 5101 Rockhill Rd., Kansas City MO 64110-2499. (816)235-1168. **Fax:** (816)235-2611. **Website:** www.newletters.org. Award has 3 categories (fiction, poetry, and creative nonfiction) with 1 winner in each. Offered annually for previously unpublished work. For guidelines, send an SASE to *New Letters*, or visit www.newletters.org. Deadline: May 18. Prize: 1st place: $1,500, plus publication; first runners-up: a copy of a recent book of poetry or fiction courtesy of our affiliate BkMk Press. Judged by regional writers of prominence and experience. Final judging by someone of national repute. Previous judges include Maxine Kumin, Albert Goldbarth, Charles Simic, and Janet Burroway.

NEW MILLENNIUM AWARDS FOR FICTION, POETRY, AND NONFICTION

New Millennium Writings, 4021 Garden Dr., Knoxville TN 37918. (865)254-4880. **Website:** www.newmillenniumwritings.com/awards. No restrictions as to style, content or number of submissions. Previously published pieces acceptable if online or under 5,000 print circulation. Simultaneous and multiple submissions welcome. Each fiction or nonfiction piece is a separate entry and should total no more than 6,000 words, except for the Short-Short Fiction Award, which should total no more than 1,000 words. (Nonfiction includes essays, profiles, memoirs, interviews, creative nonfiction, travel, humor, etc.) Each poetry entry may include up to 3 poems, not to exceed 5 pages total. All 20 poetry finalists will be published. Include name, phone, address, e-mail, and category on cover page only. Apply online via submissions manager. Send SASE or IRC for list of winners or await your book. Deadline: postmarked on or before July 31 for the Summer Awards and January 31 for the Winter Awards. Prize: $1,000 for Best Poem; $1,000 for Best Fiction; $1,000 for Best Nonfiction; $1,000 for Best Short-Short Fiction.

NEW VOICES AWARD

95 Madison Ave., Suite 1205, New York NY 10016. **Website:** www.leeandlow.com. Open to students. Annual award. Lee & Low Books is one of the few minority-owned publishing companies in the country and has published more than 100 first-time writers and illustrators. Winning titles include *The Blue Roses*, winner of a Patterson Prize for Books for Young People; *Janna and the Kings*, an IRA Children's Book Award Notable; and *Sixteen Years in Sixteen Seconds*, selected for the Texas Bluebonnet Award Masterlist. Submissions made by author. SASE for contest rules or visit website. Restrictions of media for illustrators: The author must be a writer of color who is a resident of the U.S. and who has not previously published a children's picture book. For additional information, send SASE or visit Lee & Low's website. Encourages writers of color to enter the world of children's books. Deadline: September 30. Prize: New Voices Award: $1,000 prize and standard publication contract (regardless of whether or not writer has an agent) along with an advance against royalties; New Voices Honor Award: $500 prize. Judged by Lee & Low editors.

NORTHERN CALIFORNIA BOOK AWARDS

Northern California Book Reviewers Association, c/o Poetry Flash, 1450 Fourth St. #4, Berkeley CA 94710. (510)525-5476. **E-mail:** ncbr@poetryflash.org; editor@poetryflash.org. **Website:** www.poetryflash.org. **Contact:** Joyce Jenkins, executive director. Annual Northern California Book Award for outstanding book in literature, open to books published in the current calendar year by Northern California authors. NCBR presents annual awards to Bay Area (northern California) authors annually in fiction, nonfiction, poetry and children's literature. Previously published books only. Must be published the calendar year prior to spring awards ceremony. Submissions nominated by publishers; author or agent could also nominate published work. Send 3 copies of the book to attention: NCBR. Encourages writers and stimulates interest in books and reading. Deadline: December 28. Prize: $100 honorarium and award certificate. Judging by voting members of the Northern California Book Reviewers.

OHIOANA BOOK AWARDS

Ohioana Library Association, 274 E. First Ave., Suite 300, Columbus OH 43201-3673. (614)466-3831. **Fax:** (614)728-6974. **E-mail:** ohioana@ohioana.org. **Website:** www.ohioana.org. **Contact:** David Weaver, executive director. Writers must have been born in Ohio or lived in Ohio for at least 5 years, but books about Ohio or an Ohioan need not be written by an Ohioan. Finalists announced in May and winners in July. Winners notified by mail in early summer. Offered annually to bring national attention to Ohio authors and their books, published in the last year. (Books can only be considered once.) Categories: Fiction, nonfiction, juvenile, poetry, and books about Ohio or an Ohioan. Deadline: December 31. Prize: $1,000 cash prize, certificate, and glass sculpture. Judged by a jury selected by librarians, book reviewers, writers and other knowledgeable people.

OPEN SEASON AWARDS

The Malahat Review, University of Victoria, P.O. Box 1700, Stn CSC, Victoria BC V8V 2Y2 Canada. (250)721-8524. **Fax:** (250)472-5051. **E-mail:** malahat@uvic.ca. **Website:** www.malahatreview.ca. **Contact:** John Barton, editor. The Open Season Awards accepts entries of poetry, fiction, and creative nonfiction. Winners published in spring issue of *Malahat Review* announced in winter on website, facebook page, and in quarterly e-newsletter, *Malahat lite*. Submissions must be unpublished. No simultaneous submissions. Submit up to 3 poems of 100 lines or less; 1 piece of fiction 2,500 words maximum; or 1 piece of creative nonfiction, 2,500 words maximum. No restrictions on subject matter or aesthetic approach. Include separate page with writer's name, address, e-mail, and title(s); no identifying information on mss pages. E-mail submissions now accepted: season@uvic.ca. Do not include SASE for results; mss will not be returned. Guidelines available on website. Winners and finalists will be contacted by email. Deadline: November 1. Prize: $1,000 CAD and publication in *The Malahat Review* in each category.

OREGON BOOK AWARDS

925 SW Washington St., Portland OR 97205. (503)227-2583. **Fax:** (503)241-4256. **E-mail:** la@literary-arts.org. **Website:** www.literary-arts.org. **Contact:** Susan Denning, director of programs and events. The annual Oregon Book Awards celebrate Oregon authors in the areas of poetry, fiction, nonfiction, drama and young readers' literature published between August 1 and July 31 of the previous calendar year. Awards are available for every category. See website for details. Entry fee determined by initial print run; see website for details. Entries must be previously published. Oregon residents only. Accepts inquiries by phone and e-mail. Finalists announced in January. Winners announced at an awards ceremony in November. List of winners available in April. Deadline: August 29. Prize: Grant of $2,500. (Grant money could vary.) Judged by writers who are selected from outside Oregon for their expertise in a genre. Past judges include Mark Doty, Colson Whitehead and Kim Barnes.

PEN CENTER USA LITERARY AWARDS

PEN Center USA, P.O. Box 6037, Beverly Hills CA 90212. (323)424-4939. **E-mail:** awards@penusa.org. **E-mail:** pen@penusa.org. **Website:** www.penusa.org. Offered for work published or produced in the previous calendar year. Open to writers living west of the Mississippi River. Award categories: fiction, poetry, research nonfiction, creative nonfiction, translation, children's/young adult, graphic literature, drama, screenplay, teleplay, journalism. Guidelines and submission form available on website. No anthologies, publish-on-demand, or self-published work. Deadline for book categories: 4 copies must be received by December 31. Deadline for non-book categories: 4 copies must be received by February 28. Prize: $1,000.

PNWA LITERARY CONTEST

Pacifc Northwest Writers Association, PMB 2717, 1420 NW Gilman Blvd., Suite 2, Issaquah WA 98027. (452)673-2665. **Fax:** (452)961-0768. **E-mail:** pnwa@pnwa.org. **Website:** www.pnwa.org. Annual literary contest with 12 different categories. See website for details and specific guidelines. Each entry receives 2 critiques. Winners announced at the PNWA Summer Conference, held annually in mid-July. Deadline: February 20. Prize: 1st Place: $700; 2nd Place: $300. Judged by an agent or editor attending the conference.

PRIME NUMBER MAGAZINE AWARDS

Press 53, 560 N. Trade St., Suite 103, Winston-Salem NC 27101. **E-mail:** kevin@press53.com. **Website:** www.press53.com. **Contact:** Kevin Morgan Watson, publisher. Awards $1,000 in each of 3 categories: poetry, short fiction, and creative nonficiton. Details and guidelines available online. Deadline: March 30. Submission period begins January 1. Finalists announced June 1. Winner announced on August 1. Prize: $1,000 cash. All winners receive publication in Prime Number Magazine online. Judged by industry professionals to be named when the contest begins.

PRISM INTERNATIONAL ANNUAL SHORT FICTION, POETRY, AND CREATIVENONFICTION CONTESTS

PRISM International, Creative Writing Program, UBC, Buch. E462, 1866 Main Mall, Vancouver BC V6T 1Z1 Canada. **E-mail:** promotions@prismmagazine.ca. **Website:** www.prismmagazine.ca. Offered annually for unpublished work to award the best in contemporary fiction, poetry, drama, translation, and nonfiction. Works of translation are eligible. Guidelines are available on website. Acquires first North American serial rights upon publication, and limited web rights for pieces selected for website. Open to any writer except students and faculty in the Creative Writing Department at UBC, or people who have taken a creative writing course at UBC within 2 years of the contest deadline. Entry includes subscription. Deadlines: Creative Nonfiction: November 21; Fiction and Poetry: January 23. Prize: All grand prizes are $2,000, $300 for first runner up, and $200 for second runner up. Winners are published.

THE RBC BRONWEN WALLACE AWARD FOR EMERGING WRITERS

The Writers' Trust of Canada, 460 Richmond St. W., Suite 600, Toronto ON M5C 1P1 Canada. (416)504-8222. **Fax:** (416)504-9090. **E-mail:** info@writerstrust.com. **Website:** www.writerstrust.com. **Contact:** Amanda Hopkins. Presented annually to a Canadian writer under the age of 35 who is not yet published in book form. The award, which alternates each year between poetry and short fiction, was established in memory of poet Bronwen Wallace. Deadline: Check website, to be announced. Prize: $5,000 and $1,000 to 2 finalists.

REGINA BOOK AWARD

Saskatchewan Book Awards, Inc., 315-1102 8th Ave., Regina SK S4R 1C9 Canada. (306)569-1585. **E-mail:** director@bookawards.sk.ca. **Website:** www.bookawards.sk.ca. **Contact:** Courtney Bates-Hardy, administrative director. Offered annually. In recognition of the vitality of the literary community in Regina, this award is presented to a Regina author for the best book, judged on the quality of writing. Books from the following categories will be considered: Children's; drama; fiction (short fiction by a single author, novellas, novels); nonfiction (all categories of nonfiction writing except cookbooks, directories, how-to books, or bibliographies of minimal critical content); poetry. Part of a larger group of awards, the Saskatchewan Book Awards. Deadline: November 3. Prize: $2,000 (CAD).

ROYAL DRAGONFLY BOOK AWARDS

4696 W. Tyson St., Chandler AZ 85226. (480)940-8182. **Fax:** (480)940-8787. **E-mail:** cristy@fivestarpublications.com; fivestarpublications@gmail.com. **Website:** www.fivestarpublications.com; www.fivestarbookawards.com; www.royaldragonflybookawards.com. **Contact:** Cristy Bertini. Offered annually for any previously published work to honor authors for writing excellence of all types of literature—fiction and nonfiction—in 52 categories, appealing to a wide range of ages and comprehensive list of genres. Open to any title published in English. Entry forms are downloadable at www.royaldragonflybookawards.com. Guidelines available online. Send materials to Cristy Bertini, Attn.: Five Star Book Awards, 1271 Turkey St., Ware, MA 01082. Deadline: October 1. Prize: Grand Prize winner receives $300, while another entrant will be the lucky winner of a $100 drawing. All first-place winners receive foil award seals and are included in a publicity campaign announcing winners. All first- and second-place winners and honorable mentions receive certificates.

SANTA FE WRITERS PROJECT LITERARY AWARDS PROGRAM

Santa Fe Writers Project, 369 Montezuma Ave., #350, Santa Fe NM 87501. **E-mail:** info@sfwp.com. **Website:** www.sfwp.com. **Contact:** Andrew Gifford. Annual contest seeking fiction and nonfiction of any genre. The Literary Awards Program was founded by a group of authors to offer recognition for excellence in writing in a time of declining support for writers and the craft of literature. Past judges have included Richard Currey, Jayne Anne Phillips, Chris Offutt, Lee Gutkind, and David Morrell. Deadline: December 15. Prize: $3,500 and publication.

SASKATCHEWAN FIRST BOOK AWARD

Saskatchewan Book Awards, Inc., 315-1102 8th Ave., Regina SK S4R 1C9 Canada. (306)569-1585. **E-mail:** director@bookawards.sk.ca. **Website:** www.bookawards.sk.ca. **Contact:** Courtney Bates-Hardy, administrative director. Offered annually. This award is presented to a Saskatchewan author for the best first book, judged on the quality of writing. Books from the following categories will be considered: Children's; drama; fiction (short fiction by a single author, novellas, novels); nonfiction (all categories of nonfiction writing except cookbooks, directories, how-to books, or bibliographies of minimal critical content); and poetry. Deadline: November 3. Prize: $2,000 (CAD).

THE SCARS EDITOR'S CHOICE AWARDS

829 Brian Court, Gurnee IL 60031-3155. **E-mail:** editor@scars.tv. **Website:** http://scars.tv. **Contact:** Janet Kuypers, editor/publisher (whom all reading fee checks need to be made out to). Award to showcase good writing in an annual book. Categories: short stories, poetry. Entries may be unpublished or previously published, as long as you retain the rights to your work. Open to any writer. For guidelines, visit website. Accepts inquiries by e-mail. E-mail is always preferred for inquiries and submissions. Length: "We appreciate shorter works. Shorter stories, more vivid and more real storylines in writing have a good chance." Results announced at book publication, online. Winners notified by mail when book is printed. For contest results, send SASE or e-mail or look at the contest page at website. Deadline: Revolves for appearing in different upcoming books as winners. Prize: Publication of story/essay and 1 copy of the book.

THE MONA SCHREIBER PRIZE FOR HUMOROUS FICTION & NONFICTION

3940 Laurel Canyon Blvd., #566, Studio City CA 91604. **E-mail:** brad.schreiber@att.net. **Website:** www.bradschreiber.com. **Contact:** Brad Schreiber. No SASEs. Non-US entries should enclose US currency or checks written in US dollars. Include email address. No previously published work. The purpose of the contest is to award the most creative humor writing, in any form less than 750 words, in either fiction or nonfiction, including but not limited to stories, articles, essays, speeches, shopping lists, diary entries, and anything else writers dream up. Complete rules and previous winning entries on website. Deadline: December 1. Prize: 1st Place: $500; 2nd Place: $250; 3rd Place: $100. Judged by Brad Schreiber, author, journalist, consultant, and instructor.

KAY SNOW WRITING CONTEST

Willamette Writers, Willamette Writers, 2108 Buck St., West Linn OR 97068. (503)305-6729. **Fax:** (503)344-6174. **E-mail:** reg@willamettewriters.com. **Website:** www.willamettewriters.com. Willamette Writers is the largest writers' organization in Oregon and one of the largest writers' organizations in the United States. It is a non-profit, tax-exempt Oregon corporation led by volunteers. Elected officials and directors administer an active program of monthly meetings, special seminars, workshops and annual writing conference. Continuing with established programs and starting new ones is only made possible by strong volunteer support. See website for specific details and rules. There are fivedifferent categories writers can enter: Adult Fiction, Adult Non-Fiction, Poetry, Juvenile Short Story, and Student Writer. The purpose of this annual writing contest, named in honor of Willamette Writer's founder, Kay Snow, is to help writers reach professional goals in writing in a broad array of categories and to encourage student writers. Deadline: April 23. Submission deadline begins January 15. Prize: One first prize of $300, one second place prize of $150, and a third place prize of $50 per winning entry in each of the six categories.

SOCIETY OF MIDLAND AUTHORS AWARD

Society of Midland Authors, Society of Midland Authors, P.O. Box 10419, Chicago IL 60610-0419. **E-mail:** marlenetbrill@comcast.net. **Website:** www.midlandauthors.com. **Contact:** Marlene Targ Brill, awards chair. Since 1957, the Society has presented annual awards for the best books written by Midwestern authors. The contest is open to any title published within the year prior to the contest year. Open to authors or poets who reside in, were born in, or have strong ties to a Midland state, which includes Illinois, Indiana, Iowa, Kansas, Michigan, Minnesota, Missouri, Nebraska, North Dakota, South Dakota, Ohio and Wisconsin. The Society of Midland Authors (SMA) Award is presented to one title in each of six categories: adult nonfiction, adult fiction, adult biography and memoir, children's nonfiction, children's fiction, and poetry. Books and entry forms must be mailed to the 3 judges in each category; for a list of judges and the entry form, visit the website. Do not mail books to the society's P.O. box. Deadline: January 3. Prize: cash prize of $500 and a plaque that is awarded at the SMA banquet in May in Chicago.

SOUL-MAKING KEATS LITERARY COMPETITION

The Webhallow House, 1544 Sweetwood Dr., Broadmoor Vlg CA 94015-2029. **E-mail:** SoulKeats@mail.com. **Website:** www.soulmakingcontest.us. **Contact:** Eileen Malone, award director. Annual open contest offers cash prizes in each of 13 literary categories. Competition receives 600 entries/year. Names of winners and judges are posted on website. Winners announced in January by SASE and on website. Winners are invited to read at the Koret Auditorium, San Francisco. Event is televised. Submissions in some categories may be previously published. No names or other identifying information on mss; include 3x5 card with poet's name, address, phone, fax, e-mail, title(s) of work, and category entered. Include SASE for results only; mss will not be returned. Guidelines available on website. Deadline: November 30. Prize: 1st Prize: $100; 2nd Prize: $50; 3rd Prize: $25.

THE TEXAS INSTITUTE OF LETTERS LITERARY AWARDS

E-mail: Betwx@aol.com. **Website:** www.texasinstituteofletters.org. The Texas Institute of Letters gives annual awards for books by Texas authors and writers who have produced books about Texas, including Best Books of Poetry, Fiction, and Nonfiction. Awards are also given for best Short Story, Magazine or Newspaper Article, Essay, and best Books for Children and Young Adults. Work submitted must have been published in the year stipulated, and entries may be made by authors or by their publishers. Complete guidelines and award information is available on the Texas Institute of Letters website.

TORONTO BOOK AWARDS

City of Toronto c/o Toronto Arts & Culture, Cultural Partnerships, City Hall, 9E, 100 Queen St. W., Toronto ON M5H 2N2 Canada. **E-mail:** cjones2@toronto.ca. **Website:** www.toronto.ca/book_awards. The Toronto Book Awards honor authors of books of literary or artistic merit that are evocative of Toronto. There are no separate categories; all books are judged together. Any fiction or nonfiction book published in English for adults and/or children that are evocative of Toronto are eligible. To be eligible, books must be published between January 1 and December 31 of previous year. Deadline: April 30. Prize: Each finalist receives $1,000 and the winning author receives the remaining prize money ($15,000 total in prize money available).

THE ROBERT WATSON LITERARY PRIZE IN FICTION AND POETRY

The Robert Watson Literary Prizes, *The Greensboro Review*, MFA Writing Program, 3302 MHRA Building, Greensboro NC 27402-6170. (336)334-5459. **E-mail:** jlclark@uncg.edu. **Website:** www.greensbororeview.org. **Contact:** Jim Clark, editor. Offered annually for fiction (up to 25 double-spaced pages) and poetry (up to 10 pages). Entries must be unpublished. No submissions by e-mail. Open to any writer. Guidelines available online. Deadline: September 15. Prize: $1,000 each for best short story and poem. Judged by editors of *The Greensboro Review.*

WESTERN AUSTRALIAN PREMIER'S BOOK AWARDS

State Library of Western Australia, Perth Cultural Centre, 25 Francis St., Perth WA 6000 Australia. (61) (8)9427-3151. **E-mail:** premiersbookawards@slwa.wa.gov.au. **Website:** pba.slwa.wa.gov.au. **Contact:** Karen de San Miguel. Annual competition for Australian citizens or permanent residents of Australia, or writers whose work has Australia as its primary focus. Categories: children's books, digital narrative, fiction, nonfiction, poetry, scripts, writing for young adults, West Australian history, and Western Australian emerging writers. Submit 5 original copies of the work to be considered for the awards. All works must have been published between January 1 and December 31 of the prior year. See website for details and rules of entry. Deadline: January 31. Prize: Awards $25,000 for Premier's Prize; awards $15,000 each for the Children's Books, Digital Narrative, Fiction, and Nonfiction categories; awards $10,000 each for the Poetry, Scripts, Western Australian History, Western Australian Emerging Writers, and Writing for Young Adults; awards $5,000 for People's Choice Award.

WESTERN HERITAGE AWARDS

National Cowboy & Western Heritage Museum, 1700 NE 63rd St., Oklahoma City OK 73111-7997. (405)478-2250. **Fax:** (405)478-4714. **Website:** www.nationalcowboymuseum.org. **Contact:** Jessica Limestall. The National Cowboy & Western Heritage Museum Western Heritage Awards were established to honor and encourage the legacy of those whose works in literature, music, film, and television reflect the significant stories of the American West. Accepted categories for literary entries: western novel, nonfiction book, art book, photography book, juvenile book, magazine article, or poetry book. Previously published submissions only; must be published the calendar year before the awards are presented. Requirements for entrants: The material must pertain to the development or preservation of the West, either from a historical or contemporary viewpoint. Literary entries must have been published between December 1 and November 30 of calendar year. Five copies of each published work must be furnished for judging with each entry, along with the completed entry form. Works recognized during special awards ceremonies held annually at the museum. There is an autograph party preceding the awards. Awards ceremonies are sometimes broadcast. The WHA are presented annually to encourage the accurate and artistic telling of great stories of the West through 16 categories of western literature, television, film and music; including fiction, nonfiction, children's books and poetry. See website for details and category definitions. Deadline: November 30. Prize: Awards a Wrangler bronze sculpture designed by famed western artist, John Free. Judged by a panel of judges selected each year with distinction in various fields of western art and heritage.

WESTMORELAND POETRY & SHORT STORY CONTEST

Westmoreland Arts & Heritage Festival, 252 Twin Lakes Rd., Latrobe PA 15650-9415. (724)834-7474. **Fax:** (724)850-7474. **E-mail:** info@artsandheritage.com. **Website:** www.artsandheritage.com. **Contact:** Adam Shaffer. Offered annually for unpublished work. Two categories: Poem & Short Story. Short story entries no longer than 4,000 words. Family-oriented festival and contest. Deadline: February 16. Prize: Award: $200; 1st Place: $125; 2nd Place: $100; 3rd Place: $75.

WILLA LITERARY AWARD

Women Writing the West, 8547 East Arapaho Rd., #J-541, Greenwood Village CO 80112-1436. **E-mail:** cynipid@comcast.net. **Website:** www.womenwritingthewest.org. **Contact:** Cynthia Becker. The WILLA Literary Award honors the year's best in published literature featuring women's or girls' stories set in the West. Women Writing the West (WWW), a nonprofit association of writers and other professionals writing and promoting the Women's West, underwrites and presents the nationally recognized award annually (for work published between January 1 and December 31). The award is named in honor of Pulitzer Prize winner Willa Cather, one of the country's foremost novelists. The award is given in 7 categories: historical fiction, contemporary fiction, original softcover fiction, creative nonfiction, scholarly nonfiction, poetry, and children's/young adult fiction/nonfiction. Entry forms available on the website. Deadline: November 1-February 1. Prize: $100 and a trophy. Finalist receives a plaque. Both receive digital and sticker award emblems for book covers. Notice of Winning and Finalist titles mailed to more than 4,000 booksellers, libraries, and others. Award announcement is in early August, and awards are presented to the winners and finalists at the annual WWW Fall Conference. Judged by professional librarians not affiliated with WWW.

PAUL A. WITTY OUTSTANDING LITERATURE AWARD

P.O. Box 8139, Newark DE 19714-8139. (800)336-7323. **Fax:** (302)731-1057. **Website:** www.reading.org. **Contact:** Marcie Craig Post, executive director. This award recognizes excellence in original poetry or prose written by students. Elementary and secondary students whose work is selected will receive an award. Deadline: February 2. Prize: Not less than $25 and a citation of merit.

THE WORD AWARDS

The Word Guild, Box 1243, Trenton, ON K8V 5R9 Canada. **E-mail:** info@thewordguild.com. **Website:** www.thewordguild.com. The Word Guild is an organization of Canadian writers and editors who are Christian, and who are committed to encouraging one another and to fostering standards of excellence in the art, craft, practice and ministry of writing. Memberships available for various experience levels. Yearly conference Write Canada (please see website for information) and features keynote speakers, continuing classes and workshops. Editors and agents on site. The Word Awards is for work published in the past year, in almost 30 categories including books, articles, essays, fiction, nonfiction, novels, short stories, songs, and poetry. Please see website for more information.

WORLD'S BEST SHORT-SHORT STORY CONTEST, NARRATIVE NONFICTION CONTEST & SOUTHEAST REVIEW POETRY CONTEST

The Southeast Review, English Department, Florida State University, Tallahassee FL 32306. **E-mail:** southeastreview@gmail.com. **Website:** www.southeastreview.org. **Contact:** Erin Hoover, editor. Annual award for unpublished short-short stories (500 words or less), poetry, and narrative nonfiction (6,000 words or less). Visit website for details. Deadline: March 15. Prize: $500 per category. Winners and finalists will be published in *The Southeast Review.*

WRITER'S DIGEST ANNUAL WRITING COMPETITION

Writer's Digest, a publication of F+W Media, Inc., 10151 Carver Rd., Suite 200, Cincinnati OH 45242. (715)445-4612, ext. 13430. **E-mail:** writing-competition@fwmedia.com. **Website:** www.writersdigest.com. **Contact:** Nicki Howard. Writing contest with 10 categories: Inspirational Writing (spiritual/religious, maximum 2,500 words); Memoir/Personal Essay (maximum 2,000 words); Magazine Feature Article (maximum 2,000 words); Short Story (genre, maximum 4,000 words); Short Story (mainstream/literary, maximum 4,000 words); Rhyming Poetry (maximum 32 lines); Nonrhyming Poetry (maximum 32 lines); Stage Play (first 15 pages and 1-page synopsis); TV/Movie Script (first 15 pages and 1-page synopsis). Entries must be original, in English, unpublished/unproduced (except for Magazine Feature Articles), and not accepted by another publisher/producer at the time of submission. *Writer's Digest* retains one-time publication rights to the winning entries in each category. Deadline: May (early bird); June. Prize: Grand Prize: $3,000 and a trip to the Writer's Digest Conference to meet with editors and agents; 1st Place: $1,000 and $100 of Writer's Digest Books; 2nd Place: $500 and $100 of Writer's Digest Books; 3rd Place: $250 and $100 of Writer's Digest Books; 4th Place: $100 and $50 of *Writer's Digest* Books.

WRITER'S DIGEST SELF-PUBLISHED BOOK AWARDS

Writer's Digest, 10151 Carver Rd., Suite #200, Blue Ash OH 45242. (715)445-4612, ext. 13430. **E-mail:** WritersDigestSelfPublishingCompetition@fwmedia.com. **Website:** www.writersdigest.com. **Contact:** Nicole Howard. Contest open to all English-language, self-published books for which the authors have paid the full cost of publication, or the cost of printing has been paid for by a grant or as part of a prize. Categories include: Mainstream/Literary Fiction, Genre Fiction, Nonfiction, Inspirational (spiritual/new age), Life Stories (biographies/autobiographies/family histories/memoirs), Children's Books, Reference Books (directories/encyclopedias/guide books), Poetry, and Middle-Grade/Young Adult Books. Judges reserve the right to re-categorize entries. Judges reserve the right to withhold prizes in any category. All winners will be notifed by October 12. Entrants must send a printed and bound book. Entries will be evaluated on content, writing quality, and overall quality of production and appearance. No handwritten books are accepted. Books must have been published within the past 5 years from the competition deadline. Books which have previously won awards from *Writer's Digest* are not eligible. Early bird deadline: April 1; Deadline: May 1. Prize: Grand Prize: $8,000, a trip to the Writer's Digest Conference, promotion in *Writer's Digest*, 10 copies of the book will be sent to major review houses, and a guaranteed review in *Midwest Book Review*; 1st Place (9 winners): $1,000 and promotion in *Writer's Digest*; Honorable Mentions: $50 worth of Writer's Digest Books and promotion on writersdigest.com. All entrants will receive a brief commentary from one of the judges.

WRITER'S DIGEST SELF-PUBLISHED E-BOOK AWARDS

Writer's Digest, 10151 Carver Rd., Suite #200, Blue Ash OH 45242. (715)445-4612, ext. 13430. **E-mail:** WritersDigestSelfPublishingCompetition@fwmedia.com. **Website:** www.writersdigest.com. **Contact:** Nicole Howard. Contest open to all English-language, self-published e-books for which the authors have paid the full cost of publication, or the cost of publication has been paid for by a grant or as part of a prize. Categories include: Mainstream/Literary Fiction, Genre Fiction, Nonfiction (includes reference books), Inspirational (spiritual/new age), Life Stories (biographies/autobiographies/family histories/memoirs), Children's Books, Poetry, and Middle-Grade/Young Adult Books. Judges reserve the right to re-categorize entries. Judges reserve the right to withhold prizes in any category. All winners will be notifed by December 31. Entrants must enter online. Entrants may provide a file of the book or submit entry by the Amazon gifting process. Acceptable file types include: .epub, .mobi, .ipa. Word processing documents will not be accepted. Entries will be evaluated on content, writing quality, and overall quality of production and appearance. Books must have been published within the past 5 years from the competition deadline. Books which have previously won awards from *Writer's Digest* are not eligible. Early bird deadline: August 1;

Deadline: September 19. Prize: Grand Prize: $3,000, promotion in *Writer's Digest*, a full 250-word (minimum) editorial review, $200 worth of Writer's Digest Books, and more; 1st Place (9 winners): $1,000 and promotion in *Writer's Digest*; Honorable Mentions: $50 worth of Writer's Digest Books and promotion on writersdigest.com. All entrants will receive a brief commentary from one of the judges.

WRITERS-EDITORS NETWORK INTERNATIONAL WRITING COMPETITION

CNW Publishing, P.O. Box A, North Stratford NH 03590-0167. **E-mail:** contestentry@writers-editors.com. **E-mail:** info@writers-editors.com. **Website:** www.writers-editors.com. **Contact:** Dana K. Cassell, executive director. Annual award to recognize publishable talent. Categories: Nonfiction (previously published article/essay/column/nonfiction book chapter; unpublished or self-published article/essay/column/nonfiction book chapter); fiction (unpublished or self-published short story or novel chapter); children's literature (unpublished or self-published short story/nonfiction article/book chapter/poem); poetry (unpublished or self-published free verse/traditional). Guidelines available online. Open to any writer. Maximum length: 5,000 words. Accepts inquiries by e-mail, phone and mail. Entry form online. Results announced May 31. Winners notified by mail and posted on website. Results available for SASE or visit website. Deadline: March 15. Prize: 1st Place: $100; 2nd Place: $75; 3rd Place: $50. All winners and Honorable Mentions will receive certificates as warranted. Judged by editors, librarians, and writers.

WRITERS GUILD OF ALBERTA AWARDS

Writers Guild of Alberta, Percy Page Centre, 11759 Groat Rd., Edmonton AB T5M 3K6 Canada. (780)422-8174. **Fax:** (780)422-2663. **E-mail:** mail@writersguild.ab.ca. **Website:** www.writersguild.ab.ca. **Contact:** Executive Director. Offers the following awards: Wilfrid Eggleston Award for Nonfiction; Georges Bugnet Award for Fiction; Howard O'Hagan Award for Short Story; Stephan G. Stephansson Award for Poetry; R. Ross Annett Award for Children's Literature; Gwen Pharis Ringwood Award for Drama; Jon Whyte Memorial Essay Prize; James H. Gray Award for Short Nonfiction. Eligible entries will have been published anywhere in the world between January 1 and December 31 of the current year. The authors must have been residents of Alberta for at least 12 of the 18 months prior to December 31. Unpublished mss, except in the drama and essay categories, are not eligible. Anthologies are not eligible. Works may be submitted by authors, publishers, or any interested parties. Deadline: December 31. Prize: Winning authors receive $1,500; essay prize winners receive $700.

WRITERS' LEAGUE OF TEXAS BOOK AWARDS

Writers' League of Texas, 611 S. Congress Ave., Suite 200A-3, Austin TX 78704. (512)499-8914. **Fax:** (512)499-0441. **E-mail:** wlt@writersleague.org. **E-mail:** sara@writersleague.org. **Website:** www.writersleague.org. Open to Texas authors of books published the previous year. Authors are required to show proof of Texas residency, but are not required to be members of the Writers' League of Texas. Deadline: Open to submissions from October 1 to January 15. Prize: $750, a commemorative award, and an appearance at a WLT Third Thursday panel at BookPeople in Austin, TX.

THE YOUTH HONOR AWARD PROGRAM

Skipping Stones Magazine, P.O. Box 3939, Eugene OR 97403. (541)342-4956. **E-mail:** info@skippingstones.org. **E-mail:** editor@skippingstones.org. **Website:** www.skippingstones.org. **Contact:** Arun N. Toke, Editor and Publisher. Original writing and art from youth, ages 7 to 17, should be typed or neatly handwritten. The entries should be appropriate for ages 7 to 17. Prose under 1,000 words; poems under 30 lines. Non-English and bilingual writings are welcome. To promote multicultural, international and nature awareness. Deadline: June 25. Prize: An Honor Award Certificate, a subscription to Skipping Stones and five nature and/or multicultural books. They are also invited to join the Student Review Board. Everyone who enters the contest receives the autumn issue featuring the 10 winners.

PROFESSIONAL ORGANIZATIONS

AGENTS' ORGANIZATIONS

ASSOCIATION OF AUTHORS' AGENTS (AAA), 5-8 Lower John St., Golden Square, London W1F 9HA. E-mail: anthonygoff@davidhigham.co.uk. Website: www.agentsassoc.co.uk.

ASSOCIATION OF AUTHORS' REPRESENTATIVES (AAR). E-mail: info@aar-online.org. Website: www.aar-online.org.

ASSOCIATION OF TALENT AGENTS (ATA), 9255 Sunset Blvd., Suite 930, Los Angeles CA 90069. (310)274-0628. E-mail: shellie@agentassociation.com. Website: www.agentassociation.com.

WRITERS' ORGANIZATIONS

ACADEMY OF AMERICAN POETS 584 Broadway, Suite 604, New York NY 10012. E-mail: academy@poets.org. Website: www.poets.org.

AMERICAN CRIME WRITERS LEAGUE (ACWL), 17367 Hilltop Ridge Dr., Eureka MO 63205. Website: www.acwl.org.

AMERICAN INDEPENDENT WRITERS (AIW), 1001 Connecticut Ave. NW, Suite 701, Washington DC 20036. E-mail: info@aiwriters.org. Website: americanindependentwriters.org.

AMERICAN MEDICAL WRITERS ASSOCIATION (AMWA), 30 West Gude Dr., Suite 525, Rockville MD 20850-4347. E-mail: amwa@amwa.org. Website: www.amwa.org.

AMERICAN SCREENWRITERS ASSOCIATION (ASA), 269 S. Beverly Dr., Suite 2600, Beverly Hills CA 90212. (866)265-9091. E-mail: asa@goasa.com. Website: www.asascreenwriters.com.

AMERICAN TRANSLATORS ASSOCIATION (ATA), 225 Reinekers Ln., Suite 590, Alexandria VA 22314. (703)683-6100. E-mail: ata@atanet.org. Website: www.atanet.org.

EDUCATION WRITERS ASSOCIATION (EWA), 2122 P St., NW Suite 201, Washington DC 20037. E-mail: ewa@ewa.org. Website: ewa.org.

HORROR WRITERS ASSOCIATION (HWA), 244 5th Ave., Suite 2767, New York NY 10001. E-mail: hwa@horror.org. Website: www.horror.org.

THE INTERNATIONAL WOMEN'S WRITING GUILD (IWWG), P.O. Box 810, Gracie Station, New York NY 10028. Website: www.iwwg.com.

MYSTERY WRITERS OF AMERICA (MWA), 1140 Broadway, Suite 1507, New York NY 10001. (212)888-8171. E-mail: mwa@mysterywriters.org. Website: www.mysterywriters.org.

NATIONAL ASSOCIATION OF SCIENCE WRITERS (NASW), P.O. Box 7905, Berkeley, CA 94707. (510)647-9500. E-mail: lfriedmann@nasw.org. Website: www.nasw.org.

NATIONAL ASSOCIATION OF WOMEN WRITERS (NAWW), 24165 IH-10 W., Suite 217-637, San Antonio TX 78257. Phone/Fax: (866)821-5829. Website: www.naww.org.

ORGANIZATION OF BLACK SCREENWRITERS (OBS). 1999 W. Adams Blvd., Mezzanine, Los Angeles CA 90018. Website: www.obswriter.com.

OUTDOOR WRITERS ASSOCIATION OF AMERICA (OWAA), 121 Hickory St., Suite 1, Missoula MT 59801. E-mail: krhoades@owaa.org. Website: www.owaa.org.

POETRY SOCIETY OF AMERICA (PSA), 15 Gramercy Park, New York NY 10003. Website: www.poetrysociety.org.

POETS & WRITERS, 90 Broad St., Suite 2100, New York NY 10004. (212)226-3586. Fax: (212)226-3963. Website: www.pw.org.

ROMANCE WRITERS OF AMERICA (RWA), 114615 Benfer Rd., Houston TX 77069. (832)717-5200. Fax: (832)717-5201. E-mail: info@rwanational.org. Website: www.rwanational.org.

SCIENCE FICTION AND FANTASY WRITERS OF AMERICA (SFWA), P.O. Box 877, Chestertown MD 21620. E-mail: execdir@sfwa.org. Website: www.sfwa.org.

SOCIETY OF AMERICAN BUSINESS EDITORS & WRITERS (SABEW), University of Missouri, School of Journalism, 30 Neff Annex, Columbia MO 65211. (602) 496-7862. E-mail: sabew@sabew.org. Website: www.sabew.org.

SOCIETY OF AMERICAN TRAVEL WRITERS (SATW), 7044 S. 13 St., Oak Creek WI 53154. E-mail: satw@satw.org. Website: www.satw.org.

SOCIETY OF CHILDREN'S BOOK WRITERS & ILLUSTRATORS (SCBWI), 8271 Beverly Blvd., Los Angeles CA 90048. E-mail: scbwi@scbwi.org. Website: www.scbwi.org.

WESTERN WRITERS OF AMERICA (WWA). E-mail: spiritfire@kc.rr.com. Website: www.westernwriters.org.

INDUSTRY ORGANIZATIONS

AMERICAN BOOKSELLERS ASSOCIATION (ABA), 200 White Plains Rd., Suite 600, Tarrytown NY 10591. (914)591-2665. E-mail: info@bookweb.org. Website: www.bookweb.org.

AMERICAN SOCIETY OF JOURNALISTS & AUTHORS (ASJA), 1501 Broadway, Suite 302, New York NY 10036. (212)997-0947. E-mail: director@asja.org. Website: www.asja.org.

ASSOCIATION FOR WOMEN IN COMMUNICATIONS (AWC), 3337 Duke St., Alexandria VA 22314. (703)370-7436. E-mail: info@womcom.org. Website: www.womcom.org.

ASSOCIATION OF AMERICAN PUBLISHERS (AAP), 71 5th Ave., 2nd Floor, New York NY 10003. Website: www.publishers.org.

THE ASSOCIATION OF WRITERS & WRITING PROGRAMS (AWP), Mail Stop 1E3, George Mason University, Fairfax VA 22030. Website: www.awpwriter.org.

THE AUTHORS GUILD, INC., 31 E. 32nd St., 7th Floor, New York NY 10016. E-mail: staff@authorsguild.org. Website: authorsguild.org.

CANADIAN AUTHORS ASSOCIATION (CAA), P.O. Box 581, Stn. Main Orilla ON L3V 6K5 Canada. Website: www.canauthors.org.

CHRISTIAN BOOKSELLERS ASSOCIATION (CBA), P.O. Box 62000, Colorado Springs CO 80962. Website: www.cbaonline.org.

THE DRAMATISTS GUILD OF AMERICA, 1501 Broadway, Suite 701, New York NY 10036. Website: www.dramatistsguild.com.

NATIONAL LEAGUE OF AMERICAN PEN WOMEN (NLAPW), 1300 17th St. NW, Washington DC 20036-1973. Website: www.americanpenwomen.org.

NATIONAL WRITERS ASSOCIATION (NWA), 10940 S. Parker Rd., #508, Parker CO 80134. Website: www.nationalwriters.com

NATIONAL WRITERS UNION (NWU), 256 West 38th St., Suite 703, New York, NY 10018. E-mail: nwu@nwu.org. Website: www.nwu.org.

PEN AMERICAN CENTER, 588 Broadway, Suite 303, New York NY 10012-3225. E-mail: pen@pen.org. Website: www.pen.org.

THE PLAYWRIGHTS GUILD OF CANADA (PGC), 215 Spadina Ave., Suite #210, Toronto ON M5T 2C7 Canada. E-mail: info@playwrightsguild.ca. Website: www.playwrightsguild.com.

VOLUNTEER LAWYERS FOR THE ARTS (VLA), One E. 53rd St., 6th Floor, New York NY 10022. (212)319-2787. Website: www.vlany.org.

WOMEN IN FILM (WIF), 6100 Wilshire Blvd., Suite 710, Los Angeles CA 90048. E-mail: info@wif.org. Website: www.wif.org.

WOMEN'S NATIONAL BOOK ASSOCIATION (WNBA), P.O. Box 237, FDR Station, New York NY 10150. E-mail: publicity@bookbuzz.com. Website: www.wnba-books.org.

WRITERS GUILD OF ALBERTA (WGA), 11759 Groat Rd., Edmonton AB T5M 3K6 Canada. E-mail: mail@writersguild.ab.ca. Website: writersguild.ab.ca.

WRITERS GUILD OF AMERICA-EAST (WGA), 555 W. 57th St., Suite 1230, New York NY 10019. E-mail: info@wgaeast.org. Website: www.wgaeast.org.

WRITERS GUILD OF AMERICA-WEST (WGA), 7000 W. Third St., Los Angeles CA 90048. Website: www.wga.org.

WRITERS UNION OF CANADA (TWUC), 90 Richmond St. E., Suite 200, Toronto ON M5C 1P1 Canada. E-mail: info@writersunion.ca. Website: www.writersunion.ca.

GLOSSARY

#10 ENVELOPE. A standard, business-size envelope.

ADVANCE. A sum of money a publisher pays a writer prior to the publication of a book. It is usually paid in installments, such as one-half on signing contract; one-half on delivery of complete and satisfactory manuscript.

AGENT. A liaison between a writer and editor or publisher. An agent shops a manuscript around, receiving a commission when the manuscript is accepted. Agents usually take a 10-15% fee from the advance and royalties.

ARC. Advance reader copy.

ASSIGNMENT. Editor asks a writer to produce a specific article for an agreed-upon fee.

AUCTION. Publishers sometimes bid for the acquisition of a book manuscript that has excellent sales prospects. The bids are for the amount of the author's advance, advertising and promotional expenses, royalty percentage, etc. Auctions are conducted by agents.

AVANT-GARDE. Writing that is innovative in form, style, or subject.

BACKLIST. A publisher's list of its books that were not published during the current season, but that are still in print.

BIMONTHLY. Every two months.

BIO. A sentence or brief paragraph about the writer; can include education and work experience.

BIWEEKLY. Every two weeks.

BLOG. Short for weblog. Used by writers to build platform by posting regular commentary, observations, poems, tips, etc.

BLURB. The copy on paperback book covers or hard cover book dust jackets, either promoting the book and the author or featuring testimonials from book reviewers or well-known people in the book's field. Also called flap copy or jacket copy.

BOILERPLATE. A standardized contract.

BOUND GALLEYS. Prepublication edition of book, usually photocopies of final galley proofs; also known as "bound proofs."

BYLINE. Name of the author appearing with the published piece.

CATEGORY FICTION. A term used to include all types of fiction.

CHAPBOOK. A small booklet usually paperback of poetry, ballads, or tales.

CIRCULATION. The number of subscribers to a magazine.

CLIPS. Samples, usually from newspapers or magazines, of a writer's published work.

COFFEE-TABLE BOOK. A heavily illustrated oversize book.

COMMERCIAL NOVELS. Novels designed to appeal to a broad audience. These are often broken down into categories such as western, mystery and romance. See also genre.

CONTRIBUTOR'S COPIES. Copies of the issues of magazines sent to the author in which the author's work appears.

CO-PUBLISHING. Arrangement where author and publisher share publications costs and profits of a book. Also known as cooperative publishing.

COPYEDITING. Editing a manuscript for grammar, punctuation, printing style, and factual accuracy.

COPYRIGHT. A means to protect an author's work.

COVER LETTER. A brief letter that accompanies the manuscript being sent to and agent or editor.

CREATIVE NONFICTION. Nonfictional writing that uses an innovative approach to the subject and creative language.

CRITIQUING SERVICE. An editing service in which writers pay a fee for comments on the salability or other qualities of their manuscript. Fees vary, as do the quality of the critiques.

CV. Curriculum vita. A brief listing of qualifications and career accomplishments.

ELECTRONIC RIGHTS. Secondary or subsidiary rights dealing with electronic/multimedia formats (i.e., the Internet, CD-ROMs, electronic magazines).

ELECTRONIC SUBMISSION. A submission made by modem or on computer disk.

EROTICA. Fiction that is sexually oriented.

EVALUATION FEES. Fees an agent may charge to evaluate material. The extent and quality of this evaluation varies, but comments usually concern salability of the manuscript.

FAIR USE. A provision of the copyright law that says short passages from copyrighted material may be used without infringing on the owner's rights.

FEATURE. An article giving the reader information of human interest rather than news.

FILLER. A short item used by an editor to "fill" out a newspaper column or magazine page. It could be a joke, an anecdote, etc.

FILM RIGHTS. Rights sold or optioned by the agent/author to a person in the film industry, enabling the book to be made into a movie.

FOREIGN RIGHTS. Translation or reprint rights to be sold abroad.

FRONTLIST. A publisher's list of books that are new to the current season.

GALLEYS. First typeset version of manuscript that has not yet been divided into pages.

GENRE. Refers either to a general classification of writing, such as the novel or the poem, or to the categories within those classifications, such as the problem novel or the sonnet.

GHOSTWRITER. Writer who puts into literary form article, speech, story, or book based on another person's ideas or knowledge.

GRAPHIC NOVEL. A story in graphic form, long comic strip, or heavily illustrated story; of 40 pages or more.

HI-LO. A type of fiction that offers a high level of interest for readers at a low reading level.

HIGH CONCEPT. A story idea easily expressed in a quick, one-line description.

HONORARIUM. Token payment.

HOOK. Aspect of the work that sets it apart from others and draws in the reader/viewer.

HOW-TO. Books and magazine articles offering a combination of information and advice in describing how something can be accomplished.

IMPRINT. Name applied to a publisher's specific line of books.

JOINT CONTRACT. A legal agreement between a publisher and two or more authors, establishing provisions for the division of royalties the book generates.

KILL FEE. Fee for a complete article that was assigned and then cancelled.

LEAD TIME. The time between the acquisition of a manuscript by an editor and its actual publication.

LITERARY FICTION. The general category of serious, non-formulaic, intelligent fiction.

MAINSTREAM FICTION. Fiction that transcends popular novel categories such as mystery, romance and science fiction.

MARKETING FEE. Fee charged by some agents to cover marketing expenses. It may be used to cover postage, telephone calls, faxes, photocopying or any other expense incurred in marketing a manuscript.

MASS MARKET. Non-specialized books of wide appeal directed toward a large audience.

MEMOIR. A narrative recounting a writer's (or fictional narrator's) personal or family history; specifics may be altered, though essentially considered nonfiction.

MIDDLE GRADE OR MID-GRADE. The general classification of books written for readers approximately ages 9-11. Also called middle readers.

MIDLIST. Those titles on a publisher's list that are not expected to be big sellers, but are expected to have limited/modest sales.

MODEL RELEASE. A paper signed by the subject of a photograph giving the photographer permission to use the photograph.

MULTIPLE CONTRACT. Book contract with an agreement for a future book(s).

MULTIPLE SUBMISSIONS. Sending more than one book or article idea to a publisher at the same time.

NARRATIVE NONFICTION. A narrative presentation of actual events.

NET ROYALTY. A royalty payment based on the amount of money a book publisher receives on the sale of a book after booksellers' discounts, special sales discounts and returns.

NOVELLA. A short novel, or a long short story; approximately 7,000 to 15,000 words.

ON SPEC. An editor expresses an interest in a proposed article idea and agrees to consider the finished piece for publication "on speculation." The editor is under no obligation to buy the finished manuscript.

ONE-TIME RIGHTS. Rights allowing a manuscript to be published one time. The work can be sold again by the writer without violating the contract.

OPTION CLAUSE. A contract clause giving a publisher the right to publish an author's next book.

PAYMENT ON ACCEPTANCE. The editor sends you a check for your article, story or poem as soon as he decides to publish it.

PAYMENT ON PUBLICATION. The editor doesn't send you a check for your material until it is published.

PEN NAME. The use of a name other than your legal name on articles, stories or books. Also called a pseudonym.

PHOTO FEATURE. Feature in which the emphasis is on the photographs rather than on accompanying written material.

PICTURE BOOK. A type of book aimed at preschoolers to 8-year-olds that tells a story using a combination of text and artwork, or artwork only.

PLATFORM. A writer's speaking experience, interview skills, website and other abilities which help form a following of potential buyers for that author's book.

POD. Print on demand.

PROOFREADING. Close reading and correction of a manuscript's typographical errors.

PROPOSAL. A summary of a proposed book submitted to a publisher, particularly used for nonfiction manuscripts. A proposal often contains an individualized cover letter, one-page overview of the book, marketing information, competitive books, author information, chapter-by-chapter outline, and two to three sample chapters.

QUERY. A letter that sells an idea to an editor or agent. Usually a query is brief (no more than one page) and uses attention-getting prose.

REMAINDERS. Copies of a book that are slow to sell and can be purchased from the publisher at a reduced price.

REPORTING TIME. The time it takes for an editor to report to the author on his/her query or manuscript.

REPRINT RIGHTS. The rights to republish a book after its initial printing.

ROYALTIES, STANDARD HARDCOVER BOOK. 10 percent of the retail price on the first 5,000 copies sold; 12 percent on the next 5,000; 15 percent thereafter.

ROYALTIES, STANDARD MASS PAPERBACK BOOK. 4-8 percent of the retail price on the first 150,000 copies sold.

ROYALTIES, STANDARD TRADE PAPERBACK BOOK. No less than 6 percent of list price on the first 20,000 copies; 7½ percent thereafter.

SASE. Self-addressed, stamped envelope; should be included with all correspondence.

SELF-PUBLISHING. In this arrangement the author pays for manufacturing, production and marketing of his book and keeps all income derived from the book sales.

SEMIMONTHLY. Twice per month.

SEMIWEEKLY. Twice per week.

SERIAL. Published periodically, such as a newspaper or magazine.

SERIAL FICTION. Fiction published in a magazine in installments, often broken off at a suspenseful spot.

SERIAL RIGHTS. The right for a newspaper or magazine to publish sections of a manuscript.

SHORT-SHORT. A complete short story of 1,500 words.

SIDEBAR. A feature presented as a companion to a straight news report (or main magazine article) giving sidelights on human-interest aspects or sometimes elucidating just one aspect of the story.

SIMULTANEOUS SUBMISSIONS. Sending the same article, story or poem to several publishers at the same time. Some publishers refuse to consider such submissions.

SLANT. The approach or style of a story or article that will appeal to readers of a specific magazine.

SLICE-OF-LIFE VIGNETTE. A short fiction piece intended to realistically depict an interesting moment of everyday living.

SLUSH PILE. The stack of unsolicited or misdirected manuscripts received by an editor or book publisher.

SOCIAL NETWORKS. Websites that connect users: sometimes generally, other times around specific interests. Four popular ones at the moment are Facebook, Twitter, Instagram and LinkedIn.

SUBAGENT. An agent handling certain subsidiary rights, usually working in conjuction with the agent who handled the book rights. The percentage paid the book agent is increased to pay the subagent.

SUBSIDIARY RIGHTS. All right other than book publishing rights included in a book publishing contract, such as paperback rights, book club rights and movie rights. Part of an agent's job is to negotiate those rights and advise you on which to sell and which to keep.

SUBSIDY PUBLISHER. A book publisher who charges the author for the cost to typeset and print his book, the jacket, etc., as opposed to a royalty publisher who pays the author.

SYNOPSIS. A brief summary of a story, novel or play. As part of a book proposal, it is a comprehensive summary condensed in a page or page and a half, single-spaced.

TABLOID. Newspaper format publication on about half the size of the regular newspaper page.

TEARSHEET. Page from a magazine or newspaper containing your printed story, article, poem or ad.

TOC. Table of Contents.

TRADE BOOK. Either a hardcover or softcover book; subject matter frequently concerns a special interest for a general audience; sold mainly in bookstores.

TRADE PAPERBACK. A soft-bound volume published and designed for the general public; available mainly in bookstores.

TRANSLATION RIGHTS. Sold to a foreign agent or foreign publisher.

UNSOLICITED MANUSCRIPT. A story, article, poem or book that an editor did not specifically ask to see.

YA. Young adult books

BOOK PUBLISHER SUBJECT INDEX

FICTION INDEX

Adventure

Comic Books

Confession

Contemporary/Mainstream

Erotica

Ethnic/Multicultural

Experimental

Gay/Lesbian

Historical

Horror

Humor

Juvenile/Picture Books

Literary

Military/War

Mystery/Suspense

Poetry

Religious/Spiritual

Romance

Science Fiction/Fantasy

Short Story Collections

Sports

Translation

Western

Young Adult/New Adult

NONFICTION INDEX

Agriculture

Americana

Animals

Anthropology/Archeology

Art/Architecture

Business/Economics

Child Guidance

Cinema/Film/Stage

Computers/Electronics/Software

Contemporary Culture

Cooking/Foods

Creative Nonfiction/Memoirs

Dance/Music

Education

Ethnic/Multicultural

Gardening/Horticulture

Gay/Lesbian

Government/Politics/World Affairs

Health/Nutrition

History

Hobbies

Humanities

Language

Literary Criticism/Literature

Medicine

Military/War

Money/Finance

Nature/Environment

New Age

Philosophy

Photography

Psychology

Regional

Religion/Spirituality

Science

Sex

Social Sciences/Sociology

Sports/Recreation

Translation

Travel

Women's Issues/Women's Studies

Young Adult/New Adult

GENERAL INDEX

B

C

D

E

F

G

H

I

J

K

L

M

N

Q

R

S

U

V

W

Z